Fulham

The Complete Record

Fulham

The Complete Record

1879-2007

Every game, every scorer, every player and every attendance.
FA Cup finals, complete history, pen pictures, manager profiles, appearance records

Dennis Turner

First published in Great Britain in 2007 by
The Breedon Books Publishing Company Limited
Breedon House, 3 The Parker Centre,
Derby, DE21 4SZ.

Paperback edition published in Great Britain in 2013 by DB Publishing, an imprint of JMD Media Ltd

ISBN 978-1-78091-132-8

Printed and bound by Copytech (UK) Ltd, Peterborough

Contents

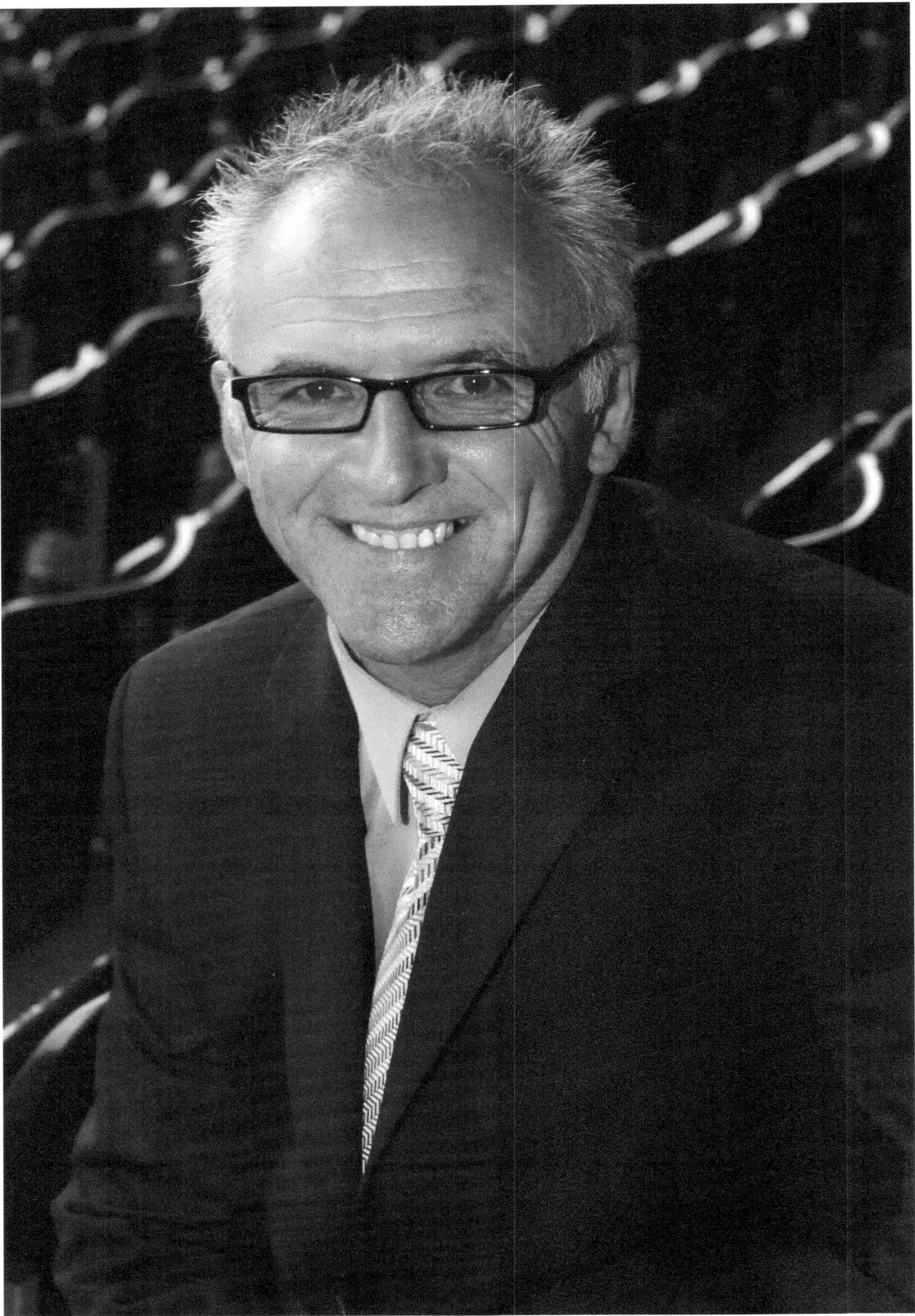

Foreword

I feel delighted and honoured to be asked to write a few words about *The Complete Record* of Fulham Football Club. Although everyone needs to look forward to a successful and stable future, we cannot forget what has gone before. We have all experienced both the tears of joy and disappointment throughout the years, and the facts and figures in this book will bring back some very memorable performances of both individuals and teams all linked to the very special friendly club we know and love.

In March of 1978 Fulham took a chance and gave me an opportunity to bridge the gap between non-League football and the then Second Division, now the Championship. For that reason alone Fulham will always be a club that is close to my heart.

A few weeks later I was making my debut away at Blackpool, and within six minutes I had given away a penalty. I was then told in no uncertain terms by my captain Ray Evans, to stay up field, never come back anywhere near the penalty area and score! All expletives from Ray's actual conversation have been left out.

Well, I actually went one better: firstly, I set up the equaliser for none other than Les Strong. Everyone who played in that game is still trying to work out what Les was actually doing that far up field on the far post to knock the ball in the net. One theory was that we did have a corner five minutes earlier, and he was still on his way back!

Les returned the compliment in the second half when he used his 'pace' to get to the byline and cross the ball to the edge of the area for my first Fulham goal on the way to the club record with a left-foot volley from 18 yards. The first headline I saw the next day read 'Fulham's Welsh Wizard'. Now I really had to start scoring some goals.

That goal started my love affair with Fulham and the fans. Even if I missed a glorious opportunity to score, and believe me there were many, the crowd would still support me. That to me typifies Fulham; that superb support and faith you had in my ability enabled me to have the confidence to go out on to the pitch and just enjoy the game. That was the one thing in my mind every game, enjoyment. That's why I always played the game with a smile. I was fortunate to set a new club scoring record and play for Wales at full international level, fulfilling a boyhood dream. Without your support I could not have done either.

There are three special memories for the older generation. Firstly, that Chesterfield goal, with outside of the left foot from near the corner flag. In another 10 years I am sure that folklore will say that I scored that goal from 'inside' the Cottage.

Next, the three epic encounters against the mighty Liverpool, 1–1 at home, 1–1 at Anfield, then only losing 1–0 in the third game. We didn't have a bad team then, did we?

Finally, the 1–1 FA Cup draw at the Cottage against the eventual winners Manchester United in front of nearly 40,000 supporters. Check the statistics on that one – 25,229 my foot! The capacity was 36,000 and we had people hanging off the pylons!

I'm sure you all have your favourite games and personalities throughout the club's illustrious history, and this book brings them all together and I am proud to have been involved in a small part of it.

I still get that special feeling, even now, when I come down to the Cottage for home games. I just hope that I have made a few of you smile or at least left you with a few good memories.

Here's to the future, but don't forget the past.

Gordon Davies (Ivor)

The History of Fulham

First steps

There has been a welter of research on the origins of Fulham FC since the first book on the Cottagers appeared 20 years ago. Thanks to the (largely unpublished) work of Alex White and Morgan Phillips and, most recently, Peter Lupson in *Thank God For Football* (SPCK Publishing, 2006), the early days of the club have emerged from the mists of late Victorian London in much sharper focus.

The prime mover in the club's early development was the church, and St Andrew's Church in Fulham Fields in particular. Opened originally as a mission church in the parish of All Saints, Fulham, in 1868, the rapid growth of the local population led to Fulham Fields being created as a separate parish in 1874 and St Andrew's a parish church. The first vicar, the Revd John Henry Cardwell, and two local families, the Murdochs and the Normans, were the key individuals in the development of the football club.

In the best traditions of muscular Christianity, 'recreation and good fellowship' were seen by Cardwell as the best way of helping channel the energies of the local youths, many of whom lived in grinding poverty. In 1879 he and 15-year-old Tom Norman formed a cricket and football club at St Andrew's. Although cricket initially took priority, and for the first three or four years the boys only played for fun among themselves, this was undoubtedly the small acorn from which the mighty oak of Fulham FC came.

Without a proper home ground, adequate financing and a formal league or cup structure, the matches were little more than the most basic park football. The first home was an area of unenclosed land adjacent to the Sunday School in Star Lane, known to the players as the 'Mud Pond'. The facilities were so basic that a school wall had to be used as one of the goals and any resemblance between those matches played by the boys of St Andrew's and what was to follow at Fulham FC just 20 years later was entirely coincidental.

A turning point

From 1883 the fledgling group of enthusiasts started down the path that before the end of the 19th century would lead to the formation of the professional Fulham Football Club. As the boys of St Andrew's got older, they took the game more seriously, and moving to a new ground indicated their intention to raise standards. First stop was the Ranelagh Club, 'a country club for wealthy gentlemen' close to the Putney Bridge railway arch, and they made use of the changing facilities at the Eight Bells public house in Fulham High Street.

At the start of 1886–87, a change of name (adding Fulham to St Andrew's Cricket and Football Club) inaugurated the most successful playing season up to then. The team won 21 of their 22 games and lifted the West London Association Cup, beating St Matthew's 2–1 in the Final. A year later they got to the last four and in 1891 were the first winners of the West London Observer Challenge Cup.

By then, the simpler name of Fulham Football Club had been adopted, a decision taken in January

1889. This was a natural transition for a club that had outgrown its origins (it had been running three teams since the 1887–88 season). Much of the personnel remained the same, although the original nickname of the Saints had to be dropped.

The Founding Fathers

Revd John Henry Cardwell

Born in Sheffield in 1842, Cardwell was a Cambridge graduate whose first appointment after ordination in 1865 was as curate at St James' Church in Clerkenwell. His next stop was St Andrew's Church in Fulham Fields in 1871, a rapidly expanding but socially deprived area of London. Although more interested in cricket than football, he was an energetic supporter of sport for his young parishioners. He remained at St Andrew's until 1890 when he took over St Anne's in Soho, where he remained until his retirement in 1914. He was living in Ealing at the time of his death, aged 78, in 1921.

Dr Patrick Murdoch

A Scot born in Dumfries in 1849, Murdoch had a successful medical practice in Lillie Road. A man of great drive and energy, he was active in St Andrew's Church (where he was elected churchwarden in 1878 and edited the parish magazine), politics (he founded the Fulham Conservative Club in 1884 and helped his friend W. Hayes Fisher, later president of Fulham FC, to win the seat in Parliament) and sport. He was a patron of the football club founded at St Andrew's in 1879 that was to become Fulham FC. He retired from his practice and returned to Scotland in the late 1890s and died in 1912, aged 63.

Tom Norman

Just 15 years old when Cardwell suggested forming a cricket and football club at St Andrew's, Tom Norman was the fourth of Edward and Lucy Norman's nine children. The father was a master house painter and the mother a Sunday School teacher (her school in Star Lane – now Greyhound Road – was the site of the club's first ground), and the family lived at Pownall Road. Born in Ipswich in 1863, Tom was three when his family moved to Fulham, and he became a master builder. In his spare time, he was secretary and principal organiser of the football club and a regular player for almost 15 years. He was married in 1891, aged 28, to a 40–year-old widow, and his last appearance for Fulham was in 1893, shortly after which all trace of him disappears.

Revd Peregrine Propert

Although it was not until May 1885 that he arrived at St Augustine's in Lillie Road (opened the previous year by St Andrew's), Propert was another significant influence on the development of the football club. A Welshman who was another Cambridge graduate, Propert was a nationally-known rower and swimmer who forsook a career in law and politics for the church. He stayed at St Augustine's until his death at the age of 78 on 1940.

Despite their growing popularity, the Fulham teams continued to pursue a nomadic existence, without a real home of their own. It was in 1891 that a ground share with Wasps Rugby Club offered the football club its first enclosed pitch, an important step because it meant that an admission fee could be charged. Since gates sometimes reached four figures, the three (old) pence charged per person offered a steady income and the prospect of financial stability.

Results on the pitch reflected this growing maturity. As well as becoming members of the newly-formed West London League in 1892–93, Fulham entered the London Senior and Middlesex Senior Cups for the first time. Although progress in the Cups was limited, the team topped the League, winning 16 and drawing two of the 18 games, and it was clear they were now a force in London football. In that championship-winning side were Jack King and Tom Norman, founder members back when the games were played at the 'Mud Pond'.

The final hurdles

As the popularity of first-class football spread south from the industrial north, so Fulham FC moved inexorably towards joining the elite that played on a full-time basis. A home of their own was the first priority, and an unusual but imaginative opportunity presented itself in 1894. A derelict site on which Lord Craven had built a cottage in about 1780 became available. The original building had been destroyed by fire in 1888 and the land was a wilderness, but it had potential!

Nobody at the time could have appreciated the significance of the acquisition of Craven Cottage as a permanent home in 1894. Not only did it offer the emerging club a much more secure base, and one that matched its ambitions, but the seven-acre site, located on the north bank of the Thames, also helped shape the character of the club over the next 100 years. It was when Fulham moved out (albeit temporarily) in 2002 to play at Loftus Road that supporters realised how inextricably the club was bound up with the ground.

It took two years to turn the site into an area suitable for football, and on 10 October 1896 Fulham won their first game at their new home, beating Minerva 4–0 in a Middlesex Senior Cup tie. Over the next nine years, the Cottage was developed into a ground that, at the time, was regarded as one of the best in the country, and was even used by England for an international against Wales in 1907. The structure created in those formative years was basically unchanged for 70 years and, even today, the work of the Edwardian architect and builders remains an integral feature of the ground.

Moving to the Cottage coincided with entry into the London League and the FA Cup. The FA Cup debut ended in a 5–0 drubbing by Swanscombe in October 1896, but in the following season, 1897–98, Fulham won the Second Division of the London League, winning 13 and drawing five of the 18 matches. It was then just a short step to adopting professionalism, the clearest signal that the club wanted to compete on a national rather than local basis. The paid professionals of Fulham FC joined the Second Division of the Southern League in 1898, and it had taken less than 20 years for the boys of St Andrew's playing on a makeshift pitch to grow into a club that was on the verge of joining the premier competition in the country.

Coming of age

Following the tentative first steps of the 1880s and the stumbling progress of the 1890s, Fulham FC was, by 1903, up and running. A professional club with its own home ground, the final step towards

A photograph of Fulham FC taken in 1901–02. Back row, left to right (players only): Meade, Head, Graham, Dwight, Lacy. Middle row: Tannahill, McNee, McKay, Miller, H. Spackman, F. Spackman. Front row: Tutthill, Stone.

maturity was taken that summer when a limited liability company was formed. The chairman, J.F. Hitchcock (whose son had once played for the club), realised that just 10 Southern League Second Division games in a season would hold back the club's development, and so, after losing yet another Test Match, 7–2 to Brentford (the third time the Cottagers had missed out on promotion in the original Play-off format), he approached the authorities to see if there was any possibility that Fulham might be admitted to the First Division. The answer was yes, on the condition the club acquired a first-class team by the end of May.

Forming a company and raising £7,500 with a share issue gave the club the means to bring in the players they needed. The money was forthcoming because 'several influential gentlemen in the district supported the scheme'. But as well as the players, a different type of person became involved in running the club, far removed from the likes of Cardwell and Murdoch. Putting the club on a more professional footing attracted prominent local businessmen and, of the eight original directors, two names stand out: John Dean and Henry Norris. They were two successful entrepreneurs and dominant personalities who spent most of the rest of their lives involved in professional football.

Chairman in the inaugural 1903–04 season, John Dean was the first of three generations of Deans to serve on the board as directors and chairmen of Fulham over three quarters of a century. The family business was Deans Blinds based in Putney, a name that was prominently displayed on matchday programmes for many years and which offered employment to a number of players once their careers were over. Dean himself was the typical Victorian businessman, imperious and demanding, and, by modern-day standards, high profile and interfering in team affairs. But his loyalty and commitment to the club were never in doubt, and neither was the question of who was in charge when he was at the helm.

John Dean was chairman until Fulham joined the League in 1907, and he left the board in 1910 after falling out with Norris. He returned in 1920 (when Norris's interests were elsewhere), took over as chairman five years later, and remained until his death in 1944. He was succeeded by his son, Charles Bradlaugh, whose own two sons (Charles and Tony) were also on the board until the late 1970s. The popular image of Fulham as a family club started in the boardroom with the Deans.

Norris was an original, a businessman and politician, charismatic and dynamic, reactionary and visionary, corrupt and ruthless. Born in 1865, he used football clubs to further his political ambitions and used political connections to promote his football schemes. He achieved a great deal, but it all turned sour as his biggest plans were on the verge of success. When his devious ways eventually caught up with him, the authorities took draconian action and he died ostracised from football.

Having made his fortune in the building industry (many of the houses around the ground were built by Allen and Norris, a firm which existed as an estate agency in the Fulham Palace Road right up to the 1990s), Norris turned his attention to politics. He was mayor of Fulham, knighted in 1917 and Conservative MP for Fulham East from 1918 to 1922, and he was a prominent freemason, rising to Grand Deacon of the United Grand Lodge of England.

Although chairman for only one season (1907–08), he was the real power at the Cottage for six seasons. In that time, Norris was instrumental in turning down an approach from Gus Mears to move Fulham into his new Stamford Bridge ground (leaving Mears to form his own club) but pushed a proposal of his own to merge Fulham with a failing south London club, Woolwich Arsenal. When he was rebuffed, he lost interest in Fulham, but, even though he became Arsenal chairman in 1910, Norris was on both boards until World War One. He stayed Fulham patron until 1924, despite the fact he was totally immersed in affairs in north London.

More than any one individual, Norris turned Arsenal into a dominant force in British football. Rescuing a near-bankrupt club, he moved it from Plumstead to a brand new Highbury Stadium in 1913, 'arranged' promotion to the top flight in 1919, although the Gunners had only finished sixth in the Second Division, and appointed Herbert Chapman to the manager's job in 1925. But he made enemies and got his comeuppance when the FA found him guilty of making illegal payments to players and of using Arsenal's accounts for personal expenses. Since illegal payments were widespread and only £125 was involved in the expenses, it seemed it was payback time for a number of people he had crossed. Norris was banned from football for life in 1929 and died in 1934.

Onwards and upwards, 1903–08

Entry into the First Division of the Southern League was the breakthrough on the playing side. Up until World War One, the Football League comprised just two divisions and so the Southern League was the Edwardian equivalent to the Third Division. The fact that Fulham's first opponents in September 1903 were Tottenham Hotspur, FA Cup winners two years earlier, shows that there had been a step change in the level of competition.

The visit of Tottenham attracted a crowd of 14,000, who saw 11 players, all new to Fulham and wearing the new white shirts, battle out a goalless draw. It was an important enough occasion to justify

Fulham FC in the Southern League, 1903–04.

the presence of a newsreel camera from Ruffle's Imperial Bioscope. Tommy Meade and William Porter were the only survivors from the previous season to play in 1903–04, and both were soon to leave the club.

Some big names were attracted to the Cottage, the biggest of which was goalkeeper Jack Fryer. A veteran of 173 First Division Football League games and three FA Cup Finals with Derby, he moved south after the 6–0 drubbing by Bury in the Final in April 1903. He was to become Fulham captain and an influential figure at the club for a number of years.

Other important acquisitions were Scottish wing-half Billy Goldie, a League champion with Liverpool, winger Albert Soar from Derby and inside-forward Harry Fletcher from Grimsby. Finishing 11th with 30 points from 34 games, and reaching the first round proper (then the last 32) of the FA Cup for the first time was a pretty good effort for the club's debut season. However, before 1903–04 was over, the Fulham board had made the signing that was to propel the Cottagers to their first silverware and then on into the Football League.

Harry Bradshaw was a football pioneer, a man who helped define the role of manager. Aged 50 when he joined Fulham, Bradshaw had been secretary, chairman and manager of Burnley (in that order) before taking over Arsenal in 1899. He transformed the ailing Gunners fortunes, making them London's first First Division side. It was something of a coup, therefore, that Fulham could persuade someone of Bradshaw's calibre to drop into non-League football in April 1904. He was not cheap, but John Dean and his fellow directors got a pretty good return on their outlay.

In Bradshaw's first season, his team jumped to sixth place in the Southern League and, remarkably, reached the last eight of the FA Cup. Luton, Manchester United, Reading (a tie which attracted the first 30,000 crowd to the Cottage) and Forest were all beaten before Fulham succumbed (they were actually thrashed 5–0) to eventual winners Aston Villa. As if this was not enough for one season, Craven Cottage was effectively rebuilt during the 1905 close season.

The new ground was unveiled in September 1905, a tame 0–0 draw against Portsmouth. This was a low-key start to a season that ended with Fulham as Southern League champions. They romped to the title, five points (only two for a win in those days) clear of Southampton, winning 19 and losing only three of the 34 matches. Bradshaw's team was built around a miserly defence, which conceded just 15 goals in the season. The title success was repeated the following season, but less emphatically. The winning margin was only two points, but the style was more adventurous, with more goals scored and conceded. Beating nearest challengers Portsmouth 2–0 in February (another 30,000 crowd) virtually assured Bradshaw's Fulham of a second Southern League title.

Captained by goalkeeper Fryer, the half-back line of Arthur 'Pat' Collins, Billy Morrison and Billy Goldie, an Englishman and two Scots, was the backbone of the team for four seasons. The three offered a mixture of grace and subtlety (Collins), gritty determination (Goldie) and inspired leadership and organisation skills (Morrison). Behind them were full-backs Harry Ross, Harry Thorpe and, in the second Championship season, Ted 'Taffa' Charlton. In Edwardian times, most teams played with two wingers, and Fulham had the ball-playing Fred Threlfall on the left and Soar or the much-travelled Bert Kingaby on the right. First Willie Wardrope, once of Newcastle, and then the university-educated Bobby Hamilton, a Scottish international from Glasgow Rangers, were the leading scorers.

All the players had been signed by Bradshaw, and most had previously been with Football League clubs. This showed not only the pedigree of the team but also that Fulham was a big enough and ambitious enough club, and Bradshaw a persuasive enough manager, to get players with top-class experience to sign. The local public responded to what was on offer at the Cottage. There were few crowds below 10,000 and one or two above 20,000.

An impressive debut: the 1907–08 season

It began very inauspiciously. At 5.00pm on a Tuesday evening in September 1907, Fulham kicked-off in the Second Division against Hull City. The visitors scored the only goal after five minutes and Bradshaw's revamped side started their League career with a defeat. But it soon got better. Derby were beaten 1–0 at the Baseball Ground four days later, Walter Freeman scoring the club's first League goal. A week later came the first home win, 6–1 against Lincoln, and in the return at Sincil Bank the next month Bob Dalrymple scored the first hat-trick in a 4–2 win. The Cottagers did not take long to find their feet.

But it was in the FA Cup that they made their mark nationally. Luton were beaten 8–3 in the first round, still the club's record Cup score, and Norwich were disposed of in round two, both at the Cottage. Then came a trip to First Division title-chasers Manchester City in round three. At the old Hyde Road ground, Fulham held on for a 1–1 draw in a match played in pouring rain and a howling wind. The replay, played in midweek, drew a record 38,000 crowd who saw Fulham over-run their top-flight opponents 3–1.

The prize was a quarter-final against League leaders (and eventual champions) Manchester United, whose star-studded side included the legendary Billy Meredith, the famous Duckworth-Roberts-Bell half-back line and the free-scoring Sandy Turnbull upfront. Another record crowd (41,000), supplemented with local dignitaries and politicians, saw Fulham's best pre-World War One performance. With two goals from Fred Harrison, they deservedly beat United 2–1 to reach the semi-final for the first time.

It proved a step too far. Against Newcastle (the outstanding side of the Edwardian era) at Anfield, Fulham crumbled. An injury in the first few minutes to goalkeeper Leslie Skene (he was kicked by Magpies centre-forward Appleyard) partly contributed to the 6–0 drubbing, still the record semi-final winning/losing margin. Disappointing as the outcome was, reaching the last four was a creditable performance, and it sparked a promotion push in the League.

An 11-match unbeaten run at the turn of the year lifted the Cottagers into the top five, but they faltered in April, losing three games. In the end, they had to settle for fourth place, three points short of promotion. However, in both competitions Fulham had achieved more than was predicted in the summer of 1907, and it was exactly 50 years (1957–58) before they were to do as well in League and Cup in the same season again. And then, just as in 1907–08, they were to miss out in both competitions.

With Fulham's first-class credentials beyond doubt, Norris's wheeling and dealing got the club elected to the Football League at the expense of Burton United in May 1907. The 28 votes he garnered were enough to overcome the objections of Chelsea to make Fulham London's fourth Football League club (after Arsenal, Chelsea and Clapton Orient). And so, with a top-class ground, a sound financial structure, a solid support base, an outstanding manager and a large and experienced squad, the club looked forward confidently to the arrival of League football at SW6.

In pursuing success on two fronts, manager Bradshaw was not afraid to chop and change the side, and he dabbled constantly in the transfer market. In 44 League and Cup matches that season he used 28 players, 17 of whom were new to the club. The Collins–Morrison–Goldie engine was still there, as were Ross and Threlfall, but there were several important additions. An injury to Fryer led to the signing of goalkeeper Leslie Skene, a Scottish international and practising doctor who, with full-back, Archie Lindsay from Reading, completed the defence. A new strikeforce of Bob Dalrymple (from Portsmouth) and Fred Harrison (from Southampton) came together and went on to score 98 goals in 240 games in their four seasons together. Dally was to be the first Fulham player to score 50 League and Cup goals.

Bill Appleyard and Jimmy Howie on the warpath for Newcastle in the 1908 FA Cup semi-final.

A period of consolidation

It must have been a huge disappointment to the supporters that the club seemed happier to consolidate their position over the next few years rather than use the promising introduction to the League as a springboard for reaching the top flight. In fact, they went down before they went up, and in 1908 First Division football was still 40 years and two world wars away. Perhaps Norris's waning interest was a factor.

Whether Bradshaw sensed this lack of ambition is not known. In 1909, however, when his five-year contract expired and another was on offer, he chose instead to leave and become secretary of the Southern League. He was, without doubt, an outstanding manager and had proved it at two clubs. His successor, Phil Kelso, was also a former Arsenal manager, who, like Bradshaw, had never been a professional player but had a wealth of experience on the administrative side of football. Kelso was to become Fulham's longest-serving manager, steering the club through the turbulence of World War One and maintaining the Second Division status. But honours were few and far between, and his tenure ended under a rather large cloud.

In the 11 seasons he was in charge, Kelso's Fulham never finished higher than sixth, dropped to 20th in his last year, but were usually to be found hovering in mid table. Consistent at Craven Cottage (only 44 of the 219 home League games in this period were lost), the away form (just 48 victories, a ratio of one win every five games) meant they were never serious promotion contenders. In the FA Cup, a run to the last eight in 1912 was as good as it got. In five of the 11 seasons, Kelso's Fulham fell at the first hurdle and in three others they only survived until the second tie.

It was not a record to set the pulses racing, yet the supporters stayed faithful. Attendances were consistently above the divisional average and only once (in the unique circumstances of 1914–15) did the average drop below five figures. Gates of around 15,000 were the norm, and in one post-war season (1921–22) the average topped 20,000. If it was not the team's success that drew the crowds, it must have been the individuals on display, and Kelso, like Bradshaw, proved a shrewd operator in the transfer market. The Fulham teams either side of World War One contained a mix of home produced talent, inexpensive signings and a handful of big names, often at the tail end of their careers. It was a formula used by many of Kelso's successors, and it seemed to produce teams that supporters wanted to watch but which were unlikely to lift the club to a higher level.

From the 120 or so players who played for Fulham during the Kelso years were some of the club's most loyal servants, a handful of British football's biggest names (with reputations usually made elsewhere) and the occasional oddity. In that final category were Hassan Hegazi (an amateur and an Egyptian, whose one game in November 1911 made him the club's first foreign player), British heavyweight boxing champion Bombardier Bill Wells (who banged the gong at the start of Rank movies and who played once in a friendly), Arthur Berry (England international, amateur, Oxford graduate and barrister) and the bespectacled Percy Fender, a reserve goalkeeper and Surrey and England cricketer.

The first of the big names to be signed by Kelso was Arthur Brown from Sunderland in 1910, capped by England when he was just 18, who had commanded a world record transfer fee of £1,600 when he moved from Sheffield United to Sunderland just two years earlier. Although only in his mid-20s, his best years were behind him, and he lasted just two years at the Cottage. The mercurial Bobby Templeton, an immensely gifted but wayward international winger, was another Kelso signing whose skills were clearly waning. The George Best of his era, in terms of both ability and personality, Templeton lived for just four years after his two seasons at Fulham ended in 1915.

Rather better value were one other pre-war and two post-war signings. Kelso signed Wattie White from Everton, and, despite losing four seasons to World War One, he went on to make over 200 appearances for Fulham until his retirement in 1923. A skilful ball-playing inside-forward or wing-half, White played in a Cup Final for Bolton and won two Scottish caps at Everton before his move. He was an excellent buy.

As was Danny Shea, one of the outstanding inside-forwards of his generation. When he was transferred from West Ham to Blackburn in 1913, it was for the first-ever £2,000 fee. He was a Championship winner at Ewood and had played twice for England before his move to Fulham in 1920. Although he was then 33, only injuries kept Shea out of the side until his departure in 1923. What he lacked in pace he made up for with guile and control, and he was a big crowd favourite. Andy Ducat was signed from Villa six months later. He was almost two years older than Shea and had won England honours at football and cricket (he was a Surrey batsman) as well as captaining Villa to FA Cup success. Like Shea, he played regularly until 1924, when he was appointed manager.

Of the players who made the breakthrough at Fulham, Arthur Reynolds, Jimmy Torrance, Frank Osborne and Frank Penn stand out in terms of their service to the club. Goalkeeper Reynolds made his debut towards the end of 1909–10 and held his place for a total of 420 games over the next 15 years. A model of consistency and loyalty, he set several club records for fewest goals conceded and most clean sheets, which stood for over 75 years. Torrance's career ran parallel with Reynolds's 357 games, also between 1910 and 1925. Club captain after the war, Torrance was a versatile player who eventually settled in defence.

Kingsley, watched by Shea, (left), Osborne and Penn (right), rises for a cross against Port Vale, 1922.

South African Osborne signed from Bromley in November 1921 and made his debut the same month. He played in only 70 games before his transfer to Spurs in 1924 but became the first Fulham player to be capped by England. When his playing career ended in the 1930s, he became a Fulham director (for which special FA permission was required), then manager and then general manager-secretary until his retirement in 1964. His was a unique Fulham career, superseded in longevity only by his old teammate Frank Penn. Joining in 1915 as a teenager, Penn stayed until he retired in 1965. He was a player up to 1934, making 459 appearances, then a club record and overhauled only twice since, before joining the training staff for the next 31 years.

On the playing side there were few highlights under Kelso before World War One. Fulham beat Chelsea in the first-ever League meeting between the two neighbours (by 1–0 in December 1910), thrashed First Division Liverpool 3–0 in the FA Cup in 1912 and crushed newly-relegated Arsenal 6–1 at the Cottage in November 1913). After signing Shea and Ducat, Fulham seemed to be making a serious push for promotion, when the club became involved in a scandal which it is generally thought led to Kelso's departure in 1924.

The most expensive signing was a relatively unknown centre-forward, £3,000 for Barney Travers from Sunderland in February 1921. He was an immediate hit with the fans and scored 29 goals in 49 games. In March 1922, with the Cottagers in fourth place, they travelled to the North East for a tricky game against South Shields. They lost 1–0, but the real story of the game was an allegation of attempted bribery by a Fulham player, Travers. Within a couple of weeks an inquiry was set up, the evidence was heard and a guilty verdict delivered to the Fulham striker. The sentence was a life ban from football.

These shameful charges and findings rocked Fulham and football, but many at the club believed that Travers was the fall guy. He acted as the messenger because he came from that part of the country, but the hapless player was only doing his manager's bidding. Not surprisingly, the promotion

In the FA Cup against Plymouth, 1922.

challenge petered out and Kelso's final two seasons were played under a cloud. It took a 1–0 victory on the last day of 1923–24, at home to Stockport, to ensure Second Division survival. Kelso left Fulham at the end of that season, aged only 53, and never worked in football again. When he died in February 1935, there was no mention of his passing in the programme, even though he was still living in the area (he was the licensee of the Rising Sun in Fulham Road).

A decade of instability

As successor, the club turned to Andy Ducat, a man of unimpeachable integrity and the first former Fulham player to become manager. But rather than ushering a period of success, Ducat's appointment marked the beginning of a period of instability. After having had just two managers in 20 years, Fulham now saw five managers come and go in the next dozen years before the arrival of Jack Peart brought back some stability to the Cottage. John Dean, back on the board and chairman again, was a hard task master.

A throwback to the Victorian era, Ducat was a genuine sportsman, cultured and articulate and rather out of place in the hurly burly of professional football. In his two seasons as manager, the team struggled in the League, but managed to hang on in Division Two and saved their best performances for the FA Cup. In 1925–26 Fulham got through to the last eight for the fourth time, beating three First Division clubs on the way. The third-round defeat of Dixie Dean's Everton was one of the most famous victories in the club's history and made a hero of teenage goalkeeper Ernie Beecham. Liverpool and Notts County were eliminated in the next rounds before Manchester United beat 10–man Fulham 2–1 at Craven Cottage. Finishing 19th in the League, however, mattered more than Cup heroics to the board, and Ducat became the first Fulham manager to be sacked.

Another former Fulham player, Joe Bradshaw, the son of former manager Harry, took over in 1926. He had cut his managerial teeth at Southend and Swansea, but he was unable to reverse the slide in League form. In 1927–28 the Cottagers were relegated for the first time in their history in what was a very bizarre season. New centre-forward Sid Elliott set a new club scoring record with 26 goals, and only divisional champions Manchester City had a better home record. Fulham lost just twice at the Cottage, scored in every match but one, kept eight clean sheets and in seven others conceded only one goal. It was the away record that cost them their Second Division status. There were two games in the space of seven days that summed up the season: at the end of January Fulham lost 8–4 at Barnsley but a week later beat Wolves 7–0 at the Cottage.

Bradshaw's side lost the first 19 of their League games that season, as well as a Cup tie at Southport. (Since they were also beaten in their final two away matches of the previous season, the losing sequence stretched to 22 games). It was at Notts County, in the 40th game of the season, that Fulham finally recorded an away win, 1–0, and by beating Reading at home the following week by the same score they gave themselves a chance of beating the drop. They had to go to Blackpool on the last day of the season knowing that the winner would stay up and the loser would be relegated. It was all over by half-time. The Cottagers were never in the game, conceding two before the break and two more after, without reply.

Despite relegation, Bradshaw saw out the third year of his contract, but when promotion was not achieved at the first attempt it was not renewed. The club decided to promote chief scout Ned Liddle to the job. He had previous managerial experience (at Southend and Queen's Park Rangers) but could not turn Fulham's fortunes around. In their first three seasons at the lower level, the club were entertaining to watch and scored plenty of goals, but, finishing in fifth, seventh and then ninth positions, were not serious promotion contenders. By Easter 1931 Dean had run out of patience with Liddle and brought in the man who finally gave supporters something to smile about. James McIntyre had taken Southampton to the Third Division South title nine years earlier and was to do the same at Fulham.

Just as managers came and went, so too did the players. In the seven seasons between Kelso's departure and the arrival of McIntyre, 96 different players were used. In only one of the seasons were fewer than 25 players used and just over a third of the 96 made 10 or fewer appearances. Some, however, stayed longer and made significantly larger contributions to Fulham over several seasons.

For much of this period, Ernie Beecham was the first-choice goalkeeper. Fearless and agile, he was immensely popular with the supporters. In November 1928 he paid a high price for his bravery when he suffered a broken neck diving at the feet of an Exeter forward (named Death). Although he came back, he was never the same player again, and the effects of that injury stayed with him for the rest of his life. Among defenders, Bert Barrett and Len Oliver stand head and shoulders above the rest. Between them they played in over 850 first-class games for Fulham between 1924 and 1936 and both were among that rare group who were capped by England while playing in the Third Division. It was Liddle who signed Manchester City's reserve centre-half Syd Gibbons in May 1930, his best piece of transfer business. Nicknamed Carnera after the heavyweight boxer, Gibbons was a tower of strength in the Fulham defence for eight seasons and with Barrett and Oliver formed a half-back line to equal the Collins–Morrison–Goldie partnership of Edwardian times.

The best of the forwards emerged later in the 1920s. Jim Hammond was one of the last players introduced by Bradshaw, in March 1929. Over the next nine years, he became the first Fulham player to score a century of goals and finished with a total of 151 in the League and Cup. Hammond was also a county cricketer for Sussex and, long after he stopped playing (in 1961), became a first-class umpire. Earlier in the 1928–29 season, Johnny Price made his debut and held his place for seven seasons until injury ended his career. A clever ball-playing inside-forward, he was compared to Arsenal's Alex James, and he contributed his fair share of goals (53 in 204 games). Finally, Jack Finch was given his chance during Liddle's final months in 1930, and he was still in the side in 1939, the only Fulham player whose career spanned the entire decade. Primarily a winger, he proved his value to the club by playing in every forward position, making almost 300 appearances.

Success at last

After getting his feet under the table in the closing weeks of 1930–31, McIntyre set about reshaping the side during the close season. Most of what he needed was in place, but he made two important signings. He went back to his previous club Coventry for right-winger Billy Richards. His runs and crosses created the chances for the two front men, and he became Fulham's first Welsh international. From Stockport, he signed centre-forward Frank 'Bonzo' Newton for a very modest fee, who, in his first season, set a new club record of 43 League goals. In all, Newton scored 81 goals in his 88 Fulham appearances, one every 98 minutes, making him the most prolific scorer in the club's history. But transfer deals involving Newton were the breaking as well as the making of McIntyre. The 'unauthorised' sale of the popular striker in September 1933 (and the expensive failure of his successor, Jack Lambert from Arsenal) led to the manager's surprising dismissal a few months later.

The first silverware: the 1931–32 season

After three seasons of deteriorating results, Fulham were starting to look like a natural Third Division South side. But in the programme for the first home game of 1931–32 the directors claimed that 'we approach the campaign with more enthusiastic belief in ourselves. The changes in the executive of the club last April were only made after careful thought and consideration, and we are of the opinion that the policy will be justified.'

New manager James McIntyre certainly believed in himself and looked to Arsenal's Herbert Chapman as his role model. In the summer he sold winger Jimmy Temple to Sunderland and centre-forward Bill Haley to Queen's Park Rangers, bringing in Bill Richards from his old club Coventry and Bonzo Newton from Stockport. Both Newton and Hammond scored twice in the 5–3 win over Coventry on the opening day, and from the start the Cottagers were among the pacesetters.

Newton was on fire all season. He was on the mark 13 times in the first nine games, he scored three hat-tricks in the season and in 11 other matches scored twice. His total of 43 goals (in 39 games) remains the club record. Hammond tried to keep pace with him, and his 31 goals also beat the previous record. In only four of the 42 games did Fulham fail to score, and their biggest wins were against Torquay (10–2) and Thames (8–0). Never out of the top three (in the days when only the champions were promoted), the Cottagers went top in February and stayed there. The title was clinched in the penultimate match, a 3–2 home win over Bristol Rovers, and the trophy was presented to John Dean after the last game, a 3–1 victory over Exeter at the Cottage. The margin over second-placed Reading was two points.

The nucleus of the side was unchanged throughout. Richards, Hammond, Newton, Price and Finch were the regular forwards, with skipper Oliver, Gibbons and Barrett behind them. Jake Iceton replaced Beecham after nine games, and the only uncertainty was with the full-back berths. Of the six players tried, Sonny Gibbon and Joe Birch (bought in October from Bournemouth) were the most used.

McIntyre's side won more and lost fewer games than any team in the Division, scoring more goals in the process. No Fulham team since has scored more in a season (111), and only Kevin Keegan's 1999 Second Division winners and Jean Tigana's team in 2001 lost fewer. The title success had been a long time coming, but was well worth the wait.

The success was as convincing as it was unexpected. From mid-table in 1931, the Cottagers claimed the Championship 12 months later with relatively few changes, and they did so in style. But there was more to come. The following season they put in a strong challenge for a second promotion and top-flight football, falling only at the final hurdle. As the season unfolded, and Fulham were among the pacesetters, McIntyre again dipped into the transfer market. He first of all signed a goalkeeper, Alf Tootill from Wolves. Nicknamed the Birdcatcher, he was a virtual ever present for the next five seasons. Days after Fulham drew 2–2 at The Dell in February, chairman Dean personally splashed out £6,500 on Saints' full-back Mike Keeping and left-winger John Arnold. This double transfer was as good a piece of transfer business as Fulham did in the inter-war period.

Although nearing the veteran stage when he was signed, Keeping was a regular until 1939 and took over as club captain. A reliable defender, renowned for his sportsmanship, he added a great stability to the back four and filled a problem position for McIntyre. Within weeks of signing, Arnold was capped by England to play against Scotland at Hampden, an international football honour to add to his Test appearance against New Zealand at Lords in 1931. He played for Hampshire in the summer and, like Hammond, was appointed a first-class umpire in the 1960s. As a footballer for Fulham, he was one of the club's most consistent performers and scored 62 goals in his 213 outings. Cricket always seemed to be his first love (when the two seasons overlapped, Hampshire took priority), and Arnold probably could have played at a higher level had he put football first.

A run of one defeat in 15 games in the spring of 1933 took Fulham to the edge of the promotion places, but after drawing 0–0 at White Hart Lane and losing both the last two games 1–0, at home to Grimsby and away at Forest, they had to settle for third place at a time when only two clubs were promoted. (Curiously, this pattern of events was repeated exactly 50 years later under Malcolm Macdonald. Fulham won promotion from the Third Division, narrowly missed out on a second promotion 12 months later, and then Macdonald, just like McIntyre, did not survive the following season.)

After two good seasons, McInytre's stock was sky high, but at the start of 1933–34 the crowd's favourite Bonzo Newton was suddenly sold to Reading for only £650. The manager said the player wanted to move because of his wife's health, and he spent £2,500 on Arsenal's veteran Jack Lambert as a replacement. It was a bad piece of business. Lambert managed only three goals in 18 games, and, with the club going nowhere in mid table, Dean used the Newton transfer as the reason for sacking McIntyre in February 1934.

His next appointment was genuinely inspired and anticipated, by 60 years or so, a practice that was to become common among the top Premiership clubs. Jimmy Hogan had been a journeyman player before World War One, and counted Fulham among his many clubs. His last appearance was in the 1908 semi-final thrashing by Newcastle. But it was as a coach that he had made his name, and in Europe. Hogan was very influential in the development of football in Holland, Hungary and Austria in particular, countries which had emerged as a force on the international scene in the 1920s. He returned to Fulham for his first managerial job in England.

With the title manager-coach, Hogan was far removed from his largely office-bound, administrative predecessors. He got involved with diets, introduced imaginative training routines and tried new tactical formations, all previously unheard of in English football generally, not just at Craven Cottage. There was some resistance from the players and the early results were mixed, despite Newton's return to Fulham from Reading. When Hogan went into hospital with appendicitis just before Christmas, Dean and his colleagues took the opportunity to end Hogan's reign, the shortest managerial term in the club's history. It was not an episode that reflected well on Fulham or John Dean personally, but Hogan went on to show his quality as a coach and manager elsewhere.

The old order restored

By the start of the 1935–36 season the chairman had in place the type of manager with whom he felt comfortable and who was to outlast him in the job. Jack Peart, a much-travelled player (nine League clubs) and experienced manager (Rochdale and Bradford City) of the old school (he preferred a three-piece worsted suit to a track suit) restored the stability that had been missing since Kelso's departure a decade earlier. It was not an orderly transition. Behind the scenes, there was friction between Peart and assistant manager Joe Edelston, a qualified coach and a disciple of Hogan and his innovative methods. It came to a head when a series of supporters' demonstrations following a poor run of

Fulham training by the seaside, 1936.

The Fulham players off duty, 1936.

results in the autumn of 1937 led to Edelston's abrupt departure. The 'ancien regime' was back in control.

Sadly, with stability came predictability. In Peart's five full League seasons (either side of seven wartime seasons) his teams never finished higher than seventh or lower than 15th, and a Cup run lasting longer than 180 minutes was the exception. Fulham were back where they were in the Kelso years, spending most of the time in the comfort of mid-table.

The major exception was in his first full season. Fulham got to the last four of the FA Cup in 1935–36 for the second time, only to be beaten by another Second Division club, Sheffield United, a club they beat twice in the League that season. The campaign came to life in the fifth round. The Cottagers squeezed past Brighton in round three and then walloped Blackpool 5–2, with centre-forward Eddie Perry scoring four times. Both victories were at the Cottage.

Next was a short journey to Stamford Bridge. The original game was postponed, and, although it was rearranged (in those pre-floodlight days) for the following Wednesday afternoon, over 52,000 still managed to attend. A bad-tempered game, in which Chelsea's Gibson was sent off, finished goalless. The replay kicked off at 3pm the next Monday, and the crowd was close to 31,000. Fulham raised their game against their First Division neighbours and stormed into a 3–0 lead, with Trevor Smith, Hammond and Arnold on the mark. Barraclough scored twice for the visitors in the last nine minutes to set up a frantic climax, but the Cottagers held on. The quarter-final was played just five days later, and Derby, second in the First Division, were the visitors to the Cottage. This was Fulham's best performance of the season. With centre-half Gibbons in inspired form, Arnold, Barrett and Smith all scored in the second half, without a Derby reply, to the delight of the 37,151 crowd.

The semi-final was anti-climatic, and a wonderful chance of reaching Wembley was squandered. The Cottagers were drawn against another Second Division side, Sheffield United, and had no injury worries for the trip to Molineux. After Arnold set up a relatively easy chance for Perry on five minutes, which the Welshman squandered, the Blades then took the initiative. They scored a goal in each half before Arnold got a consolation with five minutes remaining. Ironically, five days later, Fulham went to Bramall Lane for a Second Division match and won 1–0, to complete a League double over United.

Despite the lack of success, the closing years of the 1930s were not without interest. There were, for example, some remarkable attendances. The Cottagers made an impressive start to the last interwar season and in October 1938 faced Millwall at home. Perhaps because it was a meeting of two of the top three teams in the Division, or perhaps because it was the first home game after Prime Minister Neville Chamberlain's notorious Munich deal, there was a record crowd of 49,335 at the Cottage, an attendance never to be exceeded. Fulham won 2–1. A few weeks later, they travelled to St James' Park, where they lost 2–1 to Newcastle in front of 64,166, the largest attendance for a League match involving Fulham up to that time. Then again, a couple of months later, Stamford Bridge hosted 69,987 for a fourth-round FA Cup meeting of the West London neighbours, which Chelsea won 3–0. This was the highest attendance for any Fulham game up to that point. Ironically, Fulham played Swansea at home in the Second Division 48 hours later. The 3,155 who turned up for this 2.45pm Monday afternoon kick-off was the lowest recorded Cottage gate of the inter-war period.

Among the players, age and injury were catching up with stalwarts like Oliver, Barrett, Gibbons and Hammond. A new generation was emerging, like Ernest Hiles, Vivian Woodward, Dennis Higgins, Jimmy Tompkins and Jimmy Evans, promising players whose careers (and in two cases their lives) were cut short by the war. Peart, however, made a signing in October 1936, for a mere £300, who not only had a huge impact before the war, but was to be the star of a Championship-winning side 12

Bert Worsley fires in a shot against Chesterfield in Septmeber 1938.

years later at the age of 35.

Ronnie Rooke was a one-man goalscoring machine who was languishing in Crystal Palace reserves before Peart snapped him up. He went straight into the first team in October 1936 and scored a hat-trick on his debut, a 5–0 win over West Ham. He scored three more hat-tricks in that first season and finished top scorer with 19 goals in 22 games. He headed the scoring lists in both of the two final inter-war seasons, and in 1946–47, although he played in only 18 games before he was sold, his 13 goals was still the highest total. Even more remarkable was his haul of 212 goals in 199 wartime games. Rooke's best scoring performance, all six goals in a 6–0 win, was in a third-round Cup tie at the Cottage in January 1939, which, not surprisingly, is still a club record.

In December 1946, about halfway through the first post-war season, Peart sold Rooke to Arsenal for a nominal sum and two players. Making his First Division debut at an age most players think about retiring, he revitalised the relegation-threatened Gunners with 21 goals in 24 games. Even more remarkably, the following season he headed the Division One scoring lists, his 33 goals instrumental in Arsenal's unlikely Championship win. Fulham, meanwhile, struggled for firepower without Rooke, and not until December 1948, after Peart's death, was there a real replacement.

Perhaps Peart's major contribution was holding the club together during the seven seasons of World War Two. There were makeshift League and Cup competitions, intended as much to boost the morale of the locals as produce high-quality football. The Cottagers played a full part without winning anything, but the supporters who braved the air-raid warnings saw a virtual Who's Who of British football in Fulham colours, albeit only as guests playing on a temporary basis. Wartime football also offered the chance for a number of youngsters (Jim Taylor, Arthur Stevens and Len Quested in particular) who were to become the backbone of the post-war side to develop. Sadly they also lost valuable years, as did the likes of Joe Bacuzzi, Harry Freeman and Ernie Shepherd, who had made the breakthrough before the war but then had to put their careers on hold for seven years.

In 1945–46 the FA Cup was resumed, a year ahead of the Football League, and the third round produced a unique score in the history of the competition. Drawn against Charlton, Fulham beat the Addicks 2–1 at Craven Cottage, yet the south London side still went on to Wembley (and lost 4–1 to Derby). This was because for the only time in the history of the FA Cup, all ties from the first to the sixth rounds were played on a home and away basis. At the Valley two days earlier, Charlton had won 3–1, and so went through 4–3 on aggregate. They are the only side ever to have lost a Cup match and still got through to the Final.

The modern era begins

A 7–2 defeat at Bury in August 1946 got the post-war era underway. Fulham went into the campaign with the same manager as in 1939, a new chairman (John Dean had died in 1944 and was replaced by his son) and a largely rebuilt squad. Of the 29 players used in 1946–47, just three (Bacuzzi, Rooke and Woodward) were regulars before the war and four others were on the books (Freeman, Taylor, Cranfield and Shepherd) in 1939. Peart had virtually to build a new team, and he made some shrewd signings. Goalkeeper Ted Hinton (who was capped by Northern Ireland) and centre-half Jack Watson (who left the Cottage to coach at Real Madrid) anchored the defence, but the pick of the bunch was Pat Beasley. A vastly experienced (Arsenal and Huddersfield in the 1930s) England international, the 32-year-old was an astute and inspiring captain who got a new lease of life when he dropped back from inside-forward to wing-half.

There were signs in 1947–48 that Peart's policies were starting to pay off. Boosted by the signing of striker Bob Thomas from Plymouth for a sizeable fee of £4,000 (he scored 23 goals in his first season), Fulham unusually won as many games away from the Cottage as at home. Even more impressive was

The Fulham and Brentford teams walk out on the opening day of the 1947 season.

a run to the last eight of the FA Cup, which included a superb 1–0 win at Everton in round five in front of 71,587, the biggest attendance at a club ground for a game involving Fulham until 2006. In the sixth round, however, Stanley Matthews and First Division Blackpool were 2–0 winners at the Cottage.

Just 12 months later, the promise was fulfilled but, unfortunately, Peart was not there to see it. Just three games into the season he died, after a brief illness, a month short of his 60th birthday. Very much a safety-first manager, he had restored some equilibrium to the Cottage after a turbulent decade, and the club was undoubtedly stronger at the end of his term than at the start. It is terribly sad that he died on the brink of his greatest achievement in football.

Reaching the top: the 1948–49 season

Few people would have marked out Fulham as likely Second Division champions in August 1948. Peart's major summer signing was Jack McDonald, an outside-left from Bournemouth, for the sizeable sum of £12,000. An encouraging start (two wins and two draws in the first four games) naturally lost momentum when the manager died suddenly at the beginning of September. A period of uncertainty followed, during which only one of six games was won. When Frank Osborne took over, the Cottagers were in 17th place.

His first game in charge was a 5–0 home win over Queen's Park Rangers, with Arthur Stevens contributing a hat-trick. As important was the introduction of Doug Flack in goal and Beddy Jezzard's home debut. All the pieces were nearly in place. The missing link appeared the following week when West Brom inflicted Fulham's only home defeat of the season. The star of the Baggies 2–1 win was reserve centre-forward Arthur Rowley, who was only playing because Dave Walsh was on international duty. Although Fulham won five and drew two of the next seven games, Osborne felt Thomas needed more support up front. In December he agreed an exchange deal with Albion's Jack Smith, Rowley for Ernie Shepherd.

Rowley was Rooke's real successor, and his impact was similar to Bonzo Newton's 17 years earlier. In the second half of the season, Fulham were unstoppable. The team won 15 and lost only four of the 22 games Rowley played, and he scored 19 goals. With Thomas adding a further 23 goals in his 40 appearances, it was an irresistible strike force.

The Cottagers hit their stride early in the New Year, crushing Bury 7–2 and Plymouth 6–1 in successive weeks. By April it was a three-horse race for two places, with Fulham, West Brom and Southampton all in contention. But five wins on the trot put the Cottagers in pole position. Promotion was virtually clinched with a game to spare after a 1–1 draw with Spurs at White Hart Lane. The title followed a week later. Over 41,000 packed into the Cottage to see Rowley score once in each half to beat West Ham 2–0 and set off great scenes of celebration.

Once Rowley was signed, the team was very settled. In front of goalkeeper Flack, full-backs Bacuzzi and Freeman, and the half-back line of Quested, Taylor and skipper Beasley made 198 out of a possible 210 appearances. Stevens on the right wing was ever present, while McDonald on the left missed only one game. They carved out a hatful of chances for the inside-forward trio of Thomas, Rowley and Jezzard.

In terms of wins, goals and points, 1948–49 was not a record-breaking season. Rather it was a triumph for teamwork and consistency, for a side which started slowly but once it hit its stride kept going. In the end, the title was as merited as it seemed unlikely at the start of the season.

Not surprisingly, form dipped when Peart died. After the usual speculation and uncertainty about a new manager, Frank Osborne was persuaded to leave the boardroom for the manager's office, and a season which started in tragedy ended in triumph. Osborne took the title of secretary-manager and was assisted with team affairs by former player Eddie Perry. Frank Penn continued as trainer. The new manager claimed, when the Second Division title had been won in May 1949, that it was Jack Peart's team, but this underestimates his contribution. In his first couple of months he made three significant changes, bringing in Doug Flack in goal and Beddy Jezzard at inside-forward, but his masterstroke was the signing of West Brom's reserve centre-forward, (George) Arthur Rowley. In the second half of the season, the Cottagers were unstoppable, with Thomas (23 goals in 40 games) and Rowley (19 goals in 22 games) spearheading the successful assault on the title. In the club's 70th year, it reached the highest level of English football.

The first First Division years

Having reached the top flight for the first time in their history, the Cottagers made a few changes. There was a new programme, a facelift for the ground and a new team manager. Bill Dodgin arrived in the close season from promotion rivals Southampton. Osborne became the club secretary. There were three new additions to the squad: goalkeeper Hugh Kelly, defender Robin Lawler and winger Johnny Campbell, all signed from the bankrupt Belfast Celtic. But Kelly was the only one to get into the first team reckoning in 1949–50. The new manager kept faith with the side that had got the Cottagers into the top flight, and, on the whole, it was a creditable first year. A dreadful run of seven defeats and a draw in the last month saw them drop down to 17th from mid-table, where they spent most of the season, but the supporters seemed to enjoy it. The club's average attendance rose to a new high of 33,030, a figure that will never be beaten at Craven Cottage.

There was some serious spending in the summer of 1950. The board splashed out a new club record fee of £20,000 on Birmingham's Irish international inside-forward Bobby Brennan. The Lowe brothers, Eddie (an English international) and Reg, came from Aston Villa, and two Scottish internationals were signed, goalkeeper Ian Black from Southampton and the experienced Archie Macaulay from Arsenal, a replacement at wing-half and as captain for the departed Beasley.

No one could doubt the board's ambition or desire to stay in Division One. On paper it was as good a squad as any in the club's history, but on the pitch it failed to gel. Goalscoring was the problem, and only Thomas reached double figures (just) in 1949–50. Rowley under-performed at the highest level and moved on to Leicester in July 1950 (and on his way to a Football League scoring record), while Jezzard did not come into his own until Fulham were back in Division Two. Thomas (again) and Stevens got into double figures in 1950–51, but only two other clubs scored fewer than Fulham's 52 goals. Despite the spending, they slipped a place, to 18th.

Paradoxically, the Cottagers had their best First Division scoring season in 1951–52 but finished bottom of the pile. Relegation looked likely after they lost their opening four games. They were in the bottom two at the end of October and were never out of the drop zone. It was the home form that let them down and the five home victories remain the lowest of any Fulham team before or since. Behind the scenes, several players were becoming unsettled, and McDonald and Brennan both asked for transfers. Dodgin got the fans on his back when he allowed the popular Len Quested to move to

Bob Thomas attacks the Liverpool goal, 1949.

Huddersfield in the autumn, and he was never really forgiven. The manager's son, Bill junior, became the target for the supporters' frustration.

But the statistics do not tell the whole story. In January Fulham recorded their best win in the three First Division seasons, a 6–0 victory over Middlesbrough, with Jeff Taylor scoring the only hat-trick in these three years. Of the 23 defeats, 16 were by the odd goal, and if four had been draws the

Cottagers would have survived. Injuries, moreover, disrupted the team. Only Black, Jim Taylor, Eddie Lowe and Stevens played in more than 30 of the 42 games, and Dodgin was able to field the same team in successive games just four times. He tried to strengthen the side. Charlie Mitten and Jimmy Hill were good signings, who paid off in subsequent seasons but arrived too late to save the club's place in the First Division.

A return to the goal standard

Any hope of a quick return to the big time soon evaporated. In the opening weeks of 1952–53, the Cottagers found out just how hard Second Division life was going to be when they were beaten twice by Leicester, conceding six goals on both occasions. Ironically, former Fulham striker Rowley scored seven of the 12 goals. But it was the start of a remarkable period in the club's history, one fondly remembered by older supporters, which helped to define the modern character of the club. It took seven seasons to reclaim a place among the elite, but they were eventful, exciting years.

In the first five of the seasons, between 1952 and 1957, Fulham scored 428 goals in 210 League games, an average of more than two a game. Of the total, two thirds were scored at the Cottage (2.75 per game). The lowest total for any season was 76, while in 1953–54, Fulham's 98-goal tally was the highest in the whole of the Football League. Including the 390 goals conceded in these years means that those watching Fulham saw on average a goal every 23 minutes, a scoring rate unimaginable in the more defensively-minded modern game.

For all the attacking intent, however, eighth was the highest position the Cottagers could manage, and in 1954–55 they even slipped as low as 14th. The FA Cup was scarcely more rewarding, with progress never stretching beyond the fourth round in any of the five seasons. Yet it was a golden age, which the supporters seemed to enjoy. Gates did dip after relegation but hovered around the 20,000 in the mid-50s, well above the divisional average.

Manager Dodgin was given one full season to regain Fulham's top-flight status, and when he failed he paid the price in the autumn of 1953. There was no mention of his departure in the programme, just his name removed from the masthead. But, 40 years later, when he was in his 90s, Dodgin still felt he had been unlucky at the Cottage. A crop of promising youngsters was on the verge of developing into a very good side, and with a little more time he felt he could have succeeded. The board seemed in no rush to replace him. It was not until the early months of 1956 that Dugald Livingstone arrived from Newcastle to take over team affairs. In the two-and-a-half-year interval, Frank Osborne took on the title secretary and general manager, with former players Frank Penn, Taffy O'Callaghan and Joe Bacuzzi having responsibility for training (rather than coaching).

It was the club's hugely-talented inside-forward trio that provided so much of the excitement in those years, and Dodgin knew they had the potential to lift Fulham back in the big time. Bobby Robson, Bedford Jezzard and Johnny Haynes were at the start of wonderful careers, during which collectively they would play in 1,334 first-class games for the Cottagers, score 392 goals and win 78 England caps. All three would also manage Fulham, but with very mixed results. Arthur Stevens on the right wing and the irrepressible Charlie Mitten on the left (the only one of the five to have had League experience at another club) completed what was the club's best-ever forward line and the most talked-about strikeforce of the era.

Although he had been a first-team regular for four seasons, Jezzard only found his shooting boots

Robin Lawler breaks up a Birmingham attack in 1954, with goalkeeper Black stranded.

when Fulham returned to Division Two. He set a new club record of 154 goals (all scored in the League), 123 of which came in the four seasons between 1952 and 1956. His goal ratio in these years (0.76 per match) made him the most prolific Fulham striker other than Newton, most of whose goals were scored in the Third Division. Brave and fearless, Jezzard was an old-fashioned English centre-forward, relying more on pace and strength than subtlety. Robson had made his debut in April 1951 but took until 1952–53 to establish himself. He combined guile with an eye for goal and was ideally suited to a midfield role in the emerging 4–2–4 formation, where he starred for England alongside Haynes. But, as he showed in his second spell at the Cottage between 1962 and 1967, he was equally comfortable playing in the back four, a steadying influence who helped to bring on several younger players.

From the moment he first appeared on the national stage, as a schoolboy international in a match televised from Wembley, it was obvious that Johnny Haynes was a prodigiously gifted player. He matured into one of the finest inside-forwards of his generation, among the best passers of a ball English football has ever produced. Haynes had outstanding ball control, inspirational leadership qualities and remarkable tactical skills. His work ethic and dedication kept him playing at the highest level until well into his 30s, and his entire career was spent at Craven Cottage. His debut was on Boxing Day 1952, and by the time he was substituted against Stockport in January 1970 he had played 658 first-class games for Fulham and scored 158 goals, both new club records. Haynes was England captain between 1960 and 1962 and only the fourth player to win 50 caps, but at club level he never won a single honour or (scandalously) received any recognition from the authorities for his supreme ability, unquestioned loyalty to one club or his contribution to football.

Unfortunately, the defence was as porous as the forwards were prolific. Some of the players were very good: goalkeeper Ian Black, left-back Robin Lawler, left-half Eddie Lowe and the versatile Jimmy Hill were the equals of any in the Second Division. But there was more uncertainty about the other positions and the defence never seemed to function consistently as a unit. The emphasis was always on attack.

The tide starts to turn

After four seasons of entertaining but generally unsuccessful play, the first signs that the Cottagers were on the rise again became apparent in 1957–58. The source of the improvement can be traced back to the appointment of Dugald Livingstone as team manager in February 1956 (the job apparently did not warrant inclusion in the officials box in the matchday programme). A vastly-experienced football man (he had coached Sheffield United when they beat Fulham in the 1936 FA Cup semi-final and Newcastle when they won the Cup in 1955), he rebuilt the side in his two full seasons at the helm but had moved on before his work had paid out a dividend.

And he had to come to terms almost immediately with losing two of his three big guns. The month he took over, Robson was sold to West Brom and then, during the 1956 close season, Jezzard sustained an ankle injury on an FA tour of South Africa that ended his playing career at the age of 28. And a third member of the sparkling forward line, Charlie Mitten, moved on to manage Mansfield. In his first season Livingstone brought in Tosh Chamberlain and Roy Dwight from the reserves and signed forward Roy Bentley from Chelsea and full-back Jim Langley from Brighton.

Although 1956–57 was a classic mid-table season, 11th out of 22 clubs with 42 points from 42 games, it started to come together the next season. With just two defeats in the first 15 games, Fulham were in third place in the table at the end of October and stayed in contention for the rest of the season. But an extended Cup run, which ended in defeat in a semi-final replay, led to fixture congestion and cost the Cottagers promotion. In the 13 days from 19 April to 1 May, they had to play six Second Division fixtures, only one of which was won. In the end, they had to settle for fifth place.

Although he was offered a new contract, Livingstone (he said it was his wife) preferred to move back north (he went to Chesterfield) and Jezzard was promoted from running the youth team to first-team manager. His first acts were to sell Roy Dwight, top scorer in 1957–58, to Nottingham Forest and to buy international winger Graham Leggat from Aberdeen. From the very first game of 1958–59, a 6–1 home win over Stoke, it was clear that Fulham had promotion in their sights. The first six games were won, and they were unbeaten until the 13th match. Never out of the top two, it was a race between the Cottagers and Sheffield Wednesday for the title, which the Owls eventually claimed by two points.

The campaign was a personal triumph for skipper Haynes. Not only was he at his imperious best in midfield, but he showed the strikers the way to goal. He topped the lists with 26 goals, a personal best, which included four hat-tricks. He also scored three for England in October 1958, in a 5–0 win over Russia at Wembley. Leggat settled in very quickly. He set a new club record by scoring in the first six games of the season and finished with a total of 21 goals. The two Easter fixtures against Wednesday were vital in the promotion race. On Good Friday morning a hat-trick of headers by Jimmy Hill in the last 15 minutes, his first goals of the season, clinched an impressive 6–2 win. In the return on Easter Monday two goals from Cook earned a point, and a return to the top flight looked assured. It became a mathematical certainty a fortnight later when Barnsley were beaten 4–2 at Oakwell.

A Memorable Failure: The 1957–58 Season

There were few clues in August 1957 that Fulham were on the brink of a new era. The previous season had ended in mid-table and there were no major close-season signings. But the Cottagers got off to their customary bright start, and then, unusually, kept going. Dwight scored 13 times in the 10–match unbeaten start, but although the side stayed in the top three or four in the table Livingstone made three significant changes. In the space of a few weeks in November, George Cohen took over at right-back from the injured Lawler, Tony Macedo replaced Black in goal and Roy Bentley dropped back into defence. The changes worked, and lasted.

December was a good month and five wins and a draw put Fulham in top spot at the turn of the year. But then the Cup started, and it was a thrilling run. After brushing non-League Yeovil aside in round three, it took two games to get past fellow Second Division promotion challengers Charlton. The fifth-round tie at Upton Park was a thriller, with the lead twice changing hands before Haynes got the winner 15 minutes from time. Another Second Division side, Bristol Rovers, fell 3–1 in the quarter-finals in front of 42,000 at the Cottage.

Manchester United take the lead in the FA cup semi-final replay in 1958.

The semi-final at Villa Park, Fulham's third, paired the Cottagers with Manchester United, recently devastated by the Munich air crash. It was a classic encounter which Fulham just about shaded. Charlton gave United an early lead, but goals by Stevens and Hill (he had scored in every round) put the Cottagers 2–1 up but Charlton equalised just before the break. In the second half, the injured Langley was forced to play on the wing, and Haynes dropped back to wing-half. He and Macedo were magnificent and a draw was the least Fulham deserved. The replay at Highbury the following Wednesday was a nightmare. The Cottagers lost 5–3, but at 4–3 had what looked to be a perfectly good goal disallowed.

League form suffered, not least because of the resulting pile up in fixtures. Livingstone signed Watford centre-forward Maurice Cook in February to strengthen the promotion push (he was already Cup tied) and it looked good until the final weeks. In February, Grimsby were memorably beaten 6–0, and all five forwards were on the score sheet before half-time.

It started to go wrong with a home game against Bristol. Without Langley and Haynes (both on England duty at Hampden), Fulham were 4–0 down at half-time, and although they got back to 4–3 they dropped two valuable points. This was the first of six League games in 13 days, only one of which was won (the last game when promotion had been decided). A midweek draw against Blackburn was crucial. Without four regulars, Fulham led 1–0 until the dying moments when Macedo appeared to be fouled as Rovers scored. The referee overruled the linesman, gave the goal and another point was lost. In the end, the Cottagers finished in fifth place, four points adrift of Blackburn in second. They had won nothing but it had been a superb effort.

Jezzard had done remarkably well in his first season as manager. His team virtually picked itself, and nine players appeared in at least 30 of the games. Of the 11 that beat Stoke on the opening day, 10 played in the defeat of Rotherham in the final game. The only change was to switch Bentley to centre-half, where he excelled, and to bring in the teenage Alan Mullery at right-half, who was an instant success. The side was an effective blend of the young (Macedo, Cohen and Mullery), the experienced (Bentley, Lowe and Hill) and the stars at their peak (Haynes, Leggat and Langley). It was a mix that would serve them well in the First Division.

The halcyon years

For many older supporters, the nine First Division seasons from 1959 to 1968 were the club's high-water mark. Compared with the modern Premiership era, the 1960s were a simpler, more democratic time, when virtually every club in the Division started the season believing they could win something. All that was needed was good management, good players (many of whom were likely to be home grown) and good luck, not a shed load of money and a dressing room that reflected the General Assembly of the United Nations.

The Cottagers held on in the top flight for the best part of decade, but it was often a close-run thing. They failed to build on a very promising first season back and thereafter were too closely involved in scraps at the wrong end of the table. A couple of these were every bit as thrilling and exhilarating as a push for the title, but the lessons of an escape from relegation were not learned the following year. In three of the seven seasons between 1960 and 1967, Fulham finished 20th out of 22 clubs (when only two were relegated) and never higher than 15th. By 1967–68 their luck ran out, and when they fell they kept falling for two seasons.

Cook scores for Fulham against Preston North End, 1960.

During these years, the press often referred to Fulham as a 'Cinderella' club, and the notion that life at the Cottage was a bit of a pantomime was enhanced by the fact there was now a comedian as chairman. When Charles Dean died in December 1958, long-time director Tommy Trinder succeeded him, and his high public profile ensured the club got plenty of free publicity. But he was a hopeless businessman in an era when the maximum wage was lifted and six-figure transfer fees became the norm. The ground (with standing terraces around three sides) was a throwback to an earlier era, and the last in the top flight to have floodlights installed, in 1962. Even these were paid for by the Supporters' Club.

Rather than recognise the way football was changing and adapt to the new order, Trinder and his board retreated to their traditional ways. By the time the club was relegated in 1968, Fulham's record transfer fee was still only £35,000 (for Allan Clarke) when the record stood at £125,000. The Cottagers had to rely on a long supply line of talented youngsters to fill any gaps, and a number of very promising players emerged. But they had to grow up very quickly in the pressure-cooker atmosphere of the First Division, and not all of them fulfilled their promise. And the board was prepared to sell the club's best players if the price was right. Trinder notoriously negotiated the sale of Alan Mullery in March 1964, behind the manager's back. This was not the way ambitious clubs pushing for the top prizes behaved.

To compound these errors, Trinder and his colleagues made two other major misjudgements, which were to cost Fulham dear in the long term. Firstly, in an attempt to put the club on a more professional footing, Vic Buckingham was appointed manager early in 1965. He has a very strong claim (although there are several other challengers) to being the worst manager in Fulham's history. He came with impressive managerial credentials, from his time at West Brom in particular. But, apart from a few guest appearances as a player during the war, he had no previous experience of Fulham and, when he arrived, he tried to change everything very quickly. In so doing, he dispensed with a number of the people who helped shape its character, on and off the field, and got rid of players who still had something to offer. Results might have justified his actions, but Fulham's record deteriorated during Buckingham's three years, and it took a lot longer to recover from his lamentable legacy.

And then, at entirely the wrong time, the board took the decision to build a stand along the riverside of the ground. First mooted in the 1930s but rejected on the grounds of cost (£11,197), the extra seating capacity was undoubtedly needed. But to take on such an expensive project at a time when the club was sliding and attendances falling showed a remarkable lack of financial awareness. Since the club was in no position to fund the building work from its own resources, it incurred a substantial debt that had massive implications. Before the issue was finally resolved in 1997, ownership of Fulham changed hands several times and the team plummeted to within touching distance of Conference football. The turbulence of the quarter of a century, up to the arrival of Mohamed Al Fayed, can be traced back to the building of the stand.

A decade of two halves

All of this was some way off when Fulham resumed their life among the great and the good in August 1959. Although they got a 4–0 drubbing at Blackburn, they soon found their First Division feet. Some spirited performances and impressive results (including five straight wins in October) took them into the top six. For one brief moment in December, they might even have topped the table, but a home draw against Spurs, when the Cottagers were controversially denied a penalty, meant fifth was as high as they got. They slipped a little in the second half of the season and had to settle for 10th place, which was, nevertheless, a hugely creditable performance for the new boys. The second season was tougher, largely because of a mid-season dip in form, but again relegation was never a threat.

All this was achieved with virtually the same team that had won promotion. Alf Stokes was signed from Spurs but never really established himself, and later on, in March 1961, Bill Dodgin (junior) returned from Arsenal. Fulham were lucky that Haynes, by now the England captain, was at his most majestic, Leggat, switched from the wing to centre-forward, was a consistent goalscorer, Langley and Lowe were models of consistency, and in Macedo, Cohen and Mullery the club had three of the most coveted young defenders in the country. The team always was, however, two or three players short of being a really good Division One side, and as long as the board maintained its very frugal stance on transfers the focus of attention would always be at the bottom of the table rather than the top.

Fulham in action in the FA Cup, playing lower league Port Vale, 1962.

It nearly came unstuck in 1961–62. A dreadful run of one win and 14 defeats (including 11 on the trot) in 15 matches, between the beginning of November 1961 and the end of February 1962, left the Cottagers languishing at the foot of the table. But then an inspired run of form in the League (five wins and two draws in eight games, helped lift them into the safety of 20th place (and send Chelsea down).

This revival coincided with (or was sparked by) the first decent Cup run since 1958. Lower Division opposition in the early rounds (Hartlepools, Walsall and Port Vale) succumbed, but only after showing great resilience. In the sixth round Fulham came up against another First Division side and after trailing 2–0 at home fought back to earn a thrilling draw. Surprisingly, they won the replay at Ewood, their first away win since the previous November, when they won… at Ewood. Cook scored the only goal of the replay.

As in 1958, Fulham travelled to Villa Park for the semi-final, where they met Burnley. Leggat gave them a deserved half-time lead, but John Connelly equalised in the second half. Then, with 10 minutes remaining, came a moment of controversy. Cook fastened on to a Haynes through ball, rounded Blacklaw, but before he could put the ball in the empty net the goalkeeper's hand brought him down. The referee gave a corner not a penalty, a decision he apparently later admitted was wrong. The chance was gone, and Burnley won the replay at Filbert Street, 2–1. The Cottagers Wembley ambitions were put on hold.

Still, they had survived in the top flight and in 1962–63 looked as though they would have another relegation battle on their hands. With just four wins in the first half of the season, they were back in familiar territory, but they won eight games on the trot in the spring to ease their fears. Bobby Robson had been re-signed from West Brom in the 1962 close season, but this plus was cancelled out by the minus of a serious injury to Haynes in a car crash early in the season, which kept him out for most of it. The other new blood was provided by two more home-grown talents: Bobby Keetch and Rodney Marsh. They joined Dave Metchick and Stan Brown, already in the first team, as the main representatives of the next generation.

The long slide begins

On the surface, 1964–65 was a reasonable season. Fulham finished 15th, their second-highest placing in their first 12 top-flight seasons. The team was pretty settled, with eight players appearing in 35 of the 42 League games. But beneath the surface there were changes that heralded a new era, and changes that threatened to change the culture of the club.

It started in October 1964, with Frank Osborne's retirement at the age of 68. Beddy Jezzard, given extra responsibilities, followed him in December, and he was not even 40. Buckingham's appointment as manager in January 1965 was the catalyst for the changes, the proverbial new broom who wanted to sweep away almost everything that was there before he arrived. By the start of the next season Frank Penn had retired, Joe Bacuzzi had been sacked, and Jimmy Langley, Maurice Cook and Tosh Chamberlain had all moved on. Not long afterwards, Rodney Marsh, Graham Leggat and Bobby Keetch were also on their way.

In fairness, moving on some of the older players created room for another bunch of talented youngsters to make the breakthrough, the likes of Steve Earle, Les Barrett, Jimmy Conway, Fred Callaghan and John Dempsey. But the paucity of Buckingham's thinking is evident from his transfer dealings, when the best he could do was to bring in veterans Mark Pearson and Terry Dyson, from Sheffield Wednesday and Spurs respectively. These were not signings to inspire or lift Fulham to the next level. Only with the protracted transfer saga of Allan Clarke from Walsall in the spring of 1966 did Buckingham sign a young player on the way up rather than seasoned campaigners on the way down.

He might well have been rumbled in his first season. A dreadful start to 1965–66, just four wins in the first 23 games, left the Cottagers well and truly stranded at the foot of the table. But seven wins in eight games (among which were a 2–0 home win over champions-elect Liverpool and an unlikely 1–0 victory at high-flying Leeds) in the spring raised hopes of another escape and an incident-packed 4–2 win in front of a record crowd at Northampton, which included an Earle hat-trick, virtually assured safety. But this was not Buckingham's success. Results only picked up when Dave Sexton, recently sacked by Leyton Orient as manager, took over as coach at the turn of the year. He was the difference and his departure for Highbury in 1966 was a huge loss.

The 1966–67 season was the calm before the storm, notable primarily for the sale of Leggat to Birmingham and the emergence of Clarke as a striker of the highest quality. But from the start of 1967–68 it was clear Fulham's lease on a place in Division One was going to expire. Next to bottom in December and bottom in February, there was no fight back this time. They threw in the towel, and threw out Buckingham. When his contract expired in January 1965, he departed, unlamented, and left the luckless Bobby Robson to pick up the pieces. After retiring the previous season, Robson had gone to Canada to take a managerial job but returned to the Cottage when secretary Graham Hortop invited him to take over a sinking ship.

It was not a happy experience. The team lacked confidence, Haynes was 34 years old, injury had virtually ended Cohen's career and his own transfer dealings smacked of desperation. Robson could not be held accountable for the inevitable relegation in May 1968, but when the Cottagers found themselves bottom of the Second Division five months later the board felt he had a case to answer. It was new director, the rather shady Eric Miller, who actually pulled the trigger and sacked him in November, after just 10 months in the job. Haynes, reluctantly, took on the role of player-manager before his former playing colleague Bill Dodgin joined Fulham for a third time just before Christmas,

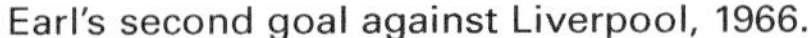

Earl's second goal against Liverpool, 1966.

but now as the club's fourth manager, in 1968. He had built an impressive reputation as a coach at Queen's Park Rangers. Working alongside Alec Stock, he had lifted Rangers from the Third to the First Division and taken them to a Wembley League Cup success.

The rot, however, had gone so deep that things got worse before they got better. Dodgin's early months were as devoid of hope as his predecessor's. It was 10 years and a day after Haynes led Fulham into the First Division that the Cottagers slipped with barely a whimper into the Third Division, a level they had last played at in 1932. The journey back to the top flight was a tortuous one and was to take over 30 years.

A break in the clouds

Changes were necessary and Dodgin was not afraid to make them. There was no clearer signal of his intentions than the ending of Johnny Haynes's magnificent career. He played his last game at home to Stockport in January 1970, after which new signing Barry Lloyd took over the number-10 shirt and the captaincy.

Dodgin did make some mistakes. He let a young Malcolm Macdonald go for a nominal fee to Luton, and it was ironic that three of the most prolific strikers and colourful personalities in English football in the 1970s, Macdonald, Clarke and Marsh, had all been at the Cottage in the 1960s, but Fulham had failed to get the most out of them.

By the end of his first full season it was clear Dodgin was on the right lines. His team lost only twice in the second half of the season and would have finished higher than fourth but for an uncertain start. It was a younger, more confident and more attacking side in which two players (Conway and Earle) topped the 20–goal mark, the first time this had happened since 1958–59. These two, along with skipper Lloyd, a couple of Bobby Robson's signings (Reg Matthewson and Vic Halom) and three other survivors from the First Division days (Callaghan, Stan Brown and Barrett), were the backbone of the side in this and the next season.

For much of 1970–71, Fulham led the Third Division and, apart from a pre-Christmas dip when they lost three successive games, they never looked like relaxing their grip on promotion. They even managed an extended League Cup run, beating Orient, Darlington and Queen's Park Rangers, before coming up against Bristol City in the quarter-finals. They squandered a great chance of going further by drawing 0–0 at the Cottage. In the replay, an early penalty gave the Robins a narrow win.

But the real goal was promotion, and in the penultimate game, away at Bradford City, two goals from George Johnson (signed by Dodgin during the season following an injury to Conway) and Lloyd secured a narrow 3–2 win and the two points needed to guarantee promotion. At home three days later, Fulham threw away the chance of winning the title by losing to Preston, the only other side that could have finished top. A draw would have been enough, but Preston won 1–0 in front of a crowd of 25,774, the biggest for a League game since the club dropped out of the First Division three years earlier.

It was a satisfying promotion, nevertheless. The turnaround had been achieved in two years without a huge outlay on new players, and the team played attractive attacking football, the only way Dodgin knew how. A prolonged stay outside of the two Divisions would have had serious financial implications. The new stand was nearing completion but attendances had dropped sharply since Division One days. Even in the promotion year of 1970–71, the average was only 12,004, compared with over 22,000 in 1967–68 and 24,000 the season before.

Halom scores against Rochdale, 1970.

The attacking philosophy that had served Dodgin so well in the Third Division was his undoing in the Second. The Cottagers never really made the adjustment to the higher level, and from the turn of the year their hard won status in Division Two was at risk. The signing of goalkeeper Peter Mellor in February made a difference, as did the controversial loan signing of Alan Mullery from Spurs in March. Protests from other relegation strugglers were overruled and the seven points taken from his six games (still only two for a win) were crucial. A rare Fred Callaghan goal at the Valley virtually assured safety, but it was close.

Too close, in fact, for Trinder, who sacked Dodgin days after the season ended. Alec Stock, who had recently resigned as Luton manager, was installed within days as the new manager. The supporters were unhappy with the chairman and, not unreasonably, had a great deal of sympathy with the outgoing manager. Trinder met the challenge head on and wound up the 'official' Supporters' Club. For a club whose core fan base was shrinking rapidly, it was a brave or stupid thing to do.

The Stock years

A vastly-experienced manager who was much more at home with smaller clubs (like Leyton Orient, Queen's Park Rangers and Luton) than he was at Arsenal and AS Roma (where his stay was measured in months), Stock spent four complete seasons in charge at the Cottage. If his brief was to consolidate Fulham's place as a mid-table Second Division side, he succeeded, literally. Between 1972 and 1976, Fulham finished between ninth and 13th out of 22 clubs, with between 40 and 44 points. The 186 goals they scored was just 10 more than they conceded. Under Stock's guidance, the Cottagers were a very average team.

He dealt shrewdly on the transfer market. Bringing Alan Mullery back from Spurs (1972) and signing Bobby Moore from West Ham (1974) were outstanding deals, and bringing Viv Busby and Alan Slough (1973) to the Cottage from his former club Luton were also good value. He also knew when to sell, as he showed when transferring Paul Went and Steve Earle for sizeable fees within weeks of each other towards the end of 1973. Stock was also lucky that several youngsters were waiting in the wings for their chance, the likes of John Lacy, John Mitchell and Les Strong.

His was a reassuring presence and in Bill Taylor had a very good coach who made the most of the material at his disposal. It was not adventurous football, but it was effective enough for Fulham to hold their own at the level at which they had spent most of their Football League career. The real drama was reserved for the FA Cup.

Nobody could have anticipated that 1975 was the year Fulham would reach Wembley. This was the fifth time the club had reached the last four and, with the possible exception of 1908, Stock's team was the least likely of the five on paper to have got through to the Final. They did it the hard way, taking more games than any previous finalist in Cup history. Every tie was won away from home, none of the five opponents were from a lower Division and three were from Division One. The fact that the Cottagers were second best against West Ham at Wembley was incidental. After the previous semi-final disappointments, especially in 1958 and 1962, being there was what mattered.

Wembley at last

Amid the sequence of mid-table (or lower) League seasons between 1971 and 1980 came Fulham's best-ever FA Cup run. In 1975 they were able to shed the unwanted record of having reached more semi-finals than any club without having reached a Final. Nobody was expecting it. It was the longest road to Wembley in the history of the competition (11 games), and home fans did not see any of the five victories. And it was not until the club had reached the sixth round that anyone took the prospect of a Cup Final seriously.

In many ways, the stiffest opposition came in the early rounds, against two other Second Division clubs. The first two games against Hull were drawn, 1–1 at the Cottage and 2–2 at Boothferry Park, before an Alan Slough goal settled the tie at Filbert Street. Nottingham Forest, under the new management of Brian Clough, were even more resilient. After two draws at the Cottage and one at the City Ground, a Viv Busby double settled the fourth meeting, in Nottingham.

Busby scores one of his goals which settles the marathon Forest tie.

Just five days later, Stock's men travelled to Goodison Park to meet First Division leaders Everton. Fulham's 2–1 win was the upset of the round and the third of three remarkable Cup wins over Everton (after 1926 and 1948). It might have been surprising, but it was thoroughly deserved, and again Busby was the hero. He scored in both halves, the first a simple tap in after 15 minutes, the second, with just six minutes remaining, was a shot on the turn from the penalty spot from a Conway cross. Kenyon had scored an equaliser for the Toffees just after the break.

In 1974–75 Carlisle were in the (old) First Division and the Cottagers travelled to Brunton Park for the sixth round. Now full of confidence and against a team struggling in the top flight, Fulham were favourites. But it took a simple goal by Les Barrett following a mix-up between goalkeeper and full-back, plus a superb display by goalkeeper Peter Mellor, to win. As at Goodison, Mullery and Moore, both former Cup winners, were magnificent, lifting the youngsters around them to new heights.

Fortunately, it was Hillsborough not the jinxed Villa Park for the semi-final against a strong Birmingham side (which included Howard Kendall, Trevor Francis and Kenny Burns). A magnificent John Mitchell strike gave the Cottagers the lead, but this was cancelled out by Gallagher. Yet again in a semi-final, Fulham had been the better team but not won. The replay at Maine Road was more finely balanced and was goalless after 90 minutes. With 29 of the 30 extra minutes played, a clearance by goalkeeper Latchford hit Mitchell and crossed the line without reaching the net. That goal was as ugly as the strike at Hillsborough had been brilliant, but it was priceless.

And so to Wembley, and a meeting with Moore's old club, West Ham. Although Fulham had beaten the Hammers in the League Cup earlier that season, there was no repeat in the FA Cup. On the day, the Cottagers acquitted themselves creditably without playing as well as they had at Everton. West Ham won it with two second-half Alan Taylor goals, but it had been a wonderful day out and a marvellous last hurrah for Mullery and Moore.

Bogged down in Clay

From Wembley, it was downhill, slowly at first but then, after a brief interlude with Malcolm Macdonald in charge, the pace of decline accelerated. This reversal of fortunes coincided with the arrival on the board of Ernest Clay. A Yorkshire businessman with no previous involvement in football, he arrived on the board in 1976 through the influence of Eric Miller, who later committed suicide when the government inspectors began to look closely at the affairs of his company, Peachey. Clay's way in was not to pay off the debt or inject new money but merely to guarantee the overdraft.

Clay was rude, crude, duplicitous, self-absorbed and acquisitive, particularly for the shares in Fulham FC. He tried to persuade those close to the club that he had the best interests of Fulham at heart but, in the end, it was clear he had one ultimate objective – to buy the freehold of the site for development purposes. Clay seemed to glory in his reputation of a buff northerner who was never afraid to speak his mind without realising that he was regarded by those in the media as an uncouth buffoon. But he not only outsmarted his critics, he also deceived his friends. He succeeded, but at Fulham's expense. Clay walked away in 1986, having bought the ground from the Church Commissioners for £972,000 in 1985 and then sold it a year later to property company Marler Estates for close to £9 million. At £367 per share, Clay's stake was valued at close on £4 million.

According to his autobiography, Stock saw through Clay from the start, which meant his days were

Slough scoring against Carlisle, 1977.

numbered. The 1975–76 season had fallen a bit flat after the excitement of the Cup run, and both coach Taylor and midfielder Conway left for Manchester City. It was a surprise (to him as well) that Mullery was not offered the job when he stopped playing in 1976. Instead Bobby Campbell came in as coach and a few months later took over as manager. Signing Best and Marsh for their 'end-of-the-pier' show that autumn was Stock's last throw of the dice, and he was gone before Christmas.

In many ways, Campbell was like Buckingham in the 1960s. Everything that was there when he arrived had to be changed. When Fulham kicked-off against Bristol Rovers in August 1978, there was only one player in the team who had played in the Cup Final three years earlier. That was Kevin Lock, and he had played for West Ham that day! All 11 Fulham players had left the club, either retired or transferred.

And, like Buckingham, Campbell left the club in a much weaker position than he found it, a division lower and sinking. He spent money, and dealt successfully in the transfer market. Richard Money and Ray Evans were bought relatively cheaply and sold for a substantial profit, while he paid modest sums for Gordon Davies, Sean O'Driscoll, Roger Brown, Ray Lewington and Kevin Lock, all of whom went on to give first-class service to Fulham. Unfortunately for the manager, they played their best football after he had been sacked. A big puzzle at the time, however, was why he paid a club record fee in February 1979 for striker Peter Kitchen from Orient and then hardly ever played him, even in a team that was losing regularly and hardly scoring.

In Campbell's first few months in 1976–77, the club sank perilously close to the relegation zone, but a Good Friday win over Chelsea led to an upturn in results and safety. There were two very average seasons (41 points from 42 games and 10th place) before it all unravelled in 1979–80. It started so well, a 3–0 half-time deficit against Birmingham was turned into a 4–3 win, but then came the slump. Bottom by December, the Cottagers were never out of the drop zone for the rest of the season. There were some very good players in the side, but they seemed not to want or to be able to play for Campbell. When they then went and lost six games on the trot in the Third Division in October 1980, he had to go.

Appointing commercial director and former player Malcolm Macdonald to his first managerial job might have been the cheap option, but it was an excellent choice. Brash and outspoken as a player, he exuded a calm, confident air, despite his relative youth and inexperience. This seemed to rub off on the players because after a while they started to play to their full potential. Never a tactician himself, Macdonald relied heavily on his coaches, initially his former colleagues Roger Thompson and George Armstrong from Arsenal and then Ray Harford, who was recruited from Colchester. The manager was very much the front man, managing the media and the chairman, but who created the right environment for the coaches and players.

It took a while to work, but after a mediocre 1980–81, the team clicked, and for two seasons the Cottage faithful were treated to the best football they had seen for 20 years. And it happened with a bunch of players who had been on the books in Campbell's time. With the exception of the experienced midfielder Peter O'Sullivan, a free transfer from Brighton, Macdonald's promotion-winning side of 1981–82 were all at the Cottage when he took over. Goalkeeper Gerry Peyton and defenders Tony Gale, Kevin Lock and Les Strong were regulars in the relegated side of two years earlier, as was striker Gordon Davies. Central-defender Roger Brown and midfielders Sean O'Driscoll and Ray Lewington were signed by Campbell but too late to make a difference, while right-back Jeff Hopkins, central-midfield player Robert Wilson and striker Dean Coney came through the juniors.

Promotion was clinched in dramatic fashion, a draw in the final game against Lincoln. On an evening of pure theatre at the Cottage, Fulham needed one point and the Imps all three to go up. Skipper Brown got the goal (his 12th of the season, a Fulham record for a defender, and one who did not take penalties), yet another header from yet another Gale free-kick, that earned the necessary draw in front of a crowd of 20,398. It need not have been that close because the quality of Fulham's football won plaudits from many neutral observers. With Harford increasingly influential, the Cottagers played a fast flowing, close passing game, with two predatory strikers, a midfield that broke quickly to support them and defence that preferred to pass the ball than lump it upfield.

After winning promotion, Macdonald banned the word 'consolidate' from the Cottage because he felt he had a side that could go on and win a second promotion. He was right. Adding only another free transfer, Ray Houghton from West Ham in place of O'Sullivan, the team took the Second Division by storm. In the first half of the season, Fulham produced a series of devastating displays (none more so than a superb 4–1 win at Macdonald's old stomping ground, St James' Park, against a Newcastle side that included Kevin Keegan) that put them in a commanding position. They lost their way in the winter months, however, and, after losing a vital home match 1–0 to challengers Leicester, went to Derby on the final day needing a win to have a chance of the third promotion place. They lost 1–0, but in circumstances that shamed Derby and the football authorities. The crowd's encroachment on to the pitch and the physical attacks on several Fulham players forced the referee to abandon the match, but Graham Kelly and his spineless colleagues at the Football League inexplicably handed the hooligans an officially sanctioned victory by allowing the result to stand.

For Fulham, 1981–83 was 1931–33 revisited, promotion from the Third Division followed by a very near miss the next season. For Macdonald, the Baseball Ground fiasco was a turning point. A poor start to the following season, relieved only by three gripping League Cup matches with Liverpool, and problems in his personal life led to his departure in the spring of 1984. Ray Harford was the obvious successor, but, for all his obvious talents as a coach, he found it difficult to cope as manager with an increasingly erratic chairman. The best players (Gale, Houghton and Davies) were sold as Clay seemed bent on asset-stripping the club and acquiring the freehold of the ground in

Derby fans invade the pitch on the last day of 1982–83. The Rams stayed up, but Fulham unsuccessfully appealed to have the game replayed when the referee had to end it with 78 seconds still to play.

order to exploit its development potential. Success for the team on the pitch appeared very low on his list of priorities.

It all fell apart in 1985. What had been a slow decline became a collapse, as Fulham suffered a club record of 26 defeats (in 42 games) and finished bottom of the table, a massive 13 points short of safety. Harford left, of course, and so did Clay, but he went with a smile on his face and a few million pounds in his pocket. The new chairman, David Bulstrode, made all the right noises, but he was a property man (Marler Estates), polished and apparently plausible. It took just months, however, for his real motives to be exposed, when he added Loftus Road, as well as Stamford Bridge and Craven Cottage, to his company's portfolio of west London football grounds.

Fulham had again been betrayed, but this time on a huge scale. Not only were they threatened with eviction from their historic home, but the existence of the club was also at risk. Bulstrode's master plan was to merge Fulham and Queen's Park Rangers (Fulham Park Rangers was one suggested name) to play at Loftus Road, while Marler had a free hand at Craven Cottage. He totally misjudged the public reaction. He was lambasted by the media, the football world as a whole and politicians, who joined forces with Fulham (and Queen's Park Rangers) supporters to try to block the proposals.

At centre stage was the ubiquitous Jimmy Hill, former Fulham player, PFA leader, Coventry manager, Charlton director and television presenter (among other things). He galvanised opposition to Marler and put together a group prepared to buy Fulham Football Club from the property company, but not the ground. He did, however, negotiate some breathing space, with the club continuing to play at the Cottage at a preferential rent, while Marler sought planning permission to build on the Cottage site. Paul Parker and Dean Coney were part of the price, leaving Fulham for Queen's Park Rangers.

Meanwhile Ray Lewington, who had returned from a season with Sheffield United to succeed Harford, was trying to stop the slide on the pitch. In the early months of 1987 there were two humiliating home defeats (5–0 by Chester and 6–0 by Port Vale), in between which was a highly-charged draw with Walsall, when there were demonstrations against the merger plans, which the visiting players and supporters wholeheartedly endorsed. Once the Hill group took over, the mood changed, the form improved and safety was achieved.

The battle for the Cottage

Few clubs are so closely identified with their grounds as Fulham with Craven Cottage. Yet the battles for ownership of the seven-acre site over the last 20 years contributed to the club's slide towards non-League football and even threatened their existence. It is a long, complicated, non-football story, but the headlines at least are an integral part of the history of the football club.

During the 1970s, Craven Cottage became a hugely attractive site, but for housing rather than football. As double-digit inflation lifted property prices sky high, the ground was valued for its development potential, and two of the club's chairmen were behind moves to get the club out. The first was Ernest Clay who, in 1984, after several years of trying, persuaded Fulham's landlords, the Church Commissioners, to sell him the freehold for £900,000. He claimed he wanted a partial development of the ground to pay off the club's debts, pay for the freehold and secure its future, but, when a planning application by a Manchester-based company (Kilroe) was rejected, Clay sold the club and the ground to Marler Estates, a company that also owned Stamford Bridge.

The original proposal exceeded permitted legal densities and many believe Clay was neither surprised nor disappointed when it was rejected. Marler paid close to £9 million which, after the £3.5 million owing Fulham's creditors, left Clay with around £5.5 million. New chairman David Bulstrode tried to reassure Fulham fans of intentions in the autumn of 1986, but in February 1987 his true colours were revealed. He bought Queen's Park Rangers and Loftus road from Jim Gregory and proposed merging them with Fulham, to play at Loftus Road and develop the Cottage.

The subsequent public outcry led to a truce rather than a settlement. Jimmy Hill and his backers (particularly Bill Muddyman) bought the club from Marler but not the ground. They remained at the Cottage, however, as tenants while the owners drew up their planning. The onset of the recession in 1989 and the purchase of Marler by another property company, John Duggan's Cabra Estates, coincided with the local council's Compulsory Purchase Order on the ground. This pushed all parties into a public inquiry.

Just before the inquiry opened, the club did a deal with Cabra, taking a large cash sum in return for a promise to vacate the Cottage voluntarily. The deal cut the ground from under the feet of the council and the CPO. But, before Fulham had to move, Cabra went under and the Royal Bank of Scotland emerged as the club's new landlords. After a protracted period of negotiation, the Bank and Fulham agreed a price for Craven Cottage, £7.5 million, with a discount negotiated by Fulham director and property expert Tom Wilson.

This took the story up to 1997. While the board was agreed on the need to purchase the Cottage, how to finance it, as well as pay for essential ground improvements and strengthening the team, led to deep divisions. Hill and Wilson favoured a partial development of the ground, but Muddyman believed a 'white knight' who could inject some new money into the club was the best route. Enter Mr Fayed; exit Mr Hill (and Mr Wilson).

Lower and lower

From the start, it was clear that Hill, the new chairman, wanted Fulham to succeed and that the club at last had a board that had the best interests of the team and supporters at heart. But the odds were stacked against them. Money was tight, the ground situation was uncertain, gates were falling and the team failed to deliver on the pitch. Lewington strengthened the squad (re-signing goalkeeper Stannard, midfielder Wilson and striker Rosenior and bringing his former teammates Clive Walker and Jeff Eckhardt to the Cottage). It was better than the previous season, but no better than mid table. They reached the Play-offs the next season, but then caved in against Bristol Rovers. An inspired run from February 1989 lifted the Cottagers into fourth. It started at Molineux, where Gordon Davies beat Johnny Haynes's club scoring record and new captain Doug Rougvie made his debut.

After this brief surge, the club started to sink. The board, for all its good intentions, made things worse with some very ill-judged appointments. Relegation to the Fourth Division was only avoided the following season with a tense draw at Cardiff in the penultimate game, a disappointing showing which led to the emergence of Alan Dicks (who had been coach at Coventry when Hill was manager) as manager, with Lewington becoming coach. Dicks did as well as anyone who had been away from English football for 10 years could have done, which was not very well at all. In fact, he was hopeless. A genuinely nice man who was out of his depth, Dicks lost the respect of the players very quickly and a home defeat by non-League Hayes in the FA Cup was the last straw, in November 1992.

Gordon Davies scores against Preston, 1990.

Appointing someone even more inept than Dicks seemed a remote possibility, but the board rose to the challenge and found Don Mackay. The Scot, who had managed Coventry and Blackburn, lacked authority over the players, who thought his training routines were naïve and his tactics confusing, and they were annoyed by his regular habit of playing them out of position. It all got too much, even for Jimmy Hill, one Sunday at Brisbane Road in March 1994. The team was 1–0 down at half-time and were so bad that Hill took over in the dressing room at the interval. A point was salvaged and Mackay was sacked the next day by vice-chairman Bill Muddyman.

The loyal Lewington was given nine games to save the club's Third Division status, but a catastrophic home defeat by Exeter left Fulham needing a win at Swansea on the last day. The 2–1 defeat was not as close as the scoreline implies, and so, for the first time in their history, the Cottagers dropped in to the League basement. Their blushes were spared a little when the divisions were renamed following the formation of the Premiership. The Third became the lowest division and so Fulham were saved the indignity of playing in the Fourth.

If there were any extenuating circumstances it was the distraction of what was going on behind the scenes. The onset of the recession in 1989, Bulstrode's death, the sale of Marler to Cabra Estates, Hammersmith and Fulham Council's compulsory purchase order on the ground and the ensuing public inquiry meant that the ground was always the dominant issue for the board. It was protracted and confusing and led to sharp divisions on the board between the chairman (Hill) and vice-chairman (Muddyman). Couple this with the incompetent management of the team and the impending relegation, and it is apparent the Cottage was not a happy place in the early 1990s.

And the team that went down was not full of bad players. Simon Morgan, Gary Brazil, Martin Pike, Sean Farrell and Jeff Eckhardt had all played at a higher level and were still only in their 20s, John Marshall and Peter Scott were experienced and proven Fulham players, while Glen Thomas, Justin

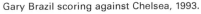

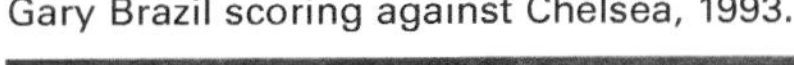
Gary Brazil scoring against Chelsea, 1993.

Skinner and Duncan Jupp were promising youngsters from the Cottagers youth scheme. On paper, it looked as though they should have been challenging for promotion, but on the field they looked a collection of strangers who did not have the heart for a battle.

Relegation led to the inevitable clear out. Lewington followed Mackay out of the door and the replacement was a very controversial choice. Ian Branfoot had endured a dreadful time at Southampton but had kept his counsel and behaved with great dignity. He had, however, a reputation as a hard man who favoured a very direct style of play. A number of players left Fulham at this time, and he built up his own squad, many with a Southampton connection. The results were unimpressive. The Cottagers could do no better than eighth in 1994–95, and in February 1996 they dropped to next to bottom place, 91st in the Football League and one position away from Conference football. This humiliation came four days after a 3–1 home defeat by Scunthorpe in front of just 2,176, the lowest official crowd for a first-class game at the Cottage. A week or two later, Branfoot handed over responsibility for team affairs to coach Micky Adams.

But the depressing facts do not do justice to the manager's achievement. Unlike Dicks and Mackay, Branfoot had the respect of the players, he restored some pride and discipline to the squad and looked after the players' interests with the board. None of this was obvious to the supporters, but, as Adams demonstrated, Branfoot was quite close to getting it right.

The revolution begins

Fulham's sojourn in the lower reaches of the Football League ended after three seasons. The fact Adams could steer Fulham to promotion in his first season shows that his inheritance was a robust one. He added some of his own ingredients, goalkeeper Mark Walton, defender Danny Cullip, veteran midfielder Glenn Cockerill and three youngsters from Gillingham, Paul Watson, Darren Freeman and Richard Carpenter.

Centre-forward Micky Conroy was on fire in the first half of the season, his 15 goals instrumental in taking Fulham to the top, with 15 wins and just four defeats in 23 games. The pace slackened after the new year, but a thrilling win at Carlisle in April virtually assured promotion, and a 0–0 draw at Mansfield days later made it a mathematical certainty. Promotion had been won with four games to spare, and had the Cottagers not carelessly lost to Northampton in the penultimate home game they would have won the title. Instead they had to settle for second place.

There was also a flurry of activity off the field, with the club at long last buying Craven Cottage, after an interminable series of twists and turns. It was a remarkable double, but there was a massive sting in the tail. Nobody could have predicted that the manager who steered Fulham to the club's first promotion in 15 years and the chairman who helped secure the purchase of the ground from the Royal Bank of Scotland would both have left the club within six months. A revolution was about to start, and its heart was the unlikely figure of Mohamed Al Fayed, the owner of Harrods in Knightsbridge.

It is still not clear why one of the country's leading businessmen with no previous football connection should have responded so positively to an invitation to buy Fulham FC. As a club, Fulham were located conveniently close to Harrods, and were a lot cheaper (if less glamorous) than Chelsea. But much needed to be done if the Cottagers' fortunes were to be restored, and it would not be cheap. Winning promotion certainly suggested that the Cottagers were at last moving in the right direction, and so the revolution really dates from Micky Adams's success. He was Kerensky to Fayed's Lenin.

Higher and higher

On taking over, the new chairman made his intentions clear (Premiership football within five years), and immediately resources appeared to make this happen. The pace of life accelerated at the Cottage and changes occurred with bewildering rapidity. Adams was an early casualty. He paid the price of not being a high profile enough name rather than an unsuccessful manager. When Kevin Keegan, a name as big in football as Fayed's was in business, came in with the clumsy title of 'Chief Operating Officer', Fulham, despite only being in the third tier of English football, suddenly became the centre of media attention in a way the club had not experienced since the Moore-Best-Marsh interlude in 1976.

Keegan appointed his old England colleague Ray Wilkins as team manager, and within weeks new players began to arrive, not from Gillingham, Wycombe Wanderers and Carlisle, but from big clubs like Arsenal, Blackburn and Sunderland. The fees, by Second Division standards and by previous Fulham standards, were breathtaking. Ian Selley cost £500,000 in October 1997, but this was doubled a week or so later when Paul Peschisolido signed, the first seven-figure transfer for the Division and for Fulham. And just to underline his commitment, Fayed sanctioned the spending of £2 million on Blackburn's Chris Coleman in November. And so it continued, with new players signing at unprecedented rates.

During the season, most of the players who had served Adams so well drifted away, or were passed over. None moved to clubs in a higher division, which implies that Keegan's judgement was not far off the mark. In the starting line up for the final game of 1997–98 were only two players who had been part of the promotion success 12 months earlier (Simon Morgan and Matt Lawrence) and one other (Steve Hayward) who had been signed by Adams.

In the Second Division, expenditure on this scale had to make a difference. It did, but not as much as was expected in that first season. The team was inconsistent, and although fourth was a good finish for a newly promoted club it did not reflect the money that had been spent. Much of the play was dull, the approach very cautious and the hoped-for excitement did not materialise. Fulham did reach the Play-offs but were second best to Grimsby. By the time of the two games against the Mariners, there had been a change at the top. Wilkins had left and Keegan was now in sole charge. The Cottagers still stumbled at the last hurdle in 1997–98, but the following season they swept all before them.

By capturing the Second Division title so emphatically, Fulham offered the proof that money made a difference. The Cottagers won more games (31) than any other team, lost fewer (7), scored the most goals (79) and conceded the least (32). They were the first team to top 100 points in the Second Division and the margin over second-placed Walsall was a record 14 points. Promotion was clinched with six games remaining and the title secured just one match later. Fulham simply blew the opposition away. On top of this, Fulham beat Southampton of the Premiership in both Cup competitions and went to Premier leaders Aston Villa in the FA Cup and won 2–0.

Yet more money was spent, because it seemed Keegan had an eye on the following season at a higher level. Stylish defender Steve Finnan was signed from Notts County, Kit Symons, who had endured a difficult time at Maine Road, slotted in alongside Coleman (and contributed a remarkable 11 goals), while upfront two strikers were added to the squad, Geoff Horsfield for a bargain £350,000 from Halifax and Barry Hayles for a substantial £2 million from Bristol Rovers

In May 1999, 50 years and a day after they had won the (old) Second Division title, the Cottagers were presented with the divisional trophy in a carefully choreographed ceremony that reflected the

Paul Moody completes his hat-trick, and his Fulham career, in the 3-0 win over Preston North End, 1999.

chairman's sense of the flamboyant. There was much to celebrate, as the team had set 11 club records that season, which showed not only their attacking prowess but also defensive strength (24 clean sheets). This was no ordinary Second Division side. Keegan's cavalier approach (a marked contrast to the safety first under Wilkins) had paid off in style.

But it all ended on a sour note. Keegan had been enticed away to manage England, a job which fell vacant following Glenn Hoddle's resignation. The press had virtually demanded he be appointed and, after a period of equivocation, he announced his acceptance of the job and his departure from the Cottage in a television interview before Fulham's final game of the season. The whole episode reflected very badly on Keegan and the FA, and, in retrospect, Fulham fans might not be the only ones to regret his decision that spring.

By appointing Paul Bracewell as Keegan's successor, the emphasis was on continuity. The England midfield player had worked with Keegan at Newcastle and was one of the manager's first signings at Fulham, where he was coaching and playing. But in terms of managerial style, it was chalk and cheese. Instead of Keegan's extrovert, adventurous attack-minded attitude, Bracewell offered a dour, safety-first, defensive approach which not only annoyed the supporters but was also not very successful. He started well enough, buying midfielder Lee Clark (and upping the Fulham transfer record by another million) and signing Arsenal's Stephen Hughes and Villa's controversial Stan Collymore on loan, both with a view to permanent deals.

It was not the manager's fault the two loan deals did not work out, and they were well worth a try. But, after the excitement of the previous season, Bracewell was guilty of something much more serious – he was boring and his teams were dull. As the season wore on, the tedium increased, and over Christmas there was a sequence of eight games (including four consecutive goalless draws) when Fulham's only goal was scored by Roberts of Tranmere. There was some consolation with a run to the last eight in the League Cup, but even this ended in huge disappointment at Filbert Street. The Cottagers led Premiership Leicester 2–0 with 10 minutes remaining, but were pegged back to 2–2. Then they led in extra-time, but it ended 3–3. In a nightmare penalty shoot-out, Fulham missed all three of their kicks and threw away the chance of reaching the semi-finals for the first time.

A French lesson for Fulham

Mercifully, the curtain came down on Bracewell's term before the season's end. German World Cup winner Karl Heinz Reidle, with help from his former Liverpool manager Roy Evans, held the fort until a permanent replacement was found. There was intense press speculation about the new manager but nobody figured on Jean Tigana, a wonderful player in the marvellous French side of the 1980s, who had built his managerial reputation at Monaco. He arrived in the spring of 2000 but did not take the reins until the close season.

He was an inspired choice, a revelation at the Cottage and a breath of fresh air for English football. He concerned himself with every aspect of the players' schedules, and with the players at every level of the club, and radically revised training routines, controlled diets and introduced a passing game that was breathtaking to watch. His alleged poor grasp of English spared him the indignity of regular media interviews, allowing him to just get on with the job. John Collins was signed from Everton. A Scottish international midfield player, he had played for Tigana at Monaco and was at the heart of the 'pass and run' style of play. Tigana also gave French striker Louis Saha a second chance in English football after his earlier disappointing time with Newcastle and further bolstered the attack with the signing of Southampton's Luis Boa Morte.

From the outset, the results were staggering. Fulham set a new club record by winning their first 11 matches and lost only once in the first half of the season. On Boxing Day nearest challengers

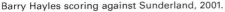

Barry Hayles scoring against Sunderland, 2001.

Watford were crushed 5–0 at the Cottage, and three weeks later Fulham completed the double, winning 3–1 at Vicarage Road. The push for the title became a procession and was all but assured with a thrilling victory at Ewood Park with seven games remaining. Blackburn had taken over as the major title threat and took a 1–0. The Cottagers cause was not helped when Rufus Brevett was sent off, but Saha got an equaliser and Sean Davis scored the winner in the final minute. Even the normally impassive Tigana did a jig along the touchline.

In the end, Fulham won the Division Championship by 10 clear points, and again they topped the century of points (101). Saha's 32 goals was the highest individual tally since Jezzard in the 1950s, and, with Boa Morte on 21 and Hayles on 19, the top three scorers managed 72 goals between them, the best since 1931–32. If only Fulham had not slipped up at home to Northampton in April 1997 they would have won three Championships in five years (and with three different managers).

It was not just the results that impressed, but the style. During the first half of the 2000–01 season, the quality of the football was the best ever seen from a Fulham side. It was fantasy football for real. Even Dario Gradi, the manager of Crewe, said that he would rather watch Fulham than Crewe after his side were beaten 2–0 at the Cottage. The number of games that were won in the closing stages was testimony not only to the players' fitness but also to the fact that the passing game wore the opposition down, making them more vulnerable as the game went on.

In terms of points earned and matches won (especially away from home), this was the club's best-ever season, putting even the Keegan season of two years earlier in the shade. There were also the fewest defeats and fewest goals conceded, emphasising that the team was the best at both ends of the pitch. To cap a brilliant season, a new club record of 14 Fulham players were selected for international duty, for countries as diverse as Portugal, Canada, Latvia, Denmark and Wales. The Championship was presented after the final home game against Wimbledon with another carefully orchestrated celebration, which was more London Palladium than Craven Cottage. A special cheer was reserved for the injured Chris Coleman, but the architect of the success, Jean Tigana, looked the most embarrassed man in the ground.

Among the internationals in 2000–01 was the captain Chris Coleman, whose career came to a very abrupt halt when he was seriously injured in a car crash in January. He suffered dreadful injuries and was lucky not to have lost more than his playing career. Coleman, however, is an immensely strong character and, as subsequent events were to show, had an even bigger contribution to make to the club. When it became obvious that Coleman would not return, Tigana signed another Frenchman who had endured a difficult time at Newcastle. Alain Goma had no impact on the promotion season, but he was to prove a top-class replacement for the injured Coleman.

For several reasons, the jump into the top flight was a leap in the dark. The survival records of promoted clubs must have made the management a little apprehensive. After all, only five years earlier, Fulham had been next-to-bottom in the whole League and there may have been worries that the club's infrastructure was not ready for the Premiership. Certainly the ground (Craven Cottage has never been a stadium) remained a throwback to an earlier, less demanding, less safety-conscious generation. There were still standing areas behind both goals at a time when all-seater grounds were obligatory. But, given the speed of Fulham's rise, the club was given special dispensation for a season to find an answer.

Whatever the solution, it was obvious that the club would never be able to compete with the majority of Premiership clubs in terms of gate receipts. With an all-seater Cottage, capacity would be around the 24,000 mark, making it one of the smallest grounds at the highest level (thus generating less revenues). If, on the other hand, Fulham had a 40,000 all-seater stadium of their own, it is unlikely they would be able to fill it. So, when faced with more expensive squads and bigger transfer fees than they had in Division One, the club had to try to generate more non-football income. In such a crowded market place, with more glamorous clubs just a Tosh Chamberlain corner-kick away, this was a tall order.

If Fulham were to be able to sustain life at the top, therefore, either someone had to be willing to write a cheque to cover any shortfall or the manager had to accept he had less to work with than his peers at Highbury, Old Trafford or St James' Park. In the six years the Cottagers have spent in the Premiership, both options seem to have been exercised and, perhaps surprisingly, they have become an established team in the top flight.

In an era of increasingly high-profile chairmen, Mohamed Al Fayed has not tried to match other football club owners for headlines. Unlike many of his peers, he was already a prominent public figure before going into football, and so he has not needed to exploit his position at the Cottage to boost his own image. There were those who questioned his commitment to Fulham and others were suspicious of his motives. But he has answered the sceptics with his actions rather than words. Despite the Dean family's long association with Fulham and the area, Tommy Trinder's undoubted love of the club, and Jimmy Hill's sterling efforts to keep the Cottagers alive at a time of imminent danger, no previous chairman has done as much for the club as Mohamed Al Fayed. His contribution has been immense on several fronts.

Spending on the team was the most obvious, in terms of transfers and wages. The big four of the Premiership apart, the Cottagers are now seen to compete on an equal footing with most other leading clubs for top-quality players. Where, during the 1980s and the 1990s (up to 1997), six-figure transfer fees were rare, seven figures has become standard since Al Fayed's arrival. With larger fees come higher wages, and, as the authoritative Deloittes' report on football club finances showed recently, Fulham's wage bill was the eighth biggest in the Premiership, bigger even than Spurs. This was disproportionate to the income from gate receipts.

Behind the scenes, Fulham now feels like a Premiership club. For the first time the Cottagers have their own training ground, the former London University facilities at Motspur Park, which also houses the administrative offices, and the ground has had a major facelift to meet the requirements of the football authorities, yet still manages to retain its unique charm. All this has happened very quickly, in fact in the time Tony Blair was Prime Minister. Younger and newer supporters who have known little else probably take it for granted. But those who have been supporting Fulham for 20 years or more realise that there is only one reason to explain Fulham's progress from near-bankruptcy in the lower reaches of the Football League to becoming an established Premiership club, one of only four London clubs in the top flight. Mohamed Al Fayed has not scored the goals or picked the team, but he has made it possible for those who do these well to do their jobs properly. No supporter could ask more of a chairman.

The manager strengthened the squad before the debut season in the Premiership. Edwin van der Sar, one of the best goalkeepers in Europe (Ajax, Juventus and Holland), was signed and he is the only serious challenger to Tony Macedo for the title of Fulham's best-ever 'keeper. It was hard, however, not to feel sorry for Maik Taylor, who had performed so splendidly in the two previous promotion successes. In Steed Malbranque, Tigana used his French connections to uncover a young, little-known midfield player who was to prove an absolute gem. And with Sylvain Legwinski, another Frenchman from Bordeaux, Fulham got an interesting character and a talented midfield player who was experienced at the highest level of European football.

There was, however, one transfer that did not work out, the most expensive in Fulham's history, and it soured the long-term relationship between Tigana and the chairman. Steve Marlet had attracted attention for his displays in the Champions League for Lyon, which had also earned him a place in the French squad. But this hardly seemed to justify the £11.5 million fee Fulham paid for him. He was fast, clever and had good control, but he was not the striker the team needed, and at times he seemed to lack the appetite for the battle. So inconsistent were his performances that it was felt Tigana only picked him because he had paid so much money for him. The transfer deal was later a source of legal contention between the club, the agents and Tigana and effectively signalled the end of the mega transfers for Fulham.

After three promotions in five seasons, playing in the Premiership was always going to be a reality check for Fulham, even playing the Tigana way. Opposing attacks were sharper and defences tighter and at times Fulham's slow, measured build up looked ponderous and laboured. Premiership defenders were prepared to retreat to their own penalty areas, let Fulham play in the middle third of the pitch but deny them space nearer goal. Too often, the Cottagers failed to break down packed defences and could not convert possession into goals. Saha, Hayles and Boa Morte, scorers of 72 goals the previous season, could only manage 17 at the higher level as the goals dropped to below one per game.

Most of the excitement in 2001–02 came in the FA Cup. The draw was kind to the Cottagers and in the first four rounds they avoided Premiership opposition, beating Wycombe, York, Walsall and West Brom to reach their sixth semi-final, where they were paired with Chelsea. With the sensitivity towards supporters for which the football authorities have become known, the tie was arranged for 7.00pm on a Sunday evening at Villa Park. This ludicrous decision reminded everyone that the interests of those who do not pay to watch live football matter far more than those who do. The supporters of Fulham (and Chelsea) were ill-served by football's Faustian Pact with television. A poor

Louis Saha scoring against Sunderland, 2003.

game was settled by a John Terry goal shortly before half-time, and Fulham again fell at the penultimate hurdle in the FA Cup stakes.

At the end of that first season, Fulham left the Cottage. The long-term plan, whether to develop the Cottage on a major scale or move to a purpose-build ground, had still not been settled, but the club had used up its special dispensation and had to find an all-seater home, albeit a temporary one. So, in August 2002 Fulham kicked-off at Loftus Road, where they were to spend the next two seasons. Although the Queen's Park Rangers staff were very hospitable, it was not home for the supporters, although the players hardly seemed to notice. Their ties to the Cottage were not so strong and they quickly adapted to the new environment, and for these two seasons the home form was crucial to the club's survival.

By the time the League campaign started, however, Fulham had already played seven matches. The club had entered the Intertoto Cup and, four days before the opening Premiership game against Bolton, they had drawn 2–2 in Bologna in the Final of this Cup. A hat-trick by Japanese star Junichi Inamoto secured a 3–1 second-leg win and a passage into the UEFA Cup. Hadjuk Split and Dinamo Zagreb were both eliminated before the Cottagers fell to Hertha Berlin in the third round. After losing 2–1 in Berlin, they were held to a goalless draw at Loftus Road.

League form was indifferent, a combination of staleness and tiredness the critics claimed, and four straight defeats in the autumn left the Cottagers in the bottom half of the table, where they spent the rest of the season. Performances were lacklustre at times, and much of the old sharpness was lost. Only once did the team manage to win two successive games (in February, home games against Villa and West Brom), and after three defeats in three games, against Manchester United, Blackburn and Liverpool, the club parted company with Tigana in April.

It was a sad end to a bold and largely successful experiment. The Frenchman had brought a new type of football to Fulham, the best ever seen at the Cottage, and managed to attract players from all over the world to the small club on the banks of the Thames. The number of players who subsequently went on to play for bigger clubs in the Premiership is a measure of the soundness of Tigana's judgement. But, as 2002–03 entered the final stages, he seemed to have lost some interest, while the team appeared at times to be going through the motions. Ironically, the foreign influence reached its peak just weeks before the manager's departure. There was not a single Englishman among the 11 who started against West Brom in February, and the two substitutes who were used were from Morocco and Latvia.

Back to basics (and the Cottage)

After the dizzying rise through the divisions and the changes it brought, life post-Tigana settled down to a new form of normality. In 2004, to the delight of the traditionalists, Fulham left Loftus Road and returned home. Talk of a new super stadium on the site had been dropped as the projected costs soared, even though planning permission had been obtained. And the idea of buying land near the White City and sharing with Queen's Park Rangers was abandoned when the owners of part of the area refused to sell to Fulham. So, it was back to the old ground, which many wanted from the start. Seating capacity and corporate boxes replaced the terracing behind each goal and the whole project was so tastefully done that Craven Cottage was substantially improved without sacrificing its original charm. The ground was modernised, but not too much.

Although still badly affected by the injuries from his car accident, the popular Chris Coleman took over on a temporary basis for the five remaining games and the 10 points that were won lifted the club into the safety of 14th position on 48 points, six clear of relegation. During the summer, Coleman indicated he would like the job on a full-time basis and there were few who argued with the decision to make the former captain the new manager. It was, however, a gamble. He would be the youngest manager in the Premiership, with no previous managerial or coaching experience. He had, moreover, been a playing colleague of most of the squad and had to make the switch from teammate to boss.

In four years at the helm, Coleman kept Fulham in the top flight, punching above their weight as some have argued. With finishes of ninth, 13th, 12th and 16th since 2003, Fulham are starting to look a Premiership club. The Cottagers may not have won anything, but nor have 15 of the other clubs in the Premiership. Only Arsenal, Manchester United, Liverpool and Chelsea have won the League or FA Cup in these seasons, such now is the dominance of the bigger, richer clubs. Coleman's achievement for three seasons was to maintain the Cottagers in the second division of the Premiership, the middle tier that is unlikely to win the major prizes but manages to hold its own at the highest level. As the manager himself said, his Fulham side beat all four of topsides (but not all in the same season) and enough others in a season to reach the magic 40–point mark with a few games to spare. Until 2006–07, that is.

Under Coleman, there was a gradual change in style. The obvious difference was a greater urgency about the play, a more direct and committed approach. All the Tigana signings have now moved on, several to bigger Premiership sides and, perhaps accepting that he has to cut his coat to suit his cloth, the type of signings have changed. Fulham no longer compete at the top end of the transfer market (a la Marlet or van der Sar) and rarely take a gamble on a young untried player (such as Malbranque). Most of Coleman's signings are experienced, usually from the Premiership rather than Europe, and there are now more players in the squad whose first language is English.

Fulham FC, 2005. Back row: Carlos Bocanagra, Brain McBride, Zat Knight, Mark Crossley, Nick Jensen, Claus Jensen, Zesh Rehman. Front row: Steed Malbranque, Moritz Volz, Thomas Radzinski, Luis Boa Morte.

In his relatively short time at the Cottage, Coleman won praise for his open and honest approach. He was admired for the way he seemed able to lift a squad without obvious stars to play above its natural level often enough in a season to get the necessary 40 points. He was clearly not at the forefront of tactical innovation, but his simple, straightforward style paid off – for a while.

In 2006–07, however, it started to unravel. With Boa Morte's surprise move to West Ham in January, the last of the Tigana signings departed. The squad was now Coleman's, and it really was not very good. Because there was virtually nothing to show from the club's youth scheme, Fulham had to buy in their players, but the Cottagers were not able to match their peers for fees in the transfer market. The fact that promising youngsters seemed not to progress beyond the promising added to the problems. The quality of the squad was declining over time, and by 2006–07 Coleman's team was getting found out.

The dreadful away record of 2005–06 (just one win) was as bad the next season and so, when the home form also dipped alarmingly, Fulham started to look vulnerable. The team became more defensive (playing one striker at home), but the defence was even more porous. Upfront, there was an over-reliance on a 30–something American to do the running, and so scoring goals became a problem as well. Players were played out of position, there was little imagination or flair from midfield and the choice of available substitutes offered little variation.

An appalling run of results in the winter and spring of 2007 saw Fulham slide towards the drop zone and, just as they had with Tigana, the board dispensed with Coleman's services with just a handful of games remaining. Only the timing of the sacking was questionable. Lawrie Sanchez, the Northern Ireland manager, took over on a 32-day contract, and one win and one draw in the final five games was enough to ensure survival. But nobody was convinced that merely changing the manager would be enough. Before the season ended, Sanchez was appointed as the permanent successor and acknowledged that a radical overhaul was needed.

His appointment was a surprise. Several other, higher-profile names, with Premiership and European experience, were linked with the job but, while superficially attractive, might not have been right for Fulham. High profile would almost certainly have meant big spending, and this is not a route the Cottagers can realistically pursue. Few managers in the Premiership will be as well placed as Sanchez to know where the talent in the Championship (and below) is located. From his time in charge of Northern Ireland, he has probably seen more of English League football than his Premiership peers.

He might not be the man to take Fulham to the next level. Such is the gap that has now emerged between the Big Four in the Premiership and the rest; however, there is no next level for the other 16 clubs whose role is primarily to make up the fixture list and fill out the television schedules. Where the Cottagers are now, playing at their much-improved traditional home in the top flight of English football, is far more than even the most loyal fan could have hoped for just 10 years ago. This is about as good as it gets.

The Craven Cottage Story

For two reasons, it was lucky that Henry Norris and his colleagues on the Fulham board decided in 1904 to commission an unknown Scottish engineer, Archibald Leitch, to turn the club's primitive Southern League home ground into a stadium worthy of top-class football. Lucky in the first place because Leitch's design created a unique environment for professional sport, the principal components of which survive in tact to this day. Few clubs have been as closely identified with their traditional home as Fulham and in an era when many leading clubs have moved, or are planning to move, to state-of-the-art grounds, Fulham supporters would resist strongly any attempt to move their club to a new home.

Secondly, the Leitch appointment was lucky because he has recently been 'discovered' by football writer and historian Simon Inglis. His most recent book on the subject, *Engineering Archie* (English Heritage, 2005) discusses at length the range of Leitch's activities, and includes a chapter on Craven Cottage. This essential volume highlights the originality of Leitch's thinking and the boldness of Norris's initiative. Between them, they created something worthwhile and lasting which has since helped to shape and define the character of the club.

As the first chapter showed, Fulham had a long journey to get to Craven Cottage, with a number of stops on the way. The nomadic early years took the club to a succession of temporary and makeshift

The original cottage, *c.*1888.

homes in the west London area until in 1894 an opportunity arose to play at a derelict site on the banks of the Thames. In the 18th century Craven Cottage had been a royal hunting lodge and later had allegedly hosted a number of famous guests (including writer Bulwer Lytton, Empress Eugenie, wife of Emperor Napoleon III of France, and Conservative politician Benjamin Disreali). In 1888, however, it was destroyed by fire and the site had been left untended for several years.

Such was the state of disrepair when Fulham took over occupancy in 1894 that it took two years to make the area usable, even for the standards of the late Victorian era. The first match took place on 10 October 1896, when Fulham defeated Minerva 4–0 in a Middlesex Senior Cup tie. Apart from the terracing, to which the excavations from the Shepherd's Bush underground station made a significant contribution, the only additional facility for spectators was a stand, built (as Inglis reveals) in 1903 by Robert Iles of Walham Green. Known at the time as the 'Rabbit Hutch', it landed Fulham in trouble with the authorities. In 1904 the club was fined a token ten shillings (50p), with four shillings (20p) costs, for a technical breach of planning procedures.

The cottage-less Craven Cottage had been home for eight years before Norris acknowledged the big-time club he wanted Fulham to become needed a modern stadium. He could have accepted the offer of another entrepreneurial builder, Gus Mears, to rent his new ground a mile or two down the road. Better served by transport links, Stamford Bridge (on which Leitch was working at the same time) seemed to offer a promising alternative, but the proposed rent (£1,500 pa) was on the high side and Norris wanted to be in control. So, while he rebuilt his existing ground, Mears started his own team.

It was the court challenge to the Rabbit Hutch that twisted Norris's arm. Doubts about the stand's licence led to Norris inviting Leitch to put forward proposals for a stadium the Fulham chairman wanted to be the best in the country. Leitch's original scheme was for a ground with a capacity of 80,000, bounded by Stevenage Road, Woodlawn Road, Kenyon Street and Greswell Street. In the autumn of 1904, a local paper reported that the scheme had received approval from the London County Council but the financing was not forthcoming.

The new Craven Cottage, 1903.

Around the same time as this scheme was floated and the court case on the Rabbit Hutch was in progress, the club secured a 99-year lease on the Cottage site and a more modest development was proposed for the summer of 1905. The original plans were discreetly dropped. Work started in May, and what emerged in time for the first game of the new season in September 1905 was a ground which clearly impressed contemporaries but which would still have been instantly recognisable to anyone who was watching Fulham as recently as the late 1960s. The total cost was £15,000, a sizeable sum for an era when Middlesbrough got a new ground for £3,000 less.

The bankings at the Putney and Hammersmith ends and along the riverside were properly terraced and fitted with Leitch's own specially designed (and later patented) crush barriers. But the centre-piece of the development was Craven Cottage (a 'pavilion') and the Stevenage Road stand. Particularly eye-catching was the ornate brick frontage of the stand, which was Norris' own contribution to the scheme. According to Inglis, Leitch optimistically claimed that the new Craven Cottage would hold 60,000 on the three sides of open terracing, 3,000 in the enclosure and 5,000 seated in the Stevenage Road stand, but in 100 years of football attendances never reached 50,000.

There was a celebratory atmosphere when the ground was officially opened, on 2 September 1905, a Southern League First Division fixture against Portsmouth. Among the estimated 20,000 crowd were a host of local dignitaries, including the Liberal and Conservative candidates for the constituency in imminent general election. The sitting MP and Fulham President, W. Hayes Fisher, officially opened the new ground. After 'a private luncheon in the club pavilion', and a performance on the pitch of the Fulham Borough Prize Band, the crowd watched two teams which would be challenging for the title battle out a goalless draw. The only slight hitch on the day was that many of those who wanted to sit in the Stevenage Road stand, or stand in the enclosure, did not realise they had to enter through separate turnstiles and so had to watch the game from the terraces.

Recognition that Fulham's impressive new structure was one of the best grounds in the country came within a couple of years when the FA selected Craven Cottage for a full England international match. In March 1907 England and Wales played out a 1–1 draw in the old Home International competition. A year later, in March 1908, the Cottage hosted its first 40,000 crowd, the visit of League champions-elect Manchester United for an FA Cup quarter-final tie.

Thereafter, there were several other 40,000+ crowds in the years up to 1939, many over 30,000, and 20,000+ soon became the norm. It was, however, on 8 October 1938 that the record attendance was recorded. Unlikely as it seems, the visitors were Millwall, and it was for a match in the (old) Second

England v Wales, Craven Cottage 1907.

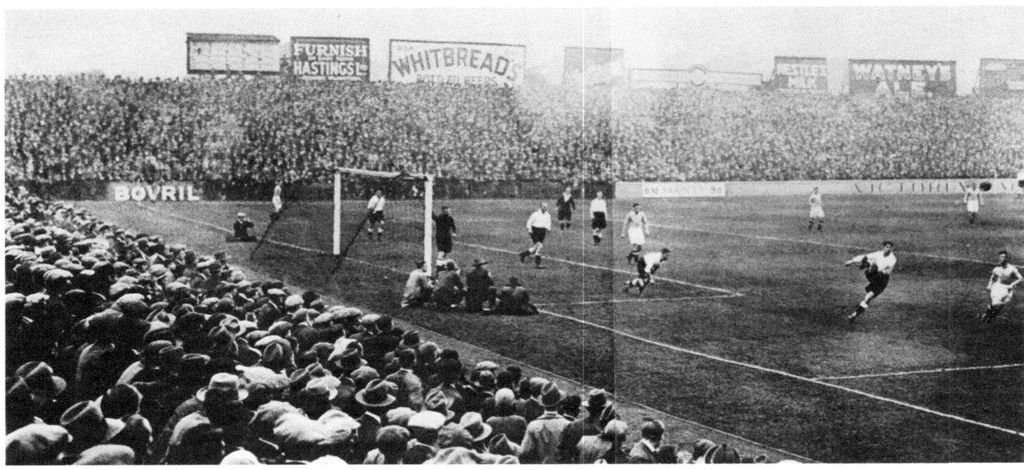

A full house at the cottage, 1932.

Division. There were special reasons why 49,335 people should have wanted to see this game. It was a local derby, and the two teams were leading the way in the table. Probably more important was the fact that this was Fulham's first home game after Prime Minister Neville Chamberlain's notorious trip to Munich and his 'Peace In Our Time' deal with Hitler. The national sense of relief that war had apparently been averted led to a jump in attendances all round the country. At the Cottage, the numbers caught Fulham officials by surprise. The kick-off had to be delayed, and the gates closed with thousands still outside. Some of Leitch's crash barriers even buckled under the strain, but there was no trouble. The Cottagers won 2–1, with Fulham players scoring all three goals, and the pitch invasion at the end was joyous rather than threatening.

A 1950s full house.

Immediately after the war, attendances generally boomed, and this coincided with Fulham's rise to the (old) First Division for the first time. Average attendances peaked at 33,030 in 1949–50, the club's debut season in the top flight. When Arthur Rowe's 'push and run' Spurs side visited the Cottage for a Good Friday game in March 1951, a post-war record crowd of 47,391 turned up to see the champions-elect win 1–0. On Easter Monday, March 1967, Manchester United, again champions-elect, drew 47,290 to the banks of the Thames, who saw a thrilling 2–2 draw.

There was just one more 40,000 crowd after that, in April 1968, when 40,154 witnessed Manchester United stroll to a 4–0 win over a doomed Fulham. Thereafter, the building of the riverside stand, increasingly stringent safety regulations and neglect by the club, steadily reduced the capacity. The Safety of Sports Ground Act of 1979 cut it to 19,830, but by the mid-1990s it was down to 14,969. The last 30,000 attendance was in October 1970, for a League Cup tie against Queen's Park Rangers. The official gate was 31,727. Fulham went from November 1985 until their first home game in the Premiership in August 2001 (a total of 406 League and Cup games) without a home crowd of at least 20,000. It was only with the arrival of Mr Fayed that Craven Cottage was once again treated as a football ground and not a potential building site.

More than half a century was to pass before there were further major improvements on the ground after Leitch's original development. There were small improvements in between, such as extending the Hammersmith End in 1961, installing floodlights in 1962 (the last First Division club to do so), and adding a roof at the rear of the Hammersmith End in 1965. But essentially, right up until 1972, only the Stevenage Road stand offered any seating capacity. Then, with an appalling sense of timing, the board agreed to build a stand along the riverside, an idea first considered in 1935 but rejected by John Dean on the grounds of cost. The £11,135 Fulham would have to have spent in the last year of George V's reign to provide cover for another 6,000 spectators, however, would have been cheaper in every way than the £464,000 debt they were left with when the stand was finally built in his granddaughter's time.

Virtually all the club's modern history, on and off the field, can be traced back to the building of this stand. Discussed when Fulham were in the top flight, and constructed while they were slipping two divisions, it opened in February 1972 (a friendly against Benfica) with the Cottagers in the (old) Second Division. It is claimed that a Fulham director (Eric Miller of the property company Peachey Estates) took responsibility for the development. He allegedly agreed with builders MacAlpine that in lieu of payment for the stand he would route work to them from Peachey which would cover the costs.

When this failed to materialise, the builders, not unreasonably, demanded payment. Fulham, however, had no money which opened the way for Ernest Clay. In 1976 he become a director and then chairman in 1977 and over the next nine years pursued his own personal agenda, which had more to do with Clay than Fulham. As the playing fortunes of the club declined in the 1980s, the condition of the ground deteriorated, and by the time ownership passed to property companies (first Marler and then Cabra) it was generally assumed that Fulham would move and the football ground would be converted to a housing development.

A combination of factors conspired to keep the club at the Cottage and the emergence of Mohamed Al Fayed led to the first serious investment in the team and the ground for a generation or more. (An estimated £750,000 was spent on cleaning and restoring the frontage of the Stevenage Road stand to its old Edwardian splendour.) As the team rose through the divisions over the last 10 years, so the need for improved facilities became imperative but, as usual, Fulham went the long way round to the right answer. The capacity when Al Fayed and Keegan arrived was little more than 20,000,

The Edwardian frontage to Craven Cottage.

although it had not been seriously tested for several years. But it was hard to see how the chairman's ambitions for the club could be realised with such a small capacity.

Plan A was to redevelop the Cottage on a grand scale and at a huge cost. Although the local council agreed to the plans, it was hard to believe that such a scheme could ever be financially viable. Even Mr Fayed's largesse had to have limits. Plan B was to move, but stay in the borough, and a site was located

Inside the ground before the modernisation to remove the terracing.

near the White City. Very plausible plans were produced for a modern 40,000 all-seater stadium which, with Queen's Park Rangers's shared involvement and the sale of Loftus Road and Craven Cottage made more financial sense. Again the local council was onside but the stumbling block was that the proposed site was owned by two different companies, only one of which was prepared to sell to Fulham.

In the meantime, the club's special dispensation to play at the Cottage in the Premiership with standing terraces along three side of the ground expired, and with neither the implementation of Plan A or Plan B imminent, the club had to find temporary accommodation. Loftus Road became Fulham's new home for two seasons between 2002 and 2004, as rent-paying tenants. While the team performed well in its new surroundings (the players after all had much less attachment to the Cottage), the supporters were homesick, and in the summer of 2004 Plan C was put into practice, a solution that delighted the hard-core Fulham faithful.

By adding all-seater stands behind the Hammersmith and Putney goals, Craven Cottage became, at a stroke, a modern football ground (thankfully, still not a 'stadium'), yet one which retained its old-style charm. The 1905 Stevenage Road stand and the Cottage were still in place and untouched, the oldest surviving examples of Leitch's work and as such a throwback to the pre-1914 era. They are, moreover, listed buildings. But the addition of the two stands behind the goals in 2004 (the responsibility of Fulham director and supporter Mark Collins) was done extremely tastefully and they have blended in very comfortably with the more traditional surroundings. The atmosphere with a full house (and the are quite a few these days in the top flight) is much better than at many more palatial grounds.

There is much that is wrong with Craven Cottage as a Premiership football arena. Entry is only possible from one side of the ground (Stevenage Road), the riverside stand which caused so many problems is hopelessly out-of-date in an era when hospitality facilities are increasingly important revenue earners, and transport access is very poor. The tube links require long walks from Putney Bridge or Hammersmith stations, motorists have to negotiate the unmentionable Fulham Palace Road and, when they get close to the ground, parking can be very difficult. (The terraced houses, built by Norris's firm at the turn of the century, have no garages and so supporters and residents have to compete for limited parking space.) And from the club's point of view, the capacity remains woefully short of the numbers that might offer Premiership financial viability.

But it is home, and it is where Fulham supporters want to be.

Fulham's Attendances

Official attendance figures were first recorded by the Football League in 1925 and reported on a regular basis by the national press only since 1938. Using the official League records for the 75 seasons since 1925–26 reveals that just over 25 million people saw the 1,601 home League games that were played up to May 2007 (including the two Play-off matches), an average of around 15,650 per game. This average has, of course, varied over time, from a high of 33,030 in the first First Division campaign of 1949–50 to a low of 4,057 in the dismal (old) Third Division season of 1990–91.

The highest attendance for one game was in October 1938, just a week or so after Prime Minister Neville Chamberlain's notorious deal with Hitler at Munich. Perhaps out of a sense of national relief that war had been avoided, attendances generally were high, but somehow 49,335 packed in the Cottage for a top-of-the-Second-Division-table clash between Fulham and Millwall, which the home side won 2–1. At the other end of the spectrum, just 2,176 bothered to turn up on a freezing Tuesday evening in January 1996 to see Fulham lose 3–1 to Scunthorpe. And it was easy to understand why so few people made the effort. A few days later, a 2–1 defeat at Torquay left the Cottagers in 91st place, the lowest point in their League history.

Attendances in any one season are determined by a number of factors: the division, the opposition, current form, ground capacity and the national trend among others. In the final two columns of the table, Fulham's average attendance for each season is related to the division in which they played,

A record crowd of 49,335 watch Fulham versus Millwall in October 1938.

ESTABLISHED 1880
Fulham Football and Athletic Co., Ltd.,
CRAVEN COTTAGE, STEVENAGE RD., FULHAM, S.W.6.
The Cottagers Journal
OFFICIAL PROGRAMME.
Nearest Stations:—
PUTNEY BRIDGE
(Underground
PUTNEY (S.R.) and
HAMMERSMITH
(Underground and Met.)
Ground Adjoins Bishop's Park.
2d.
Colours:—
WHITE SHIRTS,
BLACK KNICKERS.
L.P.T.B. TROLLEY BUS SERVICES 628, 630 and 655.
BUS ROUTES 30, 74 and 93, pass close to ground.
(Alight at Finlay Street).
FULHAM
v.
MILLWALL
Saturday, Oct. 8th, 1938
Kick off 3.30 p.m.
Football League, Div. 2.

The official programme from Fulham's game with Millwall which was watched by record numbers.

which is also a proxy for a national trend. Expressing Fulham's seasonal average as an index (percentage) of that year's divisional average gives some indication of the Cottagers performance relative to their peers.

The final column shows just how tough times have been for the club. By and large, they held their own in the Second and Third Divisions up to 1959, but in the top flight years of 1949–52 and again from 1959–68 there was a sizeable gap between Fulham's average gate and the divisional average. And the story has been the same for most of the time since, with the exception of the promotion years of 1971, 1982, 1997, 1999 and 2001. Fulham's gates are below those of the division as a whole, and the gap has never been wider than during the six Premiership seasons since 2001.

The difference between the Cottagers' gates and the rest of the Premiership has at times been less than half and never more than two thirds, which has huge implications for the financing of the club. The two seasons spent sharing with Queen's Park Rangers were the lowest point since Loftus Road is even smaller than the Cottage. But even between 2005 and 2007, with average attendances above 20,000 for the first time in 40 years, implying over 80% capacity utilisation, Fulham's gates were no more than 65% of the Premiership average.

The fact that in their first four Premiership seasons, Fulham had the lowest average gate in the division emphasises the point. And just to rub salt in the wound, in four of the six seasons (against Blackburn in 2002–03 and 2003–04, against West Brom in 2004–05 and against Birmingham in 2005–06) the lowest Premiership attendance of the season was at a Fulham home game. The Cottagers are the poor boys in a rich man's league.

In total there were 38 crowds of 40,000 or more at the Cottage, starting and ending with visits from Manchester United, in the FA Cup in 1908 and the First Division in April 1968. In the difficult years between 1985 and 1996, on the other hand, there were 20 gates of between 2,000 and 3,000 (which compares with just three gates of less than 5,000 between 1925 and 1979.)

The first official (as opposed to a reported) 40,000 crowd was in February 1926, 42,611 to see a Second Division match against Chelsea. There were 17 different clubs involved in the 38 matches, with Chelsea (six), Spurs and Manchester United (five each) leading the way. After the Millwall match, the two biggest Cottage attendances were for two First Division Easter fixtures, the 47,391 to see Spurs in March 1951 and 47,290 for the visit of Manchester United 16 years to the day later, in March 1967.

Being in the Premiership has clearly made a huge difference to attendances. The average gate in 2006–07, of 22,276, was the highest for exactly 40 years, back in the Johnny Haynes era, in 1966–67.

The lowest attendance last season, moreover (16,991), was still bigger than the highest attendance during the 13 seasons between 1984 and 1997 and better than the average attendances during the period from 1968 until 2001, 33 seasons.

Clearly, Fulham's support is better and gates have improved considerably, but can even a full Craven Cottage every match ever be enough to compete in the Premiership?

Season Attendances

SEASON	DIVISION	ATTENDANCES			DIVISIONAL	INDEX
		HIGHEST	AVERAGE	LOWEST	AVERAGE	
1907–08	Two	45,000	17,345	7,000	8,015	216
1908–09	Two	35,000	16,340	6,000	9,341	175
1909–10	Two	24,000	14,300	8,000	8,307	172
1910–11	Two	30,000	14,140	5,000	9,270	153
1911–12	Two	42,000	12,960	3,000	9,514	136
1912–13	Two	25,000	12,290	5,000	8,692	141
1913–14	Two	30,000	14,360	5,000	10,738	134
1914–15	Two	14,000	6,470	1,000	6,364	102
1919–20	Two	30,000	14,530	5,000	12,764	114
1920–21	Two	40,000	19,185	8,000	16,704	115
1921–22	Two	35,000	20,005	10,000	13,254	151
1922–23	Two	30,000	19,845	14,000	13,474	147
1923–24	Two	22,000	15,225	7,000	12,682	120
1924–25	Two	28,000	16,375	6,000	14,406	114
1925–26	Two	42,611	16,594	6,372	13,257	125
1926–27	Two	39,763	16,202	6,176	14,108	115
1927–28	Two	39,860	16,121	6,395	14,919	108
1928–29	Three South	28,349	18,250	11,069	8,614	212
1929–30	Three South	28,211	15,489	4,722	8,495	182
1930–31	Three South	18,955	10,825	7,000	6,947	156
1931–32	Three South	29,253	17,647	8,510	8,493	208
1932–33	Two	42,111	21,336	10,976	13,171	162
1933–34	Two	35,421	16,723	6,820	12,531	133
1934–35	Two	26,937	17,160	8,138	13,190	130
1935–36	Two	37,298	16,562	5,349	14,958	111
1936–37	Two	30,637	17,457	8,439	17,313	101
1937–38	Two	38,608	17,216	9,981	18,651	92
1938–39	Two	49,335	18,679	3,155	18,673	100
1946–47	Two	44,489	23,695	9,160	23,964	99
1947–48	Two	41,454	21,437	8,532	26,594	81
1948–49	Two	41,133	29,327	19,986	24,574	119
1949–50	One	45,924	33,030	21,031	37,400	88
1950–51	One	47,391	30,527	19,649	36,103	85

SEASON	DIVISION	ATTENDANCES HIGHEST	ATTENDANCES AVERAGE	ATTENDANCES LOWEST	DIVISIONAL AVERAGE	INDEX
1951–52	One	46,439	31,645	10,946	34,871	91
1952–53	Two	35,771	23,134	9,482	20,967	110
1953–54	Two	33,517	22,606	11,857	20,585	110
1954–55	Two	31,458	21,566	10,357	19,456	111
1955–56	Two	31,758	19,597	9,165	19,654	100
1956–57	Two	33,759	20,920	8,195	18,870	111
1957–58	Two	42,195	24,234	7,743	18,753	129
1958–59	Two	39,377	26,260	17,861	18,706	140
1959–60	One	44,858	30,271	17,536	31,150	97
1960–61	One	38,536	23,014	13,139	27,980	82
1961–62	One	43,355	24,401	12,639	26,106	93
1962–63	One	39,961	21,986	8,954	27,035	81
1963–64	One	41,770	21,163	12,199	27,027	78
1964–65	One	36,291	17,563	10,162	27,508	64
1965–66	One	38,960	21,138	9,735	27,014	78
1966–67	One	47,290	24,430	14,570	30,829	79
1967–68	Two	40,154	22,203	13,451	33,094	67
1968–69	Three	23,132	14,221	7,154	15,979	89
1969–70	Three	18,987	10,259	6,708	7,652	134
1970–71	Two	25,774	12,004	7,071	7,930	151
1971–72	Two	21,187	11,147	7,406	14,652	76
1972–73	Two	17,576	10,267	6,262	12,190	84
1973–74	Two	23,511	10,129	4,973	13,693	74
1974–75	Two	26,513	10,809	5,739	15,056	72
1975–76	Two	22,921	9,741	5,624	12,551	78
1976–77	Two	29,690	14,589	7,656	13,529	108
1977–78	Two	24,763	10,550	6,571	14,015	75
1978–79	Two	26,597	10,135	5,407	13,319	76
1979–80	Two	22,258	8,419	3,766	13,229	64
1980–81	Three	9,921	5,060	3,387	6,590	77
1981–82	Three	20,398	6,938	3,629	5,139	135
1982–83	Two	24,251	10,826	5,698	10,768	101
1983–84	Two	24,787	8,143	4,914	11,601	70
1984–85	Two	12,542	6,179	3,632	8,725	71
1985–86	Two	9,331	4,624	2,134	7,688	60
1986–87	Three	9,239	4,085	2,352	4,259	96
1987–88	Three	9,340	4,921	3,330	4,984	99
1988–89*	Three	10,188	5,200	3,402	5,498	95
1989–90	Three	7,141	4,484	2,652	5,079	88
1990–91	Three	6,765	4,057	2,750	5,137	79
1991–92	Three	8,671	4,492	4,531	5,423	83
1992–93	Three	9,143	4,716	3,285	6,310	75

SEASON	DIVISION	ATTENDANCES			DIVISIONAL	INDEX
		HIGHEST	AVERAGE	LOWEST	AVERAGE	
1993–94	Three	9,769	4,654	2,998	5,059	92
1994–95	Three	6,195	4,204	2,729	3,378	124
1995–96	Three	10,320	4,182	2,176	3,560	117
1996–97	Three	11,479	6,628	4,386	3,354	198
1997–98*	Two	17,114	9,175	5,096	6,364	144
1998–99	Two	17,176	11,409	7,447	7,554	151
1999–2000	One	19,623	13,069	8,688	14,149	92
2000–01	One	19,373	14,986	10,437	14,329	105
2001–02	Premier	21,159	19,545	15,885	34,324	57
2002–03	Premier	18,835	16,709	14,019	35,445	47
2003–04	Premier	18,306	16,342	13,981	35,008	47
2004–05	Premier	21,940	19,838	16,180	33,892	59
2005–06	Premier	22,486	20,340	16,550	33,873	60
2006–07	Premier	24,554	22,276	16,991	34,364	65

* Includes Play-off match

Great Fulham Teams

An Impressive Debut: 1907–08

Although the teams of 1905–06 and 1906–07 won the Southern League title, the achievement of Fulham's first League side the next year was more impressive, even if it finished empty handed in April 1908. Manager Harry Bradshaw skilfully negotiated the jump from non-League to the Second Division and his team came as close as any Fulham side for the next 50 years to a promotion and FA Cup double in the same season. In the end, the Cottagers had to settle for fourth place in the table, three points short of promotion, and defeat in the FA Cup semi-final.

A feature of the pre-World War One era was the huge turnover of players, and Bradshaw was a very active participant in the transfer market. For Fulham's debut season in the League, he signed 11 new players from other professional clubs and used 28 players in 38 games. But the 11 who played in at least half the games provided the nucleus of the side.

To start the first League campaign, the new arrivals included goalkeeper Leslie Skene from Queen's Park, a Scottish international and a doctor (who replaced the injured club captain, Jack Fryer), England international wing-half Albert Wilkes from Aston Villa, Reading full-back Archie Lindsay and Portsmouth's Scottish striker Bob Dalrymple. As the season progressed, Bradshaw made further acquisitions, the most important of whom were forwards Charlie Millington from Villa, Fred Harrison and Fred Mouncher from Southampton, inside-forward Harry Brown from Bradford and Sheffield United's England winger Bert Lipsham.

The Fulham squad at the start of the club's first campaign of 1907–08. From left to right, back row: J. Bradshaw, H. Crossthwaite, P. Waterson, H. Ross, W. Morrison, J. Hogan, J. Hindmarsh, A. Wilkes. Second row: J. Norris (assistant secretary), T. Pyne (steward), R. Armstrong, J. Hind, Mr W.G. Allen, J. Fryer, Mr J. Dean, F. Threlfall, Mr J. Watts, A. Collins, L. Skene, G. Mullet, Mr H. Bradshaw, J. Hamilton (trainer). Front row: T. Walker, W. Goldie, A. Fraser, E. Charlton, F. Bevan, A. Lindsay, T. Walker, J. Hullock. Seated on ground: E. Ward, A. Hubbard, T. Leigh, R. Dalrymple, W. Freeman, W. Thompson.

Amid the changes, there were some constants. The half-back line of the two Southern League Championship seasons, Arthur Collins, Billy Morrison and Billy Goldie, remained in tact and was the backbone of the side. Full-back Harry Ross, one of Bradshaw's first signings in 1904, was still first choice right-back, while Fred Threlfall continued to weave his intricate patterns down the right wing. This team gave notice that Fulham were a club with national rather than local aspirations.

Post-war Boom: 1921–22

During Phil Kelso's long tenure as manager (1909–24), Fulham were rarely challenging for honours, generally languishing in mid table in Division Two. But briefly there was some promise just after World War One, when an impressive run towards the end of 1920–21 held out the prospect of more the next season.

Forging a team made up of some loyal club stalwarts, a few high-profile signings and one or two youngsters, Kelso's side showed a meanness in defence (conceding just 20 goals in 42 home League games between 1920 and 1922) and a hunger for goals upfront. And they were good to watch. The fact that promotion failed to materialise was down to one moment of madness that undermined the team and brought the manager's career to a premature end.

Much of the defensive stability was attributable to Arthur Reynolds, whose goalkeeping appearances record between 1910 and 1925 was unchallenged until Jim Stannard came along.

The Fulham squad of 1921–22. From left to right, back row: Mr P. Kelso, F.R. Osborne, A. Reynolds, A. Chaplin, Sharp, Mr J. Dean. Middle row: A. Kingsley, D. Shea, B. Travers, D. Cock, H. Darvill, T. Fleming. Seated on ground: G. Martin, H. Russell, H. Bagge.

Defenders Jimmy Torrance and left-half Harry Russell also began their Fulham careers before World War One, whereas full-backs Ted Worrall and Alec Chaplin and right-half Harry Bagge were signed by Kelso in 1919. The one new defender in 1921 was the England double international Andy Ducat, a wing-half who had captained Aston Villa's 1920 Cup-winning side.

But the real difference was upfront, particularly the exciting inside-forward trio. Donald Cock had topped the club's scoring lists in both the first two post-war seasons, and in 1921 Kelso broke the club's transfer record by paying Sunderland £3,000 for a striking partner, Barney Travers. Providing the guile was the mercurial Danny Shea, an England international at the veteran stage when he signed in November 1920 but still immensely talented. On the wings, Fulham could choose between Frank Osborne and Frank Penn, two of their own discoveries who were with the club until the mid 1960s, and Scotty Kingsley, signed from Charlton.

When promotion was within touching distance, however, the Travers bribery scandal ended the striker's career, and probably Kelso's two years later, and the post-war boom was over.

The First Championship: 1931–32

It took four seasons for Fulham to regain Second Division status after the shock of relegation in 1928. In that time, they had three managers and a huge turnover of players. There were only two players who were regulars in both the relegation and promotion seasons, and it was a completely different club that went back up.

These were the days when winning promotion also meant winning the title. The architect of the

The Championship side. From left to right, back row: Oliver, Gibbon, Iceton, Birch, Penn. Front row: Richards, Hammond, Newton, Price, Finch, Gibbons.

Third Division South Championship success was manager James McIntyre in his first full season at the helm. An avowed admirer of Arsenal's Herbert Chapman, his skilful use of publicity, shrewd transfer dealings and willingness to make radical changes all combined to bring the first silverware to the Cottage in the club's 21st League season.

It took a while for the team to settle. Although Ernie Beecham started the season as first-choice goalkeeper, he made way for Jake Iceton in October after two straight defeats and never played for Fulham again. The signing of Joe Birch from Bournemouth in October 1931 solved one of the problem full-back positions, but three players, Sonny Gibbon, Arthur Tilford and Bill Hickie, shared the other berth.

The half-back line was the anchor of the side. Syd 'Carnera' Gibbons was a formidable centre-half, while wing-halves Len Oliver and Bert Barrett, both England internationals, were the survivors of the relegation season. McIntyre was lucky to have inherited from his predecessor three quality forwards, inside-forwards Johnny Price (the schemer) and Jim Hammond (the striker) and left-winger Jack Finch, who replaced the ageing Frank Penn. None of the three cost Fulham a penny in transfer fees.

But money was spent, on Bill Richards, a Welsh winger from McIntyre's old club, Coventry, and Stockport's centre-forward, Frank 'Bonzo' Newton, and it was money well spent. The sale of Jimmy Temple to Sunderland in the 1931 close season more than covered the outlay. The signing of Newton was a masterstroke for his 43 League goals in 39 games were pivotal in the Championship success, and are a club record which still stands.

The Surprising Champions: 1948–49

After two mid-table seasons following the post-war resumption of League football, it was a big surprise that Fulham emerged in May 1949 as champions of Division Two. The season started tragically, with the death of manager Jack Peart, and form was indifferent until Christmas. But a terrific run in the second half of the campaign (15 wins and only three defeats in 22 games) gave Fulham the edge over rivals Southampton and West Brom. The Cottagers won a vital clash at The Hawthorns in March, clinched promotion in the penultimate game at White Hart Lane and were crowned champions after beating West Ham in the final match.

When new manager Frank Osborne generously credited his late predecessor with the success, he was being unduly modest. While Peart had signed most of the squad, Osborne had made some crucial changes, which were the difference between mid table and champions.

The team was remarkably settled in the second half of the season, just 16 players used in 22 games, five of whom made just 11 appearances between them. Goalkeeper Doug Flack had been at the club since 1938 but it was 10 years before he made his debut. Once he had displaced Hinton in September 1948, however, he held his place. The full-backs, Harry Freeman and Joe Bacuzzi, were the only players to have played for Fulham before the war. Skipper Pat Beasley, an England international, had been an inside-forward with Arsenal and Huddersfield in the 1930s, but Peart had converted him to wing-half when he signed in 1945. Len Quested, an all-action right-half, and the stylish centre-half Jim Taylor, both came through in the first post-war season.

Of the forwards, top scorer Bob Thomas and outside-left Jack McDonald had been signed by Peart, from Brentford and Bournemouth respectively. Osborne had acquired centre-forward Rowley from West Brom in December 1948 and his 19 goals in 23 games were instrumental in the Championship

Back row, left to right: Eddie Perry (team manager), Freeman, Quested, Flack, Taylor, Bacuzzi, Beasley, Frank Penn (Trainer). Front row, left to right : Lewin, Stevens, R Thomas, Rowley, S Thomas, McDonald, Bewley.

success. The line up was completed by two one-club men, outside-right Arthur Stevens and inside-left Beddy Jezzard, who both gave Fulham loyal service through to the 1960s.

Back in the Big Time: 1958–59

During 1957–58, manager Dug Livingstone fashioned a side that came as close to winning promotion from the Second Division and reaching the Cup Final in the same season as any Fulham side for exactly 50 years. They disappointingly missed out on both prizes but the nucleus of that side, under Livingstone's successor, went on to make sure of promotion the following year and usher in what many supporters still regard as the club's halcyon years.

From the start of 1958–59, when they won nine and drew three of their first 12 games, Fulham were promotion front-runners. New manager Bedford Jezzard, appointed in the summer when Livingstone preferred to return north, was lucky with his inheritance. There was only one significant change to the squad in the summer. Roy Dwight was sold to Nottingham Forest and Scottish international Graham Leggat bought from Aberdeen for a bargain £20,000.

Otherwise it was much as the previous season. Goalkeeper Tony Macedo, only a teenager when he was given his chance just before Christmas 1957, had become the established first choice. Around the same time, George Cohen had taken over the right-back slot and started his long partnership with Jimmy Langley. Roy Bentley had been successfully converted by Livingstone from a centre-forward to a half-back to play alongside Joe Stapleton and Eddie Lowe, with Irish international Robin Lawler covering several defensive positions.

From left to right, back row: Bently, Langley, Cohen, Macedo, Cook, Mullery. Front row: Barton, Hill, Doherty, Haynes, Chamberlain.

In the forward line, Leggat occupied the right wing and the effervescent Tosh Chamberlain the left. Maurice Cook, signed the previous February, took over the centre-forward slot from the ageing Arthur Stevens. Either side of him were Jimmy Hill and skipper Johnny Haynes, at his imperious best. To his supreme distribution skills, the Maestro showed he could also score goals, finishing the season as top scorer with 26 goals, including four hat-tricks.

Several youngsters, like Brian O'Connell and Johnny Key, were used during the season, but the one significant change was made in February. Teenager Alan Mullery came in at right-half and stayed, with Bentley moving to centre-half in place of Stapleton.

Sixties Prime: 1963–64

Fulham spent the nine seasons from 1959 to 1968 in the old First Division, the club's longest run in the top flight. No honours were won in these years and several of the seasons were spent flirting with relegation, but they are still regarded as the golden years. Much of this was due to the wonderfully talented individuals at the Cottage (but not enough for a really successful team), and the apparently carefree spirit created by Beddy Jezzard and his management team, made up largely of former Fulham players.

In 1963–64, the Cottagers finished in the relative comfort of 15th, generally untroubled by thoughts of the drop. Beating Ipswich 10–1 and champions-elect Liverpool 1–0 were obvious highlights. But the club was at a crossroads. This was to be Jezzard's last season as the helm, and by the end of 1964–65 general manager Frank Osborne, trainer Frank Penn and reserve-team manager

From left to right, back row: Robson, Keetch, Mullery, Macedo, Cohen, Langley. Front row: Key, Leggat, Brown, Cook, Haynes, O'Connell.

Joe Bacuzzi had also departed. With the appointment of Vic Buckingham, the character of the club was about to change.

Stability was a feature of these years. Still regulars in 1963–64 were seven of the side that had won promotion five years earlier. Tony Macedo, George Cohen and Jimmy Langley formed the last line of defence, as they had in 1958–59. Alan Mullery, the flamboyant Bobby Keetch and England international Bobby Robson, who had returned to Fulham in 1962, made up the half-back line.

Johnny Haynes continued to reign supreme in midfield, while Graham Leggat and Maurice Cook provided the firepower upfront. On the wings were Johnny Key and Brian O'Connell, five forwards who had all played in the Second Division promotion side. But waiting on the sidelines were promising youngsters like Fred Callaghan, Rodney Marsh, Stan Brown and Steve Earle, products of the youth scheme.

The club seemed in good shape, but the transfer of Alan Mullery to Spurs in March 1964, negotiated behind the manager's back, was a turning point. When Buckingham arrived in January 1965, the decline accelerated and five years later Fulham were in the Third Division.

Wembley at Last: 1974–75

By reaching the FA Cup Final in 1975, Fulham were able to discard the unwanted record of getting to more semi-finals without ever making it through to the Final. The Cottagers had been beaten four times at the penultimate stage, and in 1958 and 1962 in particular, lost ties they should have won. But in 1975 a very ordinary Second Division side took the longest route to Wembley (11 games to win five ties), surprising themselves as much as the rest of football with their progress.

In charge was Alec Stock, giant-killer par excellence, whose previous career (especially with Yeovil, Leyton Orient and Queen's Park Rangers) was littered with unlikely Cup upsets. His Fulham side of

Fulham's 1975 Cup Final squad. Left to right, back row: John Collins, Ron Woolnough, Lloyd, Strong, Howe, Lacy, Mellor, Dowie, Busby, Mitchell, Friend, Bill Taylor. Front row: Conway, Slough, Mullery, Alec Stock, Moore, Barrett, Cutbush. Ken Coton.

1975, of ageing stars, honest journeymen and promising youngsters, swept past two Second Division and three First Division opponents to end the club's 67-year semi-final jinx.

Only 15 players were used in the Cup run of 1975, two of whom played in no more than two matches. Of the other 13, goalkeeper Peter Mellor, skipper Alan Mullery, defender Bobby Moore, midfielder Alan Slough, winger Les Barrett and striker Viv Busby played in all 12 games. Central-defender John Lacy played in 11 of the 12 FA Cup games, midfielder Jimmy Conway only missed two and full-back John Cutbush just three.

By far the unluckiest was left-back Les Strong. He had played in the 11 matches on the way to Wembley, the first 40 League games and all three League Cup ties. Then, a fortnight before Wembley, he was injured and had to sit and watch John Fraser wear his number-three shirt in the Final. The other place, and substitute spot, was a battle between three players, John Mitchell, returning from injury, Barry Lloyd and John Dowie. On the day, Mitchell appeared at Wembley, Lloyd was substitute and Dowie (who played in all but the three third-round matches against Hull) missed out.

Reaching the Final was a peak for the club. Thereafter they began a slide (interrupted only briefly in early 1980s) that at one stage looked to be terminal.

A False Dawn: 1981–82

After the Cup Final appearance in 1975, Fulham began on a long downward slide that ended in 91st place in the Football League in February 1996. The one brief ray of light in the two decades of gloom came when Malcolm Macdonald succeeded Bobby Campbell in the autumn of 1980. The club was in debt, had been relegated the previous May, and it was Macdonald's first managerial appointment. The omens were not good, but within 18 months Fulham were promoted with a young side, rich in promise, playing exciting, attacking football.

Malcolm Macdonald's promotion-winning squad at the start of the 1982–83 season. Left to right, back row: Hopkins, Tempest, O'Driscoll, Lock, Coney. Middle row: Greenway, Hatter, Peyton, Brown, Stannard, Gale, Wilson, Parker. Front row: Hartford (coach), Lewington, Houghton, Strong, Macdonald (manager), O'Sullivan, Reeves, Davies, Wright (physio).

It was achieved without spending any money. All the players who were in the promotion side were at the club during the dire Campbell era, apart from free transfer signing Peter O'Sullivan from Brighton. In goal, Irish international Gerry Peyton was in his sixth season at the club, while left-back Les Strong was signed in Bill Dodgin's time 10 years earlier. At the heart of the defence were the stylish Tony Gale and rugged Roger Brown, two players whose skills complemented each other. Brown was a Campbell signing from Norwich in the winter of 1979, whereas Gale, although still only 21 at the start of 1981–82, had already made 174 first-class appearances for Fulham. At right-back, young Jeff Hopkins came into the side and settled very quickly.

The midfield was the engine room. Sean O'Driscoll and Ray Lewington were two more Campbell signings who came good under Macdonald, young Robert Wilson came of age in these years while O'Sullivan slotted in from day one. The fact that they scored 21 times between them meant the team was not totally dependent on the front two for goals. Strikers Gordon Davies and young Dean Coney forged a wonderfully productive partnership, feeding off each other as well as linking effectively with the midfield. The two were on the mark an impressive 44 times that season.

Macdonald was lucky with his inheritance, but he (and his coaches, George Armstrong and Ray Harford) got a lot more out of them. He also had quality cover on which to draw, such as Kevin Lock in defence or midfield, Paul Parker at full-back and Dale Tempest upfront. Sadly, it all ended within a couple of seasons.

The Tide Turns: 1996–97

In the space of just five seasons, Fulham won three promotions that took them from the fourth tier of English football to the first. Of the three, the hardest earned was the first, when Micky Adams's side

The squad at the start of the 1996–97 season was back row, left to right: Angus, Blake, Walton, Cullip, Lange, Stewart, Mison. Middle row: Chris Smith (physio), Freeman, Thomas, McAree, Barkus, Honor, Hamill, Watson, Hamsher, Herrera, Scott, John Marshall (youth-team coach). Front row: Grover, Cockerill, Cusack, Len Walker (assistant manager), Micky Adams (manager), Alan Cork (reserve-team coach), Morgan, Conroy, Brooker.

climbed out of Division Three. There was no Fayed money to help him, no big names signed for huge fees, only a bunch of cheap signings and journeymen professionals who battled and scrapped for every point to win Fulham's first promotion for 15 years.

Just months before, in February 1996, when Fulham slipped to next to bottom in the Third Division, Ian Branfoot made way for Micky Adams to take over team affairs. In the summer he strengthened the squad for very modest outlay and rebuilt the confidence of the existing players. The Cottagers got off to a flyer and never looked back, winning promotion with four games to spare.

Although Adams used 28 players, there were 13 who played in at least half the games. In goal, Mark Walton, signed from non-League football, displaced Tony Lange. Paul Watson, one of three recruits from Gillingham, and Robbie Herrera, a survivor of the relegation season of 1993–94, were the regular full-backs, although late in the campaign Matt Lawrence arrived from Wycombe. In the centre of defence Mark Blake and Terry Angus were the first choices, but young Danny Cullip covered for both, and at full-back, and looked an excellent prospect.

The experience was in midfield. Nick Cusack played just in front of the back four and skipper Simon Morgan and veteran Glenn Cockerill in the middle, and these three provided the craft and know-how. The running power arrived when Richard Carpenter was signed from Gillingham in September. The engaging Darren Freeman (another Priestfield graduate) and Rob Scott offered width and support for striker Micky Conroy, who enjoyed the best scoring season of his career.

Within 12 months Adams and most of the squad were gone, replaced by Keegan and numerous expensive signings. Fulham's rapid ascent was underway, but it was the more modest squad, cheaply assembled, that started it and probably persuaded Mohamed Al Fayed to buy the club.

The Best Yet?: 2000–01

When Jean Tigana was appointed, he was an unknown quantity as a manager, but within weeks, after the team had won the first 11 games of the season, it was clear that he was an inspired choice. In a record-breaking season the Cottagers ran away with the divisional title to reclaim the place in the top flight they had lost 33 years earlier. It was not only effective, but also a joy to watch, and even older supporters conceded it was better even than in the Haynes era of the 1960s.

Although he had funds to spend, and would spend on a major scale in the Premiership, Tigana relied largely on the players he had inherited. In goal, Maik Taylor was a Kevin Keegan signing, as were full-backs Steve Finnan and Rufus Brevett and central-defenders Chris Coleman and Kit Symons. But it was manager Paul Bracewell who added his old Sunderland colleague Andy Melville to the club's defensive ranks. When skipper Coleman was seriously injured in a car crash, Tigana did splash out £4 million in March 2001 on Newcastle's Alain Goma, but his main contribution was in the Premiership.

Under Tigana, Sean Davis blossomed in midfield and he had Lee Clark and Barney Goldbaek for company. The key newcomers were in midfield or upfront. John Collins, a Tigana player in Monaco, rejoined his old boss from Everton and orchestrated the play from midfield. Luis Boa Morte, initially on loan, and Fabrice Fernandes were immensely talented wide players who were just as happy going for goal themselves as creating chances for the strikers.

Fulham paid French club Metz just over £2 million for striker Louis Saha, whose only previous experience in England was an unhappy loan spell at Newcastle. He thrived at Fulham, heading the scoring lists with 32 goals (27 in the League), the best since Jezzard in the 1950s. He was well supported by Barry Hayles (another Keegan signing) and Boa Morte, who contributed another 40 goals between them.

There had been a French Revolution at Craven Cottage, every bit as radical as Robespierre and the Jacobins in the 1790s in Paris. It was a highpoint in Fulham's 122-year history.

Fulham 2001, back row, left to right: Sam Keevill, Luke Cornwall, Elvis Hammond, Zathiath Knight, Glyn Thopson, Mailk Taylor, Marcus Hahnemann, Anthony Tucker, Kit Symons, Karl-Heinz Riedle, Bjarne Goldbaek, Simon Morgon. Middle row: Chris Smith (physiotherapist), Wayne Collins, Sean Davis, Kevin Betsy, Steve Finnan, Alan Neilson, Roger Propos (coach), Andy Melville, Paul Trollope, Louis Saha, Fabrice Fernandes, Louis Boa Morte, Alan Bevan (kit manager). Front row: Kieran McAnespie, Rufus Brevett, Lee Clark, Terry Phelan, John Collins, Jean Tigana (manager), Christian Damiano (coach), Chris Coleman, Eddie Lewis, Paul Peschisolido, Steve Hayward, Barry Hayles.

A Century of Memorable Matches

1 Fulham 4 Minerva 0 — Middlesex Senior Cup — 10 October 1896

After two years preparation, it was time for the big kick-off at 'the commodious new ground of Fulham FC on the site of Craven Cottage, Crabtree Lane near Bishop's Park' in a Middlesex Senior Cup tie. The attendance was described as 'large' for this 3.30pm start when Fulham kicked-off from 'the Bridge End'. Both sides were at full strength and Fulham made the historic breakthrough three minutes before half-time. Goalkeeper McTeare saved Harry Johnson's shot, but the ball only went back to Johnson who then passed to Jimmy Lindsey to score the first-ever goal at Craven Cottage. Lindsey added a second after 70 minutes, Jack Shrimpton made it 3–0 and Eddie Witheridge got between two defenders to shoot past the goalkeeper for the fourth 'to give the Reds a fine win'.

2 Swanscombe 5 Fulham 0 — FA Cup 2Q round — 31 October 1896

Just weeks later, a very unsettled Fulham side played in the FA Cup for the first time, in the second qualifying round against Swanscombe. A fortnight after the win over Minerva, local rivals Stanley FC visited the Cottage for a London League game and the match was played in very muddy conditions. In the first half, Fulham goalkeeper Jack May was beaten four times, including once (unusually) by a penalty. At half-time, he lodged an appeal against the conditions, which was rejected and Stanley ran out 8–0 winners. As soon as the match was over, secretary Horace Wilkins sacked May as goalkeeper and as captain and a dispirited squad travelled to Kent. It showed in the performance. Fulham were soundly beaten and they did not enter the FA Cup again for another three years, preferring the Amateur Cup in the intervening years.

3 Fulham 0 Tottenham H 0 — Southern League Division One — 5 September 1903

This is where first-class football at Fulham began, a home game in the Edwardian equivalent of the Third Division. An improved ground (with the Rabbit Hutch newly installed) and virtually a new team awaited the 14,000 who came for the opening match in the Southern League First Division. Derby goalkeeper Jack Fryer was Fulham's big-name signing, and he was the new captain. Spurs were attractive visitors, having won the FA Cup and the Southern League, and there was a great sense of occasion at the ground as the 4.00pm kick-off time approached. The game was fast and exciting but with two sound defences there were very few chances. A draw was a fair result, and the hard-earned point suggested Fulham would not be out of their depth at the higher level.

4 Fulham 12 Wellingborough 0 — Southern League Division One — 28 January 1905

This, technically, remains Fulham's biggest first-class victory and the result indicated that new manager Harry Bradshaw was close to finding the team that would bring two Southern League titles and League football to the Cottage. Days earlier, Fulham had pulled off a major surprise by beating Manchester United in the FA Cup and against Wellingborough, as one newspaper said 'the display of the team was brilliant in the extreme'. Former Newcastle players Fraser (five goals) and Wardrope (three goals) led the scoring charge, with Goldie (two), Lennie and Morrison making up the dozen. It was ample revenge for the 2–1 defeat at Wellingborough earlier in the season.

5 Aston Villa 5 Fulham 0 FA Cup round three 4 March 1905

In his first full season, manager Harry Bradshaw had put Fulham on the path to League success and had guided his Southern League charges to the last eight of the FA Cup for the first time. But a trip to mighty Aston Villa was a tie too far. Challenging for the First Division title (as usual), the Villa side contained established internationals like Bache, Spencer, Hampton and Leake, and on the day, they swept Fulham aside. As one contemporary newspaper reported, 'If asked to specify a worse exhibition of football than that served up by Fulham against Aston Villa, it would be difficult to do so'. Goals by Pearson, Hampton and Hall had killed the tie by half-time, and further strikes by Hampton and Bache just rubbed salt into the wounds. Only a heroic display by Fryer kept the score down.

6 Fulham 0 Portsmouth 0 Southern League Division One 2 September 1905

There was a party atmosphere among the 20,000 crowd when the revamped Cottage was unveiled for the opening game of 1905–06. Leitch's imaginative development had been built during the summer months and a range of local dignitaries attended the opening, the formalities of which were performed by local MP W. Hayes Fisher. Although the game lacked goals, both sides were committed to attack but the two strong defences prevailed. There was, apparently, 'much hearty cheering' and some 'rattling good sport' during the 90 minutes. Threlfall on the right wing was Fulham's most effective attacker, while Morrison marshalled the defence superbly. As the season progressed, it became clear this was a clash between two of the principal title contenders, which Fulham eventually won.

7 Bristol R 0 Fulham 1 Southern League Division One 21 April 1906

The first of six divisional titles Fulham have won in 104 years was the Southern League, clinched at Bristol with a game to spare. It was only the club's third season at this level and the success reflected manager Bradshaw's shrewd guidance. The 1–0 scoreline was typical of a season in which the defence conceded a mere 15 goals in 34 games. On a windswept Bristol pitch ('the playing area is as rough as the local crowd' claimed one report), the only goal came after 15 minutes, Freeman getting his head to a Threlfall free-kick. Although Rovers dominated possession thereafter, the Cottagers' superb half-back line of Collins, Morrison and Goldie thwarted most attacks, and behind them Fryer was in commanding form. The Championship win established Fulham as a football force in the south of England.

8 Fulham 3 Southampton 0 Southern League Division One 20 April 1907

Fulham wrapped up a second Southern League title in 12 months in their final home match of the season. The Championship was a battle between Portsmouth and the Cottagers and, with two games to go, the holders needed just two points to retain the title. The match, played at the same time as the FA Cup Final at the old Crystal Palace, attracted a disappointing crowd of 16,000. But at least they saw Fulham extend their 13-match unbeaten run and win very convincingly. After a goalless first half,

Hamilton broke the deadlock early in the second, Freeman added a second and Ross rounded it off with a penalty. Losing to West Ham the following week did not matter and did not prevent Fulham becoming a Football League club the next season.

9 Fulham 0 Hull C 1 — League Division Two — 3 September 1907

Fulham's entry into the Football League began rather curiously, at 5.00pm on a Tuesday afternoon, which probably explains why just 10,000 turned up for this historic match. Manager Harry Bradshaw had signed six players, including international goalkeeper Leslie Skene and striker Bob Dalrymple, to meet the demands of the Second Division, but the press was anxious to reassure supporters that, 'although half the team may be new, the play is still Fulham's'. Despite looking the more skilful team, and having more of the possession, the Cottagers flunked their first test. A mistake by new left-back Lindsay after eight minutes let in Hull's 'nimble brained and quick footed' inside-forward Smith to shoot past Skene. Hull then reverted to defence, and, for all their extra guile, Fulham were unable to find a way through.

10 Fulham 3 Manchester C 1 — FA Cup round three replay — 26 February 1908

By the time the FA Cup campaign got under way that first season, Fulham had found their League feet and, as well as climbing the Second Division table, were making an impression in the Cup. Relatively easy wins over Luton and Norwich took them into the last 16, where they were paired with First Division Manchester City at their old Hyde Road ground. Played in a howling gale, Fulham surprised City and, but for an error by Skene, Harrison's first-half goal would have been the winner. In the replay, the Cottagers outplayed the illustrious opponents. A huge crowd (38,000) created traffic chaos but roared Fulham on. Taking advantage of the strong wind, City led at half-time but then, with the wind to their backs, Ross, following up when 'keeper Smith only parried his penalty, Harrison and Dalrymple put Fulham into the quarter-finals.

11 Fulham 2 Manchester U 1 — FA Cup round four — 7 March 1908

This was the game that turned Fulham from a promising London club to a serious national side. Having beaten First Division Manchester City in the previous round of the FA Cup, the Cottagers drew League leaders and champions-elect Manchester United in the quarter-finals. The first-ever 40,000 crowd turned up at the Cottage to see how Harry Bradshaw's Second Division team fared against the star-studded and double-chasing United from the red side of Manchester. For once, the match lived up to the occasion and it was probably Fulham's most significant pre-World War One result.

In the United line up were the legendary Billy Meredith, the most famous footballer of his generation, the prolific Sandy Turnbull up front (who was to be killed in World War One) and a magnificent half-back line of Duckworth, Roberts and Bell. But 'amid scenes of enthusiasm without parallel in the history of local football', Fulham turned the form book on its head and deservedly beat the best team in the country. 'By tactics, Fulham overthrew the artistic Mancunians. It was a match that thrilled, a victory that gave to London the pleasure of the knowledge that the Metropolis has doughty candidates for honours in the FA Cup', as one paper put it.

It was in defence that Fulham won it. Skene was outstanding in goal and the half-back line of Collins, Morrison and Goldie dominated the United forwards and gave them no room to demonstrate

Skene, the Fulham goalkeeper, saves a Manchester United header.

their skills. Fulham took the lead with a lucky goal after 12 minutes. United full-back Burgess cleared, but the ball hit Harrison who was closing him down and flashed past Moger into the net. Although Fulham had the better of the opening exchanges, United's intricate passing and subtle runs gradually got them back in the game as half-time approached.

After the break, Fulham again had the upper hand, and Moger had to be at his best to keep the score down. But United came back and a Meredith cross was headed on by Sandy Turnbull to Jimmy Turnbull to equalise. Then, with 25 minutes remaining, Harrison got the ball just outside the penalty area and, as three defenders hesitated as to who would tackle him, hit a low drive past the 'keeper. United heads seemed to drop and Fulham finished the stronger of the teams.

After the game, both teams went off the Alhambra in Leicester Square, where they saw filmed highlights of the game, and a huge audience 'was thrilled by the incidents so truthfully and clearly set forth'. At the Saturday night 'smoking concert' which followed, speeches were made and songs sung in which the players and officials of both sides participated heartily.

Fulham: Skene; Ross, Lindsay; Collins, Morrison, Goldie; Millington, Dalrymple, Harrison, Fraser, Mouncher.

Manchester United: Moger; Stacey, Burgess; Duckworth, Roberts, Bell; Meredith, Bannister, J. Turnbull, A. Turnbull, Wall.

12 Newcastle U 6 Fulham 0 FA Cup semi-final 28 March 1908

The all-conquering Newcastle at Anfield awaited the Cottagers in the semi-final and there was a smaller than expected Fulham contingent in the 50,000 crowd (because of the high rail fares charged on Grand National weekend). Perhaps that was fortunate because this was not Bradshaw's team's finest hour. 'Fulham were painfully effete, their combination ragged, their attacks came with snatches' said one report. They were thrashed by a margin that is still today the record for a Cup semi-final and by a masterly team packed with internationals. Appleyard and Howie scored in the first half and Rutherford (2), Howie and Gardner in the second. Despite an injury restricting his mobility, goalkeeper Skene was Fulham's best player. On the day, Fulham 'lacked pace, dash and skill, never combined effectively and were really outclassed'. It was the start of a long semi-final jinx.

13 Fulham 5 Stockport C 1 — League Division Two — 5 September 1908

After a remarkably good debut season, the rest of the period up to 1915 was anti-climatic. Bradshaw left at the end of a mediocre 1908–09 season, the highlight of which was the personal achievement of centre-forward Fred Harrison scoring five goals in a League match, the first four before the interval. He owed a lot to wingers Threlfall and Lipsham, whose crosses for three of the goals required relatively easy finishes. The first goal, however, was a fluke, Dalrymple's shot hitting Harrison on the head and then diverting into the net. Stockport scored in the final minute through Martin, shortly after Proudfoot had missed a penalty for the visitors. Harrison's feat was subsequently equalled (by Jezzard, Hill and Earle) but never beaten in a League game.

14 Fulham 1 Chelsea 0 — League Division Two — 3 December 1910

The first League meeting between these closest of neighbours went Fulham's way. Although the older of the clubs, Fulham were admitted to the League after Chelsea, who were in Division One when the Cottagers gained entry to Division Two. But relegation for Chelsea in 1909–10 brought the two head-to-head in the League. Among the 35,000 crowd were the Liberal and Conservative candidates for the imminent General Election and the game was played in a Cup-tie atmosphere. Fulham scored the only goal after 20 minutes. A shot by outside-right Smith was parried by goalkeeper Molyneux, but Smith, following up, smashed the ball into the net. Although Harrison came close to adding a second before the break, Chelsea dominated territorially without threatening the goal. In the second half, played in fading light, Whittingham 'scored' from a penalty but when ordered to re-take it shot over the bar.

15 Fulham 6 W. Arsenal 1 — League Division Two — 8 November 1913

This was a meeting of two clubs with a shared director. Unthinkable today, but Henry Norris was still on the Fulham board even though he had taken over the near-bankrupt Woolwich Arsenal. The Gunners relegation in 1913, moreover, brought the Fulham manager Phil Kelso up against his former club. There was nothing to choose between the sides for an hour, but in the last 30 minutes seven goals were scored. A combination of exciting Fulham play and sloppy Arsenal defending made the Cottagers the clear masters. After Pearce had missed a sitter and Taylor had hit a post, ex-Arsenal forward Coleman and Pearce capitalised on Arsenal mistakes to score. By the time Taylor extended the lead, an injury to McKinnon reduced the Gunners to 10 men. Walker and Pearce added to the score, Stonley pulled one back, but Pearce completed the rout.

16 Fulham 5 Birmingham 0 — League Division Two — 25 March 1921

Very briefly after World War One, Fulham had a side that looked to have promotion potential. The signings of England international inside-forward Danny Shea and the bustling centre-forward Barney

Travers to play alongside Donald Cock had added some extra bite to the attack. Against Second Division leaders Birmingham on Good Friday, they gave their best display in manager Kelso's five post-war seasons. But it could have been very different. With the game still goalless, the visitors got a penalty, and Reynolds saved Jones's kick, Birmingham's seventh penalty miss of the season. Then Travers became provider, first for Cock and next for Shea, before heading the third himself. After the interval, Travers and Shea were again on the mark to complete Fulham's biggest win and Birmingham's biggest defeat of the season.

17 South Shields 0 Fulham 1 League Division Two 18 March 1922

This match was the reason the promotion potential was never fulfilled, a dark day in the history of Fulham, which ended one career and blighted the remainder of another. With 10 games to go, Fulham were in fifth place just four points behind the leaders and were looking for two points from a mid-table South Shields side. After just six minutes, Gray put the hosts ahead with a first-time shot that gave Reynolds no chance. The home team had the better of the 90 minutes, but the real story was the claim that Fulham's Travers had offered a bribe to the opposition. An inquiry was launched within days, Travers was found guilty and banned for life. But many believed he was manager Kelso's messenger and, although no charges were brought, the manager retired at the age of 53 two years later and never worked again in football.

18 Fulham 1 Everton 0 FA Cup round three replay 14 January 1926

This was the first of three remarkable FA Cup victories over Everton, all achieved when Fulham were in the Second Division and the Toffees were in the First. And this was a game in which the performance of a teenage goalkeeper became part of Fulham folklore. In the League, the Cottagers were struggling. Manager and former player Andy Ducat had succeeded Phil Kelso in 1924 but had inherited a poor squad which was slowly deteriorating. Relegation was a constant threat. When the Cup campaign began with a trip to Goodison, only a supreme optimist could have forecast that this was the start of the best run since 1912 and, in terms of higher division victims, the best run ever (only equalled in 1975).

At Goodison, Fulham had earned an unlikely draw. Dixie Dean cheered the 46,000 with his usual goal, but Teddy Craig snatched a second-half equaliser. The replay was played on a freezing cold Thursday afternoon, with snow covering the ground and terraces. 'A slipping, sliding, scrambling match seemed certain. Instead, there was one of the most interesting games of the third round. Fulham won but were lucky.'

As one newspaper said, 'If fortune proved a good 12th man for Fulham, next in order of merit came goalkeeper Beecham'. Starting the season as third choice, the 19-year-old Beecham, signed from Hertford the previous close season, had made his debut only a month earlier but, at the end of this tie, he had become a Fulham legend. 'He was here, there and everywhere. He leaped high to save, he dived wide and low to save.' On the day he was unbeatable, one of his best saves coming in the last minute in rapidly fading light. And when he was beaten, by Chedgzoy, a post came to his rescue. At full time he was carried off shoulder high by ecstatic fans.

The only goal of the game came 17 minutes into the second half. With the Toffees dominating, Fulham broke away, and Edmonds raced towards Sam Hardy's goal. The ball was cleared, but from the

Goalkeeper Beecham and centre-half McNabb keep Dixie Dean at bay.

resulting throw in the ball was crossed, defender McDonald slipped while trying to clear and Bert White scrambled the ball in. Perhaps, since Fulham had been reduced to 10 men for most of the second half because of an injury to skipper Alec Chaplin in those pre-substitute days, they deserved this bit of luck.

Fulham: Beecham; Dyer, Chaplin; Oliver, McNabb, Barrett; Harris, Craig, Edmonds, White, Penn.
Everton: Hardy; Raitt, McDonald; Peacock, Bain, Virr; Chedgzoy, Irvine, Dean, O'Donnell, Troup.

19 Fulham 3 Liverpool 1 FA Cup round four 30 January 1926

Although struggling near the foot of Division Two, Fulham disposed of another First Division Merseyside club in the fourth round of the Cup. The Reds line up included seven members of the side that had won the League title a few years earlier, including Jock McNabb, the brother of Fulham centre-half David. The two goalkeepers decided the game. For the Cottagers, Beecham was again outstanding, but Liverpool's famous international, Elisha Scott, was unusually below par. Pape opened the scoring for Fulham after four minutes, converting Harris's cross, and Harris again set up Pape's second and Fulham's third, this time a header. In between, Forshaw had equalised for Liverpool but then came Scott's error. He came out to fist a Penn lob but merely fisted thin air and the ball rolled gently into the net.

20 Fulham 1 Manchester U 2 FA Cup round six 6 March 1926

After disposing of Notts County in round five, Fulham fell at home in the quarter-finals to their fourth First Division opponents that season. The doubling of admission prices (10p to stand) backfired and the crowd was a disappointing 28,699. The game had a sensational start. United led after 90 seconds, and Beecham was at fault. He seemed to have covered a McPherson shot but took his eye off the ball and it squeezed through his grasp and over the line. But within 90 seconds, Fulham were level, Pape firing Harris's pass beyond goalkeeper Mew. The Second Division side then went on to dominate play and create the better chances in a match spoilt by a strong wind. But four minutes before the interval, United got the deciding goal. From a hotly disputed corner, Smith hooked the ball into the net.

21 Blackpool 4 Fulham 0 League Division Two 5 May 1928

After flirting with relegation for several seasons, the drop became a reality at the seaside. It was a bizarre season of solid home performances but an appalling away record. Yet, even though they had lost 19 of the first 20 games on their travels, Fulham went to Bloomfield Road for the final game knowing that a point would keep them up and send Blackpool down. Any hopes they had, however, were extinguished by half-time when they trailed 2–0. A free-kick for handball needlessly conceded by Barrett led to Hampson scoring the first, almost kicking the ball out of Beecham's hands. Oxberry scored the second and Hampson completed his hat-trick with two more after the break. Although hampered by injury to Hebden, it was a tame end to a woeful season for the Cottagers.

22 Gillingham 2 Fulham 2 Third Division South 25 August 1928

Fulham's first game in the third tier of English football began in the unprepossessing surroundings of the Priestfield Stadium in front of a crowd of just under 9,500. They had the same manager (Joe Bradshaw) but several new players (full-back Bert Rosier and inside-forwards Bill Haley and Johnny Price) following relegation the previous May. The Cottagers soon learned that life at the lower level would not necessarily be easier. Newcomer Price opened his side's account and Avey added a second before the break, but the Gills came back to equalise in the second half. That was very much the story of the season, a mix of impressive performances and careless points dropped which meant they were never in the promotion hunt.

23 Fulham 10 Torquay U 2 Third Division South 7 September 1931

In the closing weeks of the 1930–31 season, Fulham appointed a new manager, their fourth in seven years. James McIntyre was previously in charge at Southampton and Coventry and he was not short of self confidence when he arrived at the Cottage. Like his hero, Herbert Chapman, he understood the value of publicity and in his statements to the press made bold predictions about what Fulham were going to achieve with him at the helm.

He made two important signings in the close season, Bill Richards a right-winger from his previous club, Coventry (who was to become Fulham's first Welsh international), but, more importantly, centre-forward Frank 'Bonzo' Newton from Stockport. He was to set a club record which still stands of 43 League goals in a season (in 39 games). Had injury not ended his career in 1934, he might have achieved so much more.

McIntyre's side got off to a great start, winning the first two games and Newton getting five goals in the process. Then, against a Torquay team which had already conceded 14 goals in its opening three matches, the Cottagers did very much as they pleased. A head injury to full-back Webster when Fulham scored their first goal obviously weakened them, and he resumed, heavily bandaged on the left wing. But Torquay were no match for Fulham even with a full side.

By half-time they were six goals down (the last five coming in an 18–minute spell), with Newton, Finch, Proud, Hammond, Newton and Price all getting on the score sheet. After the break, Fulham's cricketing inside-forward Hammond proved to be the chief tormentor, with three on the trot. Price took the total into double figures, but the visitors salvaged some pride by scoring twice in the closing stages, through Hutchinson and Stabb.

If anyone had any doubts that Fulham were contenders for the divisional title, this mauling of Torquay by the club's then record score dispelled them. Unfortunately, this midweek game, which kicked-off early Monday evening, attracted an attendance of only 9,706.

Jim Hammond scored four times, his best scoring performance in his 10–year Fulham career.

Fulham: Beecham; Gibbon, Hickie; Oliver, Gibbons, Barrett; Proud, Hammond, Newton, Price, Finch.
Torquay United: Wright; Webster, Fowler; Clayson, Hewitt, Smith; Birkett, Trotter, Cooper, Hutchinson, Stabb.

24 Fulham 3 Bristol R 2 — Third Division South — 30 April 1932

It was not until the penultimate match that Fulham clinched the divisional title and the one available promotion place, four seasons after relegation. It was a personal triumph for manager James McIntyre in his first full season in charge. Expectations were high and the crowd of 21,000 was bettered that day only at First Division Highbury and Goodison, but Rovers ensured it was no formality. They were the better side for large parts of the game until they were depleted by injury. Rovers took a first-half lead through Cook but, with the wind behind them, and Rovers left-back hobbling on the wing, Fulham came back after the interval. They equalised through Finch and then went ahead with two goals in two minutes, headers by Barrett and Hammond. Pickering scored near the end, but Fulham held on for their first League honour.

25 Fulham 2 Tottenham H 2 — League Division Two — 10 December 1932

Months after winning the Third Division title, Fulham were contenders for a second promotion, and Spurs were also among the favourites. Fulham had new goalkeeper Alf Tootill, signed from Wolves, making his home debut. The game attracted the third largest inter-war crowd (42,111), and they got full value for money. Inspired by left-winger Finch, Fulham stormed into a two-goal lead in 25 minutes, through Richards and Newton. It should have been three by the interval, but Newton's penalty knocked goalkeeper Nicholls unconscious – and the ball stayed out. After the break, Hunt pulled the two goals back for Spurs and a thrilling derby ended all square. The visitors' day was marred, however, when their brilliant inside-forward Greenfield broke his leg in a collision with Fulham full-back Birch. At the end of the season, Spurs were promoted and Fulham just missed out.

26 Fulham 3 Chelsea 2 — FA Cup round five replay — 24 February 1936

This win over their First Division neighbours was Fulham's best performance in the 1936 Cup run. Drawn away, the first game was postponed because of fog, and when it was played on a Wednesday afternoon in those pre-floodlight days, 52,000 still managed to get to the Bridge. A bad-tempered game, in which Chelsea's Gibson was sent off for a dreadful foul on Finch, finished goalless. In the replay the following Monday (kick-off 3.00pm), Fulham raced into a 3–0 lead, through Smith in the first half and Hammond and Arnold in the second. But two Barraclough goals in the last nine minutes for the visitors set up a tense finish which kept the 30,696 crowd in suspense until the final whistle. Had a Gibson shot not got stuck in the mud after beating Fulham 'keeper Tootill, the outcome might have been different.

27 Fulham 3 Derby C 0 — FA Cup round six — 29 February 1936

Just five days after the Chelsea victory, Fulham welcomed First Division Derby to a rain-soaked Cottage for the FA Cup quarter-final. Second in the table and with six internationals in their line-up, the Rams were clear favourites to go through to the semi-finals, but the Cottagers went at them from the start. By the time Derby were disrupted by an injury to full-back Udall after 30 minutes, Fulham should have been two up, Hammond and Perry missing simple chances. But six minutes into the second half, Arnold headed the Cottagers into the lead from Finch's cross. Barrett scored a rare goal with a blistering left foot shot following an Arnold corner 20 minutes later, and Smith completed the scoring a minute later, again from an Arnold corner. The 37,151 crowd were ecstatic and the Fulham players were jubilantly carried shoulder high from the pitch.

28 Sheffield U 2 Fulham 1 — FA Cup semi-final — 21 March 1936

After beating First Division Chelsea and Derby in the previous rounds, Fulham were paired with fellow Second Division club Sheffield United in the semi-final, a team they had already beaten 3–1 in the League that season. With Arsenal playing Grimsby in the other semi-final, the draw raised the possibility of an all-London Final. Fulham and United travelled to Molineux, where 51,588 paid a ground record of £4,766 to see the game. The Blades (who had Dug Livingstone, a future Fulham manager, as coach) were the form side, unbeaten in 22 games and challenging for promotion. The Cottagers ended United's long unbeaten run that week, but sadly not at Molineux.

With the whole squad available, Fulham manager Jack Peart decided to leave out the versatile Jack Finch, who had played in all five previous Cup games and in three different positions. This was a tie the London side could and should have won but lost the game because of missed chances. The Blades settled quickest and took the initiative in midfield, where Fulham's wing halves, Barrett and Tompkins, were below par. They went a goal up after just nine minutes when Bird, in acres of space on the left, took a pass from Pickering and raced through to score before Hindson could tackle.

From Fulham's point of view, the turning point came on the half hour. Left-winger Arnold robbed Blades' full-back Hooper and crossed for Perry, standing unmarked on the edge of the six-yard box. With the goal at his mercy, he screwed the ball wide. Just 10 minutes into the second half, United doubled their lead. A headed clearance by Gibbons went to a Sheffield player and then on to centre-forward Pickering. From the edge of the box he fired past the despairing Tootill.

The Blades were clearly in control but then, inexplicably, they decided to sit back on the two-goal lead, and Fulham came more into the game. Arnold and Worsley should have done better with headers

The semi-final line up from a souvenir newspaper.

that went wide, and Smith was unlucky with a shot that hit the post. With 10 minutes remaining, the Cottagers did score, Arnold heading in a long cross from Hindson. They piled on the pressure in the closing stages, with Gibbons joining the attack, but the Blades defence held firm.

Just five days later, the teams met in a League game at Bramall Lane, and Fulham won 1–0, thanks to a Keeping penalty. As several of the players admitted 50 years later, it was no consolation.

Fulham: Tootill; Hindson, Keeping; Barrett, Gibbons, Tompkins; Worsley, Smith, Perry, Hammond, Arnold.

Sheffield United: Smith; Hooper, Cox; Jackson, Johnson, Macpherson; Barton, Barclay, Dodds, Pickering, Bird.

29 Fulham 5 West Ham U 0 League Division Two 7 November 1936

After injury ended Newton's career in 1934, Fulham lacked a goalscoring centre-forward to play alongside Hammond. When manager Jack Peart paid £300 for Crystal Palace reserve striker Ronnie Rooke, he uncovered a one-man goalscoring machine. Rooke scored three against West Ham in his first game, the first, third and fourth goals, the first Fulham player to get a hat-trick on his debut. The Hammers were reduced to 10–men after full-back Chalkley fractured a rib in a collision with his own goalkeeper, Weare, after 10 minutes trying to stop Fulham's first goal. It was an hour before the second goal went in, from Arnold, and Hammond got the fifth. This was the first of Rooke's four hat-tricks in 1936–37, and he finished with 19 goals in 22 games, the start of a remarkable career that ended at Arsenal after the war.

30 Fulham 8 Swansea T 1 League Division Two 22 January 1938

Fulham went into 1938 in the Second Division danger zone, having won just four of their first 22 games. The problems on the pitch reflected trouble behind the scenes. Weeks earlier, manager Peart had sacked the long-serving reserve-team manager Joe Edelston, who he felt was a disruptive influence. This win over Swansea was the turning point of the season and still the club's biggest-ever win in the second tier of the League. Fulham led 4–0 at half-time (scoring every 10 minutes exactly), and doubled it at full-time, Rooke leading the way with four. Hammond's goal (the third) was his 151st and last for the club. Finch (two) and O'Callaghan completed the Cottagers scoring while Millington got the Swans consolation. Fulham won 13 and lost only three games in the second half of the season and finished comfortably in the top half of the table.

31 Fulham 2 Millwall 1 League Division Two 8 October 1938

A record Craven Cottage crowd of 49,335 came to see this top-of-the-table clash between west and south London. The size of the crowd led to the kick-off being delayed and thousands were locked out. Perhaps the national sense of relief that followed Prime Minister Chamberlain's deal with Hitler at Munich the previous week was a contributory factor to the size of the crowd whose spirits were not dampened by the rain. The Lions went ahead on 38 minutes when Fulham skipper Keeping headed past his own goalkeeper. Midway through the second half came the equaliser, Woodward heading in Arnold's free-kick. With just eight minutes to go, another Arnold free-kick led to the winner by right-half Evans after goalkeeper Pearson had made a great save. The pitch invasion which followed the final whistle was celebratory and not violent.

32 Fulham 6 Bury 0 — FA Cup round three — 7 January 1939

A club record which stands to this day was set in the final inter-war season in an otherwise forgettable Cup meeting between two Second Division teams. The meagre crowd of 11,221 saw Ronnie Rooke create a bit of Fulham history by scoring six goals, a hat-trick in each half. The fact that the Shakers were down to nine fit men by half-time (Gemmell and Whitfield both hobbling with muscle injuries) helped. It was claimed that had he taken all his chances, Rooke could have beaten Joe Payne's 10–goal haul for Luton a few years earlier. The fourth and sixth goals were the pick of the bunch. It was not, however, a one-man show. O'Callaghan put on a dazzling display in midfield and Arnold, who might have scored three himself, tormented Bury down the left wing, but it was Rooke who dominated the headlines.

33 Fulham 2 Charlton A 1 — FA Cup round three — 7 January 1946

As a game of football, this third round FA Cup tie was unremarkable. A 20,000 crowd turned up for the first post-war FA Cup tie at the Cottage, played on a Monday afternoon (kick-off 2.00pm) between Second Division Fulham and Charlton of the First. All the action took place in the first 45 minutes. After 11 minutes, Tadman gave the visitors the lead and a minute later Cliff Lloyd, the Fulham left-back and later PFA Secretary, was carried off with a broken ankle. But before half-time, the irrepressible Rooke scored twice to put the 10 men ahead, which was the end of the scoring. What makes this game memorable is that the losers, Charlton, went through and on to Wembley. This was because for the only time in the history of the FA Cup, ties up to the Final were played on a two-leg basis and, 48 hours earlier, Charlton had won 3–1 at the Valley, thus going through 4–3 on aggregate.

34 Everton 0 Fulham 1 — FA Cup round five — 14 February 1948

The second part of the trilogy of outstanding Cup successes against Everton came in the second season of post-war football, when Fulham were still in the Second Division and the Toffees were once again in the top flight. After beating Doncaster and Bristol Rovers in the earlier rounds, Fulham got a home draw against Everton in round five. Eglington gave the visitors a first-half lead, but Len Quested's first goal (just after Beasley had missed an open goal) gave the Cottagers a second chance. The replay at Goodison was seven days later, on a Saturday, and attracted a crowd of 71,587, the largest attendance to see a Fulham game at a League club ground until the trip to Old Trafford in 2006.

Both teams made one change, Watson in for Wainwright for Everton, while Fulham had Bewley on the left wing in place of Grant. Those who thought the Cottagers had missed their best chance in the first game overlooked the marked improvement in the club's away record that season. From the start they took the game to their First Division hosts and, as one paper said, 'Fulham looked senior class and reduced Everton to third rate status.'

The only goal of the game was scored 17 minutes from time. Arthur Stevens's superb pass put Bob Thomas through on goal. He controlled the ball, steadied himself and slipped the ball past the advancing Sagar. It was a clinical piece of opportunism, and Thomas was mobbed by his colleagues.

But the real hero was centre-half Jim Taylor. Playing on with a huge bandage over a head wound sustained in the opening minutes, he had a magnificent game at the heart of the defence, tackling, intercepting and heading anything that came within his range. Everton were restricted to just two attempts on goal all game, a shot that the admirable Bacuzzi headed off the line and a long-range effort which Hinton tipped over. Sagar was much the busier 'keeper, and one save from a Bob Thomas header was outstanding.

Fulham seemed to be denied a blatant penalty when Saunders handled in the area, but the referee gave a free-kick on the edge of the box. But, with 10 minutes remaining, Everton's Watson clearly handled when he was on the ground, and a penalty was awarded. The normally reliable Freeman, however, blasted the spot-kick wide. There was still time for Thomas to miss another acceptable chance before the final whistle.

The Cottagers won a deserved victory, but it was as far as they went. Blackpool barred the way in the quarter-finals and Matthews and Mortensen saw the Seasiders through 2–0 at the Cottage.

Joe Bacuzzi, Jim Taylor and Bob Thomas, the stars of the win at Goodison, at a reunion in the 1980s.

Everton: Sagar; Saunders, Dugdale; Farrell, Humphreys, Watson; Grant, Boyes, Dodds, Fielding, Eglington.

Fulham: Hinton; Freeman, Bacuzzi; Quested, Taylor, Beasley; S. Thomas, R. Thomas, Stevens, Ayres, Bewley.

35 West Bromwich A 1 Fulham 2 League Division Two 5 March 1949

This was the game that persuaded Fulham fans that promotion could be achieved. Albion, the only team to have won at the Cottage that season, were second and Fulham fourth in Division Two when they played on a snow-covered Hawthorns pitch. The game was a thriller and proved decisive in May. Albion took the lead after just nine minutes when Elliott's hopeful shot was fumbled by Flack. Playing into a biting wind in the second half, Quested drove home an equaliser through a cluster of players with 20 minutes left. In the very last minute, Rowley, who had been transferred from Albion to Fulham only three months earlier, dispossessed Barlow in midfield and powered past two other defenders before beating Sanders for a dramatic winner. In the end, Fulham won the title by a point from the Albion.

36 Fulham 2 West Ham U 0 League Division Two 7 May 1949

In their 31st League season, Fulham finally won a place in the First Division, but the campaign that finished so triumphantly had started in tragedy. With just four games played, long-serving manager Jack Peart died suddenly just before his 60th birthday. Form naturally dipped and there was a hiatus before former player and current director Frank Osborne agreed to take over as manager. He made several important changes (bringing in Flack in goal and Jezzard at inside-forward) but the key move was signing West Brom's reserve centre-forward (George) Arthur Rowley just before Christmas. His 19 goals in 22 games were vital.

A civic reception for the promotion-winning Fulham team.

With Rowley, the team hit its stride and just three defeats from Christmas onwards put them in the promotion frame with West Brom and Southampton. A run of five consecutive victories in April, and a draw in the penultimate game at White Hart Lane, virtually assured promotion. At stake in the final game was the Second Division title, which would be Fulham's if they beat West Ham. A season-best crowd of 41,133 turned up to celebrate.

A newspaper claimed that, before the game, the Fulham players 'were scared stiffer than waxworks dummies' and the champagne bought by directors (even though there was rationing in those days!) was hidden in a neighbouring house until there was no doubt about the result.

There was no need to worry. The teamwork and fighting spirit that had taken them to promotion carried them to the title. And there were two more goals from Rowley. The first after 32 minutes was a left-foot drive from 20 yards, which hit the underside of the bar and bounced down over the line. He made it 2–0 and safe with 15 minutes left. When the ball bobbled in the box from Thomas's blocked shot, it ran Rowley who had escaped his marker Walker. From close range, he fired past Taylor in the Hammers goal. The visitors almost pulled a goal back but third-choice goalkeeper Larry Gage made a superb save from Robinson's powerful header.

At the final whistle, thousands of Fulham supporters raced on to the pitch, some carrying Rowley off shoulder high and others unfolding a banner which read 'Fulham forever – Division One'.

Fulham: Gage; Freeman, Bacuzzi; Quested, Taylor, Beasley; Stevens, R. Thomas, Rowley, Jezzard, McDonald.

West Ham United: Taylor; Devlin, Ford; Corbett, Walker, Moroney; Woodgate, Parsons, Robinson, McGowan, Bainbridge.

37 Fulham 1 Wolves 2 League Division One 20 August 1949

For their first game in the First Division, Fulham had a new manager (Bill Dodgin senior), a new style programme and an improved ground, but exactly the same team as had won promotion. A crowd of 41,699 attended this historic occasion. Cup-holders Wolves emerged with the points, but Fulham were not outclassed. All three goals came from long-range speculative efforts and all should have been saved. After 25 minutes Flack, in the Cottagers' goal, let Mullen's soft shot through his fingers, and a minute into the second half Hancocks on the other wing fired in a low drive and the goalkeeper seemed late going down for it. Within 10 minutes, Fulham were back in the game. Bacuzzi caught Williams, in the Wolves goal, napping from distance. It was his second and last goal in 299 games over 18 years but Fulham's first in the top flight.

38 Fulham 0 Tottenham 1 League Division One 23 March 1951

The 47,391 crowd for this game remains the highest attendance at the Cottage since 1945 and the second highest ever recorded. This Good Friday encounter was the first of two meetings between the west and north London clubs in 72 hours, and the four points that Spurs won strengthened their title challenge. Arthur Rowe's wonderful 'push and run' team had won the Second Division in style the previous season and in 1950–51 looked likely to win the club's first First Division Championship. A full strength Tottenham were too good for Fulham and a second-half Murphy goal settled the issue. He also scored the winner in the return on Easter Monday. In front of 51,862, he and Bennett scored in the first half for Spurs, and Jezzard pulled one back in the second.

39 Fulham 1 Chelsea 2 League Division One 28 April 1951

For once, the west London bragging rights belonged to Fulham. They had knocked Chelsea out of the Cup (3–0 in round four) and had spent most of the season in mid table. The Pensioners, on the other hand, had struggled and, with four games to play, were bottom of the table six points from safety (only two for a win). They beat Liverpool and Wolves at home before making the short journey to the Cottage for the penultimate game. When Jezzard's header from Lowe's free-kick gave Fulham the lead after 22 minutes, Chelsea looked doomed, but they got back on level terms through Armstrong on 32 minutes. He also scrambled the second and winner with 20 minutes to go. The crowd began singing 'Dear Old Pals' and Chelsea survived by 0.044 of a goal.

40 Fulham 3 Manchester U 3 League Division One 26 December 1951

Fulham saved the best until last. The most memorable match of their first spell in the top flight came in the season they finished bottom against the team that went on to win the title. There were 32,671 for this Boxing Day game, just 24 hours after United had narrowly won 3–2 at Old Trafford. After five minutes Fulham's Lowe went off injured but, in those pre-substitute days, he returned to play, limping, on the left wing. Rowley opened the scoring for United on 12 minutes, but Lowe equalised with the first goal seen at the Cottage direct from a corner. When Pearson and Bond scored in the first 10 minutes of the second half, the game looked safe for United, but Stevens reduced the arrears until, in the final minute, Lowe got an equaliser.

41 Fulham 1 Southampton 1 League Division Two 26 December 1952

Only in retrospect has this game assumed any significance. Fulham were meandering in mid table on their return to the Second Division. On Boxing Day, next-to-bottom Southampton were the visitors with a below-average attendance of 17,018. Inside left Brennan had been injured in the previous game and, on the morning of the Southampton match, 18-year-old Johnny Haynes was told that he was going to make his League debut. On a very heavy pitch, Fulham dominated but squandered a hatful of chances. Haynes even slipped the ball past the 'keeper, only to see it get stuck in the mud. Stevens eventually put Fulham ahead on 80 minutes, but Dudley equalised five minutes later. With two minutes to go, Mitten hit a penalty straight at Saints 'keeper Christie and so the first of the Maestro's 658 games for Fulham ended in a draw.

42 Fulham 5 Hull C 0 League Division Two 8 October 1955

Although he had eight seasons in the first team, it was only in the last four that Beddy Jezzard got into his goalscoring stride. He managed just 31 goals in his first four seasons but then 35 in the fifth alone. By the start of 1954–55, his career total stood at 127, and with Robson and Haynes either side of him he looked set to create a new scoring record. Against bottom club Hull, he helped himself to another five and so equalled Harrison's 1908 League record of goals in a game. Hull were unlucky that 'keeper Bly had to go off injured just before half-time. By then Jezzard had scored twice (six and 14 minutes), and he then put three more (67, 87 and 88) past stand-in goalie Porteus. He finished the season with a record 154 goals when injury ended his career.

43 Fulham 4 Newcastle U 5 FA Cup round four 28 January 1956

In all the polls of older Fulham fans, this is the match consistently nominated as the best-ever at the Cottage and, typically, it was a game the home team lost. On a grey January afternoon, Second Division Fulham were hosts to First Division Newcastle, Cup winners at Wembley the previous May. Ironically, Dug Livingstone, the man who had guided the Magpies to their Cup success, was poised to take over as the new manager of Fulham, who had Tosh Chamberlain on the left wing making his Cup

Newcastle score the winner in the 1956 FA Cup tie.

Chamberlain scores for Fulham.

debut. This was the game that had everything, drama, romance and controversy, and which kept the 39,200 crowd on tenterhooks until the final whistle.

After 25 minutes, the match followed the form book. Playing exhilarating football, Newcastle scored three times in 10 minutes, through Milburn (a right-foot shot from Mitchell's corner), Stokoe (again from Mitchell's pass but deflected by Wilson) and Casey (following a slick three-man move involving Mitchell). But Chamberlain gave Fulham some hope with a goal five minutes before the break and then, remarkably, scored two more (68 and 70) to level the scores. He also had a fourth questionably ruled out by a linesman in his first Cup tie, future World Cup Final referee Jack Taylor. When Jimmy Hill put Fulham 4–3 ahead in the 73rd minute, it seemed a major upset was about to happen.

But Mitchell was again Fulham's undoing. With 12 minutes remaining, he jinked down the left wing and sent over a teasing cross. Goalkeeper Black came out to catch, but both he and the ball were charged into the net by centre-forward Keeble, a legitimate tactic in those days. It was Keeble again who sealed the Geordies win in the dying minutes after a move involving Davies, Casey and…Mitchell.

There was a season's worth of drama in 90 minutes and not a dry eye in the house at the end. It was also the climax of the Robson–Jezzard–Haynes era at Fulham, for within weeks Robson was a West Brom player and in the summer Jezzard's career was ended by injury.

Fulham: Black; Wilson, Lawler; Smith, Brice, Lowe; Hill, Robson, Jezzard, Haynes, Chamberlain.

Newcastle: Simpson; Woollard, McMichael; Stokoe, Patterson, Casey; Milburn, Davies, Keeble, Curry, Mitchell.

44 Bristol C 0 Fulham 5 — League Division Two — 7 December 1957

After 18 months in charge, manager Dug Livingstone was building a side that looked like taking Fulham back to the top flight after a six-year interval. At Ashton Gate, there were clear signs it was all coming together. Just three weeks earlier, he had switched Bentley from inside-forward to wing-half and brought in the teenage Cohen at full-back to partner Langley. For the trip to Bristol, he was forced to fly 19-year-old Tony Macedo back from National Service in Germany to play in goal. That day, Fulham fielded nine of the side that was to win promotion 18 months later, and the Robins were destroyed by an outstanding display. By half-time the Cottagers led 4–0, Haynes, Dwight, Hill and Chamberlain scoring, with Dwight adding a fifth on the hour. This match was a turning point and the club's halcyon days were in sight.

45 West Ham U 2 Fulham 3 — FA Cup round five — 15 February 1958

In the epic 1958 Cup run, this was the most memorable victory. The two teams had drawn 2–2 in a thrilling Second Division promotion clash a fortnight earlier at the Cottage, and this fifth-round clash was even more exciting. A Grice goal put the Hammers ahead after just 90 seconds but, after Hill had twice gone close for Fulham and Dick headed against the bar for West Ham, Dwight equalised on 12 minutes, chipping over the advancing Gregory after being put through by Stevens. A Chamberlain 'goal' was disallowed for offside, but Hill put the visitors ahead against the run of play after 56 minutes. Just 10 minutes later, the scores were level when Bond netted a twice-taken penalty, awarded when Langley fouled Grice. The climax came on 75 minutes when Haynes fired in the winner. Promotion was West Ham's consolation.

46 Doncaster R 1 Fulham 6 — League Division Two — 15 March 1958

A week before Fulham faced Manchester United in the FA Cup semi-final, they consolidated their promotion challenge with this record away win at Belle Vue. The interest in the game lies in the fact that five of the Cottagers goals were scored by inside-forward Jimmy Hill, the first of only two occasions a Fulham player has scored five away from home. Cook opened the scoring and Hill scored twice before the interval and three times afterwards. Hill took the headlines, but it was Haynes who ran Rovers' defence ragged with inch-perfect passes all over the pitch. Higham scored a consolation for Rovers when Fulham eased up in the final 10 minutes. Rovers, who had future comedian Charlie Williams at centre-half, were relegated that season.

47 Manchester U 2 Fulham 2 — FA Cup semi-final — 22 March 1958

There can rarely have been a more emotional or drama-packed semi-final. All the nation's sympathy was with United. Just weeks earlier, eight of the brilliant young Babes had been killed in a tragic air crash at Munich. Yet the makeshift side had battled through the fifth and sixth rounds to meet a full-strength Fulham from the Second Division at Villa Park. There were almost 70,000 inside the ground at kick-off time.

It was a thrilling encounter which both sides led at one stage and which a depleted Fulham side probably shaded. There was one outstanding player on each side, Fulham's Haynes and United's Charlton, although teenage goalkeeper Macedo was not far behind. Charlton, who, along with Gregg

Macedo saves from Webster, while Cohan and Stapleton (5) look on.

and Foulkes, was a survivor of the Munich crash, was the first to get on the score sheet. Against the early run of play, he took a Taylor pass and fired into the roof of the net from the edge of the penalty area after just 12 minutes.

But it took the Cottagers less than a minute to get back on level terms. A Langley cross split the United defence and Stevens scored from close range. Haynes was becoming more dominant in midfield, and eight minutes before half-time the Second Division team took the lead. Haynes and Lawler set Dwight clear, who found Hill racing through the middle to beat Gregg, to maintain his record of scoring in every round.

But Fulham could not hold on until half-time. Langley was injured in a clash with Dawson and stretchered off. Before they had the chance to reorganise properly, Taylor fed Pearson whose shot rebounded off Cohen. The ball fell invitingly for Charlton to hammer in his second with a fierce right-foot drive.

In the second half in those pre-substitute days, Lawler dropped back to left-back and Haynes to left-half, leaving Langley to provide nuisance value down the middle. Haynes was at his most majestic and, although United piled on the pressure in the final 20 minutes, Macedo made a series of remarkable saves to keep Fulham's Wembley hopes alive.

And so to Highbury the following Wednesday, and a televised replay (there were few live televised games in those days). It all went wrong for Fulham and Macedo that day. They lost 5–3, but the result was in doubt until the final minutes. The Cottagers had what looked like a good goal disallowed when the score was 4–3, and United then went straight downfield to score the clincher. Macedo had a torrid time, and he was at fault for more than one of United's goals. For the third time, Fulham had fallen at the semi-final stage.

Fulham: Macedo; Cohen, Langley; Bentley, Stapleton, Lawler; Dwight, Hill, Stevens, Haynes, Chamberlain.

Manchester United: Gregg; Foulkes, Greaves; Goodwin, Cope, Crowther; Webster, Taylor, Dawson, Pearson, Charlton.

48 Fulham 4 Lincoln C 2 — League Division Two — 17 September 1958

After a near-promotion miss the previous season, Fulham made no mistake in 1958–59. The outstanding player in a very good team was skipper Johnny Haynes who, for the only time in his career, topped the club's scoring lists. His 26 goals included three hat-tricks and four goals in this midweek game against Lincoln. The Cottagers had made an excellent start, winning the first six and drawing the seventh game. Next came Imps, and the return of the game played at Sincil Bank the previous week, which Fulham also won 4–2. At home, Haynes scored twice in the first half, from passes by Cook and Chamberlain, before Harbertson and Chapman gave Fulham a fright by equalising early in the second half. But Haynes came back with his 10th and 11th goals of the season to seal the points for the Cottagers.

49 Fulham 6 Sheffield W 2 — League Division Two — 27 March 1959

The two teams that had dominated the Second Division promotion race all season met at the Cottage on Good Friday morning. There were 39,377 in the ground for an 11.15am kick-off and they were treated to a thriller. Harry Catterick's Wednesday led the table by a point and had played two games fewer. This was a game Fulham needed to win because Liverpool, in third place, were breathing down their necks for the second promotion place.

Leggat put Fulham ahead after six minutes, but Wilkinson equalised 15 minutes later. A Langley penalty 10 minutes before the break restored the Cottagers advantage only for Shiner to level again a minute into the second half. When Cook put Fulham 3–2 ahead, there were still 27 minutes to go, but then Hill took over.

Without a goal all season, and the crowd on his back, he had apparently had a 'clear-the-air' talk with chairman Tommy Trinder before the game, yet after 73 minutes he had still not broken his barren sequence. A right-wing corner by left-

Jimmy Hill.

winger Tosh Chamberlain changed everything. Hill was first to the ball and headed his first League goal for 11 months. In the 78th and 88th minutes he scored with two more headers to complete a hat-trick and help Fulham to a stunning victory.

The win put Fulham briefly back on top of the table. A 2–2 draw in the return on Easter Monday, courtesy of two Maurice Cook goals, virtually assured both clubs of a return to the First Division, but it was Wednesday who went up as champions.

Fulham: Macedo; Cohen, Langley; Mullery, Bentley, Lowe; Leggat, Hill, Cook, Haynes, Chamberlain.
Sheffield W: Pinner; Staniforth, Curtis; McAnearney, Swan, Kay; Wilkinson, Fantham, Shiner, Froggatt, Finney.

50 Barnsley 2 Fulham 4 League Division Two 18 April 1959

In front of a paltry crowd of just under 8,000, Fulham secured the points they needed to make a statistical certainty of the promotion that had been on the cards for most of the season. It was an anti-climatic way to regain the place in the top flight they had lost seven years earlier and to achieve what was only their third promotion in 40 seasons. The Cottagers made hard work of seeing off a team doomed to relegation. Fulham twice went ahead, through Hill (16 minutes) and Cook (55 minutes), but were twice pegged back (McCann on 49 minutes and Beaumont after 65). It took an own-goal by Beaumont a minute after the Tykes' second equaliser to give the visitors the edge and a Leggat strike four minutes from time sealed the points and promotion.

51 Wolves 9 Fulham 0 League Division One 16 September 1959

After a promising start on their return to the top flight, the Cottagers received a sharp reality check in their eighth game. A week earlier, a Haynes-less Fulham had beaten Wolves, the defending champions, 3–1 at the Cottage, but in the return they came down to earth with a thump, losing by the heaviest margin in the club's League history. Still minus Haynes (and Bentley, Cook and Chamberlain), they were tormented by Wolves left-winger Deeley, who scored four times and set up chances for his colleagues. A devastating five goals between the 58th and 74th minutes turned a defeat into a rout. The third goal in the 37th minute was the pick, England wing-half Flowers running through from midfield to hit a 30–yard drive past Macedo. The other goals were scored by Broadbent, Clamp, Mason and Murray.

52 Fulham 1 Tottenham H 1 League Division One 12 December 1959

Fulham adjusted to the demands of the First Division remarkably well and, at the halfway stage of the season, the unthinkable could have happened. If they could beat Spurs, and a couple of other results went their way, the Cottagers could have gone top of the table. But they were controversially denied it and this proved the high-water mark of their nine-year sojourn in Division One. A thrilling game began dramatically. Spurs' Jones scored from a penalty on five minutes after he had been fouled by Lampe. Just 10 minutes later, Fulham were level when Hill scored from Haynes's pass. It was Haynes who dominated the game, and he set up another chance for Hill in the second half. Mackay diverted the ball towards his own goal and full-back Baker punched it over the bar. The referee gave a corner and the chance was gone.

53 Bristol R 2 Fulham 1 — League Cup round one — 26 September 1960

Among the few First Division clubs to enter the new League Cup in 1960, Fulham travelled to Second Division Rovers on the first night of the competition. The Cottagers put out what was almost their strongest team, and the Eastville crowd was 5,000 above the average. The First Division club had the guile, while the home side had the energy and commitment. Fulham took the lead in the first half, a casually taken side-footer by Cook after a fine run on the right by Key. As the match kicked-off on the first night of the new competition, and 15 minutes before the other games, this was the first-ever goal scored in the League Cup. But Jarman equalised before the break and the winner came in the second half when Bradford fastened on to a careless Cohen back pass to score.

54 Fulham 5 Sheffield U 2 — League Division One — 17 March 1962

As spring 1962 approached, Fulham were stranded at the foot of the First Division, seven points from safety. Yet three days earlier they had beaten Blackburn in the FA Cup sixth round which sparked a revival in League form and led to eventual safety. Against the Blades, Fulham gave a display of carefree, attacking football and won their first League game since November. Cook was the unlikely hero. He opened the scoring with a powerful header from Leggat's corner and, in the second half, scored two more, one a tap in and the other walking the ball into an empty net. Cook was also the provider of Leggat's second (when the goalkeeper failed to stop his shot) and Lowe's third (from his headed pass). Kettleborough and Matthewson (later a Fulham player), on his debut, scored for United when the game was effectively over.

55 Fulham 1 Burnley 1 — FA Cup semi-final — 31 March 1962

This was Fulham's second semi-final in four years at Villa Park, where they came up against the reigning League champions and a team that had already beaten them twice in the First Division that season. The Cottagers had been lucky with the draw, eliminating lower division opposition (Hartlepools, Walsall and Port Vale) before beating Blackburn in a replay in the sixth round. But in the League they were struggling and they went into this tie very much the underdogs.

On a day when the 60,000 crowd experienced all four seasons in 90 minutes, Fulham looked more like the title challengers than the Clarets. The Cottagers could and should have had the match sewn up by the interval. They over-ran the usually elegant and efficient Burnley defence, and all they had to show for it was Leggat's 29th-minute strike. In the inside-left position, Leggat took a ball from Haynes, swivelled and volleyed it into the net from the edge of the area. He could have had two or three more.

Haynes was winning the midfield battle with McIlroy, although the Irishman seemed to be affected by an injury he received in the 14th minute. Burnley played very defensively and Fulham, inspired by Haynes, did their best to take advantage of a very subdued performance.

In the second half, Burnley came more into it, thanks to Adamson's promptings and Connelly's speed down the wing. It was just five minutes after the break that they equalised. Langley, on another attacking sortie, was caught upfield and Connelly, fed by McIlroy, took full advantage to score.

But there was controversy in the last 10 minutes. Haynes played Cook through and the centre-forward rounded Blacklaw, only for the 'keeper's hand to pull him down. To Fulham's disbelief, referee Clements gave a corner, not a penalty. As in 1958, the Cottagers had been the better side but failed to press home their advantage.

Blacklaw is beaten by Leggat's low drive.

Their best chance had gone because Burnley were not going to play as badly again. The replay was nine days later at Filbert Street and the Clarets were worth their 2–1 win. This was semi-final defeat number four in four appearances.

Burnley: Blacklaw; Angus, Elder; Adamson, Cummings, Miller; Connelly, McIlroy, Pointer, Robson, Harris.

Fulham: Macedo; Cohen, Langley; Mullery, Dodgin, Lowe; Leggat, Henderson, Cook, Haynes, O'Connell.

56 Fulham 4 Sheffield W 1 League Division One 19 September 1962

Craven Cottage was the last First Division ground to have floodlights installed. When the Supporters' Club paid the fee for Bobby Robson to return from West Brom, the club spent its available funds on floodlights. After several delays, 22,631 were present for the switch on and nobody was more switched on that evening than Maurice Cook. The first goal, however, went to Stan Brown on half an hour, a fierce shot from Chamberlain's pass. Just 10 minutes later, Cook half-volleyed past Springett from 15 yards and the next minute beat two defenders before shooting home. His hat-trick came eight minutes after the break, while the Wednesday defence appealed for offside. The Owls goal came from Layne who, with two of his teammates that evening, Swan and Kay, was later banned from football for match fixing.

57 Fulham 10 Ipswich T 1 League Division One 26 December 1963

Although this was Fulham's second 10–goal haul, it remains their biggest-ever winning margin, and it happened in the top flight against a side that 18 months earlier had won the League Championship. For Scottish international Graham Leggat, it was a personal triumph. He scored the First Division's fastest hat-trick (a record which still stands). In a dreadful piece of alliteration, one newspaper said, 'It was misty murder in the mind, torment by timetable to the accompaniment of clicking stop watches and rustling record books'.

After missing an easy chance on 12 minutes, Cook started the rout four minutes later, taking a much more difficult chance. He threw himself at Key's cross from the right for a spectacular diving header. Less than five minutes later, the visitors were 4–0 down. First, Leggat tapped in a rebound from the bar, spun in his second by a post and then hammered in his third from 25 yards. Just before half-time, Fulham got their fifth, when goalkeeper Bailey palmed in a corner by Howfield. Baker managed a consolation for Ipswich so close to half-time that there was no time to kick-off.

Graham Leggat, whose three goals in as many minutes is the fastest top-flight hat-trick.

It was more of the same after the break. Howfield got two more, in the 47th and 71st minutes, in between which Robson notched Fulham's seventh. With just two minutes remaining, and the crowd (of 19,374) urging them on, the home side continued to press forward and got to double figures. After Mullery had scored the ninth, it was Leggat appropriately who got number 10.

The scoreline did not flatter Fulham. It could have been 12 or 15, bottom-of-the-table Ipswich were that bad, Baxter and Broadfoot excepted. Their manager Jackie Milburn, who had succeeded Alf Ramsey, had nothing to say after the game. Yet two days later, virtually the same teams met for the return at Portman Road, and Ipswich won 4–2.

Fulham: Macedo; Cohen, Langley; Mullery, Keetch, Robson; Key, Cook, Leggat, Haynes, Howfield.

Ipswich Town: Bailey; Davin, Compton; Baxter, Bolton, Dougan; Broadfoot, Moran, Baker, Phillips, Blackwood.

58 Fulham 2 Liverpool 0 League Division One 26 February 1966

When Dave Sexton took over as coach in January 1966, Fulham were at the foot of the table, on 15 points, six short of safety (two points for a win) and there were only 13 games to go. With just one win in the previous 14 matches, the Cottagers position looked hopeless. But against Shankly's champions-elect, they raised their game, and kept it there for the rest of the season. Steve Earle, restored to the team by Sexton, grabbed the headlines with both goals, one in each half. The first started when Haynes swept the ball out to Leggat and Earle headed his centre past the groping Lawrence. The second came in the closing moments when Leggat again fed Earle who appeared to use his hand to control the ball before scoring. In between, Liverpool's St John was sent off after clashing with Pearson.

59 Northampton T 2 Fulham 4 League Division One 23 April 1966

The rise of Northampton through the divisions in the 1960s was as rapid as Fulham's three decades later, but, after reaching the top flight in 1965–66, the Cobblers fell back just as quickly. This First Division meeting was make or break for both clubs, with the losers almost certainly relegated. A record crowd of 24,523 packed into the old County Ground for 90 minutes of nail-biting drama that was not settled until the closing moments.

The Cottagers, with seven wins in their nine previous games, were in their best form of the season but were rocked when the predatory Hudson gave Northampton a 13th-minute lead. Goalkeeper McClelland could only palm Kiernan's shot into the centre-forward's path, and he scored from close range. Just six minutes later, left-back Nichols started the move that put Fulham back on terms. The ball was worked to Robson who flighted his shot inside the right-hand post. But Robson was at fault when the Cobblers regained the lead after 29 minutes. He failed to head the ball clear and Kiernan scored from outside the area.

Fulham, and Leggat in particular, had wasted several presentable opportunities, but in the 65th minute the visitors had a huge stroke of luck. Northampton broke clear and McClelland parried a Hudson shot which seemed to drop over the line. But the referee was stranded upfield and the linesman had slipped over as he ran down the touchline.

No goal was given, and minutes later, instead of being 3–1 up, Northampton found themselves level. Cohen raced down the right wing and slipped the ball to Earle, who scored on 65 minutes. With just two minutes left, Leggat floated the ball across and Earle, 10 yards out, placed his header perfectly. The Cobblers then pressed forward desperately and had 10 men in the Fulham area. A Haynes

The last two goals of Steve Earle's hat-trick came in the last few minutes of the match, when the score was 2–2 and Northampton were searching for a winner.

clearance found Earle 10 yards inside his own half. He had a clear run on goal and, as the 'keeper came out of his area to challenge him, Earle rounded Coe and walked the ball into the empty net.

A remarkable climax to a tense and dramatic afternoon. The result effectively ensured Fulham's survival in the top flight after a remarkable recovery in the spring. For Northampton, the odyssey was over and it was the start of a return trip back to the lower reaches of the League.

Northampton Town: Coe; Mackin, Everitt, Kurila, Branston, Kiernan, Walden, Moore, Hudson, Martin, Lines.

Fulham: McClelland; Cohen, Nichols, Robson, Dempsey, Brown, Earle, Clarke, Haynes, Pearson, Leggat.

60 Fulham 5 Aston Villa 1 League Division One 12 November 1966

This was Fulham's best result in one of the few First Division seasons in which relegation was not a constant threat. But the match is best remembered as the club's 2,000th League game and 1,000th at the Cottage, and it was celebrated in an appropriate style. It was the classic game of two halves, the second as exciting as the first, goalless, 45 minutes had been dull. In the 47th minute, Haynes and Barrett set up Pearson to open the scoring. Clarke followed a minute later with a superb individual effort, a 20–yard half volley. Although Tindall pulled one back in the 51st minute, a close-range Clarke header and 25–yard effort by Conway ended the visitors' resistance. Parmenter completed the rout five minutes from time after a poor defensive header.

61 Fulham 1 Huddersfield T 1 League Cup round five 29 November 1967

It was not until the League Cup's seventh season that Fulham had any sort of run in the competition. Ironically, it happened when they were having a terrible time in the League and were in the First Division drop zone. But, in the League Cup quarter-finals for the first time and at home to Second Division Huddersfield, they had a great chance to progress. With long-time Terriers fan and Prime Minister Harold Wilson in the 20,309 crowd, however, Fulham again disappointed. The visitors were much the better side. A Hill volley was disallowed for no obvious reason 10 minutes before Worthington took advantage of a slip by Dempsey to score after 17 minutes. Fulham controversially got back on terms through Joe Gilroy in a frantic final 10 minutes when the Huddersfield goalkeeper was distracted by an injured colleague. But Town made no mistake in the replay.

62 Fulham 0 Manchester U 4 League Division One 12 April 1968

As happened 12 months earlier, Manchester United, chasing the League title, were again Easter visitors to the Cottage. But rather than be pushed hard all the way by a committed and enthusiastic Fulham team as they had been in 1967, this time they strolled past a very dejected Cottagers side that was just awaiting the mathematical confirmation of relegation. This Good Friday match was, however, a landmark, the last 40,000 (40,154) crowd ever at the Cottage. (United were also the visitors for the first 40,000 attendance, in 1908.) The damage was done in the first half and the tormentor in chief was George Best, who started the rout after 90 seconds. He scored again on 32 minutes, and when Macedo dropped a cross Kidd was on hand to make it 3–0 five minutes before the break. Law rounded off a comfortable afternoon for the visitors three minutes from time after Aston set him up.

63 Halifax 0 Fulham 8 League Division Three 16 September 1969

Back in the Third Division for the first time in 37 years, confidence at Fulham was low and resources were scarce, and manager Bill Dodgin had a huge rebuilding job on his hands. A stuttering start came alive in the eighth game, with a record-breaking trip to the Shay. Against the then unbeaten Halifax, the Cottagers recorded the club's biggest-ever away win in the League and Steve Earle's five goals equalled Jimmy Hill's 1958 haul at Doncaster. Defensive frailties helped Fulham. Long balls down the middle led to four goals and hesitancy by left-back Burgin to another two. Luck, however, contributed the first after 12 minutes, a clearance hitting the referee, falling nicely for Horne to cross for Earle to score. After Halifax spurned a great chance to equalise, goals by Lloyd and Earle and a Conway penalty made the game safe by half-time. The second-half goals by Earle (46, 61 and 67 minutes) and Conway (60) merely rubbed salt in the wounds.

64 Fulham 1 Stockport C 1 League Division Three 17 January 1970

According to one newspaper report, 'this was a match best forgotten. It was dreary, dull, purposeless football for most of the game, and the 7,435 paying fans went home cold and disappointed'. Yet it was a milestone, the last of Johnny Haynes's 658 first-class games for Fulham. Ever-present in that, his first, Third Division season, he picked up an injury and never got back in the side. Barry Lloyd took over the number-10 shirt and the captaincy. As he had so often in the past, Haynes provided the opening from which Richardson scored Fulham's goal. He was the only real threat the Cottagers offered. Stockport, content to defend and attack on the break, got a second-half equaliser through Elgin and came closest to a winner, but Ryden hit the bar when it looked easier to score.

65 Fulham 2 Queen's Park R 0 League Cup round three 6 October 1970

In the second season back in Division Three, manager Dodgin had put together a side that looked a good promotion bet. Although the League was the priority, Fulham enjoyed a second run to the League Cup quarter-finals. The best win came against Second Division neighbours Queen's Park Rangers, who included former Fulham favourite Rodney Marsh in their line up. The game attracted the last 30,000 (31,727) crowd to the Cottage. Played in torrential rain, Dodgin's current charges dominated his previous club. Better finishing would have given Fulham more than the 1–0 half-time lead they had from Barrett's 14th-minute goal. Barrett also had a hand in the second and deciding goal in the 65th minute, when his shot was deflected past Parkes by Halom. Rangers' best effort had come moments earlier when a Venables effort was deflected on to a post by Seymour.

66 Fulham 0 Bristol C 0 League Cup round five 17 November 1970

Another League Cup quarter-final, and at home against a struggling Second Division side (managed by future Fulham boss Alan Dicks), the Cottagers spurned another great opportunity of progressing to the last four for the first time. In a match played in appalling conditions, defenders had the upper hand as torrential rain turned the pitch into a mudbath, and Fulham failed to score for the first time that season. Fulham made the mistake of playing too much down the middle where the mud and City defenders combined to prevent Earle of Halom getting going. As the game wore on, the threat from the visitors increased and reserve goalkeeper Seymour had to be very alert to keep City at bay. The closest to a goal was in the ninth minute when Sharpe was denied by a post with Seymour beaten, but City went through in the replay, winning thanks to a Sharpe penalty.

67 Bradford C 2 Fulham 3 League Division Three 28 April 1971

After sliding ignominiously from the First to the Third Divisions in successive seasons, Fulham went through a period of rebuilding under manager Bill Dodgin. It took him only two seasons to get the club moving in the right direction and the side that clinched promotion in midweek at Valley Parade contained only four players who were regulars in the last top-flight campaign two years earlier.

The Cottagers had made the running most of the season, although a midwinter dip in form saw them drop into fourth place. Going into the final month of the season, Fulham and Preston were in the promotion places, but Halifax and Aston Villa were pushing them all the way. There were just two games left when Dodgin's men travelled to West Yorkshire for a Wednesday night fixture that attracted only 6,430 people, knowing a win would take them back to Division Two.

From the kick-off, a full-strength Fulham (this was the fifth consecutive game with an unchanged team) went looking for the points they needed. The forwards, however, were very wasteful, squandering a hatful of chances, and just when they got their noses in front, the defence allowed Bradford back into the game – twice.

Earle, Barrett and Conway all missed acceptable opportunities before the Cottagers' flowing football brought them a 32nd-minute lead. George Johnston, an autumn signing from Birmingham, was on hand to fire in a loose ball. Just when it seemed they would build on their lead, Fulham conceded a soft goal on the stroke of half-time, Hall the scorer. Johnston should have got his second

George Johnston opens the scoring for Fulham after 32 minutes.

straight after the interval, but Fulham had to wait until the 55th for skipper Barry Lloyd to score with a clever lob. Again Bradford came back, and in the 70th minute Corner headed in a second equaliser. But Fulham, and Johnston, had the last word in the 75th, winning the match and promotion with a superb header.

The final game was three days later, at home to Preston, the only team that could deny them the title. In front of the biggest Cottage crowd for a League game (25,774) since the First Division days three years earlier, the Cottagers let it slip. They lost 1–0 and had to settle for second place, but promotion was the real prize.

Bradford City: Liney; Atkins, McConnell, Stowell, Corner, Cooper, Hall, Bannister, Oates, O'Neill, Middleton.

Fulham: Webster; Pentecost, Callaghan, Horne, Matthewson, Dunne, Conway, Johnston, Earle, Lloyd, Barrett.

68 Everton 1 Fulham 2 FA Cup round five 15 February 1975

This was the third of the trio of outstanding Cup victories over Everton, all achieved when the top-flight Toffees had a division advantage over the Cottagers. On this occasion, Everton were at home and were top of the First Division. Fulham, languishing in the middle of Division Two, had already taken seven games to get through to round five of the Cup, three to get past Hull and four to overcome Forest. This tie was only clinched at the City Ground five days earlier, and it was more in hope than expectation that Fulham travelled to Merseyside.

But on the day 'Fulham emerged blinking from the dark caverns of the Second Division to club Everton into oblivion in a total victory for the unsung underdog over much-vaunted sophisticated man. All afternoon, it was the bubbling Cottagers who provided nearly all the afternoon's sparkle to achieve an astonishing victory.' The result was the upset of the round, but nobody denied it was thoroughly deserved. On the day, the underdogs were much the better side and from then the supporters started believing that this could be the club's year to get to Wembley.

It was two-goal hero Viv Busby who stole the headlines. The first after 15 minutes owed much to winger Barrett's determination. He broke speedily down the left and centre-half Kenyon diverted his goalkeeper's attention from the low cross. The confusion gave Busby the chance for a simple tap in. His second, with just six minutes remaining, was decisive. This time Conway broke down the left and crossed. Busby had his back to goal when he collected the ball but turned and fired in a low shot from 12 yards.

Just after half-time, Everton had their best spell. Kenyon equalised with a header on 52 minutes and another effort by Lyons was disallowed for a foul on Mellor. But it was Fulham's day, and, while Busby stole the limelight, it was veterans Moore and Mullery who held Fulham together in defence and midfield. Not only did they do their jobs, but they also organised and controlled their younger, less experienced colleagues. The fact that Everton substituted top scorer and record signing Bob Latchford shows the grip Moore and co had on their more illustrious opponents.

Everton: Davies; Bernard, Seargeant, Clements, Kenyon, Hurst, Jones, Dobson, Lyons, Latchford (Telfer), Pearson.

Fulham: Mellor; Cutbush, Strong, Mullery, Lacy, Moore, Dowie (Lloyd), Conway, Busby, Slough, Barrett.

Busby's first goal in Fulham's shock win against Everton.

69 Fulham 1 Birmingham C 0 FA Cup semi-final replay 9 April 1975

After Everton, Fulham beat another top-flight club, Carlisle, in the sixth round to reach the semi-finals for the fifth time. Although Birmingham were in the First Division, it seemed a better draw than facing either West Ham or Ipswich and, as in 1936 and 1962, there was the possibility of an all-London Final. The Cottagers were also spared a trip to the jinxed Villa Park, the first game arranged for Hillsborough.

Many Fulham fans must have had a feeling of déjà vu at Hillsborough. They dominated the match for all but 10 minutes of the second half, but John Mitchell's superb dipping volley on 50 minutes was all they had to show for it. Then, seven minutes later, Gallagher equalised and the Cottagers must have felt their best chance had gone. It seemed unlikely that Birmingham would again be so subdued and that Fulham could raise their game once more.

A sparsely populated (35,025) Maine Road was the setting for the Wednesday night replay. For their 11th FA Cup match that season, Fulham were without Conway, for whom Dowie deputised, and

John Mitchell's dramatic winner.

the game was more evenly balanced than the first. It became something of a war of attrition, two resolute defences keeping clear goalscoring chances to a minimum. Moore was again majestic, not only with his intercepting, tackling and passing of the highest order, but his constant urging and organising of colleagues. And, if Hatton, Burns, Francis and co did get a sight of goal, Mellor was in the form he had shown in the sixth round where almost single-handedly he had kept Carlisle at bay.

Goalless after 90 minutes, it was Fulham who seemed to dig deeper and find extra reserves of energy. After 119 minutes, a third game at Highbury seemed likely until Slough, breaking down the right, crossed. Mitchell got a toe to the ball. It then struck goalkeeper Latchford in the face and bounced back to Mitchell who chested it towards goal. The ball trickled agonisingly over the line, with barely enough speed to reach the net. Fulham's joy was matched only by the despair of the Birmingham players, officials and supporters.

Mitchell's goal was as ugly as his strike in the first game was spectacular, but it was more decisive. And for Fulham, able to discard the unwanted record of more semi-final appearances without reaching the Final, it was quantity not quality that mattered.

Birmingham City: Latchford; Page, Bryant, Kendall, Gallagher, Pendrey, Hendrie, Francis, Burns, Hatton, Taylor.

Fulham: Mellor; Fraser, Strong, Mullery, Lacy, Moore, Dowie, Mitchell, Busby, Slough, Barrett.

70 West Ham U 2 Fulham 0 — FA Cup Final — 3 May 1975

After the semi-final defeats of 1908, 1936, 1958 and 1962, for many Fulham fans being there was enough. But Alec Stock said before the game 'We haven't come this far to lose'. And it had been the longest journey any club had ever had to the Final (11 games, including four which went to extra-time); all five ties had been won away from the Cottage and none were against clubs from a lower division.

This all-London Final had pitched Bobby Moore against his former club, and for the former England captain and Fulham skipper Mullery it was a last hurrah at the stadium they had graced with such distinction for club and country. Alec Stock had one big decision to make, and preferred Barry Lloyd as substitute to John Dowie who had appeared in every tie other than the three Hull games. For Les Strong, who had played in Fulham's first 54 League and Cup games that season, there was the disappointment of being injured two weeks before the Final and having to miss the Wembley game.

In the dressing room before the game.

The *Times* match report carried the headline 'Fulham Are Buried With Honours', which was an accurate summary of the 90 minutes. West Ham won with two second-half goals from scoring sensation Alan Taylor (who had scored twice in both the previous rounds, against Arsenal and Ipswich). But the Cottagers contributed to their own downfall.

After an hour, Fulham had given just about as good as they had got. Then Cutbush lost the ball on the halfway line to Holland, who fed Jennings. Mellor could only parry his shot and Taylor was on hand to finish the job. Just four minutes later, and it was effectively over as a contest. Holland fed Paddon down the left. Mellor spilled the shot and again Taylor was on the spot. The goalkeeper was even more culpable on the second goal than the first, but Fulham fans knew that without his heroics in the earlier rounds they never would have reached Wembley in the first place.

Although 2–0 down, Mullery urged his men forward and there were half chances, a Busby header and a Mitchell shot to add to the two attempts in the first half. But the match was regarded as the 'politest and friendliest' Cup Final, with Mullery and Moore showing some of their old class. 'And so in the end,' Hugh McIlvanney wrote, 'the day belonged to the favourites, but Fulham can take a measure of pride from the memory of it.'

Fulham: Mellor; Cutbush, Fraser, Mullery, Lacy, Moore, Mitchell, Conway, Busby, Slough, Barrett.

West Ham United: Day; McDowell, Lampard, Bonds, T. Taylor, Lock, Jennings, Paddon, A. Taylor, Brooking, Holland.

71 Fulham 4 Hereford U 1 League Division Two 25 September 1976

Probably the most-shown clips of a Fulham game come from the Best-Marsh end-of-the-pier-show against Hereford. To bring some glamour to the Cottage, Best and Marsh, two hugely talented but fading stars, were signed from US football. For Marsh, it was back to where it all started 15 years earlier and for Best a chance to revive a career that had been spiralling downwards. Against lowly Hereford, they showed what might have been. Turning on their full range of tricks, they gave a crowd-pleasing exhibition which encouraged their teammates to raise their game. Slough and Evanson put Fulham two up before McNeil pulled one back. In the second half, Marsh scored twice, first a simple header and then a stunning individual effort. This was as good as it got from the duo. Marsh was gone within months and Best within the year.

72 Fulham 1 Lincoln C 1 League Division Three 18 May 1982

During the turbulent two decades from the 1975 Cup Final to promotion in 1997, only Malcolm Macdonald's brief term as manager offered any hope or encouragement. An unlikely and far from unanimous choice to succeed the discredited Bobby Campbell in the autumn of 1980, the man who had been a brash, arrogant and outspoken player showed himself to be a thoughtful, bold and imaginative manager. In his first footballing role since injury ended his playing career, 'Supermac' turned a sinking club around in less than a season and put in place a structure which, if properly nurtured, could have put Fulham back in the big time. That it hit the rocks within two or three years was due to the chairman's duplicity and the manager's tendency to self-destruct.

Having steered the club to Third Division safety in his first few months at the helm, Macdonald's Fulham got off to an uneven start in August 1981, but by the autumn they had got into their stride. There was only one addition to the squad inherited from Campbell (free signing Peter O'Sullivan), but

Roger Brown's vital goal.

Macdonald (and coaches George Armstrong and the admirable Ray Harford) took a chance on youth, Jeff Hopkins, Paul Parker and Dean Coney in particular, and it paid off. Going into the spring, four clubs were fighting for three promotion places and two of them met in the Final (re-arranged) game on a Wednesday evening at a packed (20,398) Craven Cottage. Fulham needed a point to go up, Lincoln needed all three, and whichever team lost would miss out.

It was 90 minutes of pure theatre, tense, absorbing and dramatic. After a goalless first half in which the Imps had outfought and outplayed their nervous hosts, Lincoln received a double blow on 57 minutes. First, hard-tackling defender Steve Thompson was sent off for a foul on Dean Coney and then, from the resulting free-kick, skipper Roger Brown, his head bandaged to cover yet another cut, headed in Tony Gale's cleverly flighted free-kick. It was centre-half Brown's 12th League goal that season, a remarkable tally for a defender who did not take penalties.

But the 10 men got back on terms in the 72nd minute, when Dave Carr scrambled in Phil Turner's corner. From then until the final whistle, Lincoln pressed forward and only a goalline clearance by Sean O'Driscoll stopped them from taking the lead. But Fulham held on for a point and the third promotion place. As Macdonald said afterwards, 'We didn't play much football tonight, but we've produced the goods over a 46-match programme and that's what matters most.'

Fulham: Peyton; Hopkins, Strong (Tempest), O'Driscoll, Brown, Gale, Davies, Wilson, Coney, O'Sullivan, Lewington.

Lincoln City: Felgate; Carr, Neale, Cockerill, Peake, Thompson, Shipley, Turner, Hobson, Cunningham, Hibberd (Gilbert).

73 Newcastle U 1 Fulham 4 — League Division Two — 16 October 1982

After promotion in 1982, manager Malcolm Macdonald believed his team could go straight through Division Two and into the top flight. He even banned the word 'consolidation' from the Cottage. There was just one addition to the squad, free transfer Ray Houghton from West Ham replacing the previous year's free transfer signing Peter O'Sullivan in midfield.

A great start, of 10 wins and three draws in 16 games by the end of November, seemed to justify the claim. Some of the best performances came away from the Cottage and the most impressive was at St James', Macdonald's first return to his old club as a manager. Fulham's football was breathtaking that day, and free transfer signing Ray Houghton was at the heart of everything. He scored with a brilliant long-range lob after 37 minutes, spotting the 'keeper off his line. By this time Fulham were already 2–0 up, through Davies after 11 minutes (a superb interchange of passes with Coney, which was typical of the Cottagers' play) and then Coney after 22.

Ray Houghton, who scored with a spectacular chip.

The only sour notes were two disputed second-half penalties for the Magpies, 'won' by Kevin Keegan, recently signed by Newcastle and later to be a Fulham manager. An incensed Macdonald criticised Keegan afterwards, virtually accusing him of diving. Keegan himself scored from the first (just after the hour) and the immaculate Gerry Peyton saved the other.

By this time, Fulham's three-goal cushion had been restored (on 71 minutes) when Davies was the quickest to respond to goalkeeper Carr's fumbling of a Coney effort. Remarkably, Houghton's lob and Davies's first goal finished in the top three of BBC Television's Goal of the Season competition, quite an achievement for a club outside the top flight.

Newcastle United: Carr; Anderson, Saunders, Martin, Clarke, Carney, Keegan, Todd (Wharton), Varadi, McDermott and McCreery

Fulham: Peyton; Hopkins, Lock (Tempest), O'Driscoll, Brown, Gale, Davies, Wilson, Coney, Houghton and Lewington.

74 Derby C 1 Fulham 0 — League Division Two — 14 May 1983

If ever a club was cheated out of a game, and ultimately out of promotion, it was Fulham at the Baseball Ground. Although Malcolm Macdonald's young side had fallen away since the turn of the year, a win in this final match would have brought a second promotion in 12 months and a return to the top flight. In a tightly fought game, Derby took the lead late on through Davison's superb volley. As the game wore on, the crowd started to build up around the pitch until in the closing moments there were human touchlines. Several Fulham players were assaulted by the crowd and referee the said he abandoned the game with two minutes left. But Graham Kelly and his spineless administrators handed hooliganism a blank cheque by allowing the result to stand, an outcome which kept Fulham outside the promotion places.

75 Fulham 0 Liverpool 1 — League Cup round three reply — 29 November 1983

This was the last hurrah from Macdonald's fine young side. After promotion in 1982 and a controversial near miss 12 months later, Fulham struggled in the League in 1983–84. A bad run of results (six defeats and two draws in eight games) in the autumn left them in 20th place at the end of November, not the ideal time to meet Bob Paisley's outstanding Liverpool side, the reigning League champions, Division One leaders and League Cup holders.

Against all the odds, Fulham earned a deserved draw in the first game at the Cottage. Kevin Lock scored Fulham's goal from a penalty and Ian Rush was on the mark for Liverpool. And the Cottagers missed a couple of chances to clinch the tie. But the real story of the evening was the dropping of skipper Roger Brown and playing the diminutive Paul Parker at centre-half, a move that showed what a great talent Parker had. At Anfield after 120 minutes, it was 1–1 again, another immaculate Lock penalty and a goal by Dalglish. Even though Parker was carried off injured, Liverpool could not get the better of Macdonald's young side.

And so, in the days when Cup ties were played to a natural conclusion, it was back to the Cottage for a third game (Fulham won the toss). The crowd, of 20,905, was the biggest of the series, and they were treated to another 120 minutes of thrilling Cup-tie football. Still without Parker but with Coney restored upfront, Macdonald's charges again stretched the Reds to the limit. As one report put the following morning, 'Few sides can claim to have slugged it out with Liverpool toe-to-toe over nearly six hours and emerged beaten but looking fresher and with any number of reasons why the result might have gone the other way'.

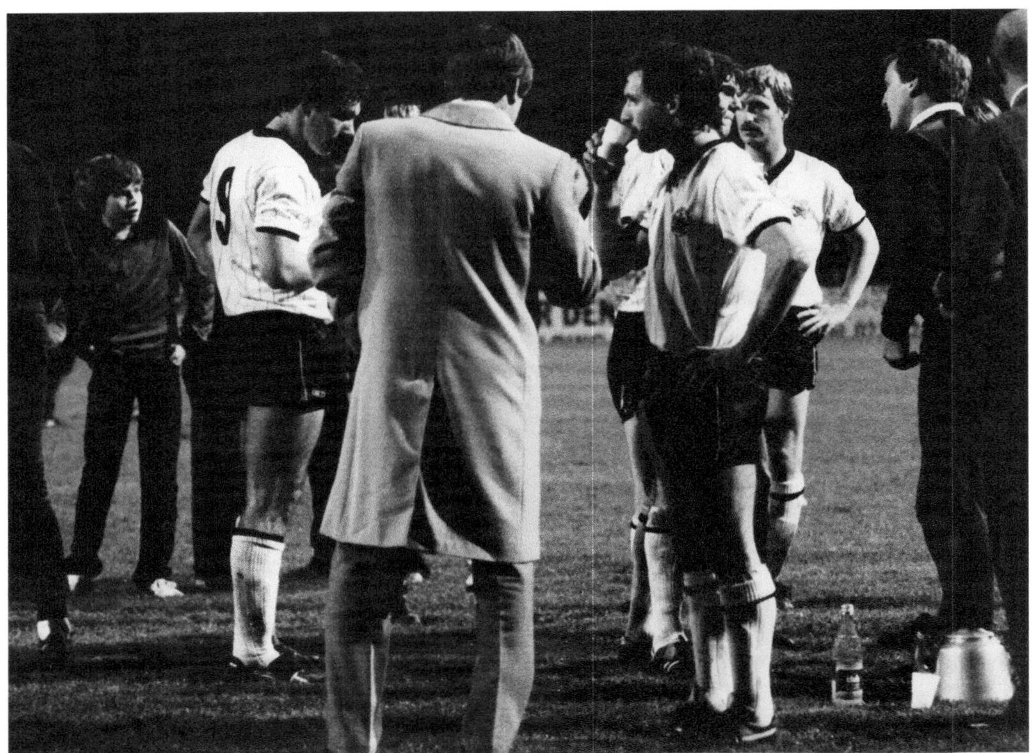

Preparing for extra-time.

Had Fulham's finishing showed the incisiveness and imagination of their approach play, Liverpool's stranglehold on the League Cup would have been loosened. Davies had a particularly frustrating evening seeing chances created by Houghton and Coney miss the target or saves by Grobbelaar. In extra-time, the Cottagers still looked the better and stronger side, but they could find no way past Neal, Lawrenson and Hansen. A Liverpool without the injured Dalglish lacked their usual cutting edge. A draw looked on the cards until six minutes from the end of extra-time when Robinson, for once, headed the ball towards goal and Johnston back headed it on for Souness to drag a low shot past Peyton.

It was yet another heroic failure against the team which would go on to retain the League title and the League Cup. For Macdonald, it was downhill thereafter. As his private life started to unravel, the chairman sacked him in the spring and he never again recaptured that early managerial promise.

Fulham: Peyton; Hopkins, Lock, Carr, Marshall, Gale, Davies, Wilson, Coney, Houghton, Lewington.

Liverpool: Grobbelaar; Neal, Kennedy, Lawrenson, Nichol, Hansen, Johnston, Lee, Rush, Robinson, Souness.

76 Portsmouth 4 Fulham 4 League Division Two 1 January 1985

This was a New Year's Day pantomime at Fratton Park, with both sides benefitting and suffering in turn from a swirling wind. By half-time, it looked all over. Portsmouth, four up, were given a standing ovation from the 18,000–crowd as they left the pitch for the break. For Fulham 'keeper Jim Stannard it was a nightmare 45 minutes. He was partly responsible for all four goals, scored by Waldron, Biley (two) and Webb. But the second half was a completely different story. Coney reduced the arrears two minutes into the second half, and then Fulham scored twice in three minutes, through Rosenior and Barnett. Pompey had less than 15 minutes to hold on, but in the 89th minute Blake fouled Carr and Lock equalised with another perfect penalty to complete the most remarkable comeback.

77 Liverpool 10 Fulham 0 — League Cup Round 2 — 23 September 1986

Just three years after playing three closely-fought League Cup games against Liverpool, a very different Fulham travelled to Anfield for another encounter in the same competition. Relegated to Division Three the previous May and sold to a property company in the summer, Ray Lewington was in charge for only his ninth game as a manager. He had played in the three memorable ties in 1983 but much else had changed by 1986. John Marshall, Dean Coney and Paul Parker were the only other survivors from that very promising young side.

It was the Cottagers' bad luck that they met a formidable Liverpool side at the height of its very considerable powers. Managed by Kenny Dalglish, the Reds had done the League and Cup double the previous season. For this game, Liverpool recalled Grobbelaar to replace Hooper in goal and gave Wark his first game of the season in place of Molby. Had they not been so profligate in front of goal, they would have beaten the club record of 11 goals they scored against the Norwegians of Stromsgodset in the Cup-winners' Cup in 1974.

Programme cover for the second leg.

The result was the Cottagers' biggest-ever first-class defeat. Fulham were simply swept aside by a ruthless Liverpool side, with four goals in the first half and six more in 18 second-half minutes. They showed no inclination to let up even when the game was in the bag. Steve McMahon was the tormentor in chief, with four goals. Rush and Wark got two a piece and Whelan and Nichol completed the rout. It could have been even worse. McMahon missed a penalty, Rush twice hit a post and a hatful of simple chances were spurned. It was a complete humiliation.

Despite conceding 10 goals that night, and 81 more in 51 other League and Cup matches, goalkeeper John Vaughan was the supporters' choice for Player of the Season in 1986–87.

Liverpool: Grobbelaar; Gillespie, Beglin, Lawrenson, Whelan, Hansen, Dalglish, Nichol, Rush, Wark, McMahon.

Fulham: Vaughan; Marshall, Cottington, Scott, Hoddy, Parker, Barnett, Achampong, Coney, Kerrins, Lewington.

78 Fulham 2 Walsall 2 — League Division Three — 28 February 1987

This was the month that the real motives of Fulham's owners, Marler Estates, were revealed. Adding Queen's Park Rangers and Loftus Road to their collection of West London football interests, they announced plans to merge Fulham and Rangers and vacate the Cottage for development. The visit of

Walsall was the first opportunity the fans had to add their disapproval to the chorus of public criticism the proposal had sparked. In an emotionally charged atmosphere, particularly the carefully planned half-time pitch invasion, the fans' response was angry but dignified and never once was violence threatened. The Walsall fans and players were also very supportive of Fulham's cause. The Cottagers needed the points following a slide down the table, and when the Saddlers went 2–0 ahead through Christie and Cross in the 65th and 68th minutes, it was an uphill struggle. But a Donnellan penalty reduced the arrears and Barnett's late equaliser from Pike's low cross salvaged a point. For all the emotion, however, the crowd was only 5,944.

79 Wolves 5 Fulham 2 League Division Three 11 February 1989

This was a most curious match. Fulham were on the wrong end of a hammering and had Clive Walker sent off, but the result proved a turning point and Gordon Davies set a new club goalscoring record. His 158th goal took him past Haynes's record, and his career total of 178 is unlikely ever to be beaten. At Molinuex, a Steve Bull hat-trick did the damage, the first two coming in the opening 14 minutes. Davies scored his breakaway goal after 21 minutes, but then a Thomas own-goal and Thompson penalty (awarded when Scott fouled Downing) gave Wolves a 4–1 lead after 31 minutes. Bull completed his treble after the break and Fulham debutant Rougvie completed the scoring a minute from time. It was his signing that sparked a run that lifted Fulham from mid table into the Play-offs.

80 Fulham 0 Hayes 2 FA Cup round one 15 November 1992

In an era when Fulham looked to be in terminal decline, this was the biggest humiliation, a Cup defeat for the first time in the modern (post-1920) era by a non-League side, and from the Diadora League at that. The fact that this was the only tie played on a Friday evening merely drew intention to Fulham's abject failure. And there was nothing fortunate about Hayes win. Fulham had the craft and the guile, but they could not match their humbler opponents for commitment and energy. After Fulham had squandered a hatful of chances, they got caught on the break in the second half. A free-kick conceded by Glen Thomas was curled over the wall and into the net by Colin Day. Hayes clinched their remarkable win when Stephen slipped Pope's left-wing cross past Stannard. The result hastened manager Dicks's departure from the Cottage.

81 Swansea C 2 Fulham 1 League Division Two 7 May 1994

After years of flirting with a drop into the fourth tier of English football for the first time, the trap door finally opened at the Vetch Field. When manager Don Mackay was sacked after the game at Leyton Orient, coach Ray Lewington was given nine games to avoid relegation. There was still a chance when the Cottagers went into the final game, as long as they beat Swansea. In the end, they failed to rise to the occasion and Jason Bowen was their undoing. He volleyed his 17th goal of the season in the 36th minute from Perrett's cross. Eckhardt missed a glorious chance to equalise before Perrett got the second after Stannard had parried Torpey's effort. Gary Brazil's last-minute goal for Fulham was too little too late, and the Cottagers went down by a point, with the unusually high total of 52 points.

82 Fulham 7 Swansea C 0 — FA Cup round one — 11 November 1995

There was little sign a quick turn-around in the club's fortunes at the lower level. With controversial new manager Ian Branfoot at the helm, League form was indifferent at best and the highlight of his brief tenure came in the FA Cup. The defeat of Second Division Swansea was the biggest win in the history of the competition by any club over a team from a higher division. Fulham were without a win in the 14 previous League games, and this seemed a very unlikely result. And it happened largely because of an injury – to a Fulham player. When Lea Barkus hobbled off after 19 minutes, he was replaced by Paul Brooker, who then ran the Swans defence ragged. Fulham were 2–0 up at the time, through Conroy (two and 16 minutes). Jupp made it three before half-time. The carnage continued after the break, with Conroy, Cusack, Brooker and Thomas piling on the misery.

83 Fulham 3 Doncaster R 1 — League Division Three — 12 October 1996

In his first few months as manager, Micky Adams had put out a team of cheap transfers, journeymen and veterans who made a flying start to the 1996–97 season and held out the prospect of Fulham's first promotion in 15 years. Walton, Watson, Cullip, Cockerill and Freeman were now becoming familiar names to Fulham fans. They topped the table with eight wins from 11 games when Doncaster came to town to celebrate 100 years of football at Craven Cottage. The display lived up to the occasion. After a goalless first half, Fulham stepped up a gear. Conroy headed home his 10th goal of the season on 51 minutes before Scott (60 minutes) and Carpenter (70 minutes) made the game safe with two superb long-range strikes. By then, Rovers' Cramb had been sent off for clashing with Angus and Birch's 82nd-minute strike was just a consolation.

84 Carlisle U 1 Fulham 2 — League Division Three — 5 April 1997

Taking Fulham from Conference candidates to promotion challengers in his first full season was Micky Adams's remarkable achievement as manager. This was the first but not last time that he was to prove himself an exceedingly good manager of smaller clubs at the lower levels. Promoted from coach to team manager in February 1996, he tweaked the squad in the summer without spending very much and rebuilt the team spirit. After getting off to a flying start in 1996–97 (11 wins in the first 14 games), the team maintained the momentum and, with Wigan and Carlisle, were involved in a three-horse race for the title. Although there were still five games remaining after this trip to Brunton Park, this was seen by the players and supporters of both clubs as a promotion decider.

Fulham travelled north, unbeaten in the previous nine games. They were without injured regulars Mark Blake, Richard Carpenter and Darren Freeman, but Danny Cullip, Rod McAree and the on-loan Christer Warren were proven replacements. With the club's first promotion for 15 years within reach, this was Fulham's biggest game since the Play-offs in 1989.

It did not get off to the best of starts when Rory Delap headed Carlisle into a first-half lead. But a rousing team talk from Adams lifted the players and they raised their game after the break. Just six minutes into the second half, McAree (preferred at the last minute to Thomas) received a short corner and crossed to the far post, where Cullip headed back for Conroy to force the ball home. Then, just four minutes later, after a flowing move, Warren knocked the ball into the path of McAree on the edge of the Carlisle box, and he hit a fierce half volley into the net to give the Cottagers the lead.

The first goal in the 2–1 victory was a dramatic close-range header from Mick Conroy (number 9 by the far post). Fulham's number 11 is Christer Warren.

The last 15 minutes were very tense. Carlisle had a reputation for scoring late goals and the visitors had their backs to the wall defending their slim lead. But they held on, and the three points lifted them back to the top after Wigan only drew. Although not a mathematical certainty (Swansea could still catch Fulham if the Cottagers lost all their remaining games and the Swans won their last four, scoring 13 more goals than Fulham), it was as good as in the bag. And for the older supporters among the 2,000 who made the 650–mile round trip, McAree's goal brought back memories of Viv Busby and Goodison in 1975. It certainly seemed as important.

Fulham: Walton; Lawrence, Cullip, Cusack, Angus, Watson; McAree, Cockerill, Morgan; Warren (Thomas), Conroy (Scott).

Carlisle United: Caig; Hopper, Archdeacon,Walling, Varty, Pounewatchy, Peacock (Thomas), Jansen (Smart), Delap, Hayward, Aspinall.

85 Aston Villa 0 Fulham 2 FA Cup round four 23 January 1999

With Kevin Keegan at the helm, Fulham were running away with the Second Division, and in style. But as if to establish their credentials for higher-grade football, they caused several Cup upsets that season. Southampton, from the top flight, were beaten in both competitions, but a trip to Premiership leaders Villa (the first Cup meeting between the teams since 1905) looked a much more daunting challenge. The day started badly for Villa (striker Stan Collymore was sent home for refusing to be a substitute and Dion Dublin was unfit) and got worse. Fulham scored twice in the first half, a Morgan header on eight minutes from Hayward's corner and a Hayward shot from a short free-kick (awarded for Southgate's foul on Collins) deflected off Peschisolido on the stroke of half-time. Ironically, both scorers had their Villa-supporting families in the 35,260 crowd. In the second half, Fulham contained the best Villa had to offer very comfortably.

86 Manchester U 1 Fulham 0 FA Cup round five 14 February 1999

This was United's year of the treble, but they never came closer to missing out on one of the three trophies than in this FA Cup game against Fulham, two divisions lower. With the fares heavily subsidised by chairman Mohamed Al Fayed, there was a large contingent of Fulham fans among the 54,798 crowd for this televised Sunday afternoon fixture. Even though the team was without Bracewell, Morgan, Peschisolido and Horsefield, for whom Lehman, Salako, Smith and Betsy deputised, they gave an excellent account of themselves and were never over-awed by the occasion. Former Fulham loan player Andy Cole (who had been bought and sold by Keegan when at Newcastle), scored the only goal after 25 minutes, getting on the end of a Solskjaer pass. Thereafter, United's class was countered by Fulham's commitment, and they were a Salako toenail away from a deserved equaliser. The only discordant note was the news that manager Keegan was a leading contender for the England job following Glenn Hoddle's departure.

87 Fulham 3 Preston NE 0 League Division Two 8 May 1999

Exactly 50 years and one day after Fulham first won the First Division Championship they were presented with it for the second time after this comprehensive victory over Preston. The day was merely a celebration of a title win that had become a statistical certainty over a fortnight earlier and which had looked very likely from the autumn onwards. Fulham headed the division by a massive 14 points and set 10 new club records in the process. In Mohamed Al Fayed's second season, Kevin Keegan had delivered on the first step of the chairman's promise to take Fulham into the top flight.

Although the title had already been won, and Preston had secured a place in the Play-offs, the best League crowd for 16 seasons (of 17,176) came to see Fulham presented with their first piece of silverware for half a century. Nearly 30 years earlier, in the final match of 1971, Preston had spoiled Fulham's party at the Cottage by winning and denying them the Third Division title. Although they were not going to prevent them from being champions this time, they made a good job of stopping them winning this match in the first 45 minutes. In the first half, the Cottagers flattered to deceive, enjoying plenty of possession but failing to turn it into chances and goals.

A second half substitution made all the difference. Off went Lehmann and on came Paul Moody, one of Micky Adams's last signings in the 1997 close season for the then sizeable fee of £200,000. A prolific scorer at Oxford, the ungainly Moody was unlucky at Fulham. He broke a leg and then fell out of favour when other strikers were signed, but with Horsefield and Peschisolido injured he made it to the bench and came on in the second half.

In less than a quarter of an hour between the 64th and 77th minutes, the old warrior scored a classic hat-trick, the first a fierce shot, the second a ferocious penalty and then a trademark header. It was enough to bury Preston and create a party mood, and was as good a way as any to end his two-year stay at Craven Cottage (he was sold to Millwall in the summer).

Substitute Moody completes his 13-minute hat-trick with a classic header.

The celebrations were elaborate and carefully choreographed, reflecting the chairman's sense of the flamboyant. All the players involved received medals and acclaim but there was one sour note. Just 48 hours earlier, after weeks of prevaricating, manager Keegan announced in a television interview that he was leaving Fulham to become England manager. The press had virtually talked him into the job. As it worked out, the Fulham supporters' disappointment that day was probably matched by the disappointment felt by Keegan himself and the England supporters a couple of years later.

Fulham: Taylor; J. Smith (McAnespie), Brevett, Morgan, Coleman, Symons, Hayward, N. Smith (Uhlenbeek), Lehmann (Moody), Collins, Hayles.

Preston North End: Lucas; Alexander, Kidd, Murdock, Jackson, Gregan, McKenna, Rankine (Darby), Macken, Harris (Basham), Appleton.

88 Fulham 3 Tottenham H 1 League Cup round four 1 December 1999

There was little about Paul Bracewell's brief managerial term that supporters recall with any fondness. After Keegan's cavaliers came Bracewell's roundheads, not only boring but ineffective. But amid the spluttering League form came some impressive Cup displays, the pick of which was this midweek destruction of a full-strength Spurs in the League Cup. The match will always be remembered as Horsfield's match because the bustling striker totally undermined Campbell and Perry at the heart of the Premiership club's defence to set up a memorable victory. Within 10 minutes, Fulham were 1–0 up, Hayles following up when goalkeeper Walker blocked Collins's shot. Although Iverson equalised after a poor clearance by Taylor, Fulham restored their lead a minute later when Collins finished off a neat three-man move. Horsefield's superb third on 76 minutes, a shot with the outside of his right foot across the goal after a run down the right wing, clinched the victory.

89 Leicester C 3 Fulham 3 League Cup round five 12 January 2000

Yet again, Fulham failed to deliver at the quarter-final stage of the League Cup and rarely can they have snatched defeat from the jaws of victory so dramatically, not just once but twice. Ahead 2–0 with just five minutes of normal time remaining, and 3–2 up in extra-time, but they still contrived to lose. Against higher division opponents and without regulars Clark and Hayles, the Cottagers went ahead in the 57th minute when clever play by Horsefield set up Peschisolido. Then, with just 15 minutes remaining, Horsefield took advantage of a defensive mistake by Walsh to make it 2–0. But, in the final five minutes, Leicester scored twice, through Marshall and Walsh. Just three minutes into extra-time, Coleman headed Fulham in front, but again Marshall pegged them back with only nine minutes left. Of the penalties, the least said the better. Leicester scored three, Fulham missed three.

90 Fulham 5 Barnsley 1 League Division One 10 September 2000

Months later, Jean Tigana's Fulham had changed beyond recognition and, with the addition of Collins, Saha and Boa Morte, the negative play of Bracewell was replaced by a sublime passing game that even won plaudits from opponents. In a record-breaking opening sequence, the Cottagers won their first 11 games playing breathtaking football, which was seen to best effect in this televised Sunday lunchtime thrashing of Barnsley. Within five minutes, a Fernandes free-kick set-up Saha to put Fulham in front. Barnsley had a goal disallowed for offside, before Saha made in 2–0 on the half hour after a Hayles effort was parried. When Goldbaek was fouled on the stroke of half-time, Saha completed his hat-trick from the penalty spot. Hayles and Boa Morte got on the score sheet in the second half, and, in between, Ward was sent off and Appleby got a consolation for the Tykes.

91 Blackburn R 1 Fulham 2 League Division One 11 April 2001

From the start of the season, Fulham were the runaway leaders of the First Division, playing a style of football that thrilled their own supporters and delighted neutrals. By the closing stages, Blackburn emerged as the Cottagers' closest challengers for the title. The teams met in midweek at Ewood Park for a televised clash that would almost certainly decide the destination of the divisional Championship.

Rovers manager Graeme Souness added some spice to occasion with his pre-match opinion that his side were currently the best team in Division One. And so it seemed after six minutes when Jansen headed the home side into an early lead. It got even worse for Fulham when, after having a good claim for a penalty for a foul on Hayles denied, left-back Rufus Brevett was sent off following a clash with Flitcroft. But they managed to claw their way back before half-time with a goal by the irrepressible Louis Saha, who made the most of a mix up between Berg and goalkeeper Friedal.

In the second half, the Cottagers' 10 comfortably contained the best that Rovers' 11 could offer and were never seriously under pressure. Then, in the dying moments, Fulham broke. The ball was played into Lee Clark, whose shot was deflected by Berg into the path of the incoming Sean Davis. Timing

Fulham players celebrate at the final whistle.

his run to perfection, he shot past the helpless Friedal to score a dramatic winner. His exaggerated celebration behind the goal was matched by the normally impassive Tigana's jig down the touchline. The title was going to London, SW6.

Blackburn Rovers: Friedal; Curtis, Short (Berkovic), Berg, Duff, (Bjornebye), Dunn, Mahon, Flitcroft, Gillespie (Hignett), Bent, Jansen.

Fulham: Taylor; Finnan, Melville, Symons, Brevett, Goldbaek, Clark, Davis, J. Collins, Hayles (Neilson), Saha.

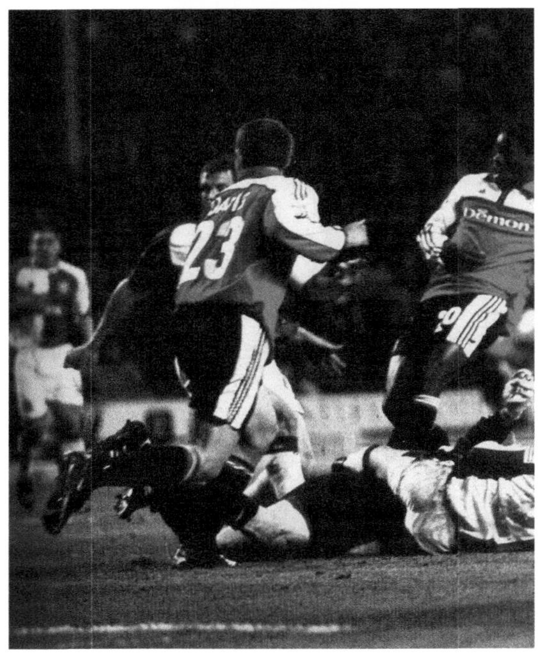

Louis Saha (right) scores Fulham's equaliser.

92 Manchester U 3 Fulham 2 — Premier League — 19 August 2001

Fulham could hardly have had a tougher Premiership baptism: a televised Sunday afternoon match at Old Trafford, home of the reigning champions. This was the ground where Tigana's Monaco had knocked United out of the European Cup quarter-final in 1998. With two future United players in their line up (van der Sar, making his Fulham debut, and Saha) and Fulham fans getting their first sight of Steed Malbranque, it was an impressive top-flight debut for the Cottagers. They took the lead in the opening minutes when Saha raced through to beat Barthez. A contentious free-kick against Finnan gave Beckham the chance to equalise just before the break, but Saha, in the first minutes after the interval, again put Fulham ahead. Van Nistlerooy was, however, on hand twice to score midway through the second period to finally see off the underdogs.

93 Chelsea 1 Fulham 0 FA Cup semi-final 14 April 2002

In many ways this was the lowest key and least satisfactory of Fulham's six semi-final appearances. The club's progress to the last four was relatively smooth, with lower division opposition Wycombe (after a replay), York, Walsall and West Brom despatched in an efficient rather than exciting manner. The semi-final draw paired the Cottagers with their nearest neighbours for only the fourth time, and the first for over 50 years.

The football authorities, however, took the edge off the semi-final as an occasion by arranging a match between two West London teams separated by a long goal kick for Villa Park at the absurd time of 7.00pm on a Sunday evening. The maximum inconvenience to supporters of both sides was the result of the FA's Faustian Pact with television.

The match itself was anti-climatic. A scrappy affair was settled by a scrappy goal, scored by John Terry following a corner just before half-time. The Cottagers were below par, as in fairness were several of Chelsea's big names, and the game never really caught fire. Legwinski brought a fine save out of Cudicini after 27 minutes from a one-two with Marlet, and Saha almost forced Desailly into conceding an own-goal on 59 minutes. Fulham probably had the better of the second half, but half chances were all they could create, and the Chelsea defence coped comfortably with the threat. As they pushed forward, however, the Cottagers left themselves vulnerable to the break, and Gudjohnsen almost took advantage.

Fulham: van der Sar; Finnan, Melville, Goma, Brevett, Collins (Boa Morte), Malbranque, Legwinski (Hayles), Davis, Marlet, Saha.

Chelsea: Cudicini; Melchiot, Desailly, Terry, Le Saux (Ferrer), Lampard, Petit, Gronkjaer, Stanic (Zenden), Gudjohnsen, Hasselbaink (Jokanavic).

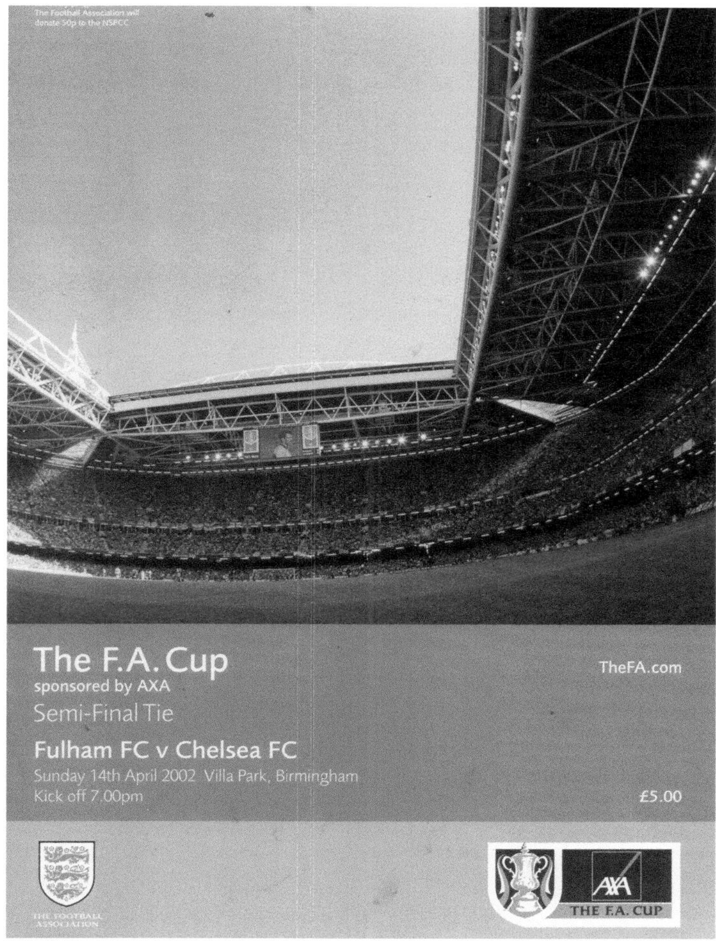

The F.A. Cup
sponsored by AXA
Semi-Final Tie
Fulham FC v Chelsea FC
Sunday 14th April 2002 Villa Park, Birmingham
Kick off 7.00pm
TheFA.com
£5.00
AXA
THE F.A. CUP

FA Cup semi final programme cover.

94 Fulham 0 FC Haka 0 — Intertoto Cup round two — 6 July 2002

Ignoring the Anglo-Italian Cup, this was Fulham's European debut, a back-door entry via the Intertoto Cup. The rules of the competition made Duckworth Lewis seem like simple arithmetic and there was no outright victor, but winning one of the three finals offered a place in the UEFA Cup. Despite the fact that Fulham had officially 'moved' to Loftus Road, this game was played at Craven Cottage when most clubs had barely started pre-season training, and less than 8,000 turned up to see it. In fact, by the time the Premiership season kicked-off, Fulham had played seven competitive matches. Against a well-organised and fit Finnish side, Fulham lacked sharpness, although they had the upper hand in terms of possession. Sava, making his debut, missed the best chance in the first half. In the end, the Cottagers went through on the away-goals rule after a 1–1 draw in Finland.

95 Fulham 3 Bologna 1 — Intertoto Cup Final — 27 August 2002

The Intertoto might be the poor relation of European club competitions, but none of the 13,756 who saw Fulham beat Serie A side Bologna at Loftus Road thought so. A 2–2 draw in Italy had set up the second leg nicely, and this was Junichi Inamoto's finest 90 minutes in a Fulham shirt. It took just 10 minutes to break the ice, Inamoto and Sava combining to create the chance for the Japanese international to score. Although Fulham dominated, the Italians equalised after half an hour when Locatelli's shot was deflected past van der Sar. An unstoppable Inamoto drive from Davis's pass in the first minute of the second half restored the Cottagers' advantage, and five minutes later the game was sealed. Marlet fed Inamoto and, although Pagliuca parried his first shot, he followed up to complete his hat-trick.

96 Fulham 3 Tottenham H 2 — Premier League — 11 September 2002

This was probably the most exciting match Fulham played in their two seasons as tenants at Loftus Road. The result turned on a substitution Tigana made (Malbranque for Boa Morte at half-time) and one Glenn Hoddle did not make (leaving Keane on the bench). Fulham, captained by van der Sar, lost Saha through injury after 20 minutes and two goals (to Richards and Etherington) by half-time. The pace picked up in the second half, and, after Spurs had an effort disallowed for offside, Fulham got back in the game on 68 minutes, Inamoto following up when Davis's shot was blocked. On 79 minutes, a Malbranque penalty, awarded by the assistant referee who saw Gardner wrestle Hayles to the ground, levelled the scores. Excitement mounted as both sides strove for the winner, and it was Legwinski, after combining with Sava, who sealed a famous win in the dying moments.

97 Fulham 3 West Bromwich A 0 — Premier League — 19 February 2003

Under Tigana, the foreign contingent at Fulham steadily rose and peaked in this midweek win over doomed Albion on a freezing cold evening at Loftus Road. The match details were quite straightforward. Fulham came to life after the break, scoring three times in five minutes. Saha broke the deadlock on 69 minutes with a stooping header, Wome added a spectacular second from 25 yards and then a Malbranque penalty. But the real story was that Fulham's starting 11 comprised two Irish internationals (one for the North and one for the Republic), a Welsh international, five Frenchmen, and players from the Cameroon, Japan and Argentina. The two substitutes used were from Latvia and

Morocco. Not one Englishman played for Fulham that evening, the first time this had ever happened. But, no sooner was the revolution completed than it ended. Tigana and Fulham parted company a few weeks later.

98 Manchester U 1 Fulham 3 Premier League 25 October 2003

Former manager Chris Coleman used to like to say that since making it to the Premiership in 2001 Fulham had beaten Manchester United, Chelsea, Arsenal and Liverpool. Not all in the same season of course, but they had shown that, on their day, the Cottagers could live with the best. Of all the victories, none was as remarkable as beating Manchester United in front of almost 68,000 people at Old Trafford, the club's first victory over United for 39 years and the first at the Theatre of Dreams since 1963.

The Cottagers travelled to Manchester just days after losing at home to Newcastle to meet a United side that had lost just once in the League and had only dropped home points in a goalless draw with Arsenal. United had left out Keane, Neville and Scholes, perhaps expecting an easy game, but after three minutes they realised they had a fight on their hands. Man-of-the-match Malbranque dispossessed Silvestre down the right and pulled back a low cross which Clark met at the near post to steer past Howard. It could have been two after 18 minutes when Volz raced down the wing, passed to Pembridge, but his shot hit the underside of the bar. Then, before the half-hour mark, both Saha and Malbranque tested Howard but the goalkeeper did well.

Almost on half-time, and against the run of play, United equalised. Van Nistlerooy and Giggs combined to set up Forlan to shoot past a stranded van der Sar. But Fulham started the second half

Manchester United 2003

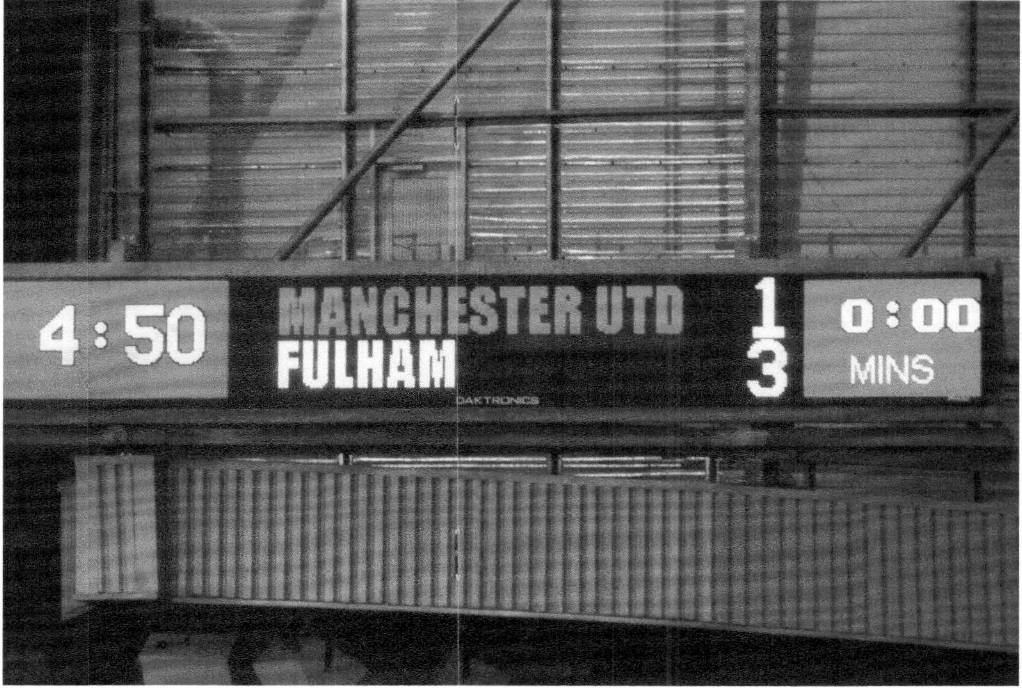

where they had left off in the first and got their reward after 66 minutes. The United defence failed to clear a Boa Morte cross and the ball fell invitingly to Malbranque, who steered a perfect shot into the bottom corner of the net.

And then, with 10 minutes left, came the best goal of the match. A wonderful pass from the left by Malbranque found substitute Inamoto, who barely checked his stride before firing a superb lofted shot into the net past the helpless Howard. Even Alex Ferguson acknowledged afterwards that Fulham were well worth the win, but he was more inclined to criticise his own players' complacency than praise Fulham's performance. He was, however, impressed enough to sign two of the Cottagers in the next couple of years.

Manchester United: Howard; G. Neville, Ferdinand, O'Shea, Silvestre (Fortune), Ronaldo (Scholes), Butt, Djemba-Djemda (Bellion), Giggs, Van Nistlerooy, Forlan.

Fulham: van der Sar; Volz, Knight, Goma, Bonnissel (Djetou), Legwinski, Malbranque, Pembridge (Inamoto), Clark, Boa Morte (Hayles), Saha.

99 Fulham 1 Chelsea 0 — Premier League — 19 March 2006

Too often, Fulham needed Premiership points in the closing months of a season to ensure survival. It was no exception when reigning champions and champions-elect Chelsea visited the Cottage in the spring of 2006. In a televised Sunday afternoon encounter, Fulham matched their neighbours' greater skills and cohesion with hard running and total commitment. When Boa Morte opened the scoring for Fulham, the ball falling kindly for him after Malbranque's shot was deflected, there were still 74 minutes remaining. The turning point came midway through the second half when the referee rightly disallowed a Drogba goal for handball. But he did not do so immediately as he could not see the incident himself and the linesman he consulted had not flagged. Strangely, the Chelsea manager objected to the decision, even though he said it was the right one. Fulham's first win over their neighbours for 27 years sparked a late-season revival, although the day was marred by some mindless crowd trouble at the final whistle.

100 Fulham 2 Arsenal 1 — Premier League — 29 November 2006

Without a win over Arsenal for over 40 years, Fulham went into this game with just one win in their previous six outings. The Cottage was packed with 24,000 on an autumnal Wednesday evening, and in a highly-charged atmosphere Fulham took the game to the Gunners from the start. Skipper Boa Morte was in inspired form against his old club and helped win the corner on six minutes which led to a goal, McBride's looping header from Jensen's cross beating Lehmann. In the 19th minute, Boa Morte beat two defenders to cross for Radzinski to score from close range. A careless free-kick conceded by Rosenior was converted spectacularly by van Persie after 35 minutes to let Arsenal back in the game, but Fulham continued to create the better chances. When Senderos was sent off after 65 minutes for hauling down Boa Morte, the advantage stayed with the Cottagers until the final whistle.

History of the Fulham Programme

Early days

Fulham have produced a programme since 1898, the year they joined the Southern League. It was a large card with the line-ups and a short editorial about the club, and the remaining space was filled with adverts. *The Cottagers' Journal* appeared for the first time on Saturday 31 August 1907 and covered the first home game against Hull City that was played the following Tuesday at the Cottage. It initially came out once a week, but this changed a year later to match days instead. It cost one old penny and contained 12–20 pages. The programme had a coloured cardboard cover full of adverts, such as houses for sale in Southfields for £350 or bicycles costing £4. 15s 0d.

The Cottagers' Journal.

OFFICIAL JOURNAL OF THE FULHAM FOOTBALL CLUB.

Edited by "MERULA."

PRESIDENT ... W. HAYES FISHER, ESQ.

Directors: Messrs. W. G. ALLEN, J. DEAN, E. D. EVANS, A. F. FOULDS, W. HALL, H. G. NORRIS (Chairman), and J. C. WATTS. Secretary-Manager: H. BRADSHAW.

No. I, Vol. I. SATURDAY, AUGUST 31, 1907. One Penny.

From the Board Room.

In presenting our official Programme in its new and enlarged form, under the more dignified title of the "Cottagers' Journal," we venture to express the hope that it will be welcomed as an improvement upon that of last season.

We could have wished that it had been possible to dispense with any advertising matter, but the cost of production is so heavy that to make it pay (and we frankly admit that we have sufficient of that much-abused commercial instinct as to desire that it should pay), advertisements are, at any rate for the current season, an absolute necessity. If, however, the sales during the season should be such as to warrant it, the space devoted to reading matter will be materially increased next season, and still further improvements added, it being our desire to make this Journal as necessary to the Fulham public as are the actual matches.

Even in its present form it challenges comparison with that issued by any other London club.

It is with more than ordinary pleasure that we are able to announce that the services of "Merula" have again been retained as Editor for the season, and in this connection it may be stated that this brilliant writer has an entirely free hand. In other words, he does not write "to order," nor are his weekly notes submitted to anyone connected with the club prior to their publication in this Journal

Before we leave the matter of the Journal, may we mention that we have made arrangements whereby a copy will be posted to any address in England each Friday night for an inclusive sum of 4s. for the full season, or any single copy for 1½d. It is thought that this innovation will be an advantage to those who cannot attend every week and yet desire to keep themselves acquainted with the current topics of Fulham in particular and the League in general. Instructions for such copies must be made to Mr. Bradshaw at Craven Cottage.

Since the close of last season the Club has withdrawn from the Southern League on its election to the Second Division of the English League, a step which we believe has met with the almost unanimous approval of the club's supporters. The change has entailed an enormous cost in the matter of transfer fees, but we are hopeful that compensation will be forthcoming in the increased attractiveness of the matches.

Having regard to the long distances the players will be called upon to travel during the season, we have thought it desirable to withdraw from the Western League, a loss in revenue which we hope will be made up by larger attendances at the Saturday matches.

The Reserves will take part in the South-Eastern League and Premier Division of the London League, and having regard to the calibre of the players who will be taking part in these matches, we earnestly appeal for a large measure of your support.

We are especially grateful for the gratifying financial success which attended the playing of our practice matches. The new Putney Hospital and other local charities will benefit largely in consequence. It is another illustration of the old proverb, "Many can help one, where one cannot help many." Mention of this proverb reminds us that it can again be brought into practice by responding to the invitation appearing on the front cover of this Journal. We shall hope to hear from many friends during the week.

Craven Cottage will next Saturday be visited by Queen's Park Rangers.

Kick-off, 3.30 p.m.

THE DIRECTORS.

The Cottages' Journal from 1907.

The editor went under the pen name of Merula, whose literary style must have made quite difficult reading for the average football fan of the time. Merula wrote at great length on previous matches, reserve games, incoming and outgoing players and other club matters, as well as poems and famous quotes. Fulham signed 13 new players and bid a 'Fond Farewell' to 11 during the summer of 1907. Bert Kingaby was one of these and, of him, Merula said 'Kingaby – he bore the quaint nickname of "Rabbit", and we can thus send him in friendly greetings, the French motto "Lapin, en avant".'

Merula fell ill shortly afterwards. He went to recuperate in Italy and was replaced by the 'Ariel', who wrote in a more straightforward way. Merula returned in the New Year and penned the following about Fulham's famous FA Cup victory over Manchester United: 'A thousand congratulations to the lads on their grand show, and for raising so loftily the prestige of the good old club. In the moment of victory one is apt to be carried beyond the ordinary bounds of reason, and to ascribe more flattering laudation than the occasion merits. I am of the opinion that the bonny boys did right gloriously, and amply merit the warmest felicitations which have been so freely tendered to them.' Weeks later Fulham lost 6–0 to Newcastle United in the semi-final, but Merula did not even mention the match in the programme! (Facsimiles of the programmes for 1907–08 and 1908–09 were produced by three Fulham supporters, Robert Fennell, Reg Weller and Ken Coton in September 2000.)

A character with the Dickensian nom de plume of 'Wilkins Macawber' took over as editor in 1910. Merula had full editorial control and some of his comments must have offended players and board members, but the new man had to be more careful about expressing his views. There was an occasional photograph of a player, together with the usual features such as line-ups, half-time scoreboards and League tables etc. Merula and Macawber had an eye for the unusual and treated the Fulham supporters to the delights of 'Football around the World', 'Ladies Football and Ladies at Football Matches', 'The Evils of Betting', 'Faulty Refereeing', 'Sport and Decadence' as well as articles on boxing. Copies of Fulham programmes from 1907–1915 can be read at the British Newspaper Library at Colindale (although the set for 1913 was stolen a few years ago), or at the Hammersmith and Fulham Archive (mostly 1907–1910).

When Wilkins Macawber took over the editing of the programme in 1910, it became instantly more readable and the material and style were aimed at the average football fan. The format of the programme remained very much the same in the years leading up to World War One. 'Tales of the Cottagers' was the title given to the news and views of the club. Other features were 'Through the Glasses' written by 'The Flag Lieutenant'. This looked at the most important football topics of the day, such as Woolwich Arsenal's move from Plumstead to Highbury in 1913. Another new feature was 'Do You Know That', which had snippets of news and information about other teams and their players, i.e. transfer rumours.

Most programmes had large, single cartoons, but if they were supposed to be funny then humour has changed a great deal. There are a few articles that make very strange reading today. Written by guest writers, among the most peculiar was by Dr W. Chappell, called 'Football and Physique - The Importance of Being Fit'. These were four of its golden rules: A) ascertain whether you are free from organic defect or disease; B) if you are not in training, play gingerly and avoid overstrain and violence; C) have a cold bath as soon as possible after a game, ignoring perspiration and bodily heat, and finally D) take no alcoholic beverage either before or after a game.

Controversially, the normal League fixture programme was maintained in 1914–15, despite the war raging in Europe. As the season progressed, more players and supporters departed for foreign fields with the various services. As a consequence, the matchday programmes were greatly reduced in size as attendances fell away. As would be expected, the wartime programmes were full of patriotic and jingoistic comments. Footballers and spectators were called to arms as many responded to Lord Kitchener's request for recruits with the slogan 'Your Country Needs You'. Interestingly, players in the forces were referred to by rank on the team sheet.

Interwar blandness

Inflationary pressures led to a doubling of admission and programme prices, to 1/- and 2d respectively, after the war. The 'Baker's Man' became the editor from 1919 to 1928. During his time, however, the contents of the programme deteriorated, probably because newspaper coverage, especially in the national press, improved enormously. An obviously posed individual action picture of the players appeared in 1923–24, and the programme doubled in size from 1924 as Britain's economy began to recover from the effects of war and recession, but the contents changed little. The news and information section was still called 'Tales of the Cottagers' and players' profiles were called 'Cameos'. The team line-ups also appeared on the centre pages for the first time, surrounded by adverts.

A 1929 programme.

There were one or two innovations in 1926–27, such as a list of goalscorers and a cartoon of one of the opposing players, but not until 1928 did the programme again start to be as interesting as it had been before the war. A photograph of the Stevenage Road stand taken from the road was introduced to the cover, which lasted until 1945, and the layout was much improved. The details of the club and the opposition's name were printed in bold letters on the cover for the first time and it also included information about local LCC tramway services (26, 28 and 82) which passed near the ground. 'Tales of the Cottagers' was re-titled 'Cottage Pie' and a new editor, whose nom de plume was 'The Pieman', took over. The visitors' column was renamed 'Our Friends The Enemy' a title that was kept through to the early 1950s. Details of away travel appeared for the first time, and Thomas Cook (the travel agency) supplied the tickets. A game at Bournemouth, for instance, cost 6/6d (about 32p) return.

The club produced a souvenir programme for the final match of 1931–32 against Exeter City to celebrate winning the Third Division South Championship. It was printed on glossy paper and contained portraits of the directors, the manager and the players, and also contained a review of the successful season. When Jimmy Hogan took over as manager in 1934, he became the first manager to write his own column in the programme. He once complained about 'the meanness of anonymous letters', and that he never read them because he was too busy. The editorial comment was not impartial but could sometimes be constructive and critical. Defeats, however, were often met with comments on how unlucky the boys were or that the ball just would not go in the net.

Adverts for Chelsea Palace Theatre regularly appeared, sometimes with famous names like Gracie Fields, George Formby and Ted Ray. The most novel and interesting feature of the programme during the 1930s was the cartoon page, which usually covered the previous home game. There was a series of six or seven small drawings over a whole page about these matches. There was also a warning to spectators not to buy pirate programmes that were sold outside the ground at the time and right up to the late 1960s.

Wartime improvisation

League football was suspended for the duration of the war in September 1939, and the Home Office closed Craven Cottage. Within weeks, however, the authorities had responded to the changed conditions and football was organised on a regional basis, with the Cottage once again being opened. The first game in the war competitions was played on 21 October 1939. The programme thanked the players for giving up their afternoon off to play for Fulham since many were in the police force or

OFFICIAL PROGRAMME. TWOPENCE

FULHAM FOOTBALL CLUB

FULHAM FOOTBALL & ATHLETIC Co. Ltd
Registered Office: CRAVEN COTTAGE, Stevenage Rd., FULHAM, S.W.6

Chairman—C. B. DEAN
Directors—E. D. EVANS N. A. D'AMATO F. R. OSBORNE. T. TRINDER.
Medical Officer—Dr. J. WILSON CLYNE, M.B. Secretary-Manager—J. G. PEART.
Telephone—PUTNEY 3621. Telegrams—"FULHAMISH, WALGREEN, LONDON."

FULHAM v. CHELSEA
FOOTBALL LEAGUE, SOUTH
SATURDAY, APRIL 6th, 1946 Kick off 3.15 p.m.

CLUB CHATTER

Last Saturday's game against Brentford provided a perfect illustration of the truth of that old adage "A game is never lost until it is won." On the day's play I am certain our Brentford friends would agree that we were the superior side.

The Brentford players are entitled to full credit for persevering on what appeared to be a hopeless task, and in the closing minutes their efforts were rewarded with two of the most weird goals I have ever seen scored in one match.

During the first half our side gave a splendid display of first class football. The injury sustained by Viv Woodward, which caused a shuffling of the forward line, had an adverse effect on their second half display.

However, despite this handicap they continued to dominate the proceedings, but several excellent chances were allowed to go abegging. It was a big disappointment to our players to lose fifty per cent. of their Bonus, when it looked to be in the bag.

To-day we welcome our neighbours Chelea, and we are sorry that International Tommy Lawton will be absent from their side.

Having players of International class has its drawbacks, but it does seem rather curious that Lawton should be called upon to play in a Trial match.

A splendid victory at Villa Park and honours even at the Valley against Charlton must warn our players that they are in for a very busy afternoon.

Peter Buchanan has been looking forward to this match, we are hoping he will produce his very best form against his old clubmates.

The ankle injury sustained by Viv Woodward keeps him out of to-day's match.

Our Combination team are playing very well at present and a very entertaining match should be seen at the Cottage next Saturday when they meet Millwall Reserves in the Combination Cup, kick-off 3.15.

Our Junior side have won their way into the Final of the Brentford Hospital Cup. The Final-Tie is to be played at Craven Cottage on Thursday, 2nd May.

Our postponed League fixture against West Ham will be played at Upton Park on Monday, 29th April.

Our Home fixture versus Birmingham has not yet been arranged.

On behalf of the Football League we thank our patrons for their generous contribution of £103/0/2 collected at our match last Saturday.

NEXT HOME MATCH
SATURDAY, APRIL 13th, 1946 Kick off 3.15 p.m.
FULHAM v. MILLWALL
LONDON COMBINATION CUP

A 1946 programme.

working in ammunition factories. As well as reporting on the fortunes of players in the various services, the programme also carried regular air-raid warnings, along the following lines: 'In the event of an air raid, all exits will be opened. Cover is also provided under the Stand. Public shelter space is limited, so please obtain shelter elsewhere.'

Initially, the programme followed the pre-war format, but, as the war began to bite, it got smaller, and by 1942 it was just a single sheet that contained the line-ups and fixtures only. Fulham could rarely field one of their own players, and the teams were made up almost entirely of guests who were serving locally. A new warning appeared in 1944: 'Danger from Flying Bombs – Spotters will be stationed to give warning of imminent danger.' Bombings played havoc at some grounds, but most bombs hit the pitch, although one blew a big hole in the centre of the Stevenage Road Stand. The programme called this 'Hitler's Christmas Present'.

The club received many letters from Fulham players serving abroad and printed these in the programme. Corporal Vivian Woodward, an inside-forward from the late 1930s, and a driver with the RAOC, wrote that at top speed he could not keep up with the Nazi retreat. The pre-war programme format was reintroduced in February 1945 with the usual photograph of the Stevenage Road stand on the cover.

When the League programme was resumed in August 1946, the programme underwent a major change. Many items, including paper, were in short supply, but nevertheless the club managed to produce a programme which was much reduced from the pre-war format. For the first three post-war seasons, it comprised eight pages but was not very good value. The old title, *The Cottagers Journal*, used since 1907, was dropped, and it just became the plain *official programme*. Only three quarters of one page was given over to information or news about the club, and the rest was advertisements, the line-ups and the season's fixture lists.

A biased view of life

The programme's quality improved significantly after Fulham's rise to the First Division in 1949, but its price was increased by 50 percent. The number of pages rose to 12, and the page size also increased. Colour was used (red and green) on the cover for the first time, which showed two players chasing a ball towards goal. The pace of change was much slower in those days, and people did not expect a new cover each season so the style of cover remained the same until 1961.

The programme for the first First Division match against Wolves in August 1949 was the template during this period. It included such features as 'Club Notes', 'Our Friends The Enemy' (a history of the visitors and a photograph of one of their leading players) and a profile of one of the Fulham players. This issue listed 32 professionals and 23 amateurs on the club's books and also carried a team photograph. When Fulham were relegated to the Second Division in 1952, the colour of the cover changed and the price rose again, to four old pence. It had therefore doubled in three years, but some interesting new features appeared between 1952 and 1954. An in-depth question and answer article, in which each of the players revealed much about their background and early career before their arrival at the Cottage, was particularly interesting.

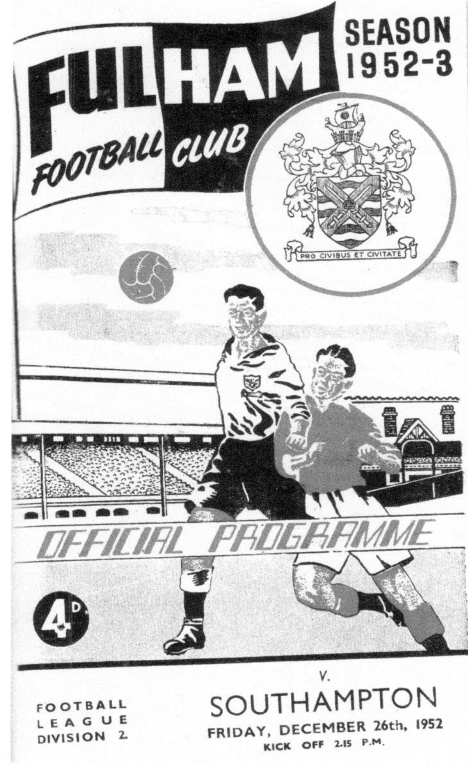

A 1952 programme of Haynes's first match for Fulham.

During the 1950s, the opening article, called 'Inside The Cottage', gave an absurdly biased account of recent games. It usually had a ridiculously partisan editorial with frequent references being made to 'the greatest save we have ever seen', or that the (opposing) goalkeeper was very lucky to keep the score down with lucky saves. The referee always seemed to blow for time when Fulham were about to score, and the home players were always in devastating form. Another regular feature was 'Cottage Crumbs'. This was a round up of snippets about events at the club, such as representative honours, new arrivals and recent departures and injury news. It also included inane comments such as how Ian Black lost his new shoes at a Bristol hotel.

The programme made its first attempt at a history page in 1956. A series of articles on former players appeared, which highlighted their Fulham careers, discussed what they were doing presently and even gave their addresses so that supporters could write to them. Information on the reserves and juniors increased during this period, and by 1960 'Focus on Youth' had appeared. It featured promising youngsters like Fred Callaghan, Dave Metchick and Brian Nichols. There were, however, signs that the programme was deteriorating. It was printed on poor quality paper, contained few photographs and little reading material.

While Arsenal and Chelsea were producing magazines full of action shots and interesting articles, the Fulham programme compared very unfavourably with the club's First Division peers. The cover was changed in 1961 for the first time since 1948, to a picture of the ground taken from the Hammersmith end. The exception came in May 1962 when Johnny Haynes won his 50th international cap and his picture took pride of place on the cover. Although many of the old features survived, they were less prominent and not so entertainingly written. There were few innovations and the programme showed a distinct lack of originality. Line-ups for the previous games first appeared in 1961, and a team photograph was used in 1963 for the first time in 15 years. There was also a very small column on the programme of 40 years ago and a Supporters' Club page.

Not until 1964–65 was an effort made to raise the programme's standard. The cover was more imaginative, a disguised black-and-white action photograph of four players jumping for a ball. Ken Coton's action photographs appeared for the first time, but they were not very well reproduced due to the poor quality of paper that was used. The first action picture was of Brian O'Connell challenging West Ham's Jim Standen in the opening League match of the season.

Catch up at last

The programme was completely revamped for 1965–66, probably due to the efforts of new secretary Graham Hortop. It was completely overhauled, looked modern and stylish, and was very well produced on glossy paper. A new green cover was introduced, showing the legs of players and the club's crest. Inside, the 'Voice of Fulham' included club gossip and news. There were some excellent action shots and lots of interesting and original picture-based articles, such as a spotlight on players, like how Rodney Marsh felt when he played in goal in an emergency.

Programme sales began to boom, and from average sales of 9,200 programmes per match in 1964–65, this rose to nearly 20,000 during 1966–67. The peak for sales was established in April 1967 when a post-war attendance record of 47,290 watched visitors Manchester United and bought 32,500 programmes. A sign of the times was a request to all the Alf Garnetts at the Hammersmith end to mind their language. The following season, colour action shots were introduced for the first time, and new ideas included supporters' questions to players and an occasional history article. There was also a cartoon character called 'Freddie Fulham', a mythical supporter who came out with such gems as 'Frank Large is such a danger man we expect defences to make an extra charge for Large.' However, centre-forward Large proved to be a disastrous flop that, after playing as a centre-half in the reserves, he was soon sold at a greatly reduced fee.

Like many other clubs, Fulham adopted a magazine style, larger format programme in 1973 but resisted the practice of using inserts about football in general that were produced by an outside agency for clubs in general. The most outstanding feature were Ken Coton's photographs, although the reading material was a bit thin. There were few regular features, other than the season's statistics and line-ups, and generally the programme seemed to be thrown together rather than planned. The club appeared to be completely unaware of its history at this time and once asked supporters for match details of games played during season 1964–65, just a decade earlier.

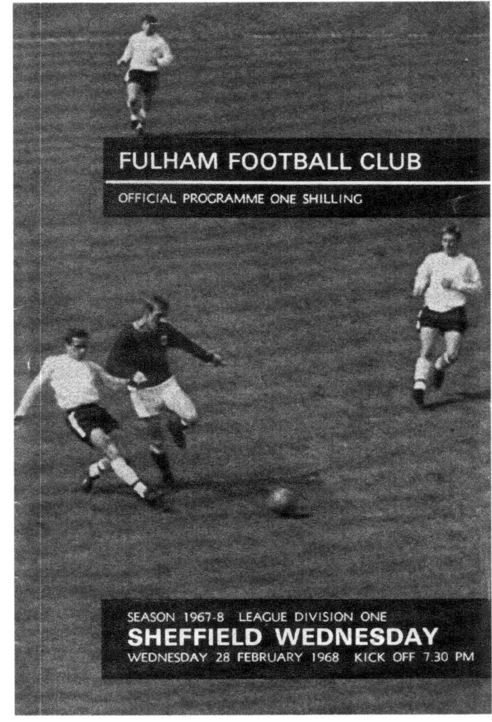

A 1968 programme.

There were some oddities during the 1970s. For

a match against AS Roma in the Anglo-Italian Cup in 1972–73, no magazine at all was produced. Instead, spectators were expected to buy an expensive competition brochure. The Preston Cup-tie programme in January 1974, played during the Three-day week, comprised only four pages. There was a colour souvenir programme issued for the Benfica game, played to mark the opening of the Riverside Stand in 1972, and the Manchester United Cup-tie issue in January 1979 also contained colour photographs. Another innovation from 1977 was the history article on old players and past matches. Reserve and youth-team reports began to appear thanks to Keith Evemy, probably Fulham's most ardent fan.

Supporters take over

After 1981, the editorial content was now entirely in the hands of a small group of Fulham supporters, rather than professional writers as it had been previously. They tried to cover the items that they would like to see as fans. Dennis Turner took over as editor and new features began to appear in the programme. The 'Cottage Diary' was a round up of snippets of information about the club, 'This Week' highlighted reports of matches from the past, and the 'Manager by Manager' spot had articles on all of Fulham's managers up to that time. In 1982–83, articles appeared on the 'Missing Seasons' (The Southern League and War Years) and the History of the Fulham programme, plus items on 'Position by Position' – the best players over the years in each playing position. There were also features on 'Behind the Scenes' at Fulham, Colin Gibson of the *Daily Telegraph* interviewed the current squad, while Jim Sims wrote delightfully idiosyncratic features on old players. In other words, it became more of a supporters' magazine. Ken Coton's photographs continued to grace the programme, but he was soon to leave and be replaced by Gary Pierce, Mike Floyd and Phil Wardle, who continued to supply excellent action shots including photographs of goals.

In 1986 Chris Mason took over as editor of the programme for a while. The austere black-and-white cover of the 1986–87 programme reflected what was going on inside the club. Ernest Clay had sold out to property developer David Bulstrode, and the club was on the point of folding. The programme editorial became more and more difficult to write and was very evasive, which encouraged David Lloyd to launch the fanzine *TOOFIF* in 1988. This was a clearer expression of supporters' views but had little 'official' information.

From November 1990 programme production went back 'in house' to the staff

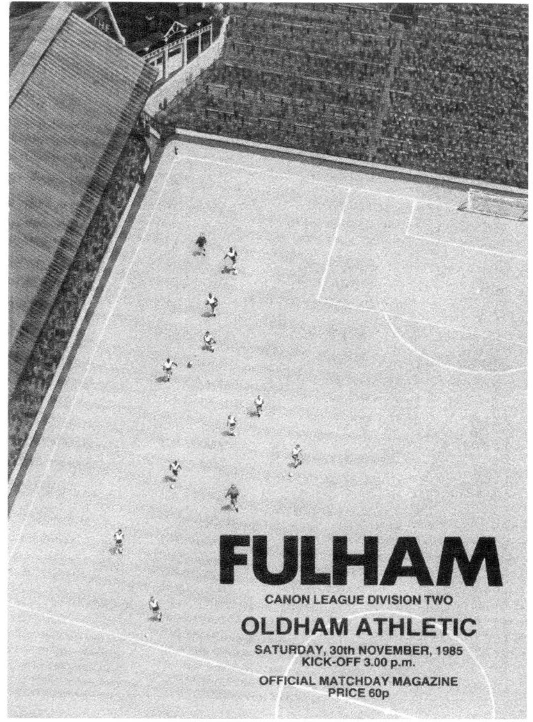

A 1985 programme.

at the Cottage, and the supporters' group which had been responsible for the articles disbanded. The content was never quite as interesting, although the introduction of colour photography helped to soften the blow. Unfortunately, the commercial side and adverts began to dominate the content of the programme, but there were some interesting new ideas over the next few seasons. Production values steadily improved, the price climbed, but the content was very variable and, overall, the programme was rather shapeless.

1994 programme.

There were some memorable pieces. The Fulham players who appeared in the 1975 FA Cup Final were tracked down and interviewed for the programme in 1990–91, and colour action and portrait shots began to appear for the first time in the second half of the season. There was an 'Armchair Critic' review of various things such as books and videos. In 1992–93 a feature called 'My First Time' appeared, in which Fulham players and supporters talked about their first game or visits to Craven Cottage. Jimmy Hill wrote a regular article called 'View at the Top' in 1993–94, and Simon Morgan penned an often very funny piece about the goings on inside the club, but the quality of the photographs deteriorated.

Modern times

As the club moved through the divisions, so the programme got bigger and more expensive. Production techniques had improved markedly, and it looked more and more like the magazines available on news stands. The advertising and 'corporate' element increased, as did generic football articles rather than exclusively Fulham features. The photographs of the players are much 'artier', but the action pictures (where the photographer's skill still counts and technology does not really make a difference) are not up to the standard of the 1960s and 1970s. But the Fulham programme, like every other programme, has to compete with so many more information sources. For many years it was only the press, but now it is the fanzine, television and the internet. The programme is no longer the sole source of information on the club for supporters, and it is probably more important to the club as a means of reaching supporters, primarily for marketing purposes.

The last home game of 2006-07, against Liverpool, Lawrie Sanchez's first in charge and the result that kept Fulham in the Premier League.

Programme Values

Pre-World War Two programmes are very expensive to buy. Their present values are between £50 and £100 for the 1919–1939 period, and older ones will go for £100 plus. Most World War Two issues were single-sheet affairs and will cost between £25 and £60 depending on the opposition. Games against the more successful London clubs, such as Arsenal, Chelsea and Spurs, appear to be more expensive. Most home programmes since the war are relatively easy to buy, especially after 1966, as ebay seems to have opened up the market considerably. However, there are some very rare post-war issues that will cost up to £50 per programme.

Rarest home programmes (Value over £20):

14/12/1946	v	Nottingham Forest (match abandoned)
01/03/1947	v	Manchester City (single sheet) – First game played after the great freeze and hastily arranged
10/05/1947	v	Chesterfield
17/04/1948	v	Millwall
11/02/1950	v	Brentford – Friendly (single sheet)
18/02/1953	v	Rotherham United
18/01/1954	v	Grimsby Town (FA Cup) – the single sheet produced for the second replayed match is the rarity
23/04/1956	v	Luton Town (Reg Lowe's testimonial)

Plus two matches from the Olympic Games at Craven Cottage in August 1948:
Great Britain v France
Luxembourg v Yugoslavia

Programmes from Postponed Games:

01/02/1947	v	Chesterfield
17/02/1951	v	Portsmouth
25/05/1956	v	Nottingham Forest
05/01/1997	v	Swansea City

There are also various match programmes that cost a little more than the regular cost, such as the League Cup programme against Northampton Town in October 1965 and the four-page insert against Lincoln City in May 1982, when only 5,000 programmes were printed but over 20,000 fans turned up on the night.

Fulham's Greatest Players

ARNOLD, John

Born: *Cowley, Oxford, 30 November 1907*
Died: *Southampton, Hampshire 3 April 1984*

One of the few double internationals at football and cricket, John Arnold played cricket for England against New Zealand at Lords in 1931, and his only football cap came in April 1933 for England against Scotland at Hampden Park. The winger's first club was Oxford City, where his father Fred had kept goal. He moved to Southampton in September 1928 and was soon a regular in the side on the left wing, and he went on to hit 46 goals in 120 appearances for the Saints before his move to Craven Cottage, alongside teammate Mike Keeping, for a joint fee of £6,500. John helped Fulham reach the semi-final of the FA Cup in 1936, with excellent performances against Chelsea and Derby County during the Cup run. The clever winger scored Fulham's consolation goal as they went down 2–1 to Sheffield United in the semi-final at Molineux. Arnold carried on playing for the Whites until November 1944, appearing in every round as Fulham reached the semi-final of the Football League War Cup in 1940, where they lost 4–3 to the Hammers at Stamford Bridge. John had spent the early years of the war packing cigarettes and tobacco for the troops, and he also played football for Walsall, Southampton, Bristol City and Cowley as a guest. The Hampshire cricketer played 396 matches and hit over 21,000 runs, including 37 centuries, for the County between 1929 and 1950. He was an opening right-hand batsman, an occasional slow bowler and also an excellent deep fielder. Arnold returned to senior cricket as a first-class umpire in 1961 and sometimes officiated at county matches with his former Fulham colleague Jim Hammond. Arnold died jusst a week afer his old Southampton and Fulham teammate Mike Keeping.

Appearances:

	Football League		FA Cup		GRAND TOTAL	
SEASON	Apps	Goals	Apps	Goals	Apps	Goals
1932–33	13	6	-	-	13	6
1933–34	31	6	2	1	33	7
1934–35	34	8	1	1	35	9
1935–36	24	9	4	3	28	12
1936–37	36	12	1	-	37	12
1937–38	30	8	1	-	31	8
1938–39	34	8	2	-	36	8
TOTAL	202	57	11	5	213	62

BACUZZI, Joe

Born: *Clerkenwell, London, 25 September 1916*
Died: *Clerkenwell, London, 1 February 1995*

Joe's parents came from Milan in Italy, but he was born and brought up in the Clerkenwell area of London, and he won an English Schools Shield winners' medal in 1930 with Islington

Schools. After a trial with Arsenal, he signed for Fulham in June 1935 and from 1937 was a regular at right-back. He was a stylish full-back who liked to attack and was an excellent passer and had good control over the ball. Joe played 13 times for England in wartime internationals, making his debut against Wales in November 1939, and played a number of times at Wembley, experiencing some great victories over the Scots. He was called up by the army and saw service in North Africa and Italy but managed 104 wartime games for Fulham. Joe appeared for Chelsea and Arsenal against the famous Russian side Moscow Dynamo during November 1945, and the match at Stamford Bridge attracted a huge crowd. The swarthy full-back also scored Fulham's first ever goal in Division One with a fortunate shot against Wolves in August 1949. He was 39 when he played his last game for the club against Bury in December 1955.

Bacuzzi was appointed as Fulham's reserve-team trainer in 1956, a post he held until 1965, then he worked in a factory making eyeglasses. He lived in the Clerkenwell area until his death in February 1995. His son David played for Arsenal, Manchester City and Reading.

Appearances:

	Football League		FA Cup		GRAND TOTAL	
SEASON	Apps	Goals	Apps	Goals	Apps	Goals
1936–37	2	-	-	-	2	-
1937–38	26	1	-	-	26	1
1938–39	42	-	2	-	44	-
1945–46	-	-	2	-	2	-
1946–47	18	-	-	-	18	-
1947–48	39	-	5	-	44	-
1948–49	41	-	1	-	42	-
1949–50	38	1	1	-	39	1
1950–51	34	-	5	-	39	-
1951–52	26	-	-	-	26	-
1952–53	15	-	-	-	15	-
1953–54	-	-	-	-	-	-
1954–55	1	-	-	-	1	-
1955–56	1	-	-	-	1	-
TOTAL	283	2	16	-	299	2

BARNETT, Gary

Born: Stratford-upon-Avon, Warwickshire, 11 March 1963

Barnett was a regular during the dark days of the late 1980s. A great trier, but sometimes inconsistent, Fulham fans either loved him or loathed, him but he had his moments in a Fulham shirt. 'Barney' was skilful on the ball and had a good shot and was viewed as a good model by the various managers that he played under. His best season at the Cottage was 1986–87 when he scored nine goals during a traumatic season in which the club nearly went out of existence. Gary eventually played over 200 games for Fulham before moving north to sign for Huddersfield Town, where he made 120+15 appearances. He moved on to Leyton Orient in 1993. He appeared for Coventry City, Oxford United and Wimbledon before his arrival at the Cottage, and when he left Brisbane Road in 1995 he had played 433+51 games, scoring 67 goals, during his League career. Under Barnett's management, Barry Town played in the European Cup-winners' Cup in 1996 and eventually lost to Aberdeen after a good run.

They won the League of Wales in 1997–98 without losing a match and the Welsh Cup in 1997. Barny was assistant manager of Kidderminster Harriers when they gained entry to the League in 2000 and made a couple of League appearances for the club in an emergency. Gary moved to Hull City as assistant manager but was sacked after only six months. After playing for Evesham United, he returned to Aggborough as assistant manager in October 2003.

Appearances:

	Football League		FA Cup		League Cup		GRAND TOTAL	
SEASON	Apps	Goals	Apps	Goals	Apps	Goals	Apps	Goals
1984–85	0+2	1	1	-	-	-	1+2	1
1985–86	34+2	6	1	-	4	2	39+2	8
1986–87	42	9	4	1	4	-	50	10
1987–88	39+3	9	1	-	4	1	44+3	10
1988–89	28	5	1	-	2	-	31	5
1989–90	24+8	1	1+1	-	3	-	28+9	1
TOTAL	167+15	31	9+1	1	17	3	193+16	35

BARRETT, Bert

Born: *West Ham, London, 11 November 1903*
Died: *Cape Town, South Africa, 8 December 1989*

Described as 'a clean, neat player who is a real football artiste', Bert Barrett was easily recognisable on the pitch before the days of numbers due to his blond hair. He gained a Schoolboy cap against Scotland in 1917 and helped West Ham Schools to three English Schools Shield victories. Bert played for Leytonstone, West Ham United and Southampton, where he remained an amateur while he studied to become an accountant. Barrett gained four amateur international caps and also played for the Amateurs against the Professionals in October 1924 and vice versa in October 1929.

Bert played for the full England side in the 3–0 victory over Ireland in 1930 when Fulham were a Third Division club.

Barrett was a great club servant and was an automatic choice for 10 years, playing over 400 games at either full or half-back. He gained a Third Division South Championship medal in 1931–32 and played in Fulham's FA Cup semi-final defeat against Sheffield United in 1936. He also helped the Whites to third place in the Second Division in 1932–33 and for a time was Fulham's main penalty taker.

After a brief spell as the coach at Leytonstone, Bert was the secretary of a wholesale firm in Romford market and emigrated to South Africa in 1954 and coached Camps Bay (Cape Town) in November 1958.

Appearances:

	Football League		FA Cup		GRAND TOTAL	
SEASON	Apps	Goals	Apps	Goals	Apps	Goals
1925–26	36	2	4	-	40	2
1926–27	31	-	2	-	33	-
1927–28	39	-	1	-	40	-
1928–29	31	-	2	-	33	-
1929–30	34	1	5	4	39	5
1930–31	42	5	4	-	46	5
1931–32	30	5	3	-	33	5
1932–33	41	2	1	-	42	2
1933–34	40	1	2	-	42	1
1934–35	42	-	1	-	43	-
1935–36	19	-	5	1	24	1
1936–37	4	-	-	-	4	-
TOTAL	389	16	30	5	419	21

BARRETT, Les

Born: *Chelsea, London, 22 October 1947*

Les Barrett was a very fast winger who loved to take on and beat full-backs and send over dangerous crosses for the other forwards. On his day he was a real crowd pleaser, who scored 90 goals for Fulham. Les came into the side at the start of the 'Great Escape' of 1966, when Fulham managed to avoid what was thought to be certain relegation. He gained an Under-23 cap for England against Greece in 1967 and helped a Young England side beat England 5–0. Fulham dropped from the First to the Third Division, but Barrett and Jimmy Conway tore Third Division defences to shreds as Fulham clinched promotion back to the Second Division in 1970–71, with Les finishing the season as top scorer with 15 League goals. He also appeared in every game in Fulham's run to the FA Cup Final in 1975 and scored the winning goal in the sixth-round win at Carlisle United. The speedy winger appeared in two losing League Cup quarter-finals with Fulham in 1967 and 1970. Les left Fulham in October 1977 for Millwall, where he made only eight appearances as he lost his speed when he reached 30, and later played as a sweeper in non-League football, making 175+4 appeaances for Woking, including a couple of local Cup Finals. Barrett presently runs a small market garden at Earlsfield.

Appearances:

	Football League		FA Cup		League Cup		GRAND TOTAL	
SEASON	Apps	Goals	Apps	Goals	Apps	Goals	Apps	Goals
1965–66	12+2	4	-	-	-	-	12+2	4
1966–67	33	8	3	-	3	1	39	9
1967–68	40	8	3	-	6	2	49	10
1968–69	29	2	2	-	1	-	32	2
1969–70	44	7	1	-	2	-	47	7
1970–71	46	15	1	-	6	3	53	18
1971–72	42	8	3	-	2	-	47	8
1972–73	39	6	1	-	4	-	44	6
1973–74	42	7	3	1	4	3	49	11
1974–75	41	5	12	1	3	2	56	8
1975–76	32+1	1	1	-	1	-	34+1	1
1976–77	20	4	1+1	1	4	1	25+1	6
TOTAL	420+3	75	31+1	3	36	12	487+4	90

BEASLEY, Pat

Born: *Stourbridge, Worcestershire, 27 July 1913*
Died: *Taunton, Somerset, 27 February 1986*

Beasley began his career on the left wing with Arsenal and Huddersfield Town. After missing out on two FA Cup Finals for the Gunners, Pat played in the 1938 Final with the Terriers, but they lost to an extra-time penalty against Preston. Regarded as Alex James's deputy, he gained League Championship medals with the Gunners in 1933–34 and 1934–35, and he

gained his only England cap against Scotland in 1939 when he scored in a 2–1 victory at Hampden Park. He gained two caps in wartime internationals and played as a guest for many clubs including Fulham.

By the time Beasley joined Fulham permanently in December 1945, he had been converted into an inspirational half-back and captained the side that won the Second Division title in 1948–49. After just one season in the top flight with Fulham, he left to become the player-manager with Bristol City in July 1950. He retired as a player in May 1952 and then took City to the Third Division South Championship in 1954–55. After managing Birmingham City (1958–60) and Dover (1961–64) and a season as chief scout at Fulham from 1960, Beasley retired to live in Chard, Somerset, where he also coached the local club from July 1964.

Appearances:

	Football League		FA Cup		GRAND TOTAL	
SEASON	Apps	Goals	Apps	Goals	Apps	Goals
1945–46	-	-	2	-	2	-
1946–47	40	9	1	-	41	9
1947–48	36	3	5	-	41	3
1948–49	39	1	1	-	40	1
1949–50	37	-	2	-	39	-
TOTAL	152	13	11	-	163	13

BEECHAM, Ernie

Born: *Hertford, Hertfordshire, 23 July 1906*
Died: *Hertford, Hertfordshire, August 1985*

A brave and fearless goalkeeper, Ernie Beecham never fully recovered from a terrible injury he received playing for Fulham and was affected by his injuries for the rest of his life. Life was a struggle for him as he was often unable to work and the club was often generous and helped out their former 'keeper financially.

Beecham was diving at the feet of an Exeter City player called Bill Death when he received a serious spinal injury. He managed to play again for a while with Queen's Park Rangers (95

appearances), Brighton and Swindon Town but was never quite the same 'keeper.

Beecham had joined Fulham in May 1925 after playing for Ward End Works and Hertford Town and was outstanding during Fulham's 1926 FA Cup run, especially in a Cup tie at the Cottage against Everton. He was selected to play in an England trial match during his Cottage days and might have gone on to great things, but he missed the game due to the injury, and in March 1936 he retired from playing.

Appearances:

	Football League		FA Cup		GRAND TOTAL	
SEASON	Apps	Goals	Apps	Goals	Apps	Goals
1925–26	25	-	5	-	30	-
1926–27	42	-	2	-	44	-
1927–28	42	-	1	-	43	-
1928–29	13	-	-	-	13	-
1929–30	37	-	5	-	42	-
1930–31	6	-	-	-	6	-
1931–32	9	-	-	-	9	-
TOTAL	174	-	13	-	187	-

BENTLEY, Roy

Born: Bristol, Somerset, 17 May 1924

Bentley played for both Bristol clubs before joining Newcastle United in June 1946 for a fee of £8,500. He moved on to Chelsea in early 1948 and was converted from inside to centre-forward with great success.

His acceleration and strength in the air helped Roy score nine goals in his 12 appearances for England, appearing for them in the disastrous 1950 World Cup side that lost to the US in Brazil. Roy also represented Great Britain against the Rest of Europe in August 1955, he won two B international caps and played for the Football League three times.

Bentley was the Chelsea captain when they took the League title for the first time in 1954–55 under the management of Ted Drake. He moved to Fulham in September 1956 and hit 14 goals during his first season. In November 1957 he was converted into a right-half and a centre-half from October 1958, and he mastered both these positions with great success. He came close to a Wembley Final in

1958, but the Whites lost to Manchester United at the semi-final stage, and appeared 35 times as Fulham gained promotion to the top flight in 1958–59.

The England international went on to score 208 goals in 656 appearances, including 150 goals in 367 games for Chelsea, in an outstanding career. Roy Bentley managed both Reading (1963–69) and Swansea City (1969–72) successfully then managed Thatcham Town and was the secretary at Reading (1977–84), Aldershot (1984–86) and the Shrivenham Golf Club. Roy lives in retirement in the Reading area and recently returned to Stamford Bridge as guest of honour when they celebrated their Premiership title success.

Appearances:

	Football League		FA Cup		League Cup		GRAND TOTAL	
SEASON	Apps	Goals	Apps	Goals	Apps	Goals	Apps	Goals
1956–57	32	14	2	1			34	15
1957–58	31	7	7	1			38	8
1958–59	35	-	4	-			39	-
1959–60	29	2	2	-			31	2
1960–61	15	-	-	-	1	-	16	-
TOTAL	142	23	15	2	1	-	158	25

BLACK, Ian

Born: Aberdeen, 27 March 1924

One of Fulham's greatest goalkeepers, Ian Black recently visited the Cottage for the first time since he left the club in 1959. He joined Aberdeen in July 1944 and moved to Southampton in December 1947, where he was working as a mechanic after his demobilisation. He made his one and only appearance for Scotland against England in April 1948 in a 2–0 defeat.

The Saints narrowly missed promotion three seasons on the trot as Black missed just five games between signing and leaving The Dell. His manager at Southampton, Bill Dodgin, moved to take over at Fulham in 1950, and Black was one of his first signings.

The Scottish international goalkeeper was a tall, stylish 'keeper with safe, reliable hands, good anticipation and considerable courage, but was sometimes vulnerable on crosses. Black became the first Fulham goalkeeper to score a goal, after injury forced him to play at centre-forward, when he headed home Stevens's cross against Leicester City in August 1952. He missed much of 1954–55 after being hit by a series of injuries including a broken arm, but he was mainly the first-choice 'keeper until he lost his place to Tony Macedo in November 1957. In July 1959 Black moved to Bath City and then on to Canterbury City from 1962–64. He was youth-team manager at Brentford in the 1960s and worked for Redhill in 1969 as an advisor. Black has now retired and continues to live in the Tolworth area.

Appearances:

	Football League		FA Cup		GRAND TOTAL	
SEASON	Apps	Goals	Apps	Goals	Apps	Goals
1950–51	42	-	5	-	47	-
1951–52	39	-	1	-	40	-
1952–53	37	1	1	-	38	1
1953–54	32	-	3	-	35	-
1954–55	27	-	-	-	27	-
1955–56	34	-	2	-	36	-
1956–57	37	-	2	-	39	-
1957–58	15	-	-	-	15	-
TOTAL	263	1	14	0	277	1

BLAKE, Mark

Born: Portsmouth, Hampshire, 19 December 1967

Good in the air and on the ground, Mark Blake was Fulham's main penalty taker and hit 20 goals for the club. The England Youth international began his career with Southampton but did not play regular first-team football until he joined Shrewsbury Town in 1990, where he made 177+3 appearances and won a Third Division Championship medal in 1993–94. He was released by the Shrews in May 1994 and, after a brief spell playing for Rangers of Hong Kong, was signed by Fulham manager Ian Branfoot in September 1994 as a replacement for the departing Glen Thomas. He soon became a crowd favourite and was voted Fulham's Player of the Year in 1995, and he played a leading role as Fulham gained promotion as runners up from the Third Division in 1996–97. However, the following

season he struggled to find a regular place in the side, and he decided to move to France to play for AS Cannes in July 1998.

Blake signed for Aldershot Town in April 2000, later playing non-League football for Andover in April 2001, Bashley in October 2001, Winchester City in March 2002 and Eastleigh in January 2005, while studying for a degree in Business Studies, and today he works as a sales manager for an IT firm. Mark played in an FA Vase Final for Winchester City in May 2004 when they beat AFC Sudbury at St Andrews, Birmingham, after beating Robbie Herrera's Bideford in the two-leg semi-final.

Appearances:

	Football League		FA Cup		League Cup		GRAND TOTAL	
SEASON	Apps	Goals	Apps	Goals	Apps	Goals	Apps	Goals
1994–95	34+1	3	4	1	2	1	40+1	5
1995–96	35+3	5	3	-	4	-	42+3	5
1996–97	40+1	7	1	-	4	-	45+1	7
1997–98	24+3	2	2	1	-	-	26+3	3
TOTAL	133+8	17	10	2	10	1	153+8	20

BOA MORTE, Luis

Born: Lisbon, Portugal, 8 April 1977

A player with terrific pace and a powerful shot, Luis Boa Morte joined Arsenal from Sporting Lisbon in June 1997 but was mainly a reserve, although he did pick up some silverware, including two Charity Shield medals and a Premiership medal in 1997–98 when he appeared 4+11 times. He moved to Southampton in August 1999 for £500,000 but made little impact at The Dell, and in July 2000 he was loaned to Fulham for a year. Luis was soon cracking in the goals for the Whites as he formed deadly partnerships up front with Louis Saha and Barry Hayles.

He eventually signed for Fulham in June for £1.6 million after helping the club win the First Division title in 2000–01, scoring 21 goals, and manager Jean Tigana used him as a speedy wide midfield player. He showed the more negative side of his temperament by being sent off twice for spitting and diving in the area.

Luis has appeared for Portugal at full, Under-23 and Youth levels and played for them against England in February 2004 in the Algarve. Boa Morte has the ability to change games and was made club captain by Chris Coleman. However, he seemed to lose his drive and enthusiasm during 2006–07 and was sold to West Ham in January 2007 for a £5.5 million fee.

Appearances:

	Football League		FA Cup		League Cup		GRAND TOTAL	
SEASON	Apps	Goals	Apps	Goals	Apps	Goals	Apps	Goals
2000–01	21+18	18	1	-	5+1	3	27+19	21
2001–02	15+8	1	2+1	-	2+1	1	19+10	2
2002–03	25+4	2	2+1	-	0+1	1	27+6	3
2003–04	32+1	9	5	1	1	-	38+1	10
2004–05	29+2	8	5	1	3	-	37+2	9
2005–06	35	6	1	-	1	1	37	7
2006–07	12+3	-	-	-	-	-	12+3	-
TOTAL	169+36	44	16+2	2	12+3	6	197+41	52

BRAZIL, Gary

Born: *Tunbridge Wells, Kent, 19 September 1962*

Gary Brazil is remembered for his industrious displays first in midfield and then as a striker partnering Sean Farrell in the Fulham attack. He made his name at Sheffield United and Preston, helping them to promotion. Gary had an excellent scoring record at Preston with 69 goals in 186+3 appearances. Newcastle United spent £100,000 on him, but he struggled to make the first team and was happy when Fulham came in and signed him in September 1990.

Gary played in a striking role but had a poor first season when he scored only five goals. He was ever present the following season, however, and was top scorer with 14 goals. However, another 14 goals from him in 1993–94 were not enough to save Fulham from relegation.

During his latter days at the Cottage, Gary often played in midfield, and he became youth-team coach from January 1996. After appearing for Cambridge United and Barnet, he moved into non-League soccer, playing for Slough Town. Sam Allardyce appointed Gary as a coach at Notts County in May 1998, and he was manager of the club for two spells and was also coach at Doncaster Rovers before returning to the Cottage in January 2007 as the Under-18 coach.

Appearances:

	Football League		FA Cup		League Cup		GRAND TOTAL	
SEASON	Apps	Goals	Apps	Goals	Apps	Goals	Apps	Goals
1990–91	41+1	4	3	1	-	-	44+1	5
1991–92	46	14	1	-	2	2	49	16
1992–93	27+3	7	-	-	-	-	27+3	7
1993–94	46	14	1	-	4	1	51	15
1994–95	30+2	7	2	-	4	-	36+2	7
TOTAL	190+6	46	7	1	10	3	207+6	50

BREVETT, Rufus

Born: *Derby, 24 September 1969*

An uncompromising defender, Rufus began his career with Doncaster Rovers and made 125+4 appearances for the Yorkshire club before his move to Queen's Park Rangers in February 1991 for a £250,000 fee. He had helped the unfashionable Rovers get to the Final of the FA Youth Cup in 1988. At Loftus Road he kept Robbie Herrera out of the side as he claimed the left-back berth as his own, making 158+12 appearances before his move to Fulham for £375,000 in January 1998.

The formidable Brevett helped Fulham to

defensive records in the Second Division Championship season of 1998–99 with his ruthless tackling and also scored a very important goal against Stoke City at the Cottage early in the Championship campaign. He was adaptable and was used by Kevin Keegan as a wing-back. His marauding runs down the left flank became a feature of the team, but under Jean Tigana he played a more conventional defensive full-back role in a flat back four. He appeared 39 times as Fulham took the First Division title in 2000–01, and fans who thought he would struggle in the top flightwere proved wrong when he maintained his place in the side until his transfer to West Ham United in January 2003. This included playing in Europe, in the Inter Toto and UEFA Cups, as well as helping Fulham reach an FA Cup semi-final in 2002. Since leaving the Cottage, Rufus has played for Plymouth Argyle, Leicester City on loan and Oxford United.

Appearances:

	Football League		FA Cup		League Cup		GRAND TOTAL	
SEASON	Apps	Goals	Apps	Goals	Apps	Goals	Apps	Goals
1997–98	13	-	-	-	-	-	13	-
1998–99	45	1	5	-	5	-	55	1
1999–2000	22+1	-	2	-	6+1	-	30+2	-
2000–01	39	-	1	-	2	-	42	-
2001–02	34+1	-	6	-	1+1	1	41+2	1
2002–03	20	-	-	-	-	-	20	-
TOTAL	173+2	1	14	-	14+2	1	201+4	2

BROWN, Roger

Born: Tamworth, Staffordshire, 12 December 1952

Big and as brave as a lion, Roger Brown is fondly remembered by most Fulham supporters for his many brilliant displays. After failing to make the grade as a youngster with Walsall, he worked as a production manager in an engineering firm. Bournemouth signed him from A.P. Leamington in February 1978, and he soon impressed with some commanding displays. First Division Norwich City signed him in July 1979. Brown moved on to Fulham the following March for £100,000 but was injured on his debut against Chelsea and missed the rest of the season as

Fulham were relegated. Ever present during 1981–82, as Fulham won promotion, he also scored 12 goals, a record for a defender in a season. The blood-splattered Brown scored the vital equaliser that earned a 1–1 draw with Lincoln City in the match that clinched promotion. Brown did not miss a game the following season as Fulham narrowly missed promotion again. He formed an excellent partnership with Tony Gale in the centre of the Whites defence. However, soon afterwards he fell out with manager Malcolm MacDonald and was transferred back to Bournemouth in December 1983, before serving Weymouth as player-coach and Poole Town as player-manager.

Brown was the manager of Colchester United from 1987–88 but resigned after a defeat at Leyton Orient. Roger presently works for the Probation Service, managing a Community Service Project in Walsall.

Appearances:

	Football League		FA Cup		League Cup		GRAND TOTAL	
SEASON	Apps	Goals	Apps	Goals	Apps	Goals	Apps	Goals
1979–80	1	-	-	-	-	-	1	-
1980–81	39	2	3	-	2	-	44	2
1981–82	46	12	2	-	6	-	54	12
1982–83	42	4	3	-	4	1	49	5
1983–84	13	-	-	-	-	-	13	-
TOTAL	141	18	8	-	12	1	161	19

BROWN, Stan

Born: *Lewes, Sussex, 15 September 1941*

Stan Brown began his Fulham career as a centre-forward but was soon performing as a wing-half in Fulham's First Division side of the 60s. His teammates appreciated the hard work and

consistency that Stan brought to the side, and he was surprisingly good in the air for his size as well as being an excellent tackler who used the ball well. His first goal for the Whites in September 1962 proved to be the winner against eventual champions Everton, a 1–0 victory at the Cottage.

Brown played in the 'Great Escape' side of 1966 but also experienced two relegations from the First to the Third Division. Fulham reached two League Cup quarter-finals in 1967 and 1970, and he played in both of these, but they were lost to Huddersfield Town and Bristol City after replays. He was ever present in 1969–70 and played in most games the following season as Fulham finished as runners-up in the Third Division.

Rarely selected by new manager Alec Stock, Stan Brown left Fulham for Colchester United in December 1972 after a loan spell with Brighton. Since leaving the Football League, he has played for, or managed, non-League Haywards Heath, Burgess Hill, Ringmer Southwick and Burgess Hill and today lives in retirement in the Lewes area.

Appearances:

	Football League		FA Cup		League Cup		GRAND TOTAL	
SEASON	Apps	Goals	Apps	Goals	Apps	Goals	Apps	Goals
1960–61	1	-	-	-	-	-	1	-
1962–63	34	7	2	-	3	1	39	8
1963–64	15	-	-	-	-	-	15	-
1964–65	35	1	2	-	3	-	40	1
1965–66	36	3	1	-	2	-	39	3
1966–67	40	-	3	-	3	-	46	-
1967–68	42	1	3	-	6	-	51	1
1968–69	35+1	-	2	2	1	-	38+1	2
1969–70	44+2	3	1	-	3	-	48+2	3
1970–71	35+1	1	1	-	5	-	41+1	1
1971–72	28+1	-	-	-	1	-	29+1	-
1972–73	3	-	-	-	2	-	5	-
TOTAL	348+5	16	15	2	29	1	392+5	19

BUSBY, Viv

Born: *High Wycombe, Buckinghamshire, 19 June 1949*

Enigmatic during his Fulham career, Busby could score wonderful goals, show his brilliant ball skills and speed in some games yet in others he looked mediocre to say the

least. He only managed 38 goals for Fulham despite being a regular in the side for three seasons.

Busby started his career at Wycombe Wanderers before turning professional with Luton Town in January 1970, and he played alongside Fulham reject Malcolm MacDonald. Alec Stock was his manager at Luton, and he also signed him when he took over at Fulham.

Busby played for Fulham in the 1975 FA Cup Final, which they lost 2–0 to the Hammers, and scored some vital goals on the way at Nottingham Forest and Everton. However, he struggled to find the net the following season and should have scored in the two-leg Anglo-Scottish Cup Final defeat against Middlesbrough.

After the arrival of Rodney Marsh, Busby was sold to Norwich City for £50,000 in September 1976, and he later played for Stoke City, Sheffield United, Tulsa Roughnecks Blackburn Rovers and York City and eventually scored 83 goals in a total of 294+49 appearances during his career.

He formed a successful management team with Denis Smith at York City and Sunderland and had a nine-month spell in charge at Hartlepool United before being sacked for financial reasons. He has subsequently coached at Sheffield United and Everton before he returned to Craven Cottage as reserve-team manager in December 1999. After this he coached at Swindon Town and York City and was caretaker manager there in 2004.

Busby was diagnosed with leukaemia in 2002 but has recovered from the illness.

Appearances:

	Football League		FA Cup		League Cup		GRAND TOTAL	
SEASON	Apps	Goals	Apps	Goals	Apps	Goals	Apps	Goals
1973–74	34+4	12	2	-	2	-	38+4	12
1974–75	38	11	12	6	3	1	53	18
1975–76	37	6	1	1	3	-	41	7
1976–77	5	-	-	-	2	-	7	-
TOTAL	114+4	29	15	7	10	1	139+4	37

CALLAGHAN, Fred

Born: Parsons Green, London, 19 December 1944

A great memory of the 60s was Fred's storming runs down the wing to make well-hit crosses into the box, which earned him the nickname of the Tank. He made the breakthrough when Alan Mullery was transferred to Spurs in 1964 and appeared regularly at left-back or left-half for Fulham over the next eight seasons.

Unfortunately, Fulham dropped from the First to the Third Division in the late 60s, but Callaghan was one of the few survivors, and he later played a vital role in the club's promotion as runners-up in the Third Division in 1970–71. He did not score often but one of his most vital goals came at The Valley in April 1972 to earn a 2–2 draw, which ultimately sent Charlton down to the Third Division instead of Fulham. His

playing career came to a premature end in May 1974 when he suffered a slipped disc. After spells in charge at Enfield (1974–77) and Woking (1977–80), Callaghan took over at Brentford in March 1980 and did well for a while but was sacked in 1984.

He is one of the many Fulham players of the 60s who took the 'knowledge' and became a taxi driver, but he also worked in non-League football as assistant manager at Woking and Kingstonian before becoming the manager at Basingstoke Town (1991–93) and Wealdstone (1993–95). This was followed by spells as the general manager of Walton & Hersham and Carshalton Athletic. For the last few seasons, Fred has been working on the hospitality side at Fulham, a job he seems to relish.

Appearances:

	Football League		FA Cup		League Cup		GRAND TOTAL	
SEASON	Apps	Goals	Apps	Goals	Apps	Goals	Apps	Goals
1963–64	8	-	-	-	-	-	8	-
1964–65	12	-	-	-	2	-	14	-
1965–66	9	-	-	-	1	-	10	-
1966–67	34+1	3	3	1	3	1	40+1	5
1967–68	35	-	3	-	6	1	44	1
1968–69	40	2	2	-	1	-	43	2
1969–70	28+1	1	1	-	2	-	31+1	1
1970–71	45	-	1	-	6	-	52	-
1971–72	42	3	3	-	2	-	47	3
1972–73	38+1	-	1	-	4	-	43+1	-
1973–74	0+1	-	-	-	-	-	0+1	
TOTAL	291+4	9	14	1	27	2	332+4	12

CHAMBERLAIN, Tosh

Born: Camden Town, London, 11 July 1934

A legendary Fulham character, Tosh is still a very popular visitor to the Cottage. He could hit a ball as hard as any player in the club's history, but it did not always go where he wanted it to go.

Tosh played for Middlesex, London, and England Schools and also gained Youth international honours. On his Fulham debut he was on target with his first shot against Lincoln City in November 1954 and later scored a memorable hat-trick in an amazing Cup tie with Newcastle United in January 1956, which Fulham lost 5–4. He hit 15 goals in 1956–57 and 13 goals the following season, but the highlight

of his career came in 1958 when Fulham played Manchester United in the FA Cup semi-final. Chamberlain also played in Fulham's promotion side of 1958–59 but was not a first-team regular after February 1960.

The cockney legend left Fulham for Dover in the summer of 1965 and joined Gravesend & Northfleet the following year. He was the main reason that Johnny Haynes came to the Cottage, as they had played in the same District sides during their school days. He had a love/hate relationship with Johnny on the pitch, but they were great friends off it, and it was fitting that Tosh should lay a wreath to Johnny on the Cottage pitch upon his death in October 2005.

Appearances:

	Football League		FA Cup		League Cup		GRAND TOTAL	
SEASON	Apps	Goals	Apps	Goals	Apps	Goals	Apps	Goals
1954–55	6	1	-	-			6	1
1955–56	21	11	1	3			22	14
1956–57	39	15	2	-			41	15
1957–58	27	13	6	1			33	14
1958–59	24	7	-	-			24	7
1959–60	27	6	2	1			29	7
1960–61	11	1	1	-	1	-	13	1
1961–62	14	2	-	-	2	-	16	2
1962–63	3	-	-	-	1	-	4	-
1963–64	7	2	-	-	-	-	7	2
1964–65	8	1	1	-	-	-	9	1
TOTAL	187	59	13	5	4	-	204	64

CHAPLIN, Alec

Born: Dundee, Angus, 6 February 1892
Died: Fulham, London, 9 March 1986

Like his brother-in-law Jimmy Sharp, Chaplin was a cool and calm full-back who loved to play himself out of difficult situations. He rarely panicked and was Fulham's regular left-back for five seasons after World War One, and before the change in the offside law in the mid-20s Fulham's defence was one of the tightest in the Second Division.

The resolute Scotsman came south to seek work in a munitions factory called Napier's at the start of the war, having previously appeared for Dundee Hibernian from May 1914. After the war ended, he was made captain of Fulham and missed only eight games between his debut in August 1919 and March 1924. Chaplin played in the Fulham side that lost 2–1 to Manchester United at the Cottage in a quarter-final, but the club was often struggling against relegation at this time.

Alec and his family lived in the Cottage for some years until the Whites released him in November 1926. He then became Northfleet's player-coach and he appeared in two Kent Senior Cup Finals. They beat Sheppey United at Maidstone in 1927 before a 10,000 crowd. He left the game in 1929 and later became a Labour councillor on Fulham Borough Council from 1944–59 and was also vice-chairman of the Housing Committee.

A proud and independent man, Alec watched games at the Cottage right up until his death. He had two brothers who were also professional – Jack of Spurs, Dundee and Manchester City and George of Dundee, Bradford City and Coventry City.

Appearances:

	Football League		FA Cup		GRAND TOTAL	
SEASON	Apps	Goals	Apps	Goals	Apps	Goals
1919–20	39	-	1	-	40	-
1920–21	39	-	5	-	44	-
1921–22	41	-	3	-	44	-
1922–23	41	-	1	-	42	-
1923–24	36	1	3	-	39	1
1924–25	34	-	1	-	35	-
1925–26	29	-	3	-	32	-
TOTAL	259	1	17	-	276	1

CHARLTON, Ted

Born: Southwick, Co. Durham, 15 January 1888
Died: Sutton, Surrey, January qtr, 1978

Fulham's first player to reach 200 Football League appearances, Ted Charlton was a no-frills full-back who gave his opponents a hard time with his tough tackling and speed. He was also good at starting attacks with his accurate passes out of defence. Ted began his career with Southwick FC of Sunderland in May 1904, where he represented the Wearside League and joined Fulham in May 1906, winning a Southern League Championship medal during his first season at the Cottage. Charlton almost left the club for Glossop when he lost his place to the newly-signed Archie Lindsay in 1907, but the League refused permission for this transfer. The Wearsider soon gained his place back in the side the following

season, and he went from strength to strength in Fulham's defence. Ted missed only three games between August 1909 and April 1912 and played in the Whites excellent FA Cup run of 1911–12 when they beat Burnley and Liverpool before losing in the quarter-final at The Hawthorns. 'Taffa', as he was often called, appeared in an international trial match at the Cottage in January 1909 for the South versus the North but never made the full international side. Charlton played in the first post-war season and moved to Robert Thompson Munitions Works in August 1920, where he also worked. He later played for Carlisle United from January 1922. His elder brother Bill appeared for Newport County.

Appearances:

	Southern League		Football League		FA Cup		GRAND TOTAL	
SEASON	Apps	Goals	Apps	Goals	Apps	Goals	Apps	Goals
1906–07	20	-			4	-	24	-
1907–08			9	-	-	-	9	-
1908–09			28	4	2	-	30	4
1909–10			37	2	3	-	40	2
1910–11			37	1	1	-	38	1
1911–12			29	-	4	-	33	-
1912–13			13	-	-	-	13	-
1913–14			24	-	1	-	25	-
1914–15			34	-	2	-	36	-
1919–20			18	-	1	-	19	-
TOTAL	20	-	229	7	18	-	267	7

CLARK, Lee

Born: Wallsend-upon-Tyne, 27 October 1972

The £3 million manager Paul Bracewell paid Sunderland for Lee Clark proved to be a good deal. He was an all-action midfielder who defended well and was a fine passer of the ball. He often inspired the rest of the team and proved to be a very important player as Fulham climbed to the top flight. If he had a weakness it was his lack of pace, and but for that he may have won full England honours. As it was, he gained 11 Under-21 caps and also represented his country at Youth and Schools level.

Newcastle United spotted him when he was only nine years old playing for Wallsend Boys Club, and he made his debut for the Magpies when only 17 and later helped United back into the top flight in 1992–93 as champions. He struggled to hold his place in the Premiership and was transferred to near-neighbours Sunderland in June 1997 for £2.75 million, where he picked up another First Division medal in 1998–99.

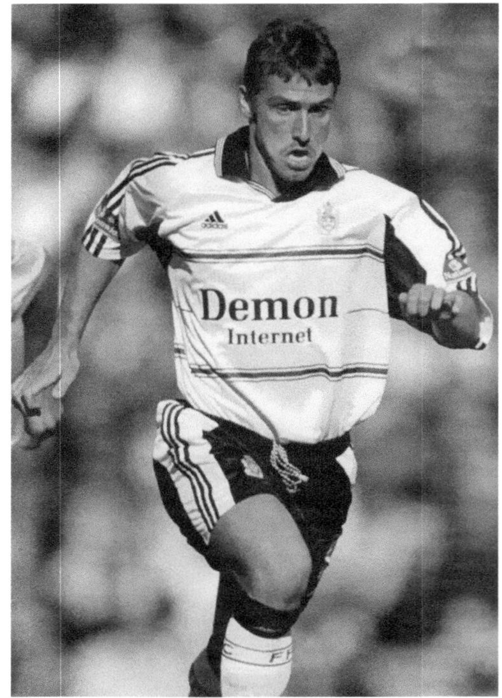

After being caught on camera attending the 1999 FA Cup Final wearing a derogatory shirt about Sunderland, the Geordie midfielder was sold to Fulham for a record £3 million. Lee ended his first season at the Cottage as top scorer in the League and played an important role in helping Fulham to win the First Division title in 2000–01 (his third such medal), returning the club to the top flight for the first time in 33 years. After missing much of 2001–03 due to injury, Clark regained a regular first-team spot in 2003–04. He rejoined Newcastle United in August 2005 on a free transfer and is currently working for the club as a coach.

Appearances:

	Football League		FA Cup		League Cup		GRAND TOTAL	
SEASON	Apps	Goals	Apps	Goals	Apps	Goals	Apps	Goals
1999–2000	42	8	4	-	6	1	52	9
2000–01	47	7	1	-	4	-	52	7
2001–02	5+4	-	-	-	3	-	8+4	-
2002–03	9+2	2	-	-	2	1	11+2	3
2003–04	25	2	1	-	1	-	27	2
2004–05	15+2	1	4+1	-	-	-	19+3	1
TOTAL	143+8	20	10+1	-	16	2	169+9	22

CLARKE, Allan

Born: Short Heath near Willenhall, Staffordshire, 31 July 1946

Allan Clarke came from a family of footballers, and his brothers Frank, Derek, Kelvin and Wayne all played League football. He began his career with Walsall, and the Fulham manager Vic Buckingham took some time to entice Allan to join the club and eventually paid £35,000 for the player. He hit 29 goals during 1966–67, as Fulham finished well clear of the relegation zone, and on his call up to the England Under-23 team he hit four goals in an 8–0 victory over Wales. 'Sniffer' scored twice for the Football League when they beat the Scottish League 3–0 at Hampden Park in March 1967 but did not win his first England cap until after he had left the Cottage. He eventually played 18 times for his country on top of his six caps at Under-23 level. His unique way of celebrating goals, raising his right arm in gladiator style, was to become familiar to Fulham fans and, despite playing for a relegated side, he managed to score 27 goals in 1967–68, including four goals in a 6–2 League Cup victory over Workington. Sadly, Fulham were forced to sell Clarke after their relegation as he insisted on First Division football, and he was sold to Leicester City in June 1968 for a record £150,000. Despite reaching the FA Cup Final, where they lost to Manchester City, the Foxes were also relegated the following season and 'Sniffer' moved to Leeds for another record fee of £165,000 in July 1969. Clarke was to gain many medals at Elland Road as Leeds won the League Championship in 1973–74, and he played in three FA Cup Finals, winning only one against Arsenal in 1973 when he scored the winning goal with a superb header. He also played in the 1975 European Cup Final, but they lost 2–0 to Bayern Munich.

When Allan retired from playing in 1980, he had scored 297 goals in a career total of 641+6 games for Walsall, Fulham, Leeds United and Barnsley. He became the player-manager at Barnsley in 1978 and returned to Elland Road as manager in October 1980 but had little success. Later, he subsequently managed Scunthorpe United, Barnsley (again) and Lincoln City before running his own soccer school in the Scunthorpe area.

Appearances:

	Football League		FA Cup		League Cup		GRAND TOTAL	
SEASON	Apps	Goals	Apps	Goals	Apps	Goals	Apps	Goals
1965–66	7+1	1	-	-	-	-	7+1	1
1966–67	42	24	3	3	2	2	47	29
1967–68	36	20	3	2	6	5	45	27
TOTAL	85+1	45	6	5	8	7	99+1	57

COHEN, George

Born: Kensington, London, 22 October 1939

Fulham's chairman Mohamed Al Fayed invested close on £60,000 to make sure that Fulham FC maintained George Cohen's World Cup-winners' medal from 1966. He was the club's sole representative as the England team beat West Germany in the Final 4–2 after extra-time.

George went on to gain 37 England caps, appeared eight times at Under-23 level and represented the Football League on four occasions. His razor sharp tackling and his strength and speed made him a formidable opponent and his quick recovery helped him retrieve what sometimes looked like lost situations. He loved to go forward but his crosses sometimes let him down.

At the tender age of 17, George was thrown in at the deep end when he made his Fulham debut, and he soon proved the saying that if you are good enough you are old enough. The quicksilver full-back helped Fulham back into the top flight in 1959 and also appeared in two FA Cup semi-finals in 1958 and 1962, but he was on the losing side on both occasions.

Cohen missed only 18 games between 1957 and 1966. A terrible injury received against Liverpool at the Cottage in December 1967, when he injured his kneeeffectively ended his career. He never fully recovered and was forced to retire in March 1969.

Cohen ran Fulham's youth team for two seasons, managed Tonbridge in 1974 and also became a building and property developer. After his successful fight against cancer in the 1980s, George returned to the Cottage to work in hospitality for the club.

Appearances:

	Football League		FA Cup		League Cup		GRAND TOTAL	
SEASON	Apps	Goals	Apps	Goals	Apps	Goals	Apps	Goals
1956–57	1	-	-	-			1	-
1957–58	26	-	7	-			33	-
1958–59	41	1	4	-			45	1
1959–60	42	-	2	-			44	-
1960–61	41	-	1	-	1	-	43	-
1961–62	41	1	8	-	2	-	51	1
1962–63	38	-	2	-	1	-	41	-
1963–64	41	1	2	-	1	-	44	1
1964–65	40	2	2	-	2	-	44	2
1965–66	39	-	1	-	3	-	43	-
1966–67	35	1	3	-	3	-	41	1
1967–68	17	-	-	-	5	-	22	-
1968–69	6	-	1	-	-	-	7	-
TOTAL	408	6	33	-	18	-	459	6

COLEMAN, Chris

Born: Swansea, Glamorgan, 10 June 1970

Welsh international Chris Coleman's playing career was ended by a horrific car crash in January 2001 when he was at the height of his career. He started playing football with Swansea City in 1987, after a period as a trainee at

Manchester City. In 1989 and 1991 Chris gained two Welsh Cup-winners' medals with the Swans before being transferred to Crystal Palace for £275,000 in July 1991. In his early days, he often appeared at full-back, but at Selhurst Park he was converted into a central-defender and helped them to the First Division title in 1993–94. The cultured defender later joined Blackburn Rovers for £2.8 million in December 1995, but he suffered an Achilles tendon injury and struggled to regain his first-team place when he recovered.

Chris became Fulham's most expensive signing when he joined from Ewood in November 1997 for £1.9 million. He looked Premiership quality playing two divisions below his standard, and he had an outstanding season in 1998–99 as he captained Fulham to the Second Division Championship title. He partnered his Welsh international colleagues Kit Symons and later Andy Melville in the Fulham defence. In 2001–02, despite missing half the season due to the car crash, Chris had played enough games to win a First Division Championship medal in 2001–02, but he never appeared for the club again and retired in October 2002. However, Coleman played one more time for Wales in a 1–0 victory over Germany, in May 2002, when he came on as substitute in the last minute and, after gained 32 caps for his country in total and also represented them at Under-21, Youth and Schools level.

Coleman became Fulham's manager in May 2003 after a period as a club coach. (See Managers' section)

Appearances:

	Football League		FA Cup		League Cup		GRAND TOTAL	
SEASON	Apps	Goals	Apps	Goals	Apps	Goals	Apps	Goals
1997–98	28	1	1	-	-	-	29	1
1998–99	45	4	7	-	5	1	57	5
1999–2000	40	3	3	1	7	1	50	5
2000–01	25	-	-	-	1	-	26	-
TOTAL	138	8	11	1	13	2	162	11

COLLINS, Arthur 'Pat'

Born: *Chesterfield, Derbyshire, 29 May 1882*
Died: *Balham, London, 6 February 1953*

Women apparently swooned in the presence of 'King' Arthur as this dapper Edwardian dandy gained popularity with the female fans of Fulham. A cultured and elegant player, Arthur 'Pat' Collins formed a superb half-back line at the Cottage, along with Billy Morrison and Billy Goldie, as Fulham won two Southern League Championships between 1905–07. With entry into the Football League, Collins played a leading role as the club reached the semi-final of the FA Cup in 1907–08, where they lost to

Newcastle United, and just missed out on promotion. He represented the Professionals versus the Amateurs at the Cottage in January 1906 and the South against the North at Stamford Bridge in January 1907 in trial matches, but he was never selected for the full England side.

Collins came from a wealthy background and had begun his career with Leicester Fosse in September 1901, where his father Tom was on the board of directors. Primarily a right-half, Collins also played at centre-half towards the end of his playing career and was on the management committee of the Players' Union from 1909. He played a total of 392 League and Cup games during his career with Leicester Fosse, Fulham and Norwich City (who he joined in May 1914) before returning to Leicester Fosse in September 1915, retiring in December 1917.

Appearances:

	Southern League		Football League		FA Cup		GRAND TOTAL	
SEASON	Apps	Goals	Apps	Goals	Apps	Goals	Apps	Goals
1905–06	31	-			2	1	33	1
1906–07	32	-			4	-	36	-
1907–08			32	-	6	-	38	-
1908–09			34	-	2	1	36	1
1909–10			36	1	3	-	39	1
1910–11			32	-	1	-	33	-
1911–12			30	4	-	-	30	4
1912–13			28	3	1	-	29	3
1913–14			5	1	-	-	5	1
TOTAL	63	-	197	9	19	2	279	11

CONEY, Dean

Born: Dagenham, Essex, 18 September 1963

A skilful and clever player with a supply of deft and subtle touches around the box, Dean 'Dixie' Coney scored 73 goals in 250 appearances for Fulham, not a bad return considering he once went 15 months without a League goal. He developed an excellent partnership with Gordon Davies, giving 'Ivor' a steady stream of chances. The big target-man scored 19 goals as Fulham clinched promotion to the Second Division in 1981–82, but then the goals dried up. Dean stayed in the side despite this, and Fulham just missed promotion the following season.

Not blessed with great speed, Coney nevertheless was Fulham's top scorer with 12 goals in 1985–86, but the Whites were relegated at the end of that season. He had gained four England Under-21 caps before moving to Queen's Park Rangers in June 1987, along with Paul Parker, as part of the deal that enabled the club to re-form as Fulham (1987) Ltd.

He was later transferred to Norwich City in March 1989 for £350,000 but had an unhappy spell at the club and was forced to retire from League football in 1991 due to cruciate ligament problems.

After a period playing in Hong Kong, 'Dixie' signed for Farnborough Town in November 1991 and featured in some very good FA Cup runs with them in a more defensive role. After a season with Carshalton Athletic, Dean retired in May 1998 and joined Farnborough Town again as coach and was later caretaker and assistant manager at the club. He was assistant manager to Jim Stannard at Redbridge early in 2005.

Appearances:

	Football League		FA Cup		League Cup		GRAND TOTAL	
SEASON	Apps	Goals	Apps	Goals	Apps	Goals	Apps	Goals
1980–81	7	3	-	-	-	-	7	3
1981–82	42	13	2	2	7	4	51	19
1982–83	37	4	3	2	4	1	44	7
1983–84	26+1	7	-	-	2	-	28+1	7
1984–85	24	7	1	-	3	2	28	9
1985–86	37	12	1	-	4	1	42	13
1986–87	36+1	10	4	2	4	2	44+1	14
TOTAL	209+2	56	11	6	24	10	244+2	72

CONWAY, Jimmy

Born: Dublin, Ireland, 10 August 1946

Jimmy Conway represented the League of Ireland against the Irish League in May 1964 as a 17-year-old and joined Fulham two years later from his club Bohemians of Dublin for £12,000. He scored a cracking goal on his debut against Wolves in the League Cup five months later, playing as a half-back. A flexible player, Conway also appeared at right-back for Fulham during 1968–69, but for the second successive season he played in a relegated side. Manager Bill Dodgin placed him on the right wing when Fulham went down into the Third Division, and he terrorised opposition defences and was joint top scorer with 23 goals (which included eight goals in five games during September) during 1969–70. He was not so prolific the following season, but Fulham gained promotion as runners-up.

As his career developed he played in a more withdrawn midfield role, but he became injury prone and missed much of the 1971–72 and 1972–73 seasons because of this. Conway appeared at Wembley in the FA Cup Final in 1975 after playing in most games of the Cup run but moved to Manchester City in August 1976,

joining former Fulham coach Bill Taylor at Maine Road. He won 19 caps for the Republic of Ireland and also represented them at Schoolboy, Youth and amateur levels.

Cohen ended his career as a player with Portland Timbers in the North America Soccer League and still lives in Oregon today, and when he visited the Cottage in February 2005 he told the crowd that he was coaching for Portland Timbers. Jimmy came from a family of 17, and his brother John also played for Fulham in the early 70s. His son Paul later played for Carlisle United and Northampton Town during the 1990s.

Appearances:

	Football League		FA Cup		League Cup		GRAND TOTAL	
SEASON	Apps	Goals	Apps	Goals	Apps	Goals	Apps	Goals
1966–67	30	3	3	-	1	1	34	4
1967–68	42	4	3	-	6	-	51	4
1968–69	34+1	5	1	-	1	-	36+1	5
1969–70	46	21	1	-	3	2	50	23
1970–71	29	8	-	-	2	2	31	10
1971–72	22	8	3	1	-	-	25	9
1972–73	13+1	4	1	-	-	-	14+1	4
1973–74	25+2	3	2	-	-	-	27+2	3
1974–75	32	4	10	1	3	-	45	5
1975–76	39	7	1	1	3	1	43	9
TOTAL	312+4	67	25	3	19	6	356+4	76

COOK, Maurice

Born: Berkhamsted, Hertfordshire, 10 December 1931
Died: Berkhamsted, Hertfordshire, 31 December 2006

Maurice Cook was a great servant to both Watford and Fulham during his 12-year League career. He joined Watford from his local side Berkhamsted in May 1953 and was a very versatile player for the Hornets, appearing in every position, even as an emergency goalkeeper. Cook missed just three matches in four seasons and scored 77 goals in 218 appearances for Watford, and he also represented the Third Division South.

Cook signed for Fulham in January 1958 for £12,000 but was Cup tied and could not play in the FA Cup run that season, but he did not miss any of the 1962 Cup run when Fulham lost to Burnley in the semi-final. The

hardworking striker scored 17 goals during Fulham's promotion season of 1958–59 and hit the historic first ever goal in the Football League Cup at Bristol Rovers in September 1960. He was an integral part of the team of the early 60s, and the big, bustling centre-forward was joint top scorer in 1961–62 with 15 goals and was again top scorer the following season with 15 goals, but this was his last season as first choice. His contribution was often underrated, but he was a hard, direct and brave forward who, although lacking speed and control, had an abundance of perseverance. The arrival of manager Vic Buckingham led to Cook's departure to Reading in May 1965, where he stayed for just one season before playing for Banbury United in the Southern League. He appeared for local side Potter's End from September 1969 then retired to become a publican in Berkhamsted and Boxmoor and later worked in security at the Oval in the 1990s. Ironically, he died on the eve of the Fulham versus Watford Premiership match on New Year's day 2007.

Appearances:

	Football League		FA Cup		League Cup		GRAND TOTAL	
SEASON	Apps	Goals	Apps	Goals	Apps	Goals	Apps	Goals
1957–58	15	9	-	-			15	9
1958–59	41	17	4	-			45	17
1959–60	17	8	2	1			19	9
1960–61	32	12	1	-	1	1	34	13
1961–62	35	15	8	4	2	-	45	19
1962–63	35	15	2	-	2	-	39	15
1963–64	29	5	2	1	1	-	32	6
1964–65	17	8	-	-	2	1	19	9
TOTAL	221	89	19	6	8	2	248	97

DAVIES, Gordon

Born: Merthyr Tydfil, Mid Glamorgan, 8 August 1955

Fulham's record goalscorer, Gordon 'Ivor' Davies scored 178 goals for the club in the main competitions. The Welshman had failed to make the grade at Maine Road and went off to Madeley College in 1973 to become a qualified geography and PE teacher and played regularly for Merthyr Tydfil. Then Fulham gave him a fresh chance as a full-time professional and signed him from the Welsh Valleys club for £4,000 in March 1978, at the age of 22.

Manager Bobby Campbell helped 'Ivor' to quickly develop into an excellent striker, one who was quick on the turn and had a natural eye for goal. His goals helped Fulham rise from Third Division mediocrity to being on the brink of promotion to the top flight. He gained 18 caps for Wales but surprisingly scored only once against Northern Ireland in May 1983.

After a wage dispute, 'Ivor' moved to neighbours Chelsea in November 1984 but made only 13+2 appearances for the Blues. He rejoined Manchester City in October 1985 for £70,000 and scored 14 goals in 42 games before returning to the Cottage for a second spell in October 1986, when manager Ray Lewington signed him for £45,000. By then, though, Davies had lost some of his sharpness and suffered a number of injuries during his second spell with the club but broke the club's scoring record at at Molineux in February 1989. He left the club to join Wrexham in 1991, and they pulled off an FA Cup sensation when they beat the mighty Arsenal in January 1992. When he left the

Racecourse Ground, Davies had scored 204 goals in 512+35 appearances during his Football League career.

After a brief spell managing Tornedo in Norway, 'Ivor' returned to England to sign for Northwich Victoria in August 1992 and scored a hat-trick when they beat Wycombe Wanderers 3–2 in the Drinkwise Cup Final in 1993. Today, Davies runs his own pest control company and helps out on the hospitality side at Fulham, and he remains ever popular with the fans.

Appearances:

	Football League		FA Cup		League Cup		GRAND TOTAL	
SEASON	Apps	Goals	Apps	Goals	Apps	Goals	Apps	Goals
1977–78	4+1	1	-	-	-	-	4+1	1
1978–79	32	9	3	1	2	1	37	11
1979–80	39	15	2	-	2	1	43	16
1980–81	45	18	6	3	2	1	53	22
1981–82	41	24	2	-	7	1	50	25
1982–83	38	19	3	-	3	1	44	20
1983–84	35+1	23	2	-	5	3	42+1	26
1984–85	10+1	5	-	-	3	1	13+1	6
1986–87	18+3	6	3	3	-	-	21+3	9
1987–88	35+4	13	1	-	3	2	39+4	15
1988–89	31+5	14	0+1	-	0+1	-	31+7	14
1989–90	19+4	6	-	-	1	-	20+4	6
1990–91	19+11	6	2	1	-	-	21+11	7
TOTAL	366+30	159	24+1	8	28+1	11	418+32	178

DAVIS, Sean

Born: Battersea, London, 20 September 1979

The only player to appear for Fulham in all four divisions, Sean Davis made his debut in October 1996 as a substitute against Cambridge United at the Cottage at the age of 17 years and 25 days. Sean did not blossom until Jean Tigana became manager and his excellent coaching brought out the best in his performances in midfield.

A fiercely competitive player, Davis is also an excellent passer of the ball and scored some vital goals during his time at Craven Cottage, his most memorable being the winner at Blackburn Rovers in 2001, which virtually brought Fulham the First Division title. He also scored some memorable long-range goals at Preston and West Brom that season. During March 2001, Davis appeared twice for the England Under-21 side in victories over Finland and Albania in March 2001, and he played in the European Under-21 Championship in Switzerland two months later. He was selected for the full England squad against Australia in February 2003 but was an unused substitute. After Fulham's promotion to the Premiership in 2001 Davis was a regular in midfield for three seasons and helped the club reach an FA Cup semi-final

and also to win the Inter-Toto Cup and thus gain entry into the UEFA Cup in 2002. He nearly moved to Middlesbrough and Everton before his transfer to Tottenham Hotspur in July 2004 for a fee of £3.5 million. He became surplus to requirements at White Hart Lane and moved to Portsmouth in January 2006 for £2.5 million and was outstanding as Pompey had a great season in the Premiership in 2006–07 after narrowly missing relegation the previous term.

Appearances:

	Football League		FA Cup		League Cup		GRAND TOTAL	
SEASON	Apps	Goals	Apps	Goals	Apps	Goals	Apps	Goals
1996–97	0+1	-	-	-	-	-	0+1	-
1997–98	-	-	-	-	-	-	-	-
1998–99	1+5	-	1	-	1+1	-	3+6	-
1999–2000	15+11	-	1+1	1	2+2	2	18+14	3
2000–01	37+3	6	1+1	-	2	1	40+4	7
2001–02	25+5	-	3+1	-	3	-	31+6	-
2002–03	28	3	4	-	0+1	-	32+1	3
2003–04	22+1	5	6	1	-	-	28+1	6
TOTAL	128+26	14	16+3	2	8+4	3	152+33	19

DEMPSEY, John

Born: Hampstead, London, 15 March 1946

John Dempsey replaced Bobby Keetch in the Fulham side in September 1965 and quickly made the centre-half position his own and did not miss another game until April 1968, just before Fulham were finally relegated from the First Division. One of the highlights of his time at the Cottage was scoring a hat-trick against Northampton Town in the League Cup in October 1965, when it was decided to try him at centre-forward. John established himself that season and played a major role as Fulham managed to beat the drop.

Dempsey qualified to play for the Republic of Ireland, despite being born in London, as his parents were Irish. He made his debut against Spain in Valencia in December 1966 but was on the losing side in a two-goal defeat. He went on to gain 21 caps for his country.

Fulham manager Bill Dodgin sold Dempsey to Chelsea for £70,000 in January 1969. With the Blues he enjoyed FA Cup success in 1970, beating Leeds United in the replay 2–1 at Old Trafford. The following May he scored when he

hit an excellent volley as Chelsea beat Real Madrid in the replayed Final of the European Cup-winners' Cup 2–1 in Athens.

Dempsey appeared at Wembley again in 1972, but Chelsea lost 2–1 to Stoke City in the Football League Cup Final. After this he was hit by a spate of injuries and had appeared in just over 200 games for the Pensioners before departing to the United States in March 1978 to play for Philadelphia Fury. He later managed Maidenhead United, Athlone Town and Egham Town during the 1980s and qualified as a Physical Education Instructor. He worked at the Broadfields Centre for people with physical and mental handicaps at Edgware for many years.

Appearances:

	Football League		FA Cup		League Cup		GRAND TOTAL	
SEASON	Apps	Goals	Apps	Goals	Apps	Goals	Apps	Goals
1964–65	4	-	1	-	-	-	5	-
1965–66	38	2	1	1	4	3	43	6
1966–67	42	-	3	-	3	-	48	-
1967–68	38	1	3	-	6	-	47	1
1968–69	27	1	-	-	1	-	28	1
TOTAL	149	4	8	1	14	3	171	8

EARLE, Steve

Born: Feltham, Middlesex, 1 November 1945

A prolific goalscorer during much of his time at Fulham, Steve Earle was missed when he was sold to Leicester City for £70,000 to ease the club's financial problems caused by the massive outlay on the Riverside Stand. Combining pace and skill rather than physical strength, he scored over 100 goals for Fulham in 11 seasons, and he was especially prolific during the 'Great Escape' season of 1965–66 when he hit 11 goals in only 15 appearances, including a match-winning hat-trick at Northampton Town that sent the Cobblers down instead of Fulham.

He partnered Allan Clarke up front from 1966–68, and they were both regularly on target despite the team's struggles against relegation. The Feltham-born Earle completely lost his form during 1968–69, due to a succession of injuries, and became the target of the boo-boys.

However, he was 'red hot' the following season and hit a total of 23 goals including five in the record away 8–0 victory at Halifax in September 1969, to share the Fulham record for goals in one game along with Fred Harrison, Bedford Jezzard and Jimmy Hill.

Earle was awarded a belated testimonial match in October 1975 against his new club Leicester City, but fewer than 2,000 attended the match. He helped Leicester reach an FA Cup semi-final during his first season at Filbert Street, after beating Fulham on the way, but Liverpool beat them 3–1 in a replay. After that he was in and out of the side but scored 26 goals in 107+8 appearances for the Foxes in total.

After leaving Leicester, Earle played in the States for Detroit Express, Tulsa Roughnecks and Wichita Wings as well as brief spells with Peterborough United and Telford United. The former Fulham striker is an occasional visitor to the Cottage but lives in Tulsa, Oklahoma, where he has coached youngsters.

Appearances:

	Football League		FA Cup		League Cup		GRAND TOTAL	
SEASON	Apps	Goals	Apps	Goals	Apps	Goals	Apps	Goals
1963–64	12	5	-	-	-	-	12	5
1964–65	4	2	-	-	-	-	4	2
1965–66	15	11	-	-	-	-	15	11
1966–67	36+2	12	3	-	2	1	41+2	13
1967–68	26+1	5	3	-	5	3	34+1	8
1968–69	13+2	-	2	-	-	-	15+2	-
1969–70	41	22	1	-	2	1	44	23
1970–71	42	13	1	-	6	1	49	14
1971–72	41	11	3	-	2	3	46	14
1972–73	40	15	1	-	3	-	44	15
1973–74	15+1	2	-	-	2	1	17+1	3
TOTAL	285+6	98	14	-	22	10	321+6	108

ECKHARDT, Jeff

Born: Sheffield, Yorkshire, 7 October 1965

Eckhardt was a utility player who appeared at right-back, central-defence, midfield and even as a striker for Fulham during his six seasons at the club, and he became a great favourite with the crowd for his 100 percent effort in whatever role he was given by his various Fulham managers. He used his heading ability to great effect and was a feared tackler. At Bramall Lane, Jeff had played with Ray Lewington, and it was

'Lew' who signed him in November 1987 for £50,000. He had felt it was time to seek pastures new and over the next seven seasons played almost 300 games for the Cottagers. He helped them reach the Third Division Play-offs in 1989 where they lost to Bristol Rovers, but the club usually struggled during his time with them. His final appearance came when Fulham lost at Swansea City and were relegated to the bottom division for the first time in May 1994. Eckhardt decided to move to Stockport County in July 1994, and, after scoring 12 goals in 69+8 games, he moved on to Cardiff City in August 1996 where he hit 16 goals in 150+14 games. He became their player-coach in August 2000, helping them to win promotion from Division Three in 1998–99. When he left Ninian Park to move to non-League Newport County in July 2001, Eckhardt's Football League career total of appearances was 581+28, in which he scored 58 goals for his four clubs. Jeff also appeared for Merthyr Tydfil from 2004 and was their player-caretaker manager during 2006, before moving to Risca United as coach, and then player-manager in 2007.

Appearances:

	Football League		FA Cup		League Cup		GRAND TOTAL	
SEASON	Apps	Goals	Apps	Goals	Apps	Goals	Apps	Goals
1987–88	29	1	-	-	-	-	29	1
1988–89	45	2	1	-	2	-	48	2
1989–90	39+1	2	2	-	3	-	44+1	2
1990–91	28+1	2	0+1	-	2	-	30+2	2
1991–92	43	7	-	-	2	-	45	7
1992–93	30	6	1	-	2	-	33	6
1993–94	33+2	5	1	-	2	-	36+2	5
TOTAL	247+4	25	5+1	-	13	-	265+5	25

FINCH, Jack

Born: *West Ham, London, 3 February 1909*
Died: *Worthing, Sussex, 15 November 1993*

The fast and skilful Jack Finch created chances for his teammates with a stream of accurate crosses throughout the 30s for Fulham. He worked as a motor mechanic while playing for Walthamstow Avenue but moved to Lowestoft Town in September 1929 when offered a coach-driving job in the town.

After a trial with Aston Villa, Finch signed as a professional for Fulham in November 1930 and was soon a regular in the side. He appeared in Fulham's 10–2 victory over Torquay United in September 1931, gained a Third Division South Championship medal at the end of that season, scoring 11 goals in 39 appearances, and was ever present in 1932–33 as Fulham finished third in the Second Division.

The highlight of his career was helping the Whites to an FA Cup semi-final in 1936, but he missed the match itself, which the team lost 2–1 to Sheffield United at Molineux. His only representative honour came when he appeared for the London Combination against Diables Rouges of Belgium in February 1937. Finch appeared regularly for Fulham (making 79 wartime appearances scoring 11 goals) and also played as a guest for Spurs and Brentford, until he joined Sittingbourne as player-manager in 1943. After a brief spell with Colchester United in August 1946 he seems to have retired from playing. Jack coached a Nigerian touring side in 1949 and managed Valur (Iceland) from April 1950 before working as a freelance reporter in West Ham and the Barking area.

Appearances:

	Football League		FA Cup		GRAND TOTAL	
SEASON	Apps	Goals	Apps	Goals	Apps	Goals
1930–31	18	1	-	-	18	1
1931–32	39	11	5	-	44	11
1932–33	42	6	1	-	43	6
1933–34	36	7	2	-	38	7
1934–35	39	8	1	1	40	9
1935–36	30	10	5	-	35	10
1936–37	21	1	-	-	21	1
1937–38	34	4	1	-	35	4
1938–39	21	2	-	-	21	2
TOTAL	280	50	15	1	295	51

FINNAN, Steve

Born: Limerick, Ireland, 20 April 1976

One of the classiest full-backs to appear for Fulham in recent years, Steve Finnan is a good reader of the game and an excellent tackler who loves going forward and sending over accurate crosses. After starting his career as Welling United's first ever trainee in July 1993, Steve moved on to Birmingham City in June 1995 for £100,000 but, being unable to hold down a regular spot, moved to Notts County in 1996 and helped them to the Third Division title in 1997–98.

One of Kevin Keegan's many excellent signings, Finnan joined Fulham in November 1998 for a £500,000 fee, and by the close of the

season he had won a Second Division Championship medal with the Whites. His direct runs down the right flank had become a feature of his play, and he had an excellent season during 2000–01 as Fulham won the First Division Championship.

Continuing to impress in the Premiership the following season, he was outstanding in the club's run to the FA Cup semi-final in 2002. Steve is a regular in the Republic of Ireland side after gaining eight Under-21 caps, and he shone at the 2002 World Cup Finals in South Korea and Japan.

Since moving to Liverpool in June 2003 for £4 million, Finnan has won many honours. The highlights have been two European Champions League Finals in 2005 (beating AC Milan on penalties after coming from three down to draw 3–3) and in 2007 (losing 2–1 to AC Milan), an FA Cup-winners' medal in 2006 (the Reds winning a penalty shoot-out after a 3–3 draw over West Ham), a runners'-up League Cup medal in 2005 (lost 3–2 to Chelsea), a European Super Cup-winners' medal in August 2005 (a 3–1 victory over

CSKA Moscow in Monaco) and also a FIFA World Club Championship runners'-up medal in 2005 (losing to Sao Paulo (Brazil) 1–0 in Yokohama).

Appearances:

	Football League		FA Cup		League Cup		GRAND TOTAL	
SEASON	Apps	Goals	Apps	Goals	Apps	Goals	Apps	Goals
1998–99	21+1	2	4	-	-	-	25+1	2
1999–2000	35	2	4	1	6	-	45	3
2000–01	45	2	1	-	1+1	-	47+1	2
2001–02	38	-	6	-	3	-	47	-
2002–03	32	-	3	-	1	-	36	-
TOTAL	171+1	6	18	1	11+1	-	200+2	7

FREEMAN, Harry

Born: *Woodstock, Oxfordshire, 4 November 1918*
Died: *Woodstock, Oxfordshire, 19 March 1997*

A dour and taciturn defender, Harry Freeman had excellent anticipation, which made up for his lack of pace, and he could read a game well. With his immensely powerful shooting, he scored some memorable goals from long free-kicks, including a brilliant goal against Tottenham Hotspur in 1946 when he shot home from 45 yards.

Former goalkeeper Les Skene's brother recommended Freeman to Fulham, and he joined the club in May 1937 from Woodstock Town. He made his debut for Fulham against Newcastle United in March 1939 and later appeared in 111 wartime games for the Whites while a member of the Royal Fusiliers. He did not miss a game between January 1946 and March 1948 and gained a Second Division Championship medal in 1948–49 (37 appearances). He toured Spain in 1949 and the US and Canada in 1951 with Fulham and also represented the FA against the RAF in 1948.

After leaving the Cottage in October 1952, Harry had a brief spell at Walsall before joining Dover as player-manager in 1953 and later appeared for Ashford United in 1954. After a short spell on Fulham's ground staff in the mid-50s, Harry was player-coach at Windsor & Eton in 1956 and entered the bakery trade after returning to his hometown of Woodstock to manage his local club in October 1957.

Appearances:

	Football League		FA Cup		GRAND TOTAL	
SEASON	Apps	Goals	Apps	Goals	Apps	Goals
1938–39	1	-	-	-	1	-
1945–46	-	-	2	-	2	-
1946–47	42	3	1	-	43	3
1947–48	30	1	5	-	35	1
1948–49	37	1	1	-	38	1
1949–50	41	1	2	1	43	2
1950–51	18	1	-	-	18	1
1951–52	10	-	-	-	10	-
TOTAL	179	7	11	1	190	8

FRYER, Jack

Born: *Cromford, Derbyshire, April 1877*
Died: *Westminster, London, 22 December 1933*

Fulham's star performer during the club's Southern League days, Jack Fryer was very agile and quick and had great anticipation and courage. He was already well known when he joined the club from Derby County in May 1903 and had signed for the Rams from Clay Cross Juniors in September 1896 and played in three FA Cup Finals for the club, but ended on the losing side on each occasion. They lost to Nottingham Forest 3–1 in 1898, to Sheffield United 4–1 in 1899 and lost by a record 6–0 to

Bury in 1903, all Finals being played at the Crystal Palace ground. Fryer should never have played in the 1903 Final as he was suffering from a groin injury.

Oddly, the 1901 census described him as a carpenter rather than a footballer, but Fryer had made 200 appearances for the Rams before his move to the Cottage and his fine goalkeeping helped the defence to concede only 96 goals in the 123 Southern League appearances he made over the next four seasons.

A very popular individual, Jack was made club captain and quickly impressed with some brilliant displays. He won two Southern League Championship medals between 1905–07 but broke his arm just above the wrist in April 1907 diving at the feet of a Reading forward in a friendly match, and he was never the quite the same 'keeper. He bravely fought his way back to fitness after missing over a year out injured and was awarded a benefit match in March 1909 when Fulham played Clapton Orient in a Second Division fixture. The popular Fryer received £630 from his benefit match, and he soon retired to become a publican. He played cricket for the Ind Coope Brewery cricket club for many years and was running a public house close to the Stamford Bridge ground when he died in 1933.

Appearances:

	Southern League		Football League		FA Cup		GRAND TOTAL	
SEASON	Apps	Goals	Apps	Goals	Apps	Goals	Apps	Goals
1903–04	27	-			7	-	34	
1904–05	31	-			9	-	40	-
1905–06	30	-			1	-	31	-
1906–07	35	-			4	-	39	-
1908–09			11	-	2	-	13	-
1909–10			8	-	3	-	11	-
TOTAL	123	-	19	-	26	-	168	-

GALE, Tony

Born: Pimlico, London, 19 November 1959

An elegant central-defender, Tony Gale was probably at his best partnering Roger Brown during his time with Fulham. It was apparent straightaway that Fulham had found a great talent when he made his first-team debut at just 16 years and eight months old in an Anglo-Scottish tie at Orient. He soon gained eight England Youth caps, later earning an Under-21 cap against Poland in 1982, and he should have gained full international honours but may have been let down by his lack of pace.

Gale replaced the retiring Bobby Moore in the Fulham side in 1977, but Fulham were relegated to the Third Division in 1979–80 as Tony's, and a number of other players, form dipped, but he was soon leading the Whites to promotion in 1981–82. He played 44 times during the promotion season despite being dropped for the first match against Brentford after a bust up with manager Malcolm MacDonald. He went on to show some of the best form of his career that season and the next as Fulham went close to promotion again.

In August 1984 Gale was transferred to First Division West Ham for a fee of £200,000 and on three occasions came close to playing in Wembley Finals. They lost at the semi-final stage in the League Cup in 1989 and 1990 and lost 4–0 to Nottingham Forest in an FA Cup

semi-final in 1991 when Gale was harshly sent off for a professional foul after only 26 minutes. He scored seven goals in 259+9 appearances for the Hammers before his move to Blackburn Rovers when he rejoined his old Fulham manager Roy Harford. Despite appearing only 15 times for Rovers during 1994–95, Tony won a Premiership champions medal, the highlight of his career. After a spell with Crystal Palace, Tony appeared for Maidenhead before retiring in late 1997, and today he can be seen regularly on Sky Sports and is director of football at Walton Casuals.

Appearances:

	Football League		FA Cup		League Cup		GRAND TOTAL	
SEASON	Apps	Goals	Apps	Goals	Apps	Goals	Apps	Goals
1977–78	38	8	1	-	2	-	41	8
1978–79	36	2	2	-	2	-	40	2
1979–80	42	4	2	-	2	-	46	4
1980–81	40	1	5	-	2	1	47	2
1981–82	44	1	2	-	7	-	53	1
1982–83	42	2	3	-	4	1	49	3
1983–84	35	1	2	-	5	-	42	1
TOTAL	277	19	17	-	24	2	318	21

GIBBONS, Syd

Born: *Darlaston, Staffordshire, 24 March 1907*
Died: *Woodnesborough, Kent, 17 July 1953*

Described as a robust player with a real Corinthian charge, Syd Gibbons was the strong man of Fulham's defence during the 1930s and was nicknamed 'Carnera' after a famous heavyweight boxer of the time. He attended the

Central School in Darlaston and represented Darlaston and Birmingham Schools before playing for Green Old Boys, Cradley Heath, Wolves and Walsall, while working as a foundry hand, when he signed for Manchester City in April 1927, he had gained an England Junior international cap against Scotland in 1926. He was reserve to Sam Cowan at Maine Road and only played five times as City took the Second Division title in 1927–28.

Fulham manager Ned Liddell saw Gibbons's huge potential and signed him in May 1930 for a fee of only £500. This proved a real bargain and his rugged all-action style was soon influencing the rest of the team. He formed a superb half-back line with Bert Barrett and Len Oliver, which helped Fulham win the Third Division South title in 1931–32 and helped the club to remain in the Second Division during the 1930s. Between December 1930 and January 1938 Gibbons missed just eight games for Fulham and also helped the club reach an FA Cup semi-final in 1936, but they lost to Sheffield United 2–1. He is the only defender in Fulham's history to score a hat-trick, which came against Southampton in November 1934 with Fulham 3–0 down. He was then pushed up to join the attack, and he scored three goals in the last 20 minutes to earn a 3–3 draw.

Gibbons left Fulham to become the player-manager of Worcester City in June 1938, and they won the Southern League Cup in 1940. After the war, he ran a tobacconist shop in Putney and scouted for Fulham and was aged only 46 when he died in July 1953.

Appearances:

	Football League		FA Cup		GRAND TOTAL	
SEASON	Apps	Goals	Apps	Goals	Apps	Goals
1930–31	32	-	3	2	35	2
1931–32	42	-	5	-	47	-
1932–33	42	3	1	-	43	3
1933–34	38	3	2	-	40	3
1934–35	42	5	1	-	43	5
1935–36	39	1	6	-	45	1
1936–37	42	1	1	-	43	1
1937–38	22	-	-	-	22	-
TOTAL	299	13	19	2	318	15

GOLDIE, Billy

Born: Hurlford, Ayrshire, 22 January 1878
Died: Hurlford, Ayrshire, 3 February 1952

A dour and tenacious left-half, Billy Goldie was feared by many of his opponents. He began his career at home-town club Hurlford Thistle in 1895, where he won two Ayrshire Cup medals, then played at Clyde briefly, before joining Liverpool in November 1897. His brother Archie also played at Anfield, and Billy initially played at full-back for the club. Liverpool were runners-up in the First Division in 1899–1900, and Billy was ever present as they took the League Championship the following season, playing 119 consecutive games during this period, but he was suspended in August 1903 when he became involved in an illegal transfer scam between Liverpool and Portsmouth.

When the suspension was over, he joined Fulham in January 1904 and helped the club to two Southern League titles between 1905–07. The fearsome Scotsman played in every game during Fulham's FA Cup run to the quarter-final in 1905, where they lost 5–0 to Aston Villa, and their run to the semi-final in 1908, where they lost to Newcastle United. Between January 1904 and April 1908, Goldie missed just four games

for the club and gained a Western League runners'-up medal in 1906–07. Goldie's strong Scottish accent made him unintelligible to the Fulham management, and he needed an interpreter when he went before the FA disciplinary commission.

Billy moved to Leicester Fosse in August 1908, just after his younger brother, John, joined Fulham from Hurlford Thistle, and appeared 88 times for the Midlands club. He became a publican in 1911 and played occasionally for Leicester Imperial and later returned to Hurlford where he worked as a road surfaceman.

Appearances:

	Southern League		Football League		FA Cup		GRAND TOTAL	
SEASON	Apps	Goals	Apps	Goals	Apps	Goals	Apps	Goals
1903–04	18	-			1	-	19	-
1904–05	30	4			9	-	39	4
1905–06	34	-			2	-	36	-
1906–07	38	1			4	-	42	1
1907–08			36	-	6	-	42	-
TOTAL	120	5	36	-	22	-	178	5

HAMMOND, Jim

Born: *Hove, Sussex, 7 November 1907*
Died: *Hove, Sussex, 16 June 1985*

Forceful in the air, difficult to shake off the ball and possessing a strong shot in either foot, Jim Hammond held Fulham's goalscoring record for many years with 151 goals until Bedford Jezzard in the 1950s. Herbert Edward Hammond, better known as 'Jim', was only 16 and playing for Robins' Athletic when he represented his county, Sussex, against Surrey at football in February 1926. He also won an England Amateur cap against Wales in 1928 when still working as a clerk in a Brighton wine office.

Hammond joined Fulham in April 1928 and scored five goals in his first six matches for the club, hit 18 goals in 1929–30 and scored 33 League and Cup goals during 1931–32, when Fulham won the Third Division South title. He hit seven hat-tricks for the Lilliewhites, which included scoring four goals against Torquay United in a 10–2 victory in September 1931 and versus Sheffield United in a 7–2 victory in April 1935. He played a key role in the FA Cup run to the semi-finals in 1936, where they lost to

Sheffield United. He never won a full cap but was selected as reserve when England played Austria in December 1932 and also represented the FA against the Army, Royal Navy and the Royal Marines. Also a fine cricketer, he usually missed the start and end of most seasons due to his football commitments, but played 196 matches for Sussex between 1928 and 1946, scoring 4,000 runs and taking 428 wickets during his career.

After serving in the RAF during the war, Hammond coached cricket in Holland for a year in 1946 then had a similar job at Cheltenham Boys College until becoming a first-class umpire in 1961. He coached at Brighton College after this, until his retirement in 1972, and he lived in the town until his death in 1985, just a week after his old strike partner at Fulham, Ronnie Rooke.

Appearances:

	Football League		FA Cup		GRAND TOTAL	
SEASON	Apps	Goals	Apps	Goals	Apps	Goals
1928–29	8	5	-	-	8	5
1929–30	31	17	5	1	36	18
1930–31	36	14	4	2	40	16
1931–32	42	31	5	2	47	33
1932–33	38	10	1	-	39	10
1933–34	41	15	2	1	43	16
1934–35	40	22	1	-	41	22
1935–36	40	15	6	3	46	18
1936–37	21	7	1	-	22	7
1937–38	19	6	1	-	20	6
TOTAL	316	142	26	9	342	151

HAYLES, Barry

Born: *Lambeth, London, 17 May 1972*

Barry Hayles unusually is a Jamaican international who has also represented England at semi-professional level. A late starter in the game, Hayles began his career as an 18-year-old playing for Willesden Hawkeye in the Middlesex Senior League before moving to Conference League Stevenage Borough in July 1993. He won a Conference League medal in 1995–96, when he scored 29 goals in 38 games, and earned two England semi-pro caps. He moved into the League with Bristol Rovers at the age of 25, who saw his potential and paid £250,000 for his services in June 1997, and he soon rewarded

their outlay with 37 goals in 74+2 appearances for the Pirates.

Hayles was Fulham's record signing at £2 million when Kevin Keegan signed him in November 1998 but he struggled at first to live down his huge price tag. He showed flashes of what was to come with some outstanding goals, but it was not until the arrival of Jean Tigana in 2000 that Fulham fans saw Barry's best form. His 18 goals helped Fulham to the top spot in the First Division in 2000–01, but he found goals harder to come by in the top flight. His fast, direct style and close dribbling skills created openings and he could score from all angles with his head and feet.

After leaving the Cottage, Barry had a brief spell at Bramall Lane before joining Millwall in August 2004. After two seasons at The Den, he joined Plymouth Argyle in July 2006 for £100,000 and continues to find the net regularly.

Appearances:

	Football League		FA Cup		League Cup		GRAND TOTAL	
SEASON	Apps	Goals	Apps	Goals	Apps	Goals	Apps	Goals
1998–99	26+4	8	4	1	-	-	30+4	9
1999–2000	21+14	5	3+1	2	3+1	2	27+16	9
2000–01	28+7	18	-	-	3+1	1	31+8	19
2001–02	27+8	8	2+3	2	3	2	32+11	12
2002–03	4+10	1	-	-	1	-	5+10	1
2003–04	10+16	4	3+3	1	-	-	13+19	5
TOTAL	116+59	44	12+7	6	10+2	5	138+68	55

HAYNES, Johnny

Born: *Edmonton, Middlesex, 17 October 1934*
Died: *Edinburgh, Midlothian, 18 October 2005*

Johnny Haynes was unquestionably Fulham's greatest-ever player. He dictated most games with his magnificent tactical brain, control and passing ability, and he was a perfectionist who was as hard on himself as he was on his teammates when they did not meet his demanding standards.

Haynes holds the club's aggregate appearance record and was the leading aggregate goalscorer until Gordon Davies surpassed his record. He followed his boyhood friend Tosh Chamberlain to Fulham in 1950

rather than accept offers from Spurs and Arsenal, and over the next 20 years he remained loyal to the club despite the many offers from other clubs, both at home and abroad. He hit 18 goals during his first full season in 1953–54 and 19 goals two seasons later, but his best season came in 1958–59 when he scored 26 goals in only 38 appearances as Fulham won promotion to the First Division. He never played for Fulham at Wembley but appeared in two losing FA Cup semi-finals in 1958 against Manchester United and in 1962 when Burnley were the opposition.

The maestro won 56 England caps, thwe last 22 as captain. He played in two World Cup Finals in 1958 and 1962. He also gained eight Under-23 caps, five B caps and won Youth and Schools international honours and played 14 times for the Football League representative side, scoring seven goals. He became Britain's first ever £100–per-week player and remained at his best until he was involved in a car crash in Blackpool in August 1962. His serious injuries meant he lost some of his pace when he eventually recovered.

As Haynes's career was going into decline, things also went downhill at Fulham, who were relegated from the First to the Third Division in consecutive seasons in the late 1960s. Haynes played his last game for the club in January 1970 against Stockport County in the Third Division. He was caretaker manager of Fulham in November 1968 after the sacking of Bobby Robson but had no desire to take the job on a permanent basis.

After his Fulham contract ended in June 1970, Haynes went to play in South Africa, living there for many years, and was 40 when he retired from playing in 1974 after appearing for three Durban clubs. During the 1980s, John returned to the UK to live in Edinburgh and was an occasional visitor to Craven Cottage until his death the day after his 71st birthday.

Appearances:

	Football League		FA Cup		League Cup		GRAND TOTAL	
SEASON	Apps	Goals	Apps	Goals	Apps	Goals	Apps	Goals
1952–53	18	1	1	-			19	1
1953–54	41	16	3	2			44	18
1954–55	37	8	1	1			38	9
1955–56	40	18	2	1			42	19
1956–57	33	5	2	-			35	5
1957–58	38	15	7	1			45	16
1958–59	34	26	4	-			38	26
1959–60	31	10	2	-			33	10
1960–61	39	9	1	-	1	-	41	9
1961–62	38	5	6	1	1	-	45	6
1962–63	8	-	1	-	-	-	9	-
1963–64	40	8	2	-	1	-	43	8
1964–65	39	5	2	-	2	-	43	5
1965–66	33	6	1	-	4	1	38	7
1966–67	36	6	3	1	2	-	41	7
1967–68	34	5	3	1	5	1	42	7
1968–69	28	1	2	1	1	-	31	2
1969–70	27	3	1	-	3	-	31	3
TOTAL	594	147	44	9	20	2	658	158

HERRERA, Robbie

Born: Torquay, Devon, 12 June 1970

A reliable full-back who often pushed up into attack, Robbie Herrera sent over many crosses and created chances for his forwards. His swarthy looks came from his father, who had been a professional footballer in Spain. He

began his career at Queen's Park Rangers and made his Football League debut against Liverpool at Anfield in April 1990 but failed to get a regular place the their side and was eventually third choice behind Clive Wilson and Rufus Brevett. He had two loan spells at Torquay during 1992 and one with Fulham from October 1993 to January 1994, before Fulham director Cyril Swain paid his transfer fee of £40,000 from his own pocket in March 1994.

Herrera probably played at his best under manager Micky Adams. He used him as a wing-back, making the most of his natural inclination to make attacking runs down the left flank and his ability to recover quickly when caught out of position. His only goal for Fulham came at Leyton Orient in March 1994 when he appeared on the left side of midfield in a 2–2 draw. He had an excellent season as Fulham finished as runners up in Division Three in 1996–97 until he injured his shoulder playing at Torquay in January. The following season he was hit by injury again, and by the time he had recovered Rufus Brevett had been signed from Queen's Park Rangers and taken his place in the side. Herrera was sold to Torquay United for £35,000 in August 1998 but was released by them in June 2001 after a season full of injury.

When Roy McFarland took over from Wes Saunders as Torquay's manager, he had another look at Herrera and signed him on monthly contracts until he moved to Leyton Orient in October. After leaving Brisbane Road, Robbie signed for Merthyr Tydfil in December 2001 and later played for Taunton Town, Bideford and was player-manger at Torrington from March 2006. Robbie played in an FA Vase semi-final for Bideford in 2004 when they lost to Winchester City 7–3 on aggregate.

Appearances:

	Football League		FA Cup		League Cup		GRAND TOTAL	
SEASON	Apps	Goals	Apps	Goals	Apps	Goals	Apps	Goals
1993–94	23	1	-	-	-	-	23	1
1994–95	26+1	-	4	-	3	-	33+1	-
1995–96	42+1	-	5	-	4	-	51+1	-
1996–97	26	-	1	-	4	-	31	-
1997–98	26	-	3	-	4	-	33	-
TOTAL	143+2	1	13	-	15	-	171+2	2

HILL, Jimmy

Born: *Balham, London, 22 July 1928*

Former player Jimmy Hill played a vital role in saving the club during the late 1980s when he became the chairman of the newly-formed Fulham (1987). He had played for Fulham for most of the 1950s and his hard-working style enabled some of his more talented colleagues to shine. He appeared briefly for Fulham juniors in 1943 but did not become a professional until May 1949 when he signed for Brentford, and he went on to score 10 goals in 86 appearances for the Bees, most of which were at wing-half.

Hill was transferred to Craven Cottage in March 1952 as a half-back, and when Bobby Robson was sold to West Bromwich Albion in 1956 Jimmy moved to the inside-right position. His finest moments came helping Fulham reach an FA Cup semi-final against Manchester United in 1958, scoring in every round. The next season he made 32 appearances as the Cottagers returned to the First Division in 1958–59. His five goals at Doncaster Rovers in March 1958 equalled the club record for goals in

a single game. Jimmy gained a lot of publicity as the PFA chairman fighting for the abolition of the maximum wage, which was finally achieved in 1961.

Hill was forced to retire from playing in June 1961 due to a knee injury. In November he became the manager of Coventry City and had six very successful years at Highfield Road, taking them from the Third to the First Division. He was offered a lucrative job with London Weekend Television in 1967 and helped to revamp the way football was presented on television. During the 1970s, Hill became involved in the NASL but lost money when Detroit Express went bankrupt and was the commercial manager at Fulham for a while.

When property speculators tried to merge Fulham with Queen's Park Rangers in 1987, he helped form the consortium that saved the club. Somehow Fulham held on to Craven Cottage but struggled to find success on the pitch until Mohamed Al Fayed replaced Hill as the chairman of Fulham in 1997. Despite a brush with cancer he continues to be involved in media work in his late 70s.

Appearances:

	Football League		FA Cup		GRAND TOTAL	
SEASON	Apps	Goals	Apps	Goals	Apps	Goals
1951–52	6	1	-	-	6	1
1952–53	30	-	1	-	31	-
1953–54	33	2	3	1	36	3
1954–55	32	1	1	-	33	1
1955–56	31	4	2	1	33	5
1956–57	37	5	2	-	39	5
1957–58	37	16	7	6	44	22
1958–59	32	6	4	2	36	8
1959–60	25	5	1	1	26	6
1960–61	13	1	-	-	13	1
TOTAL	276	41	21	11	297	52

HOPKINS, Jeff

Born: Swansea, Mid Glamorgan, 11 April 1964

A wholehearted, enthusiastic and determined defender, Jeff Hopkins helped Fulham to promotion from the Third Division, missing just one game during his first full season (1981–82) in the first team. He was one of many young players developed by the club at this time. Beginning his Whites career as a

right-back, he was moved to centre-half when Roger Brown moved to Bournemouth and Paul Parker emerged as a more natural right-back.

Hopkins made his international debut for Wales when only 19 years old and gained 14 of his 16 caps while at Craven Cottage. He also gained five Under-21 and youth caps for his country.

Hopkins was beset by a series of injuries from 1985. After joining Crystal Palace for £240,000 in August 1988, his injury problems continued and he missed the FA Cup Final in 1990. He was almost forced to give up the game, but the Welshman made a comeback on loan with Plymouth Argyle in 1991 and later made 148+8 appearances for Reading, helping them to the Championship of the Second Division in 1993–94. Jeff went on to make a career total of 507+18 appearances, scoring 12 goals, before being released by the Berkshire club in May 1997. Hopkins played for Selangor

(Malaysia) in June 1997 and moved to Australia the following year to play for Gippsland Falcons and then coached Eastern Pride from 2000–01.

Appearances:

	Football League		FA Cup		League Cup		GRAND TOTAL	
SEASON	Apps	Goals	Apps	Goals	Apps	Goals	Apps	Goals
1980–81	1	-	-	-	-	-	1	-
1981–82	31+4	-	2	-	7	1	40+4	1
1982–83	41	1	3	-	4	-	48	1
1983–84	31+2	-	2	-	5	-	38+2	-
1984–85	40	2	1	-	3	1	44	3
1985–86	23	-	1	-	-	-	28	-
1986–87	20	1	3	-	-	-	23	1
1987–88	26	-	-	-	3	-	29	-
TOTAL	213+6	4	12	-	26	2	251+6	6

HOUGHTON, Ray

Born: Glasgow, 9 January 1962

Ray Houghton must be Fulham's best-ever free transfer signing, when he joined from West Ham in June 1982. He possessed great dribbling ability, was an excellent passer and scored some wonderful goals for the club.

After some great performances, Fulham almost won promotion to the old First Division at the end of his first season at the Cottage, but sadly he became one of the many stars to be sold off to help balance the books for a paltry fee of £147,000 in September 1985 and Oxford United got a real bargain.

Ray hit the headlines after his superb performances at St James' Park, Newcastle, in October 1982 when he scored with a brilliant lob from 25 yards out in a 4–1 victory. His 11 goals in

1984–85 included a last-minute winner in a very exciting 3–2 victory over Manchester City during the Christmas period. Houghton made 145 appearances before his move to Oxford United, and he won a League Cup-winners' medal in 1986 when he scored one of the goals that helped Oxford beat Queen's Park Rangers in the Wembley Final. Anfield was Ray's next stop, where he gained many honours, including FA Cup winners' medals in 1989 and 1992 and two League Championship medals in 1987–88 and 1989–90. He became a regular in the Republic of Ireland side and eventually winning 73 caps, despite his strong Glaswegian accent, as Houghton qualified to play for them via his father's nationality. He was in the team when Ireland reached the quarter-final of the World Cup in 1990, where they lost narrowly by a single goal to host nation Italy in Rome.

Ray moved from Anfield to Villa Park in July 1992 and to Crystal Palace in March 1995, where he was later coach for eight months from August 2000. When Houghton left Reading for Stevenage Borough in October 1999 he had appeared in 675+40 League and Cup games and scored 94 goals. He is now an analyst on Talk Sport.

Appearances:

	Football League		FA Cup		League Cup		GRAND TOTAL	
SEASON	Apps	Goals	Apps	Goals	Apps	Goals	Apps	Goals
1982–83	42	5	3	1	4	1	49	7
1983–84	40	3	-	-	5	-	45	3
1984–85	42	8	1	2	3	1	46	11
1985–86	5	-	-	-	-	-	5	-
TOTAL	129	16	4	3	12	2	145	21

JEZZARD, Bedford

Born: Clerkenwell, London, 19 October 1927
Died: London, 21 May 2005

An archetypal English centre-forward of the post-war era, Jezzard could shoot with both feet and was a powerful header of the ball. 'Beddy' terrorised Second Division defences in the early 1950s and held Fulham's aggregate goalscoring record with 154 goals until Johnny Haynes surpassed his total in the late 1960s.

Jezzard attended Durrant Senior School in Watford and joined the local club as an amateur

in December 1944 after turning out for the Croxley Boys Club. He went to Fulham from Watford in July 1948 and made 30 appearances as the Lilliewhites won promotion as Second Division champions in 1948–49. However, he struggled to find the net during Fulham's four-year spell in the top flight but hit over 20 goals a season from 1953–56 in the Second Division. His 38 goals in 1953–54 remains Fulham's best post-1945 total in a season. He formed a brilliant inside formation with Bobby Robson and Johnny Haynes and scored four goals against Derby in October 1953 and versus Barnsley in August 1955, but his best performance came against Hull City in October 1955 when he scored five goals.

Despite playing in the Second Division, 'Beddy' gained two England caps in a 7–1 defeat in Hungary and in a 3–0 victory over Northern Ireland in October 1955, in the same side as Johnny Haynes. He also represented the Football League on three occasions, including scoring two goals in a 4–0 victory over the Scottish League in April 1954. The England international's playing career came to a premature end when he broke his leg on a tour of South Africa with the FA in the summer of 1956, and he was appointed as the youth-team coach at Fulham in August 1957, then manager in June 1958 with Frank Osborne as general manager (See Managers' section). Jezzard ran a public house in Stamford Brook near Hammersmith for many years after leaving football.

Appearances:

	Football League		FA Cup		GRAND TOTAL	
SEASON	Apps	Goals	Apps	Goals	Apps	Goals
1948–49	30	6	1	-	31	6
1949–50	39	8	2	-	41	8
1950–51	35	9	3	-	38	9
1951–52	27	8	1	-	28	8
1952–53	42	35	1	-	43	35
1953–54	42	39	3	-	45	39
1954–55	39	23	1	-	40	23
1955–56	38	27	2	-	40	27
TOTAL	292	155	14	-	306	155

KEEPING, Mike

Born: Milford-on-Sea, Hampshire, 22 August 1902

Died: Milford-on-Sea, Hampshire, 28 March 1984

Mike Keeping played for Ringwood Collegiate and Milford FC before signing for Southampton in December 1920. He did not make his debut until October 1924 and was a regular in the side from 1925–26. The Saints reached an FA Cup semi-final in March 1926 but lost 2–1 to Arsenal at Stamford Bridge with Keeping at left-back. He toured Canada in 1926 and South Africa and Rhodesia in 1929 with the Football Association, represented the Football League against the Irish League in September 1931 and played in two England trial games for the Professionals against the Amateurs in 1926 and 1929. His manager at the Dell, Jim McIntyre, signed him when he was

manager of Fulham in February 1933, a classy and sporting left-back who joined the club in a joint transfer with outside left Johnny Arnold. They cost a total of £5,100 but proved great signings and were first-team regulars up until the outbreak of war in 1939.

Mike appeared in every game in Fulham's FA Cup run to the semi-final in 1936, where they lost to fellow Second Division side Sheffield United at Molineux. They nearly reached Wembley again in 1940, getting to the semi-final of the League War Cup before losing 4–3 to West Ham United at Stamford Bridge. He had played a total of 498 games (scoring 18 goals) for Southampton and Fulham between 1924 and 1939 and made another 46 appearances for the Whites during 1939–40, after which he retired.

Keeping became the coach at Real Madrid in February 1949, then coached at HBS and Ermelo in Holland and also coached in Denmark, France and North Africa before taking charge at Poole Town in 1959. He helped his brother run two garages in Milford and flew for a seaplane manufacturer in Southampton.

Appearances:

	Football League		FA Cup		GRAND TOTAL	
SEASON	Apps	Goals	Apps	Goals	Apps	Goals
1932–33	14	-	-	-	14	-
1933–34	17	-	1	-	18	-
1934–35	26	-	1	-	27	-
1935–36	35	3	6	-	41	3
1936–37	40	2	1	-	41	2
1937–38	37	-	1	-	38	-
1938–39	36	2	2	-	38	2
TOTAL	205	7	12	-	217	7

KEY, Johnny

Born: Chelsea, London, 5 November 1937

Fast, direct and an accurate crosser of the ball, Johnny Key played most of his games for Fulham in the First Division. When Key signed in May 1956, he was already a good athlete having won the Southern AAA long jump championship after attending the Latymer Upper Grammar School and playing for the Chelsea Boys club. He appeared six times (two goals) as Fulham won promotion to the top flight in 1959, and he was soon appearing

regularly in the Fulham side at either outside-right or left but missed most of the club's FA Cup run in 1962 and was in and out of the side over the next four seasons.

One of Key's best performances for Fulham came against Spurs in January 1965 when he scored two excellent goals in a 4–1 victory. He was one of the many experienced players released by Fulham manager Vic Buckingham and Coventry City manager Jimmy Hill signed him in May 1966. He then helped City to the Second Division Championship in 1966–67 but, after scoring their first ever First Division goal, lost his place in the side and was transferred to Orient in March 1968. The wingman became injury prone and was forced to retire the following year and, like many other former players, became a London taxi driver for many years and lived in the same street as Bedford Jezzard. A grandchild of Johnny's now works at Fulham's Motspur Park Offices.

Appearances:

	Football League		FA Cup		League Cup		GRAND TOTAL	
SEASON	Apps	Goals	Apps	Goals	Apps	Goals	Apps	Goals
1957–58	-	-	1	1	-	-	1	1
1958–59	6	2	1	-			7	2
1959–60	25	4	-	-			25	4
1960–61	28	5	1	-	1	-	30	5
1961–62	9	-	1	1	1	-	11	1
1962–63	22	4	1	-	2	3	25	7
1963–64	27	5	1	-	1	1	29	6
1964–65	26	4	2	1	1	1	29	6
1965–66	20	5	-	-	4	-	24	5
TOTAL	163	29	8	3	10	5	181	37

LACY, John

Born: Liverpool, 14 August 1951

Lacy competed with Ernie Howe for the centre-half berth at Fulham during the 1970s and won thanks partially to the great influence Bobby Moore had on his career as his partner in the heart of the defence. Very tall and well built, Lacy was terrific in the air but was not so comfortable when playing on the ground. He played for Marine and Kingstonian while studying for a BSc at the London School of Economics. Discovered by youth-team manager George Cohen playing for the London University side in 1970, he was signed as a professional by Fulham in July 1971.

One of the highlights for Lacy was playing at Goodison Park in the fifth roundof Fulham's 1975 FA Cup run, a club that he supported as a boy. They won 2–1 at Everton but eventually lost in the Final to West Ham. His other honour while at the Cottage came in the Anglo-Scottish Cup Final when he played in the second leg that ended 0–0, and the Whites lost 1–0 on aggregate.

Lacy moved on to White Hart Lane in July 1978 for a fee of £200,000, joining the club at the same time as Argentinean stars Ossie Ardilles

and Ricky Villa. He was in and out of the Spurs side and sometimes found the pace of Division One hard to handle. The highlight of his time at Spurs was appearing at Wembley in the 1982 FA Charity Shield, where they lost 1–0 to Liverpool.

Lacy joined Crystal Palace in August 1983 but injuries took their toll, and he played his last League match for Palace against Blackburn in May 1984 at the age of 32. John moved to Stavangstadt of Norway in November 1984 and also played for Barnet and St Albans City, taking over as their player-manager in July 1987. He moved to Wivenhoe in 1988 where he ended his playing career in 1991. In recent years, Lacy has been working in double glazing, first as a sales rep and more recently as a sales manager.

Appearances:

	Football League		FA Cup		League Cup		GRAND TOTAL	
SEASON	Apps	Goals	Apps	Goals	Apps	Goals	Apps	Goals
1972–73	3+1	-	-	-	-	-	3+1	-
1973–74	32+1	-	3	-	3	1	38+1	1
1974–75	39	2	11	-	2	-	52	2
1975–76	26+1	1	1	-	-	-	27+1	1
1976–77	26+1	2	-	-	1	-	27+1	2
1977–78	38	2	1	-	2	-	41	2
TOTAL	164+4	7	16	-	8	1	188+4	8

LANGLEY, Jim

Born: Kilburn, London, 7 February 1929

Jim Langley was a flamboyant left-back with a wide range of tricks, such as bicycle-kicks, overhead-kicks, an enormous throw in and a superb slide tackle, which made him a great favourite with the Fulham crowd. He played as an amateur for Yiewsley, Hounslow Town, Uxbridge, Hayes, Brentford and Ruislip before signing as a professional with Guildford City in August 1948. He moved to Leeds United in June 1948 and appeared as an outside-left at Elland Road before signing for Brighton in July 1953, where he found regular first-team football at left-back.

Langley gained honours representing the Third Division South in 1955, gained a B international cap against West Germany in March 1955 and also played for the Football League against the Irish League at Newcastle in

October 1956. He moved to Fulham in February 1957. He won three caps for England, but had the misfortune to miss a penalty at Wembley. He played in the Final of the Inter Cities Fairs Cup for a London Representative side that lost 6–0 to Barcelona in 1960. He was in both of Fulham's FA Cup semi-final sides of 1958 and 1962, and missed just two games in the club's promotion season of 1958–59. In fact, he did not miss a game from February 1959 to November 1961, he was ever present three times. He was given a free transfer by Fulham manager Vic Buckingham in May 1965, few Fulham fans could make sense of the decision.

Jim moved to Queen's Park Rangers in July 1965, and he helped the Hoops to the Third Division title and Football League Cup Final victory over West Brom at Wembley in 1966–67. The England international became player-manager of Hillingdon Borough in September 1967 and played at Wembley again in 1971, at the age of 42, in a FA Trophy Final. He made a grand total of 647+1 appearances, scoring 63 goals, for his four League clubs. He now lives in retirement in Hillingdon.

Appearances:

	Football League		FA Cup		League Cup		GRAND TOTAL	
SEASON	Apps	Goals	Apps	Goals	Apps	Goals	Apps	Goals
1956–57	12	1	-	-			12	1
1957–58	38	4	7	-			45	4
1958–59	40	7	2	-			42	7
1959–60	42	3	2	-			44	3
1960–61	42	5	1	-	1	-	44	5
1961–62	35	2	5	2	2	-	42	4
1962–63	42	4	2	-	3	-	47	4
1963–64	31	1	2	-	1	-	34	1
1964–65	41	4	2	-	3	-	46	4
TOTAL	323	31	23	2	10	0	356	33

LAWLER, Robin

Born: *Drumcondra, Dublin, 28 February 1925*
Died: *Fulham, London, 17 April 1998*

Robin Lawler arrived at Fulham from Belfast Celtic in March 1949, along with Johnny Campbell and Hugh Kelly, but it took him until 1952–53 to gain a regular first-team spot. He played mainly at left-back or left-half during his Fulham career and developed into a good all round defender with a long throw.

Robin had made his name in the Irish League, winning an Irish Cup-winners' medal in 1947, and represented that League against the Scottish League in January and November 1948.

Robin, whose real name was Joseph Frederick, joined Home Farm (Dublin) in 1942, played for Distillery in 1943 then moved back to Dublin to play for Transport FC in 1944 and Drumcondra in 1945 before moving north again to join Belfast Celtic in 1946. His first cap for the Republic of Ireland came in March 1953 against Austria, and he might have made more than eight appearances for his country but club commitments took precedence over country. He played in Fulham's run to an FA Cup semi-final in 1958 and played 29 games as the club finished runners-up in the Second Division in 1958–59

Lawler left Fulham for Yiewsley (later Hillingdon Borough) in July 1962 and worked for Deans Blinds for 21 years before retiring due to ill health. His brother James played at Southend United for many years. Robin was also the club's snooker champion for many years.

Appearances:

	Football League		FA Cup		GRAND TOTAL	
SEASON	Apps	Goals	Apps	Goals	Apps	Goals
1949–50	2	-	-	-	2	-
1950–51	4	-	-	-	4	-
1951–52	5	-	-	-	5	-
1952–53	33	-	-	-	33	-
1953–54	42	-	3	-	45	-
1954–55	39	-	1	-	40	-
1955–56	37	-	2	-	39	-
1956–57	41	-	2	-	43	-
1957–58	25	-	6	-	31	-
1958–59	29	-	4	-	33	-
1959–60	16	-	-	-	16	-
1959–60	7	-	-	-	7	-
1960–61	1	-	-	-	1	-
TOTAL	281	0	18	-	299	0

LEGGAT, Graham

Born: Aberdeen 20 June 1934

Scottish international Graham Leggat started his career at Aberdeen in 1953 and played a major role as the Dons took the Scottish League Championship in 1954–55 and won two Cup medals at Pittodrie, a runners'-up medal in the 1954 Scottish Cup Final and a winners' medal in the Scottish League Cup Final of 1956, Graham scoring the winner when they beat St Mirren 2–1. He won the first of his 18 Scottish caps against England in April 1956, represented the

Scottish League on five occasions and appeared in the Scottish Under-23 side.

Leggat scored 92 goals in 151 appearances for the Dons before moving to Fulham in August 1958 for a fee of £20,000. Very fast and extremely brave, he scored in his first six matches for the club, eventually helping Fulham into the top flight, scoring 21 goals. He hit eight hat-tricks for Fulham in all, scored 23 goals in 1960–61 and the following season helped the club reach the semi-final of the FA Cup. He scored a hat-trick in three minutes during the 10–1 demolition of Ipswich Town on Boxing Day 1963 and was again Fulham's top scorer in 1963–64 with 15 goals from only 25 appearances. Graham could score goals from all angles and is the only Fulham player to score a century of goals in the top flight. After hitting five goals in two games in late December 1966 the Fulham manager Vic Buckingham surprised and angered the fans when he sold him to Birmingham City for £20,000. Leggat made only 19+3 appearances (three goals) before being transferred to Rotherham United in July 1968. Next was Aston Villa in 1969 as coach, before joining Bromsgrove Rovers the following March. Leggat moved to Canada in 1971 where he managed Toronto Metros and became a sports journalist and commentator with TSN, a Sports TV network in Ontario, where he worked for over 30 years, until his reitirement.

Appearances:

	Football League		FA Cup		League Cup		GRAND TOTAL	
SEASON	Apps	Goals	Apps	Goals	Apps	Goals	Apps	Goals
1958–59	36	21	4	1			40	22
1959–60	28	18	2	2			30	20
1960–61	36	23	-	-	-	-	36	23
1961–62	31	13	8	1	-	-	39	14
1962–63	33	10	1	-	1	-	35	10
1963–64	25	15	2	1	1	-	28	16
1964–65	17	4	-	-	2	-	19	4
1965–66	32+1	15	1	-	3	-	36+1	15
1966–67	13+2	8	-	-	1	2	14+2	10
TOTAL	251+3	127	18	5	8	2	277+3	134

LEWINGTON, Ray

Born: Lambeth, London, 7 September 1956

The grafter of the side whose ball-winning skills enabled others to play their natural game, Ray Lewington started his career at Chelsea, and he played in their side that won promotion from the Second Division in 1976–77. He moved to NASL club Vancouver Whitecaps in March 1979 and was loaned to Wimbledon the following September. He joined Fulham in March 1980 for a £50,000 fee, but he could not prevent the Cottagers from being relegated that season. He played an important role in the Cottager's promotion in 1981–82 and was ever present as the club just missed another promotion the following season.

Lewington was sold to Sheffield United in July 1985 for £40,000, but a year later he returned to the Cottage to become Fulham's youngest-ever manager at only 29 years and 10 months. (See Managers' section.) He retired from playing in June 1990 but had appeared mainly for the reserves since 1988. He made a total of 429+10 appearances (28 goals) for his five League clubs plus 35+1 games (three goals) for Vancouver Whitecaps.

As well as managing at the Cottage, Lewington was also in charge at Brentford (2000–01) and Watford (2002–05), chief coach at Fulham, Crystal Palace and Brentford and returned to the Cottage again in July 2005 to look after the reserves.

Appearances:

	Football League		FA Cup		League Cup		GRAND TOTAL	
SEASON	Apps	Goals	Apps	Goals	Apps	Goals	Apps	Goals
1979–80	10	1	-	-	-	-	10	1
1980–81	19+1	-	2+1	-	2	-	23+2	-
1981–82	31	4	2	-	7	1	40	5
1982–83	42	10	3	1	4	-	49	11
1983–84	32+1	-	2	-	4	1	38+1	1
1984–85	38	5	1	-	3	-	42	5
1986–87	25	-	-	-	4	-	29	-
1987–88	31	1	1	-	3	-	35	1
1988–89	-	-	-	-	-	-	-	-
1989–90	2+2	-	3	-	-	-	5+2	-
TOTAL	230+4	21	14+1	1	27	2	271+5	24

LLOYD, Barry

Born: Hillingdon, Middlesex, 19 February 1949

Barry Lloyd joined Fulham as part of the deal that took John Dempsey to Chelsea in February 1969. Unable to break through at Stamford Bridge, the move was a good one for Lloyd as he found regular first-team football at Craven Cottage. Manager Bill Dodgin made Lloyd captain, and the side won promotion from the Third Division in 1970–71, and he scored at

Bradford City on the night that they clinched promotion. The club also reached the quarter-finals of the League Cup that season before going down 1–0 at Bristol City. Barry was ever present that season, and, in fact, missed only one game between December 1969 and December 1972.

The blond-haired midfielder lost his regular place halfway through the 1974–75 season but was chosen as substitute for the 1975 FA Cup Final side, having played in some of the earlier rounds. Manager Bobby Campbell sold him to Hereford United in October 1976, but he struggled at Edgar Street and moved to Brentford at the end of the season, where he again played under the management of Bill Dodgin. After a brief spell with Houston Hurricane in the US, Lloyd took over at Yeovil Town from July 1978 until July 1981 when he became manager of Worthing, taking them from the Second Division to runners-up in the Premier Division of the Isthmian League. This earned him the assistant manager's post at Brighton in May 1986, and he took full control at the club the following January and stayed until December 1993. He later had two further spells at Worthing in 1996 and 2001.

Appearances:

	Football League		FA Cup		League Cup		GRAND TOTAL	
SEASON	Apps	Goals	Apps	Goals	Apps	Goals	Apps	Goals
1968–69	15	3	-	-	-	-	15	3
1969–70	30+4	7	-	-	0+2	-	30+6	7
1970–71	46	9	1	-	6	-	53	9
1971–72	42	3	3	-	2	-	47	3
1972–73	32+1	1	-	-	4	1	36+1	2
1973–74	34+2	2	2	-	4	-	40+2	2
1974–75	25+1	1	2+2	-	3	-	30+3	1
1975–76	25	3	-	-	2	-	27	3
TOTAL	249+8	29	8+2	-	21+2	1	278+12	30

LOCK, Kevin

Born: Plaistow, London, 27 December 1953

Good in the air and an excellent passer out of defence, Kevin Lock was a free-kick and penalty specialist at Craven Cottage and scored a remarkable 29 goals from the left-back position. He had joined the Hammers as an apprentice in July 1969, signing professional forms in December 1971, and gained four England Under-23 caps and a European Youth Championship-winners' medal in 1972 in his early days at Upton Park. He took over from Bobby Moore for the Hammers when the former England captain moved to Fulham in 1974. Kevin was the man of the match for West Ham against his future employers Fulham in the 1975 FA Cup Final. He had made 151+12 appearances for the Hammers when he moved to Fulham in May 1978 for a £60,000 fee. Initially playing at the centre of the Cottagers defence, he was moved to left-back where he was more effective.

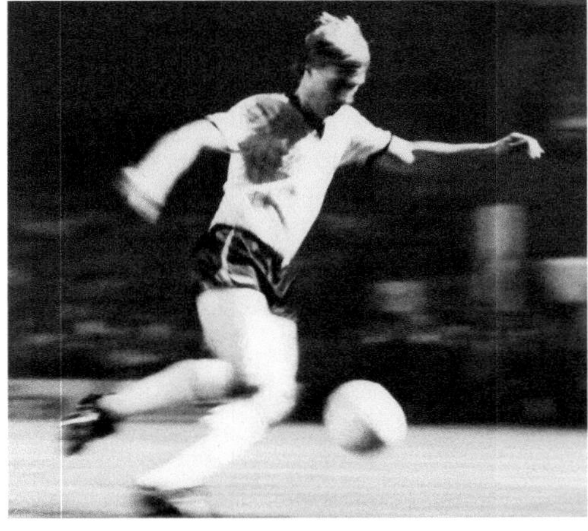

Helping the Lilliewhites to promotion in 1981–82, Lock missed the last few weeks of the season due to injury and later in his Fulham career seemed to be hit by a succession of muscle problems and strains. Among his 29 goals, 'Locky' scored with penalties at Anfield and the Cottage in the epic League Cup encounters with Liverpool in 1983.

After leaving Fulham, Kevin played briefly for Southend United before becoming their youth coach from 1985–92, and was a coach at Millwall and Chelsea before taking over as Brentford's assistant manager from June 1993 to June 1998.

Appearances:

	Football League		FA Cup		League Cup		GRAND TOTAL	
SEASON	Apps	Goals	Apps	Goals	Apps	Goals	Apps	Goals
1978–79	39	3	3	-	2	-	44	3
1979–80	38	5	-	-	2	-	40	5
1980–81	29	5	6	-	1	-	36	5
1981–82	25+1	5	0+1	-	0+1	-	25+3	5
1982–83	34	2	-	-	3	-	37	2
1983–84	15	2	-	-	3	2	18	4
1984–85	30	5	1	-	2	-	33	5
TOTAL	210+1	27	10+1	-	13+1	2	233+3	29

LOWE, Eddie

Born: Halesowen, Worcestershire, 11 July 1925

An influential half-back who was good in the air and a strong tackler, Eddie Lowe played as an amateur for Millwall, Finchley and Walthamstow Avenue during wartime football before signing for Aston Villa from Birmingham works side Kynoch's in September 1945. Eddie was soon a first-team regular and gained three England caps during May 1947, against France at Highbury, in Zurich against Switzerland then played in a 10–0 victory over Portugal in Lisbon. Unfortunately, he never appeared for his country again despite some great displays for Fulham. Transferred to Fulham in May 1950 for £10,000 to help bolster the defence, Eddie helped Fulham to reach the FA Cup quarter-finals, where they lost 1–0 at Blackpool. The following season, however, they were relegated from the top flight.

For the next seven seasons Eddie plied his trade in the Second Division and, despite forming an excellent half-back line with Jimmy Hill and Gordon Brice, the defence continued to

leak many goals. This period came to an end when Fulham finished runners-up in the Second Division in 1958–59 and returned to the top flight. Lowe missed most of Fulham's 1958 FA Cup run due to injury but appeared in all games during the 1962 run, which also ended in semi-final defeat, this time against Burnley.

Lowe made his last appearance for the Lilliewhites during May 1963 in a 3–3 draw with Birmingham City at the Cottage. He took over as player-manager at Notts County in July 1963, but after two seasons of limited success he moved on to become a purchasing manager for a central heating company in Nottingham. He still lives in Nottingham in retirement.

Appearances:

	Football League		FA Cup		League Cup		GRAND TOTAL	
SEASON	Apps	Goals	Apps	Goals	Apps	Goals	Apps	Goals
1950–51	40	-	5	-			45	-
1951–52	39	4	1	-			40	4
1952–53	36	-	1	-			37	-
1953–54	39	1	3	-			42	1
1954–55	36	-	1	-			37	-
1955–56	39	-	2	-			41	-
1956–57	42	-	2	1			44	1
1957–58	35	1	1	-			36	1
1958–59	32	-	4	-			36	-
1959–60	33	-	2	-			35	-
1960–61	34	-	1	-	1	-	36	-
1961–62	40	2	8	1	2	-	50	3
1962–63	28	-	2	-	2	-	32	-
TOTAL	473	8	33	2	5	-	511	10

MACEDO, Tony

Born: *Gibraltar, 22 February 1938*

Tony Macedo was one of Fulham's best-ever goalkeepers and was unlucky not to win full England honours after playing 10 times for the Under-23 side. Spectacular, brave and acrobatic, the Gibraltar-born goalkeeper was more like a continental 'keeper than a typically English one. He was good on crosses, had safe hands and could distribute the ball quickly and accurately. He replaced Ian Black in goal from December 1957 and appeared in every match during the 1958 FA Cup run but had an off day in the semi-final replay at Highbury, letting in five goals against Manchester United.

Macedo missed just five games in 1958–59 as Fulham clinched promotion back to the First Division, and the following season he was in great form when Fulham finished 10th. He was first choice until mid 1965–66, although he missed much of 1963–64 due to injury, and he played throughout Fulham's FA Cup run of 1962. He had an excellent season in 1966–67 but became rather injury prone after this and was transferred to Colchester United in September 1968 for £5,000, where he made 40 appearances. He later moved to South Africa to play for Durban City and Highlands Park and is still living in Johannesburg today. Tony was the son of a Spanish international who played for San Sebastian and Real Madrid in the 1930s.

Appearances:

	Football League		FA Cup		League Cup		GRAND TOTAL	
SEASON	Apps	Goals	Apps	Goals	Apps	Goals	Apps	Goals
1957–58	23	-	7	-			30	-
1958–59	37	-	3	-			40	-
1959–60	39	-	2	-			41	-
1960–61	31	-	-	-	-	-	31	
1961–62	38	-	8	-	2	-	48	-
1962–63	42	-	2	-	3	-	47	-
1963–64	24	-	2	-	-	-	26	-
1964–65	40	-	2	-	2	-	44	-
1965–66	21	-	-	-	3	-	24	-
1966–67	33	-	2	-	1	-	36	-
1967–68	18	-	3	-	3	-	24	-
TOTAL	346	-	31	-	14	-	391	-

MALBRANQUE, Steed

Born: *Mouscron, Belgium, 6 January 1980*

It was a great loss when Fulham manager Chris Coleman was forced to sell Steed Malbranque to Spurs in August 2006. The club should have got more than the £2.5m they obtained for him, but there was only a year to go on his contract. When Steed played well so did Fulham. A clever player who was full of skills and tricks, Malbranque was sometimes inconsistent and frustrating.

Although born in Belgium, Steed became a French Under-21 international who helped his country to the 2002 European Under-21 Championship Final. The busy player made over 50 appearances for Lyon and assisted them to the runners'-up spot in the French League and to the quarter-finals of the UEFA Cup.

Fulham manager Jean Tigana signed Steed for £5 million in August 2001, and the all-action player quickly made a big impression and became a major influence in the Fulham side. Steed has been very unlucky not to be selected

for the full French side after many impressive performances for Fulham. He helped the club win the Inter Toto Cup in 2002–03 to gain entry into the UEFA Cup, where they eventually lost to Hertha Berlin. He remained a regular in the Fulham midfield, scoring some spectacular goals, until his move to Spurs.

Appearances:

	Football League		FA Cup		League Cup		GRAND TOTAL	
SEASON	Apps	Goals	Apps	Goals	Apps	Goals	Apps	Goals
2001–02	33+4	8	6	1	1+2	1	40+6	10
2002–03	35+2	6	4	4	-	-	39+2	10
2003–04	38	6	6	2	-	-	44	8
2004–05	22+4	6	1	-	4	1	27+4	7
2005–06	32+2	6	-	-	1	-	33+2	6
TOTAL	160+12	32	17	7	6+2	2	183+14	41

MARSHALL, John

Born: Balham, London, 18 August 1964

A versatile and consistent player, John Marshall spent 25 years at Fulham as a player, coach and chief scout. He started his Fulham career as a central-defender in the juniors, appeared as a striker in an emergency during 1983–84 and later appeared at right-back and as a right-sided midfield player for the Whites. He scored some spectacular goals but also set up many chances for his teammates. He was ever present during 1985–86, when Fulham were relegated to the Third Division. His best season was 1988–89 when they reached the Third Division Play-offs but lost to Bristol Rovers. His speed on the right wing tested most Third Division defences, and at one time it looked as though he might break Johnny Haynes's aggregate appearance record, but he broke his leg in two places against Gillingham in April 1995 and never fully

recovered. He was awarded a joint testimonial with Peter Scott in 1990 against Chelsea and Everton. Marshall became a youth coach in May 1996 and rarely appeared for the first team after this, before retiring in June 1998. He was appointed as chief scout in November 1999, in succession to Arthur Cox, and held this post until June 2005, when he left the club almost unnoticed. After a spell as chief scout at Leicester City, Marshall left for a job outside football in October 2006.

Appearances:

	Football League		FA Cup		League Cup		GRAND TOTAL	
SEASON	Apps	Goals	Apps	Goals	Apps	Goals	Apps	Goals
1983–84	21+4	-	2	-	3	-	26+4	-
1984–85	29+3	1	-	-	2	-	31+3	1
1985–86	42	3	1	-	4	-	47	3
1986–87	29	4	4	2	4	-	37	6
1987–88	24+1	2	-	-	4	1	28+1	3
1988–89	41+2	7	1	-	-	-	42+2	7
1989–90	34+2	4	3	1	3	-	40+2	5
1990–91	34+1	2	0+1	-	2	-	36+2	2
1991–92	41	-	1	-	2	-	44	-
1992–93	40+1	2	1	-	2	-	43+1	2
1993–94	21	1	1	-	2	-	24	1
1994–95	25+2	2	4	-	4	-	33+2	2
1995–96	14+2	-	-	-	2	-	16+2	-
1996–97	-	-	-	-	0+1	-	0+1	-
TOTAL	395+18	28	18+1	3	34+1	1	447+20	32

MELLOR, Peter

Born: Prestbury, Cheshire, 20 November 1947

A terrific shot-stopper and very brave when diving at the feet of opponents, Peter Mellor would sometimes flap at crosses but usually had a safe pair of hands. He was an England Youth international but failed to make the grade at

Manchester City and moved to Witton Albion in 1968. Burnley rescued his career when they signed him from the non-League side in April 1969. After 77 appearances for the Turf Moor club, Mellor lost his form in a struggling side and was signed by Fulham manager Bill Dodgin in February 1972 for £25,000. The eccentric 'keeper played a very important role as Fulham saved themselves from relegation that season. He was outstanding during the club's FA Cup run of 1975 and almost single-handedly kept Carlisle United at bay in a 1–0 quarter-final victory at Brunton Park. Mellor was also in excellent form for the two semi-final matches with Birmingham City, but he took a lot of the blame for the defeat in the Final against West Ham as his mistakes led to two goals for Hammers' Alan Taylor.

The fair-haired 'keeper picked up a runners'-up medal when Fulham lost in the Final of the Anglo-Scottish Cup, later that year, to Middlesbrough 1–0 on aggregate. However, Whites manager Bobby Campbell never forgave him for a poor display in a 5–1 defeat by Notts County in November 1976, in which he was carried off, and he never played in the first team

again and was transferred to Hereford United in September 1977. His career was revived at Edgar Street, and he joined Portsmouth in July 1978 and played 146 games for Pompey, helping them to promotion to Division Three in 1979–80.

Mellor made a total of 488 appearances during his career, plus 27 for the Edmonton Drillers in Canada. He lived in the United States after retiring from playing and presently lives in Florida and has been the goalkeeping coach for Florida State and the US national side.

Appearances:

	Football League		FA Cup		League Cup		GRAND TOTAL	
SEASON	Apps	Goals	Apps	Goals	Apps	Goals	Apps	Goals
1971–72	13	-	-	-	-	-	13	-
1972–73	42	-	1	-	4	-	47	-
1973–74	38	-	3	-	2	-	43	-
1974–75	42	-	12	-	3	-	57	-
1975–76	42	-	1	-	3	-	46	-
1976–77	13	-	-	-	5	-	18	-
TOTAL	190	-	17	-	17	-	224	-

MITCHELL, John

Born: *St Albans, Hertfordshire, 12 March 1952*

A striker remembered for his goals during Fulham's FA Cup run of 1975, John Mitchell was an enigma. He seemed to spend a lot of time on the ground and could look a clumsy player, but was capable of achieving the spectacular and was always a brave battler in attack. 'Mitch' won an FA County Youth Cup medal in 1970 when he played in the Hertfordshire side that beat Cheshire 2–1 while playing for Carlton Youth Club. He played for Hertford Town and St Albans City before moving to Fulham in February 1972 for £3,000. Mitchell scored 11 goals in his first season but then lost his form and suffered a series of injuries. The highlight of his career at the Cottage was scoring in both FA Cup semi-final matches against Birmingham City in 1975. His last-minute winner at Maine Road in the replay took the Cottagers to Wembley for the first time in their history. The goal was as fortunate and scrappy as his goal at Hillsborough in the first game had been breathtakingly brilliant. He had a terrific season in 1977–78 as he scored 22 goals, including four

against Orient at the Cottage in May 1977, and he formed an excellent partnership in attack with Teddy Maybank. John was transferred to Millwall for £100,000 in June 1978 but was again beset by injuries, which eventually forced him to retire from the game at the age of 30, after scoring 21 goals in 87+3 appearances for the Lions.

A successful businessman since leaving the game, 'Mitch' has been manager of St Albans on two occasions and also their club chairman. In recent years he was on the board of directors at Luton Town and is currently the chief executive.

Appearances:

	Football League		FA Cup		League Cup		GRAND TOTAL	
SEASON	Apps	Goals	Apps	Goals	Apps	Goals	Apps	Goals
1972–73	36	11	1	-	-	-	37	11
1973–74	11+2	2	1	-	4	-	16+2	2
1974–75	8+8	5	5+1	2	0+1	-	13+10	7
1975–76	26+1	10	1	-	2+1	-	29+2	10
1976–77	38	19	2	-	3	2	43	21
1977–78	39	9	1	-	2	-	42	9
TOTAL	158+11	56	11+1	2	11+2	2	180+14	60

MITTEN, Charlie

Born: *Rangoon, Burma, 17 January 1921*
Died: *Stockport, Cheshire, 2 January 2002*

An elegant and sophisticated outside-left, Charlie Mitten was a star at both Manchester United and Fulham during the post-war period. He played for Dunblane Rovers and Strathalen Hawthorne before joining Manchester United as an amateur in August 1936. His early career was greatly affected by the war, but he played in his first Wembley Wartime Cup Final in 1945 as a guest for Chelsea in a 2–0 victory over Millwall. He helped United beat Blackpool 4–2 in the 1948 FA Cup Final and once hit a hat-trick of penalties for United against Aston Villa in March 1950.

Mitten became disillusioned with his financial situation at Old Trafford and was attracted by the lure of the money offered to him to play in Bogota for the Sante Fe club. When he returned to England, he was given a six-month ban by the Football Association and was also released by United manager Matt Busby. Fulham were only too happy to sign the cultures wingman, and he joined the club in December 1951 and entertained the Craven Cottage crowd for the next five seasons. Playing his part in a star-studded forward line, he made an immediate impact when he scored twice in a 6–0 win over Middlesbrough, but

unfortunately the Cottagers were relegated at the end of his first season.

Mitten was usually Fulham's main penalty taker during his time at Craven Cottage, and he formed a brilliant left-wing partnership with the young Johnny Haynes. He departed the Cottage to become the player-manager of Mansfield Town in February 1956 and moved on to manage Newcastle United in June 1958. During the 1960s Charlie was in charge of the White City Greyhound Stadium in Manchester and Altrincham FC, and he was also a licensed FIFA agent. His sons John and Charles both played professional football and his grandson Andy is a leading light in United's Supporters' Club.

Appearances:

	Football League		FA Cup		GRAND TOTAL	
SEASON	Apps	Goals	Apps	Goals	Apps	Goals
1951–52	16	6	-	-	16	6
1952–53	40	7	1	1	41	8
1953–54	41	9	3	-	44	9
1954–55	36	6	1	-	37	6
1955–56	21	4	1	-	22	4
TOTAL	154	32	6	1	160	33

MONEY, Richard

Born: Lowestoft, Suffolk, 13 October 1955

Richard Money performed in midfield when he first came to Fulhamfrom Scunthorpe United for £50,000, in December 1977. He replaced departing John Lacy at centre-half in 1978–79 and initially did very well in this position, but he struggled the following season and was moved to right-back in an attempt to fill another gap created by the sale of Ray Evans to Stoke City.

Money became the Fulham skipper during the relegation season of 1979–80 and played for the England B side against New Zealand in October 1979, a match played at Brisbane Road. He moved to Anfield in April 1980 for a Fulham record fee of £333,333, a record that remained until Tony Thorpe was sold to Bristol City for £1 million during the summer of 1998. He had big problems trying to displace the likes of Phil Thompson, Alan Hansen and Mark Lawrenson from the Liverpool side and played only 17 times for the Reds. Richard appeared in a European Cup semi-

final in a 1–1 draw at Bayern Munich, as the Reds reached the Final on the away-goals rule, but did not appear in the Final. 'Mr Versatility' had a loan spell at Derby County before joining Luton Town in March 1982 for £100,000. He moved to Portsmouth in August 1983 for a fee of £55,000 but had a miserable time at Fratton Park, being hit by a succession of serious injuries before returning to his first club Scunthorpe United as player-coach in 1985.

Money worked at Aston Villa as a youth-team coach and became the manager at Scunthorpe United from January 1993 to March 1994. Subsequently, he was assistant manager at Nottingham Forest and Manchester City, academy manager at Coventry City before moving to Sweden to manage AIK Stockholm and Vasterai SK. This was followed by a spell as manager at Newcastle United Jets in Australia. He returned to the UK in May 2006 to take charge at Walsall, and they were Champions of League Two by 2007.

Appearances:

	Football League		FA Cup		League Cup		GRAND TOTAL	
SEASON	Apps	Goals	Apps	Goals	Apps	Goals	Apps	Goals
1977–78	23	2	-	-	-	-	23	2
1978–79	42	1	3	-	2	-	47	1
1979–80	41	-	2	1	2	-	45	1
TOTAL	106	3	5	1	4	-	115	4

MOORE, Bobby

Born: Barking, Essex, 12 April 1941
Died: Kingston Vale, Surrey, 24 February 1993

One of the greats of English football, Fulham fans were fortunate to see Bobby Moore grace the side during the mid 1970s. Moore was voted Footballer of the Year when he skippered the Hammers to victories in the FA Cup Final of 1964 and the European Cup-winners' Cup of 1965. However, his greatest achievement was captaining England to the World Cup in 1966 when they beat West Germany in the Final at Wembley. Bobby won a record 108 caps for his country, plus caps at Under-23 and Youth levels, and represented the Football League.

After 642 appearances and 27 goals for the Hammers, the Fulham manager Alec Stock sent his captain Alan Mullery to Upton Park to sign him in March 1974 for a fee of £20,000. Moore and Mullery were soon instilling a new confidence and belief into the younger players. Fulham's march to the FA Cup Final in 1975 took 12 games and Bobby played in all of them. After the semi-final victory over Birmingham, the *Times* newspaper headline was 'Two old men on the way to Wembley', and it described it as Moore's last chance of glory, and to add to the fairytale his former club West Ham would be the opposition. Sadly, the Hammers won the Final 2–0, despite a superb performance from Bobby. The following season he picked up another losers' medal when Fulham lost to Middlesbrough in the Final of the Anglo-Scottish Cup. His final season, 1976–77, saw the arrival at Craven Cottage of George Best and Rodney Marsh, but Fulham struggled against relegation despite the star names.

Moore had played 1,045 games, including internationals, when he retired from League football in May 1977. He later played for Seattle Sounders in the US and was player-coach for Henning Fremond (Denmark). Moore managed Oxford City and Eastern AA (Hong Kong) before becoming the chief executive at Southend United and was later a manager and director at Roots Hall. The former England captain worked as a football commentator and journalist until his untimely death from cancer.

Appearances:

	Football League		FA Cup		League Cup		GRAND TOTAL	
SEASON	Apps	Goals	Apps	Goals	Apps	Goals	Apps	Goals
1973–74	10	1	-	-	-	-	10	1
1974–75	41	-	12	-	3	-	56	-
1975–76	33	-	1	-	3	-	37	-
1976–77	40	-	2	-	5	-	47	-
TOTAL	124	1	15	-	11	-	150	1

MORGAN, Simon

Born: Birmingham, 5 September 1966

A great crowd favourite at Craven Cottage, Simon Morgan appeared for the club at full-back, as a central-defender and also in midfield during his 11 seasons at the Cottage. He began his career at Leicester City as an apprentice in July 1983 and was capped twice by England at Under-21 level, against Sweden and Yugoslavia, in the autumn of 1986. Simon was a regular at left-back until a succession of managerial changes saw him out of favour at Filbert Street.

Having appeared 168+4 times in the Foxes side, Morgan moved to Fulham in October 1990 for £100,000 and was the outstanding performer in some very poor teams that appeared for the Whites during the early 1990s. He was unable to prevent the club's relegation to the basement division, for the first time in its history, in 1993–94 but skippered Fulham when they were promoted as Third Division runners-up three seasons later. After this experience, he wrote an entertaining book called *On Song for Promotion*. Simon gained a Second Division Championship medal in 1998–99 and scored one of the goals that helped Fulham to a shock FA Cup victory at Aston Villa that season. A serious knee injury the following season restricted his appearances, but he had a testimonial match against Tottenham Hotspur in August 2000 when over 12,000 fans attended his big game.

Morgan moved to Brighton in June 2001 and helped them (and Micky Adams again) win the Second Division Championship during 2001–02, but he retired when he was appointed as Fulham's community development manager in June 2002, a post he held until his move to the role of Head of Community Development for the Premier League in 2007.

Appearances:

	Football League		FA Cup		League Cup		GRAND TOTAL	
SEASON	Apps	Goals	Apps	Goals	Apps	Goals	Apps	Goals
1990–91	32	1	3	-	-	-	35	1
1991–92	34+2	3	1	-	2	-	37+2	3
1992–93	38+1	8	1	-	2	-	41+1	8
1993–94	36+1	6	-	-	4	-	40+1	6
1994–95	42	11	4	-	4	-	50	11
1995–96	41	6	3	-	3	-	47	6
1996–97	44	8	1	-	4	1	49	9
1997–98	21+1	1	1	-	4	-	26+1	1
1998–99	32+2	5	3	2	5	1	40+2	8
1999–2000	26+2	-	2	-	5	-	33+2	-
2000–01	0+1	-	-	-	-	-	0+1	-
TOTAL	346+10	49	19	2	33	2	398+10	53

MULLERY, Alan

Born: Notting Hill, London, 23 November 1941

Another Fulham great, Alan Mullery started and ended his playing career with the Cottagers, winning many honours on the way. Making his debut as a 17-year-old in February 1959, Alan remained in the side for the rest of the season as the Lilliewhites won promotion back to Division One as runners-up. He won the first of his three Under-23 caps against Italy in November 1960 and later gained full caps after his move to Spurs. The West Londoner was superb as Fulham reached the FA Cup semi-final in 1962, but they lost to Burnley after a replay.

Spurs manager Bill Nicholson paid £72,500 for Mullery in December 1964, and soon after Alan won his first England cap against Holland. He played 35 times for his country, including playing in the 1970 World Cup Finals in Mexico, where they lost to West Germany in the quarter-finals. Mullery won an FA Cup-winners' medal in 1967, a League Cup-winners' medal in 1971 and a UEFA Cup-winners' medal in 1972, when Spurs beat Wolves in the Final.

Alec Stock signed Mullery on a permanent basis for £65,000 in August 1972, after a loan spell, and made him club captain. 'Mullers' scored some tremendous goals over the next few seasons, and his most famous one came against Leicester City in the FA Cup in January 1974. Stock sent him to Upton Park to sign Bobby Moore from West Ham, and most people expected him to take over at Fulham after Stock,

but this never happened. Mullery and Moore were inspirational as Fulham got to Wembley in 1975, and Alan was voted Footballer of the Year and later awarded an MBE. After retiring from playing he was disappointed and the fans surprised when he was not offered the job of coach in succession to the departed Bill Taylor and instead he was appointed as manager of Brighton in July 1976. The England international also managed Charlton Athletic, Crystal Palace, Queen's Park Rangers, Brighton again, Southwick and Barnet. He was appointed as consultant at Crawley Town in September 2005 and continues to appear on Sky Sports on a regular basis.

Appearances:

	Football League		FA Cup		League Cup		GRAND TOTAL	
SEASON	Apps	Goals	Apps	Goals	Apps	Goals	Apps	Goals
1958–59	14	-	-	-			14	-
1959–60	36	2	2	-			38	2
1960–61	37	1	1	-	-	-	38	1
1961–62	40	6	7	-	2	-	49	6
1962–63	38	1	2	-	2	-	42	1
1963–64	34	3	2	1	1	-	37	4
1971–72	6	1	-	-	-	-	6	1
1972–73	40	8	1	-	2	-	43	8
1973–74	40	2	3	1	4	1	47	4
1974–75	42	9	12	-	3	1	57	10
1975–76	36+1	4	1	-	3	1	40+1	5
TOTAL	363+1	37	31	2	17	3	411+1	42

O'CONNELL, Brian 'Pat'

Born: Earls Court, London, 13 September 1937

One of Fulham's unsung heroes of the 1960s, O'Connell was a versatile player who appeared at outside-left, inside-forward and finally at left-back for the club during their First Division days. When he finally broke into the side in 1960–61, he scored 10 goals in his 28 appearances and missed just one game during the 1962 FA Cup run, appearing as an outside-left in the two semi-final matches with Burnley. He played at left-back during 1965–66 but lost his place in the side before the club's great revival that season. Maybe, he should have scored more often than his modest 28 goals, but Pat provided important cover in most positions in the side, during the days when Fulham carried a small squad. He was one of the many experienced players released by Fulham manager Vic Buckingham, when he was transferred to Crystal Palace on a free transfer in July 1966. and was one of Bobby Robson's first signings when he took charge of Vancouver Royals during the summer of 1967, but he returned to England in 1969 to play in the Southern League with the now defunct Brentwood. They reached the FA Cup third round

in 1969–70, beating Reading on the way. O'Connell later played for Dover before joining Epsom & Ewell as player-manager during the summer of 1973. They were finalists in the first ever FA Vase in 1975, but they lost to Hoddesdon Town 2–1.

Pat became a London taxi cab driver when his playing days were over but has suffered from back problems in recent years.

Appearances:

	Football League		FA Cup		League Cup		GRAND TOTAL	
SEASON	Apps	Goals	Apps	Goals	Apps	Goals	Apps	Goals
1958–59	1	-	-	-			1	-
1959–60	6	2	-	-			6	2
1960–61	26	10	1	-	1	-	28	10
1961–62	31	8	7	-	1	-	39	8
1962–63	31	2	-	-	2	-	33	2
1963–64	13	1	-	-	-	-	13	1
1964–65	24	1	1	-	2	1	27	2
1965–66	20	2	1	-	2	1	23	3
TOTAL	152	26	10	-	8	2	170	28

OLIVER, Len

Born: *Fulham, London, 1 August 1905*
Died: *Letchworth, Hertfordshire, August 1967*

Len Oliver was described in the *Topical Times* of 1933 as 'a big-hearted player and a clever dribbler who set his forwards going with instinctive passes out of defence.' He was a fixture in the team from 1924–34, missing just four games between September 1924 and November 1929, and captained the side for seven of these years.

Young Len worked as a clerk at a West End store while playing as an amateur for Alma Athletic and Tufnell Park, before joining Fulham as a professional in June 1924. He featured in Fulham's excellent FA Cup run of 1926 when they beat Everton and Liverpool before going out to Manchester United at the quarter-final stage. Oliver and Bert Barrett were two constants in an ever-changing Fulham defence during the late 1920s.

Even though the Lilliewhites languished in the Third Division, Len won an England cap against Belgium in May 1929, in a 5–1 victory in Brussels, and was also reserve when his country played Scotland in 1931. He made 39 appearances, alongside Bert Barrett and Syd Gibbons, in the half-back line as Fulham took the Third Division South title in 1931–32, and he was ever present the following season when they went close to promotion again.

Other honours came his way when Len toured Canada with the Football Association in 1931, and he also represented the Football League against the Army in October 1926. The clever wing-half left Fulham to become the coach at Cliftonville in July 1938 and was a physical training instructor during the war, after which he lived in Letchworth and coached local side Arlesley Town.

Appearances:

	Football League		FA Cup		GRAND TOTAL	
SEASON	Apps	Goals	Apps	Goals	Apps	Goals
1924–25	38	-	2	-	40	-
1925–26	41	-	5	-	46	-
1926–27	42	1	2	-	44	1
1927–28	41	-	1	-	42	-
1928–29	42	1	3	-	45	1
1929–30	28	-	3	-	31	-
1930–31	40	1	4	-	44	1
1931–32	39	-	4	-	43	-
1932–33	42	-	1	-	43	-
1933–34	40	-	2	-	42	-
1934–35	13	-	1	-	14	-
TOTAL	406	3	28	-	434	3

Paul PARKER

Born: West Ham, London, 4 April 1964

With his great athleticism and the ability to recover very quickly when beaten by a forward, Paul Parker belied his slight build. He was also excellent in the air for such a small man and could out-jump players much taller than himself. He established himself in the first team during 1983–84 and made his debut for the England Under-21 side in a 2–0 victory over Finland, at The Dell, in October 1984. Paul went on to win eight caps at that level on top of his three Youth international caps gained earlier in his Fulham career. He lived through all the trials and tribulations of the Fulham Park Rangers saga, when the chairman David Bulstrode wanted to amalgamate Fulham and Queen's Park Rangers, and he moved to Loftus Road with Dean Coney for a joint fee of £500,000, as part of the deal that enabled the new consortium, led by Jimmy Hill, to create a new club – Fulham (1987).

Parker looked instantly at ease in the top flight and soon won his first England cap, eventually appearing 19 times for his country. The Rangers man played in England's run to the 1990 World Cup semi-final, where they lost a penalty shoot-out to Germany. An established England international when he moved to

Manchester United for £2 million in August 1991, he was to play a key role in their all-conquering side over the next few years. They won the League title in 1992–93, the League and FA Cup double in 1993–94, and Paul also played in the 1992 and 1994 League Cup Finals at Wembley. He came to Fulham for a second spell in January 1997 but quickly moved on to Golden Club (Hong Kong), Chelsea and Heybridge Swifts. After retiring from playing, Paul was director of football at Ashford Town, manager at Chelmsford City and Welling United, and consultant at Folkestone Invicta before working for MUTV.

Appearances:

	Football League		FA Cup		League Cup		GRAND TOTAL	
SEASON	Apps	Goals	Apps	Goals	Apps	Goals	Apps	Goals
1980–81	1	-	-	-	-	-	1	-
1981–82	2+3	-	-	-	-	-	2+3	-
1982–83	6+11	-	3	-	2	-	11+11	-
1983–84	34	-	2	-	4	-	40	-
1984–85	36	-	1	-	3	-	40	-
1985–86	30	-	1	-	3	-	34	-
1986–87	31	2	4	-	4	1	39	3
1996–97	3	-	-		-		3	-
TOTAL	143+14	2	11	-	16	1	170+14	3

PENN, Frank

Born: Edmonton, Middlesex, 15 April 1896
Died: St Pancras, London, 19 December 1966

Joining Fulham as a teenager in 1915, Frank Penn spent 50 years as a player and a trainer and worked under 12 managers at the Cottage. Playing for the Vicar of Wakefield FC and Alston Rangers, he qualified as an engineer and mechanic, and he served with the Royal Flying Corp during the war. He also made 73 appearances for the Lilliewhites, scoring five goals, in wartime football, including gaining a runners'-up medal in the 1919 Victory Cup Final against Chelsea.

Penn was usually first choice at outside-left after 1919 but lost his place to Harvey Darvill for a while during 1921–22. He played on the left wing and at left-half during Fulham's run to an FA Cup quarter-final in 1926, which included victories over Liverpool's two main clubs. The lively winger played in a trial match for England

in April 1919 when he represented the South against the North and also appeared for the FA against the Army in October 1926, at The Den.

Between August 1926 and September 1929, Penn missed just three games for the Lilliewhites but eventually lost his place to Jack Finch after September 1931. His final game was over Easter 1934 and Frank held the appearance record for Fulham with 460 first-class appearances. Eddie Lowe overtook it in the 1960s. Penn became the assistant trainer in 1934, suceeding Bill Voisey as chief trainer five years later, and qualifying as a physiotherapist. He remained as the Fulham trainer until 1965 when he retired but died soon afterwards. His son Frank (Junior) played a few games for Fulham during World War Two.

Appearances:

	Football League		FA Cup		GRAND TOTAL	
SEASON	Apps	Goals	Apps	Goals	Apps	Goals
1919–20	23	1	-	-	23	1
1920–21	36	2	5	-	41	2
1921–22	23	-	-	-	23	-
1922–23	41	1	1	-	42	1
1923–24	36	2	3	-	39	2
1924–25	40	2	2	-	42	2
1925–26	27	5	5	1	32	6
1926–27	41	7	2	-	43	7
1927–28	40	3	1	-	41	3
1928–29	42	10	3	1	45	11
1929–30	38	6	5	3	43	9
1930–31	30	6	3	2	33	8
1931–32	9	-	2	-	11	-
1933–34	1	-	-	-	1	-
TOTAL	427	45	32	7	459	52

PESCHISOLIDO, Paul

Born: Scarborough, Canada, 25 May 1971

A Canadian international with over 50 caps for his country, Peschisolido joined Birmingham City from Toronto Blizzard in November 1992 for £25,000. He moved to Stoke City in August 1994 then had a second spell at St Andrew's, where his wife Karen Brady was the chief executive. Fulham's first million-pound signing, Peschisolido joined Fulham from West Bromwich Albion in October 1997 for a record fee of £1.1 million. He was among new management team Ray Wilkins and Kevin Keegan's first signings and, he had a terrific first season at the Cottage, scoring 13 goals in 34 appearances. He always looked dangerous with his fast darting runs, and he rarely missed the target when he had an opportunity to score.

However, Peschisolido struggled to maintain this form the following season, being hit by suspension and injuries, but he won a Second Division Championship medal at the end of 1998–99. New manager Jean Tigana decided that he was surplus to requirements when he took over in 2000, and Paul had loan spells with Queen's Park Rangers, Sheffield

United and Norwich City during 2000–01 and was finally sold to Sheffield United for a cut price £125,000 in July 2001. Surprisingly, he was rarely a first-team regular at Bramall Lane and moved on to Derby County in March 2004, and played when they beat West Bromwich Albion in the First Division Play-off Final at Wembley in May 2007.

Appearances:

	Football League		FA Cup		League Cup		GRAND TOTAL	
SEASON	Apps	Goals	Apps	Goals	Apps	Goals	Apps	Goals
1997–98	34	13	3	-	-	-	37	13
1998–99	19+14	7	5	2	1+1	1	25+15	10
1999–2000	18+12	4	1+1	-	4	3	23+13	7
2000–01	-	-	-	-	2	-	2	-
TOTAL	71+26	24	9+1	2	7+1	4	87+28	30

PEYTON, Gerry

Born: Birmingham, 20 May 1956

A goalkeeper who made difficult saves look easy and was consistent and reliable, Gerry Peyton quickly became a firm favourite with the Fulham faithful after his move to the Cottage in December 1976 for a £35,000 fee. Despite failing to make the grade at Aston Villa, he moved to Atherstone Town where he was spotted by Burnley and joined the club in May 1975.

Gerry missed just three games for the Cottagers between January 1977 and October 1980 but picked up a serious injury at the beginning of 1981 and was replaced by the up-and-coming Jim Stannard. The following season, he was first choice again as Fulham finished runners-up in the Third Division.

The Birmingham-born goalkeeper won the first of his 33 caps for the Republic of Ireland against Spain in 1979 after Don Revie had tried to call him up for the England Under-21 side, but he decided to play for the country of his parents. Most (22) of his caps came while he was at the Cottage, and he was in the 1988 European Championship and the 1990 World Cup Finals squad but was not selected to play.

Peyton went on loan to Southend United in 1983–84 but returned later to reclaim his place in the side. The Eire international moved to Bournemouth on a free transfer in July 1986 and returned to the Cottage in triumph when his new club clinched the Third Division title with a 3–1 victory in May 1997. He had been ever present for the Cherries that season and went on to make 238 appearances for the south-coast club over the next five seasons. Everton paid £80,000 for services in July 1991, and he subsequently played on loan for Bolton Wanderers, Norwich City and Chelsea then signed for Brentford and West Ham. He coached in Japan with Vissel Kobe from January 1994 and with AIK Stockholm in 1999 before returning as goalkeeping coach with Fulham in May 2001. After two seasons with the Cottagers, Gerry moved to Arsenal in a similar role, where he continues to work today.

Appearances:

	Football League		FA Cup		League Cup		GRAND TOTAL	
SEASON	Apps	Goals	Apps	Goals	Apps	Goals	Apps	Goals
1976–77	23	-	2	-	-	-	25	-
1977–78	42	-	1	-	2	-	45	-
1978–79	40	-	3	-	2	-	45	-
1979–80	31	-	2	-	2	-	35	-
1980–81	28	-	6	-	2	-	36	-
1981–82	44	-	2	-	7	-	53	-
1982–83	42	-	3	-	4	-	49	-
1983–84	27	-	2	-	2	-	31	-
1984–85	32	-	-	-	3	-	35	-
1985–86	36	-	1	-	4	-	41	-
TOTAL	345	-	22	-	28	-	395	-

PIKE, Martin

Born: South Shields, Tyneside, 21 October 1964

A good tackler and composed player who loved to attack, Martin Pike failed to make the grade at West Brom and joined Peterborough United in August 1983 as a midfield player. He was quickly converted into a full-back and attracted the attention of Sheffield United, whom he joined for £20,000 in August 1986. He helped United to promotion from Division Three in 1988–89, but after losing his place at Bramall Lane he had loan spells at Tranmere Rovers and Bolton Wanderers. He joined Fulham in February 1990 for £55,000 and missed just two games between his debut and October 1993, after which he was hit by a serious injury that kept him out of the side for some time. Robbie Herrera was signed on loan as cover, but when Pike returned, his form dipped, and he was released shortly after Fulham were relegated to the Third Division. He joined Rotherham United in August 1994, but his spell at Millmoor was unhappy as his continued to be plagued by injuries. Pikey was released and joined Northern League Durham City in August 1996 and later played for Blyth Spartans before joining Bedlington Terriers in the summer of 1998. He helped them to two Northern League titles, and he played at Wembley in the 1999 FA Vase Final, where the Terriers lost 1–0 to Tiverton Town. Pike is presently Fulham's North East scout after a spell working for Sunderland's youth academy.

Appearances:

	Football League		FA Cup		League Cup		GRAND TOTAL	
SEASON	Apps	Goals	Apps	Goals	Apps	Goals	Apps	Goals
1989–90	20	2	-	-	-	-	20	2
1990–91	45+1	3	3	1	2	-	50+1	4
1991–92	45	2	1	-	2	-	48	2
1992–93	46	6	1	-	2	-	49	6
1993–94	31+2	1	-	-	4	-	35+2	1
TOTAL	187+3	14	5	1	10	-	202+3	15

PRICE, Johnny

Born: Mhow, Madyha Pradesh, India, 4 December 1903
Died: Southsea, Hampshire, 22 June 1987

Price was one of Fulham manager Joe Bradshaw's best-ever signings and appeared on a regular basis at inside-left for the Cottagers from August 1928 until December 1934. During the 1920s, he served with the 10th Royal Hussars and Coldstream Guards, represented the Army at football, and his regiment won the Cavalry Cup in 1924 and 1926. He won three England amateur caps while with Woking and scored 66 goals in 74 games for the Cards. He played in two Surrey Senior Cup Finals and also represented the Isthmian League, the Surrey County FA and toured with the Middlesex Wanderers.

Price appeared once for Brentford as an amateur before joining Fulham as a professional on leaving the army in June 1928, at the age of 25. He went straight into the first team and scored 14 goals in 32 League and Cup appearances during the 1928–29 season. A goalscoring inside-left when he first signed for Fulham, he later played in a deeper role, after 1931, playing more as a schemer then a striker. He played in a full England trial in March 1929 for the Rest versus England and also toured South Africa with the Football Association during the summer of 1929. Johnny won a Third Division South Championship medal in 1931–32 but played only eight games for the club

after December 1934, mainly due to injuries. A hip injury was to end his career shortly after he joined Port Vale, and he went to Wimbledon as coach in November 1937. He stayed at Plough Lane until 1955 when he became Yiewsley as coach while also working in an engineering factory's accounts office in Colnbrook, close to where he lived at nearby Wraysbury.

Renowned in the greyhound-racing world, Price would regularly bring his greyhounds into the Cottage for treatment from Fulham's physiotherapists. He was assistant secretary at Fulham in the early 1960s but later lived in retirement at Southsea for many years.

Appearances:

	Football League		FA Cup		GRAND TOTAL	
SEASON	Apps	Goals	Apps	Goals	Apps	Goals
1928–29	29	13	3	1	32	14
1929–30	25	9	4	1	29	10
1930–31	19	6	1	1	20	7
1931–32	32	4	5	1	37	5
1932–33	30	6	1	-	31	6
1933–34	26	4	-	-	26	4
1934–35	23	4	1	-	24	4
1935–36	4	2	-	-	4	2
1936–37	2	1	-	-	2	1
TOTAL	190	49	15	4	205	53

QUESTED, Len

Born: Folkestone, Kent, 9 January 1925

The engine room of the side, Len Quested never stopped working and running for the team and would be described today as a midfield dynamo. He attended St Peter's School (Folkestone) and represented Folkestone and Kent Schools before playing for Invicta FC and Folkestone Town while serving in the Royal Navy during the war.

Len joined Fulham in 1943 and made his debut in January 1944, just before his 19th birthday, scoring two goals in a 6–3 victory at Brighton. After his demobilisation, the effervescent wing-half signed as a professional in August 1946 and became a regular first-team performer from May 1947. He played in Fulham's FA Cup run of 1948, which included an excellent 1–0 victory at Goodison Park. Len, alongside Jim Taylor and Pat Beasley, formed the backbone of the side that took Fulham to the Second Division Championship in 1948–49, and his first League goal came in a dramatic and vital 2–1 victory over main rivals West Brom at The Hawthorns in March 1949.

Len did not look out of place in the top flight, and he won an England B cap against Holland in February 1950, at St James' Park,

Newcastle. Ever present during Fulham's first season in the top flight, Len played in an additional losing FA Cup quarter-final in 1951, and the club really missed his power and enthusiasm when he was strangely exchanged for Huddersfield's Jeff Taylor in November 1951. The fans were angered by his departure and vented their anger on manager Bill Dodgin and his son Bill (jnr).

Quested captained the Terriers to promotion back to the top flight in 1952–53, and he also toured South Africa with the Football Association side during the summer of 1956. Len emigrated to Australia in 1957 and played for Hakoah, Auburn and Awaba before coaching Auburn and managing Canterbury (Sydney).

Appearances:

	Football League		FA Cup		GRAND TOTAL	
SEASON	Apps	Goals	Apps	Goals	Apps	Goals
1946–47	6	-	-	-	6	-
1947–48	36	-	5	1	41	1
1948–49	39	1	1	-	40	1
1949–50	42	1	2	-	44	1
1950–51	39	4	5	-	44	4
1951–52	13	-	-	-	13	-
TOTAL	175	6	13	1	188	7

REYNOLDS, Arthur

Born: Dartford, Kent, 24 January 1887
Died: London, January qtr 1971

Given a testimonial by Fulham against Chelsea in April 1923, Arthur Reynolds was described in the programme as 'a quiet and unassuming fellow who is popular with all at the club and is a very consistent goalkeeper whose off-days are few.' He was one of the greatest goalkeepers in the club's history and unlucky not to gain more honours during his illustrious career. He held the appearance record for Fulham goalkeepers of 420 League and Cup games before Jim Stannard surpassed this total 70 years later. This was despite losing four seasons to World War One when he was often away on war work.

Reynolds started his career with Dartford and moved to the Cottage in April 1910, was ever present during his first two seasons, and played in the club's FA Cup run to the quarter-finals in 1912. He represented London against Birmingham in October 1913 and also the Football League against the Southern League in October 1914. Six years later, he appeared in an international trial match for the South versus England at Craven Cottage but never made the full England side despite being one of the best 'keepers in the country.

Reynolds was always difficult to beat, and he had six clean sheets on the trot during 1921–22 and 1922–23 and went nine home games without conceding a goal from March–October 1920. Missing only three games between September 1919 and February 1925, Reynolds left Fulham for Orient in August 1925 but was reported to have retired after three games for their reserves.

A year later, Arthur made a comeback with his home-town club Dartford and signed many former Fulham players when he became player-manager in September 1926. He was still playing for the club in season 1928–29 at the age of 41 and was a regular visitor to Craven Cottage up until his death. It has recently been discovered that he was called Arthur William Reynolds and was born in 1887 and not 1889 as previously thought.

Appearances:

	Football League		FA Cup		GRAND TOTAL	
SEASON	Apps	Goals	Apps	Goals	Apps	Goals
1909–10	2	-	-	-	2	-
1910–11	38	-	1	-	39	-
1911–12	38	-	4	-	42	-
1912–13	36	-	1	-	37	-
1913–14	30	-	1	-	31	-
1914–15	19	-	-	-	19	-
1919–20	38	-	1	-	39	-
1920–21	40	-	5	-	45	-
1921–22	42	-	3	-	45	-
1922–23	42	-	1	-	43	-
1923–24	41	-	3	-	44	-
1924–25	33	-	1	-	34	-
TOTAL	399	-	21	-	420	-

ROBSON, Sir Bobby

Born: Sacriston, Co. Durham, 18 February 1933

It was in October 1950 that Fulham beat off strong competition from Sunderland and Newcastle United to sign Bobby from Langley Park, a small club in County Durham. He helped form a great inside-forward trio with Beddy Jezzard and Johnny Haynes scoring 19 goals in 1952–53 and 23 in 1954–55. Fulham had many offers for his services before Bobby moved to The Hawthorns for £25,000 in March 1956. Robson won 20 England caps, but none while with Fulham, and also played for the Under-23 and B sides and five times for the Football League.

After 257 appearances and 61 goals for Albion, Robson moved back to Craven Cottage for a second spell and played in a more defensive position in the Fulham side. A cultured player, he gave the Whites another five seasons of excellent service before retiring in May 1967, when his career total was 627 appearances, in which he scored 141 goals.

Robson moved to North America to coach Vancouver Royals but the following January returned to Fulham as the club's manager. It was an unhappy time, and he was sacked 10 months later with Fulham close to the bottom of the Second Division. Robson was soon given another chance when he was appointed as manager of Ipswich Town in January 1969. It was the start of a highly-successful 13 years in charge at Portman

Road. Ipswich should have won the League title in 1980–81 but were pipped by Aston Villa, and that season they won the UEFA Cup, beating AZ Alkmaar over two legs in an exciting Final. His greatest triumph came in the 1978 FA Cup Final when Ipswich beat Arsenal.

Robson succeeded another former Fulham player, Ron Greenwood, as the England manager in July 1982. His highlight as England boss came in the 1990 World Cup Finals. He took England to the semi-final where they were unfortunate to lose to West Germany on penalties after a 1–1 draw. They reached the quarter-finals of the 1986 World Cup but lost 2–1 to Argentina. Since leaving the England job, Robson has managed PSV Eindhoven twice, Sporting Lisbon, Porto, Barcelona (1998–99) and Newcastle United (1999–2004) with plenty of success. Bobby never seems to want to retire, and in September 2006 he became consultant to the Republic of Ireland despite suffering from ill health.

Appearances:

	Football League		FA Cup		League Cup		GRAND TOTAL	
SEASON	Apps	Goals	Apps	Goals	Apps	Goals	Apps	Goals
1950–51	1	-	-	-	-	-	1	-
1951–52	16	3	-	-	-	-	16	3
1952–53	35	19	1	-	-	-	36	19
1953–54	33	13	1	1	-	-	34	14
1954–55	42	23	1	-	-	-	43	23
1955–56	25	10	2	-	-	-	27	10
1962–63	34	1	2	1	2	-	38	2
1963–64	39	1	2	-	1	-	42	1
1964–65	42	1	2	-	3	1	47	2
1965–66	36	6	-	-	3	-	39	6
1966–67	41	-	3	-	3	-	47	-
TOTAL	344	77	14	2	12	1	370	80

ROOKE, Ronnie

Born: *Guildford, Surrey, 7 December 1912*
Died: *Bedford, 9 June 1985*

One of the great goalscorers in Fulham's history, Ronnie Rooke was a clinical and ruthless finisher with either foot and was just as effective with his head. He played for Guildford City and Woking before being signed by Crystal Palace in March 1933 and became a prolific goalscorer in their reserves (scoring over 50 goals during 1933–34) but was rarely selected for the first team.

Fulham manager Jack Peart picked up a great bargain when he paid just £300 for Rooke's services in October 1936, and he scored a hat-trick on his debut against West Ham. His best tally was 27 goals in 1938–39, which included all six in a 6–0 victory over Bury in the FA Cup in January 1939, but his career was to be greatly affected by the war. The bandy-legged forward scored 212 goals in 199 wartime games for Fulham between 1939 and 1946 while serving in the RAF. However, he gained just one wartime cap against Wales in October 1942 and failed to shine in a 2–1 defeat. He played for an Arsenal XI against Moscow Dynamo in November 1945 and was surprisingly transferred to the Gunners in December 1946 for £1,000 plus Dave Nelson and Cyril Grant. The reasons for his transfer remain a mystery. The following season Rooke helped the Gunners to clinch the League Championship

when he scored 33 goals. He was player-manager at Crystal Palace from 1949–50 and may have been the first manager to ever be sent off when he got his marching orders in a match with Millwall during the 1950–51 season. He had two spells as manager of Bedford Town during the 1950s, was player-coach for Haywards Heath from June 1955 and also turned out for Addlestone. In later life he worked as a PRO for Whitbread's Brewery and as a porter at Luton Airport.

Appearances:

	Football League		FA Cup		GRAND TOTAL	
SEASON	Apps	Goals	Apps	Goals	Apps	Goals
1936–37	22	19	-	-	22	19
1937–38	27	17	1	-	28	17
1938–39	38	21	2	6	40	27
1945–46	-	-	2	2	2	2
1946–47	18	13	-	-	18	13
TOTAL	105	70	5	8	110	78

ROSS, Harry

Born: *Brechin, Angus, 4 April 1881*
Died: *Brechin, Angus, 28 November 1953*

A tough tackling full-back who was rarely beaten by an opposing winger, Harry Ross was

an excellent passer and became Fulham's penalty and free-kick exponent. He joined Burnley from Brechin Harp in May 1899 and went on to play 111 League and Cup games in the Second Division for the Clarets before joining Fulham in May 1904. He cost a fee of £230, but the club did not have to pay this until they joined the Football League in 1907, as there were no formal transfer arrangements between the Football and Southern Leagues.

Harry was the regular right-back as Fulham won two Southern League Championships between 1905–07. He kept his place during the club's first season in the Football League and appeared in every game during Fulham's run to an FA Cup semi-final in 1908. He was dropped after a poor performance against Glossop in September 1908 and was transferred to St Mirren a month later. He signed for both Southport Central and Darwen in October 1909, but the consequence of this was that he was not allowed to play for either club and returned to his home town to play for Brechin City in November 1910. Harry was trainer to St Augustine's FC at Lawrence, Massachusetts, in 1929 when his son David joined Burnley, but he failed to make the grade at Turf Moor. Harry returned to the Scotland after the war to live in Brechin and died there after an accidental fall in 1953.

Appearances:

	Southern League		Football League		FA Cup		GRAND TOTAL	
SEASON	Apps	Goals	Apps	Goals	Apps	Goals	Apps	Goals
1904–05	28	2			7	1	35	3
1905–06	33	1			2	-	35	1
1906–07	37	6			4	-	41	6
1907–08			28	2	6	2	34	4
1908–09			1	1	-	-	1	1
TOTAL	98	9	29	3	19	3	146	15

SAHA, Louis

Born: Paris, France, 8 August 1978

A forward with everything, Louis Saha has lightning pace, is good in the air, has close control and can score goals with ease. He became the first player since Bedford Jezzard to score 30 goals in a season as Fulham clinched the First Division title in 2000–01. He was one

of Jean Tigana's first signings when he joined Fulham from French club Metz during June 2000 for a £2.1 million fee. He quickly started to hit the net, and by Christmas he had already scored 20 goals and formed excellent striking partnerships with Barry Hayles and Luis Boa Morte as Fulham ran away with the First Division title. A great timer of his runs into the box, he often leaves defences in his wake as he explodes into the penalty area to score goals, but he did not score so often during his first season in the Premiership and was plagued by a series of injuries during 2002–03. However, he was back to his best the following season and had scored 15 goals in just 22 appearances when Sir Alex Ferguson came into the picture and signed him for Manchester United in January 2004 for £12.82 million. The French Under-21 international had played on loan at Newcastle United prior to coming to Craven Cottage but did not show his best form. Since moving to Old Trafford, the Frenchman has become very injury prone and missed the 2004 and 2005 FA Cup Finals but played in the 2006 Carling Cup Final, in which United beat Wigan Athletic 4–0 at Cardiff, and had a long run in the side as the Reds won the Premiership title in 2006–07.

Louis appeared for France in Euro 2004 and the World Cup Finals of 2006 and was a playing substitute in the quarter and semi-finals but did not play in the Final against Italy, where the French lost on penalties after a 1–1 draw.

Appearances:

	Football League		FA Cup		League Cup		GRAND TOTAL	
SEASON	Apps	Goals	Apps	Goals	Apps	Goals	Apps	Goals
2000–01	39+4	27	1	-	3+1	5	43+5	32
2001–02	28+8	8	5+1	-	0+2	1	33+11	9
2002–03	13+4	5	3	1	-	-	16+4	6
2003–04	20+1	13	1	2	-		21+1	15
TOTAL	100+17	53	10+1	3	3+3	6	113+21	62

SCOTT, Peter

Born: Notting Hill, London, 1 October 1963

Peter Scott came through Fulham's youth scheme after representing Berkshire Schools and developed into a hard-working midfielder who gained a regular place in the side from August

1985. Despite 'Scotty' scoring twice in a 3–1 victory over Leeds United in the first game of 1985–86, Fulham were relegated that season.

Peter appeared in the record 10–0 defeat at Anfield in the League Cup in September 1986 and played through the dark days of 1987 when the club nearly went out of existence. His best season at the Cottage was 1988–89 when Fulham reached the Third Division Play-offs, but he was sent off against Bristol Rovers at the Cottage after a rash challenge.

Scott had a joint testimonial with John Marshall in 1990 with matches against Chelsea and Everton. Despite playing most games during 1991–92, Fulham manager Don Mackay released him, and he moved to Bournemouth in August 1992. He was hit by a succession of injuries at Dean Court, and he was released and given a free transfer again. After a trial with Woking, Peter signed for Barnet in November 1993 and captained the side for the next two and a half seasons, making 88+8 appearances. Scott dropped down into non-League football after this and appeared for Hayes, Aylesbury United, and he ended his playing career with Beaconsfield SYCOB where he later became assistant manager and manager.

Appearances:

	Football League		FA Cup		League Cup		GRAND TOTAL	
SEASON	Apps	Goals	Apps	Goals	Apps	Goals	Apps	Goals
1981–82	1	-	-	-	-	-	1	-
1982–83	-	-	-	-	0+1	-	0+1	-
1983–84	31+1	4	2	-	2	1	35+1	5
1984–85	17+2	1	1	-	1+1	-	19+3	1
1985–86	32	5	1	-	4	-	37	5
1986–87	30	6	1	-	4	3	35	9
1987–88	22+1	2	-	-	-	-	22+1	2
1988–89	36+3	3	1	-	-	-	37+3	3
1989–90	41	3	1	1	4	2	46	6
1990–91	23	2	1	-	2	-	26	2
1991–92	37+2	1	1	-	1	-	39+2	1
TOTAL	270+9	27	9	1	18+2	6	297+11	34

SHARP, Jimmy

Born: Jordanstone, Alsyth, 11 October l880
Died: Fulham, London, 18 November 1949

A classic Scottish full-back, Jimmy Sharp was not the quickest but possessed great positional sense and superb anticipation. The Scottish international gained five caps and also represented the Scottish League against the Football League in March 1903. Sharp joined Dundee from local side East Craigie in August 1899 and had five seasons at Dens Park before moving south to join Fulham in May 1904. He had to compete with Harry Thorpe for the left-back berth during 1904–05 and joined Woolwich Arsenal, where he played in two losing FA Cup semi-finals, to Newcastle United 2–0 at the Victoria Ground, Stoke, in 1906 and to Sheffield Wednesday 3–1 at St Andrews, Birmingham, in 1907. Sharp moved north again to join Glasgow Rangers in April 1908 but stayed for only nine months before rejoining Fulham, who equalled their record transfer fee when they paid £1,000 for him. He moved to the US in July 1910 but returned four months later to reclaim the left-back berth. He played in Fulham's 1912 FA Cup run to the quarter-finals where they lost to West Bromwich Albion, but with the emergence of Tommy Burns Fulham

decided to sell Sharp to Chelsea in November 1912, where he made 64 appearances before he left the club in 1915.

Sharp joined Dundee United in September 1915 and retired from playing the following April. He returned to the Cottage for a third time in 1919 as the club's trainer and scored his first goal for Fulham in his final match in April 1920 when he was forced to play as Harold Crockford missed the team bus to Bury for a Second Division match. He moved with Jimmy Torrance to Walsall as trainer in June 1926 and moved onto Cliftonville as coach in August 1929. He worked in the building industry from the 1930s and was a regular visitor to the Cottage.

Appearances:

	Southern League		Football League		FA Cup		GRAND TOTAL	
SEASON	Apps	Goals	Apps	Goals	Apps	Goals	Apps	Goals
1904–05	18	-			1	-	19	-
1908–09			15	-	2	-	17	-
1909–10			28	-	3	-	31	-
1910–11			16	-	1	-	17	-
1911–12			25	-	4	-	29	-
1912–13			11	-	-	-	11	-
1919–20			1	1	-	-	1	1
TOTAL	18	-	96	1	11	-	125	1

SLOUGH, Alan

Born: Luton, Bedfordshire, 24 September 1947

Alan Slough was a 100 percent trier and was the engine room of the Fulham side in the mid-1970s. He started his career at Luton Town in May 1965 and helped the Hatters to the Fourth Division title in 1967–68 with promotion again two seasons later playing 301+10 games for the Hatters before joining Fulham in August 1973. His manager at Kenilworth Road was Alec Stock, and it was Alec who signed him for Fulham, along with Viv Busby, in August 1973 for a £45,000 fee. Stock initially selected him at left-back, but Alan later moved into midfield for the Whites. The high point of his career was playing at Wembley with Fulham in the 1975 FA Cup Final, and he played in every game during the Cup run and scored the vital goal that beat Hull City in the third-round second replay at Filbert Street. He was on the losing side again in the Anglo-Scottish Cup Final in December 1975 against Middlesbrough.

Alec Stock appointed him as captain after the departure of Alan Mullery in 1976, but he did not get on so well with Bobby Campbell and was sold to Peterborough United as player-coach in July 1977, where he scored a hat-trick of penalties against Chester and made 127+1 appearances for the Posh.

Slough moved to Torquay United in August 1982 and after this was player-coach with Weymouth, Yeovil Town and Minehead. Alan was player-manager of Christians in Sport (Torbay) from 1993–99, and he currently runs his own cleaning company and soccer schools in the Torbay area.

Appearances:

	Football League		FA Cup		League Cup		GRAND TOTAL	
SEASON	Apps	Goals	Apps	Goals	Apps	Goals	Apps	Goals
1973–74	33	2	3	-	4	-	40	2
1974–75	39	2	12	2	3	1	54	5
1975–76	40	5	1	-	3	-	44	5
1976–77	42	4	2	-	5	-	49	4
TOTAL	154	13	18	2	15	1	187	16

STANNARD, Jim

Born: Harold Hill, Essex, 6 October 1962

During the gloomy times of the early 1990s, one player stood out above the rest and that was Jim Stannard. Well built, some would say overweight, Jim was very brave and extremely agile for such a large man and it was often only Stannard who stood between Fulham and defeat. Joining the club from Ford United in June 1980, 'Big Jim' went straight from the South East Counties side into the first team when he made his debut against Swindon Town in January 1981 and went on to replace the injured Gerry Peyton for the rest of the season. When he later became disillusioned with reserve-team football, Stannard had two loan spells, at Southend United and at Charlton Athletic, before signing for the Shrimpers in July 1985 for £12,000. Fulham manager Ray Lewington brought him back to the Cottage in

August 1987 for a fee of £50,000 after 124 appearances for Southend. Some sources state that Jim scored a goal direct from a dropped kick at Crewe Alexandra in September 1989, but Andy Sayer touched the ball just before it entered the net.

Between August 1987 and April 1995, Stannard missed just 14 League and Cup games for the Whites. Fulham manager Ian Branfoot thought Jim was past his best, and he moved to Gillingham in June 1995, but he was proved wrong as Stannard broke a number of records in his first season at Priestfield. He was ever present in 1995–96 and let in only 20 goals all season, including only 14 away from home (a new Football League record), and this included 29 clean sheets, also a record. He was voted Gillingham's Player of the Year and selected for the PFA Divisional team of the Year. He became a goalkeeping coach with the Gills in 1998 and retired in May 1999 with a grand total of 697 appearances with his four clubs. He has since coached at Millwall and Brentford for two spells as well as managing Redbridge FC in 2005.

Appearances:

	Football League		FA Cup		League Cup		GRAND TOTAL	
SEASON	Apps	Goals	Apps	Goals	Apps	Goals	Apps	Goals
1980–81	17	-	-	-	-	-	17	-
1981–82	2	-	-	-	-	-	2	-
1982–83	-	-	-	-	-	-	-	-
1983–84	15	-	-	-	3	-	18	-
1984–85	7	-	1	-	-	-	8	-
1987–88	46	-	1	-	4	-	51	-
1988–89	47	-	1	-	2	-	50	-
1989–90	44	-	3	-	4	-	51	-
1990–91	42	-	2	-	-	-	44	-
1991–92	46	-	1	-	2	-	49	-
1992–93	43	-	1	-	2	-	46	-
1993–94	46	-	1	-	4	-	51	-
1994–95	36	-	3	-	4	-	43	-
TOTAL	391	-	14	-	25	-	430	-

STEVENS, Arthur

Born: Battersea, London, 13 January 1921
Died: Epsom, Surrey, January 2007

A very fast and direct outside-right or centre-forward, Arthur Stevens would centre accurately at great speed and often cut in for a shot at goal. He represented Battersea & Wandsworth Schools before playing for Wimbledon from 1937, scoring 38 goals in just 42 appearances, and he later joined Brentford and Sutton United before appearing for Fulham for the first time in 1941.

Arthur Stevens served Fulham for 25 years as player, trainer-coach and caretaker manager after signing professional forms with the club in December 1943. He served in the Royal Artillery and was involved in the D-Day landings in June 1944. He was not a regular first-team player until 1948–49 when he was ever present as Fulham won the Second Division title in the 1948–49 season, during which he scored 12 goals. After Fulham's relegation in 1952, he continued to score regularly in the Second Division and was part of a great forward line that also included Bobby Robson, Bedford Jezzard, Johnny Haynes and Charlie Mitten. His best season for goals scored was 1956–57 when he hit 17. He played in two losing FA Cup quarter-final defeats against Blackpool in 1948 and 1951 and came even closer to a Wembley Cup Final in 1958 when, after playing in all seven games of the Cup run, scored in both semi-finals against Manchester United, but

Fulham eventually lost to the Reds 5–3 in the replay at Highbury.

The following season, he lost his place to Graham Leggat but remained on the coaching staff after his retirement in 1960 and was caretaker manager between Jezzard and Buckingham.

After leaving the Cottage in January 1968, Arthur and his wife ran a grocer's store in Banstead, and he later lived in Epsom until his recent death. His tally of 124 goals is remarkable considering much of his career was spent on the right wing.

Appearances:

	Football League		FA Cup		GRAND TOTAL	
SEASON	Apps	Goals	Apps	Goals	Apps	Goals
1946–47	16	5	-	-	16	5
1947–48	23	11	5	4	28	15
1948–49	42	12	1	-	43	12
1949–50	39	5	2	-	41	5
1950–51	42	11	5	1	47	12
1951–52	39	7	1	-	40	7
1952–53	36	13	-	-	36	13
1953–54	32	10	3	1	35	11
1954–55	22	8	1	1	23	9
1955–56	30	9	-	-	30	9
1956–57	40	15	2	2	42	17
1957–58	22	4	7	5	29	9
1958–59	3	-	-	-	3	-
TOTAL	386	110	27	14	413	124

STRONG, Les

Born: Streatham, London, 3 July 1953

A real Fulham character, Les Strong needed a sense of humour, as he was the only player to survive the troublesome management period of Bobby Campbell. When 'Strongy' joined Fulham, he was a pencil thin right-winger, and by the time it ended he was a stocky full-back. He had been converted into a left-back by December 1973, and he took his fair share of stick from the characters in the Stevenage Road enclosure. Strong improved greatly, playing alongside Bobby Moore in defence, and played in every game during the 1975 FA Cup run but sadly missed the Final due to an injury. He had a special medal struck for him by the FA. Strong scored an unfortunate own-goal in the Anglo-Scottish Cup Final of 1975 at Ayresome Park and this proved to be the winning goal of a two-leg Final. Missing only six games between April 1976 and September 1982, Strong captained the side to promotion in 1981–82 and earned a well-deserved testimonial against an England team in May 1982. He played his last game for Fulham shortly after this and moved to Brentford on loan in December 1982. He signed for Crystal Palace on a free transfer in August

1983 and ended his career with one appearance for Rochdale in October 1984. He was catering manager at Fulham from 1985–87 and has been a coach with Walton Casuals since 2003 and part of Fulham's hospitality team.

Appearances:

	Football League		FA Cup		League Cup		GRAND TOTAL	
SEASON	Apps	Goals	Apps	Goals	Apps	Goals	Apps	Goals
1972–73	18+2	2	-	-	-	-	18+2	2
1973–74	17+1	-	3	-	-	-	20+1	-
1974–75	40	-	11	-	3	-	54	-
1975–76	36	-	-	-	3	-	39	-
1976–77	42	-	2	-	5	-	49	-
1977–78	41	1	1	-	2	-	44	1
1978–79	41	1	3	-	2	-	46	1
1979–80	41	-	1	-	2	-	44	-
1980–81	45	1	5	-	2	1	52	2
1981–82	46	-	2	-	7	-	55	-
1982–83	3	-	-	-	-	-	3	-
TOTAL	370+3	5	28	-	26	1	424+3	6

SYMONS, Kit

Born: Basingstoke, Hampshire, 8 March 1971

A solid all-round central-defender who was good in the air and sound on the floor, Kit Symons nearly broke Fulham's goalscoring record for a defender in 1998–99 but was one short of Roger Brown's record of 12 goals. Kit had many ups and downs during his playing career, and as a 21-year-old he played in a losing FA Cup semi-final for Portsmouth against Liverpool in 1992. After gaining Welsh Youth caps, two Under-21 and one B cap, Symons won 33 full Welsh caps, often playing alongside Chris Coleman and Andy Melville. Manchester City paid Portsmouth £1.6 million when they signed Symons in August 1995. After starting 1997–98 as captain, it gradually became a nightmare for him, ending in relegation to the Second Division and Kit being given a free transfer by manager Joe Royle. Some people wondered whether he could recover from this experience, but he was soon forming a great central-defensive partnership with Chris Coleman at Fulham, and they took the Cottagers to the Second Division title in 1998–99.

With the arrival of Andy Melville in the summer of 1999, Kit's appearances became less frequent, but he remained an important member of Fulham's squad. After Chris Coleman's dreadful car accident in January 2001, He returned to the side and performed outstandingly well as Fulham clinched the First Division Championship. However, with the signings of Alain Goma and Abdesalam Ouaddou by Jean Tigana, his chances of first-team action greatly diminished, and he was sold to Crystal Palace in December 2001 for £400,000. Kit was caretaker manager at Palace during November 2003 and has been their assistant manager since then.

Appearances:

	Football League		FA Cup		League Cup		GRAND TOTAL	
SEASON	Apps	Goals	Apps	Goals	Apps	Goals	Apps	Goals
1998–99	45	11	7	-	5	-	57	11
1999–2000	27+2	2	4	-	5+1	-	36+3	2
2000–01	22+2	-	1	-	5	-	28+2	-
2001–02	2+2	-	-	-	-	-	2+2	-
TOTAL	96+6	13	12	-	15+1	-	123+7	13

TAYLOR, Jim

Born: Cowley near Uxbridge, Middlesex, 5 November 1917
Died: Reading, Berkshire, 6 March 2001

Good in the air and quick in the tackle, Jim Taylor had sound positional play and good

distribution. After playing for Lowe Sawyer FC and Hillingdon British Legion, he joined Fulham in March 1938. During the war he served with the Royal Navy and played 88 wartime games, scoring six goals, for Fulham and also appeared as a guest for Brentford, Chelsea, Burnley, Luton Town and St Mirren.

Taylor made his debut in a friendly at Luton Town on 7 October 1939 and helped the club reach the semi-finals of the National War Cup, where they lost 4–3 to West Ham at Stamford Bridge in June 1940. He did not make his League debut until August 1946 in the disastrous 7–2 defeat at Bury at the age of 28, and then missed only six games until February 1950. He formed an excellent half-back line with Len Quested and Pat Beasley as Fulham became the Second Division Champions of 1948–49.

Taylor was 33 when he made his debut for England against Argentina in a 2–1 victory at Wembley in May 1951 and his other cap came against Portugal the same month. After touring Canada with the Football Association, he was drafted into the England squad that played in the ill-fated 1950 World Cup Finals in Brazil but was not selected to play. He played three times for the Football League between 1948–51 and also represented the London FA. A Fulham regular until April 1953, Taylor moved to Loftus Road, where he made 44 appearances, then became player-manager of Tunbridge Wells Rangers in May 1954 and was later the manager of Yiewsley and Uxbridge. He lived in retirement at Spencer's Wood, Reading, having worked as a painter and decorator at Windsor Castle.

Appearances:

	Football League		FA Cup		GRAND TOTAL	
SEASON	Apps	Goals	Apps	Goals	Apps	Goals
1945–46	-	-	2	-	2	-
1946–47	42	3	1	-	43	3
1947–48	36	2	5	-	41	2
1948–49	42	-	1	-	43	-
1949–50	35	-	2	-	37	-
1950–51	37	-	4	-	41	-
1951–52	33	-	1	-	34	-
1952–53	36	-	1	-	37	-
TOTAL	261	5	17	-	278	5

TAYLOR, Maik

Born: Hildesheim, Germany, 4 September 1971

An underrated goalkeeper who was often spectacular but also did the basics very well, the safe and reliable Maik Taylor was very unlucky to lose his place to van der Sar when Fulham reached the Premiership in 2001. After serving in the British Army, Taylor played for Petersfield United, Basingstoke Town, and Farnborough Town before signing for League club Barnet for £700 in June 1995 at the age of 23. The Barnet manager was former England 'keeper Ray Clemence, who helped greatly to improve Maik as a goalkeeper. He was later sold to Southampton in January 1997 for £500,000 after 84 appearances for the Bees, but he was unable to gain a regular place in the side with the Saints.

The Fulham management team of Ray Wilkins and Kevin Keegan paid a bargain £800,000 when they signed Taylor in November 1997. He had a great season in 1998–99, as Fulham finished as Second Division Champions. Not only was he ever present, but he also kept 24 clean sheets in 46 League appearances for the club. He was soon capped for Northern Ireland and has mainly been their first-choice 'keeper ever since. He had another fine season as Fulham

won the First Division title in 2000–01 and, having missed very few games since joining the club, found himself a reserve when manager Jean Tigana signed Edwin van der Sar during the summer of 2001. Maik was forced to watch from the substitutes bench for much of the next two seasons. He became fed up with playing second fiddle and so moved to Birmingham City on a year's loan in August 2003. He signed for the club the following March for £1.3 million and was one of their goalkeepers as they won promotion back to the Premiership in 2007.

Appearances:

	Football League		FA Cup		League Cup		GRAND TOTAL	
SEASON	Apps	Goals	Apps	Goals	Apps	Goals	Apps	Goals
1997–98	30	-	2	-	-	-	32	-
1998–99	46	-	7	-	5	-	58	-
1999–2000	46	-	4	-	7	-	57	
2000–01	44	-	1	-	5	-	50	-
2001–02	1	-	2	-	3	-	6	-
2002–03	18+1	-	4	-	2	-	24+1	-
TOTAL	185+1	-	20	-	22	-	227+1	-

THOMAS, Glen

Born: Hackney, London, 6 October 1967

Involved with Fulham from the age of 10, Glen Thomas spent 10 years as a professional at Craven

Cottage but left after a dispute over his contract with Ian Branfoot. A naturally left-footed footballer who played at either left-back or as a central-defender for the Whites, he struggled against the faster players but was a good tackler and sometimes commanding in the air. He gained a regular place in the side during 1988–89 as Fulham had a great run in to reach the Third Division Play-offs but lost to Bristol Rovers over two legs. Injury kept him out for much of the following season, but he missed just a handful of games over the next couple of seasons. Rumours about a possible move to West Ham United in 1993 never materialised, but Glen remained unsettled after this. When new manager Ian Branfoot could not persuade him to sign a new contract, he was released on a free transfer after almost 300 games for Fulham and was quickly replaced by Mark Blake. After training with Crystal Palace, Glen signed for Peterborough United in November 1994 but struggled to gain a regular place in the side, and he moved on to Barnet in March 1995. Glen seemed to lose his form after leaving the Cottage and also struggled when he moved to Gillingham in January 1996 for a £15,000 fee. He was unlucky with injuries while at Priestfield and nearly lost an eye during a training accident, and he decided to retire after a loan spell at Brighton when it became clear he would never be fit enough to play first-class football again. Thomas made a comeback with non-League Barking in March 1999 then played for Aveley, Bishop's Stortford and Ford United, where he was also joint caretaker manager during 2002.

Appearances:

	Football League		FA Cup		League Cup		GRAND TOTAL	
SEASON	Apps	Goals	Apps	Goals	Apps	Goals	Apps	Goals
1986–87	1	-	-	-	-	-	1	-
1987–88	27	-	1	-	3	-	31	-
1988–89	40+2	1	1	-	2	-	43+2	1
1989–90	16+1	1	-	-	4	-	20+1	1
1990–91	32+2	1	2	-	3	-	37+2	1
1991–92	45	3	1	-	2	-	48	3
1992–93	43	-	1	-	2	-	46	-
1993–94	37	-	1	-	4	-	42	-
1994–95	7	-	-	-	2	-	9	-
TOTAL	248+5	6	7	-	22	-	277+5	6

THOMAS, Bob

Born: *Stepney, London, 2 August 1919*
Died: *Sutton, Surrey, March 1990*

Bob Thomas managed a goal every three games in League soccer during a career that was greatly affected by the war when he was a youngster. A penalty box striker who was good at getting into scoring positions, the East London-born striker maybe should have scored more often as his shooting could sometimes be wayward, which earned him the nickname of 'Over the bar Bob'. Thomas took a job as a copy boy at the *Daily Express* and appeared as an amateur for Romford, Hayes and Golders Green before becoming a professional with Brentford in May 1939. Serving in the Royal Navy on HMS *Kelvin*, Bob was a guest player at Arsenal, Cardiff City, Charlton

Athletic, Fulham, Luton Town, Southampton and West Ham during the war years. He joined his brother David at Plymouth Argyle in April 1946, where he hit 18 goals in 42 appearances.

Manager Jack Peart paid £4,000 to bring him to Craven Cottage in June 1947, and he scored 23 goals during Fulham's Second Division Championship season of 1948–49. He got into double figures for goals over the next two seasons but lost his place in the side during 1951–52 and moved south of the river to join Crystal Palace in September 1952, where he scored 31 goals in 96 appearances, before being surprisingly released during the summer of 1955. Thomas had a short spell with Tunbridge Wells Rangers, who were managed by his former Fulham colleague Jim Taylor, before moving to the Tommy Lawton-managed Kettering Town in November 1955. Bob won a Southern League Championship medal in his second season at Kettering and eventually poached 56 goals in 72 games for the Poppies. He won another Southern League medal with Gravesend & Northfleet the following season and was Clacton's top scorer as they won the First Division title in 1959–60. After giving up playing, Bob returned to work in Fleet Street for the *Financial Times* and finally retired from working in 1981 after a heart attack.

Appearances:

	Football League		FA Cup		GRAND TOTAL	
SEASON	Apps	Goals	Apps	Goals	Apps	Goals
1947–48	36	5	5	1	41	6
1948–49	40	23	1	-	41	23
1949–50	42	10	2	1	44	11
1950–51	37	14	1	-	38	14
1951–52	12	3	-	-	12	3
TOTAL	167	55	9	2	176	57

TOMPKINS, Jim

Born: Edmonton, Middlesex, May 1914
Died: Normandy, France, 10 July 1944

One of the most heroic and tragic figures to play for Fulham, Jimmy Tompkins was the Cottagers regular left-half from 1935–39 and, but for the war and his untimely death, would have gone on to play many more games for the club. He was a tight marking, fierce tackling left-half who was cool, stylish and mature beyond his years and always the epitome of fairness. He attended St Walter St Johns School in Battersea, and when he left school he worked as an insurance broker. He

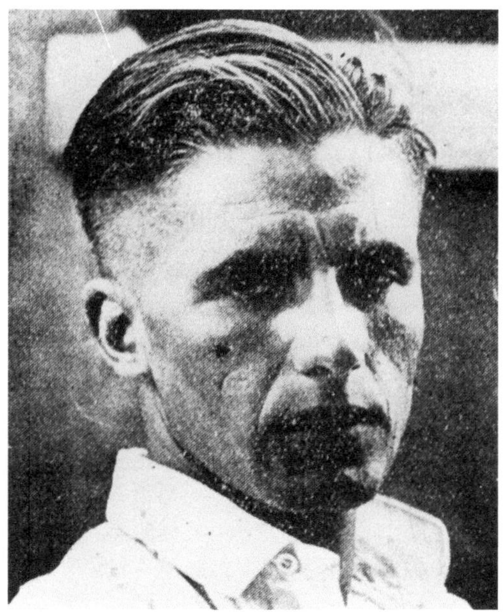

was still at school when he played for Woking in April 1930, where he scored three goals in 34 appearances for the Cards. He was on Arsenal's ground staff when he signed amateur forms for Fulham in March 1932, and this led to a dispute between the two clubs who both wanted him. Fulham won the battle, but Jim was not an overnight sensation, and he did not become a regular in the side until 1935–36, just in time for Fulham's FA Cup run to the semi-finals, where they lost to Sheffield United at Molineux. Once he had filled out his lightweight frame, Tompkins was the regular left-half until the outbreak of war in 1939; in fact, he did not miss a match from March 1936 until the outbreak of war. Tompkins played in the three lost games of 1939–40 and saw war action very early due to his experience with the Territorial Army. He joined the Royal Fusiliers (City of London Regiment) in 1939 and soon obtained his first stripe. By 1944 he was a major seconded to the 7th Battalion of the Hampshire Regiment but was killed on 10 July shortly after the D-Day landings. His death is commemorated at the Bayeux Memorial, as he has no known grave and there are no details about how he was killed. To add to the tragedy, his wife Cecilia died months later and their only son, Maurice, who was on Fulham's ground staff during the 1950s, also lost his life serving in the army.

Appearances:

	Football League		FA Cup		GRAND TOTAL	
SEASON	Apps	Goals	Apps	Goals	Apps	Goals
1933–34	5	-	-	-	5	-
1934–35	1	-	-	-	1	-
1935–36	29	-	6	-	35	-
1936–37	35	-	1	-	36	-
1937–38	42	1	1	-	43	1
1938–39	42	4	2	-	44	4
TOTAL	154	5	10	-	164	5

TOOTILL, Alf

Born: Ramsbottom, Lancashire, 12 November 1908
Died: Chichester, Sussex, 31 August 1975

It is not clear why Alf Tootill had the nickname of 'the Birdcatcher', but although on the small side he was an acrobatic and intelligent

goalkeeper who had a safe pair of hands. He was discovered by Accrington Stanley playing for local side Ramsbottom United and was soon offered a trial and signed by the club as an amateur in November 1926. He joined the professional ranks a year later and soon established himself as the first-choice 'keeper in 1928–29. He was soon spotted by a Wolves scout and moved to Molineux in March 1929 for a fee of £450, where he went on to make 143 appearances for the Black Country club and was ever present as the Wolves took the Second Division Championship in 1931–32. However, the unforgiving Wolves manager Major Frank Buckley was very unhappy when he let in seven goals against Arsenal and immediately decided to sell him. The Fulham manager Jim McIntyre signed him for £1,000 in November 1932, and he immediately replaced Jake Iceton as the Cottagers' goalkeeper. He missed just four games between March 1933 and May 1937 and the highlight was helping the Whites reach the FA Cup semi-final in 1936 where they lost 2–1 to Sheffield United.

Fed up with playing second fiddle to Hugh Turner at the Cottage, Tootill moved to Crystal Palace in November 1938 but played only one first-team game during 1938–39. However, during the war years Tootill played regularly for Palace (159 appearances), helping them to two war League Championships in 1939–40 and 1940–41. The 'Birdcatcher' also appeared as a guest for Aldershot, Brighton and Ipswich Town during these years. He was good enough to play Lancashire League cricket with Ramsbottom from 1927–35 and scored two centuries. After retiring from playing in 1945, Alf worked for an engineering firm until his death at the age of 66.

Appearances:

	Football League		FA Cup		GRAND TOTAL	
SEASON	Apps	Goals	Apps	Goals	Apps	Goals
1932–33	23	-	1	-	24	-
1933–34	40	-	2	-	42	-
1934–35	42	-	1	-	43	-
1935–35	41	-	6	-	47	-
1936–37	41	-	1	-	42	-
1937–38	16	-	-	-	16	-
TOTAL	203	-	11	-	214	-

TORRANCE, Jimmy

Born: *Coatbridge, Scotland, 28 July 1889*
Died: *Friern Barnet, Middlesex, 2 July 1949*

A marvellous one-club man, Jimmy Torrance had a curious build for a footballer. He was on the short side, and seemed all body and no legs, but the Coatbridge man may well have topped Fulham's appearances record but for the war. He was working as a boilermaker and playing for Rob Roy (Coatbridge) in 1908 and Ashfield (Glasgow) when he was signed by Fulham manager Phil Kelso in September 1910. Originally an inside or centre-forward when he first joined the club. Torrance was in and out of the side until March 1913 when he was switched to wing-half, and over the next 12 seasons he

became a permanent fixture in the side, sometimes as an attacking centre-half. Torrance also appeared 135 times for the Cottagers in wartime football, scoring 15 goals, and therefore played in almost 500 games for the club. His only Fulham medal, a runners'-up medal, came in the 1919 Victory Cup Final which Fulham lost 3–0 to Chelsea at Highbury. Between September 1919 and September 1924, Jimmy missed just 10 games for the Lilliewhites before finally losing his place to the upcoming Bert Barrett. He went on to play a further 41 games for Walsall after joining the club in March 1926 and was appointed player-manager from February 1927 to May 1928 but found little success. He worked for a telephone company called Std Telephones & Cables (Hendon) and became a permit player for its works side. The Scotsman had a sad life off the field, having an unhappy marriage and his only child, a son, dying in his teens. He spent many years in the Friern Barnet mental hospital before dying of lung cancer just before his 60th birthday.

Appearances:

	Football League		FA Cup		GRAND TOTAL	
SEASON	Apps	Goals	Apps	Goals	Apps	Goals
1910–11	12	1	-	-	12	1
1911–12	17	4	-	-	17	4
1912–13	18	5	1	-	19	5
1913–14	13	-	1	-	14	-
1914–15	36	4	2	-	38	4
1919–20	38	2	1	-	39	2
1920–21	42	3	5	-	47	3
1921–22	39	4	3	-	42	4
1922–23	38	4	1	-	39	4
1923–24	40	3	3	-	43	3
1924–25	38	3	2	-	40	3
1925–26	7	-	-	-	7	-
TOTAL	338	33	19	-	357	33

VAN DER SAR, Edwin

Born: Voorhout, Holland, 29 October 1970

A goalkeeper with great reflexes and agility for such a big man, Fulham were very fortunate to have Edwin van der Sar, one of the best 'keepers in the world, playing for the club for four seasons. Often spectacular, he could also do the basics very well and is a superb technical 'keeper. He won honours galore before his arrival at Craven Cottage. These include playing in two European Cup Finals for Ajax, beating AC Milan 1–0 in 1995, and losing to Juventus on penalties the following year. He also appeared in a World Club Championship match in Tokyo in November 1995, where Ajax beat Porto Alegre on penalties. On top of this, Edwin has four Dutch League medals and two Cup-winners' medals and a European Super Cup-winners' medal. He has played over 100 times for Holland, and he helped them reach the semi-final in the 1998 World Cup, where they lost to Brazil on penalties, and they did the same when they lost to Italy in Euro 2000. Van der Sar was the first non-Italian to appear in goal for Juventus when he joined them from Ajax in July 1999 for £7 million, but he lost his place when they signed Gianluigi Buffon from Parma for £32 million.

Jean Tigana pulled off a coup with he signed van der Sar from Juventus for a new club record £7 million in August 2001. His excellent performances helped Fulham consolidate their place in the Premiership during 2001–02, and

they reached an FA Cup semi-final where they lost 1–0 to Chelsea at Villa Park. Edwin helped the club win their section of the Inter Toto Cup and gain entry to the UEFA Cup in 2002–03, where they finally went out to Hertha Berlin. the Dutchman was in great form over the next two seasons before his move to Old Trafford in June 2005 for a cut price £2 million. In his first season with Manchester United they won only the League Cup, beating Wigan Athletic 4–0 in the Final at Cardiff, but in 2007 he won an FA Premiership Championship medal as United held off Chelsea to win the title.

Appearances:

	Football League		FA Cup		League Cup		GRAND TOTAL	
SEASON	Apps	Goals	Apps	Goals	Apps	Goals	Apps	Goals
2001–02	37	-	4	-	-	-	41	-
2002–03	19	-	-	-	-	-	19	-
2003–04	37	-	6	-	-	-	43	-
2004–05	33+1	-	5	-	1	-	39+1	-
TOTAL	126+1	-	15	-	1	-	142+1	-

WALKER, Willie

Born: *Darlington, Co. Durham, April qtr 1891*
Died: *Darlington, Co. Durham, 13 March 1968*

A fast and direct winger, Willie Walker was an excellent crosser of the ball at speed. He began

his career with Darlington Forge Albion, with whom he won a Durham Junior Cup and League medals, and had a trial with Darlington before joining Darlington St Augustine. He moved to Fulham, along with another future star, Alf Marshall, in September 1909. He played in 17 League games during his first season at the Cottage and was in the London Challenge Cup Final side, when the Lilliewhites beat Spurs 4–1 at Stamford Bridge before a 20,000 crowd. The following season Fulham lost to Spurs 2–1 in the Final with Willie on the left wing again. Walker finally fought off Bert Lipsham and Fred Mouncher to claim the left-wing berth as his own and gave Fulham great service, except for the war years when he was mostly away on national work. The only blot on a burgeoning career was being the first Fulham player to be sent off (for retaliation) in a Football League encounter at Bradford in February 1913. He was injured when Fulham played at West Brom in a losing FA Cup quarter-final in 1912 but scored nine goals during 1912–13. Walker had competition for the outside-left position from Scottish international Bobby Templeton from

1913–15, and he eventually lost his place to the promising Frank Penn in 1920–21. Walker moved to Lincoln City in August 1921 but by May 1922 went out of the game for 18 months due to severe appendix problems. He had a brief trial with Lincoln in January 1924 but was not signed.

Appearances:

	Football League		FA Cup		GRAND TOTAL	
SEASON	Apps	Goals	Apps	Goals	Apps	Goals
1909–10	17	5	-	-	17	5
1910–11	30	2	-	-	30	2
1911–12	25	3	3	-	28	3
1912–13	32	9	1	-	33	9
1913–14	24	2	1	-	25	2
1914–15	15	-	2	1	17	1
1919–20	25	2	1	-	26	2
1920–21	2	-	-	-	2	-
TOTAL	170	23	8	1	178	24

WHITE, Walter

Born: *Hurlford, Ayrshire, 15 May 1882*
Died: *Fulham, London, 8 July 1950*

A diminutive and skilful ball-player whose ball control was always a feature of his play, Walter White was a very steady player, equally effective at inside-forward or left-half. He played in a more defensive role with Fulham and was as much at home stopping players as he had been at scoring and creating goals earlier in his career.

'Wattie' joined Bolton Wanderers from Hurlford Thistle in June 1902 and played for the Trotters in the 1904 FA Cup Final against Manchester City at Crystal Palace. The Trotters were disappointed to lose 1–0 to a goal from the great Billy Meredith that looked offside. The following season, Bolton finished as runners-up of the Second Division, with White scoring 24 goals (including three hat-tricks) in only 33 appearances. He helped to develop a triangular wing game at Burnden Park along with McEwan and Marshall to such a high pitch of perfection that it was later copied by other clubs.

'Wattie' won his first Scottish cap against England in April 1907 in a 1–1 draw at St James' Park, Newcastle, and a year later gained his second and last cap in another 1–1 draw between the old enemies at Hampden Park before a crowd of 125,000.

After scoring 93 goals in 217 appearances for Bolton Wanderers, White was sold to Everton in November 1908 and came close to another Cup Final appearance in 1910, but the Toffees lost to Barnsley 3–0 in a semi-final replay at Old Trafford. The Scottish international joined Fulham in November 1910 and remained at Craven Cottage for 13 seasons. He made few appearances after January 1920 and became a father figure to the reserves in the early 1920s. He is the oldest player to have played for Fulham, at the age of 40 years nine months, when he appeared in his last game at Bury in February 1923. He retired in the summer of 1923 and had a benefit match against Queen's Park Rangers in January 1926.

Appearances:

	Football League		FA Cup		GRAND TOTAL	
SEASON	Apps	Goals	Apps	Goals	Apps	Goals
1910–11	31	4	1	-	32	4
1911–12	37	2	4	-	41	2
1912–13	31	2	1	-	32	2
1913–14	36	3	1	-	37	3
1914–15	33	4	2	-	35	4
1919–20	16	3	-	-	16	3
1920–21	6	-	3	-	9	-
1922–23	1	-	-	-	1	-
TOTAL	191	18	12	-	203	18

WILSON, Robert

Born: Fulham, London, 5 June 1961

An attacking midfielder who liked to score goals, Robert Wilson's strengths were his tackling, the timing of his runs into the penalty area to score vital goals and orchestrating clever one-touch moves. He represented West London and Inner London School and joined Fulham as an apprentice in July 1977 and turned professional almost two years later. He started his career as a right-back but was later converted into an attacking midfield player. During 1981–82, 'Willo' made 42+1 appearances as Fulham finished as Third Division runners-up and they reached the fourth round of the League Cup where they lost narrowly at Spurs 1–0. He missed just two games and scored 11 goals the following season as Fulham went close to promotion again. The Fulham-born player won two Republic of Ireland Under-21 caps in the Toulon Trophy in June 1983, playing against USSR and France. A serious gas accident at his new Berkshire home nearly ended Robert, and his wife's, life in December 1983. He was Fulham's leading scorer with 11 goals during 1984–85 and soon became one of the many players to leave Fulham due to their severe financial position. He was transferred to Millwall in August 1985 for £57,500 before rejoining his former manager Ray Harford at Luton Town in August 1986. Fulham manager Ray Lewington re-signed Wilson in September 1987, but he missed most of the club's run-in to reach the Third Division Play-offs during 1988–89 and joined Huddersfield Town in July 1989 for £20,000. He ended his League career at

Rotherham United and had played a career total of 374+27 games, scoring 69 goals. Wilson joined Farnborough Town in August 1992 and also appeared for Altrincham, Ossett Albion and finally Accrington Stanley in 1994, and was the youth development office at Huddersfield Town in 1999.

Appearances:

	Football League		FA Cup		League Cup		GRAND TOTAL	
SEASON	Apps	Goals	Apps	Goals	Apps	Goals	Apps	Goals
1979–80	2	-	2	-	-	-	4	-
1980–81	31+4	4	-	-	0+2	-	31+6	4
1981–82	42+1	5	2	-	7	3	51+1	8
1982–83	40	11	3	-	2	-	45	11
1983–84	14+2	3	-	-	4	-	18+2	3
1984–85	39	11	-	-	3	-	42	11
1987–88	18+2	3	1	-	1	1	20+2	4
1988–89	25+3	1	1	-	2	-	28+3	1
TOTAL	211+12	38	9	-	19+2	4	239+14	42

Fulham's Managers

Harry Bradshaw (1904–09)

Born: Burnley, Lancashire
Player: None
Manager: Burnley, Woolwich Arsenal, Fulham
Died: London, September 1924

It was something of a coup when, in April 1904, the Fulham board announced the appointment of Harry Bradshaw as the club's first manager. A highly-respected football pioneer, Bradshaw was secretary and chairman of Burnley in the 1890s, taking them to third place in Division One, before moving to Woolwich Arsenal in 1899. Described by one authoritative writer as the best Gunners manager until Herbert Chapman, he rescued the ailing club from bankruptcy and transformed them into a top-flight footballing force in his five years at Plumstead.

At the Cottage, he enhanced his reputation. In only his second season, Fulham won the Southern League Championship (effectively the Edwardian Third Division), and after retaining the title the club was elected to the Football League in 1907. The debut campaign showed that Bradshaw's Fulham were not out of their depth. They reached the semi-final of the FA Cup and were just three points short of a promotion place. And on top of this, he oversaw the rebuilding of the Cottage in 1905.

Although a remote, administrative figure, Bradshaw knew the sort of player he wanted, and at Fulham, as at Arsenal, he had a preference for Scottish players, noted for their control, dribbling and passing skills. The turnover of players was high, and he was always active in the transfer market. In all, he used 70 players in five seasons (including his sons, Will and Joe) and never fewer than 21 in a season.

By 1909, Bradshaw had had enough. Although offered a new contract by Fulham, he preferred to become Secretary of the Southern League, a post he held until his retirement in 1921. He was still living in Putney (Chelverton Road) at the time of his death in September 1924.

Phil Kelso (1909–24)

Born: Largs, Scotland, 1871
Player: None
Manager: Hibernian, Woolwich Arsenal, Fulham
Died: London, February 1935

Still Fulham's longest-serving manager, Phil Kelso succeeded Bradshaw at Fulham, just as he had at Arsenal in 1904. A Scot, born in Largs in 1871, (like Bradshaw) he was never a professional player but had managed Hibernian before going south to Woolwich. After taking the Gunners to two FA Cup semi-finals, he returned to Scotland to run a hotel in his home town, but the Fulham board persuaded him back to football, and London.

After the initial excitement of the Southern League titles and Football League entry under Bradshaw, Kelso's Fulham became a consistent mid-table Second Division side, better at home than away. He was a noted disciplinarian, with strong views on smoking and drinking, he expected players to live close to London and often took the team away the night before a game. Kelso also dealt regularly in the transfer market and several times he signed big-name players who might bring some glamour to the Cottage, internationals like Arthur Brown, Bobby Templeton, Andy Ducat and Danny Shea.

Steering Fulham through the difficult years of World War One was a considerable achievement, but all Kelso's good work and credibility as a manger was undermined in March 1922. As the Cottagers mounted their first serious promotion challenge in Kelso's time, the club was charged and found guilty of trying to bribe an opponent before a game against South Shields. Centre-forward Barney Travers carried the can, but he was widely believed to have been doing Kelso's bidding.

In 1923–24, the team struggled and only avoided relegation with a 1–0 win on the final day of the season. Kelso then retired, aged only 53, and never worked in football again. He became the landlord of The Grove in Hammersmith and then The Rising Sun in the Fulham Road and was 64 when he died in February 1935.

Andy Ducat (1924–26)

Born: Brixton, London, February 1886
Player: Southend, Woolwich Arsenal, Aston Villa, Fulham, England
Manager: Fulham
Died: Lord's, July 1942

There followed a decade of instability when five managers came and went before Jack Peart's appointment in 1935. First up was Andy Ducat, the first former player to manage the club and the first manager to be sacked. After the scandal of the Kelso years, Ducat was a man of unimpeachable integrity. A Londoner from Brixton, he was among the most distinguished sportsmen in England, one of the handful who had played for England at both football and cricket.

Like his two managerial predecessors, Ducat had been with Arsenal, but as a player, signed by Kelso in 1905. In 1912 he was transferred to Aston Villa and captained the 1920 FA Cup-winning side. When the Villa board tried to insist he lived nearer the club, he decided to move on, and in May 1921 Kelso signed him for a second time. Appointing him manager was a popular decision but, in the end, the wrong one.

Kelso's legacy was a struggling team and, despite making wholesale changes, Ducat was not the man to revive the club's fortunes. Beating three First Division sides on the way to the last eight of the FA Cup in 1926 was his major achievement, and although Fulham avoided relegation it was too close for comfort.

After he was sacked at the end of 1925–26, the gentlemanly Ducat was reinstated as an amateur and turned out for Casuals while still continuing to play cricket for Surrey, coaching at Eton and reporting for a national newspaper. This was more appropriate for Ducat, a throwback to the old Victorian values of sportsmanship, than the hurly burly of League management. In July 1942, while batting for the Army at Lord's, he collapsed and died just after lunch. He was just 56. Wisden, apparently, had a lengthy debate as to whether he was 'not out, 29' or 'retired, dead, 29'.

Joe Bradshaw (1926–29)

Born: Burnley, Lancashire, 1880
Player: Woolwich Arsenal, Fulham, Chelsea, Queen's Park Rangers, Southend
Manager: Southend, Swansea, Fulham, Bristol City
Died: Not known

Another former Fulham player followed Ducat into the manager's office. Joe Bradshaw had made a handful of appearances on the right wing when his father was manager 20 years earlier. His pre-Fulham career was spent with Southampton and Arsenal (again with his father) and, after leaving the Cottage, he played for Chelsea, Queen's Park Rangers and Southend.

It was at Southend in 1911 that Bradshaw got started as a manager, initially as player-manager but, from 1913, on a full-time basis. After the war, he stepped up into the Football League with Swansea and spent seven years in South Wales before returning to the Cottage. His inheritance was a poisoned chalice. Bradshaw managed to keep Fulham in the Second Division in 1926–27, but it was a struggle and the following season the trapdoor opened. In a really strange season in which the Cottagers had one of the best home records in the division but lost their first 20 away games (including a Cup tie), they needed a point a Blackpool to stay up. They lost 4–0 and were relegated for the first time.

Surprisingly, he kept his job the next season, but after a mediocre showing at the lower level his contract was not renewed. But he got another chance, Second Division Bristol City appointing him manager in the 1929 close season. As at Fulham, he had a constant battle against relegation at Ashton Gate, winning in his first two seasons (once by just 0.1 of a goal), but in 1931–32, with City rock bottom and facing the drop, Bradshaw resigned in February and left football.

Ned Liddell (1929–31)

Born: Whitburn, County Durham, May 1878
Player: Sunderland, Southampton, Gainsborough Town, Clapton Orient, Southend, Arsenal
Manager: Southend, Queen's Park Rangers, Fulham, Luton
Died: Essex, November 1968

The very experienced Ned Liddell, Fulham's 51-year-old chief scout, was the board's choice to succeed his old boss, Bradshaw, but his was to prove the shortest managerial term to date. Liddell was an experienced football man. His career began as a player in his native North East at the turn of the century and lasted in some form or another until he died at the age of 90 in 1968.

As a player before World War One, Liddell had spells with Sunderland, Southampton, Gainsborough, Clapton Orient, Southend and Arsenal. He first succeeded Bradshaw as manager of Southend and then was in charge of Queen's Park Rangers (1920–24) before joining Fulham as a scout. He therefore knew football generally and the club very well, and his promotion to manager in 1929 made sense. But, it was an unhappy experience. Fulham slipped further down the Third Division and Liddell was as relieved as anyone when he reverted to scouting over Easter 1931 and James McIntyre came in as manager.

Although results were not impressive, most of the squad that won promotion the following season were at the club under Liddell. He signed goalkeeper Iceton, defender Gibbon and winger Finch, while inside-forwards Price and Hammond came good in Liddell's time. But while he could spot talent as a scout, he was not a good manager of teams and he willingly stepped aside and stayed on to help his successor.

When Liddell did leave the Cottage, he scouted for West Ham and then had a second crack at management with Luton from 1936–38. In the post-1945 period, his was scouting again and spent over 20 years with Spurs up to the time of his death.

James Mcintyre (1931–34)

Born: Walsall, Staffordshire, 1881
Player: Walsall, Notts County, Northampton, Reading, Coventry
Manager: Southampton, Coventry, Fulham
Died: Surrey, 1954

Just before the end of 1930–31, a manager with a proven record in the Third Division became Fulham's fourth manager in seven years, and the most successful for 25 years. James McIntyre was a journeyman player with his home-town club Walsall and then Notts County and Reading. He retired in 1907 and joined the training staff at Coventry, moving on to Southampton in 1912. After World War One, he became manager at The Dell and guided the Saints to the Third Division South title in 1922. He retired two years later and, like Kelso, went to run a hotel in Scotland, but he was lured back by Coventry in 1928, from where Fulham recruited him.

Aged 50, McIntyre was a man unencumbered by self-doubt, who openly acknowledged that his role model was Arsenal's Herbert Chapman. He was more accessible to the press and a shrewd operator in the transfer market. But his best signing, Stockport's prolific scorer Frank 'Bonzo' Newton, was not only key to Fulham's Third Division Championship success in McIntyre's first full season, but he was also the manager's undoing.

The title success in 1932 was followed by a near-miss the following season. But when McIntyre sold Newton to Reading in September 1933 for just £650, and replaced him with Arsenal veteran Jack Lambert for £2,500, he lost the confidence of the board and the supporters. Lambert was not a success, and in February 1934 the manager was sacked, the Newton transfer cited as the reason.

It was an unfortunate end to a successful term as Fulham manager. It was very surprising that McIntyre did not get another job in football and ended his working life in a factory in Southampton, working for Follands. He died in Surrey in 1954, aged 72.

Jimmy Hogan (1934–35)

Born: Nelson, Lancashire, October 1882
Player: Rochdale, Nelson, Burnley, Fulham, Swindon, Bolton
Manager: Austria (national side), Fulham, Aston Villa
Died: Lancashire, January 1974

In a move as bold and as imaginative, but not as successful, as the appointment of Jean Tigana in 2000, Fulham went for Jimmy Hogan in the 1934 close season. A Fulham player in Edwardian times (his last game was the 1908 semi-final), Hogan had a long and uneventful playing career, and counted Burnley, Swindon and Bolton among his numerous clubs. But it was as a coach rather than a player that he made his mark, and it was on the continent rather than in England that he won acclaim for his innovative training methods and tactics.

Hogan was a football missionary who blazed a trail in Europe and made a significant contribution to the game's development either side of World War One. In his case, he worked in Hungary, Switzerland, Germany and Holland, but it was in Austria that he enjoyed his greatest success, coaching an outstanding national side. For chairman John Dean, appointing Hogan as Fulham manager was a step into the unknown, a complete break with the past, and he probably had no idea what to expect.

Hogan's first coaching job in England lasted months rather than years. Unlike the secretary-managers or trainers of the day, he involved himself in every aspect of the players' routines, ball skills and diets as well as fitness and team tactics. An innovative thinker, he disliked the 'third game' popularised by Herbert Chapman, preferring the close passing game he saw at the Cottage in his playing days.

The results were mixed at best, and many senior players did not warm to his methods. At the turn of 1935, Hogan went into hospital with appendicitis and, when he was recovering, the board sacked him, an appallingly insensitive act. He returned to Europe and Austria and, after more success, spent the last three inter-war seasons managing Aston Villa. In the post-war era, he was coach at Villa Park, and at Celtic and Brentford. Hogan's long and eventful life ended, at the age of 91, in January 1974, a prophet without honour in his own country.

Jack Peart (1935–48)

Born: South Shields, Tyneside, October 1888
Player: Sheffield United, Stoke, Newcastle, Notts County, Birmingham, Derby, Port Vale, Norwich
Manager: Rochdale, Bradford City, Fulham
Died: London, September 1948

After Joe Edelston stepped in as 'caretaker' manager (as he had done after McIntyre's dismissal), the board reverted to type and picked the 46-year-old, pipe-smoking Jack Peart in the spring of 1935, on an annual salary of £600. It was a 'safety first' appointment. Happier in a worsted suit than tracksuit, Peart was the archetypal administrator who, after the turbulence of the previous decade, brought some stability to the club.

When his long, nomadic and injury-riddled playing career, which included spells at Sheffield United, Stoke, Newcastle, Notts County and Derby (he played in every division of the Football League as well as the Southern and Welsh Leagues), ended, Peart began his managerial career with Ebbw Vale in 1920. He then had seven years in charge of Rochdale and five at Bradford City before moving to the Cottage. A knowledgeable, thoughtful man, Peart's Fulham once again became a solid, mid-table Second Division side. Operating on a tight budget, he had a good eye for bargain signings (Rooke, Beasley and Bob Thomas were probably the best) and he was prepared to encourage home-grown talent (Bacuzzi, Stevens and Taylor especially).

Peart's greatest success in his long tenure (the second longest of any Fulham manager) came in his first season, with a Cup run that stopped just 90 minutes short of Wembley. The war, however, accounted for seven of his 13 seasons and he had the thankless task of keeping the club going during the makeshift wartime competitions. Ironically, it all came right in 1948–49 when the Cottagers won the Second Division Championship. Sadly, Peart had died in September 1948 after a brief illness when the season was just four games old. He was just short of his 60th birthday, but he left the club in better shape than he had found it.

Frank Osborne (1948–64)

Born: Wynberg, South Africa, October 1896
Player: Fulham, Tottenham Hotspur, Southampton, England
Manager: Fulham
Died: Surrey, March 1988

After the usual speculation, the Board asked one of its own to succeed Peart as manager. Frank Osborne, a Fulham player in the 1920s (and first to win an England cap), had become a director in the 1930s, while working for chairman John Dean's company. So Osborne reluctantly started on a managerial career that lasted, in one form or another, until his retirement at the age of 68 in 1964.

To start with, he was assisted by Eddie Perry, Fulham's former centre-forward, as team manager. After just a few months in the job, the Cottagers won the Second Division title, a success to which Osborne made a significant contribution. During the 1949 close season, Bill Dodgin was appointed manager and Osborne became secretary or general manager. This arrangement was repeated when Dug Livingstone and Beddy Jezzard became team managers in the 1950s, with Osborne holding the fort in the intervals.

For the first 20 years of the post-1945 era, Osborne was the key figure at Craven Cottage. He had an excellent relationship with the board, knew the club inside out and offered continuity during a period when Fulham changed division, manager and even chairman. Along with trainer Frank Penn, who had joined the club in 1915, six years before Osborne, he shaped the character of Fulham FC, even though he was not technically responsible for team affairs.

Osborne's career, as a player, director, manager and secretary, is unique in the history of the club and, in terms of length of service, has been bettered only by Penn. It was appropriate that the two left within six months of each other. Osborne went of his own accord in October 1964, and never returned to the club thereafter. He lived quietly at his Epsom home and died, at the age of 91, in March 1988.

Bill Dodgin (1949–53)

Born: Gateshead, Tyneside, April 1909
Player: Huddersfield, Lincoln, Charlton, Bristol Rovers, Clapton Orient, Southampton
Manager: Southampton, Fulham, Brentford, Sampdoria, Bristol Rovers
Died: Surrey, October 1999

When Fulham won the Second Division title in 1949, they pipped West Brom to it and both clubs pipped Southampton to promotion. But Saints manager Bill Dodgin was in charge of a top-flight club in 1949 because Fulham appointed him as team manager that summer. Aged 39, he was not only one of the Cottagers youngest managers (Kelso and Ducat were a similar age) but one of the youngest in the First Division.

He had, however, plenty of experience. Before the war, he had been a wing-half with Huddersfield, Lincoln, Charlton, Bristol Rovers, Clapton Orient and Southampton, and it was at The Dell that he started his managerial career in 1946. The success he had with the Saints impressed the Fulham board sufficiently for them to offer him the job of leading the club in its debut at the highest level.

Dodgin did not have an easy time. The squad was probably not quite good enough for the top flight and, although he had money to spend in 1950, he had three years of struggle in Division One, the third of which ended in relegation. When there was no serious challenge for promotion in the club's first season back in Division Two, Fulham and Dodgin parted company. Strangely, his departure was not even mentioned in the programme.

In some ways, Dodgin made a rod for his own back, selling the popular Quested and playing his own son. He was also unlucky because youngsters he had signed, like Robson and Haynes, were just starting to blossom. But Dodgin was a cheerful character who did not bear grudges, and he went on to work for Brentford, Sampdoria and, from 1961 until his retirement in 1972, with Bristol Rovers. He was 90 when he died in 1999.

Dugald Livingstone (1956–58)

Born: Alexandra, Dumbartonshire, February 1898
Player: Celtic, Everton, Plymouth Argyle, Aberdeen, Tranmere Rovers
Manager: Sparta Rotterdam, Republic of Ireland and Belgium national sides, Newcastle, Fulham, Chesterfield
Died: Bucks, February 1981

It was over two years before Dodgin was replaced, and his successor is probably the most underrated of all Fulham's managers. Almost 58 when he was appointed in January 1956, Scotsman Dug Livingstone had a long footballing pedigree that went back to Celtic, Aberdeen and Everton as a player in the 1920s. But his coaching CV was more impressive. He had coached in Holland and was in charge of the Belgium national side in the 1954 World Cup Finals. Back in Britain, he was coach of the Sheffield United and Newcastle sides that reached the FA Cup Finals in 1936 and 1955 respectively, and had worked at Exeter and Manchester City.

His reward for steering Newcastle to FA Cup success was to be stripped of team selection duties. Livingstone left and in two years at the Cottage steered the club successfully through a period of transition. Within months of taking over, two of the club's prized inside-forward trio were gone, Robson to West Brom and Jezzard to injury. But the easy-going Livingstone made some shrewd signings and subtle positional changes that were to take Fulham back into the top flight.

During his tenure, Macedo and Cohen got into the side, Langley and Cook were signed, as was inside-forward Bentley who was successfully converted to half-back. It started to gel in his second full season (1957–58), only for the Cottagers to narrowly miss out on promotion and lose a thrilling FA Cup semi-final. The club was anxious to keep him, but Livingstone's wife wanted to go back north, and in the summer of 1958 he took over at Chesterfield. He had, however, left Fulham in good shape. Livingstone stayed at Saltergate until his retirement in 1962 and died in Marlow in 1981, 10 days short of his 83rd birthday.

Beddy Jezzard (1958–64)

Born: Clerkenwell, London, October 1927
Player: Fulham, England
Manager: Fulham
Died: London, May 2005

When Livingstone went north, Fulham kept the manager's job in the family by promoting internally. Club-record scorer Beddy Jezzard had been youth-team manager after his playing career was prematurely ended in the 1956 close season. It was his first managerial job, but he had Osborne and trainer Frank Penn alongside and he inherited a very good squad. Signing Graham Leggat during the summer of 1958 was the last piece of the jigsaw and the team won promotion in the new manager's first season.

For the next five seasons, Jezzard kept Fulham in the top flight, sometimes with very little to spare, and came within a whisker of reaching the FA Cup Final. He did it by spending virtually no money. In his final full season, 1963–64, seven of the promotion side were still regulars, only the returning Bobby Robson and Watford's Bobby Howfield had cost (modest) fees and the rest came through the juniors. Jezzard was a quiet, unassuming man who kept a very low public profile. But he undoubtedly helped to create a great spirit among the players because, while there were few new signings, very few wanted to leave.

It was one particular transfer, however, of Alan Mullery to Spurs in March 1964, that marked the beginning of the end for Jezzard. The deal (Fulham's record fee) was negotiated by chairman Trinder behind the manager's back, and Mullery told Jezzard and his teammates of his impending move at half-time during a First Division match against Liverpool. When his mentor, Osborne, retired in October 1964 the club wanted to give Jezzard full control, but, just weeks later, he decided it was not for him and resigned. Still not yet 40, he left football for good and went to run the family pub not far from Hammersmith, thus ending a remarkable Fulham career.

After leaving football, he kept in touch with many of his former colleagues and was an occasional visitor to the Cottage. Sadly, in his later years he suffered from multi-infarct dementia and died in 2005, aged 77.

Vic Buckingham (1965–68)

Born: Greenwich, London, October 1915
Player: Tottenham Hotspur
Manager: Bradford, West Brom, Ajax, Sheffield Wednesday, Fulham, Ethnikos
Died: Sussex, January 1995

Chairman Trinder wanted to make Fulham a more 'professional' club and looked outside for a new manager while coach Arthur Stevens held the fort. The choice of Viv Buckingham was very unfortunate. In a relatively short space of time, his radical changes left the club facing relegation from the First to the Third Divisions in successive seasons. Despite the strong competition, he has a very good claim to being Fulham's worst manager.

Yet he arrived at the Cottage in January 1965 with very impressive credentials. As a player, he was a classy wing-half with Spurs in a war-affected career. He then earned his coaching stripes with Pegasus before going into management with Bradford (1951–53), West Brom (1953–59), Ajax (1959–61) and Sheffield Wednesday (1961–64). At The Hawthorns, his Albion side almost did the League and Cup double, in Amsterdam he allegedly discovered Cruyff and his three seasons at Hillsborough all finished in the top half of the First Division, but were tainted by match-fixing allegations.

At Fulham, his attempts to change too much too soon ended in tears. Long-serving trainer Penn retired and reserve-team manager Bacuzzi was sacked within months, and players like Cook, Langley, Keetch, Leggat, O'Connell, Key and Marsh were all moved on. A clear out might have been justified but not to have replaced them with veterans like Terry Dyson and Mark Pearson, both well past their 'buy-by' dates. Relegation was only avoided in his first full season by the appointment of the outstanding Dave Sexton as coach at the turn of 1966. There was a breathing space the following year before the relegation trapdoor opened in 1967–68.

By the time the drop was confirmed, Buckingham had gone. He left, unlamented, in January 1968 when his three-year contract expired. Thereafter, he coached briefly in Greece and Spain and died in Chichester in January 1995, aged 79.

Bobby Robson (1968)

Born: Sacriston, County Durham, February 1933
Player: Fulham, West Brom, England
Manager: Vancouver Royals, Fulham, Ipswich, England national side, PSV Eindhoven, Sporting Lisbon, Porto, Barcelona, Newcastle

For any manager, taking over Fulham in January 1968 was a poisoned chalice, but for a former player in his first job it was Mission Impossible. Robson (who ironically had been signed by Buckingham for West Brom) had retired from playing in May 1967 after 370 games for the Cottagers. When a manager's job in Canada did not work out as he had hoped, Fulham secretary Graham Hortop was pushing at an open door when he telephoned Robson about returning to the Cottage. On reflection, he might have felt discretion was the better part of valour.

By the time he arrived, the damage was done, and it was too late to save Fulham's top-flight status. But some of Robson's signings smacked of panic (Johnny Byrne) or naivety (Frank Large in for Allan Clarke). And galvanising a group of dispirited players who were very recently former teammates was asking a lot of an untried manager. Nobody blamed Robson for relegation in 1968, but when Fulham dropped straight to the foot of Division Two the next season, the alarm bells started to ring.

It was not clear why the team did so badly in the autumn of 1968. Most had First Division experience and there were youngsters like Malcolm Macdonald with obvious potential. But the board was impatient and Eric Miller (later to commit suicide amid allegations of business corruption) sacked Robson after just 10 months in the job. It proved to be Fulham's loss.

From a torrid baptism in SW6, Robson went on to prove himself among the best managers of his generation in England and in Europe, and at club as well as international level. Now in his 70s, and knighted, he is a national treasure and, despite the sour experience of his first job in management, is still obviously in love with football.

Bill Dodgin junior (1968–72)

Born: Wardley, County Durham, November 1931
Player: Fulham, Arsenal
Manager: Queen's Park Rangers, Fulham, Northampton, Brentford
Died: Surrey, June 2000

For a few weeks after Robson's sacking, Johnny Haynes stepped in as a reluctant player-manager. It was his suggestion that the board appoint his old teammate, and son of a former Fulham manager, on a permanent basis. Dodgin became the club's fourth manager in the 'annus horriblis' of 1968. Things, however, were to get worse before they got better.

A very average centre-half, Dodgin had two spells as a player with Fulham either side of eight years at Highbury. When a broken leg ended his career in 1963, he began coaching, with Millwall and then with Queen's Park Rangers. At Loftus Road, with manager Alec Stock, he helped take Rangers from the Third to the First Divisions in successive seasons and a League Cup success at Wembley.

At Craven Cottage, he took 18 months to turn the club around. There was another relegation in 1969, and some promise in 1969–70, before Fulham won promotion from the Third Division in 1971. And they did it playing the only way Dodgin knew how – by open, attacking football. The manager was well served by the likes of Callaghan, Brown, Conway, Earle and Barrett, who were already on the books, but added some of his own signings, Dunne, Webster and Lloyd in particular. His attacking approach did not work so well back in the Second Division, and when relegation was avoided only by the narrowest of margins chairman Trinder sacked Dodgin in May 1972, much to the supporters' annoyance.

Among his subsequent jobs were spells in charge of Northampton and (again like his father) Brentford. Dodgin also returned for a fourth spell at Fulham, as Youth Development Officer in 1994. He was, sadly, a victim of Alzheimers, and died in Chertsey in June 2000, just eight months after his father. He was 68.

Alec Stock (1972–76)

Born: Peasedown St John, Somerset, March 1917
Player: Charlton, Queen's Park Rangers
Manager: Leyton O, AS Roma, Queen's Park Rangers, Luton, Fulham, Bournemouth
Died: Dorset, April 2001

Days before Dodgin's sacking, Alec Stock (his old mentor at Queen's Park Rangers and a playing colleague of his father at Charlton) resigned as Luton manager. A vastly-experienced manager, Stock was not a popular choice but gradually won over the supporters and, while never really promotion challengers, he consolidated Fulham's position in Division Two and steered the club to its first-ever FA Cup Final.

Stock was an unlikely manager. An army major who had been a journeyman player before the war, he was smart, fastidious, a bit deaf and asthmatic. Much happier at smaller clubs, he had enjoyed success at Yeovil, Leyton Orient, Queen's Park Rangers and Luton, but could not settle during his brief spells at Arsenal or AS Roma. Wherever he worked, he was clearly 'The Boss' in the old sense of the word, a man-manager who was much respected by his players but who left coaching and tactics to others.

His record at Fulham defined consistency. In four complete seasons, the club won between 40 and 44 points from 42 games, finishing between ninth and 13th. Getting to Wembley in 1975 was, however, the crowning achievement, not just of his time at the Cottage but probably also of his whole career. He was prepared to give youngsters a chance (Strong, Mitchell and Lacy), sold well (Earle and Went) and bought shrewdly (Slough, Busby and especially Mullery and Moore).

The unravelling of the club's finances, the emergence of Ernest Clay on the board and the appointment of Bobby Campbell as coach in the summer of 1976 meant Stock's days were numbered. From the start, he questioned Clay's motives and knew he could not work with him. He went in December 1976, and was with Queen's Park Rangers and then Bournemouth until his retirement. The original 'Ron Manager' died in Dorset, aged 84, in April 2001.

Bobby Campbell (1976–80)

Born: Liverpool, April 1937
Player: Liverpool, Wigan A, Portsmouth, Aldershot
Manager: Fulham, Portsmouth, Chelsea

The board went over Stock's head when coach Bill Taylor left for Manchester City in the summer of 1976, preferring to replace him with Bobby Campbell rather than Alan Mullery. When Stock went, Campbell got the nod and at the age of 39 became a manager for the first time.

Campbell the player had been with Liverpool (just 14 games), Wigan, Portsmouth and Aldershot. Campbell the coach had started at Portsmouth and then moved on to Queen's Park Rangers and Arsenal before joining Fulham. Campbell the manager had a torrid time at the Cottage where change and instability were the hallmarks of his tenure, just as consistency had characterised the Stock years.

It began badly (a 12-match run without a win in the winter of 1976) and ended dreadfully (relegation in 1979–80 and then six consecutive Third Division defeats in the autumn of 1980). In between, there was very little to cheer.

The manager's own brusque personality did little to endear him to supporters. Campbell seemed (publicly at least) to have a very short fuse and, like Buckingham, he tried to change too much. When Fulham kicked-off the 1978–79 season, only Kevin Lock had played in the Cup Final three years earlier – and he had played for West Ham. Les Strong was the only player to survive the whole Campbell era. If change, and the manager's almost compulsive dealing in the transfer market (at which he was very good), had led to improvements, it would have been justified. But Fulham were relegated.

An unhappy and unsuccessful interlude was thankfully ended when he and his assistant Mike Kelly were sacked in October 1980. Campbell went to continue his career, with a couple of promotion successes, at Portsmouth and Chelsea (chairman Ken Bates was his son's godparent), plus spells coaching back at Aldershot and Queen's Park Rangers.

Malcolm Macdonald (1980–84)

Born: Fulham, London, January 1950
Player: Fulham, Luton, Newcastle, Arsenal, England
Manager: Fulham, Huddersfield

It was far from clear that the club had got it right when commercial director and former player Malcolm Macdonald was given the manager's job. A brash, arrogant striker, who never doubted his own ability and was never short of a controversial comment, he seemed an unlikely saviour. But he was a breath of fresh air. Thoughtful, imaginative and bold, he first lifted the spirits of supporters and staff, and then lifted the team back up the table and to within touching distance of the top flight. And he did it essentially with the players who were already at the club when he took over.

As a manager, Macdonald knew his limitations. He defined his job as creating the environment for others (coaches and players) to do their jobs, to keep the erratic chairman off everyone's backs and raise Fulham's profile publicly. He succeeded far sooner and to a greater extent than anyone could reasonably have expected. He was shrewd in his choice of coaches (Roger Thompson and George Armstrong, colleagues from his Arsenal days, the then unknown Ray Harford from Colchester and Terry Mancini). The teams, bolstered only by one free transfer signing each year, O'Sullivan in 1981–82 and Houghton in 1982–83, played positive attacking football, which got results. Promotion in 1982 was followed by a very near miss 12 months later.

The Macdonald years were, however, an isolated upturn in Fulham's long downward slide. Sadly, it was not built on very firm foundations, and the manager had a tendency in these years to self-destruct. When his private life became of more interest to the press than the performance of the team in the spring of 1984, the chairman took the opportunity to sack him. After a brief spell at Huddersfield, he left football and, after some well-publicised personal difficulties, Macdonald now seems to have got his life back on track, working for the media in the North East.

Ray Harford (1984–86)

Born: Halifax, Yorkshire, June 1945
Player: Charlton, Exeter, Lincoln, Mansfield, Port Vale, Colchester
Manager: Fulham, Luton, Wimbledon, Blackburn, West Brom, Queen's Park Rangers
Died: London, August 2003

The obvious successor was Macdonald's coach Ray Harford, and five wins in six games in the spring of 1984 assured him of the job. Harford had been at the Cottage as a coach since 1981, prior to which he had coached at Colchester and made over 350 appearances for six lower division clubs. Yet, for all this experience, the reaction generally was Ray Who?

In just a few years at Fulham, Harford had built a reputation as an outstanding coach, and the ease with which many youngsters slotted into the team was testimony to his methods. But he was not a man who courted or welcomed publicity, appearing to believe that football was a private business between him and the players. Privately, he was a very engaging personality with a droll sense of humour, but to supporters he could appear dour and uncommunicative.

He was given the job at the wrong time. Fulham's financial problems became more pressing and the chairman more irascible, and Harford was not the man to take him on. The best players were sold, the supply of juniors was exhausted and there was a limit to the number of times the manager could pull a rabbit out of a hat. The reckoning came in 1985–86 when Fulham never recovered from a bad start. Easily the worst team in the Second Division, they finished bottom, a massive 13 points short of safety. Harford left in June 1986.

But he was not out of work for long, and managed Luton and Wimbledon before teaming up with Kenny Dalglish in 1991 to take Blackburn from the Second Division to the Premiership title. After that, he was in managerial roles at West Brom, Queen's Park Rangers and Oxford. It was while coaching at Millwall that Harford, a non-smoker, was diagnosed with lung cancer. He died in August 2003 at the relatively young age of 58.

Ray Lewington (1986–94)

Born: Lambeth, London, September 1956
Player: Chelsea, Vancouver Whitecaps, Wimbledon, Fulham, Sheffield United
Manager: Fulham, Crystal Palace, Brentford, Watford

Few managers can have experienced such a torrid debut season as Ray Lewington. The popular former player returned to the Cottage as Harford's replacement in the summer of 1986 after a year at Sheffield United. He came back to a club that was newly relegated and had new owners, Marler Estates, a property company whose real motives were far from transparent.

The new manager had few resources at his disposal and the team struggled to make an impact in the Third Division. With results going against him, Lewington then had to endure the furore that surrounded the merger proposals with Queen's Park Rangers in the winter of 1987 and the uncertainty of another takeover. He and the team both survived in Division Three and in 1988–89 reached the Play-offs, but this was about as good as it got. After a struggle against relegation the following season, Lewington made way as manager, first for Alan Dicks and then Don Mackay, but stayed at Fulham as number two. He was given nine games in the spring of 1994 to save the Cottagers from relegation after Mackay was sacked, but, when the club dropped into the fourth tier of English football for the first time, he left.

Nobody doubted Lewington's commitment or integrity, and he retained the backing of the supporters throughout a difficult period. But he had little to work with and, even as manager, was still one of the best players at the club. While his coaching skills were widely recognised, moreover, he seemed to lack a nasty side that the best managers need to have. At times, his loyalty was taken for granted, and he played second fiddle to managers with much less ability.

But he was a respected figure in football, particularly in the South East, outside the top flight. After Fulham, he worked at Crystal Palace, Brentford and Watford, before returning to the Cottage in 2005 as reserve-team coach.

Alan Dicks (1990–91)

Born: Kennington, London, August 1934
Player: Chelsea, Southend, Coventry
Manager: Bristol City, Fulham

The takeover of Fulham by Jimmy Hill and his colleagues was wholeheartedly endorsed by supporters. After making the Play-offs in 1989, however, enthusiasm cooled as events at the Cottage at times took on an element of farce. When the club was struggling close to the drop zone in 1990, Alan Dicks arrived at Hill's behest to 'help' Lewington. Initially he was a 'consultant', but by the start of the next season he was installed as manager.

It was not long before the sceptics who thought Dicks was out of his depth were proved right. As a player, he had been with Chelsea and Southend before moving to Coventry. At Highfield Road, he became coach with Hill as manager and the two took Coventry into the First Division. Dicks then went to Bristol City as manager and took them into the top flight but, as the slide back down the divisions got underway, he left Ashton Gate with the Robins facing bankruptcy and went to work abroad.

Managing Fulham was Dicks's first job in English football for a decade, and it showed. He was completely out of touch with players, opponents and tactics. Simon Morgan, who played more games for Fulham in the 1990s than anyone else, wrote about the lack of discipline, shambolic training sessions and confusing tactics under Dicks. He was liked as a person, but the players had no respect for him as a manager.

This was reflected in the results. In his only full season, Fulham finished 21st but were spared relegation because only three clubs went down. And they got six fewer points (46) than when they were finally relegated three years later. A humiliating FA Cup defeat at home to Hayes, six divisions lower, in November was the end for Dicks, and weeks later he left Fulham and football.

Don Mackay (1991–94)

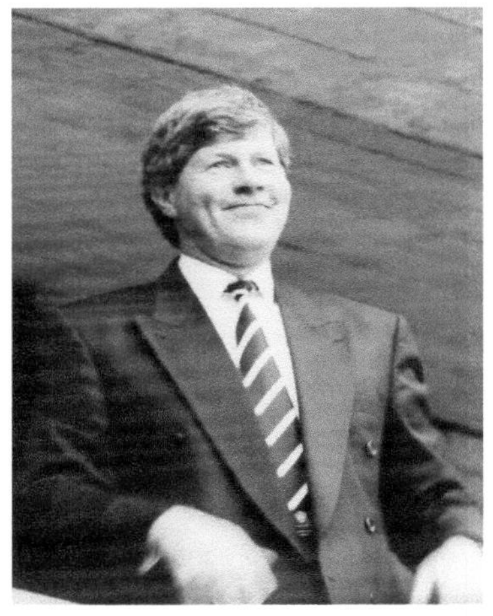

Born: Partick, Glasgow, March 1940
Player: Forfar, Dundee United, Southend
Manager: Dundee, Coventry, Blackburn, Fulham

The popular view that things could only get better after Dicks was soon disproved. Don Mackay talked a good game and put on a show of exaggerated animation from the touchline, but this was principally for the benefit of supporters. Basically, he was clueless and confirmed the old adage that goalkeepers (and a Scottish one at that) do not make good managers.

Born in Perth in 1940, Mackay played for Forfar, Dundee United and Southend between 1958 and 1974. His first managerial job in Britain was back in Dundee, but in 1984 he came south (via Sweden) to Coventry (1984–86) and Blackburn (1987–91). The arrival of Jack Walker to Ewood meant Mackay was displaced by Dalglish and Harford. He was not out of work for very long and with just under half the 1991–92 season gone he arrived at the Cottage.

His one full season in charge (1992–93) was spent largely in mid-table, but the following season it all went pear shaped. After just two wins in the first 16 games, the Cottagers were in the bottom four and spent the rest of the season trying to get out of the drop zone. Losing the final match at Swansea meant the League basement for the first time in the club's history. By then, Mackay had gone, effectively sacked in the dressing room at half-time at Leyton Orient in March. Lewington stepped in for the final nine games.

The players found Mackay weak and confusing and the squad was divided into small cliques. A familiar sight at home games was chairman Jimmy Hill leaving the Directors' Box, going down to the dugout and then, minutes later, seeing a substitution made. It hardly inspired confidence in the manager. His post-Cottage career included a brief spell in charge at Aidrieonians in 2001 and scouting for Middlesbrough.

Ian Branfoot (1994–96)

Born: Gateshead, Tyneside, January 1947
Player: Sheffield Wednesday, Doncaster, Lincoln
Manager: Reading, Southampton, Fulham, Swansea

After Lewington's vain efforts to save Fulham from the drop in the spring of 1994, the board decided on a huge shake up, and 47-year-old Ian Branfoot was the less than popular choice to implement it. He managed the way he played. As a full-back with Sheffield Wednesday, Doncaster and Lincoln, and a manager at Reading, he was tough, uncompromising and competitive. It was something of a surprise when he jumped into the top flight with Southampton, and he suffered appalling personal abuse from so-called supporters but conducted himself with great dignity.

It was Branfoot's no-nonsense approach which the Fulham board felt could stop the rot at the Cottage. He certainly wielded the axe among the players. He moved on from the likes of Stannard, Pike, Eckhardt and Glen Thomas and replaced them with a number of players who Southampton on their CVs. The players were much more committed but results did not go the way the club hoped.

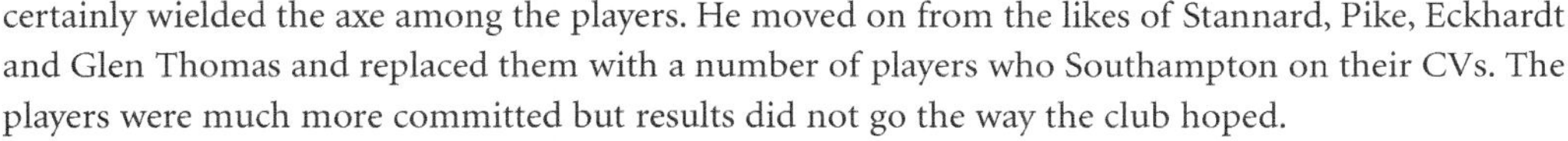

Mid-table was all Fulham could manage in Branfoot's first season and it got worse in the second. Defeat at Torquay in February 1996 saw the club drop to 91st place in the League, the lowest in Fulham's history. This came days after a 3–1 home defeat by Scunthorpe which attracted the smallest official crowd ever to a first-class game at the Cottage, just 2,176. Just over a week later, Branfoot was made general manager and coach Micky Adams took over team affairs.

On the surface, Branfoot was a failure, but Simon Morgan compared him very favourably with his predecessors, believing he brought some pride back to the club. It was the small things that made the difference, such as getting proper training kit and taking the players' side with the board. And Adams could not have succeeded almost immediately had he not had a decent inheritance.

Micky Adams (1996–97)

Born: Sheffield, Yorkshire, November 1961
Player: Gillingham, Coventry, Leeds, Southampton, Stoke, Fulham
Manager: Fulham, Swansea, Brentford, Brighton, Leicester, Coventry

Despite the fact he had been at the Cottage for 18 months as a player, Adams was something of an unknown quantity to supporters. Injuries had restricted his appearances and he had never managed before. In his first few months he lifted the club away from the Third Division basement and in the 1996 close season put together a squad for very little outlay that would bring the club's first promotion for 15 years. And there is no doubt that Adams's motivational skills were instrumental in the success.

Aged 35, Adams had previously played for Gillingham, Coventry, Leeds, Southampton and Stoke, which included almost 250 First Division appearances. At Fulham he made several cheap or free signings

(Watson, Freeman, Carpenter, Cockerill and Cullip) and squeezed a bit more out of some of the players already at the club (Morgan, Angus, Blake and especially Conroy). The team got off to a flying start and kept going, clinching promotion with four games to spare.

At the same time, the club was negotiating to buy the ground from the Royal Bank of Scotland, a deal which was to cost the management team their jobs. The existing board lacked the resources to strengthen the squad and improve the ground, while promotion had made the Cottagers a more attractive proposition. Enter Mohamed Al Fayed and exit Messrs Adams, Branfoot and assistant manager Alan Cork. Adams had hardly been a failure, but the new chairman wanted a high-profile manager who would put Fulham back on the map.

Adams's post-Fulham managerial career was as nomadic as his pre-Fulham playing days. To date, it has taken in Swansea, Brentford, Forest, Brighton, Leicester and Coventry. Branfoot has scouted for Swansea and Leeds and run the Sunderland academy while Cork worked again with Adams at Swansea and Leicester and was at Cardiff in between.

Ray Wilkins (1997–98)

Born: Hillingdon, Middlesex, September 1956
Player: Chelsea, Manchester United, AC Milan, Paris St Germain, Rangers, Queen's Park Rangers, Crystal Palace, Wycombe Wanderers, Hibernian, Millwall, Leyton Orient, England
Manager: Queen's Park Rangers, Fulham

There were few more high-profile personalities in English football than Kevin Keegan. The former Scunthorpe, Liverpool, Hamburg, Southampton, Newcastle and England player had been out of football since leaving the manager's job at St James' eight months earlier. He was persuaded back, taking the clumsy title of chief operating officer, and the first thing he did was to appoint his old England colleague Ray Wilkins as team manager.

It was a strange choice. Where Keegan was exciting to the point of recklessness, Wilkins was boring and predictable. In a long career, he had played for seven English clubs, AC Milan, Paris St-Germain, Glasgow Rangers and Hibernian. While he was a cultured midfield player, his spell as manager at Loftus Road resulted in Rangers being relegated.

The Keegan-Wilkins duo took up the challenge from Al Fayed, spent money and got some big-name players to drop down a division or two to join Fulham. But results were slow to improve and performances were uninspiring. Slowly, the Cottagers climbed the table, but it was not very exciting to watch. It was a poor return on the record amounts spent (by the standards of Fulham and the third tier of English football). This was Wilkins rather than Keegan, and even stumbling into the Play-offs was not really good enough. Just before the first Play-off game against Grimsby, Wilkins went, clearly sacked by his old friend.

The acrimonious parting of the ways was necessary. Adams's team was much better to watch and it had only cost a fraction of the new squad. Wilkins resumed his tour around the football clubs of Britain (Chelsea, Watford and Millwall as a coach), but he has never been given another chance as a manager. An exceedingly nice and unfailingly courteous man, he was probably not cut out for the rough and tumble of management.

Kevin Keegan (1998–99)

Born: Armthorpe, Yorkshire, February 1951
Player: Scunthorpe, Liverpool, SV Hamburg, Southampton, Newcastle, England
Manager: Newcastle, Fulham, England (national side), Manchester City

When Wilkins went, Keegan took over team duties himself, and from the start Fulham set the pace in the Second Division. As the season wore on, club records (defensive as well as attacking) tumbled and in many statistical respects this was Fulham's best-ever season. The Fayed Revolution at the Cottage was officially launched.

Even though Fulham were racing away with the divisional title, Keegan continued to spend money, but it seemed as if he was preparing for a higher division. The likes of Steve Finnan, Barry Hayles and Geoff Horsefield were clearly capable of playing at a higher level, while cameos from former Newcastle stars Peter Beardsley and Philippe Albert added to the glamour that the Fayed-Keegan partnership was creating. Success in the two Cup competitions against Premiership opponents confirmed the club's potential.

But just as it all seemed to be going well, Glenn Hoddle's ill-advised remarks in a *Times* interview injected a discordant note into Fulham's procession to the title. When the England manager resigned, Keegan was the 'Peoples' Choice' as successor, largely as a result of a media campaign. The fact that Keegan wanted the job was entirely understandable. What upset the Fulham fans was the uncertainty he created by saying he did not want to leave Fulham and that he could do both jobs, and then, when he decided to go, announcing it on a television programme days before the celebrations to mark the title win.

It was an unfortunate end to what had been a thrilling and successful phase, one that had taken Adams's work to the next level and encouraged the chairman to believe that his ambitions for Fulham were achievable. Keegan had brought excitement and style to the Cottage but, as at Newcastle, England and Manchester City, he did not stay long enough to see the job he had started through to a conclusion.

Paul Bracewell (1999–2000)

Born: Heswall, Cheshire, July 1962
Player: Stoke, Sunderland, Everton, Newcastle, Fulham, England
Manager: Fulham, Halifax

To liken Bracewell's succession to the dustcarts after the Lord Mayor's Show may be a bit harsh, but for Fulham fans the first season back in the second tier of English football for 13 years was anti-climatic. It was even worse than that – it was seriously boring. Bracewell's appointment was understandable. Despite a catalogue of appalling injuries, he had been an efficient and highly-regarded midfield player with Stoke, the outstanding Everton side of the mid-1980s, Newcastle (with Keegan) and Sunderland.

Although he was 35 years old, he was one of Keegan's first signings in the autumn of 1997, combining playing with coaching. When Keegan left, Bracewell offered the prospect of continuity, but the two were like chalk and cheese. His early forays into the transfer market were imaginative but only Lee Clark really worked out. While mid table was a satisfactory record for most clubs in their first season at a higher level, Fulham's expectations were higher and, after Keegan, supporters were more demanding, wanting exciting rather than ultra-cautious football.

Apart from a brief flourish in the League Cup, Bracewell's Fulham disappointed, and eight successive games in December 1999, in which the only Fulham goal was an own-goal by a Tranmere full-back, just about summed up his brief tenure. As a player, Bracewell was hardworking rather than sparkling; as a manager, he lacked his predecessor's charisma, and his teams seemed more concerned with avoiding defeat than winning. Fulham's fourth manager in less than three seasons bit the dust in the spring after a dismal 1–0 defeat at Ipswich.

A Bracewell signing, German World Cup winner Karl-Heinz Reidle (assisted by former Liverpool manager Roy Evans), stepped into the breach in the closing weeks of the season. Bracewell himself was manager at lowly Halifax the following season and then had two years with the FA as a national coach.

Jean Tigana (2000–01)

Born: Bamako, Mali, June 1955
Player: Sporting Toulon, Lyonnais, Bordeaux, Marseilles, France
Manager: Lyonnais, AS Monaco, Fulham, Besiktas JK

The board broke new ground with the appointment of Tigana in the spring of 2000. In the speculation that followed Bracewell's sacking, nobody had the 45-year-old Frenchman on their radar, but his selection proved as inspired as it was surprising. The brilliant midfield player (for Toulon, Lyon and especially Bordeaux, as well as Platini's wonderful national side of the 1980s) had become an innovative and successful manager (in particular with Monaco from 1995 to 1999) before he got the call from Fulham.

A totally unknown quantity on his arrival, he took about 90 minutes to persuade Fulham supporters that something special was about to happen, the length of time it took to demolish Crewe in the opening game of 2000–01. Another 10 straight victories followed as the Cottagers cruised to the First Division title playing a sublime passing game that made this the most attractive Fulham side in living memory.

Life in the Premiership was, unsurprisingly, much harder, but Tigana's players were not out of their depth. Such was his standing in Europe, and so comprehensive his network, that a steady stream of previously unknown players made their way to SW6 (Legwinski and Malbranque) as well as a top international goalkeeper like van der Sar. It was a surreal time at the Cottage, playing the biggest clubs with major stars just five years on from Micky Adams and what was in reality the Fourth Division.

In the club's second season back in the top flight, Tigana seemed to lose his way, or perhaps lose interest. Relations with the board were soured by the purchase of Steve Marlet, who showed very little evidence of being worth even half the reported £11 million fee Fulham paid. With relegation a possibility, the board sacked the manager with just a handful of games remaining, a sad end to a wonderful phase.

Chris Coleman (2003–07)

Born: Swansea, Glamorgan, June 1970
Player: Swansea, Crystal Palace, Blackburn, Fulham, Wales
Manager: Fulham, Real Sociedad

Chris Coleman symbolised the Fayed Revolution at the Cottage. Among the first signings for a record £1.9 million from Blackburn in November 1997, he was a natural leader who he captained the side to the Second Division title 18 months later. He was also Tigana's captain as Fulham romped away with the First Division two years later. But Coleman's contribution was sadly cut short in January 2001 when a dreadful car crash ended his playing career.

Highly regarded at the Cottage, the former Welsh international central-defender became more involved in coaching as his recovery progressed. Although still not 100% fit, he took on the caretaker manager's role when Tigana went in April 2003 and was appointed permanently after this successful 'trial' period. He was the youngest manager in the Premiership (33) and Fulham's youngest full-time manager.

He got off to a great start, steering the Cottagers to their highest-ever top-flight placing. He had a pretty good inheritance from Tigana, but added excellent motivational skills and so squeezed a bit extra out of some of the squad than his more illustrious predecessor. As the turnover among the squad increased, however, shortcomings started to emerge. When key players moved on, their replacements were often of lesser ability. Without Tigana's reputation and network, moreover, Coleman too often turned to players he knew, from Blackburn or Wales.

It worked for a while but, in his fourth season, the cracks were starting to show. As the quality of the squad dipped, and the tactics became more predictable and sterile, the supporters (for so long totally behind him) got restless when a long winless run in the winter of 2007 brought Fulham to the brink of relegation. The board acted, as it did with Tigana, by dispensing with the manager's services. Sadly, had Coleman left in the summer of 2006, he would have been regarded as an outstanding manager.

Lawrie Sanchez (2007-)

Born: Lambeth, England, 22 October 1959
Player: Reading, Wimbledon, Swindon Town, Sligo Rovers, Northern Ireland
Manager: Sligo Rovers, Wimbledon (reserve-team coach), Wycombe Wanderers, Northern Ireland, Fulham

With five games left at the end of the 2006–07 season, Sanchez was given the task of making sure that Fulham avoided relegation. Sanchez managed to guide Fulham to one draw and then a win over Liverpool in the final game of the season to ensure that Fulham missed the drop.

As a player, the highlight of his career was scoring the winning goal in Wimbledon's shock victory over Liverpool in the 1988 FA Cup Final. He also scored the goal that helped Wimbledon to win promotion to the First Division in 1986. Sanchez left the Dons in 1994 for Swindon Town, where he played for a season, before ending his career as player-manager for Sligo Rovers. He also gained three international caps for Northern Ireland.

Sanchez's managerial career began at Wycombe Wanderers, starting out as reserve team coach and eventually being appointed as manager in 1999. In 2001 Sanchez guided Wycombe to the FA Cup semi-final, which they lost to Liverpool 2–1, having held them to 0–0 for most of the match. He was appointed as manager of Northern Ireland in January 2004, taking over from Sammy McIlroy, and saw his side beat England 1–0 in the World Cup 2006 Qualifiers, as well as enjoying a 3–2 victory over Spain in a Euro 2008 qualifying match. When Sanchez resigned from the Northern Ireland job on 11 May 2007, his team was top of their Euro 2008 Qualifying group. With high stakes and everything to play for, only time will tell whether Sanchez can prove himself as a Premiership Manager.

Fulham's League/Premiership Record Against Other Clubs

Up to end of 2006–07 season. Play-offs and Test Matches not included

		HOME					AWAY					POINTS*	
Opponents	P	W	D	L	F	A	W	D	L	F	A	Total	% of wins
Aldershot	4	1	0	1	6	3	2	0	0	5	1	9	75
Arsenal	40	6	4	10	31	37	0	2	18	17	53	24	20
Aston Villa	46	11	9	3	42	28	4	7	12	24	41	61	44
Barnet	8	3	1	0	10	1	1	2	1	4	5	15	63
Barnsley	76	17	13	8	65	37	5	10	23	40	82	89	39
Barrow	2	1	0	0	2	1	0	0	1	1	3	3	50
Birmingham C	68	12	11	11	50	39	8	11	15	51	59	82	40
Blackburn R	68	14	12	8	65	47	8	5	21	31	59	83	41
Blackpool	98	23	16	10	70	43	10	13	26	51	86	128	44
Bolton W	66	15	9	9	54	39	7	8	18	34	47	83	42
Bournemouth	24	4	5	3	16	12	2	3	7	14	22	26	36
Bradford C	36	7	8	3	27	13	3	7	8	16	22	45	42
Bradford PA	34	10	4	3	36	21	7	5	5	25	22	60	59
Brentford	40	8	8	4	35	21	9	4	7	26	31	63	53
Brighton & HA	34	13	0	4	37	12	3	3	11	14	34	51	50
Bristol C	50	14	6	5	43	22	9	6	10	29	33	81	54
Bristol R	54	15	5	7	60	41	5	7	15	30	51	72	44
Burnley	80	23	9	8	77	47	5	6	29	33	86	99	41
Bury	68	18	9	7	68	35	6	11	17	35	55	92	45
Cambridge U	16	3	1	4	11	10	1	2	5	2	11	15	31
Cardiff C	48	12	3	9	47	41	9	4	11	30	31	70	49
Carlisle U	32	9	1	6	27	15	4	3	9	19	31	43	45
Charlton A	54	13	8	6	35	29	6	10	11	31	43	75	46
Chelsea	56	5	6	17	31	51	2	10	16	22	45	37	22
Chester C	22	7	2	2	18	11	5	3	3	14	17	41	62
Chesterfield	36	10	7	1	29	14	4	5	9	15	25	54	50
Colchester U	10	3	1	1	8	4	1	1	3	8	12	14	47
Coventry C	34	9	5	3	31	15	6	2	9	21	28	52	51
Crewe A	8	3	1	0	8	2	2	2	0	7	5	18	75
Crystal P	38	10	6	3	32	19	5	7	7	23	28	58	51
Darlington	14	6	1	0	24	5	3	2	2	7	10	30	71
Derby C	44	10	8	4	38	24	3	6	13	27	52	53	40
Doncaster R	34	9	4	4	35	18	5	6	6	20	23	52	51
Everton	38	12	4	3	29	17	0	4	15	14	45	44	39

Opponents	P	HOME W	D	L	F	A	AWAY W	D	L	F	A	POINTS* Total	% of wins
Exeter C	26	6	5	2	24	14	6	1	6	21	18	42	54
Gainsborough T	10	4	0	1	18	2	2	2	1	6	6	20	67
Gillingham	32	9	4	3	26	15	4	2	10	16	27	45	47
Glossop NE	16	5	1	2	18	9	3	2	3	6	7	27	56
Grimsby T	52	14	5	7	50	31	8	5	13	36	35	76	49
Halifax T	4	2	0	0	5	2	1	0	1	9	2	9	75
Hartlepool U	12	4	1	1	8	5	3	0	3	7	6	22	61
Hereford U	8	2	2	0	6	2	0	2	2	1	3	10	42
Huddersfield T	56	15	8	5	44	28	6	5	17	29	51	76	45
Hull C	76	17	13	8	61	25	8	11	19	33	61	99	43
Ipswich T	16	3	4	1	20	8	4	1	3	14	12	26	54
Leeds U	62	17	4	10	56	39	9	7	15	31	48	89	48
Leicester C	72	22	9	5	75	39	15	5	16	54	69	125	58
Leyton O	82	18	14	9	66	41	11	11	19	38	51	112	46
Lincoln C	44	15	4	3	53	22	7	4	11	27	46	74	56
Liverpool	40	7	6	7	26	25	0	5	15	15	53	32	27
Luton T	48	16	3	5	49	27	8	1	15	28	44	76	53
Macclesfield T	2	1	0	0	1	0	1	0	0	1	0	6	100
Manchester C	44	9	6	7	44	38	4	4	14	26	55	49	37
Manchester U	54	8	10	9	41	45	2	3	22	23	61	43	27
Mansfield T	26	5	6	2	16	12	4	4	5	15	18	37	47
Merthyr T	4	2	0	0	9	4	1	0	1	5	7	9	75
Middlesbrough	52	14	3	9	40	36	7	4	15	33	52	70	45
Millwall	36	10	4	4	25	14	5	6	7	20	24	55	51
Nelson	2	0	1	0	0	0	0	1	0	1	1	2	33
Newcastle U	50	14	5	6	52	39	7	7	11	35	46	75	50
Newport C	14	5	0	2	15	8	2	3	2	13	12	24	57
Northampton T	26	5	4	4	21	22	4	3	6	19	23	34	44
Norwich C	32	7	4	5	33	20	6	5	5	22	21	48	50
Nottingham F	82	24	11	6	74	33	9	13	19	48	74	123	50
Notts C	58	22	3	4	80	33	6	10	13	28	53	97	56
Oldham A	48	13	6	5	37	22	6	5	13	27	39	68	47
Oxford U	18	3	4	2	8	8	1	2	6	6	12	18	33
Peterborough U	2	0	0	1	0	1	0	0	1	1	4	0	0
Plymouth A	52	14	7	5	59	35	3	7	16	31	60	65	42
Portsmouth	44	6	7	9	27	29	4	7	11	23	41	44	33
Port Vale	46	12	6	5	54	30	8	7	8	25	37	73	53
Preston NE	58	16	4	9	42	29	9	6	14	35	41	85	49
Queen's Park R	22	4	1	6	15	15	2	3	6	7	14	22	33
Reading	30	6	5	4	20	17	5	2	8	17	18	40	44
Rochdale	10	3	2	0	11	2	4	1	0	8	4	24	80
Rotherham U	42	12	6	3	41	19	6	6	9	27	34	66	52

		HOME					AWAY					POINTS*	
Opponents	**P**	**W**	**D**	**L**	**F**	**A**	**W**	**D**	**L**	**F**	**A**	**Total**	**% of wins**
Scarborough	6	2	0	1	6	2	1	1	1	5	5	10	56
Scunthorpe U	8	2	1	1	5	5	3	0	1	9	6	16	67
Sheffield U	54	14	6	7	61	35	5	6	16	22	45	69	43
Sheffield W	60	18	5	7	61	35	4	9	17	32	59	80	44
Shrewsbury T	20	7	1	2	19	8	2	4	4	9	15	32	53
Southampton	54	15	10	2	42	25	1	7	19	26	63	65	40
Southend U	18	5	2	2	14	12	4	3	2	11	9	32	59
Southport	2	1	0	0	3	2	1	0	0	2	0	6	100
South Shields	18	4	3	2	13	8	0	1	8	5	19	16	30
Stockport C	42	17	1	3	54	14	8	3	10	28	29	79	63
Stoke C	60	14	7	9	56	40	10	7	13	32	50	86	48
Sunderland	42	9	4	8	32	30	4	7	10	22	32	50	40
Swansea C	56	22	2	4	81	28	6	7	15	38	63	93	55
Swindon T	22	7	2	2	25	11	3	4	4	17	22	36	55
Thames A	4	2	0	0	12	2	0	2	0	0	0	8	67
Torquay U	20	8	1	1	30	8	3	2	5	15	19	36	60
Tottenham H	56	7	10	11	37	43	2	11	15	25	49	48	29
Tranmere R	14	4	1	2	10	6	3	2	2	11	6	24	57
Walsall	28	9	5	0	33	12	4	7	3	21	22	51	61
Watford	18	5	2	2	25	8	3	3	3	17	18	29	54
West Bromwich A	62	13	7	11	42	27	7	6	18	36	73	73	39
West Ham U	70	16	8	11	61	43	8	7	20	43	70	87	41
Wigan A	28	8	4	2	22	10	4	4	6	14	16	44	52
Wimbledon	8	2	1	1	8	5	2	1	1	7	3	14	58
Wolverhampton W	66	14	8	11	50	37	5	10	18	34	64	75	38
Wrexham	12	2	2	2	3	4	2	3	1	9	6	17	47
Wycombe W	4	1	1	0	2	0	0	1	1	1	3	5	42
York C	14	3	2	2	10	8	3	1	3	10	8	21	50

* Three points for a win throughout

Summary of Fulham's League Seasons

	HOME					AWAY					TOTAL							
Season	W	D	L	F	A	W	D	L	F	A	P	W	D	L	F	A	Pts	Pos
SOUTHERN LEAGUE																		
Division One																		
1903–04	7	6	4	23	14	2	6	9	11	22	34	9	12	13	34	36	30	11
1904–05	10	5	2	32	9	4	5	8	14	25	34	14	10	10	46	34	38	6
1905–06	10	7	0	22	6	9	5	3	22	9	34	19	12	3	44	15	50	1
1906–07	13	5	1	34	12	7	8	4	24	20	38	20	13	5	58	32	53	1
FOOTBALL LEAGUE																		
Division Two																		
1907–08	12	2	5	50	14	10	3	6	32	35	38	22	5	11	82	49	49	4
1908–09	8	4	7	39	26	5	7	7	19	22	38	13	11	14	58	48	37	10
1909–10	9	7	3	28	13	5	6	8	23	30	38	14	13	11	51	43	41	7
1910–11	12	3	4	35	15	3	4	12	17	33	38	15	7	16	52	48	37	10
1911–12	10	3	6	42	24	6	4	9	24	34	38	16	7	15	66	58	39	8
1912–13	13	5	1	47	16	4	0	15	18	39	38	17	5	16	65	55	39	9
1913–14	10	3	6	31	20	6	3	10	15	23	38	16	6	16	46	43	38	11
1914–15	12	0	7	35	20	3	7	9	18	27	38	15	7	16	53	47	37	12
1919–20	11	6	4	36	18	8	3	10	25	32	42	19	9	14	61	50	47	6
1920–21	14	4	3	33	12	2	6	13	10	35	42	16	10	16	43	47	42	9
1921–22	14	5	2	41	8	4	4	13	16	30	42	18	9	15	57	38	45	7
1922–23	10	7	4	29	12	6	5	10	14	20	42	16	12	14	43	32	44	10
1923–24	9	8	4	30	20	1	6	14	15	36	42	10	14	18	45	56	34	20
1924–25	11	6	4	26	15	4	4	13	15	41	42	15	10	17	41	56	40	12
1925–26	8	6	7	32	29	3	6	12	14	48	42	11	12	19	46	77	34	19
1926–27	11	4	6	39	31	2	4	15	19	61	42	13	8	21	58	92	34	18
1927–28	12	7	2	46	22	1	0	20	22	67	42	13	7	22	68	89	33	21
Division Three South																		
1928–29	14	3	4	60	31	7	7	7	41	40	42	21	10	11	101	71	52	5
1929–30	12	6	3	54	33	6	5	10	33	50	42	18	11	13	87	83	47	7
1930–31	15	3	3	49	21	3	4	14	28	54	42	18	7	17	77	75	43	9
1931–32	15	3	3	72	27	9	6	6	39	35	42	24	9	9	111	62	57	1
Division Two																		
1932–33	12	5	4	46	31	8	5	8	32	34	42	20	10	12	78	65	50	4
1933–34	13	3	5	29	17	2	4	15	19	50	42	15	7	20	48	67	37	16
1934–35	15	3	3	62	26	2	9	10	14	30	42	17	12	13	76	56	46	7
1935–36	11	6	4	58	24	4	8	9	18	28	42	15	14	13	76	52	44	9
1936–37	11	5	5	43	24	4	8	9	28	37	42	15	13	14	71	61	43	11
1937–38	10	7	4	44	23	6	4	11	17	34	42	16	11	15	61	57	43	8
1938–39	12	5	4	35	20	5	5	11	26	35	42	17	10	15	61	55	44	12

	HOME					AWAY					TOTAL							
Season	**W**	**D**	**L**	**F**	**A**	**W**	**D**	**L**	**F**	**A**	**P**	**W**	**D**	**L**	**F**	**A**	**Pts**	**Pos**
1946–47	12	4	5	40	25	3	5	13	23	49	42	15	9	18	63	74	39	15
1947–48	6	9	6	24	19	9	1	11	23	27	42	15	10	17	47	46	40	11
1948–49	16	4	1	52	14	8	5	8	25	23	42	24	9	9	77	37	57	1
Division One																		
1949–50	8	6	7	24	19	2	8	11	17	35	42	10	14	18	41	54	34	17
1950–51	8	5	8	35	37	5	6	10	17	31	42	13	11	18	52	68	37	18
1951–52	5	7	9	38	31	3	4	14	20	46	42	8	11	23	58	77	27	22
Division Two																		
1952–53	14	1	6	52	28	3	9	9	29	43	42	17	10	15	81	71	44	8
1953–54	12	3	6	62	39	5	7	9	36	46	42	17	10	15	98	85	44	8
1954–55	10	5	6	46	29	4	6	11	30	50	42	14	11	17	76	79	39	14
1955–56	15	2	4	59	27	5	4	12	30	52	42	20	6	16	89	79	46	9
1956–57	13	1	7	53	32	6	3	12	31	44	42	19	4	19	84	76	42	11
1957–58	13	5	3	53	24	7	7	7	44	35	42	20	12	10	97	59	52	5
1958–59	18	1	2	65	26	9	5	7	31	35	42	27	6	9	96	61	60	2
Division One																		
1959–60	12	4	5	42	28	5	6	10	31	52	42	17	10	15	73	80	44	10
1960–61	8	8	5	39	39	6	0	15	33	56	42	14	8	20	72	95	36	17
1961–62	8	3	10	38	34	5	4	12	28	40	42	13	7	22	66	74	33	20
1962–63	8	6	7	28	30	6	4	11	22	41	42	14	10	18	50	71	38	16
1963–64	11	8	2	45	23	2	5	14	13	42	42	13	13	16	58	65	39	15
1964–65	10	5	6	44	32	1	7	13	16	46	42	11	12	19	60	78	34	20
1965–66	9	4	8	34	37	5	3	13	33	48	42	14	7	21	67	85	35	20
1966–67	8	7	6	49	34	3	5	13	22	49	42	11	12	19	71	83	34	18
1967–68	6	4	11	27	41	4	3	14	29	57	42	10	7	25	56	98	27	22
Division Two																		
1968–69	6	7	8	20	28	1	4	16	20	53	42	7	11	24	40	81	25	22
Division Three																		
1969–70	12	9	2	43	26	8	6	9	38	29	46	20	15	11	81	55	55	4
1970–71	15	6	2	39	12	9	6	8	29	29	46	24	12	10	68	41	60	2
Division Two																		
1971–72	10	7	4	29	20	2	3	16	16	48	42	12	10	20	45	68	34	20
1972–73	11	6	4	32	16	5	6	10	26	33	42	16	12	14	58	49	44	9
1973–74	11	4	6	26	20	5	6	10	13	23	42	16	10	16	39	43	42	13
1974–75	9	8	4	29	17	4	8	9	15	22	42	13	16	13	44	39	42	9
1975–76	9	8	4	27	14	4	6	11	18	33	42	13	14	15	45	47	40	12
1976–77	9	7	5	39	25	2	6	13	15	36	42	11	13	18	54	61	35	17
1977–78	9	8	4	32	19	5	5	11	17	30	42	14	13	15	49	49	41	10
1978–79	10	7	4	35	19	3	8	10	15	28	42	13	15	14	50	47	41	10
1979–80	6	4	11	19	28	5	3	13	23	46	42	11	7	24	42	74	29	20
Division Three																		
1980–81	8	7	8	28	29	7	6	10	29	35	46	15	13	18	57	64	43	13

	HOME					AWAY					TOTAL							
Season	**W**	**D**	**L**	**F**	**A**	**W**	**D**	**L**	**F**	**A**	**P**	**W**	**D**	**L**	**F**	**A**	**Pts**	**Pos**
1981–82	12	9	2	44	22	9	6	8	33	29	46	21	15	10	77	51	78	3
Division Two																		
1982–83	13	5	3	36	20	7	4	10	28	27	42	20	9	13	64	47	69	4
1983–84	9	6	6	35	24	6	6	9	25	29	42	15	12	15	60	53	57	11
1984–85	13	3	5	35	26	6	5	10	33	38	42	19	8	15	68	64	65	9
1985–86	8	3	10	29	32	2	3	16	16	37	42	10	6	26	45	69	36	22
Division Three																		
1986–87	8	8	7	35	41	4	9	10	24	36	46	12	17	17	59	77	53	18
1987–88	10	5	8	36	24	9	4	10	33	36	46	19	9	18	69	60	66	9
1988–89	12	7	4	42	28	10	2	11	27	39	46	22	9	15	69	67	75	4
1989–90	8	8	7	33	27	4	7	12	22	39	46	12	15	19	55	66	51	20
1990–91	8	8	7	27	22	2	8	13	14	34	46	10	16	20	41	56	46	21
1991–92	11	7	5	29	16	8	6	9	28	37	46	19	13	14	57	53	70	9
Division Two*																		
1992–93	9	9	5	28	22	7	8	8	29	33	46	16	17	13	57	55	65	12
1993–94	7	6	10	20	23	7	4	12	30	40	46	14	10	22	50	63	52	21
Division Three																		
1994–95	11	5	5	39	22	5	9	7	21	32	42	16	14	12	60	54	62	8
1995–96	10	9	4	39	26	2	8	13	18	37	46	12	17	17	57	63	53	17
1996–97	13	5	5	41	20	12	7	4	31	18	46	25	12	9	72	38	87	2
Division Two																		
1997–98	12	7	4	31	14	8	3	12	29	29	46	20	10	16	60	43	70	6
1998–99	19	3	1	50	12	12	5	6	29	20	46	31	8	7	79	32	101	1
Division One																		
1999–2000	13	7	3	33	13	4	9	10	19	28	46	17	16	13	52	41	67	9
2000–01	16	5	2	49	14	14	6	3	41	18	46	30	11	5	90	32	101	1
FA Premiership																		
2001–02	7	7	5	21	16	3	7	9	15	28	38	10	14	14	36	44	44	13
2002–03	11	3	5	26	18	2	6	11	15	32	38	13	9	16	41	50	48	14
2003–04	9	4	6	29	21	5	6	8	23	25	38	14	10	14	52	46	52	9
2004–05	8	4	7	29	26	4	4	11	23	34	38	12	8	18	52	60	44	13
2005–06	13	2	4	31	21	1	4	14	17	37	38	14	6	18	48	58	48	12
2006–07	7	7	5	18	18	1	8	10	20	42	38	8	15	15	38	60	39	16

*Due to the introduction of the Premier League, Division Three became known as Division Two.

Fulham's League Totals

	HOME					AWAY						TOTAL					
	W	D	L	F	A	W	D	L	F	A	P	W	D	L	F	A	Pts
PREMIER/DIV ONE																	
	156	94	116	597	505	63	90	213	394	741	732	219	184	329	991	1246	841
DIV ONE/TWO																	
	561	244	233	1947	1078	238	255	545	1112	1794	2076	799	499	778	3059	2872	2896
DIV TWO/THREE																	
	207	114	85	720	430	129	102	175	535	644	812	336	216	260	1255	1074	1224
DIV THREE																	
	34	19	14	119	68	19	24	24	70	87	134	53	43	38	189	155	202
SOUTHERN LEAGUE																	
	40	23	7	111	41	22	24	24	71	76	140	62	47	31	182	117	233
TOTAL																	
	998	494	455	3494	2122	471	495	981	2182	3342	3894	1469	989	1436	5676	5464	5396

1896-97

London League Division Two

No		Date	V	Opponents	R	H-T	F-T	Scorers	Attend
1	O	3	A	Brentford	L	1-2	1-6	Scorer Unknown	
2		24	H	Stanley	L	0-4	0-8		
3	N	21	H	Brentford	L	0-2	0-2		
4		28	H	Harrow A	W	1-0	5-0	Hollands 2, Shrimpton, J. Johnson,Surman	
5	J	9	A	Forest Swifts	L	0-1	1-8	Laird	
6		30	A	Hammersmith A	L	1-1	2-4	Lindsey, (O`Brien og)	
7	F	6	H	Forest Swifts	W	0-1	2-1	Pearce, Cadley	
8		13	A	West Croydon	D	1-0	1-1	Moon	
9		27	A	Harrow A	W	1-0	1-0	Aylott	
10	M	6	H	Queen's Park R	L	1-0	1-2	Moon	
11		13	A	Stanley	L	0-1	0-2		
12		20	A	Bromley	L	1-1	1-2	Aylott	
13		27	H	Bromley	D	0-0	0-0		
14	A	10	H	Hammersmith A	D		1-1		
15		17	H	West Croydon	D		1-1	Moon	
16		?	A	Queen's Park R	L		0-2		

F.A. Cup

No		Date	V	Opponents	R	H-T	F-T	Scorers
2Q	O	31	A	Swanscombe	L	0-3	0-5	

Middlesex Senior Cup

No		Date	V	Opponents	R	H-T	F-T	Scorers
1Q	O	10	H	Minerva	W	1-0	4-0	Lindsey, Surman 2, Witheridge
2Q	N	14	H	Enfield	W	1-0	3-0	Aylott 2, Hollands
1	J	16	H	London Welsh	L	0-1	1-3	Robertson (Fulham later awarded tie)
2	F	20	H	Ealing	L	0-1	1-3	Moon

London Senior Cup

No		Date	V	Opponents	R	H-T	F-T	Scorers
1Q	O	17	A	Woodford	L	1-2	1-4	Lindsey

Taylor, G.	Humphries	Shrimpton, H.	Peet	Pearce	Shrimpton, J.	Robertson	Frame	Lindsey	Surman	Hollands	May	Jackson	Johnson	Witheridge	Kingsbury	Shrimpton, T.	Laird	Aylott	Cox	Hooper	Cadley	Moon	Steers	Davey	Mitchell	Atkinson	Cherrett	Harris	Williams	
1	2	3	4	5	6	7	8	9	10	11																				1
	3	2				7	6	9	10	11	1	4	5	8																2
		3			6	7	10	9		11			5		1	2	4	8												3
		3			6	7	8	9	10	11			5		1	2	4													4
		2			3	7			10	11		9	5		1		6		4											5X
1					6	7	2	8		11			5				3	9	4	10										6
1				7	6		2		11				5				3	9	4	10	8									7
1				3	6	7	2		11				5					9	4		8	10								8
1					6	11	2						5				3	8	4			10	7	9						9
1				8	6	11	2						5						4			10	7	9	3					10
1				7	6				11				5				3					10	9		2	4	8			11
1				8	6	11							5					9				10	7		2	3	4			12
1				6		11			10				5						4			9	7		2	3	8			13
1				6		11			10										4			9	7		2	3	5	8		14
1				6		11			10										4			9	7		2	3	5	8		15
Team Unknown																														16

Taylor, G.	Humphries	Shrimpton, H.	Peet	Pearce	Shrimpton, J.	Robertson	Frame	Lindsey	Surman	Hollands	May	Jackson	Johnson	Witheridge	Kingsbury	Shrimpton, T.	Laird	Aylott	Cox	Hooper	Cadley	Moon	Steers	Davey	Mitchell	Atkinson	Cherrett	Harris	Williams	
	3	2			6	7	4	9	10	11			5	8	1															2Q

Taylor, G.	Humphries	Shrimpton, H.	Peet	Pearce	Shrimpton, J.	Robertson	Frame	Lindsey	Surman	Hollands	May	Jackson	Johnson	Witheridge	Kingsbury	Shrimpton, T.	Laird	Aylott	Cox	Hooper	Cadley	Moon	Steers	Davey	Mitchell	Atkinson	Cherrett	Harris	Williams	
1	3	2			6	7	4	9	10	11			5	8																1Q
		3			6	7	10			11			5	8	1	2		9	4											2Q
1					6	7	9		10	11			5			2		8	4										3	1
1					6	7	2		11				5	9				3	4		8	10								2

Taylor, G.	Humphries	Shrimpton, H.	Peet	Pearce	Shrimpton, J.	Robertson	Frame	Lindsey	Surman	Hollands	May	Jackson	Johnson	Witheridge	Kingsbury	Shrimpton, T.	Laird	Aylott	Cox	Hooper	Cadley	Moon	Steers	Davey	Mitchell	Atkinson	Cherrett	Harris	Williams	
1	3	2			6	7	4	9	10	11			5	8																1Q

X Ten men only

1897-98

London League Division Two

No		Date	V	Opponents	R	H-T	F-T	Scorers	Atten
1	S	25	H	Forest Swifts	W	2-0	9-0	Moon 3, Witheridge 2, Mitchell, Taylor, Aylott, Robertson	
2	O	2	H	Orient	W	3-0	6-0	Freeman 3, Moon 2, Aylott	
3	N	13	H	West Croydon	W	1-0	3-1	Aylott, Steers, Robertson	
4		20	A	Metropolitan Railway	W	1-0	1-0	Surman	
5	J	8	A	Harrow A	W	3-0	4-0	Ives, Freeman 2, Robertson	
6		15	H	Harrow A	W	8-0	13-0	Ives 5, Freeman 3, Taylor 2, Davies 2, Robertson	
7	F	5	H	Metropolitan Railway	D	0-2	2-2	Freeman pen, Robertson	
8		12	A	Barnet	D	1-0	1-1	Freeman	
9		19	A	2nd Life Guards	W		Scr	Fulham 2 pts	
10		26	A	Hammersmith A	W	1-0	2-0	Freeman 2	
11	M	12	H	2nd Life Guards	W	1-0	1-0	Ives	
12		16	A	West Croydon	D	1-0	2-2	Ives, Freeman	
13		26	H	Barnet	D	0-0	0-0		
14	A	2	A	West Hampstead	W	2-0	3-0	Freeman 2, Davies	
15		9	A	Orient	W	2-0	4-2	Freeman 3, Ives	
16		11	A	Forest Swifts	W	2-0	4-0	Freeman 2, Robertson, Bowker (at Craven Cottage)	
17		16	H	Hammersmith A	W	1-0	3-0	Ives 2 (1 pen), Freeman	
18		23	H	West Hampstead	D	0-0	2-2	Freeman 2 (1 pen)	

App

Goal

London Senior Cup

No		Date	V	Opponents	R	H-T	F-T	Scorers
1	O	9	H	Westminster	W	2-0	4-1	Freeman 2, Moon, Taylor
2	N	6	H	Wandsworth	W	0-0	1-0	Freeman pen.
3		27	H	Metropolitan Railway	W	1-0	2-0	Robertson, Aylott
4	J	1	A	Q.P.R.	W	1-1	4-3	Freeman 2, Ives, A.N. Other
5		22	A	Barking Woodville	D	0-0	0-0	
5R		29	H	Barking Woodville	L	0-1	0-1	

F.A. Amateur Cup

No		Date	V	Opponents	R	H-T	F-T	Scorers
1Q	O	16	H	Eversleigh	W	2-0	3-0	Robertson, Freeman 2
2Q		30	A	Southall	L	0-1	0-1	

Middlesex Senior Cup

No		Date	V	Opponents	R	H-T	F-T	Scorers
1	O	23	A	Pemberton	L	0-4	0-5	

	Kingsbury	Mitchell	Shrimpton, H.	Cox	Taylor	Peet	Steers	Witheridge	Moon	Aylott	Robertson	Freeman	Osbaldton	McPherson	Maile, A.	Knight	Surmon	Shrimpton, J.	Jennings	Pask	Ives	Cherrett	Davies	Wright	Harris, W.	Stevens	Alexander, W.	Stone, A.	Rock	Bowker	Simpson	Bowden	May
1	1	2	3	4	5	6	7	8	9	10	11																						
2	1	2	3	4	5		7		9	10		8	11	6																			
3		2	3	4	5		7			10	11	8			1	6	9																
4			3	4	5		7			10	11	8			1	2	9	6															
5			2		5		10			6	11	8			1	4			3	7	9												
6			3		5		4				11	8			1				2	7	9	6	10										
7			3	4	5						11	8		9	1	6			2				7	10									
8			3		5					6	11	8		9	1	4			2				7	10									
9																																	
10			3		5					4	11	8			1	6			2		9		7		10								
11					5					4	11	8			1	6			2		9		7			3	10						
12										4	11	8			1	3			2		9	6	7		10			5					
13			3		5					4	11	8			1	6					9		7		10	2							
14			3		5					4	11	8			1	6			2		9		7		10								
15					5		11			2	6	8			1	3					9		7		10				4				
16			3		5					4	11	8			1	6	2				9		7							10			
17			3		5					4	11	8			1	6					9		7								2	10	
18			3		5					6	11	8			1	4			2		9		7									10	
A	2	3	14	5	16	1	7	1	2	15	16	16	1	3	15	14	3	1	9	2	11	2	12	2	5	2	1	1	1	1	1	2	-
G		1			3		1	2	5	3	6	23		1			1				11		3							1			-

	Kingsbury	Mitchell	Shrimpton, H.	Cox	Taylor	Peet	Steers	Witheridge	Moon	Aylott	Robertson	Freeman	Osbaldton	McPherson	Maile, A.	Knight	Surmon	Shrimpton, J.	Jennings	Pask	Ives	Cherrett	Davies	Wright	Harris, W.	Stevens	Alexander, W.	Stone, A.	Rock	Bowker	Simpson	Bowden	May
1	1	2	3	4	5		7		9	10	11	8				6																	
2		2	3	4			7			10	11	8			1	6	5												9				
3			3	4	5		7	10		9	11	8			1	2	6																
4			2		5		7			6	11	8			1	4			3		9		10										
5			3	4	5						11	8			1	6			2	7	9		10										
5R			3	4	5						11	8			1	6			2	7	9		10										

	Kingsbury	Mitchell	Shrimpton, H.	Cox	Taylor	Peet	Steers	Witheridge	Moon	Aylott	Robertson	Freeman	Osbaldton	McPherson	Maile, A.	Knight	Surmon
1Q		2		4	5		7	10	9	3	11	8			1	6	
2Q		2	3	4			7		9	10	11	8			1	6	5

	Kingsbury	Mitchell	Shrimpton, H.	Cox	Taylor	Peet	Steers	Witheridge	Moon	Aylott	Robertson	Freeman	Osbaldton	McPherson	Maile, A.	Knight	Surmon	Shrimpton, J.	Jennings	Pask	Ives	Cherrett	Davies	Wright	Harris, W.	Stevens	Alexander, W.	Stone, A.	Rock	Bowker	Simpson	Bowden	May
1		2	3	4	5		7		9	10	11	8				6																	1

1898-99

Southern League Division Two

	P	W	D	L	F	A	Pts
Thames Ironworks	22	19	1	2	64	16	39
Wolverton L & NW Rly	22	13	4	5	88	43	30
Watford	22	14	2	6	62	35	30
Brentford	22	11	3	8	59	39	25
Wycombe Wanderers	22	10	2	10	55	57	22
Southall	22	11	0	11	44	55	22
Chesham	22	9	2	11	45	62	20
St Albans	22	8	3	11	45	59	19
Shepherds Bush	22	7	3	12	37	53	17
Fulham	22	6	4	12	36	44	16
Uxbridge	22	7	2	13	29	48	16
Maidenhead	22	3	2	17	33	86	8

No		Date	V	Opponents	R	H-T	F-T	Scorers	Atten
1	S	10	A	Maidenhead	W	2-0	3-0	Alexander 2 Ives	
2		17	H	Brentford	L	0-3	1-4	Alexander	
3	O	1	A	Uxbridge	L	1-0	1-2	Freeman	
4			A	Chesham T	L	0-2	1-2	Freeman	
5	N	12	H	Maidenhead	D	1-1	2-2	Brown Craney	
6	D	3	A	Thames Ironworks	L	0-2	1-2	Freeman	
7		10	H	St Albans	D	1-1	2-2	Craney 2	
8		17	H	Wycombe W	W	0-0	3-1	Sherran 2 Hobart	
9	J	14	A	Southall	L	0-0	0-2		
10		21	H	Uxbridge	D	1-0	1-1	Stapley	
11		28	A	Watford	L	0-3	3-6	Sherran 2 Pask	
12	F	4	H	Wolverton & LNWR	L	0-2	1-3	Sherran	
13		11	H	Shepherd's Bush	W	2-0	3-2	Sherran Hobart Mayes	
14		26	A	Brentford	L	0-1	1-2	Hopkinson	
15	M	4	A	St Albans	L	0-2	1-3	Hopkinson	
16		18	H	Chesham T	W	2-0	2-1	Hopkinson 2	
17		22	H	Watford	W	1-0	2-0	Robertson Hopkinson	
18		25	A	Wolverton & LNWR	D	2-0	2-2	Sherran Hopkinson	
19		31	A	Shepherd's Bush	L	0-0	0-1		
20	A	8	H	Thames Ironworks	L	0-1	0-1		
21		12	A	Wycombe W	L	1-1	1-4	Sherran (pen)	
22		29	H	Southall	W	1-1	5-1	Hopkinson 3 Sherran Bowden	

App

Goa

FA AMATEUR CUP

1Q	O	15	H	2nd Coldstream Guards	W	3-0	4-0	Freeman (pen) Brown 2 Mandry
2Q		29	A	3rd Grenadiers	W	4-1	8-1	Brown 2 Craney 2 Park Robertson Freeman (1 og)
3Q	N	19	A	Hammersmith A	L	0-0	0-1	

LONDON SENIOR CUP

1	O	8	A	Civil Service	W	2-0	5-0	Freeman 3 Brown 2
2	N	5	H	Old St Mark's	L	0-1	0-1	

	aile AJ	Aylott	Johnson	Taylor	Bowden	Alexander	Freeman	Ives	Craney	Robertson	Simpson	Maile T	Ballantyne	Mandry	Pask	Brown	Sherran	Love	Hobart	Curling	Tutthill	Stapley	Mackie	Mayes	Humphries	Walker	Hopkinson	Hounsell	Turrill	Woodham	Surmon	Craig	Dawson	Bull	Holley	Lewis	Waite	Rose	Reed
1		3	4	5	6	7	8	9	10	11	2																												
2		3	4	5	6	7	8	9	10	11	2																												
3		3		5	6	7	8		10	11				9																2	4								
4		4		5			8		10	11	2	3		6	7	9																							
5		4			6		8		10	11	2	3			7	9																5							
6		4			6		8				2	3	5		7																		9	10	11				
7		4			6		8		10	11	2	3	5		7		9																						
8		4			6						2	3	5				9	8	10																	7	11		
9		4			11							2			7		9	8	10	1		6	3																
10		4		5	6							2			7		10		8	1		11	3															9	
11				5	6							2			7		10		8			4	3	9	11														
12				5	6							2			4		10		8				3	9	11	7													
13		4		5								2					10		7			6	3	8	10	11													
14				5	6							2			7		10					4	3		8	11	9												
15				5	6							2			7		10		8				3		4	11	9												
16		4		5	6							2			7		10		8			11	3				9												
17				5	6					11		2			7		10					4	3				9	8											
18		4		5	6							2			7		10					11	3				9	8											
19		4		5								2			7		10					6	3			11	9	8											
20				5	6										7		10				2	4	3				9	8	11										
21				5	6										7		10		8		2	4	3				9		11										
22		4		5	8										7		10				6	2	3				9												11
A		15	2	18	19	3	7	2	6	7	7	16	3	2	17	2	16	2	9	2	3	12	14	3	5	5	9	4	2	1	1	1	1	1	1	1	1	1	1
G		-	-	-	1	3	3	1	3	1	-	-	-	-	1	1	9	-	2	-	-	1	-	1	-	-	9	-	-	-	-	-	-	-	-	-	-	-	-

	aile AJ	Aylott	Johnson	Taylor	Bowden	Alexander	Freeman	Ives	Craney	Robertson	Simpson	Maile T	Ballantyne	Mandry	Pask	Brown	Sherran	Love	Hobart	Curling	Tutthill	Stapley	Mackie	Mayes	Humphries	Walker	Hopkinson	Hounsell	Turrill	Woodham	Surmon	Craig	Dawson	Bull	Holley	Lewis	Waite	Rose	Reed
		4		5	6		8		10		2	3		11	7	9														1Q									
		4			6		8		10	11	2	3			7	9														2Q									
		4			6		8		10	11	2	3			7	9														3Q									

	aile AJ	Aylott	Johnson	Taylor	Bowden	Alexander	Freeman	Ives	Craney	Robertson	Simpson	Maile T	Ballantyne	Mandry	Pask	Brown	Sherran	Love	Hobart	Curling	Tutthill	Stapley	Mackie	Mayes	Humphries	Walker	Hopkinson	Hounsell	Turrill	Woodham	Surmon	Craig	Dawson	Bull	Holley	Lewis	Waite	Rose	Reed
			4	5	6		8		10			3		11	7	9														1									
			4		6				10		2	3			7	9														2									

eshire played No 2 v Civil Service
rimpton was No 8 v Old St Mark's
rmon was No 11 v Old St Mark's

1899-1900

Southern League Division Two

	P	W	D	L	F	A	Pts
Watford	20	14	2	4	57	25	30
Fulham	20	10	4	6	44	23	24
Chesham Town	20	11	2	7	43	37	24
Wolverton L & NW Rly	20	9	6	5	46	36	24
Greys United	20	8	6	6	63	29	22
Shepherds Bush	20	9	4	7	45	37	22
Dartford	20	8	3	9	36	44	19
Wycombe Wanderers	20	8	3	9	35	50	19
Brentford	20	5	7	8	31	48	17
Southall	20	6	3	11	21	44	15
Maidenhead	20	1	2	17	16	64	4

No		Date	V	Opponents	R	H-T	F-T	Scorers	Att
1	S	2	H	Southall	W	2-0	3-0	Sherran Lloyd 2	
2		16	H	Maidenhead	W	2-0	4-1	Hopkinson 3 Shrran	
3	O	7	A	Dartford	W	1-1	2-1	Read Lloyd	
4		21	A	Wolverton & LNR	L	1-3	3-4	Lloyd 2 Tuttill	
5	N	4	A	Brentford	D	1-2	3-3	Lloyd Tuttill Powell	
6		11	H	Dartford	W	1-0	4-3	Reed 3 Lloyd	
7	D	2	H	Chesham T*	D	0-0	1-1	Lloyd	
8		30	H	Brentford	W	4-0	5-0	Lloyd Powell 2 Reed Johnson	
9	J	6	A	Watford	L	1-1	1-2	Reed	
10		13	H	Shepherd's Bush	W	1-0	2-0	Johnson 2	
11		20	H	Wolverton & LNR	L	0-1	0-1		
12		27	A	Maidenhead	D	0-1	1-1	Spackman (F)	
13	F	17	H	Grays U	W	1-0	3-1	Ambrose Reed 2	
14	M	3	H	Watford	L	0-1	0-1		
15		10	A	Chesham T	L	0-0	0-1		
16		24	A	Southall	W	1-1	4-1	Tuttill Newlands Johnson Lloyd	
17	A	7	A	Grays U	D	0-0	0-0		
18		13	A	Shepherd's Bush	L	0-1	0-1		
19		14	H	Wycombe W	W	0-1	2-1	Ives Lloyd	
20		25	A	Wycombe W	W	4-0	6-0	Ives 2 Lloyd 2 Frewin Anderson	
TM	A	30	N	Thames Ironworks	L	1-4	1-5	Lloyd (at Tottenham)	

* Abandoned after 80 minutes but the result stood

Ap

Goa

FA Cup

1Q	S	30	A	Queen's Park R	L	0-2	0-3

	Maile	Howland	Morton	Stubbs	Taylor	Tutthill	Johnson	Lloyd	Hopkinson	Sherran	Reed	Curling	Spackman H	Pask	Aylott	Bowden	Powell	Drury	Angus	Janes	Spackman F	Head	McMorran	Ambrose	Windust	Frewin	Newlands	Newbiggin	Humphries	Ives	Davis	Charratt	Anderson
1	1	2	3	4	5	6	7	8	9	10	11																						
2	1	2	3	4	5	6	7	8	9	10	11																						
3			3	4	5	6	7	8	9	10	11	1	2																				
4			3	4	5	6		8			9	1	2	7	10	11																	
5			3	4	5	6	7	8			10	1	2				9	11															
6	1		3	4	5	6	7	8			11		2				9		10														
7	1		3	4	5	6		8			11		2				9			7	10												
8		3		4	5	6	7	8			11						9				10	1	2										
9		3		4	5	6	7	8			11		2				9				10	1											
10		3		4	5	6	7	8			11		2				9				10	1											
11		3		4	5	6	7	8			11		2				9				10	1											
12		3		4	5	6	7	8					2				9				11	1	10										
13		3		4	5	6	7	8			11		2								10	1		9									
14		3		4	5	6	7	8			11		2								10	1		9									
15		3	2	4	5	6	7	8			11											1		9	10								
16		3		4	5	6	7	8			11											1	2			9	10						
17		3		4	5	6	7	8														1				9	10	11	2				
18		3		4	5	6	7	8														1				9		10	2	11			
19		3		4	5	6	7	8														1				10		11	2	9			
20					5	6		8														1	2			9		10		11	3	4	7
TM		3		4	5	6	7	8														1				9		10	2	11			
A	4	15	8	20	21	21	18	21	3	3	15	3	11	1	1	1	8	1	1	1	8	14	4	3	1	6	2	5	4	4	1	1	1
G	-	-	-	-	-	3	4	14	3	2	8	-	-	-	-	-	3	-	-	-	1	-	-	1	-	1	1	-	-	3	-	-	1

	Maile	Howland	Morton	Stubbs	Taylor	Tutthill	Johnson	Lloyd	Hopkinson	Sherran	Reed	Curling	Spackman H
1Q	1		3	4	5	6	7	8	9	10	11		2

1900-01

Southern League Division Two

	P	W	D	L	F	A	Pts
Brentford	16	14	2	0	63	11	30
Grays United	16	12	2	2	62	12	26
Sheppey United	16	8	1	7	44	26	17
Shepherds Bush	16	8	1	7	30	30	17
Fulham	16	8	0	8	38	26	16
Chesham Town	16	5	1	10	26	39	11
Maidenhead	16	4	1	11	21	49	9
Wycombe Wanderers	16	4	1	11	23	68	9
Southall	16	4	1	11	22	68	9

No		Date	V	Opponents	R	H-T	F-T	Scorers	Atten
1	S	8	A	Southall	L	0-0	0-1		
2		29	H	Brentford	L	0-2	1-2	(Smith og)	
3	O	6	A	Maidenhead	W	2-1	3-2	Robertson, Lloyd, Anderson	
4	N	17	A	Chesham T	L	1-2	1-3	Lloyd	
5	D	8	A	Grays U	L	0-1	0-1		
6		26	H	Shepherd's Bush	L	0-1	0-3		
7	F	9	A	Sheppey U	L	0-2	0-2		
8		16	H	Grays U	L	0-2	0-2		
9		23	H	Chesham T	W	2-1	5-2	Meade 2, Taylor, Spackman (F), McKay	
10	M	2	A	Brentford	L	0-4	1-5	Tutthill	
11		16	H	Wycombe W	W	3-0	5-0	Levy, Meade, McKay, Spackman (F), Ferne	
12		30	H	Sheppey U	W	1-0	3-0	Spackman (F), Meade, Ferne	
13	A	5	A	Shepherd's Bush	W	1-0	3-0	Spackman (F), Meade, (Milestone og)	
14		9	H	Southall	W	1-0	3-1	Miller 2, Levy	
15		18	H	Maidenhead	W	4-0	9-0	Meade 3, Ferne 3, Spackman (F), McKay, Tutthill	
16		29	A	Wycombe W	W	2-0	3-2	Stone, Holmes, Lloyd	

App

Goals

FA Cup

3Q	N	3	A	Queen's Park R	L	0-4	0-7	

London League Division One

17	S	1	H	Brentford	W	0-0	2-0	Lloyd 2
18		22	A	Tottenham H Res	L	0-1	1-2	Lloyd
19	O	13	H	Lower Clapton Imp	W	4-1	5-1	Levy 2, Molyneux, Stubbs, Lloyd
20		25	A	Brentford	D	0-1	2-2	Molyneux, Lloyd
21		27	H	Woolwich A Res	L	1-1	1-2	Gray
22	N	10	H	Wandsworth	W	2-0	4-0	Levy, Gray, Robertson 2
23		24	A	Deptford T	L	0-1	0-2	
24	D	1	H	Deptford T	W	1-0	1-0	Lloyd
25		15	A	Woolwich A Res	L	0-3	1-4	Molyneux
26		22	H	Clapton O	W	2-1	3-1	Meade 2, Turner
27		25	A	Millwall Res	L	0-3	0-11	
28		29	H	Wandsworth	W	2-0	4-0	Levy, Meade, Ferne, Lloyd
29	J	5	A	Q.P.R. Res	L	0-0	0-1	
30		26	A	Clapton O	D	0-1	1-1	Meade
31	M	23	A	Lower Clapton Imp	W	3-1	6-1	Taylor, McKay 2 (1 pen), Meade 2, Ferne
32	A	6	H	Tottenham H Res	W	5-2	5-2	Levy 2, Meade 2, Tutthill
33		8	H	Millwall Res	D	0-1	1-1	McKay pen
34		13	H	Q.P.R. Res	L		0-1	
35		27	H	West Ham U Res	L	0-1	0-1	
36			A	West Ham U Res	L			

Match awarded opposition 2-0

App

Goals

head	Steven	Engelfield	Stubbs	Taylor	Tutthill	Johnson	Lloyd	Levy	Holmes	Howland	Molyneux	Spackman F	Anderson	Robertson	McMorran	Miller	Gray	Spackman H	Stone	Meade	Turner	Ferne	Nobbs	McKay	Underwood			
	2	3	4	5	6	7	8	9	10	11																		1
	2	3	4	5	6	7	8	10	11		9																	2
	2	3		5	6		8	10			9	4	7	11														3
		3		5	6		8	10				11	7		2	4	9											4
		3		5	6		8	10			9					4	7	2	11									5
		3		5	6			10								4		2		9	8	11	7					6
		3		5	6			7								4		2		9	10	11		8				7
		3		5	6			11			7					4		2		9	10			8				8
		3		5	6			7				10				4				9	2	11		8				9
		3		5	6			7				10				4				9	2	11		8				10
		3		5	6			7				10				4				9	2	11		8				11
		3		5	6			7				10				4				9	2	11		8				12
				5	6			7				10				4		2		9	3	11		8				13
				5	6		3	7								9			11		2	10		8	4			14
				5	6		1		7			10				4		2		9	3	11		8				15
				5	6		8	7	9									2	10		3	11			4			16
5	3	12	2	16	16	2	8	15	4	1	4	8	2	1	1	12	2	7	3	9	11	10	1	9	2	-	-	A
	-	-	-	1	2	-	3	2	1	-	-	5	1	1	-	2	-	-	1	8	-	5	-	3	-	-	-	G
	2	3	4	5	6		8	10					7	11			9											30a
	2		4	5	6	7	8	9	10	3				11														17
	2	3	4	5	6	7	8	9	10					11														18
	2	3	4	5	6		8	10			9		7	11														19
	2	3	4	5	6		8	10			9		7	11														20
	2	3	4	5	6		8	10					7	11			9											21
	2	3		5	6		8	10					7	11		4	9											22
				5	6		8	10	11				7			4	9	2										23X
		3		5	6		8	10			9					4	7	2								11		24
		3		5	6		8	10			9					4	11	2					7					25
		3		5	6			10			9					4		2			8	11	7					26
				5	6		8	10			9					4		2			3	11	7					27
				5	6		8	10								4		2		9	3	11	7					28
				5	6		8	10								4		2		9	3	11	7					29
				5	6			8	10		7					4		2		9	3	11						30
		3		5	6			7				10				4				9	2	11		8				31
				5	6			7				10				4		2		9	3	11		8				32
				5	6			7				10				4		2		9	3	11		8				33
				5	6			7				10				4		2		9	3	11		8			1	34
				5	6			7				10				4		2		9	3	11		8				35
atch not played																											36	
3	6	9	5	19	19	2	12	19	4	1	7	5	5	6	-	14	5	12	-	8	10	10	5	5	-	1	1	A
	-	-	1	1	1	-	7	6	-	-	3	-	-	2	-	-	2	-	-	8	1	2	-	3	-	-	-	G

10 men only

1901-02

Southern League Division Two

	P	W	D	L	F	A	Pts
Fulham	16	13	0	3	51	19	26
Grays United	16	12	1	3	49	14	25
Brighton & Hove Albion	16	11	0	5	34	17	22
Wycombe Wanderers	16	7	3	6	36	30	17
West Hampstead	16	6	4	6	39	29	16
Shepherds Bush	16	6	1	9	31	31	13
Southall	16	5	2	9	28	52	12
Maidenhead	16	3	1	12	23	59	7
Chesham Town	16	2	2	12	24	64	6

No		Date	V	Opponents	R	H-T	F-T	Scorers	Att
1	S	14	H	Southall	W	1-0	2-1	Meade 2	
2		28	H	Grays U	L	0-1	0-2		
3	O	12	H	Maidenhead	W	4-0	5-2	Meade, McKay, Tannahill 2, McNee	
4		19	A	Wycombe W	W	1-0	2-1	McKay 2	
5	N	30	A	Brighton & HA	L	0-2	0-2		
6	D	21	H	West Hampstead	W	3-0	4-2	Tannahill 2, Meade, Slaughter	
7		26	H	Shepherd's Bush	W		3-1	McKay 2 (pens), Stone	
8	J	11	A	Grays U	L	0-3	1-6	Tannahill	
9	F	22	A	Chesham T	W		5-2	Dwight (F), McKay, Meade 2, Sherran	
10	M	8	A	Maidenhead	W	2-0	2-1	Meade 2	
11		22	H	Brighton & HA	W	2-1	2-1	Meade, (1 og)	
12		28	A	Shepherd's Bush	W		2-0	Tannahill, Tutthill	
13		29	H	Chesham T	W		8-0	McKay 3, Hopkinson 2, Tutthill, Reed 2	
14	A	5	A	Southall	W	2-0	5-0	Meade 4, Sherran	
15		12	H	Wycombe W	W		8-0	Sherran 2, Porter 2, McKay 3, Tannahill	
16		19	A	West Hampstead	W	1-0	2-0	Sherran, Tannahill	
TM	A	30	N	Swindon T	L	0-2	1-3	Meade (at Reading)	

App
Goa

FA Cup

No		Date	V	Opponents	R	H-T	F-T	Scorers	Att
P	S	21	A	Chiswick	W		3-2	McKay, Tannahill, Meade	
1Q	O	5	A	Crouch End V	L		2-4	Tannahill, Meade	

London League Division One

No		Date	V	Opponents	R	H-T	F-T	Scorers	Att
17	S	7	H	Woolwich A Res	W	1-1	3-1	Tutthill, McNee, Meade	
18	N	2	A	Clapton Or	D	1-2	2-2	Tutthill, McKay	
19	N	9	H	Deptford T	W	2-0	4-1	Meade 2, Spackman, F., Tutthill	
20	N	16	A	Tottenham H Res	L	1-4	2-8	Meade 2	
21	N	23	H	Q.P.R. Res	D	2-0	2-2	Tutthill, McKay pen.	
22	D	14	A	Q.P.R. Res	L	1-3	1-5	Stone	
23	D	25	A	Millwall Res	L		0-2		
24	D	27	A	West Ham U Res	L	1-2	2-3	Miller, Tannahill	
25	J	4	H	Excelsior (G.P.O.)	W	1-0	3-1	Meade 2, Slaughter	
26	J	18	H	Clapton O	L	1-2	1-2	Meade	
27	J	25	A	Deptford T	W		2-0	Meade, Sherran	
28	F	1	H	West Ham U Res	W		2-0	Miller, Stone	
29	F	8	A	Wandsworth	W	2-0	3-1	Tutthill 2, Sherran	
30	F	15	H	Wandsworth	W	0-0	1-0	Tutthill	
31	M	15	A	Woolwich A Res	L	1-4	2-5	Meade, Porter	
32	M	31	H	Millwall Res	W	0-0	3-0	Meade 3	
33	A	2	A	Excelsior (G.P.O.)				scratched	
34	A	25	H	Tottenham H Res	W	3-0	3-0	Miller, Sherran, Meade	

App
Goa

Head	Graham	Dwight C	Miller	Tutthill	Spackman F	Tannahill	McKay	Meade	McNee	Dwight F	Spackman H	Underwood	Stone	Lacey	Pickett	Rance	Slaughter	Sherran	Porter	Reed	Hopkinson	McAvoy	Low	Roland	Howland	
1	2	3	4	5	6	7	8	9	10	11																1
1	6	3	4	5		7	8	9	11	10	2															2
1	6	3	4			7	8	9	10		2	5	11													3
		3	4			7	8	9	10		2		11	5	6	1										4
		3	4	6		7	8	9			2		11	5		1	10									5
1		3	4	6		7	8	9			2		11	5			10									6
1		3	4	6		7	8	9			2		11	5			10									7
1		3	2	6		7	8	9					11	5			10									8x
1	2	3	4	6		7	8	9						5				10	11							9x
1		3	4	6		7	8	9			2			5				10								10
1	2	3	4			7	8	9					6	5				10	11							11
1	2	3	4	6		7	8	9						5				10	11							12
1	2	3	4	6			8			11			10	5						7	9					13
1	2	3	4	6		7	8	9						5				10	11							14
1	2	3	4	6		7	8	9						5				10	11							15
1	2	3	4	6		7	8	9						5				10	11							16
1	2	3	4	6		7	8	9						5				10	11							TM
5	11	17	17	14	1	16	17	16	4	3	7	1	8	14	1	2	4	8	7	1	1	-	-	-	-	A
-	-	-	-	1	-	9	13	15	1	1	-	-	1	-	-	-	1	5	2	2	2	-	-	-	-	G

X 10 men in both matches

Head	Graham	Dwight C	Miller	Tutthill	Spackman F	Tannahill	McKay	Meade	McNee	Dwight F	Spackman H	Underwood	Stone	Lacey	Pickett	Rance	Slaughter	Sherran	Porter	Reed	Hopkinson	McAvoy	Low	Roland	Howland	
1		3	4	5	6	7	8	9	10	11	2															P
1	5	3	4			7	8	9	10		2		11		6											1Ω

Head	Graham	Dwight C	Miller	Tutthill	Spackman F	Tannahill	McKay	Meade	McNee	Dwight F	Spackman H	Underwood	Stone	Lacey	Pickett	Rance	Slaughter	Sherran	Porter	Reed	Hopkinson	McAvoy	Low	Roland	Howland	
1		3	4	5	6	7	8	9	10	11	2															17
	6	3	4	10		7	8	9			2		11	5		1										18
		3	4	6	10	7	8	9			2		11			1						5				19
		3	4	6		7	8	9			2		11`	5		1						10				20
		3	4	6		7	8	9			2		11	5		1	10									21
		3	4	6		7	8	9			2		11	5			10						1			22
1	2	3	4		11	7	8	9			6			5			10									23
1		3	4	6		7	8	9					11	5			10							2		24
1		3	4	6			8	9			2		11	5			10	7								25
1	2	3	4	6		7	8	9					11	5			10									26
1	2	3	4	6		7	8	9					11	5			10									27
1	2	3	4	6		7	8	9					11	5			10									28
1	4	3	5	9		7	8				2		11					10							6	29
1		3	2	6		7	8	9					4	5				10	11							30
1		3	4	6		7	8	9			2			5				10	11							31
1	2	3	4	6		7	8	9					11	5				10								32
match void																										33
1	2	3	4	6		7	8	9						5				10	11							34
2	8	17	17	16	3	16	17	16	1	1	10	-	13	14	-	4	8	6	3	-	-	2	1	1	1	A
-	-	-	3	7	1	1	2	14	1	-	-	-	2	-	-	-	1	3	1	-	-	-	-	-	-	G

1902-03

Southern League Division Two

	P	W	D	L	F	A	Pts
Fulham	10	7	1	2	27	7	15
Brighton & Hove Albion	10	7	1	2	34	11	15
Grays United	10	7	0	3	28	12	14
Wycombe Wanderers	10	3	3	4	13	19	9
Chesham Town	10	2	1	7	9	37	5
Southall	10	1	0	9	10	35	2

No		Date	V	Opponents	R	H-T	F-T	Scorers	Atter
1	O	11	H	Brighton & HA	W	0-0	1-0	Tannahill	
2		25	H	Wycombe W	W	2-0	5-0	Tutthill, Meade 2, Hopkinson 2	
3	D	13	A	Southall	W	1-0	2-0	Hopkinson, Meade	
4		20	H	Chesham T	W	4-0	6-0	Meade 2, Hopkinson 2, Porter, Tutthill	
5	J	31	A	Brighton & HA	L	1-1	1-3	Lloyd	
6	M	2	A	Chesham T	W	0-2	6-2	Tutthill 2, Sherran 2, Hopkinson, Tannahill	
7	A	4	H	Southall	W	2-0	4-0	Dwight (pen), Lloyd, Tannahill, (Reed og)	
8		11	H	Grays U	W	0-0	1-0	Tutthill	
9		14	A	Wycombe W	D	0-0	0-0		
10		22	A	Grays U	L		1-2	Tannahill	
TM	A	28	N	Brentford	L	1-4	2-7	Meade, Lloyd	(at Shepherd's Bush
									App
									Goal

FA Cup

No		Date	V	Opponents	R	H-T	F-T	Scorers	
P	S	20	A	Civil Service	W	1-0	2-0	Meade, Lloyd	(at Craven Cottage
1Q	O	4	H	Crouch End V	W	1-0	4-0	Tutthill, Meade, Porter 2	
2Q		18	A	Willesden T	D	0-0	0-0		(at Craven Cottage
R		23	H	Willesden T	W	2-0	5-0	Meade 3, Lloyd, Dwight	
3Q	N	1	A	Watford	D	0-1	1-1	Meade	
R		6	H	Watford	W		3-0	Meade 2, Sherran	
4Q		15	H	Luton A	W	2-1	4-1	Lloyd, Meade, Tannahill, Hopkinson	
5Q		29	A	Luton T	L		1-5	Cowan	

London League Division One

No		Date	V	Opponents	R	H-T	F-T	Scorers	
12	S	27	H	Woolwich A Res	L	0-0	0-2		
13	N	8	A	Q.P.R. Res	L		2-4	Lloyd 2	
14		22	H	West Ham U Res	W	3-2	4-4	Hopkinson, Cowan, Sherran 2	
15	D	6	A	Deptford T	L	0-1	0-3		
16		25	A	Leyton	L		1-2	Scorer Unknown	
17	J	3	A	West Ham U Res	L	1-2	1-3	Spackman, F.	
18		10	H	Deptford T	D		1-1	Tutthill	
19	F	7	A	Wandsworth	W	3-1	6-2	Lloyd 2, Sherran 2, Meade, Spackman, F.	
20		21	H	Millwall Res	D	1-1	1-1	Meade	
21		28	H	Tottenham Res	D		1-1	Dwight pen.	
22	M	7	A	Woolwich A Res	L		1-6	Scorer Unknown	
23		14	A	Millwall Res	W		2-0	Meade, Dwight pen.	
24		21	H	Q.P.R. Res	W		1-0	Spackman, F.	
25	A	1	H	Clapton O Res	W		4-0	Lacey, Lloyd, Stone 2	
26		18	H	Wandsworth	W	1-0	3-0	Sherran, Dwight pen, Lloyd	
27		25	H	Leyton	D		1-1	Hopkinson	
28		27	A	Tottenham H Res	L		0-3		
29		30	A	Clapton O Res	W		2-0	Scorers Unknown	
									App
									Goal

Head	Graham	Dwight	Spackman	Lloyd	Tutthill	Tannahill	Cowan	Meade	Hopkinson	Sherran	Lacey	Charratt	Porter	Hilsdon	Easter	Brown	Stone	Mills	Robinson	
	2	3	4	5	6	7	8	9	10	11										1
	2	3	11	5	6	7	8	9	10		4									2
	2	3			6	7	8	9	10	11	5	4								3
	2	3	4		6	7		10	9	8	5		11							4
	2	3	11	5	6	7		10	8		4			9						5
	2			5	6	7			8	10	4			9	11	3				6
		3	11	5	6	7		8	2	10	4			9						7
	2	3	11	5	6	7		10	8		4			9						8
	2	3	11	5	6	7		9	8		4						10			9
	2	3	11	5	6	7		9	8	10	4									10
	2	3	11	5	6	7		9	8	10	4									TM
1	10	10	9	9	11	11	3	10	11	7	10	1	1	4	1	1	1	-	-	A
	-	1	-	3	5	4	-	6	6	2	-	-	1	-	-	-	-	-	-	G

Head	Graham	Dwight	Spackman	Lloyd	Tutthill	Tannahill	Cowan	Meade	Hopkinson	Sherran	Lacey	Charratt	Porter	Hilsdon	Easter	Brown	Stone	Mills	Robinson	
	2	3		8	6	7		9		10	5	4	11							P
	2	3	4		6	7	8	9	10		5		11							1Q
	2	3	11	5	6	7	4	9	10	8										2Q
	2	3		5	6	7	8	9	10		4		11							R
	2	3	11	5	6	7	8	10	9		4									3Q
	2	3		5	6	7	8	10	9	11	4									R
	2	3	4	5	6	7	8	10	9	11										4Q
	2	3	4		6	7	8	10	9		5		11							5Q

Head	Graham	Dwight	Spackman	Lloyd	Tutthill	Tannahill	Cowan	Meade	Hopkinson	Sherran	Lacey	Charratt	Porter	Hilsdon	Easter	Brown	Stone	Mills	Robinson	
	2	3		8	6	7		9		10	5	4	11							12
	2	3		5	6	7	8	10	9	11	4									13
	2	3		5	6	7	8	11	9	10	4									14
	2		3		6	7	8	10	9	11		4						5		15
	2	3	4		6	7		10	9	8	5		11							16
	2		10	5	6	8		9			4				11	3			7	17
	2		8	5	6	7		10	9		4				11	3				18
	2	3	11	5		7		9	4	10	6			8						19
		3	11	5	6	7		9	2	10	4			8						20
	2	3		5	6	7		9	11	10	4			8						21
	2	3		5	6	7		9	11	10	4			8						22
	2	3	11	5	6	7		9	10	8	4									23
	2	3	10	5	6	7		9	8		4						11			24
		3		5	6	7			2	10	4			9	8		11			25
	2	3	11	5	6	7		9	8	10	4									26
	2	3	11	5	6	7		8	9	10	4									27
	2	3	11	5	6	7		8	9	10	4									28
	2	3	11	5	6	7		8	9	10	4									29
8	16	15	12	16	17	18	3	17	16	15	17	2	2	5	3	2	2	1	1	A
	-	3	3	6	1	-	1	3	2	5	1	-	-	-	-	-	2	-	-	G

1903-04

Southern League Division One

	P	W	D	L	F	A	Pts
Southampton	34	22	6	6	75	30	50
Tottenham Hotspur	34	16	11	7	54	37	43
Bristol Rovers	34	17	8	9	64	42	42
Portsmouth	34	17	8	9	41	38	42
Queens Park Rangers	34	15	11	8	53	37	41
Reading	34	14	13	7	48	35	41
Millwall	34	16	8	10	64	42	40
Luton Town	34	14	12	8	38	33	40
Plymouth Argyle	34	13	10	11	44	34	36
Swindon Town	34	10	11	13	30	42	31
Fulham	34	9	12	13	34	36	30
West Ham United	34	10	7	17	39	44	27
Brentford	34	9	9	16	34	48	27
Wellingborough	34	11	5	18	44	63	27
Northampton Town	34	10	7	17	36	60	27
New Brompton	34	6	13	15	26	43	25
Brighton & Hove Albion	34	6	12	16	46	69	24
Kettering Town	34	6	7	21	39	76	19

No		Date	V	Opponents	R	H-T	F-T	Scorers	Atte
1	S	5	H	Tottenham H	D	0-0	0-0		14,0
2		12	A	Luton T	D	0-0	0-0		3,0
3		19	H	New Brompton	W		1-0	Lawrence	7,0
4		26	A	Kettering T	L	0-1	0-1		2,0
5	O	3	H	Southampton	D	1-2	2-2	Hogan, May	17,5
6		10	A	Swindon T	D	0-1	2-2	Soar, Lawrence	4,0
7		17	A	Millwall A	W	1-0	2-1	Fletcher, May	8,0
8		24	H	Queen's Park R	D	2-2	2-2	Soar, Fletcher	15,1
9	N	7	H	Reading	L	0-0	0-1		12,0
10		11	A	Plymouth A	L	0-0	0-1		4,0
11		21	H	Bristol R	L	0-1	0-1		8,0
12	D	26	A	Brentford	D	1-1	1-1	Soar	15,0
13		28	A	West Ham U	L	0-0	0-2		2,0
14		30	A	Wellingborough	W	2-1	3-2	Axcell, Hunt, Fletcher	3,0
15	J	2	A	Tottenham H	L		0-1		12,0
16		9	H	Luton T	W	0-0	1-0	Fletcher	17,0
17		16	A	New Brompton	D	0-0	0-0		4,0
18		27	H	Kettering T	W	2-0	4-1	Axcell 2, Gray, Fletcher	1,2
19		30	A	Southampton	L		0-2		3,0
20	F	13	H	Millwall A	L		1-2	Fletcher	9,5
21		20	A	Queen's Park R	D		1-1	Fletcher	12,0
22		24	A	Brighton & HA	L	1-1	1-2	Connor	3,0
23		27	H	Plymouth A	W		1-0	Meade	13,0
24	M	5	A	Reading	L		0-3		4,0
25		12	H	Wellingborough	W		2-0	Axcell, Soar	9,0
26		19	A	Bristol R	L		0-1		3,0
27		21	A	Northampton T	L	1-1	1-2	Soar	2,0
28		26	H	Brighton & HA	W		3-0	Fletcher 3	8,0
29	A	2	A	Portsmouth	D	0-0	0-0		8,0
30		5	H	Swindon T	L		1-3	Fletcher	4,0
31		9	H	Northampton T	W		2-0	Soar, Fletcher	9,0
32		16	H	Brentford	D	0-0	0-0		12,5
33		18	H	Portsmouth	D		2-2	Hunt 2	3,0
34		23	H	West Ham U	D		1-1	Fletcher	7,0
									Ap
									Goa

Fryer	Orr	Turner	Green	Hamilton	Robotham	Fletcher	May	Davidson	Fisher	Lawrence	Soar	Meade	Hunt	Biggar	Gray	Hogan	Connor	McQueen	Waterson	Colville	Porter	Axcell	Miecznikowski	Goldie	Harwood	Anderson	Storey	Stephenson	Farnfield (PH)	Farnfield (HV)	Farnfield (GS)	
1	2	3	4	5	6	7	8	9	10	11																						1
1	2	3	4	5	6		8			11	7	9	10																			2
	2	3	4	5	6	8	10			11	7		9	1																		3
	2	3	4	5	6	8	10			11	7		9	1																		4
1	2	3		4	6	8	10			11	7				5	9																5
1	2	3		4	6	8	10			11	7				5	9																6
1	2	3		4	6	8	10			11	7	9			5																	7
1	2	3		4	6	8	10			11	7				5		9															8
	2	3	4	5	6	8				11	7			1			9	10														9
1	2	3		4	6	8				11	7				5		9	10														10
1	2	3			6	8				11	7	10			5		9		4													11
1	2	3	6			8				11	7		9		5		10			4												12
1	2	3			6	8				11			9		5		10			4	7											13
1	2	3	6	5		8					7		9						4			10	11									14
1	2	3	6			8					7		9		5					4		10	11									15
1	2	3			6	8				11	7				5		9			4		10										16
	2	3				8				11	7			1	5		9			4		10		6								17
1		3			4	8					7		9		5							10		6	2	11						18
1		3			4	8				11	7				5		9					10		6	2							19
1	2	3			4	8					7				5			10				9		6		11						20
1		2			4	10					7	9	8		5									6	3	11						21
1		2			4	10					7		8		5		9							6	3	11						22
1	2	3			4	10					7	9	8		5									6		11						23
1	2	3			4	8					7	9			5									6		11	10					24
1	2				4						7		8		5			11				10		6	3		9					25
1	2				4						7		8		5			11				10		6	3		9					26
	2				4	8					7		9	1	5			11				10		6	3							27
	2				4	8					7		9	1	5			11				10		6	3							28
1	2	3			4	8					7		9		5			11				10		6								29
1		3	4			8					7		9		5			11				10		6	2							30
1		3				8				10	7				5		9			4		11		6	2							31
1	2	3		4		8					7	9			5		10					11		6								32
					4	7				11			8	1	5			10	3			9		6				2				33
1		3			4	8					7		9											6	2				5	10	11	34
27	26	29	9	12	27	31	8	1	1	18	31	7	19	7	27	2	12	10	3	6	1	16	2	18	11	6	3	1	1	1	1	A
-	-	-	-	-	-	13	2	-	-	2	6	1	3	-	1	1	1	-	-	-	-	4	-	-	-	-	-	-	-	-	-	G

Secretary Herbert Jackson who later committed suicide.

1903-04

Cont.

No		Date	V	Opponents	R	H-T	F-T	Scorers	Atter
FA Cup									
1Q	S	19	H	Hampstead	W	2-0	3-0	Lloyd 2, Meade	N
2Q	O	3	A	Crouch End V	W	4-0	5-0	Meade 3, Fisher, Tannahill	N
3Q		17	H	Civil Service	D	1-1	3-3	Green (pen), Connor, Tannahill	5,000
R		22	A	Civil Service	W		3-0	Fisher, Connor, Fletcher	2,000
4Q		31	A	Queen's Park R	D	0-0	1-1	Fletcher	20,000
R	N	4	H	Queen's Park R	W	2-1	3-1	Fletcher, McQueen, Connor	10,000
5Q		16	H	West Norwood	W	1-0	4-0	Connor 3, Fletcher	5,000
6Q		28	H	Luton T	W	2-1	3-1	Connor, Lawrence, Robotham	10,000
7Q	D	12	A	West Ham U	W	1-0	1-0	Fletcher	14,000
1	F	6	A	Woolwich Arsenal	L	0-1	0-1		15,000

London League Premier Division

No		Date	V	Opponents	R	H-T	F-T	Scorers	Atter
35	S	1	A	Q.P.R.	L		0-2		3,000
36		7	A	Woolwich A	L		0-2		3,000
37		14	A	Tottenham H	L	0-2	1-2	Hunt	3,500
38	O	19	H	Millwall	L	1-1	1-4	Hogan	1,000
39	J	11	H	West Ham U	L		1-2	Connor	1,200
40	F	15	A	Millwall	L	1-4	1-8	Hamilton	500
41	M	7	A	West Ham U	L		1-3	Axcell	12,000
42	A	1	H	Brentford	W	1-0	2-1	Meade, Fletcher	
43		4	A	Brentford	W	0-0	1-0	Meade	
44		11	H	Tottenham H	L		1-5	Anderson	
45		25	H	Q.P.R.	D	0-0	0-0		
46		30	H	Woolwich A	W	0-0	1-0	Fletcher	10,000
									App
									Goa

Fryer	Orr	Turner	Green	Hamilton	Robotham	Fletcher	May	Davidson	Fisher	Lawrence	Soar	Meade	Hunt	Biggar	Gray	Hogan	Connor	McQueen	Waterson	Colville	Porter	Axcell	Mierczinkowski	Goldie	Harwood	Anderson	Nidd	Tannahill	Tutthill	Lloyd	Spackman	
								9	10			8		1	5				4						2		3	7		6	11	1Q
			5						10			9	8	1					4						2		3	7		6	11	2Q
			5						10				8	1			9	11	4						2		3	7		6		3Q
	2		4			8			10	11					5		9								3			7	6			R
	2	3		4	6	8	10			11	7				5		9															4Q
	2	3	4		6	8				11	7				5		9	10														R
	2	3				8	9			11	7				5		10		4										6			5Q
	2	3			6	8				11	7				5		9	10	4													6Q
	2	3				8				11	7				5		9	10	4										6			7Q
	2	3			4	8				11	7				5		9					10		6								1
	2	3		4	6	7	8	9	10	11					5																	35
	2	3	4	5	6		8	9		11	7					10																36
		3			6	8	10			11	7		9	1	5				4						2							37
	2	3	5		6		11				7		10	1		9			4						8							38
	2	3				8				11	7			1	5		9			4		10		6								39
			4	5	9						7			1			8			6		10			2	11	3					40
	2	3	6	5		7				11							8			4		10									X	41
				6	4	8						9		1	5				2						3	11		7			Y	42
	2				4	8					7	9		1	5			11		3		10		6								43
		3		4		8					7		9		5									6	2	11					Y	44
	2	3		4		7							8		5			10				11			9				6			45
	2	3			4	8					7		9		5			10				11		6								46
	8	9	4	5	8	9	4	2	1	5	8	2	5	6	8	2	3	3	3	4	-	6	-	4	6	3	1	1	1	-	-	A
	-	-	-	1	-	2	-	-	-	-	-	2	1	-	-	1	1	-	-	-	-	1	-	-	-	1	-	-	-	-	-	G

is 9 Storey   Y is 10 Wales

1904-05

Southern League Division One

	P	W	D	L	F	A	Pts
Bristol Rovers	34	20	8	6	74	36	48
Reading	34	18	7	9	57	38	43
Southampton	34	18	7	9	54	40	43
Plymouth Argyle	34	18	5	11	57	39	41
Tottenham Hotspur	34	15	8	11	53	34	38
Fulham	34	14	10	10	46	34	38
Queens Park Rangers	34	14	8	12	51	46	36
Portsmouth	34	16	4	14	61	56	36
New Brompton	34	11	11	12	40	40	33
Watford	34	15	3	16	44	45	33
West Ham United	34	12	8	14	48	42	32
Brighton & Hove Albion	34	13	6	15	44	45	32
Northampton Town	34	12	8	14	43	54	32
Brentford	34	10	9	15	33	38	29
Millwall	34	11	7	16	38	47	29
Swindon Town	34	12	5	17	41	59	29
Luton Town	34	12	3	19	45	54	27
Wellingborough	34	5	3	26	25	107	13

Manager: Harry Bradshaw

No		Date	V	Opponents	R	H-T	F-T	Scorers	Atte
1	S	3	A	Tottenham H	W	1-0	1-0	Wardrope (pen)	20,0
2		10	H	Luton T	D	0-0	0-0		15,0
3		17	A	Swindon T	L	1-0	1-2	Bell	5,0
4		24	H	New Brompton	D	0-1	1-1	Morrison	15,0
5	O	1	A	Wellingborough	L	1-2	1-2	Fletcher	2,0
6		8	H	Southampton	D	0-0	0-0		20,0
7		15	H	Brighton & HA	W	0-0	1-0	Goldie	12,0
8		22	A	Watford	L	0-0	1-2	Bell	5,8
9		29	H	Plymouth A	D	0-0	0-0		16,0
10	N	5	A	West Ham U	D	0-0	0-0		8,0
11		12	H	Reading	W	1-0	2-0	Wardrope 2	20,0
12		19	A	Bristol R	L	0-3	1-4	Bell	5,0
13	D	3	A	Portsmouth	L	0-1	0-1		7,0
14		17	A	Queen's Park R	L	0-1	0-2		14,0
15		24	H	Millwall A	W	2-0	2-1	Lennie, Wardrope	20,0
16		31	H	Tottenham H	W		1-0	Wardrope	19,0
17	J	7	A	Luton T	L		0-6		5,0
18		21	A	New Brompton	L		0-3		6,0
19		28	H	Wellingborough	W	6-0	12-0	Fraser 5, Wardrope 3, Goldie 2, Lennie, Morrison	12,0
20	F	11	A	Brighton & HA	W	2-1	4-1	Bradshaw (W), Harwood 2, Bell	5,0
21		22	H	Watford	W	0-1	2-1	Lennie, Wardrope	2,0
22		25	A	Plymouth A	D	0-1	1-1	Wardrope	10,0
23	M	11	A	Reading	D	0-0	0-0		3,0
24		18	H	Bristol R	D	0-0	0-0		11,0
25		23	A	Northampton T	D	0-0	0-0		2,0
26		25	H	Northampton T	W		4-1	Wardrope, Ross (pen), Bell, Bradshaw	8,0
27	A	1	H	Portsmouth	W	1-0	2-0	Fraser 2	12,0
28		3	H	Swindon T	W	1-0	3-0	Ross, Wardrope, Holmes	2,0
29		8	A	Brentford	D		1-1	Wardrope	10,0
30		15	H	Queen's Park R	L		1-2	Wardrope	12,0
31		17	H	West Ham U	L		0-3		2,0
32		22	A	Millwall A	W		2-0	Goldie, Wardrope	7,0
33		24	A	Southampton	W		1-0	Wardrope	10,0
34		29	H	Brentford	W	1-0	1-0	Fraser	12,0

Ap

Goa

FA Cup

6Q	D	10	H	Luton T	W	2-0	4-0	Wardrope, Lennie, Ross (pen), Fraser	16,0
7Q	J	14	A	Manchester U	D	1-1	2-2	Fraser, Wardrope	17,0
R		18	H	Manchester U	D	0-0	0-0		20,0
2R		23	N	Manchester U	W	0-0	1-0	Graham (at Villa Park)	8,0
1	F	4	H	Reading	D	0-0	0-0		30,0
R		8	A	Reading	D	0-0	0-0		13,5
2R		13	N	Reading	W	0-0	1-0	Fraser (at White Hart Lane)	22,0
2		18	H	Nottingham F	W	1-0	1-0	Wardrope	18,0
3	M	4	A	Aston Villa	L	0-3	0-5		47,0

Fryer	Ross	Sharp	Haworth	Gray	Goldie	Soar	Fletcher	Wardrope	Graham	Bell	Morrison	Pratt	Robotham	Clutterbuck	Lennie	Hunt	Fraser	Thorpe	Bradshaw W	Bradshaw J	Harwood	Waterson	Axcell	Phillipson	Holmes	Kirby	
1	2	3	4	5	6	7	8	9	10	11																	1
1	2	3	4	5	6	7	8	9	10	11																	2
1	2	3	4	5	6	7	8	9	10	11																	3
1	2	3	4		6		7	9	10	11	5	8															4
1	2	3		5		7	8		10	11	4	9	6														5
	2	3	4			7	8		10		5	9	6	1	11												6
1	2	3	4		6	7	8	9	10		5				11												7
	2	3	4		6		7		10	9	5			1	11	8											8
1	2	3	4	5	6	7		10	8	11		9															9
1	2	3	4		6	7	8	10		11	5						9										10
1	2		4		6	7		10	8	11	5						9	3									11
1	2		4		6	7		10	8	11	5						9	3									12
1	2		4	5	6				8						11		9	3	7	10							13
1	2		4	5	6	7		10	8						11		9	3									14
1	2		4	5	6	7		10	8						11		9	3									15
1	2		4	5	6	7		10	8						11		9	3									16
1	2		4	5	6	7		10	8	11							9	3									17
1			4	5	6	7		10	8	11	2						9				3						18
1		3	4		6	7		10	8		5				11		9	2									19
1		3		5						11			6			8			7	10	9	2	4				20
1		3	4	5	6	7		10		8					11		9	2									21
1	2	3	4	5	6	7		10	8	9					11												22
1	2	3	4	5	6	7				8					11		9							10			23
1	2		4		6				8	11	5							3	7	10	9						24
1		3	4					10	8		5		6				9	2	7	11							25
1	2				6			10		8	5		4		11		9	3	7								26
1	2		4	5	6	7		10		8					11		9	3									27
1	2	3			6	7		10	8	9	5		4												11		28
1	2		4		6	7		10		8	5				11		9	3									29
1	2		4		6	7		10		8	5				11		9	3									30
		3	4		6	7		10	8	11	5			1			9	2									31
1	2		4		6			10	8	11	5						9	3								7	32
1	2		4		6	7		10		8	5				11		9	3									33
1	2		4		6	7		10		8	5				11		9	3									34
31	28	18	30	16	30	26	9	27	24	26	20	4	6	3	17	2	21	19	5	4	3	1	1	1	1	1	A
-	2	-	-	-	4	-	1	16	-	5	2	-	-	-	3	-	8	-	2	-	2	-	-	-	1	-	G

Fryer	Ross	Sharp	Haworth	Gray	Goldie	Soar	Fletcher	Wardrope	Graham	Bell	Morrison	Pratt	Robotham	Clutterbuck	Lennie	Hunt	Fraser	Thorpe	Bradshaw W	Bradshaw J	Harwood	Waterson	Axcell	Phillipson	Holmes	Kirby	
1	2		4	5	6	7		10	8						11		9	3									6Q
1		2	4		6	7		10	8		5				11		9	3									7Q
1			3		6	7		10	8		5		4		11		9	2									R
1	2		4		6	7		10	8		5				11		9	3									2R
1	2		4		6	7		10	8		5				11		9	3									1
1	2		4		6	7		10	8		5				11		9	3									R
1	2		4		6	7		10	8		5				11		9	3									2R
1	2		4		6	7		10		8	5				11		9	3									2
1	2		4		6	7		10	8		5				11		9	3									3

Alex Fraser.

1904-05

Cont.

No		Date	V	Opponents	R	H-T	F-T	Scorers	Atten
Western League									
1	S	5	A	West Ham U	D	2-0	2-2	Wardrope, Gray	5,00
2		14	A	Portsmouth	L	0-2	0-2		4,00
3		19	H	Brentford	D		1-1	Fletcher	3,00
4		26	H	West Ham U	W	3-2	3-2	Pratt 3	3,00
5	O	5	A	Reading	W	0-0	1-0	Wardrope	1,20
6		10	A	Southampton	L	1-1	1-2	Wardrope	2,00
7		17	H	Portsmouth	L	1-1	1-2	Fitchie	3,00
8		31	A	Bristol R	L	0-2	0-5		1,50
9	N	14	H	Tottenham H	D	0-0	0-0		4,00
10		21	A	Brentford	L	0-1	0-1		
11	D	26	H	Queen's Park R	W	2-0	4-0	Wardrope 2, Graham 2	12,00
12		27	A	Millwall	L	0-2	1-3	Wardrope	3,00
13	J	2	A	Tottenham H	W		5-0	Fraser 2, Graham 2, o.g. Morgan	
14	F	27	H	Bristol R	L		0-2		1,50
15	M	13	H	Plymouth A	L	0-2	0-4		2,00
16		20	H	Southampton	L	0-0	0-1		3,00
17		29	A	Plymouth A	W		1-0	Bradshaw, W.	
18	A	10	H	Reading	W	3-0	3-2	Lennie, Graham 2	
19		21	A	Q.P.R.	L		1-2	Ross pen.	12,00
20		25	H	Millwall	W	3-0	5-1	Wardrope 4, Lennie	2,00

Fryer	Ross	Sharp	Haworth	Gray	Goldie	Soar	Fletcher	Wardrope	Graham	Bell	Morrison	Pratt	Robotham	Clutterbuck	Lennie	Hunt	Fraser	Thorpe	Bradshaw W	Bradshaw J	Harwood	Waterson	Axcell	Phillipson	Holmes	Kirby	Pegg	Fitchie	Head	Bryant	Martin	
1	2	3	4	5	6	7	8	9	10	11																						1
1	2	3	4	5	6		8	10		11									7								9					2
1	2	3	4		6		7	9	10	11	5	8																				2
1	2		4			7	8			11	5	9	6					3										10				4
1	2		4				7	10	8		5	9	6		11						3											5
	2	3	4				8	9	10	7	5			1	11								6									6
	2		4					11		9	5					8		3	7				6					10	1			7
1	2		4		6		7	10	8	11	5	9									3											8
1	2		4		6		8				5				11		9	3	7									10				9
1	2		4		6			10	8	11	5						9	3	7													10
1	2		4	5	6	7		10	8						11		9	3														11
1	2																	3														12
1	2		4	5	6	7		10	8	11							9	3														13
		3								11			6	1		8				10	2	7	4							5	9	14
	2	3	4	5	6	7		10		8					11		9												1			15
1	2		4		6				8	11	5						10	3	7	9												16
Not Known																																17
1	2		4		6	7			8	10	5				11		9	3														18
1	2		4		6	7			8	10	5						9	3	11													19
1		3	4	5	6	7		10		8					11		9	2														20

1905-06

Southern League Division One

	P	W	D	L	F	A	Pts
Fulham	34	19	12	3	44	15	50
Southampton	34	19	7	8	58	39	45
Portsmouth	34	17	9	8	61	35	43
Luton Town	34	17	7	10	64	40	41
Tottenham Hotspur	34	16	7	11	46	29	39
Plymouth Argyle	34	16	7	11	52	33	39
Norwich City	34	13	10	11	46	38	36
Bristol Rovers	34	15	5	14	56	56	35
Brentford	34	14	7	13	43	52	35
Reading	34	12	9	13	53	46	33
West Ham United	34	14	5	15	42	39	33
Millwall	34	11	11	12	38	41	33
Queens Park Rangers	34	12	7	15	58	44	31
Watford	34	8	10	16	38	57	26
Swindon Town	34	8	9	17	31	52	25
Brighton & Hove Albion	34	9	7	18	30	55	25
New Brompton	34	7	8	19	20	62	22
Northampton Town	34	8	5	21	32	79	21

Manager: Harry Bradshaw

No		Date	V	Opponents	R	H-T	F-T	Scorers	Atte
1	S	2	H	Portsmouth	D	0-0	0-0		20,00
2		9	A	Swindon T	W	1-0	4-1	Edgley (pen), Wardrope, Wood, Threlfall	6,00
3		16	H	Millwall A	D		1-1	Threlfall	20,00
4		23	A	Luton T	W		1-0	Edgley	9,00
5		30	H	Tottenham H	D	0-0	0-0		25,00
6	O	7	A	Brentford	W		2-0	Fraser, Threlfall	12,00
7		14	H	Norwich C	W		2-1	Threlfall 2	15,00
8		21	A	Plymouth A	D	0-0	0-0		12,00
9		28	H	Southampton	D		1-1	Morrison	25,00
10	N	4	A	Reading	L		0-1		5,00
11		11	H	Watford	D	0-0	0-0		10,00
12		18	A	Brighton & HA	W		2-1	Threlfall, Wardrope	5,00
13		25	H	West Ham U	W		1-0	(1 og)	15,00
14	D	2	A	Northampton T	W		3-1	Edgley 2, Morrison	3,00
15		9	A	Queen's Park R	W		3-1	Wardrope 2, Edgley	12,00
16		16	H	Bristol R	W		1-0	Wardrope	16,00
17		23	A	New Brompton	W		3-0	Fraser, Wardrope 2	4,00
18		30	A	Portsmouth	L		0-1		8,0
19	J	6	H	Swindon T	D	0-1	1-1	Fraser	5,00
20		20	A	Millwall A	D	0-1	1-1	Wardrope	8,00
21		27	H	Luton T	W	1-0	3-0	Morrison, Fraser, Wood	14,00
22	F	10	H	Brentford	W	1-0	2-0	Wardrope, Fraser	10,00
23		12	A	Tottenham H	W	1-0	1-0	Fraser	20,00
24		17	A	Norwich C	D	0-0	0-0		9,00
25		24	H	Plymouth A	W	1-0	3-1	Freeman, Wardrope, Bell	15,00
26	M	3	A	Southampton	L	1-1	1-2	Wardrope	8,00
27		10	H	Reading	D	0-0	0-0		20,00
28		17	A	Watford	D	0-0	0-0		5,00
29		24	H	Brighton & HA	W	2-0	2-0	Wardrope, Wheatcroft	9,00
30		31	A	West Ham U	D	0-0	0-0		12,0
31	A	7	H	Northampton T	W	2-0	3-1	Wardrope, Fraser, Wheatcroft	15,00
32		14	H	Queen's Park R	W	0-0	1-0	Fraser	20,0
33		21	A	Bristol R	W	1-0	1-0	Freeman	6,00
34		25	H	New Brompton	W		1-0	Ross	3,0

App

Goa

FA Cup

No		Date	V	Opponents	R	H-T	F-T	Scorers	Atte
1	J	13	H	Queen's Park R	W	1-0	1-0	Collins	27,0
2	F	3	H	Nottingham F	L	0-2	1-3	Fraser	31,00

Western League

No		Date	V	Opponents	R	H-T	F-T	Scorers	Atte
1	S	6	H	West Ham U	W	1-1	2-1	Soar Edgley	2,00
2		11	A	West Ham U	L	0-1	0-1		
3		20	A	Portsmouth	L	1-0	1-2	Catterall	5,00
4		25	H	Portsmouth	W	0-0	1-0	Soar Edgley	2,5
5	O	2	H	Bristol R	W	1-0	3-0	Wardrope Morrison (pen) Fraser	4,00
6		9	H	Millwall	D	0-0	0-0		6,0
7		16	A	Tottenham H	L	0-0	0-1		6,00
8		23	A	Bristol R	L	0-3	0-5		
9		30	H	Reading	W	1-0	2-0	Hogan Edgley	
10	N	13	H	Plymouth A	D	1-0	2-2	Edgley 2	3,0
11		20	H	Tottenham H	L	0-1	0-3		2,0
12	D	4	H	Southampton	L		2-3	Trelfall Edgley	3,00
13		25	H	Queen's Park R	L	1-1	1-2	Fraser (pen)	25,0
14		26	A	Brentford	L	0-2	2-3	Fraser (Riley og)	
15	J	15	A	Southampton	L		0-2		2,00
16		24	A	Plymouth A	D		1-1	Soar	
17	M	21	A	Reading	D	1-2	3-3	Waterson Edgley 2	
18	A	13	A	Queen's Park R	D	0-1	1-1	Catterall	
19		16	H	Brentford	W	1-1	2-1	Ross (pen) Fraser	7,0
20		17	A	Millwall	L		0-1		

Fryer	Ross	Thorpe	Haworth	Morrison	Goldie	Soar	Wood	Edgley	Wardrope	Threlfall	Collins	Robotham	Fraser	Bell	Kirby	Waterson	Hogan	Thomas	Thompson	Fitchett	Freeman	Wheatcroft	Fidler	Catterall	Fitchie	Harwood	
1	2	3	4	5	6	7	8	9	10	11																	1
1	2	3	4	5	6	7	8	9	10	11																	2
1	2	3	4		6	7	8	9	10	11	5																3
1	2	3		5	6	7	8	9	10	11		4															4
1	2	3		5	6	7	8	9	10	11	4																5
1	2	3		5	6	7			10	11	4		9	8													6
1	2	3		5	6	7			10	11	4		9	8													7
1	2	3		5	6	7			10	11	4		9	8													8
1	2	3		5	6				10	11	4		9	8	7												9
1		3		5	6			9		11	4				7	2	8	10									10
1	2	3		5	6				10	11	4		9	7			8										11
	2	3		5	6		8	9	10	11	4			7					1								12
	2	3		5	6	7		9	10	11	4			8					1								13
1	2	3		5	6			9	10	11	4			7			8										14
	2	3		5	6			9	10	11	4		8	7					1								15
	2	3		5	6	7			10	11	4		9	8					1								16
1	2	3		5	6		8		10	11	4		9	7													17
1	2	3		5	6				10	11	4		9	7			8										18
1	2	3		5	6				10	11	4		9	7			8										19
1	2	3		5	6		8		10	11	4		9	7													20
1	2	3		5	6		8		10	11	4		9	7													21
1	2			5	6	7			10	11	4		9	8						3							22
1	2			5	6	7				11	4		10	8						3	9						23
1	2	3		5	6	7				11	4		10	8							9						24
1	2	3		5	6				10	11	4		9	7							8						25
1	2	3		5	6				10	11	4		9	7							8						26
1	2	3		5	6	7			10	11	4										8	9					27
1	2	3		5	6				10	11	4			7							8	9					28
1	2	3		5	6			10	11	8	4			7								9					29
1	2	3		5	6			9	10	11	4				7							8					30
1	2	3		5	6				10	11	4		9	7								8					31
1	2	3		5	6				10	11	4		9	7								8					32
1	2	3		5	6				10	11	4		9	7							8						33
1	2	3		5	6				10	11	4		9	7							8						34
30	33	32	3	33	34	14	9	12	31	34	31	1	21	26	3	1	5	1	4	2	8	6	-	-	-	-	A
-	1	-	-	3	-	-	2	5	13	6	-	-	8	1	-	-	-	-	-	-	2	2	-	-	-	-	G

Fryer	Ross	Thorpe	Haworth	Morrison	Goldie	Soar	Wood	Edgley	Wardrope	Threlfall	Collins	Robotham	Fraser	Bell	Kirby	Waterson	Hogan	Thomas	Thompson	Fitchett	Freeman	Wheatcroft	Fidler	Catterall	Fitchie	Harwood	
1	2	3		5	6		8		10	11	4		9	7													1
	2			5	6		8		10	11	4		9	7					1	3							2

Fryer	Ross	Thorpe	Haworth	Morrison	Goldie	Soar	Wood	Edgley	Wardrope	Threlfall	Collins	Robotham	Fraser	Bell	Kirby	Waterson	Hogan	Thomas	Thompson	Fitchett	Freeman	Wheatcroft	Fidler	Catterall	Fitchie	Harwood	
1	2	3	4			7	8	9	10	11	5	6															1
1	2	3	4	5	6		8	9	10	11				7													2
1	2				6	7				11	5		9	8						4			3	10			3
	2	3		5		7	8	9	10	11	6								1	4							4
1	2	3		5	6	7			10	11	4		9	8													5
1		3		5	6	7				11	4		9	8		2								10			6
1	2	3		5		7	8	9		11	4	6		10													7
1		3		5			8			11	4	6	9		7		10						2				8
		3		5			8	9			6				7	2	10	11	1	4							9
1	2	3		5	6		8	9	10	11	4			7													10
	2	3	4	5	6			9		11				7			8		1						10		11
	2	3		5				9	10	11		4		7			8		1	6							12
	2	3		5	6		8		10	11	4		9	7					1								13
	2	3	4	5	6								8	7					1		9			10		11	14
1	2	3		5	6	7											8			4				10		9	15
			4	5		7			10							6	8		1	3			2	11		9	16
Team unknown																											17
	2	3		5	6	7		9	11		4								1		8			10			18
1	2			5	6			9	10	11	4						7				8		3				19
Team Unknown																											20

Star centre half Billy Morrison.

1906-07

Southern League Division One

	P	W	D	L	F	A	Pts
Fulham	38	20	13	5	58	32	53
Portsmouth	38	22	7	9	64	36	51
Brighton & Hove Albion	38	18	9	11	53	43	45
Luton Town	38	18	9	11	52	52	45
West Ham United	38	15	14	9	60	41	44
Tottenham Hotspur	38	17	9	12	63	45	43
Millwall	38	18	6	14	71	50	42
Norwich City	38	15	12	11	57	48	42
Watford	38	13	16	9	46	43	42.
Brentford	38	17	8	13	57	56	42
Southampton	38	13	9	16	49	56	35
Reading	38	14	6	18	57	47	34
Leyton	38	11	12	15	38	60	34
Bristol Rovers	38	12	9	17	55	54	33
Plymouth Argyle	38	10	13	15	43	50	33
New Brompton	38	12	9	17	47	59	33
Swindon Town	38	11	11	16	43	54	33
Queens Park Rangers	38	11	10	17	47	55	32
Crystal Palace	38	8	9	21	46	66	25
Northampton Town	38	5	9	24	29	88	19

Manager: Harry Bradshaw

No	Date		V	Opponents	R	H-T	F-T	Scorers	Atter
1	S	1	A	Norwich C	D	0-0	0-0		8,00
2		8	H	Luton T	D	0-0	0-0		20,00
3		15	A	Crystal Palace	W	2-0	3-0	Wheatcroft, Hamilton, Thompson	8,00
4		22	H	Brentford	W		1-0	Ross (pen)	20,00
5		24	A	Tottenham H	L		1-5	Ross (pen)	15,00
6		29	A	Millwall A	D		2-2	Hamilton, Kingaby	12,00
7	O	3	A	Swindon T	D	0-2	2-2	Wheatcroft, Hamilton	2,00
8		6	H	Leyton	W		3-1	Ross (pen), Edgley, Thompson	13,00
9		13	A	Portsmouth	D	0-0	0-0		14,00
10		20	H	New Brompton	W		2-1	Wheatcroft, Fraser	17,00
11		27	A	Plymouth A	D	0-1	1-1	Fraser	10,00
12		29	H	Tottenham H	W		2-1	Threlfall, Freeman	20,00
13	N	3	H	Brighton & HA	W		2-0	Fraser, Ross	16,00
14		10	A	Reading	W		1-0	Wheatcroft	8,00
15		17	H	Watford	D	0-0	0-0		10,00
16		24	A	Northampton T	W	2-0	4-0	Freeman 2, Wheatcroft 2	3,00
17	D	1	H	Queen's Park R	D	0-0	1-1	Morrison	21,00
18		8	H	Bristol R	W		3-0	Hamilton, Thelfall 2	10,00
19		15	A	Southampton	W		2-1	Freeman, Hamilton	10,00
20		22	H	West Ham U	L		1-4	Hamilton	12,00
21		29	H	Norwich C	D	1-1	1-1	Hogan	12,00
22	J	5	A	Luton T	L	0-1	0-2		7,00
23		19	H	Crystal Palace	W	0-0	2-1	Hamilton, Goldie	12,00
24		26	A	Brentford	L	0-1	0-1		15,00
25	F	9	A	Leyton	D	1-1	1-1	Wheatcroft	6,00
26		16	H	Portsmouth	W	0-0	2-0	Hamilton, Kingaby	30,00
27		23	A	New Brompton	D	0-1	1-1	Threlfall	6,00
28	M	2	H	Plymouth A	W	1-0	2-0	Threlfall, Freeman	16,00
29		9	A	Brighton & HA	D	0-0	0-0		10,00
30		16	H	Reading	W	2-0	2-1	Hogan, Morrison	17,00
31		23	A	Watford	W	1-0	1-0	Freeman	8,00
32		29	H	Swindon T	W	3-0	4-0	Threlfall 2, Freeman 2	14,00
33		30	H	Northampton T	W	2-0	3-1	Hamilton, Ross (pen), Hogan	10,00
34	A	2	H	Millwall A	D	0-0	0-0		12,00
35		6	A	Queen's Park R	W	1-0	2-0	Freeman, Hogan	14,00
36		13	A	Bristol R	W	1-0	2-0	Hogan, Kingaby	8,00
37		20	H	Southampton	W	0-0	3-0	Hamilton, Freeman, Ross (pen)	16,00
38		27	A	West Ham U	L	0-2	1-4	Hamilton	10,00

App

Goal

FA Cup

No	Date		V	Opponents	R	H-T	F-T	Scorers	Atter
1	J	12	A	Stockport C	D	0-0	0-0	(at Craven Cottage)	30,00
R		16	H	Stockport C	W	1-0	2-1	Freeman, Threlfall	10,00
2	F	2	H	Crystal Palace	D	0-0	0-0		30,00
R		6	A	Crystal Palace	L	0-0	0-1		20,00

Western League

No	Date		V	Opponents	R	H-T	F-T	Scorers	Atter
1	S	3	H	Chelsea	D	0-0	0-0		12,00
2		10	A	Queen's Park R	W		1-0	Fraser	
3	O	8	H	Bristol R	W		4-1	Freeman 2 Fraser Hindmarsh	
4		22	A	Brentford	L		0-5		
5	N	5	A	Bristol R	W		1-0	Freeman 2 Fraser Hindmarsh	
6		12	H	Brentford	W	1-0	3-1	Hamilton 2 Freeman	4,00
7		21	A	Reading	W	1-0	1-0	Threlfall	
8		26	H	Reading	W		3-0	Hamilton Threlfall Morrison	
9	D	25	H	Queen's Park R	W	2-0	2-0	Freeman Fraser	17,00
10		26	A	Chelsea	L		1-2	Hamilton	25,00

Title Decider

No	Date		V	Opponents	R	H-T	F-T	Scorers	Atter
TD	A	15	N	West Ham U	L		0-1	(at Stamford Bridge)	10,00

Fryer	Ross	Thorpe	Waterson	Morrison	Goldie	Bell	Edgley	Hamilton	Wheatcroft	Threlfall	Collins	Kingaby	Fraser	Thompson	Hindmarsh	McIntyre	Freeman	Charlton	Hogan	Horne			
1	2	3	4	5	6	7	8	9	10	11													1
1	2	3		5	6	7	8	9	10	11	4												2
1	2	3		5	6			9	10		4	7	8	11									3
1	2	3		5	6			9	10		4	7	8	11									4
1	2	3		5	6	7		9			4		8	11	10								5
1	2	3		5	6			9	10	11		7	8			4							6
1	2	3		5	6	7		9	10		4		8	11									7
1	2	3		5	6		9		10		4	7	8	11									8
1	2	3		5	6			9	10			7	8	11		4							9
1	2	3		5	6				10		4	7	9	11			8						10
1	2			5	6			9		11	4	7	10				8	3					11
1	2			5	6				9	11	4	7	10				8	3					12
1	2			5	6				10	11	4	7	9				8	3					13
1	2			5	6				10	11	4	7	9				8	3					14
1	2			5	6				10	11	4	7	9				8	3					15
1	2			5	6				10	11	4	7	9				8	3					16
1	2			5	6			9	10	11	4	7					8	3					17
1	2	3		5	6			9		11		7	10			4	8						18
1	2			5	6			9		11		7	10			4	8	3					19
1	2			5	6			9			4	7	10	11			8	3					20
1	2	3		5	6	8				11	4	7					9		10				21
		3		5	6			9		11	4	7					8	2	10	1			22
1	2			5	6			9		11	4	7	10				8	3					23
1	2			5	6	11			10			7	9			4	8	3					24
1	2			5	6			9	8	11	4	7	10					3					25
1	2			5	6			9		11	4	7	10				8	3					26
1	2			5	6			9		11	4	7	10				8	3					27
1	2			5	6			9		11	4	7	10				8	3					28
1	2			5	6			9		11	4	7	10				8	3					29
	2			5	6			9		11	4		10				8	3	7	1			30
1	2			5	6			9		11	4	7	10				8	3					31
1	2			5	6			9		11	4	7	10				8	3					32
1	2	3		5	6			9		11	4	7					8		10				33
1	2	3		5	6			9		11	4	7					8		10				34
1	2	3		5	6			9		11	4	7					8		10				35
1	2	3		5	6			9		11	4	7					8		10				36
1	2	3		5	6			9		11	4	7					8		10				37
	2	3		5	6			9		11	4	7					8		10	1			38
5	37	19	1	38	38	6	3	29	17	29	32	33	27	8	1	5	28	20	9	3			A
-	6	-	-	2	1	-	1	11	7	7	-	3	3	2	-	-	10	-	5	-			G

Fryer	Ross	Thorpe	Waterson	Morrison	Goldie	Bell	Edgley	Hamilton	Wheatcroft	Threlfall	Collins	Kingaby	Fraser	Thompson	Hindmarsh	McIntyre	Freeman	Charlton	Hogan	Horne			
1	2			5	6			9	10	11	4	7					8	3					1
1	2			5	6			9	10	11	4	7					8	3					R
1	2			5	6			9	10	11	4	7					8	3					2
1	2			5	6			9	10	11	4	7					8	3					R

Fryer	Ross	Thorpe	Waterson	Morrison	Goldie	Bell	Edgley	Hamilton	Wheatcroft	Threlfall	Collins	Kingaby	Fraser	Thompson	Hindmarsh	McIntyre	Freeman	Charlton	Hogan	Horne			
		3		5	6	7		9	10	11						4	8	2					1
	2	3		5	6	7					4		9	11					8		10		2
		3		5	6	4							9	11	10		8	2	7				3
	2	3		5	6								9	11	10	4	8		7			1	4
	2	3				7		9		11							8		10				5
	2			5				9		11	4		7			6	10	3	8				6
	2			5	6			9		11	4		10				8	3	7	1			7
	2			5	6			9		11	4		10				8	3	7				8
	2			5	6			9		11	4	7	10				8	3					9
	2	3		5	6			9		11	4	7	10				8			1			10

Fryer	Ross	Thorpe	Waterson	Morrison	Goldie	Bell	Edgley	Hamilton	Wheatcroft	Threlfall	Collins	Kingaby	Fraser	Thompson	Hindmarsh	McIntyre	Freeman	Charlton	Hogan	Horne			
	2	3		5	6			9		11	4	7					8		10				TD

Fred Threlfall, the exciting outside right.

1907-08

Division Two

	P	W	D	L	F	A	Pts
Bradford City	38	24	6	8	90	42	54
Leicester Fosse	38	21	10	7	72	47	52
Oldham Athletic	38	22	6	10	76	42	50
Fulham	38	22	5	11	82	49	49
West Bromwich Albion	38	19	9	10	61	39	47
Derby County	38	21	4	13	77	45	46
Burnley	38	20	6	12	67	50	46
Hull City	38	21	4	13	73	62	46
Wolverhampton W	38	15	7	16	50	45	37
Stoke	38	16	5	17	57	52	37
Gainsborough Trinity	38	14	7	17	47	71	35
Leeds City	38	12	8	18	53	65	32
Stockport County	38	12	8	18	48	67	32
Clapton Orient	38	11	10	17	40	65	32
Blackpool	38	11	9	18	51	58	31
Barnsley	38	12	6	20	54	68	30
Glossop	38	11	8	19	54	74	30
Grimsby Town	38	11	8	19	43	71	30
Chesterfield	38	6	11	21	46	92	23
Lincoln City	38	9	3	26	46	83	21

Manager: Harry Bradshaw

Did you know that?

The 6-0 defeat inflicted on Fulham by Newcastle in the FA Cup semi final is still the biggest winning margin at this stage in the history of the competition. In November 1907, Fulham paid their first £1,000 transfer fee, for Fred Harrison from Southampton.

No		Date	V	Opponents	R	H-T	F-T	Scorers	Atte
1	S	3	H	Hull C	L	0-1	0-1		10,0
2		7	A	Derby C	W	1-0	1-0	Freeman	7,0
3		14	H	Lincoln C	W	3-0	6-1	Threlfall 2, Hubbard, Freeman, Bevan, Dalrymple	10,0
4		21	H	Grimsby T	L	0-1	0-1		20,0
5		28	A	Barnsley	L	0-3	0-6		7,0
6	O	5	H	Chesterfield	W	2-0	5-0	Dalrymple 2, Millington 2, Fraser	13,0
7		12	A	Burnley	W	1-0	1-0	Dalrymple	8,0
8		16	A	Lincoln C	W	2-2	4-2	Dalrymple 3, Millington	3,0
9		19	H	Oldham A	L	0-0	1-2	Fraser	25,0
10		26	A	Clapton O	W	0-0	1-0	Dalrymple	15,0
11	N	2	H	Leeds C	W	1-0	2-0	Fraser, Threlfall	20,0
12		9	A	Wolverhampton W	L	0-0	0-2		10,0
13		16	H	Gainsborough T	W	5-0	6-0	Lee, Fraser, Millington, Dalrymple 3	15,0
14		23	A	Stockport C	L	0-0	0-2		8,0
15		30	H	Glossop	W	4-1	6-1	Millington 4, Harrison, Mouncher	13,0
16	D	7	A	Leicester F	W	1-0	3-2	Harrison 2, Threlfall	10,0
17		14	H	Blackpool	W	0-0	3-0	Millington, Mouncher, Wilkes	7,0
18		21	A	Stoke	L	1-2	1-6	Dalrymple	5,0
19		26	A	Bradford C	W	2-1	3-1	Millington, Harrison, Mouncher	25,0
20		28	H	West Bromich A	D	1-0	1-1	Ross pen	20,0
21	J	1	A	Chesterfield	D	0-1	1-1	Millington	8,0
22		4	H	Derby C	D	0-0	0-0		18,0
23		18	A	Grimsby T	W	3-0	4-0	Harrison, Ross (pen), Millington, Mouncher	5,0
24		25	H	Barnsley	W	1-0	2-0	Harrison, Mouncher	12,0
25	F	8	H	Burnley	W	2-0	2-1	Millington, Harrison	15,0
26		15	A	Oldham A	D	0-2	3-3	Harrison 2, Dalrymple	12,0
27		29	A	Leeds C	W	0-0	1-0	Dalrymple	10,0
28	M	14	A	Gainsborough T	D	1-2	3-3	Mouncher, Morrison, Fraser	5,0
29		18	H	Clapton O	W	1-0	4-0	Dalrymple 3, Harrison	8,0
30		21	H	Stockport C	L	0-1	0-1		20,0
31	A	1	H	Wolverhampton W	W	0-1	2-1	Suart, Dalrymple	8,0
32		4	H	Leicester F	W	1-0	5-1	Harrison, Dalrymple, Carter, Brown 2	30,0
33		11	A	Blackpool	L	0-0	1-2	Lipsham	4,0
34		17	H	Bradford C	L	0-1	0-2		45,0
35		18	H	Stoke	W	2-1	5-1	Brown 3, Carter 2	15,0
36		20	A	Hull C	W	1-0	2-1	Harrison, Carter	14,0
37		25	A	West Bromich A	L	0-2	1-3	Carter	6,9
38		29	A	Glossop	W	1-0	2-1	Carter, (Gettins og)	5

Ap

Goa

FA Cup

1	J	11	A	Luton T	W	5-2	8-3	Dalrymple 2, Harrison 2, Millington 2, Ross, Morrison	5,5
2	F	1	A	Norwich C	W	2-0	2-1	Millington, Threlfall (at Craven Cottage)	19,0
3		22	A	Manchester C	D	1-0	1-1	Harrison	23,0
R		26	H	Manchester C	W	0-1	3-1	Ross (pen), Harrison, Dalrymple	38,0
4	M	7	H	Manchester U	W	1-0	2-1	Harrison 2	41,0
SF		28	N	Newcastle U	L	0-2	0-6	(at Anfield)	50,0

1	Dalrymple, Lindsay and Skene debuts Millington debut
12	Lee debut
14	Harrison and Mouncher debuts
30	Fraser's last game
31	Suart debut
32	H. Brown and Lipsham debuts
37	Goldie's last game

Skene	Ross	Lindsay	Collins	Morrison	Goldie	Dalrymple	Freeman	Bevan	Hubbard	Threlfall	Wilkes	Fraser	Hogan	Millington C	Hind	Ward	Lee	Harrison	Mouncher	Charlton	Crossthwaite	Carter	Suart	Brown	Lipsham	Waterson	Bradshaw J	
1	2	3	4	5	6	7	8	9	10	11																		1
1	2	3	4	5	6	7	8	9	10	11																		2
1	2	3	4	5	6	7	8	9	10	11																		3
1	2	3	4	5	6	7	8	9	10	11																		4
1	2	3	5		6	7	8	9	10	11	4																	5
1		3	5	2	6	8				11	4	10	7	9														6
1		3	5	2	6	8				11	4	10	7	9														7
1		3	5	2	6	8				11	4	10	7	9														8
1		3	5	2	6	8				11	4	10	7	9														9
1		3	5	2	6	8				11		10		9	4	7												10
1		3	5	2	6	8				11	4	10		9		7												11
1		3	5	2	6	8				7	4	10		9			11											12
1		3	5	2	6	8				7	4	10		9			11											13
1		3	5	2	6	8				7	4			10				9	11									14
1	2		5		6	8				7	4			10				9	11	3								15
1	2		5		6	8				7	4			10				9	11	3								16
1	2		5		6	8				7	4			10				9	11	3								17
1	2		5		6	8				7	4			10				9	11	3								18
1	2	3	5		6	8				7	4			10				9	11									19
1	2	3	4	5	6	8				7				10				9	11									20
1	2	3	4	5	6	8				7				10				9	11									21
1	2	3	5		6	8				7	4			10				9	11									22
1	2		4	5	6	8				7				10				9	11	3								23
1	2	3	4	5	6	8				7				10				9	11									24
	2	3	4	5	6	8				7				10				9	11		1							25
1	2	3	4	5	6	8				7				10				9	11									26
1	2	3	4	5	6	8				7				10				9	11									27
1	2	3	4	5	6	8						10		7				9	11									28
1	2	3		5	6	8								10	4	7		9	11									29
1	2	3		5	6	8						10		9	4	7			11									30
1	2	3		5	6	8								10				9	11			7	4					31
1	2	3		5	6	8												9				7	4	10	11			32
1	2	3		5	6	8												9				7	4	10	11			33
1	2	3	4	5	6									8				9				7		10	11			34
1	2				6									8				9	11	3		7	5	10		4		35
1	2		4	5										8				9		3		7	6	10	11			36
1	2		4	5	6									8				9		3		7		10	11			37
		2	4	5														9	11	3	1	7	6	10			8	38
36	28	30	32	30	36	33	5	5	5	27	15	10	4	30	3	4	2	24	20	9	2	8	6	7	5	1	1	A
-	2	-	-	1	-	19	2	1	1	4	1	5	-	13	-	-	1	12	6	-	-	6	1	5	1	-	-	G

Skene	Ross	Lindsay	Collins	Morrison	Goldie	Dalrymple	Freeman	Bevan	Hubbard	Threlfall	Wilkes	Fraser	Hogan	Millington C	Hind	Ward	Lee	Harrison	Mouncher	Charlton	Crossthwaite	Carter	Suart	Brown	Lipsham	Waterson	Bradshaw J	
1	2	3	4	5	6	8				7				10				9	11									1
1	2	3	4	5	6	8				7				10				9	11									2
1	2	3	4	5	6	8				7				10				9	11									3
1	2	3	4	5	6	8				7				10				9	11									R
1	2	3	4	5	6	8						10		7				9	11									4
1	2	3	4	5	6	8							7	10				9	11									SF

0 points v	Stockport C	0 points
1 point v	Oldham A, West Bromwich A	2 points
2 points v	Barnsley, Blackpool, Bradford C, Grimsby T, Hull C, Stoke, Wolves	14 points
3 points v	Derby C, Chesterfield, Gainsboro T	9 points
4 points v	Burnley, Clapton O, Glossop, Leeds C, Leicester F, Lincoln C	24 points

Bob Dalrymple, top scorer.

1908-09

Division Two

	P	W	D	L	F	A	Pts
Bolton Wanderers	38	24	4	10	59	28	52
Tottenham Hotspur	38	20	11	7	67	32	51
West Bromwich Albion	38	19	13	6	56	27	51
Hull City	38	19	6	13	63	39	44
Derby County	38	16	11	11	55	41	43
Oldham Athletic	38	17	6	15	55	43	40
Wolverhampton W	38	14	11	13	56	48	39
Glossop	38	15	8	15	57	53	38
Gainsborough Trinity	38	15	8	15	49	70	38
Fulham	38	13	11	14	58	48	37
Birmingham	38	14	9	15	58	61	37
Leeds City	38	14	7	17	43	53	35
Grimsby Town	38	14	7	17	41	54	35
Burnley	38	13	7	18	51	58	33
Clapton Orient	38	12	9	17	37	49	33
Bradford Park Avenue	38	13	6	19	51	59	32
Barnsley	38	11	10	17	48	57	32
Stockport County	38	14	3	21	39	71	31
Chesterfield	38	11	8	19	37	67	30
Blackpool	38	9	11	18	46	68	29

Manager: Harry Bradshaw

Did you know that?

Left back Jimmy Sharp played for Scotland against Wales at Wrexham in March 1909, the first of only two Fulham players to win full Scottish caps. (Graham Leggat was the other.)

1 Morrison and Ross finales
15 Threlfall's last game
29 Smith debut
38 Freeman and Millington finales

No		Date	V	Opponents	R	H-T	F-T	Scorers	Atter
1	S	2	H	Glossop	L	1-2	2-3	Carter, Ross (pen)	10,00
2		5	H	Stockport C	W	4-0	5-1	Harrison 5	25,00
3		12	A	West Bromich A	D	1-0	1-1	Brown	14,52
4		19	H	Birmingham	D	1-1	1-1	Dalrymple	30,00
5		26	A	Gainsborough T	D	0-1	1-1	Harrison	20,00
6	O	3	H	Grimsby T	W	2-1	5-2	Brown 2, Harrison, Dalrymple, (Wheelhouse og)	16,00
7		10	A	Bolton W	D	0-0	0-0		12,00
8		17	A	Burnley	W	1-0	3-1	Charlton (pen), Harrison, Lipsham	7,00
9		24	H	Bradford	W	2-0	3-1	Dalrymple, Brown, Charlton (pen)	20,00
10		31	A	Wolverhampton W	W	0-0	1-0	Millington	10,00
11	N	7	H	Oldham A	W	1-0	3-2	Brown, Charlton (pen), Harrison	12,00
12		14	A	Clapton O	D	0-0	1-1	Millington	15,00
13		21	H	Leeds C	L	0-0	0-1		18,00
14		28	A	Barnsley	W	1-0	2-1	Harrison, Brown	6,00
15	D	5	H	Tottenham H	L	1-0	2-3	Dalrymple, Lipsham	35,00
16		12	A	Hull C	L	0-0	0-2		10,00
17		19	H	Derby C	L	0-2	1-2	Lipsham	15,00
18		25	H	Chesterfield	D	0-0	0-0		12,00
19		26	A	Blackpool	L	0-1	0-2		5,00
20	J	1	A	Chesterfield	L	0-2	1-2	Millington	6,00
21		2	A	Stockport C	W	1-1	2-1	Freeman, Harrison	7,00
22		9	H	West Bromich A	W	1-0	2-0	Dalrymple, Millington	30,00
23		23	A	Birmingham	W	2-1	3-1	Freeman 2, Parsonage	9,00
24		30	H	Gainsborough T	W	2-0	4-0	Freeman 2, Dalrymple, Millington	10,00
25	F	13	H	Bolton W	L	1-2	1-2	Freeman	18,00
26		27	A	Bradford	D	1-1	1-1	Parsonage	9,00
27	M	6	H	Wolverhampton W	D	1-0	1-1	Lee	6,00
28		13	A	Oldham A	L	0-0	0-1		15,00
29		20	H	Clapton O	L	0-1	1-2	Dalrymple	25,00
30		25	A	Grimsby T	D	1-1	2-2	Freeman 2	3,00
31		27	A	Leeds C	L	0-1	0-2		10,00
32		31	H	Burnley	W	3-0	3-0	Charlton (pen), Dalrymple 2	5,00
33	A	3	H	Barnsley	D	2-0	2-2	Dalrymple, Harrison	16,00
34		9	A	Glossop	D	0-0	0-0		5,00
35		10	A	Tottenham H	L	0-1	0-1		30,00
36		12	H	Blackpool	W	2-0	3-0	Harrison, Dalrymple, Parsonage	7,00
37		17	H	Hull C	L	0-1	0-3		15,00
38		24	A	Derby C	L	1-2	1-2	Dalrymple	5,00
									App
									Goal

FA Cup

No		Date	V	Opponents	R	H-T	F-T	Scorers		Atter
1	J	16	A	Carlisle U	W	3-0	4-1	Millington, Freeman 2, Collins	(at Craven Cottage)	18,00
2	F	6	A	Tottenham H	L	0-0	0-1			33,00

	Skene	Ross	Charlton	Collins	Morrison	Wilkes	Carter	Dalrymple	Harrison	Millington C	Lipsham	Lindsay	Parsonage	Suart	Threlfall	Brown	Wyllie	Goldie J	Fryer	Freeman	Leigh	Sharp	Mouncher	Lee	McCourt	Smith	Millington B	Littlewort	Waterson	Bradshaw
1		2	3	4	5	6	7	8	9	10	11																			
2			2	4				8	9		11	3	5	6	7	10														
3			2	4					9	8	11	3	5	6	7	10														
4			2	4				8	9		11	3	5	6	7	10														
5			2	4				8	9		11	3	5	6	7	10														
6			2	4				8	9		11	3	5	6	7	10														
7			2	4				8	9	7	11	3	5	6		10														
8			2	4				8	9	7	11	3	5	6		10														
9			2	4				8	9	7	11	3	5	6		10														
10			2	4				8	9	7	11	3	5	6		10														
11			2	4				8	9	7	11	3	5	6		10														
12			2	4				8	9	7	11	3	5	6		10														
13			2	4				8	9	7	11	3	5	6		10														
14			2	4				8	9	7	11	3	5	6		10														
15			2	4				8	9		11	3	5	6	7	10														
16			2	4			7	8	10		11	3	5	6			9													
17			2	4				8	7	9	11	3		5		10		6												
18			2	4				8	7	10	11	3	5	6			9		1											
19			2	4					8	7	11	3	5	6		10	9													
20			2					8	7	10	11			4			5	6	1	9	3									
21				4				8	7	10	11	3		5				6	1	9	2									
22			2	4				8	7	10				5				6	1	9		3	11							
23			2	4					7	8			5			10		6	1	9		3	11							
24			2	4				8	7	10	11			5				6	1	9		3								
25			2	4				8	7	10	11		5	6					1	9		3								
26			2	4						9			5	6		10			1	8		3	11	7						
27				4						9	11	2		5		10			1	8		3	6	7						
28				4							11	2		5			9			8		3	6	7	10					
29				4				8	9		11	2		5					1			3	6		10	7				
30				4				8	7		11	2		5						9		3	6				10			
31				4				8		10	11	2		5						9		3	6			7				
32			3					10	9	7	11	2		6				4		8								5		
33			2	4				10	9	7	11			6						8		3						5		
34											11	3	5				9	4	1	10	2			7					6	8
35			2	4				10	9	7	11			5						8		3	6							
36				4				10	9	8	11	2	5	6								3				7				
37				4				10			11	2		6			9					3		7				5		8
38								10		8	11	2		4						9		3	6			7		5		
A	7	1	28	34	1	1	2	31	31	27	35	29	22	35	6	19	7	8	11	16	3	15	10	5	2	4	1	4	1	2
G		1	4	-	-	-	1	12	13	5	3	-	3	-	-	6	-	-	-	8	-	-	-	1	-	-	-	-	-	-

	Skene	Ross	Charlton	Collins	Morrison	Wilkes	Carter	Dalrymple	Harrison	Millington C	Lipsham	Lindsay	Parsonage	Suart	Threlfall	Brown	Wyllie	Goldie J	Fryer	Freeman	Leigh	Sharp	Mouncher	Lee	McCourt	Smith	Millington B	Littlewort	Waterson	Bradshaw
1			2	4				8	7	10			5					6	1	9		3	11							
2			2	4				8	7	10	11			5				6	1	9		3								

0 points v	Derby C, Hull C, Leeds C, Tottenham H	0 points
1 point v	Bolton W, Chesterfield, Clapton O, Glossop	4 points
2 points v	Blackpool, Oldham A	4 points
3 points v	Barnsley, Birmingham, Bradford , Gainsboro T, Grimsby T, West Bromwich A, Wolves	21 points
4 points v	Burnley, Stockport C	8 points

Fred Harrison, scored 5 goals against Stockport.

1909-10

Division Two

	P	W	D	L	F	A	Pts
Manchester City	38	23	8	7	81	40	54
Oldham Athletic	38	23	7	8	79	39	53
Hull City	38	23	7	8	80	46	53
Derby County	38	22	9	7	72	47	53
Leicester Fosse	38	20	4	14	79	58	44
Glossop	38	18	7	13	64	57	43
Fulham	38	14	13	11	51	43	41
Wolverhampton W	38	17	6	15	64	63	40
Barnsley	38	16	7	15	62	59	39
Bradford Park Avenue	38	17	4	17	64	59	38
West Bromwich Albion	38	16	5	17	58	56	37
Blackpool	38	14	8	16	50	52	36
Stockport County	38	13	8	17	50	47	34
Burnley	38	14	6	18	62	61	34
Lincoln City	38	10	11	17	42	69	31
Clapton Orient	38	12	6	20	37	60	30
Leeds City	38	10	7	21	46	80	27
Gainsborough Trinity	38	10	6	22	33	75	26
Grimsby Town	38	9	6	23	50	77	24
Birmingham	38	8	7	23	42	78	23

Manager: Phil Kelso

Did you know that?

Fulham centre half George Parsonage was suspended from football for allegedly asking for an illegal payment as part of a proposed transfer to Chesterfield. He had claimed he was only joking.

1	Maven debut
7	Walker debut
32	Marshall debut
33	Skene final match
34	Lipsham final match
36	Fryer final match
37	Reynolds debut
38	H. Brown finale

No		Date	V	Opponents	R	H-T	F-T	Scorers	Att
1	S	4	A	Stockport C	W	0-0	2-0	Harrison, Charlton (pen)	10,0
2		11	H	Glossop	W	1-0	2-0	Harrison, Collins	20,0
3		13	H	Blackpool	L	0-1	0-1		8,0
4		18	A	Birmingham	D	1-0	1-1	Brown	12,0
5		25	H	West Bromich A	L	0-0	0-2		18,1
6	O	2	A	Oldham A	W	1-0	1-0	Harrison	10,0
7		4	A	Blackpool	D	0-1	1-1	Charlton (pen)	5,0
8		9	H	Barnsley	W	2-0	3-0	Harrison, Brown, Maven	20,0
9		16	H	Bradford	W	0-0	3-1	Dalrymple 2, Lipsham	10,0
10		23	A	Burnley	L	0-1	0-2		3,0
11		30	H	Leeds C	W	3-0	5-1	Harrison 3, Brown 2	15,0
12	N	6	A	Wolverhampton W	D	1-1	1-1	Dalrymple	5,0
13		13	H	Gainsborough T	L	0-0	0-1		12,0
14		20	A	Grimsby T	W	2-0	2-0	McLaughlin, Brown	4,0
15		27	H	Manchester C	D	0-1	1-1	Walker	12,0
16	D	4	A	Leicester F	W	2-1	3-2	Dalrymple 2, Maven	4,0
17		11	H	Lincoln C	D	0-1	1-1	Brown	12,0
18		18	A	Clapton O	D	0-0	0-0		10,0
19		25	H	Hull C	W	2-0	3-1	Walker 2, Harrison	24,0
20		27	A	Hull C	L	1-1	2-3	Brown, Dalrymple	16,0
21	J	1	A	Derby C	L	0-1	1-3	Brown	8,0
22		8	H	Stockport C	W	0-0	2-0	Harrison, Brown	10,0
23		22	A	Glossop	W	0-0	1-0	Dalrymple	4,0
24		29	H	Birmingham	D	0-0	0-0		10,0
25	F	12	H	Oldham A	D	1-0	1-1	Walker	15,0
26		24	A	Barnsley	L	0-1	1-2	Walker	3,0
27		26	A	Bradford	L	0-0	0-3		12,0
28	M	5	H	Burnley	W	0-1	2-1	Malcolm, Harrison	12,0
29		12	A	Leeds C	D	1-1	2-2	Harrison, Maven	4,0
30		19	H	Wolverhampton W	D	0-0	0-0		14,0
31		25	H	Derby C	D	0-0	0-0		20,0
32		26	A	Gainsborough T	L	0-1	0-2		3,0
33		29	A	West Bromich A	L	1-1	2-3	Burns, Lindsay (pen)	11,7
34	A	2	H	Grimsby T	W	2-0	3-2	Smith, Harrison, Flanagan	10,0
35		9	A	Manchester C	L	1-0	1-3	Mouncher	16,0
36		16	H	Leicester F	W	1-0	2-0	Brown, Smith	14,0
37		23	A	Lincoln C	D	1-1	2-2	Harrison 2	4,0
38		30	H	Clapton O	D	0-0	0-0		12,0
									Ap
									Goa

FA Cup

No		Date	V	Opponents	R	H-T	F-T	Scorers	Att
1	J	15	A	Chesterfield	D	0-0	0-0		9,0
R		19	H	Chesterfield	W	1-1	2-1	Dalrymple, Harrison	8,0
2	F	5	A	Newcastle U	L	0-1	0-4		35,8

Skene	Charlton	Sharp	Collins	Maven	Suart	Berry	Dalrymple	Harrison	Brown	Lipsham	Flanagan	Goldie	Smith	Walker	Lindsay	McLaughlin	O'Donnell	Prout	Burns	Fryer	Leigh	Malcolm	Marshall	Mouncher	Dixon	Reynolds	
1	2	3	4	5	6	7	8	9	10	11																	1
1	2	3	4	5	6	7	8	9	10	11																	2
1	2	3	4	5	6	7		9	10	11	8																3
1	2	3	4	5	6	7	8	9	10	11																	4
1	2	3	4	5	6	7	8	9	10	11																	5
1	2	3	4	5	6	7	8	9	10	11																	6
1	2	3	4	5			8	9	10			6	7	11													7
1	2	3	4	5		7	8	9	10	11		6															8
1	2	3	4	5	6	7	8	9	10	11																	9
1	2		4	5	6	7	8	9	10	11					3												10
1	2	3	4	5	6	7	8	9	10					11													11
1	2	3	4	5	6		8	9	10	11			7														12
1	2		4	5	6	7	8	9	10	11					3												13
1	2	3	4	5	6		8		10				7	11		9											14
1	2		4	5	6		8	9	10				7	11	3												15
1	2	3	4	5	6		8	9	10				7	11													16
1	2	3	4	5	6		8	9	10				7	11													17
1	2	3	4	5	6		8		10				7	11		9											18
1	2	3	4	5	6		8	9	10				7	11													19
	2	3	4	5	6		8	9	10				7	11			1										20
	2	3	4	5	6		8	9	10				7	11			1										21
	2	3	4	5	6	7		9	10	11							1	8									22
	2	3	4	5	6		8	10					7	11					9	1							23
	2	3	4	5	6		8	10		11			7						9	1							24
	2	3	4	5	6		8		10				7	11				9		1							25
	2		4	5	6		8	10					7	11				9		1	3						26
	2		4		6		8	9					7	11						1	3	10	5				27
1	2			5	6		8	10		11			7		3			4				9					28
1	2	3	4	5	6		8	9					7									10		11			29
1	2	3	4	5			8	9	10			6	7											11			30
1	2	3	4	5	6		8	9			10		7											11			31
1	2		4		5			9		11		6	7		3							10	8				32
1	2		4	5				9				6	7		3			8	10						11		33
	2		5					9		11	8	6	7		3			4	10	1							34
		3		5	4			9			10	6	7		2			8		1				11			35
	2	3	4		5			9	10		8	6	7	11						1							36
	2		4		5			9	10		8	6	7	11							3					1	37
	2	3	4		5			9	10		8	6	7	11												1	38
25	37	28	36	32	33	12	29	35	27	16	7	10	26	17	8	2	3	7	4	8	3	4	2	4	1	2	A
-	2	-	1	3	-	-	7	14	10	1	1	-	2	5	1	1	-	-	1	-	-	1	-	1	-	-	G

Skene	Charlton	Sharp	Collins	Maven	Suart	Berry	Dalrymple	Harrison	Brown	Lipsham	Flanagan	Goldie	Smith	Walker	Lindsay	McLaughlin	O'Donnell	Prout	Burns	Fryer	Leigh	Malcolm	Marshall	Mouncher	Dixon	Reynolds	
	2	3	4	5	6			9	10				7					8		1				11			1
	2	3	4	5	6		8	9		11	10		7							1							R
	2	3	4	5	6		8	9	10	11			7							1							2

0 points v	West Bromwich A Gainsboro T,	0 points
1 point v	Blackpool, Manchester C, Derby C,	3 points
2 points v	Birmingham, Barnsley, Bradford, Burnley, Wolves, Lincoln C, Clapton O, Hull C	16 points
3 points v	Oldham A, Leeds C,	6 points
4 points v	Stockport C, Glossop, Grimsby T, Leicester F	16 points

THE COTTAGERS' JOURNAL.

Fulham v. Chelsea

SATURDAY, December 3rd, 1910.

Kick-Off : : 2.30 p.m.

FULHAM.

1 Reynolds

2 Charlton 3 Sharp

4 Collins 5 Mavin 6 Suart

7 Smith 8 White 9 Harrison 10 Brown 11 Walker

O

12 McEwan 13 V. J. Woodward 14 Evan Jones 15 Whittingham 16 Brawn

17 Taylor 18 McConnell 19 Warren

20 Cameron 21 Bettridge

22 Molyneux

L CHELSEA. R

Referee - - H. S. BAMLETT.

Linesmen - - A. GREEN & C. BRADLEY.

From the programme for the first ever Fulham v Chelsea match.

1910-11

Division Two

	P	W	D	L	F	A	Pts
West Bromwich Albion	38	22	9	7	67	41	53
Bolton Wanderers	38	21	9	8	69	40	51
Chelsea	38	20	9	9	71	35	49
Clapton Orient	38	19	7	12	44	35	45
Hull City	38	14	16	8	55	39	44
Derby County	38	17	8	13	73	52	42
Blackpool	38	16	10	12	49	38	42
Burnley	38	13	15	10	45	45	41
Wolverhampton W	38	15	8	15	51	52	38
Fulham	38	15	7	16	52	48	37
Leeds City	38	15	7	16	58	56	37
Bradford Park Avenue	38	14	9	15	53	55	37
Huddersfield Town	38	13	8	17	57	58	34
Glossop	38	13	8	17	48	62	34
Leicester Fosse	38	14	5	19	52	62	33
Birmingham	38	12	8	18	42	64	32
Stockport County	38	11	8	19	47	79	30
Gainsborough Trinity	38	9	11	18	37	55	29
Barnsley	38	7	14	17	52	62	28
Lincoln City	38	7	10	21	28	72	24

Manager: Phil Kelso

Did you know that?

In his first full season, goalkeeper Arthur Reynolds did not miss a game, the first of four seasons (he also did it in 1911-12, 1921-22 and 1922-23) in which he was ever-present. Syd Gibbons equalled the feat in the 1930s, but since 1945, the best has been three seasons (Jim Langley, Les Barrett, Peter Mellor and Jim Stannard).

4	Torrance debut
6	Dalrymple finale
7	White debut
9	A Brown debut
11	Lindsay finale
18	Harrison's 50th goal
19	Collins 200th game
33	Harrison finale
37	Mouncher and Suart finale

No		Date	V	Opponents	R	H-T	F-T	Scorers	Atten
1	S	3	H	Birmingham	W	1-0	3-0	Smith 2, Maven	25,00
2		10	A	West Bromich A	L	1-0	1-2	Dalrymple	10,14
3		17	H	Hull C	L	0-0	0-1		20,00
4		24	A	Bolton W	L	0-2	0-2		5,00
5	O	1	A	Bradford	L	0-0	0-1		20,00
6		8	H	Burnley	W	0-0	3-0	Harrison, Torrance, Dalrymple	10,00
7		15	A	Gainsborough T	W	0-0	1-0	Smith	6,00
8		22	H	Leeds C	W	1-1	2-1	Harrison, Maven	10,00
9		29	A	Stockport C	D	1-0	1-1	White	5,00
10	N	5	H	Derby C	W	3-1	3-1	Maven, Brown 2	17,00
11		12	A	Barnsley	L	1-4	2-4	Walker, Smith	5,00
12		19	H	Leicester C	W	2-1	3-1	Smith, White, Maven	15,00
13		26	A	Wolverhampton W	L	0-3	1-5	Smith	9,00
14	D	3	H	Chelsea	W	1-0	1-0	Smith	30,00
15		10	A	Clapton O	L	0-0	0-1		15,00
16		17	H	Blackpool	W	2-1	2-1	Harrison, Smith	14,00
17		24	A	Glossop	L	1-0	1-2	Mouncher	2,00
18		26	H	Huddersfield T	W	2-0	2-1	Harrison, White	25,00
19		31	A	Birmingham	D	0-1	1-1	Maven (pen)	14,00
20	J	7	H	West Bromich A	L	0-0	0-1		20,00
21		21	A	Hull C	D	0-0	0-0		8,00
22		28	H	Bolton W	W	0-0	2-0	Harrison, Maven	15,00
23	F	11	A	Burnley	L	0-1	0-1		10,00
24		13	H	Bradford	W	2-0	4-0	Walker, Harrison, Smith 2	5,00
25		18	H	Gainsborough T	W	0-0	1-0	Spink	7,00
26		25	A	Leeds C	L	1-1	1-3	Maven (pen)	6,00
27		28	A	Huddersfield T	W	0-0	2-1	White, Burns	4,00
28	M	4	H	Stockport C	W	4-0	6-2	Burns 3, Smith, Maven, Harrison	8,00
29		15	A	Derby C	D	1-1	2-2	Harrison, Burns	2,00
30		18	H	Barnsley	L	0-1	0-2		8,00
31		25	A	Leicester F	L	0-1	2-3	Maven, Brown	6,00
32	A	1	H	Wolverhampton W	L	0-0	0-1		10,00
33		8	A	Chelsea	L	0-1	0-2		40,00
34		14	A	Lincoln C	L	0-0	0-1		10,00
35		15	H	Clapton O	D	0-0	1-1	Charlton (pen)	16,00
36		17	H	Lincoln C	D	0-0	0-0		8,00
37		22	A	Blackpool	W	1-1	2-1	Brown, Mouncher	5,00
38		29	H	Glossop	D	1-0	2-2	Maven (pen), Burns	8,00
									App
									Goal

FA Cup

1	J	14	A	West Bromich A	L	0-3	1-4	Mouncher	18,03

Reynolds	Charlton	Lindsay	Collins	Maven	Goldie	Smith	Dalrymple	Harrison	Flanagan	Walker	Torrance	Suart	White	Kirkwood	Brown A	Sharp	Moucher	Marshall	Burns R	Redwood	Spink	Borland	Burns T	Horton	
	2	3	4	5	6	7	8	9	10	11															1
	2	3	4	5	6	7	8	9	10	11															2
	2	3	4	5	6	7	8	9	10	11															3
	2	3	4	5	6	7	8	10		11	9														4
	2	3	4	5		7		9	8	11	10	6													5
	2	3	4	5		7	8	9		11	10	6													6
	2	3	4	5		7		9		11	10	6	8												7
		3	4	5		7		9		11	10	6	8	2											8
	2	3	4	5		7		9		11		6	8		10										9
	2	3	4	5		7		9		11		6	8		10										10
	2	3	4	5		7		9		11		6	8		10										11
	2		4	5		7		9		11		6	8		10	3									12
	2		4	5		7		9		11		6	8		10	3									13
	2		4	5		7		9		11		6	8		10	3									14
	2		4		6	7		9		11		5	8		10	3									15
	2		4	5		7		9		11		6	8		10	3									16
	2			5		7		9				6	8		10	3	11	4							17
	2		4	5		7		9				6	8		10	3	11								18
	2		4	5		7		9				6	8		10	3	11								19
	2			5	6	7		9				4	8		10	3	11								20
	2			5	6	7					10		8			3	11	4	9						21
	2		4	5		7		10				6	8				11		9	3					22
	2		4	5				10				6	8				11		9	3	7				23
	2		4	5		7		10		11		6	8						9	3					24
	2		4	5		7		10		11		6							9	3	8				25
	2		4	5	6	7		10		11			8						9	3					26
	2		4	5	6	7		10		11			8						9	3					27
	2		4	5		7		10		11		6	8						9	3					28
	2	3	4	5	6	7		10		11			8						9						29
	2		4	5	6	7		10		11			8			3			9						30
	2		4	5		7				11			10		9	3		6	8						31
	2		4	5		7				11	10	6	8			3			9						32
	2		4	5		7		9		11			10			3		6	8						33
	2	3	4			7				11	10		8		9			6				5			34
	2		4			7				11	10		8		9			6				5	3		35
	2				4	7				11	10		8					6				5	3	9	36
	2			5		7					10	6	8		9	3	11	4							37
	2			5	6	7				11	10		8			3		4	9						38
[illegible]	37	13	32	34	13	37	5	30	4	30	12	23	31	1	16	16	8	9	14	7	2	3	2	1	A
	1	-	-	10	-	11	2	8	-	2	1	-	4	-	4	-	2	-	6	-	1	-	-	-	G

Reynolds	Charlton	Lindsay	Collins	Maven	Goldie	Smith	Dalrymple	Harrison	Flanagan	Walker	Torrance	Suart	White	Kirkwood	Brown A	Sharp	Moucher	Marshall	Burns R	Redwood	Spink	Borland	Burns T	Horton	
	2		4	5		7		10				6	8		9	3	11								1

0 points v	Barnsley, West Bromwich A, Wolves	0 points
1 point v	Clapton O, Glossop, Hull C, Lincoln C	4 points
2 points v	Bolton W, Bradford, Burnley, Chelsea, Leeds C, Leicester F	12 points
3 points v	Birmingham, Derby C, Stockport C	9 points
4 points v	Blackpool, Gainsboro T, Huddersfield T	12 points

Fred Maven, scored ten goals from centre half.

1911-12

Division Two

	P	W	D	L	F	A	Pts
Derby County	38	23	8	7	74	28	54
Chelsea	38	24	6	8	64	34	54
Burnley	38	22	8	8	77	41	52
Clapton Orient	38	21	3	14	61	44	45
Wolverhampton W	38	16	10	12	57	33	42
Barnsley	38	15	12	11	45	42	42
Hull City	38	17	8	13	54	51	42
Fulham	38	16	7	15	66	58	39
Grimsby Town	38	15	9	14	48	55	39
Leicester Fosse	38	15	7	16	49	66	37
Bradford Park Avenue	38	13	9	16	44	45	35
Birmingham	38	14	6	18	55	59	34
Bristol City	38	14	6	18	41	60	34
Blackpool	38	13	8	17	32	52	34
Nottingham Forest	38	13	7	18	46	48	33
Stockport County	38	11	11	16	47	54	33
Huddersfield Town	38	13	6	19	50	64	32
Glossop	38	8	12	18	42	56	28
Leeds City	38	10	8	20	50	78	28
Gainsborough Trinity	38	5	13	20	30	64	23

Manager: Phil Kelso

Did you know that?

When Egyptian amateur and Cambridge graduate Hassan Hegazi played (and scored) in the 3-1 win over Stockport in November 1911, he was the first foreigner to play first class football for Fulham.

1	Coleman and Pearce debuts
32	Gray debut
38	A Brown finale

No		Date	V	Opponents	R	H-T	F-T	Scorers	Atte
1	S	2	A	Bristol C	L	0-1	0-1		7,0
2		9	H	Birmingham	W	1-1	2-1	Pearce 2	12,00
3		16	A	Huddersfield T	L	0-2	0-2		7,00
4		23	H	Blackpool	W	2-0	3-0	Pearce, Torrance, Smith	10,0
5		30	A	Glossop	D	1-0	1-1	Collins	2,00
6	O	7	H	Hull C	L	0-1	0-1		10,0
7		14	A	Barnsley	D	1-1	2-2	Pearce, Maven	7,0
8		21	H	Bradford	W	1-0	2-0	Coleman, Smith	20,0
9		28	H	Burnley	L	0-2	3-4	White, Coleman, Maven	15,0
10	N	4	A	Derby C	L	1-3	1-6	Pearce	12,0
11		11	H	Stockport C	W	2-0	3-1	Hegazi, Coleman, Collins	8,0
12		18	A	Leeds C	W	2-0	2-0	Coleman, Brown	8,0
13		25	H	Wolverhampton W	D	1-0	1-1	Pearce	10,0
14	D	2	A	Leicester F	W	2-0	5-2	Pearce 2, Coleman, Collins, Walker	8,0
15		9	H	Gainsborough T	W	4-0	7-1	Coleman 2, Maven 2 (2 pens), Brown, Pearce 2	10,0
16		16	A	Grimsby T	L	0-1	0-1		5,0
17		23	H	Nottingham F	W	1-0	2-0	Collins, Pearce	10,0
18		25	H	Chelsea	L	0-1	0-1		42,0
19		26	A	Chelsea	L	0-0	0-1		35,0
20		30	H	Bristol C	W	1-0	2-1	Coleman 2	10,0
21	J	6	A	Birmingham	W	1-1	3-1	Walker 2, Maven	7,0
22		20	H	Huddersfield T	W	0-1	3-1	Maven, Pearce 2	11,0
23		27	A	Blackpool	L	1-2	1-3	White	4,0
24	F	10	A	Hull C	W	2-2	3-2	Brown 2 Torrance	10,0
25		17	H	Barnsley	D	2-2	2-2	Coleman, Maven	20,0
26	M	2	A	Burnley	L	0-3	1-5	Pearce	20,0
27		16	A	Stockport C	L	1-1	1-2	Maven	6,0
28		23	H	Leeds C	W	2-2	7-2	Pearce 3, Coleman 2, Maven 2 (1 pen)	5,0
29		27	A	Bradford	W	1-0	2-0	Torrance, Coleman	4,0
30		30	A	Wolverhampton W	D	0-0	0-0		11,0
31	A	1	H	Glossop	L	0-2	0-2		3,0
32		5	H	Clapton O	L	0-0	0-2		20,0
33		6	H	Leicester F	W	3-1	4-1	Pearce 3, Coleman	9,0
34		8	A	Clapton O	L	0-2	0-4		17,0
35		13	A	Gainsborough T	W	0-0	1-0	Torrance	3,0
36		15	H	Derby C	D	0-0	0-0		20,0
37		20	H	Grimsby T	L	1-1	1-3	Pearce	8,0
38		27	A	Nottingham F	D	0-0	1-1	Brown	3,0
									Ap
									Go

FA Cup

No		Date	V	Opponents	R	H-T	F-T	Scorers	Atte
1	J	13	H	Burnley	W	1-1	2-1	Coleman, Brown	13,1
2	F	3	H	Liverpool	W	1-0	3-0	Coleman 2, Pearce	30,0
3		24	H	Northampton T	W	1-0	2-1	Brown 2	32,0
4	M	9	A	West Bromich A	L	0-2	0-3		50,0

Reynolds	Charlton	Sharp	Collins	Maven	Marshall	Smith	Coleman	Pearce	White	Walker	Torrance	Burns	Duncan	McIntosh	Spink	Clifford	Brown	Hegazi	Gray	Wood	
1	2	3	4	5	6	7	8	9	10	11											1
1	2	3	4	5	6	7	8	9	10	11											2
1	2	3	4	5	6	7	8	9	10	11											3
1	2	3	4	5		7	8	9	6	11	10										4
1	2		4	5		7	8	9	6	11		3	10								5
1	2	3	4	5		7	8	9	6	11	10										6
1	2		4	5			8	9	6		10	3		11	7						7
1	2	3	4		5	7	8	9	6		10			11							8
1	2		4	5		7	8	9	6		10			11		3					9
1			2	5	4	7	8	9	6	10			11			3					10
1	2	3	4	5		7	8		6	11							10	9			11
1	2	3	4	5		7	8	9	6	11							10				12
1	2	3	4	5		7	8	9	6	11							10				13
1	2	3	4	5		7	8	9	6	11							10				14
1	2		4	5		7	8	9	6	11						3	10				15
1	2	3	4	5		7	8		6	11	9						10				16
1	2	3	4	5		7	8	9	6	11							10				17
1	2	3	4	5		7	8	9	6	11							10				18
1	2	3		5			8	9	6	11					7	4	10				19
1	2	3		5		7	8	9	6					11		4	10				20
1	2	3		5		7		9	6	11	8					4	10				21
1	2	3		5	4	7	8	9	6	11							10				22
1	2	3		5	4	7	8	9	6	11							10				23
1	2	3		5		7		9	6	11	8					4	10				24
1	2	3		5	4	7	8	9		11						6	10				25
1	2	3	4	5		7		9	6	11	8						10				26
1	2	3	4	5		7	8	9	6					11			10				27
1	2	3	4	5		7	8	9	6				11				10				28
1	2	3	4	5		7	8		6		9		11				10				29
1	2		4	5		7		9	6		8	3	11				10				30
1		3	4	5		7		9	6		8	2	11				10				31
1			4	5			8	9	6	11	10	3			7				2		32
1			4	5			8	9	6	11		3			7		10		2		33
1			4	5				9	6	11		3			7		10		2	8	34
1			4	5				9	6		10	3	11		7				2	8	35
1			4	5			8	9	6		11	3			7		10		2		36
1				5	4		8	9	6		10	3	11		7				2		37
1			4	5			8		6		10	3		11	7		9		2		38
38	29	25	30	37	9	29	31	34	37	25	17	11	8	6	9	8	25	1	7	2	A
-	-	-	4	10	-	2	14	21	2	3	4	-	-	-	-	-	5	1	-	-	G

1	2	3		5	4	7	8	9	6	11							10				1
1	2	3		5	4	7	8	9	6	11							10				2
1	2	3		5	4	7	8	9	6	11							10				3
1	2	3		5	4	7	8	9	6					11			10				4

0 points v	Burnley, Chelsea, Clapton O, Grimsby T	0 points
1 point v	Derby C, Glossop	2 points
2 points v	Barnsley, Blackpool, Bristol C, Huddersfield T, Hull C, Stockport C, Wolves	14 points
3 points v	Nottingham F	3 points
4 points v	Birmingham , Bradford, Gainsboro T, Leeds C, Leicester F	20 points

Bert Pearce, top scorer.

1912-13

Division Two

	P	W	D	L	F	A	Pts
Preston North End	38	19	15	4	56	33	53
Burnley	38	21	8	9	88	53	50
Birmingham	38	18	10	10	59	44	46
Barnsley	38	19	7	12	57	47	45
Huddersfield Town	38	17	9	12	66	40	43
Leeds City	38	15	10	13	70	64	40
Grimsby Town	38	15	10	13	51	50	40
Lincoln City	38	15	10	13	50	52	40
Fulham	38	17	5	16	65	55	39
Wolverhampton W	38	14	10	14	56	54	38
Bury	38	15	8	15	53	57	38
Hull City	38	15	6	17	60	55	36
Bradford Park Avenue	38	14	8	16	60	60	36
Clapton Orient	38	10	14	14	34	47	34
Leicester Fosse	38	13	7	18	49	65	33
Bristol City	38	9	15	14	46	72	33
Nottingham Forest	38	12	8	18	58	59	32
Glossop	38	12	8	18	49	68	32
Stockport County	38	8	10	20	56	78	26
Blackpool	38	9	8	21	39	69	26

Manager: Phil Kelso

Did you know that?

At Bradford in February 1913, outside left Willie Walker retaliated after being continually fouled and was given his marching orders, the first Fulham player to be sent off in the League.

No		Date	V	Opponents	R	H-T	F-T	Scorers	Attend
1	S	7	H	Leeds C	W	4-0	4-0	Walker 2, Pearce, Coleman	20,000
2		9	A	Birmingham	L	1-0	1-2	Collins	12,000
3		14	A	Grimsby T	L	1-1	1-2	Coleman	6,000
4		16	H	Huddersfield T	W	1-0	2-0	Walker 2	7,000
5		21	H	Bury	W	1-0	3-1	Pearce 2, Collins	20,000
6		28	A	Blackpool	L	0-1	0-2		5,000
7	O	5	A	Barnsley	L	0-0	1-2	Maven	7,000
8		12	H	Bradford	W	2-1	3-1	Pearce, Coleman, Collins	12,000
9		19	A	Wolverhampton W	L	1-1	1-2	Pearce	12,000
10		26	H	Leicester F	D	0-0	1-1	Pearce	6,000
11	N	2	A	Stockport C	L	0-1	0-1		5,000
12		9	H	Preston NE	W	2-0	3-1	Fitchie, Coleman, Walker	15,000
13		16	A	Burnley	L	0-2	0-5		12,000
14		23	H	Hull C	W	1-0	2-0	Pearce, Coleman	12,000
15		30	A	Leicester F	L	0-0	0-1		9,000
16	D	7	H	Clapton O	D	1-1	1-1	Coleman	20,000
17		21	H	Nottingham F	D	0-0	0-0		10,000
18		25	A	Bristol C	L	0-0	1-2	Maven	10,000
19		28	A	Leeds C	W	1-1	3-2	Torrance 2, Walker	10,000
20	J	2	A	Glossop	L	0-2	0-2		2,000
21		4	H	Grimsby T	L	0-1	0-1		7,000
22		18	A	Bury	L	0-1	0-1		7,000
23		25	H	Blackpool	W	1-1	4-2	Torrance 2, Fitchie, Coleman	7,000
24	F	8	H	Barnsley	D	0-1	1-1	Coleman	15,000
25		15	A	Bradford	W	1-2	3-2	Maven, Lee, Pearce	8,000
26		22	H	Wolverhampton W	W	2-0	4-2	Coleman 3, Torrance	15,000
27	M	8	H	Stockport C	W	2-0	7-0	Pearce 3, Coleman 3, Lee	8,000
28		15	A	Preston NE	L	0-1	0-1		11,000
29		21	A	Lincoln C	L	0-1	0-3		5,000
30		22	H	Burnley	W	4-0	4-2	White, Walker, Smith, Coleman	25,000
31		24	H	Birmingham	W	2-1	3-2	Coleman , Lee 2	8,000
32		25	A	Huddersfield T	L	1-1	1-5	Lee	10,500
33		29	A	Hull C	W	1-0	1-0	White	7,000
34	A	5	H	Glossop	W	0-0	2-0	Lee, Walker	7,000
35		7	H	Bristol C	D	0-0	0-0		5,000
36		12	A	Clapton O	L	1-1	1-2	Coleman	14,000
37		19	H	Lincoln C	W	2-0	3-1	Coleman 2, Walker	8,000
38		26	A	Nottingham F	W	1-2	4-2	Lee 2, Coleman, Taylor	3,000
									Apps
									Goals

FA Cup

No		Date	V	Opponents	R	H-T	F-T	Scorers	Attend
1	J	11	H	Hull C	L	0-0	0-2		10,000

18 Nixon debut
23 Coquet debut
31 Russell debut
37 Taylor debut

Reynolds	Charlton	Sharp	Collins	Maven	White	Smith	Coleman	Pearce	Torrance	Walker	Gray	Marshall	Burns	Wood	Forrest	Fitchie	Lee	Nixon	Weir	Overend	Coquet	Crossley	Winship	Russell	Stewart	Bowering	Taylor	Champion	
1	2	3	4	5	6	7	8	9	10	11																			1
1	2	3	4	5	6	7	8	9	10	11																			2
1		3	4	5	6	7	8	9	10	11	2																		3
1		3	4	5	6	7	8	9	10	11	2																		4
1	2	3	4	5		7	8	9	10	11		6																	5
1	2		4	5	6	7	8	9	10	11			3																6
1	2			5	6	7		9	10	11		4	3	8															7
1	2	3	5		6	7	10	9		11		4		8															8
1	2	3	6			7	8	9	10	11		4			5														9
1		3	4	5	6	7	8	9		11			2			10													10
1	2	3	4	5	6	7	8	9								10	11												11
1	2	3			6	7	8	9		11		4			5	10													12
1	2	3			6		8	9		11		4			5	10	7												13
1	2		4	5	6	7	8	9		11			3			10													14
1	2		4	5	6	7	8	9		11			3			10													15
1			4	5	6	7	8	9		11	2		3			10													16
1			4	2	6	7	8	9	10	11			3		5														17
				5	6	7	8	9	10	11	2	4	3					1											18
			4	5	10	7	8		9	11	2	6	3					1											19
1			4	5	10	7	8		9	11	2	6	3																20
1	2		4	5	6	7	8		10	11			3						9										21
1			4		10				9	11	2	6	3	8	5					7									22
1			4		6	7	8		9				3		5	10					2	11							23
1			4	5	6	7	8	9	10				3				11				2								24
1			4	5	6		8	9	10	11	3						7				2								25
1			4	5			8	9	10	11	3	6					7				2								26
1			4	5			8	9		11	3	6		10			7				2								27
1			4	5			8	9			3	6		10			7				2		11						28
1			4	5			8	9		11		6	3	10			7				2								29
1			4	5	10	7	8			11		6	3				9				2								30
1			4		10	7	8			11		6	3				9				2			5					31
1			4		10	7	8			11		6	3				9				2			5					32
1					10	7	8			11		6	3				9				2			5	4				33
1					10	7	8			11		6	3				9				2			5	4				34
1				5	10		8				3	6					9			7	2		11		4				35
1				5	10	7	8			11		6	3				9				2				4				36
1				5			8			11	3						9			7	2				4	6	10		37
1				5	6	7	8						3				9				2				4		10	11	38
36	13	11	28	28	31	29	36	24	18	32	13	21	22	6	6	8	17	2	1	3	16	1	2	4	6	1	2	1	A
-	-	-	3	3	2	1	20	11	5	9	-	-	-	-	-	2	8	-	-	-	-	-	-	-	-	-	1	-	G

Reynolds	Charlton	Sharp	Collins	Maven	White	Smith	Coleman	Pearce	Torrance	Walker	Gray	Marshall	Burns	Wood	Forrest	Fitchie	Lee	Nixon	Weir	Overend	Coquet	Crossley	Winship	Russell	Stewart	Bowering	Taylor	Champion	
1			4	5	10	7	8		9	11	2	6	3																1

0 points v	Grimsby T	0 points
1 point v	Barnsley, Bristol C, Clapton O, Leicester F,	4 points
2 points v	Birmingham, Blackpool, Burnley, Bury, Glossop, Huddersfield T, Lincoln C, Preston NE, Stockport C, Wolves	20 points
3 points v	Nottingham F	3 points
4 points v	Bradford, Hull C, Leeds C	12 points

Tim Coleman, top scorer.

1913-14

Division Two

	P	W	D	L	F	A	Pts
Notts County	38	23	7	8	77	36	53
Bradford Park Avenue	38	23	3	12	71	47	49
Woolwich Arsenal	38	20	9	9	54	38	49
Leeds City	38	20	7	11	76	46	47
Barnsley	38	19	7	12	51	45	45
Clapton Orient	38	16	11	11	47	35	43
Hull City	38	16	9	13	53	37	41
Bristol City	38	16	9	13	52	50	41
Wolverhampton W	38	18	5	15	51	52	41
Bury	38	15	10	13	39	40	40
Fulham	38	16	6	16	46	43	38
Stockport County	38	13	10	15	55	57	36
Huddersfield Town	38	13	8	17	47	53	34
Birmingham	38	12	10	16	48	60	34
Grimsby Town	38	13	8	17	42	58	34
Blackpool	38	9	14	15	33	44	32
Glossop	38	11	6	21	51	67	28
Leicester Fosse	38	11	4	23	45	61	26
Lincoln City	38	10	6	22	36	66	26
Nottingham Forest	38	7	9	22	37	76	23

Manager: Phil Kelso

Did you know that?

Fulham beat Chelsea 3-2 in a friendly at Stamford Bridge, and one of the goals was scored by a guest player, 'Bombardier' Billy Wells, one-time British heavyweight boxing champion and the second man to bang the gong in the introduction to Rank films.

1 Templeton debut
9 Maven finale
15 Collins finale
24 Charlton's 200th game
34 Coleman finale

No		Date	V	Opponents	R	H-T	F-T	Scorers	Atten
1	S	1	H	Bury	D	1-0	1-1	Maven	8,00
2		6	A	Clapton O	L	0-1	0-1		18,00
3		13	H	Huddersfield T	W	0-0	1-0	Coleman	25,00
4		20	A	Glossop	W	1-0	1-0	White	2,00
5		27	H	Lincoln C	W	3-0	4-0	Maven, Lee 2, Coleman	15,00
6	O	4	A	Stockport C	W	2-1	3-1	Maven, White, (Wood og)	6,00
7		11	H	Blackpool	D	0-0	0-0		6,00
8		18	A	Bradford	L	0-0	0-1		12,00
9		25	H	Nottingham F	W	1-0	2-0	Pearce 2	15,00
10	N	1	A	Notts C	L	0-2	0-4		12,00
11		8	H	Woolwich A	W	0-0	6-1	Coleman 2, Pearce 2, Taylor, Walker	30,00
12		15	A	Leicester F	L	0-1	0-3		10,00
13		22	H	Grimsby T	D	2-0	2-2	Coleman, Collins	15,00
14		29	A	Wolverhampton W	L	0-0	0-1		12,00
15	D	6	H	Birmingham	W	0-0	1-0	Taylor	10,00
16		13	A	Hull C	D	1-0	1-1	Pearce	8,00
17		20	H	Bristol C	W	1-0	3-1	Pearce, Coleman 2	12,00
18		25	A	Leeds C	L	0-2	1-2	Pearce	17,00
19		26	H	Leeds C	L	0-0	0-1		25,00
20		27	H	Clapton O	W	1-0	2-0	Coleman, Taylor	20,00
21	J	1	A	Bury	L	0-0	0-1		12,00
22		3	A	Huddersfield T	L	0-1	1-3	Pearce	6,00
23		17	H	Glossop	W	2-1	2-1	Pearce, Coleman	9,00
24		24	A	Lincoln C	W	1-0	1-0	Lee	5,00
25	F	7	H	Stockport C	W	2-0	2-0	Walker, Coleman	5,00
26		14	A	Blackpool	D	1-0	1-1	Coleman	5,00
27		21	H	Bradford	L	1-3	1-6	Pearce	8,00
28		28	A	Nottingham F	D	0-1	1-1	Pearce	6,00
29	M	7	H	Notts C	L	0-1	1-2	Pearce	18,00
30		14	A	Woolwich A	L	0-1	0-2		30,00
31		21	H	Leicester C	L	1-1	1-2	Coleman	6,00
32		28	A	Grimsby T	W	1-0	3-0	White, Pearce, Lee	8,00
33	A	4	H	Wolverhampton W	W	0-0	1-0	Pearce	10,00
34		10	H	Barnsley	L	0-0	1-2	Russell pen	25,00
35		11	A	Birmingham	W	1-0	1-0	Lee	20,00
36		13	A	Barnsley	L	0-0	0-1		10,00
37		18	H	Hull C	L	0-0	0-1		10,00
38		25	A	Bristol C	W	1-0	1-0	Wood	7,00
									App
									Goal

FA Cup

No		Date	V	Opponents	R	H-T	F-T	Scorers	Atten
1	J	10	A	Manchester C	L	0-2	0-3		25,34

Reynolds	Coquet	Houghton	Stewart T	Maven	White	Curtis	Coleman	Pearce	Lee	Templeton	Russell	Torrance	Marshall	Smith	Walker	Forrest	Charlton	Taylor	McDonald	Collins	Wood	Garvey	Champion	Maughan	Laws	
1	2	3	4	5	6	7	8	9	10	11																1
1	2	3	4	5	6	7	8	9			10	11														2
1	2	3		5	6		8	9			10		4	7	11											3
1	2	3		5	10		8		9		6		4	7	11											4
1	2	3		5	10		8		9		6		4	7	11											5
1	2	3		5	10		8		9		6	11		7		4										6
1	2	3	4	5	10		8		9		6	11		7												7
1		3	4	5	10		8	9			6			7	11		2									8
1		3	4	5	10		8	9			6			7	11		2									9
1	2	3	4		6		8	9			5			7	11			10								10
	2	3			6		8	9			5			7	11			10	1	4						11
	2	3			6		8	9			5			7	11			10	1	4						12
	2	3			6		8				5	9		7	11			10	1	4						13
	2	3			6				9		5			7	11			10	1	4	8					14
		3			6			9			5			7	11		2	10	1	4	8					15
		3			6			9			5		4	7	11		2	10	1		8					16
		3			6		8	9			5		4	7	11		2	10	1							17
		3			6		8	9	7		5		4		11		2	10	1							18
1		3			6		8	9			5		4	7	11		2	10								19
1		3			6		8	9			5		4	7	11		2	10								20
1		3			6			9		11	5	8	4	7			2	10								21
1		3						9		11	5	8	4	7			2	10				6				22
1		3			6		8	9			5		4	7			2	10					11			23
1		3			6		8		9		5		4	7	11		2	10								24
1		3			6		8		9		5		4	7	11		2	10								25
1		3					8	9			5		4	7	11		2	10				6				26
1		3			6		8	9			5		4	7	11		2	10								27
1		3			6		8	9			5		4	7	11		2	10								28
1		3			6		8	9			5		4	7	11		2	10								29
1		3			6		8	9			5		4	7	11		2	10								30
1		3			6		8	9			5			7	11		2	10						4		31
1		3	10		6			9	7	11	5	4									8				2	32
1		3	10		6			9	7	11	5	4									8				2	33
1		3	10		6		8	9	7	11	5	4					2									34
1		3			10				9	11	5	6		7			2				8				4	35
1		3			10				9	11	5	6		7			2				8				4	36
1		3			10				9	11	5	6		7			2				8				4	37
1		3			10				9	11	5	6		7			2				8				4	38
30	12	38	9	9	36	2	27	26	16	10	37	13	18	32	24	1	24	22	8	5	9	2	1	1	6	A
-	-	-	-	3	3	-	12	14	5	-	1	-	-	-	2	-	-	3	-	1	1	-	-	-	-	G

1		3			6		8	9			5	10	4	7	11		2									1

0 points v	Barnsley, Bradford, Leeds C, Leicester F, Notts C	0 points
1 point v	Bury, Hull C	2 points
2 points v	Blackpool, Clapton O, Huddersfield T, Wolves, Woolwich A	10 points
3 points v	Grimsby T, Nottingham F	6 points
4 points v	Birmingham, Bristol C, Glossop, Lincoln C, Stockport C	20 points

Arthur 'Pat' Collins, first Fulham player to 200 appearances, moves to Leicester.

1914-15

Division Two

	P	W	D	L	F	A	Pts
Derby County	38	23	7	8	71	33	53
Preston North End	38	20	10	8	61	42	50
Barnsley	38	22	3	13	51	51	47
Wolverhampton W	38	19	7	12	77	52	45
Arsenal	38	19	5	14	69	41	43
Birmingham	38	17	9	12	62	39	43
Hull City	38	19	5	14	65	54	43
Huddersfield Town	38	17	8	13	61	42	42
Clapton Orient	38	16	9	13	50	48	41
Blackpool	38	17	5	16	58	57	39
Bury	38	15	8	15	61	56	38
Fulham	38	15	7	16	53	47	37
Bristol City	38	15	7	16	62	56	37
Stockport County	38	15	7	16	54	60	37
Leeds City	38	14	4	20	65	64	32
Lincoln City	38	11	9	18	46	65	31
Grimsby Town	38	11	9	18	48	76	31
Nottingham Forest	38	10	9	19	43	77	29
Leicester Fosse	38	10	4	24	47	88	24
Glossop	38	6	6	26	31	87	18

Manager: Phil Kelso

Did you know that?

In the match at home to Grimsby in February 1915, 21-year-old Ernie Thompson was No. 3 and 22-year-old William Maughan, No. 4. Both were to die in the trenches in the next two years.

18	Gray finale
FAC2	Pearce 50th goal
21	Peace finale
30	Templeton finale
38	Coquet, Lee and Smith finales

No		Date	V	Opponents	R	H-T	F-T	Scorers	Atten
1	S	2	A	Leeds C	W	1-0	1-0	Lee	8,00
2		5	H	Clapton O	W	3-0	4-0	Lee 2, Simons 2	12,00
3		9	H	Leeds C	W	1-0	1-0	Slade	5,00
4		12	A	Arsenal	L	0-1	0-3		10,00
5		19	H	Derby C	W	0-0	2-0	Russell, Lee	14,00
6		26	A	Lincoln C	L	1-2	1-3	Cannon	6,00
7	O	3	H	Birmingham	L	0-1	2-3	Cannon, Simons	12,00
8		10	A	Grimsby T	D	0-1	1-1	Slade	8,00
9		17	H	Huddersfield T	L	0-0	2-3	Simons, Russell	10,00
10		24	A	Bristol C	D	0-0	0-0		7,00
11		31	H	Bury	W	4-1	6-3	White 2, Slade 2, Russell, Lee	8,00
12	N	7	A	Preston NE	L	0-0	1-2	Russell	9,00
13		14	H	Nottingham F	W	1-0	2-1	Lee, White	8,00
14		21	A	Leicester F	W	2-0	2-0	Lee 2	4,00
15		28	H	Barnsley	W	2-0	2-0	Russell, Lee	1,00
16	D	5	A	Glossop	L	0-1	0-1		50
17		12	H	Wolverhampton W	L	0-1	0-1		4,00
18		19	A	Blackpool	D	2-0	2-2	Pearce 2	3,00
19		26	H	Stockport C	W	1-0	1-0	Bellamy	5,00
20	J	2	A	Clapton O	L	1-1	1-2	Taylor	10,00
21		16	H	Arsenal	L	0-0	0-1		10,00
22		23	A	Derby C	D	0-1	1-1	Russell	6,00
23	F	13	H	Grimsby T	W	0-1	2-1	Cannon, Taylor	3,00
24		20	A	Huddersfield T	D	1-0	2-2	Torrance 2	6,00
25		27	H	Bristol C	L	0-1	1-2	Torrance	4,00
26	M	1	A	Birmingham	L	0-1	0-1		5,00
27		6	A	Bury	L	0-1	0-1		4,00
28		13	H	Preston NE	L	0-0	0-2		6,00
29		20	A	Nottingham F	D	1-0	2-2	Lee 2	5,00
30		27	H	Leicester F	W	0-0	1-0	Maughan	4,00
31		29	H	Lincoln C	W	2-0	3-1	Lee 3	1,80
32	A	2	A	Stockport C	W	2-0	2-0	Taylor, Torrance	4,00
33		3	A	Barnsley	D	1-2	2-2	Taylor, Lee	4,50
34		5	A	Hull C	L	0-1	0-2		6,00
35		6	H	Hull C	W	2-1	4-1	Slade, Lee, White, Smith	2,00
36		10	H	Glossop	W	0-0	2-0	Cannon 2	6,00
37		17	A	Wolverhampton W	L	0-2	0-2		7,50
38		24	H	Blackpool	L	0-0	0-1		5,00
									App
									Goa

FA Cup

1	J	9	A	South Shields	W	0-1	2-1	Taylor, Walker	15,00
2		30	H	Southampton	L	2-1	2-3	Taylor, Pearce	8,89

	Reynolds	Charlton	Houghton	Torrance	Russell	White	Bellamy	Slade	Lee	Simons	Templeton	Forrest	Cannon	Pearce	Marshall	Smith	Gray	Coquet	Nixon	Wood	Taylor	Maughan	Walker	Thompson	Nicholl	Miller
1		2	3	4	5	6	7	8	9	10	11															
2		2	3	4	5	6	7	8	9	10	11															
3		2	3	4	5	6	7	8	9	10	11															
4		2	3	4	5	6	7	8	9	10	11															
5		2	3	4	5	6	7	8	9	10	11															
6		2	3	4		6	7			10	11	5	8	9												
7		2	3	5		6			9	10	11		8		4	7										
8		2	5	6			4	8	7	10	11			9			3									
9		2	3	6	5		4	8	7	10	11		9													
10		2		6	5	10	4	8	9		11					7	3									
11		2		6	5	10	4	8	9		11					7	3									
12		2		6	5	10	4	8	9		11					7		3								
13		2		6	5	10	4	8	9		11					7		3								
14		2		6	5	10	4		9		11					7		3	1	8						
15		2		6	5	10	4		9		11					7		3	1	8						
16		2		6	5	10	4				11					7		3	1	8	9					
17		2		6	5	10	7				11							3	1	8	9	4				
18		2		6	5	8					11			9		7	3		1		10	4				
19		2		6	5	8	4							9		7		3	1		10		11			
20		2		6	5	8								9		7		3	1		10	4	11			
21		2		6	5	8								9		7		3	1		10	4	11			
22		2		6	5	8			9		11					7		3	1		10	4				
23		2		6	5			8					9			7			1		10	4	11	3		
24		2		9	5			8							6	7		3			10	4	11			
25		2		9	5			8							6	7		3			10	4	11			
26			2	9	5	6		8								7		3			10	4	11			
27			2	9	5	6		8								7		3			10	4	11			
28			2	6	5	8					11		9			7		3				4			10	
29			2	8	5	6			9		11					7		3	1			4			10	
30		2	3	8	5	6			9		11					7			1			4			10	
31		2	3	8	5	6			9										1		10	4	11			7
32		2	3	8	5	6			9										1		10	4	11			7
33		2	3	8	5	6			9										1		10	4	11			7
34		2	3	8	5	6			9										1		10	4	11			7
35		2	3		5	6		8	9							7			1		10	4				11
36		2			5	6			9				8			7		3	1		10	4	11			
37		2		8	5	6			9									3	1		10	4	11			7
38		2		8	5	6			9							7		3			10	4	11			
A	9	34	19	36	35	33	17	17	25	9	22	1	6	6	3	24	4	19	19	4	20	21	15	1	3	6
G		-	-	4	6	4	1	5	16	4	-	-	5	2	-	1	-	-	-	-	4	1	-	-	-	-

	Reynolds	Charlton	Houghton	Torrance	Russell	White	Bellamy	Slade	Lee	Simons	Templeton	Forrest	Cannon	Pearce	Marshall	Smith	Gray	Coquet	Nixon	Wood	Taylor	Maughan	Walker	Thompson	Nicholl	Miller
1		2		6	5	8								9		7		3	1		10	4	11			
2		2		6	5	8								9		7		3	1		10	4	11			

0 points v	Arsenal, Birmingham, Preston NE, Wolves	0 points
1 point v	Blackpool, Bristol C, Huddersfield T	3 points
2 points v	Bury, Clapton O, Glossop, Hull C, Lincoln C	10 points
3 points v	Barnsley, Derby C, Grimsby T, Nottingham F	12 points
4 points v	Leeds C, Leicester F, Stockport C	12 points

Top scorer, Harry Lea.

1915-16

London Combination

Principal Tournament

	P	W	D	L	F	A	Pts
Chelsea	22	17	3	2	71	18	37
Millwall	22	12	6	4	46	24	30
The Arsenal	22	10	5	7	43	46	25
West Ham Utd	22	10	4	8	47	35	24
Fulham	22	10	4	8	45	37	24
Tottenham Hotspur	22	8	8	6	38	35	24
Brentford	22	6	8	8	36	40	20
Queen's Park Ranger	22	8	3	11	27	41	19
Crystal Palace	22	8	3	11	35	55	19
Watford	22	8	1	13	37	46	17
Clapton Orient	22	4	6	1	22	44	14
Croydon Common	22	3	5	14	24	50	11

Supplementary Tournament

	P	W	D	L	F	A	Pts
Chelsea	14	10	1	3	50	15	21
West Ham Utd	14	9	2	3	32	16	20
Tottenham Hotspur	14	8	3	3	32	22	19
Fulham	14	9	0	5	38	19	18
Millwall	14	8	2	4	30	22	18
Crystal Palace	14	8	2	4	41	29	18
Watford	14	5	3	6	22	20	13
Brentford	14	5	2	7	29	33	12
Croydon Common	14	4	3	7	28	27	11
Clapton Orient	14	3	4	7	17	27	10
The Arsenal	14	3	4	7	19	31	10
Luton Town	14	4	1	9	31	44	9
Queen's Park Ranger	14	2	5	7	14	37	9
Reading	14	2	2	9	23	64	8

Manager: Phil Kelso

No		Date	V	Opponents	R	H-T	F-T	Scorers	Atte
1	S	4	A	Watford	W	2-0	4-2	Taylor 2, Cannon 2	4,0
2		11	H	Millwall	L	0-0	1-2	Taylor	8,0
3		18	A	Croydon C	L	0-1	2-3	Pearce, Taylor	2,6
4		25	H	Arsenal	W	1-0	4-3	White 2, Pearce, Sheldon	8,0
5	O	2	A	Brentford	D		2-2	Taylor, Cannon	2,9
6		9	H	West Ham U	W	1-0	1-0	Cannon	7,0
7		16	A	Tottenham H	L	0-0	1-3	Wheatcroft	4,2
8		23	H	Crystal Palace	W	0-0	5-0	Taylor 2, White 2, Cannon	5,0
9		30	A	Queen's Park R	L	1-1	1-2	Taylor	8,0
10	N	6	H	Chelsea	L	0-2	0-3		14,0
11		13	H	Watford	W	3-1	4-3	Shields 3, Taylor	3,5
12		20	A	Millwall	D	0-0	0-0		5,0
13		27	H	Croydon C	W	2-0	2-0	Allan 2	1,5
14	D	4	A	Arsenal	L	1-2	1-2	Niblo	3,0
15		11	H	Brentford	W	4-0	4-3	Shields, Slade 2, Taylor	3,0
16		18	A	West Ham U	W	3-2	3-2	White, Taylor, Shields (pen)	3,0
17		25	H	Clapton O	W	1-0	4-0	White, Taylor 2, Slade	2,5
18		27	A	Clapton O	W		3-1	Taylor, Slade, Torrance	4,0
19	J	1	H	Tottenham H	L	0-1	0-2		5,5
20		8	A	Crystal Palace	D	2-1	2-2	Cannon, Taylor	8
21		15	H	Queen's Park R	L	0-1	0-1		5,0
22		22	A	Chelsea	D	1-1	1-1	Shields	25,0

Supplementary Tournament

No		Date	V	Opponents	R	H-T	F-T	Scorers	Atte
23	F	5	H	Reading	W	2-0	6-0	White 2, Smith 2, Taylor 2	4,5
24		12	A	Clapton O	W	1-0	3-0	Taylor, Shields, Bresname	2,5
25		19	H	Tottenham H	W	1-1	3-1	Shields 2, Taylor	3,0
26		26	A	Millwall	W	4-1	7-1	Taylor, White 3, Shields 2, Smith	3,5
27	M	4	H	Chelsea	L	0-1	0-1		11,5
28		11	A	Watford	L	0-0	0-2		1,0
29		18	H	Clapton O	W	2-0	4-0	Nicholl, White 2, Shields	4,5
30		25	A	Tottenham H	L	0-1	0-4		5,0
31	A	1	H	Millwall	W	3-1	4-2	Shields, White 3	8,0
32		8	A	Chelsea	L	0-3	3-6	Shields 2, White	16,0
33		15	H	Watford	W	2-0	2-0	Taylor 2	4,5
34		21	A	Brentford	L	1-1	1-2	Walden	5,0
35		24	H	Brentford	W	1-0	1-0	Shields	4,0
36		29	A	Reading	W	2-0	4-0	Shields 2, White 2	1,0

Ap

Goa

Reynolds	Bellamy	Bullock	Tull	Russell	White	Wood	Cannon	Pearce	Taylor	Torrance	Sheldon	Galt	Grossart	Blackman	Martin G	Wheatcroft	Bell	Coquet	Maughan	Walker	Marshall	Shields	Allan	Niblo	Nichol	Slade	Bresname	Bull	Stapley	Smith	Weller	Pike	Whittley	Darrell	Walden	Martin J	Lee	Urwin	
1	2	3	4	5	6	7	8	9	10	11																														1
1	2	3	4	5	6		7	8	10	11	7																													2
1	2		4	3			7	9	10	6	7	5	6																											3
1	4	3		6	8			9	10	11	7	5		2																										4
1		3		6	8			8	10	4	7	5		2	11																									5
1				6	8	7	11		10	4		5	3	2		9																								6
1					6	8	11		10	4		5	3	2		9	7																							7
1				5	8	7	11	9	10	4			6	2				3																						8
1					8	7		9	10	6		5	3	2					4	11																				9
1				5	8	7	4	9	10	6			3							11	2																			10
1				3	6	7		9	10	5									4	11	2	8																		11
1				3	7				10	6		5			11				4		2	9	8																	12
1				5	6	7			10	4			3				2						9	8	11																13
1						8		5	6	4		5	3				7				2			11	6															14
1				3	6		7		10	5				2							4	9		11		8														15
1				6	8				10	4		5	3	2					7			9		11																16
1				3	8				10	5				2						11	4				6	9	7														17
1	2				6		7		10	5										11	3				4	9	7														18
1				3	6				10	5				2						11		9				8	7	4													19
1				3	6		11		10	5				2							4	9				8	7														20
1					6				10	5				2					4	11		9		7		8			3												21
1				3	8				10	4		5	6	2						11		9					7														22
1				3	8				10	11		5	6	2					4								7			9										23
1				5	8				10	4			6	3								9					7			11	2									24
1				6	8				10	4		5		2								9					7			11	3									25
1					8				10	4		5	6	2								9					7			11	3									26
1				3	8				10	4		5	6	2								9					7			11										27
1				4						11		5	6	2								9				8	7				3	10								28
				6						4		5		2						11		9			10		7				3		1						29
1					8				10	4		5	6	2								9	11				7				3								30
1				3	8				10	4				2						11		9			6		7		5										31
1				5	10				8	6				3						7		9			4									2	11				32
1				5	8				10	4				2						11		9					7								3		6			33
1					8	10				4				2			3					5			6										7		9	11	34
1						8			6	4				2			3				5	9															6	7	11	35
1				5	8					4				2								9								10	3				7	6		11	36
35	4	4	3	29	35	14	9	7	30	35	4	17	16	27	2	2	5	1	6	12	9	22	3	5	7	7	15	1	3	6	6	1	1	2	3	3	2	3	
-	-	-	-	-	20	-	6	2	21	1	1	1	1	-	-	1	-	-	-	-	-	18	2	1	1	4	1	-	-	-	3	-	-	-	-	-	-	-	

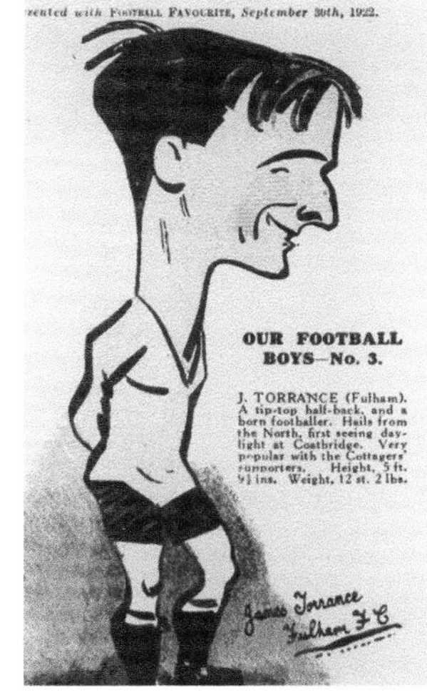

...ented with FOOTBALL FAVOURITE, September 30th, 1922.
OUR FOOTBALL BOYS—No. 3.
J. TORRANCE (Fulham). A tip-top half-back, and a born footballer. Hails from the North, first seeing daylight at Coatbridge. Very popular with the Cottagers' supporters. Height, 5 ft. 9½ ins. Weight, 12 st. 2 lbs.
James Torrance
Fulham F.C.

A cartoon of James Torrance.

1916-17

London Combination

	P	W	D	L	F	A	Pts
West Ham Utd.	40	30	5	5	110	45	65
Millwall Athletic	40	26	6	8	85	48	58
Chelsea	40	24	5	11	93	48	53
Tottenham Hotspur	40	24	5	11	112	64	53
The Arsenal	40	19	10	11	62	47	48
Fulham	40	21	3	16	102	63	45
Luton	39	20	3	16	101	82	43
Crystal Palace	38	14	7	17	68	72	35
Southampton	39	13	8	18	57	80	34
Queen's Park Rangers	39	10	9	20	48	86	29
Watford	40	8	9	2	69	115	25
Brentford	40	9	7	24	56	99	25
Portsmouth	40	9	4	27	58	117	22
Clapton Orient	40	6	7	27	49	104	19

Manager: Phil Kelso

Frank Penn, the start of 50 years at the Cottage.

No		Date	V	Opponents	R	H-T	F-T	Scorers	Atten
1	S	2	H	Reading	W	5-0	9-0	Hoare 5, Martin (G), Mordue, White 2	3,00
2		9	A	Millwall	L	1-0	2-3	Hoare, Martin (G)	6,00
3		16	H	Watford	W	2-0	7-0	Hoare 3, Gordon, White, Galt 2 (1 pen)	4,00
4		23	A	Clapton O	W	2-0	3-0	Galt (pen), White, Martin (G)	4,00
5		30	A	Southampton	L	0-2	3-4	Taylor, Torrance 2	4,00
6	O	7	H	Queen's Park R	W	0-0	2-0	Taylor, Hoare	5,00
7		14	A	West Ham U	L	0-1	0-2		10,00
8		21	H	Tottenham H	W	0-1	2-1	Gibson, Hoare	4,00
9		28	A	Crystal Palace	L	0-0	0-1		1,20
10	N	4	H	Brentford	W	2-0	2-0	Taylor, Hoare	4,00
11		11	A	Chelsea	L	0-1	0-4		15,00
12		18	H	Arsenal	W	1-0	2-0	Hoare, Martin (G)	1,50
13		25	A	Portsmouth	W	2-1	4-3	Bateman, Gibson 3	4,00
14	D	2	H	Millwall	L	0-1	0-1		4,00
15		9	A	Watford	W	4-0	8-2	Martin (G) 3, Gibson, Taylor 2, Mordue 2	2,00
16		23	H	Southampton	W	5-0	8-1	Hampton 3, Tufnell 3, Mordue 2	2,00
17		25	A	Luton T	L		0-1		4,00
18		26	H	Luton T	W		5-1	Hampton 3, Gordon 2	5,00
19		30	A	Queen's Park R	W	1-1	7-1	Hoare, Handley, Gordon, Martin (G) 2, Watson, Gibson	3,00
20	J	6	H	West Ham U	L	0-0	0-2		8,00
21		13	A	Tottenham H	L	0-1	0-1	(at Homerton)	4,00
22		20	H	Crystal Palace	W	2-0	4-3	Hoare 2, Martin (G), Tufnell	1,50
23		27	A	Brentford	D	0-0	1-1	Cannon	2,00
24	F	3	H	Chelsea	W	1-0	2-0	Hoare, Gordon	6,00
25		10	A	Arsenal	L	1-0	2-3	Martin (G), McIntyre	4,80
26		17	H	Luton T	W	3-0	4-2	Hoare 3, Tufnell	4,00
27		24	A	Brentford	W	3-0	4-1	McIntyre, Hoare 3	2,00
28	M	3	H	Queen's Park R	D	0-0	0-0		3,00
29		10	A	Chelsea	L	0-2	1-3	Torrance	5,00
30		17	H	Southampton	W	2-0	3-1	Tufnell, Martin (G) 2 (1 pen)	4,00
31		24	H	Watford	W	4-1	7-2	Gibson 2, Martin (J) 3, Hutchins, Smith (A)	4,00
32		31	A	Luton T	W	2-1	3-2	Martin (G) 2, Gibson	1,50
33	A	6	H	Millwall	D	0-0	1-1	Smith	10,00
34		7	H	Brentford	L	0-2	0-2		5,00
35		9	A	Millwall	L	0-1	0-2		6,00
36		10	H	Clapton O	W	2-1	2-1	Black, Holley	3,00
37		14	A	Queen's Park R	L	0-1	0-2		1,50
38		18	A	Watford	L	1-3	2-4	Platts, Penn	1,00
39		21	H	Chelsea	L	0-0	0-4		8,00
40		28	A	Southampton	W	1-1	2-1	Gibson, Brown	3,00
									App
									Goal

ms	Houghton	Russell	Gordon	Galt	Martin J	Mordue	White	Hoare	Martin G	Walker	Torrance	Blackman	Bresname	Reynolds	McMaster	Taylor W	Marshall	Grossart	Wood	Nicholl	Gibson	Taylor E	Green	Handley	Low	Bateman	Shaw	Dix	Noble	Cannon	Watson	Kennedy	Holley	Hampton	Tufnell	Fox	Charlton	Flavers	Ross	Watson	Wilding	McIntyre	Smith W	Catterson	Orr	Jefferson	Dorrington	Hutchins	Johnson	Smith A	Quinn	Robinson	Agarth	Thompson	Pitt	Humphries	Black	Penn	Gibbs	Platts	Jackson	Greenaway	Brown	Howie	Rutherford	Smith J	
	2	3	4	5	6	7	8	9	10	11																																																								1
	3	2	6	5		11	10	9	8	7	4																																																							2
	3		4	5	6		8	9	10		11	2	7																																																				3
		3	4	5	6		8	9	10		11	2	7	1																																																			4
		3	6	5		7	8				9	2		1	4	10	11																																																5
			4		5	7	6	9		11		2				10		3	8																																															6
		3		5	6		8		10	11	4	2	7	1						9																																														7
		3	4	5	6	7		9		11	10	2		1							8																																													8
	3		4	5	6	7		9	8		11	2							8																																															9
	3			5		7		9		11	4	2			6	10					8																																													10
	3			5		7	8	9		11	6	2			4						10	1																																												11
	3					7		9	10		5	2			6						8	1	4	11																																										12
	3							9			4	2			6						8				5	7	10	11																																						13
	3	4		5		7	10				6	2				9						1							8	11																																				14
	3					11			10		6	2			7	8					9				5						4																																			15
	3					7					5	2			6																	4	8	9	10	11																														16
	3					7					5				11						8										6	4	10	9			2																													17
	3		4			7					5										8										6		10	9		11	2																													18
		3	4				5	9	8			2									7			11							6				10																															19
	3		4					8			5	2				10					9	1								11	6							7																												20
	3		4					8			7	2			11						9				5						6				10																															21
	3		4					8	10		5	2			11						7										6				9																															22
	3		4						8		5	2			6						7									9					10				1	11																										23
	3	4	9					8			10	2									7			11	5						6																																			24
	3							8	9		4	2						6				1								7						11					5	10																								25
								8			5	2			6									11											10							9	1	3	4	7																					26
								8			4	2			6			3			7	1								11					10							9			5																						27
				5				8			4	2						6			9			11											10								1		3	7																					28
		6						10			8	3			4						11				5											7						9			2		1																				29
									8	11	5	2			6			4			7														10							9			3		1																				30
										6	5	2			6						8																					10	1		3			4	7	9																	31
									9		5	2			6						8																					10			3			4		7	11	1															32
							9				4	3			6						9				5								10												2					7		1	11														33
											4	2			6						7				5								8									10		3						11		1		9													34
							9				5	2			6			3			7												9		10	11																		4	1												35
															6			3			7												8		5															11				2	1	4	9	10									36
												2												11											8	6						4	1		3					7								10	5	9							37
												2						5																	8				1						3					11				4				10		9	6	7					38
												2						6			8			11																		10	1						4	9		1										7	3	5			39
												2						3			9				5																	6																10				7	11		4	8	40
5	19	10	15	12	8	14	11	23	13	8	32	35	3	4	22	6	1	10	2	1	27	4	1	8	7	1	1	1	1	5	9	2	7	3	13	6	2	1	2	9	1	11	5	2	10	2	2	2	2	8	1	4	1	4	2	1	1	4	1	2	1	3	2	1	1	1	
	1	-	5	3	3	5	4	23	15	-	3	-	-	-	-	5	-	-	-	-	10	-	-	1	1	1	-	-	-	1	1	-	1	6	6	-	-	-	-	1	-	2	-	-	-	-	-	-	-	-	-	-	-	-	-	-	1	1	-	1	-	-	1	-	-	-	

1917-18

London Combination

	P	W	D	L	F	A	Pts
Chelsea	36	21	8	7	82	39	50
West Ham Utd.	36	30	9	7	103	51	49
Fulham	36	20	7	9	75	60	47
Tottenham Hotspur	36	22	2	12	86	56	46
The Arsenal	36	15	5	15	76	56	37
Brentford	36	16	3	17	81	94	35
Crystal Palace	36	13	4	19	54	83	30
Queen's Park Rangers	36	14	2	20	48	73	30
Millwall	36	12	4	20	52	74	28
Clapton Orient	36	2	4	30	34	104	8

Manager: Phil Kelso

Danny Shea, wartime guest and post war signing.

No		Date	V	Opponents	R	H-T	F-T	Scorers	Atte
1	S	1	A	West Ham U	L	0-1	1-6	Morris	8,0
2		8	H	Crystal Palace	W	4-1	7-1	Simms 3, Morris 3, Low	4,5
3		15	H	Queen's Park R	W	1-0	2-1	Edwards 2	4,0
4		22	A	Clapton O	W	2-1	5-1	Howie 2, Morris 3	2,0
5		29	H	Millwall	W	2-1	3-1	Russell, Torrance, Greenaway	5,0
6	O	6	A	Tottenham H	L	0-1	0-1	(at Highbury)	7,0
7		13	H	Chelsea	D	0-1	1-1	Morris	8,0
8		20	A	Brentford	W	2-1	3-1	Morris 2, Cumming	4,0
9		27	H	West Ham U	D	0-1	1-1	Howie	8,0
10	N	3	A	Crystal Palace	L	1-1	1-2	McIntyre	1,2
11		10	A	Queen's Park R	W	2-1	3-2	Morris 2, Cumming	3,0
12		17	H	Clapton O	W	1-0	3-0	Morris 3	3,0
13		24	A	Millwall	L	1-0	1-2	Morris	4,5
14	D	1	H	Tottenham H	W	2-1	4-3	Morris 3, McIntyre	6,0
15		8	A	Chelsea	D	1-0	2-2	Morris, Hoare	10,0
16		15	H	Brentford	W	1-0	2-0	Morris, Howie	4,0
17		22	A	West Ham U	W	1-0	3-0	McIntyre 2, Cumming	8,0
18		25	H	Arsenal	D		1-1	Torrance	7,0
19		26	A	Arsenal	D		1-1	Morris	7,0
20		29	H	Crystal Palace	D	0-1	1-1	Torrance (pen)	3,0
21	J	5	H	Queen's Park R	W	0-0	1-0	Penn	5,0
22		12	A	Clapton O	D	0-1	1-1	Howie	1,5
23		19	H	Millwall	W	1-1	4-2	Morris 2, Torrance 2	5,0
24		26	A	Tottenham H	W	0-0	1-0	Shea (at Highbury)	14,0
25	F	2	H	Chelsea	L	0-2	0-2		6,0
26		9	A	Arsenal	W	3-0	3-0	McIntyre 2, Cannon	8,0
27		16	H	West Ham U	W	3-1	3-1	Shea 2, Maven	8,0
28		23	A	Crystal Palace	L	1-3	2-5	McIntyre 2	3,0
29	M	2	A	Queen's Park R	W	1-0	1-0	Crockford	3,5
30		9	H	Clapton O	W	2-1	3-2	Taylor 2, Gordon	4,0
31		16	A	Millwall	W	1-0	2-0	Elliott 2	5,0
32		23	H	Tottenham H	L	0-1	0-3		12,0
33		29	A	Brentford	W	1-1	3-2	Torrance 2, Shea	6,0
34		30	A	Chelsea	L	0-5	0-7		7,0
35	A	1	H	Brentford	L	2-4	4-6	Shea 3 (1 pen), Bassett	4,0
36		6	H	Arsenal	W	2-1	2-1	McIntyre, Shea	2,0
									App
									Goa

Bailey	Blackman	Grimsdell	Hall	Torrance	Brown	Late	Edwards	Morris	Taylor	McIntyre	Drabble	Russell	Low	Simms	Handley	Howie	Greenaway	Penn	Smith T	Maven	Wigmore	Cumming	Elliott	Harding	Bradley	Green	Carr	Reynolds	Smythe	Brandham	Burke	Hoare	Holley	Smith W	Crockford	Shea	Nicholl	Martin G	McMaster	Cannon	Johnson	Gordon	Bassett	Dodds	Bell	Symes	Wood	Bethune	
1	2	3	4	5	6	7	8	9	10	11																																							1
	2	3				5	8	10		6	1	4	5	9	11																																		2
	2	3		11			8	10			1	4		9		5	7																																3
	2	3	4	5			8	9		6	1					10	7	11																															4
	2	3		5			8	9		6	1	4				10	7	11																															5
	2	3		5			8	9		6	1	4						11	7	10																													6
	2	3		5				9		8	1	4				10		11			6	7																											7
	2	3		4				10		8	1	6	5					11				7	9																										8
	2	3	4	5				9		8	1					10		11			6	7																											9
	2	3	4	5						9	1					8		10						6	7	11																							10
	2	3	6	4				9		10	1							8		5		11					7																						11
		3						9		8						2		11		5		10						1	4	6	7																		12
	2	3	5					9		8	1					10		11		5		7								6																			13
	2	3	5					9		8	1					10		11		5		7								6																			14
	2	3	5					9		8	1							11		5		7								6		10																	15
	2	3	5					9		8	1					10		11		5		7								6																			16
	2	3	5					9		8	1					10		11		5		7								6																			17
	2	3		6				9		8	1		5			4		11													7		10																18
	2	3		6				9		8	1		5			4		11													7		10																19
	2	3	4	6				9		8						5		11				7											10	1															20
	2	3		4				9		6	1					10		11		5		7													8														21
	2	3	7	4				9		6	1					10		11		5																8													22
		3	4	10				9		6						2		11		5		7												1		8													23
	2	3	4	9						6	1							11		5																8	7	10											24
	2	3		9						6	1					10		11		5																8	7		4										25
	2	3		7						6	1							11		5															10	8			4	9									26
		3		9						6								11		5														1	9	8	7		4		2								27
	2	3		9				9		6	1							11		5																8	7		4										28
	2	3	4							9	1							11		5															10	8	7		6										29
		3							10	6	1					2		11		5																8	7		4			9							30
		3	4	2						6	1							11		5			9									10				8							7						31
		2		4						10	1							11		5															9	8			6				7	3					32
		3	6	8						10								11		5														1		8							7	2	4				33
	3		11	8							1							7		5																10							11	2		6	8		34
	2	3		8						6	1		5					11																		8							7			4	10		35
	2			6						9	1							11		5																8							7			4	10	3	36
1	29	34	12	33	1	2	6	23	2	36	30	6	5	2	1	19	3	33	1	23	2	13	2	1	1	1	1	1	1	6	3	2	3	4	5	15	6	1	7	1	1	1	6	3	1	3	3	1	
-	-	-	-	-	-	-	2	24	2	9	-	1	1	3	-	4	1	1	-	1	-	3	2	-	-	-	-	-	-	-	-	2	-	-	1	8	-	-	-	1	-	1	1	-	-	-	-	-	

1918-19

London Combination

	P	W	D	L	F	A	Pts
Brentford	36	20	9	7	94	48	49
The Arsenal	36	20	5	11	85	56	45
West Ham Utd.	36	17	7	12	65	51	41
Fulham	36	17	6	13	70	55	40
Queen's Park Rangers	36	16	7	13	69	60	39
Chelsea	36	13	11	12	70	53	37
Crystal Palace	36	14	6	16	66	73	34
Tottenham Hotspur	36	13	8	15	52	72	34
Millwall Athletic	36	10	9	17	50	67	29
Clapton Orient	36	3	6	27	35	123	12

Manager: Phil Kelso

Arthur Reynolds was restricted to occastional wartime appearances.

No	Date		V	Opponents	R	H-T	F-T	Scorers		Atter
1	S	7	H	Tottenham H	D	2-0	2-2	Bassett, Torrance		9,00
2		14	A	Chelsea	L	1-1	2-4	Maven, Hampton		8,00
3		21	H	Arsenal	L	1-1	1-2	Shea		8,00
4		28	A	Crystal Palace	L	0-0	0-1			6,00
5	O	5	H	Queen's Park R	D	2-2	3-3	Shea, Bassett, Torrance		4,00
6		12	A	Millwall	W	0-0	1-0	White		4,00
7		19	A	Clapton O	W	2-0	4-1	McIntyre 3, Shea		2,00
8		26	H	West Ham U	D	1-1	2-2	Shea, Penn		4,00
9	N	2	A	Tottenham H	L	0-1	0-1		(at Homerton)	6,00
10		9	H	Chelsea	L	0-1	1-2	McIntyre		10,00
11		16	A	Arsenal	W	2-0	3-1	Hampton 2, Shea		5,00
12		23	H	Crystal Palace	W	1-1	5-1	Higginbottam, McIntyre, Shea, Hampton 2		7,00
13		30	A	Queen's Park R	W	1-0	3-0	McIntyre 2, Hampton		6,00
14	D	7	H	Millwall	L	0-1	0-1			7,00
15		14	H	Clapton O	W	2-1	5-1	Shea 3, Harris 2		3,00
16		21	A	West Ham U	L	0-1	1-2	Harris		10,50
17		25	A	Brentford	L	1-0	1-2	Wood		10,80
18		26	H	Brentford	L	1-2	1-4	McIntyre		20,00
19		28	H	Tottenham H	W	1-0	3-1	McIntyre, Elliott (pen), Penn		7,00
20	J	4	A	Chelsea	L	0-3	0-3			25,00
21		11	H	Arsenal	W	2-1	3-1	Hampton, McIntyre, Martin		10,00
22		18	A	Crystal Palace	W	1-1	4-1	Bassett, McIntyre 2, Pearce		6,00
23		25	H	Queen's Park R	W	0-0	1-0	McIntyre		12,00
24	F	1	A	Millwall	D	0-1	1-1	Harris		10,00
25		8	A	Clapton O	W	1-0	4-0	Harris, Bassett, Tee 2		5,00
26		15	H	Brentford	W	2-0	3-2	Harris 2, Bassett		25,00
27		22	A	Tottenham H	W	1-0	2-0	McIntyre, Harris	(at Homerton)	6,00
28	M	1	H	Chelsea	W	3-2	6-2	Torrance (pen), McIntyre, Harris 3, (Middleboe og)		26,00
29		8	A	Arsenal	L	0-1	0-5			22,00
30		15	H	Crystal Palace	D	0-1	1-1	Torrance		15,00
31		22	A	Queen's Park R	W	0-0	1-0	Harris		11,00
32		29	H	Millwall	W	1-0	2-0	McIntyre, Taylor		15,00
33	A	5	H	Clapton O	W	1-0	2-0	Farnfield, Harris		12,00
34		12	A	Brentford	L	0-2	0-5			15,00
35		18	H	West Ham U	D	1-1	1-1	Walker		20,00
36		21	A	West Ham U	L	1-2	1-2	Harris		15,00
										App
										Goa

Victory Cup

1	M	24	H	Munitions League	W	0-0	3-0	Penn, Torrance 2		3,00
2		31	A	Arsenal	W	2-0	4-1	McIntyre, Elliott 2, Whittingham		22,00
SF	A	19	A	Tottenham H	W	0-0	2-0	Whittingham 2	(at Stamford Bridge)	45,00
F		26	N	Chelsea	L	0-1	0-3		(at Highbury)	36,00

ith W	Blackman F	Blackman S	Bratley	Low	McIntyre	Bassett	Shea	Cannon	Torrance	Penn	Molyneux	Maven	Hampton	Wood A	Coquet	Russell	Marshall	Hall	Crockford	Higginbottom	Fender	White	Hatfield	Symes	Kelso	Wilson S	Simms	Reynolds	Hogg	Hall	Orr	Harris	McNeal	Elliott	McCracken	Brown	Martin	Langtry	Pearce	Jennings	Walker	Tee	Taylor	Grimsdell	Nixon	Bagge	Grossart	Farnfield E	Charlton	Wallace	Morris	Jones	Wood	Pitts	Lynes	Hunter	Carr	Whittingham	
	2	3	4	5	6	7	8	9	10	11																																																	1
	2	3	6		4		10		8	7	1	5	9	11																																													2
	3				6	7	8		10	11		5	9		2	4																																											3
	2				6	7	8		10	11	1	5					3	4	9																																								4
	2	3	4	5	6	7	8		10	11										9																																							5
	2	3	4		6	7	8		11			5	9								1	10																																					6
	2	3	4		10	7	8		6	11		5	9								1																																						7
	2	3			10	7	8		6	11		5	9										1	4																																			8
	2	4			10	7			6	11		5											1		4	8	9																																9
	2	3	4	5	10		8		6	11			9							7								1																															10
	2					6		8		6	11		5	9	7											3			1	4																													11
	2	3	4	5	10		8		6	11			9							7								1																															12
	2	3		5	10		8		6	11			9							7				4				1																															13
	2		4		10	7	8		6	11		5															9				3																												14
	2				10	7	8		6	11	1	5												4							3	9																											15
	2	3		5	10	7	8		6	11																			1			9	4																										16
	3			5	10	7			4	11				8													9		1		3		4																										17
	2			5	10	7			6	11				8										4			9		1		3																											18
	2			3	8	7			6	11		5							10					4					1					9																									19
	2						7		4	11		5																					4	8	3	9	10																						20
	2					7	6			11		5	9			4															3		4				10																						21
						7	6		5	11						4			10												3		4					2	9																					22
	2					7	6		5							3																9	4				10			4	11																			23
	2					7			5	11						3																9	4				10		8	4																				24
	2				10	7			5	11						3																8	4							4		9																		25
	2				8	7			5	11						3			10													9	4							4																				26
	2				8	7			5	11						3																9	4							4			10																		27
	2				8	7			5	11						3																9	4							4			10																		28
	2				8	7			5	11						3								4								9	4										10																		29
	2				10	7			6	11						3																9	4						8	4																				30
	2				8	7		10		11						4												1				9	4										3																	31
	2				8				10	11		5		7		4																	4										9	3																	32
				10	8					11						2																9					7							3	1	4	6	10													33
					6					11		5				4																9					7							2	1				3	8	10									34
	2													10			5															9									11					4	6		3	8		7								35
					10									7		6	5															9									11			2		4			3	8										36
	31	11	9	9	33	25	2	32	32	3	6	15	7	1	1	17	3	1	4	4	2	1	2	6	1	2	4	3	6	4	6	15	15	2	1	1	6	1	3	7	3	1	4	5	2	3	2	1	3	3	1	1	-	-	-	-	-	-	
	-	-	-	-	16	5	9	-	4	2	-	1	7	1	-	-	-	-	-	1	-	1	-	-	-	-	-	-	-	-	-	14	-	1	-	-	1	-	1	-	-	2	1	-	-	-	-	-	-	-	-	-	-	-	-	-	-	-	

ith W	Blackman F	Blackman S	Bratley	Low	McIntyre	Bassett	Shea	Cannon	Torrance	Penn	Molyneux	Maven	Hampton	Wood A	Coquet	Russell	Marshall	Hall	Crockford	Higginbottom	Fender	White	Hatfield	Symes	Kelso	Wilson S	Simms	Reynolds	Hogg	Hall	Orr	Harris	McNeal	Elliott	McCracken	Brown	Martin	Langtry	Pearce	Jennings	Walker	Tee	Taylor	Grimsdell	Nixon	Bagge	Grossart	Farnfield E	Charlton	Wallace	Morris	Jones	Wood	Pitts	Lynes	Hunter	Carr	Whittingham	
									8	11		5				2																9					7							3		6							1	4	10				1
	2			10	10				5	11						3																	6	9																						4	7	8	2
	2				10					11			9			5																7	6													4			3									8	SF
	2			10	10				5	11						4																7	6	9															3								8		F

1919-20

Division Two

	P	W	D	L	F	A	Pts
Tottenham Hotspur	42	32	6	4	102	32	70
Huddersfield Town	42	28	8	6	97	38	64
Birmingham	42	24	8	10	85	34	56
Blackpool	42	21	10	11	65	47	52
Bury	42	20	8	14	60	44	48
Fulham	42	19	9	14	61	50	47
West Ham United	42	19	9	14	47	40	47
Bristol City	42	13	17	12	46	43	43
South Shields	42	15	12	15	58	48	42
Stoke	42	18	6	18	60	54	42
Hull City	42	18	6	18	78	72	42
Barnsley	42	15	10	17	61	55	40
Port Vale	42	16	8	18	59	62	40
Leicester City	42	15	10	17	41	61	40
Clapton Orient	42	16	6	20	51	59	38
Stockport County	42	14	9	19	52	61	37
Rotherham County	42	13	8	21	51	83	34
Nottingham Forest	42	11	9	22	43	73	31
Wolverhampton W	42	10	10	22	55	80	30
Coventry City	42	9	11	22	35	73	29
Lincoln City	42	9	9	24	44	101	27
Grimsby Town	42	10	5	27	34	75	25

Manager: Phil Kelso

Did you know that?

Trainer Jimmy Sharp scored his only goal for Fulham in the last of his 125 games for the club. When centre forward Harold Crockford missed the bus for an away game at Bury in April 1920, 39-year-old Sharp had to play. He scored the first goal in a 2-2 draw and is also still the oldest player to have played for Fulham in the League.

No	Date		V	Opponents	R	H-T	F-T	Scorers	Atte
1	A	30	H	South Shields	W	1-0	1-0	McIntyre	20,00
2	S	4	A	Clapton O	W	0-0	1-0	Torrance	9,00
3		6	A	South Shields	L	0-0	0-2		20,00
4		13	A	Leicester C	L	1-2	2-3	Cock 2	12,00
5		15	H	Clapton O	W	2-1	2-1	Cock 2	7,00
6		20	H	Leicester C	W	4-0	5-0	Cock 3, McIntyre 2	16,00
7		29	H	Rotherham C	W	1-0	3-0	McIntyre, Cock 2	5,00
8	O	4	A	Bristol C	W	2-0	3-0	Cock 2, McIntyre	20,00
9		11	A	Coventry C	W	1-0	1-0	White	14,00
10		13	H	Bristol C	D	1-0	1-1	McDonald	14,00
11		18	H	Coventry C	D	0-0	0-0		16,00
12		25	H	Huddersfield T	D	0-1	2-2	Cock 2	14,00
13	N	1	A	Huddersfield T	L	0-1	0-1		3,00
14		8	H	Blackpool	L	0-1	1-2	White	12,00
15		15	A	Blackpool	D	1-0	1-1	Cock	6,00
16		22	H	West Ham U	L	0-1	1-2	White	18,00
17		29	A	West Ham U	W	1-0	1-0	McIntyre	15,00
18	D	6	H	Tottenham H	L	0-1	1-4	Cock	30,00
19		13	A	Tottenham H	L	0-2	0-4		45,00
20		25	H	Grimsby T	W	1-0	2-1	McIntyre, Walker	12,0
21		27	A	Rotherham C	D	1-0	1-1	Cock	5,0
22	J	1	A	Port Vale	W	4-0	4-3	Cock 2, Banks, (Perry og)	8,00
23		3	H	Stoke	D	0-0	0-0		12,0
24		17	A	Stoke	L	0-0	0-1		8,0
25		24	H	Wolverhampton W	D	0-1	1-1	Cock	12,0
26	F	7	H	Hull C	W	0-0	1-0	McIntyre	18,0
27		14	A	Hull C	L	0-0	0-2		10,0
28		21	H	Stockport C	W	2-0	4-1	Walker, Cock 2, Torrance	8,0
29		23	A	Wolverhampton W	L	1-2	1-2	McIntyre	10,0
30		28	A	Stockport C	L	0-1	1-2	Cock	6,0
31	M	6	A	Barnsley	L	1-2	1-4	Banks	6,0
32		13	H	Barnsley	D	1-0	1-1	Banks	15,0
33		20	A	Nottingham F	W	2-0	3-0	Banks 2, Bertram	8,0
34		27	H	Nottingham F	W	1-0	1-0	McDonald	10,0
35	A	2	A	Grimsby T	W	1-0	2-0	Crockford 2	10,0
36		3	A	Lincoln C	W	1-0	1-0	Crockford	9,0
37		5	H	Birmingham	L	0-0	1-2	Crockford	18,0
38		6	A	Birmingham	L	0-2	0-2		20,0
39		10	H	Lincoln C	W	2-0	3-0	Bertram, Banks, Crockford	13,0
40		17	A	Bury	D	1-1	2-2	Sharp, Cock	12,0
41		24	H	Bury	W	0-0	1-0	Crockford	7,0
42	M	1	H	Port Vale	W	1-0	4-0	Cock 2, Crockford, Penn	6,0

Ap

Goa

FA Cup

1	J	10	H	Swindon T	L	1-2	1-2	Hoare	30,0

1	Debuts for Bagge, Chaplin, McIntyre and Penn
4	Cock debut
6	McDonald debut
16	Worrall debut
21	Banks debut
23	Charlton finale
32	McIntyre finale
33	Reynolds's 200th game
40	Sharp finale
42	Marshall finale

	Nixon	Charlton	Chaplin	Russell	Torrance	Bagge	Nash	McIntyre	Taylor	Martin	Penn	Walker	Marshall	Cock	Coates	Reynolds	McDonald	White	Bertram	Hall	Worrall	Houghton J	Houghton JH	Banks	Hoare GR	Papworth	Crockford	Sharp	Marrable
1	1	2	3	4	5	6	7	8	9	10	11																		
2	1	2	3	4	5	6	7	8		10	11	9																	
3	1	2	3	4		6	7			10	11	9	5	8															
4	1	2	3	4		6				8	10	11	5	9	7														
5		2	3	5		6				8	10	11	4	9	7	1													
6		2	3	4	5			10			11		6	9		1	7	8											
7		2	3	4	5			10			11		6	9		1	7	8											
8		2	3	4	5			10			11		6	9		1	7	8											
9		2	3	4	5			10			11		6	9		1	7	8											
10		2	3	4	5			10			11		6	9		1	7	8											
11		2	3	4	5			10			11		6	9		1	7	8											
12		2	3	4	5						10	11	6	9		1	7	8											
13		2	3	6	5						10	11	4	9		1	7		8										
14		2	3	4	5			8				11	6	9		1	7	10											
15		2	3	5	4							11	6	9		1	7	8	10										
16				3	5							11	6	9		1	7	8	10	4	2								
17			10	3	4			8			11		6	9		1	7					2	5						
18				3	4			8			11		6	9		1	7	10				2	5						
19			3		5	4		8				11	6	9		1	7	10				2							
20		2			5	4		8				11	6	9		1	7	10				3							
21		2	3		5			6				11	4	9		1	7							8	10				
22			3		5			6				11	4	9		1	7		10		2			8					
23		2	3		5			6				11	4	9		1	7	10						8					
24			3		5			6			11		4	9		1	7		10		2			8					
25			3		5			6			11		4	9		1	7				2			8	10				
26			3	6	5			10				11	4	9		1	7				2			8					
27			3	6	5			10			11		4	9		1	7				2			8					
28			3	6	5			10				11	4	9		1	7				2			8					
29			3		6			10				11	4	9		1	7				2			8		5			
30			3		6			10				11	4	9		1	7				2			8		5			
31			3		4			6				11		10		1	7				2			8		5	9		
32			3	5	4			6				11		9		1	7				2			8			10		
33			3	5	6							11	4			1	7		10		2			8			9		
34			3	5	6							11	4			1	7		10		2			8			9		
35			3		6							11	4			1	7		10		2			8		5	9		
36			3		4							7	6			1	11		8		2			10		5	9		
37			3	5	6							11	4			1	7		10		2			8			9		
38			3	2	6						11		4	9		1	7							8		5	10		
39			3	5	6						11		4			1	7		10		2			8			9		
40			3		6						11		4	9		1	7		8		2					5		10	
41			3	6							11		4	9		1	7	8			2						10		5
42			3	5	6						11		4	9		1	7	8			2						10		
A	4	18	39	29	38	7	3	25	1	5	23	25	38	34	2	38	37	16	12	1	20	4	2	19	2	7	11	1	1
G	-	-	-	-	2	-	-	9	-	-	1	2	-	25	-	-	2	3	2	-	-	-	-	6	-	-	7	1	-

	Nixon	Charlton	Chaplin	Russell	Torrance	Bagge	Nash	McIntyre	Taylor	Martin	Penn	Walker	Marshall	Cock	Coates	Reynolds	McDonald	White	Bertram	Hall	Worrall	Houghton J	Houghton JH	Banks	Hoare GR	Papworth	Crockford	Sharp	Marrable
1		2	3		5			6				11	4	9		1	7							8	10				

0 points v	Birmingham, Tottenham H	0 points
1 point v	Barnsley, Blackpool, Huddersfield T, Stoke, Wolves	5 points
2 points v	Hull C, Leicester C, South Shields, Stockport, West Ham U	10 points
3 points v	Rotherham C, Bristol C, Bury, Coventry C	12 points
4 points v	Clapton O, Grimsby T, Lincoln C, Nottingham F, Port Vale	20 points

Harry Bagge, a debutant in 1919–20.

1920-21

Division Two

	P	W	D	L	F	A	Pts
Birmingham	42	24	10	8	79	38	58
Cardiff City	42	24	10	8	59	32	58
Bristol City	42	19	13	10	49	29	51
Blackpool	42	20	10	12	54	42	50
West Ham United	42	19	10	13	51	30	48
Notts County	42	18	11	13	55	40	47
Clapton Orient	42	16	13	13	43	42	45
South Shields	42	17	10	15	61	46	44
Fulham	42	16	10	16	43	47	42
Sheffield Wednesday	42	15	11	16	48	48	41
Bury	42	15	10	17	45	49	40
Leicester City	42	12	16	14	39	46	40
Hull City	42	10	20	12	43	53	40
Leeds United	42	14	10	18	40	45	38
Wolverhampton W	42	16	6	20	49	66	38
Barnsley	42	10	16	16	48	50	36
Port Vale	42	11	14	17	43	49	36
Nottingham Forest	42	12	12	18	48	55	36
Rotherham County	42	12	12	18	37	53	36
Stoke	42	12	11	19	46	56	35
Coventry City	42	12	11	19	39	70	35
Stockport County	42	9	12	21	42	75	30

Manager: Phil Kelso

Did you know that?

For the second successive season, Donald Cock was Fulham's top scorer while his brother Jack headed Chelsea's scoring lists.

12	Walker finale
15	Edelston debut
17	Shea debut
18	Gavigan debut
27	Travers debut
40	Finales for Banks and Nixon

No		Date	V	Opponents	R	H-T	F-T	Scorers	Atten
1	A	28	H	Wolverhampton W	W	1-0	2-0	Banks, Cock	25,00
2		30	H	Stockport C	W	1-0	3-1	Penn, Morris, Banks	12,00
3	S	4	A	Wolverhampton W	L	0-0	0-1		25,00
4		11	H	West Ham U	D	0-0	0-0		30,00
5		13	A	Stockport C	D	0-1	1-1	Crockford	9,00
6		18	A	West Ham U	L	0-0	0-2		20,00
7		25	H	Notts C	W	1-1	3-1	Banks 2, Crockford	18,00
8	O	2	A	Notts C	L	1-2	1-2	Banks	14,00
9		9	H	Cardiff C	L	0-0	0-3		28,00
10		16	A	Cardiff C	L	0-2	0-3		25,00
11		23	A	Leicester C	D	0-0	1-1	Torrance	19,00
12		30	H	Leicester C	D	1-0	1-1	Banks	18,00
13	N	6	A	Blackpool	L	0-1	0-1		8,00
14		13	H	Blackpool	L	1-1	1-2	Cock	12,00
15		20	A	Sheffield W	L	0-1	0-3		20,00
16		27	H	Sheffield W	W	1-0	2-0	Hall, Cock	8,00
17	D	4	A	Clapton O	L	0-0	0-3		20,00
18		11	H	Clapton O	W	1-0	1-0	Cock	25,00
19		18	A	Stoke	W	0-0	2-1	Cock, Hall	8,00
20		25	A	Leeds U	D	0-0	0-0		25,00
21		27	H	Leeds U	W	1-0	1-0	Hall	30,00
22	J	1	H	Stoke	L	1-0	1-3	Cock	10,00
23		15	A	Bury	D	0-0	1-1	Cock	10,00
24		22	H	Bury	D	0-0	0-0		20,00
25	F	5	A	Coventry C	W	0-0	2-0	Morris, Torrance (pen)	18,00
26		12	A	Bristol C	L	0-1	0-2		16,00
27		26	A	Barnsley	L	0-3	1-3	Cock	12,00
28		28	H	Bristol C	W	0-0	3-0	Travers 2, Shea	10,00
29	M	5	H	Barnsley	W	0-0	1-0	Cock	20,00
30		12	A	Nottingham F	L	0-2	1-5	Travers	9,00
31		14	H	Coventry C	W	1-0	2-0	Torrance, Penn	15,00
32		19	H	Nottingham F	W	0-0	2-1	Travers 2	15,00
33		25	H	Birmingham	W	3-0	5-0	Cock, Shea 2, Travers 2	40,00
34		26	H	Rotherham C	W	0-0	1-0	Travers	26,00
35		29	A	Birmingham	L	0-1	0-1		30,00
36	A	2	A	Rotherham C	L	0-1	0-2		10,00
37		9	H	Port Vale	W	0-0	1-0	Travers	20,00
38		16	A	Port Vale	D	0-0	0-0		10,00
39		23	H	South Shields	D	0-0	0-0		16,00
40		30	A	South Shields	L	0-3	0-3		16,00
41	M	2	H	Hull C	W	1-0	3-0	Travers 2, Shea	10,00
42		7	A	Hull C	D	0-0	0-0		8,00
									App
									Goa

FA Cup

1	J	8	A	Blackburn R	D	1-1	1-1	Cock	45,00
R		13	H	Blackburn R	W	0-0	1-0	McDonald	23,21
2		29	A	Lincoln C	D	0-0	0-0		14,00
R	F	7	H	Lincoln C	W	1-0	1-0	Morris	18,00
3		19	H	Wolverhampton W	L	0-0	0-1		27,53

	Reynolds	Worrall	Chaplin	Bagge	Marrable	Torrance	McDonald	Banks	Cock	Crockford	Penn	Morris	Martin	Taylor	Russell	Houghton	Hall	Papworth	Walker W	Symes	White	Bertram	Edelston	Shea	Gavigan	Travers	Walker JH	Nixon
1		2	3	4	5	6	7	8	9	10	11																	
2		2	3	4	5	6	7	8		10	11	9																
3		2	3	4	5	6	7	8		10	11	9																
4		2	3	4	5	6	7	8	9	10	11																	
5		2	3	4		5	7	8	9	11			6	10														
6		2	3	4		6	7	8	9	10	11				5													
7		2	3	4		5	7	8	9	11			6	10														
8			3	4		5	7	8	9	11			6	10		2												
9			3	4	5	6	7	8	9	11				10		2												
10			3	4	5	6	7	8		9	11				2		10											
11		2	3	4		5	7	8		9							10	6	11									
12		2	3	4		5	7	8		9									11	6	10							
13		2	3	4		5		8	9	10	11									6		7						
14		2	3	4	5	6		8	9		11	10										7						
15		2	3	4		5		8	9	10	11											7	6					
16		2	3	4		7		8	9		11				5		10						6					
17		2	3	4		7			9		11				5		10						6	8				
18		2	3	4		5			9		11						10						6	8	7			
19		2	3	4		5			9		11						10						6	8	7			
20		2	3	4		5					11	9					10						6	8	7			
21		2	3	4		5					11	9					10				8		6		7			
22		2	3	4		5			9		11						10				8		6		7			
23		2	3	4		5	7	8	9		11				6						10							
24		2	3	4		5	7		9		11				6						10			8				
25		2	3	4		5		10			11	9			6									8	7			
26			3	4		5				9	11				2						10		6	8	7			
27		2		4		5			9		11				3								6	8	7	10		
28		2		4		5			10		11				3								6	8	7	9		
29		2	3	4		5			10		11												6	8	7	9		
30		2	3			5	7		10		11												6	8		9	4	
31		2	3			5	7		10		11												6	8		9	4	
32		2				5	7		10		11				3								6	8		9	4	
33		2	3			5	7		10		11												6	8		9	4	
34		2	3			5	7		10		11												6	8		9	4	
35		2	3			5	7		10		11												6	8		9	4	
36		2	3			5	7		10		11												6	8		9	4	
37		2	3	4		5	7				11												6	8		9	10	
38		2	3	4		5	7	10			11												6	8		9		1
39		2	3	4		5	7	10			11												6	8		9		
40		2	3	4		5	7	10			11												6	8		9		1
41		2	3	4		5	7		10		11												6	8		9		
42		2	3	4		5	7		10		11												6	8		9		
A	0	38	39	35	7	42	27	21	29	15	36	6	3	4	11	2	9	1	2	2	6	3	25	23	10	16	8	2
G		-	-	-	-	3	-	6	10	2	2	2	-	-	-	-	3	-	-	-	-	-	-	4	-	11	-	-

	Reynolds	Worrall	Chaplin	Bagge	Marrable	Torrance	McDonald	Banks	Cock	Crockford	Penn	Morris	Martin	Taylor	Russell	Houghton	Hall	Papworth	Walker W	Symes	White	Bertram	Edelston	Shea	Gavigan	Travers	Walker JH	Nixon
1		2	3	4		5	7		9		11						10				8		6					
R		2	3	4		5	7	8	9		11						10						6					
2		2	3	4		5	7		9		11										10		6	8				
R		2	3	4		5		10			11	9			6									8	7			
3		2	3	4		5			9		11										10		6	8	7			

0 points v	Blackpool, Cardiff C	0 points
1 point v	South Shields, West Ham U	2 points
2 points v	Barnsley, Birmingham, Bristol C, Bury, Clapton O, Leicester C, Nottingham F, Notts C, Rotherham C, Sheffield W, Stoke, Wolves	24 points
3 points v	Hull C, Leeds U, Port Vale, Stockport C	12 points
4 points v	Coventry	4 points

Top scorer Donald Cock.

1921-22

Division Two

	P	W	D	L	F	A	Pts
Nottingham Forest	42	22	12	8	51	30	56
Stoke	42	18	16	8	60	44	52
Barnsley	42	22	8	12	67	52	52
West Ham United	42	20	8	14	52	39	48
Hull City	42	19	10	13	51	41	48
South Shields	42	17	12	13	43	38	46
Fulham	42	18	9	15	57	38	45
Leeds United	42	16	13	13	48	38	45
Leicester City	42	14	17	11	39	34	45
Sheffield Wednesday	42	15	14	13	47	50	44
Bury	42	15	10	17	54	55	40
Derby County	42	15	9	18	60	64	39
Notts County	42	12	15	15	47	51	39
Crystal Palace	42	13	13	16	45	51	39
Clapton Orient	42	15	9	18	43	50	39
Rotherham County	42	14	11	17	32	43	39
Wolverhampton W	42	13	11	18	44	49	37
Port Vale	42	14	8	20	43	57	36
Blackpool	42	15	5	22	44	57	35
Coventry City	42	12	10	20	51	60	34
Bradford Park Avenue	42	12	9	21	46	62	33
Bristol City	42	12	9	21	37	58	33

Manager: Phil Kelso

Did you know that?

In November 1921, in the 4-1 win at Sheffield Wednesday, Frank Osborne and Harvey Darvill, both making their League debuts, were amongst the scorers, the only time two debutants were on the same scoresheet.

3	Ducat debut
13	Osborne and Darvill debuts
16	Torrance's 200th game
26	Fleming debut
32	Croal debut
33	Travers finale

No		Date	V	Opponents	R	H-T	F-T	Scorers	Atte
1	A	27	H	Coventry C	W	1-0	5-0	Cock 2, Torrance (pen), Travers, Shea	25,0
2		29	A	Leicester C	W	0-0	2-1	Shea, Cock	16,0
3	S	3	A	Coventry C	L	0-1	0-2		20,0
4		5	H	Leicester C	D	0-0	0-0		15,0
5		10	A	Hull C	L	1-0	1-2	Travers	10,0
6		17	H	Hull C	W	1-0	6-0	Travers 3, Shea, Cock 2	20,0
7		24	A	Notts C	L	0-2	0-3		17,0
8	O	1	H	Notts C	W	2-0	4-0	Travers 2, Shea, (Marriott og)	20,0
9		8	A	Crystal Palace	L	0-0	0-2		20,0
10		15	H	Crystal Palace	D	1-1	1-1	Travers	30,0
11		22	H	Rotherham C	W	2-0	4-0	Travers 2, Shea, Cock	20,0
12		29	A	Rotherham C	L	0-1	0-1		10,0
13	N	5	A	Sheffield W	W	1-0	4-1	Shea, Darvill, Travers, Osborne	16,0
14		12	H	Sheffield W	W	1-0	3-1	Travers 2, Osborne	16,0
15		19	A	Bradford	W	1-1	2-1	Osborne, Travers	9,0
16		26	H	Bradford	W	1-1	2-1	Shea, Travers	19,0
17	D	3	A	Blackpool	W	2-0	2-0	Torrance, (Tulloch og)	7,0
18		10	H	Blackpool	W	1-0	1-0	Gavigan	35,0
19		17	H	Clapton O	W	1-0	2-0	Shea 2 (1 pen)	25,0
20		24	A	Clapton O	L	0-2	2-4	Travers, Osborne	20,0
21		26	H	Stoke	W	2-1	2-1	Shea, Torrance	30,0
22		27	A	Stoke	L	0-2	0-3		20,0
23		31	A	Derby C	D	0-0	1-1	Travers	12,0
24	J	14	H	Derby C	D	0-2	2-2	Cock, Shea	18,0
25		21	H	Barnsley	D	0-0	0-0		12,0
26	F	4	H	Wolverhampton W	W	1-0	1-0	Darvill	12,0
27		11	A	Wolverhampton W	D	0-0	0-0		15,0
28		25	A	Nottingham F	D	0-0	0-0		16,0
29		28	H	Nottingham F	W	2-0	2-0	Kingsley, Cock	20,0
30	M	4	H	Bristol C	D	0-0	0-0		20,0
31		6	A	Barnsley	L	1-1	1-2	Boland	9,0
32		11	A	Bristol C	L	0-1	0-1		20,0
33		18	A	South Shields	L	0-1	0-1		12,0
34		25	H	South Shields	W	1-0	3-0	Osborne, Croal 2	20,0
35	A	1	A	Port Vale	D	1-1	1-1	Osborne	10,0
36		8	H	Port Vale	W	1-0	1-0	Torrance	15,0
37		14	A	Leeds U	L	0-1	0-2		18,0
38		15	A	West Ham U	L	0-1	0-1		25,0
39		17	H	Leeds U	L	0-1	0-1		20,0
40		22	H	West Ham U	W	0-0	2-0	Osborne 2	10,0
41		29	A	Bury	L	0-1	0-1		5,0
42	M	6	H	Bury	L	0-1	0-1		15,0
									Ap
									Goa

FA Cup

No		Date	V	Opponents	R	H-T	F-T	Scorers	Atte
1	J	7	A	Plymouth A	D	1-1	1-1	Travers	29,9
R		11	H	Plymouth A	W	0-0	1-0	Shea	28,3
2		28	A	Leicester C	L	0-1	0-2		30,0

	Reynolds	Worrall	Symes	Bagge	Torrance	Russell	Gavigan	Shea	Travers	Cock	Penn	Chaplin	Ducat	Edelston	Osborne	Darvill	McDonald	Martin	Kingsley	Fleming	Boland	Croal
1	1	2	3	4	5	6	7	8	9	10	11											
2	1	2		4	5	6	7	8	9	10	11	3										
3	1	2			5	6	7	8	9	10	11	3	4									
4	1	2			5	6	7	8	9	10	11	3	4									
5	1	2		4		5	7	8	9	10	11	3		6								
6	1	2			5	6	7	8	9	10	11	3	4									
7	1	2			5	6	7	8	9	10	11	3	4									
8	1	2		6	5		7	8	9	10	11	3	4									
9	1	2		6	5		7	8	9	10	11	3	4									
10	1	2		6	5		7	8	9	10	11	3	4									
11	1	2		6	5		7	8	9	10	11	3	4									
12	1	2		6	5		7	8	9	10	11	3	4									
13	1	2		6		5	7	8	9			3	4		10	11						
14	1	2		6	5		7	8	9			3	4		10	11						
15	1	2		6	5		7	8	9			3	4		10	11						
16	1	2		6	5	4	7	8	9		11	3			10							
17	1	2		6	5	4	7	8	9			3			10	11						
18	1	2		6	5	4	7	8	9			3			10	11						
19	1	2		6	5	4	7	8	9			3			10	11						
20	1	2		6	5	4		8	9			3			10	11	7					
21	1	2		6	5	4	7	8	9			3			10	11						
22	1	2		6	5	4	7	8	9			3			10	11						
23	1	2		4	5		7	8	9			3			10	11		6				
24	1	2			5			8	9	10	11	3	4					6	7			
25	1	2		6	5			8	9	10		3	4			11			7			
26	1			6	5			8	9	10		3	4			11			7	2		
27	1			4		5		8	9	10		3				11		6	7	2		
28	1				4	5		8		10		3			9	11		6	7	2		
29	1				5			8		10		3	4		9	11		6	7	2		
30	1				5			8		10		3	4		9	11		6	7	2		
31	1			4	5			8	9			3				11		6	7	2	10	
32	1			6	5			8	9			3	4			11			7	2		10
33	1				5			8	9			3	4			11		6	7	2		10
34	1				5			8			11	3	4		9			6	7	2		10
35	1				5			8			11	3	4		9			6	7	2		10
36	1			6	5			8			11	3	4		9				7	2		10
37	1			6	5						11	3	4		9				7	2	8	10
38	1			6	5			8			11	3	4		9				7	2		10
39	1			6	5			8		9	11	3	4				7			2		10
40	1			4	5					9	11	2			8			6	7	3		10
41	1			4	5					9	11	2			8			6	7	3		10
42	1			4	5					9	11	2			8			6	7	3		10
A	42	25	1	31	39	17	22	38	30	23	23	41	25	1	22	19	2	13	18	17	2	11
G	-	-	-	-	4	-	1	11	17	8	-	-	-	-	8	2	-	-	1	-	1	2

	Reynolds	Worrall	Symes	Bagge	Torrance	Russell	Gavigan	Shea	Travers	Cock	Penn	Chaplin	Ducat	Edelston	Osborne	Darvill	McDonald	Martin	Kingsley	Fleming	Boland	Croal
1	1	2		4	5		7	8	9			3			10	11		6				
R	1	2		4	5			8	9	7		3			10	11		6				
2	1	2		6	5			8	9	10		3	4			11			7			

0 points v	Bury, Leeds U	0 points
1 point v	Barnsley, Bristol C, Crystal Palace	3 points
2 points v	Clapton O, Coventry C, Derby C, Hull C, Notts C, Rotherham C, South Shields, Stoke, West Ham U	18 points
3 points v	Leicester C, Nottingham F, Port Vale, Wolves	12 points
4 points v	Blackpool, Bradford, Sheffield W	12 points

Barney Travers, banned for a bribery attempt.

1922-23

Division Two

	P	W	D	L	F	A	Pts
Notts County	42	23	7	12	46	34	53
West Ham United	42	20	11	11	63	38	51
Leicester City	42	21	9	12	65	44	51
Manchester United	42	17	14	11	51	36	48
Blackpool	42	18	11	13	60	43	47
Bury	42	18	11	13	55	46	47
Leeds United	42	18	11	13	43	36	47
Sheffield Wednesday	42	17	12	13	54	47	46
Barnsley	42	17	11	14	62	51	45
Fulham	42	16	12	14	43	32	44
Southampton	42	14	14	14	40	40	42
Hull City	42	14	14	14	43	45	42
South Shields	42	15	10	17	35	44	40
Derby County	42	14	11	17	46	50	39
Bradford City	42	12	13	17	41	45	37
Crystal Palace	42	13	11	18	54	62	37
Port Vale	42	14	9	19	39	51	37
Coventry City	42	15	7	20	46	63	37
Clapton Orient	42	12	12	18	40	50	36
Stockport County	42	14	8	20	43	58	36
Rotherham County	42	13	9	20	44	63	35
Wolverhampton W	42	9	9	24	42	77	27

Manager: Phil Kelso

Did you know that?

After only 33 League and Cup appearances, Frank Osborne played centre forward in England's 2-0 win over Northern Ireland at the Hawthorns in October 1922, the first Fulham player to play for England.

1	Reynolds's 300th game
4	Cock finale
13	McDonald finale
16	Worrall finale
28	White finale
42	Shea finale

No		Date	V	Opponents	R	H-T	F-T	Scorers	Atten
1	A	26	A	Port Vale	W	0-0	1-0	Shea	10,00
2		28	H	Wolverhampton W	W	2-0	2-0	Osborne 2	14,00
3	S	2	H	Port Vale	D	0-0	1-1	Shea	23,00
4		4	A	Wolverhampton W	D	0-0	0-0		12,00
5		9	A	Crystal Palace	D	0-0	0-0		12,00
6		16	H	Crystal Palace	W	0-0	2-1	Osborne 2	26,00
7		23	A	Hull C	L	0-1	0-1		8,00
8		30	H	Hull C	D	0-0	0-0		22,00
9	O	7	A	Sheffield W	L	0-1	0-1		10,00
10		14	H	Sheffield W	W	0-0	1-0	Torrance	22,00
11		21	A	Manchester U	D	1-0	1-1	Shea	18,00
12		28	H	Manchester U	D	0-0	0-0		20,00
13	N	4	H	Barnsley	L	0-0	0-1		19,00
14		11	A	Barnsley	W	0-0	1-0	Osborne	12,00
15		18	H	Blackpool	D	1-1	1-1	Papworth	16,00
16		25	A	Blackpool	L	0-1	0-3		10,00
17	D	9	H	Coventry C	W	1-0	4-0	Torrance 2 (2 pens), Osborne 2	15,00
18		11	A	Coventry C	L	0-1	0-1		5,00
19		16	A	Bradford C	L	1-2	1-2	Darvill	10,00
20		23	H	Bradford C	D	0-0	0-0		15,00
21		25	A	Notts C	L	0-0	0-1		14,00
22		26	H	Notts C	W	1-0	2-1	Darvill, Smith	25,00
23		30	A	Southampton	L	0-2	0-2		8,00
24	J	6	H	Southampton	D	1-1	1-1	Osborne	25,00
25		20	A	Derby C	L	0-2	0-2		11,00
26		27	H	Derby C	W	1-0	3-1	Papworth 2, Croal	18,00
27	F	10	H	Bury	W	1-0	3-0	Papworth 2 (2 pens), Osborne	12,00
28		14	A	Bury	W	1-0	1-0	Penn	7,00
29		17	A	Rotherham C	W	0-1	3-1	Kingsley, Shea, Papworth	9,00
30		24	H	Rotherham C	L	1-1	1-2	Croal	15,00
31	M	3	A	Clapton O	W	0-0	2-0	Osborne, Croal	20,00
32		10	H	Clapton O	D	0-0	0-0		22,00
33		17	H	Stockport C	W	1-0	3-0	Shea 3	16,00
34		24	A	Stockport C	W	1-0	2-0	McKay, Croal	8,00
35		30	H	Leicester C	W	0-0	2-0	Shea, McKay	28,00
36		31	H	Leeds U	W	2-0	3-0	Torrance (pen), McKay 2	20,00
37	A	2	A	Leicester C	D	1-0	1-1	McKay	24,00
38		7	A	Leeds U	D	1-0	1-1	Darvill	10,00
39		14	H	West Ham U	L	0-1	0-2		30,00
40		21	A	West Ham U	L	0-1	0-1		20,00
41		28	H	South Shields	L	0-0	0-1		14,00
42	M	5	A	South Shields	L	0-2	0-2		6,00
									App
									Goal

FA Cup

No		Date	V	Opponents	R	H-T	F-T	Scorers	Atten
1	J	13	A	Leicester C	L	0-1	0-4		25,87

	Reynolds	Fleming	Chaplin	Bagge	Torrance	Martin	McDonald	Shea	Osborne	Darvill	Penn	Cock	Kingsley	Symes	Russell	Croal	Ducat	Worrall	Papworth	Gavigan	McKay	Smith	Edelston	Thomas	White
1	1	2	3	4	5	6	7	8	9	10	11														
2	1	2	3	4	5	6	7	8	9	10	11														
3	1	2	3	4	5	6	7	8	9	10	11														
4	1	2	3	4	5	6	7	8		10	11	9													
5	1	2	3	4	5	6	7	8	9	10	11														
6	1	2	3	4	5	6	7	8	9	10	11														
7	1	2	3	4	5	6		8	9	10	11		7												
8	1	2	3	4	5	6		8	9	10	11			7											
9	1	2	3	4		6		8	9	11				7	5	10									
10	1	2	3	6	5		7	8	9		11					10	4								
11	1	2	3	5	9	6		8		10	11			7			4								
12	1		3		5	6	7	8	9		11					10	4	2							
13	1		3		5	6	7	8	9		11					10	4	2							
14	1		3		5	6		8	10		11		7				4	2	9						
15	1		3		5	6		8	10		11		7				4	2	9						
16	1		3		5	6		8	10		11		7				4	2	9						
17	1	2	3		5	6		8	9	10	11						4			7					
18	1	2	3		5	6		8		10	11						4		9	7					
19	1	2	3		5	6		8		10	11						4			7	9				
20	1	2	3		5	6		8	9	10	11						4			7					
21	1	2	3	4	5	6			8	10	11									7		9			
22	1	2	3	4	5	6		8		10	11		7									9			
23	1	2	3	4	5	6		8		10	11		7									9			
24	1	2	3	4	5	6			8	10	11		7									9			
25	1	2	3	10	5	6		8	7		11						4					9			
26	1	2	3	4	5			8	7		11					10			9				6		
27	1	2	3	4	5			8	7		11					10			9				6		
28	1	2	3			6		8			11						4		9				5	7	10
29	1	2	3		5			8			11		7			10	4		9				6		
30	1	2	3		5						11		7			10	4		8		9		6		
31	1	2	3	4	5			8	7		11					10			9				6		
32	1	2	3	4	5			8			11					10				7	9		6		
33	1	2	3	4	5			8			11					10				7	9		6		
34	1	2	3	4	5			8			11					10				7	9		6		
35	1	2	3	4	5			8	7		11					10					9		6		
36	1	2	3	4	5			8	7		11					10					9		6		
37	1	2		4		5		8	7		11					10	3				9		6		
38	1	2	3	4	5			8		10	11		7								9		6		
39	1	2	3	4	5			8	7		11					10					9		6		
40	1	2	3	4				8	7		11				5	10					9		6		
41	1	2	3	4	5			8	7		11					10					9		6		
42	1	2	3	4	5			8			11		7			10					9		6		
A	2	37	41	30	38	26	9	39	28	19	41	1	11	3	2	19	16	5	10	8	13	5	17	1	1
G	-	-	-	-	4	-	-	8	10	3	1	-	1	-	-	4	-	-	6	-	5	1	-	-	-

	Reynolds	Fleming	Chaplin	Bagge	Torrance	Martin	McDonald	Shea	Osborne	Darvill	Penn	Cock	Kingsley	Symes	Russell	Croal	Ducat	Worrall	Papworth	Gavigan	McKay	Smith	Edelston	Thomas	White
1	1	2	3	6	5			8	9	10	11		7				4								

0 points v	South Shields, West Ham U	0 points
1 point v	Blackpool, Bradford C, Hull C, Southampton	4 points
2 points v	Barnsley, Coventry C, Derby C, Manchester U, Notts C, Rotherham C, Sheffield W	14 points
3 points v	Clapton O, Crystal Palace, Leeds U, Leicester C, Port Vale, Wolves	18 points
4 points v	Bury, Stockport C	8 points

Frank Osborne, Fulham's first England cap.

1923-24

Division Two

	P	W	D	L	F	A	Pts
Leeds United	42	21	12	9	61	35	54
Bury	42	21	9	12	63	35	51
Derby County	42	21	9	12	75	42	51
Blackpool	42	18	13	11	72	47	49
Southampton	42	17	14	11	52	31	48
Stoke	42	14	18	10	44	42	46
Oldham Athletic	42	14	17	11	45	52	45
Sheffield Wednesday	42	16	12	14	54	51	44
South Shields	42	17	10	15	49	50	44
Clapton Orient	42	14	15	13	40	36	43
Barnsley	42	16	11	15	57	61	43
Leicester City	42	17	8	17	64	54	42
Stockport County	42	13	16	13	44	52	42
Manchester United	42	13	14	15	52	44	40
Crystal Palace	42	13	13	16	53	65	39
Port Vale	42	13	12	17	50	66	38
Hull City	42	10	17	15	46	51	37
Bradford City	42	11	15	16	35	48	37
Coventry City	42	11	13	18	52	68	35
Fulham	42	10	14	18	45	56	34
Nelson	42	10	13	19	40	74	33
Bristol City	42	7	15	20	32	65	29

Manager: Phil Kelso

Did you know that?

Goalkeeper Arthur Reynolds missed the trip to Leicester in March 1924, thus ending a record run of 124 consecutive League and Cup appearances.

12	Edmonds debut
23	Osborne finale
32	Torrance's 300th game
33	Ducat finale
35	Croal finale

No		Date	V	Opponents	R	H-T	F-T	Scorers	Atte
1	A	25	H	South Shields	L	0-0	2-3	Heard, Torrance (pen)	22,00
2		27	A	Bury	L	1-1	1-2	Penn	10,00
3	S	1	A	South Shields	L	0-1	0-1		12,00
4		3	H	Bury	L	0-0	0-2		14,00
5		8	A	Crystal Palace	D	1-0	1-1	Papworth	12,00
6		15	H	Crystal Palace	W	1-0	1-0	Doyle	11,00
7		22	A	Sheffield W	L	0-0	1-2	Doyle	12,00
8		29	H	Sheffield W	W	2-0	4-1	Doyle 3, Papworth	18,00
9	O	6	A	Coventry C	L	0-1	0-3		16,00
10		13	H	Coventry C	D	0-0	1-1	Papworth	10,00
11		20	A	Bristol C	W	1-0	1-0	Papworth	12,00
12		27	H	Bristol C	D	1-1	1-1	Papworth	12,00
13	N	3	A	Southampton	L	0-0	0-1		14,00
14		10	H	Southampton	W	1-0	3-2	Torrance (pen), Doyle, Papworth	16,00
15		17	H	Derby C	W	1-2	3-2	Edmonds 2, Torrance (pen)	15,00
16		24	A	Derby C	D	1-3	3-3	Penn, Edmonds, Doyle	14,00
17	D	1	H	Blackpool	L	2-1	2-3	Doyle, Edmonds	17,00
18		8	A	Blackpool	L	0-1	0-3		8,00
19		15	H	Nelson	D	0-0	0-0		13,00
20		22	A	Nelson	D	1-0	1-1	Papworth	6,00
21		25	H	Hull C	D	0-0	1-1	Doyle	22,00
22		26	A	Hull C	L	1-2	2-4	Papworth 2	13,00
23		29	H	Oldham A	D	0-0	0-0		15,0
24	J	5	A	Oldham A	L	0-1	1-2	Papworth	12,00
25		19	H	Manchester U	W	1-1	3-1	Edmonds 3	12,00
26		26	A	Manchester U	D	0-0	0-0		25,00
27	F	9	A	Barnsley	L	0-1	1-2	Heard	6,00
28		16	H	Bradford C	D	0-0	1-1	Edmonds	15,00
29		23	A	Bradford C	L	0-1	0-1		15,00
30	M	1	H	Port Vale	D	0-0	0-0		15,00
31		8	A	Port Vale	L	0-1	1-3	Edmonds	10,00
32		10	H	Barnsley	W	1-0	3-0	Darvill, Edmonds 2	7,00
33		15	A	Leeds U	L	0-1	0-3		18,00
34		22	H	Leeds U	L	0-2	0-2		17,00
35		29	A	Leicester C	L	1-2	1-2	Chaplin	14,00
36	A	5	H	Leicester C	W	1-0	1-0	Edmonds	17,00
37		12	H	Clapton O	D	0-0	0-0		10,00
38		19	A	Clapton O	D	0-0	0-0		18,00
39		21	H	Stoke	W	3-0	3-0	Edmonds, Heard, Bagge	15,0
40		22	A	Stoke	D	0-0	0-0		6,00
41		26	A	Stockport C	L	0-1	1-2	Darvill	8,00
42	M	3	H	Stockport C	W	1-0	1-0	Linfoot	20,00
									App
									Goa

FA Cup

1	J	12	H	Llanelly	W	2-0	2-0	Edmonds 2	14,00
2	F	2	A	Burnley	D	0-0	0-0		23,50
R		7	H	Burnley	L	0-0	0-1		31,00

Reynolds	Fleming	Chaplin	Bagge	Torrance	Edelston	Osborne	Heard	McKay	Doyle	Penn	Gavigan	Croal	Papworth	Darvill	Aimer	London	Ducat	Edmonds	Riddell	Reid	Lafferty	Linfoot	Whalley	Martin	
1	2	3	4	5	6	7	8	9	10	11															1
1	2	3	4	5	6		8	9	10	11	7														2
1	2	3	4	5	6	7	8	9	10	11															3
1	2	3	4	5	6	9	8		10	11	7														4
1	2	3	4	5	6	7			10			8	9	11											5
1	2	3	4	5	6	7			10			8	9	11											6
1	2	3	4	5	6	7			10	11		8	9												7
1	2	3	4	5		7			10	11	8		9		6										8
1	2	3	4	5		7			10	11	8		9		6										9
1		3	6	5					10	11	7	8	9			2	4								10
1		3	6	5		7	8		10	11			9			2	4								11
1		3	6	5		7			10	11			9			2	4	8							12
1	2	3	6	5		7			10	11	8		9				4								13
1	2	3	6	5			8		10	11	7		9				4								14
1		3	6	5			8		10	11	7					2	4	9							15
1		3	6	5			8		10	11	7					2	4	9							16
1		3	6	5		8			10	11	7					2	4	9							17
1		3	6	5		8			10	11	7					2	4	9							18
1	2		6	5			8			11	7			10	3		4	9							19
1		3	6	4		7			10	11	8		9				2		5						20
1		3	6	4		7			10	11	8		9				2		5						21
1	2	3	6	5		7			10	11		8	9				4								22
1		3	6	4		7			10	11			8				2		5	9					23
1		3	6	4					10	11	7		8				2		5	9					24
1		3	6	4						11	7		9	10			2	8	5						25
1		3	6	4						11	7		9	10			2	8	5						26
1	2	3			4		8		10	11	7							9	5		6				27
1		3	6	4			8		10	11	7						2	9	5						28
1		3	6		4		7			11			9	10			2	8	5						29
1		3	6	4						11	7		9	10			2	8	5						30
1		3	8	5	6					11	7			10			2	9	4						31
1		3	8	5	6					11	7			10			2	9	4						32
1		3	8	5	6					11				10			2	9	4			7			33
1	2	3	6	5						11	8			10				9	4			7			34
	2	9	4	5	6						7	10		11	3			8					1		35
1	2		4	10	6		8							11	3			9	5			7			36
1	2	10		5	4		8							11	3			9				7		6	37
1	2	10	4	5	6		8							11	3			9				7			38
1	2		4	5	6		8			10				11	3			9				7			39
1	2		4	5	6		8	9		11				10	3							7			40
1	2		4	5	6		8			11	7			10	3			9							41
1	2		4	5	6		8			11				10	3			9				7			42
41	23	36	40	40	20	17	19	4	25	36	25	6	19	19	11	7	23	23	15	2	1	8	1	1	A
-	-	1	1	3	-	-	3	-	9	2	-	-	10	2	-	-	-	13	-	-	-	1	-	-	G

Reynolds	Fleming	Chaplin	Bagge	Torrance	Edelston	Osborne	Heard	McKay	Doyle	Penn	Gavigan	Croal	Papworth	Darvill	Aimer	London	Ducat	Edmonds	Riddell	Reid	Lafferty	Linfoot	Whalley	Martin	
1		3	6	4					10	11	7						2	8	5	9					1
1		3	6	4						11	7		9	10			2	8	5						2
1		3	6	4						11	7		9	10			2	8	5						R

0 points v	Blackpool, Bury, Leeds U, South Shields	0 points
1 point v	Bradford C, Coventry C, Hull C, Oldham A, Port Vale	5 points
2 points v	Barnsley, Clapton O, Leicester C, Nelson, Sheffield W, Southampton, Stockport C	14 points
3 points v	Crystal Palace, Coventry C, Derby C, Manchester U, Stoke	15 points
4 points v		0 points

New signing from Wolves, centre forward George Edmonds.

1924-25

Division Two

	P	W	D	L	F	A	Pts
Leicester City	42	24	11	7	90	32	59
Manchester United	42	23	11	8	57	23	57
Derby County	42	22	11	9	71	36	55
Portsmouth	42	15	18	9	58	50	48
Chelsea	42	16	15	11	51	37	47
Wolverhampton W	42	20	6	16	55	51	46
Southampton	42	13	18	11	40	36	44
Port Vale	42	17	8	17	48	56	42
South Shields	42	12	17	13	42	38	41
Hull City	42	15	11	16	50	49	41
Clapton Orient	42	14	12	16	42	42	40
Fulham	42	15	10	17	41	56	40
Middlesbrough	42	10	19	13	36	44	39
Sheffield Wednesday	42	15	8	19	50	56	38
Barnsley	42	13	12	17	46	59	38
Bradford City	42	13	12	17	37	50	38
Blackpool	42	14	9	19	65	61	37
Oldham Athletic	42	13	11	18	35	51	37
Stockport County	42	13	11	18	37	57	37
Stoke	42	12	11	19	34	46	35
Crystal Palace	42	12	10	20	38	54	34
Coventry City	42	11	9	22	45	84	31

Manager: Andy Ducat

Did you know that?

Just days after helping Fulham to a 2-0 home win over Coventry in November 1924, 28-year-old inside forward Harvey Darvill died from a burst blood vessel in his stomach.

1	Prouse debut
2	Russell finale
4	Oliver debut
14	Darvill finale
14	Reynolds' 400th game
22	Craig debut
29	Edelston finale
31	Penn's 200th game
40	Reynolds finale
41	Gavigan finale

No		Date	V	Opponents	R	H-T	F-T	Scorers	Atten
1	A	30	A	Bradford C	D	0-1	1-1	Prouse	20,00
2	S	6	H	South Shields	D	0-0	1-1	Darvill	18,00
3		8	A	Port Vale	W	0-0	1-0	Prouse	10,00
4		13	A	Derby C	L	1-3	1-5	Prouse	17,00
5		20	H	Blackpool	W	1-0	1-0	Darvill	22,00
6		27	A	Hull C	L	0-2	0-3		9,00
7	O	4	H	Portsmouth	D	0-0	0-0		23,00
8		11	A	Chelsea	D	0-0	0-0		45,00
9		18	A	Wolverhampton W	L	1-0	1-2	Richards	18,00
10		25	H	Stockport C	W	0-0	2-0	Torrance (pen), Prouse	17,00
11	N	1	A	Manchester U	L	0-1	0-2		20,00
12		8	H	Leicester C	D	0-0	2-2	Prouse 2	18,00
13		15	A	Stoke	D	1-1	1-1	Darvill	10,00
14		22	H	Coventry C	W	1-0	2-0	Prouse 2	16,00
15		29	A	Oldham A	D	0-0	0-0		8,00
16	D	1	H	Middlesbrough	D	0-0	0-0		8,00
17		6	H	Sheffield W	W	1-1	2-1	Torrance 2 (1 pen)	15,00
18		13	A	Clapton O	L	0-2	0-3		15,00
19		20	H	Crystal Palace	W	2-1	3-1	Prouse 3	18,00
20		26	A	Southampton	L	0-1	0-1		18,00
21		27	H	Bradford C	D	1-1	1-1	Richards	8,00
22	J	1	A	Middlesbrough	W	2-1	3-1	Wood 2, Craig	10,00
23		17	H	Derby C	L	0-1	0-2		25,00
24		24	A	Blackpool	L	0-1	1-4	Prouse	8,00
25	F	7	A	Portsmouth	L	0-0	0-3		12,00
26		9	H	Hull C	W	2-0	4-0	Linfoot, Penn, Edmonds, Prouse	6,00
27		14	H	Chelsea	L	0-1	1-2	Linfoot	28,00
28		21	H	Wolverhampton W	W	1-0	1-0	Prouse	20,00
29		25	A	South Shields	L	0-2	1-2	Prouse	6,00
30		28	A	Stockport C	L	0-0	1-4	Pilkington	10,00
31	M	7	H	Manchester U	W	1-0	1-0	Edmonds	16,00
32		14	A	Leicester C	L	0-2	0-4		22,00
33		21	H	Stoke	W	0-0	1-0	Penn	16,00
34		28	A	Coventry C	W	1-0	1-0	Prouse	13,00
35	A	4	H	Oldham A	W	1-0	1-0	Edmonds	12,00
36		10	H	Southampton	W	1-0	1-0	Edmonds	20,00
37		11	A	Sheffield W	L	0-2	1-3	Edmonds	14,00
38		13	A	Barnsley	L	0-0	0-1		11,00
39		14	H	Barnsley	L	1-1	1-2	Craig	6,00
40		18	H	Clapton O	L	0-1	0-2		16,00
41		25	A	Crystal Palace	W	1-1	2-1	Edmonds, Wolfe	10,00
42	M	2	H	Port Vale	D	1-1	1-1	Edmonds	10,00
									App
									Goa

FA Cup

No		Date	V	Opponents	R	H-T	F-T	Scorers	Atten
1	J	10	A	Swindon T	W	1-1	2-1	Edmonds, Richards	20,30
2		31	A	Cardiff C	L	0-1	0-1		20,00

Reynolds	Russell	Chaplin	Bagge	Torrance	Lafferty	Linfoot	Prouse	Edmonds	Darvill	Penn	Brooks	Oliver	Riddell	Aimer	Fleming	Richards	Gavigan	Kennedy	Papworth	Packham	Wood	Craig	Whalley	Edelston	Pilkington	Wolfe	Doyle	McKenna	
	2	3	4	5	6	7	8	9	10	11																			1
	2	3	4	5	6	7	8	9	10	11																			2
		3	4	5	6	7	8	9	10	11	2																		3
		3	6			7	8	9	10	11		4	5	2															4
		3	6			7	8	9	10	11		4	5		2														5
		3	6				8	9	10	11		4	5		2	7													6
			6	5			8	9	10	11		4		3	2	7													7
		3	6	5				9	8	11		4			2	10	7												8
		3	6	5			8			11		4	9		2	10	7												9
		3	6	5			8			11		4	9		2	10	7												10
		3		5			8		10			4	6		2	11	7	9											11
		3		5			8		9	11		4	6		2	10	7												12
		3		5		7	8		9	11		4	6		2	10													13
		3		5		7	8		9	11		4	6		2	10													14
		3		5		7	8			11		4	6		2	10			9										15
		3		5		7	8			11	2	4	6			10			9										16
		3	8	5		7	9			11		4	6		2	10													17
		3	8	5			9			11		4	6		2	10				7									18
		3		5			8			11		4	6		2	10				7	9								19
		3		5			8			11		4	6		2	10				7	9								20
		3		5			8			11		4	6		2	10				7	9								21
				5			8			11		4	6	3	2	7					9	10							22
		3	4	5			8	9		11			6		2	7						10							23
				5			8	9		11		4	6	3	2	7						10							24
				5			8	9		11		4	6	3	2	7						10	1						25
				5		7	8	9		11	3	4			2							10	1	6					26
				5		7	8	9		11	3	4			2							10	1	6					27
				5		7	8	9		11	3	4			2							10	1	6					28
				5		7	8	9		11	3	4			2							10		6					29
		3	6	5		7		9		11		4			2							10			8				30
		3	6	5		7	8	9		11		4			2							10	1						31
		3	6	5		7	8	9		11		4			2							10	1						32
		3	6	5		7	8			11		4			2							10	1			9			33
		3	6	5		7	8			11		4			2							10				9			34
		3	6	5		7	8	9		11	2	4										10							35
		3	6	5		7		9		11	2	4										8					10		36
		3	6	5		7		9		11	2	4										8					10		37
		3	6			7		9				4				11		5							2	10	8		38
		3	6	5		7		9		11		4										8			2		10		39
		3	6	5				9		11		4			2		7					8					10		40
		3	6	5				9		11		4			2		7					8				10		1	41
		3	6	5		7		9		11		4			2							8				10		1	42
3	2	34	26	38	3	25	33	26	12	40	9	38	20	5	32	21	7	2	2	4	4	20	7	4	3	5	5	2	A
	-	-	-	3	-	2	16	7	3	2	-	-	-	-	-	2	-	-	-	-	2	2	-	-	1	1	-	-	G

Reynolds	Russell	Chaplin	Bagge	Torrance	Lafferty	Linfoot	Prouse	Edmonds	Darvill	Penn	Brooks	Oliver	Riddell	Aimer	Fleming	Richards	Gavigan	Kennedy	Papworth	Packham	Wood	Craig	Whalley	Edelston	Pilkington	Wolfe	Doyle	McKenna	
		3		5			8	9		11		4	6		2	7						10							1
				5			8	9		11		4	6	3	2	7						10	1						2

0 points v	Derby C, Clapton O, Barnsley,	0 points
1 point v	South Shields, Portsmouth, Chelsea, Leicester C	4 points
2 points v	Bradford C, Blackpool, Hull C, Wolves, Stockport C, Manchester U, Sheffield W, Southampton	16 points
3 points v	Port Vale, Stoke, Oldham A, Middlesbrough	12 points
4 points v	Coventry C, Crystal Palace	8 points

Harvey Darvill, who died tragically days after the home game against Coventry.

1925-26

Division Two

	P	W	D	L	F	A	Pts
Sheffield Wednesday	42	27	6	9	88	48	60
Derby County	42	25	7	10	77	42	57
Chelsea	42	19	14	9	76	49	52
Wolverhampton W	42	21	7	14	84	60	49
Swansea Town	42	19	11	12	77	57	49
Blackpool	42	17	11	14	76	69	45
Oldham Athletic	42	18	8	16	74	62	44
Port Vale	42	19	6	17	79	69	44
South Shields	42	18	8	16	74	65	44
Middlesbrough	42	21	2	19	77	68	44
Portsmouth	42	17	10	15	79	74	44
Preston North End	42	18	7	17	71	84	43
Hull City	42	16	9	17	63	61	41
Southampton	42	15	8	19	63	63	38
Darlington	42	14	10	18	72	77	38
Bradford City	42	13	10	19	47	66	36
Nottingham Forest	42	14	8	20	51	73	36
Barnsley	42	12	12	18	58	84	36
Fulham	42	11	12	19	46	77	34
Clapton Orient	42	12	9	21	50	65	33
Stoke City	42	12	8	22	54	77	32
Stockport County	42	8	9	25	51	97	25

Manager: Andy Ducat

No		Date	V	Opponents	R	H-T	F-T	Scorers	Atte
1	A	29	A	Sheffield W	L	0-1	0-3		21,17
2		31	H	Swansea T	L	0-0	0-1		13,75
3	S	5	H	Stoke C	L	2-3	2-4	Edmonds, White	15,60
4		12	A	Oldham A	L	0-2	0-4		13,66
5		19	H	Stockport C	W	0-0	1-0	Edmonds	7,02
6		21	A	Swansea T	L	0-1	0-6		16,62
7		26	A	Chelsea	L	0-1	0-4		49,37
8	O	3	A	South Shields	L	1-3	2-5	Kennedy, Penn	7,32
9		5	H	Wolverhampton W	L	1-1	1-2	Penn	6,37
10		10	H	Preston NE	W	1-0	2-1	Pape 2	19,89
11		17	H	Clapton O	L	0-2	0-2		26,47
12		24	A	Barnsley	D	1-1	2-2	Prouse, Pape	8,30
13		31	H	Darlington	W	2-0	4-0	Pape 2, Ferguson 2	19,39
14	N	7	A	Hull C	L	0-1	0-1		6,99
15		14	H	Derby C	D	0-0	1-1	Harris	12,69
16		21	A	Nottingham F	D	1-1	2-2	Craig, Barrett	6,48
17		28	H	Southampton	D	0-0	1-1	Craig	13,27
18	D	5	A	Blackpool	L	0-1	0-2		6,78
19		12	H	Port Vale	D	0-1	3-3	Ferguson, Barrett, Craig	11,45
20		19	A	Bradford C	D	0-0	0-0		7,79
21		25	H	Middlesbrough	W	1-0	2-0	Pape, Penn	19,61
22		26	A	Middlesbrough	L	0-3	0-4		17,4
23	J	2	H	Shefield W	W	2-0	3-0	Pape, McNabb, Penn	17,62
24		16	A	Stoke C	L	0-1	0-5		7,61
25		23	H	Oldham A	W	0-0	2-1	McNabb, Craig	13,78
26	F	6	H	Chelsea	L	0-2	0-3		42,61
27		9	A	Stockport C	W	1-0	2-1	Harris, Prouse	4,24
28		13	H	South Shields	W	0-0	2-1	Pape, McNabb	22,33
29		27	A	Clapton O	D	0-0	1-1	Craig	20,65
30	M	13	A	Darlington	W	1-1	2-1	Linfoot, Pape	7,76
31		20	H	Hull C	D	1-0	1-1	Pape	14,60
32		25	A	Preston NE	L	0-0	1-2	Pape	6,02
33		27	A	Derby C	L	1-2	1-3	Edmonds	13,60
34	A	2	A	Portsmouth	D	0-0	0-0		20,75
35		3	H	Nottingham F	L	0-1	0-2		19,34
36		5	H	Portsmouth	L	1-1	2-3	Prouse 2	13,04
37		10	A	Southampton	L	0-1	0-2		7,46
38		12	A	Wolverhampton W	D	0-0	0-0		8,85
39		17	H	Blackpool	D	1-1	1-1	Craig	14,68
40		19	H	Barnsley	D	2-0	2-2	Prouse 2	7,12
41		24	A	Port Vale	W	1-0	1-0	Prouse	9,2
42	M	1	H	Bradford C	W	2-0	2-0	Craig, Penn	17,77
									App
									Goa

FA Cup

No		Date	V	Opponents	R	H-T	F-T	Scorers	Atte
3	J	9	A	Everton	D	0-1	1-1	Craig	46,00
R		14	H	Everton	W	0-0	1-0	White	20,1
4		30	H	Liverpool	W	2-1	3-1	Pape 2, Penn	36,38
5	F	20	A	Notts C	W	0-0	1-0	Prouse	33,0
6	M	6	H	Manchester U	L	1-1	1-2	Pape	28,6

Did you know that?

Teenage goalkeeper Ernie Beecham made his debut against Blackpool in December 1925. He then went on to make 130 consecutive appearances, beating Reynolds' record. It remains today a record for the consecutive appearances from a debut. Beecham's run was ended by a broken neck sustained diving at the feet of an Exeter forward named Death in November 1928.

2	Fleming finale
3	Dyer debut
4	Barrett debut
11	Torrance finale
12	McNabb debut
18	Beecham debut
36	Bagge finale
40	Edmonds finale
41	Chaplin finale

Boot	Fleming	Chaplin	Oliver	Torrance	Bagge	McCree	Prouse	White	Craig	Penn	Wolfe	Dyer	Edmonds	Packham	Riddell	Barrett	McKenna	Kennedy	Ferguson	Garnish	Harris	Pape	Probert	McNabb	Beecham	Linfoot	Caesar	Moseley	Gregory	
1	2	3	4	5	6	7	8	9	10	11																				1
1	2	3	4	5	6	7	8	9		11	10																			2
1		3	4	5	6			8		11	10	2	9	7																3
		3	4					8	11	7	10	2	9		5	6	1													4
		3	8		4		7		10	11		2	9		5	6	1													5
		3	8		4		7		10			2	9			6	1	5	11											6
		3	5		4		8		10	7		2	9			6	1		11											7
		3	5	6	4		8		10	11		2					1	9		7										8
		3	5	6	4		8	9	7	11		2	10				1													9
		3	5	6				8		11			10			4	1				7	9	2							10
		3	4	5						11	10	2	8			6	1				7	9								11
1		3	6				8				10	2				4			11		7	9		5						12
1		3	6				8				10	2				4			11		7	9		5						13
1		3	6				8				10	2				4			11		7	9		5						14
1		3	6								10	2	8			4			11		7	9		5						15
1		3	4						8		10	2				6			11		7	9		5						16
1		3	4						10		8	2				6			11		7	9		5						17
		3	4						8		10	2				6			11		7	9		5	1					18
		3	4						8			2	10			6			11		7	9		5	1					19
		3	4						8	11		2	10			6					7	9		5	1					20
		3	4						8	11		2	10			6					7	9		5	1					21
			4						8	11		2	10			6					7	9	3	5	1					22
		3	4				10		8	11		2				6					7	9		5	1					23
			4					10	8	11		2	9			6					7		3	5	1					24
			4						8	11		2	10			6					7	9	3	5	1					25
					4		10		8	6						3			11		7	9	2	5	1					26
			4				10		8	6						3			11		7	9	2	5	1					27
			4				10		8	11		2				6					7	9	3	5	1					28
			4				10		8	6		2				3			11		7	9		5	1					29
		3	4				10		8	6		2									7	9		5	1	11				30
		3	4						8	10		2				6					7	9		5	1	11				31
			4				10		8	6		2				3			11		7	9		5	1					32
			4				10		8	11		2	9			6					7		3	5	1					33
		3	4						8	11	10					6						9	2	5	1	7				34
		3	4						8		10					6			11			9	2	5	1	7				35
		3	4		7		10		8							6			11			9	2	5	1					36
			4				10		8			2				6			11			9	3	5	1	7				37
			4						10			2				6			11		7	9	3		1		5	8		38
			4				8		10	11		2				6					7	9	3	5	1					39
		3	4				8		11			2	10			6		9						5	1	7				40
		10	4				8		11			2				6		9						5	1	7			3	41
			4				8		10	11		2				6					7	9		5	1				3	42
9	2	29	41	7	10	2	24	7	34	27	13	34	17	1	2	36	8	4	18	1	27	29	14	30	25	7	1	1	2	A
-	-	-	-	-	-	-	7	1	7	5	-	-	3	-	-	2	-	1	3	-	2	11	-	3	-	1	-	-	-	G

Boot	Fleming	Chaplin	Oliver	Torrance	Bagge	McCree	Prouse	White	Craig	Penn	Wolfe	Dyer	Edmonds	Packham	Riddell	Barrett	McKenna	Kennedy	Ferguson	Garnish	Harris	Pape	Probert	McNabb	Beecham	Linfoot	Caesar	Moseley	Gregory	
		3	4				10		8	11		2				6					7	9		5	1					3
		3	4					10	8	11		2	9			6					7			5	1					R
			4				10		8	11		2				6					7	9	3	5	1					4
			4				10		8	6		2				3			11		7	9		5	1					5
		3	4						8	6		2	10						11		7	9		5	1					6

0 points v	Chelsea, Stoke C, Swansea T	0 points
1 point v	Blackpool, Clapton O, Derby C, Hull C, Nottingham F, Portsmouth, Southampton Wolves	8 points
2 points v	Barnsley, Middlesbrough, Oldham A, Preston NE, Sheffield W, South Shields	12 points
3 points v	Bradford C, Port Vale	6 points
4 points v	Darlington, Stockport C	8 points

John Dean, back on the board as Chairman.

1926-27

Division Two

	P	W	D	L	F	A	Pts
Middlesbrough	42	27	8	7	122	60	62
Portsmouth	42	23	8	11	87	49	54
Manchester City	42	22	10	10	108	61	54
Chelsea	42	20	12	10	62	52	52
Nottingham Forest	42	18	14	10	80	55	50
Preston North End	42	20	9	13	74	72	49
Hull City	42	20	7	15	63	52	47
Port Vale	42	16	13	13	88	78	45
Blackpool	42	18	8	16	95	80	44
Oldham Athletic	42	19	6	17	74	84	44
Barnsley	42	17	9	16	88	87	43
Swansea Town	42	16	11	15	68	72	43
Southampton	42	15	12	15	60	62	42
Reading	42	16	8	18	64	72	40
Wolverhampton W	42	14	7	21	73	75	35
Notts County	42	15	5	22	70	96	35
Grimsby Town	42	11	12	19	74	91	34
Fulham	42	13	8	21	58	92	34
South Shields	42	11	11	20	71	96	33
Clapton Orient	42	12	7	23	60	96	31
Darlington	42	12	6	24	79	98	30
Bradford City	42	7	9	26	50	88	23

Manager: Joe Bradshaw

Did you know that?

Jimmy Temple made his debut in January 1927. A fast, goalscoring winger, he jumped two divisions in May 1931 to sign for First Division Sunderland. Only two other Fulham players were sold to top-flight clubs during the entire inter-war period.

25 Temple debut
35 Prouse finale

No		Date	V	Opponents	R	H-T	F-T	Scorers	Atter
1	A	28	A	Manchester C	L	2-3	2-4	Tonner, McNabb (pen)	35,11
2		30	H	Nottingham F	W	0-1	2-1	Craig, Wolfe	12,16
3	S	4	H	Darlington	W	2-1	2-1	Harris, McNabb	22,30
4		11	A	Portsmouth	L	0-2	0-2		15,23
5		13	H	Barnsley	W	0-0	1-0	Tonner	9,85
6		18	H	Oldham A	D	1-1	1-1	Tonner	18,57
7		25	A	Chelsea	D	2-2	2-2	McNabb, Tonner	46,08
8	O	2	A	Grimsby T	L	0-2	0-2		12,16
9		7	A	Nottingham F	L	0-1	0-2		7,48
10		9	H	Blackpool	W	1-0	1-0	McNabb	16,23
11		16	H	South Shields	D	1-1	2-2	Smith, (Phizackles og)	19,50
12		23	A	Preston NE	D	1-2	2-2	Penn, Prouse	17,22
13		30	H	Bradford C	D	1-1	1-1	Smith	15,30
14	N	6	A	Southampton	L	0-0	1-4	Smith	8,39
15		13	H	Port Vale	W	2-1	6-2	McNabb 2, Prouse 2, Tonner, Smith	3,10
16		20	A	Middlesbrough	L	0-3	1-6	Tonner	15,75
17		27	H	Clapton O	W	1-0	2-0	Prouse, Tonner	18,85
18	D	4	A	Notts C	L	0-2	0-4		9,48
19		11	H	Wolverhampton W	W	2-1	4-1	Penn 2, Prouse, Craig	17,55
20		18	A	Hull C	L	0-1	0-2		11,10
21		25	A	Reading	L	0-1	0-2		14,54
22		27	H	Reading	L	1-0	1-2	McNabb	39,76
23		28	A	Barnsley	L	0-1	0-5		5,47
24	J	15	H	Manchester C	L	0-2	2-5	Penn, Craig	20,50
25		22	A	Darlington	L	0-2	0-5		6,84
26	F	5	A	Oldham A	W	0-0	3-2	Craig 2, Temple	10,94
27		12	H	Chelsea	L	1-0	1-2	Pape	31,50
28		19	H	Grimsby T	L	0-2	0-5		6,61
29		26	A	Blackpool	D	0-0	0-0		7,95
30	M	5	A	South Shields	D	1-1	1-1	Hoyland	4,29
31		12	H	Preston NE	L	0-0	0-1		16,15
32		14	H	Portsmouth	D	0-0	0-0		6,17
33		19	A	Bradford C	L	0-0	0-1		10,45
34		28	H	Southampton	W	1-0	3-0	Prouse 2, Penn	7,79
35	A	2	A	Port Vale	L	1-3	1-7	Smith	7,64
36		9	H	Middlesbrough	L	0-0	0-3		12,17
37		15	H	Swansea T	W	2-2	4-3	Tonner 2, Oliver, Penn	24,55
38		16	A	Clapton O	W	2-1	3-2	Tonner, Smith, Penn	16,92
39		18	A	Swansea T	L	1-2	2-4	Tonner 2	11,31
40		23	H	Notts C	W	3-0	3-0	Hoyland 2, Temple	12,64
41		30	A	Wolverhampton W	L	1-1	1-2	McNabb	8,59
42	M	7	H	Hull C	W	2-0	3-1	Smith, Tonner, McNabb	8,91
									App
									Goal

FA Cup

No		Date	V	Opponents	R	H-T	F-T	Scorers	Atter
3	J	8	H	Chesterfield	W	3-2	4-3	Tonner 2, Pape, Craig	16,57
4		29	H	Burnley	L	0-2	0-4		23,56

Beecham	Dyer	Barrett	Oliver	McNabb	Wolfe	Harris J	Craig	Pape	Tonner	Penn	Scullion	Prouse	Pike	Probert	Gregory	Walters	Smith	Brown	Johnson	Temple	Pilkington	Moseley	Harris G	Hoyland	
	2	3	4	5	6	7	8	9	10	11															1
	2	3	4	5	6	7	8		10	11	9														2
	2	3	4	5	6	7	10		9	11		8													3
	2	3	4	5	6	7	8	9	10	11															4
	2	3	4	5	6	7	8	9	10	11															5
	2	3	4	5	6	7	10	9	8	11															6
	2	3	4	5	6		10	9	8	11			7												7
		3	4	5	6		10	9	8	11			7	2											8
			4	5		11	10		8	6		9	7	2	3										9
	2		4	5		7	10		8	11		9			3	6									10
	2		4	5		7	10		8	11					3	6	9								11
	2		4	6		7	10			11		8			3	5	9								12
	2		4	6		7	10			11		8			3	5	9								13
	2		4	6		7	11		10			8			3	5	9								14
	2		4	6		7			10	11		8			3	5	9								15
	2		4	6		7			10	11		8			3	5	9								16
			4	5			7		10	11		8			3	6	9	2							17
			4	5			7		10	11		8			3	6	9	2							18
		6	4	10			7			11		8			3	5	9	2							19
		6	4	5			7		10	11		8			3		9	2							20
		6	4	5			7		10	11		8			3		9	2							21
		6	4	10			7			11		8			3	5	9	2							22
	3	6	4		10		7	9	8	11						5		2							23
	2	3	4	5			7	9	10	11		8				6									24
			4			11		9		6		10			3		8	2	5	7					25
		6	4	5			8	9	10	11					3			2		7					26
		6	4				8	9	10	11					3	5		2		7					27
		6	4				8	9	10	11					3	5		2		7					28
	2	3	4	5				9		11							10			7	6	8			29
	2	6	4	5			8			11							9			7			3	10	30
	2	6	4	5			8			11							9			7			3	10	31
	2	6	4	5			8			11							9			7			3	10	32
	2	6	4	5			8			11		10					9			7			3		33
	2	6	4	5			8			11		10					9			7			3		34
	2	3	4	5			8			11		10				6	9			7					35
	2	6	4	5			8		10	11					3		9			7					36
	2	6	4	5			8		10	11					3		9			7					37
	2	6	4	5			8		10	11					3		9			7					38
	2	6	4	5			8		10	11					3		9			7					39
	2	6	4	5			8			11					3		9			7				10	40
	2	6	4	5			8			11					3		9			7				10	41
	2	6	4	5			8		10	11					3		9			7					42
2	30	31	42	38	9	15	38	13	28	41	1	19	3	2	25	16	27	11	1	18	1	1	5	5	A
	-	-	1	9	1	1	5	1	13	7	-	7	-	-	-	-	7	-	-	2	-	-	-	3	G

Beecham	Dyer	Barrett	Oliver	McNabb	Wolfe	Harris J	Craig	Pape	Tonner	Penn	Scullion	Prouse	Pike	Probert	Gregory	Walters	Smith	Brown	Johnson	Temple	Pilkington	Moseley	Harris G	Hoyland	
		3	4	5			7	9	10	11		8				6		2							3
		6	4				7	9	10	11		8			3	5		2							4

0 points v	Grimsby T, Manchester C, Middlesbrough, Reading	0 points
1 point v	Bradford C, Chelsea, Portsmouth, Preston NE	4 points
2 points v	Barnsley, Darlington, Hull C, Nottingham F, Notts C, Port Vale, South Shields, Southampton, Swansea, Wolves	20 points
3 points v	Blackpool, Oldham A	6 points
4 points v	Clapton O	4 points

David 'Jock' McNabb, centre half signed from Portsmouth.

1927-28

Division Two

	P	W	D	L	F	A	Pts
Manchester City	42	25	9	8	100	59	59
Leeds United	42	25	7	10	98	49	57
Chelsea	42	23	8	11	75	45	54
Preston North End	42	22	9	11	100	66	53
Stoke City	42	22	8	12	78	59	52
Swansea Town	42	18	12	12	75	63	48
Oldham Athletic	42	19	8	15	75	51	46
West Bromwich Albion	42	17	12	13	90	70	46
Port Vale	42	18	8	16	68	57	44
Nottingham Forest	42	15	10	17	83	84	40
Grimsby Town	42	14	12	16	69	83	40
Bristol City	42	15	9	18	76	79	39
Barnsley	42	14	11	17	65	85	39
Hull City	42	12	15	15	41	54	39
Notts County	42	13	12	17	68	74	38
Wolverhampton W	42	13	10	19	63	91	36
Southampton	42	14	7	21	68	77	35
Reading	42	11	13	18	53	75	35
Blackpool	42	13	8	21	83	101	34
Clapton Orient	42	11	12	19	55	85	34
Fulham	42	13	7	22	68	89	33
South Shields	42	7	9	26	56	111	23

Manager: Joe Bradshaw

Did you know that?

In January 1928, Fulham lost 8-4 at Barnsley, an aggregate score for a match that has only been equalled once since, the 10-2 win over Torquay in September 1931.

1	Debuts for Elliott and Steele
16	Penn's 300th game
25	Oliver's 200th game
41	Avey debut
42	Elliott finale

No		Date	V	Opponents	R	H-T	F-T	Scorers	Atte
1	A	27	H	Preston NE	D	2-2	2-2	Elliott 2	25,6
2		29	A	Nottingham F	L	0-4	0-7		11,4
3	S	3	A	Swansea T	L	0-2	1-2	Elliott	14,6
4		10	H	Chelsea	D	0-1	1-1	McKenna	39,8
5		15	H	Nottingham F	W	2-0	2-0	McKenna, Elliott	9,4
6		17	H	Barnsley	W	2-1	3-1	Elliott, Craig, Devan	16,9
7		24	A	Wolverhampton W	L	0-2	1-3	McKenna	11,6
8	O	1	H	Port Vale	W	1-0	4-0	Hoyland, McKenna, Elliott, McNabb	10,5
9		8	A	South Shields	L	0-2	1-2	Devan	6,2
10		15	H	Leeds U	D	1-0	1-1	Craig	16,7
11		22	A	Bristol C	L	0-2	0-3		7,7
12		29	H	West Bromich A	W	0-1	3-1	Elliott 2, Temple	20,5
13	N	5	A	Clapton O	L	1-2	2-3	Elliott, Harris	15,8
14		12	H	Stoke C	L	1-0	1-5	Temple	10,7
15		19	A	Southampton	L	1-2	2-5	Elliott 2	4,6
16		26	H	Grimsby T	D	2-0	2-2	McKenna, Elliott	6,3
17	D	3	A	Oldham A	L	2-3	2-4	Elliott 2	10,1
18		10	H	Notts C	W	1-0	2-1	Elliott, Craig	11,5
19		17	A	Reading	L	0-1	1-2	McKenna	8,4
20		24	H	Blackpool	D	2-1	2-2	Penn, Elliott	10,8
21		27	A	Hull C	L	0-3	2-3	McNabb (pen), McKenna	14,0
22		31	A	Preston NE	L	0-1	0-1		14,8
23	J	7	H	Swansea T	W	2-1	3-2	Elliott, McKenna, Craig	15,0
24		21	A	Chelsea	L	1-1	1-2	Elliott	42,2
25		28	A	Barnsley	L	1-5	4-8	Craig, Elliott 2, Johnson	4,5
26	F	4	H	Wolverhampton W	W	4-0	7-0	Elliott 3, McKenna, Craig, Temple 2	12,9
27		11	A	Port Vale	L	0-3	1-4	Penn	7,5
28		18	H	South Shields	W	0-0	2-0	Craig, Smith	15,6
29		25	A	Leeds U	L	0-0	1-2	Temple	17,3
30	M	3	H	Bristol C	W	3-0	5-0	Elliott 3, Craig, Temple	18,5
31		10	A	West Bromich A	L	0-1	0-4		17,6
32		17	H	Clapton O	W	0-0	2-0	McKenna, Penn	21,4
33		24	A	Stoke C	L	1-3	1-5	Craig	10,1
34		26	H	Hull C	L	0-1	0-2		7,0
35		31	H	Southampton	W	1-0	1-0	Smith	9,3
36	A	6	A	Manchester C	L	1-2	1-2	McNabb	50,6
37		7	A	Grimsby T	L	0-1	0-1		9,0
38		9	H	Manchester C	D	1-1	1-1	Temple	25,9
39		14	H	Oldham A	D	1-0	1-1	Ferguson	14,3
40		21	A	Notts C	W	0-0	1-0	Ferguson	7,6
41		28	H	Reading	W	0-0	1-0	Craig	18,9
42	M	5	A	Blackpool	L	0-2	0-4		14,4
									Ap
									Goa

FA Cup

3	J	14	A	Southport	L	0-1	0-3		8,0

Beecham	Barrett	Harris	Oliver	McNabb	Steele	Temple	Craig	Elliott	Hoyland	Penn	Dyer	Devan	McKenna	Lowe	Johnson	Gregory	Horler	Hebden	Sparke	Smith	Walters	Lawson	Ferguson	Avey	
1	2	3	4	5	6	7	8	9	10	11															1
1	2	3	4	5	6	7	8	9	10	11															2
1	3		4	5	6	7	8	9			2	11	10												3
1	3		4	5	6		10	9		11	2	7	8												4
1	3		4	5	6		10	9		11	2	7	8												5
1	3		4	5	6		10	9		11	2	7	8												6
1	3		4	5	6		10	9		11	2	7	8												7
1	3		4	5	6			9	10	11	2	7	8												8
1	3		4		6			9	10	11	2	7	8	5											9
1	3		4		6	7	10	9		11	2		8	5											10
1	3		4	5	6	7	10	9		11	2		8												11
1	3		4	5	6	7	10	9		11	2		8												12
1	3	2	4	5		7	10	9	8	11					6										13
1	3		4	5		7	10	9		11	2		8		6										14
1	3		4	5	6		7	9	10	11			8			2									15
1	3		4	5	6		7	9	10	11	2		8												16
1	3		4	5	6		7	9	10	11	2		8												17
1			4	5	6		7	9	10	11	2		8			3									18
1			4	5	6		7	9	10	11	2		8			3									19
1			4	5	6		7	9	10	11	2		8				3								20
1	6		4	5			7	9	10	11			8				3	2							21
1	6		4	5			7	9	10				8				3	2	11						22
1	6		4	5			7	9	10	11			8				3	2							23
1	6		4	5	8		7	9	10	11							3	2							24
1	6				8		7	9	10	11				5	4		3	2							25
1	6		4	5		7	8	9		11			10			3		2							26
1	6		4	5		7	8	9		11						3		2		10					27
1	6		4	5			8	9	7	11						3		2		10					28
1	6		4	5	10	7	8	9		11						3		2							29
1	6		4	5		7	8	9		11			10			3		2							30
1	4		6	5		7	8	9		11						3		2	10						31
1	6		4	5		7	8	9		11			10				3	2							32
1	6		4	5		7	8	9		11			10				3	2							33
1	6		4	5		7	8	9		11			10			3		2							34
1	3		4	5	6	7	8	10		11								2		9					35
1	3		4	5	6	7	8	10		11								2		9					36
1	3		4		6	7	8	10		11								2		9	5				37
1	3		4	5		7	8	10		11								2		9		6			38
1	3		4	5		7		9		10								2		8		6	11		39
1	3		8	5	4	7	10	9		6								2					11		40
1	3		4	5		7	10	9		6								2					11	8	41
1	3		4	5		7	10	9		6								2					11	8	42
42	39	3	41	38	25	24	39	42	17	40	16	7	25	3	3	10	8	22	2	7	1	2	4	2	A
-	-	1	-	3	-	7	10	26	1	3	-	2	10	-	1	-	-	-	-	2	-	-	2	-	G

Beecham	Barrett	Harris	Oliver	McNabb	Steele	Temple	Craig	Elliott	Hoyland	Penn	Dyer	Devan	McKenna	Lowe	Johnson	Gregory	Horler	Hebden	Sparke	Smith	Walters	Lawson	Ferguson	Avey	
1	6		4	5			7	9	10	11			8				3	2							3

0 points v	Hull C, Stoke C	0 points
1 point v	Blackpool, Chelsea, Grimsby T, Leeds U, Manchester C, Oldham A, Preston NE	7 points
2 points v	Barnsley, Bristol C, Clapton O, Nottingham F, Port Vale, Reading, South Shields, Southampton, Swansea T, West Bromwich A, Wolves	22 points
3 points v		0 points
4 points v	Notts C	4 points

Centre forward Sid Elliot broke the club's scroring record even though Fulham were relegated.

1928-29

Division Three South

	P	W	D	L	F	A	Pts
Charlton Athletic	42	23	8	11	86	60	54
Crystal Palace	42	23	8	11	81	67	54
Northampton Town	42	20	12	10	96	57	52
Plymouth Argyle	42	20	12	10	83	51	52
Fulham	42	21	10	11	101	71	52
Queen's Park Rangers	42	19	14	9	82	61	52
Luton Town	42	19	11	12	89	73	49
Watford	42	19	10	13	79	74	48
Bournemouth	42	19	9	14	84	77	47
Swindon Town	42	15	13	14	75	72	43
Coventry City	42	14	14	14	62	57	42
Southend United	42	15	11	16	80	75	41
Brentford	42	14	10	18	56	60	38
Walsall	42	13	12	17	73	79	38
Brighton & Hove Albion	42	16	6	20	58	76	38
Newport County	42	13	9	20	69	86	35
Norwich City	42	14	6	22	69	81	34
Torquay United	42	14	6	22	66	84	34
Bristol Rovers	42	13	7	22	60	79	33
Merthyr Town	42	11	8	23	55	103	30
Exeter City	42	9	11	22	67	88	29
Gillingham	42	10	9	23	43	83	29

Manager: Joe Bradshaw

Did you know that?

Fulham left half Alex Steele added to the two caps he won while at Charlton when he played for Northern Ireland against Wales at Wrexham in February 1929, the Cottagers' first Irish international since joining the League.

1 Debuts for Haley, Price and Rosier
30 Hammond debut
32 Gibbon debut

No	Date		V	Opponents	R	H-T	F-T	Scorers	Attend
1	A	25	A	Gillingham	D	1-2	2-2	Price, Avey	9,457
2	S	1	H	Plymouth A	W	3-0	5-2	Temple, Avey, Haley, Price, Penn	21,556
3		5	A	Crystal Palace	L	1-0	1-2	Temple	15,005
4		8	A	Bournemouth	L	0-0	0-1		8,031
5		10	H	Crystal Palace	D	2-2	2-2	Haley 2	11,239
6		15	A	Queen's Park R	L	1-1	1-2	Price	21,805
7		22	H	Bristol R	W	3-0	6-1	Avey 2, Price, Temple, Penn, McNabb	15,730
8		29	A	Watford	W	2-0	6-2	Price 3, Haley 2, Temple	15,011
9	O	6	H	Walsall	W	3-1	5-1	Temple, Oliver, Haley 2, Price	19,214
10		13	A	Newport C	D	1-2	3-3	Haley, Temple, Avey	6,994
11		20	H	Merthyr T	W	3-0	4-0	McNabb 2, Haley, Temple	16,515
12		27	A	Southend U	W	1-0	1-0	Temple	8,843
13	N	3	H	Exeter C	D	0-0	0-0		19,474
14		10	A	Brighton & HA	L	0-1	0-2		10,351
15		17	H	Norwich C	W	0-1	2-1	Temple, Price	15,050
16	D	1	H	Northampton T	W	0-1	2-1	Penn, Lawson	16,952
17		15	H	Luton T	W	3-2	4-2	McNabb, Temple 2, Penn	11,069
18		22	A	Brentford	W	0-0	2-1	Avey, Craig	8,876
19		25	H	Torquay U	W	1-0	2-1	Haley, McNabb (pen)	20,327
20		26	A	Torquay U	D	1-1	1-1	Penn	6,028
21		29	H	Gillingham	W	3-0	4-2	Temple, Haley, Avey 2	16,816
22	J	5	A	Plymouth A	L	1-1	2-4	Haley, Temple	15,508
23		12	A	Coventry C	W	0-1	2-1	Temple, Haley	18,088
24		19	H	Bournemouth	W	0-0	3-0	Haley 2, McNabb (pen)	17,356
25		26	H	Queen's Park R	W	2-0	5-0	Haley 2, Temple 2, Price	26,743
26	F	2	A	Bristol R	L	1-1	3-5	Craig, Temple 2	5,272
27		9	H	Watford	L	2-1	2-3	Haley, Price	19,430
28		16	A	Walsall	D	0-2	2-2	Temple, Price	5,999
29		23	H	Newport C	L	1-1	2-3	Allen, Temple	15,361
30	M	2	A	Merthyr T	L	0-1	1-4	Penn	2,987
31		9	H	Southend U	L	2-0	2-4	Hammond, Temple	16,189
32		16	A	Exeter C	W	2-1	4-1	Avey 3, Hammond	5,231
33		23	H	Brighton & HA	W	0-0	3-1	Penn, Avey, Hammond	17,183
34		29	H	Swindon T	W	1-0	2-0	Price, Penn	26,868
35		30	A	Norwich C	D	1-2	2-2	Hammond 2	7,737
36	A	1	A	Swindon T	W	0-1	2-1	Temple, Gibbon	6,540
37		6	H	Charlton A	L	0-2	2-5	Avey, Temple	28,349
38		13	A	Northampton T	D	0-2	3-3	Temple 2, Avey	9,436
39		17	A	Charlton A	D	0-0	0-0		14,071
40		20	H	Coventry C	D	0-1	2-2	Temple, Penn	15,300
41		27	A	Luton T	W	1-0	3-1	Penn, Haley, Avey	13,463
42	M	4	H	Brentford	W	0-0	1-0	Craig	16,524
									App
									Goals

FA Cup

No	Date		V	Opponents	R	H-T	F-T	Scorers	Attend
1	N	24	A	Coventry C	W	2-1	4-1	Temple 2, Price, Penn	28,000
2	D	8	H	Luton T	D	0-0	0-0		19,78
R		13	A	Luton T	L	0-2	1-4	Temple	11,25

Beecham	Barrett	Rosier	Oliver	McNabb	Steele	Temple	Avey	Haley	Price	Penn	Dyer	Craig	Lawson	Mason	Bird	Allen	Hammond	Meeson	Hebden	Gibbon	Binks	
1	2	3	4	5	6	7	8	9	10	11												1
1	2	3	4	5	6	7	9	8	10	11												2
1	2	3	4	5	6	7	9	8	10	11												3
1	2	3	4	5	6	7	8	9	10	11												4
1	3		4	5	6	7	9	8	10	11	2											5
1	3		4	5		7	9	8	10	6	2	11										6
1	2	3	4	5	6	7	9	8	10	11												7
1	3	2	4	5	6	7	9	8	10	11												8
1	3	2	4	5	6	7	8	9	10	11												9
1	3	2	4	5	6	7	8	9	10	11												10
1	3	2	4	5	6	7	9	8	10	11												11
1	2	3	4	5	6	7	8	9	10	11												12
1	2	3	4	5		7	9	8	10	11			6									13
	2	3	4	5		7	9	8	10	11			6	1								14
	4	2	5			7	9	8	10	11			6	1	3							15
	3	2	5		4	7	9	8	10	11			6	1								16
			4	5		7	9	8		11	2	10	6	1	3							17
			4	5		7	9	8		11	2	10	6	1	3							18
			4	5		7	9	8		11	2	10	6	1	3							19
			5		4	7	9	8		11	2	10	6	1	3							20
			4	5		7	9	8		11	2	10	6	1	3							21
			4	5		7	9	8		11	2	10	6	1	3							22
			4	5	6	7	9	8	10	11	2			1	3							23
			4	5		7	9	8	10	11	2		6	1	3							24
			4	5		7	9	8	10	11	2		6	1	3							25
			4	5		7	9		8	11	2	10	6	1	3							26
	3	2	4	5		7	10	9	8	11			6	1								27
	3	2	5		4	7		8	10	11			6	1		9						28
	6	2	4	5		7		8	10	11				1	3	9						29
	3	2	5		4	7	9	8		11			6	1			10					30
	3		4	5	6	7	8	9		11							10	1	2			31
	3		4			7	9		10	11			6	1			8			2	5	32
	3		4			7	9		8	11			6	1			10			2	5	33
	3		4			7		8	10	11			6	1			9			2	5	34
	3		4			7		8	10	11			6	1			9			2	5	35
	3		4		8	7			10	11	2		6	1						9	5	36
	3		4			7	9	8	10	11			6	1						2	5	37
	6		4	5	8	7	9			11	2	10		1	3							38
	6		4	5		7	9			11	2	8		1	3		10					39
	6		4	5		7	9			11	2	8		1	3		10					40
	6		4	5		7	9	8		11	2	10		1	3							41
		2	4		5	7	9	10		11		8	6	1	3							42
3	31	19	42	30	20	42	37	35	29	42	17	13	23	28	17	2	8	1	1	6	6	A
-	-	-	1	6	-	26	15	19	13	10	-	3	1	-	-	1	5	-	-	1	-	G

Beecham	Barrett	Rosier	Oliver	McNabb	Steele	Temple	Avey	Haley	Price	Penn	Dyer	Craig	Lawson	Mason	Bird	Allen	Hammond	Meeson	Hebden	Gibbon	Binks	
	3	2	5		4	7	9	8	10	11			6	1								1
	3	2	5		6	7	9	8	10	11			4	1								2
		2	5	9	4	7		8	10	11			6	1	3							R

0 points v		0 points
1 point v	Charlton A, Crystal Palace, Newport C	3 points
2 points v	Bournemouth, Brighton & HA, Bristol R, Merthyr T, Plymouth A, Queen's Park R, Southend U, Watford	16 points
3 points v	Coventry C, Exeter C, Gillingham, Northampton T, Norwich C, Torquay U, Walsall	21 points
4 points v	Brentford, Luton T, Swindon T	12 points

Jimmy Temple, top scorer from the right wing.

1929-30

Division Three South

	P	W	D	L	F	A	Pts
Plymouth Argyle	42	30	8	4	98	38	68
Brentford	42	28	5	9	94	44	61
Queen's Park Rangers	42	21	9	12	80	68	51
Northampton Town	42	21	8	13	82	58	50
Brighton & Hove Albion	42	21	8	13	87	63	50
Coventry City	42	19	9	14	88	73	47
Fulham	42	18	11	13	87	83	47
Norwich City	42	18	10	14	88	77	46
Crystal Palace	42	17	12	13	81	74	46
Bournemouth	42	15	13	14	72	61	43
Southend United	42	15	13	14	69	59	43
Clapton Orient	42	14	13	15	55	62	41
Luton Town	42	14	12	16	64	78	40
Swindon Town	42	13	12	17	73	83	38
Watford	42	15	8	19	60	73	38
Exeter City	42	12	11	19	67	73	35
Walsall	42	13	8	21	71	78	34
Newport County	42	12	10	20	74	85	34
Torquay United	42	10	11	21	64	94	31
Bristol Rovers	42	11	8	23	67	93	30
Gillingham	42	11	8	23	51	80	30
Merthyr Town	42	6	9	27	60	135	21

Manager: Ned Liddell

Did you know that?

Bert Barrett played for England in the 3–0 win over Northern Ireland in Belfast in October 1929, just months after his wing-half partner Len Oliver was in the England side which beat Belgium 5–1 in Brussels. Remarkably, Fulham had two players capped for England while a Third Division club.

4	Dyer finale
FAC4	Penn's 400th game
27	Temple's 50th goal
29	Craig finale
32	Steele finale
36	Rosier finale
39	McNabb finale

No		Date	V	Opponents	R	H-T	F-T	Scorers	Atte
1	A	31	A	Norwich C	W	3-0	4-0	Temple 2, Haley, Avey	15,77
2	S	2	H	Bournemouth	D	1-2	3-3	Price 2, Haley	12,99
3		7	H	Crystal Palace	L	1-2	1-2	Avey	23,27
4		11	A	Bournemouth	L	0-3	0-5		6,84
5		14	A	Gillingham	W	0-0	1-0	Avey	7,90
6		16	A	Queen's Park R	D	0-0	0-0		12,49
7		21	H	Northampton T	W	0-0	1-0	Avey	20,40
8		28	A	Exeter C	L	0-1	1-2	Avey	5,89
9	O	5	H	Southend U	D	0-2	2-2	Temple, Craig	21,57
10		12	A	Luton T	L	1-1	1-4	Allen	10,05
11		19	H	Brentford	W	2-0	2-0	Hammond, Allen	25,89
12		26	A	Clapton O	W	1-1	4-2	Hammond 3, Barrett (pen)	15,59
13	N	2	H	Coventry C	W	1-0	2-0	Price, Hammond	15,31
14		9	A	Watford	D	0-0	0-0		12,44
15		16	H	Newport C	W	1-1	2-1	Penn, Avey	28,21
16		23	A	Torquay U	W	0-1	4-2	Price, Temple 3	4,38
17	D	7	A	Plymouth A	L	0-0	1-3	Hammond	15,65
18		21	A	Brighton & HA	L	0-2	0-5		4,20
19		25	H	Bristol R	W	4-1	6-2	Haley 3, Penn 2, Price	15,35
20		26	A	Bristol R	L	1-1	1-4	Allen	16,78
21		28	H	Norwich C	D	1-1	3-3	Haley 3	12,41
22	J	1	H	Swindon T	W	2-0	4-1	Temple 2, Haley 2	5,54
23		4	A	Crystal Palace	L	1-1	3-4	Allen, Temple, Hammond	17,73
24		18	H	Gillingham	W	1-1	2-1	Haley, Craig	15,19
25	F	1	H	Exeter C	D	1-1	2-2	Hammond, Penn	10,09
26		3	H	Merthyr T	W	4-1	5-4	Temple 2, Haley, Lawson, Penn	4,72
27		8	A	Southend U	W	2-0	2-1	Hammond, Temple	6,20
28		15	H	Luton T	D	1-0	1-1	Allen	13,73
29		22	A	Brentford	L	0-3	1-5	Hammond	21,96
30	M	1	H	Clapton O	D	2-2	2-2	Temple, Allen	17,01
31		8	A	Coventry C	L	1-2	1-3	Hammond	12,65
32		13	A	Northampton T	L	0-0	1-3	Murphy	4,72
33		15	H	Watford	W	1-1	6-1	Haley 4, Cox, Price	10,52
34		22	A	Newport C	D	0-1	1-1	Penn	4,62
35		29	H	Torquay U	W	1-0	1-0	Price	11,03
36	A	5	A	Merthyr T	W	2-1	4-3	Haley 3, Hammond	1,72
37		12	H	Plymouth A	L	0-0	1-3	Hammond	22,99
38		19	A	Swindon T	D	0-0	1-1	Avey	2,30
39		21	H	Walsall	W	2-1	3-2	Hammond, Price, Avey	11,44
40		22	A	Walsall	D	1-2	2-2	Temple, Haley	4,99
41		26	H	Brighton & HA	W	2-0	5-1	Haley, Hammond 3, Price	10,51
42	M	3	H	Queen's Park R	L	0-1	0-2		17,03
									App
									Goa

FA Cup

No		Date	V	Opponents	R	H-T	F-T	Scorers	Atte
1	N	30	H	Thames A	W	1-0	4-0	Penn, Avey, Barrett 2	13,99
2	D	14	A	Leyton	W	2-1	4-1	Penn 2, Barrett (pen), Hammond	14,00
3	J	11	H	Bournemouth	D	1-0	1-1	Price	21,80
R		15	A	Bournemouth	W	1-0	2-0	Haley, Barrett (pen)	12,38
4		25	A	Nottingham F	L	0-0	1-2	Haley	31,25

Beecham	Gibbon	Rosier	Oliver	McNabb	Barrett	Temple	Haley	Avey	Price	Penn	Cox	Dyer	Brown	Hammond	Regan	Craig	Binks	Allen	Steele	Henderson	Murphy	Lawson	Keeble	Bird	Mason	Boland	Bradley	
1	2	3	4	5	6	7	8	9	10	11																		1
1	2	3	4		6	7	8	9	10	11	5																	2
1	2	3	4	5	6	7	8	9	10	11																		3
1		3	4	5	6	7	9		10	11		2	8															4
1	2	3	4	5	6	7	8	9		11				10														5
1	2	3	4	5	6	7	8	9		11				10														6
1	3	2		5	6	7	8	9		11				10	4													7
1	3	2	4	5	6	7	8	9		11						10												8
1	3	2	4	5	6	7	8			11						10	9											9
1	3	2	4		6	7			10	11				8			5	9										10
1	3	2	4			7			10	11				8			5	9	6									11
1	3	2	4		6	7			10	11				8			5	9										12
1	3	2	4		6	7			10	11				8			5	9										13
1	3	2	4		6	7			10	11				8			5	9										14
1	3	2	4		6	7		9	10	11				8			5											15
1	3	2	4		6	7		9	10	11				8			5											16
1	3	2			6	7		9	10	11				8			5			4								17
1	3	2			6	7	8	9		11				10			5			4								18
1	3	2			6		8		10	11				9			5	7		4								19
1		2			6		8		7	11						10	5	9	3	4								20
1		2			6		9		10	11				8		7	5		3	4								21
1		2		5	6	7	9		10	11							3	8		4								22
1		3	4		2	7				11				10		8	5	9		6								23
1	3		4	5	2	7	9			11						8				6	10							24
1	3			5	2	7	9			11				8						4	10	6						25
1	3			5	2	7	8			11										4	10	6	9					26
1	3	2		5	6	7	8			11				10				9		4								27
1	3	2		5	6	7	8			11				10				9		4								28
1	3	2	4	5	6	7	9			11				10		8												29
1		2		5		7	8			11	6			10				9		4				3				30
	3	2		5		7	8				6			9						4	10				1	11		31
		2		5		7					4		8	9					6		10				1	11	3	32
1		2	4	5		7	9		10	11	6			8										3				33
1	3	2	4	5		7	9		10	11				8						6								34
1	3	2	4			7	9		10	11				8			5			6								35
1	3	2	4			7	9		10	11				8			5			6								36
1	3		4		6	7	9		10	11				8			5										2	37
1			4	5	3	7		9	10	6				8												11	2	38
			4	5	3	7		9	10	6				8											1	11	2	39
			8		3	7	9		10								5			4		6			1	11	2	40
			4		3	7	9		10					8			5					6			1	11	2	41
1			4		2	7	8	9		11				10			5					6		3				42
37	29	33	28	22	34	39	30	14	25	38	5	1	2	31	1	7	21	12	4	18	5	5	1	3	5	6	6	A
-	-	-	-	-	1	14	21	8	9	6	1	-	-	17	-	2	-	6	-	-	1	1	-	-	-	-	-	G

Beecham	Gibbon	Rosier	Oliver	McNabb	Barrett	Temple	Haley	Avey	Price	Penn	Cox	Dyer	Brown	Hammond	Regan	Craig	Binks	Allen	Steele	Henderson	Murphy	Lawson	Keeble	Bird	Mason	Boland	Bradley	
1	3	2			6	7		9	10	11				8			5			4								1
1	3	2			6	7		9	10	11				8			5			4								2
1	2		4	5	3	7	9		8	11				10						6								3
1	2		4	5	3	7	9		8	11				10						6								R
1	2		4	5	3	7	9			11				10					8	6								4

0 points v	Crystal Palace, Plymouth A	0 points
1 point v	Bournemouth, Exeter C, Luton T, Queen's Park R	4 points
2 points v	Brentford, Brighton & HA, Bristol R, Coventry C, Northampton T	10 points
3 points v	Clapton O, Newport C, Norwich C, Southend U, Swindon T, Walsall, Watford	21 points
4 points v	Gillingham, Merthyr T, Torquay U	12 points

Teddy Craig played the last of his 161 games for Fulham in February.

1930-31

Division Three South

	P	W	D	L	F	A	Pts
Notts County	42	24	11	7	97	46	59
Crystal Palace	42	22	7	13	107	71	51
Brentford	42	22	6	14	90	64	50
Brighton & Hove Albion	42	17	15	10	68	53	49
Southend United	42	22	5	15	76	60	49
Northampton Town	42	18	12	12	77	59	48
Luton Town	42	19	8	15	76	51	46
Queen's Park Rangers	42	20	3	19	82	75	43
Fulham	42	18	7	17	77	75	43
Bournemouth	42	15	13	14	72	73	43
Torquay United	42	17	9	16	80	84	43
Swindon Town	42	18	6	18	89	94	42
Exeter City	42	17	8	17	84	90	42
Coventry City	42	16	9	17	75	65	41
Bristol Rovers	42	16	8	18	75	92	40
Gillingham	42	14	10	18	61	76	38
Walsall	42	14	9	19	78	95	37
Watford	42	14	7	21	72	75	35
Clapton Orient	42	14	7	21	63	91	35
Thames	42	13	8	21	54	93	34
Newport County	42	11	6	25	69	111	28
Norwich City	42	10	8	24	47	76	28

Manager: Ned Liddell / James McIntyre

Did you know that?

Sunderland sent a scout to watch one of Fulham's promising youngsters in September 1930. But rather than Wally Hammond, the Gloucestershire and England batsman and one-time Bristol Rovers winger he thought he was going to watch, the scout saw Jim Hammond, the Sussex all-rounder and Fulham inside forward.

1	Gibbons and Iceton debuts
15	Barrett's 200th game
FAC1	Penn's 50th goal
17	Finch debut
31	Haley's 50th goal
31	Avey finale
41	Haley finale
42	Temple finale

No		Date	V	Opponents	R	H-T	F-T	Scorers	Atten
1	A	30	H	Watford	W	2-1	3-2	Penn, Haley, Allen	14,12
2	S	1	H	Coventry C	D	0-0	0-0		8,64
3		6	A	Notts C	L	1-2	1-6	Penn	10,16
4		8	H	Brentford	D	1-1	1-1	Haley	12,24
5		13	H	Clapton O	W	1-0	2-0	Hammond, Temple	7,31
6		17	A	Brentford	L	1-2	1-4	(Salt og)	9,56
7		20	A	Thames	D	0-0	0-0		4,07
8		27	H	Norwich C	W	0-0	1-0	Penn	13,66
9	O	4	A	Queen's Park R	W	1-0	2-0	Hammond, Avey	14,28
10		11	H	Walsall	W	2-0	5-2	Temple 2, Hammond, Avey, Penn	14,24
11		18	A	Crystal Palace	L	0-2	2-5	Temple, Barrett (pen)	21,11
12		25	H	Southend U	W	0-0	1-0	Barrett	10,83
13	N	1	A	Luton T	L	0-2	0-5		8,38
14		8	H	Bristol R	W	1-2	6-2	Avey 3, Price, Thompson, Temple	11,05
15		15	A	Newport C	W	2-0	3-1	Penn, Price, Hammond	4,08
16		22	H	Gillingham	D	1-1	1-1	Thompson	9,06
17	D	6	H	Brighton & HA	L	0-0	0-1		8,74
18		17	A	Torquay U	L	1-2	1-3	Hammond	2,84
19		20	H	Northampton T	W	3-2	4-2	Hammond 2, Watkins 2	9,64
20		25	A	Swindon T	L	0-2	1-4	Barrett	4,67
21		26	H	Swindon T	W	3-0	6-1	Watkins 2, Finch, Hammond, Temple, Haley	7,24
22		27	A	Watford	D	2-2	2-2	Haley, Dowden	7,24
23	J	3	H	Notts C	W	1-0	3-1	Watkins, Temple 2	11,60
24		14	A	Exeter C	L	0-2	2-3	Watkins, (Miller og)	2,66
25		17	A	Clapton O	L	0-1	0-2		7,98
26		24	H	Thames	W	1-0	4-2	Hammond 3, Price	9,06
27		31	A	Norwich C	D	1-0	1-1	Hammond	8,49
28	F	7	H	Queen's Park R	L	0-1	0-2		18,95
29		14	A	Walsall	L	0-0	0-2		5,53
30		21	H	Crystal Palace	W	1-0	2-0	Haley, (Crilley og)	15,43
31		28	A	Southend U	W	2-1	4-2	Proud, Haley, Penn, Oliver	5,35
32	M	7	H	Luton T	W	2-1	2-1	Watkins 2	7,00
33		14	A	Bristol R	L	0-2	1-2	Barrett (pen)	7,57
34		21	H	Newport C	L	0-1	0-1		10,12
35		28	A	Gillingham	L	1-2	2-3	Haley 2	4,89
36	A	3	H	Bournemouth	W	0-0	1-0	Hammond	7,37
37		4	H	Exeter C	W	2-1	4-2	Haley 2, Barrett (pen), Temple	12,09
38		6	A	Bournemouth	L	1-1	1-2	Murphy	4,57
39		11	A	Brighton & HA	D	0-1	1-1	Hammond	6,70
40		18	H	Torquay U	W	2-0	3-0	Watkins 2, Webb	8,84
41		25	A	Northampton T	L	0-0	2-4	Price 2	2,75
42	M	2	A	Coventry C	L	1-0	1-2	Price	5,95
									App
									Goa

FA Cup

1	N	29	H	Wimbledon	D	1-1	1-1	Price	13,30
R	D	3	A	Wimbledon	W	1-0	6-0	Penn 2, Gibbons 2, Watkins, Hammond	12,14
2		13	H	Halifax T	W	3-0	4-0	Haley 2, Watkins, Hammond	18,00
3	J	10	H	Portsmouth	L	0-0	0-2		27,51

	eton	Gibbon	Lilley	Oliver	Gibbons	Barrett	Temple	Haley	Allen	Price	Penn	Beecham	Hammond	Murphy	Griffiths	Watkins	Reid	Dudley	Avey	Thompson	Baillie	Finch	Bird	Dowden	Proud	Kelly	Webb
1		2	3	4	5	6	7	8	9	10	11																
2		2	3	4	5	6	7	8	9	10	11																
3		2	3	4	5	6	7	8			11	1	9	10													
4		2	3	4	5	6	7	8		10	11		9														
5		2	3	4	5	6	7			10	11		8		9												
6		2	3	4	5	6	7				11		10		9	8											
7		2		4		6	7				11		10			8	3	5	9								
8		2		4		6	7			10	11	1	8				3	5	9								
9		2		4		6	7			10	11		8				3	5	9								
10		2		4		6	7			10	11		8				3	5	9								
11		2		4		6	7			10	11		8				3	5	9								
12		2		4		6	7	9		10	11		8				3	5									
13		2		4		6	7			10	11		8				3	5		9							
14		2				3	7			10	6		8					5	11	9	4						
15		2		4		3	7			10	6		8					5	11	9							
16		2		4		3	7	8		10	6							5	11	9							
17		2	3	4	10	6					11		8			9		5				7					
18		2		4	5	6	7	8			11		10			9							3				
19		2		4	5	6	7	8			11		10			9							3				
20		2		4	5	6	7	8				1	10			9						11	3				
21		2		4	5	6	7	8				1	10			9						11	3				
22		2		4	5	6	7	8				1	10									11	3	9			
23		2		4	5	6	7	8					10			9						11	3				
24		2		4	5	6	7			10			8			9						11	3				
25		2		4	5	6		8					10			9						11	3		7		
26		2		4	5	6	7	8		10			9									11	3				
27		2		4	5	6	7	8		10			9									11	3				
28		2		4	5	6	7	8		10			9									11	3				
29		2		4	5	3	7				6		10			9						11				8	
30		2		4	5	6		8			11		10			9							3		7		
31		2		4	5	6		8			11		10						9				3		7		
32		2		4	5	6		8			11		10			9							3		7		
33		2		4	5	6	7	8			11		10			9							3				
34		2		4	5	6	7	8			11		10			9							3				
35		2			5	6	7	9					10	8							4	11	3				
36		2		4	5	6	7	9					10	8								11	3				
37		2		4	5	6	7	9					10	8								11	3				
38		2		4	5	6		9			11		10	8								7	3				
39		2		4	5	6		9			11		10	8								7	3				
40		2		4	5	3		8			11			10		9						7					6
41		2		4	5	6		9		10	11											8	3		7		
42		2		4	5	3	7			10	11	1		8		9											6
A	6	42	7	40	32	42	33	28	2	19	30	6	36	8	2	17	7	11	9	4	2	18	22	1	5	1	2
G		-	-	1	-	5	9	10	1	6	6	-	14	1	-	10	-	-	5	2	-	1	-	1	1	-	1

	eton	Gibbon	Lilley	Oliver	Gibbons	Barrett	Temple	Haley	Allen	Price	Penn	Beecham	Hammond	Murphy	Griffiths	Watkins	Reid	Dudley	Avey	Thompson	Baillie	Finch	Bird	Dowden	Proud	Kelly	Webb
1		2		4		3	7			10	6		8					5	11	9							
R		2	3	4	10	6	7				11		8			9		5									
2		2		4	5	6	7	8			11		10			9							3				
3		2		4	5	6	7	8					10			9			11				3				

0 points v		0 points
1 point v	Brentford, Brighton & HA, Coventry C, Gillingham	4 points
2 points v	Bournemouth, Bristol R, Clapton O, Crystal Palace, Exeter C, Luton T, Newport C, Northampton T, Notts C, Queen's Park R, Swindon T, Torquay U,	26 points
3 points v	Norwich C, Thames, Watford	9 points
4 points v	Southend U	4 points

Fred Avey's last game for Fulham was in February 1931.

1931-32

Division Three South

	P	W	D	L	F	A	Pts
Fulham	42	24	9	9	111	62	57
Reading	42	23	9	10	97	67	55
Southend United	42	21	11	10	77	53	53
Crystal Palace	42	20	11	11	74	63	51
Brentford	42	19	10	13	68	52	48
Luton Town	42	20	7	15	95	70	47
Exeter City	42	20	7	15	77	62	47
Brighton & Hove Albion	42	17	12	13	73	58	46
Cardiff City	42	19	8	15	87	73	46
Norwich City	42	17	12	13	76	67	46
Watford	42	19	8	15	81	79	46
Coventry City	42	18	8	16	108	97	44
Queen's Park Rangers	42	15	12	15	79	73	42
Northampton Town	42	16	7	19	69	69	39
Bournemouth	42	13	12	17	70	78	38
Clapton Orient	42	12	11	19	77	90	35
Swindon Town	42	14	6	22	70	84	34
Bristol Rovers	42	13	8	21	65	92	34
Torquay United	42	12	9	21	72	106	33
Mansfield Town	42	11	10	21	75	108	32
Gillingham	42	10	8	24	40	82	28
Thames	42	7	9	26	53	109	23

Manager: James McIntyre

Did you know that?

Fulham beat Coventry 5-3 on the opening day and drew the return in January 5-5. The 18 goals scored in the two games is Fulham's highest aggregate score against another club in a season, challenged only by the 17 with Ipswich in 1963–64 (10–1 and 2–4).

1	Newton and Richards debuts
9	Beecham finale
10	Oliver's 300th game
10	Birch debut
11	Hammond's 50th goal
19	Perry debut
23	Hindson debut

No		Date	V	Opponents	R	H-T	F-T	Scorers	Atte
1	A	29	H	Coventry C	W	3-1	5-3	Newton 2, Barrett, Hammond 2	17,2
2	S	2	A	Exeter C	W	0-0	3-0	Newton 3	7,7
3		5	A	Gillingham	L	0-1	1-2	Richards	7,3
4		7	H	Torquay U	W	6-0	10-2	Hammond 4, Newton 2, Price 2, Finch, Proud	9,7
5		12	H	Luton T	W	1-1	3-2	Hammond, Newton, Proud	8,5
6		16	A	Torquay U	W	2-1	3-2	Hammond, Newton, Finch	5,0
7		19	A	Cardiff C	W	2-0	3-0	Hammond 2, Newton	13,2
8		26	H	Northampton T	L	0-2	1-3	Newton	19,7
9	O	3	A	Reading	L	0-1	2-4	Newton 2	11,9
10		10	H	Southend U	D	0-0	1-1	Barrett	28,7
11		17	H	Clapton O	W	0-0	5-1	Hammond 2, Price, Newton, Barrett (pen)	16,9
12		24	A	Swindon T	D	0-2	2-2	Newton, Price	4,9
13		31	H	Norwich C	W	2-0	4-0	Hammond, Finch, Newton, Richards	16,4
14	N	7	A	Brighton & HA	W	2-2	3-2	Hammond, Newton 2	10,3
15		14	H	Mansfield T	W	1-1	2-1	Finch, Barrett	16,9
16		21	A	Watford	L	0-1	1-3	Newton	14,1
17	D	5	A	Bournemouth	W	3-0	3-0	Finch, Newton 2	5,5
18		19	A	Bristol R	D	1-1	2-2	Hammond 2	5,1
19		25	A	Brentford	D	0-0	0-0		26,1
20		26	H	Brentford	W	1-0	2-1	Richards, Perry	29,2
21		28	H	Queen's Park R	L	0-1	1-3	Newton	22,2
22	J	2	A	Coventry C	D	2-1	5-5	Newton 3, Hammond, Finch	11,0
23		16	H	Gillingham	L	0-1	0-2		11,9
24		18	H	Crystal Palace	W	3-0	4-0	Hammond, Newton 2, Richards	8,4
25		23	A	Luton T	W	3-0	3-1	Newton 3	6,3
26		30	H	Cardiff C	W	1-0	4-0	Hammond, Newton 2, Richards	14,6
27	F	6	A	Northampton T	W	1-0	1-0	Newton	6,2
28		13	H	Reading	D	1-2	3-3	Hammond 2, (Richardson og)	18,7
29		20	A	Southend U	L	1-3	1-4	Hammond	6,3
30		27	A	Clapton O	W	1-0	1-0	Newton	11,0
31	M	5	H	Swindon T	D	0-0	2-2	Newton, Wood	17,5
32		12	A	Norwich C	D	1-2	2-2	Finch, Peters	11,7
33		19	H	Brighton & HA	W	0-0	3-0	Finch, Hammond, Wrightson	20,4
34		25	A	Thames	D	0-0	0-0		4,8
35		26	A	Mansfield T	W	1-1	2-1	Wrightson, Richards	5,9
36		28	H	Thames	W	2-0	8-0	Hammond 3, Richards 2, Finch, Newton 2	19,8
37	A	2	H	Watford	W	3-0	5-0	Finch, Newton 2, Hammond 2	22,5
38		9	A	Crystal Palace	L	0-1	0-2		21,3
39		16	H	Bournemouth	W	1-0	3-0	Wrightson, Newton 2 (pen)	14,5
40		23	A	Queen's Park R	L	0-1	1-3	Hammond	21,5
41		30	H	Bristol R	W	0-1	3-2	Finch, Barrett, Hammond	20,4
42	M	7	H	Exeter C	W	1-1	3-1	Hammond, Newton 2	15,5
									Ap
									Goa

FA Cup

1	N	28	H	Guildford	W	1-0	2-0	Hammond 2	12,0
2	D	12	H	Yeovil & Petters U	D	0-0	0-0		15,1
R		17	A	Yeovil & Petters U	W	1-1	5-2	Newton 3, Price, Richards	8,0
3	J	9	A	Watford	D	0-0	1-1	Newton	15,9
R		14	H	Watford	L	0-1	0-3		23,1

Beecham	Gibbon	Hickie	Oliver	Gibbons	Barrett	Richards	Hammond	Newton	Price	Penn	Webb	Proud	Finch	Iceton	Birch	Bird	Dudley	Perry	Hindson	Molloy	Tilford	Wood	Peters	Wrightson	Keen	
1	2	3	4	5	6	7	8	9	10	11																1
1	2	3		5	6	7	8	9	10	11	4															2
1	2	3		5	6	7	8	9	10	11	4															3
1	2	3	4	5	6		8	9	10			7	11													4
1	2	3	4	5	6		8	9	10			7	11													5
1	2	3	4	5	6		8	9	10			7	11													6
1	2	3	4	5	6		8	9	10			7	11													7
1	2	3	4	5	6		8	9	10			7	11													8
1	2	3	4	5	6		8	9	10			7	11													9
	2		4	5	6		8	9	10			7	11	1	3											10
	2		4	5	6	7	8	9	10				11	1	3											11
	2		4	5	6	7	8	9	10				11	1	3											12
	2		4	5	6	7	8	9	10				11	1	3											13
	2		4	5	6	7	8	9	10				11	1	3											14
	2		4	5	6	7	8	9	10				11	1	3											15
	2		4	5	6	7	8	9	10				11	1		3										16
	2		4	5	6	7	8	9	10				11	1	3											17
	2			5		7	8	9	10	6			11	1	3		4									18
	2		4	5		7	8		10	6			11	1	3			9								19
	2		4	5		7	8		10	6			11	1	3			9								20
	2		4	5		7	8	9	10	6			11	1	3											21
	2		4	5		7	8	9	10	6			11	1	3											22
			4	5			8	9	10	11			7	1	3		6		2							23
			4	5		7	8	9	10				11	1	3		6		2							24
			4	5		7	8	9	10				11	1	3				2	6						25
			4	5		7	8	9	10				11	1	3				2	6						26
			4	5		7	8	9	10				11	1	3				2	6						27
			4	5		7	8	9	10				11	1	3				2	6						28
			4	5	6	7	8	9	10				11	1	2						3					29
			4	5	6	7	8	9	10				11	1	2						3					30
			4	5	6	7	8	9					11	1	2						3	10				31
			4	5	6		8		10				11	1	2			9			3		7			32
			4	5	6	7	10	9					11	1	2						3			8		33
			4	5	6	7	10	9					11	1	2						3			8		34
			4	5		7	10	9			6		11	1	2						3			8		35
			4	5	6	7	10	9					11	1	2						3			8		36
			4	5	6	7	10	9					11	1	2						3			8		37
			4	5	6	7	10	9	8				11	1	2						3					38
			4	5	6	7	10	9					11	1	2						3			8		39
			4	5	6	7	10	9					11	1	2						3			8		40
			4	5	6	7	10	9					11	1	2						3			8		41
			4	5	6	7	10	9					11	1	2						3			8		42
9	22	9	39	42	30	33	42	39	32	9	3	7	39	33	32	1	3	3	6	4	14	1	1	9	-	A
-	-	-	-	-	5	8	31	43	4	-	-	2	11	-	-	-	-	1	-	-	-	1	1	3	-	G

Beecham	Gibbon	Hickie	Oliver	Gibbons	Barrett	Richards	Hammond	Newton	Price	Penn	Webb	Proud	Finch	Iceton	Birch	Bird	Dudley	Perry	Hindson	Molloy	Tilford	Wood	Peters	Wrightson	Keen	
	2		4	5	6	7	8	9	10				11	1	3											1
	2			5	6	7	8	9	10				11	1	3										4	2
	2		4	5		7	8	9	10	6			11	1	3											R
	2		4	5	6	7	8	9	10				11	1	3											3
			4	5		7	8	9	10	6			11	1	3				2							R

0 points v	Gillingham, Queen's Park R	0 points
1 point v	Reading, Southend U	2 points
2 points v	Crystal Palace, Northampton T, Swindon T, Watford	8 points
3 points v	Brentford, Bristol R, Coventry C, Norwich C, Thames	15 points
4 points v	Bournemouth, Brighton & HA, Cardiff C, Clapton O, Exeter C, Luton T, Mansfield T, Torquay U	32 points

Full back Joe Birch was signed from Bournemouth in October 1931.

1932-33

Division Two

	P	W	D	L	F	A	Pts
Stoke City	42	25	6	11	78	39	56
Tottenham Hotspur	42	20	15	7	96	51	55
Fulham	42	20	10	12	78	65	50
Bury	42	20	9	13	84	59	49
Nottingham Forest	42	17	15	10	67	59	49
Manchester United	42	15	13	14	71	68	43
Millwall	42	16	11	15	59	57	43
Bradford Park Avenue	42	17	8	17	77	71	42
Preston North End	42	16	10	16	74	70	42
Swansea Town	42	19	4	19	50	54	42
Bradford City	42	14	13	15	65	61	41
Southampton	42	18	5	19	66	66	41
Grimsby Town	42	14	13	15	79	84	41
Plymouth Argyle	42	16	9	17	63	67	41
Notts County	42	15	10	17	67	78	40
Oldham Athletic	42	15	8	19	67	80	38
Port Vale	42	14	10	18	66	79	38
Lincoln City	42	12	13	17	72	87	37
Burnley	42	11	14	17	67	79	36
West Ham United	42	13	9	20	75	93	35
Chesterfield	42	12	10	20	61	84	34
Charlton Athletic	42	12	7	23	60	91	31

Manager: James McIntyre

Did you know that?

Outside right Bill Richards became Fulham's first Welsh international when he played in the 4-1 win over Northern Ireland at Wrexham in December 1932. A couple of months after signing for Fulham, John Arnold played for England against Scotland at Hampden Park in April, adding a football cap to his Test appearance at Lord's the previous summer.

No		Date	V	Opponents	R	H-T	F-T	Scorers	Atten
1	A	27	A	Bradford C	L	0-1	0-2		17,23
2	S	3	H	Swansea T	W	2-0	3-1	Haddleton 2, Hammond	14,77
3		5	H	Chesterfield	D	2-2	2-2	Finch, Gibbons (pen)	10,97
4		10	A	Notts C	W	1-1	2-1	Haddleton 2	10,16
5		17	H	Port Vale	D	1-1	1-1	Price	21,27
6		24	A	Millwall	L	1-1	1-2	Newton	19,56
7	O	1	H	Southampton	W	2-2	4-2	Newton 2, Hammond, Richards	17,11
8		8	A	Bury	D	1-0	1-1	Price	5,10
9		15	H	Lincoln C	W	1-0	3-2	Price, Newton 2	25,50
10		22	A	Burnley	D	2-0	3-3	Newton 2, Gibbons	6,60
11		29	H	Bradford	W	2-2	5-2	Newton 2, Richards, Price, Finch	20,32
12	N	5	A	Plymouth A	W	0-1	3-2	Newton 2, Finch	24,02
13		12	H	Oldham A	W	1-0	1-0	Newton	18,50
14		19	A	Manchester U	L	2-3	3-4	Price, Richards, Newton	28,80
15		26	H	Stoke C	L	0-1	1-3	Newton	25,87
16	D	3	A	Charlton A	W	0-1	2-1	Newton, Hammond	15,31
17		10	H	Tottenham H	D	2-0	2-2	Richards, Newton	42,11
18		17	A	Grimsby T	L	0-1	0-1		6,00
19		24	H	Nottingham F	L	0-1	0-1		16,83
20		26	H	West Ham U	W	1-1	4-2	Hammond 2, Wrightson, Barrett	26,93
21		27	A	West Ham U	D	0-0	1-1	Richards	32,23
22		31	H	Bradford C	W	1-0	1-0	Hammond	22,31
23	J	2	A	Chesterfield	L	0-2	2-3	Gibbons, Wrightson	11,39
24		7	A	Swansea T	L	0-1	0-3		8,58
25		21	H	Notts C	L	3-2	3-4	Hammond, Newton 2	14,79
26		28	A	Port Vale	W	1-1	2-1	Newton, Finch	5,38
27	F	4	H	Millwall	D	1-0	1-1	Newton	17,70
28		11	A	Southampton	D	1-0	2-2	Richards, Newton	8,58
29		18	H	Bury	D	0-1	3-3	Arnold, Barrett, Perry	21,40
30	M	8	H	Burnley	W	2-0	2-1	Wood, (Bellis og)	11,50
31		11	A	Bradford	W	1-0	4-1	Newton 2, Hammond, Arnold	10,47
32		18	H	Plymouth A	W	1-1	3-1	Arnold, Newton 2	23,77
33		25	A	Oldham	W	1-0	3-1	Arnold 2, Hammond	11,42
34	A	1	H	Manchester U	W	1-1	3-1	Newton, Finch, Hammond	21,47
35		5	A	Lincoln C	L	0-1	0-3		8,02
36		8	A	Stoke C	W	1-0	1-0	Price	22,06
37		14	H	Preston NE	W	0-0	1-0	Arnold	21,30
38		15	H	Charlton A	W	2-0	3-1	Wood 2, Newton	25,08
39		17	A	Preston NE	W	1-0	2-1	Finch, Rounce	14,27
40		22	A	Tottenham H	D	0-0	0-0		44,31
41		29	H	Grimsby T	L	0-1	0-1		17,46
42	M	6	A	Nottingham F	L	0-0	0-1		3,84
									App
									Goal

FA Cup

3	J	14	A	Chester	L	0-3	0-5		14,32

7	Newton's 50th goal
16	Tootill debut
29	Arnold and Keeping debuts
36	Barrett's 300th game

…eton	Birch	Tilford	Oliver	Gibbons	Barrett	Richards	Wrightson	Newton	Hammond	Finch	Haddleton	Price	Tootill	Webb	Gibbon	Hindson	Keeping	Perry	Arnold	Wood	Rounce	
	2	3	4	5	6	7	8	9	10	11												1
	2	3	4	5	6	7			8	11	9	10										2
	2	3	4	5	6	7			8	11	9	10										3
	2	3	4	5	6	7			8	11	9	10										4
	2	3	4	5	6	7			8	11	9	10										5
	2	3	4	5	6	7		9	8	11		10										6
	2	3	4	5	6	7		9	8	11		10										7
	2	3	4	5	6	7		9	8	11		10										8
	2	3	4	5	6	7		9	8	11		10										9
	2	3	4	5	6	7		9	8	11		10										10
	2	3	4	5	6	7		9	8	11		10										11
	2	3	4	5	6	7		9	8	11		10										12
	2	3	4	5	6	7		9	8	11		10										13
	2	3	4	5	6	7		9	8	11		10										14
	2	3	4	5	6	7	10	9	8	11												15
	2	3	4	5	6	7	8	9	10	11			1									16
	2	3	4	5	6	7		9	8	11		10	1									17
	2	3	4	5	6	7		9	8	11		10	1									18
	2	3	4	5	6	7		9	8	11		10	1									19
	2	3	4	5	6	7	9		8	11		10	1									20
	2	3	4	5	6	7	9		8	11		10	1									21
	2	3	4	5	6	7	9		8	11		10	1									22
	2		4	5	6	7	9		8	11		10	1	3								23
	2		4	5	6	7	9		8	11		10	1	3								24
	3		4	5	6	7		9	8	11		10	1		2							25
	2		4	5	6	7		9	8	11		10				3						26
	2		4	5	6	7		9	8	11		10				3						27
	2		4	5	6	7		9	8	11		10				3						28
	2		4	5	6				8	7		10					3	9	11			29
	2		4	5	6			9	8	7			1				3		11	10		30
	2		4	5	6			9	8	7			1				3		11	10		31
	2		4	5				9	8	7			1				3		11	6	10	32
	2		4	5	6			9	8	7			1				3		11		10	33
	2		4	5	6	7		9	8	11			1				3				10	34
	2		4	5	6			9		7		10	1				3		11	8		35
			4	5	6			9		7		10	1			2	3		11	8		36
			4	5	6			9		7		10	1			2	3		11	8		37
			4	5	6			9		7		10	1			2	3		11	8		38
			4	5	6			9	8	7			1			2	3		11		10	39
			4	5	6				8	7			1			2	3		11	9	10	40
			4	5	6			9	8	7			1			2	3		11		10	41
			4	5	6			9	8	7			1			2	3		11		10	42
9	35	22	42	42	41	29	8	31	38	42	4	30	23	2	1	10	14	1	13	8	7	A
	-	-	-	3	2	6	2	27	10	6	4	6	-	-	-	-	-	1	6	3	1	G

	2	3	4	5	6	7	9		8	11		10	1									3

0 points v	Grimsby T, Nottingham F	0 points
1 point v	Chesterfield, Millwall	2 points
2 points v	Bradford C, Bury, Lincoln C, Manchester U, Notts C, Stoke C, Swansea T, Tottenham H	16 points
3 points v	Burnley, Port Vale, Southampton, West Ham U	12 points
4 points v	Bradford, Charlton A, Oldham A, Plymouth A, Preston NE	20 points

Eddie Perry scored in his only game of the season.

1933-34

Division Two

	P	W	D	L	F	A	Pts
Grimsby Town	42	27	5	10	103	59	59
Preston North End	42	23	6	13	71	52	52
Bolton Wanderers	42	21	9	12	79	55	51
Brentford	42	22	7	13	85	60	51
Bradford Park Avenue	42	23	3	16	86	67	49
Bradford City	42	20	6	16	73	67	46
West Ham United	42	17	11	14	78	70	45
Port Vale	42	19	7	16	60	55	45
Oldham Athletic	42	17	10	15	72	60	44
Plymouth Argyle	42	15	13	14	69	70	43
Blackpool	42	15	13	14	62	64	43
Bury	42	17	9	16	70	73	43
Burnley	42	18	6	18	60	72	42
Southampton	42	15	8	19	54	58	38
Hull City	42	13	12	17	52	68	38
Fulham	42	15	7	20	48	67	37
Nottingham Forest	42	13	9	20	73	74	35
Notts County	42	12	11	19	53	62	35
Swansea Town	42	10	15	17	51	60	35
Manchester United	42	14	6	22	59	85	34
Millwall	42	11	11	20	39	68	33
Lincoln City	42	9	8	25	44	75	26

Manager: James McIntyre /
Joe Edelston

Did you know that?

In the final game of the season, at home to Oldham in May 1934, amateur Bernard Joy played his only game for Fulham. He then played for Arsenal and England (the last amateur to win a full cap). He later became a journalist for the London Evening Standard, wrote the one of the best histories of Arsenal (Forward Arsenal) and 'ghosted' Bobby Campbell's column in the Fulham programme in the 1970s.

5	Tompkins debut
6	Newton finale
10	Lambert debut
23	Oliver's 400th game
28	Hammond's 200th game
36	Penn finale
37	Iceton finale
42	Gibbon and Richards finales

No		Date	V	Opponents	R	H-T	F-T	Scorers	Atte
1	A	26	H	Port Vale	W	2-0	3-0	Finch, Newton 2	21,0
2		28	H	Blackpool	W	0-0	1-0	Price	14,9
3	S	2	A	Notts C	L	0-3	1-4	Arnold	14,7
4		4	A	Blackpool	L	2-4	3-4	Abel, Hammond, (Watson og)	20,7
5		9	H	Swansea T	W	1-0	1-0	Arnold	19,9
6		16	A	Millwall	W	0-0	1-0	Hammond	20,3
7		23	H	Lincoln C	W	0-0	1-0	Price	13,6
8		30	A	Bury	D	0-3	3-3	Price, Hammond 2	8,4
9	O	7	H	Hull C	D	1-0	1-1	Finch	22,8
10		14	A	Burnley	L	1-1	1-2	Arnold	9,8
11		21	H	Brentford	D	0-0	1-1	Lambert	35,4
12		28	A	Bolton W	L	0-0	1-3	Lambert	14,1
13	N	4	H	Manchester U	L	0-1	0-2		17,0
14		11	A	Plymouth A	L	0-1	0-4		18,9
15		18	H	West Ham U	W	2-0	3-1	Price, Arnold, Hammond	18,1
16		25	A	Nottingham F	L	0-0	0-2		9,5
17	D	2	H	Grimsby T	W	0-0	1-0	Finch	14,6
18		9	A	Bradford	L	1-3	1-3	Finch	8,0
19		16	H	Preston NE	W	1-0	1-0	Wood	11,4
20		23	A	Oldham A	D	1-1	2-2	Wood, Hammond	6,6
21		25	H	Southampton	W	0-0	1-0	Lambert	21,7
22		26	A	Southampton	L	0-1	0-2		24,7
23		30	A	Port Vale	D	1-1	2-2	Hammond 2	8,1
24	J	6	H	Notts C	W	2-0	3-0	Wood 2, Finch	15,0
25		20	A	Swansea T	L	0-0	0-1		8,3
26		29	H	Millwall	W	1-0	2-0	Gibbons (pen), Hammond	7,4
27	F	3	A	Lincoln C	L	0-2	0-5		5,3
28		10	H	Bury	W	0-0	2-1	Hammond, Barrett	18,7
29		17	A	Hull C	D	0-0	0-0		7,9
30		24	H	Burnley	D	0-0	1-1	Arnold	15,0
31	M	3	A	Brentford	W	1-0	2-1	Gibbons 2 (2 pens)	25,1
32		10	H	Bolton W	L	0-1	0-2		18,6
33		17	A	Manchester U	L	0-0	0-1		17,5
34		24	H	Plymouth A	W	2-1	3-2	Hammond 2, Arnold	12,4
35		30	H	Bradford C	L	0-0	0-1		23,1
36		31	A	West Ham U	L	1-3	1-5	Finch	22,5
37	A	2	A	Bradford C	L	0-0	0-1		11,8
38		7	H	Nottingham F	W	1-0	3-1	Hammond 2, Lambert	11,6
39		14	A	Grimsby T	L	1-1	1-3	Hammond	9,3
40		21	H	Bradford	L	0-1	0-2		11,1
41		28	A	Preston NE	L	0-1	0-2		12,4
42	M	5	H	Oldham A	L	1-2	1-2	Finch	6,8

Ap

Goa

FA Cup

No		Date	V	Opponents	R	H-T	F-T	Scorers	Atte
3	J	13	A	Liverpool	D	1-1	1-1	Lambert	45,6
R		17	H	Liverpool	L	1-0	2-3	Hammond, Arnold	28,0

Tootill	Hindson	Keeping	Oliver	Gibbons	Barrett	Richards	Hammond	Newton	Price	Finch	Arnold	Tilford	Abel	Tompkins	Birch	Lambert	Rounce	Wood	Diaper	Iceton	Gibbon	Perry	Murray	Penn	Joy	
1	2	3	4	5	6	7	8	9	10	11																1
1	2	3	4	5	6	7	8	9	10	11																2
1	2	3	4	5	6		8	9	10	7	11															3
1	2		4	5	6		8		10	7	11	3	9													4
1		3	4		6		8		10	7	11		9	5	2											5
1		3	4	5	6		8	9	10	7	11				2											6
1		3	4	5	6		8		10	7	11		9		2											7
1		3	4	5	6		8		10	7	11		9		2											8
1		3	4	5	6		8		10	7	11		9		2											9
1		3	4	5	6		8		10	7	11				2	9										10
1		3	4	5	6		8		10	7	11				2	9										11
1		3	4	5	6		8			7	11				2	9	10									12
1		3	4	5	6		8		10	7	11				2	9										13
1		3	4	5	6	7	8		10	11					2	9										14
1		3	4	5	6		8		10	7	11				2	9										15
1		3	4	5	6		8		10	7	11				2	9										16
1		3	4	5	6		8			7	11				2	9	10									17
1			4	5	3		8		6	7	11				2	9	10									18
1			4	5	6		10			7	11	3			2	9		8								19
1				5	6		10			7	11	3			2	9		8	4							20
1			4	5	6	7	10				11	3			2	9		8								21
1			4		6	7	10				11	3		5	2	9		8								22
	3		4		6		10			11			7	5	2	9		8		1						23
1	3		4	5	6		10			7	11				2	9		8								24
1	3		4	5	6		10				11		7		2	9		8								25
1	3		4	5	6		10			7	11				2	9		8								26
1		3	4	5	6		10			7	11				2	9		8								27
1	3		4	9	6		10			7	11		8	5	2											28
1			4	5	6		8		10	7	11				3	9					2					29
1			4	5	6		8		10	7	11				3	9					2					30
1			4	5	6		8		10	7	11				3						2	9				31
1	3		4	5	6		8				11		7			10					2	9				32
1	3		4	5	6		8			7	11				2		10				9					33
1	3		4	5	6	7	8		10		11				2						9					34
1	3		4	5		7	8		10		11				2						9		6			35
1	3		4			7	8		10	11				5	2						9			6		36
	3			5	6	7	8			11						9	10		4	1	2					37
1	3		4	5	6	7	9		10	11						8					2					38
1	3		4	5	6	7	9		10	11						8					2					39
1	3		4	5	6	7	9		10	11						8					2					40
1	3		4	5	10	7	9			11						8			6		2					41
1	3		4	5	10	7			8	11											2	9			6	42
40	20	17	40	38	40	14	41	4	26	36	31	5	9	5	31	26	5	9	3	2	14	3	1	1	1	A
-	-	-	-	3	1	-	15	2	4	7	6	-	1	-	-	4	-	4	-	-	-	-	-	-	-	G

Tootill	Hindson	Keeping	Oliver	Gibbons	Barrett	Richards	Hammond	Newton	Price	Finch	Arnold	Tilford	Abel	Tompkins	Birch	Lambert	Rounce	Wood	Diaper	Iceton	Gibbon	Perry	Murray	Penn	Joy	
1		3	4	5	6		10			7	11				2	9		8								3
1	3		4	5	6		10			7	11				2	9		8								R

0 points v	Bolton W, Bradford, Bradford C, Manchester U	0 points
1 point v	Burnley, Oldham A	2 points
2 points v	Blackpool, Grimsby T, Hull C, Lincoln C, Nottingham F, Notts C, Plymouth A, Preston NE, Southampton, Swansea T, West Ham U	22 points
3 points v	Brentford, Bury, Port Vale	9 points
4 points v	Millwall	4 points

Assistant Manager Joe Edelston took over temporarily when James McIntyre was sacked in February 1934.

1934-35

Division Two

	P	W	D	L	F	A	Pts
Brentford	42	26	9	7	93	48	61
Bolton Wanderers	42	26	4	12	96	48	56
West Ham United	42	26	4	12	80	63	56
Blackpool	42	21	11	10	79	57	53
Manchester United	42	23	4	15	76	55	50
Newcastle United	42	22	4	16	89	68	48
Fulham	42	17	12	13	76	56	46
Plymouth Argyle	42	19	8	15	75	64	46
Nottingham Forest	42	17	8	17	76	70	42
Bury	42	19	4	19	62	73	42
Sheffield United	42	16	9	17	79	70	41
Burnley	42	16	9	17	63	73	41
Hull City	42	16	8	18	63	74	40
Norwich City	42	14	11	17	71	61	39
Bradford Park Avenue	42	11	16	15	55	63	38
Barnsley	42	13	12	17	60	83	38
Swansea Town	42	14	8	20	56	67	36
Port Vale	42	11	12	19	55	74	34
Southampton	42	11	12	19	46	75	34
Bradford City	42	12	8	22	50	68	32
Oldham Athletic	42	10	6	26	56	95	26
Notts County	42	9	7	26	46	97	25

Manager: Jimmy Hogan / Joe Edelston

Did you know that?

Welsh full back Samuel 'Sonny' Gibbon was killed in a motor cycle accident near Deal in Kent in April 1935. He was just 25 years of age and had played 127 games for Fulham.

1	Hammond's 100th goal
1	Clarke debut
5	Hiles debut
9	Newton's return
17	Price's 50th goal
17	Newton's finale
21	Lambert finale
28	Oliver finale
34	JT Smith debut
34	Gibbons' 200th game

No		Date	V	Opponents	R	H-T	F-T	Scorers	Atten
1	A	25	H	Plymouth A	W	1-0	3-0	Hammond 3	21,74
2		27	H	Brentford	D	1-1	2-2	Hammond, Gibbons (pen)	26,65
3	S	1	A	Norwich C	D	0-0	0-0		19,37
4		5	A	Brentford	L	0-0	0-1		11,79
5		8	H	Newcastle U	W	2-0	3-2	Finch, Hammond 2	26,93
6		15	A	West Ham U	L	0-2	1-2	Hammond	17,95
7		22	H	Blackpool	W	3-0	4-1	Hammond, Price, Clarke, Finch	10,31
8		29	A	Bury	L	0-2	0-2		5,90
9	O	6	H	Hull C	W	2-0	4-0	Gibbons, Hammond, (Quantick Woodhead ogs)	20,48
10		13	A	Nottingham F	D	0-1	1-1	Price	12,59
11		20	H	Bradford C	W	1-0	3-1	Price, Arnold, Newton	21,08
12		27	A	Notts C	D	0-1	1-1	Newton	11,64
13	N	3	H	Southampton	D	0-1	3-3	Gibbons 3	19,70
14		10	A	Bolton W	L	0-1	0-4		19,61
15		17	H	Oldham A	W	0-0	3-1	Newton, Arnold 2	14,63
16		25	A	Burnley	L	0-2	1-3	Arnold	11,26
17	D	1	H	Swansea T	W	2-1	4-1	Newton 2, Hammond, Price	13,68
18		8	A	Manchester U	L	0-1	0-1		25,70
19		15	H	Port Vale	W	0-0	2-0	Finch, Arnold	8,13
20		22	A	Barnsley	L	0-0	0-2		2,99
21		25	A	Bradford	D	0-0	0-0		11,79
22		26	H	Bradford	D	1-0	2-2	Wood, Arnold (pen)	26,90
23		29	A	Plymouth A	L	1-2	1-3	Hammond	17,88
24	J	5	H	Norwich C	L	0-2	1-3	Hammond	16,56
25		19	A	Newcastle U	D	0-0	1-1	Perry	24,54
26		26	H	West Ham U	W	0-0	3-0	Finch, Perry 2	22,58
27	F	2	A	Blackpool	D	1-0	1-1	Hammond	11,03
28		9	H	Bury	L	0-1	1-2	Perry	16,32
29		16	A	Hull C	W	0-0	2-1	Finch 2	5,06
30		23	H	Nottingham F	W	1-0	2-1	Perry 2	14,99
31	M	2	A	Bradford C	D	0-0	0-0		7,81
32		9	H	Notts C	W	2-0	7-0	Perry 3, Arnold 2, Finch, Hammond	8,63
33		16	A	Southampton	D	1-1	1-1	Hammond	8,94
34		23	H	Bolton W	W	2-1	2-1	Hammond, Perry	21,74
35		30	A	Oldham A	L	1-0	1-2	Perry	6,04
36	A	6	H	Burnley	W	0-0	2-0	Smith, Hammond	14,17
37		13	A	Swansea T	L	0-1	0-2		6,73
38		19	H	Sheffield U	W	4-0	7-2	Hammond 4, Perry 2, Finch	14,36
39		20	H	Manchester U	W	2-1	3-1	Perry, Warburton, Hammond	11,05
40		22	A	Sheffield U	W	1-1	2-1	Warburton, (Barke og)	11,64
41		27	A	Port Vale	D	0-1	1-1	Warburton	3,86
42	M	4	H	Barnsley	L	1-1	1-3	Perry	9,62
									App
									Goal

FA Cup

3	J	12	A	Sunderland	L	1-2	2-3	Finch, Arnold	40,10

	Tootill	Birch	Keeping	Oliver	Gibbons	Barrett	Clarke	Lambert	Hammond	Price	Finch	Hiles	Arnold	Newton	Hindson	Perry	Fabian	Wood	Warburton	Smith	Allen	Buckley	Tompkins	Mayes
1	1	2	3	4	5	6	7	8	9	10	11													
2	1	2	3	4	5	6	7	8	9	10	11													
3	1	2	3	4	5	6	7	8	9	10	11													
4	1	2	3	4	5	6	7		8	10		9	11											
5	1	2	3	4	5	6	8		9	10	7		11											
6	1	2	3	4	5	6	8		9	10	7		11											
7	1	2	3	4	5	6	8		9	10	7		11											
8	1	2	3	4	5	6	8		9	10	7		11											
9	1	2	3		5	6	4	7	8	10			11	9										
10	1	2			5	6	4		8	10	7		11	9	3									
11	1	2			5	6	4		8	10	7		11	9	3									
12	1	2			5	6	4		8	10	7		11	9	3									
13	1	2			5	6	4		8	10	7		11	9	3									
14	1	2			5	6	4		8	10	7		11	9	3									
15	1	2	3		5	6	4		8	10	7		11	9										
16	1	2	3		5	6	4	8	10		7		11	9										
17	1	2	3		5	6	4		8	10	7		11	9										
18	1	2			5	6	4		8	10	7		11		3	9								
19	1	2			5	6	4	9	8	10	7		11		3									
20	1	2	3		5	6	4	9	8	10	7		11											
21	1	2	3		5	6	4	8	9	10			11				7							
22	1	2			5	6	4		9	10	7		11		3			8						
23	1	2	3	4	5	6	8		9		10		11				7							
24	1	2			5	6	4		8	7	10		11		3			9						
25			3	4	5	6	7		8		10		11		2	9								
26			3	4	5	6	7		8		10		11		2	9								
27			3	4	5	6	7		8		10		11		2	9								
28			3	4	5	6			8		10		11		2	9	7							
29			3		5	6	4		8		10		11		2	9			7					
30			3		5	6	4		8		10		11		2	9			7					
31			3		5	6	4		8		10		11		2	9			7					
32			3		5	6	4		8		10		11		2	9			7					
33		2			5	6	4		8		10		11		3	9		7						
34			3		5	6	4		8		10		11		2	9				7				
35		2			5	6	4		8		10		11		3	9				7				
36			3		5	6	4		8		10		11		2	9				7				
37			3		5	6	4		8		10		11		2	9				7				
38					5	6	4		8		10				2	9			7		11	3		
39					5	6	4		8		10				2	9			7		11	3		
40		2			5	4				8	10				3	9			7		11		6	
41		2			5	6	4		8		10				3	9			7	11				
42		2			5	6	4				10				3	9		8	7					11
A	2	29	26	13	42	42	40	8	40	23	39	1	34	9	27	19	3	3	10	5	3	2	1	1
G	-	-	-	-	5	-	1	-	22	4	8	-	8	5	-	15	-	1	3	1	-	-	-	-

	Tootill	Birch	Keeping	Oliver	Gibbons	Barrett	Clarke	Lambert	Hammond	Price	Finch	Hiles	Arnold
3	1	2	3	8	5	6	4		9	7	10		11

0 points v	Barnsley, Bury	0 points
1 point v	Brentford, Norwich C	2 points
2 points v	Bolton W, Bradford, Burnley, Manchester U, Oldham A, Plymouth A, Southampton, Swansea T, West Ham U	18 points
3 points v	Blackpool, Bradford C, Newcastle U, Nottingham F, Notts C, Port Vale	18 points
4 points v	Hull C, Sheffield U	8 points

A debut for South African half wing Bruce Clarke.

1935-36

Division Two

	P	W	D	L	F	A	Pts
Manchester United	42	22	12	8	85	43	56
Charlton Athletic	42	22	11	9	85	58	55
Sheffield United	42	20	12	10	79	50	52
West Ham United	42	22	8	12	90	68	52
Tottenham Hotspur	42	18	13	11	91	55	49
Leicester City	42	19	10	13	79	57	48
Plymouth Argyle	42	20	8	14	71	57	48
Newcastle United	42	20	6	16	88	79	46
Fulham	42	15	14	13	76	52	44
Blackpool	42	18	7	17	93	72	43
Norwich City	42	17	9	16	72	65	43
Bradford City	42	15	13	14	55	65	43
Swansea Town	42	15	9	18	67	76	39
Bury	42	13	12	17	66	84	38
Burnley	42	12	13	17	50	59	37
Bradford Park Avenue	42	14	9	19	62	84	37
Southampton	42	14	9	19	47	65	37
Doncaster Rovers	42	14	9	19	51	71	37
Nottingham Forest	42	12	11	19	69	76	35
Barnsley	42	12	9	21	54	80	33
Port Vale	42	12	8	22	56	106	32
Hull City	42	5	10	27	47	111	20

Manager: Jack Peart

Did you know that?

In a cricket County Championship match in the 1936 close season, Hampshire's John Arnold was caught by George Cox of Sussex off the bowling of Jim Hammond. All three were Fulham footballers at the time.

7	Dennison debut
11	Worsley debut
19	Barrett's 400th game
29	Higgins debut
30	Woodward debut
41	Hammond's 300th game

No		Date	V	Opponents	R	H-T	F-T	Scorers	Atte
1	A	31	A	Hull C	D	1-0	1-1	Perry	11,65
2	S	2	H	Nottingham F	W	4-0	6-0	Finch 2, Hammond 3, Smith	12,62
3		7	H	Barnsley	D	1-0	1-1	Perry	22,57
4		11	A	Nottingham F	D	1-0	1-1	Perry	10,25
5		14	A	Plymouth A	L	0-1	0-2		17,66
6		18	H	Burnley	D	0-1	2-2	Price, Hammond	10,18
7		21	H	Bradford C	W	3-0	5-1	Perry 3, Hammond, Johnston	17,17
8		28	A	Newcastle U	L	1-3	2-6	Price, Hammond	24,73
9	O	5	H	Tottenham H	L	0-0	1-2	Perry	37,29
10		12	A	Manchester U	L	0-1	0-1		27,72
11		19	H	Norwich C	D	0-1	1-1	Arnold	17,03
12		26	A	Southampton	W	1-0	2-1	Finch, Worsley	14,99
13	N	2	H	Sheffield U	W	3-1	3-1	Perry, Worsley, Smith	14,96
14		9	A	Bradford	D	1-1	1-1	Finch	8,90
15		16	H	Leicester C	W	2-0	2-0	Hammond, Perry	13,94
16		23	A	Blackpool	D	0-0	1-1	Worsley	12,35
17		30	H	West Ham U	W	0-1	4-2	Smith, Perry, Finch 2	23,44
18	D	7	A	Bury	D	0-0	0-0		7,00
19		14	H	Doncaster R	L	0-1	1-3	Hammond	15,88
20		21	A	Swansea T	W	1-0	2-0	Smith, Arnold	6,55
21		25	H	Charlton A	D	0-0	0-0		24,38
22		26	A	Charlton A	L	1-1	1-2	Worsley	27,80
23		28	H	Hull C	W	0-0	3-0	Hammond 3	13,08
24	J	4	A	Barnsley	L	0-1	0-2		8,85
25		18	H	Plymouth A	D	1-0	2-2	Worsley, Gibbons	15,32
26	F	1	H	Newcastle U	W	3-0	3-1	Worsley, Smith, (Fairhurst og)	24,88
27		8	A	Tottenham H	D	2-1	2-2	Worsley 2	45,27
28		22	A	Norwich C	L	0-1	0-1		11,30
29	M	4	H	Bury	W	4-0	7-0	Keeping (pen), Hammond 2, Arnold 2, Higgins, Smith	5,34
30		7	A	Leicester C	L	1-0	2-5	Smith 2	12,75
31		14	H	Bradford	W	2-0	4-1	Arnold, Perry, Hammond, Keeping	16,79
32		26	A	Sheffield U	W	1-0	1-0	Keeping (pen)	10,51
33		28	H	Blackpool	W	2-0	4-2	Hammond, Arnold, Finch 2	18,25
34	A	1	H	Manchester U	D	2-0	2-2	Finch 2	11,13
35		4	A	West Ham U	D	0-0	0-0		32,00
36		10	A	Port Vale	L	0-1	0-1		11,97
37		11	H	Southampton	L	0-1	0-2		14,15
38		13	H	Port Vale	W	5-0	7-0	Arnold 2, Perry, Smith, Worsley, (Heywood, Griffiths ogs)	9,95
39		18	A	Doncaster R	D	0-0	0-0		10,80
40		25	H	Swansea T	L	0-0	0-1		9,30
41		29	A	Bradford C	L	0-0	0-1		4,33
42	M	2	A	Burnley	W	2-0	2-0	Perry, Arnold	4,70
									App
									Goa

FA Cup

3	J	11	H	Brighton & HA	W	1-0	2-1	Worsley, Hammond	29,32
4		25	H	Blackpool	W	2-1	5-2	Hammond, Perry 4	20,71
5	F	19	A	Chelsea	D	0-0	0-0		52,09
R		24	H	Chelsea	W	1-0	3-2	Smith, Hammond, Arnold	30,65
6		29	H	Derby C	W	0-0	3-0	Arnold, Barrett, Smith	37,15
SF	M	21	N*	Sheffield U	L	0-1	1-2	Arnold (at Molineux)	51,50

Tootill	Hindson	Keeping	Clarke	Gibbons	Barrett	Smith	Hammond	Perry	Finch	Allen	Arnold	Price	Johnston	Dennison	Tompkins	Warburton	Worsley	Birch	Higgins	Woodward	Edelston	Dodds	Pitts	Hiles	Mayes	Brooks	
1	2	3	4	5	6	7	8	9	10	11																	1
1	2	3	4	5	6	7	8	9	10	11																	2
1	2	3	4	5	6	7	8	9	10		11																3
1	2	3	4	5	6	7	8	9	10	11																	4
1	2	3	4	5	6	7	8	9	10	11																	5
1	2	3	4	5	6		8	9		11		10	7														6
1	2	3	4	5			8	9	10	11			7	6													7
1	2	3	4	5			8	9	10			11	7	6													8
1	2	3	4	5	6		8	9	10		11	7															9
1	2	3		5			8	9	10		11		7		6	4											10
1	2	3	4				9		8		11			10	5	6	7										11
1	2	3	4	5		8	10		11					9	6		7										12
1	2	3	4	5		8	10	9	11						6		7										13
1	2	3	4	5		8	10	9	11						6		7										14
1	2	3	4	5		8	10	9	11						6		7										15
1	2	3	4	5		8	10	9	11						6		7										16
1	2		4	5	3	8	10	9	11						6		7										17
1	2	3	4	5		8	10	9	11						6		7										18
1	2	3	4	5	6	8	10	9	11								7										19
1	2	3		5	6	8	9		10		11					4	7										20
1	2	3		5	6	8	9		10		11					4	7										21
1	2	3		5		8	9		10		11				6	4	7										22
1		3		5		8	9		10		11				6	4	7	2									23
1	2	3		5		8	9		10		11				6	4	7										24
1	2	3		5		8	9		10		11				6	4	7										25
1	2	3		5	4	8	10	9	11						6		7										26
1	2	3	4	5		8	10	9	11						6		7										27
1		3		5	4	8	10	9	7		11				6			2									28
1		3	4			8	10	9			11			5	6			2	7								29
1	3			5	4	8		9			11			6				2		7	10						30
1	2	3		5	4	8	10	9			11				6		7										31
1	2	3		5	4	8	10	9			11				6		7										32
1	2	3		5	4	8	10		9		11				6		7										33
1	2	3		5	4	8	10		9		11				6		7										34
1	2	3		5	4	8	10			11					6		7					9					35
1	2	3	4	5		8	10	9			11				6		7										36
1		3	4	5		8	10		9		11				6		7	2									37
1			4			8	10	9			11				6		7	2					3	5			38
1				5		8	9				11				6	4	7	2					3		10		39
			4	5		8	10				11				6		7	2		9			3			1	40
1			4	5		8	10	9			11				6		7	2					3				41
1			4	5		8		9			11	10			6		7	2					3				42
1	33	35	26	39	19	36	40	28	30	7	24	4	4	6	29	9	29	10	1	2	1	1	5	1	1	1	A
-	-	3	-	1	-	9	15	13	10	-	9	2	1	-	-	-	9	-	1	-	-	-	-	-	-	-	G

Tootill	Hindson	Keeping	Clarke	Gibbons	Barrett	Smith	Hammond	Perry	Finch	Allen	Arnold	Price	Johnston	Dennison	Tompkins	Warburton	Worsley	Birch	Higgins	Woodward	Edelston	Dodds	Pitts	Hiles	Mayes	Brooks	
1	2	3		5		8	9		10		11				6	4	7										3
1	2	3		5	4	8	10	9	11						6		7										4
1	2	3		5	4	8	10	9	11						6		7										5
1	2	3		5	4	8	10	9	7		11				6												R
1	2	3		5	4	8	10	9	7		11				6												6
1	2	3		5	4	8	10	9			11				6		7										SF

0 points v		0 points
1 point v	Barnsley, Charlton A, Doncaster R, Manchester U, Norwich C, Plymouth A, Tottenham H	7 points
2 points v	Bradford C, Leicester C, Newcastle U, Port Vale, Southampton, Swansea T	12 points
3 points v	Blackpool, Bradford, Burnley, Bury, Hull C, Nottingham F, West Ham U	21 points
4 points v	Sheffield U	4 points

New signing Bob Dennison works out with trainer Bill 'Doc' Voisey.

1936-37

Division Two

	P	W	D	L	F	A	Pts
Leicester City	42	24	8	10	89	57	56
Blackpool	42	24	7	11	88	53	55
Bury	42	22	8	12	74	55	52
Newcastle United	42	22	5	15	80	56	49
Plymouth Argyle	42	18	13	11	71	53	49
West Ham United	42	19	11	12	73	55	49
Sheffield United	42	18	10	14	66	54	46
Coventry City	42	17	11	14	66	54	45
Aston Villa	42	16	12	14	82	70	44
Tottenham Hotspur	42	17	9	16	88	66	43
Fulham	42	15	13	14	71	61	43
Blackburn Rovers	42	16	10	16	70	62	42
Burnley	42	16	10	16	57	61	42
Barnsley	42	16	9	17	50	64	41
Chesterfield	42	16	8	18	84	89	40
Swansea Town	42	15	7	20	50	65	37
Norwich City	42	14	8	20	63	71	36
Nottingham Forest	42	12	10	20	68	90	34
Southampton	42	11	12	19	53	77	34
Bradford Park Avenue	42	12	9	21	52	88	33
Bradford City	42	9	12	21	54	94	30
Doncaster Rovers	42	7	10	25	30	84	24

Manager: Jack Peart

Did you know that?

Centre forward Ronnie Rooke scored a hat-trick in the 5-0 win over West Ham in November 1936 (one of four hat-tricks he scored that season). He was the first of only two Fulham players to score a hat-trick on their debuts. (Doug McGibbon in January 1947 was the other.)

3	Price finale
12	Barrett finale
13	Perry finale
14	Rooke debut
25	Bacuzzi debut

No		Date	V	Opponents	R	H-T	F-T	Scorers	Atter
1	A	29	H	Plymouth A	D	1-1	2-2	Smith, Price	21,97
2	S	5	A	Nottingham F	L	1-3	3-5	Cox 2, Keeping (pen)	13,49
3		7	A	Burnley	W	0-0	2-0	Smith, Arnold	9,99
4		12	H	Chesterfield	W	1-0	1-0	Perry	15,28
5		14	A	Coventry C	D	1-1	1-1	Worsley	18,18
6		19	A	Aston Villa	W	1-0	3-0	Perry 2, Arnold	48,58
7		21	H	Burnley	W	1-0	2-0	Perry, Arnold	9,96
8		26	H	Bradford C	L	0-0	0-1		20,35
9	O	3	A	Swansea T	L	0-1	0-3		13,54
10		10	H	Southampton	W	0-0	2-0	Worsley, Arnold	20,06
11		17	A	Blackburn R	W	1-0	2-0	Perry, Hammond	8,57
12		24	H	Bury	D	1-0	1-1	Perry	30,63
13		31	A	Leicester C	L	0-1	0-2		12,70
14	N	7	H	West Ham U	W	1-0	5-0	Rooke 3, Arnold, Hammond	22,28
15		14	A	Norwich C	L	0-0	0-3		12,94
16		21	H	Newcastle U	L	1-3	3-4	Smith, Keeping (pen), Finch	23,63
17		28	A	Bradford	D	1-0	1-1	Hammond	10,19
18	D	5	H	Barnsley	W	1-0	1-0	Rooke	11,95
19		12	A	Sheffield U	L	0-1	0-2		16,61
20		19	H	Tottenham H	D	1-2	3-3	Hammond 2, Woodward	20,49
21		25	H	Blackpool	L	0-0	0-3		22,85
22		26	A	Plymouth A	W	1-0	3-0	Cox, Smith, Hammond	37,05
23		28	A	Blackpool	L	0-2	1-3	Smith	13,18
24	J	2	H	Nottingham F	W	3-1	5-2	Smith, Arnold, Woodward 2, (Munro og)	11,01
25		9	A	Chesterfield	L	1-1	1-4	Woodward	10,09
26		23	H	Aston Villa	W	2-1	3-2	Rooke 3	15,84
27		30	A	Bradford C	D	1-1	1-1	Rooke	4,26
28	F	6	H	Swansea T	W	2-0	5-0	Rooke 2 (1 pen), Arnold, Warburton 2	16,10
29		13	A	Southampton	D	1-1	3-3	Rooke 3	14,31
30		20	H	Blackburn R	D	1-1	1-1	Hammond	20,05
31		27	A	Bury	D	1-0	1-1	Arnold	7,83
32	M	6	H	Leicester C	W	0-0	2-0	Woodward, Smith	19,53
33		13	A	West Ham U	D	1-2	3-3	Arnold 2, Rooke	29,40
34		20	H	Norwich C	L	2-0	2-3	Rooke, Smith	18,54
35		26	A	Doncaster R	L	0-0	1-2	Gibbons	14,01
36		27	A	Newcastle U	D	1-0	1-1	Smith	10,16
37		29	H	Doncaster R	W	1-0	1-0	Arnold	16,05
38	A	3	H	Bradford	D	0-0	0-0		12,81
39		10	A	Barnsley	L	0-1	0-1		9,12
40		17	H	Sheffield U	W	2-0	4-0	Rooke 3 (1 pen), Arnold	8,43
41		24	A	Tottenham H	D	0-0	1-1	Rooke	21,13
42	M	1	H	Coventry C	L	0-1	0-2		8,69
									App
									Goa

FA Cup

3	J	16	A	Millwall	L	0-2	0-2		32,49

ootill	Hindson	Keeping	Clarke	Gibbons	Tompkins	Worsley	Smith	Finch	Price	Allen	Cox	Arnold	Barrett	Perry	Birch	Warburton	Pitts	Hammond	Rooke	Dennison	Woodward	Brooks	Bacuzzi	Targett	Higgins	
	2	3	4	5	6	7	8	9	10	11																1
	2	3	4	5	6	7	8	10			9	11														2
	2	3	4	5		7	8		10		9	11	6													3
	2	3	4	5	6	7	8	10				11		9												4
		3	4	5	6	7	8					11		9	2	10										5
		3	4	5	6	7	8					11		9	2	10										6
			4	5	6	7	8					11		9	2	10	3									7
		3	4	5	6	7	8					11		9	2	10										8
		3	4	5	6	7	8					11		9	2			10								9
		3	4	5		7	8					11	6	9	2			10								10
		3	4	5		7	8					11	6	9	2			10								11
		3	4	5		7	8					11	6	9	2			10								12
		3	4	5	6	7	8					11		9	2			10								13
		3	4	5	6		8	7				11			2			10	9							14
		3	4	5	6		8	7				11			2			10	9							15
		3	4	5	6	7	8	10				11			2				9							16
		3	4	5		7	8					11			2			10	9	6						17
		3	4	5		7	8	11							2			10	9	6						18
		3	4	5	6	7	8	10				11			2				9							19
		3	4	5	6		7	10				11			2			8			9					20
		3	4	5	6		10	7				11					2	8			9					21
		3	4	5	6		7	11			9				2			10			8					22
		3		5	6		7	11			9				2	4		10			8					23
		3		5	4		8				9	11			2			10		6	7	1				24
		3		5	4		8	7				11						10			9		2	6		25
		3	4	5	6		8	7				11			2	10			9							26
		3	4	5	6		8	7				11			2	10			9							27
		3	4	5	6		8	7				11			2	10			9							28
		3	4	5	6			7				11			2	10		8	9							29
		3	4	5	6			7				11			2	10		8	9							30
		3	4	5	6	7						11			2	10		8	9							31
		3	4	5	6		8					11			2	10			9		7					32
		3	4	5	6		8					11			2	10			9		7					33
		3	4	5			8					11			2	10			9	6	7					34
		3	4	5	6		8					11			2	10			9		7					35
		3	4	5	6		8	11							2	10			9		7					36
		3	4	5	6	7	8					11			2			10	9							37
		3	4	5	6	7	8					11			2	10			9							38
			4	5	6	7	8	10				11					2				9		3			39
		3	4	5	6	7						11			2			10	9		8					40
		3	4	5	6	7	8					11			2			10	9							41
		3	4	5	6		8	11							2	10			9						7	42
	4	40	39	42	35	23	38	21	2	1	5	36	4	10	35	18	3	21	22	4	13	1	2	1	1	A
	-	2	-	1	-	2	9	1	1	-	3	12	-	6	-	2	-	7	19	-	5	-	-	-	-	G

ootill	Hindson	Keeping	Clarke	Gibbons	Tompkins	Worsley	Smith	Finch	Price	Allen	Cox	Arnold	Barrett	Perry	Birch	Warburton	Pitts	Hammond	Rooke	Dennison	Woodward	Brooks	Bacuzzi	Targett	Higgins	
		3	4	5	6		8				9	11			2			10			7					3

0 points v	Blackpool, Norwich C	0 points
1 point v	Bradford C, Coventry C, Newcastle U	3 points
2 points v	Barnsley, Bradford, Bury, Chesterfield, Doncaster R, Leicester C, Nottingham F, Sheffield U, Swansea T, Tottenham H	20 points
3 points v	Blackburn R, Plymouth A, Southampton, West Ham U	12 points
4 points v	Aston Villa, Burnley	8 points

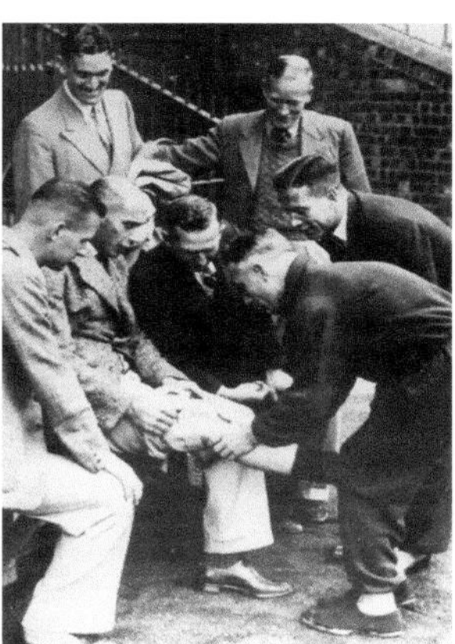

Clarke, Hammond, Finch and Barrett watch 'Doc' Voisey check Gibbons injury.

1937-38

Division Two

	P	W	D	L	F	A	Pts
Aston Villa	42	25	7	10	73	35	57
Manchester United	42	22	9	11	82	50	53
Sheffield United	42	22	9	11	73	56	53
Coventry City	42	20	12	10	66	45	52
Tottenham Hotspur	42	19	6	17	76	54	44
Burnley	42	17	10	15	54	54	44
Bradford Park Avenue	42	17	9	16	69	56	43
Fulham	42	16	11	15	61	57	43
West Ham United	42	14	14	14	53	52	42
Bury	42	18	5	19	63	60	41
Chesterfield	42	16	9	17	63	63	41
Luton Town	42	15	10	17	89	86	40
Plymouth Argyle	42	14	12	16	57	65	40
Norwich City	42	14	11	17	56	75	39
Southampton	42	15	9	18	55	77	39
Blackburn Rovers	42	14	10	18	71	80	38
Sheffield Wednesday	42	14	10	18	49	56	38
Swansea Town	42	13	12	17	45	73	38
Newcastle United	42	14	8	20	51	58	36
Nottingham Forest	42	14	8	20	47	60	36
Barnsley	42	11	14	17	50	64	36
Stockport County	42	11	9	22	43	70	31

Manager: Jack Peart

Did you know that?

After a very poor start to the season, a Fulham director was told to wait outside Hammersmith Palais during the week in October 1937 to see whether certain first team players were keeping late nights and drinking too much. He found the suspicions groundless.

1	Evans and Turner debuts
4	Gibbons' 300th game
11	O'Callaghan debut
19	Hammond's 150th goal
19	Hindson finale
22	Birch, Smith and Tootill finales
34	Gibbons finale
39	Hammond finale

No		Date	V	Opponents	R	H-T	F-T	Scorers	Atte
1	A	28	A	Plymouth A	L	0-1	0-4		23,66
2	S	2	A	Sheffield W	L	0-2	1-2	Rooke	16,51
3		4	H	Chesterfield	D	0-1	1-1	Woodward	16,71
4		6	H	Sheffield W	D	0-0	0-0		11,35
5		11	A	Swansea T	L	0-1	0-2		11,64
6		18	H	Norwich C	L	2-2	3-4	Woodward 2 (1 pen), Finch	17,0
7		20	A	Blackburn R	D	1-1	2-2	Woodward, Hammond	12,50
8		25	A	Aston Villa	L	0-1	0-2		42,2
9	O	2	H	Bradford	D	0-0	1-1	Woodward	15,1
10		9	A	West Ham U	D	0-0	0-0		33,2
11		16	H	Tottenham H	W	2-0	3-1	Rooke 2, Woodward (pen)	29,5
12		23	A	Sheffield U	L	0-1	1-2	Woodward	14,9
13		30	H	Manchester U	W	1-0	1-0	Woodward	17,3
14	N	6	A	Stockport C	L	0-1	0-2		15,2
15		13	H	Barnsley	D	0-0	0-0		13,2
16		20	A	Nottingham F	W	1-0	1-0	Hammond	11,7
17		27	H	Newcastle U	L	1-1	1-2	Warburton	12,3
18	D	4	A	Luton T	L	0-2	0-4		13,5
19		11	H	Coventry C	L	2-1	3-4	Hammond 3	14,0
20		25	A	Burnley	L	0-1	0-1		27,5
21		27	H	Burnley	W	1-1	2-1	O'Callaghan, Arnold	18,0
22	J	1	H	Plymouth A	L	2-1	2-3	Worsley, O'Callaghan	13,2
23		15	A	Chesterfield	W	1-0	2-0	Evans, O'Callaghan	6,6
24		22	H	Swansea T	W	4-0	8-1	Rooke 4, O'Callaghan, Finch 2, Hammond	15,1
25		29	A	Norwich C	W	1-0	2-1	Woodward 2	10,0
26	F	5	H	Aston Villa	D	0-1	1-1	Finch	38,6
27		12	A	Bury	L	2-3	2-4	Tompkins, Rooke	8,9
28		16	A	Bradford	W	0-1	2-1	Arnold, (Ross og)	6,3
29		19	H	West Ham U	D	1-0	1-1	Arnold	22,8
30		26	A	Tottenham H	D	1-1	1-1	Rooke	34,0
31	M	5	H	Sheffield U	D	1-0	1-1	Woodward	23,1
32		12	A	Manchester U	L	0-1	0-1		30,3
33		19	H	Stockport C	W	1-0	2-0	Woodward, Arnold	16,4
34		26	A	Barnsley	D	0-0	0-0		9,3
35	A	2	H	Nottingham F	W	1-0	2-0	Arnold, Rooke	15,2
36		9	A	Newcastle U	W	1-0	2-1	Woodward, Arnold	12,4
37		15	H	Southampton	W	0-0	1-0	Arnold	13,1
38		16	H	Luton T	W	2-0	4-1	Woodward 2, Bacuzzi, Rooke	17,2
39		18	A	Southampton	L	0-2	0-4		14,8
40		23	A	Coventry C	W	1-0	1-0	Arnold	28,3
41		30	H	Bury	W	3-0	4-0	Rooke 3, Higgins	9,9
42	M	7	H	Blackburn R	W	2-0	3-1	Rooke 3	11,7
									App
									Goa

FA Cup

3	J	8	A	Brentford	L	1-2	1-3	O'Callaghan	29,8

Turner	Birch	Keeping	Evans	Gibbons	Tompkins	Finch	Smith	Rooke	Hammond	Arnold	Worsley	Woodward	Bacuzzi	Higgins	Warburton	Dennison	Clarke	Edelston	Tootill	O'Callaghan	Hindson	Buckley	Hiles	Pitts	
1	2	3	4	5	6	7	8	9	10	11															1
1	2	3	4	5	6		8	9	10	11	7														2
1	2	3	4	5	6	10	7	9		11		8													3
1		3	4	5	6	11	8	9			7	10	2												4
1		3	4	5	6	11						9	2	7	8	10									5
1		3	6		5	11			8		7	9	2				4	10							6
		3		5	6	11	8		10		7	9	2				4		1						7
	2	3		5	6				8	11	7	9			10		4		1						8
	2	3	4	5	6	10	8	9		11		7							1						9
	2	3	4	5	6	11	8	9				7						10	1						10
	2	3	4	5	6	7		9		11		8							1	10					11
	2	3	4	5	6	11		9				8		7					1	10					12
	2	3	4	5	6	7	8			11		9							1	10					13
	2	3		5	6	11	8				7	9					4		1	10					14
		3		5	6	7	8			11		9	2				4		1	10					15
				5	6	10			9	11	7		3		4				1	8	2				16
		3		5	6	10			9	11	7				4				1	8	2				17
		3		5	6	10		9		11	7				4				1	8	2				18
				5	6	7	8		9	11					4				1	10	2	3			19
	2			5	6		8		9	11	7				4				1	10		3			20
	2			5	6		8		9	11	7				4				1	10		3			21
	2	3		5	6		8		9	11	7				4				1	10					22
1		3	4		5	7		9	8	11		6	2							10					23
1		3	4		6	11		9	8			7	2			5				10					24
1		3	4		6	11		9	8			7	2			5				10					25
1		3	4		6	11		9	8			7	2			5				10					26
1		3	4		6	11		9	8			7	2			5				10					27
1		3	4		6	7		9		11		8	2			5				10					28
1		3	4		6	7		9		11		8	2			5				10					29
1		3	4	5	6	7		9		11		8	2							10					30
1		3	4		6	7		9		11		8	2			5				10					31
1		3	4		6	7		9		11		8	2			5				10					32
1		3	4		6	7		9		11		8	2							10			5		33
1		3	4		6	7				11	8	9	2							10			5		34
1		3	4		6	7		9		11		8	2							10			5		35
1		3	4		6			9	8	11	7	10	2										5		36
1		3	4		6			9	8	11	7	10	2										5		37
1		3	4		6	7		9		11	8	10	2										5		38
1			4		6	7			9	11		10	2							8			5	3	39
1		3	4		6	7		9		11	8	10	2										5		40
1		3	4		6			9		11	8	10	2	7									5		41
1		3	4		6	11		9			8	10	2	7									5		42
26	13	37	31	22	42	34	14	27	19	30	19	33	26	4	9	9	5	2	16	26	4	3	10	1	A
-	-	-	1	-	1	4	-	17	6	8	1	15	1	1	1	-	-	-	-	4	-	-	-	-	G

1		3	4		6	7		9	8	11						5				10	2				3

0 points v	Plymouth A	0 points
1 point v	Sheffield W, Aston Villa, Sheffield U	3 points
2 points v	Swansea T, Norwich C, West Ham U, Manchester U, Stockport C, Barnsley, Burnley, Southampton, Bury, Newcastle U, Luton T, Coventry C	24 points
3 points v	Chesterfield, Blackburn R, Bradford, Tottenham H	12 points
4 points v	Nottingham F	4 points

Welsh international and former Spurs inside-forward Taffy O'Callaghan signed in October 1937.

1938-39

Division Two

	P	W	D	L	F	A	Pts
Blackburn Rovers	42	25	5	12	94	60	55
Sheffield United	42	20	14	8	69	41	54
Sheffield Wednesday	42	21	11	10	88	59	53
Coventry City	42	21	8	13	62	45	50
Manchester City	42	21	7	14	96	72	49
Chesterfield	42	20	9	13	69	52	49
Luton Town	42	22	5	15	82	66	49
Tottenham Hotspur	42	19	9	14	67	62	47
Newcastle United	42	18	10	14	61	48	46
West Bromwich Albion	42	18	9	15	89	72	45
West Ham United	42	17	10	15	70	52	44
Fulham	42	17	10	15	61	55	44
Millwall	42	14	14	14	64	53	42
Burnley	42	15	9	18	50	56	39
Plymouth Argyle	42	15	8	19	49	55	38
Bury	42	12	13	17	65	74	37
Bradford Park Avenue	42	12	11	19	61	82	35
Southampton	42	13	9	20	56	82	35
Swansea Town	42	11	12	19	50	83	34
Nottingham Forest	42	10	11	21	49	82	31
Norwich City	42	13	5	24	50	91	31
Tranmere Rovers	42	6	5	31	39	99	17

Manager: Jack Peart

Did you know that?

Within 72 hours in January 1939, Fulham played in front of the biggest and smallest officially recorded crowds in the club's history up to that point. On a Saturday, 69,987 were at Stamford Bridge for a Cup tie against Chelsea and the following Monday afternoon, just 3,155 were at the Cottage for a Second Division match against Swansea.

- 1 Finch's 50th goal
- FAC3 Rooke's 50th goal
- 32 Freeman debut
- 33 Finch finale
- 36 Dennison finale
- 40 Evans finale
- 41 O'Callaghan finale
- 42 Finales for Arnold, Clarke, Higgins, Hiles, Keeping, Tompkins, Turner and Worsley

No		Date	V	Opponents	R	H-T	F-T	Scorers	Atten
1	A	27	H	West Ham U	W	2-2	3-2	Finch, Arnold, Worsley	24,56
2		29	A	Bury	W	0-0	2-0	Arnold, Tompkins	9,47
3	S	3	A	Tranmere R	W	1-0	1-0	Woodward	12,84
4		5	A	Burnley	L	0-0	0-2		13,89
5		10	H	Chesterfield	W	1-0	2-0	Worsley, Rooke	18,80
6		12	H	Burnley	D	0-0	0-0		11,96
7		17	A	Swansea T	D	1-1	1-1	Rooke	6,31
8		24	H	Bradford	W	3-0	4-0	Rooke 2, Arnold, Finch	17,60
9	O	1	A	Manchester C	W	3-2	5-3	Rooke 4, Arnold	29,67
10		8	H	Millwall	W	0-1	2-1	Woodward, Evans	49,33
11		15	A	Tottenham H	L	0-1	0-1		46,67
12		22	H	Southampton	D	0-1	1-1	Evans	21,42
13		29	A	Plymouth A	D	0-0	0-0		23,99
14	N	5	H	Nottingham F	D	0-0	2-2	Keeping (pen), Worsley	18,71
15		12	A	Newcastle U	L	0-2	1-2	Rooke (pen)	64,16
16		19	H	West Bromich A	W	0-0	3-0	Arnold 2, Woodward	22,66
17		26	A	Norwich C	D	2-1	3-3	Tompkins 2, Rooke	10,22
18	D	3	H	Luton T	W	1-1	2-1	Higgins, Keeping	19,44
19		10	A	Coventry C	L	0-3	1-3	Evans	21,82
20		17	H	Sheffield U	L	1-1	1-2	Rooke	15,68
21		24	A	West Ham U	L	0-1	0-1		10,39
22		27	A	Sheffield W	L	0-2	1-5	Evans	46,55
23		31	H	Tranmere R	W	1-0	1-0	Rooke	12,15
24	J	23	H	Swansea T	W	0-0	1-0	Rooke	3,15
25		28	A	Bradford	W	3-1	5-1	Higgins 3, Rooke 2	8,72
26	F	4	H	Manchester C	W	2-0	2-1	Arnold, Rooke	24,66
27		11	A	Millwall	D	1-0	1-1	O'Callaghan	32,48
28		18	H	Tottenham H	W	0-0	1-0	O'Callaghan (pen)	26,46
29		25	A	Southampton	L	0-1	1-2	Higgins	12,51
30	M	4	H	Plymouth A	L	0-1	1-2	Rooke	10,36
31		11	A	Nottingham F	D	0-1	1-1	Higgins	9,34
32		18	H	Newcastle U	D	1-1	1-1	Woodward	20,18
33		25	A	West Bromich A	L	0-1	0-3		19,65
34	A	1	H	Norwich C	W	0-0	2-0	Higgins 2	12,67
35		7	H	Blackburn R	L	2-2	2-3	Higgins, Rooke,	28,53
36		8	A	Luton T	L	0-0	1-2	Woodward	16,32
37		10	A	Blackburn R	L	1-1	1-2	Higgins	23,46
38		15	H	Coventry C	W	0-0	1-0	Arnold	15,09
39		18	H	Sheffield W	D	0-2	2-2	Tompkins, Rooke	11,04
40		22	A	Sheffield U	L	0-1	0-2		21,90
41		24	A	Chesterfield	W	0-0	1-0	Rooke	8,54
42		29	H	Bury	L	1-2	1-2	Rooke	7,72
									App
									Goal

FA Cup

No		Date	V	Opponents	R	H-T	F-T	Scorers	Atten
3	J	7	H	Bury	W	3-0	6-0	Rooke 6	11,22
4		21	A	Chelsea	L	0-0	0-3		69,98

urner	Bacuzzi	Keeping	Evans	Hiles	Tompkins	Finch	Worsley	Rooke	Woodward	Arnold	Higgins	Dennison	O'Callaghan	Buckley	Easson	Freeman	Miller	Clarke	Tuckett	
	2	3	4	5	6	7	8	9	10	11										1
	2	3	4	5	6	7	8	9	10	11										2
	2	3	4	5	6	7	8	9	10	11										3
	2	3	4	5	6	11	8	9	10		7									4
	2	3	4		6	11	8	9	10			5	7							5
	2	3	4		6	11	8	9	7			5	10							6
	2	3	4	5	6	7	8	9	10	11										7
	2	3	4	5	6	7	8	9	10	11										8
	2	3	4	5	6	7	8	9	10	11										9
	2	3	4	5	6	7	8	9	10	11										10
	2	3	4	5	6	7	8	9	10	11										11
	2	3	4	5	6	7	8	9	10	11										12
	2	3	4	5	6	7	8	9	10	11										13
	2	3	4	5	6		7	9	10	11			8							14
	2	3	4	5	6	7	8	9		11		10								15
	2		4	5	6		8	9	10	11	7	3								16
	2		4	5	6		8	9	10	11	7	3								17
	2	3	4	5	6		8	9	10	11	7									18
	2		4	5	6	10	8		9	11	7	3								19
	2		4	5	6	7	8	9	10	11		3								20
	2	3	4	5	6	7		9	10	11			8							21
	2	3	4	5	6	7			10	11		9	8							22
	2		4		6	7	8	9	10	11		5		3						23
	2	3	4		6		8	9		11	7	5	10							24
	2	3	4	5	6		8	9		11	7		10							25
	2	3	4	5	6		8	9		11	7		10							26
	2	3	4	5	6		8	9		11	7		10							27
	2	3	4	5	6		8	9		11	7		10							28
	2	3	4	5	6		8	9			7	11	10							29
	2	3	4	5	6		8	9		11	7		10							30
	2	3	4	5	6			9	8	11	7				10					31
	2		4	5	6	10		9	8	11	7					3				32
	2	3	4	5	6	10		9	8	11	7									33
	2	3	4	5	6		8	9	10		7						11			34
	2	3	4	5	6			9	8		7				10		11			35
	2	3	4	5	6		8		10		7	9					11			36
	2	3	4	5	6		8		9		7				10		11			37
	2	3	4	5	6		10	9	8	11	7									38
	2	3	4	5	6		10	9	8	11	7									39
	2	3	4	5	6		10	9	8	11	7									40
	2	3			6			9	8	11	7		10					4	5	41
	2	3		5	6		8	9	10	11	7							4		42
2	42	36	40	37	42	21	35	38	34	34	24	12	13	1	3	1	4	2	1	A
	-	2	4	-	4	2	3	21	5	8	10	-	2	-	-	-	-	-	-	G

urner	Bacuzzi	Keeping	Evans	Hiles	Tompkins	Finch	Worsley	Rooke	Woodward	Arnold	Higgins	Dennison	O'Callaghan	Buckley	Easson	Freeman	Miller	Clarke	Tuckett	
	2	3	4		6		8	9		11	7	5	10							3
	2	3	4		6		8	9		11	7	5	10							4

0 points v	Blackburn R, Sheffield U	0 points
1 point v	Burnley, Newcastle U, Plymouth A, Sheffield W, Southampton,	5 points
2 points v	Bury, Coventry C, Luton T, Nottingham F, Tottenham H, West Bromwich A, West Ham U	14 points
3 points v	Millwall, Norwich C, Swansea T	9 points
4 points v	Bradford, Chesterfield, Manchester C, Tranmere R	16 points

All eyes on Arnold as he pots in the old snooker room, upstairs in the Cottage.

1939-40

Division Two

No		Date	V	Opponents	R	H-T	F-T	Scorers	Att
1	A	26	A	Bury	L		1-3	Woodward	9,0
2		28	A	West Ham U	L		1-2	Rooke	15,2
3	S	2	H	Luton T	D	0-1	1-1	Rooke	8,0

South B

	P	W	L	D	F	A	Pts
B'mouth & BA	18	12	4	2	49	26	26
Chelsea	18	11	5	2	52	37	24
Reading	18	9	4	5	43	37	23
Fulham	18	7	7	4	42	41	18
Portsmouth	18	7	9	2	37	42	16
Aldershot	18	5	9	4	38	49	14
Brighton & HA	18	5	12	1	42	53	11
Southampton	18	4	14	0	41	63	8

South C

	P	W	L	D	F	A	Pts
Tottenham	18	11	3	4	43	30	26
West Ham	18	10	4	4	53	28	24
Arsenal	18	9	4	5	41	26	23
Brentford	18	8	6	4	42	34	20
Millwall	18	7	6	5	36	30	19
Charlton	18	7	7	4	39	56	18
Fulham	18	8	9	1	38	42	17
Southampton	18	5	10	3	28	55	13
Chelsea	18	4	11	3	33	53	11
Portsmouth	18	3	12	3	26	45	9

Manager: Jack Peart

Football League South B

No		Date	V	Opponents	R	H-T	F-T	Scorers	Att
1	O	21	H	Portsmouth	W	0-0	2-1	Rooke 2	6,4
2		28	A	Queen's Park R	D	1-1	2-2	Rooke 2	5,0
3	N	4	H	Aldershot	W	0-1	3-1	Fisher 2, Finch	5,0
4		11	A	Bournemouth	L	1-0	1-2	Arnold	3,0
5		18	H	Chelsea	L	0-3	1-3	Perry	8,0
6		25	A	Southampton	L	0-2	2-5	Arnold, Woodward	4,0
7	D	2	H	Brighton & HA	W	4-2	7-4	Perry 4, Burgess, Tompkins, Woodward	5,0
8		9	A	Reading	L	0-2	1-6	Muttitt	3,0
9		16	H	Brentford	L	1-1	2-4	Woodward, Burgess	5,0
10		23	A	Portsmouth	L	0-2	1-3	Mills	1,9
11		25	H	Queen's Park R	L		3-8	Mills, Woodward, Thomas (DS)	6,0
12		26	A	Aldershot	D	0-2	3-3	Arnold 2, Thomas DS	3,0
13		30	H	Bournemouth	W	2-1	5-2	Taylor, Thomas (DWJ), Woodward 2, Wilkins	3,0
14	J	6	A	Chelsea	D	1-1	1-1	Rooke	6,2
15		13	H	Southampton	W	2-1	4-1	Arnold, Rooke 2, Woodward	1,7
16		20	A	Brighton & HA	D	1-1	1-1	Rooke	1,3
17	F	14	A	Brentford	W		5-2	Woodward, Rooke 3, Arnold	1,8
18	M	13	H	Reading	W		6-2	Rooke 3, Woodward, Ottewell, (1 og)	1,5

Football League South C

No		Date	V	Opponents	R	H-T	F-T	Scorers	Att
19	F	10	H	Portsmouth	W	3-1	3-2	Finch, Rooke, Arnold	3,8
20		17	A	Millwall	L	0-0	0-2		3,8
21		24	A	Southampton	W	4-0	4-0	Taylor, Arnold, Woodward, Rooke	3,0
22	M	2	H	Arsenal	D	1-0	1-1	Woodward	8,0
23		9	A	West Ham U	L	0-1	0-5		8,0
24		16	H	Charlton A	W	2-0	2-0	Woodward, Arnold	6,6
25		22	A	Chelsea	W	2-0	4-1	Rooke 2, Woodward, (1 og)	15,0
26		23	H	Tottenham H	L	1-1	2-3	Arnold, (1 og)	8,0
27		25	H	Chelsea	W	0-2	4-3	Rooke, Cranfield 2, (1 og)	10,0
28		30	A	Brentford	L	0-3	0-5		6,9
29	A	6	A	Portsmouth	W	1-0	3-0	McCormick, Woodward 2	5,0
30		10	A	Tottenham H	L		1-3	Rooke	2,0
31		13	H	Millwall	W	0-0	2-0	Rooke, McCormick	8,0
32		18	A	Charlton A	L		5-7	Rooke 2, Woodward 3	7
33	M	22	A	Arsenal	L		1-2	Ottewell	6,0
34		27	H	West Ham U	W		2-1	Rooke, McCormick	4,0
35	J	3	H	Brentford	L		3-5	Ottewell 2, Rooke	
36		6	H	Southampton	L		1-2	Ottewell	1,0

League War Cup

No		Date	V	Opponents	R	H-T	F-T	Scorers	Att
1/1	A	20	H	Brentford	W	0-1	4-1	Thomas DS, Arnold 2, Rooke	12,0
1/2		27	A	Brentford	W	0-1	2-1	Woodward, Jones	7,8
2/1	M	4	A	Norwich C	D	0-1	1-1	Rooke	6,0
2/2		11	H	Norwich C	W	1-0	1-0	McCormick	8,2
3		18	H	Nottingham F	W		2-0	Rooke, (1og)	8,7
4		25	H	Everton	W	3-1	5-2	Woodward 2, Rooke, McCormick, Arnold	14,7
SF	J	1	N	West Ham U	L	0-2	3-4	Woodward, Rooke 2 (1 pen) (at Stamford Bridge)	32,7

PLAYER	A	G	PLAYER	A	G	PLAYER	A	G
J Arnold	36	10	G Green	2	-	R Rooke	35	27
Bacuzzi	18	-	J Griffiths	7	-	A Rozier	1	-
F Boulton	11	-	D Higgins	2	-	H Scott	1	-
Brown	3	-	E Hiles	40	-	E Shepherd	1	-
H Burgess	7	2	L Jones	4	-	J Smith	1	-
H Cann	19	-	M Keeping	44	-	R Stuart	2	-
A Chesters	1	-	W Mason	1	-	J Taylor	42	2
H Cothliff	1	-	J McCormick	10	3	DS Thomas	6	3
F Cox	4	-	R McCormick	4	-	DWJ Thomas	3	-
H Cranfield	3	2	G Mills	4	2	J Tompkins	25	1
R Dennison	1	-	E Muttitt	1	1	H Turner	3	-
J Evans	42	-	E O'Callaghan	3	-	S Weaver	2	-
D Flack	7	-	S Ottewell	5	5	W Whatley	1	-
J Finch	34	2	E Perry	5	5	G Wilkins	2	1
L Fisher	2	2	H Pitts	1	-	V Woodward	43	19
H Freeman	7	-	E Reay	3	-	H Worsley	6	-
						Own Goals		4

Includes the three Division Two fixtures in the aborted 1939-40 season plus the 43 wartime League and Cup games.

Jim Taylor, future England centre half combined football with naval duties.

1940-41

South Regional League

	P	W	D	L	F	A	GA
Crystal Palace	27	16	4	7	86	44	1.954
West Ham United	25	14	6	5	70	39	1.794
Coventry City	10	5	3	2	28	16	1.750
Arsenal	19	10	5	4	66	38	1.736
Cardiff City	24	12	5	7	75	50	1.500
Reading	26	14	5	7	73	51	1.431
Norwich City	19	9	2	8	73	55	1.327
Watford	35	15	6	14	96	73	1.315
Portsmouth	31	16	2	13	92	71	1.296
Tottenham Hotspur	23	9	5	9	53	41	1.293
Millwall	31	16	5	10	73	57	1.280
Walsall	32	14	7	11	100	80	1.250
West Bromwich Albion	28	13	5	10	83	69	1.202
Leicester City	33	17	5	11	87	73	1.191
Northampton Town	30	14	3	13	84	71	1.183
Bristol City	20	10	2	8	55	48	1.145
Mansfield	29	12	6	11	77	68	1.132
Charlton Athletic	19	7	4	8	37	34	1.088
Aldershot	24	14	2	8	73	68	1.073
Brentford	23	9	3	11	51	51	1.000
Chelsea	23	10	4	9	57	58	0.981
Birmingham	16	7	1	8	38	43	0.883
Fulham	30	10	7	13	62	73	0.849
Luton town	35	11	7	17	82	100	0.820
Stoke City	36	9	9	18	76	96	0.791
Queens Park Rangers	23	8	3	12	47	60	0.783
Brighton & Hove Albion	25	8	7	10	51	75	0.680
Nottingham Forest	25	7	3	15	50	77	0.649
Bournemouth & Boscombe Athletic	27	9	3	15	59	92	0.641
Notts County	21	8	3	10	42	66	0.636
Southend United	29	12	4	13	64	101	0.633
Southampton	31	4	4	23	53	111	0.477
Swansea Town	10	2	1	7	12	33	0.363
Clapton Orient	15	1	3	11	19	66	0.287

* Final placings were decided on goal average

Manager: Jack Peart

No		Date	V	Opponents	R	H-T	F-T	Scorers	Atten
1	A	31	H	Queen's Park R	W	1-1	3-1	Woodward Rooke 2	3,000
2	S	7	A	Arsenal	L	0-3	0-5		3,000
3		14	H	Arsenal	L	0-1	0-1		1,000
4		21	A	Millwall	L	0-2	1-4	Woodward	600
5		28	H	Luton T	D	0-1	3-3	Woodward Rooke Richfield	800
6	O	5	A	Charlton A	L	0-1	0-3		500
7		12	H	Clapton O	W	2-0	3-1	Birkett Thomas 2	400
8		19	A	Brentford	L	0-5	3-8	Miller 2 Thomas	1,000
9		26	H	Reading	D	0-0	1-1	Finch	300
10	N	2	A	Reading	L	0-1	1-2	Rooke	2,000
11		9	H	Charlton A	L	1-1	1-2	Finch	150
12		16	A	Queen's Park R	W	1-0	5-2	Thomas 2 Rooke 2 Taylor	1,000
13		23	H	Brentford	W	2-0	3-0	Thomas 2 Rooke	600
14	D	7	H	Millwall	L	1-2	3-5	Woodward Thomas Rooke	600
15		14	A	Luton T	W	1-1	4-3	Thomas Fisher 2 Hiles	400
16		21	H	West Ham U	L	1-1	1-2	Woodward	1,000
17		25	A	Chelsea	L		2-5	Woodward Osborne	3,441
18		28	A	West Ham U	L	1-1	1-2	Rooke	2,500
19	M	8	A	Norwich C	L		0-2		1,38
20		29	A	Crystal P	D	0-1	1-1	Rooke	3,000
21	A	5	A	Portsmouth	D	3-3	3-3	Rooke 3	3,099
22		13	A	Millwall	D	0-0	0-0		5,000
23		26	A	West Ham U	W	1-0	1-0	Rooke	3,000
24	M	3	A	Aldershot	D	0-1	3-3	Rooke 2 Revell	2,00
25		10	A	Brentford	W	0-1	3-2	O'Callaghan Revell Woodward	2,670
26		17	H	Millwall	W	2-1	4-1	Revell Rooke 2 Woodward	2,14
27		24	H	Southend U	W	3-1	8-2	McCormick Revell Rooke 4 Halton 2	1,000
28		31	A	Millwall	L	0-3	0-6		1,800
29	J	2	H	Queen's Park R	W		3-2	Miller Rooke 2	2,50
30		9	A	Tottenham H	L	1-0	1-2	Revell	4,000

London Cup (Group A)

A	J	4	H	Queen's Park R	W	2-1	4-1	Revell Rooke Keeping (1 og)	1,000
A		11	A	Queen's Park R	W	1-3	7-5	Rooke 4 Woodward Evans Robson	2,256
A		25	A	Crystal Palace	L	0-2	2-5	Revell Beasley	2,000
A	F	1	H	Brentford	W	3-0	4-1	Revell Rooke Beasley O'Callaghan	2,40
A		8	A	Brentford	L	1-4	4-7	O'Callaghan 2 Keeping Smith	2,00
A	M	1	A	Crystal Palace	L	0-1	1-4	Robinson	2,50
A		15	A	Aldershot	L	1-2	1-3	Freeman	3,00
A		22	A	Aldershot	L	0-1	2-4	Rooke Cullen	3,50
A	A	11	H	Chelsea	W	1-0	4-0	Woodward 2 Rooke O'Callaghan	5,00
A		19	A	Chelsea	L	2-1	3-4	Rooke 2 Wooward	2,71

League War Cup

1/1	F	15	A	Watford	L	0-3	1-4	Robson	5,00
1/2		22	H	Watford	W	0-1	2-1	O'Callaghan Rooke	2,50

PLAYER	A	G	PLAYER	A	G	PLAYER	A	G
Arnold	2	-	R Halton	3	2	W Pavitt	1	-
Bacuzzi	10	-	R Hammond	1	-	F Penn	1	-
Bastin	1	-	E Hiles	31	1	J Poulter	1	-
Birkett	3	1	S Hobbus	4	-	C Revell	14	5
Bonass	1	-	W Hughes	2	-	M Richfield	2	1
Boulton	12	-	J Jobling	1	-	G Robinson	2	-
Briggs	5	-	P Joslin	8	-	R Rodger	2	-
Buckham	1	-	W Kay	1	-	R Rooke	27	24
Cardwell	3	-	M Keeping	2	-	A Rozier	1	-
Collett	1	-	G Lunn	1	-	G Scaife	14	-
Cranfield	2	-	S Malpass	7	-	JT Smith	2	-
Cullis	9	-	G Matthewson	5	-	R Spence	3	-
Duke	1	-	J McCormick	1	1	J Taylor	7	1
Evans	7	-	R McCormick	3	-	DWJ Thomas	14	9
Finch	17	2	J Miller	6	3	J Thomson	1	-
Fisher	11	2	R Morris	5	-	G Trewick	1	-
Flack	7	-	E Muttitt	10	-	S Weaver	3	-
Freeman	7	-	E O'Callaghan	9	1	W Whittaker	3	-
V Griffiths	1	-	V O'Leary	15	-	J Wilson	1	-
Grundy	5	-	J Osborne	2	1	V Woodward	29	8

Jim McCormack, a wartime guest who signed full-time in 1945.

1941-42

London League

	P	W	D	L	F	A	Pts
Arsenal	30	23	2	5	108	43	48
Portsmouth	30	20	2	8	105	59	42
West Ham United	30	17	5	8	81	44	39
Aldershot	30	17	5	8	85	56	39
Tottenham Hotspur	30	15	8	7	61	41	38
Crystal Palace	30	14	6	10	70	53	34
Reading	30	13	8	9	76	58	34
Charlton Athletic	30	14	5	11	72	64	33
Brentford	30	14	2	14	80	76	30
Queens Park Rangers	30	11	3	16	52	59	25
Fulham	30	10	4	16	79	99	24
Brighton & Hove Albion	30	9	4	17	71	108	22
Chelsea	30	8	4	18	56	88	20
Millwall	30	7	5	18	53	82	19
Clapton Orient	30	5	7	18	42	94	17
Watford	30	6	4	20	47	114	16

Manager: Jack Peart

No		*Date*	*V*	*Opponents*	*R*	*H-T*	*F-T*	*Scorers*	*Atte*
1	A	30	H	Aldershot	L	1-2	2-6	Rooke 2	3,50
2	S	6	A	Millwall	W	1-0	4-2	Muttitt, Cranfield, Rooke 2	5,00
3		13	H	Arsenal	L	0-3	2-5	Cranfield, Rooke	10,47
4		20	A	Queen's Park R	W	3-1	5-2	Sibley, Rooke 4	5,50
5		27	H	Reading	D	2-1	2-2	Rooke 2	6,01
6	O	4	H	Brighton & HA	L	1-3	2-3	McCormick, Morgan	2,50
7		11	H	Brentford	W	1-0	4-3	Gallacher 2, Hiles 2	6,00
8		18	A	Crystal Palace	L	0-2	1-3	Hiles	5,00
9		25	A	Clapton O	L	1-0	1-2	Jones (E)	2,00
10	N	1	H	Tottenham H	D	2-1	2-2	Rooke 2	6,00
11		8	A	Portsmouth	L	1-3	3-5	Gallacher, Richardson, Rooke	6,32
12		15	H	Chelsea	L	0-2	1-4	Freeman	4,99
13		22	A	Charlton A	D	2-2	3-3	Rooke 2, Gallacher	3,06
14		29	H	West Ham U	L	0-3	1-3	Jones (L)	4,46
15	D	6	A	Watford	W	1-0	5-3	Thomas, Gallacher 2, Conley 2	1,00
16		13	A	Aldershot	L	0-4	3-4	Rampling, Rooke 2	3,00
17		20	H	Millwall	W	3-0	4-3	Rooke 4	1,00
18		25	A	Arsenal	L		0-2		10,57
19		27	H	Queen's Park R	L	0-3	0-3		3,77
20	J	3	A	Reading	L	1-2	1-4	Gallacher	4,00
21		10	A	Brighton & HA	W	4-1	7-3	Dean, Finch 2, Gallacher2, Rooke 2	2,50
22		17	A	Brentford	W	2-1	3-2	Dean 3	3,00
23		31	H	Clapton O	W	3-0	5-1	Dean, Conley 3, Finch	1,92
24	F	14	H	Portsmouth	L	0-2	2-7	Conley 2	4,40
25		21	A	Chelsea	W	2-1	5-1	Rooke 2, Gallacher, Finch, Woodward	3,25
26		28	H	Charlton A	L	2-1	4-7	Dean 2, Rooke, Gallacher	3,09
27	M	7	A	West Ham U	D	0-0	1-1	Kiernan	2,50
28		14	H	Watford	L	1-1	1-3	Finch	2,46
29	M	2	A	Tottenham H	L	1-4	1-7	Conley	3,75
30		23	H	Crystal Palace	W	0-3	4-3	Conley 4	3,00

London War Cup

Q	M	21	A	Portsmouth	L	1-2	1-9	Kiernan	6,21
Q		28	H	Chelsea	W	0-0	1-0	Conley	5,88
Q	A	4	H	Portsmouth	W	1-0	2-1	Conley 2	5,16
Q		6	A	Chelsea	D		2-2	Conley 2	10,98
Q		11	H	Crystal Palace	W	1-0	4-1	Woodward 2, Conley, Gallagher	6,00
Q		16	A	Crystal Palace	W	3-1	4-3	Rooke 3, Foxall	3,37

PLAYER	A	G	PLAYER	A	G	PLAYER	A	G
Abel	1	-	J Holliday	2	-	J Richardson	6	1
Bacuzzi	10	-	L Howe	1	-	R Rooke	25	30
Beasley	1	-	E Jones	7	1	G Scaife	2	-
Bonass	2	-	L Jones	24	1	Sharp	3	-
Briggs	1	-	P Joslin	4	-	A Sibley	12	1
Briggs	1	-	E Keen	2	-	G Skinner	1	-
Buckingham	1	-	L Kelly	1	-	E Smith	2	-
Compton	1	-	T Kiernan	5	2	C Smith	1	-
Conley	20	18	F Lester	2	-	W Sneddon	1	-
Cranfield	6	2	Lodge	1	-	A Stevens	1	-
Cullis	9	-	G Ludford	1	-	F Swift	5	-
Cumner	2	-	J McCormick	6	1	F Taylor	4	-
Dean	14	7	Mackie	1	-	DWJ Thomas	4	1
Duffy	6	-	S Malpass	7	-	S Tickridge	1	-
Duke	25	-	F Marsden	1	-	J Tompkins	10	-
Evans	3	-	G Matthewson	18	-	E Tuckett	1	-
Finch	10	5	J Milsom	1		H Wallbanks	1	-
Ford	1	-	G Milton	1	-	Walsh	1	-
Foxall	5	1	Morgan	1	1	R Ward	1	-
Freeman	13	1	E Muttitt	7	1	W Whatley	11	
Gallacher	29	12	H Neary	1	-	Whitfield	6	-
Gibbons	1	-	E Nichols	1	-	J Wilson	1	-
W Griffiths	2	-	O Parry	1	-	V Woodward	2	3
V Hamilton	1	-	G Poland	1	-	A Young	1	-
Hiles	24	3	R Pryde	2	-			
Holley	1	-	D Rampling	4	1			

Ronnie Rooke, who scored a remarkable 212 goals in 199 wartime appearances.

1942-43

Football League South

	P	W	D	L	F	A	Pts
Arsenal	30	21	1	6	102	40	43
Tottenham Hotspur	30	16	6	6	68	28	38
Queens Park Rangers	30	18	2	8	64	49	38
Portsmouth	30	16	3	9	66	52	35
Southampton	30	14	5	9	86	58	33
West Ham United	30	14	5	9	80	66	33
Chelsea	30	14	4	10	52	45	32
Aldershot	30	14	2	12	87	77	30
Brentford	30	12	5	11	64	63	29
Charlton Athletic	30	13	3	12	68	75	29
Clapton Orient	30	11	5	12	54	72	27
Brighton & Hove Albion	30	10	5	13	65	73	25
Reading	30	9	6	13	67	74	24
Fulham	30	10	2	16	69	78	22
Crystal Palace	30	7	5	16	49	75	19
Millwall	30	6	5	17	66	88	17
Watford	30	7	2	19	51	88	16
Luton Town	30	4	6	18	43	100	14

Manager: Jack Peart

No		Date	V	Opponents	R	H-T	F-T	Scorers	Atter
1	A	29	A	Luton T	L	1-1	1-3	Freeman	2,00
2	S	5	H	Brentford	W	0-0	3-1	Conley, Thomas, Gallacher	4,60
3		12	A	Reading	L	0-3	1-4	Martin	4,00
4		19	H	Millwall	W	2-0	4-1	Rooke, Dean 2, Conley	4,50
5		26	A	Chelsea	L	1-1	2-4	Jones, Rooke	10,63
6	O	3	H	Arsenal	L	2-1	3-4	Rooke, Dean, Conley	11,00
7		10	A	Crystal Palace	W	1-1	4-2	Finch, Conley, Rooke, Dean	4,60
8		17	H	Charlton A	L	1-3	2-4	Holliday, Muttitt	5,50
9		24	A	Southampton	L	1-1	2-4	Arnold, Conley	7,00
10		31	H	West Ham U	L	1-2	2-3	Conley, Rooke	5,50
11	N	7	A	Portsmouth	D	0-0	1-1	Tompkins	5,84
12		14	H	Watford	W	2-0	2-0	Rooke 2	3,00
13		21	A	Clapton O	L	2-3	2-4	Neary, Freeman	2,50
14		28	H	Luton T	W	4-1	6-2	Thomas, Leyfield 3, Rooke, Driver	1,50
15	D	5	A	Brentford	L	1-2	2-4	Conley, Finch	5,20
16		12	H	Reading	W	2-1	5-2	Driver 2, Rooke 2, Leyfield	3,00
17		19	A	Millwall	W	3-0	6-1	Dean, Broadhurst 3, Ottewell, Conley	3,00
18		25	A	Queen's Park R	L		1-2	Conley	4,00
19		26	H	Queen's Park R	W	2-0	4-2	Thomas 2, Rooke, Conley	7,91
20	J	2	H	Chelsea	W	1-1	3-1	Rooke 2, Conley	9,80
21		9	A	Arsenal	L	1-3	2-7	Rooke, Conley	8,33
22		16	H	Crystal Palace	L	1-2	1-2	Ottewell	3,82
23		23	A	Charlton A	L	0-2	0-2		3,50
24		30	H	Southampton	L	1-3	2-8	Conley 2	2,51
25	F	6	A	West Ham U	L	0-1	1-2	Conley	5,20
26		13	H	Portsmouth	L	0-4	2-6	Rooke 2	4,83
27		20	A	Watford	W	3-1	4-1	Rooke, Dean 2, Ottewell	2,50
28		27	H	Clapton O	D	0-0	1-1	Holley	4,00

League War Cup South

No		Date	V	Opponents	R	H-T	F-T	Scorers	Atter
Q	M	6	H	Charlton A	W	1-0	3-1	Jones L 2, Rooke	5,03
Q		13	A	Aldershot	L	1-3	1-4	Rooke	5,00
Q		20	H	Portsmouth	D	1-1	2-2	Rooke 2	5,81
Q		27	A	Charlton A	L	0-4	1-6	Rooke	4,50
Q	A	3	H	Aldershot	D	1-1	2-2	Rooke, Hobbis	7,72
Q		10	A	Portsmouth	W	2-0	3-1	Thomas 2, Conley	7,26

LAYER	A	G	PLAYER	A	G	PLAYER	A	G
Arnold	1	1	T Holley	20	1	S Pilkington	1	-
Bacuzzi	13	-	J Holliday	2	1	H Pitts	1	-
Broadhurst	1	3	L Jones	29	3	D Rampling	1	-
Buckley	6	-	N Kirkman	1	-	R Rooke	26	23
Bush	12	-	F Kurz	1	-	A Rozier	2	-
Conley	32	16	F Lester	5	-	L Salmon	1	-
Conway	1	-	C Leyfield	7	4	R Savage	1	-
V Copping	2	-	C Lloyd	5	-	C Smith	1	-
V Costello	1	-	G Ludford	1	-	JT Smith	2	-
Davie	1	-	S Malpass	7	-	W Sneddon	2	-
Dean	14	7	D Martin	1	1	W Sperrin	1	-
Drake	2	-	O McCulloch	1	-	A Stevens	2	-
Driver	5	3	J McInnes	4	-	DWJ Thomas	10	6
Duke	34	-	G Merrett	1	-	J Thomson	3	-
Evans	19	-	G Milton	5	-	J Tompkins	4	1
Farmer	1	-	A Muir	3	-	E Tuckett	4	-
Ferrier	1	-	E Muttitt	6	1	J Watson	1	-
Finch	18	2	H Neary	2	1	W Whitfield	2	-
Freeman	20	2	W Nicholson	1	-	J Wilson	2	-
Gallacher	3	1	F O'Donnell	3	-	V Woodward	1	-
Hiles	3	-	S Ottewell	9	3			
Hobbis	1	1	R Palmer	1	-			

Joe Bacuzzi, who won an England cap in the wartime internationals.

1943-44

Football League South

	P	W	D	L	F	A	Pts
Tottenham Hotspur	30	19	8	3	71	36	46
West Ham United	30	17	7	6	74	39	41
Queens Park Rangers	30	14	12	4	69	54	40
Arsenal	30	14	10	6	72	42	38
Crystal Palace	30	16	5	9	75	53	37
Portsmouth	30	16	5	9	68	59	37
Brentford	30	14	7	9	71	51	35
Chelsea	30	16	2	12	79	55	34
Fulham	30	11	9	10	80	73	31
Millwall	30	13	4	13	70	66	30
Aldershot	30	12	6	12	64	73	30
Reading	30	12	3	15	73	62	27
Southampton	30	10	7	13	67	88	27
Charlton Athletic	30	9	7	14	57	73	25
Watford	30	6	8	16	58	80	20
Brighton & Hove Albion	30	9	2	19	55	82	20
Clapton Orient	30	4	3	23	32	87	11
Luton Town	30	3	5	22	42	104	11

Manager: Jack Peart

No		Date	V	Opponents	R	H-T	F-T	Scorers	Atte
1	A	28	A	Luton T	D	1-1	2-2	Thomas (DWJ), Leyfield	4,00
2	S	4	H	Brentford	W	2-2	4-3	Stamps 2, Thomas (DWJ), Rooke	7,73
3		11	A	Aldershot	D	1-1	2-2	Rooke, Dean	6,00
4		18	H	Millwall	W	2-1	4-1	Rooke 2, Stamps, Leyfield	
5		25	A	Chelsea	L	0-3	0-3		11,71
6	O	2	H	Arsenal	L	1-3	3-4	Rooke 2, Thomas (DWJ)	17,99
7		9	H	Crystal Palace	L	2-2	4-5	Rooke 3, Leyfield	8,00
8		16	A	Charlton A	D	1-0	1-1	Conley	8,00
9		23	A	Southampton	W	1-1	3-2	Stamps, Rooke 2	7,00
10		30	H	West Ham U	L	1-2	2-6	Stamps, Rooke	10,00
11	N	6	H	Brighton & HA	W	2-2	6-2	Thomas (DWJ), Rooke 2, Conley, Malpass, Jones (L)	5,00
12		13	H	Watford	D	0-0	0-0		3,90
13		20	A	Clapton O	W	1-0	3-1	Rooke, Duggan 2	2,00
14		27	H	Luton T	W	1-1	4-1	Stamps 2, Thomas (DWJ), Stevens	1,00
15	D	4	A	Brentford	D	0-0	1-1	Stamps	7,51
16		11	H	Aldershot	D	1-1	2-2	Stamps 2	3,00
17		18	H	Queen's Park R	D	1-2	2-2	Rooke, Stamps	6,00
18		25	A	Tottenham H	L		0-2		16,62
19		27	H	Tottenham H	L		0-2		
20	J	1	A	Millwall	L	1-3	1-5	Rooke (at Selhurst Park)	3,97
21		8	A	Brighton & HA	W	2-2	6-3	Taylor, Quested 2, Rooke 3	3,00
22		22	A	Arsenal	D	1-0	1-1	O'Callaghan	8,11
23		29	A	Crystal Palace	L	0-4	2-6	Rooke, Muttitt	7,00
24	F	5	H	Charlton A	W		5-1	Rooke 3, Conley, Jones (L)	5,00
25		12	H	Southampton	W	3-2	6-2	Conley 2, Holley 2, Kiernan 2	5,00
26	A	1	A	West Ham U	L	0-2	2-3	Kiernan, Rooke	5,00
27		10	H	Chelsea	L		2-3	Kiernan 2	
28		22	A	Queen's Park R	D	1-1	3-3	Stamps, Kiernan 2	4,00
29		29	A	Watford	W	2-1	6-3	Stamps 2, Kiernan 3, Rampling	2,19
30	M	6	H	Clapton O	W	1-0	3-1	Conley 2, Kiernan	2,00

League War Cup South

Q	F	19	A	Reading	L	0-2	0-3		4,00
Q		26	H	Luton T	W	2-0	2-0	Rooke, Kiernan	3,00
Q	M	4	A	Clapton O	W	2-0	4-0	Stevens, Rooke, Flack, Devlin	2,00
Q		11	H	Reading	L	2-2	3-4	Rooke, Devlin 2	7,00
Q		18	A	Luton T	L	1-1	2-3	Rooke 2	3,00
Q		25	H	Clapton O	L	2-3	4-5	Kiernan 2, Rooke 2	5,00

PLAYER	A	G	PLAYER	A	G	PLAYER	A	G
Allen	2	-	T Holley	20	2	L Quested	1	2
Bowpitt	3	-	J Horton	1	-	D Rampling	4	1
H Brophy	1	-	J Humphreys	1	-	R Rooke	32	32
J Brown	8	-	P Humphreys	2	-	R Royston	1	-
V Buchan	7	-	J James	1	-	D Sears	1	-
W Chick	1	-	L Jones	31	2	E Shepherd	3	-
W Cobley	1	-	V Jones	2	-	J Stamps	15	14
W Copping	2	-	P Joslin	5	-	A Stevens	8	2
J Conley	30	7	T Kiernan	11	14	J Summers	4	-
R Cowan	7	-	D Kinnear	1	-	J Taylor	1	-
A Cox	18	-	F Laing	1	-	T Taylor	8	1
C Dean	3	1	F Lester	8	-	DWJ Thomas	11	5
Devlin	4	3	C Leyfield	15	3	RA Thomas	2	-
E Duggan	1	2	C Lloyd	16	-	J Tompkins	4	-
H Duke	23	-	W Lumby	1	-	H Wallbanks	1	-
Evans	11	-	S Malpass	7	1	J Wallbanks	1	-
W Flack	6	1	D Mangnall	1	-	T Ward	1	-
H Freeman	4	-	T Manley	6	-	J Watson	1	-
C Fuller	1	-	J Millbanks	2	-	JF Watson	3	-
R Halton	1	-	G Milton	2	-	S Weaver	1	-
Henley	1	-	E Muttitt	3	1	W Whittaker	2	-
A Hickman	3	-	E O'Callaghan	10	1	J Wilson	3	-
E Hiles	1	-	H Phipps	1	-	V Woodward	1	-

Vivian Woodward, was the forward who played for Fulham before, during and after the war.

1944-45

Football League South

	P	W	D	L	F	A	Pts
Tottenham Hotspur	30	23	6	1	81	30	52
West Ham United	30	22	3	5	96	47	47
Brentford	30	17	4	9	87	57	38
Chelsea	30	16	5	9	100	55	37
Southampton	30	17	3	10	96	69	37
Crystal Palace	30	15	5	10	74	70	35
Reading	30	14	6	10	78	68	34
Arsenal	30	14	3	13	77	67	31
Queens Park Rangers	30	10	10	10	70	61	30
Watford	30	11	6	13	66	84	28
Fulham	30	11	4	15	79	83	26
Portsmouth	30	11	4	15	56	61	26
Charlton Athletic	30	12	2	16	72	81	26
Brighton & Hove Albion	30	10	2	18	66	95	22
Luton Town	30	6	7	17	56	104	19
Aldershot	30	7	4	19	44	85	18
Millwall	30	5	7	18	50	84	17
Clapton Orient	30	5	7	18	39	86	17

Manager: Jack Peart

No	Date		V	Opponents	R	H-T	F-T	Scorers	Atten
1	A	26	H	Chelsea	W	5-0	7-4	Rooke 4, Potts 2, O'Callaghan	10,00
2	S	2	A	Reading	L	2-2	4-5	Conley 2, Rooke 2	4,00
3		9	H	Queen's Park R	D	2-1	2-2	Thomas (R), Rooke	8,00
4		16	A	Brighton & HA	W	4-1	7-1	Rooke 4, Leyfield, Potts 2	4,50
5		23	H	Crystal Palace	W	3-2	6-2	Rooke 4, Flack, O'Callaghan	8,00
6		30	A	Watford	W	1-1	2-1	Potts 2	4,84
7	O	7	H	Southampton	W	1-3	4-3	Rooke 3, Leyfield	8,00
8		14	H	Arsenal	D	1-2	4-4	Arnold, Thomas (R) 2, (Field og)	16,00
9		21	A	Charlton A	W	0-0	3-1	Potts, Rooke 2	7,00
10		28	H	Clapton O	W	1-1	5-2	Cheetham 3, Potts 2	6,00
11	N	4	H	Brentford	L	0-2	0-2		25,00
12		11	H	West Ham U	L	2-3	4-7	Potts 2, Arnold, Lowes	10,35
13		18	H	Portsmouth	L	0-0	0-2		8,98
14		25	A	Tottenham H	L	0-0	1-2	Jones (L)	14,30
15	D	2	A	Chelsea	L	0-2	0-2		18,00
16		9	H	Reading	L	1-2	2-3	Lowes, Wilson (J)	8,00
17		16	A	Queen's Park R	D	2-2	4-4	Dodds 2 (1 pen), Watson, Lowes	10,00
18		23	H	Luton T	W	3-1	3-2	Dodds 3	5,00
19		26	A	Luton T	L		1-3	(1 og)	5,00
20		30	H	Brighton & HA	L	2-2	2-3	O'Callaghan, Dodds	4,00
21	J	6	A	Crystal Palace	W	2-0	2-0	Gallacher, Jessop	6,00
22		13	H	Watford	L	0-0	0-2		4,00
23		20	A	Southampton	L	0-0	0-3		6,00
24		27	A	Arsenal	L	0-2	3-8	Dodds 2, Lowes (at White Hart Lane)	5,24
25	M	24	A	Clapton O	D	0-0	0-0		2,50
26		31	A	Brentford	W	2-2	3-2	Sloan 3	8,78
27	A	14	A	West Ham U	L	0-0	2-3	Rooke, Lowes	8,00
28		21	A	Portsmouth	L	1-0	1-3	(1 og)	7,98
29		28	H	Tottenham H	L	2-2	2-4	Rooke 2	8,00
30	M	5	H	Charlton A	W	1-2	5-3	Rooke 2, Steele 2, Weston	1,50

League War Cup South

Q	F	3	H	Millwall	L	0-1	1-3	Sloan	8,00
Q		10	A	Brighton & HA	W	2-0	3-1	Sloan 2, Rooke	7,00
Q		17	H	Brentford	W	0-0	1-0	Rooke	15,00
Q		24	A	Millwall	L	0-1	0-1		9,00
Q	M	3	H	Brighton & HA	W	1-1	5-2	Dodds 3, Livingstone 2	9,00
Q		10	H	Brentford	W	3-1	5-2	Lowes, Jones L, Kippax 3	10,38

LAYER	A	G	PLAYER	A	G	PLAYER	A	G
Abel	1	-	H Hollis	2	-	E Muttitt	3	-
Adams	1	-	I Hopkins	2	-	H Neary	2	-
Arnold	7	2	A Hudgell	1	-	E O'Callagan	10	3
Bacuzzi	18	-	D Hunt	1	-	H Potts	10	11
Bewley	2	-	D Jarvis	2	-	J Preskett	2	-
Blair	1	-	W Jessop	8	1	D Rampling	2	-
Borrows	1	-	C Jones	1	-	R Redfern	1	-
Boulter	6	-	E Jones	2	-	H Rickett	10	-
Bowpitt	1	-	F Jones	2	-	A Robson	1	-
Briggs	2	-	G Jones	1	-	R Rooke	15	27
Briscoe	1	-	L Jones	33	2	E Shepherd	1	-
Buchanan	1	-	S Jones	3	-	J Sloan	11	6
Buckingham	7	-	V Jones	1	-	J Smith	3	-
Buckton	1	-	J Jordan	1	-	L Smith	1	-
Cheetham	6	3	T Kiernan	1	-	A Squires	1	-
Chitty	1	-	F Kippax	5	3	F Steele	1	2
Conley	3	2	W Laws	1	-	J Taylor	3	-
Cowan	15	-	C Leyfield	9	2	A Tennant	1	-
Cox	1	-	A Livingstone	4	2	DWJ Thomas	2	-
Cunliffe	2	-	C Lloyd	12	-	RA Thomas	4	3
Dawes	1	-	A Lowes	20	6	E Toser	1	-
Dawes	3	-	J Mallett	1	-	E Tunnicliffe	2	-
Dodds	9	11	J McCormick	3	-	H Wallbanks	1	-
Duke	18	-	H McCluskey	1	-	JF Watson	26	1
Flack	10	1	J Meadows	1	-	A Weston	1	1
Freeman	20	-	J Millbank	2	-	R White	1	-
Gage	2	-	J Miller	3	-	W Whittaker	1	-
Gallacher	2	1	K Moody	1	-	J Wilson	3	1
Gibson	3	-	N Moore	1	-	H Wright	1	-
Hamilton	1	-	J Norris	1	-			
Hiles	1	-	M Muir	1	-	Own Goals		3

Scottish international winger Pete Buchanan guested during the war and was transfered from Chelsea in March 1946.

1945-46

Football League South

	P	W	D	L	F	A	Pts
Birmingham	42	28	5	9	96	45	61
Aston Villa	42	25	11	6	106	58	61
Charlton Athletic	42	25	10	7	92	45	60
Derby County	42	24	7	11	101	62	55
West Bromwich Albion	42	22	8	12	104	69	52
Wolverhampton Wanderers	42	20	11	11	75	48	51
West Ham United	42	20	11	11	94	76	51
Fulham	42	20	10	12	93	73	50
Tottenham Hotspur	42	22	3	17	78	81	47
Chelsea	42	19	6	17	92	80	44
Arsenal	42	16	11	15	76	73	43
Millwall	42	17	8	17	79	105	42
Coventry City	42	15	10	17	70	69	40
Brentford	42	14	10	18	82	72	38
Nottingham Forest	42	12	13	17	72	73	37
Southampton	42	14	9	19	97	105	37
Swansea Town	42	15	7	20	90	112	37
Luton Town	42	13	7	22	60	92	33
Portsmouth	42	11	6	25	66	87	28
Leicester City	42	8	7	27	57	101	23
Newport County	42	9	2	31	52	125	20
Plymouth Argyle	42	3	8	31	39	120	14

Manager: Jack Peart

FAC3 Debuts for Beasley and Taylor

No		Date	V	Opponents	R	H-T	F-T	Scorers	Atte
1	A	25	A	Derby C	L	1-3	2-5	Rooke 2	15,0
2		30	A	Newport C	W		5-1	Rooke 3 Bewley Wardle	5,0
3	S	1	H	Derby C	W	0-0	2-1	Sargent, McCormick	20,0
4		8	H	Leicester C	W	0-0	1-0	Taylor	18,0
5		12	A	Nottingham F	D	0-0	1-1	Wardle	14,0
6		15	A	Leicester C	W		1-0	Taylor	14,0
7		22	A	Coventry C	L	0-1	1-3	Rooke (1 pen)	14,1
8		29	H	Coventry C	W	1-0	2-0	Rooke, McCormick	17,8
9	O	6	H	Luton T	W	2-0	4-1	Buchanan 2, Wardle, Rooke	15,0
10		13	A	Luton T	D	2-0	2-2	Rooke 2 (1 pen)	10,0
11		20	A	Aston Villa	L	0-2	0-3		15,0
12		27	H	Aston Villa	L	0-0	1-4	Rooke	32,5
13	N	3	H	Arsenal	W		5-2	Rooke 3, Jessop, Shepherd	30,0
14		10	A	Arsenal	L	0-1	0-2	(at White Hart Lane)	19,0
15		17	A	Charlton A	L	2-1	2-4	Rampling, Rooke	20,0
16		24	H	Charlton A	L		2-4	Shepherd 2	35,0
17	D	1	H	Swansea T	W	3-0	5-2	Shepherd 3, McCormick, Miller	18,0
18		8	A	Swansea T	D	0-2	2-2	Shepherd, Rooke	15,0
19		15	H	Plymouth A	W	0-0	4-0	Rampling 2, Rooke, Shepherd	15,0
20		22	A	Plymouth A	W	1-0	2-0	Rooke, Rampling	2,0
21		25	A	Portsmouth	D		2-2	Freeman, Rooke	11,8
22		26	H	Portsmouth	W	3-1	5-2	Rooke 4, Shepherd	22,3
23		29	H	Nottingham F	D	0-2	3-3	McCormick, Freeman 2 (1 pen)	20,0
24	J	12	H	Wolverhampton W	W	2-1	3-1	Woodward 2, Shepherd	34,0
25		19	A	Wolverhampton W	L	0-1	0-2		18,0
26	F	2	H	West Ham U	L	0-0	0-1		30,0
27		9	H	West Bromich A	L	0-2	1-4	(1 og)	15,1
28		16	A	West Bromich A	L		1-3	Beasley	20,0
29		23	A	Birmingham C	L		0-2		25,0
30	M	9	H	Tottenham H	D	0-0	1-1	Rooke	30,0
31		16	A	Tottenham H	W		3-1	Beasley, Buchanan 2	23,2
32		23	A	Brentford	W		2-1	Buchanan, Rooke	23,4
33		30	H	Brentford	D	2-0	2-2	Rooke, Beasley	27,4
34	A	6	H	Chelsea	W	2-2	3-2	Shepherd, Beasley, McCormick	35,0
35		13	A	Chelsea	D	0-0	0-0		35,0
36		15	H	Birmingham C	W	1-0	3-2	Taylor (pen), Buchanan, Woodward	14,0
37		19	A	Millwall	W	1-0	1-0	Shepherd	25,0
38		20	H	Southampton	W	1-1	3-1	Woodward 2, Beasley	15,0
39		22	H	Millwall	W	1-0	7-0	Rooke 2, Woodward 2, Buchanan 2, Shepherd	18,7
40		27	A	Southampton	D	1-0	1-1	Shepherd	10,0
41		29	A	West Ham U	W		5-3	Rooke 3, Shepherd 2	8,0
42	M	4	H	Newport C	W	3-0	3-1	Buchanan, Woodward, Beasley	15,0

FA Cup

No		Date	V	Opponents	R	H-T	F-T	Scorers	Atte
3/1	J	5	A	Charlton A	L		1-3	Rampling	30,0
3/2		7	H	Charlton A	W	2-1	2-1	Rooke 2	20,0

PLAYER	A	G	PLAYER	A	G	PLAYER	A	G
J Bacuzzi	37	-	G Holben	2	-	H Rickett	17	-
A Beasley	24	6	D Hunt	1	-	R Rooke	41	33
D Bewley	12	1	D Jarvis	7	-	J Sanders	1	-
G Bremner	1	-	W Jessop	1	1	F Sargent	1	1
A Brown	1	-	E Jones	9	-	E Shepherd	35	16
P Buchanan	25	9	A Little	1	-	A Stevens	1	-
J Chisholm	2	-	C Lloyd	15	-	J Taylor	37	3
W Collins	1	-	A Lowes	1	-	DS Thomas	1	-
J Evans	8	-	A Machin	1	-	H Wallbanks	28	-
D Evans	13	-	S Malpass	4	-	C Wardle	4	3
H Ferrier	4	-	J McCormick	31	5	JF Watson	25	-
H Freeman	42	3	J McDermott	3	-	G Wilkins	1	-
G Frost	2	-	J Miller	4	1	V Woodward	16	8
A Gage	4	-	J Morris	1	-	H Worsley	1	-
E Hiles	1	-	E O'Callaghan	1	-	Own Goals		1
F Hindle	1	-	D Rampling	15	5			

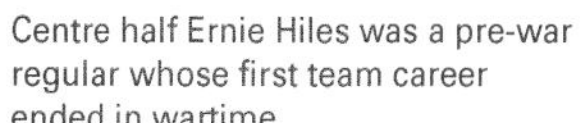

Centre half Ernie Hiles was a pre-war regular whose first team career ended in wartime.

1946-47

Division Two

	P	W	D	L	F	A	Pts
Manchester City	42	26	10	6	78	35	62
Burnley	42	22	14	6	65	29	58
Birmingham City	42	25	5	12	74	33	55
Chesterfield	42	18	14	10	58	44	50
Newcastle United	42	19	10	13	95	62	48
Tottenham Hotspur	42	17	14	11	65	53	48
West Bromwich Albion	42	20	8	14	88	75	48
Coventry City	42	16	13	13	66	59	45
Leicester City	42	18	7	17	69	64	43
Barnsley	42	17	8	17	84	86	42
Nottingham Forest	42	15	10	17	69	74	40
West Ham United	42	16	8	18	70	76	40
Luton Town	42	16	7	19	71	73	39
Southampton	42	15	9	18	69	76	39
Fulham	42	15	9	18	63	74	39
Bradford Park Avenue	42	14	11	17	65	77	39
Bury	42	12	12	18	80	78	36
Millwall	42	14	8	20	56	79	36
Plymouth Argyle	42	14	5	23	79	96	33
Sheffield Wednesday	42	12	8	22	67	88	32
Swansea Town	42	11	7	24	55	83	29
Newport County	42	10	3	29	61	133	23

Manager: Jack Peart

Did you know that?

The controversial sale of Ronnie Rooke to Arsenal in December 1946 was instigated by Fulham. Jack Peart, the Fulham manager, knew it would be unpopular and advised Arsenal's Tom Whittaker to park his car a few streets away from the Cottage or else the supporters would turn it over if they knew he was there.

No		Date	V	Opponents	R	H-T	F-T	Scorers	Atter
1	A	31	A	Bury	L	0-2	2-7	Rooke 2	12,84
2	S	2	A	West Ham U	L	1-2	2-3	Beasley, Rooke	28,01
3		7	H	Luton T	W	2-0	2-1	Shepherd, Rooke	26,03
4		9	H	West Ham U	W	3-2	3-2	Wallbanks, Rooke, Shepherd	19,90
5		14	A	Plymouth A	D	1-1	2-2	Beasley 2	24,53
6		16	A	Sheffield W	D	1-0	1-1	Rooke	20,47
7		21	H	Leicester C	W	3-1	4-2	Stevens, Shepherd, McCormick, Rooke	25,37
8		28	A	Chesterfield	D	1-0	1-1	Rooke	16,81
9	O	5	H	Millwall	W	3-2	3-2	Stevens, Rooke, Beasley	30,99
10		12	A	Bradford	W	1-1	2-1	Taylor, Watson	9,66
11		19	H	Barnsley	W	3-0	6-1	Rooke 2, Beasley 2, Shepherd, McCormick	37,22
12		26	A	Burnley	L	0-2	0-2		26,90
13	N	2	H	Tottenham H	D	0-1	1-1	Freeman	40,76
14		9	A	Swansea T	W	0-0	2-0	Rooke 2	21,32
15		16	H	Newcastle U	L	0-0	0-3		44,48
16		23	A	West Bromich A	L	1-3	1-6	Thomas	20,85
17		30	H	Birmingham C	L	0-1	0-1		20,79
18	D	7	A	Coventry C	L	0-1	0-1		17,01
19		25	A	Newport C	L	2-1	2-4	Beasley, Taylor	13,86
20		26	H	Newport C	W	2-1	4-1	Nelson, Buchanan, Shepherd 2	20,09
21		28	H	Bury	W	1-0	2-0	Grant, Nelson	20,36
22	J	1	A	Manchester C	L	0-2	0-4		49,44
23		4	A	Luton T	L	0-1	0-2		17,34
24		18	H	Plymouth A	W	2-0	3-1	McGibbon 3	24,10
25	M	1	H	Manchester C	D	0-2	2-2	Ayres, Beasley	32,12
26		8	A	Tottenham H	D	0-1	1-1	Shepherd	27,71
27		15	H	Swansea T	W	1-0	3-0	Ayres 2, McGibbon	17,60
28		22	A	Newcastle U	W	2-0	3-1	Stevens 2, McGibbon	43,64
29		29	H	West Bromich A	L	0-0	0-1		25,71
30	A	5	A	Birmingham C	L	1-1	1-2	McGibbon	28,19
31		7	H	Sheffield W	L	0-2	1-2	Freeman	26,65
32		12	H	Coventry C	W	1-0	2-0	Nelson (pen), Stevens	16,75
33		19	A	Nottingham F	L	1-1	1-2	Ayres	20,30
34		26	H	Southampton	D	0-0	0-0		14,08
35	M	3	A	Barnsley	L	0-0	1-4	McGibbon	12,32
36		10	H	Chesterfield	W	1-1	2-1	Freeman, Taylor	10,26
37		17	H	Burnley	W	0-0	1-0	Beasley	25,43
38		24	A	Southampton	L	0-1	0-2		10,36
39		26	H	Nottingham F	D	0-0	1-1	Grant	9,16
40		31	H	Bradford	L	0-2	0-3		9,66
41	J	7	A	Leicester C	L	0-0	0-2		8,89
42		14	A	Millwall	D	0-1	1-1	McGibbon	10,57

App

Goal

FA Cup

3	J	11	H	Birmingham C	L	0-2	1-2	Watson	22,39

1 Shepherd and Watson debuts
2 Hinton debut
5 Stevens debut
13 S. Thomas debut
18 Rooke and Woodward finales
24 McGibbon debut
37 Quested debut

Evans	Freeman	Lloyd	Wallbanks	Watson	Taylor	Buchanan	Woodward	Rooke	Beasley	Shepherd	Hinton	Malpass	McCormick	Lewin	Stevens	Cranfield	Thomas	Hudson	Radcliffe	Hughes	Nelson	Grant	McGibbon	Bacuzzi	Ayres	Quested	Bewley	Hinshelwood	
	2	3	4	5	6	7	8	9	10	11																			1
	2	3	4	5	6	7	8	9	10	11	1																		2
	2		4	5	6	7	8	9	10	11	1	3																	3
	2		4	5	6	7		9	10	11	1	3	8																4
	2		4	5	6		8	9	10	11	1			3	7														5
	2		4	5	6	7		9	10	11	1		8	3															6
	2		4	5	6			9	10	11	1		8	3	7														7
	2		4	5	6			9	10	11	1		8	3	7														8
	2		4	5	6			9	10		1		8	3	7	11													9
	2		4	5	6			9	10	11	1		8	3	7														10
	2		4	5	6	7		9	10	11	1		8	3															11
	2		4	5	6	7	11	9	10		1		8	3															12
	2		4	5	6		10	9	11		1		8	3			7												13
	2		4	5	6	10	8	9	11		1			3			7												14
	2		4	5	6		8	9	10	11	1			3			7												15
	2		4	5	6			9	10	11	1			3			7	8											16
	2		4	5	6		8	9	10	11	1			3			7												17
	2			5	6		8	9	10	11				3			7		1	4									18
	2		4	5	6	7			10	11				3					1		8	9							19
	2		4	5	6	7			10	11				3					1		8	9							20
	2		4	5	6	7			10	11				3					1		8	9							21
	2		4	5	6	7			10	11				3					1		8	9							22
	2		4	5	6	7			10	11				3					1		8	9							23
	2		4	5	6	7			10	11				3					1		8		9						24
	2			5	6	7			4	11									1		8		9	3	10				25
	2		4	5	6					11	1				7						8		9	3	10				26
	2			5	4				6	11	1				7						10		9	3	8				27
	2			5	6				4	11	1				7						10		9	3	8				28
	2			5	4				6	11	1				7						10		9	3	8				29
	2			5	4				6	11	1				7						10		9	3	8				30
	2			5	4				6	11	1				7						10		9	3	8				31
	2			5	4				6	11	1				7						10		9	3	8				32
	2			5	4				6		1				7		8				11		9	3	10				33
	2			5	4	7			6		1				11						10		9	3	8				34
	2			5	4	7			6	11	1										10		9	3	8				35
	2		4	5	6				8	11	1				9						7		10	3					36
	2			5	6	7			10	11	1										8		9	3		4			37
	2			5	6				10	11	1						7				8	9		3		4			38
	2			5	6	7			10	11	1										8		9	3		4			39
	2		4	5	6					11	1				7						10	9		3		8			40
	2				5				10	11							8		1				9	3		4	6	7	41
	2			5	6	7			10										1		11		9	3	8	4			42
	42	2	26	41	42	20	10	18	40	35	31	2	9	20	16	1	9	1	10	1	23	7	17	18	12	6	1	1	A
	3	-	1	1	3	1	-	13	9	7	-	-	2	-	5	-	1	-	-	-	3	2	8	-	4	-	-	-	G

Evans	Freeman	Lloyd	Wallbanks	Watson	Taylor	Buchanan	Woodward	Rooke	Beasley	Shepherd	Hinton	Malpass	McCormick	Lewin	Stevens	Cranfield	Thomas	Hudson	Radcliffe	Hughes	Nelson	Grant	McGibbon	Bacuzzi	Ayres	Quested	Bewley	Hinshelwood	
			4	5	6	7			10	11			8	3					1		9								3

0 points v	Birmingham C, West Bromwich A	0 points
1 point v	Manchester C, Nottingham F, Sheffieild W, Southampton	4 points
2 points v	Barnsley, Bradford, Burnley, Bury, Coventry C, Leicester C, Luton T, Newcastle U, Newport C, Tottenham H, West Ham U	22 points
3 points v	Chesterfield, Millwall, Plymouth A	9 points
4 points v	Swansea T	4 points

Ted Hinton and Jim Taylor pulling a roller along.

1947-48

Division Two

	P	W	D	L	F	A	Pts
Birmingham City	42	22	15	5	55	24	59
Newcastle United	42	24	8	10	72	41	56
Southampton	42	21	10	11	71	53	52
Sheffield Wednesday	42	20	11	11	66	53	51
Cardiff City	42	18	11	13	61	58	47
West Ham United	42	16	14	12	55	53	46
West Bromwich Albion	42	18	9	15	63	58	45
Tottenham Hotspur	42	15	14	13	56	43	44
Leicester City	42	16	11	15	60	57	43
Coventry City	42	14	13	15	59	52	41
Fulham	42	15	10	17	47	46	40
Barnsley	42	15	10	17	62	64	40
Luton Town	42	14	12	16	56	59	40
Bradford Park Avenue	42	16	8	18	68	72	40
Brentford	42	13	14	15	44	61	40
Chesterfield	42	16	7	19	54	55	39
Plymouth Argyle	42	9	20	13	40	58	38
Leeds United	42	14	8	20	62	72	36
Nottingham Forest	42	12	11	19	54	60	35
Bury	42	9	16	17	58	68	34
Doncaster Rovers	42	9	11	22	40	66	29
Millwall	42	9	11	22	44	74	29

Manager: Jack Peart

Did you know that?

In the 1948 close season, manager Jack Peart paid Fulham's first five-figure fee (£12,000) for Bournemouth's outside left Jack McDonald.

1 R Thomas debut
41 Watson finale
42 McGibbon finale

No		Date	V	Opponents	R	H-T	F-T	Scorers	Atte
1	A	23	H	Brentford	W	2-0	5-0	Beasley, Thomas (R), McGibbon 3	32,82
2		27	A	West Bromich A	L	0-1	1-2	McGibbon	23,06
3		30	A	Leicester C	W	2-0	2-0	McGibbon 2	25,34
4	S	3	H	West Bromich A	L	0-0	0-1		24,71
5		6	H	Leeds U	W	3-0	3-2	Beasley, Thomas (S), Shepherd	26,24
6		10	A	Barnsley	W	1-1	2-1	Thomas (R), Shepherd	18,01
7		13	A	Bury	L	0-1	0-1		14,48
8		17	H	Barnsley	L	0-0	0-1		18,09
9		20	A	Coventry C	L	0-3	2-5	Grant, Stevens	20,21
10		27	H	Newcastle U	W	2-0	3-0	Shepherd, Thomas (S), Grant	41,45
11	O	4	A	Birmingham C	L	1-0	1-3	Watson	39,75
12		11	H	Southampton	L	0-1	0-2		24,43
13		18	A	Doncaster R	W	0-0	1-0	Taylor	22,18
14		25	H	Nottingham F	D	0-0	0-0		20,14
15	N	1	A	Bradford	L	0-2	0-3		16,39
16		8	H	Cardiff C	W	2-1	4-1	Thomas (R), Beasley, Stevens 2	34,77
17		15	A	Sheffield W	L	0-1	0-2		32,20
18		22	H	Tottenham H	L	0-1	0-2		36,14
19		29	A	Millwall	W	2-1	2-1	Shepherd, Thomas (R)	18,39
20	D	6	H	Chesterfield	D	0-0	0-0		9,81
21		13	A	West Ham U	L	0-2	0-3		27,33
22		20	A	Brentford	W	2-0	2-0	McGibbon, Taylor	20,71
23		25	H	Plymouth A	D	1-1	1-1	Shepherd	17,0
24		27	A	Plymouth A	L	1-1	2-3	Stevens, (Oakes og)	24,46
25	J	3	H	Leicester C	W	2-0	3-1	Stevens 2, Freeman	17,67
26		17	A	Leeds U	W	0-0	1-0	Stevens	29,64
27		31	H	Bury	D	1-1	1-1	Stevens	18,53
28	F	21	H	Birmingham C	D	1-1	1-1	Stevens	13,1
29	M	6	H	Doncaster R	D	0-0	0-0		17,15
30		13	A	Nottingham F	W	1-0	2-0	Stevens 2	20,91
31		20	H	Bradford	D	0-0	0-0		16,89
32		26	A	Luton T	W	3-0	3-0	McGibbon, Bewley, Ayres	18,03
33		27	A	Cardiff C	D	0-0	0-0		33,78
34		29	H	Luton T	D	0-1	1-1	McGibbon	20,15
35	A	3	H	Sheffield W	L	0-0	0-2		22,79
36		10	A	Tottenham H	W	1-0	2-0	McGibbon, Shepherd	32,49
37		14	A	Newcastle U	L	0-0	0-1		54,0
38		17	H	Millwall	W	1-0	1-0	Thomas (R)	13,83
39		21	A	Southampton	L	0-0	0-1		15,31
40		24	A	Chesterfield	L	0-1	0-1		9,03
41		28	H	Coventry C	L	0-1	0-2		8,5
42	M	1	H	West Ham U	D	0-0	1-1	Ayres	15,79

App
Goa

FA Cup

3	J	10	H	Doncaster R	W	1-0	2-0	Ayres, Stevens	16,1
4		24	H	Bristol R	W	3-2	5-2	Ayres 2, Stevens 3	20,0
5	F	7	H	Everton	D	0-1	1-1	Quested	37,5
R		14	A	Everton	W	0-0	1-0	Thomas (R)	71,5
6		28	H	Blackpool	L	0-1	0-2		40,0

Hinton	Freeman	Bacuzzi	Quested	Watson	Taylor	Thomas S	Thomas R	McGibbon	Beasley	Shepherd	Grant	Stevens	Radcliffe	Lewin	Jones	Wallbanks	Ayres	Hinshelwood	Edwards	Bewley	Rampling	
1	2	3	4	5	6	7	8	9	10	11												1
1	2	3	4	5	6	7	8	9	10	11												2
1	2	3	4	5	6	7	8	9	10	11												3
1	2	3	4	5	6	7	8	9	10	11												4
1	2	3	4	5	6	7	8	9	10	11												5
1	2	3	4	5	6	7	8	9	10	11												6
1	2	3	4	5	6	7	8	9	10	11												7
1	2	3	4	5	6	7	8	9	10	11												8
1	2	3	4	5	6		8	10	11		9	7										9
1	2	3	4	5	6	8			10	11	9	7										10
	2	3	4	5	6		8		10	11	9	7	1									11
1	2	3		5	6	8	10		4	11	9	7										12
1	2	3	4	5	6	8		9	10	11		7										13
1	2	3	4	5	6	8	9		10	11		7										14
1	2	3	4	5	6	8		9	10	11		7										15
1	2	3	4	5	6	7	8		10	11		9										16
1	2	3	4	5	6	7	8		10	11		9										17
1	2	3	4	5	6	7	8		10	11		9										18
1	2		4	5	6		8		10	11	9	7		3								19
1	2		4	5	6		8		10	11	9	7		3								20
1	2	3	4	5	6		8			11	9	7			10							21
1	2	3		5	6		8	9		11		7				4	10					22
1	2	3		5	6		8	9		11		7				4	10					23
1	2	3	8		5			9	6	11		7				4	10					24
1	2	3			5		7		6	11		9				4	10	8				25
1	2	3	4		5	7	8		6			9					10		11			26
1	2	3	4		5	7	8		10			9						11		6		27
1	2	3	4		5	7	8		6			9					10		11			28
1		3	4		5	7	8		6	11		9		2			10					29
1		3	4		5	7	8			11		9		2			10			6		30
1		3	4		5	7	8			11		9		2			10			6		31
1		3	4		5	7	8	9		11				2			10			6		32
1		3	4		5	7	8	9	6	11				2			10					33
1		3	4		5	7	8	9	11					2			10			6		34
1		3	4	5		7	8	9	11					2			10			6		35
1		3	4	5		7		9	10	11				2			8			6		36
1		3	8	5		7		9	10	11				2		4				6		37
1		3		5		7	8	9	10	11				2		4				6		38
1	2	3		5	4	7	8	9	6							11	10					39
1		3	4	5		7	8	9	10	11				2						6		40
1		3	4	5			8	9	6	11				2			10				7	41
1	2		4		5		8	9	6	11				3			10				7	42
41	30	39	36	30	36	31	36	25	36	35	7	23	1	15	1	7	17	2	2	10	2	A
-	1	-	-	1	2	2	5	10	3	6	2	11	-	-	-	-	2	-	-	1	-	G

Hinton	Freeman	Bacuzzi	Quested	Watson	Taylor	Thomas S	Thomas R	McGibbon	Beasley	Shepherd	Grant	Stevens	Radcliffe	Lewin	Jones	Wallbanks	Ayres	Hinshelwood	Edwards	Bewley	Rampling	
1	2	3	8		5		7		6			9				4	10		11			3
1	2	3	4		5	7	8		6			9			11		10					4
1	2	3	4		5	7	8		6		11	9					10					5
1	2	3	4		5	7	8		6			9					10			11		R
	2	3	4		5	7	8		6	11		9	1				10					6

0 points v	Coventry C, Sheffield W, Southampton, West Bromwich A	0 points
1 point v	Birmingham C, Bradford, Bury, Chesterfield, Plymouth A, West Ham U	6 points
2 points v	Barnsley, Newcastle U, Tottenham H	6 points
3 points v	Cardiff C, Doncaster R, Luton T, Nottingham F	12 points
4 points v	Brentford, Leeds U, Leicester C, Millwall	16 points

Len Quested prepares for training.

1948-49

Division Two

	P	W	D	L	F	A	Pts
Fulham	42	24	9	9	77	37	57
West Bromwich Albion	42	24	8	10	69	39	56
Southampton	42	23	9	10	69	36	55
Cardiff City	42	19	13	10	62	47	51
Tottenham Hotspur	42	17	16	9	72	44	50
Chesterfield	42	15	17	10	51	45	47
West Ham United	42	18	10	14	56	58	46
Sheffield Wednesday	42	15	13	14	63	56	43
Barnsley	42	14	12	16	62	61	40
Luton Town	42	14	12	16	55	57	40
Grimsby Town	42	15	10	17	72	76	40
Bury	42	17	6	19	67	76	40
Queen's Park Rangers	42	14	11	17	44	62	39
Blackburn Rovers	42	15	8	19	53	63	38
Leeds United	42	12	13	17	55	63	37
Coventry City	42	15	7	20	55	64	37
Bradford Park Avenue	42	13	11	18	65	78	37
Brentford	42	11	14	17	42	53	36
Leicester City	42	10	16	16	62	79	36
Plymouth Argyle	42	12	12	18	49	64	36
Nottingham Forest	42	14	7	21	50	54	35
Lincoln City	42	8	12	22	53	91	28

Manager: Jack Peart / Frank Osborne

Did you know that?

During the thrilling battle for promotion in the spring of 1949, goalkeeper Doug Flack was injured with just three vital games remaining. Since reserve Ted Hinton was also injured, third choice Larry Gage had to play. Fulham won two and drew one to take the title. Gage earned rave reviews but they were his only appearances for Fulham.

1	McDonald debut
7	Shepherd finale
10	Hinton finale
10	Jezzard debut
11	Flack debut
21	Rowley debut

No		Date	V	Opponents	R	H-T	F-T	Scorers	Atten
1	A	21	A	Grimsby T	W	3-0	3-2	Jinks, Ayres, Thomas (R)	19,271
2		25	H	Barnsley	D	0-0	1-1	Stevens	21,00
3		28	H	Nottingham F	W	4-0	4-0	Jinks 2, Stevens 2	27,82
4	S	1	A	Barnsley	D	0-1	1-1	McDonald	17,84
5		4	A	Bury	L	0-1	0-2		18,68
6		8	H	Southampton	W	1-0	1-0	Stevens	24,70
7		11	A	Plymouth A	L	0-3	1-3	Thomas (R)	24,20
8		15	A	Southampton	L	0-1	0-3		24,65
9		18	H	Blackburn R	D	1-0	1-1	Ayres	27,19
10		25	A	Cardiff C	L	0-2	1-2	McDonald	38,42
11	O	2	H	Queen's Park R	W	1-0	5-0	Thomas (R) 2, Stevens 3	38,66
12		9	H	West Bromich A	L	1-1	1-2	Thomas (R)	31,63
13		16	A	Chesterfield	W	1-0	1-0	Thomas (R)	16,48
14		23	H	Lincoln C	W	2-1	2-1	Stevens, McDonald	24,76
15		30	A	Sheffield W	W	1-0	2-1	Thomas (R), Jezzard	34,09
16	N	6	H	Coventry C	W	1-0	1-0	Jezzard	24,31
17		13	A	Leeds U	D	0-0	1-1	Thomas (R)	26,75
18		20	H	Leicester C	W	0-0	1-0	Thomas (R)	23,87
19	D	4	H	Tottenham H	D	0-1	1-1	Freeman	36,24
20		11	A	West Ham U	L	0-0	0-1		22,68
21		18	H	Grimsby T	W	1-1	3-1	McDonald, Thomas (R), Beasley	19,99
22		25	A	Bradford	D	0-1	1-1	Stevens	20,74
23		27	H	Bradford	W	2-0	2-0	McDonald 2	22,24
24	J	1	A	Nottingham F	W	0-0	2-0	Rowley, McDonald	19,791
25		15	H	Bury	W	3-2	7-2	Rowley 4, Thomas (R) 2, McDonald	19,89
26		22	H	Plymouth A	W	4-1	6-1	Rowley 3, Stevens, Thomas (R), Jezzard	29,71
27	F	5	A	Blackburn R	L	0-0	0-1		22,58
28		19	H	Cardiff C	W	3-0	4-0	Jezzard, Stevens, Thomas (R) 2	40,79
29		26	A	Queen's Park R	L	0-1	0-1		27,44
30	M	5	A	West Bromich A	W	0-1	2-1	Quested, Rowley	27,59
31		12	H	Chesterfield	W	0-0	2-1	Thomas (R) 2	29,09
32		19	A	Lincoln C	W	2-0	3-0	Jezzard, Rowley 2	13,19
33		26	H	Sheffield W	D	1-1	1-1	Thomas (R)	34,03
34	A	2	A	Coventry C	L	0-0	0-1		26,36
35		6	A	Brentford	D	0-0	0-0		29,16
36		9	H	Leeds U	W	0-0	1-0	Rowley	23,96
37		15	H	Luton T	W	2-0	4-1	Rowley 2, Stevens, Thomas (R)	35,62
38		16	A	Leicester C	W	1-0	3-0	Jezzard, Thomas (R), Rowley	34,65
39		18	A	Luton T	W	2-1	3-1	Rowley, McDonald, Thomas (R)	20,12
40		23	H	Brentford	W	1-1	2-1	Rowley, Thomas (R)	39,14
41		30	A	Tottenham H	D	0-1	1-1	Thomas (R)	50,13
42	M	7	H	West Ham U	W	1-0	2-0	Rowley 2	41,13
									App
									Goals

FA Cup

3	J	8	H	Walsall	L	0-0	0-1		32,00

Hinton	Freeman	Bacuzzi	Quested	Taylor	Beasley	Stevens	Thomas R	Jinks	Ayres	McDonald	Shepherd	Thomas S	Bewley	Jezzard	Flack	Hinshelwood	Lewin	Rowley	Gage	
1	2	3	4	5	6	7	8	9	10	11										1
1	2	3	4	5	6	7	8	9	10		11									2
1	2	3	4	5	6	8		9	10	11		7								3
1	2	3	4	5	6	8		9	10	11		7								4
1	2	3	4	5	6	7	8	9	10	11										5
1	2	3	4	5	6	7	8	9	10	11										6
1	2	3	4	5		7	8	9		10	11		6							7
1	2	3	4	5	6	7	8	9	10	11										8
1	2	3	4	5	6	7	8	9	10	11										9
1	2	3	4	5	6	9	8			11		7		10						10
	2	3	4	5	6	9	8			11		7		10	1					11
	2	3	4	5	6	9	8			11		7		10	1					12
	2	3	4	5		9	8			11		7	6	10	1					13
	2	3	4	5	6	9	8			11				10	1	7				14
	2	3	4	5	6	9	8			11		7		10	1					15
	2	3	4	5	6	9	8			11		7		10	1					16
	2	3	4	5	6	9	8			11		7		10	1					17
		3	4	5		9	8			11		7	6	10	1		2			18
	2	3		5	6	9	8			11		7	4	10	1					19
	2	3		5	6	9	8			11		7	4	10	1					20
	2		4	5	6	7	8			11				10	1		3	9		21
	2	3	4	5	6	7	8			11				10	1			9		22
	2	3	4	5	6	7	8			11				10	1			9		23
	2	3	4	5	6	7	8			11				10	1			9		24
	2	3	4	5	6	7	8			11				10	1			9		25
	2	3	4	5	6	7	8			11				10	1			9		26
	2	3	4	5	6	7	8			11				10	1			9		27
	2	3	4	5	6	7	8			11				10	1			9		28
	2	3	4	5	6	7	8			11				10	1			9		29
	2	3	4	5	6	7	8			11				10	1			9		30
	2	3	4	5	6	7	8			11				10	1			9		31
	2	3	4	5	6	7	8			11				10	1			9		32
	2	3	4	5	6	7	8			11				10	1			9		33
	2	3	4	5	6	7	8		10	11					1			9		34
	2	3	4	5	6	8	10			11		7			1			9		35
	2	3		5	6	8	10			11		7	4		1			9		36
		3	4	5	6	7	8			11				10	1		2	9		37
		3	4	5	6	7	8			11				10	1		2	9		38
		3	4	5	6	7	8			11				10	1		2	9		39
		3	4	5	6	7	8			11				10			2	9	1	40
	2	3	4	5	6	7	8			11				10				9	1	41
	2	3	4	5	6	7	8			11				10				9	1	42
0	37	41	39	42	39	42	40	9	9	41	2	14	6	30	29	1	6	22	3	A
-	1	-	1	-	1	12	23	3	2	9	-	-	-	6	-	-	-	19	-	G

	2	3	4	5	6	7	8			11				10	1			9		3

0 points v		0 points
1 point v	Blackburn R	1 point
2 points v	Barnsley, Bury, Cardiff C, Coventry C, Plymouth A, Queen's Park R, Southampton, Tottenham H, West Bromwich A, West Ham U	20 points
3 points v	Bradford, Brentford, Leeds U, Sheffield W	12 points
4 points v	Chesterfield, Grimsby T, Leicester C, Lincoln C, Luton T, Nottingham F	24 points

Ted Hinton, Irish international goalkeeper who lost his place in September.

1949-50

Division One

	P	W	D	L	F	A	Pts
Portsmouth	42	22	9	11	74	38	53
Wolverhampton Wanderers	42	20	13	9	76	49	53
Sunderland	42	21	10	11	83	62	52
Manchester United	42	18	14	10	69	44	50
Newcastle United	42	19	12	11	77	55	50
Arsenal	42	19	11	12	79	55	49
Blackpool	42	17	15	10	46	35	49
Liverpool	42	17	14	11	64	54	48
Middlesbrough	42	20	7	15	59	48	47
Burnley	42	16	13	13	40	40	45
Derby County	42	17	10	15	69	61	44
Aston Villa	42	15	12	15	61	61	42
Chelsea	42	12	16	14	58	65	40
West Bromwich Albion	42	14	12	16	47	53	40
Huddersfield Town	42	14	9	19	52	73	37
Bolton Wanderers	42	10	14	18	45	59	34
Fulham	42	10	14	18	41	54	34
Everton	42	10	14	18	42	66	34
Stoke City	42	11	12	19	45	75	34
Charlton Athletic	42	13	6	23	53	65	32
Manchester City	42	8	13	21	36	68	29
Birmingham City	42	7	14	21	31	67	28

Manager: Bill Dodgin

Did you know that?

In the club's first season in the First Division, Fulham's average home attendance exceeded 30,000 for the first time. The 33,030 average has never been bettered. The range was a high of 45,924 (against Chelsea) to a low of 21,031 (against Middlesbrough).

8	Kelly debut
10	Campbell debut
25	Lawler debut
26	Pavitt debut
33	S Thomas finale
42	Beasley, Kelly and Rowley finales

No		Date	V	Opponents	R	H-T	F-T	Scorers	Atten
1	A	20	H	Wolverhampton W	L	0-1	1-2	Bacuzzi	41,69
2		24	A	Huddersfield T	D	0-0	2-2	Rowley, Thomas (R)	21,80
3		27	A	Aston Villa	L	0-2	1-3	Quested	47,78
4		31	H	Huddersfield T	W	1-0	4-1	Rowley 2, Jezzard, (Hepplewhite og)	24,26
5	S	3	H	Charlton A	L	0-2	1-2	McDonald	37,51
6		7	A	Middlesbrough	W	2-0	2-1	Thomas (R) 2	36,79
7		10	A	Manchester C	L	0-2	0-2		42,30
8		17	H	Chelsea	D	0-1	1-1	Freeman	45,92
9		24	H	Newcastle U	W	0-1	2-1	Thomas (R), Jezzard	39,00
10	O	1	A	Blackpool	D	0-0	0-0		33,34
11		9	A	Stoke C	W	0-0	2-0	Thomas (R), Jezzard	24,62
12		15	H	Burnley	W	1-0	1-0	Rowley	34,31
13		22	A	Sunderland	L	0-1	0-2		46,25
14		29	H	Liverpool	L	0-1	0-1		41,87
15	N	5	A	Arsenal	L	0-0	1-2	Jezzard	40,59
16		12	H	Bolton W	W	2-0	3-0	Jezzard, Thomas (R), Rowley	30,19
17		19	A	Birmingham C	D	0-0	1-1	Stevens	20,16
18		26	H	Derby C	D	0-0	0-0		36,81
19	D	3	A	West Bromich A	L	1-2	1-4	Jezzard	30,88
20		10	H	Manchester U	W	1-0	1-0	Jezzard	35,36
21		17	A	Wolverhampton W	D	0-1	1-1	Rowley	32,39
22		24	H	Aston Villa	W	2-0	3-0	Rowley, McDonald 2	30,66
23		26	A	Everton	D	1-1	1-1	Stevens	54,72
24		27	H	Everton	D	0-0	0-0		36,02
25		31	A	Charlton A	L	0-1	1-2	McDonald	32,64
26	J	14	H	Manchester C	W	1-0	1-0	McDonald	29,28
27		21	A	Chelsea	D	0-0	0-0		52,25
28	F	4	A	Newcastle U	L	1-0	1-3	Thomas (R)	41,12
29		18	H	Blackpool	W	0-0	1-0	Thomas (R)	32,13
30		25	H	Stoke C	D	0-1	2-2	Thomas (R) 2	27,49
31	M	4	A	Burnley	D	0-0	0-0		19,85
32		11	H	Birmingham C	D	0-0	0-0		24,97
33		18	A	Derby C	L	1-0	1-2	Thomas (S)	18,97
34		25	H	Arsenal	D	2-0	2-2	Campbell, Stevens	35,70
35	A	1	A	Bolton W	L	0-2	1-2	Jezzard	23,65
36		7	A	Portsmouth	L	0-1	0-3		38,93
37		8	H	Sunderland	L	0-1	0-3		39,54
38		10	H	Portsmouth	L	0-1	0-1		24,81
39		15	A	Liverpool	D	1-0	1-1	Stevens	36,27
40		22	H	West Bromich A	L	0-0	0-1		25,02
41		29	A	Manchester U	L	0-1	0-3		11,96
42	M	6	H	Middlesbrough	L	1-0	1-2	Stevens (pen)	21,03
									App
									Goa

FA Cup

3	J	9	A	Charlton A	D	1-1	2-2	Thomas (R), Freeman	51,97
R		11	H	Charlton A	L	0-1	1-2	McDonald	41,16

Flack	Freeman	Bacuzzi	Quested	Taylor	Beasley	Stevens	Thomas R	Rowley	Jezzard	McDonald	Kelly	Campbell	Thomas S	Summers	Lawler	Pavitt	Jinks	Hinshelwood	
1	2	3	4	5	6	7	8	9	10	11									1
1	2	3	4	5	6	7	8	9	10	11									2
1	2	3	4	5	6	7	8	9	10	11									3
1	2	3	4	5	6	7	8	9	10	11									4
1	2	3	4	5	6	7	8	9	10	11									5
1	2	3	4	5	6	7	8	9	10	11									6
1	2	3	4	5	6	7	8	9	10	11									7
	2	3	4	5	6	7	8	9	10	11	1								8
	2	3	4	5	6	7	8	9	10	11	1								9
	2	3	4	5	6	7	10	9	11		1	8							10
	2	3	4	5	6	7	10	9	11		1	8							11
	2	3	4	5	6	7	10	9	11		1	8							12
	2	3	4	5	6	7	10	9	11		1	8							13
	2	3	4	5	6	7	8	9	10		1		11						14
	2	3	4	5	6	8	11	9	10		1		7						15
	2	3	4	5	6	7	8	9	10		1			11					16
	2	3	4	5	6	7	8	9	10		1			11					17
	2	3	4	5	6	7	8	9	10		1			11					18
	2	3	4	5	6	7	8	9	10		1			11					19
	2	3	4	5	6	7	8	9	10	11	1								20
1	2	3	4	5	6	7	8	9	10	11									21
	2	3	4	5	6	7	8	9	10	11	1								22
	2	3	4	5	6	7	8	9	10	11	1								23
	2	3	4	5	6	7	8	9	10	11	1								24
	2	3	4	5		7	8	9	10	11	1				6				25
	2		4	5		7	8	9	10	11	1				6	3			26
1	2		4	5	6	7	8	9	10	11						3			27
1	2		4	5	6	7	8	9	10	11						3			28
1	2	3	4		6	7	8		10							5	9	11	29
1	2	3	4		6	7	8		10							5	9	11	30
	2	3	4		6	7	8		10		1	9				5		11	31
1	2	3	4		6	7	8		10			9				5		11	32
1	2	3	4		6		8		10			9	7			5		11	33
1	2	3	4		6	7	8		10			9				5		11	34
	2	3	4		6	7	8		10		1	9				5		11	35
	2	3	4	5	6	7	8		10		1	9						11	36
		3	4	5	6		10	9		11	1	8				2		7	37
1	2	3	4	6			10	9		11		8				5		7	38
	2	3	4	6		7	8	9	10	11	1					5			39
1	2	3	4	6		7	8	9	10	11						5			40
	2		4	5	6	7	8	9	10	11	1					3			41
	2	3	4	5	6	7	10	9		11	1	8							42
7	41	38	42	35	37	39	42	34	39	24	25	13	3	4	2	15	2	10	A
-	1	1	1	-	-	5	10	7	8	5	-	1	1	-	-	-	-	-	G

Flack	Freeman	Bacuzzi	Quested	Taylor	Beasley	Stevens	Thomas R	Rowley	Jezzard	McDonald	Kelly	Campbell	Thomas S	Summers	Lawler	Pavitt	Jinks	Hinshelwood	
	2	3	4	5	6	7	8	9	10	11	1								3
	2		4	5	6	7	8	9	10	11	1					3			R

0 points v	Charlton A, Portsmouth, Sunderland, West Bromwich A	0 points
1 point v	Arsenal, Derby C, Liverpool, Wolves	4 points
2 points v	Aston Villa, Birmingham C, Bolton W, Chelsea, Everton, Manchester C, Manchester U, Middlesbrough, Newcastle U	18 points
3 points v	Blackpool, Burnley, Huddersfield T, Stoke C	12 points
4 points v		0 points

Centre forward Jimmy Jinks was signed from Millwall in August 1948 but was not a success.

1950-51

Division One

	P	W	D	L	F	A	Pts
Tottenham Hotspur	42	25	10	7	82	44	60
Manchester United	42	24	8	10	74	40	56
Blackpool	42	20	10	12	79	53	50
Newcastle United	42	18	13	11	62	53	49
Arsenal	42	19	9	14	73	56	47
Middlesbrough	42	18	11	13	76	65	47
Portsmouth	42	16	15	11	71	68	47
Bolton Wanderers	42	19	7	16	64	61	45
Liverpool	42	16	11	15	53	59	43
Burnley	42	14	14	14	48	43	42
Derby County	42	16	8	18	81	75	40
Sunderland	42	12	16	14	63	73	40
Stoke City	42	13	14	15	50	59	40
Wolverhampton Wanderers	42	15	8	19	74	61	38
Aston Villa	42	12	13	17	66	68	37
West Bromwich Albion	42	13	11	18	53	61	37
Charlton Athletic	42	14	9	19	63	80	37
Fulham	42	13	11	18	52	68	37
Huddersfield Town	42	15	6	21	64	92	36
Chelsea	42	12	8	22	53	65	32
Sheffield Wednesday	42	12	8	22	64	83	32
Everton	42	12	8	22	48	86	32

Manager: Bill Dodgin

Did you know that?

In a spending spree in preparation for their second season in top flight, the Fulham board paid a club record £20,000 to Birmingham for Irish inside forward Bobby Brennan.

1 Black, Brennan, Macaulay and E Lowe debuts
5 R Lowe debut
32 R Thomas' 50th goal
38 Robson debut

No		Date	V	Opponents	R	H-T	F-T	Scorers	Atte
1	A	19	A	Manchester U	L	0-1	0-1		45,85
2		23	H	Charlton A	L	0-2	1-3	Stevens	31,57
3		26	H	Wolverhampton W	W	2-1	2-1	Stevens, Quested	42,01
4		30	A	Charlton A	D	0-0	0-0		28,99
5	S	2	A	Sunderland	W	0-0	1-0	Macaulay	43,08
6		4	A	Blackpool	L	0-1	0-4		28,05
7		9	H	Aston Villa	W	2-1	2-1	Jezzard, Thomas	35,81
8		13	H	Blackpool	D	2-2	2-2	Jezzard, Thomas	39,76
9		16	A	Derby C	L	0-3	2-3	Jezzard, Freeman	25,32
10		23	H	Liverpool	W	0-1	2-1	Jezzard, Thomas	42,95
11		30	A	Portsmouth	L	0-1	0-1		32,18
12	O	7	H	Everton	L	0-4	1-5	Hinshelwood	29,44
13		14	A	Stoke C	D	1-0	1-1	Quested	26,65
14		21	H	Huddersfield T	D	1-1	1-1	Stevens	31,62
15		28	A	Middlesbrough	D	0-1	1-1	Jezzard	34,11
16	N	4	H	West Bromich A	L	0-0	0-1		21,13
17		11	A	Newcastle U	W	1-1	2-1	Thomas, Stevens	54,23
18		18	H	Sheffield W	W	2-1	4-2	McDonald, Thomas 2, Macaulay	26,35
19		25	A	Arsenal	L	0-3	1-5	Thomas	41,34
20	D	2	H	Burnley	W	2-0	4-1	Thomas, Jezzard, Stevens, (Cummings og)	25,25
21		9	A	Chelsea	L	0-2	0-2		43,83
22		16	H	Manchester U	D	2-0	2-2	Stevens 2	19,64
23		23	A	Wolverhampton W	D	1-0	1-1	Stevens	29,22
24		25	H	Bolton W	L	0-1	0-1		21,71
25		26	A	Bolton W	W	0-0	1-0	Campbell	43,11
26		30	H	Sunderland	D	0-0	1-1	Brennan	33,61
27	J	13	A	Aston Villa	L	0-1	0-3		39,99
28		20	H	Derby C	L	2-4	3-5	Stevens, Brennan 2	28,86
29	F	3	A	Liverpool	L	0-1	0-2		33,33
30		28	A	Everton	L	0-0	0-1		19,90
31	M	3	H	Stoke C	W	0-0	2-0	Stevens, Bowie	26,06
32		10	A	Huddersfield T	W	1-0	2-1	Jezzard, Thomas	19,65
33		17	H	Middlesbrough	W	0-0	2-0	Bowie, Quested	29,44
34		23	H	Tottenham H	L	0-0	0-1		47,39
35		24	A	West Bromich A	D	0-0	0-0		23,69
36		26	A	Tottenham H	L	0-2	1-2	Jezzard	51,86
37		31	H	Newcastle U	D	1-1	1-1	Campbell	28,10
38	A	7	A	Sheffield W	D	1-2	2-2	Thomas, Bowie	32,35
39		14	H	Arsenal	W	0-1	3-2	Quested, Thomas 2	34,11
40		21	A	Burnley	W	0-0	2-0	Thomas 2	19,92
41		28	H	Chelsea	L	1-1	1-2	Jezzard	24,89
42	M	2	H	Portsmouth	L	1-3	1-4	Stevens	21,27
									App
									Goal

FA Cup

3	J	6	H	Sheffield W	W	0-0	1-0	Brennan	29,20
4		27	A	Millwall	W	1-0	1-0	Campbell	42,17
5	F	10	A	Chelsea	D	0-1	1-1	Campbell	69,43
R		14	H	Chelsea	W	1-0	3-0	Brennan 2, Stevens	29,94
6		24	A	Blackpool	L	0-1	0-1		32,00

	Black	Freeman	Bacuzzi	Macaulay	Taylor	Lowe E	Stevens	Quested	Jezzard	Brennan	McDonald	Thomas	Hinshelwood	Lowe R	Campbell	Pavitt	Lawler	Bowie	Robson
1		2	3	4	5	6	7	8	9	10	11								
2		2	3	4	5	6	7	8	9	10		11							
3		2	3	8	5	6	7	4	9	10		11							
4		2	3	8	5	6	7	4	9			10	11						
5		2		8	5	6	11	4	9			10		3	7				
6		2		8	5	6	11	4	9			10		3	7				
7		2		8	5	6	11	4	9			10		3	7				
8		2	3	8	5	6	11	4	9			10			7				
9		2	3	8	5	6	11	4	9			10			7				
10			3	8	5	6	11	4	9			10			7	2			
11			3	8	5	6	11	4	9	10					7	2			
12			3	8	5	6	11	4	9			10	7			2			
13		2		4	5	6	11	8	9			10	7			3			
14		2		4	5	6	11	7	9	10		8				3			
15		2	3	4	5	6	11	7	9	10		8							
16		2	3	4	5	6	11	7	9	10		8							
17		2	3	8	5	6	7	4		10	11	9							
18		2	3	8	5	6	7	4		10	11	9							
19			3	8	5	6	7	4		10	11	9				2			
20			2	8	5	6	7	4	11	10		9		3					
21			2	8	5	6	7	4	11	10		9		3					
22			2	8	5	6	7	4	11	10		9		3					
23			2	8	5	6	7	4	11	10		9		3					
24			2	8	5	6	7	4	11	10		9		3					
25			2	8		6	7			10		9		3	11	5	4		
26			2	8		6	7			10		9		3	11	5	4		
27			2	8			7	4		10		9		3	11	5	6		
28			2	8			7	4	9	10				3	11	5	6		
29			2	4		6	7		9	10				3	11	5		8	
30			2		5	6	7	4	10	9				3	11			8	
31			2		5	6	7	4		10		9		3	11			8	
32			2		5	6	7	4	10			9		3	11			8	
33			2		5	6	7	4	10			9		3	11			8	
34			2		5	6	7	4	10			9		3	11			8	
35			2		5	6	7	4	10			9		3	11			8	
36			2		5	6	7	4	10			9		3	11			8	
37			2		5	6	7	4	10			9		3	11			8	
38			2		5	6	7	4	11			9		3				8	10
39			2		5	6	7	4	10			9		3	11			8	
40		2			5	6	7	4	10			9		3	11			8	
41		2			5	6	7	4	10			9		3	11			8	
42		2			5	6	7	4	10		11	9		3				8	
A	2	18	34	29	37	40	42	39	35	22	5	37	3	26	23	11	4	14	1
G		1	-	2	-	-	11	4	9	3	1	14	1	-	2	-	-	3	-

	Black	Freeman	Bacuzzi	Macaulay	Taylor	Lowe E	Stevens	Quested	Jezzard	Brennan	McDonald	Thomas	Hinshelwood	Lowe R	Campbell	Pavitt	Lawler	Bowie	Robson
3			2	8		6	7	4		10		9		3	11	5			
4			2	8	5	6	7	4	9	10				3	11				
5			2	10	5	6	7	4		9				3	11			8	
R			2		5	6	7	4	10	9				3	11			8	
6			2		5	6	7	4	10	9				3	11			8	

0 points v	Chelsea, Derby C, Everton, Portsmouth, Tottenham H	0 points
1 point v	Blackpool, Charlton A, Manchester U, West Bromwich A	4 points
2 points v	Arsenal, Aston Villa, Bolton W, Liverpool	8 points
3 points v	Huddersfield T, Middlesbrough, Newcastle U, Sheffield W, Stoke C, Sunderland, Wolves	21 points
4 points v	Burnley	4 points

Archie Macaulay, an experienced Scottish international, was signed from Arsenal to replace Pat Beasley.

1951-52

Division One

	P	W	D	L	F	A	Pts
Manchester United	42	23	11	8	95	52	57
Tottenham Hotspur	42	22	9	11	76	51	53
Arsenal	42	21	11	10	80	61	53
Portsmouth	42	20	8	14	68	58	48
Bolton Wanderers	42	19	10	13	65	61	48
Aston Villa	42	19	9	14	79	70	47
Preston North End	42	17	12	13	74	54	46
Newcastle United	42	18	9	15	98	73	45
Blackpool	42	18	9	15	64	64	45
Charlton Athletic	42	17	10	15	68	63	44
Liverpool	42	12	19	11	57	61	43
Sunderland	42	15	12	15	70	61	42
West Bromwich Albion	42	14	13	15	74	77	41
Burnley	42	15	10	17	56	63	40
Manchester City	42	13	13	16	58	61	39
Wolverhampton Wanderers	42	12	14	16	73	73	38
Derby County	42	15	7	20	63	80	37
Middlesbrough	42	15	6	21	64	88	36
Chelsea	42	14	8	20	52	72	36
Stoke City	42	12	7	23	49	88	31
Huddersfield Town	42	10	8	24	49	82	28
Fulham	42	8	11	23	58	77	27

Manager: Bill Dodgin

Did you know that?

On Boxing Day 1951, Fulham's first goal in the 3-3 draw with Manchester United was scored by Eddie Lowe, the first goal at the Cottage direct from a corner.

---

5 Stevens' 50th goal
12 McDonald finale
15 Quested finale
16 Jeff Taylor debut
23 Dodgin debut
26 Freeman finale
FAC3 Stevens' 200th game
27 Mitten debut
33 Hill debut
37 R Thomas finale

No		Date	V	Opponents	R	H-T	F-T	Scorers	Atte
1	A	18	H	Preston NE	L	1-1	2-3	Bowie, Jezzard	38,33
2		20	A	Tottenham H	L	0-1	0-1		48,76
3		25	A	Burnley	L	0-1	0-1		18,79
4		29	H	Tottenham H	L	1-1	1-2	Thomas	33,92
5	S	1	H	Charlton A	D	0-2	3-3	Stevens, Jezzard, McDonald	29,07
6		3	A	Stoke C	D	1-1	1-1	Newcombe	21,22
7		8	A	Chelsea	L	0-1	1-2	McDonald	47,58
8		12	H	Stoke C	W	1-0	5-0	Jezzard 2, Macaulay 2, Bowie	16,72
9		15	A	Middlesbrough	L	0-1	0-2		23,62
10		22	H	West Bromich A	W	0-0	1-0	Bowie	26,13
11		29	A	Newcastle U	W	0-0	1-0	McDonald	55,53
12	O	6	H	Portsmouth	L	1-1	2-3	McDonald, Bowie	41,01
13		13	A	Liverpool	L	0-2	0-4		36,79
14		20	H	Blackpool	L	0-2	1-2	Brennan	43,50
15		27	A	Arsenal	L	0-2	3-4	Stevens 2, Brennan	51,17
16	N	3	H	Manchester C	L	1-1	1-2	Stevens	33,58
17		10	A	Derby C	L	0-0	0-5		20,54
18		17	H	Aston Villa	D	0-2	2-2	Pavitt, Brennan	15,39
19		24	A	Sunderland	D	1-1	2-2	Robson, Brennan	34,01
20	D	1	H	Wolverhampton W	D	1-0	2-2	Taylor (Jeff), Brennan	33,82
21		8	A	Huddersfield T	L	0-1	0-1		8,26
22		15	A	Preston NE	W	0-0	1-0	Lowe	25,70
23		22	H	Burnley	L	0-2	1-2	Campbell	20,10
24		25	A	Manchester U	L	0-0	2-3	Thomas 2	35,69
25		26	H	Manchester U	D	1-1	3-3	Lowe 2, Stevens	32,67
26		29	A	Charlton A	L	0-1	0-3		19,58
27	J	5	H	Chelsea	L	0-2	1-2	Jezzard	43,88
28		19	H	Middlesbrough	W	3-0	6-0	Mitten 2, Taylor (Jeff) 3, Jezzard	28,94
29		26	A	West Bromich A	W	0-0	2-0	Taylor (Jeff), (Barlow og)	24,22
30	F	9	H	Newcastle U	D	0-0	1-1	Lowe	46,43
31		16	A	Portsmouth	L	0-2	0-4		33,76
32	M	1	H	Liverpool	D	0-1	1-1	Mitten (pen)	36,75
33		8	A	Blackpool	L	0-1	2-4	Mitten, Hill	18,60
34		15	H	Arsenal	D	0-0	0-0		44,08
35		22	A	Manchester C	D	0-1	1-1	Mitten (pen)	31,03
36	A	5	A	Aston Villa	L	0-2	1-4	Stevens	17,25
37		11	H	Bolton W	L	1-0	1-2	Mitten	38,3
38		12	H	Sunderland	L	0-0	0-1		29,62
39		14	A	Bolton W	L	1-0	1-2	Stevens	29,46
40		19	A	Wolverhampton W	D	1-2	2-2	Brennan, Robson	19,98
41		26	H	Huddersfield T	W	0-0	1-0	Jezzard	21,29
42	M	1	H	Derby C	W	1-0	3-0	Jezzard, Brennan, Robson	10,94
									App
									Goa

FA Cup

3	J	12	H	Birmingham C	L	0-0	0-1		26,0

Black	Bacuzzi	Lowe R	Quested	Taylor Jim	Lowe E	Stevens	Bowie	Jezzard	Brennan	Campbell	Thomas	Newcombe	Pavitt	McDonald	Macaulay	Freeman	Robson	Flack	Taylor Jeff	Lawler	Dodgin	Mitten	Hill	Hinshelwood	
1	2	3	4	5	6	7	8	9	10	11															1
1	2	3	4	5	6	7	8	9		11	10														2
1	2	3		4	6		8	9	10	7		11	5												3
1	2	3		4	6	8		10	9		7	11	5												4
1	2		4	5	6	7	8	10				11	3	9											5
1	2		4	5	6		8	10		11		7	3	9											6
1	2		4	5	6	7		10		11			3	9	8										7
1	3		4		6	7	10	9		11			5		8	2									8
1	3		4		6	7	10	9	8	11			5			2									9
1	3		4		6	7	10	9	8	11			5			2									10
1	3		4		6	7	8			11			5	9		2	10								11
1	3		4		6	7	8			11			5	9		2	10								12
1	3		4		6	7	8			11	9		5			2	10								13
1	3		4		6	7			9	11			5		8	2	10								14
	3		4		6	9			10	11		7	5		8	2		1							15
	3			4	6	7	10			11			5		8	2		1	9						16
	2	3		4	6	7	10		8	11			5					1	9						17
1	2	3		4	6	11			8		7		5				10		9						18
1	2	3		5	4	7			8	11							10		9	6					19
1	3			5	6	7			10	11	4		2				8		9						20
1	3			5	6	7		11	8		4		2				10		9						21
1	2			5	6	7	8			11	4						10		9		3				22
1	2			5	6	7	10			11	4						8		9		3				23
1	2			5	6			9		7	8				4		11		10		3				24
1	2			5	6	7		9		11	8				4				10		3				25
1				5		7		9		11	8				4	2			10	6	3				26
1	2			5	6	7		9	10						4				8		3	11			27
1		3		5	6	7	8	9							4				10		2	11			28
1		3		5	6	7	8	9							4				10		2	11			29
1		3		5	6	7	8	9							4				10		2	11			30
1		3		5	6	7	8	9							4				10		2	11			31
1		3		5	6	7	8	9							4				10		2	11			32
1		3		5	6	7				9					8				10		2	11	4		33
1		3		5	6	7		9							8				10		2	11	4		34
1		3		5	6	7		9		8									10		2	11	4		35
1		3		5	4	7		10		8									9		2	11	6		36
1		3		5	4	7		9	10		8										2	11	6		37
1		3		5	6	9			10						4		8				2	11		7	38
1		3			6	9			10				5		4		8				2	11		7	39
1		3		5		7		9	10						4		8			6	2	11			40
1		3		5		7		9	10								8			6	2	11	4		41
1		3		5	4	7		9	10								8			6	2	11			42
'9	26	22	13	33	39	39	20	27	19	25	12	5	19	5	19	10	16	3	21	5	21	16	6	2	A
-	-	-	-	-	4	7	4	8	7	1	3	1	1	4	2	-	3	-	5	-	-	6	1	-	G

1		3		5	6	7	8	9	10	11					4						2				3

0 points v	Blackpool, Bolton W, Burnley, Chelsea, Portsmouth, Tottenham H	0 points
1 point v	Arsenal, Aston V, Charlton A, Liverpool, Manchester C, Manchester U, Sunderland	7 points
2 points v	Derby C, Huddersfield T, Middlesbrough, Preston NE, Wolves	10 points
3 points v	Newcastle U, Stoke C	6 points
4 points v	West Bromwich A	4 points

Bill Dodgin broke Fulham's transfer record to sign Irish international inside forward Bobby Brennan.

1952-53

Division Two

	P	W	D	L	F	A	Pts
Sheffield United	42	25	10	7	97	55	60
Huddersfield Town	42	24	10	8	84	33	58
Luton Town	42	22	8	12	84	49	52
Plymouth Argyle	42	20	9	13	65	60	49
Leicester City	42	18	12	12	89	74	48
Birmingham City	42	19	10	13	71	66	48
Nottingham Forest	42	18	8	16	77	67	44
Fulham	42	17	10	15	81	71	44
Blackburn Rovers	42	18	8	16	68	65	44
Leeds United	42	14	15	13	71	63	43
Swansea Town	42	15	12	15	78	81	42
Rotherham United	42	16	9	17	75	74	41
Doncaster Rovers	42	12	16	14	58	64	40
West Ham United	42	13	13	16	58	60	39
Lincoln City	42	11	17	14	64	71	39
Everton	42	12	14	16	71	75	38
Brentford	42	13	11	18	59	76	37
Hull City	42	14	8	20	57	69	36
Notts County	42	14	8	20	60	88	36
Bury	42	13	9	20	53	81	35
Southampton	42	10	13	19	68	85	33
Barnsley	42	5	8	29	47	108	18

Manager: Bill Dodgin

Did you know that?

When the Cottagers were beaten 6-1 at Leicester in August 1952, their goal was scored by Ian Black, the only Fulham goalkeeper to have scored in a first class game. He was injured in the first half and in those pre-substitute days, he returned to play up front, with Bobby Brennan going in goal. Early in the second half, Black scored a consolation goal with a header.

2	Macaulay finale
10	Campbell finale
13	Wilson debut
23	Haynes debut
25	Jezzard's 50th goal
25	N Smith debut
26	R Lowe finale
28	Flack finale
35	Pavitt finale
38	Jim Taylor finale
39	Brice debut
42	Brennan finale

No		Date	V	Opponents	R	H-T	F-T	Scorers	Atten
1	A	23	H	Bury	W	1-0	2-0	Stevens, Robson	29,34
2		25	A	Leicester C	L	0-3	1-6	Black	24,60
3		30	A	Birmingham C	W	1-0	4-1	Robson 2, Brennan, Stevens	29,57
4	S	3	H	Leicester C	L	1-3	4-6	Stevens, Jezzard 2, Mitten (pen)	22,39
5		6	H	Luton T	W	1-0	2-0	Robson 2	28,68
6		11	A	Notts C	D	0-1	1-1	Robson	18,50
7		13	A	Leeds U	L	0-2	0-2		18,37
8		17	H	Notts C	W	3-0	6-0	Jezzard, Robson 2, Stevens 2, Brennan	14,07
9		20	H	Plymouth A	W	1-1	2-1	Jezzard 2	35,77
10		27	A	Rotherham U	L	0-0	0-1		16,69
11	O	4	H	Lincoln C	W	2-1	4-2	Stevens, Jezzard 2, Robson	24,80
12		11	A	Hull C	L	0-2	1-3	Robson	30,16
13		18	H	Blackburn R	W	1-1	2-1	Jezzard, Stevens	29,07
14		25	A	Nottingham F	W	1-0	1-0	Robson	20,97
15	N	1	H	Everton	W	0-0	3-0	Jezzard, Mitten, Stevens	26,77
16		8	A	Brentford	D	1-0	2-2	Jezzard, Robson	29,24
17		15	H	Doncaster R	L	1-2	1-3	Jezzard	20,71
18		22	A	Swansea T	D	0-1	1-1	Stevens	20,11
19		29	H	Huddersfield T	L	0-1	0-2		24,00
20	D	6	A	Sheffield U	L	1-0	1-2	Jezzard	29,59
21		13	H	Barnsley	W	2-1	3-1	Jezzard, Brennan, Mitten	13,65
22		20	A	Bury	D	0-0	1-1	Jezzard	6,08
23		26	H	Southampton	D	0-0	1-1	Stevens	17,01
24		27	A	Southampton	L	2-3	3-5	Jezzard 2, Taylor (Jeff)	21,89
25	J	3	H	Birmingham C	W	2-0	3-1	Jezzard 2, Robson	21,50
26		17	A	Luton T	L	0-2	0-2		21,40
27		24	H	Leeds U	W	1-0	2-1	Jezzard, Mitten	21,21
28		31	A	Doncaster R	D	0-0	0-0		10,72
29	F	7	A	Plymouth A	L	1-2	1-3	Mitten	21,65
30		18	H	Rotherham U	W	3-1	4-1	Jezzard 3, Stevens	9,48
31		21	A	Lincoln C	D	1-2	2-2	Jezzard 2	15,04
32		28	H	Hull C	W	1-0	2-1	Jezzard, Mitten	24,99
33	M	7	A	Blackburn R	D	0-1	2-2	Mitten, Jezzard	23,55
34		14	H	Nottingham F	L	0-1	0-1		22,89
35		25	A	Everton	D	2-1	3-3	Stevens, Jezzard 2	10,82
36		28	H	Brentford	W	2-0	5-0	Jezzard 2, Robson 2, Stevens	25,55
37	A	3	A	West Ham U	W	0-0	2-1	Jezzard 2	24,59
38		6	H	West Ham U	L	0-2	2-3	Haynes, Newcombe	19,27
39		11	H	Swansea T	W	2-0	3-1	Robson 2, Jezzard	26,07
40		18	A	Huddersfield T	L	2-1	2-4	Robson 2	23,59
41		25	H	Sheffield U	L	1-0	1-2	Jezzard	28,52
42		29	A	Barnsley	D	1-0	1-1	Jezzard	3,20
									App
									Goal

FA Cup

3	J	14	A	Bolton W	L	1-2	1-3	Mitten	32,23

Black	Dodgin	Bacuzzi	Lowe E	Taylor Jim	Hill	Stevens	Robson	Jezzard	Brennan	Mitten	Lawler	Macaulay	Flack	Lowe R	Campbell	Wilson	Taylor Jeff	Healey	Haynes	Smith	Pavitt	Newcombe	Brice	
	2	3	4	5	6	7	8	9	10	11														1
	2		3	5		7	8	9	10	11	6	4												2
	2		3	5	4	7	8	9	10	11	6		1											3
	2		3	5	4	7	8	9	10	11	6		1											4
	2		3	5	4	7	8	9	10	11	6													5
	2		3	5	4	7	8	9	10	11	6													6
	2		3	5	4	7	8	9	10	11	6													7
	2		4	5		7	8	9	10	11	6			3										8
	2		4	5		7	8	9	10	11	6			3										9
	2		4	5			8	9	10	11	6			3	7									10
	2		4	5		7	8	9	10	11	6			3										11
	2		4	5		7	8	9	10	11	6			3										12
	5		4			7	8	9	10	11	6			3		2								13
	5		4			7	8	9	10	11	6			3		2								14
			4	5		7	8	9	10	11	6			3		2								15
			4	5		7	8	9	10	11	6			3		2								16
			4	5		7		9	10	11	6			3		2	8							17
			4	5	8	7		9	10	11	6			3		2								18
			4	5		7	8	9	10	11	6			3		2								19
		2	4	5	6	7	8	9	10	11				3										20
		2	4	5	6	7	8	9	10	11				3										21
		2	4	5	6	7	8	9	10	11								3						22
			4	5	6	7	8	9		11				3		2			10					23
			4	5	6	7		9	10	11				3		2	8							24
				5	6		8	9	7	11				3		2			10	4				25
			4	5	6	7	8	9	10	11			1	3							2			26
			4	5	6		8	9	7	11	3		1						10		2			27
			4	5	6		8	9	7	11	3		1						10		2			28
			4	5	6		8	9	7	11	3								10		2			29
		2		5	6	7	8	9			3								10	4		11		30
		2		5	6	7	8	9		11	3								10	4		11		31
		2		5	6	7	8	9		11	3								10	4				32
		2		5	6	7		9	8	11	3								10	4				33
		2		5	6	7		9	8	11	3								10	4				34
			3	5	6	7	8	9		11									10	4	2			35
			4	5	6	7	8	9		11	3					2			10					36
		2	4	5	6	7	8	9		11	3								10					37
		2	4	5	6		8	9		11	3								10			7		38
		2	4		6	7	8	9		11	3								10				5	39
		2	4		6	7	8	9		11	3								10				5	40
		2	4		6	7		9	8	11	3								10				5	41
		2	4		6	7		9	8	11	3								10				5	42
7	14	15	36	36	30	36	35	42	32	40	33	1	5	18	1	11	2	1	18	7	5	3	4	A
	-	-	-	-	-	13	19	35	3	7	-	-	-	-	-	-	1	-	1	-	-	1	-	G

Black	Dodgin	Bacuzzi	Lowe E	Taylor Jim	Hill	Stevens	Robson	Jezzard	Brennan	Mitten	Lawler	Macaulay	Flack	Lowe R	Campbell	Wilson	Taylor Jeff	Healey	Haynes	Smith	Pavitt	Newcombe	Brice	
			3	5	6		8	9	7	11						2			10	4				3

0 points v	Huddersfield T, Leicester C, Sheffield U	0 points
1 point v	Doncaster R, Southampton	2 points
2 points v	Hull C, Leeds U, Luton T, Nottingham F, Plymouth A, Rotherham U, West Ham U	14 points
3 points v	Barnsley, Blackburn R, Brentford, Bury, Everton, Lincoln C, Notts C, Swansea T	24 points
4 points v	Birmingham C	4 points

Full back and future Fulham director Tom Wilson made his debut in October 1952.

1953-54

Division Two

	P	W	D	L	F	A	Pts
Leicester City	42	23	10	9	97	60	56
Everton	42	20	16	6	92	58	56
Blackburn Rovers	42	23	9	10	86	50	55
Nottingham Forest	42	20	12	10	86	59	52
Rotherham United	42	21	7	14	80	67	49
Luton Town	42	18	12	12	64	59	48
Birmingham City	42	18	11	13	78	58	47
Fulham	42	17	10	15	98	85	44
Bristol Rovers	42	14	16	12	64	58	44
Leeds United	42	15	13	14	89	81	43
Stoke City	42	12	17	13	71	60	41
Doncaster Rovers	42	16	9	17	59	63	41
West Ham United	42	15	9	18	67	69	39
Notts County	42	13	13	16	54	74	39
Hull City	42	16	6	20	64	66	38
Lincoln City	42	14	9	19	65	83	37
Bury	42	11	14	17	54	72	36
Derby County	42	12	11	19	64	82	35
Plymouth Argyle	42	9	16	17	65	82	34
Swansea Town	42	13	8	21	58	82	34
Brentford	42	10	11	21	40	78	31
Oldham Athletic	42	8	9	25	40	89	25

Manager: Bill Dodgin / Frank Osborne

Did you know that?

Bedford Jezzard's 39 League goals in 1953-54 remains a post-war record and second only to Bonzo Newton's 43 goals in 1931-32. This included scoring in a record nine consecutive games between Christmas Day and 27th February.

1 Chenhall debut
19 Jezzard's 200th game
36 Jeff Taylor finale
37 Jezzard's 100th goal
42 Barton debut

No		Date	V	Opponents	R	H-T	F-T	Scorers	Atte
1	A	20	H	Bristol R	D	1-1	4-4	Robson 2, Stevens, Haynes	23,58
2		22	H	Stoke C	L	0-0	0-1		26,63
3		24	A	Leicester C	D	1-0	2-2	Haynes, Jezzard	19,81
4		29	A	Brentford	L	0-1	1-2	Mitten (pen)	21,68
5	S	2	H	Leicester C	D	0-0	1-1	Mitten (pen)	16,90
6		5	A	West Ham U	L	0-2	1-3	Jezzard	30,10
7		7	A	Rotherham U	L	1-2	2-3	Jezzard, Haynes	14,42
8		12	H	Leeds U	L	1-1	1-3	Taylor	26,04
9		16	H	Rotherham U	L	2-3	2-4	Taylor, Mitten	11,85
10		19	A	Birmingham C	D	2-2	2-2	Jezzard 2	21,13
11		26	H	Nottingham F	W	0-1	3-1	Jezzard 2, Robson	24,25
12	O	3	A	Luton T	W	0-1	2-1	Lowe, Jezzard	18,61
13		10	H	Derby C	W	2-0	5-2	Jezzard 4, Mitten	25,52
14		17	A	Blackburn R	L	1-3	1-5	Robson	25,79
15		24	H	Doncaster R	L	0-1	1-2	Hill	25,23
16		31	A	Bury	W	1-1	3-1	Jezzard 2, Robson	9,39
17	N	7	H	Oldham A	W	3-1	3-1	Mitten, Jezzard 2	18,28
18		14	A	Everton	D	2-0	2-2	Jezzard, Stevens	36,09
19		21	H	Hull C	W	1-1	5-1	Robson 2, Haynes 2, Jezzard	21,71
20		28	A	Notts C	D	0-0	0-0		19,33
21	D	5	H	Lincoln C	W	3-0	4-1	Robson, Jezzard 2, Haynes	18,72
22		12	A	Bristol R	L	1-1	1-2	Stevens	22,83
23		19	A	Stoke C	W	0-0	3-1	Mitten (pen), Haynes, Robson	13,91
24		25	H	Plymouth A	W	1-0	3-1	Jezzard 3	17,29
25		26	A	Plymouth A	D	0-1	2-2	Jezzard, Mitten	15,28
26	J	2	H	Brentford	W	2-1	4-1	Robson, Hill, Stevens, Jezzard	24,37
27		16	H	West Ham U	L	3-2	3-4	Stevens, Jezzard, Haynes	30,45
28		23	A	Leeds U	W	0-1	2-1	Stevens, Jezzard	20,17
29	F	6	H	Birmingham C	W	3-0	5-2	Jezzard, Robson 2, Haynes, Stevens	20,54
30		13	A	Nottingham F	L	1-2	1-4	Jezzard	25,14
31		20	H	Luton T	W	3-0	5-1	Jezzard, Haynes 3, Taylor	26,98
32		27	A	Derby C	D	2-2	3-3	Jezzard, Taylor, Stevens	13,40
33	M	6	H	Blackburn R	L	1-0	2-3	Taylor 2	29,07
34		13	A	Doncaster R	D	2-1	2-2	Mitten, Taylor	10,02
35		20	H	Bury	W	2-0	3-0	Taylor, Jezzard 2	18,01
36		27	A	Hull C	L	0-1	1-2	Haynes	16,94
37	A	3	H	Notts C	W	1-3	4-3	Jezzard 2, Stevens, Mitten	17,79
38		10	A	Oldham A	W	3-1	3-2	Robson, Haynes 2	13,96
39		16	A	Swansea T	L	0-1	0-2		19,60
40		17	H	Everton	D	0-0	0-0		33,51
41		19	H	Swansea T	W	3-0	4-3	Jezzard 3, Stevens	17,90
42		24	A	Lincoln C	L	2-2	2-4	Haynes, Jezzard	11,81
									App
									Goa

FA Cup

No		Date	V	Opponents	R	H-T	F-T	Scorers	Atte
3	J	9	A	Grimsby T	D	3-3	5-5	Taylor 3, Stevens, Hill	14,76
R		18	H	Grimsby T	W	2-0	3-1	Taylor, Haynes 2	18,72
4		30	A	Leyton O	L	0-2	1-2	Robson	25,80

Black	Chenhall	Lawler	Hill	Brice	Lowe	Stevens	Robson	Jezzard	Haynes	Mitten	Smith	Newcombe	Taylor	Ronson	Elliott	Cronin	Barton	
1	2	3	4	5	6	7	8	9	10	11								1
1	2	3	4	5	6	7	8	9	10	11								2
1	2	3	6	5			8	9	10	11	4	7						3
1	2	3	4	5	6		8	9	10	11		7						4
1	2	3	6	5	4		8	9	10	11		7						5
1	2	3		5	6		8	9	10	11	4	7						6
1	2	3		5	6			9	10	11	4	7	8					7
1	2	3		5	6	7		9	10		4	11	8					8
1	2	3		5	6		8	9		11	4	7	10					9
1	2	3		5	6	7	8	9	10	11	4							10
1	2	3		5	6	7	8	9	10	11	4							11
1	2	3		5	6	7	8	9	10	11	4							12
1	2	3		5	6	7	8	9	10	11	4							13
1	2	3		5	6	7	8	9	10	11	4							14
1	2	3	4	5	6	7	8	9	10	11								15
1	2	3	4	5	6	7	8	9	10	11								16
1	2	3	4	5	6	7	8	9	10	11								17
1	2	3	4	5	6	7	8	9	10	11								18
1	2	3	4	5	6	7	8	9	10	11								19
1	2	3	4	5	6	7	8	9	10	11								20
1	2	3	4	5	6	7	8	9	10	11								21
1	2	3	4	5	6	7	8	9	10	11								22
1	2	3	4	5	6	7	8	9	10	11								23
1	2	3	4	5	6	7	8	9	10	11								24
1	2	3	4	5	6	7	8	9	10	11								25
1	2	3	4	5	6	7	8	9	10	11								26
1	2	3	4	5	6	7		9	10	11			8					27
1	2	3	4	5	6	7	8	9	10	11								28
1	2	3	6	5		7	8	9	10	11	4							29
1	2	3	6	5		7	8	9	10	11	4							30
1	2	3	4	5	6	7		9	10	11			8					31
1	2	3	4	5	6	7		9	10	11			8					32
	2	3	4	5	6	7		9	10	11			8	1				33
	2	3	4	5	6			9	10	11		7	8	1				34
	2	3	4	5	6			9	10	11		7	8		1			35
	2	3	4	5	6		7	9	10	11			8		1			36
	2	3	8	5	6	7		9	10	11					1	4		37
	2	3	4	5	6	7	8	9	10	11					1			38
	2	3	4	5	6	7	8	9	10	11					1			39
	2	3	4	5	6	7	8	9	10	11					1			40
	2	3	4	5	6	7	8	9	10	11					1			41
	2	3	4	5	6		8	9	10	11					1		7	42
32	42	42	33	42	39	32	33	42	41	41	12	9	10	2	8	1	1	A
-	-	-	2	-	1	10	13	39	16	9	-	-	8	-	-	-	-	G

Black	Chenhall	Lawler	Hill	Brice	Lowe	Stevens	Robson	Jezzard	Haynes	Mitten	Smith	Newcombe	Taylor	Ronson	Elliott	Cronin	Barton	
1	2	3	4	5	6	7		9	10	11			8					3
1	2	3	4	5	6	7		9	10	11			8					R
1	2	3	4	5	6	7	8	9	10	11								

0 points v	Blackburn R, Rotherham U, West Ham U	0 points
1 point v	Bristol R, Doncaster R	2 points
2 points v	Brentford, Everton, Hull C, Leeds U, Leicester C, Lincoln C, Nottingham F, Stoke C, Swansea T	18 points
3 points v	Birmingham C, Derby C, Notts C, Plymouth A	12 points
4 points v	Bury, Luton T, Oldham A	12 points

Robin Lawler and Johnny Haynes lead Ian Black and Tom Wilson trails.

1954-55

Division Two

	P	W	D	L	F	A	Pts
Birmingham City	42	22	10	10	92	47	54
Luton Town	42	23	8	11	88	53	54
Rotherham United	42	25	4	13	94	64	54
Leeds United	42	23	7	12	70	53	53
Stoke City	42	21	10	11	69	46	52
Blackburn Rovers	42	22	6	14	114	79	50
Notts County	42	21	6	15	74	71	48
West Ham United	42	18	10	14	74	70	46
Bristol Rovers	42	19	7	16	75	70	45
Swansea Town	42	17	9	16	86	83	43
Liverpool	42	16	10	16	92	96	42
Middlesbrough	42	18	6	18	73	82	42
Bury	42	15	11	16	77	72	41
Fulham	42	14	11	17	76	79	39
Nottingham Forest	42	16	7	19	58	62	39
Lincoln City	42	13	10	19	68	79	36
Port Vale	42	12	11	19	48	71	35
Doncaster Rovers	42	14	7	21	58	95	35
Hull City	42	12	10	20	44	69	34
Plymouth Argyle	42	12	7	23	57	82	31
Ipswich Town	42	11	6	25	57	92	28
Derby County	42	7	9	26	53	82	23

Manager: Frank Osborne

Did you know that?

In October 1954, Johnny Haynes won the first of his 56 England caps, against Northern Ireland in Belfast. He thus completed the set of England representative honours from schoolboy through to full cap before the age of 21. The next month, his old school friend, Tosh Chamberlain, scored with his first touch of the ball on his debut against Lincoln.

- 14 Stevens' 300th game
- 18 Chamberlain debut
- 18 Robson's 50th goal
- 29 Greenwood debut
- 33 Dwight debut
- 37 Lowe's 200th game
- 39 Stapleton debut

No		Date	V	Opponents	R	H-T	F-T	Scorers	Atten
1	A	21	H	Blackburn R	W	4-0	5-1	Stevens, Jezzard, Mitten 2, Haynes	31,14
2		25	A	Derby C	W	2-2	4-3	Jezzard, Haynes 2, Robson	18,65
3		28	A	Bury	W	1-1	3-1	Jezzard, Stevens, Haynes	18,17
4	S	1	H	Derby C	W	1-0	2-0	Jezzard, Haynes	26,24
5		4	A	Swansea T	D	2-1	2-2	Robson, Jezzard	27,02
6		8	H	Doncaster R	W	1-1	5-2	Robson 2, Jezzard 2, Mitten	19,99
7		11	H	Notts C	W	3-0	3-1	Haynes, Jezzard, Mitten	26,61
8		15	A	Doncaster R	L	0-1	0-4		15,09
9		18	A	Liverpool	L	0-1	1-4	Robson	44,37
10		25	H	Bristol R	L	1-2	2-3	Jezzard 2	31,45
11	O	2	A	Plymouth A	L	2-2	2-3	Stevens, Robson	23,20
12		9	H	Birmingham C	W	2-0	2-1	Stevens, Robson	30,29
13		16	A	Ipswich T	W	3-1	4-2	Robson 2, Stevens, Jezzard	20,05
14		23	H	Luton T	W	0-0	3-1	Stevens 2, Robson	30,63
15		30	A	Rotherham U	W	0-2	3-2	Robson, Jezzard 2	19,31
16	N	6	H	Stoke C	D	0-0	2-2	Mitten (pen), Stevens	30,47
17		13	A	Middlesbrough	L	0-2	2-4	Robson, Jezzard	21,73
18		20	H	Lincoln C	W	3-0	3-2	Chamberlain, Robson 2	21,02
19		27	A	Hull C	D	0-0	0-0		17,86
20	D	4	H	Nottingham F	D	1-0	1-1	Robson	20,06
21		11	A	Leeds U	D	0-0	1-1	Newcombe	30,71
22		18	A	Blackburn R	L	1-2	1-3	Haynes	25,63
23		25	H	Port Vale	W	2-0	3-1	Haynes, Robson, Jezzard	17,51
24		27	A	Port Vale	L	0-1	0-4		29,41
25	J	1	H	Bury	D	0-0	0-0		17,23
26	F	5	H	Liverpool	L	1-2	1-2	Brice	21,72
27		12	A	Bristol R	L	1-2	1-4	Jezzard	19,33
28		19	H	Plymouth A	L	2-2	2-3	Robson 2	10,41
29	M	5	H	Ipswich T	W	2-0	4-1	Jezzard, Barton, Hill, Robson	17,17
30		12	A	Luton T	L	0-1	0-3		17,96
31		19	H	Rotherham U	D	1-1	1-1	Jezzard	16,45
32		26	A	Stoke C	D	0-0	1-1	Mitten (pen)	7,05
33		30	A	Birmingham C	L	1-1	2-3	Robson, Dwight	9,68
34	A	2	H	Middlesbrough	L	0-0	1-2	Dwight	17,77
35		8	A	West Ham U	L	1-2	1-2	Jezzard	34,23
36		9	A	Lincoln C	D	2-1	2-2	Jezzard, Robson	12,41
37		11	H	West Ham U	D	0-0	0-0		21,61
38		16	H	Hull C	L	0-0	0-1		13,25
39		20	H	Swansea T	W	3-0	5-1	Robson, Jezzard 3, Barton	10,35
40		23	A	Nottingham F	L	0-1	0-2		10,02
41		27	A	Notts C	D	0-0	0-0		8,23
42		30	H	Leeds U	L	1-0	1-3	Robson	21,40
									App
									Goal

FA Cup

No		Date	V	Opponents	R	H-T	F-T	Scorers	Atten
3	J	8	H	Preston NE	L	1-1	2-3	Haynes, Stevens	24,76

Elliott	Chenhall	Lawler	Hill	Brice	Lowe	Stevens	Robson	Jezzard	Haynes	Mitten	Smith	Gibson	Cronin	Black	Bacuzzi	Chamberlain	Fisher	Newcombe	Wilson	Greenwood	Barton	Dwight	Stapleton	
	2	3	4	5	6	7	8	9	10	11														1
	2	3	4	5	6	7	8	9	10	11														2
	2	3	4	5	6	7	8	9	10	11														3
	2	3	4	5	6	7	8	9	10	11														4
	2	3	4	5	6	7	8	9	10	11														5
	2	3		5	6	7	8	9	10	11	4													6
	2	3		5	6	7	8	9	10	11	4													7
	2	3	4	5	6	7	8	9	10	11														8
	2	3	4	5	6	7	8	9	10	11														9
	2	3	6	5		7	8	9	10	11	4													10
	2	3	6			7	8	9		11	4	5	10											11
	2	3	5		6	7	8	9	10	11	4			1										12
	2	3	4	5	6	7	8	9	10	11				1										13
	2	3		5	6	7	8	9	10	11	4			1										14
	2	3		5	6	7	8	9	10	11	4			1										15
	2			5	6	7	8	9	10	11	4			1	3									16
	2	3		5	6	7	8	9	10	11	4			1										17
		3	10	5	6		8	9			4			1		11	2	7						18
		3	10	5	6		8	9		11	4			1			2	7						19
		3		5	6		8	9	10	11	4			1			2	7						20
		3	4	5	6		8	9	10	11				1			2	7						21
	2	3	4	5	6		8	9	10	11				1				7						22
	2	3	4	5	6	7	8	9	10	11				1										23
	2	3	4	5	6	7	8	9	10	11														24
		3	4	5	6	7	8	9	10	11									2					25
			4	5	6	7	8	9	10	11							3		2					26
		3	4	5	6	7	8	9	10	11									2					27
				5	6		8	9	10		4			1		11	3	7	2					28
	2	6	10		4		8	9		11				1			3			5	7			29
	2	6	10		4		8	9		11				1			3			5	7			30
		3	4		6		8	9	10	11				1					2	5	7			31
		3	4	9	6		8		10	11				1					2	5	7			32
		3	4		6		8		10	11				1					2	5	7	9		33
		3	4		6		8		10					1		11			2	5	7	9		34
		3	4		6		8	9	10					1		11			2	5	7			35
		3	4		6		8	9	10					1		11			2	5		7		36
		3	4		6		8	9	10	11				1					2	5	7			37
		3	4		6		8	9	10					1		11			2	5		7		38
		3	4				8	9	10	11				1					2	5	7		6	39
		3	4				8	9	10	11				1					2	5	7		6	40
		3					8	9	10	11	4			1					2	5	7		6	41
		3					8	9	10	11	4			1					2	5	7		6	42
5	22	39	32	27	36	22	42	39	37	36	15	1	1	27	1	6	8	6	16	14	12	4	4	A
-	-	-	1	1	-	8	23	23	8	6	-	-	-	-	-	1	-	1	-	-	2	2	-	G

		3	4	5	6	7	8	9	10	11									2					3

0 points v	Bristol R, Liverpool, Middlesbrough, Plymouth A	0 points
1 point v	Hull C, Leeds U, Nottingham F, West Ham U	4 points
2 points v	Birmingham C, Blackburn R, Doncaster R, Luton T, Port Vale, Stoke C,	12 points
3 points v	Bury, Lincoln C, Notts C, Rotherham U, Swansea T	15 points
4 points v	Derby C, Ipswich T	8 points

Defender Joe Stapleton made his debut in April 1955.

1955-56

Division Two

	P	W	D	L	F	A	Pts
Sheffield Wednesday	42	21	13	8	101	62	55
Leeds United	42	23	6	13	80	60	52
Liverpool	42	21	6	15	85	63	48
Blackburn Rovers	42	21	6	15	84	65	48
Leicester City	42	21	6	15	94	78	48
Bristol Rovers	42	21	6	15	84	70	48
Nottingham Forest	42	19	9	14	68	63	47
Lincoln City	42	18	10	14	79	65	46
Fulham	42	20	6	16	89	79	46
Swansea Town	42	20	6	16	83	81	46
Bristol City	42	19	7	16	80	64	45
Port Vale	42	16	13	13	60	58	45
Stoke City	42	20	4	18	71	62	44
Middlesbrough	42	16	8	18	76	78	40
Bury	42	16	8	18	86	90	40
West Ham United	42	14	11	17	74	69	39
Doncaster Rovers	42	12	11	19	69	96	35
Barnsley	42	11	12	19	47	84	34
Rotherham United	42	12	9	21	56	75	33
Notts County	42	11	9	22	55	82	31
Plymouth Argyle	42	10	8	24	54	87	28
Hull City	42	10	6	26	53	97	26

Manager: Frank Osborne / Dug Livingstone

Did you know that?

Both Johnny Haynes and Bedford Jezzard were in the England side which beat Northern Ireland 3-0 at Wembley in November. Despite being a Second Division club, Fulham had two players in the England team. It happened again, with Haynes and Jimmy Langley, against Scotland, Portugal and Yugoslavia in the spring of 1958.

22	Jezzard's 150th goal
22	Bacuzzi finale
27	Mitten finale
32	Robson finale
34	Jezzard's 300th game
39	Brice finale
42	Greenwood and Jezzard finales

No		Date	V	Opponents	R	H-T	F-T	Scorers	Atte
1	A	20	A	Bury	W	2-0	5-1	Haynes 2, Jezzard 2, Stevens	13,57
2		24	H	Blackburn R	W	2-0	3-0	Stevens, Haynes, Jezzard	18,31
3		27	H	Barnsley	W	2-0	5-1	Jezzard 4, Robson	21,64
4		29	A	Blackburn R	L	0-1	0-1		24,38
5	S	3	A	Middlesbrough	D	0-0	1-1	Mitten	26,27
6		7	H	Notts C	D	0-0	1-1	Stevens	16,45
7		10	H	Bristol C	W	1-0	3-0	Haynes, Jezzard 2	25,87
8		15	A	Notts C	W	2-1	4-3	Haynes 3, Mitten	9,56
9		17	A	West Ham U	L	1-1	1-2	Jezzard	25,73
10		24	H	Port Vale	L	1-1	1-4	Mitten	25,36
11	O	1	A	Rotherham U	W	2-1	3-2	Robson, Jezzard 2	12,87
12		8	H	Hull C	W	3-0	5-0	Jezzard 5	21,20
13		15	A	Nottingham F	L	0-1	0-1		16,02
14		22	H	Leicester C	W	1-0	3-2	Robson 2, Jezzard	17,97
15		29	A	Doncaster R	L	1-0	2-4	Robson, Haynes	14,12
16	N	5	H	Bristol R	L	1-2	3-5	Jezzard 2, Stevens	31,75
17		12	A	Stoke C	W	1-0	2-1	Hill, Robson	18,94
18		19	H	Plymouth A	W	0-0	2-1	Jezzard, Mitten (pen)	22,85
19		26	A	Liverpool	L	0-3	0-7		34,99
20	D	3	H	Sheffield W	L	1-1	1-2	Hill	23,28
21		10	A	Lincoln C	L	1-3	1-6	Barton	11,63
22		17	H	Bury	W	1-1	3-1	Jezzard 2, Haynes	12,05
23		24	A	Barnsley	L	0-0	0-3		15,01
24		26	H	Swansea T	W	0-0	4-1	Haynes 2 (1 pen), Chamberlain, Jezzard	18,78
25		27	A	Swansea T	L	0-2	0-2		21,05
26		31	H	Middlesbrough	W	2-0	4-1	Hill, Chamberlain, Robson 2	18,47
27	J	14	A	Bristol C	L	0-0	1-2	Haynes	27,79
28		21	H	West Ham U	W	2-1	3-1	Chamberlain, Hill, Jezzard	24,32
29	F	4	A	Port Vale	L	0-2	1-2	Robson	13,23
30		11	H	Rotherham U	D	1-0	1-1	Haynes	9,16
31		18	A	Plymouth A	D	0-0	0-0		17,13
32	M	3	A	Leicester C	L	0-1	1-2	Robson	35,51
33		10	H	Lincoln C	W	1-0	3-0	Jezzard, Chamberlain, Haynes	19,19
34		17	A	Bristol R	D	0-1	2-2	Haynes (pen), Stevens	21,82
35		24	H	Stoke C	W	0-0	2-0	Stevens, Chamberlain	15,94
36		30	H	Leeds U	L	1-1	1-2	Chamberlain	25,45
37		31	A	Hull C	D	1-0	2-2	Haynes 2	12,68
38	A	2	A	Leeds U	L	1-3	1-6	Haynes	20,11
39		7	H	Liverpool	W	2-0	3-1	Dwight 3	15,66
40		14	A	Sheffield W	W	2-0	3-2	Stevens, Dwight, Chamberlain	26,94
41		21	H	Doncaster R	W	4-0	4-0	Chamberlain 3, Stevens	17,75
42	M	2	H	Nottingham F	W	3-2	4-3	Stevens, Dwight, Jezzard, Chamberlain	9,97
									App
									Goa

FA Cup

3	J	7	A	Notts C	W	1-0	1-0	Haynes	21,50
4		28	H	Newcastle U	L	1-3	4-5	Chamberlain 3, Hill	39,20

Black	Chenhall	Lawler	Stapleton	Greenwood	Lowe	Stevens	Robson	Jezzard	Haynes	Mitten	Barton	Hill	Hewkins	Chamberlain	Elliott	Bacuzzi	Smith	Wilson	Brice	Collins	Dwight	Hall	
1	2	3	4	5	6	7	8	9	10	11													1
1	2	3	4	5	6	7	8	9	10	11													2
1	2	3	4	5	6	7	8	9	10	11													3
1	2	3	4	5	6	7	8	9	10	11													4
1	2	3	4	5	6	9	8		10	11	7												5
1	2	3	4	5	6	9	8		10	11	7												6
1	2	3	4	5	6	7	8	9	10	11													7
1	2	3	4	5	6	7		9	10	11		8											8
1	2	3	4	5	6			9	10	11	7	8											9
1	2	3	4	5	6	7	8	9	10	11													10
1	2	3	4	5	6	7	8	9	10	11													11
1	2	3	4	5			8	9	10	11	7	6											12
1	2	3	4	5			8	9	10	11	7	6											13
1	2	3	4	5		7	8	9	10	11		6											14
1	2	3		5	6	7	8	9	10	11		4											15
1	2	3		5	6	7	8	9	10	11		4											16
	2	3	4	5	6	7	8	9		11		10	1										17
	2	3		5	6	7	8	9	10	11		4	1										18
	2	3		5	6	7	8	9	10			4	1	11									19
	2	3	4	5	6		7	9	8	11		10			1								20
	2	3		5	6		8	9	10	11	7	4			1								21
1		3		5	6	7		9	10			8		11		2	4						22
1		3		5	6			9	10		7	8		11			4	2					23
1		3			6	7		9	10			8		11			4	2	5				24
1		3			6	7		9	10			8		11			4	2	5				25
1		3			6		8	9	10			7		11			4	2	5				26
1		3			6		8	9	10	11		7					4	2	5				27
1		3			6	7		9	10			8		11			4	2	5				28
1		3			6		8	9	10			7		11			4	2	5				29
1		3			6		8	9	10			7		11			4	2	5				30
1		3			6		8	9	10			7		11			4	2	5				31
1					6		8	9	10			7		11			4	2	5	3			32
1					6	7		9	10			8		11			4	2	5	3			33
1					6	7		9	10			8		11			4	2	5	3			34
1		2			6	7		9	10			8		11			4		5	3			35
1		2			6	7		9	10			8		11			4		5	3			36
1				5	6	7		9	10			8		11			4	2		3			37
1				5	6	7		9	10			8		11			4	2		3			38
1		3			6	7			10			8		11			4	2	5		9		39
		3		5	6	7						8	1	11			4	2			9	10	40
		3	2	5	6	7		9	10				1	11			4				8		41
		3	2	5	6	7		9	10				1	11			4				8		42
34	21	37	18	28	39	30	25	38	40	21	7	31	6	21	2	1	21	16	14	7	4	1	A
-	-	-	-	-	-	-	9	10	27	18	4	1	4	-	11	-	-	-	-	-	-	5	G

Black	Chenhall	Lawler	Stapleton	Greenwood	Lowe	Stevens	Robson	Jezzard	Haynes	Mitten	Barton	Hill	Hewkins	Chamberlain	Elliott	Bacuzzi	Smith	Wilson	Brice	Collins	Dwight	Hall	
1		3			6		8	9	10	11		7					4	2	5				3
1		3			6		8	9	10			7		11			4	2	5				4

0 points v	Leeds U, Port Vale	0 points
1 point v	Bristol R	1 point
2 points v	Barnsley, Blackburn R, Bristol C, Doncaster R, Leicester C, Lincoln C, Liverpool, Nottingham F, Sheffield W, Swansea T, West Ham U	22 points
3 points v	Hull C, Middlesbrough, Notts C, Plymouth A, Rotherham U	15 points
4 points v	Bury, Stoke C	8 points

Giant South African goalkeeper Ken Hewkins was signed from Clyde in November 1955.

1956-57

Division Two

	P	W	D	L	F	A	Pts
Leicester City	42	25	11	6	109	67	61
Nottingham Forest	42	22	10	10	94	55	54
Liverpool	42	21	11	10	82	54	53
Blackburn Rovers	42	21	10	11	83	75	52
Stoke City	42	20	8	14	83	58	48
Middlesbrough	42	19	10	13	84	60	48
Sheffield United	42	19	8	15	87	76	46
West Ham United	42	19	8	15	59	63	46
Bristol Rovers	42	18	9	15	81	67	45
Swansea Town	42	19	7	16	90	90	45
Fulham	42	19	4	19	84	76	42
Huddersfield Town	42	18	6	18	68	74	42
Bristol City	42	16	9	17	74	79	41
Doncaster Rovers	42	15	10	17	77	77	40
Leyton Orient	42	15	10	17	66	84	40
Grimsby Town	42	17	5	20	61	62	39
Rotherham United	42	13	11	18	74	75	37
Lincoln City	42	14	6	22	54	80	34
Barnsley	42	12	10	20	59	89	34
Notts County	42	9	12	21	58	86	30
Bury	42	8	9	25	60	96	25
Port Vale	42	8	6	28	57	101	22

Manager: Dug Livingstone

Did you know that?

When Fulham beat Port Vale 6-3 at home in February 1957, the goals were shared equally between Roy Bentley and Roy Dwight. Only once before, in March 1913 against Stockport (Bert Pearce and Tim Coleman), and once since, against Ipswich on Boxing Day 1963 (Graham Leggat and Bobby Howfield), have two Fulham players scored hat-tricks in the same game.

1	Lampe debut
5	Doherty debut
7	Stevens 100th goal
10	Bentley debut
12	N Smith finale
18	Wilson finale
21	Haynes' 50th goal
31	Langley debut
33	Cohen debut

No		Date	V	Opponents	R	H-T	F-T	Scorers	Atter
1	A	18	H	West Ham U	L	1-0	1-4	Dwight	25,80
2		20	A	Sheffield U	L	1-3	2-5	Stapleton, Dwight	22,74
3		25	A	Nottingham F	L	0-2	1-3	Dwight	21,49
4		29	H	Sheffield U	L	1-2	1-2	Dwight	8,19
5	S	1	H	Huddersfield T	W	1-0	1-0	Dwight	17,60
6		4	A	Bristol C	W	3-0	3-0	Dwight, Chamberlain, Stevens	22,67
7		8	H	Swansea T	W	2-2	7-3	Dwight 3, Chamberlain, Stevens 2 (1 pen), (King og)	25,37
8		12	H	Bristol C	W	1-1	2-1	Chamberlain, Hill	15,11
9		15	A	Lincoln C	L	0-1	0-1		11,47
10		22	H	Rotherham U	W	2-0	3-1	Bentley, Chamberlain, Stevens	31,10
11		29	A	Port Vale	L	0-1	1-2	Stevens	21,28
12	O	6	A	Bury	W	1-0	1-0	Dwight	11,85
13		13	H	Grimsby T	W	2-0	3-1	Stevens 3 (2 pens)	31,72
14		20	A	Liverpool	L	2-2	3-4	Chamberlain 2, Haynes	36,73
15		27	H	Stoke C	W	1-0	1-0	Stevens	29,47
16	N	3	A	Middlesbrough	L	0-3	1-3	Hill	29,20
17		10	H	Leicester C	D	0-1	2-2	Bentley 2	33,75
18		17	A	Bristol R	L	0-1	0-4		24,65
19		24	H	Notts C	W	2-0	5-1	Dwight 3, Stevens 2	15,36
20	D	1	A	Doncaster R	L	0-3	0-4		13,14
21		8	H	Leyton O	W	0-1	3-1	Dwight, Haynes 2	26,84
22		15	A	West Ham U	L	1-2	1-2	Bentley	18,11
23		22	H	Nottingham F	L	0-0	0-1		12,49
24		25	A	Blackburn R	L	0-1	0-2		23,88
25		26	H	Blackburn R	W	2-1	7-2	Chamberlain 3, Dwight 2, Bentley 2	8,23
26		29	A	Huddersfield T	D	0-1	1-1	Dwight	16,50
27	J	12	A	Swansea T	W	3-0	5-4	Dwight 3, Chamberlain 2	17,90
28		19	H	Lincoln C	L	0-1	0-1		17,05
29	F	2	A	Rotherham U	L	2-2	3-4	Haynes, Bentley, Dwight	10,55
30		9	H	Port Vale	W	2-1	6-3	Bentley 3, Dwight 3	13,96
31		16	H	Bury	L	1-1	1-3	Haynes	26,44
32		23	A	Grimsby T	L	1-1	1-3	Watson	13,30
33	M	2	H	Liverpool	L	0-1	1-2	Dwight	26,92
34		9	A	Stoke C	W	2-0	2-0	Bentley 2	24,78
35		16	H	Middlesbrough	L	0-2	1-2	Chamberlain	20,45
36		23	A	Leicester C	W	0-1	3-1	Bentley, Hill, Langley (pen)	36,45
37		30	H	Bristol R	W	2-1	3-2	Chamberlain, Hill, Stapleton	21,99
38	A	6	A	Notts C	D	0-0	0-0		17,12
39		13	H	Doncaster R	W	3-0	3-0	Hill, Stevens, Bentley	14,41
40		19	H	Barnsley	W	1-0	2-0	Stevens, Chamberlain	16,99
41		20	A	Leyton O	W	0-0	2-0	Stevens 2	17,73
42		22	A	Barnsley	D	0-1	1-1	Chamberlain	8,53
									App
									Goal

FA Cup

3	J	5	A	Ipswich T	W	2-1	3-2	Stevens 2, Dwight	22,21
4		26	A	Blackpool	L	2-3	2-6	Lowe, Bentley	26,24

Black	Chenhall	Lawler	Smith	Lampe	Lowe	Stevens	Stapleton	Dwight	Haynes	Chamberlain	Barton	Hill	Collins	Doherty	Bentley	Edwards	Wilson	Hewkins	Langley	Watson	Cohen	
	2	3	4	5	6	7	8	9	10	11												1
	2	3	4	5	10	8	6	9		11	7											2
	2	3	4	5	6	7	8	10		11		9										3
		3		5	6	7	4	9	10	11		8	2									4
		3		5	6	7	4	9	10			8	2	11								5
		3		5	6	7	4	9	10	11		8	2									6
		3		5	6	7	4	9	10	11		8	2									7
		3		5	6	7	4	9	10	11		8	2									8
		3		5	6	7	4	9		11		8	2	10								9
		3		5	6	7	4	9		11		8	2		10							10
		3	4		5	7				11		8	2	10	9	6						11
		3	4	5	6	7		9		11		8	2	10								12
		3		5	6	7		9	10	11		4	2		8							13
		3		5	6	7	4		10	11		8	2		9							14
		3		5	6	7	4		10	11		8	2		9							15
		3		5	6	7	4		10	11		8	2		9							16
		3		5	6	7		9	10	11		4			8		2					17
		3		5	6	7		9		11		4		10	8		2					18
		3		5	6	7		9	10	11		4	2		8							19
		3		5	6	7	4	9		11		10	2		8							20
		3		5	6	7		9	10	11		4	2		8							21
		3		5	6	7		9	10	11		4	2		8							22
		3		5	6	7		9		11		4	2	8	10							23
		3		5	6	7		9	10	11		4	2		8							24
		3		5	6	7		9	10	11		4	2		8							25
		3		5	6	7		9	10	11		4	2		8							26
	2	3		5	6	7		9	10	11		4			8							27
	2	3		5	6	7		9	10	11		4			8							28
		3		5	6	7		9	10	11		4	2		8			1				29
		3		5	6	7	2	9	10	11		4			8			1				30
		2		5	6	7		9	10	11		4			8			1	3			31
		2			5			9	10	11		4			8	6		1	3	7		32
				5	6	11		9	10			4			8			1	3	7	2	33
		2		5	6	11	4	7	10			8			9				3			34
		2		5	6		4	7	10	11		8			9				3			35
		2		5	6	7	4		10	11		8			9				3			36
		2		5	6	7	4		10	11		8			9				3			37
		2		5	6	7	4		10	11		8			9				3			38
		2		5	6	7	4		10	11		8			9				3			39
		2		5	6	7	4	9	10	11					8				3			40
		2		5	6	7	4	9	10	11					8				3			41
		2		5	6	7	4	9	10	11					8				3			42
7	5	41	5	40	42	40	24	34	33	39	1	37	22	6	32	2	2	5	12	2	1	A
	-	-	-	-	-	15	2	25	5	15	-	5	-	-	14	-	-	-	1	1	-	G

Black	Chenhall	Lawler	Smith	Lampe	Lowe	Stevens	Stapleton	Dwight	Haynes	Chamberlain	Barton	Hill	Collins	Doherty	Bentley	Edwards	Wilson	Hewkins	Langley	Watson	Cohen	
	2	3		5	6	7		9	10	11		4			8							1
		3		5	6	7		9	10	11		4	2		8							2

0 points v	Lincoln C, Liverpool, Middlesbrough, Nottingham F, Sheffield U, West Ham U	0 points
1 point v		0 points
2 points v	Blackburn R, Bristol R, Bury, Doncaster R, Grimsby T, Port Vale, Rotherham U	14 points
3 points v	Barnsley, Huddersfield T, Leicester C, Notts C	12 points
4 points v	Bristol C, Leyton O, Stoke C, Swansea T	16 points

The injured Bobby Jezzard was replaced by Roy Dwight, Elton John's cousin, who was top scorer with 25 goals.

1957-58

Division Two

	P	W	D	L	F	A	Pts
West Ham United	42	23	11	8	101	54	57
Blackburn Rovers	42	22	12	8	93	57	56
Charlton Athletic	42	24	7	11	107	69	55
Liverpool	42	22	10	10	79	54	54
Fulham	42	20	12	10	97	59	52
Sheffield United	42	21	10	11	75	50	52
Middlesbrough	42	19	7	16	83	74	45
Ipswich Town	42	16	12	14	68	69	44
Huddersfield Town	42	14	16	12	63	66	44
Bristol Rovers	42	17	8	17	85	80	42
Stoke City	42	18	6	18	75	73	42
Leyton Orient	42	18	5	19	77	79	41
Grimsby Town	42	17	6	19	86	83	40
Barnsley	42	14	12	16	70	74	40
Cardiff City	42	14	9	19	63	77	37
Derby County	42	14	8	20	60	81	36
Bristol City	42	13	9	20	63	88	35
Rotherham United	42	14	5	23	65	101	33
Swansea Town	42	11	9	22	72	99	31
Lincoln City	42	11	9	22	55	82	31
Notts County	42	12	6	24	44	80	30
Doncaster Rovers	42	8	11	23	56	88	27

Manager: Dug Livingstone

Did you know that?

All five forwards (Dwight, Hill, Cook. Haynes and Chamberlain) scored before half time in Fulham's 6-0 home win over Grimsby. Dwight completed the scoring in the second half.

17	Black finale
17	Lowe's 300th game
20	Macedo debut
22	Dwight's 50th goal
23	Haynes' 200th game
FAC3	Key debut
27	Stevens' 400th game
28	Cook debut
37	Chenhall finale
39	Dwight finale

No		Date	V	Opponents	R	H-T	F-T	Scorers	Atte
1	A	24	H	Derby C	W	1-0	2-0	Haynes, Dwight	27,16
2		29	A	Notts C	W	2-1	5-1	Dwight 2, Haynes, Chamberlain 2	18,23
3		31	A	Swansea T	D	3-2	4-4	Dwight 2, Hill, Bentley	26,54
4	S	4	H	Notts C	W	1-0	1-0	Dwight	14,60
5		7	H	Liverpool	D	1-2	2-2	Chamberlain, Haynes	32,82
6		11	A	Ipswich T	D	0-0	1-1	Langley	19,64
7		14	H	Barnsley	D	0-0	1-1	Haynes	24,44
8		18	H	Ipswich T	D	0-0	0-0		16,22
9		21	A	West Ham U	L	2-1	2-3	Dwight, Bentley	23,85
10		28	H	Sheffield U	W	3-1	6-3	Dwight 4, Bentley, Stevens	26,13
11	O	5	A	Blackburn R	D	1-1	1-1	Stevens	25,80
12		12	A	Middlesbrough	L	0-1	0-2		31,75
13		19	H	Leyton O	W	0-0	3-1	Dwight, Hill, Bentley	26,56
14		26	A	Charlton A	D	0-2	2-2	Stevens, Langley (pen)	29,66
15	N	2	H	Doncaster R	W	1-0	4-1	Hill, Haynes, Stevens, (Williams og)	21,28
16		9	A	Rotherham U	L	1-2	1-3	Bentley	8,78
17		16	H	Huddersfield T	W	1-0	2-1	Haynes 2	18,24
18		23	A	Grimsby T	L	0-1	1-3	Barton	15,11
19		30	H	Stoke C	L	0-1	3-4	Dwight, Hill, Bentley	19,72
20	D	7	A	Bristol C	W	4-0	5-0	Dwight 2, Haynes, Hill, Chamberlain	16,98
21		14	H	Cardiff C	W	1-0	2-0	Hill, (Malloy og)	16,02
22		21	A	Derby C	D	3-1	3-3	Dwight 2, Bentley	21,99
23		25	A	Lincoln C	W	0-0	1-0	Dwight	8,02
24		26	H	Lincoln C	W	3-1	4-1	Haynes 2, Chamberlain, Hill	18,97
25		28	H	Swansea T	W	0-0	2-0	Doherty, Haynes	24,78
26	J	11	A	Liverpool	L	0-1	1-2	Chamberlain	51,70
27		18	A	Barnsley	L	0-0	0-1		14,33
28	F	1	H	West Ham U	D	1-1	2-2	Haynes, Langley	42,19
29		22	H	Grimsby T	W	5-0	6-0	Dwight 2, Haynes, Hill, Cook, Chamberlain	21,31
30	M	8	H	Charlton A	W	2-1	3-1	Haynes, Hill, Chamberlain	34,06
31		13	A	Leyton O	W	1-0	3-1	Dwight, Cook, Lowe	12,37
32		15	A	Doncaster R	W	3-0	6-1	Cook, Hill 5	15,18
33		29	A	Huddersfield T	W	1-0	3-0	Haynes, Cook, Chamberlain	19,21
34	A	4	A	Bristol R	D	1-2	2-2	Hill, Dwight	31,01
35		7	H	Bristol R	W	2-0	3-0	Chamberlain, Langley, Cook	31,31
36		12	A	Stoke C	W	1-0	2-1	Chamberlain, Cook	19,11
37		19	H	Bristol C	L	0-4	3-4	Cook, Barton 2	27,04
38		21	H	Middlesbrough	L	0-1	0-1		26,14
39		23	H	Blackburn R	D	1-0	1-1	Chamberlain	32,10
40		26	A	Cardiff C	L	0-2	0-3		11,84
41		28	A	Sheffield U	D	1-0	1-1	Hill	15,98
42	M	1	H	Rotherham U	W	3-1	3-1	Chamberlain, Cook 2	7,74
									App
									Goa

FA Cup

3	J	4	H	Yeovil T	W	0-0	4-0	Hill 2, Key, Doherty		24,82
4		25	H	Charlton A	D	0-0	1-1	Hill		39,58
R		29	A	Charlton A	W	0-0	2-0	Bentley, Stevens		43,09
5	F	15	A	West Ham U	W	1-1	3-2	Dwight, Hill, Haynes		37,50
6	M	1	H	Bristol R	W	3-0	3-1	Hill, Stevens 2		42,0
SF		22	N	Manchester U	D	2-2	2-2	Stevens, Hill	(at Villa Park)	69,74
R		26	N	Manchester U	L	2-3	3-5	Dwight, Stevens, Chamberlain	(at Highbury)	38,25

Black	Lawler	Langley	Edwards	Stapleton	Lowe	Stevens	Bentley	Dwight	Haynes	Chamberlain	Hill	Weir	Taylor	Lampe	Watson	Hewkins	Forbes	Doherty	Cohen	Barton	Macedo	Cook	Chenhall	Collins	Key	
1	2	3	4	5	6	7	8	9	10	11																1
1	2	3	4	5	6		9	7	10	11	8															2
1	2	3	4	5	6		9	7	10	11	8															3
1	2	3	4	5	6		9	7	10	11	8															4
1	2	3	4	5	6		9	7	10	11	8															5
1	2	3	4	5	6	7	8	9	10			11														6
1	2	3	4	5	6		8	7	10			11	9													7
1	2	3	4	5	6		9	7	10		8	11														8
1	2	3	6	4		11	10	9	8					5	7											9
	2	3		4		11	8	9	10				7	5		1	6									10
	2	3	4			11	6	9	10		8		7	5		1										11
1	2	3	4	5	6	11	9		10		8		7													12
1	2	3	4	5	6	11	9	7			8							10								13
1	2	3	4	5	6	11	9	7	10		8															14
1	2	3	4	5	6	11	9	7	10		8															15
1	2	3		4	6	11	9	7	10		8			5												16
1		3		5	6	11	4	9	10		8								2	7						17
		3		5	6	11	4	9	10		8					1			2	7						18
		3		5	6	11	4	9	10		8					1			2	7						19
		3			6		4	9	10	11	8			5					2	7	1					20
		3			6		4	9	10	11	8			5					2	7	1					21
		3			6		4	9	10	11	8			5					2	7	1					22
		3			6	11	4	9	10		8			5					2	7	1					23
		3			6	7	4		10	11	8			5				9	2		1					24
		3			6	7	4		10	11	8			5				9	2		1					25
		3			6	7	4		10	11	8			5				9	2		1					26
	3				6	7	9			11	8			5			4	10	2		1					27
	6	3					4	7	10	11	8			5					2		1	9				28
	6	3		5			4	7	10	11	8								2		1	9				29
	6	3		5	4			7	10	11	8								2		1	9				30
	6	3		5	4			7	10	11	8								2		1	9				31
	6	3		5			4	7	10	11	8								2		1	9				32
	6	3		5	4			7	10	11	8								2		1	9				33
	6	3		5	4			7	10	11	8								2		1	9				34
	6	3		5	4	7			10	11	8								2		1	9				35
		3		5	6				10	11	8						4		2	7	1	9				36
				5	6	7				11	10						4		2	8	1	9	3			37
		3		5	6		4		10	11	8								2	7	1	9				38
			6	5				7	10	11	4								2	8	1	9		3		39
		3	6	5	4				10	11	8								2	7	1	9				40
		3	6	5	4	7			10	11	8								2		1	9				41
			6	5	4	7				11	10								2	8	1	9		3		42
5	25	38	18	32	35	22	31	30	38	27	37	3	4	13	1	4	4	5	26	13	23	15	1	2		A
-	-	4	-	-	1	4	7	22	15	13	16	-	-	-	-	-	-	1	-	3	-	9	-	-		G

Black	Lawler	Langley	Edwards	Stapleton	Lowe	Stevens	Bentley	Dwight	Haynes	Chamberlain	Hill	Weir	Taylor	Lampe	Watson	Hewkins	Forbes	Doherty	Cohen	Barton	Macedo	Cook	Chenhall	Collins	Key	
		3			6	7	4		10		8			5				9	2		1				11	3
	6	3		5		7	4	9	10	11	8								2		1					4
	6	3				7	4	9	10	11	8			5					2		1					R
	6	3		5		9	4	7	10	11	8								2		1					5
	6	3		5		9	4	7	10	11	8								2		1					6
	6	3		5		9	4	7	10	11	8								2		1					SF
	6	3		5		9	4	7	10	11	8								2		1					R

0 points v	Middlesbrough	0 points
1 point v	Barnsley, Liverpool, West Ham U	3 points
2 points v	Blackburn R, Bristol C, Cardiff C, Grimsby T, Ipswich T, Rotherham U, Stoke C	14 points
3 points v	Bristol R, Charlton A, Derby C, Sheffield U, Swansea T	15 points
4 points v	Doncaster R, Huddersfield T, Leyton O, Lincoln C, Notts C	20 points

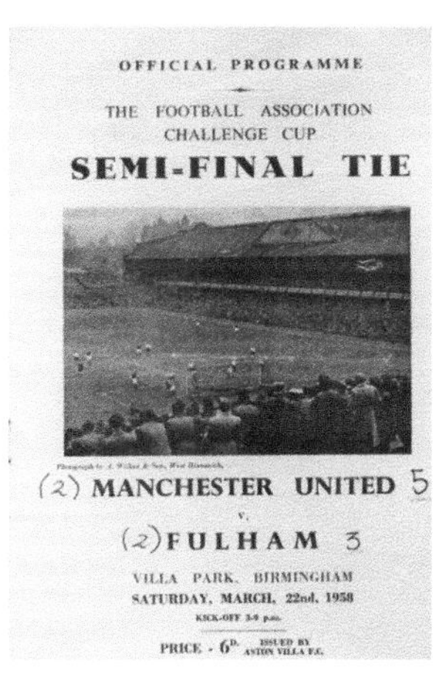

FA Cup semi-final programme covers.

1958-59

Division Two

	P	W	D	L	F	A	Pts
Sheffield Wednesday	42	28	6	8	106	48	62
Fulham	42	27	6	9	96	61	60
Sheffield United	42	23	7	12	82	48	53
Liverpool	42	24	5	13	87	62	53
Stoke City	42	21	7	14	72	58	49
Bristol Rovers	42	18	12	12	80	64	48
Derby County	42	20	8	14	74	71	48
Charlton Athletic	42	18	7	17	92	90	43
Cardiff City	42	18	7	17	65	65	43
Bristol City	42	17	7	18	74	70	41
Swansea Town	42	16	9	17	79	81	41
Brighton & Hove Albion	42	15	11	16	74	90	41
Middlesbrough	42	15	10	17	87	71	40
Huddersfield Town	42	16	8	18	62	55	40
Sunderland	42	16	8	18	64	75	40
Ipswich Town	42	17	6	19	62	77	40
Leyton Orient	42	14	8	20	71	78	36
Scunthorpe United	42	12	9	21	55	84	33
Lincoln City	42	11	7	24	63	93	29
Rotherham United	42	10	9	23	42	82	29
Grimsby Town	42	9	10	23	62	90	28
Barnsley	42	10	7	25	55	91	27

Manager: Bedford Jezzard

Did you know that?

On Boxing Day 1958, two of Fulham's goals in the 3-1 home win over Brighton were scored by full backs George Cohen and Jimmy Langley, and both were from open play. The return the next day attracted the record crowd of 36,747 to Brighton's old Goldstone Ground.

1	Leggat debut
12	Chamberlain's 50th goal
13	Stevens finale
22	O'Connell debut
29	Mullery debut
39	Barton finale

No	Date	V	Opponents	R	H-T	F-T	Scorers	Atten
1	A 23	H	Stoke C	W	4-0	6-1	Cook 3, Haynes, Leggat, Chamberlain	31,84
2	27	A	Sunderland	W	2-0	2-1	Leggat, Chamberlain	37,77
3	30	A	Swansea T	W	1-0	2-1	Haynes, Leggat	25,21
4	S 3	H	Sunderland	W	1-2	6-2	Haynes 3, Chamberlain, Leggat, Langley	26,39
5	6	H	Ipswich T	W	2-2	3-2	Haynes, Cook, Leggat	33,71
6	10	A	Lincoln C	W	0-2	4-2	Leggat 2, Chamberlain, Haynes	13,09
7	13	A	Bristol R	D	0-0	0-0		30,00
8	17	H	Lincoln C	W	2-0	4-2	Haynes 4	20,59
9	20	H	Derby C	W	1-2	4-2	Haynes 2, Langley, Cook	31,75
10	27	A	Leyton O	W	1-0	2-0	Chamberlain, Cook	24,43
11	O 4	H	Scunthorpe U	D	0-0	1-1	Leggat	24,56
12	11	A	Grimsby T	D	0-2	2-2	Langley, Chamberlain	16,77
13	18	H	Liverpool	L	0-0	0-1		43,92
14	25	A	Middlesbrough	W	3-1	3-2	Leggat 3	31,97
15	N 1	H	Sheffield U	W	1-1	4-2	Key, Haynes, Cook, Leggat	32,05
16	8	A	Bristol C	D	1-1	1-1	Haynes	32,37
17	15	H	Cardiff C	W	1-0	2-1	Cook, Chamberlain	24,07
18	22	A	Huddersfield T	L	0-0	1-2	Key	19,77
19	29	H	Barnsley	W	1-0	5-2	Leggat 2, Doherty, Cook, (Houghton og)	18,52
20	D 6	A	Rotherham U	L	0-2	0-4		7,43
21	13	H	Charlton A	W	0-0	2-1	Johnson 2	18,54
22	20	A	Stoke C	L	0-3	1-4	Barton	18,47
23	26	H	Brighton & HA	W	1-0	3-1	Johnson, Cohen, Langley	28,63
24	27	A	Brighton & HA	L	0-1	0-3		36,34
25	J 3	H	Swansea T	L	0-1	1-2	Cook	27,61
26	17	A	Ipswich T	W	1-0	2-1	Cook, Haynes	15,96
27	31	H	Bristol R	W	1-0	1-0	Cook	23,82
28	F 7	A	Derby C	L	0-2	0-2		21,67
29	14	H	Leyton O	W	3-1	5-2	Leggat, Doherty, Haynes 3	20,47
30	21	A	Scunthorpe U	W	0-1	2-1	Langley (pen), Haynes	10,08
31	28	H	Bristol C	W	1-0	1-0	Leggat	26,89
32	M 7	A	Liverpool	D	0-0	0-0		43,92
33	14	H	Middlesbrough	W	1-0	3-2	Leggat, Haynes, Barton	26,80
34	21	A	Sheffield U	L	0-1	0-2		17,82
35	27	H	Sheffield W	W	2-1	6-2	Leggat, Langley (pen), Cook, Hill 3	39,37
36	28	H	Grimsby T	W	1-0	3-0	Haynes, Leggat, Langley (pen)	25,05
37	30	A	Sheffield W	D	1-1	2-2	Cook 2	32,05
38	A 4	A	Cardiff C	W	0-1	2-1	Leggat, Haynes	23,21
39	11	H	Huddersfield T	W	1-0	1-0	Cook	20,90
40	18	A	Barnsley	W	1-0	4-2	Hill, Cook, Leggat, (Bartlett og)	8,06
41	23	A	Charlton A	L	0-1	1-2	Hill	22,12
42	25	H	Rotherham U	W	2-0	4-0	Haynes 3 (1 pen), Hill	17,86
								App
								Goal

FA Cup

No	Date	V	Opponents	R	H-T	F-T	Scorers	Atten
3	J 10	H	Peterborough U	D	0-0	0-0		31,90
R	24	A	Peterborough U	W	1-0	1-0	Johnson	21,40
4	28	A	Birmingham C	D	1-0	1-1	Hill	42,67
R	F 4	H	Birmingham C	L	2-2	2-3	Leggat, Hill	27,52

Macedo	Cohen	Langley	Bentley	Stapleton	Lowe	Leggat	Hill	Cook	Haynes	Chamberlain	Lawler	Stevens	Doherty	Key	Barton	Lampe	Johnson	O'Connell	Hewkins	Collins	Mullery	Edwards	
	2	3	4	5	6	7	8	9	10	11													1
	2	3	4	5	6	7	8	9	10	11													2
	2	3	4	5	6	7	8	9	10	11													3
	2	3		5	6	7	8	9	10	11	4												4
	2	3		5	6	7	8	9	10	11	4												5
	2	3		5	6	7	8	9	10	11	4												6
	2	3	4	5	6	7	8	9	10	11													7
	2	3	4	5	6	7	8	9	10	11													8
	2	3	4	5		7	8	9	10	11	6												9
	2	3	4	5			8	9	10	11	6	7											10
	2	3	4	5		7	8	9		11	6	10											11
	2	3	4	5		7		9	10	11	6		8										12
	2	3	4	5				9	10		6	11		7	8								13
	2	3	5		4	7		9	10		6			11	8								14
	2	3	5		6	7		9	10		4			11	8								15
	2	3	5		6	11	8	9	10		4			7									16
	2	3			4	7	8	9		11	6		10			5							17
	2	3	5		4		8	9		11	6		10	7									18
	2	3	5		4	7	8	9		11	6		10										19
	2	3		5	4	7	8	9		11	6		10										20
	2	3	5		4		8	9			6		10		7		11						21
	2	3	5		4			9			6		10		7		11	8					22
	2	3	5		4	7		9	10		6				8		11						23
	2	3	5		4	7		9	10		6				8		11						24
	2	3	5		4	7	8	9	10		6						11						25
	2	3		5	4	7	8	9	10		6						11						26
	2		4	5	6	7	8	9	10		3			11					1				27
	2	11	5		4	7		9	10		6				8				1	3			28
	2		5		6	11	8		10		3		9		7				1		4		29
		3				11		7	10		2		9		8	5			1		4	6	30
	2	3	5			11		7	10		6		9		8				1		4		31
	2	3	5			11	8	9	10		6				7						4		32
	2	3	5		6	11	8	9	10						7						4		33
	2	3	5		6	11	8	9	10						7						4		34
	2	3	5		6	7	8	9	10	11											4		35
	2	3	5			7	8	9	10	11	6										4		36
	2	3	5			7	8	9	10	11	6										4		37
	2	3	5		6	7	8	9	10	11											4		38
	2	3	5		6		8	9		11			10		7						4		39
	2	3	5		6	7	8	9	10	11											4		40
	2	3	5		6	7	8	9	10	11											4		41
	2	3	5		6	7	8	9	10	11											4		42
7	41	40	35	16	32	36	32	41	34	24	29	3	11	6	15	2	6	1	5	1	14	1	A
	1	7	-	-	-	21	6	17	26	7	-	-	2	2	2	-	3	-	-	-	-	-	G

Macedo	Cohen	Langley	Bentley	Stapleton	Lowe	Leggat	Hill	Cook	Haynes	Chamberlain	Lawler	Stevens	Doherty	Key	Barton	Lampe	Johnson	O'Connell	Hewkins	Collins	Mullery	Edwards	
	2	3	5		4	7	8	9	10		6						11						3
	2	3	5		4	7	8	9	10		6						11						R
	2		4	5	6	7	8	9	10		3						11						4
	2		4	5	6	7	8	9	10		3			11					1				R

0 points v		0 points
1 point v	Liverpool	1 point
2 points v	Brighton & HA, Charlton A, Derby C, Huddersfield T, Rotherham U, Sheffield U, Stoke C, Swansea T	16 points
3 points v	Bristol C, Bristol R, Grimsby T, Scunthorpe U, Sheffield W	15 points
4 points v	Barnsley, Cardiff C, Ipswich T, Leyton O, Lincoln C, Middlesbrough, Sunderland	28 points

Left winger Mike Johnson, making his debut, scored both the goals in Fulham's 2–1 over Charlton in December 1958.

1959-60

Division One

	P	W	D	L	F	A	Pts
Burnley	42	24	7	11	85	61	55
Wolverhampton W	42	24	6	12	106	67	54
Tottenham Hotspur	42	21	11	10	86	50	53
West Bromwich Albion	42	19	11	12	83	57	49
Sheffield Wednesday	42	19	11	12	80	59	49
Bolton Wanderers	42	20	8	14	59	51	48
Manchester United	42	19	7	16	102	80	45
Newcastle United	42	18	8	16	82	78	44
Preston North End	42	16	12	14	79	76	44
Fulham	42	17	10	15	73	80	44
Blackpool	42	15	10	17	59	71	40
Leicester City	42	13	13	16	66	75	39
Arsenal	42	15	9	18	68	80	39
West Ham United	42	16	6	20	75	91	38
Everton	42	13	11	18	73	78	37
Manchester City	42	17	3	22	78	84	37
Blackburn Rovers	42	16	5	21	60	70	37
Chelsea	42	14	9	19	76	91	37
Birmingham City	42	13	10	19	63	80	36
Nottingham Forest	42	13	9	20	50	74	35
Leeds United	42	12	10	20	65	92	34
Luton Town	42	9	12	21	50	73	30

Manager: Bedford Jezzard

Did you know that?

At the end of the season, Newcastle's George Eastham began his long campaign to be allowed to move to another club. The Players Union leaders were Jimmy Hill and Cliff Lloyd, a current and former Fulham player, the Newcastle manager was Charlie Mitten, another former Fulham player, and Eastham was given a job by a family friend whilst on 'strike', Ernest Clay, a future Fulham chairman.

FAC3 Hill's 50th goal
26 Haynes 100th goal
33 Stapleton finale

No		Date	V	Opponents	R	H-T	F-T	Scorers	Atte
1	A	22	A	Blackburn R	L	0-2	0-4		30,23
2		26	H	Manchester C	W	4-1	5-2	Haynes 2, Leggat 2, Mullery	26,81
3		29	H	Blackpool	W	1-0	1-0	Leggat	42,58
4	S	2	A	Manchester C	L	1-1	1-3	Stokes	37,48
5		5	A	Everton	D	0-0	0-0		31,98
6		9	H	Wolverhampton W	W	2-0	3-1	Doherty, Cook, Stokes	32,15
7		12	H	Luton T	W	2-1	4-2	Leggat 2, Hill, Doherty	30,01
8		16	A	Wolverhampton W	L	0-3	0-9		41,69
9		19	A	Bolton W	L	1-1	2-3	Cook 2	24,75
10		26	H	Chelsea	L	1-0	1-3	Chamberlain	40,81
11	O	3	H	Nottingham F	W	0-1	3-1	Stokes 2, Cook	29,23
12		10	A	West Bromich A	W	3-0	4-2	Chamberlain 2, Cook, Stokes	20,39
13		17	H	Newcastle U	W	3-1	4-3	Key, Cook, Hill, Haynes	36,29
14		24	A	Birmingham C	W	3-0	4-2	Cook 2, Key, Langley (pen)	26,69
15		31	H	West Ham U	W	0-0	1-0	Stokes	44,85
16	N	7	A	Manchester U	D	2-1	3-3	Leggat 3	44,30
17		14	H	Preston NE	L	0-0	1-2	Haynes	26,43
18		21	A	Leicester C	W	0-0	1-0	Chamberlain	24,26
19		28	H	Burnley	W	1-0	1-0	Hill	29,58
20	D	5	A	Leeds U	W	1-1	4-1	Leggat 2, Chamberlain, Haynes	18,84
21		12	H	Tottenham H	D	1-1	1-1	Hill	36,77
22		19	H	Blackburn R	L	0-1	0-1		17,53
23		26	A	Sheffield W	D	1-0	1-1	Leggat	49,40
24		28	H	Sheffield W	L	0-0	1-2	Langley (pen)	36,85
25	J	2	A	Blackpool	L	0-2	1-3	Sullivan	17,04
26		16	H	Everton	W	0-0	2-0	Haynes, Mullery	21,22
27		23	A	Luton T	L	1-1	1-4	Hill	17,87
28	F	6	H	Bolton W	D	1-0	1-1	Jones	24,74
29		13	A	Chelsea	L	0-3	2-4	Haynes, Bentley	38,68
30		20	A	Nottingham F	D	2-1	2-2	Key, Leggat	23,17
31		27	H	Leeds U	W	0-0	5-0	Leggat 4, Langley (pen)	23,35
32	M	5	A	Newcastle U	L	1-2	1-3	Bentley	33,99
33		12	H	Birmingham C	D	1-2	2-2	Leggat 2	25,20
34		19	A	Tottenham H	D	1-0	1-1	Haynes	52,18
35		26	H	Manchester U	L	0-2	0-5		38,25
36	A	2	A	Preston NE	L	0-3	1-4	Haynes	15,00
37		9	H	Leicester C	D	1-1	1-1	Johnson	18,26
38		15	A	Arsenal	L	0-0	0-2		37,65
39		16	A	West Ham U	W	1-1	2-1	Chamberlain, O'Connell	34,08
40		18	H	Arsenal	W	1-0	3-0	Key, Jones, O'Connell	31,05
41		23	H	West Bromich A	W	1-0	2-1	Jones, Haynes	23,63
42		30	A	Burnley	D	0-0	0-0		30,8
									Ap
									Goa

FA Cup

No		Date	V	Opponents	R	H-T	F-T	Scorers	Atte
3	J	9	H	Hull C	W	2-0	5-0	Leggat 2, Chamberlain, Cook, Hill	22,1
4		30	A	Leicester C	L	1-1	1-2	(Cunningham og)	31,00

Macedo	Cohen	Langley	Mullery	Bentley	Cook	Leggat	Hill	Doherty	Haynes	Chamberlain	Lawler	Stokes	Key	Johnson	Stapleton	Lampe	Lowe	Sullivan	Hewkins	Jones	Stratton	O'Connell	
1	2	3	4	5	6	7	8	9	10	11													1
1	2	3	4	5		7	8	9	10	11	6												2
1	2	3	4	5		7	8	9	10	11	6												3
1	2	3	4	5	9	7		8		11	6	10											4
1	2	3	4	5	8			9		11	6	10	7										5
1	2	3	4	5	8	7		9			6	10		11									6
1	2	3	4	5		7	8	9			6	10		11									7
1	2	3	4			7	8	9			6	10		11	5								8
1	2	3	4		10		8	9					7	11		5	6						9
1	2	3	4		10	7	8	9		11						5	6						10
1	2	3	4	5	10		8			11		9	7				6						11
1	2	3	4	5	10		8			11		9	7				6						12
1	2	3	4	5	9		8		10	11			7				6						13
1	2	3	4	5	9		8		10	11			7				6						14
1	2	3	4	5	9				10	11		8	7				6						15
1	2	3	4	5		9	8		10	11			7				6						16
1	2	3	4	5		9	8		10	11			7				6						17
1	2	3	4			7	8		10	11		9				5	6						18
1	2	3	4			9	8		10	11			7			5	6						19
1	2	3	4			9	8		10	11			7			5	6						20
1	2	3	4			9	8		10	11			7			5	6						21
1	2	3			9	7	8		10	11	4					5	6						22
1	2	3	4			7	8		10	11		9				5	6						23
1	2	3	4			11	8		10			9	7		5		6						24
1	2	3	4	5	9	7	8			11							6	10					25
1	2	3	4	5	9	7	8		10	11							6						26
	2	3	4	5		7	8	9	10	11							6		1				27
	2	3	4	5				7	10	11		8					6		1	9			28
1	2	3		5		7			10		4	8					6			9	11		29
1	2	3				11			10		6	8	7			5	4			9			30
1	2	3			8	11			10		6		7			5	4			9			31
1	2	3		9	8	11			10		4		7			5	6						32
1	2	3			8	11			10		4		7		5		6			9			33
1	2	11	4	9			8		10		3		7			5	6						34
1	2	11	4	9		7	8		10		3					5	6						35
	2	3	4	5		11		9	10			8	7				6		1				36
1	2	3	4	5				9					7	11			6	8				10	37
1	2	3	4	5		9			10				7	11			6					8	38
1	2	3	4	9					10	11	6		7			5						8	39
1	2	3	4	5					10	11			7				6			9		8	40
1	2	3	4	5					10	11			7				6			9		8	41
1	2	3	4	5				9	10	11			7				6					8	42
39	42	42	36	29	17	28	25	15	31	27	16	15	25	6	3	14	33	2	3	7	1	6	A
-	-	3	2	2	8	18	5	2	10	6	-	6	4	1	-	-	-	1	-	3	-	2	G

Macedo	Cohen	Langley	Mullery	Bentley	Cook	Leggat	Hill	Doherty	Haynes	Chamberlain	Lawler	Stokes	Key	Johnson	Stapleton	Lampe	Lowe	Sullivan	Hewkins	Jones	Stratton	O'Connell	
1	2	3	4	5	9	7	8		10	11							6						3
1	2	3	4	5	9	7		8	10	11							6						4

0 points v	Blackburn R, Chelsea, Preston NE	0 points
1 point v	Bolton W, Manchester U, Sheffield W	3 points
2 points v	Arsenal, Blackpool, Luton T, Manchester C, Newcastle U, Tottenham H, Wolves	14 points
3 points v	Birmingham C, Burnley, Everton, Leicester C, Nottingham F	15 points
4 points v	Leeds U, West Bromwich A, West Ham U	12 points

In February 1960, centre forward Allan Jones scored in the first minute of his debut, a 1–1 draw with Bolton.

1960-61

Division One

	P	W	D	L	F	A	Pts
Tottenham Hotspur	42	31	4	7	115	55	66
Sheffield Wednesday	42	23	12	7	78	47	58
Wolverhampton W	42	25	7	10	103	75	57
Burnley	42	22	7	13	102	77	51
Everton	42	22	6	14	87	69	50
Leicester City	42	18	9	15	87	70	45
Manchester United	42	18	9	15	88	76	45
Blackburn Rovers	42	15	13	14	77	76	43
Aston Villa	42	17	9	16	78	77	43
West Bromwich Albion	42	18	5	19	67	71	41
Arsenal	42	15	11	16	77	85	41
Chelsea	42	15	7	20	98	100	37
Manchester City	42	13	11	18	79	90	37
Nottingham Forest	42	14	9	19	62	78	37
Cardiff City	42	13	11	18	60	85	37
West Ham United	42	13	10	19	77	88	36
Fulham	42	14	8	20	72	95	36
Bolton Wanderers	42	12	11	19	58	73	35
Birmingham City	42	14	6	22	62	84	34
Blackpool	42	12	9	21	68	73	33
Newcastle United	42	11	10	21	86	109	32
Preston North End	42	10	10	22	43	71	30

Manager: Bedford Jezzard

Did you know that?

In the first season of the League Cup, Maurice Cook scored Fulham's goal in the 2-1 First Round defeat at Bristol Rovers. It was the first goal ever scored in the history of the competition.

- 6 Haynes' 300th game
- 10 Lowe's 400th game
- 11 Langley's 200th game
- 14 Leggat's 50th goal
- 20 Bentley finale
- 27 S Brown debut
- 32 Hill finale

No		Date	V	Opponents	R	H-T	F-T	Scorers	Atten
1	A	20	H	Cardiff C	D	0-2	2-2	Leggat, Haynes	30,91
2		24	A	Newcastle U	L	1-5	2-7	Key, Doherty	23,49
3		27	A	West Bromich A	W	0-2	4-2	Leggat 2, Cook, Haynes	20,69
4		31	H	Newcastle U	W	3-1	4-3	Key 2, Haynes 2	21,27
5	S	3	H	Birmingham C	W	1-0	2-1	O'Connell, Cook	19,29
6		10	A	Sheffield W	L	0-1	0-2		25,84
7		14	H	Nottingham F	W	0-0	1-0	Leggat	13,63
8		17	H	Chelsea	W	2-0	3-2	Leggat, O'Connell, Haynes	37,42
9		21	A	Nottingham F	L	1-3	2-4	Cook, O'Connell	15,11
10		24	H	Preston NE	W	2-0	2-0	Langley (pen), Cook	23,77
11	O	1	A	Burnley	L	0-2	0-5		19,96
12		8	A	Blackpool	W	2-1	5-2	Cook 2, Langley (pen), O'Connell, Leggat	20,62
13		15	H	Everton	L	2-1	2-3	Key, Langley	30,60
14		22	A	Bolton W	W	0-0	3-0	Leggat 3	19,81
15		29	H	West Ham U	D	1-1	1-1	Leggat	20,94
16	N	5	A	Tottenham H	L	0-2	1-5	Leggat	56,27
17		12	H	Leicester C	W	2-2	4-2	Leggat 3, Key	16,24
18		19	A	Aston Villa	L	1-1	1-2	Leggat	31,50
19		26	H	Wolverhampton W	L	0-2	1-3	Haynes	23,98
20	D	3	A	Blackburn R	L	1-2	1-5	O'Connell	12,91
21		10	H	Manchester U	D	3-2	4-4	Brown 2, Mullery, O'Connell	23,62
22		17	A	Cardiff C	L	0-1	0-2		16,80
23		24	A	Manchester C	L	1-2	2-3	Leggat, Cook	18,46
24		26	H	Manchester C	W	0-0	1-0	Chamberlain	20,24
25		31	H	West Bromich A	L	1-2	1-2	Haynes	18,08
26	J	14	A	Birmingham C	L	0-1	0-1		23,26
27		21	H	Sheffield W	L	1-4	1-6	O'Connell	17,92
28	F	4	A	Chelsea	L	1-2	1-2	Leggat	39,18
29		11	A	Preston NE	L	0-1	0-2		8,69
30		22	H	Burnley	L	0-0	0-1		13,13
31		25	H	Blackpool	W	2-1	4-3	Cook, Hill, Johnson, Leggat	19,34
32	M	4	A	Everton	L	0-0	0-1		35,84
33		11	H	Bolton W	D	2-1	2-2	Johnson, Leggat	18,79
34		18	A	West Ham U	W	1-1	2-1	Cook, Langley (pen)	18,74
35		25	H	Tottenham H	D	0-0	0-0		38,53
36		31	H	Arsenal	D	0-1	2-2	Haynes 2	35,47
37	A	1	A	Manchester U	L	1-1	1-3	O'Connell	24,93
38		3	A	Arsenal	L	0-2	2-4	Langley (pen), Leggat	20,01
39		8	H	Aston Villa	D	0-1	1-1	Leggat	23,04
40		15	A	Leicester C	W	1-0	2-1	O'Connell, Leggat	30,99
41		22	H	Blackburn R	D	0-1	1-1	Leggat	17,02
42		29	A	Wolverhampton W	W	2-0	4-2	Cook 3, O'Connell	24,85
									App
									Goal

FA Cup

3	J	7	A	Newcastle U	L	0-3	0-5		36,03

League Cup

1	S	26	A	Bristol R	L	1-1	1-2	Cook	20,02

	Cohen	Langley	Mullery	Lampe	Bentley	Leggat	O'Connell	Hill	Haynes	Key	Doherty	Cook	Lowe	Hewkins	Edwards	Brown R	Chamberlain	Watson	Lawler	Brown S	Johnson	Dodgin
1	2	3	4	5	6	7	8	9	10	11												
2	2	3	4	5	6	11		8	10	7	9											
3	2	3	4	5	6	11		8	10	7		9										
4	2	3	4	5		11	8		10	7		9	6									
5	2	3	4	5		11	8		10	7		9	6									
6	2	3	4			11	8		10	7	9	6	5									
7	2	3	4	5		11	8		10	7		9	6									
8	2	3	4	5		11	8		10	7		9	6									
9	2	3	4		5	11	8		10	7		9	6									
10	2	3	4		5	11	8		10	7		9	6									
11	2	3			5	11	8		10	7		9	6	1	4							
12	2	3	4		5	11	8	10		7		9	6	1								
13	2	3	4		5	11		8	10	7		9	6	1								
14	2	3	4		5	11		8	10	7				1	6	9						
15	2	3	4		5	11		8	10	7					6	9						
16	2	3	4		5	11		8	10	7		9			6							
17		3			5	10	8		6	7		9	4		2		11					
18	2	3			5	10	8		6	7		9	4				11					
19	2	3			5	10	8		6	7		9	4				11					
20	2	3	4		5	11	8		10	7			6	1		9						
21	2	3	4	5		7	8		10	11				1	6	9						
22	2	3	4				8		10	11			5	1	6	9		7				
23	2	3	4			9			10			8	5	1	6		11	7				
24	2	3	4			9			10			8	5	1	6		11	7				
25	2	3	4			9			10			8	5	1	6		11	7				
26	2	11	4				8		10	7		9	5		6				3			
27	2	11	4				8			7		9	5		6				3	10		
28	2	3	4			11		8	10	7		9	5						6			
29	2	3	4			7		8	10			9	5				11		6			
30	2	3	4	5				8	10			9	6					7			11	
31	2	3	4	5		7		8	10			9	6								11	
32	2	3	4	5		9		8	10				6					7			11	
33	2	3	4			8			10	7	9		5						6		11	
34	2	3	4			8			10			9	6					7			11	5
35	2	3	4			7	8		10			9	6								11	5
36	2	3	4			7	8		10			9	6								11	5
37	2	3					8		10			9	6					7	4		11	5
38	2	3	4			7	8		10			9	6				11					5
39	2	3	4			7	8		10			9		1					6		11	5
40	2	3	4			8	10			7		9	6				11					5
41	2	3	4			9	8		10	7			6				11					5
42	2	3	4				8		10		9	7	6				11					5
A	41	42	37	11	15	36	26	13	39	28	4	32	34	11	12	5	11	8	7	1	9	9
G	-	5	1	-	-	23	10	1	9	5	1	12	-	-	-	2	1	-	-	-	2	-

	Cohen	Langley	Mullery	Lampe	Bentley	Leggat	O'Connell	Hill	Haynes	Key	Doherty	Cook	Lowe	Hewkins	Edwards	Brown R	Chamberlain	Watson	Lawler	Brown S	Johnson	Dodgin
3	2	3	4				8		10	7		9	5	1	6		11					

	Cohen	Langley	Mullery	Lampe	Bentley	Leggat	O'Connell	Hill	Haynes	Key	Doherty	Cook	Lowe	Hewkins	Edwards	Brown R	Chamberlain	Watson	Lawler	Brown S	Johnson	Dodgin
1	2	3			5		8		10	7		9	6	1	4		11					

0 points v	Burnley, Everton, Sheffield W	0 points
1 point v	Arsenal, Aston Villa, Blackburn R, Cardiff C, Manchester U, Tottenham H	6 points
2 points v	Birmingham C, Chelsea, Manchester C, Newcastle U, Nottingham F, Preston NE, West Bromwich A, Wolves	16 points
3 points v	Bolton W, West Ham U	6 points
4 points v	Blackpool, Leicester C	8 points

Talented sriker John Doherty made 51 appearances between 1956 and 1962.

1961-62

Division One

	P	W	D	L	F	A	Pts
Ipswich Town	42	24	8	10	93	67	56
Burnley	42	21	11	10	101	67	53
Tottenham Hotspur	42	21	10	11	88	69	52
Everton	42	20	11	11	88	54	51
Sheffield United	42	19	9	14	61	69	47
Sheffield Wednesday	42	20	6	16	72	58	46
Aston Villa	42	18	8	16	65	56	44
West Ham United	42	17	10	15	76	82	44
West Bromwich Albion	42	15	13	14	83	67	43
Arsenal	42	16	11	15	71	72	43
Bolton Wanderers	42	16	10	16	62	66	42
Manchester City	42	17	7	18	78	81	41
Blackpool	42	15	11	16	70	75	41
Leicester City	42	17	6	19	72	71	40
Manchester United	42	15	9	18	72	75	39
Blackburn Rovers	42	14	11	17	50	58	39
Birmingham City	42	14	10	18	65	81	38
Wolverhampton W	42	13	10	19	73	86	36
Nottingham Forest	42	13	10	19	63	79	36
Fulham	42	13	7	22	66	74	33
Cardiff City	42	9	14	19	50	81	32
Chelsea	42	9	10	23	63	94	28

Manager: Bedford Jezzard

Did you know that?

During the 1961 close season, two former Fulham forwards from the 1930s, Jim Hammond and John Arnold, were both appointed first-class cricket umpires. The 11 consecutive defeats suffered between 2nd December and 24th February is Fulham's longest-ever losing sequence.

4	Metchick debut
LC1	Keetch debut
10	Cook's 50th goal
12	Mealand debut
18	Lawler finale
25	Henderson debut
30	Cohen's 200th game
31	Doherty finale

No		Date	V	Opponents	R	H-T	F-T	Scorers	Atte
1	A	19	A	Birmingham C	L	1-1	1-2	O'Connell	25,38
2		23	H	Manchester C	L	3-0	3-4	O'Connell, Langley (pen), Mullery	16,28
3		26	H	Everton	W	2-1	2-1	Cook, Doherty	23,12
4		30	A	Manchester C	L	1-0	1-2	Brown R	36,77
5	S	2	A	Chelsea	D	0-0	0-0		37,99
6		6	H	Bolton W	D	1-1	2-2	Brown R, (Stanley og)	12,63
7		9	A	Sheffield W	D	1-0	1-1	Metchick	33,85
8		16	H	Leicester C	W	0-1	2-1	Leggat, Chamberlain	19,83
9		20	A	Bolton W	W	1-0	3-2	Mullery 2, O'Connell	16,74
10		23	A	Ipswich T	W	1-1	4-2	Cook, Cohen, Haynes, O'Connell	23,05
11		30	H	Burnley	L	2-3	3-5	Cook 2, Leggat	30,66
12	O	7	H	Aston Villa	W	1-0	3-1	Leggat, Cook, Metchick	22,22
13		14	A	Nottingham F	D	1-1	1-1	Leggat	21,70
14		21	H	West Ham U	W	1-0	2-0	Mullery, Leggat	32,37
15		28	A	Sheffield U	D	1-1	2-2	Cook, Mullery	19,60
16	N	4	H	Cardiff C	L	0-1	0-1		20,07
17		11	A	Tottenham H	L	2-3	2-4	Leggat, Haynes	35,66
18		18	H	Blackpool	L	0-0	0-1		18,59
19		25	A	Blackburn R	W	0-0	2-0	Cook, (Woods og)	12,89
20	D	2	H	Wolverhampton W	L	0-0	0-1		22,10
21		9	A	Manchester U	L	0-1	0-3		22,19
22		16	H	Birmingham C	L	0-1	0-1		12,73
23		23	A	Everton	L	0-2	0-3		30,39
24		26	A	Arsenal	L	0-1	0-1		32,95
25	J	13	H	Chelsea	L	0-1	3-4	Leggat, Chamberlain, Lowe	35,64
26		20	H	Sheffield W	L	0-1	0-2		19,96
27	F	3	A	Leicester C	L	1-1	1-4	Haynes	20,27
28		10	H	Ipswich T	L	1-1	1-2	Mullery	25,20
29		20	A	Burnley	L	0-1	1-2	Henderson	25,60
30		24	A	Aston Villa	L	0-0	0-2		24,72
31	M	3	H	Nottingham F	D	1-0	1-1	Henderson	18,41
32		17	H	Sheffield U	W	3-0	5-2	Cook 3, Leggat, Lowe	22,70
33		23	A	Cardiff C	W	2-0	3-0	Cook, Henderson, Leggat	16,75
34	A	7	A	Blackpool	L	1-0	1-2	Haynes	10,64
35		11	H	Arsenal	W	4-0	5-2	Cook 2, Leggat, Henderson, O'Connell	26,51
36		14	H	Blackburn R	W	1-0	2-0	O'Connell, Leggat	20,51
37		17	H	Tottenham H	D	1-0	1-1	O'Connell	43,35
38		21	A	Wolverhampton W	W	2-1	3-1	Leggat 2, O'Connell	21,02
39		23	H	West Bromich A	L	0-1	1-2	Haynes	29,33
40		24	A	West Bromich A	L	0-1	0-2		22,02
41		28	H	Manchester U	W	1-0	2-0	Cook, Leggat	40,11
42		30	A	West Ham U	L	1-2	2-4	Langley, Henderson	24,73
									App
									Goa

FA Cup

No		Date	V	Opponents	R	H-T	F-T	Scorers		Att
3	J	6	H	Hartlepools U	W	3-0	3-1	Cook 2, Key		18,04
4		27	H	Walsall	D	0-2	2-2	Cook, Henderson		30,03
R		30	A	Walsall	W	1-0	2-0	Lowe, Metchick		24,04
5	F	17	H	Port Vale	W	0-0	1-0	Langley (pen)		29,55
6	M	10	H	Blackburn R	D	0-1	2-2	Haynes, (Woods og)		29,99
R		14	A	Blackburn R	W	0-0	1-0	Cook		34,09
SF		31	N	Burnley	D	1-0	1-1	Leggat	(at Villa Park)	59,98
R	A	9	N	Burnley	L	0-1	1-2	Langley	(at Filbert Street)	35,00

League Cup

No		Date	V	Opponents	R	H-T	F-T	Scorers	Att
1	S	13	H	Sheffield U	D	0-0	1-1	Brown M	5,51
R		25	A	Sheffield U	L	0-2	0-4		8,82

Macedo	Cohen	Langley	Mullery	Dodgin	Lowe	Leggat	O'Connell	Doherty	Haynes	Chamberlain	Key	Cook	Johnson	Brown R	Metchick	Brown M	Mealand	Lawler	Hewkins	Edwards	Henderson	Lampe	Keetch	
1	2	3	4	5	6	7	8	9	10	11														1
1	2	3	4	5	6		8		10	11	7	9												2
1	2	3	4	5	6		8	9	10			7	11											3
1	2	3	4	5	6			8	10			7		9	11									4
1	2	3	4	5	6			8	10			7		9	11									5
1	2	3	4	5	6				10	11		7		9	8									6
1	2	3	4	5	6				10	11		9			8	7								7
1	2	3	4	5	6	7	8		10	11		9												8
1	2	3	4	5	6	7	8		10	11		9												9
1	2	3	4	5	6		8		10	11	7	9												10
1	2	3	4	5	6	7	8		10	11		9												11
1		3	4	5	6	7	8		10			9			11		2							12
1	2	3	4	5	6	7	8					9			11	10								13
1	2	3	4	5	6	7			10	11		9			8									14
1	2	3	4	5	6	7			10	11		9			8									15
1	2	3	4	5	6	7	8		10	11		9												16
1	2	3	4	5	6	7	8		10	11		9												17
1	2		4	5	6	7	8	9	10						11			3						18
1	2	3	4	5	6		8		10		7	9			11									19
1	2	3	4	5	6	7	8		10			9			11									20
	2	3	4	5		8	10				7	9			11				1	6				21
	2	3	4	5	6	8			10		7	9			11				1					22
1	2		4	5	6	8			10		7	9			11		3							23
1	2		4	5	6	9	8		10		7				11		3							24
	2		4	5	6	8			10	11	7						3		1		9			25
1	2		4		6	8			10	11	7						3				9	5		26
1	2		4				8		10				7		11		3			6	9	5		27
	2		4	5	6	8			10			7			11		3		1		9			28
1	2	3	4		6		10	9				7			11						8	5		29
1	2	3	4		6		11	9	10			7									8	5		30
1	2	3	4		6	7	11	9	10												8	5		31
1	2	3	4	5	6	7	11		10			9									8			32
1	2	3	4	5	6	7	11		10			9									8			33
1	2	3	4	5	6	7	11		10			9									8			34
1	2	3	4	5	6	7	11		10			9									8			35
1	2	3	4	5	6	7	11					9			10						8			36
1	2	3	4	5	6	7	11		10			9									8			37
1	2	3	4	5	6	7	11		10			9									8			38
1	2	3		5	6	7	11		10			9								4	8			39
1	2	3		5	6	7	11		10			9								4	8			40
1	2	3	4	5	6	7	11		10			9									8			41
1	2	3	4	5	6	7	11		10			9									8			42
8	41	35	40	37	40	31	31	8	38	14	9	35	2	3	19	2	7	1	4	4	18	5	-	A
-	1	2	6	-	2	14	8	1	5	2	-	14	-	2	2	-	-	-	-	-	5	-	-	G

Macedo	Cohen	Langley	Mullery	Dodgin	Lowe	Leggat	O'Connell	Doherty	Haynes	Chamberlain	Key	Cook	Johnson	Brown R	Metchick	Brown M	Mealand	Lawler	Hewkins	Edwards	Henderson	Lampe	Keetch	
1	2			5	6	8	10				7	9	11				3			4				3
1	2		4		6	7	8		10			9					3				11	5		4
1	2		4		6	8			10			7			11		3				9	5		R
1	2	3	4		6	8	10					7			11						9	5		5
1	2	3	4	5	6	7	11		10			9									8			6
1	2	3	4	5	6	7	11		10			9									8			R
1	2	3	4	5	6	7	11		10			9									8			SF
1	2	3	4	5	6	7	11		10			9									8			R

Macedo	Cohen	Langley	Mullery	Dodgin	Lowe	Leggat	O'Connell	Doherty	Haynes	Chamberlain	Key	Cook	Johnson	Brown R	Metchick	Brown M	Mealand	Lawler	Hewkins	Edwards	Henderson	Lampe	Keetch	
1	2	3	4		6				10	11		9			8	7							5	1
1	2	3	4	5	6		8			11	7	9			10									R

0 points v	Birmingham C, Blackpool, Burnley, Manchester C, West Bromwich A	0 points
1 point v	Chelsea, Sheffield W, Tottenham H	3 points
2 points v	Arsenal, Aston Villa, Cardiff C, Everton, Ipswich T, Leicester C, Manchester U, Nottingham F, West Ham U, Wolves	20 points
3 points v	Bolton W, Sheffield U,	6 points
4 points v	Blackburn R	4 points

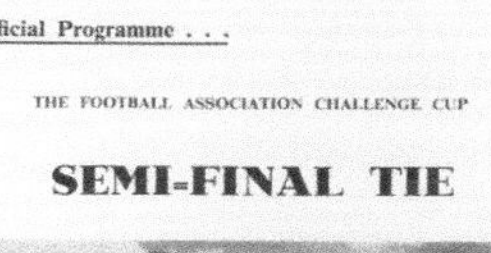

Semi-final programme covers.

1962-63

Division One

	P	W	D	L	F	A	Pts
Everton	42	25	11	6	84	42	61
Tottenham Hotspur	42	23	9	10	111	62	55
Burnley	42	22	10	10	78	57	54
Leicester City	42	20	12	10	79	53	52
Wolverhampton W	42	20	10	12	93	65	50
Sheffield Wednesday	42	19	10	13	77	63	48
Arsenal	42	18	10	14	86	77	46
Liverpool	42	17	10	15	71	59	44
Nottingham Forest	42	17	10	15	67	69	44
Sheffield United	42	16	12	14	58	60	44
Blackburn Rovers	42	15	12	15	79	71	42
West Ham United	42	14	12	16	73	69	40
Blackpool	42	13	14	15	58	64	40
West Bromwich Albion	42	16	7	19	71	79	39
Aston Villa	42	15	8	19	62	68	38
Fulham	42	14	10	18	50	71	38
Ipswich Town	42	12	11	19	59	78	35
Bolton Wanderers	42	15	5	22	55	75	35
Manchester United	42	12	10	20	67	81	34
Birmingham City	42	10	13	19	63	90	33
Manchester City	42	10	11	21	58	102	31
Leyton Orient	42	6	9	27	37	81	21

Manager: Bedford Jezzard

Did you know that?

The eight consecutive victories between the end of February and the beginning of April just as the Big Freeze was thawing remains Fulham's best winning sequence in the top flight.

---

10 Macedo's 200th game
19 Lampe finale
FAC3 Lowe's 500th game
29 Marsh debut
39 Lowe finale

No		Date	V	Opponents	R	H-T	F-T	Scorers	Atten
1	A	18	H	Leicester C	W	1-1	2-1	Leggat 2	27,16
2		22	A	Sheffield U	L	0-2	0-2		19,89
3		25	A	Bolton W	L	0-0	0-1		16,66
4		29	H	Sheffield U	D	1-1	2-2	Cook 2	16,35
5	S	1	H	Everton	W	1-0	1-0	Brown	30,58
6		8	A	West Bromich A	L	1-3	1-6	Henderson	17,89
7		12	A	Sheffield W	L	0-1	0-1		20,06
8		15	H	Arsenal	L	0-2	1-3	Mullery	31,54
9		19	H	Sheffield W	W	3-0	4-1	Brown, Cook 3	22,62
10		22	A	Birmingham C	L	0-3	1-4	Langley (pen)	20,43
11		29	H	Leyton O	L	0-2	0-2		26,50
12	O	6	A	Nottingham F	L	1-1	1-3	Langley	23,72
13		13	H	Ipswich T	D	0-1	1-1	Brown	22,96
14		20	A	Blackpool	D	0-0	0-0		17,11
15		27	H	Blackburn R	D	0-0	0-0		18,09
16	N	3	A	Aston Villa	W	1-0	2-1	Henderson, Brown	28,98
17		10	H	Tottenham H	L	0-0	0-2		39,96
18		17	A	West Ham U	D	0-0	2-2	Leggat, Langley	17,66
19		24	H	Manchester C	L	2-3	2-4	Brown, Leggat	17,67
20	D	1	A	Liverpool	L	0-0	1-2	Langley (pen)	38,56
21		8	H	Wolverhampton W	L	0-2	0-5		17,45
22		15	A	Leicester C	W	2-1	3-2	Leggat, Brown, Cook	18,84
23		26	H	Manchester U	L	0-0	0-1		23,33
24	F	16	A	Leyton O	D	0-0	1-1	Cook	16,93
25		23	H	Nottingham F	W	2-1	3-1	Robson, Key, (Palmer og)	15,78
26	M	2	A	Ipswich T	W	1-0	1-0	Leggat	18,22
27		9	H	Blackpool	W	1-0	2-0	Leggat, Cook	8,95
28		16	A	Blackburn R	W	0-0	1-0	Cook	9,85
29		23	H	Aston Villa	W	0-0	1-0	Marsh	22,50
30		29	A	Manchester C	W	1-1	3-2	Cook 2, O'Connell	12,78
31	A	1	A	Manchester U	W	1-0	2-0	O'Connell, Leggat	28,12
32		6	H	West Ham U	W	0-0	2-0	Cook, Key	26,87
33		12	A	Burnley	L	0-2	0-4		22,40
34		13	A	Tottenham H	D	0-0	1-1	Leggat	45,95
35		15	H	Burnley	D	1-0	1-1	Key	25,86
36		20	H	Liverpool	D	0-0	0-0		18,89
37		27	A	Wolverhampton W	L	0-1	1-2	Cook	18,89
38	M	1	H	Bolton W	W	2-0	2-1	Leggat, Brown	10,89
39		4	H	Birmingham C	D	1-1	3-3	Cook, (Smith Green ogs)	20,17
40		11	A	Everton	L	1-3	1-4	Key	60,57
41		14	A	Arsenal	L	0-1	0-3		17,38
42		18	H	West Bromich A	L	0-1	1-2	Cook	17,48
									App
									Goal

FA Cup

No		Date	V	Opponents	R	H-T	F-T	Scorers	Atten
3	F	4	A	West Ham U	D	0-0	0-0		21,00
R		20	H	West Ham U	L	0-1	1-2	Robson	20,64

League Cup

No		Date	V	Opponents	R	H-T	F-T	Scorers	Atten
2	S	26	H	Bournemouth	W	3-0	4-0	Key 2, Brown, Henderson	7,02
3	O	17	A	Hull C	W	0-1	2-1	Key, Metchick	20,30
4	N	14	A	Norwich C	L	0-0	0-1		17,55

	Macedo	Cohen	Langley	Mullery	Dodgin	Lowe	Leggat	Robson	Henderson	Haynes	O'Connell	Cook	Metchick	Brown S	Brown M	Watson	Key	Mealand	Chamberlain	Keetch	Lampe	Stratton	Marsh
1		2	3	4	5	6	7	8	9	10	11												
2		2	3	4	5	6	7	8	9	10	11												
3		2	3	4	5	6	7		8		11	9	10										
4		2	3	4	5	6	7		10			8	11	9									
5		2	3	4	5	6	7		10			8	11	9									
6		2	3		5	6	7		10			4	11	9	8								
7		2	3		5	6			10			8	11	9		4	7						
8			3	4	5	6		8	10			7	11	9				2					
9			3	4	5			6	10			8		9			7	2	11				
10			3	4	5			6	10			8		9			7	2	11				
11			3	4	5			6	10			8		9			7		11	2			
12		2	3	4	5			6	10		11	8		9			7						
13		2	3	4	5	6	7		10		11	8		9									
14		2	3	4	5	6	7		10		11	8		9									
15		2	3	4	5	6	7		10		11		8	9									
16		2	3	4	5	6	7	8	10		11			9									
17		2	3	4		6	7	8	10		11			9							5		
18		2	3			6	7	4	10		11		8	9							5		
19		2	3			6	7	4	10		11		8	9							5		
20		2	3	4		5	7	6	10		11	8		9									
21		2	3	4		5	7	6	10		11	8		9									
22		2	3	4		6	7	10				8		9						5		11	
23		2	3	4			7	10				8		9		6				5		11	
24		2	3	4		5	7	6		10		8		9								11	
25		2	3	4		5	8	6		10	11	9					7						
26		2	3	4		5	8	6		10	11	9					7						
27		2	3	4		5	8	6	10		11	9					7						
28		2	3	4		5	8	6	10		11	9					7						
29		2	3	4		5	8	6			11	9					7						10
30		2	3	4		5	8	6			11	9		10			7						
31		2	3	4			8	6			11	9		10			7			5			
32		2	3	4		5	8	6			11	9		10			7						
33		2	3	4		5	8	6			11	9		10			7						
34		2	3	4			8	6			11	9		10			7			5			
35		2	3	4			8	6			11	9		10			7			5			
36		2	3	4			8	6			11	9		10			7			5			
37		2	3	4			8	6			11	9		10			7			5			
38		2	3	4			8	6			11	9		10			7			5			
39		2	3	4		5	8	6			11	9		10			7						
40		2	3	4				6		10	11	9		8			7			5			
41		2	3	4				6		10	11	9		8			7			5			
42		2	3	4				6		10	11	9		8	7					5			
A	2	38	42	38	16	28	33	34	23	8	31	35	9	34	2	2	22	3	3	12	3	3	1
G		-	4	1	-	-	10	1	2	-	2	15	-	7	-	-	4	-	-	-	-	-	1

	Macedo	Cohen	Langley	Mullery	Dodgin	Lowe	Leggat	Robson	Henderson	Haynes	O'Connell	Cook	Metchick	Brown S	Brown M	Watson	Key	Mealand	Chamberlain	Keetch	Lampe	Stratton	Marsh
3		2	3	4		5	7	6	10			8		9								11	
R		2	3	4		5		6		10		8	11	9			7						

	Macedo	Cohen	Langley	Mullery	Dodgin	Lowe	Leggat	Robson	Henderson	Haynes	O'Connell	Cook	Metchick	Brown S	Brown M	Watson	Key	Mealand	Chamberlain	Keetch	Lampe	Stratton	Marsh
2			3	4	5			6	10			8		9			7		11	2			
3			3	4	5	6					11	8	10	9			7			2			
4		2	3			6	7	4	10		11		8	9							5		

0 points v	Arsenal, West Bromwich A, Wolves	0 points
1 point v	Birmingham C, Burnley, Leyton O, Liverpool, Sheffield U, Tottenham H	6 points
2 points v	Bolton W, Everton, Manchester C, Manchester U, Nottingham F, Sheffield W	12 points
3 points v	Blackburn R, Blackpool, Ipswich T, West Ham U	12 points
4 points v	Aston Villa, Leicester C	8 points

The talented but injury prone centre half Derek Lampe made the last of his 96 appearances in November 1962.

1963-64

Division One

	P	W	D	L	F	A	Pts
Liverpool	42	26	5	11	92	45	57
Manchester United	42	23	7	12	90	62	53
Everton	42	21	10	11	84	64	52
Tottenham Hotspur	42	22	7	13	97	81	51
Chelsea	42	20	10	12	72	56	50
Sheffield Wednesday	42	19	11	12	84	67	49
Blackburn Rovers	42	18	10	14	89	65	46
Arsenal	42	17	11	14	90	82	45
Burnley	42	17	10	15	71	64	44
West Bromwich Albion	42	16	11	15	70	61	43
Leicester City	42	16	11	15	61	58	43
Sheffield United	42	16	11	15	61	64	43
Nottingham Forest	42	16	9	17	64	68	41
West Ham United	42	14	12	16	69	74	40
Fulham	42	13	13	16	58	65	39
Wolverhampton W	42	12	15	15	70	80	39
Stoke City	42	14	10	18	77	78	38
Blackpool	42	13	9	20	52	73	35
Aston Villa	42	11	12	19	62	71	34
Birmingham City	42	11	7	24	54	92	29
Bolton Wanderers	42	10	8	24	48	80	28
Ipswich Town	42	9	7	26	56	121	25

Manager: Bedford Jezzard

Did you know that?

In the 10-1 hammering of Ipswich on Boxing Day 1963, Graham Leggat scored three goals in three minutes, which is still the fastest hat-trick ever scored in the top flight.

5	Robson's 200th game
7	Dodgin finale
10	Haynes' 400th game
18	Mullery's 200th game
24	Leggat's 100th goal
30	Langley's 300th game
31	Earle debut
31	Henderson finale
34	Mullery finale
35	Callaghan debut
39	Cohen's 300th game

No		Date	V	Opponents	R	H-T	F-T	Scorers	Atte
1	A	24	A	Everton	L	0-1	0-3		49,52
2		28	H	Sheffield W	W	2-0	2-0	Mullery, Haynes	20,87
3		31	H	Birmingham C	W	1-0	2-1	Chamberlain 2 (1 pen)	21,26
4	S	4	A	Sheffield W	L	0-0	0-3		20,94
5		7	A	West Bromich A	L	0-1	0-3		17,99
6		10	A	Burnley	L	0-2	1-4	Leggat	19,34
7		14	H	Arsenal	L	1-1	1-4	Leggat	34,93
8		18	H	Burnley	W	1-1	2-1	Haynes, Leggat	17,28
9		21	A	Leicester C	W	0-0	1-0	Marsh	26,54
10		28	H	Bolton W	W	2-0	3-1	Cook, Haynes, Langley (pen)	17,34
11		30	A	Blackpool	L	0-0	0-1		13,75
12	O	5	A	Blackburn R	L	0-0	0-2		13,61
13		12	H	Nottingham F	D	0-0	0-0		23,55
14		19	A	Stoke C	D	1-0	1-1	Leggat	24,73
15		26	H	Chelsea	L	0-0	0-1		32,94
16	N	2	A	Tottenham H	L	0-0	0-1		42,02
17		9	H	Aston Villa	W	0-0	2-0	Cohen, Key	15,06
18		16	A	Liverpool	L	0-0	0-2		38,47
19		23	H	Sheffield U	W	2-1	3-1	Cook, Leggat, Howfield	22,24
20		30	A	West Ham U	D	1-0	1-1	Leggat	23,17
21	D	7	H	Wolverhampton W	W	2-1	4-1	Haynes, Cook, Key, Leggat	19,30
22		14	H	Everton	D	0-1	2-2	Keetch, Cook	17,86
23		21	A	Birmingham C	D	0-0	0-0		13,91
24		26	H	Ipswich T	W	5-1	10-1	Leggat 4, Howfield 3, Cook, Mullery, Robson	19,37
25		28	A	Ipswich T	L	1-2	2-4	Leggat, Key	15,80
26	J	11	H	West Bromich A	D	1-0	1-1	Mullery	16,39
27		18	A	Arsenal	D	0-1	2-2	Howfield, Haynes	35,89
28	F	1	H	Leicester C	W	2-0	2-1	Metchick, Key	17,58
29		8	A	Bolton W	L	1-1	1-2	Howfield	9,61
30		19	H	Blackburn R	D	0-0	1-1	Key	12,26
31		22	A	Nottingham F	L	0-0	0-2		14,71
32		29	H	Blackpool	D	0-0	1-1	Earle	12,19
33	M	7	A	Chelsea	W	2-0	2-1	O'Connell, Earle	26,24
34		14	H	Liverpool	W	0-0	1-0	Stratton	14,02
35		21	A	Aston Villa	D	0-1	2-2	Leggat 2	11,42
36		27	H	Manchester U	D	1-2	2-2	Earle, Haynes	41,77
37		28	H	Tottenham H	D	0-1	1-1	Haynes	30,38
38		30	A	Manchester U	L	0-1	0-3		42,49
39	A	4	A	Sheffield U	L	0-1	0-1		15,15
40		11	H	West Ham U	W	1-0	2-0	Keetch, Haynes	22,02
41		18	A	Wolverhampton W	L	0-3	0-4		16,43
42		25	H	Stoke C	D	1-1	3-3	Earle 2, Leggat	15,74
									App
									Goa

FA Cup

3	J	4	H	Luton T	W	0-0	4-1	Mullery, Leggat, Cook, Howfield	18,08
4		25	A	Blackburn R	L	0-1	0-2		24,31

League Cup

2	S	25	A	Colchester U	L	1-3	3-5	Metchick 2, Key	7,77

Macedo	Cohen	Keetch	Mullery	Dodgin	Robson	Leggat	Brown S	Cook	Haynes	Chamberlain	Underwood	Key	Langley	Marsh	Townsend	Metchick	Stratton	Watson	Howfield	Drake	Henderson	O'Connell	Earle	Edwards	Callaghan	Mealand	
1	2	3	4	5	6	7	8	9	10	11																	1
	2	3	4	5	6		8	9	10	11	1	7															2
	2	3	4	5	6		8	9	10	11	1	7															3
	2	3	4	5	6		8	9	10	11	1	7															4
	2		4	5	6			9	10	11	1	7	3	8													5
	2		4	5	6	8	9		10			7	3		1	11											6
	2		4	5	6	8		9	10			7	3		1		11										7
	2	5	4		6	11		9	10		1	7	3	8													8
	2	5	4		6	11		9	10		1	7	3	8													9
	2	5	4			11	8	9	10		1	7	3					6									10
	2	5	4				8	9	10		1	7	3				11	6									11
	2	5	4		6		8	9	10		1	7	3					11									12
	2	5	4		6	7	8	9	10		1		3					11									13
	2	5	4		6	11	8	9	10		1	7	3														14
	2	5	4		6	11	8	9	10		1	7	3														15
	2	5	4		6		8	9	10	11	1	7	3														16
	2	5	4		6		9	8	10	11	1	7	3														17
	2	5	4		6		9	8	10		1	7	3						11								18
1	2	5	4		6	9		8	10			7	3						11								19
1	2	5	4		6	9		8	10			7							11	3							20
1	2	5	4		6	9		8	10			7							11	3							21
1	2	5	4		6	9		8	10			7							11	3							22
1	2	5	4		6	9		8	10			7							11	3							23
1	2	5	4		6	9		8	10			7	3						11								24
1	2	5	4		6	9		8	10			7	3						11								25
1	2	5	4		6	9		8	10			7	3						11								26
1	2	5	4		6			8	10			7					9		11	3							27
1	2	5	4		6							7	3			8			11		9	10					28
1	2	5	4		6				10				3			8			7		9	11					29
1	2	5	4		6				10			7	3			8			11		9						30
1	2	5	4		6				10				3	8					11		9		7				31
1	2	5	4		6	8			10				3				9					11	7				32
1	2	5	4		6	8			10				3				9					11	7				33
1	2	5	4		6	8			10				3				9					11	7				34
1	2	5				8			10				3				9					11	7	4	6		35
1	2	5			4	8			10				3				9					11	7		6		36
1	2	5			4			8	10				3				9					11	7		6		37
	2				5		4	8	10		1						9			3		11	7		6		38
1	2	5			4			8								10	9			3		11	7		6		39
1		5			4	9			10				3			8						11	7		6	2	40
1	2	5			4	9			10				3			8						11	7		6		41
1	2	5			4	9			10				3			8						11	7		6		42
24	41	38	34	7	39	25	15	29	40	7	16	27	31	4	2	8	11	4	14	7	4	13	12	1	8	1	A
-	1	2	3	-	1	15	-	5	8	2	-	5	1	1	-	1	1	-	6	-	-	1	5	-	-	-	G

Macedo	Cohen	Keetch	Mullery	Dodgin	Robson	Leggat	Brown S	Cook	Haynes	Chamberlain	Underwood	Key	Langley	Marsh	Townsend	Metchick	Stratton	Watson	Howfield	Drake	Henderson	O'Connell	Earle	Edwards	Callaghan	Mealand	
1	2	5	4		6	9		8	10			7	3						11								3
1	2	5	4		6	9		8	10				3			7			11								4

Macedo	Cohen	Keetch	Mullery	Dodgin	Robson	Leggat	Brown S	Cook	Haynes	Chamberlain	Underwood	Key	Langley	Marsh	Townsend	Metchick	Stratton	Watson	Howfield	Drake	Henderson	O'Connell	Earle	Edwards	Callaghan	Mealand	
	2	5	4		6	11		9	10			7	3		1	8											2

0 points v		0 points
1 point v	Arsenal, Blackburn R, Blackpool, Everton, Manchester U, Nottingham F, Tottenham H, West Bromwich A	8 points
2 points v	Bolton W, Burnley, Chelsea, Ipswich T, Liverpool, Sheffield U, Sheffield W, Stoke C, Wolves	18 points
3 points v	Aston Villa, Birmingham C, West Ham U	9 points
4 points v	Leicester C	4 points

Bill Dodgin's playing career ended against his old club Arsenal in September 1963, but he was to return to the Cottage as manager.

1964-65

Division One

	P	W	D	L	F	A	Pts
Manchester United	42	26	9	7	89	39	61
Leeds United	42	26	9	7	83	52	61
Chelsea	42	24	8	10	89	54	56
Everton	42	17	15	10	69	60	49
Nottingham Forest	42	17	13	12	71	67	47
Tottenham Hotspur	42	19	7	16	87	71	45
Liverpool	42	17	10	15	67	73	44
Sheffield Wednesday	42	16	11	15	57	55	43
West Ham United	42	19	4	19	82	71	42
Blackburn Rovers	42	16	10	16	83	79	42
Stoke City	42	16	10	16	67	66	42
Burnley	42	16	10	16	70	70	42
Arsenal	42	17	7	18	69	75	41
West Bromwich Albion	42	13	13	16	70	65	39
Sunderland	42	14	9	19	64	74	37
Aston Villa	42	16	5	21	57	82	37
Blackpool	42	12	11	19	67	78	35
Leicester City	42	11	13	18	69	85	35
Sheffield United	42	12	11	19	50	64	35
Fulham	42	11	12	19	60	78	34
Wolverhampton W	42	13	4	25	59	89	30
Birmingham City	42	8	11	23	64	96	27

Manager: Bedford Jezzard / Vic Buckingham

Did you know that?

Fulham's home game against Manchester United in September 1964 was the Cottagers' first appearance on the new BBC2 programme, Match Of The Day. Manchester United were also the opponents six years earlier when Fulham first appeared in a live televised match, the FA Cup semi-final replay at Highbury.

12 Metchick finale
FAC3 Chamberlain finale
FAC3 Dempsey debut
35 Macedo's 300th game
42 Cook and Langley finales

No		Date	V	Opponents	R	H-T	F-T	Scorers	Atten
1	A	22	H	West Ham U	L	0-1	1-2	Metchick	31,218
2		26	A	Birmingham C	D	0-1	2-2	Metchick, Langley (pen)	20,719
3		29	A	West Bromich A	D	2-1	2-2	Metchick, Cohen	18,709
4	S	2	H	Birmingham C	W	1-0	3-1	Metchick 3	13,100
5		5	H	Manchester U	W	0-1	2-1	Haynes, (Brennan og)	36,291
6		9	A	Sheffield U	D	1-1	1-1	Marsh	20,379
7		12	A	Chelsea	L	0-1	0-1		41,472
8		16	H	Sheffield U	L	1-2	1-2	Marsh	12,415
9		19	A	Nottingham F	W	1-1	3-2	Langley, Marsh 2	22,307
10		26	H	Stoke C	L	0-2	1-4	Marsh	15,167
11		30	A	Leeds U	D	1-1	2-2	Leggat, Marsh	31,260
12	O	5	A	Tottenham H	L	0-3	0-3		32,908
13		10	H	Leicester C	W	2-1	5-2	Marsh 2, Leggat 2, O'Connell	14,300
14		17	A	Sunderland	D	0-0	0-0		38,297
15		24	H	Wolverhampton W	W	2-0	2-0	Marsh, Cohen	14,671
16		31	A	Aston Villa	L	0-1	0-2		14,845
17	N	7	H	Liverpool	D	1-0	1-1	Haynes	18,637
18		14	A	Sheffield W	D	0-0	1-1	Earle	17,794
19		21	H	Blackpool	D	2-1	3-3	Earle, Chamberlain, Howfield	16,587
20		28	A	Blackburn R	L	0-1	0-2		12,434
21	D	5	H	Arsenal	L	2-1	3-4	Marsh, Brown, Cook	13,764
22		12	A	West Ham U	L	0-1	0-2		21,985
23		19	H	West Bromich A	W	2-0	3-1	Marsh, Howfield, Haynes	10,39
24		26	A	Burnley	L	0-1	0-4		15,602
25		28	H	Burnley	L	0-1	0-1		10,16
26	J	16	H	Chelsea	L	0-1	1-2	Cook	26,400
27		23	H	Nottingham F	W	2-1	4-1	Howfield, Cook, Marsh, Key	15,82
28	F	6	A	Stoke C	L	1-1	1-3	Marsh	28,60
29		13	H	Tottenham H	W	0-0	4-1	Key 2, Cook, Marsh	27,708
30		20	A	Arsenal	L	0-2	0-2		22,10
31		24	A	Leicester C	L	1-4	1-5	Haynes	16,77
32		27	H	Sunderland	W	1-0	1-0	Cook	16,86
33	M	13	H	Leeds U	D	1-1	2-2	Langley (pen), Cook	24,704
34		15	A	Manchester U	L	1-2	1-4	Marsh	45,63
35		20	A	Liverpool	L	2-1	2-3	Marsh, Cook	28,46
36		27	H	Sheffield W	W	2-0	2-0	Leggat, Cook	12,14
37		30	A	Wolverhampton W	D	0-0	0-0		18,96
38	A	3	A	Blackpool	L	0-2	0-3		11,97
39		9	H	Blackburn R	W	0-1	3-2	Robson, Haynes, Marsh	11,65
40		16	A	Everton	L	0-1	0-2		38,53
41		19	H	Everton	D	0-1	1-1	Key	13,32
42		24	H	Aston Villa	D	0-0	1-1	Langley	13,494
									App
									Goal

FA Cup

3	J	9	H	Millwall	D	2-1	3-3	Key, Stratton 2	21,31
R		11	A	Millwall	L	0-0	0-2		35,00

League Cup

2	S	23	H	Oxford U	W	1-0	2-0	Key, O'Connell	8,334
3	O	14	A	Reading	D	1-0	1-1	Cook	13,87
R		19	H	Reading	L	0-1	1-3	Robson	5,27

Macedo	Cohen	Langley	Robson	Keetch	Callaghan	Earle	Metchick	Leggat	Haynes	O'Connell	Key	Marsh	Brown	Underwood	Cook	Howfield	Chamberlain	Drake	Mealand	Dempsey	Stratton	Parmenter	Jones	
1	2	3	4	5	6	7	8	9	10	11														1
1	2	3	4	5	6		8		10	11	7	9												2
1	2	3	4	5	6		8			11	7	9	10											3
1	2	3	4	5	6		8		10	11	7	9												4
1	2	3	4	5	6		8		10	11	7	9												5
1	2	3	4	5	6		8		10	11	7	9												6
1	2	3	4	5	6		8		10	11	7	9												7
1	2	3	4	5	6		8	7	10	11		9												8
	2	3	4	5			8		10	11	7	9	6	1										9
	2	3	4	5	6				10	11	7	9	8	1										10
1	2	3	4	5			8	7	10	11		9	6											11
1	2	3	4	5			8	7	10	11		9	6											12
1	2	3	4	5				7	10	11		9	6		8									13
1	2	3	4	5				7	10	11		9	6		8									14
1	2	3	4	5				7	10	11		9	6		8									15
1	2	3	4	5	6			7	10	11		9	8											16
1	2	3	4	5		7			10			9	6			8	11							17
1	2	3	4	5		7			10			9	6			8	11							18
1	2	3	4	5		7			10			9	6			8	11							19
1	2		4	5						10		9	6		7	8	11	3						20
1	2	3	4	5						10		9	6		7	8	11							21
1		3	4	5	8				10			9	6			7	11		2					22
1	2	3	4	5					10			9	6		8	7	11							23
1	2	3	4	5					10	8		9	6			7	11							24
1	2	3	4	5					10	8	7	9	6			11								25
1	2	3	6						10		7	8	4		9	11				5				26
1	2	3	6						10		7	8	4		9	11				5				27
1	2	3	6					9	10		7	8	4			11				5				28
1	2	3	6					11	10		7	8	4		9					5				29
1	2	3	6	5				11	10		7	8	4								9			30
1	2	3	6	5				11	10		7	8	4								9			31
1	2	3	4	5					10		7	8	6		9						11			32
1	2	3	4	5					10		7	8	6		9						11			33
1	2	3	4	5				11	10		7	8	6		9									34
1	2	3	4	5					10		7	8	6		9							11		35
1	2	3	4	5				11	10		7	8	6		9									36
1	2	3	4	5				11	10		7	8	6								9			37
1	2	3	4	5				11	10		7	8	6								9			38
1		3	4		5				10	11	7	8	6		9				2					39
1	2	3	4	5				9	10	11	7	8	6											40
1	2	3	4	5					10	11	7	8	6		9									41
1	2	3	6	5					10	11	7	8	4		9									42
0	40	41	42	37	12	4	11	17	39	24	26	41	35	2	17	12	8	1	2	4	6	1	-	A
-	2	4	1	-	-	2	6	4	5	1	4	17	1	-	8	3	1	-	-	-	-	-	-	G

Macedo	Cohen	Langley	Robson	Keetch	Callaghan	Earle	Metchick	Leggat	Haynes	O'Connell	Key	Marsh	Brown	Underwood	Cook	Howfield	Chamberlain	Drake	Mealand	Dempsey	Stratton	Parmenter	Jones	
1	2	3	4	5					10	11	7		6			8					9			3
1	2	3	4						10		7	8	6				11			5	9			R

Macedo	Cohen	Langley	Robson	Keetch	Callaghan	Earle	Metchick	Leggat	Haynes	O'Connell	Key	Marsh	Brown	Underwood	Cook	Howfield	Chamberlain	Drake	Mealand	Dempsey	Stratton	Parmenter	Jones	
1	2	3	4	5	6				10	11	7	9	8	1										2
1	2	3	4	5	6			7		11		9	10		8									3
1		3	4	5				7	10				6		9	11			2				8	R

0 points v	Arsenal, Burnley, Chelsea, Stoke C, West Ham U	0 points
1 point v	Aston Villa, Blackpool, Everton, Liverpool, Sheffield U	5 points
2 points v	Blackburn R, Leeds U, Leicester C, Manchester U, Tottenham H	10 points
3 points v	Birmingham C, Sheffield W, Sunderland, West Bromwich A, Wolves	15 points
4 points v	Nottingham F	4 points

Dave Metchick got off to a flying start to the season with six goals in the first four games but by December he was an Orient player.

1965-66

Division One

	P	W	D	L	F	A	Pts
Liverpool	42	26	9	7	79	34	61
Leeds United	42	23	9	10	79	38	55
Burnley	42	24	7	11	79	47	55
Manchester United	42	18	15	9	84	59	51
Chelsea	42	22	7	13	65	53	51
West Bromwich Albion	42	19	12	11	91	69	50
Leicester City	42	21	7	14	80	65	49
Tottenham Hotspur	42	16	12	14	75	66	44
Sheffield United	42	16	11	15	56	59	43
Stoke City	42	15	12	15	65	64	42
Everton	42	15	11	16	56	62	41
West Ham United	42	15	9	18	70	83	39
Blackpool	42	14	9	19	55	65	37
Arsenal	42	12	13	17	62	75	37
Newcastle United	42	14	9	19	50	63	37
Aston Villa	42	15	6	21	69	80	36
Sheffield Wednesday	42	14	8	20	56	66	36
Nottingham Forest	42	14	8	20	56	72	36
Sunderland	42	14	8	20	51	72	36
Fulham	42	14	7	21	67	85	35
Northampton Town	42	10	13	19	55	92	33
Blackburn Rovers	42	8	4	30	57	88	20

Manager: Vic Buckingham

Did you know that?

Rodney Marsh was named as Fulham's first substitute, against Blackpool in August 1965. A week later, at Chelsea, Graham Leggat became the first to come on as a substitute when he replaced the injured Johnny Haynes. It was not until March 1967 at Old Trafford, that a substitute, Steve Earle, scored.

8	Pearson debut
11	Nichols debut
14	Robson's 300th gme
25	Jezzard's 50th goal
25	N Smith debut
26	R Lowe finale
28	Flack finale
35	Pavitt finale
38	Jim Taylor finale
39	Brice debut
42	Brennan finale

No		*Date*	*V*	*Opponents*	*R*	*H-T*	*F-T*	*Scorers*	*Atten*
1	A	21	A	Blackpool	D	0-0	2-2	Key Haynes	15,28
2		25	H	Blackburn R	W	4-0	5-2	Brown 2 Key 2 Dyson	14,48
3		28	H	Chelsea	L	0-3	0-3		34,02
4	S	1	A	Blackburn R	L	1-2	2-3	Brown O'Connell	10,49
5		4	H	Tottenham H	L	0-1	0-2		28,71
6		8	H	Sheffield U	D	0-0	0-0		9,73
7		11	A	Liverpool	L	0-1	1-2	Key	46,38
8		15	A	Sheffield U	L	0-0	0-2		17,96
9		18	H	Aston Villa	L	1-2	3-6	Leggat 3	12,63
10		25	A	Sunderland	D	1-1	2-2	O'Connell Robson	39,09
11	O	2	H	West Ham U	W	0-0	3-0	Haynes Leggat (Charles og)	22,31
12		9	A	Arsenal	L	1-1	1-2	Dyson	32,32
13		16	H	Everton	W	2-1	3-2	Dempsey Dyson Pearson	18,11
14		23	A	Manchester U	L	0-1	1-4	Dempsey	34,41
15		30	H	Newcastle U	W	0-0	2-0	Key Leggat	19,22
16	N	6	A	West Bromich A	L	0-1	2-6	Leggat Robson	20,02
17		13	H	Nottingham F	D	1-0	1-1	Marsh	13,86
18		20	A	Sheffield W	L	0-1	0-1		14,23
19		27	H	Northampton T	L	1-2	1-4	Haynes	11,38
20	D	4	A	Stoke C	L	0-1	2-3	Marsh 2	14,87
21		11	H	Burnley	L	1-2	2-5	Haynes Pearson	12,09
22		18	A	Everton	L	0-2	0-2		20,67
23		28	A	Leicester C	L	0-1	0-5		20,17
24	J	1	H	Arsenal	W	0-0	1-0	Leggat	25,80
25		8	A	Burnley	L	0-1	0-1		17,20
26		15	H	Manchester U	L	0-1	0-1		33,01
27		29	H	Blackpool	D	0-0	0-0		12,09
28	F	5	A	Chelsea	L	0-2	1-2	Leggat	34,24
29		19	A	Tottenham H	L	3-4	3-4	Earle Leggat Barrett	32,24
30		26	H	Liverpool	W	1-0	2-0	Earle 2	31,61
31	M	12	A	Aston Villa	W	2-1	5-2	Earle 2 Leggat 2 Barrett	13,79
32		19	H	Sunderland	W	3-0	3-0	Leggat 2 (Hurley og)	20,91
33		26	A	West Ham U	W	1-0	3-1	Earle Leggat Barrett	18,99
34	A	2	H	West Bromich A	W	2-1	2-1	Haynes 2	20,42
35		8	H	Leeds U	L	0-1	1-3	Robson	38,96
36		12	A	Leeds U	W	0-0	1-0	Pearson	33,96
37		16	H	Sheffield W	W	1-2	4-2	Barrett Earle Leggat Robson	20,98
38		18	H	Leicester C	L	0-2	0-4		18,01
39		23	A	Northampton T	W	1-2	4-2	Earle 3 Robson	24,52
40		26	A	Nottingham F	W	2-1	2-1	Leggat Pearson	19,73
41		30	H	Stoke C	D	0-1	1-1	Clarke	25,49
42	M	7	A	Newcastle U	D	1-0	1-1	Robson	18,81
									App
									Goa

FA Cup

3	J	22	A	Sheffield U	L	0-1	1-3	Dempsey	18,00

League Cup

2	S	22	A	Wrexham	W	2-0	2-1	O'Connell Dyson	12,00
3	O	13	H	Northampton T	W	3-0	5-0	Dempsey 3 Dyson 2	7,83
4	N	3	H	Aston V	D	1-0	1-1	Haynes	10,08
R		8	A	Aston V	L	0-0	0-2		18,53

Macedo	Cohen	Mealand	Brown	Keetch	Robson	Key	O'Connell	Leggat	Haynes	Dyson	Marsh	Dempsey	Callaghan	Pearson	Nichols	McClelland	Ryan	Parmenter	Hill	Earle	Barrett	Clarke	Drake	
1	2	3	4	5	6	7	8	9	10	11	S													1
1	2	3	4	5	6	7	8		10	11	9		S											2
1	2	3	4	5	6	7	8	12	**10**	11	9													3
1	2	3	4	5	6	7	8	10		11	9		S											4
1	2	S	4	3	6	7	8			11	9	5	10											5
1	2		4	3	6	7	10	9		11	8	5												6
1	2		4	3	6	7	10	9		11	8	5												7
1	2		4	3	6	7			10	11	9	5		8										8
1	2		4	3	6	7	8	9	10	11		5		S										9
1	2	3	6		4	7	8	9	10	11		5												10
1		3		6	4	7	8	9	10	11		5	S		2									11
1	2	**3**		6	4	7	8		10	11	9	5		12										12
1	2			5	6	7	S		10	11	8	9		4	3									13
1	2		S	5	6	7			10	11	8	9		4	3									14
1	2		S	5	6	7		8	10	11		9		4	3									15
1	2		4	5	6	7		8	10	11		9			3									16
1	2		4	S			10	7	8	11	9	5	6		3									17
1	2		4				10	7	8	11	9	5	6		3									18
1	2		4	5		7	11		10	12	8	9	6		3									19
	2		4			7			9		8	5	6		3	1	10	11						20
	2						8	7	10		9	5	6	4	3	1		11	S					21
	2		6		4			7	8	11	9	5		10	3	1								22
	2		4		6	S	3	7	8	11	9	5		10		1								23
	2		6	4		7	3	9	10			5		8	S	1		11						24
1	2		6	4	8	S	3	7	10	11		5		9										25
1	2		6	8	4	7	3	9	10		S	5						11						26
	2		9		**4**							5	6	10	3	1	12	11		7	8			27
	2		9	S	4			7				5	6	10	3	1		11			8			28
	2		6		4			11	9			5	S	10	3	1				7	8			29
	2		6		4			8	9			5	S	10	3	1				7	11			30
	2		6		4			8	9			5	S	10	3	1				7	11			31
	2		6		4			8	9			5	S	10	3	1				7	11			32
	2		6		4			8	9			5		10	3	1				7	11	S		33
			6		4		2	8	9			5		10	3	1				7	11	S		34
	2		6		4			8	**9**			5		10	3	1				7	11	12		35
	2		6		4			8				5	S	10	3	1				7	11	9		36
	2		6		4			8				5	S	10	3	1				7	11	9		37
	2		6		4			8				5	S	10	3	1				7	11	9		38
	2		6		4			11	9			5		10	3	1				7	S	8		39
	2		4		6			11	**9**			5		10	3	1				7	12	8		40
	2		4		6			11	9			5		10	3	1				7	12	8		41
			4		6			11	8			5	10		3	1				7	S	9	2	42
21	39	7	36	19	36	20	20	32	33	21	17	38	9	24	27	21	1	6	-	15	12	7	1	A
-	-	-	-	-	-	-	-	1	-	1	-	-	-	1	-	-	1	-	-	-	2	1	-	S
-	-	-	3	-	6	5	2	16	6	3	3	2	-	4	-	-	-	-	-	10	4	1	-	G

Macedo	Cohen	Mealand	Brown	Keetch	Robson	Key	O'Connell	Leggat	Haynes	Dyson	Marsh	Dempsey	Callaghan	Pearson	Nichols	McClelland	Ryan	Parmenter	Hill	Earle	Barrett	Clarke	Drake	
	2		6	4		S	3	9	8	11	7	5		10		1								3

Macedo	Cohen	Mealand	Brown	Keetch	Robson	Key	O'Connell	Leggat	Haynes	Dyson	Marsh	Dempsey	Callaghan	Pearson	Nichols	McClelland	Ryan	Parmenter	Hill	Earle	Barrett	Clarke	Drake	
1	2	3	4		6	7	8	9	10	11		5												2
1	2			5	6	7			10	11	8	9		4	3									3
1	2			5	6	7		8	10	11		9		4	3									4
			6	2		7	10	9	8	11		5	4		3	1								R

0 points v	Burnley, Chelsea, Leicester C, Manchester U, Tottenham H	0 points
1 point v	Sheffield U, Stoke C	2 points
2 points v	Arsenal, Aston Villa, Blackburn R, Blackpool, Everton, Leeds U, Liverpool, Northampton T, Sheffield W, West Bromwich A	20 points
3 points v	Newcastle U, Nottingham F, Sunderland	9 points
4 points v	West Ham U	4 points

Irish international goalkeeper Jack McClelland, signed from Arsenal, took over from Tony Macedo in the battle against relegation.

1966-67

Division One

	P	W	D	L	F	A	Pts
Manchester United	42	24	12	6	84	45	60
Nottingham Forest	42	23	10	9	64	41	56
Tottenham Hotspur	42	24	8	10	71	48	56
Leeds United	42	22	11	9	62	42	55
Liverpool	42	19	13	10	64	47	51
Everton	42	19	10	13	65	46	48
Arsenal	42	16	14	12	58	47	46
Leicester City	42	18	8	16	78	71	44
Chelsea	42	15	14	13	67	62	44
Sheffield United	42	16	10	16	52	59	42
Sheffield Wednesday	42	14	13	15	56	47	41
Stoke City	42	17	7	18	63	58	41
West Bromwich Albion	42	16	7	19	77	73	39
Burnley	42	15	9	18	66	76	39
Manchester City	42	12	15	15	43	52	39
West Ham United	42	14	8	20	80	84	36
Sunderland	42	14	8	20	58	72	36
Fulham	42	11	12	19	71	83	34
Southampton	42	14	6	22	74	92	34
Newcastle United	42	12	9	21	39	81	33
Aston Villa	42	11	7	24	54	85	29
Blackpool	42	6	9	27	41	76	21

Manager: Vic Buckingham

Did you know that?

In his penultimate game for Fulham in December 1966, Graham Leggat scored a hat-trick at home to Leicester. This brought his total to 13 goals in the 12 matches he had played against Leicester since 1959, and all were scored against the great Gordon Banks.

10	Cohen's 400th game
LC3	Conway debut
24	Leggat finale
35	Seymour debut
40	Pentecost debut
42	Robson finale

No	Date	V	Opponents	R	H-T	F-T	Scorers	Atten
1	Aug 20	H	Everton	L	0-0	0-1		21,63
2	23	A	Burnley	L	0-1	0-3		18,34
3	27	A	Stoke C	W	0-1	2-1	Leggat, Clarke	26,33
4	29	H	Burnley	D	0-0	0-0		15,02
5	Sep 3	H	Sheffield U	L	0-0	0-1		14,88
6	6	A	Nottingham F	L	0-1	1-2	Earle	22,12
7	10	A	West Bromich A	L	0-1	1-5	Earle	18,00
8	17	H	Leeds U	D	1-1	2-2	Leggat, Earle	19,91
9	24	A	Newcastle U	D	1-0	1-1	Earle	20,33
10	Oct 1	H	Tottenham H	L	2-2	3-4	Clarke, Earle, Leggat	28,62
11	8	A	Liverpool	D	2-2	2-2	Clarke 2	44,02
12	15	H	West Ham U	W	2-1	4-2	Clarke 2, Earle, (Burnett og)	34,82
13	22	A	Sheffield W	D	1-1	1-1	Haynes	20,04
14	29	H	Chelsea	L	0-1	1-3	Barrett	43,14
15	Nov 5	A	West Ham U	L	1-1	1-6	Callaghan	22,26
16	12	H	Aston Villa	W	0-0	5-1	Clarke 2, Conway, Pearson, Parmenter	16,07
17	19	A	Arsenal	L	0-1	0-1		25,75
18	26	H	Manchester C	W	1-0	4-1	Clarke 2, Haynes, Cohen	14,57
19	Dec 3	A	Blackpool	W	0-0	1-0	Earle	13,51
20	10	H	Southampton	W	2-1	3-1	Clarke 2, Conway	19,87
21	17	A	Everton	L	0-3	2-3	Clarke, Barrett	31,39
22	26	A	Leicester C	W	1-0	2-0	Callaghan, Barrett	26,93
23	27	H	Leicester C	W	2-2	4-2	Leggat 3, Haynes	25,17
24	31	H	Stoke C	W	2-1	4-1	Leggat 2, Clarke, (Skeels og)	24,85
25	Jan 7	A	Sheffield U	L	0-2	0-4		15,00
26	14	H	West Bromich A	D	0-1	2-2	Callaghan, Barrett	20,68
27	21	A	Leeds U	L	0-1	1-3	Barrett	32,01
28	Feb 4	H	Newcastle U	W	2-0	5-1	Clarke 3, Haynes, Earle	21,61
29	11	A	Tottenham H	L	2-2	2-4	Haynes, Clarke	43,96
30	25	H	Liverpool	D	1-0	2-2	Barrett, (Yeats og)	37,48
31	Mar 4	A	Chelsea	D	0-0	0-0		46,78
32	18	H	Sheffield W	L	0-0	1-2	Barrett	21,77
33	25	A	Southampton	L	1-1	2-4	Earle, Clarke	27,94
34	27	H	Manchester U	D	1-1	2-2	Clarke, Barrett	47,29
35	28	A	Manchester U	L	0-0	1-2	Earle	51,67
36	Apr 1	H	Sunderland	W	1-1	3-1	Clarke, Pearson, Earle	22,72
37	8	A	Aston Villa	D	1-1	1-1	Haynes	13,71
38	19	H	Arsenal	D	0-0	0-0		27,49
39	22	A	Manchester C	L	0-2	0-3		22,75
40	29	H	Blackpool	D	1-0	2-2	Clarke 2	14,86
41	May 6	A	Sunderland	L	0-2	1-3	Conway	18,60
42	13	H	Nottingham F	L	1-2	2-3	Clarke, Earle	20,41
								App
								Su
								Goal

FA Cup

3	Jan 28	A	Bradford	W	2-1	3-1	Clarke 2, Haynes	14,71
4	Feb 18	H	Sheffield U	D	0-0	1-1	Clarke	32,65
R	Mar 1	A	Sheffield U	L	0-2	1-3	Callaghan	33,27

League Cup

2	Sep 13	H	Crystal Palace	W	0-0	2-0	Leggat 2 (1pen)	9,90
3	Oct 5	H	Wolverhampton W	W	2-0	5-0	Clarke 2, Barrett, Earle, Conway	14,32
4	26	A	Blackpool	L	1-3	2-4	Callaghan, Parmenter	15,34

Match	McClelland	Cohen	Nichols	Robson	Dempsey	Brown	Earle	Leggat	Clarke	Pearson	Barrett	Haynes	Macedo	Callaghan	Conway	Drake	Parmenter	Seymour	Dyson	Pentecost	Cunningham	Ryan
1		2	3	4	5	6	7	8	9	10	11			S								
2		2	3	4	5	6	7	11	8	10	S	9										
3		2	3	4	5	6	7	11	8	10	S	9	1									
4		2	3	4	5	6	7	11	8	10	S	9	1									
5		2	3	6	5	4	7	11	8	10		9	1	S								
6		2	**3**	6	5	4	7	11	8	10	9		1	12								
7		2		4	5	6	7	11	8	10	9	S	1	3								
8		2		6	3	4	9	11	10	8	S	7	1	5								
9		2		6	3	4	9	11	10	8		7	1	5								
10		2		6	3	4	9	11	10	8	S	7	1	5								
11		2		4	3	8	9		10	S	11	7		5	6							
12		2		4	3	8	9	S	10		11	7		5	6							
13				4	3	8	9	6	10	12	11	**7**		5		2						
14		2	5	4	3	7	9		10	6	11			8			S					
15		2		4	3	6	9		10	S	11	7		5	8							
16		2		4	3	S			10	8	9	7	1	5	6		11					
17		2		4	3	8	7		10		9		1	5	6		11		S			
18		2		4	3	8	9		10		11	7	1	5	6		S					
19		2		4	3	8	9	S	10		11	7	1	5	6							
20		2		**4**	3	8	9	12	10		11	7	1	5	6							
21		2	5		3	8	9		10		11	7	1	4	6							
22		**2**		4	3	8	9	12	10		11	7	1	5	6							
23				4	3	8		9	10	S	11	7	1	5	6	2						
24				4	3	8	S	9	10		11	7	1	5	6	2						
25				4	3	8	9		10	S	11	7	1	5	6	2						
26				4	3	8	9		10		11	7	1	5	6	2					S	
27		2		4	3	8	9		10		11	7	1	5	6	S						
28		2		4	3	8	**9**		10	12	11	7	1	5	6							
29		2		4	3	8	9		10	S	11	7	1	5	6							
30		2		4	3	8	9		10	S	11	7		5	6							
31		2	S	4	3	5	9		10	8	11	7	1		6							
32		2	S	4	3	5	9		10	8	11	7	1		6							
33		2	S	4	3	6	9		10	8	11		1	5	7							
34		2		4	3	8	S		10	9	11	7	1	5	6							
35		2		4	3	8	12		10	**9**	11	7		5	6			1				
36		2		4	3	8	12		10	9	**11**	7	1	5	6							
37		2		4	3	8	11		10	9		7	1	5	6				S			
38		2		4	3	9	11		10	**8**		7	1	5	6				12			
39			2	4	3	8	9		10		11	7	1	5	6				S			
40			2	4	3		9		10		11	7	1	5	6	S				8		
41		2	S	4	3	8	9		10		11	7	1	5	6							
42		2	S	4	3	8	9		10		11	7	1	5	6							
A		35	10	41	42	40	35	13	42	21	33	36	33	34	30	5	2	1	-	1	-	-
S		-	-	-	-	-	2	2	-	2	-	-	-	1	-	-	-	-	1	-	-	-
G		1	-	-	-	-	12	8	24	2	8	6	-	3	3	-	1	-	-	-	-	-

Round	McClelland	Cohen	Nichols	Robson	Dempsey	Brown	Earle	Leggat	Clarke	Pearson	Barrett	Haynes	Macedo	Callaghan	Conway	Drake	Parmenter	Seymour	Dyson	Pentecost	Cunningham	Ryan
3		**2**		4	3	8	9		10	12	11	7	1	5	6							
4		2		4	3	8	9		10	S	11	7		5	6							
R		2		4	3	8	9		10	S	11	7	1	5	6							

Round	McClelland	Cohen	Nichols	Robson	Dempsey	Brown	Earle	Leggat	Clarke	Pearson	Barrett	Haynes	Macedo	Callaghan	Conway	Drake	Parmenter	Seymour	Dyson	Pentecost	Cunningham	Ryan
2		2		6	3	4	9	11		8	10	7	1	5	S							
3		2		4	3	8	9	S	10		11	7		5	6							
4		2	5	4	3	7			10	6	9			8			11					S

0 points v	Sheffield U, Nottingham F, Everton, Tottenham H	0 points
1 point v	Arsenal, Burnley, Chelsea, Leeds U, Manchester U, Sheffield W, West Bromwich A	7 points
2 points v	Liverpool, Manchester C, Southampton, Sunderland, West Ham U	10 points
3 points v	Aston Villa, Blackpool, Newcastle U	9 points
4 points v	Leicester C, Stoke C,	8 points

Former Busby Babe, Mark Pearson, was signed by manager Buckingham from his former club, Sheffield Wednesday.

1967-68

Division One

	P	W	D	L	F	A	Pts
Manchester City	42	26	6	10	86	43	58
Manchester United	42	24	8	10	89	55	56
Liverpool	42	22	11	9	71	40	55
Leeds United	42	22	9	11	71	41	53
Everton	42	23	6	13	67	40	52
Chelsea	42	18	12	12	62	68	48
Tottenham Hotspur	42	19	9	14	70	59	47
West Bromwich Albion	42	17	12	13	75	62	46
Arsenal	42	17	10	15	60	56	44
Newcastle United	42	13	15	14	54	67	41
Nottingham Forest	42	14	11	17	52	64	39
West Ham United	42	14	10	18	73	69	38
Leicester City	42	13	12	17	64	69	38
Burnley	42	14	10	18	64	71	38
Sunderland	42	13	11	18	51	61	37
Southampton	42	13	11	18	66	83	37
Wolverhampton W	42	14	8	20	66	75	36
Stoke City	42	14	7	21	50	73	35
Sheffield Wednesday	42	11	12	19	51	63	34
Coventry City	42	9	15	18	51	71	33
Sheffield United	42	11	10	21	49	70	32
Fulham	42	10	7	25	56	98	27

Manager: Vic Buckingham / Bobby Robson

Did you know that?

In the 1968 close season, Fulham received their first six figure transfer fee when Bobby Robson sold Allan Clarke to Leicester City.

14	Gilroy debut
16	S Brown's 200th game
23	Pearson finale
26	Matthewson debut
26	Haynes' 150th goal
26	Clarke's 50th goal
40	Nichols finale
41	Clarke and Macedo finales
42	Mealand finale

No		Date	V	Opponents	R	H-T	F-T	Scorers	Atte
1	A	19	H	Wolverhampton W	L	0-1	1-2	Nichols	27,87
2		23	A	Sunderland	L	0-1	0-3		30,06
3		26	A	Chelsea	D	0-1	1-1	Brown	38,40
4		28	H	Sunderland	W	1-0	3-2	Barrett 2, Haynes	19,59
5	S	2	A	Leeds U	L	0-2	0-2		27,76
6		6	A	Sheffield W	L	1-0	2-4	Clarke 2	26,33
7		9	H	Everton	W	0-0	2-1	Moss, Barrett	25,36
8		16	A	Leicester C	W	1-0	2-1	Clarke, Haynes	16,44
9		23	H	West Ham U	L	0-2	0-3		29,23
10		30	A	Burnley	L	0-0	0-2		14,22
11	O	7	H	West Bromich A	L	0-1	1-2	Clarke	17,31
12		14	A	Newcastle U	L	1-0	1-2	Clarke	27,66
13		21	H	Manchester C	L	0-0	2-4	Earle, Conway	22,10
14		28	A	Arsenal	L	2-3	3-5	Dempsey, Conway, Clarke	29,97
15	N	11	A	Coventry C	W	2-0	3-0	Clarke 2, Gilroy	31,31
16		18	H	Nottingham F	W	1-0	2-0	Clarke 2	22,41
17		25	A	Stoke C	W	0-0	1-0	Haynes	19,34
18	D	2	H	Liverpool	D	0-0	1-1	Clarke	29,33
19		16	A	Wolverhampton W	L	1-2	2-3	Gilroy, Moss	25,95
20		23	H	Chelsea	D	1-2	2-2	Gilroy, Moss	33,49
21		26	A	Tottenham H	D	1-2	2-2	Gilroy, Pearson	34,77
22		30	H	Tottenham H	L	1-1	1-2	Barrett	30,05
23	J	6	H	Leeds U	L	0-3	0-5		24,41
24		20	H	Leicester C	L	0-0	0-1		16,60
25	F	3	A	West Ham U	L	1-3	2-7	Clarke, Earle	32,23
26		10	H	Burnley	W	1-0	4-3	Clarke 2, Earle, Haynes	15,31
27		24	A	West Bromich A	L	0-2	1-2	Barrett	18,50
28		28	H	Sheffield W	W	0-0	2-0	Clarke, Earle	15,39
29	M	8	A	Southampton	L	0-1	1-2	Haynes	29,05
30		13	H	Sheffield U	L	0-0	0-1		15,38
31		16	A	Manchester C	L	1-2	1-5	Clarke	30,77
32		23	H	Arsenal	L	0-0	1-3	Barrett	20,61
33	A	6	H	Coventry C	D	0-0	1-1	Earle	20,86
34		12	H	Manchester U	L	0-3	0-4		40,15
35		13	A	Nottingham F	D	1-2	2-2	Barrett, Clarke	20,63
36		15	A	Manchester U	L	0-2	0-3		60,46
37		20	H	Newcastle U	W	2-0	2-0	Clarke 2	14,67
38		23	A	Sheffield U	W	0-1	3-2	Barrett, Gilroy, Conway	20,64
39		27	A	Liverpool	L	1-2	1-4	Clarke	32,42
40	M	1	H	Stoke C	L	0-1	0-2		14,64
41		4	H	Southampton	D	1-0	2-2	Gilroy 2	13,45
42		21	A	Everton	L	1-3	1-5	Conway	38,33
									App
									Su
									Goa

FA Cup

3	J	27	H	Macclesfield T	W	1-2	4-2	Clarke 2, Gilroy, Haynes	23,67
4	F	17	H	Portsmouth	D	0-0	0-0		39,38
R		21	A	Portsmouth	L	0-1	0-1		43,96

League Cup

2	S	13	H	Tranmere R	W	0-0	1-0	Barrett	10,17
3	O	11	A	Workington	D	1-0	2-2	Haynes, Earle	11,35
R		16	H	Workington	W	2-1	6-2	Clarke 4, Callaghan, Barrett	8,61
4	N	1	H	Manchester C	W	2-0	3-2	Earle 2, Clarke	11,73
5		29	H	Huddersfield T	D	0-1	1-1	Gilroy	20,30
R	D	12	A	Huddersfield T	L	1-0	1-2	Gilroy	23,57

Macedo	Cohen	Dempsey	Brown	Nichols	Conway	Haynes	Callaghan	Barrett	Earle	Parmenter	Seymour	Pearson	Clarke	Ryan	Moss	O'Connor	McClelland	Mealand	Gilroy	Cunningham	Drake	Matthewson	Byrne	Salvage	Mullen	Pentecost	Murray	Kerrigan	Dyson	
1	2	3	4	5	6	7	8	9	10	11		S																		1
	2	3	4	5	6	10		8		11	1	7	9	S																2
	2	3	4	5	6	7		9		11	1	8	10							S										3
	2	3	4	5	6	7		9		11	1	8	10	S																4
	2	3	4	5	6			8		11	1	7	9	10												S				5
	2	3	7	S	6		5	11			1		10	4	8	9														6
	2	3	7		6		5	11	9		1		10	4	8	S														7
	2	3	7		6	10	5	11					9	4	8		1									S				8
	2	3	7		6	10	5	11	12				9	4	8		1													9
		3	7		6	10	5	11			1		9	4	8			2								S				10
	2	3	7		6	10	5	11	8		1		9	4				S												11
	2	3	7		6	10	8	11			1		9	4	S			5												12
		3	7		6	10	5	11	8		1	S	9	4				2												13
	2	3	7		6	10	5	11			1		9	4					8					S						14
1	2	3	4		6	7	5		**8**	11		12	9						10											15
1	2	3	4		6	7	5	11	8	S			9						10											16
1	2	3	4		6	7	5	11	8	S			9						10											17
1	**2**	3	4		6	7	5	10	8	11		12	9																	18
1		3	4		2	7	5	11	9			6			8				10										S	19
1		3	4		2	**7**	5	11				6	9	12	8				10											20
1		3	4		2	7	5	11	8			6	9		S				10											21
1		3	4		2	**7**	5	11	8			6	9		12				10											22
1		**3**	4		2	7	5	11	8			6	9	12					10											23
1	**2**	3	7		6		5	10	8	11				4					9	12										24
1		3	4		6	7		11	8	S			9	5					10		2									25
1		3	2		6	7	5	11	8				10	12					**9**			4								26
1		3	2	5	6	7	8	11	10				9	S								4								27
		3	2	5	6	7	8	11	9		1		10	S								4								28
		3	2	**5**	6	7	8	11	9		1			12	10							4								29
		3	2	5	6	7	8	11	9		1		10									4						S		30
		3	2	5	6	7	8	11	9		1		10									4						S		31
		3	2		6	7	5	11	8				10	S			1					4	9							32
1		3	6		2	7	5	10	8					S								4	9	11						33
1		3	7		2	6	5	10					8	4				S					9	11						34
1		3	7		2	6	5	10					8	4				12					**9**	11						35
		3	6	12	7		**5**	10	9		1		8	4				2	11											36
		3	7		2	6	5	11	8				9	4			1		**10**						12					37
			6	2	7		4	11	8				9	3			1	5	10									S		38
			6	2	7	8	4	11	9				10	3			1	5	S											39
			4	**2**	7	8	6	11					9	3			1	5	10				12							40
1			4		7	S		8					10	3					9			5		11		2	6			41
		3	7		8												1	**5**	9			4		11	12	2	6	10		42
8	17	38	42	13	42	34	35	40	26	8	16	9	36	20	8	1	8	8	18	-	1	10	4	5	-	2	2	1		A
-	-	-	-	1	-	-	-	-	1	-	-	2	-	4	1	-	-	1	-	1	-	-	1	-	2	-	-	-		S
-	-	1	1	1	4	5	-	8	5	-	-	1	20	-	3	-	-	-	7	-	-	-	-	-	-	-	-	-		G

Macedo	Cohen	Dempsey	Brown	Nichols	Conway	Haynes	Callaghan	Barrett	Earle	Parmenter	Seymour	Pearson	Clarke	Ryan	Moss	O'Connor	McClelland	Mealand	Gilroy	
1		3	4		6	7	**5**	11	8	12			9	2					10	3
1		3	10	2	7	6	5	11	8	S			9	4						4
1		3	2	12	6	7	5	11	8				10	4					**9**	R

Macedo	Cohen	Dempsey	Brown	Nichols	Conway	Haynes	Callaghan	Barrett	Earle	Parmenter	Seymour	Pearson	Clarke	Ryan	Moss	O'Connor	McClelland	Mealand	Gilroy	Cunningham	
	2	3	7		6		5	11	9				10	4	8		1			S	2
	2	3	7		6	10	5	11	8		1		9	4				S			3
	2	3	7		6	10	8	11			1		9	4	S			5			R
1	2	3	4		6	10	5	11	8			7	9	S							4
1	2	3	4		6	7	5	11	8				9	S					10		5
1		3	4		2	7	5	11	8	S		6	9						10		R

0 points v	Arsenal, Leeds U, Manchester C, Manchester U, West Bromwich A, West Ham U, Wolves	0 points
1 point v	Liverpool, Southampton, Tottenham H	3 points
2 points v	Burnley, Chelsea, Everton, Leicester C, Newcastle U, Sheffield U, Sheffield W, Stoke C, Sunderland	18 points
3 points v	Coventry C, Nottingham F	6 points
4 points v		0 points

Dempsey and Pearson under starters orders.

1968-69

Division Two

	P	W	D	L	F	A	Pts
Derby County	42	26	11	5	65	32	63
Crystal Palace	42	22	12	8	70	47	56
Charlton Athletic	42	18	14	10	61	52	50
Middlesbrough	42	19	11	12	58	49	49
Cardiff City	42	20	7	15	67	54	47
Huddersfield Town	42	17	12	13	53	46	46
Birmingham City	42	18	8	16	73	59	44
Blackpool	42	14	15	13	51	41	43
Sheffield United	42	16	11	15	61	50	43
Millwall	42	17	9	16	57	49	43
Hull City	42	13	16	13	59	52	42
Carlisle United	42	16	10	16	46	49	42
Norwich City	42	15	10	17	53	56	40
Preston North End	42	12	15	15	38	44	39
Portsmouth	42	12	14	16	58	58	38
Bristol City	42	11	16	15	46	53	38
Bolton Wanderers	42	12	14	16	55	67	38
Aston Villa	42	12	14	16	37	48	38
Blackburn Rovers	42	13	11	18	52	63	37
Oxford United	42	12	9	21	34	55	33
Bury	42	11	8	23	51	80	30
Fulham	42	7	11	24	40	81	25

Manager: Bobby Robson / Bill Dodgin

Did you know that?

Fulham went from the third minute of the match against Aston Villa on 17th August to the 13th minute of the game at home to Palace on 13th September, a total of 660 minutes, without scoring a goal.

4	Haynes' 600th game
10	Gilroy finale
17	Halom debut
27	Dempsey finale
28	Lloyd debut
30	Horne debut
31	Cohen and Ryan finales
41	Moreline debut
42	McClelland finale

No		Date	V	Opponents	R	H-T	F-T	Scorers	Atten
1	A	10	H	Bristol C	W	1-0	1-0	Gilroy	16,57
2		17	A	Aston Villa	D	1-0	1-1	Conway	21,45
3		21	H	Hull C	D	0-0	0-0		15,07
4		24	H	Bolton W	L	0-1	0-2		12,83
5		27	A	Sheffield U	L	0-1	0-1		17,93
6		31	A	Millwall	L	0-0	0-2		18,37
7	S	7	A	Oxford U	L	0-1	0-1		13,75
8		13	H	Crystal Palace	W	1-0	1-0	Macdonald	23,13
9		18	A	Derby C	L	0-1	0-1		26,77
10		21	A	Blackpool	D	1-1	2-2	Conway 2	15,76
11		28	H	Blackburn R	D	0-0	1-1	Macdonald	12,96
12	O	5	A	Birmingham C	L	0-3	4-5	Macdonald, Large 2, (Robinson og)	27,51
13		9	H	Sheffield U	D	1-1	2-2	Macdonald, Kerrigan	12,79
14		12	H	Norwich C	L	0-1	1-3	Macdonald	17,74
15		19	A	Middlesbrough	L	0-2	0-2		23,23
16		26	H	Bury	D	0-0	0-0		11,41
17	N	9	H	Portsmouth	D	0-0	2-2	Callaghan, Dempsey	14,60
18		16	A	Carlisle U	L	0-1	0-2		9,64
19		23	H	Huddersfield T	W	2-1	4-3	Halom, Jones, Byrne, Conway	11,39
20		25	A	Preston NE	D	0-0	0-0		11,72
21		30	A	Charlton A	L	1-4	3-5	Halom, Byrne, Ryan	17,27
22	D	7	H	Cardiff C	L	1-2	1-5	Barrett	13,19
23		14	A	Norwich C	L	0-0	0-2		13,02
24		21	H	Middlesbrough	L	0-0	0-3		13,33
25		26	H	Birmingham C	W	2-0	2-0	Callaghan, Halom	13,19
26		28	A	Bury	L	0-1	1-5	Jones	8,83
27	J	18	A	Portsmouth	L	1-2	1-3	Haynes	20,52
28	F	1	H	Carlisle U	L	0-0	0-2		12,86
29		15	H	Charlton A	L	0-0	0-1		14,92
30		19	H	Preston NE	W	1-1	2-1	Lloyd 2	11,72
31	M	1	A	Bristol C	L	0-4	0-6		15,34
32		8	H	Aston Villa	D	0-1	1-1	Dear	15,50
33		15	A	Bolton W	L	2-3	2-3	Dear, Lloyd	8,42
34		22	H	Millwall	W	1-0	2-0	Barrett, Conway	15,56
35		24	A	Cardiff C	W	2-0	2-0	Dear 2	20,74
36		29	H	Oxford U	L	0-1	0-1		14,85
37	A	2	H	Derby C	L	0-0	0-1		18,17
38		5	A	Blackburn R	D	1-0	2-2	Dear 2	7,86
39		7	A	Hull C	L	0-3	0-4		10,85
40		12	H	Blackpool	D	0-0	0-0		7,15
41		15	A	Huddersfield T	L	0-0	0-3		5,83
42		19	A	Crystal Palace	L	2-0	2-3	Dear, Large	36,52
									App
									Su
									Goal

FA Cup

No		Date	V	Opponents	R	H-T	F-T	Scorers	Atten
3	J	4	A	Sunderland	W	4-1	4-1	Mullen 2, Brown, Haynes	27,09
4		25	H	West Bromich A	L	1-1	1-2	Brown	31,20

League Cup

No		Date	V	Opponents	R	H-T	F-T	Scorers	Atten
2	S	3	A	Orient	L	0-1	0-1		12,90

Seymour	Ryan	Dempsey	Matthewson	Callaghan	Brown	Haynes	Conway	Large	Gilroy	Barrett	Pentecost	Kerrigan	Salvage	Macdonald	McClelland	Byrne	Jones	Halom	Murray	Earle	Parmenter	Williamson	Cohen	Mullen	Lloyd	Horne	Tranter	Dear	Roberts	Moreline	
	2	3	4	5	6	**7**	8	9	10	11	12																				1
	2	3	4	5	6	7	8	9	10	11		S																			2
	2	3	4	5	6	7	8	9	10	11									S												3
	2	3	4	5	6	7	8	9	**10**	11		12																			4
	5	3	4	7	6	8		9		10	**2**		11	12																	5
	2	3	4	5	6	7	8	**9**		10		12	11																		6
		3	4	5	6	7	8	9		11	2	S		10																	7
		3	4	5	6	7	8	9	12	11	2			**10**																	8
	S	3	4	5	6	7	8	9		11	2			10																	9
	2	3	4	5	**6**	7	8	9	10	11				12	1																10
	S	3	4	5	6	7	8	9		11	2			10	1																11
	5	3	4	**7**	6			9		11	2	8		10	1									S							12
		3	4	5	6	7		9		11	2	8		10										S							13
		3	4	5	6	7				10	2	**8**		9		12	11														14
	5	3	**4**	6	12		7	9		11	2			10			8														15
	5	3		6	4	10	7	**9**		11	2			12			8														16
	5	3		6	4		7	9		11	2			S	1		8	10													17
	5	3		6	4	8	7				2			S		9	11	10													18
	5	3		6	4	8	7				2					9	**11**	10	12												19
	5	3		6	4	8	7				2					9		10	S	11											20
	5	3		6	4	8	2	12								9		10		7	**11**										21
	5	3		6	4	8	7			11	2					9		10	S												22
		3	4	5		8	7	12		11	**2**				1	9		6		10											23
		3	4	5		8	7	12						11		**9**		6		10		1	2								24
	2	5	6	3	4	10	7	S									11	8		9		1									25
	2	5	6	3	4	**10**	7									12	11	8		9		1									26
		5	6	3	11	10		4		7								S		9		1	2	8							27
			6	3	4	**10**	12	5						9			11			7		1	2		8						28
	3		5	6	4	10	11	12								9				7		1	2		**8**						29
	3		5		11	10											7			S		1	2		8	4	6	9			30
	3		**5**		11	10											7			12		1	2		8	6	4	9			31
				3	10		2												6	7		1		11	8	4	S	9	5		32
				3	10		2			11							7		**6**			1			8	4	12	9	5		33
				3	10		6			7					1		11			S					8	4	2	9	5		34
				3	10		6			7					1		11			12					8	4	2	**9**	5		35
				3	10		6			7					1		11			S					8	4	2	9	5		36
				3	10		6			11					1					7				S	8	4	2	9	5		37
				3	10		6			11					1					7				S	8	4	2	9	5		38
				3	S		10			11					1	6				7					8	4	2	9	5		39
				3			10			7					1	6	11			S					8	4	2	9	5		40
				3			10			7					1	6	11								8	4	S	9	5	2	41
				3			11	9		S					1	6	7								8	4		10	5	2	42
8	21	27	24	40	35	28	34	19	5	29	16	3	2	10	14	12	18	10	2	13	1	10	6	2	15	13	9	13	11	2	A
	-	-	-	-	1	-	1	4	1	-	1	2	-	3	-	2	-	-	1	2	-	-	-	-	-	-	1	-	-	-	S
-	1	1	-	2	-	1	5	3	1	2	-	1	-	5	-	2	2	3	-	-	-	-	-	-	3	-	-	7	-	-	G

Seymour	Ryan	Dempsey	Matthewson	Callaghan	Brown	Haynes	Conway	Large	Gilroy	Barrett	Pentecost	Kerrigan	Salvage	Macdonald	McClelland	Byrne	Jones	Halom	Murray	Earle	Parmenter	Williamson	Cohen	Mullen	Lloyd	Horne	Tranter	Dear	Roberts	Moreline	
	2		6	3	4	10		5		7							S?		S?	9	11	1		8							3
			4	3	11	10	8	5		7								6		9		1	2	S							4

Seymour	Ryan	Dempsey	Matthewson	Callaghan	Brown	Haynes	Conway	Large	Gilroy	Barrett	Pentecost	Kerrigan	Salvage	Macdonald	McClelland	Byrne	Jones	Halom	Murray	Earle	Parmenter	Williamson	Cohen	Mullen	Lloyd	Horne	Tranter	Dear	Roberts	Moreline	
	2	3	4	5	6	7	8	9		11		10	S																		2

0 points v	Bolton W, Carlisle U, Charlton A, Derby C, Middlesbrough, Norwich C, Oxford U	0 points
1 point v	Bury, Hull C, Portsmouth, Sheffield U	4 points
2 points v	Aston Villa, Birmingham C, Blackburn R, Blackpool, Bristol C, Cardiff C, Crystal Palace, Huddersfield T, Millwall	18 points
3 points v	Preston NE	3 points
4 points v		0 points

Manager Bill Dodgin's three new signings (l-r) Wilf Tranter, Brian Dear and Stan Horne.

1969-70

Division Three

	P	W	D	L	F	A	Pts
Orient	46	25	12	9	67	36	62
Luton Town	46	23	14	9	77	43	60
Bristol Rovers	46	20	16	10	80	59	56
Fulham	46	20	15	11	81	55	55
Brighton & Hove Albion	46	23	9	14	57	43	55
Mansfield Town	46	21	11	14	70	49	53
Barnsley	46	19	15	12	68	59	53
Reading	46	21	11	14	87	77	53
Rochdale	46	18	10	18	69	60	46
Bradford City	46	17	12	17	57	50	46
Doncaster Rovers	46	17	12	17	52	54	46
Walsall	46	17	12	17	54	67	46
Torquay United	46	14	17	15	62	59	45
Rotherham United	46	15	14	17	62	54	44
Shrewsbury Town	46	13	18	15	62	63	44
Tranmere Rovers	46	14	16	16	56	72	44
Plymouth Argyle	46	16	11	19	56	64	43
Halifax Town	46	14	15	17	47	63	43
Bury	46	15	11	20	75	80	41
Gillingham	46	13	13	20	52	64	39
Bournemouth	46	12	15	19	48	71	39
Southport	46	14	10	22	48	66	38
Barrow	46	8	14	24	46	81	30
Stockport County	46	6	11	29	27	71	23

Manager: Bill Dodgin

Did you know that?

There was a family reunion when Fulham, managed by Bill Dodgin junior, played Bristol Rovers, managed by his father Bill, himself a former Fulham manager (in the 1950s). Honours were even, with both sides winning on their own grounds.

5 Richardson debut
11 Earle's 50th goal
21 Webster debut
27 Haynes finale
29 S Brown's 300th game

No		Date	V	Opponents	R	H-T	F-T	Scorers	Atte
1	A	9	H	Bradford C	D	0-0	0-0		9,94
2		16	A	Bury	L	0-1	0-1		5,64
3		23	H	Gillingham	W	1-1	2-1	Haynes, Conway (pen)	8,64
4		27	H	Southport	W	1-0	3-2	Conway 2 (1 pen), Brown	9,14
5		30	A	Barrow	L	0-2	1-3	Richardson	5,66
6	S	6	H	Shrewsbury T	W	1-0	3-1	Conway 2 (1 pen), Barrett	8,99
7		13	A	Bristol R	L	2-1	2-3	Conway, Earle	10,63
8		16	A	Halifax T	W	4-0	8-0	Earle 5, Conway 2 (1 pen), Lloyd	5,80
9		20	H	Plymouth A	W	2-1	4-3	Conway 2, Lloyd, Haynes	12,84
10		27	A	Stockport C	W	2-0	4-1	Earle 3, Conway	4,23
11		29	A	Orient	L	1-1	1-3	Earle	18,86
12	O	4	H	Doncaster R	D	0-1	1-1	Brown	13,53
13		8	H	Bury	L	1-2	2-4	Conway, Lloyd	11,72
14		11	A	Bournemouth	D	1-1	2-2	Conway, Earle	8,42
15		18	A	Rotherham U	D	0-0	0-0		7,69
16		25	H	Barnsley	D	0-0	0-0		10,51
17	N	1	A	Brighton & HA	L	1-1	1-2	Haynes	17,76
18		8	H	Torquay U	D	0-1	1-1	Earle	10,00
19		22	H	Mansfield T	D	0-1	1-1	Conway	8,03
20		25	A	Luton T	L	0-0	0-1		16,48
21	D	13	H	Bristol R	W	1-0	3-1	Richardson 2, Earle	6,74
22		20	A	Shrewsbury T	D	0-0	1-1	Earle	3,84
23		26	A	Gillingham	L	0-2	0-2		8,26
24		27	H	Barrow	W	1-0	2-1	Richardson, Lloyd	9,55
25	J	2	H	Orient	D	0-0	1-1	Conway	12,30
26		10	A	Plymouth A	L	0-1	0-2		9,66
27		17	H	Stockport C	D	1-1	1-1	Richardson	7,43
28		27	A	Walsall	W	2-1	3-1	Lloyd, Halom, Earle	6,25
29		31	A	Doncaster R	W	0-0	1-0	Conway	8,18
30	F	6	H	Bournemouth	D	0-1	1-1	Earle	9,71
31		14	A	Bradford C	D	0-0	0-0		9,61
32		21	A	Barnsley	D	1-0	3-3	Conway, Earle, Gilchrist	9,67
33		28	H	Rotherham U	W	2-0	3-2	Halom, Lloyd, Barrett	8,14
34	M	14	H	Rochdale	W	2-0	2-0	Halom 2	6,70
35		18	H	Walsall	W	2-0	4-0	Earle 2, Halom, Brown	7,30
36		21	A	Reading	W	3-0	4-0	Halom 2, Barrett, Earle	16,43
37		27	A	Torquay U	D	1-0	1-1	Barrett	7,93
38		28	H	Tranmere R	D	0-0	1-1	Barrett	10,31
39		30	H	Brighton & HA	W	3-0	4-1	Barrett, Callaghan, Halom, Conway (pen)	17,93
40	A	3	A	Southport	W	1-0	2-0	Barrett, Conway	3,43
41		6	A	Mansfield T	W	0-2	3-2	Conway, Halom, Lloyd	10,32
42		8	H	Luton T	L	0-1	0-1		18,98
43		15	H	Halifax T	W	0-1	2-1	Conway, Halom	7,07
44		18	A	Rochdale	W	1-0	1-0	Halom	5,07
45		20	H	Reading	W	1-0	2-1	Earle 2	9,71
46		27	A	Tranmere R	L	0-0	0-1		5,66
									App
									Su
									Goa

FA Cup

No		Date	V	Opponents	R	H-T	F-T	Scorers	Atte
1	N	15	A	Exeter C	L	0-0	0-2		9,18

League Cup

No		Date	V	Opponents	R	H-T	F-T	Scorers	Atte
1	A	13	A	Orient	D	0-0	0-0		8,67
R		18	H	Orient	W	1-0	3-1	Conway 2 (1 pen), Earle	11,42
2	S	3	H	Leeds U	L	0-1	0-1		20,44

Seymour	Gilchrist	Callaghan	Horne	Roberts	Matthewson	Conway	Lloyd	Halom	Haynes	Jones	Brown	Large	Pentecost	Earle	Barrett	Williamson	Richardson	O'Leary	Tranter	Webster	Moreline	
1	2	3	4	5	6	7	**8**	9	10	11	12											1
1	2	3	4	5		7	12	9	10	**11**	6	8										2
1	2		4	5	6	7	S		10		8		3	9	11							3
	2	6	4	5		7	12		10		8		3	**9**	11	1						4
	2	6	4	5		7	S		10		9		3		11	1	8					5
1	2		4	5	6	**7**			**10**	8	12		3	9	11							6
1	2		4		5	7	8		**10**		3			9	11		6	12				7
1		3	4	12	5	7	8		**10**		2			9	11		6					8
1		3	4		5	7	8	S	10		2			9	11		6					9
1		3	4	5		7	8		**10**		2		12	9	11		6					10
1		3	4	S		7	8		10		6		2	9	11		5					11
1		3	4		5	7	8		10		2		12	**9**	11		6					12
1	S	3		5		7	8	9	10		4		2		11		6					13
1	2	6	S		5	7			10	8	3			9	11		4					14
1	2	6			5	7	8		10	S	3			9	11		4					15
1	2	6			5	7	8		10	9	3				11		4		S			16
1	2	6	S		5	7	8		10		3			9	11		4					17
1	2	3	6		5	7			10	S	8			9	11		4					18
1	2	3	6		5	7			10		8			9	11		4		S			19
1		6	4		5	7	S		10		3			9	11		8		2			20
	2	6	4		5	7			10	12	3			**9**	11		8			1		21
	2	3	4		5	7			10	12	6			**9**	11		8			1		22
	2	6	**4**		5	7			10		3			9	11		8		12	1		23
	2	6			5	7	12		10		3			9	11		**8**		4	1		24
	2	6	4		5	7	**8**	12	10		3			9	11					1		25
	2	**6**	4			7	12	8	10		3			9	11		5			1		26
	2		4	5	6	7	S		10		3			9	11		8			1		27
	S		4		6	7	10	8			3		2	9	11		5			1		28
	12		4		6	7	10	8			3		2	9	**11**		5			1		29
	12	6	4		5	**7**	10	8			3		2	9	11					1		30
	S		4		5	7	10	8			3		2	9	11		6			1		31
	12		4		5	7	**8**	10			3		2	9	11		6			1		32
	S		4		5	7	8	10			3		2	9	11		6			1		33
		S	4		5	7	10	8			3		2	9	11		6			1		34
			4		**5**	7	10	8			3		2	9	11		6			1	12	35
		S			5	7	10	8			4		2	9	11		6			1	3	36
			S		5	7	10	8			3		2	9	11		6			1	4	37
		12			5	7	10	8			4		2	9	11		**6**			1	3	38
		10	S		5	7		8			4		2	9	11				6	1	3	39
		6			5	7	10	8			4		2	9	11				S	1	3	40
		3			5	7	10	8			4		2	9	11				S	1	6	41
		3			5	7	10	8			4		2	9	11				S	1	6	42
			S		5	7	10	8			4		2	9	11				3	1	6	43
			S		5	7	10	8			4		2	9	11				3	1	6	44
			S		5	7	10	8			4		2	9	11				3	1	6	45
					5	7	10	8			4		2	9	11		S		3	1	6	46
8	20	28	29	9	39	46	30	23	27	5	44	1	25	41	44	2	31	-	7	26	11	A
-	3	1	-	1	-	-	4	1	-	2	2	-	2	-	-	-	-	1	1	-	1	S
-	1	1	-	-	-	21	7	11	3	-	3	-	-	22	7	-	5	-	-	-	-	G

Seymour	Gilchrist	Callaghan	Horne	Roberts	Matthewson	Conway	Lloyd	Halom	Haynes	Jones	Brown	Large	Pentecost	Earle	Barrett	Williamson	Richardson	O'Leary	Tranter	Webster	Moreline	
1	**2**	3	6		5	7			10		8			9	11		4		12			1

Seymour	Gilchrist	Callaghan	Horne	Roberts	Matthewson	Conway	Lloyd	Halom	Haynes	Jones	Brown	Large	Pentecost	Earle	Barrett	Williamson	Richardson	O'Leary	Tranter	Webster	Moreline	
1	2	3	4	5		7	S	9	10	11	6	8										1
1	2	6	4	5		7	12		**10**		8		3	9	11							R
1	2		4	5	6	7	12		10		**8**		3	9	11							2

0 points v	Bury, Luton T	0 points
1 point v	Orient, Tranmere R	2 points
2 points v	Barnsley, Barrow, Bournemouth, Bradford C, Brighton & HA, Bristol R, Gillingham, Plymouth A, Torquay U	18 points
3 points v	Doncaster R, Mansfield T, Rotherham U, Shrewsbury T, Stockport C	15 points
4 points v	Halifax T, Reading, Rochdale, Southport, Walsall	20 points

Goalkeeper Malcom Webster arrived from Arsenal in December 1969.

1970-71

Division Three

	P	W	D	L	F	A	Pts
Preston North End	46	22	17	7	63	39	61
Fulham	46	24	12	10	68	41	60
Halifax Town	46	22	12	12	74	55	56
Aston Villa	46	19	15	12	54	46	53
Chesterfield	46	17	17	12	66	38	51
Bristol Rovers	46	19	13	14	69	50	51
Mansfield Town	46	18	15	13	64	62	51
Rotherham United	46	17	16	13	64	60	50
Wrexham	46	18	13	15	72	65	49
Torquay United	46	19	11	16	54	57	49
Swansea City	46	15	16	15	59	56	46
Barnsley	46	17	11	18	49	52	45
Shrewsbury Town	46	16	13	17	58	62	45
Brighton & Hove Albion	46	14	16	16	50	47	44
Plymouth Argyle	46	12	19	15	63	63	43
Rochdale	46	14	15	17	61	68	43
Port Vale	46	15	12	19	52	59	42
Tranmere Rovers	46	10	22	14	45	55	42
Bradford City	46	13	14	19	49	62	40
Walsall	46	14	11	21	51	57	39
Reading	46	14	11	21	48	85	39
Bury	46	12	13	21	52	60	37
Doncaster Rovers	46	13	9	24	45	66	35
Gillingham	46	10	13	23	42	67	33

Manager: Bill Dodgin

Did you know that?

Liverpool-born winger Alan Mansley became Fulham's first loan player following the introduction on the modern arrangements. He played just one game in December 1970 before returning to Brentford.

1 Dunne debut
8 Callaghan's 200th game
17 Barrett's 200th game
22 Seymour finale
28 Earle's 200th game
41 Barrett's 50th goal
44 Conway's 200th game

No		Date	V	Opponents	R	H-T	F-T	Scorers	Atten
1	A	15	A	Barnsley	W	0-0	1-0	Barrett	8,80
2		22	H	Swansea C	W	2-1	4-1	Earle 2, Halom, Dunne	10,38
3		29	A	Walsall	L	2-2	2-3	Halom, Lloyd	6,17
4	S	2	H	Bradford C	W	2-0	5-0	Halom, Earle, Lloyd, Conway, Barrett	10,32
5		5	H	Chesterfield	W	1-0	2-0	Earle, Lloyd	13,17
6		12	A	Rochdale	W	1-1	2-1	Barrett, Conway	4,79
7		19	H	Doncaster R	D	1-0	1-1	Conway	13,64
8		23	H	Brighton & HA	W	0-0	1-0	Lloyd	13,85
9		26	A	Preston NE	D	0-0	1-1	Dunne	12,10
10		28	H	Tranmere R	W	2-0	2-0	Halom, Brown	10,96
11	O	3	H	Plymouth A	D	0-0	1-1	Earle	13,33
12		10	A	Shrewsbury T	W	1-0	1-0	Barrett	6,41
13		17	H	Barnsley	D	0-1	1-1	Lloyd	12,95
14		21	A	Reading	D	0-0	1-1	Halom	14,16
15		24	H	Halifax T	W	2-0	3-1	Lloyd, Morton, Earle	10,74
16		31	A	Torquay U	L	0-0	1-3	Johnston	7,59
17	N	7	H	Bury	W	1-0	2-1	Lloyd, Barrett	9,39
18		9	A	Port Vale	W	1-0	1-0	Lloyd	8,29
19		14	A	Rotherham U	D	0-1	1-1	Johnston	9,39
20		28	H	Aston Villa	L	0-0	0-2		16,02
21	D	5	A	Mansfield T	L	0-1	0-1		8,05
22		19	A	Swansea C	L	0-2	1-4	Johnston	10,62
23		28	H	Gillingham	W	1-0	1-0	Halom	7,07
24	J	2	A	Wrexham	D	2-0	2-2	Barrett, (Ingle og)	9,71
25		8	A	Tranmere R	W	3-0	3-0	Barrett 2, Halom	4,61
26		16	H	Reading	D	0-1	1-1	Earle	10,14
27		30	A	Aston Villa	L	0-0	0-1		33,34
28	F	6	H	Mansfield T	D	0-0	0-0		9,37
29		13	A	Bristol R	W	0-0	1-0	Conway	18,87
30		20	H	Port Vale	W	2-1	4-1	Barrett 2, Earle 2	10,38
31		26	H	Torquay U	W	2-0	4-0	Barrett 2, Conway, Matthewson	13,01
32	M	2	H	Bristol R	W	0-0	2-1	Johnston, Earle	15,87
33		6	A	Halifax T	L	1-0	1-2	Johnston	8,01
34		10	A	Brighton & HA	L	2-2	2-3	Conway, Johnston	14,41
35		13	H	Rotherham U	W	0-0	1-0	Earle	9,62
36		17	H	Wrexham	W	0-0	1-0	Barrett	8,85
37		20	A	Bury	L	0-1	0-2		4,12
38		26	A	Chesterfield	D	0-0	0-0		13,37
39	A	3	H	Walsall	W	0-0	1-0	Barrett	8,42
40		7	H	Rochdale	W	0-0	2-0	Earle, Conway (pen)	10,05
41		10	A	Gillingham	W	0-1	3-1	Barrett, Johnston, Conway	9,36
42		12	A	Plymouth A	D	1-0	1-1	Halom	11,71
43		17	H	Shrewsbury T	D	0-0	0-0		12,70
44		24	A	Doncaster R	W	0-0	1-0	Earle	4,39
45		28	A	Bradford C	W	1-1	3-2	Johnston 2, Lloyd	6,43
46	M	1	H	Preston NE	L	0-1	0-1		25,77
									App
									Su
									Goal

FA Cup

1	N	21	H	Bristol R	L	0-0	1-2	Johnston	13,92

League Cup

1	A	19	H	Orient	W	0-0	1-0	Conway	10,97
2	S	9	A	Darlington	W	2-0	4-0	Barrett 2, Halom, Conway (pen)	9,32
3	O	6	H	Queen's Park R	W	1-0	2-0	Barrett, Halom	31,72
4		27	H	Swindon T	W	1-0	1-0	Earle	22,57
5	N	17	H	Bristol C	D	0-0	0-0		16,28
R		24	A	Bristol C	L	0-1	0-1		23,24

	Webster	Moreline	Callaghan	Brown	Matthewson	Dunne	Conway	Halom	Earle	Lloyd	Barrett	Seymour	Richardson	Pentecost	Davidson	Horne	Morton	Johnston	Roberts	Mansley	Tranter
1		2	3	4	5	6	7	8	9	10	11			S							
2		2	3	4	5	6	7	8	9	10	11										S
3		2	3	4	5	6	7	8	9	10	11					S					
4		2	3	4	5	6	7	8	9	10	11								S		
5		2	3	4	5	6	7	8	9	10	11			S							
6		2	3	4	5	6	7	8	9	10	11					S					
7		2	3	4	5	6	7	8	9	10	11	1							S		
8		2	3	4	5	6	7	8	9	10	11	1	S								
9		2	3	7	5	6		8	9	10	11	1	4			S					
10		2	3	4	5	6	7	8	9	10	11	1	S								
11			3	2	5	6	**7**	8	9	10	11	1	4	12							
12			3		5	6		8	9	10	11	1	4	2	7	S					
13			3	**7**	5	6		8	9	10	11	1	4	2		12					
14			3	7	5	6		8	9	10	11	1	4	2		S					
15			3	4	12	6		8	9	10	11		5	2			**7**				
16			3	4	S	6		8	9	10	7		5	2				11			
17		12	3	4	6			8	9	10	11		**5**	2				7			
18		S	3	4	5	6		8	9	10	11			2				**7**			
19		8	3	**4**	5	6		12	9	10	11			2				7			
20			3	4	5	6		8	9	10	11	1		2		S		7			
21		2	3	4	5	6		**8**	9	10	11	1				7		12			
22		2	**3**	12		6			9	8	10	1				4		7	5	11	
23		2	8	4	5	6		9	7	10	11			3		S					
24		2	8	4	5	6		9	7	10	11			3							S
25		2	8	4	5	6		9	7	10	11			3							S
26		2	6		5	4		8	9	10	11		12	3				**7**			
27		4	3		5	6	**7**	9	10	8	11		12								2
28		4	3		**5**	6	7	12	9	10	11							8			2
29		4	3	2	5	6	7	S	9	10	11							8			
30		4	3	2	5	6	7		9	10	11		S					8			
31		4	3	2	5	6	7		9	10	11		S					8			
32		4	3	2	5	6	7		9	10	11		S					8			
33		3	4	2	5	6	7		9	10	11					S		8			
34		4	3	2	5	6	7		9	10	11		S					8			
35		2	3	**7**	5	4		12	9	10	11		6					8			
36		2	3	4	5	6	7		9	10	11		12					**8**			
37		2	3	4	5	6	7		9	10	11		12					**8**			
38				4	5	6	7	8	9	10	11		S	3							2
39			3	4	5	6	7	9		10	11			2		S		8			
40			3	4	5	6	7	S	9	10	11			2				8			
41			3		5	6	7	9		10	11		12	2		4		**8**			
42			3		5	6	7	**9**		10	11		12	2		4		8			
43			3		5	6	7	**9**		10	11		12	2		4		8			
44			3		5	6	7	12	9	10	11			2		4		**8**			
45			3		5	6	7	S	9	10	11			2		4		8			
46			3		5	6	7	12	9	10	11			2		4		**8**			
A		28	45	35	43	45	29	30	42	46	46	11	9	22	1	8	1	25	1	1	3
S		1	-	1	1	-	-	5	-	-	-	-	7	1	-	1	-	1	-	-	-
G		-	-	1	1	2	8	8	13	9	15	-	-	-	-	-	1	9	-	-	-

	Webster	Moreline	Callaghan	Brown	Matthewson	Dunne	Conway	Halom	Earle	Lloyd	Barrett	Seymour	Richardson	Pentecost	Davidson	Horne	Morton	Johnston	Roberts	Mansley	Tranter
1			3	4	5	6		8	9	10	11	1		2		S		7			

	Webster	Moreline	Callaghan	Brown	Matthewson	Dunne	Conway	Halom	Earle	Lloyd	Barrett	Seymour	Richardson	Pentecost	Davidson	Horne	Morton	Johnston	Roberts	Mansley	Tranter
1		2	3	4	5	6	7	8	9	10	11			S							
2		2	3	**4**	5	6	7	8	9	10	11				12						
3			3		5	6		8	9	10	11	1	4	2	S		7				
4			3	4	S	6		8	9	10	11		5	2			7				
5		**7**	3	4	5	6		8	9	10	11	1		2			12				
R			3	4	5	6		8	9	10	11	1		2		7			S		

0 points v	Aston Villa	0 points
1 point v	Mansfield T, Preston NE	2 points v
2 points v	Brighton & HA, Bury, Halifax T, Plymouth A, Reading, Swansea C, Torquay U, Walsall	16 points
3 points v	Barnsley, Chesterfield, Doncaster R, Rotherham U, Shrewsbury T, Wrexham	18 points
4 points v	Bradford C, Bristol R, Gillingham, Port Vale, Rochdale, Tranmere R	24 points

Father and son, Bill Dodgin and Bill junior, managers of Bristol Rovers and Fulham, before the FA Cup tie in November 1970.

1971-72

Division Two

	P	W	D	L	F	A	Pts
Norwich City	42	21	15	6	60	36	57
Birmingham City	42	19	18	5	60	31	56
Millwall	42	19	17	6	64	46	55
Queen's Park Rangers	42	20	14	8	57	28	54
Sunderland	42	17	16	9	67	57	50
Blackpool	42	20	7	15	70	50	47
Burnley	42	20	6	16	70	55	46
Bristol City	42	18	10	14	61	49	46
Middlesbrough	42	19	8	15	50	48	46
Carlisle United	42	17	9	16	61	57	43
Swindon Town	42	15	12	15	47	47	42
Hull City	42	14	10	18	49	53	38
Luton Town	42	10	18	14	43	48	38
Sheffield Wednesday	42	13	12	17	51	58	38
Oxford United	42	12	14	16	43	55	38
Portsmouth	42	12	13	17	59	68	37
Orient	42	14	9	19	50	61	37
Preston North End	42	12	12	18	52	58	36
Cardiff City	42	10	14	18	56	69	34
Fulham	42	12	10	20	45	68	34
Charlton Athletic	42	12	9	21	55	77	33
Watford	42	5	9	28	24	75	19

Manager: Bill Dodgin

Did you know that?

The signing of Alan Mullery on loan in March 1972 created a furore amongst Fulham's relegation rivals. And he made a difference, the club winning two and drawing two during his six-game stay, points that helped them beat the drop. Mullery signed permanently in the summer, the third time he had signed for the Cottagers.

3	Halom finale
6	Cross debut
15	Fraser debut
30	Mellor debut

No		Date	V	Opponents	R	H-T	F-T	Scorers	Atte
1	A	14	H	Watford	W	2-0	3-0	Earle 2, Johnston	13,56
2		21	A	Preston NE	L	0-2	0-2		16,42
3		28	H	Norwich C	D	0-0	0-0		10,66
4		31	H	Queen's Park R	L	0-0	0-3		21,18
5	S	4	A	Middlesbrough	L	0-0	0-2		20,68
6		11	H	Burnley	L	0-1	0-2		10,66
7		18	A	Swindon T	L	0-2	0-4		13,97
8		25	H	Orient	W	1-0	2-1	Barrett, Earle	9,15
9		28	A	Luton T	L	0-1	0-2		14,01
10	O	2	A	Sheffield W	L	0-1	0-4		14,98
11		9	H	Hull C	W	1-0	1-0	Earle	8,35
12		12	H	Oxford U	D	1-1	1-1	Callaghan	7,53
13		16	A	Watford	W	1-1	2-1	Conway, (Eddy og)	9,30
14		23	A	Portsmouth	L	0-2	3-6	Conway 2 (1 pen), Barrett	14,17
15		30	H	Blackpool	W	1-1	2-1	Conway, Lloyd	11,02
16	N	6	A	Bristol C	W	2-0	2-1	Cross, Barrett	17,26
17		13	H	Cardiff C	W	2-2	4-3	Conway 2, Earle, Cross	10,70
18		20	H	Charlton A	W	1-0	1-0	Barrett	13,35
19		27	A	Birmingham C	L	1-2	1-3	Conway	25,67
20	D	4	H	Carlisle U	L	0-1	0-1		8,10
21		11	A	Sunderland	L	1-0	1-2	Barrett	11,80
22		18	H	Middlesbrough	D	1-1	2-2	Cross, Barrett	7,57
23		27	A	Millwall	L	0-1	1-4	Lloyd	21,39
24	J	1	H	Swindon T	L	2-2	2-4	Earle 2	7,40
25		8	A	Norwich C	L	1-1	1-2	Earle	21,87
26		22	H	Luton T	W	2-0	3-1	Barrett, Johnston 2	11,32
27		29	A	Oxford U	L	0-1	0-1		8,11
28	F	12	H	Portsmouth	D	1-0	1-1	Cross	8,39
29		19	A	Blackpool	L	1-2	1-2	Conway	11,48
30		26	H	Bristol C	W	0-0	2-0	Callaghan, Earle	9,27
31	M	4	A	Cardiff C	L	0-1	0-1		13,12
32		11	A	Hull C	L	0-2	0-4		11,11
33		18	H	Preston NE	D	0-0	0-0		9,07
34		25	A	Burnley	D	1-0	1-1	Lloyd	10,08
35		28	H	Sheffield W	W	1-0	4-0	Cross 2, Earle, Mullery (pen)	7,94
36	A	1	H	Millwall	W	1-0	1-0	Barrett	20,15
37		3	A	Orient	L	0-1	0-1		16,02
38		8	A	Charlton A	D	1-1	2-2	Earle, Callaghan	9,05
39		18	H	Birmingham C	D	0-0	0-0		16,55
40		22	A	Carlisle U	L	0-1	1-3	Cross	6,06
41		25	A	Queen's Park R	D	0-0	0-0		20,60
42		29	H	Sunderland	D	0-0	0-0		12,36
									App
									Su
									Goa

FA Cup

3	J	15	A	Queen's Park R	D	1-0	1-1	Conway	23,7
R		18	H	Queen's Park R	W	1-0	2-1	Cross 2	24,18
4	F	5	A	Huddersfield T	L	0-2	0-3		18,3

League Cup

1	A	17	H	Cambridge U	W	2-0	4-0	Halom, Earle 3	8,3
2	S	7	A	Sheffield U	L	0-0	0-3		24,2

	Webster	Pentecost	Callaghan	Brown	Matthewson	Dunne	Johnston	Halom	Earle	Lloyd	Barrett	Horne	Moreline	Carlton	Conway John	Cross	Richardson	Conway Jim	Fraser	Stephenson	Mellor	Tranter	Mullery
1	1	2	3	4	5	6	7	**8**	9	10	11	12											
2	1	2	3	4	5	6	7	8	9	10	11	S											
3	1	2	3	4	5	6	7	**8**	9	10	11	12											
4	1	2	3	**4**	5	6	7		9	10	11		12	8									
5	1	2	3		5	6	7		9	10	11	S	4	8									
6	1	**2**	3		5	6			9	10	11	12	4		7	8							
7	1		3		5		S		9	10	11	4	2			8	6	7					
8	1		3	2	5	6			9	10	11		S			8	4	7					
9	1		3	2	5	**6**			9	10	11		12			8	4	7					
10	1		3	2	5	6	12		9	10	11					**8**	4	7					
11	1		3	2	5	6	12		9	10	11					**8**	4	7					
12	1	2	3		5	6	S		9	10	11					8	4	7					
13	1	2	3		5	6	S		9	10	11					8	4	7					
14	1	2	3		5	6	8		9	10	11			S			4	7					
15	1		3	4	6				9	10	11					8	S	7	2	5			
16	1		3	4	5				9	10	11		S			8	6	7	2				
17	1		3	4	6				9	10	11					**8**	12	7	2	5			
18	1		3	4	6				9	10	11					8	S	7	2	5			
19	1		3	2	6				9	10	11		S	4		8		7		5			
20	1		3	2					9	10	11		6	4		8	S	7		5			
21	1		3	4		6			9	10	11		S			8		7	2	5			
22	1		3	4	12	6			9	10	11					8		7	**2**	5			
23	1		3	12	4	6			9	10	**11**					8		7	2	5			
24	1		3		**4**	6			9	10	11			12		8		7	2	5			
25	1		3	7	6	4			9	10	11		S			8			2	5			
26	1		3		6	4	7		9	10	11		2			8	5			S			
27	1		3		5	4	12		9	10	**11**		2			8	6	7					
28	1		3	4	6				9	10	11	S	2			8	5	7					
29	1		3	4	5	S			9	10	11		2			8	6	7					
30			3	4	5				9	10	11		2	S		8	6	7			1		
31			3	2	5				9	10	11	7				8	6		S		1	4	
32			3	2	5				9	10	11	7				**8**	6				1	12	4
33			3	2	5	6			9	10	11	7		S		8					1		4
34			3	2	5	6			9	10	11	7		S		8					1		4
35			3	2	5	6			9	10	11	7		S		8					1		4
36			3	2	5	6			9	10	11	7		12		**8**					1		4
37			3	2	5	6			9	10	11	7		12		**8**					1		4
38		2	3		5	6	7		9	10	11	4		8			S				1		
39		2	4		5	6	12		**9**	10	11	7	3			8					1		
40		2	11	4	5	6	12			**10**	9	7	3			8					1		
41		2	4		5	6	S		9	10	11	7	3			8					1		
42		2	6		5	4	S		9	10	11	7	3			8					1		
A	29	14	42	28	39	30	8	3	41	42	42	13	13	5	1	35	16	22	9	10	13	1	6
S	-	-	-	1	1	-	5	-	-	-	-	3	2	3	-	-	1	-	-	-	-	1	-
G	-	-	3	-	-	-	3	-	11	3	8	-	-	-	-	7	-	8	-	-	-	-	1

	Webster	Pentecost	Callaghan	Brown	Matthewson	Dunne	Johnston	Halom	Earle	Lloyd	Barrett	Horne	Moreline	Carlton	Conway John	Cross	Richardson	Conway Jim	Fraser	Stephenson	Mellor	Tranter	Mullery
3	1		3		5	4	12		9	10	11	2			**8**	6	7						
R	1		3		5	4	S		9	10	11		2			8	6	7					
4	1		3		5	4			9	10	11	S	2			8	6	7					

	Webster	Pentecost	Callaghan	Brown	Matthewson	Dunne	Johnston	Halom	Earle	Lloyd	Barrett	Horne	Moreline	Carlton	Conway John	Cross	Richardson	Conway Jim	Fraser	Stephenson	Mellor	Tranter	Mullery
1	1		3	4	5	6		8	9	10	11	12		**7**								2	
2	1	2	3		5	6	12		9	10	11		4	8	**7**								

0 points v	Carlisle U, Swindon T	0 points
1 point v	Birmingham C, Burnley, Middlesbrough, Norwich C, Oxford U, Portsmouth, Preston NE, Queen's Park R, Sunderland	9 points
2 points v	Blackpool, Cardiff C, Hull C, Luton T, Millwall, Orient, Sheffield W	14 points
3 points v	Charlton A	3 points
4 points v	Bristol C, Watford	8 points

Defender Jimmy Browne, capped by the Republic of Ireland in May 1971.

1972-73

Division Two

	P	W	D	L	F	A	Pts
Burnley	42	24	14	4	72	35	62
Queen's Park Rangers	42	24	13	5	81	37	61
Aston Villa	42	18	14	10	51	47	50
Middlesbrough	42	17	13	12	46	43	47
Bristol City	42	17	12	13	63	51	46
Sunderland	42	17	12	13	59	49	46
Blackpool	42	18	10	14	56	51	46
Oxford United	42	19	7	16	52	43	45
Fulham	42	16	12	14	58	49	44
Sheffield Wednesday	42	17	10	15	59	55	44
Millwall	42	16	10	16	55	47	42
Luton Town	42	15	11	16	44	53	41
Hull City	42	14	12	16	64	59	40
Nottingham Forest	42	14	12	16	47	52	40
Orient	42	12	12	18	49	53	36
Swindon Town	42	10	16	16	46	60	36
Portsmouth	42	12	11	19	42	59	35
Carlisle United	42	11	12	19	50	52	34
Preston North End	42	11	12	19	37	64	34
Cardiff City	42	11	11	20	43	58	33
Huddersfield Town	42	8	17	17	36	56	33
Brighton & Hove Albion	42	8	13	21	46	83	29

Manager: Alec Stock

Did you know that?

Les Barrett's club record-breaking run of 168 consecutive appearances ended when injury kept him out of the game at home to Portsmouth in November 1972.

1	Matthewson finale
4	S Brown finale
6	Mitchell debut
8	Callaghan's 300th game
10	Strong debut
13	Cross finale
17	Barrett's 300th game
19	Lacy debut
24	Pentecost finale
27	Earle's 100th goal
34	Richardson finale
38	Earle's 300th game
42	Horne finale

No		Date	V	Opponents	R	H-T	F-T	Scorers	Atten
1	A	12	A	Sheffield W	L	0-2	0-3		23,10
2		19	H	Burnley	D	0-1	1-1	Went	10,28
3		26	A	Middlesbrough	W	1-0	2-1	Cross, Barrett	11,41
4	S	2	H	Preston NE	L	0-1	1-3	Richardson	7,64
5		9	A	Brighton & HA	L	1-2	1-2	Earle	15,61
6		16	H	Huddersfield T	D	0-1	1-1	Mullery	7,07
7		20	H	Hull C	W	1-0	2-0	Earle, Mullery	7,68
8		23	A	Millwall	W	1-1	3-1	Mitchell, Lloyd, Earle	12,24
9		26	A	Bristol C	D	1-0	1-1	Earle	14,21
10		30	H	Orient	D	1-1	1-1	Earle	10,99
11	O	7	H	Aston Villa	W	1-0	2-0	Mullery, Mitchell	17,57
12		14	A	Carlisle U	L	1-0	1-2	Mitchell	6,22
13		17	H	Queen's Park R	L	0-2	0-2		17,00
14		21	H	Blackpool	W	0-0	2-0	Strong, Earle	8,64
15		28	A	Sunderland	D	0-0	0-0		11,61
16	N	4	H	Bristol C	W	2-1	5-1	Earle, Mitchell 2, Strong, (Merrick og)	8,98
17		11	A	Hull C	D	2-1	2-2	Mitchell 2	9,40
18		18	H	Portsmouth	D	0-0	0-0		9,62
19		25	A	Cardiff C	L	0-1	1-3	Mullery	9,69
20	D	9	A	Oxford U	D	0-0	0-0		8,34
21		16	H	Nottingham F	W	1-1	3-1	Mitchell, Barrett, Mullery (pen)	8,25
22		23	A	Swindon T	D	1-1	2-2	Earle, (Potter og)	9,48
23		26	H	Millwall	W	1-0	1-0	Conway (Jim)	16,90
24		30	A	Burnley	D	1-1	2-2	Went, Conway (Jim)	15,47
25	J	6	H	Middlesbrough	W	0-0	2-1	Mullery, Conway (Jim)	9,69
26		20	A	Preston NE	W	3-0	3-0	Earle 2, Barrett	5,75
27		27	H	Brighton & HA	W	2-1	5-1	Earle 2, Mitchell, Barrett, Conway (Jim)	12,00
28	F	10	A	Huddersfield T	L	0-0	0-1		6,46
29		17	H	Sheffield W	W	0-0	1-0	Earle	11,68
30		24	A	Nottingham F	L	0-2	1-2	Earle	8,81
31	M	3	A	Aston Villa	W	0-1	3-2	Barrett, Mitchell, Went	24,00
32		10	H	Carlisle U	W	0-0	1-0	Mitchell	9,83
33		17	A	Blackpool	L	0-0	0-2		8,01
34		24	H	Sunderland	L	1-1	1-2	Mullery	9,64
35		27	H	Luton T	L	0-1	0-1		7,44
36		31	H	Cardiff C	D	1-1	1-1	Conway (John)	6,26
37	A	7	A	Luton T	L	0-1	0-1		8,43
38		14	H	Oxford U	W	0-0	2-0	Earle, (Lowe og)	6,35
39		20	H	Swindon T	D	0-0	0-0		8,51
40		21	A	Portsmouth	W	2-1	2-1	Conway (John) 2	9,19
41		23	A	Orient	L	1-1	2-3	Barrett, Mullery	9,95
42		28	A	Queen's Park R	L	0-1	0-2		22,18
									App
									Su
									Goal

FA Cup

No		Date	V	Opponents	R	H-T	F-T	Scorers	Atten
3	J	13	A	Sheffield W	L	0-1	0-2		21,02

League Cup

No		Date	V	Opponents	R	H-T	F-T	Scorers	Atten
1	A	16	A	Reading	D	1-0	1-1	Richardson	8,88
R		23	H	Reading	D	0-0	1-1	Went	5,63
2R		28	A	Reading	W	1-0	1-0	Lloyd	8,17
2	S	5	A	Hull C	L	0-0	0-1		6,35

Mellor	Pentecost	Moreline	Mullery	Matthewson	Dunne	Conway (Jim)	Horne	Cross	Lloyd	Barrett	Callaghan	Went	Brown	Richardson	Earle	Cutbush	Conway (John)	Mitchell	Strong	Carlton	Lacy	Fraser	Pinkney	Shrubb	
	2	3	4	5	6	**7**	8	9	10	11	12														1
		2	4		6			9	10	11	3	5	7	8		S									2
		2			6			9	10	11	3	5	7	4	8	S									3
		2			6			**8**	10	11	3	5	7	4	9	12									4
			8		6		4		**10**	11	3	5		9	7	2	12								5
			4		6		S		10	11	3	5			8	2	7	9							6
			4		6				10	11	3	5		12	8	2	**7**	9							7
			4		6				10	11	3	5		S	8	2	7	9							8
			4		6				10	11	3	5		12	8	2	**7**	9							9
			4		6		S		10	11	3	5			8	2		9	7						10
			4		6		12		10	11	3	5			8	2		9	**7**						11
			4		6		12		10	11	3	5			8	2		9	**7**						12
			4		6			12	10	11	3	5			8	2		9	**7**						13
		S	4		6				10	11	3	5			8	2		9	7						14
		S	4		6				10	11	3	5			8	2		9	7						15
			4		6				10	11	3	5			8	**2**		9	7	12					16
			4		6				10	11	3	5			8	2		9	7		S				17
		12	4		6				10		3	5			8	2	7	9	**11**						18
			4		6				10		3	5			8	2	**7**	9	11		12				19
			4		6	7			10	11	3	5			8	2		9			S				20
			4		6	7			10	11	3	5			8	2		9			S				21
	12		4		6	7			10	11	**3**				8	2		9			5				22
			4		6	7			10	11	3				8	2		9	S		5				23
	12		4		6	7			**10**	11	3	5			8	2		9							24
			4		6	7	10			11	3	5			8			9	S			2			25
			4		6	7				11	3	5			8			9	S			2	10		26
			4		6	7				11	3	5			8			9	S			2	10		27
		12	4		6	**7**				11	3	5			8			9				2	10		28
			4		6					11	3	5			8	2		9	7			S	10		29
			4		6					11	3	5			8	2	12	9	**7**				10		30
		S	4		6					11	3	5			8	2		9	7				10		31
			4		**6**					11	3	5			8	2		9	7			12	10		32
			4						10	11	3	5			8	2		9	12		**6**		7		33
			4						10	11	3	5		6	8	2		9	**7**				12		34
			4						12	11	3	5			8	2		9	7				**10**	6	35
			4				6			11	3	5			8	2	7	**9**	12				10		36
			6				4		10		3	5			8	2	12	9	11				**7**		37
			4			7	6		10	11	3	5			8	2	12		**9**						38
			4			**7**	6		10	11	3	5			8	2	12	9							39
		3	4			S	6		10	11		5			8	2	**7**	9							40
		3	4			12	6		10	11		5			8	2	7	**9**							41
		3	4			7	6		10	11		5			8	2	12	**9**							42
2	1	7	40	1	32	13	10	4	32	39	38	39	3	5	40	34	9	36	18	-	3	4	11	1	A
	2	2	-	-	-	1	2	1	1	-	1	-	-	2	-	1	6	-	2	1	1	1	1	-	S
	-	-	8	-	-	4	-	1	1	6	-	3	-	1	15	-	3	11	2	-	-	-	-	-	G

Mellor	Pentecost	Moreline	Mullery	Matthewson	Dunne	Conway (Jim)	Horne	Cross	Lloyd	Barrett	Callaghan	Went	Brown	Richardson	Earle	Cutbush	Conway (John)	Mitchell	Strong	Carlton	Lacy	Fraser	Pinkney	Shrubb	
		12	4		6	7	**10**			11	3	5			8			9				2			3

Mellor	Pentecost	Moreline	Mullery	Matthewson	Dunne	Conway (Jim)	Horne	Cross	Lloyd	Barrett	Callaghan	Went	Brown	Richardson	Earle	Cutbush	Conway (John)	Mitchell	Strong	Carlton	Lacy	Fraser	Pinkney	Shrubb	
		2	4		6		S	8	10	11	3	5		9		7									1
		2	4		6			9	10	11	3	5	7		8	S									R
		2			6			9	10	11	3	5	7	4	8	S									2R
	S				6		4		10	11	3	5		9	8	2	7								2

0 points v	Luton T, Queen's Park R	0 points
1 point v	Cardiff C, Huddersfield T, Orient, Sunderland	4 points
2 points v	Blackpool, Brighton & HA, Burnley, Carlisle U, Nottingham F, Preston NE, Sheffield W, Swindon T	16 points
3 points v	Bristol C, Hull C, Oxford U, Portsmouth	12 points
4 points v	Aston Villa, Middlesbrough, Millwall	12 points

Defender Reg Matthewson played the last of his 172 games in August 1972.

1973-74

Division Two

	P	W	D	L	F	A	Pts
Middlesbrough	42	27	11	4	77	30	65
Luton Town	42	19	12	11	64	51	50
Carlisle United	42	20	9	13	61	48	49
Orient	42	15	18	9	55	42	48
Blackpool	42	17	13	12	57	40	47
Sunderland	42	19	9	14	58	44	47
Nottingham Forest	42	15	15	12	57	43	45
West Bromwich Albion	42	14	16	12	48	45	44
Hull City	42	13	17	12	46	47	43
Notts County	42	15	13	14	55	60	43
Bolton Wanderers	42	15	12	15	44	40	42
Millwall	42	14	14	14	51	51	42
Fulham	42	16	10	16	39	43	42
Aston Villa	42	13	15	14	48	45	41
Portsmouth	42	14	12	16	45	62	40
Bristol City	42	14	10	18	47	54	38
Cardiff City	42	10	16	16	49	62	36
Oxford United	42	10	16	16	35	46	36
Sheffield Wednesday	42	12	11	19	51	63	35
Crystal Palace	42	11	12	19	43	56	34
Preston North End	42	9	14	19	40	62	31
Swindon Town	42	7	11	24	36	72	25

Manager: Alec Stock

Did you know that?

Fulham's Second Division match at Millwall in January 1974 was played during the Three Day Week and was the first first-class game ever played on a Sunday.

1	Slough and Busby debuts
10	Earle and Webster finales
19	Moreline and Went finales
FAC3	Dowie debut
FAC4	Mullery's 300th game
33	Moore debut
36	Callaghan finale
39	Howe debut
39	Dunne finale

No		Date	V	Opponents	R	H-T	F-T	Scorers	Atte
1	A	25	H	Millwall	W	1-0	2-0	Barrett, Conway (Jim)	12,07
2	S	1	A	Middlesbrough	W	0-0	2-0	Barrett, Earle	14,97
3		8	H	Orient	L	0-1	0-3		10,98
4		12	H	Blackpool	D	0-0	0-0		9,30
5		15	A	Cardiff C	D	0-0	0-0		11,25
6		19	A	Aston Villa	D	0-0	1-1	Slough	30,16
7		22	H	Bolton W	W	1-0	1-0	Busby	9,56
8		29	A	Oxford U	D	0-0	0-0		8,04
9	O	2	H	Aston Villa	W	0-0	1-0	Mitchell	11,77
10		6	H	Preston NE	D	0-0	0-0		10,52
11		13	A	Notts C	L	0-0	1-2	Earle	11,97
12		20	H	Sunderland	L	0-1	0-2		14,97
13		22	A	Blackpool	L	0-0	0-2		5,52
14		27	A	Carlisle U	L	0-2	0-3		7,14
15	N	3	H	Bristol C	W	0-0	2-1	Conway (John), Busby	9,61
16		10	A	Nottingham F	L	0-1	0-3		10,51
17		17	H	Portsmouth	W	1-0	2-0	Mitchell, Barrett	8,40
18		24	A	West Bromich A	L	0-1	0-2		12,68
19	D	1	H	Hull C	D	0-0	0-0		5,63
20		8	A	Swindon T	D	1-0	1-1	Mullery	5,58
21		15	A	Sheffield W	W	2-0	3-0	Conway (John), Barrett, Busby	7,92
22		22	H	Oxford U	W	0-0	3-1	Cutbush, Busby, Slough	4,97
23		26	A	Luton T	D	0-1	1-1	Conway (John)	15,26
24		29	A	Orient	L	0-0	0-1		13,66
25	J	12	H	Cardiff C	L	0-0	0-1		7,41
26		20	A	Millwall	L	0-1	0-1		15,13
27	F	2	H	Sheffield W	W	2-1	4-1	Busby 3, Barrett	6,58
28		16	H	Notts C	W	0-0	2-0	Conway (Jim), Busby	7,51
29		23	A	Preston NE	W	0-0	1-0	Slough	9,54
30	M	5	H	Luton T	W	0-0	2-1	Lloyd 2	10,07
31		9	H	Carlisle U	L	0-1	0-2		6,73
32		16	A	Sunderland	L	0-1	0-1		30,43
33		19	H	Middlesbrough	L	0-1	0-4		18,11
34		23	H	Nottingham F	W	1-0	2-0	Busby, Conway (Jim)	9,88
35		30	A	Bristol C	W	0-0	1-0	Mullery	10,94
36	A	2	A	Bolton W	D	0-0	0-0		18,63
37		6	H	West Bromich A	D	0-0	0-0		9,49
38		12	H	Crystal Palace	L	0-3	1-3	Moore	23,51
39		13	A	Portsmouth	L	0-1	0-3		12,05
40		16	A	Crystal Palace	W	0-0	2-0	Busby, Barrett	32,12
41		20	H	Swindon T	W	1-1	4-1	Cutbush, Howe, Barrett, Busby	7,08
42		27	A	Hull C	L	0-0	0-2		5,73

App

Su

Goa

FA Cup

3	J	5	H	Preston NE	W	1-0	1-0	Conway (John)	6,93
4		26	H	Leicester C	D	1-1	1-1	Mullery	26,23
R		30	A	Leicester C	L	0-0	1-2	Barrett	37,13

League Cup

2	O	10	A	Oxford U	D	0-1	1-1	Barrett	7,1
R		16	H	Oxford U	W	1-0	3-0	Went, Lacy, Barrett	6,43
3		31	H	Ipswich T	D	2-1	2-2	Mullery, Barrett	8,9
R	N	14	A	Ipswich T	L	1-0	1-2	Earle	21,4

Mellor	Cutbush	Slough	Mullery	Went	Dunne	Conway Jim	Earle	Busby	Lloyd	Barrett	Moreline	Mitchell	Lacy	Conway John	Webster	Fraser	Strong	Friend	Dowie	Moore	Callaghan	Howe	Shrubb	
1	2	3	4	5	6	7	8	9	10	11											S			1
1	2	3	4	5	6	7	8	9	10	11	S													2
1	2	3	4	5	6	7	9	**8**	10	11	12													3
1	2	3	4	5	6	7	8	S	10	11		9												4
1	2	3	4	5	7		8	S	10	11		9	6											5
1	2	3	4	5	7		**8**	12	10	11		9	6											6
1	2	7	4	5		12		8	10	11	3	**9**	6											7
1	2	3	4	5	7		8	9	10	11		S	6											8
1	2	3	4	5	7		8	**9**	10	11		12	6											9
1	2	3	4	5			**8**	12	10	11		9	6	7										10
1	2	3	4	5	8		9	12	**10**	11		7	6											11
1	2	3	4	5	7		8	12	**10**	11		9	6											12
1	2	3	4	5	7			8	10	11	S	9	6											13
1	2	3	4	5	7		12	8	10	11		**9**	6											14
	2	3	4	5			8	9	10	11			6	7	1	S								15
	2	3	4	5	12		8	**9**	10	11			6	7	1									16
	2	3	4	5	6		8		10	11		9		7	1		S							17
	2	3	4	5	6		8		10	11	S	9		7	1									18
1	2	10	4	5	8			9		11	3		6	7		S								19
1	2	10	4		6	8		9		11			5	7		3			S					20
1	2	10	4		6	8		9	S	11			5	7		3								21
1	2	10	4		6	8		9	S	11			5	7		3								22
1	2	10	4		6	8		9	S	11			5	7		3								23
1	**2**	10	4		6	8		9	12	11			5	7		3								24
1		10	4		6	8		9		11		12	5	**7**		2	3							25
1		8	4		6	7		9	10	11			5			2	3		S					26
1		8	4		6	7		9	10	11		S	5			2	3							27
1		8	4		6	7		9	10	11			5			2	3		S					28
1		8	4		6	**7**		9	10	11			5			2	3	12						29
1		8	4		6			9	10	11	S		5			2	3	7						30
1		4			5	7		9	10	11			6	12		2	3	**8**						31
1		4			6	7		9	10	11			5			2	3	S	8					32
1	2	**3**	8		6	7		9	10	11			5				12			4				33
1	2		8		6	7		9	10	11			5	S			3			4				34
1	2		4		6	7		9	10	11			5				3			8	S			35
1	2		8		6	7		**9**	10	11			5				3			4	12			36
1	2		4		6	**7**		9	10	11			5	12			3			8				37
1	2		8		6	12		9	10	11			**5**	7			3			4				38
1	8		4		**3**	7		9	12	11						5	2			10		6		39
1	**7**		4			8		9	10	11				S		2	3			6		5		40
1	7		4			8		9	10	11						2	3		S	6		5		41
1	**8**		4			7		9	10	11			12			2	3			6		5		42
38	34	33	40	19	35	25	15	34	34	42	2	11	32	13	4	17	17	2	1	10	-	4		A
-	-	-	-	-	1	2	1	4	2	-	1	2	1	2	-	-	1	1	-	-	1	-		S
-	2	3	2	-	-	3	2	11	2	7	-	2	-	3	-	-	-	-	-	1	-	1		G

Mellor	Cutbush	Slough	Mullery	Went	Dunne	Conway Jim	Earle	Busby	Lloyd	Barrett	Moreline	Mitchell	Lacy	Conway John	Webster	Fraser	Strong	Friend	Dowie	Moore	Callaghan	Howe	Shrubb	
1		10	4		6					11		9	5	7		2	3		8				S	3
1		8	4		6	7		9	10	11			5			2	3		S					4
1		8	4		6	7		9	10	11			5			**2**	3		12					R

Mellor	Cutbush	Slough	Mullery	Went	Dunne	Conway Jim	Earle	Busby	Lloyd	Barrett	Moreline	Mitchell	Lacy	Conway John	Webster	Fraser	Strong	Friend	Dowie	Moore	Callaghan	Howe	Shrubb	
1	2	3	4	5	8			7	10	11		9	6			S								2
1	2	3	4	5	7		8	S	10	11		9	6											R
	2	3	4	5				8	10	11	12	**9**	6	7	1									3
	2	3	4	5	6		8		10	11		9	S	7	1									R

0 points v	Carlisle, Orient, Sunderland	0 points
1 point v	Blackpool, Cardiff C, Hull C, West Bromich A	4 points
2 points v	Crystal Palace, Middlesbrough, Millwall, Nottingham F, Notts C, Portsmouth	12 points
3 points v	Aston Villa, Bolton W, Luton T, Oxford U, Preston NE, Swindon T	18 points
4 points v	Bristol C, Sheffield W	8 points

The unlucky midfield player John Dowie had the first of his 50 team outings in January 1974.

1974-75

Division Two

	P	W	D	L	F	A	Pts
Manchester United	42	26	9	7	66	30	61
Aston Villa	42	25	8	9	79	32	58
Norwich City	42	20	13	9	58	37	53
Sunderland	42	19	13	10	65	35	51
Bristol City	42	21	8	13	47	33	50
West Bromwich Albion	42	18	9	15	54	42	45
Blackpool	42	14	17	11	38	33	45
Hull City	42	15	14	13	40	53	44
Fulham	42	13	16	13	44	39	42
Bolton Wanderers	42	15	12	15	45	41	42
Oxford United	42	15	12	15	41	51	42
Orient	42	11	20	11	28	39	42
Southampton	42	15	11	16	53	54	41
Notts County	42	12	16	14	49	59	40
York City	42	14	10	18	51	55	38
Nottingham Forest	42	12	14	16	43	55	38
Portsmouth	42	12	13	17	44	54	37
Oldham Athletic	42	10	15	17	40	48	35
Bristol Rovers	42	12	11	19	42	64	35
Millwall	42	10	12	20	44	56	32
Cardiff City	42	9	14	19	36	62	32
Sheffield Wednesday	42	5	11	26	29	64	21

Manager: Alec Stock

Did you know that?

It took Fulham four games, or seven hours (420 minutes), to overcome Nottingham Forest in the Fourth Round FA Cup tie, the longest tie in the Cottagers' history.

25 Barrett's 400th game
FAC4 Conway's 300th game
42 Bullivant debut

No		Date	V	Opponents	R	H-T	F-T	Scorers	Atten
1	A	17	A	West Bromich A	W	0-0	1-0	Busby	11,40
2		20	A	Notts C	D	0-0	1-1	Mullery (pen)	9,36
3		24	H	Cardiff C	W	3-0	4-0	Conway (Jim) 2, Busby 2	8,11
4		28	H	Notts C	W	1-0	3-0	Slough, Conway (Jim), Busby	9,37
5		31	A	Millwall	L	0-1	0-2		9,93
6	S	7	H	York C	L	0-1	0-2		7,62
7		14	A	Orient	D	0-0	0-0		8,92
8		21	H	Norwich C	W	2-0	4-0	Busby, Fraser, Barrett, Lacy	9,41
9		25	H	Bristol R	D	0-0	0-0		8,70
10		28	A	Oldham A	L	0-0	0-1		12,75
11	O	5	H	Manchester U	L	0-1	1-2	Busby	26,51
12		12	A	Portsmouth	D	0-0	0-0		12,52
13		19	H	Bristol C	D	0-1	1-1	Mullery	8,96
14		26	A	Oxford U	L	1-1	1-2	Barrett	8,71
15	N	2	H	Aston Villa	W	1-0	3-1	Lacy, Busby, Lloyd	10,97
16		9	A	Hull C	L	0-1	1-2	Cutbush	7,57
17		16	H	Sunderland	L	0-3	1-3	Mullery	14,19
18		23	A	Sheffield W	L	0-0	0-1		12,37
19		30	H	Blackpool	W	0-0	1-0	Mullery	6,41
20	D	7	A	Nottingham F	D	0-1	1-1	Belfitt	10,05
21		11	A	Cardiff C	D	0-0	0-0		8,48
22		14	H	West Bromich A	W	0-0	1-0	Mullery	6,73
23		21	A	Southampton	D	0-0	0-0		13,56
24		26	H	Orient	D	0-0	0-0		9,60
25		28	A	Bolton W	D	0-0	0-0		4,70
26	J	11	H	Nottingham F	L	0-0	0-1		9,15
27		18	A	Blackpool	L	0-1	0-1		6,71
28	F	1	H	Hull C	D	1-1	1-1	Dowie	5,73
29		8	A	Aston Villa	D	1-0	1-1	Busby	28,53
30		22	A	Sunderland	W	0-1	2-1	Busby 2	33,41
31		25	H	Sheffield W	W	1-0	2-1	Barrett, Mullery	8,55
32	M	4	H	Millwall	D	0-0	0-0		13,31
33		11	A	Bristol R	W	2-1	2-1	Mullery (pen), Mitchell	11,76
34		15	H	Oldham A	D	0-0	0-0		13,18
35		22	A	York C	L	2-2	2-3	Slough, Busby	7,82
36		24	H	Southampton	W	2-0	3-2	Conway (Jim), Mullery (pen), Barrett	11,93
37		28	H	Bolton W	W	1-0	2-1	Dowie, Mullery	9,45
38		31	A	Norwich C	W	1-1	2-1	Mitchell 2	29,90
39	A	12	A	Manchester U	L	0-1	0-1		52,97
40		19	H	Portsmouth	D	1-0	2-2	Mitchell 2	17,58
41		22	H	Oxford U	D	0-0	0-0		11,30
42		26	A	Bristol C	L	1-0	1-3	Barrett	11,53
									App
									Su
									Goal

FA Cup

No		Date	V	Opponents	R	H-T	F-T	Scorers		Atten
3	J	4	H	Hull C	D	1-0	1-1	Conway (Jim)		8,89
R		7	A	Hull C	D	0-0	2-2	Busby 2		11,85
2R		13	N	Hull C	W	1-0	1-0	Slough	(at Filbert Street)	4,92
4		28	H	Nottingham F	D	0-0	0-0			14,84
R	F	3	A	Nottingham F	D	1-0	1-1	Dowie		26,36
2R		5	H	Nottingham F	D	1-0	1-1	Slough		11,92
3R		10	A	Nottingham F	W	1-0	2-1	Busby 2		23,24
5		15	A	Everton	W	1-0	2-1	Busby 2		45,23
6	M	8	A	Carlisle U	W	0-0	1-0	Barrett		21,57
SF	A	5	N	Birmingham C	D	0-0	1-1	Mitchell	(at Hillsborough)	55,00
R		9	N	Birmingham C	W	0-0	1-0	Mitchell	(at Maine Road)	35,10
F	M	3	N	West Ham U	L	0-0	0-2		(at Wembley)	100,00

League Cup

No		Date	V	Opponents	R	H-T	F-T	Scorers	Atten
2	S	11	A	Wolverhampton W	W	0-1	3-1	Barrett 2, Busby	16,15
3	O	8	H	West Ham U	W	0-1	2-1	Mullery, Slough	29,61
4	N	13	A	Newcastle U	L	0-0	0-3		23,22

Match	Mellor	Cutbush	Strong	Mullery	Lacy	Moore	Conway Jim	Slough	Busby	Lloyd	Barrett	Fraser	Mitchell	Howe	Belfitt	Conway John	Dowie	Scrivens	Bullivant	Dunne
1		2	3	4	5	6	7	8	9	10	11									S
2		2	3	4	5	6	7	8	9	10	11									S
3		2	3	4	5	6	7	8	9	10	11						S			
4		2	3	4	5	6	7	8	9	10	11		S							
5		2	3	4	5	6	7	8	9	10	11	S								
6			3	4	5	6	7	8	9	**10**	11	2	12							
7			3	4	5	6	7	8	9	10	11	2								S
8			3	4	5	6	7	8	9	10	11	2				S				
9			3	4	5	6	7	8	9	10	11	2					S			
10			3	4	5	6	7	**8**	9	10	11	2	12							
11			3	4	5	6	7	8	9	10	11	2	12							
12		2	3	**4**	5	6	7	8	9	10	11		12							
13		2	3	4	5	6	7	8	9	10	11		S							
14		2	3	4	5	6	7	8	**9**	10	11		12							
15		2	3	4	5	6	7	8	9	10	11		S							
16		2	3	4	5	6	7	8	9	10	11		S							
17		2	3	4		6	7	8	9	10	11			5			S			
18			3	4		6		8	9	10	11	2	7	5			S			
19			3	4	5	6		8	7	10	11	2	S		9					
20		2	3	4	5	6	S	8	7	10	11				9					
21		2	3	4	5	6	8	10	S		11				9	7				
22		2	3	4	5	6	8	10	S		11				9	7				
23		2	3	4	5		8	6		10	11		S		9	7				
24		2	3	4	5	6	8	10		S	11				9	7				
25		2	3	4	5	6	8	10	9		11		S			7				
26		2	3	4		6	8	10	9	S	11			5		7				
27		2	3	4	5	6			9	10			11	S		7	8			
28		2	3	4	5	6	7	10	9		11		S				8			
29		2	3	4	5	6	8	10	9		11		S				7			
30		2	3	4	5	6	8	10	9	12	11						**7**			
31			3	4	5	6	8	10	9	7	11	**2**	12							
32			3	4	5	6	8	10	9		11	2	S				7			
33			3	4	5	6		10	9	S	11	2	8				7			
34			3	4	5	6	8	10	9		11	2	12				**7**			
35			3	4	5	6		10	9	S	11	2	8				7			
36			3	4	5	6	8	10	9		11	**2**	12				7			
37			3	4	5	6	8	10	**9**		11	2	12				7			
38		S	3	4	5	6		10	9		11	2	8				7			
39			3	4	5	6		10	9	S	11	2	8				7			
40		12	**3**	4	5	6		10	9		11	2	8				7			
41		2		4	5	6	**8**		9	10	11	3	7				12			
42		2		4	5	6			9	10	11	3					**8**	7	12	
A	2	24	40	42	39	41	32	39	38	25	41	20	8	3	6	7	14	1	-	-
S		1	-	-	-	-	-	-	-	1	-	-	8	-	-	-	1	-	1	-
G		1	-	9	2	-	4	2	11	1	5	1	5	-	1	-	2	-	-	-

Round	Mellor	Cutbush	Strong	Mullery	Lacy	Moore	Conway Jim	Slough	Busby	Lloyd	Barrett	Fraser	Mitchell	Howe	Belfitt	Conway John	Dowie	Scrivens	Bullivant	Dunne
3		2	3	4	5	6	8	10	9		11		12			**7**				
R		2	3	4		6	8	10	9		11		S	5		7				
2R		2	3	4	5	6	8	10	9	S	11		7							
4		2	**3**	4	5	6		8	9	10	11		7				12			
R		2	3	4	5	6	8	10	9	S	11						7			
2R		2	3	4	5	6	8	10	9		11		S				7			
3R		2	3	4	5	6	8	10	9		11		S				7			
5		2	3	4	5	6	8	10	9	12	11						**7**			
6			3	4	5	6	**8**	10	9	12	11	2					7			
SF			3	4	5	6	**8**	10	9		11	2	7				12			
R			3	4	5	6		10	9	S	11	2	8				7			
F		2		4	5	6	8	10	9	S	11	3	7							

Round	Mellor	Cutbush	Strong	Mullery	Lacy	Moore	Conway Jim	Slough	Busby	Lloyd	Barrett	Fraser	Mitchell	Howe	Belfitt	Conway John	Dowie	Scrivens	Bullivant	Dunne
2			3	4	5	6	7	8	9	10	11	2	S							
3		2	3	4	5	6	7	8	9	10	11		S							
4		2	3	4		6	7	8	9	**10**	11		12	5						

0 points v	York C, Manchester U	0 points
1 point v	Millwall, Oldham A, Bristol C, Oxford U, Hull C, Nottingham F	6 points
2 points v	Orient, Portsmouth, Sheffield W, Sunderland, Blackpool	10 points
3 points v	Notts C, Cardiff C, Bristol R, Aston Villa, Southampton, Bolton W	18 points
4 points v	West Bromwich A, Norwich C	8 points

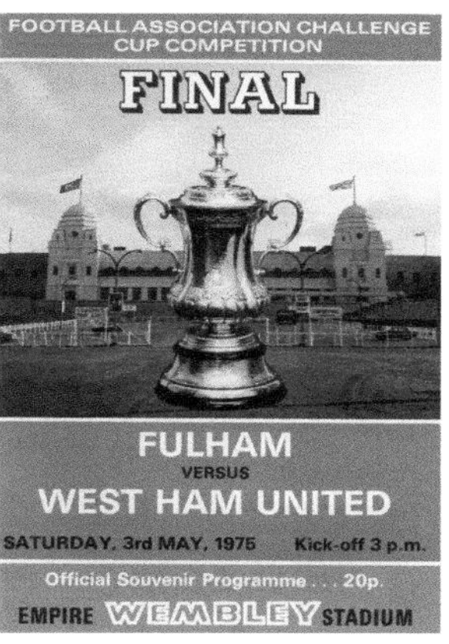

FA Cup final programme and ticket.

1975-76

Division Two

	P	W	D	L	F	A	Pts
Sunderland	42	24	8	10	67	36	56
Bristol City	42	19	15	8	59	35	53
West Bromwich Albion	42	20	13	9	50	33	53
Bolton Wanderers	42	20	12	10	64	38	52
Notts County	42	19	11	12	60	41	49
Southampton	42	21	7	14	66	50	49
Luton Town	42	19	10	13	61	51	48
Nottingham Forest	42	17	12	13	55	40	46
Charlton Athletic	42	15	12	15	61	72	42
Blackpool	42	14	14	14	40	49	42
Chelsea	42	12	16	14	53	54	40
Fulham	42	13	14	15	45	47	40
Orient	42	13	14	15	37	39	40
Hull City	42	14	11	17	45	49	39
Blackburn Rovers	42	12	14	16	45	50	38
Plymouth Argyle	42	13	12	17	48	54	38
Oldham Athletic	42	13	12	17	57	68	38
Bristol Rovers	42	11	16	15	38	50	38
Carlisle United	42	12	13	17	45	59	37
Oxford United	42	11	11	20	39	59	33
York City	42	10	8	24	39	71	28
Portsmouth	42	9	7	26	32	61	25

Manager: Alec Stock

Did you know that?

The season after reaching the FA Cup final, Fulham lost 1-0 to Middlesbrough over two legs in the final of the Anglo-Scottish Cup.

25	Mullery's 400th game
39	Mullery finale
41	Conway and Fraser finales
42	Lloyd finale
42	Margerrison debut

No		Date	V	Opponents	R	H-T	F-T	Scorers	Atte
1	A	16	H	Blackpool	D	0-0	0-0		8,86
2		20	H	Carlisle U	W	1-0	3-0	Conway, Barrett, Slough	7,43
3		23	A	Bolton W	D	2-1	2-2	Busby, Mitchell	8,78
4		26	A	Sunderland	L	0-2	0-2		25,45
5		30	H	West Bromich A	W	2-0	4-0	Mitchell, Howe 2, Busby	9,91
6	S	6	A	Oxford U	W	2-0	3-1	Conway, Busby, Mitchell	7,31
7		13	H	Bristol R	L	0-0	0-2		11,51
8		20	A	Hull C	W	0-1	2-1	Busby, Lloyd	8,47
9		27	H	Chelsea	W	0-0	2-0	Howe, Conway	22,92
10	O	4	A	Blackburn R	W	1-0	1-0	Howe	10,19
11		11	H	Nottingham F	D	0-0	0-0		10,14
12		18	A	Luton T	L	0-1	0-1		14,08
13		25	H	Orient	D	0-1	1-1	Howe	10,46
14	N	1	A	Portsmouth	W	0-0	1-0	Slough	11,44
15		8	H	Charlton A	D	1-0	1-1	Lloyd	15,46
16		15	A	York C	L	0-1	0-1		3,41
17		22	H	Luton T	W	1-0	2-0	Conway 2	9,62
18		29	H	Bristol C	L	0-2	1-2	Mullery	11,40
19	D	6	A	Oldham A	D	0-1	2-2	Howe, Conway	8,74
20		13	H	Bolton W	L	1-1	1-2	Slough	8,74
21		20	A	Blackpool	D	0-1	1-1	Mullery	6,37
22		26	H	Notts C	W	1-0	3-2	Mitchell 2, Slough	11,88
23		27	A	Plymouth A	L	0-4	0-4		24,05
24	J	10	A	Bristol R	L	0-0	0-1		7,86
25		17	H	Oxford U	D	1-0	1-1	Mitchell	6,78
26		31	A	Carlisle U	D	1-2	2-2	Mitchell 2	6,41
27	F	7	H	Sunderland	W	1-0	2-0	Busby 2	11,89
28		17	A	Charlton A	L	0-1	2-3	Mullery 2	11,53
29		21	H	York C	W	1-0	2-0	Lloyd, Slough	6,68
30		24	A	Southampton	L	1-1	1-2	Lacy	24,85
31		28	A	Orient	L	0-1	0-2		7,55
32	M	6	H	Portsmouth	L	0-0	0-1		6,92
33		9	H	Southampton	W	1-0	1-0	Mitchell	8,73
34		13	A	Nottingham F	L	0-0	0-1		11,44
35		20	A	Bristol C	D	0-0	0-0		19,93
36		27	H	Oldham A	W	1-0	1-0	Conway	5,85
37	A	6	A	Chelsea	D	0-0	0-0		23,60
38		10	H	Hull C	D	0-1	1-1	Mitchell	5,62
39		14	A	West Bromich A	L	0-2	1-3	Scrivens	18,26
40		17	A	Notts C	L	0-2	0-4		8,81
41		19	H	Plymouth A	D	0-0	0-0		6,91
42		24	H	Blackburn R	D	0-1	1-1	Howe	5,91
									Ap
									Su
									Goa

FA Cup

3	J	3	H	Huddersfield T	L	1-1	2-3	Conway, Busby	10,29

League Cup

2	S	9	A	West Bromich A	D	0-1	1-1	Conway	10,87
R		24	H	West Bromich A	W	0-0	1-0	Mullery	9,36
3	O	8	H	Peterborough U	L	0-0	0-1		9,80

Mellor	Cutbush	Strong	Mullery	Howe	Moore	Conway	Mitchell	Busby	Lloyd	Barrett	Dowie	Slough	James	Kerslake	Lacy	Fraser	Camp	Bullivant	Scrivens	Margerrison	
1	2	3	4	5	6	7	**8**	9	10	11	12										1
1	2	3	4	5	6	7		9	S	11	8	10									2
1	2	3	4	5	6	7	11	9	S		8	10									3
1	2	3	4	5	6	8	12	9	**7**	11		**10**									4
1	2	3	4	5	6	8	7	9		11	S	10									5
1	2	3	4	5	6	**7**	11	9			8	10				S					6
1	2	3	4	5	6	7	8	9		11	S	10									7
1	2	3	4	5	6	**7**	11	9	8			10				S					8
1	2	3	4	5	6	8		9	7	11	S	10									9
1	2	3	4	5	6	8		9	7	11	S	10									10
1	2	3	4	5	6	8	7	9	S	11		10									11
1			4	5	6	8	**7**	9	10	11	12	3	2								12
1			4	11	6	7		9	10		8	2	S	3	5						13
1		3	4		6	7		9	S	11	8	10	2		5						14
1			4	S	6	7		9	10	11	8	3	2		5						15
1		3	4	10	6	7		9	8	11	S	2			5						16
1		3	4	5	6	7		9	S	11	8	10				2					17
1		3	4	5	6	8		9	S	11	7	10				2					18
1		3	4	5	6	7		9		11	**8**	10			12	2					19
1		**3**	4	2	6	8		9		11	7	10			5		12				20
1	2	3	4		6	8				11	7	**10**	12		5		9				21
1	2	3	4		6	8	7	9		11	S	10			5						22
1	2	3	4	12	**6**	7	8	9		11		10			5						23
1	2	3	4		6	7	8	9		11	S	10			5						24
1	2	3	4	12	6	8	7	9		**11**		10			5						25
1	2		4	5	6	7	8	9	10	11			3					S			26
1		3	4		6	8		9	7	11		10	2		5		S				27
1		3	4		6	8	S	9	7	11		10	2		5						28
1		3	4		6	8	9		7	**11**		10	2		5			12			29
1		3	4		6	8	9		7	11	S	10	2		5						30
1		3	4		6	**8**		9	7	11		10	2		5			12			31
1	2	**8**	4		6		7	9	10	11	12	3			5						32
1	2	3	4	S	6	8	7	9	11			10			5						33
1	2	3	4	6			8	**9**	7	11	12	10			5						34
1	2	3	4	6		7	8	9	S	11		10			5						35
1	2	3		6		8	10	9	**7**	11	S	4			5						36
1		3	4	6		8	7	9	10	S		11	2		5						37
1		3		6		**7**	8	9	10			11	2		5			**4**	12		38
1		**3**	12	6		8	7	9	4			10	2		5				11		39
1				6		8	**7**	9	4	11	10	3	S		5	2					40
1				6		**8**	7		4	12	11	10	2		5	3	9				41
1		3		6			**9**		4		10	8	2		5		**7**		11	12	42
2	22	36	36	28	33	39	26	37	25	32	14	40	14	1	26	5	3	1	2	-	A
-	-	-	1	2	-	-	1	-	-	1	4	-	1	-	1	-	1	2	1	1	S
-	-	-	4	7	-	7	10	6	3	1	-	5	-	-	1	-	-	-	1	-	G

Mellor	Cutbush	Strong	Mullery	Howe	Moore	Conway	Mitchell	Busby	Lloyd	Barrett	Dowie	Slough	James	Kerslake	Lacy	Fraser	Camp	Bullivant	Scrivens	Margerrison	
1	2		4		6	8	7	9		11	**10**	3	12		5						3

Mellor	Cutbush	Strong	Mullery	Howe	Moore	Conway	Mitchell	Busby	Lloyd	Barrett	Dowie	Slough	James	Kerslake	Lacy	Fraser	Camp	Bullivant	Scrivens	Margerrison	
1		3	4	5	6	8	7	9	S		11	10				2					2
1	2	3	4	5	6	8	7	9	11	S		10									R
1	2	3	4	5	6	8	12	9	**7**	11		10									3

0 points v	Bristol R	0 points
1 point v	Bolton W, Bristol C, Charlton A, Nottingham F, Orient, Plymouth A	6 points
2 points v	Blackpool, Luton T, Notts C, Portsmouth, Southampton, Sunderland, West Bromwich A, York C	16 points
3 points v	Blackburn R, Carlisle U, Chelsea, Hull C, Oldham A, Oxford U	18 points
4 points v		0 points

Outstanding coach Bill Taylor left at the end of the season for Manchester City.

1976-77

Division Two

	P	W	D	L	F	A	Pts
Wolverhampton W	42	22	13	7	84	45	57
Chelsea	42	21	13	8	73	53	55
Nottingham Forest	42	21	10	11	77	43	52
Bolton Wanderers	42	20	11	11	75	54	51
Blackpool	42	17	17	8	58	42	51
Luton Town	42	21	6	15	67	48	48
Charlton Athletic	42	16	16	10	71	58	48
Notts County	42	19	10	13	65	60	48
Southampton	42	17	10	15	72	67	44
Millwall	42	15	13	14	57	53	43
Sheffield United	42	14	12	16	54	63	40
Blackburn Rovers	42	15	9	18	42	54	39
Oldham Athletic	42	14	10	18	52	64	38
Hull City	42	10	17	15	45	53	37
Bristol Rovers	42	12	13	17	53	68	37
Burnley	42	11	14	17	46	64	36
Fulham	42	11	13	18	54	61	35
Cardiff City	42	12	10	20	56	67	34
Orient	42	9	16	17	37	55	34
Carlisle United	42	11	12	19	49	75	34
Plymouth Argyle	42	8	16	18	46	65	32
Hereford United	42	8	15	19	57	78	31

Manager: Alec Stock /
Bobby Campbell

Did you know that?

The 6-0 interval lead Fulham built up over Orient in the final home game equalled the club's best-ever first half performance (against Torquay in 1931), and John Mitchell's four goals equalled Fred Harrison's first-half tally against Stockport in 1908.

2	Evanson debut
LC2	Marsh debut
4	Best debut
5	Busby finale
12	Dowie finale
12	Mahoney debut
13	Greenaway debut
15	Mellor finale
16	Maybank debut
17	Peyton debut
25	Cutbush finale
29	Marsh finale
30	Barrett finale
31	Evans debut
41	Mitchell's 50th goal
42	Moore and Slough finales

No		Date	V	Opponents	R	H-T	F-T	Scorers	Atten
1	A	21	H	Nottingham F	D	2-1	2-2	Lacy, Barrett	9,43
2		24	A	Burnley	L	1-2	1-3	Barrett	11,48
3		28	A	Charlton A	D	1-0	1-1	Bullivant	10,69
4	S	4	H	Bristol R	W	1-0	1-0	Best	21,12
5		11	H	Wolverhampton W	D	0-0	0-0		25,79
6		18	A	Luton T	W	1-0	2-0	Barrett, Marsh	19,92
7		25	H	Hereford U	W	2-1	4-1	Slough, Evanson, Marsh 2	18,93
8	O	2	A	Southampton	L	0-1	1-4	Mitchell	28,48
9		16	A	Sheffield U	D	0-1	1-1	Mitchell	28,79
10		23	H	Hull C	D	0-0	0-0		18,67
11		30	A	Bolton W	L	0-0	1-2	Best	24,22
12	N	6	H	Cardiff C	L	0-1	1-2	Best	12,36
13		13	A	Plymouth A	D	1-1	2-2	Mitchell, Howe	25,33
14		16	H	Carlisle U	W	1-0	2-0	Marsh 2	9,21
15		20	H	Notts C	L	0-3	1-5	Slough	12,19
16		27	A	Blackpool	L	0-2	2-3	Mitchell 2	16,77
17	D	4	H	Oldham A	W	1-0	5-0	Mitchell 2, Maybank 2, Best	14,32
18		11	A	Orient	D	0-0	0-0		11,23
19		14	H	Blackburn R	W	0-0	2-0	Maybank, Best	8,54
20		27	A	Chelsea	L	0-0	0-2		55,00
21		28	H	Millwall	L	0-1	2-3	Mitchell, Howe	18,07
22	J	1	A	Cardiff C	L	0-2	0-3		20,26
23		3	H	Bolton W	L	0-0	0-2		12,59
24		15	H	Burnley	D	1-2	2-2	Slough, Barrett	8,81
25		22	A	Nottingham F	L	0-0	0-3		24,71
26	F	5	H	Charlton A	D	1-0	1-1	Mitchell	14,95
27		12	A	Bristol R	L	1-1	1-2	Mitchell	11,14
28		19	A	Wolverhampton W	L	0-1	1-5	Mitchell	25,86
29		26	H	Luton T	L	1-2	1-2	Warboys	11,07
30	M	5	A	Hereford U	L	0-0	0-1		6,59
31		11	H	Southampton	D	0-1	1-1	Lacy	13,40
32		19	A	Carlisle U	W	0-0	2-1	Slough, Mitchell	6,24
33		26	H	Sheffield U	W	2-0	3-2	Mitchell, Maybank 2	12,45
34	A	2	A	Hull C	L	0-0	0-1		6,15
35		8	H	Chelsea	W	2-0	3-1	Warboys, Best, Mitchell	29,69
36		9	A	Millwall	D	0-0	0-0		11,00
37		11	H	Plymouth A	W	0-0	2-0	Mitchell, Maybank	11,71
38		16	A	Notts C	D	0-0	0-0		14,84
39		23	H	Blackpool	D	0-0	0-0		10,95
40		30	A	Oldham A	L	0-0	0-1		9,46
41	M	7	H	Orient	W	6-0	6-1	Mitchell 4, Maybank 2	7,65
42		14	A	Blackburn R	L	0-0	0-1		9,40
									App
									Su
									Goal

FA Cup

No		Date	V	Opponents	R	H-T	F-T	Scorers	Atten
3	J	8	H	Swindon T	D	1-3	3-3	Marsh, Howe, Barrett	16,46
R		11	A	Swindon T	L	0-2	0-5		23,88

League Cup

No		Date	V	Opponents	R	H-T	F-T	Scorers	Atten
2	A	31	H	Peterborough U	D	1-0	1-1	Barrett	10,22
R	S	7	A	Peterborough U	W	1-0	2-1	Best, Slough	16,47
3		22	H	Bolton W	D	1-1	2-2	Best, Mitchell	14,96
R	O	5	A	Bolton W	D	2-1	2-2	Mitchell, Howe	15,01
2R		18	N	Bolton W	L	0-0	1-2	(Nicholson og) (at St Andrew's)	9,31

eale	Cutbush	Strong	Slough	Lacy	Howe	Mitchell	Bullivant	Busby	Dowie	Barrett	Evanson	Mellor	Moore	Best	Marsh	James	Mahoney	Greenaway	Maybank	Peyton	Digweed	Camp	Jump	Margerrison	Warboys	Storey	Evans	Gale	Kerslake	Lloyd	
	2	3	4	5	6	7	8	9	10	11			S																		1
	2	3	4	5	6	10	7	9	**8**	11	12																				2
	2	3	4		5	10	7	9	S	11	8	1	6																		3
	2	3	4		5		S	9		11	8	1	6	7	10																4
	2	3	4		5		S	9		11	8	1	6	7	10																5
	2	3	4		5	9	S			11	8	1	6	7	10																6
	2	3	4		5	9	S			11	8	1	6	7	10																7
		3	4		5	9	2			11	8	1	6	7	**10**	12															8
	2	3	4		5	9	12			**11**	8	1	6	7	10																9
	2	3	4		5	9	11		S		8	1	6	7	10																10
		3	4	2	5	9	11		S		8	1	6	7	10																11
		3	2	4	5	9	S		11		8	1	6	7			10														12
		3	4		5	9	**11**				8	1	6	7	10	2		12													13
		3	4		5	9	11				8	1	6	7	10	2		S													14
		3	4		5	9	11				8	**1**	6	7	10	2		12													15
	2	3	4		5	9				11	8		6	7				S	10												16
	2	3	4		5	9				11	8		6	7				S	10	1											17
	2	3	4	5		9				11	8		6	7		S			10	1											18
	2	3	4	5		9				11	8		6	7		S			10	1											19
		3	4	5	2	9				11	10		6	7				8		1								S			20
	2	3	4	10	5	9				11	8		6				12	7													21
	2	3	4	10	5	9			S	11	8		6					7													22
	2	3	4		5	9			S	11	8		6	7				10			1										23
	2	3	4	12	5		8			11			6	7	10					1		**9**									24
	12	2	4	5		9	11				**8**		6	7	10					1			3								25
		2	4	5		9	11				8		6	7	10			S		1			3								26
		2	4	5		9	11			S	8		6	7						1			3	10							27
		2	3	5		8	4				11		6	7	10					1				S	9						28
		2	3	5		**8**	4			7	11		6		10					1				12	9						29
		3	2	5		8	4			11	10		6							1				S	9	7					30
		3	8	5		10					11		6						7	1				S	9	4	2				31
		3	10	5		11							6						7	1				8	9	4	2	S			32
		3	8		5	10	S						6						7	1				11	9	4	2				33
		3	10	5		11	S						6	7					8	1					9	4	2				34
		3	11	5		10					S		6	7					8	1					9	4	2				35
		3	10	5		11					S		6	7					8	1					9	4	2				36
		3	11	5		10					S		6	7					8	1					9	4	2				37
		3	10	5		11	8						6	7						1				S	9	4	2				38
		3	10	5		11					12		6	**7**					8	1					9	4	2				39
		3	11	5		10	S						6	7					8	1					9	4	2				40
		3	11	5		10					S		6	7					8	1					9	4	2				41
		3	4	5			11				8		6	7					10	1				S	9		2				42
	17	42	42	26	23	38	18	5	3	20	29	13	40	32	16	3	1	4	15	23	1	1	3	3	15	12	12				A
	1	-	-	1	-	-	1	-	-	-	2	-	-	-	-	1	1	2	-	-	-	-	-	1	-	-	-				S
	-	-	4	2	2	19	1	-	-	4	1	-	-	6	5	-	-	-	8	-	-	-	-	-	2	-	-				G

eale	Cutbush	Strong	Slough	Lacy	Howe	Mitchell	Bullivant	Busby	Dowie	Barrett	Evanson	Mellor	Moore	Best	Marsh	James	Mahoney	Greenaway	Maybank	Peyton	Digweed	Camp	Jump	Margerrison	Warboys	Storey	Evans	Gale	Kerslake	Lloyd	
	2	3	4		5	9				11	8		6	7	10			12		1											3
	2	3	4		5	9	11			12	**8**		6	7	10					1											R

eale	Cutbush	Strong	Slough	Lacy	Howe	Mitchell	Bullivant	Busby	Dowie	Barrett	Evanson	Mellor	Moore	Best	Marsh	James	Mahoney	Greenaway	Maybank	Peyton	Digweed	Camp	Jump	Margerrison	Warboys	Storey	Evans	Gale	Kerslake	Lloyd	
	2	3	4		5		7	9	S	11	8	1	6		10																2
	2	3	4		5		S	9		11	8	1	6	7	10																R
	2	3	4		5	9	S			11	8	1	6	7	10																3
		3	4	10	5	9	2		7	11	8	1	6																	S	R
	2	3	4		5	9	11		S		8	1	6	7	10																2R

0 points v	Bolton W, Cardiff C	0 points
1 point v	Blackpool, Burnley, Hull C, Millwall, Nottingham F, Notts C, Southampton , Wolves	8 points
2 points v	Blackburn R, Bristol R, Charlton A, Chelsea, Hereford U, Luton T, Oldham A	14 points
3 points v	Orient, Plymouth A, Sheffield U	9 points
4 points v	Carlisle U	4 points

George Best signs and scores on his debut in September 1976.

1977-78

Division Two

	P	W	D	L	F	A	Pts
Bolton Wanderers	42	24	10	8	63	33	58
Southampton	42	22	13	7	70	39	57
Tottenham Hotspur	42	20	16	6	83	49	56
Brighton & Hove Albion	42	22	12	8	63	38	56
Blackburn Rovers	42	16	13	13	56	60	45
Sunderland	42	14	16	12	67	59	44
Stoke City	42	16	10	16	53	49	42
Oldham Athletic	42	13	16	13	54	58	42
Crystal Palace	42	13	15	14	50	47	41
Fulham	42	14	13	15	49	49	41
Burnley	42	15	10	17	56	64	40
Sheffield United	42	16	8	18	62	73	40
Luton Town	42	14	10	18	54	52	38
Orient	42	10	18	14	43	49	38
Notts County	42	11	16	15	54	62	38
Millwall	42	12	14	16	49	57	38
Charlton Athletic	42	13	12	17	55	68	38
Bristol Rovers	42	13	12	17	61	77	38
Cardiff City	42	13	12	17	51	71	38
Blackpool	42	12	13	17	59	60	37
Mansfield Town	42	10	11	21	49	69	31
Hull City	42	8	12	22	34	52	28

Manager: Bobby Campbell

Did you know that?

John Lacy played the last of his 192 games for Fulham in April 1978. The £200,000 fee for his transfer to Spurs was one of the very first to be decided by a League tribunal rather than direct negotiation between the clubs.

1	Gale debut
15	Best finale
16	Maybank finale
18	Money debut
18	Strong's 200th game
19	Howe finale
20	Hatter debut
34	Davies debut
42	Lacy and Mitchell finales

No		Date	V	Opponents	R	H-T	F-T	Scorers	Att
1	A	20	H	Charlton A	D	0-0	1-1	Maybank	9,8
2		23	A	Oldham A	L	0-1	0-2		7,2
3		27	A	Bristol R	D	0-0	0-0		6,4
4	S	3	H	Blackburn R	D	0-0	0-0		10,0
5		10	A	Tottenham H	L	0-0	0-1		31,9
6		17	H	Notts C	W	1-0	5-1	Mitchell 3, Maybank, Evanson	6,6
7		24	A	Cardiff C	L	0-1	1-3	Maybank	8,8
8	O	1	A	Crystal Palace	W	2-1	3-2	Maybank 2, Gale	28,3
9		4	H	Burnley	W	1-0	4-1	Mitchell 2, Mahoney, Best	6,8
10		8	H	Blackpool	D	0-1	1-1	Mahoney	9,1
11		15	A	Luton T	L	0-1	0-1		12,8
12		22	H	Orient	L	0-2	1-2	Gale	9,1
13		29	A	Sheffield U	L	1-1	1-2	Gale	16,7
14	N	5	H	Sunderland	D	2-1	3-3	Mitchell, Best, Maybank	10,5
15		12	A	Stoke C	L	0-2	0-2		14,1
16		19	H	Hull C	W	1-0	2-0	Lacy, Gale	6,6
17		26	A	Southampton	L	0-0	0-2		21,0
18	D	3	H	Bolton W	W	0-0	2-0	Gale, Evans	8,2
19		10	A	Millwall	W	2-0	3-0	Gale, Evans, (Moore og)	7,6
20		17	H	Stoke C	W	2-0	3-0	Evanson, Evans, Bullivant	8,0
21		26	A	Mansfield T	L	1-0	1-2	Mitchell	8,4
22		28	H	Brighton & HA	W	2-0	2-1	Money, Margerrison	21,6
23		30	H	Oldham A	L	0-1	0-2		10,0
24	J	2	A	Charlton A	W	0-0	1-0	Greenaway	14,5
25		14	H	Bristol R	D	1-1	1-1	Mitchell	8,4
26	F	4	H	Tottenham H	D	0-1	1-1	Greenaway	24,7
27		25	H	Crystal Palace	D	0-1	1-1	Evanson	14,0
28	M	7	H	Cardiff C	W	1-0	1-0	Gale	6,5
29		10	H	Luton T	W	1-0	1-0	Mahoney	7,9
30		15	A	Blackburn R	L	0-1	0-4		9,1
31		17	A	Orient	D	0-0	1-1	Margerrison	7,9
32		24	H	Sheffield U	W	1-0	2-0	Money, (Franks og)	8,9
33		25	A	Brighton & HA	L	0-1	0-2		24,6
34		27	H	Mansfield T	L	0-1	0-2		7,0
35	A	1	A	Sunderland	D	0-1	2-2	Margerrison, Mitchell	11,9
36		4	A	Notts C	D	0-1	1-1	Gale	7,3
37		7	H	Southampton	D	1-1	1-1	Lacy	16,9
38		15	A	Hull C	W	1-0	1-0	Evans	3,9
39		18	A	Blackpool	W	1-1	2-1	Strong, Davies	4,6
40		22	H	Millwall	L	0-1	0-1		10,7
41		25	A	Burnley	L	0-0	0-2		9,4
42		29	A	Bolton W	D	0-0	0-0		34,1
									Ap
									S
									Goa

FA Cup

3	J	7	A	Burnley	L	0-0	0-1		11,1

League Cup

1/1	A	13	H	Orient	L	0-0	0-2		4,6
1/2		16	H	Orient	W	1-0	2-1	Maybank 2	4,3

	Peyton	Evans	Strong	Storey	Lacy	Gale	Margerrison	Mitchell	Warboys	Maybank	Bullivant	Evanson	Greenaway	Best	Howe	Mahoney	Kerslake	James	McCurdy	Money	Hatter	Lovell	Davies	Mason	Gray
1	1	2	3	4	5	6	7	**8**	9	10	11	12													
2	1	2	3	4	5	6	11		9	10	7	8			S										
3	1	2	3	4	5	6	**7**		9	10	11	8	12												
4	1	2	3	4	5	6	S	8	9	10	7			11											
5	1	2	3	4	5	6	S	8		9	11	10	7												
6	1	2	3		5	6	8	9		10	4	11	7			S									
7	1	2	3		5	6	7	9		10	4	8		11	S										
8	1	2	3		5	6	8	9		10	S	11		**7**	4										
9	1	2	3		**5**	6	8	9			12	11		7	4	10									
10	1	2	3		5		4	8		9	**11**	10		7	6	12									
11	1	2	3		5	6	11	9			S	10		7	4	8									
12	1	2	3		5	6	11	9			12	8		7	**4**	10									
13	1	2	3		5	6	8	9			4	11		7		**10**	12								
14	1	2	3		5		8	9		10	4	11	S	**7**				6							
15	1	2	3		5		8	9		10	4	11		7	6			S							
16	1	2	3		**5**	6	8	9		10	4	12	7		11										
17	1	2	3			6	11	9			4	8	7		5		12		**10**						
18	1	2	3		6	8	10	9			S	11	7		5					4					
19	1	2	3		6	8	11	9			S	10	7		5					4					
20	1	2	3		6	8	11	9			12	10	**7**							4	5				
21	1	2	3		5	8	11	9			**7**	10				12				4	6				
22	1	2	3		5	8	11	9				10	7			12				**4**	6				
23	1	2	3		5	8	11	9				10	7			S				4	6				
24	1	2	3		5		11	9			8	10	7			S				4	6				
25	1	2	3		5	6	11	9			8	10	7			S				4					
26	1	2	3		5	8	11	9			**4**	10	7			12				6					
27	1	2	3		5	8	11	9			4	10	7			S				6					
28	1	2	3		5	8	11				4	10	7			9				6					S
29	1	2	3		5	8	11	9				10	7			4				6					S
30	1	2	3		5	8	11	9			4	10	S			7				6					
31	1	2	3		5	8	11	9			4	10	S			7				6					
32	1	2	3		5	8	11	9			4	10	S			7				6					
33	1	2	3			5	11	9			4	**10**	7			8				6		12			
34	1	2	3			5	11	9			4	10				7				6		**8**	12		
35	1	2	3			5	11	9			4	10	7			8				6		S			
36	1	2	3		5	6	11	9			4	10	7			8						S			
37	1	2	3		5	6	11	9			4	10	7			S				8					
38	1	2	3		5	6	11	9			4	10	7			S				8					
39	1	2	3		5	6	11	9			4	10	8									S	7		
40	1		3		5	6	11	9			4	10	8							2		S	**7**		
41	1		3		5	6	11	9			4	10				S				2		7	8		
42	1				5	6	11	**9**			4	10	7							2		12	8	3	
A	42	39	41	5	38	38	40	39	4	12	32	39	23	10	10	13	-	1	1	23	5	2	4	1	
S	-	-	-	-	-	-	-	-	-	-	3	2	1	-	-	4	2	-	-	-	-	2	1	-	
G	-	4	1	-	2	8	3	9	-	6	1	3	2	2	-	3	-	-	-	2	-	-	1	-	

	Peyton	Evans	Strong	Storey	Lacy	Gale	Margerrison	Mitchell	Warboys	Maybank	Bullivant	Evanson	Greenaway	Best	Howe	Mahoney	Kerslake	James	McCurdy	Money	Hatter	Lovell	Davies	Mason	Gray
3	1	2	3		5	8	11	9			4	10	7			S					6				

	Peyton	Evans	Strong	Storey	Lacy	Gale	Margerrison	Mitchell	Warboys	Maybank	Bullivant	Evanson	Greenaway	Best	Howe	Mahoney	Kerslake	James	McCurdy	Money	Hatter	Lovell	Davies	Mason	Gray
1/1	1		3	2	5	6	7	8	9	10	4	**11**			12										
1/2	1		3	2	5	6	7	8	9	10	4	**11**			12										

0 points v	Mansfield, Oldham A	0 points
1 point v	Blackburn R, Orient, Southampton, Tottenham H,	4 points
2 points v	Brighton & HA, Bristol R, Burnley, Cardiff C, Luton T, Millwall, Sheffield U, Stoke C, Sunderland	18 points
3 points v	Blackpool, Bolton W, Charlton A, Crystal Palace, Notts C	15 points
4 points v	Hull C	4 points

Ernest Clay takes over as chairman, a turning point for the club.

1978-79

Division Two

	P	W	D	L	F	A	Pts
Crystal Palace	42	19	19	4	51	24	57
Brighton & Hove Albion	42	23	10	9	72	39	56
Stoke City	42	20	16	6	58	31	56
Sunderland	42	22	11	9	70	44	55
West Ham United	42	18	14	10	70	39	50
Notts County	42	14	16	12	48	60	44
Preston North End	42	12	18	12	59	57	42
Newcastle United	42	17	8	17	51	55	42
Cardiff City	42	16	10	16	56	70	42
Fulham	42	13	15	14	50	47	41
Orient	42	15	10	17	51	51	40
Cambridge United	42	12	16	14	44	52	40
Burnley	42	14	12	16	51	62	40
Oldham Athletic	42	13	13	16	52	61	39
Wrexham	42	12	14	16	45	42	38
Bristol Rovers	42	14	10	18	48	60	38
Leicester City	42	10	17	15	43	52	37
Luton Town	42	13	10	19	60	57	36
Charlton Athletic	42	11	13	18	60	69	35
Sheffield United	42	11	12	19	52	69	34
Millwall	42	11	10	21	42	61	32
Blackburn Rovers	42	10	10	22	41	72	30

Manager: Bobby Campbell

Did you know that?

Fulham set a new club transfer record when they paid £150,000 for Orient striker Peter Kitchen in February 1979.

1	Lock debut
7	Guthrie debut
10	Beck debut
36	Evanson finale
37	Margerrison finale
42	Evans finale

No		Date	V	Opponents	R	H-T	F-T	Scorers	Attend
1	A	19	A	Bristol R	L	0-1	1-3	Margerrison	5,950
2		22	H	Wrexham	L	0-0	0-1		6,135
3		26	H	Burnley	D	0-0	0-0		5,407
4	S	2	A	West Ham U	W	1-0	1-0	Margerrison	25,778
5		9	H	Sheffield U	W	0-0	2-0	Mahoney, Margerrison	6,672
6		16	A	Sunderland	D	0-0	1-1	Margerrison	17,976
7		23	H	Millwall	W	0-0	1-0	Greenaway	8,917
8		30	A	Oldham A	W	0-0	2-0	Guthrie, Davies	6,972
9	O	7	H	Stoke C	W	1-0	2-0	Greenaway, Gale	12,531
10		14	A	Brighton & HA	L	0-1	0-3		24,576
11		21	H	Preston NE	W	2-2	5-3	Davies, Money, Lock, Guthrie, (Baxter og)	8,719
12		28	A	Crystal Palace	W	0-0	1-0	Greenaway	28,733
13	N	3	H	Blackburn R	L	1-1	1-2	Evans	12,583
14		10	H	Bristol R	W	0-0	3-0	Guthrie 2, Beck	10,296
15		18	A	Burnley	L	2-2	3-5	Evanson, Guthrie, Gale	10,566
16		21	H	West Ham U	D	0-0	0-0		26,597
17		25	A	Charlton A	D	0-0	0-0		11,440
18	D	2	H	Notts C	D	1-0	1-1	Guthrie	7,591
19		16	H	Newcastle U	L	1-2	1-3	Guthrie	8,575
20		23	A	Cardiff C	L	0-1	0-2		5,558
21		26	H	Cambridge U	W	2-0	5-1	Davies, Margerrison, Guthrie 3	7,814
22		30	H	Luton T	W	1-0	1-0	(Aizlewood og)	8,591
23	J	20	H	Sunderland	D	0-1	2-2	Davies, Guthrie	11,260
24	F	6	A	Sheffield U	D	0-1	1-1	Margerrison	12,451
25		10	H	Oldham A	W	1-0	1-0	Davies	6,942
26		24	H	Brighton & HA	L	0-0	0-1		18,464
27	M	3	A	Preston NE	D	1-2	2-2	Kitchen, Guthrie	10,890
28		10	H	Crystal Palace	D	0-0	0-0		16,564
29		21	A	Leicester C	L	0-0	0-1		10,396
30		24	A	Wrexham	D	1-0	1-1	Kitchen	9,046
31		27	A	Orient	L	0-1	0-1		6,610
32		31	H	Charlton A	W	1-0	3-1	Kitchen, Davies, Evans	6,955
33	A	4	A	Stoke C	L	0-0	0-2		15,243
34		7	A	Notts C	D	0-1	1-1	Guthrie	9,485
35		11	H	Cardiff C	D	2-2	2-2	Kitchen, Lock	6,067
36		14	A	Cambridge U	L	0-1	0-1		6,523
37		16	H	Orient	D	1-1	2-2	Davies, Lock	8,052
38		21	A	Newcastle U	D	0-0	0-0		11,916
39		24	A	Millwall	D	0-0	0-0		7,397
40		28	H	Leicester C	W	2-0	3-0	Strong, Davies 2	7,00
41	M	5	A	Luton T	L	0-1	0-2		9,11
42		9	A	Blackburn R	L	1-1	1-2	Kitchen	4,684
									App
									Su
									Goal

FA Cup

No		Date	V	Opponents	R	H-T	F-T	Scorers	Attend
3	J	9	H	Queen's Park R	W	1-0	2-0	Margerrison, Davies	21,19
4		31	H	Manchester U	D	0-1	1-1	Margerrison	25,22
R	F	12	A	Manchester U	L	0-0	0-1		41,02

League Cup

No		Date	V	Opponents	R	H-T	F-T	Scorers	Attend
2	A	29	H	Darlington	D	2-2	2-2	Mahoney, Davies	3,89
R	S	5	A	Darlington	L	0-0	0-1		5,06

Peyton	Evans	Strong	Money	Banton	Lock	Bullivant	Gale	Margerrison	Evanson	Davies	Mahoney	Boyd	Guthrie	Greenaway	Beck	Lovell	Marinello	Kitchen	Mason	Hatter	Digweed	
1	2	3	4	5	6	7	8	9	10	11		S										1
1	2	3	10	5	4	7	6		**11**	8	9	12										2
1	2	3	10	5	4	7	6	S	11	8	9											3
1		2	4	5	3	7	6	10	11	8	9	S										4
1	2	3	4	**5**	10	7	6	12	11	8	9											5
1	2	3	5		4	7	6	10	11	8	9			S								6
1	2	3	5		4	7	6	10	**11**	8			9	12								7
1	2	3	5		4	7	6	10	S	8			9	11								8
1	2	3	5		4	7	**6**	10	12	8			9	11								9
1	2	3	5		4	7	6		S	8			9	11	10							10
1	2	3	5		4	**7**	6		12	8			9	11	10							11
1	2	3	5		4	7	6		12	**8**			9	11	10							12
1	2	3	**5**		4	7	6	12	8				9	11	10							13
1	2	3	5		4	**7**	6	12	8				9	11	10							14
1	2	3	5	S	4		6		8				9	11	10	7						15
1	2	3	5		4		6	7	8				9	11	10	S						16
1	2	3	5		4		6	S	11	8			9	7	10							17
1	2	3	5		4	8	6	S		7			9	11	10							18
1	2	3	5		4	8		12	**10**	7			9	11	6							19
1	2	3	5		4	8		6	S	7			9	11	10							20
1	2	3	5		4	8		6	12	7			9		**10**		11					21
1	2	3	5		**4**	8		10	6	7			9	12			11					22
1		**2**	5	3		4	6	10	12	7			9		8		11					23
1		2	5	6	3	4		10	S	7			9		8		11					24
1	2	3	5		6	4		10	S	7			9		8		11					25
1	2	3	5			4	6	7	S				9		8		11	10				26
1	2	3	5		4	11	6		S				9		8		7	10				27
1		2	5		3	4	6		S				9		8		7	10				28
1	2	3	5		11	4	6	7	12		**9**				8			10				29
1	2	3	5		7	4	6	12	8		**9**				11			10				30
1	2	3	5		7	4	6		S				9	11	8			10				31
1	2	3	5		4		6	8	S	7			9		11			10				32
1	2	3	5		4		6	11	S	7			9		8			10				33
1	2	3	5		4		6	**11**		7		12	9		8			10				34
1	2		5		4		6	12		7		**11**	9		8			10	3			35
1	2	3	5		4		6	11	12	7			9		8			**10**				36
1	2	3	5		4		6	11	S	7			9		8			10				37
1		2	5		4		6		S	7			9		8			10	3	11		38
		2	5				6			7			9	S	8	4		10	3	11		39
		2	5		4		6			7			9		8	S		10	3	11		40
	2	3	5		4		6			7			9		8	S		10		11	1	41
	2	3	5		7		6			4			9		8		12	**10**		11	1	42
0	35	41	42	7	39	28	36	20	16	32	7	1	34	14	32	2	8	17	4	5	2	A
-	-	-	-	-	-	-	-	6	7	-	-	2	-	2	-	-	1	-	-	-	-	S
-	2	1	1	-	3	-	2	6	1	9	1	-	13	3	1	-	-	5	-	-	-	G

Peyton	Evans	Strong	Money	Banton	Lock	Bullivant	Gale	Margerrison	Evanson	Davies	Mahoney	Boyd	Guthrie	Greenaway	Beck	Lovell	Marinello	Kitchen	Mason	Hatter	Digweed	
1		2	5		3	4	6	10	S	7			9		8		11					3
1	2	3	5		6	4		10	S	7			9		8		11					4
1	2	3	5		6	4	10	12		**7**			9		8		11					R

Peyton	Evans	Strong	Money	Banton	Lock	Bullivant	Gale	Margerrison	Evanson	Davies	Mahoney	Boyd	Guthrie	Greenaway	Beck	Lovell	Marinello	Kitchen	Mason	Hatter	Digweed	
1		2	4	5	3	7	6	**10**	11	8	9	12										2
1		2	4	5	3	7	6	10	11	8	9	S										R

0 points v	Blackburn R, Brighton & HA	0 points
1 point v	Burnley, Cardiff C, Newcastle U, Orient, Wrexham	5 points
2 points v	Bristol R, Cambridge U , Leicester C, Luton T, Notts C, Stoke C, Sunderland	14 points
3 points v	Charlton A, Crystal Palace, Millwall, Preston NE, Sheffield U, West Ham U	18 points
4 points v	Oldham A	4 points

Midfielder John Beck is signed from Coventry in October 1978.

1979-80

Division Two

	P	W	D	L	F	A	Pts
Leicester City	42	21	13	8	58	38	55
Sunderland	42	21	12	9	69	42	54
Birmingham City	42	21	11	10	58	38	53
Chelsea	42	23	7	12	66	52	53
Queen's Park Rangers	42	18	13	11	75	53	49
Luton Town	42	16	17	9	66	45	49
West Ham United	42	20	7	15	54	43	47
Cambridge United	42	14	16	12	61	53	44
Newcastle United	42	15	14	13	53	49	44
Preston North End	42	12	19	11	56	52	43
Oldham Athletic	42	16	11	15	49	53	43
Swansea City	42	17	9	16	48	53	43
Shrewsbury Town	42	18	5	19	60	53	41
Orient	42	12	17	13	48	54	41
Cardiff City	42	16	8	18	41	48	40
Wrexham	42	16	6	20	40	49	38
Notts County	42	11	15	16	51	52	37
Watford	42	12	13	17	39	46	37
Bristol Rovers	42	11	13	18	50	64	35
Fulham	42	11	7	24	42	74	29
Burnley	42	6	15	21	39	73	27
Charlton Athletic	42	6	10	26	39	78	22

Manager: Bobby Campbell

Did you know that?

Keith Castle, Britain's first heart transplant patient and Fulham supporter, had his operation on the opening day of the season, when Fulham were at Birmingham. When he went into the theatre, the Cottagers trailed 3-0 at half time. When he came round, he learned Fulham had won 4-3. 'Now you know why I'm in here,' he is alleged to have quipped to doctors.

2	Peters debut
15	Bullivant finale
21	Maybank 'debut'
FAC3	Wilson debut
25	Guthrie finale
27	Strong's 300th game
30	O'Driscoll debut
31	Brown debut
33	Lewington debut
40	Maybank finale
41	Money finale

No		Date	V	Opponents	R	H-T	F-T	Scorers	Atte
1	A	18	A	Birmingham C	W	0-3	4-3	Davies 3, Guthrie	19,1
2		22	H	Orient	D	0-0	0-0		9,1
3		25	A	Sunderland	L	0-0	1-2	Gale	25,3
4	S	1	H	Preston NE	W	1-0	1-0	Marinello	7,9
5		8	A	Queen's Park R	L	0-0	0-3		17,1
6		15	H	Burnley	W	1-1	3-1	Davies 2, Lock	6,5
7		22	A	Leicester C	D	2-3	3-3	Davies 3	14,8
8		29	H	Luton T	L	0-1	1-3	Lock	9,9
9	O	6	H	Wrexham	L	0-2	0-2		7,0
10		9	A	Orient	L	0-0	0-1		5,0
11		13	A	Swansea C	L	1-3	1-4	Beck	12,9
12		20	H	Notts C	L	1-1	1-3	Davies	6,2
13		27	A	Chelsea	W	0-0	2-0	Beck, Davies	30,5
14	N	3	H	Birmingham C	L	1-2	2-4	Davies, Lock	8,2
15		10	H	West Ham U	L	0-0	1-2	Davies	16,4
16		17	A	Oldham A	W	1-0	1-0	Greenaway	5,4
17		24	H	Watford	D	0-0	0-0		10,1
18	D	1	A	Newcastle U	L	0-1	0-2		23,4
19		8	H	Shrewsbury T	W	2-1	2-1	Guthrie, Gale	5,3
20		15	A	Cambridge U	L	0-3	0-4		4,7
21		26	A	Cardiff C	L	0-0	0-1		8,1
22		29	H	Sunderland	L	0-0	0-1		9,5
23	J	12	A	Preston NE	L	0-0	2-3	Davies, Gale	7,9
24		19	H	Queen's Park R	L	0-1	0-2		11,5
25	F	2	A	Burnley	L	0-0	1-2	Gale	6,9
26		9	H	Leicester C	D	0-0	0-0		8,6
27		16	A	Luton T	L	0-3	0-4		9,1
28		23	H	Swansea C	L	1-1	1-2	Lock	6,1
29		26	H	Bristol R	D	1-1	1-1	Maybank	4,8
30	M	1	A	Notts C	D	0-0	1-1	Maybank	6,9
31		8	H	Chelsea	L	0-1	1-2	Lock	22,2
32		15	A	Wrexham	D	0-1	1-1	Davies	6,1
33		22	A	West Ham U	W	3-2	3-2	Maybank, Banton 2	30,0
34		28	H	Oldham A	L	0-1	0-1		5,8
35	A	4	A	Bristol R	L	0-0	0-1		7,2
36		8	A	Charlton A	W	0-0	1-0	(Berry og)	4,9
37		12	H	Newcastle U	W	0-0	1-0	Davies	7,2
38		15	H	Cardiff C	W	2-1	2-1	Lewington, (Grapes og)	5,1
39		19	A	Watford	L	0-3	0-4		15,8
40		22	H	Charlton A	W	1-0	1-0	O'Driscoll	3,7
41		26	H	Cambridge U	L	1-1	1-2	Mahoney	4,9
42	M	3	A	Shrewsbury T	L	0-2	2-5	Kitchen, Mahoney	6,3
									App
									Su
									Goa

FA Cup

3	J	8	A	Blackburn R	D	1-1	1-1	Money	9,8
R		15	H	Blackburn R	L	0-1	0-1		5,6

League Cup

2/1	A	29	A	West Bromich A	D	0-1	1-1	Davies	13,6
2/2	S	15	H	West Bromich A	L	0-1	0-1		11,5

Digweed	Strong	Mason	Bullivant	Money	Gale	Marinello	Beck	Guthrie	Lock	Davies	Peyton	Peters	Banton	Mahoney	Kitchen	Greenaway	Hatter	Maybank	Wilson	Gayle	O'Driscoll	Brown	Lewington	
1	2	3	4	5	6	7	8	9	10	11			S											1
	3		4	5	6	7	8	9	10	11	1	2	S											2
	3		4	5	6	7	8	9	10	11	1	2	S											3
	3		4	5	6	7	8	9	10	11	1	2	S											4
	3		4	**5**	6	7	8	9	10	11	1	2	12											5
	3		4	5	6	7	8		10	11	1	2		9	S									6
	3		4	5	6		8		10	11	1	2	S	9	7									7
	3		4	5	6	7	8		10	11	1	2		9	12									8
	3		4	5	6	7	8	9		11	1	2		10	S									9
	3		4	5	6	**7**	8		10	11	1	2		9	12									10
	3		4	**5**	6		8		7	11	1	2		10		12	9							11
	3		4	5	6	7	8	9	10	11	**1**	2				12								12
1	3		4	5	6	7	8	9	10	11		2			S									13
1	3		4	5	6	7	8	9	10	11		**2**			12									14
1	3		4	5	6	7	8	9	10	11		2			S									15
1	3			5	6		8	9	10	11		2		S		7	4							16
1	3			4	6		8	9	10	11		2		S		7	5							17
1	3			4	6		8	9	10	11		2		S		7	5							18
1	3			4	6		8	9	10	11		2		S		7	5							19
	3			4	6		8	9	10	11	1	2		S		7	5							20
	3			4	6		8		10	11	1	2	5			7		9	S					21
	3			4	6	7	8		**11**	9	1	2	5			12		10						22
	3			4	6		8			9	1	2	5			S		10	7	11				23
	3			4	6		8			9	1	2	5			11		10	S	7				24
	3			4	6		8	12		**9**	1	2	5			11		10		7				25
	3			4	6	S	8		11		1	2	5		9			10		7				26
	3			**4**	6	12	8		11		1	2	5		9			10		7				27
	3			**2**	6	11	8		4	9	1	12	5					10		7				28
	3			2	6	11	8		4	9	1		5					10		7	S			29
	3			2	6	S			11	9	1		5					10	4	7	8			30
	3			2	6	8			4	9	1							10	S	7	11	5		31
	3			2	6		8		4	9	1		5					10	S	7	11			32
	3			2	6		8		4	9	1		5					10		7	S		11	33
	3			2	6		8		4	9	1		5					10		7	S		11	34
	3			2	6		8		4	9	1		5					**10**		7	12		11	35
	3			2	6		8		4	9	1		5	10						7	S		11	36
	3			2	6		8		4	9	1		5	**7**				10			12		11	37
	3			2	6		8		4	9	1		5	S				10			7		11	38
				3	6		8		4	9	1	**2**	5	12				10			7		11	39
1	3			2	6		8		4	9			5	S				10			7		11	40
1	3			2	6		8		**4**	10			5	9		12					7		11	41
1	3				6		8		4			**2**	5	10	9	12					7		11	42
11	41	1	15	41	42	17	40	15	38	39	31	28	21	10	4	8	6	19	2	14	8	1	10	A
-	-	-	-	-	-	1	-	1	-	-	-	1	1	1	3	5	-	-	-	-	2	-	-	S
-	-	-	-	-	4	1	2	2	5	15	-	-	2	2	1	1	-	3	-	-	1	-	1	G

Digweed	Strong	Mason	Bullivant	Money	Gale	Marinello	Beck	Guthrie	Lock	Davies	Peyton	Peters	Banton	Mahoney	Kitchen	Greenaway	Hatter	Maybank	Wilson	Gayle	O'Driscoll	Brown	Lewington	
		3		4	6		8			9	1	2	5			7	S	10	11					3
	3			4	6		8			9	1	**2**	5	12		11		10	7					R

Digweed	Strong	Mason	Bullivant	Money	Gale	Marinello	Beck	Guthrie	Lock	Davies	Peyton	Peters	Banton	
	3		4	5	6	7	8	9	10	11	1	2	S	2/1
	3		4	5	6	7	8	9	10	11	1	2	S	2/2

0 points v	Cambridge U, Luton T, Queen's Park R, Sunderland, Swansea C	0 points
1 point v	Bristol R, Notts C, Orient, Watford, Wrexham	5 points
2 points v	Birmingham C, Burnley, Cardiff C, Chelsea, Leicester C, Newcastle U, Oldham A, Preston NE, Shrewsbury T, West Ham U	20 points
3 points v		0 points
4 points v	Charlton A	4 points

Nomadic striker Chris Guthrie's Fulham career ended in February at Burnley.

1980-81

Division Three

	P	W	D	L	F	A	Pts
Rotherham United	46	24	13	9	62	32	61
Barnsley	46	21	17	8	72	45	59
Charlton Athletic	46	25	9	12	63	44	59
Huddersfield Town	46	21	14	11	71	40	56
Chesterfield	46	23	10	13	72	48	56
Portsmouth	46	22	9	15	55	47	53
Plymouth Argyle	46	19	14	13	56	44	52
Burnley	46	18	14	14	60	48	50
Brentford	46	14	19	13	52	49	47
Reading	46	18	10	18	62	62	46
Exeter City	46	16	13	17	62	66	45
Newport County	46	15	13	18	64	61	43
Fulham	46	15	13	18	57	64	43
Oxford United	46	13	17	16	39	47	43
Gillingham	46	12	18	16	48	58	42
Millwall	46	14	14	18	43	60	42
Swindon Town	46	13	15	18	51	56	41
Chester	46	15	11	20	38	48	41
Carlisle United	46	14	13	19	56	70	41
Walsall	46	13	15	18	59	74	41
Sheffield United	46	14	12	20	65	63	40
Colchester United	46	14	11	21	45	65	39
Blackpool	46	9	14	23	45	75	32
Hull City	46	8	16	22	40	71	32

Manager: Bobby Campbell / Malcolm Macdonald

Did you know that?

Roger Brown played his second game for Fulham at Rotherham in the Third Division on the opening day of the season. His first was against Second Division Chelsea the previous March, days after he had been signed from First Division Norwich. In three consecutive games, therefore, Brown played in the First, Second and Third Divisions.

28	Hatter finale
30	Stannard debut
35	Tempest debut
39	Coney debut
45	Parker debut
46	Hopkins debut
46	Greenaway and Mahoney finales
46	Davies' 50th goal

No		Date	V	Opponents	R	H-T	F-T	Scorers	Attend
1	A	16	A	Rotherham U	D	1-1	2-2	Beck, Lock	4,436
2		20	H	Colchester U	W	0-0	1-0	Lock	4,155
3		23	A	Swindon T	W	1-2	4-3	Davies 2, Wilson, Mahoney	6,544
4		29	H	Hull C	D	0-0	0-0		4,592
5	S	5	H	Blackpool	L	1-2	1-2	Davies	4,940
6		13	A	Brentford	W	1-1	3-1	O'Driscoll, Brown, Davies	11,610
7		17	A	Exeter C	L	0-0	0-1		5,300
8		20	H	Walsall	W	1-0	2-1	Davies, Lock	4,573
9		27	A	Portsmouth	L	0-0	0-1		15,460
10	O	1	H	Exeter C	L	0-0	0-1		4,509
11		4	H	Burnley	L	0-1	0-2		4,673
12		7	A	Plymouth A	L	1-2	1-2	Beck	11,647
13		11	A	Gillingham	L	0-1	0-1		4,730
14		18	H	Oxford U	L	0-2	0-4		3,832
15		22	H	Millwall	D	1-0	1-1	Davies	4,095
16		25	A	Chester	W	0-0	1-0	Davies	5,126
17		28	A	Newport C	L	0-2	1-2	Beck	6,029
18	N	1	H	Chesterfield	D	1-0	1-1	Wilson	4,706
19		4	H	Plymouth A	D	0-0	0-0		3,507
20		8	A	Carlisle U	D	0-1	2-2	Beck, Hatter	3,665
21		11	A	Colchester U	L	1-2	2-3	Beck, Davies	2,543
22		15	H	Rotherham U	D	0-1	1-1	O'Driscoll	4,008
23		29	A	Barnsley	D	2-1	2-2	Peters, Goodlass	9,940
24	D	6	H	Huddersfield T	D	1-0	2-2	Davies 2	4,513
25		20	A	Reading	D	0-0	0-0		4,455
26		26	H	Sheffield U	W	1-0	2-1	Lock, Davies	6,323
27		27	A	Charlton A	D	0-1	1-1	Greenaway	11,067
28	J	10	A	Millwall	L	1-1	1-3	Davies	6,002
29		16	H	Barnsley	L	1-1	2-3	Mahoney, Wilson	5,263
30		31	H	Swindon T	W	0-0	2-0	Davies, Mahoney	4,785
31	F	7	H	Brentford	D	1-0	1-1	Beck	8,721
32		14	A	Blackpool	W	1-0	2-0	Mahoney, Goodlass	3,792
33		21	H	Portsmouth	W	1-0	3-0	Davies, Lock, (Doyle og)	9,921
34	M	1	A	Walsall	W	2-1	2-1	Beck, Peters	4,958
35		7	A	Burnley	L	0-2	0-3		5,472
36		14	H	Gillingham	W	1-1	3-2	Davies 2, Gale	5,445
37		17	H	Chester	L	0-1	0-1		3,387
38		21	A	Oxford U	L	0-1	0-2		3,646
39		28	H	Newport C	W	1-0	2-1	Davies, Wilson	4,570
40	A	4	A	Chesterfield	D	0-0	0-0		6,756
41		7	A	Hull C	W	0-0	1-0	Brown	3,263
42		11	H	Carlisle U	L	1-1	2-3	Banton, Coney	4,193
43		18	H	Charlton A	W	1-0	1-0	Coney	7,102
44		21	A	Sheffield U	W	1-0	2-1	Coney, Greenaway	10,898
45		25	H	Reading	L	0-1	1-2	Strong	4,60
46	M	2	A	Huddersfield T	L	1-2	2-4	Beck, Davies	6,965
									Apps
									Sub
									Goals

FA Cup

No		Date	V	Opponents	R	H-T	F-T	Scorers	Attend
1	N	22	A	Reading	W	0-0	2-1	Davies, Mahoney	7,485
2	D	13	H	Brentford	W	1-0	1-0	Greenaway	11,261
3	J	3	A	Bury	D	0-0	1-1	Mahoney	5,36
R		6	H	Bury	D	0-0	0-0		6,58
2R		12	N	Bury	W	0-0	1-0	Davies (at The Hawthorns)	2,46
4		24	H	Charlton A	L	0-1	1-2	Davies	17,05

League Cup

No		Date	V	Opponents	R	H-T	F-T	Scorers	Attend
1/1	A	9	A	Peterborough U	L	1-0	2-3	Strong, Gale	3,66
1/2		12	H	Peterborough U	D	0-0	1-1	Davies	3,47

Peyton	Peters	Strong	Beck	Brown	Gale	Greenaway	Wilson	O'Driscoll	Davies	Lock	Mahoney	Hatter	Goodlass	Clement	Digweed	Corner	Banton	Lewington	Stannard	Day	Tempest	Coney	Parker	Hopkins	Mason	Scott	
1	2	3	4	5	6	7	8	9	10	11															S		1
1	2	3	4	5	6	7	8	9	10	11	S																2
1	2	3	4	5	6	S	10	8	9	11	7																3
1	2	3	4	5	6	S	10	8	9	11	**7**																4
1	2	3	4	5	6	12	10	8	9	**11**	7																5
1	2	3	4	5	6	10		8	9	11	**7**	12															6
1	2	3	4	**5**	6	12	10	8	9	11	7																7
1	2	3	4	5	6	S	10	8	9	11	7																8
1	**2**	3	4	5	6	12	10	8	9	11	7																9
1	**2**	3	4	5	6	12		8	9	10	7		11														10
1		3	4	5	6	S		8	9	10	7		11	2													11
1		3	4	5	7	12		8	9	**10**		6	11	2													12
1		3	4	5	6	S	10	8	9		7		11	2													13
1		3	4	5	9	10	2	7	8	6			11													S	14
1		3	4	5	9	12	**10**	7	8	6			11	2													15
1	S	3	4	5	6	9	10	7	8				11	2													16
	12	3	4	5	6	**9**	10	7	8				11	2	1												17
1	12	2	4	5	6		10	7	8	3	**9**		11														18
1	9	3	4	5	6	12	10	7	8				11	**2**													19
1	2	3	4	5	9		10	8	7			**6**	11			12											20
1	2	3	**4**	5	9		10	7	8			6	11			12											21
1	2	3	4	5	9		8	10	7	S			11			6											22
1	9	2	4	5	10		12	8		3	7	**6**	11														23
1	9	2		5	4	10	S	8	7	3		6	11														24
1	9	2			4	10		8	**7**	3		6	11				5	12									25
1	12	2			4	10		8	7	3	5	6	**11**				9										26
1	S	2			4	10		8	7	3	9	6					5	11									27
1		2					S	8	**7**	3	9	6	11	4			5	10									28
1		6		5	4		12	8	7	**3**	9		11	2				10									29
	3		4	5	6	11	12	**8**	7		9			2				10	1								30
	2	3	4	5	6	**11**	12	8	7		9							10	1								31
	12	3	4	5	6		10	8	7	**2**	9		11						1								32
	12	2	4	5	6		10		7	3	9			**8**				11	1								33
	8	3	4	5	6		10	9	**7**	2								11	1	12							34
	8	3	4	5	6		10	**9**	7									11	1	2	12						35
	8	3	4	5	6		10	**9**	7					2				11	1	12							36
	8	3	4	5	6		10	9	7					2				**11**	1	12							37
	4	3		5	6		10	8	7		**9**			2				11	1	12							38
		3		5	6	4	10	**8**	7	2								11	1	12		9					39
		3	8	5	6	4	10	S	7	2								11	1			9					40
		3	8	5	**6**	4	10		7	2				12				11	1			9					41
	2	3	8			4	10	S	7					6			5	11	1			9					42
	4	3	8	5			10	12	7	**2**				6				11	1			9					43
	8	3		5		4	10	12	7					2			6	11	1			**9**					44
	6	3	4			8		**10**	7				12				5	11	1			9	2				45
	6	3	4			8		12	7		9		**10**				5	11	1					2			46
8	29	45	37	39	40	19	31	39	45	29	22	9	21	17	1	1	8	19	17	1	-	7	1	1			A
-	5	-	-	-	-	7	4	3	-	-	-	1	1	1	-	2	-	1	-	5	1	-	-	-			S
-	2	1	8	2	1	2	4	2	18	5	4	1	2	-	-	-	1	-	-	-	-	3	-	-			G

Peyton	Peters	Strong	Beck	Brown	Gale	Greenaway	Wilson	O'Driscoll	Davies	Lock	Mahoney	Hatter	Goodlass	Clement	Digweed	Corner	Banton	Lewington	Stannard	Day	Tempest	Coney	Parker	Hopkins	Mason	Scott	
	2	3		5	9		S	8	7	4	10	6	11														1
	9	2			4	10		**8**	7	3		6	11				5			12							2
		2			8	7		6	10	5	11	3	9				4	S									3
		2			4	**10**		8	7	3	9	6	11				5	12									R
		6		5	4			8	7	3	9		11	2			S	10									2R
			4	5		11	12	8	7	**3**	9			2			6	10									4

Peyton	Peters	Strong	Beck	Brown	Gale	Greenaway	Wilson	O'Driscoll	Davies	Lock	Mahoney	Hatter	Goodlass	Clement	Digweed	Corner	Banton	Lewington	Stannard	Day	Tempest	Coney	Parker	Hopkins	Mason	Scott	
	2	3	4	5	6	7		**8**	10		9	12						11									1/1
	2	3	4	5	6	7	12		10	11	9							**8**									1/2

0 points v	Burnley, Exeter C, Oxford U	0 points
1 point v	Barnsley, Carlisle U, Huddersfield T, Millwall, Plymouth A, Reading	6 points
2 points v	Blackpool, Chester, Chesterfield, Colchester U, Gillingham, Newport C, Portsmouth, Rotherham U	16 points
3 points v	Brentford, Charlton A, Hull C	9 points
4 points v	Sheffield U, Swindon T, Walsall	12 points

Ted Drake in the dugout (with physio Ron Woolnough) as acting manager against Millwall on the day Bobby Campbell was sacked in October 1980.

1981-82

Division Three

	P	W	D	L	F	A	Pts
Burnley	46	21	17	8	66	45	80
Carlisle United	46	23	11	12	65	50	80
Fulham	46	21	15	10	77	51	78
Lincoln City	46	21	14	11	66	40	77
Oxford United	46	19	14	13	63	49	71
Gillingham	46	20	11	15	64	56	71
Southend United	46	18	15	13	63	51	69
Brentford	46	19	11	16	56	47	68
Millwall	46	18	13	15	62	62	67
Plymouth Argyle	46	18	11	17	64	56	65
Chesterfield	46	18	10	18	57	58	64
Reading	46	17	11	18	67	75	62
Portsmouth	46	14	19	13	56	51	61
Preston North End	46	16	13	17	50	56	61
Bristol Rovers	46	18	9	19	58	65	61
Newport County	46	14	16	16	54	54	58
Huddersfield Town	46	15	12	19	64	59	57
Exeter City	46	16	9	21	71	84	57
Doncaster Rovers	46	13	17	16	55	68	56
Walsall	46	13	14	19	51	55	53
Wimbledon	46	14	11	21	61	75	53
Swindon Town	46	13	13	20	55	71	52
Bristol City	46	11	13	22	40	65	46
Chester	46	7	11	28	36	78	32

Manager: Malcolm Macdonald

Did you know that?

Central defender Roger Brown scored 12 League goals in 46 games, and none was from a penalty or direct from a free kick. The previous best for a defender was 10 by Fred Maven in 1910-11 and 1911-12, but he was the club's penalty taker.

1	O'Sullivan debut
9	Scott debut
11	Peyton's 200th game
14	Peters's finale
19	Gale's 200th game
25	Strong's 400th game
31	Beck finale

No		Date	V	Opponents	R	H-T	F-T	Scorers	Atter
1	A	29	H	Brentford	L	1-2	1-2	Davies	7,67
2	S	5	A	Lincoln C	D	0-0	1-1	Beck	3,03
3		12	H	Bristol C	W	0-1	2-1	Davies, Brown	4,16
4		19	A	Chesterfield	L	0-0	0-3		4,01
5		22	A	Wimbledon	W	1-0	3-1	Coney 2, Davies	5,55
6		26	H	Chester	W	2-0	2-0	O'Driscoll, Lewington	3,62
7		29	H	Southend U	W	0-1	2-1	Davies, Wilson	4,55
8	O	3	A	Oxford U	L	0-1	0-2		4,24
9		10	A	Huddersfield T	L	0-1	0-1		8,25
10		17	H	Newport C	W	1-1	3-1	Davies 2, Lewington	3,91
11		20	H	Exeter C	W	2-1	4-1	Davies 2, O'Driscoll, Brown	4,50
12		24	A	Burnley	D	0-2	2-2	Davies 2	4,22
13		31	H	Portsmouth	D	0-0	1-1	Wilson	7,54
14	N	3	A	Plymouth A	L	0-1	1-3	Davies	4,91
15		7	A	Carlisle U	W	2-0	2-1	Davies, Coney	4,38
16		14	H	Walsall	D	1-1	1-1	Brown	6,16
17		28	H	Millwall	D	0-0	0-0		8,34
18	D	5	A	Bristol R	W	1-0	2-1	Coney, Davies	4,48
19		30	A	Swindon T	W	2-0	4-1	Davies 2, Lock, O'Driscoll	5,64
20	J	20	A	Reading	W	2-0	3-0	Gale, Coney, Lewington	3,76
21		23	A	Brentford	W	0-0	1-0	O'Sullivan	10,83
22		30	H	Chesterfield	W	1-0	1-0	Davies	9,21
23	F	6	A	Bristol C	D	0-0	0-0		9,22
24		9	H	Wimbledon	W	1-0	4-1	Coney 2, Wilson, (Downes og)	7,80
25		19	A	Southend U	D	0-0	0-0		7,71
26		23	H	Oxford U	D	0-0	0-0		5,95
27		27	H	Huddersfield T	D	0-1	2-2	Coney, Lock	5,96
28	M	7	A	Newport C	W	0-0	3-1	Brown, Wilson, Coney	5,17
29		10	A	Exeter C	L	0-0	0-1		3,36
30		13	H	Burnley	D	1-1	1-1	Davies	7,12
31		16	H	Plymouth A	L	1-2	1-3	Tempest	5,10
32		20	A	Portsmouth	D	0-1	1-1	Lock	10,71
33		27	H	Carlisle U	W	3-0	4-1	Brown 2, Davies, O'Driscoll	7,47
34	A	3	A	Walsall	D	0-0	1-1	O'Driscoll	3,12
35		6	H	Doncaster R	W	1-1	3-1	Coney, Davies, Brown	5,08
36		10	A	Gillingham	L	0-1	0-2		9,98
37		13	H	Swindon T	W	2-0	2-0	Brown 2	6,65
38		17	H	Bristol R	W	2-0	4-2	Davies, Lock, Brown, O'Driscoll	6,84
39		20	A	Preston NE	W	1-1	3-1	Davies 2, Lock	6,00
40		25	A	Millwall	L	0-2	3-4	Brown, O'Driscoll, (Stevens og)	6,48
41	M	1	H	Reading	D	0-1	2-2	Wilson, Lewington	6,77
42		5	A	Chester	W	1-0	2-0	Coney, Tempest	1,17
43		8	A	Doncaster R	L	1-1	1-2	Coney	4,72
44		11	H	Gillingham	D	0-0	0-0		7,17
45		15	H	Preston NE	W	2-0	3-0	Davies 2, Coney	7,58
46		18	H	Lincoln C	D	0-0	1-1	Brown	20,39
									App
									Su
									Goa

FA Cup

1	N	21	A	Bristol R	W	0-0	2-1	Coney 2	6,49
2	J	2	A	Hereford U	L	0-1	0-1		4,61

League Cup

1/1	S	1	A	Bournemouth	W	1-0	1-0	Davies	3,93
1/2		15	H	Bournemouth	W	0-0	2-0	Beck, Wilson	3,58
2/1	O	7	A	Newcastle U	W	0-0	2-1	Wilson, Coney	20,24
2/2		27	H	Newcastle U	W	1-0	2-0	Lewington, Coney	7,21
3	N	10	A	Oldham A	D	0-1	1-1	Wilson	6,61
R		17	H	Oldham A	W	2-0	3-0	Coney 2, Hopkins	6,98
4	D	2	A	Tottenham H	L	0-1	0-1		30,12

Peyton	Hopkins	Strong	Beck	Brown	Banton	Davies	Day	Coney	O'Sullivan	Lewington	Wilson	Gale	O'Driscoll	Scott	Tempest	Peters	Lock	Reeves	Parker	Stannard	
1	2	3	4	5	6	7	**8**	9	10	11	12										1
1	2	3	4	5		7	S	9	10	11	8	6									2
1	2	3	4	5		7		9	10	11	8	6						S			3
1	2	3	4	5		7	S	9	10	11	8	6									4
1	2	3		5		7	S	9	10	11	8	6	4								5
1	2	3		5		7	S	9	10	11	8	6	4								6
1	2	3		5		7	S	9	10	11	8	6	4								7
1	2	3		5		7	12	9	10	11	8	6	**4**								8
1	2	3		5		7	12	9	10		8	6	**4**	11							9
1	2	3		5		7	S	9	10	11	8	6	4								10
1	2	3		5		7	S	9	10	11	8	6	4								11
1	2	3		5		7	S		10	11	8	6	4		9						12
1	2	3		5		7	S	9	10	11	8	6	4								13
1	2	3		5		7		9	10	11	8	6	**4**			12					14
1	2	3		5		7		9	10	11	8	6	4						S		15
1	2	3		**5**		7	12	9	10	11	8	6	4								16
1	2	3		5		7		9	10	11	8	6	4				S				17
1	2	3		5		7		9	10	11	8	6	4				S				18
1	2	3		5		7		**9**	10	11	8	6	4				12				19
1		3		5		**7**		9	10	11		6	4				2	8	12		20
1		3		5				9	10	11		6	4		7		2	8	S		21
1		3		5		**7**		9	10	11	8	6	4		12		2				22
1		3		5				9	10	11	8	6	4		7		2	S			23
1		3		5		7		9	10	11	8	6	4		S		2				24
1	12	3		5		7		9	10	**11**	8	6	4				2				25
1		3		5		7		9	10		8	6	**4**				2	11	12		26
1	S	3		5		7		9	10		8	6	4				2	11			27
1	S	3		5		7		9	10		8	6	4				2	11			28
1	S	3		5		7		9	10		8	6	4				2	11			29
1	12	3		5		7		9	10		8	6	4				2	**11**			30
1	2	3	12	5		7			10		8		**4**		9		6		11		31
1	2	3		5		7			10		8	6	4		**9**		11		12		32
1	2	3		5		7			10		8	6	4		9		11		S		33
1	2	3		5		7		9			8	6	4		S		11		10		34
1	2	3		5		7		9	10		8	6	4		S		11				35
1	2	3		5		7		9	10		8	6	4		S		11				36
1	2	3		5		7		9	10		8	6	4		S		11				37
1	2	3		5		7		9	10		8	6	4		S		11				38
	2	3		5		7		9	10		8	6	4		S		11			1	39
	2	3		**5**		7		9	10	8		6	4		12		11			1	40
1		2		5		**7**		9	10	11	8	6	4		12		3				41
1	12	2		5				9	10	11	8	**6**	4		**7**		3				42
1	S	2		5				9	10	11	8	6	4		7		3				43
1	12	2		5				9	10	11	8	6	4		7		**3**				44
1	2	**3**		5		7		9	10	11	8	6	4		12						45
1	2	**3**		5		7		9	10	11	8	6	4		12						46
44	31	46	4	46	1	41	1	42	45	31	42	44	42	1	9	-	25	7	2	2	A
-	4	-	1	-	-	-	3	-	-	-	1	-	-	-	5	1	1	-	3	-	S
-	-	-	1	12	-	24	-	13	1	4	5	1	7	-	2	-	5	-	-	-	G

Peyton	Hopkins	Strong	Beck	Brown	Banton	Davies	Day	Coney	O'Sullivan	Lewington	Wilson	Gale	O'Driscoll	Scott	Tempest	Peters	Lock	Reeves	Parker	Stannard	
1	2	**3**		5		7		9	10	11	8	6		4			12				1
1	2	3		5		7		9	10	11	8	6		4			S				2

Peyton	Hopkins	Strong	Beck	Brown	Banton	Davies	Day	Coney	O'Sullivan	Lewington	Wilson	Gale	O'Driscoll	Scott	Tempest	Peters	Lock	Reeves	Parker	Stannard	
1	2	3	4	5		7	S	9	10	11	8	6									1/1
1	2	3	4	5		7	S	9	10	11	8	6									1/2
1	2	3		5		7		9	10	**11**	8	6		4			12				2/1
1	2	3		5		7	S	9	10	11	8	6		4							2/2
1	2	3		5		7		9	10	11	8	6		4			S				3
1	2	3				7	S	9	10	11	8	6		4				5			R
1	2	3		5		7		9	10	11	8	6		4			S				4

0 points v	Plymouth A	0 points
1 point v	Gillingham, Huddersfield T, Millwall, Oxford U	4 points
2 points v	Burnley, Lincoln C, Portsmouth, Walsall	8 points
3 points v	Brentford, Chesterfield, Doncaster R, Exeter C	12 points
4 points v	Bristol C, Reading, Southend U	12 points
6 points v	Bristol R, Carlisle U, Chester, Newport C, Preston NE, Swindon T, Wimbledon	42 points

Free transfer signing Peter O'Sullivan from Brighton was a key member of Malcolm Macdonald's promotion side.

1982-83

Division Two

	P	W	D	L	F	A	Pts
Queen's Park Rangers	42	26	7	9	77	36	85
Wolverhampton W	42	20	15	7	68	44	75
Leicester City	42	20	10	12	72	44	70
Fulham	42	20	9	13	64	47	69
Newcastle United	42	18	13	11	75	53	67
Sheffield Wednesday	42	16	15	11	60	47	63
Oldham Athletic	42	14	19	9	64	47	61
Leeds United	42	13	21	8	51	46	60
Shrewsbury Town	42	15	14	13	48	48	59
Barnsley	42	14	15	13	57	55	57
Blackburn Rovers	42	15	12	15	58	58	57
Cambridge United	42	13	12	17	42	60	51
Derby County	42	10	19	13	49	58	49
Carlisle United	42	12	12	18	68	70	48
Crystal Palace	42	12	12	18	43	52	48
Middlesbrough	42	11	15	16	46	67	48
Charlton Athletic	42	13	9	20	63	86	48
Chelsea	42	11	14	17	51	61	47
Grimsby Town	42	12	11	19	45	70	47
Rotherham United	42	10	15	17	45	68	45
Burnley	42	12	8	22	56	66	44
Bolton Wanderers	42	11	11	20	42	61	44

Manager: Malcolm Macdonald

Did you know that?

Fulham finished fourth, just missing out on promotion, but above Chelsea in 18th. This was the last of only six times in 89 seasons of League football that Fulham finished above their West London neighbours, and by the widest margin. The other seasons were 1950–51, 1959–60, 1961–62, 1962–63 and 1966–67.

1	Houghton debut
2	O'Sullivan finale
3	Strong finale
10	Davies' 200th game
11	Carr debut
17	Rosenior debut

No		Date	V	Opponents	R	H-T	F-T	Scorers	Atten
1	A	28	H	Rotherham U	D	1-1	1-1	Davies	7,02
2	S	4	A	Shrewsbury T	W	0-0	1-0	Wilson	3,52
3		7	H	Queen's Park R	D	0-0	1-1	Lewington	15,00
4		11	H	Bolton W	W	2-0	4-0	Coney 2, Lewington, Houghton	5,68
5		18	A	Middlesbrough	W	2-1	4-1	Davies 2, Lewington, Houghton	6,44
6		25	H	Leeds U	W	1-1	3-2	Davies 2, Coney	12,79
7		28	A	Charlton A	L	0-0	0-3		6,79
8	O	2	A	Barnsley	L	3-1	3-4	Hopkins, Wilson, Davies	12,58
9		9	H	Blackburn R	W	2-1	3-1	Davies, Lewington, Wilson	5,69
10		16	A	Newcastle U	W	3-0	4-1	Davies 2, Coney, Houghton	29,49
11		23	H	Burnley	W	1-1	3-1	Lewington 2, Houghton	9,04
12		30	A	Crystal Palace	D	1-0	1-1	O'Driscoll	14,91
13	N	6	H	Oldham A	L	0-2	0-3		6,89
14		13	A	Grimsby T	W	2-0	4-0	Davies 2, Wilson, Gale	6,95
15		20	A	Wolverhampton W	W	1-2	4-2	Lewington, Davies 2, Wilson	14,44
16		27	H	Sheffield W	W	1-0	1-0	Davies	13,86
17	D	4	A	Leicester C	L	0-0	0-2		9,08
18		11	H	Derby C	W	1-0	2-1	Thomas, Carr	7,85
19		18	A	Carlisle U	L	1-0	2-3	Lewington, O'Driscoll	4,85
20		27	H	Cambridge U	D	0-1	1-1	Brown	9,10
21		28	A	Chelsea	D	0-0	0-0		29,79
22	J	1	H	Wolverhampton W	L	1-2	1-3	Lewington	17,19
23		3	H	Shrewsbury T	W	0-1	2-1	Davies, Thomas	7,78
24		15	A	Rotherham U	W	1-0	1-0	Brown	7,66
25		22	H	Middlesbrough	W	1-0	1-0	Wilson	8,43
26	F	5	A	Bolton W	W	0-0	1-0	O'Driscoll	6,74
27		19	A	Blackburn R	D	0-0	0-0		6,14
28		26	H	Newcastle U	D	1-2	2-2	Davies, Lock	14,27
29	M	5	A	Burnley	L	0-1	0-1		8,82
30		12	H	Crystal Palace	W	1-0	1-0	Brown	11,23
31		19	A	Oldham A	L	0-0	0-1		6,18
32		26	H	Grimsby T	W	2-0	4-0	Wilson 2, Lewington, Davies	8,09
33	A	2	H	Chelsea	D	1-1	1-1	Lock	15,24
34		5	A	Cambridge U	L	0-0	0-1		6,24
35		9	H	Charlton A	W	0-0	2-1	Davies, Brown	9,03
36		16	A	Leeds U	D	0-1	1-1	Houghton	24,32
37		19	H	Barnsley	W	0-0	1-0	Gale	9,00
38		23	H	Leicester C	L	0-0	0-1		24,25
39		30	A	Sheffield W	L	0-0	1-2	Wilson	12,53
40	M	2	A	Queen's Park R	L	0-2	1-3	Davies	24,43
41		7	H	Carlisle U	W	1-0	2-0	Wilson 2	10,04
42		14	A	Derby C	L	0-0	0-1		21,12
									App
									Su
									Goal

FA Cup

3	J	8	A	Oldham A	W	0-0	2-0	Houghton, Coney	8,08
4		29	A	Watford	D	0-0	1-1	Coney	24,57
R	F	1	H	Watford	L	0-1	1-2	Lewington	22,20

League (Milk) Cup

1/1	S	1	A	Southend U	L	0-1	0-1		2,67
1/2		14	H	Southend U	W	1-0	4-2	Coney, Houghton, Davies, (Yates og)	4,64
2/1	O	5	H	Coventry C	D	2-2	2-2	Gale, Brown	6,23
2/2		26	A	Coventry C	D	0-0	0-0		8,21

Peyton	Hopkins	Strong	O'Driscoll	Brown	Gale	Davies	Wilson	Coney	Houghton	Lewington	O'Sullivan	Parker	Lock	Tempest	Carr	Thomas	Rosenior	McDermott	Reeves	Scott	
	2	3	4	5	6	7	8	9	10	11		S									1
	2	3	4	5	6	7	8	9	10	**11**	12										2
	2	3	4	5	6	7	8	9	10	11		12									3
	2		4	5	6	7	**8**	9	10	11		12	3								4
	2		4	5	6	7	8	9	10	11		12	3								5
	2		4	5	6	7	8	9	10	11		S	3								6
	2		4	**5**	6	7	8	9	10	11		12	3								7
	2		4	5	6	7	8	9	10	11		S	3								8
	2		4	5	6	7	8	9	10	11		S	3								9
	2		4	5	6	7	8	9	10	11			**3**	12							10
	2		4	5	6	**7**		9	10	11		3		8	12						11
	2		4	5	6			9	10	11		8	3		7					S	12
	2		4	5	6		8	9	10	11		12	3		**7**						13
	2		4	5	6	7	8	9	10	11		S	3								14
	2		4	5	6	7	8	9	10	11		S	3								15
	2		4	5	6	7	8	**9**	10	11		12	3								16
	2		4	5	6		8		10	11		12	3			7	**9**				17
	2		4	5	6		8		10	**11**		12	3		**7**	9					18
	2		4	5	6	7	8		10	11		S	3			9					19
	2		4	5	6	7	8	9	10	11		S	3								20
	2		4	5	6	7	8	9	10	11		S	3								21
	2		4	5	6	7	8	9	10	11		S	3								22
	2		4	5	6	7	8	9	10	11			**3**			12					23
	2		4	5	6	7	8	9	10	11		3				S					24
	2		4	5	6	7	8	9	10	11		3				S					25
	2		4	5	6	7	8	9	10	11		3			S						26
	2		4	5	6	7	8		10	11				9	3					S	27
	2		4	5	6	7	8	9	10	11			3	S							28
	2		4	5	6	7	8		10	11			3	**9**	12						29
	2		4	5	6	7	8	**9**	10	11			3					12			30
	2		4	5	6	7	**8**	9	10	11			3					12			31
	2		4	5	6	7	8	9	10	11			3					S			32
	2		4	5	6	7	8	9	10	11			3					S			33
	2		4	5	6	**7**	8	9	10	11			3					12			34
	2		4	5	6	7	8	9	10	11			3					S			35
	2		4	5	6	7	8	9	10	11		12	3								36
	2		4	5	6	7	8	9	10	11		S	3								37
	2		4	5	6	7	8	**9**	10	11		12	3								38
	2		4	5	6	7	8	9	10	11		12	3								39
			4	5	6	7	8	9	10	11		2	**3**						12		40
	2		4	5	6	7	8	9	10	11			3	S							41
	2		**4**	5	6	7	8	9	10	11			3						12		42
2	41	3	42	42	42	38	40	37	42	42	-	6	34	3	4	3	1	-	-	-	A
	-	-	-	-	-	-	-	-	-	-	1	11	-	1	2	1	-	3	2	-	S
	1	-	3	4	2	19	11	4	5	10	-	-	2	-	1	2	-	-	-	-	G

Peyton	Hopkins	Strong	O'Driscoll	Brown	Gale	Davies	Wilson	Coney	Houghton	Lewington	O'Sullivan	Parker	Lock	Tempest	Carr	Thomas	Rosenior	McDermott	Reeves	Scott	
	2		4	5	6	7	8	9	10	11		3			S						3
	2		4	5	6	7	8	9	10	11		3			S						4
	2		4	5	6	7	8	9	10	11		3			S						R

Peyton	Hopkins	Strong	O'Driscoll	Brown	Gale	Davies	Wilson	Coney	Houghton	Lewington	O'Sullivan	Parker	Lock	Tempest	Carr	Thomas	Rosenior	McDermott	Reeves	Scott	
	2		4	5	6	7	8	9	10	11		S	3								1/1
	2		4	5	6	7		9	10	11		8	3	S							1/2
	2		4	5	6	7	8	9	10	11		S	3								2/1
	2		4	5	6			9	10	11		3			8				**7**	12	2/2

0 points v	Leicester C, Oldham A	0 points
1 point v	Cambridge U, Queen's Park R	2 points
2 points v	Chelsea	2 points
3 points v	Barnsley, Burnley, Carlisle U, Charlton A, Derby C, Sheffield W, Wolves	21 points
4 points v	Blackburn R, Crystal Palace, Leeds U, Newcastle U, Rotherham U	20 points
6 points v	Bolton W, Grimsby T, Middlesbrough, Shrewsbury T	24 points

In the 3–1 home win over Burnley on October 1982, diminutive full back and future captain Cliff Carr made the first of his 192 appearances.

1983-84

Division Two

	P	W	D	L	F	A	Pts
Chelsea	42	25	13	4	90	40	88
Sheffield Wednesday	42	26	10	6	72	34	88
Newcastle United	42	24	8	10	85	53	80
Manchester City	42	20	10	12	66	48	70
Grimsby Town	42	19	13	10	60	47	70
Blackburn Rovers	42	17	16	9	57	46	67
Carlisle United	42	16	16	10	48	41	64
Shrewsbury Town	42	17	10	15	49	53	61
Brighton & Hove Albion	42	17	9	16	69	60	60
Leeds United	42	16	12	14	55	56	60
Fulham	42	15	12	15	60	53	57
Huddersfield Town	42	14	15	13	56	49	57
Charlton Athletic	42	16	9	17	53	64	57
Barnsley	42	15	7	20	57	53	52
Cardiff City	42	15	6	21	53	66	51
Portsmouth	42	14	7	21	73	64	49
Middlesbrough	42	12	13	17	41	47	49
Crystal Palace	42	12	11	19	42	52	47
Oldham Athletic	42	13	8	21	47	73	47
Derby County	42	11	9	22	36	72	42
Swansea City	42	7	8	27	36	85	29
Cambridge United	42	4	12	26	28	77	24

Manager: Malcolm Macdonald / Ray Harford

Did you know that?

Fulham played the first of four League Cup ties against Liverpool in November 1983 (the others were in 1986, 1993 and 1998), all of which they lost. Conversely, the Cottagers have met Merseyside neighbours Everton four times in the FA Cup (1926, 1948, 1975 and 2004) and won each time.

2 Marshall debut
9 Davies' 100th goal

No		Date	V	Opponents	R	H-T	F-T	Scorers	Atte
1	A	27	A	Barnsley	L	0-1	0-3		9,8
2	S	3	H	Portsmouth	L	0-1	0-2		10,6
3		7	A	Manchester C	D	0-0	0-0		23,3
4		11	A	Crystal Palace	D	1-0	1-1	Tempest	11,3
5		17	H	Leeds U	W	0-0	2-1	Lock, Tempest	10,0
6		24	A	Grimsby T	L	1-1	1-2	Davies	5,7
7		27	H	Middlesbrough	W	1-1	2-1	Houghton, Tempest	6,4
8	O	1	H	Swansea C	W	1-0	5-0	Gale, Davies 2, Houghton, Tempest	7,2
9		8	H	Chelsea	L	2-2	3-5	Davies 3	24,7
10		15	A	Carlisle U	L	0-2	0-2		3,7
11		22	A	Shrewsbury T	D	0-0	0-0		4,7
12		31	H	Cardiff C	L	0-0	0-2		5,9
13	N	5	A	Newcastle U	L	1-1	2-3	Wilson 2	31,5
14		11	H	Sheffield W	D	0-1	1-1	Davies	9,6
15		19	A	Huddersfield T	L	0-0	0-2		8,9
16		26	H	Blackburn R	L	0-0	0-1		5,6
17	D	3	A	Cambridge U	D	1-1	1-1	Lock	3,0
18		10	H	Charlton A	L	0-0	0-1		6,1
19		17	A	Oldham A	L	0-1	0-3		4,5
20		26	H	Derby C	D	0-0	2-2	Rosenior 2	7,4
21		27	A	Brighton & HA	D	0-0	1-1	Sealy	15,0
22		31	A	Portsmouth	W	2-1	4-1	Carr, Davies 2, Rosenior	15,6
23	J	2	H	Grimsby T	D	1-0	1-1	Carr	7,3
24		14	H	Barnsley	W	0-0	1-0	Carr	5,0
25		21	A	Leeds U	L	0-1	0-1		11,4
26	F	5	A	Swansea C	W	0-0	3-0	Davies 2, Coney	7,3
27		11	H	Crystal Palace	D	0-0	1-1	Davies	9,1
28		19	A	Cardiff C	W	2-0	4-0	Coney 2, Rosenior 2	7,1
29		25	H	Shrewsbury T	W	0-0	3-0	Coney, Davies, Rosenior	5,1
30	M	3	H	Newcastle U	D	2-1	2-2	Scott, Davies	12,2
31		7	A	Sheffield W	D	0-0	1-1	Rosenior	20,4
32		17	H	Manchester C	W	4-0	5-1	Davies 4, Rosenior	9,6
33		24	A	Middlesbrough	W	0-0	2-0	Davies, Coney	5,4
34		31	H	Carlisle U	D	0-0	0-0		6,0
35	A	7	A	Chelsea	L	0-3	0-4		31,9
36		14	H	Huddersfield T	L	0-2	0-2		5,2
37		21	A	Derby C	L	0-1	0-1		12,1
38		23	H	Brighton & HA	W	3-0	3-1	Scott, Davies, Coney	7,7
39		29	A	Blackburn R	W	0-0	1-0	Davies	4,3
40	M	5	H	Cambridge U	W	0-0	1-0	Wilson	4,9
41		7	A	Charlton A	W	2-2	4-3	Scott, Houghton, Carr, Davies	6,1
42		12	H	Oldham A	W	2-0	3-0	Davies, Coney, Scott	5,0
									Ap
									S
									Goa

FA Cup

No		Date	V	Opponents	R	H-T	F-T	Scorers	Atte
3	J	7	H	Tottenham H	D	0-0	0-0		23,3
R		11	A	Tottenham H	L	0-2	0-2		32,8

League (Milk) Cup

No		Date	V	Opponents	R	H-T	F-T	Scorers	Atte
2/1	O	5	A	Doncaster R	W	2-1	3-1	Tempest, Davies, Scott	4,8
2/2		26	H	Doncaster R	W	2-0	3-1	Davies 2, Lewington	3,8
3	N	8	H	Liverpool	D	0-0	1-1	Lock	20,1
R		22	A	Liverpool	D	0-0	1-1	Lock	15,7
2R		29	H	Liverpool	L	0-0	0-1		20,9

Stannard	Hopkins	Lock	O'Driscoll	Brown	Gale	Tempest	Wilson	Coney	Houghton	Parker	Carr	Marshall	Davies	Scott	Lewington	Peyton	Tapley	Rosenior	Sealy	Foley	Reeves	Cottington	
1	**2**	3	4	5	6	7	8	9	10	11	12												1
1		3		5	6	12	8	**9**	10	2		4	7	11									2
1		**3**		5	6	9	8		10	2	12	4	7	11									3
1			12	5	6	**9**	8		10	2	3	4	7	11									4
1	S	3		5	6	9			10	2	8	4	7	11									5
1	12	3		5	6	9			10	2	8	**4**	7	11									6
1		**3**	4	5	6	9	8		10	2	12		7	11									7
1	12		4	**5**	6	9	8		10	2	3		7	11									8
1			4	5	6	9	**8**		10	2	3		7	11	12								9
1			4	5	6	**9**	8	12	10	2	3		7	11									10
1	5		4		6		**8**	9	10	2	3		7	12	11								11
1	5	6	4					**9**	10	2	3	12	7	8	11								12
1	4	6		5			8	**9**	10	2	3	12	7		11								13
1		3	S	5	6		8		10	2	4	9	7		11								14
1		3	S	5	6		8	7	10	2	4	9			11								15
	2	3			6		8		10		4	**9**	7		11	1	5	12					16
	2	3	6				8	9	10		4	5	7	S	11	1							17
	5	3	4		6			9	10		8	2	7		11	1		S					18
	5	3			6				10		4	2		S	11	1		9	7	8			19
	5	**3**			6				10		4	2		8	11	1		9	7	12			20
	5				6				**10**		3	2	12	8	11	1		9	7	4			21
	5				6				10		3	2	4	8	11	1		9	7	S			22
	5				6			7	**10**		3	2	4	8	11	1		9			12		23
	5		4		6			S		2	3	7		8	11	1		9			10		24
	5		12		6					2	3	4		8	11	1		9	7		**10**		25
	5				6			11	9	2	3		4	7	10	1		8			S		26
	5				6			8	10	2	3		7	4	11	1		9			S		27
	5				6			8	11	2	3		7	4	10	1		9				S	28
	5				6		S	8	10	2	3		7	4	11	1		9					29
	5				6		12	8	10	2	3		7	4	11	1		**9**					30
	5				6		S	8	10	2	3		7	4	11	1		9					31
	5				6	12		8	10	2	3		7	4	**11**	1		9					32
	5				6	S		8	10	2	3		7	4	11	1		9					33
	5				6	S		8	10	2	3		7	4	11	1		9					34
	5				6	4		8	10	2	3	S	7		11	1		9					35
	5				6	**4**		8	10	2	3		7		11	1		9				12	36
	5				6			8	**10**	2	3	12	7	4	11	1		9					37
	5				**6**			8	10	2	3	12	7	4	11	1		9					38
	5							8	10	2	3	6	7	4	11	1		9				S	39
	5						12	8	10	2	3	6	7	4	11	1		**9**					40
	5					9	S	8	10	2	3	6	7	4	11	1							41
	5					9	S	8	10	2	3	6	7	4	11	1							42
5	31	15	10	13	35	13	14	26	40	34	38	21	35	31	32	27	1	22	5	2	2	-	A
-	2	-	2	-	-	2	2	1	-	-	3	4	1	1	1	-	-	1	-	1	1	1	S
-	-	2	-	-	1	4	3	7	3	-	4	-	23	4	-	-	-	8	1	-	-	-	G

Stannard	Hopkins	Lock	O'Driscoll	Brown	Gale	Tempest	Wilson	Coney	Houghton	Parker	Carr	Marshall	Davies	Scott	Lewington	Peyton	Tapley	Rosenior	Sealy	Foley	Reeves	Cottington	
	5		S		6					2	3	7	4	8	11	1		9			10		3
	5		12		6					2	3	7	4	8	11	1		9			**10**		R

Stannard	Hopkins	Lock	O'Driscoll	Brown	Gale	Tempest	Wilson	Coney	Houghton	Parker	Carr	Marshall	Davies	Scott	Lewington	Peyton	Tapley	Rosenior	Sealy	Foley	Reeves	Cottington	
	5		4		6	9	8		10	2	3	S	7	11									2/1
	5		**4**		6			9	10	2	3		7	8	11							12	2/1
	2	3	S		6		8		10	5	4	9	7		11								3
	2	3	12		6		8		10	**5**	4	9	7		11	1							R
	2	3	S		6		8	9	10		4	5	7		11	1							2R

0 points v	Chelsea, Huddersfield T	0 points
1 point v	Carlisle U, Derby C, Grimsby T, Newcastle U	4 points
2 points v	Crystal Palace, Sheffield W	4 points
3 points v	Barnsley, Blackburn R, Cardiff C, Charlton A, Leeds U, Oldham A, Portsmouth	21 points
4 points v	Brighton & HA, Cambridge U, Manchester C, Shrewsbury T	16 points
6 points v	Middlesbrough, Swansea C	12 points

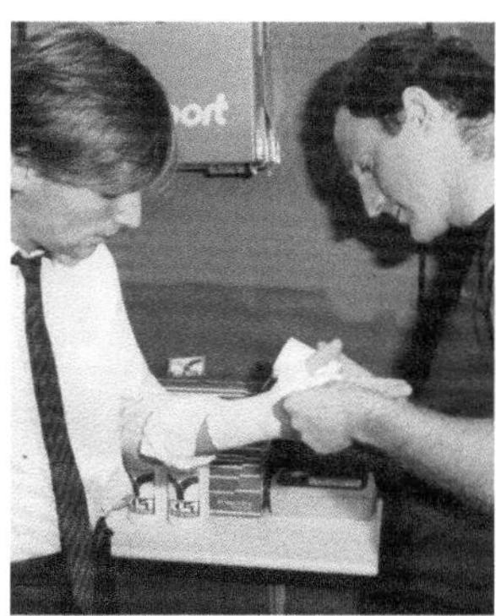

Physio Derek Wright treats Peter Scott.

1984-85

Division Two

	P	W	D	L	F	A	Pts
Oxford United	42	25	9	8	84	36	84
Birmingham City	42	25	7	10	59	33	82
Manchester City	42	21	11	10	66	40	74
Portsmouth	42	20	14	8	69	50	74
Blackburn Rovers	42	21	10	11	66	41	73
Brighton & Hove Albion	42	20	12	10	54	34	72
Leeds United	42	19	12	11	66	43	69
Shrewsbury Town	42	18	11	13	66	53	65
Fulham	42	19	8	15	68	64	65
Grimsby Town	42	18	8	16	72	64	62
Barnsley	42	14	16	12	42	42	58
Wimbledon	42	16	10	16	71	75	58
Huddersfield Town	42	15	10	17	52	64	55
Oldham Athletic	42	15	8	19	49	67	53
Crystal Palace	42	12	12	18	46	65	48
Carlisle United	42	13	8	21	50	67	47
Charlton Athletic	42	11	12	19	51	63	45
Sheffield United	42	10	14	18	54	66	44
Middlesbrough	42	10	10	22	41	57	40
Notts County	42	10	7	25	45	73	37
Cardiff City	42	9	8	25	47	79	35
Wolverhampton W	42	8	9	25	37	79	33

Manager: Ray Harford

Did you know that?

Both Kenny Achampong and Jeff Hopkins were sent of at Huddersfield in March 1985, the first time two Fulham players were dismissed in one match.

7	Elkins debut
13	Davies finale
15	Kerrins debut
22	Barnett debut
FAC3	Stannard finale
27	Achampong debut
35	Lock finale
42	Lewington and Wilson finale

No		Date	V	Opponents	R	H-T	F-T	Scorers	Atte
1	A	25	H	Shrewsbury T	L	1-0	1-2	Lock	4,89
2		27	A	Leeds U	L	0-0	0-2		14,20
3	S	1	A	Manchester C	W	2-1	3-2	Coney, Sealy, Wilson	21,07
4		4	H	Birmingham C	L	0-0	0-1		6,03
5		8	H	Blackburn R	W	2-1	3-2	Coney, Houghton, Wilson	4,43
6		15	A	Oxford U	L	1-1	2-3	Carr, Scott	8,08
7		22	H	Middlesbrough	W	0-1	2-1	Coney, Lewington	4,73
8		29	A	Brighton & HA	L	0-0	0-2		12,39
9	O	6	H	Huddersfield T	W	1-0	2-1	Davies, Houghton	4,37
10		13	A	Charlton A	W	1-0	2-1	Coney, Davies	6,61
11		20	H	Cardiff C	W	2-1	3-2	Davies, Lock, Wilson	5,35
12		27	A	Crystal Palace	D	2-2	2-2	Carr, Davies	8,03
13	N	10	H	Wimbledon	W	1-1	3-1	Carr, Coney, Davies	8,83
14		17	A	Grimsby T	W	2-2	4-2	Rosenior 3, Wilson	6,78
15		20	A	Carlisle U	L	0-1	0-3		2,99
16		24	H	Wolverhampton W	L	1-0	1-2	Houghton	7,04
17	D	1	A	Barnsley	L	0-1	0-1		6,74
18		7	H	Oldham A	W	1-0	3-1	Coney, Lewington, Wilson	4,47
19		16	A	Notts C	L	1-1	1-2	Marshall	4,91
20		22	H	Manchester C	W	1-1	3-2	Houghton, Lewington, Wilson	6,74
21		26	H	Sheffield U	W	0-0	1-0	Lewington	6,27
22		29	A	Birmingham C	D	1-0	2-2	Hopkins, Wilson	11,82
23	J	1	A	Portsmouth	D	0-4	4-4	Coney, Rosenior, Barnett, Lock	17,63
24		26	A	Shrewsbury T	L	1-1	1-3	Tapley	3,17
25	F	2	H	Brighton & HA	W	0-0	2-0	Houghton, Wilson	6,99
26		9	A	Blackburn R	L	0-1	1-2	Carr	11,02
27		19	H	Oxford U	W	0-0	1-0	Achampong	6,63
28		23	H	Carlisle U	W	1-0	3-2	Achampong 2, Rosenior	5,22
29	M	2	H	Crystal Palace	D	1-2	2-2	Hopkins, Lock	7,65
30		9	A	Cardiff C	W	1-0	2-0	Lock, Wilson	4,39
31		16	H	Charlton A	D	0-0	0-0		6,91
32		23	A	Huddersfield T	D	2-0	2-2	Houghton 2	4,84
33		30	H	Leeds U	L	0-0	0-2		7,90
34	A	6	A	Sheffield U	W	1-0	1-0	Rosenior	11,11
35		8	H	Portsmouth	L	0-2	1-3	Rosenior	12,54
36		13	A	Middlesbrough	L	0-1	0-2		4,44
37		16	A	Wimbledon	D	0-1	1-1	Wilson	5,81
38		20	H	Grimsby T	W	1-1	2-1	Sealy 2	3,63
39		27	A	Wolverhampton W	W	3-0	4-0	Houghton, Sealy 3	6,17
40	M	4	H	Barnsley	D	1-1	1-1	Wilson	3,72
41		6	A	Oldham A	L	1-1	1-2	Sealy	2,75
42		11	H	Notts C	W	0-0	1-0	Lewington	4,88
									App
									Su
									Goa

FA Cup

No		Date	V	Opponents	R	H-T	F-T	Scorers	Atte
3	J	5	H	Sheffield W	L	1-2	2-3	Houghton 2	11,43

League (Milk) Cup

No		Date	V	Opponents	R	H-T	F-T	Scorers	Atte
2/1	S	25	H	Carlisle U	W	0-0	2-0	Coney 2	3,34
2/2	O	9	A	Carlisle U	W	0-1	2-1	Davies, Houghton	2,81
3		30	A	Sheffield W	L	1-1	2-3	Carr, Hopkins	15,66

Parker	Lock	Scott	Hopkins	Marshall	Davies	Wilson	Coney	Houghton	Rosenior	Sealy	Cottington	Carr	Lewington	Elkins	Kerrins	Stannard	Barnett	Hesford	Tapley	Achampong	Lee	Reeves	
2	3	4	5	6	7	8	**9**	10	11	12													1
2	3	4	5	6	7	8	9	10		11	S												2
2	3	4	5	6	7	8	9	10		11	S												3
2	**3**	4	5	6	7	8	9	10		11	12												4
2		4	5	6		8	9	10	7		12	3	**11**										5
2		4	5	**6**		8	9	10	7		12	3	11										6
		4	5	6	12	8	9	10	**7**			3	11	2									7
2		4	5	12	7	**8**	9	10				3	11	6									8
2		4	5	S	7		9	10	8			3	11	6									9
2	6	S	5	4	7	8	9	10				3	11										10
2	6		5	4	7	8	9	10	S			3	11										11
2	6	S	5	4	7	8	9	10				3	11										12
2	6		5	4	7	8	9	10				3	11		S								13
2	6		5	4		8	9	10	7		S	3	11										14
2	6		5	**4**		8	9	10	7			3	11		12								15
2	**6**		5	4		8	9	10	7			3	11		12								16
2	6	S	5	4		8	9	10	7			3	11			1							17
2	6	4	5	S		8	9	10	7			3	11			1							18
2	6	4	5	7		8	9	10	S			3	11			1							19
2	6	4	5	12		8	9	10	**7**			3	11			1							20
2	6		5	4		8	9	10	7			3	11			1	S						21
2	**6**		5	4		8	9	10	7			3	11			1	12						22
2	6		5	4		**8**	9	10	7			3	11			1	12						23
2	6	8	5	12			**9**	10	7			3	11					1	4				24
	6	8	5	9		4		10	7		S	3	11	2				1					25
8	6	S	5	9		4		10	7			3	11	2				1					26
2	6		5	S		8		10	9			3	11	4						7			27
2	6		5	S		8		10	9			3	11	4						7			28
2	6		5	S		8		10	9			3	11	4						7			29
2	6		5	S		8		10	9			3	11	4						7			30
2	6	8	5					10	**9**	12		3	11	4						7			31
2	6		5			8		10	**9**	12		3	11	4						7			32
	6	12	5	2		8		10				3	11	4						7	**9**		33
	6	7		5		8		10	9		2	3	11	4								S	34
	6	7		5		8		10	9		2	3	11	4								12	35
2			5			8		10		7	**6**	3	11	4						8		12	36
2		S	5			8		10	9	7		3	11	4						6			37
		12	5	2		8		10		9	**4**	3	11	6						7			38
4			5	2		8		10	9	7		3	11	6						S			39
2		S	5	4		8		10	9	7		3	11	6									40
2			5	4		8		10	9	7		3	11	6						S			41
2			5	4		8		10	9	7		3	11	6						S			42
36	30	17	40	29	10	39	24	42	30	10	4	38	38	21	-	7	-	3	1	10	1	-	A
-	-	2	-	3	1	-	-	-	-	3	3	-	-	-	2	-	2	-	-	-	-	2	S
-	5	1	2	1	5	11	7	8	7	7	-	4	5	-	-	-	1	-	1	3	-	-	G

Parker	Lock	Scott	Hopkins	Marshall	Davies	Wilson	Coney	Houghton	Rosenior	Sealy	Cottington	Carr	Lewington	Elkins	Kerrins	Stannard	Barnett	Hesford	Tapley	Achampong	Lee	Reeves	
2	6	8	5	S			9	10	7			3	11			1	4						3

Parker	Lock	Scott	Hopkins	Marshall	Davies	Wilson	Coney	Houghton	Rosenior	Sealy	Cottington	Carr	Lewington	Elkins	Kerrins	Stannard	Barnett	Hesford	Tapley	Achampong	Lee	Reeves	
2		4	5		7	8	9	10	S			3	11	6									2/1
2	6		5	4	7	8	9	10	S			3	11										2/2
2	**6**	12	5	4	7	8	9	10				3	11										3

0 points v	Leeds U, Shrewsbury T	0 points
1 point v	Barnsley, Birmingham C, Portsmouth	3 points
2 points v	Crystal Palace	2 points
3 points v	Blackburn R, Brighton & HA, Carlisle U, Middlesbrough, Notts C, Oldham A, Oxford U, Wolves	24 points
4 points v	Charlton A, Huddersfield T, Wimbledon	12 points
6 points v	Cardiff C, Grimsby T, Manchester C, Sheffield U	24 points

Paul Parker receives his Player of the Year award.

1985-86

Division Two

	P	W	D	L	F	A	Pts
Norwich City	42	25	9	8	84	37	84
Charlton Athletic	42	22	11	9	78	45	77
Wimbledon	42	21	13	8	58	37	76
Portsmouth	42	22	7	13	69	41	73
Crystal Palace	42	19	9	14	57	52	66
Hull City	42	17	13	12	65	55	64
Sheffield United	42	17	11	14	64	63	62
Oldham Athletic	42	17	9	16	62	61	60
Millwall	42	17	8	17	64	65	59
Stoke City	42	14	15	13	48	50	57
Brighton & Hove Albion	42	16	8	18	64	64	56
Barnsley	42	14	14	14	47	50	56
Bradford City	42	16	6	20	51	63	54
Leeds United	42	15	8	19	56	72	53
Grimsby Town	42	14	10	18	58	62	52
Huddersfield Town	42	14	10	18	51	67	52
Shrewsbury Town	42	14	9	19	52	64	51
Sunderland	42	13	11	18	47	61	50
Blackburn Rovers	42	12	13	17	53	62	49
Carlisle United	42	13	7	22	47	71	46
Middlesbrough	42	12	9	21	44	53	45
Fulham	42	10	6	26	45	69	36

Manager: Ray Harford

Did you know that?

The 26 defeats in 42 League games is the most in a season in Fulham's League history.

1	Donnellan debut
5	Houghton finale
16	Coney's 50th goal
42	Peyton finale

No		Date	V	Opponents	R	H-T	F-T	Scorers	Atte
1	A	17	H	Leeds U	W	0-1	3-1	Scott 2, Coney	5,77
2		24	A	Middlesbrough	L	0-0	0-1		5,36
3		26	H	Grimsby T	W	1-1	2-1	Sealy 2	4,87
4		31	A	Barnsley	L	0-1	0-2		5,19
5	S	7	H	Portsmouth	L	0-0	0-1		9,33
6		14	A	Crystal Palace	D	0-0	0-0		6,38
7		17	H	Sheffield U	L	1-0	2-3	Coney, Sealy	4,25
8		21	A	Blackburn R	L	0-0	0-1		5,24
9		28	H	Brighton & HA	W	0-0	1-0	Carr	5,86
10	O	5	H	Shrewsbury T	W	0-0	2-1	Marshall, Pike	3,41
11		12	A	Wimbledon	L	0-0	0-1		5,95
12		19	H	Stoke C	W	1-0	1-0	Pike	4,00
13	N	2	H	Sunderland	L	1-0	1-2	Coney	5,79
14		9	A	Hull C	L	0-3	0-5		6,12
15		23	A	Huddersfield T	W	1-1	3-1	Barnett 2, Carr	4,65
16		30	H	Oldham A	D	0-1	2-2	Coney 2	3,54
17	D	7	H	Bradford C	W	1-0	4-1	Barnett, Marshall, Achampong, Carr	3,72
18		14	A	Leeds U	L	0-0	0-1		9,9
19		21	H	Middlesbrough	L	0-2	0-3		3,5
20		28	A	Sheffield U	L	0-1	1-2	Barnett	10,4
21	J	1	H	Norwich C	L	0-0	0-1		7,4
22		11	A	Portsmouth	D	1-0	1-1	Coney	13,6
23		18	H	Barnsley	W	0-0	2-0	Carr, Scott	3,5
24	F	1	A	Grimsby T	L	0-0	0-1		3,5
25		18	A	Stoke C	L	0-1	0-1		6,4
26	M	8	A	Shrewsbury T	L	0-2	1-2	Barnett	2,5
27		11	H	Blackburn R	D	1-0	3-3	Barnett, Marshall, Coney	2,5
28		15	H	Wimbledon	L	0-2	0-2		6,2
29		18	A	Millwall	D	0-0	1-1	Achampong	5,6
30		22	H	Crystal Palace	L	1-0	2-3	Coney 2	4,9
31		29	A	Norwich C	L	1-2	1-2	Coney	17,3
32		31	H	Millwall	L	0-1	1-2	Pike	4,5
33	A	2	A	Bradford C	L	1-1	1-3	Burvill	5,5
34		5	A	Sunderland	L	0-3	2-4	Coney, Burvill	11,3
35		8	H	Carlisle U	L	0-1	0-1		2,1
36		12	H	Hull C	D	0-0	1-1	Achampong	2,7
37		16	A	Brighton & HA	W	1-1	3-2	Brathwaite, Dreyer, Pike	6,2
38		19	A	Carlisle U	L	1-2	1-2	Dreyer	3,8
39		22	H	Charlton A	L	0-1	0-3		5,5
40		26	H	Huddersfield T	W	1-1	2-1	Scott 2	2,8
41		29	A	Charlton A	L	0-0	0-2		9,3
42	M	3	A	Oldham A	L	0-0	1-2	Coney	2,5
									Ap
									S
									Goa

FA Cup

3	J	13	A	Sheffield U	L	0-0	0-2		7,0

League (Milk) Cup

2/1	S	24	H	Notts C	D	0-1	1-1	Barnett	2,3
2/2	O	7	A	Notts C	W	0-2	4-2	Barnett, Marshall, Pike, Coney	3,0
3		29	A	Chelsea	D	0-0	1-1	Carr	19,6
R	N	6	H	Chelsea	L	0-1	0-1		20,1

	Peyton	Cottington	Carr	Scott	Hopkins	Parker	Marshall	Donnellan	Sealy	Coney	Houghton	Achampong	Hicks	Batty	Elkins	Grew	Barnett	Pike	Kerrins	Fishenden	Gore	Dreyer	Burvill	Brathwaite	Smith	Hoddy
1		2	3	4	5	6	7	8	9	10	11	S														
2		2	3	**4**		6	7	8	9	10	11	12	5													
3		2	3	4		6	7	8	9	10	11	S	5	1												
4		2	3	4	5	6	7		9	10	11	12		1	**8**											
5		**2**	3	4	5	6	7	12	9	10	11	8				1										
6		2	3	4	5		7		9	10		8			6	1	11	S								
7		2	3	4	5		7		9	10		8			6	1	**11**	12								
8		2	3	4	5		7			10		8			6	1	11	12	**9**							
9		2	3		5		7			9		8	6		12		4	10	**11**							
10		2	3		5	4	7			**9**		8	6				11	10	12							
11		2	3	4	5	6	7			9		12	**8**				11	10								
12		2	3	4	5	6	7			9		8					11	10	S							
13		2	3	4	5	6	7			9		8					11	10	S							
14		2			5	6	7					8	4		3		11	10	9							S
15		2	10	4	5	6	7			9		8			3		11		S							
16		2	10	4	5	6	7			9		8			3				11					S		
17		2	10	4	5	6	7			9		8			3		11		S							
18		**2**	10	4	5	6	7			9		8			3		11		12							
19		2	10	4	5	6	7	S		9		8			3		11									
20		2	10	4	5	6	7	S				8	9		3		11									
21		2	10	4	5	6	7	11				8			**3**		12			9						
22		2	10	4	5	6	7	3		9		8					11			S						
23		2	10	4	5	6	7	3		9		8					11			S						
24		2	3		5	6	7	10		9		8					11		S	4						
25		2	3		5	6	7	10		9		8					**11**	12		4						
26		2	3	4		6	7	8		9			**5**				11	10	12							
27		2	3	4		6	7	10		9		12	**5**				11	8								
28		2	3	4		6	7	8		9		12					11	10			**5**					
29		2	3	4		**6**	5	8		9		7					11	10	12							
30		2	3	4		6	5	**8**		9		7					11	10	12							
31		2	3	4		**6**	5	7		9		8					11	12				10				
32		2	3	**4**			5			9		8	6				11	12				10	7			
33		2					5	**8**		9							11	10	3		6	7	4	12		
34		2	3				5	12		9		8					11	10			**6**	4	7			
35		2	3				5	**4**		9		7					11	12			6	10	8			
36		2	3				5	4				7					11	9	10			6	8	S		
37		2	**3**				5	4				7					11	9	10			6	8	12		
38		2		**7**		3	5	**4**		11							12	9	10			6	8			
39		2		4			7	3		9		S					11	10	8			5	6			
40		2		4		3	5			9		7					11	10	S			6	8			
41		2		4		3	5	**8**		9							7	10	11			6		12		
42		2		4			5			9		**8**					**7**	10	11		6	3			12	
A	6	42	35	32	23	30	42	21	7	37	5	30	10	2	12	4	34	20	11	3	5	12	9	-	-	
S	-	-	-	-	-	-	-	2	-	-	-	5	-	-	1	-	2	6	5	-	-	-	-	3	1	
G	-	-	4	5	-	-	3	-	3	12	-	3	-	-	-	-	6	4	-	-	-	2	2	1	-	

	Peyton	Cottington	Carr	Scott	Hopkins	Parker	Marshall	Donnellan	Sealy	Coney	Houghton	Achampong	Hicks	Batty	Elkins	Grew	Barnett	Pike	Kerrins	Fishenden	Gore	Dreyer	Burvill	Brathwaite	Smith	Hoddy
3		2	10	4	5	6	7	**3**		9		8			12		11									

	Peyton	Cottington	Carr	Scott	Hopkins	Parker	Marshall	Donnellan	Sealy	Coney	Houghton	Achampong	Hicks	Batty	Elkins	Grew	Barnett	Pike	Kerrins	Fishenden	Gore	Dreyer	Burvill	Brathwaite	Smith	Hoddy
2/1		2	3	4	5		7			10		8			6		11	12	**9**							
2/2		2	3	4	5	6	7			9		8					11	10	S							
3		2	3	4	5	6	7			9		8					11	10	S							
R		2	3	4	5	6	7			9		8			S		11	10								

0 points v	Carlisle U, Charlton A, Middlesbrough, Norwich C, Sheffield U, Sunderland, Wimbledon	0 points
1 point v	Blackburn R, Crystal Palace, Hull C, Millwall, Oldham A, Portsmouth	6 points
2 points v		0 points
3 points v	Barnsley, Bradford C, Grimsby T, Leeds U, Shrewsbury T, Stoke C	18 points
4 points v		0 points
6 points v	Brighton & HA, Huddersfield T	12 points

Manager Ray Harford meets Fulham's oldest player, 93 year-old Alec Chaplin, who was captain in the 1920s.

1986-87

Division Three

	P	W	D	L	F	A	Pts
Bournemouth	46	29	10	7	76	40	97
Middlesbrough	46	28	10	8	67	30	94
Swindon Town	46	25	12	9	77	47	87
Wigan Athletic	46	25	10	11	83	60	85
Gillingham	46	23	9	14	65	48	78
Bristol City	46	21	14	11	63	36	77
Notts County	46	21	13	12	77	56	76
Walsall	46	22	9	15	80	67	75
Blackpool	46	16	16	14	74	59	64
Mansfield Town	46	15	16	15	52	55	61
Brentford	46	15	15	16	64	66	60
Port Vale	46	15	12	19	76	70	57
Doncaster Rovers	46	14	15	17	56	62	57
Rotherham United	46	15	12	19	48	57	57
Chester City	46	13	17	16	61	59	56
Bury	46	14	13	19	54	60	55
Chesterfield	46	13	15	18	56	69	54
Fulham	46	12	17	17	59	77	53
Bristol Rovers	46	13	12	21	49	75	51
York City	46	12	13	21	55	79	49
Bolton Wanderers	46	10	15	21	46	58	45
Carlisle United	46	10	8	28	39	78	38
Darlington	46	7	16	23	45	77	37
Newport County	46	8	13	25	49	86	37

Manager: Ray Lewington

Did you know that?

Fulham lost their first-ever penalty shoot out. In the Second Round of the Freight Rover Cup, they went out 11-10 at Aldershot. The scores were level 1-1 after 120 minutes.

1	Lewington returns
1	Vaughan debut
4	Oakes debut
14	Davies returns
29	Skinner debut
29	Davies' 300th game
35	Thomas debut
36	Cottington finale
44	Vaughan finale
45	Coney and Parker finales
46	Carr finale

No		Date	V	Opponents	R	H-T	F-T	Scorers	Atten
1	A	23	A	Rotherham U	D	0-0	0-0		3,27
2		30	H	Blackpool	L	0-1	0-1		3,90
3	S	6	A	Chester C	D	0-1	2-2	Parker, Scott	2,56
4		13	H	Brentford	L	1-1	1-3	Donnellan	4,79
5		16	H	Bolton W	W	0-1	4-2	Coney 2, Achampong, Scott	2,43
6		20	A	Notts C	W	2-0	3-2	Achampong 2, Coney	4,45
7		27	H	Middlesbrough	D	2-2	2-2	Scott 2	3,85
8		30	A	Walsall	D	1-1	1-1	Scott	4,11
9	O	4	A	Port Vale	W	1-0	1-0	Barnett	3,81
10		11	H	Swindon T	L	0-1	0-2		4,70
11		18	A	Wigan A	L	0-0	0-2		2,49
12		21	H	Bristol R	D	0-2	2-2	Oakes, Achampong	2,36
13		25	H	Bury	W	1-0	2-1	Marshall, Barnett	2,68
14	N	1	A	Doncaster R	L	0-2	1-2	Marshall	2,25
15		4	A	Chesterfield	L	0-1	1-3	Davies	2,24
16		8	H	Bristol C	L	0-2	0-3		4,45
17		22	A	Carlisle U	W	0-0	3-1	Coney 2, Davies	2,46
18		29	H	Darlington	W	1-0	3-1	Coney 2, Davies	3,36
19	D	13	H	Mansfield T	D	1-0	1-1	Davies	3,56
20		20	A	York C	D	0-1	1-1	Oakes	2,57
21		26	H	Gillingham	D	1-1	2-2	Marshall, Davies	5,88
22		27	A	Bournemouth	L	2-1	2-3	Kerrins, Barnett	6,67
23	J	1	A	Newport C	D	0-0	0-0		2,38
24		3	H	Carlisle U	W	0-0	3-0	Marshall, Coney, Barnett	3,70
25		24	H	Chester C	L	0-0	0-5		3,06
26	F	1	A	Brentford	D	2-1	3-3	Scott, Achampong, Carr	5,43
27		7	A	Bolton W	L	0-1	2-3	Hoddy, Achampong	4,12
28		14	H	Notts C	W	2-0	3-1	Barnett, Hicks, (Goodwin og)	3,05
29		17	H	Rotherham U	D	0-1	1-1	Oakes	2,35
30		21	A	Middlesbrough	L	0-1	0-3		9,36
31		28	H	Walsall	D	0-0	2-2	Barnett, Donnellan	5,94
32	M	3	H	Doncaster R	D	0-0	0-0		4,15
33		7	A	Bury	L	1-0	1-2	Cottington	2,15
34		18	A	Bristol R	D	0-0	0-0		2,44
35		21	A	Swindon T	L	0-0	0-2		7,42
36		28	H	Port Vale	L	0-2	0-6		3,79
37	A	4	A	Bristol C	D	0-0	0-0		8,55
38		7	A	Blackpool	L	0-1	0-1		1,90
39		11	H	Chesterfield	W	2-1	3-1	Coney, Barnett, Parker	4,52
40		18	H	Newport C	W	1-0	2-0	Coney, (Compton og)	4,23
41		20	A	Gillingham	L	0-1	1-4	Donnellan	6,12
42		25	H	York C	W	1-0	1-0	Barnett	4,10
43		28	H	Wigan A	D	1-1	2-2	Brathwaite, Barnett	3,60
44	M	2	A	Darlington	W	0-0	1-0	Donnellan	1,26
45		4	H	Bournemouth	L	0-0	1-3	Hopkins	9,23
46		9	A	Mansfield T	D	0-1	1-1	Davies	2,75
									App
									Su
									Goal

FA Cup

1	N	15	A	Hereford U	D	2-2	3-3	Barnett, Marshall, Coney	3,77
R		24	H	Hereford U	W	2-0	4-0	Marshall, Davies 2, Coney	3,59
2	D	6	H	Newport C	W	2-0	2-0	Oakes, Davies	4,05
3	J	10	H	Swindon T	L	0-1	0-1		7,07

League (Littlewoods) Cup

1/1	A	26	A	Aldershot	W	0-1	3-1	Achampong, Scott, Coney	2,18
1/2	S	3	H	Aldershot	W	2-0	2-0	Scott, Parker	2,09
2/1		23	A	Liverpool	L	0-4	0-10		13,49
2/2	O	7	H	Liverpool	L	1-3	2-3	Scott, Coney	7,86

aughan	Marshall	Gore	Scott	Steggles	Parker	Barnett	Achampong	Coney	Kerrins	Lewington	Cottington	Oakes	Donnellan	Brathwaite	Hoddy	Hicks	Hopkins	Davies	Carr	Pike	Elkins	Skinner	Thomas	Batty	Langley	Harlow	
	2	3	4	5	6	7	8	9	10	11	S																1
	2	**3**	4	5	6	7	8	9	10	11	12																2
	2	**3**	4	5	6	7	8	9	10	11	12																3
	2		4		6		8	9	10	11	5	3	**7**	12													4
	2		4		6		8	9	10	11	5	3		7	S												5
	2	5			6	7	8	9	10	**11**	4	3			12												6
	2		4		6	**7**	8	9	10	11	3	5			12												7
	2		4		6	7	8	9		11	5	3		S	10												8
	2	10	4		6	7	8	9		11	5	3				S											9
	2		4			7	8	9		**11**	3	5	12		10	6											10
	2		4				8	9	10	11	3	5			7	6										S	11
	2		4		6	7	8	9	10	11		5			S	3											12
	2		4		6	7	8	9	10	**11**	3	5			12												13
	2		4		6	7	8	9	10		S	5					3	11									14
	2		4		6	7		9	10		S	5			8		3	11									15
	2		**4**		6	7	12	9	10			5			8		3	11									16
	2				6	7		9	10		S	5	4		8		3	11									17
	2				6	7		9	10			5	4		8	3		11	S								18
	2				6	7		9	10			5	**4**		8		3	11	12								19
	2		4		6	7	9		10			5	8				3	11	S								20
	2		4		6	7		**9**	10			5	8				3	11	12								21
	2		4		6	7		9	10			5	8				3	11	S								22
	2		4		6	7		9	10			5	8				3	**11**	12								23
	2		4		6	7		9	10			5	8		12		**3**		11								24
	2	3	4			**7**	8	9	10		6	5	12		11												25
	2		4			7	8	**9**	10		6	5			11	3			12								26
	2		4			7	8	9			6	5	12		**11**	3			10								27
	2					7			10		6	5	4			3		S	8	9	11						28
						7					6	5	4			3		9	10	8	11	2				S	29
						7			2		6	5	4			3		9	10	8	11	S					30
						7	5		2		6		4			3		9	10	8	11	S					31
					5	**7**			2		6		4	12		3		9	10	8	11						32
					6				2		**7**	5	4			3		9	10	8	11	12					33
						2			12	6	7	5	4			3		9	10	8	**11**						34
		4				**7**		12	8	11	2	5	6						10	9			3				35
	7					**11**	12	9		4	2	5	8			6			3	10							36
					2	7		9		4		5				6	8		3	10	11	S					37
					2	7		9		4		5	12			6	8		3	10	**11**						38
					8	7	S	9		4		5	10	11		2	6		3								39
			2		6	7	S	9		4		5	10	11			8		3								40
			2		6	7		9		4		5	10	**11**			8		3	12							41
			2			7		9		4		5	10	**11**		6	8	12	3								42
			8			7		9		4		5	10	**11**		2	6	12	3								43
			8		11	7		9		4		5	10			**2**	6	12	3								44
			2		6	7		9		4		5	12	**11**			8	10	3					1			45
			8			7	S					5	11				6	10	3	9		4		1	2		46
4	29	7	30	3	31	42	19	36	29	25	21	41	25	7	11	20	20	18	21	12	9	2	1	2	1		A
	-	-	-	-	-	-	2	1	1	-	2	-	5	2	4	-	-	3	4	1	-	1	-	-	-		S
	4	-	6	-	2	9	6	10	1	-	1	3	4	1	1	1	1	6	1	-	-	-	-	-	-		G

aughan	Marshall	Gore	Scott	Steggles	Parker	Barnett	Achampong	Coney	Kerrins	Lewington	Cottington	Oakes	Donnellan	Brathwaite	Hoddy	Hicks	Hopkins	Davies	Carr	Pike	Elkins	Skinner	Thomas	Batty	Langley	Harlow	
	2				6	7	S	9	10		12	5	4		**8**		3	11									1
	2				6	7	S	9	10		12	5	4		8		**3**	11									R
	2				6	7	S	9	10			5	4		8		3	11	S								2
	2	3	4		6	7	12	9	10			5	**8**		11							S					3

aughan	Marshall	Gore	Scott	Steggles	Parker	Barnett	Achampong	Coney	Kerrins	Lewington	Cottington	Oakes	Donnellan	Brathwaite	Hoddy	Hicks	Hopkins	Davies	Carr	Pike	Elkins	Skinner	Thomas	Batty	Langley	Harlow	
	2	3	4		6	7	10	9	8	11	5		S			S											1/1
	2	3	4		6	7	10	9	8	11	5		S	S													1/2
	2		4		6	7	8	9	10	11	3			S	5							S					2/1
	2		4		6	7	8	9		11	3		12	S	**10**	5											2/2

0 points v	Blackpool, Bournemouth, Swindon T	0 points
1 point v	Brentford, Bristol C, Chester C, Doncaster R, Gillingham, Middlesbrough, Wigan A	7 points
2 points v	Bristol R, Mansfield T, Rotherham U, Walsall	8 points
3 points v	Bolton W, Bury, Chesterfield, Port Vale	12 points
4 points v	Newport C, York C	8 points
6 points v	Carlisle U, Darlington, Notts C	18 points

Property developer David Bulstrode becomes the new chairman.

1987-88

Division Three

	P	W	D	L	F	A	Pts
Sunderland	46	27	12	7	92	48	93
Brighton & Hove Albion	46	23	15	8	69	47	84
Walsall	46	23	13	10	68	50	82
Notts County	46	23	12	11	82	49	81
Bristol City	46	21	12	13	77	62	75
Northampton Town	46	18	19	9	70	51	73
Wigan Athletic	46	20	12	14	70	61	72
Bristol Rovers	46	18	12	16	68	56	66
Fulham	46	19	9	18	69	60	66
Blackpool	46	17	14	15	71	62	65
Port Vale	46	18	11	17	58	56	65
Brentford	46	16	14	16	53	59	62
Gillingham	46	14	17	15	77	61	59
Bury	46	15	14	17	58	57	59
Chester City	46	14	16	16	51	62	58
Preston North End	46	15	13	18	48	59	58
Southend United	46	14	13	19	65	83	55
Chesterfield	46	15	10	21	41	70	55
Mansfield Town	46	14	12	20	48	59	54
Aldershot	46	15	8	23	64	74	53
Rotherham United	46	12	16	18	50	66	52
Grimsby Town	46	12	14	20	48	58	50
York City	46	8	9	29	48	91	33
Doncaster Rovers	46	8	9	29	40	84	33

Manager: Ray Lewington

Did you know that?

When Fulham beat Bristol Rovers at home in September 1987, five of the team (Stannard, Lewington, Wilson, Rosenior and Davies) were in their second spells at the Cottage having previously been transferred to Southend, Sheffield United, Millwall, QPR and Chelsea respectively.

1	Rosenior and Stannard return
9	Wilson returns
12	Walker debut
18	Eckhardt debut
32	Davies' 150th goal
38	Cole debut
44	Achampong finale
46	Hopkins and Oakes finales

No		Date	V	Opponents	R	H-T	F-T	Scorers	Att
1	A	15	A	Walsall	W	0-0	1-0	Rosenior	4,6
2		22	H	Doncaster R	W	3-0	4-0	Rosenior 2, Davies 2	4,1
3		29	A	Brighton & HA	L	0-1	0-2		8,7
4	S	1	H	Notts C	D	0-0	0-0		4,7
5		4	A	Mansfield T	W	0-0	2-0	Rosenior, Davies	3,5
6		12	H	Gillingham	L	0-0	0-2		7,4
7		16	A	Chester C	W	1-1	2-1	Rosenior 2	2,4
8		19	A	Port Vale	D	1-0	1-1	Skinner	3,8
9		26	H	Bristol R	W	0-1	3-1	Davies, Barnett, Rosenior	4,6
10		29	H	Sunderland	L	0-1	0-2		6,9
11	O	3	A	Blackpool	L	0-1	1-2	Wilson	4,9
12		10	H	York C	W	2-1	3-1	Walker 2, Davies	4,0
13		17	A	Wigan A	W	2-0	3-1	Rosenior 2, Walker	2,8
14		20	A	Southend U	W	1-0	2-0	Davies, Rosenior	3,4
15		24	H	Aldershot	L	1-2	1-2	Davies	6,5
16	N	3	H	Grimsby T	W	3-0	5-0	Skinner 2, Davies, Barnett, Rosenior	3,4
17		7	H	Northampton T	D	0-0	0-0		6,7
18		21	A	Rotherham U	W	1-0	2-0	Davies, Walker	3,4
19		28	H	Preston NE	L	0-1	0-1		5,3
20	D	12	A	Bury	D	1-1	1-1	Rosenior	2,6
21		15	A	Bristol C	L	0-3	0-4		6,1
22		19	H	Chesterfield	L	1-1	1-3	Barnett	4,0
23		26	A	Bristol R	L	1-1	1-3	Rosenior	4,7
24		28	H	Brentford	D	0-0	2-2	Wilson, Scott	9,3
25	J	1	H	Brighton & HA	L	1-0	1-2	Davies	6,5
26		2	A	Gillingham	D	2-1	2-2	Rosenior 2	6,0
27		9	A	Doncaster R	D	1-0	2-2	Rosenior, Davies	1,8
28		16	H	Port Vale	L	1-0	1-2	Lewington	3,7
29		30	A	Notts C	L	1-2	1-5	Walker	6,1
30	F	6	H	Mansfield T	D	0-0	0-0		3,3
31		14	A	Brentford	L	0-1	1-3	Wilson	8,7
32		20	H	Walsall	W	1-0	2-0	Rosenior, Davies	3,7
33		27	H	Blackpool	W	1-0	3-1	Scott, Rosenior, Walker	4,0
34	M	1	A	Sunderland	L	0-2	0-2		11,3
35		5	H	Wigan A	W	3-2	3-2	Rosenior, Skinner, Walker	3,8
36		12	A	York C	W	2-1	3-1	Walker, Rosenior, Davies	2,5
37		19	H	Bristol C	D	0-0	0-0		4,8
38		26	A	Aldershot	W	1-0	3-0	Marshall, Achampong, Barnett	4,4
39	A	2	A	Northampton T	L	1-1	2-3	Skinner, Barnett	6,2
40		4	H	Rotherham U	W	2-0	3-1	Barnett 2, Skinner	4,4
41		9	A	Grimsby T	W	1-0	2-0	Achampong, Marshall	3,1
42		15	H	Chester C	W	0-0	1-0	Cole	4,1
43		23	H	Southend U	W	1-0	3-1	Achampong, Eckhardt, Barnett	5,0
44		30	A	Preston NE	L	0-1	1-2	Barnett	4,1
45	M	2	H	Bury	L	0-1	0-1		5,2
46		7	A	Chesterfield	L	0-1	0-1		3,0
									Ap
									S
									Goa

FA Cup

1	N	14	A	Gillingham	L	0-2	1-2	Rosenior	6,4

Littlewoods Cup

1/1	A	18	H	Colchester U	W	0-1	3-1	Davies, Rosenior, Marshall	2,7
1/2		25	A	Colchester U	W	0-0	2-0	Barnett, Davies	1,5
2/1	S	22	H	Bradford C	L	0-2	1-5	Skinner	4,3
2/2	O	7	A	Bradford C	L	1-1	1-2	Wilson	6,4

Stannard	Langley	Thomas	Lewington	Hopkins	Oakes	Marshall	Skinner	Rosenior	Davies	Barnett	Kerrins	Donnellan	Achampong	Hicks	Elkins	Wilson	Walker	Eckhardt	Pike	Scott	Hoddy	Gore	Cole	Greaves	Brathwaite	Donovan	
1	2	3	**4**	5	6	7	8	9	10	11	12											S					1
1	2	3	**4**	5	6	7	8	9	10	11	12	14															2
1	2	3	4	5	6	7	**8**	9	10	11	12	14															3
1	2	3	4	5	6	7	**8**	9	10	11	12	14															4
1		3	**4**	5	6	7	8	9	10	11	2	12		S													5
1		3	**4**	5	6	**7**	8	9	10	11	2	12	14														6
1		3	4	5	6	7	8	9	**10**	11	2	12													S		7
1		3	4	5		7	8	9	**10**	11	2	12		6											S		8
1		3	**4**	5	6		8	9	10	11	12	S			2	7											9
1		3	4	5	6		**8**	9	10	11	S	12			2	7											10
1		3	4	5	6		8	9	10	11					2	7					S					S	11
1		3	4	5	6	8	S	9	**10**	12					2	7	11										12
1		3	4	5	6	8		9	10		S	S			2	7	11										13
1		3	4	5	6	7		9	10		S	S			2	8	11										14
1			4	**5**	6	8	14	9	10		3	12			2	7	11										15
1	3		**4**		5	7	8	9	10	11	14	12		6	2												16
1	2	3	4		5	7	8	9	10	11		S		6	S												17
1	2	3	**4**				12	9	10	7				6	S	8	11	5									18
1	2	3	**4**					9	10	7		12		6	S	8	11	5									19
1	2	3	4				S	9	10	7				6		8	11	5			S						20
1	2	3	4				**7**	9	10					6		8	11	5	12		S						21
1	2	3	4				10	9		7			14	6		8	11	5			S						22
1	2	3	**4**					9	10	7				S	6	8	11	5		12							23
1	2	3	**4**					9	10	12			S		6	8	11	5		7							24
1	2	3	4					9	**10**	7			14		6	8		5	12	11							25
1	**2**	3	4					9		7	8		10	12	6			5	14	11							26
1		3	4					9	10	7	2		S	6			11	5		8	S						27
1		3	4		5		8		10	7	6		14	S			11	2			9						28
1		3	4		6		9		10	7	S		14				11	2		8		5					29
1			4		6		14	9	**10**	7					3	12	11	2		8		5					30
1			4		6		**10**	9	12	7					3	14	11	2		8		5					31
1					5		S	9	10	7			S		3	4	11	2		8		6					32
1					5		12	9	10	7			14		3	**4**	11	2		8		6					33
1			S		5		12	9	**10**	7					3	4	11	2		8		6					34
1				S	5	S	4	9	10	7					3		11	2		8		6					35
1				6	5	12	4	9	10	**7**					3		11	2		8		S					36
1				6	5	9	4			**7**			10		3		11	2		8	14	12					37
1				6	5	9	4			**7**			10		3			2		8	14	S	11				38
1				6	5	9	4		12	7			**10**		3			2		8		S	11				39
1				6	5	9	4		S	**7**			10		3			2		8	S		11				40
1				6	5	9			S	7			10		3			2		8	4	S	11				41
1				6	5	9	**4**			**7**			10		3		12	2		8	S		11				42
1				6	5	9	4		12	7			**10**		3		S	2		8			11				43
1				6	5	10	**4**		14	12			9		3		7	2		8			11				44
1				6	5	9			**10**	7					3		4	2		8	12		11	S			45
1				6	**5**	9	S		10	7					3		4	2		8			11	12			46
46	15	27	31	26	35	24	27	34	35	39	8	-	9	9	29	18	25	29	-	22	2	7	9	-			A
-	-	-	-	-	-	1	5	-	4	3	6	11	6	1	-	2	1	-	3	1	3	1	-	1			S
-	-	-	1	-	-	2	6	20	13	9	-	-	3	-	-	3	8	1	-	2	-	-	1	-			G

Stannard	Langley	Thomas	Lewington	Hopkins	Oakes	Marshall	Skinner	Rosenior	Davies	Barnett	Kerrins	Donnellan	Achampong	Hicks	Elkins	Wilson	Walker	Eckhardt	Pike	Scott	Hoddy	Gore	Cole	Greaves	Brathwaite	Donovan	
1	2	3	4		**5**		S	9	10	7				6	12	8	11										1

Stannard	Langley	Thomas	Lewington	Hopkins	Oakes	Marshall	Skinner	Rosenior	Davies	Barnett	Kerrins	Donnellan	Achampong	Hicks	Elkins	Wilson	Walker	Eckhardt	Pike	Scott	Hoddy	Gore	Cole	Greaves	Brathwaite	Donovan	
1	2	3	4	5	6	7	8	9	10	11	S														S		1/1
1	2	3	**4**	5	6	7	8	9	10	11	12	14															1/2
1			**4**			2	8	9		11	7	10	12	5	6				S						3		2/1
1		3	S	5	6	4	8	9	10	11					2	7					S						2/2

0 points v	Brighton & HA, Chesterfield, Preston NE, Sunderland	0 points
1 point v	Brentford, Bristol C, Bury, Gillingham, Northampton T, Notts C, Port Vale	7 points
2 points v		0 points
3 points v	Aldershot, Blackpool, Bristol R	9 points
4 points v	Doncaster R, Mansfield T	8 points
6 points v	Chester C, Grimsby T, Rotherham U, Southend U, Walsall, Wigan A, York C	42 points

Jimmy Hill led the campaign to save Fulham and returned as chairman.

1988-89

Division Three

	P	W	D	L	F	A	Pts
Wolverhampton W	46	26	14	6	96	49	92
Sheffield United	46	25	9	12	93	54	84
Port Vale	46	24	12	10	78	48	84
Fulham	46	22	9	15	69	67	75
Bristol Rovers	46	19	17	10	67	51	74
Preston North End	46	19	15	12	79	60	72
Brentford	46	18	14	14	66	61	68
Chester City	46	19	11	16	64	61	68
Notts County	46	18	13	15	64	54	67
Bolton Wanderers	46	16	16	14	58	54	64
Bristol City	46	18	9	19	53	55	63
Swansea City	46	15	16	15	51	53	61
Bury	46	16	13	17	55	67	61
Huddersfield Town	46	17	9	20	63	73	60
Mansfield Town	46	14	17	15	48	52	59
Cardiff City	46	14	15	17	44	56	57
Wigan Athletic	46	14	14	18	55	53	56
Reading	46	15	11	20	68	72	56
Blackpool	46	14	13	19	56	59	55
Northampton Town	46	16	6	24	66	76	54
Southend United	46	13	15	18	56	75	54
Chesterfield	46	14	7	25	51	86	49
Gillingham	46	12	4	30	47	81	40
Aldershot	46	8	13	25	48	78	37

Manager: Ray Lewington

Did you know that?

Peter Scott was sent off in the second leg of the play off against Bristol Rovers. This was his third dismissal (he also saw red at Crystal Palace in September 1985 and at Chesterfield in November 1986). Duncan Jupp emulated this three red card trick in the 1990s.

1	Sayer debut
5	Peters returns
6	Mauge debut
30	Kerrins finale
37	Marshall's 200th game
P/O2	Wilson finale

No		Date	V	Opponents	R	H-T	F-T	Scorers	Atten
1	A	27	A	Cardiff C	W	0-1	2-1	Sayer, Elkins	6,02
2	S	3	H	Southend U	W	0-0	1-0	Davies	4,75
3		10	A	Mansfield T	L	0-2	1-3	Sayer	2,73
4		17	H	Bury	W	1-0	1-0	Cole	3,75
5		20	A	Bolton W	L	1-1	2-3	Sayer, Peters	4,23
6		24	H	Wigan A	D	0-1	1-1	Sayer	3,43
7	O	1	A	Huddersfield T	L	0-0	0-2		4,57
8		5	H	Wolverhampton W	D	0-1	2-2	Wilson, Skinner	4,82
9		8	A	Bristol C	W	2-0	5-1	Peters, Sayer 2, Eckhardt, Marshall	8,16
10		15	H	Aldershot	W	2-0	5-1	Sayer 2, Marshall, Barnett, Eckhardt	5,10
11		22	A	Swansea C	L	0-1	0-2		4,73
12		25	H	Northampton T	W	1-1	3-2	Skinner, Barnett, (Thomas og)	5,51
13		29	A	Notts C	W	1-0	1-0	Walker	5,51
14	N	5	H	Blackpool	D	0-0	1-1	Gordon	4,76
15		8	H	Reading	W	1-1	2-1	Barnett, Sayer	6,93
16		12	A	Sheffield U	L	0-1	0-1		11,08
17		26	A	Port Vale	L	0-1	0-3		5,09
18	D	3	H	Bristol R	L	0-1	0-2		4,46
19		17	H	Preston NE	W	1-0	2-1	Skinner, Walker	3,86
20		26	A	Gillingham	W	0-0	1-0	Davies	5,87
21		31	A	Chesterfield	L	0-2	1-4	Walker	3,08
22	J	2	H	Brentford	D	2-2	3-3	Scott, Davies 2	8,02
23		7	H	Chester C	W	3-0	4-1	Scott, Walker, Barnett, Davies	4,19
24		13	A	Southend U	D	0-0	0-0		4,84
25		21	H	Mansfield T	D	1-1	1-1	Davies	4,14
26		28	A	Bury	L	0-1	1-3	Barnett	3,58
27	F	4	H	Huddersfield T	L	0-0	1-2	Walker	4,08
28		11	A	Wolverhampton W	L	1-4	2-5	Davies, Rougvie	15,62
29		18	H	Bristol C	W	1-1	3-1	Walker, Davies, Marshall	4,46
30		28	A	Northampton T	L	1-2	1-2	Skinner	3,94
31	M	4	H	Swansea C	W	0-0	1-0	Marshall	4,71
32		11	A	Blackpool	W	0-0	1-0	Skinner	3,01
33		14	H	Notts C	W	1-0	2-1	Davies 2	3,40
34		18	H	Cardiff C	W	1-0	2-0	Marshall, Skinner	4,26
35		24	A	Brentford	W	0-0	1-0	Cole	10,85
36		27	H	Gillingham	L	0-0	1-2	Marshall	6,47
37	A	1	A	Preston NE	W	2-1	4-1	Davies 2, Walker, Gordon	8,19
38		5	A	Chester C	L	0-2	0-7		2,12
39		8	H	Chesterfield	W	0-0	2-1	Marshall, Sayer	4,25
40		15	H	Bolton W	D	0-0	1-1	Skinner	4,95
41		22	A	Wigan A	W	0-0	1-0	Thomas	3,05
42		25	A	Aldershot	W	0-0	2-1	Walker, Davies	3,84
43		29	H	Sheffield U	D	1-1	2-2	Scott, Davies	7,99
44	M	1	A	Reading	W	1-0	1-0	Skinner	5,15
45		6	A	Bristol R	D	0-0	0-0		7,30
46		13	H	Port Vale	L	1-0	1-2	Cole	6,25
P/O		21	A	Bristol R	L	0-0	0-1		9,02
P/O		25	H	Bristol R	L	0-0	0-4		10,18
									App
									Su
									Goal

FA Cup

1	N	19	A	Colchester U	L	0-1	0-1		4,48

Littlewoods Cup

1/1	A	30	H	Brentford	D	1-1	2-2	Skinner, Sayer	5,48
1/2	S	6	A	Brentford	L	0-0	0-1		7,70

Eckhardt	Elkins	Skinner	Thomas	Langley	Sayer	Wilson	Barnett	Cole	Walker	Hoddy	Davies	Marshall	Scott	Peters	Mauge	Gore	Gordon	Kerrins	Cawley	Donnellan	Rougvie	Batty	
2	3	4	5	6	7	8	9	10	11	S								S					1
3	5	7	6	2	8	4	**9**	10	11	12	14												2
5	3	8	6	2	9	4	7	10	**11**	12								S					3
5	3	8	6	2	9	4	7	10	**11**		S	12											4
5	3	8	6	2	**9**	4	7	10			12		11	14									5
5	3	8	6	2	**9**	4	7	10			14			12	11								6
5		8	6		9	4	7	10			12	14		2	**11**	3							7
5	S	**8**	6		9	4	7				10	3	12	2	11								8
5		8	6	3	9	4	11					7	S	2	12		**10**						9
5		8	6	3	9	4	11		S		S	7		2			10						10
5		8	6	**3**	9	4	11		14			7	12	2			10						11
5		**8**	6	3	9	4	11		14			7	12	2			10						12
6			3		**9**	4	7		11		S	2	8			5	10	12					13
6			3		**9**	4	7		11		12	2	8	S		5	10						14
6			3		9	4	7		11		S	2	8	S		5	10						15
6	S	12	3		9	4	**7**		11			2	8	5			10						16
6	S	12			9	4	**7**		11			2	8			5	10	3					17
6	12				9	**4**	7	14	11			2	8			5	10	3					18
6	3	4		S	S		7	9	11		10	2	8						5				19
6	3	4	5	S	S		7	9	11		10	2	8										20
6	3	S	4		12		**7**	9	11		10	2	8						5				21
6	3	**4**	14		12		7	9	11		10	2	8						5				22
6	3		**5**			4	7	9	11		10	2	8						12	14			23
6	3		**5**			4	7	9	11		10	2	8						14	12			24
6	3	S		5		4	**7**	9	11		10	2	8							12			25
6	3	14	5			4	7	**9**	11		10	2	8				12						26
6	3	14	5			4	7	**9**	11		10	2	8				12						27
	3	S	5		S	4	7	9	11		10	2	8								6		28
	3	4	6	2	S			9	11		10	7	8							14	5		29
	3	4	6	2	12			9			10	7	8				14	**11**			5		30
6	S	4	3	2	11	S		9			10	7	8								5		31
6		4	3	2		S		9	11		10	7	8				S				5		32
6		4	3	2		S		9	11		10	7	8				S				5		33
6		4	3	2		S		9	11		10	7	8				S				5		34
6		4	3	2		S		9	11		10	7	8				14				5	1	35
6		4	3	2	12	**8**		9	11		10	7					14				5		36
6		4			S	S		9	11		10	7	8		2		3				5		37
6		**4**	14			12		9	11		10	7	8		2		3				5		38
6	5	4	3		12	S		9	11		**10**	7	8		2								39
6		4	3		12	S		**9**	11		10	7	8		2						5		40
6	S	4	3			S		9	11		10	7	8		2						5		41
6		4	3		12	14		9	11		**10**	7	8		2						5		42
6		4	3		12	S		**9**	11		10	7	8		2						5		43
6	S	4	3			S		9	11		10	7	8		2						5		44
6	14	4	3			S		9	11		10	7	8		2						5		45
6	2	4	3		12	S		9	11		**10**	7	8								5		46
6	S	4	3			S		9	11		10	7	8		2						5		P/O
6		4+	3		12	14		9	11		10	7	8		**2**						5		P/O
45	20	35	41	19	19	25	28	37	38	-	31	41	36	7	14	6	12	3	3	-	20	1	A
-	2	4	2	-	10	3	-	1	2	2	5	2	3	2	1	-	5	1	2	4	-	-	S
2	1	8	1	-	10	1	5	3	8	-	14	7	3	2	-	-	2	-	-	-	1	-	G

6			3		9	4	7		11		14	2	8	**5**		12	10						1

3	5	7	6	2	8	4	9	10	**11**	12								S					1/1
5	3	7	6	2	8	4	9	10	**11**		12					14							1/2

0 points v	Huddersfield T, Port Vale	0 points
1 point v	Bolton W, Bristol R, Mansfield T, Sheffield U, Wolves	5 points
2 points v		0 points
3 points v	Bury, Chester C, Chesterfield, Gillingham, Northampton T, Swansea	18 points
4 points v	Blackpool, Brentford, Southend U, Wigan A	16 points
6 points v	Aldershot, Bristol C, Cardiff C, Notts C, Preston NE, Reading	36 points

Manager Ray Lewington's former Chelsea teammate Clive Walker added some flair down the left flank.

1989-90

Division Three

	P	W	D	L	F	A	Pts
Bristol Rovers	46	26	15	5	71	35	93
Bristol City	46	27	10	9	76	40	91
Notts County	46	25	12	9	73	53	87
Tranmere Rovers	46	23	11	12	86	49	80
Bury	46	21	11	14	70	49	74
Bolton Wanderers	46	18	15	13	59	48	69
Birmingham City	46	18	12	16	60	59	66
Huddersfield Town	46	17	14	15	61	62	65
Rotherham United	46	17	13	16	71	62	64
Reading	46	15	19	12	57	53	64
Shrewsbury Town	46	16	15	15	59	54	63
Crewe Alexandra	46	15	17	14	56	53	62
Brentford	46	18	7	21	66	66	61
Leyton Orient	46	16	10	20	52	56	58
Mansfield Town	46	16	7	23	50	65	55
Chester City	46	13	15	18	43	55	54
Swansea City	46	14	12	20	45	63	54
Wigan Athletic	46	13	14	19	48	64	53
Preston North End	46	14	10	22	65	79	52
Fulham	46	12	15	19	55	66	51
Cardiff City	46	12	14	20	51	70	50
Northampton Town	46	11	14	21	51	68	47
Blackpool	46	10	16	20	49	73	46
Walsall	46	9	14	23	40	72	41

Manager: Ray Lewington

Did you know that?

On-loan (from Luton) striker Iain Dowie managed to score and get sent off at Chester in September 1989.

2	Nebbeling debut
25	Donnellan finale
27	Pike debut
27	Sayer finale
31	Newson debut
37	Peters finale
44	Elkins finale
45	Mauge finale
46	Barnett, Lewington and Walker finales

No		Date	V	Opponents	R	H-T	F-T	Scorers	Att
1	A	19	H	Tranmere R	L	0-1	1-2	Eckhardt	4,8
2		26	A	Bolton W	D	0-0	0-0		5,5
3	S	2	H	Mansfield T	W	0-0	1-0	Skinner	4,5
4		9	A	Crewe A	W	0-0	3-2	Walker, Sayer 2	3,3
5		16	H	Swansea C	W	0-0	2-0	Thomas, Sayer	4,5
6		23	A	Walsall	D	0-0	0-0		3,9
7		26	H	Huddersfield T	D	0-0	0-0		4,4
8		30	A	Chester C	W	1-0	2-0	Dowie, Marshall	2,1
9	O	7	A	Bristol R	L	0-0	0-2		5,8
10		14	H	Rotherham U	D	0-0	1-1	Marshall	4,3
11		17	A	Reading	L	0-1	2-3	Skinner, Sayer	4,7
12		21	H	Bury	D	0-0	2-2	Walker, Marshall	3,5
13		28	A	Brentford	L	0-2	0-2		7,9
14		31	H	Northampton T	D	1-1	1-1	Mauge	3,5
15	N	5	A	Leyton O	D	1-0	1-1	Sayer	5,8
16		11	H	Cardiff C	L	1-3	2-5	Milton, Skinner	4,0
17		25	H	Wigan A	W	1-0	4-0	Scott, Walker 2, Sayer	3,1
18	D	2	A	Notts C	L	0-1	0-2		5,1
19		16	A	Blackpool	W	1-0	1-0	Walker	2,6
20		26	H	Bristol C	L	0-1	0-1		6,0
21		30	H	Shrewsbury T	W	1-1	2-1	Walker 2	3,6
22	J	1	A	Birmingham C	D	0-0	1-1	Scott	8,9
23		6	A	Preston NE	L	0-1	0-1		5,0
24		13	H	Bolton W	D	2-2	2-2	Milton, Skinner	4,5
25		19	A	Tranmere R	L	0-0	1-2	Walker	6,1
26		27	H	Crewe A	D	0-0	1-1	Marshall	3,9
27	F	10	A	Swansea C	L	1-3	2-4	Walker, Milton	3,4
28		13	A	Mansfield T	L	0-0	0-3		2,2
29		17	H	Notts C	W	1-1	5-2	Milton 2, Mauge, Scott, Davies	4,6
30		24	A	Wigan A	L	0-0	1-2	Davies	2,1
31	M	3	H	Preston NE	W	1-0	3-1	Pike, Davies, Walker	4,2
32		6	H	Chester C	W	0-0	1-0	Walker	3,8
33		10	A	Huddersfield T	W	0-0	1-0	Walker	4,7
34		17	H	Bristol R	L	0-0	1-2	Walker	5,6
35		20	A	Rotherham U	L	1-0	1-2	Barnett	4,5
36		24	H	Reading	L	0-0	1-2	Davies	4,8
37		31	A	Bury	D	0-0	0-0		3,0
38	A	4	H	Walsall	D	0-0	0-0		2,6
39		7	A	Northampton T	D	1-0	2-2	Davies, Elkins	2,8
40		10	H	Brentford	W	1-0	1-0	Milton	6,7
41		14	H	Birmingham C	L	0-1	1-2	Milton	4,5
42		16	A	Bristol C	L	1-2	1-5	Eckhardt	16,1
43		21	H	Blackpool	D	0-0	0-0		3,8
44		24	A	Shrewsbury T	L	0-2	0-2		2,8
45		28	A	Cardiff C	D	1-1	3-3	Milton 2, Davies	3,9
46	M	5	H	Leyton O	L	1-0	1-2	Pike	7,1
									Ap
									S
									Go

FA Cup

1	N	19	A	Bath C	D	0-0	2-2	Peters, Walker	4,2
1/R		22	H	Bath C	W	1-1	2-1	Marshall, Watson	3,5
2	D	9	A	Bristol C	L	1-0	1-2	Scott	7,6

Littlewoods Cup

1/1	A	23	H	Oxford U	L	0-1	0-1		3,3
1/2		30	A	Oxford U	W	2-2	5-3	Scott 2, Skinner 2, Walker	3,8
2/1	S	19	A	Sunderland	D	1-1	1-1	Watson	11,4
2/2	O	3	H	Sunderland	L	0-2	0-3		6,3

Stannard	Mauge	Kimble	Skinner	Eckhardt	Thomas	Marshall	Bremner	Watson	Davies	Sayer	Walker	Lewington	Barnett	Nebbeling	Scott	Dowie	Langley	Donnellan	Elkins	Milton	Vertannes	Burns	Peters	Dowson	Pike	Newson	Batty	Cole	Ferney	
1	2	3	4	5	6	7	8	9	10	**11**	12	14																		1
1	2	14	4		6	**7**	12	9		10	11		**3**	5	8															2
1	2	14	4		6	7	12	9		10	**11**		3	5	8															3
1	2		4	14	3	6	12	**9**		10	11		**7**	5	8															4
1	2		4	6	3	7	12			10	**11**		S	5	8	9														5
1	2		4	6			3	S		10	11		7	5	8	9		S												6
1	2		4	6	3	**7**	12			10	11		14	5	8	9														7
1	2		4	6	3	7	S	S		10	11			5	8	9														8
1	2		**4**	6	3	7	12	S		10	11			5	8	9														9
1	2		4	6	**3**	7		9		10	11			5	8		12	14												10
1	2		4	6		7	S		12	10	**11**			5	8		3	9												11
1	2		4	6		7		S	S	10	11			5	8		3	9												12
1			4	6		7			9	**10**	11			5	8		2	14	3	12										13
1	10		4			6			**7**	9	11		14	5	8		2		3	12										14
1			4			6		S		9	11		7	5	8		2		**3**	10	12									15
1	8		4			6		14		**9**	11		7	5			2		3	10	12									16
1			4	6		7				9	11	S		5	8		2	S	3	10										17
1	3		4	6		7				9	11	14		5	8		12	**2**		10										18
1			4	6		7		10		9	11			5	8			2		14		**3**	12							19
1	12		**4**	6		7		10		9	11			5	8			2		14		3								20
1	4			6		7		10		**9**	11		S	5	8			2		12		3								21
1	**4**			6		7		10		9	11		12	5	8			2		14		3								22
1			4	6		7		12		9	11		14	5	**8**			2		10		3								23
1			**4**	6		7	12	10			11		14	5	8					9		2		3						24
1	4			6		7	2	10			**11**		14	5	8			12		9				3						25
1	4			6		7	2	**10**		9	11		S	5	8					12				3						26
1	4			6		7	14			**9**	11		12	5	8					10				2	3					27
1	**4**			6		7	2		12		11		10	5	8					9			S		3					28
1	4			6			2		7	S	11		10	5	8					9			S		3					29
1	4			6			2		7		11	S	10	5	8					9					3				S	30
1	4			6		12	S		7		11		10	**5**	8					9					3	2				31
1	4			6		5	S		7		11		10		8					9					3	2			S	32
	4			6		5	12		7		11		10		8					**9**					3	2	1		S	33
	4			6		**10**	S		7		11		12	5	8					9					3	2	1			34
1	4		S	6		5	S		7		11		10		8					9					3	2				35
1	4		12	6		5			7		**11**		10		8		S			9					3	2				36
1	4		12	6		5			**7**		11		10		8					9			14		3	2				37
1	4		8	6		**2**			7		11		10				12		14	9					3	5				38
1	4		14		6				**7**		12	8	10				2		11	9					3	5				39
1	4		S	2	6				7		S		10		8				11	9					3	5				40
1	4		14	2	6				7		12		10		8				**11**	9					3	5				41
1			4	2	6				14		12		10	11	8					9					3	5		**7**		42
1	**4**		S	2	12				7		11		10	6	8					9					3	5				43
1			S	2	6				12		11		10	4	8				**7**	9					3	5				44
1	14		12	2	**4**				7		11		10	6	8					9					3	5				45
1			12	2	4	14			7		11	**8**	10	6						9					3	5				46
4	35	1	24	39	16	34	7	12	19	25	41	2	24	36	41	5	8	8	9	27	-	6	-	4	20	16	2	1		A
-	2	2	6	1	1	2	9	2	4	-	4	2	8	-	-	-	3	3	1	7	2	-	2	-	-	-	-	-		S
-	2	-	4	2	1	4	-	-	6	6	13	-	1	-	3	1	-	-	1	9	-	-	-	-	2	-	-	-		G

Stannard	Mauge	Kimble	Skinner	Eckhardt	Thomas	Marshall	Bremner	Watson	Davies	Sayer	Walker	Lewington	Barnett	Nebbeling	Scott	Dowie	Langley	Donnellan	Elkins	Milton	Vertannes	Burns	Peters	Dowson	Pike	Newson	Batty	Cole	Ferney	
1			4	10		6		S		9	11	8	**7**	5				12	3				2							1
1			4	6		7		10		9	11	**8**	S	5				12	3				2							R
1	**3**		12			7		10		9		4	14	5	8		11	2					6							2

Stannard	Mauge	Kimble	Skinner	Eckhardt	Thomas	Marshall	Bremner	Watson	Davies	Sayer	Walker	Lewington	Barnett	Nebbeling	Scott	Dowie	Langley	Donnellan	Elkins	Milton	Vertannes	Burns	Peters	Dowson	Pike	Newson	Batty	Cole	Ferney	
1	2	3	4	**5**	6	7		9	10	S	12		11		8															1/1
1	2	12	4		6	**7**	14	**9**		10	11		3	5	8															1/2
1	2		4	6	**3**	7	12	9		10	11		S	5	8															2/1
1	2		4	6	3	5	S	9		10	11		**7**		8			12												2/2

0 points v	Bristol C, Bristol R, Reading, Tranmere R	0 points
1 point v	Birmingham C, Cardiff C, Leyton O, Rotherham U	4 points
2 points v	Bolton W, Bury, Northampton T, Walsall	8 points
3 points v	Brentford, Mansfield T, Notts C, Preston NE, Shrewsbury T, Swansea C, Wigan A	21 points
4 points v	Blackpool, Crewe A, Huddersfield T	12 points
6 points v	Chester C	6 points

Talented midfield player Justin Skinner, a product of Fulham's youth scheme, was one of the club's best-ever penalty taker.

1990-91

Division Three

	P	W	D	L	F	A	Pts
Cambridge United	46	25	11	10	75	45	86
Southend United	46	26	7	13	67	51	85
Grimsby Town	46	24	11	11	66	34	83
Bolton Wanderers	46	24	11	11	64	50	83
Tranmere Rovers	46	23	9	14	64	46	78
Brentford	46	21	13	12	59	47	76
Bury	46	20	13	13	67	56	73
Bradford City	46	20	10	16	62	54	70
Bournemouth	46	19	13	14	58	58	70
Wigan Athletic	46	20	9	17	71	54	69
Huddersfield Town	46	18	13	15	57	51	67
Birmingham City	46	16	17	13	45	49	65
Leyton Orient	46	18	10	18	55	58	64
Stoke City	46	16	12	18	55	59	60
Reading	46	17	8	21	53	66	59
Exeter City	46	16	9	21	58	52	57
Preston North End	46	15	11	20	54	67	56
Shrewsbury Town	46	14	10	22	61	68	52
Chester City	46	14	9	23	46	58	51
Swansea City	46	13	9	24	49	72	48
Fulham	46	10	16	20	41	56	46
Crewe Alexandra	46	11	11	24	62	80	44
Rotherham United	46	10	12	24	50	87	42
Mansfield Town	46	8	14	24	42	63	38

Manager: Alan Dicks

Did you know that?

Between September and December 1990, striker Leroy Rosenior played 11 games while on loan from West Ham. It was his third spell at the Cottage as player, having previously played from 1982 until his transfer to QPR in 1985 and again from 1987 until his transfer to West Ham in 1988.

1	Kelly debut
2	Cole finale
3	Brazil and Ferney debuts
5	Stannard's 200th game
10	Davies' 400th game
13	Morgan debut
20	Rosenior finale
35	Davies finale
40	Onwere debut
46	Skinner finale

No		Date	V	Opponents	R	H-T	F-T	Scorers	Atter
1	A	25	A	Crewe A	D	0-0	1-1	Marshall	4,14
2	S	1	H	Cambridge U	L	0-1	0-2		4,14
3		8	A	Shrewsbury T	D	0-1	2-2	Pike, Haag	2,92
4		15	H	Huddersfield T	D	0-0	0-0		3,85
5		18	H	Wigan A	L	1-1	1-2	Thomas	3,04
6		22	A	Preston NE	L	0-0	0-1		4,69
7		29	A	Bournemouth	L	0-1	0-3		5,85
8	O	2	H	Birmingham C	D	1-2	2-2	Brazil, Rosenior	4,01
9		6	H	Rotherham U	W	2-0	2-0	Rosenior, Davies	3,49
10		13	A	Stoke C	L	0-1	1-2	Rosenior	12,39
11		20	A	Swansea C	D	0-2	2-2	Brazil, Davies	4,50
12		23	H	Bury	W	0-0	2-0	Newson, Morgan	3,43
13		27	H	Exeter C	W	1-2	3-2	Pike, Davies 2	4,52
14	N	4	A	Leyton O	L	0-1	0-1		6,16
15		10	A	Southend U	D	0-1	1-1	Brazil	5,80
16		24	H	Tranmere R	L	0-1	1-2	Davies	4,19
17	D	1	A	Reading	L	0-1	0-1		4,07
18		15	H	Bolton W	L	0-0	0-1		3,46
19		22	A	Mansfield T	D	1-0	1-1	Eckhardt	2,83
20		26	H	Bradford C	D	0-0	0-0		3,02
21		29	H	Chester C	W	1-0	4-1	Skinner 2, Scott, Brazil	3,08
22	J	1	A	Grimsby T	L	0-0	0-3		7,49
23		12	A	Cambridge U	L	0-0	0-1		5,08
24		19	H	Crewe A	W	1-0	2-1	Eckhardt, Davies	3,47
25		26	A	Huddersfield T	L	0-1	0-1		4,36
26	F	2	A	Wigan A	L	0-1	0-2		2,25
27		5	H	Preston NE	W	0-0	1-0	Stant	2,75
28		16	A	Tranmere R	D	1-1	1-1	Stant	5,21
29		23	H	Southend U	L	0-2	0-3		5,11
30	M	2	H	Reading	D	1-1	1-1	Stant	4,47
31		9	A	Bolton W	L	0-2	0-3		7,31
32		12	A	Birmingham C	L	0-1	0-2		8,08
33		16	H	Bournemouth	D	0-0	1-1	Talbot	4,08
34		19	H	Stoke C	L	0-0	0-1		3,13
35		23	A	Rotherham U	L	0-3	1-3	Scott	3,18
36		30	A	Bradford C	D	0-0	0-0		6,20
37	A	1	H	Mansfield T	W	0-0	1-0	Stant	3,55
38		6	A	Chester C	L	0-1	0-1		1,04
39		9	H	Shrewsbury T	W	0-0	4-0	Skinner 2, Baker, Marshall	3,41
40		13	H	Grimsby T	D	0-0	0-0		5,46
41		16	A	Brentford	W	1-0	2-1	Haag, Stant	7,83
42		20	H	Swansea C	D	0-0	1-1	Haag	4,20
43		23	H	Brentford	L	0-1	0-1		6,76
44		27	A	Bury	D	1-1	1-1	Pike	3,21
45	M	4	A	Exeter C	W	1-0	1-0	Skinner	3,79
46		11	H	Leyton O	D	0-1	1-1	Onwere	6,59
									App
									Su
									Goa

FA Cup

1	N	17	H	Farnborough	W	1-0	2-1	Pike, Brazil	4,99
2	D	7	H	Cambridge U	D	0-0	0-0		5,92
R		11	A	Cambridge U	L	1-1	1-2	Davies	4,96

Rumbelows League Cup

1/1	A	28	H	Peterborough U	L	1-1	1-2	Joseph	2,73
1/2	S	4	A	Peterborough U	L	0-1	0-2		2,96

atty	Newson	Pike	Skinner	Eckhardt	Thomas	Baker	Kelly	Joseph	Milton	Marshall	Cole	Scott	Stannard	Ferney	Haag	Brazil	Davies	Rosenior	Langley	Cobb	North	Morgan	Gray	Nebbeling	Stant	Parks	Finch	Talbot	Onwere	Gore	
	2	3	4	5	6	7	8	9	**10**	11	12								S												1
	2	3	14	6	5	**8**	7	9	10	11	12	4																			2
	2	3	14	6	5	8	7	12		11			1	4	**9**	10															3
	2	3	S	6	5	8	7			11			1	4	9	**10**	12														4
	2	3	8	6	5		7		14	11			1	**4**	9	10	12														5
	2	3	14	**6**	5		7	12		11		4	1		9	10	8														6
	2	3			5	6	7			11		**4**	1		8	10	12	9	14												7
	2	3			5		7			11			1	4	**8**	10	12	9	14	6											8
	2	3					7			11			1	4	12	10	**8**	9	S	6	5										9
	2	3					7		14	11			1	**4**		10	8	9		12	5	6									10
	2	3	S				7		**11**				1	4		10	8	9		12	5	6									11
	2	3	12				**7**		14				1	4		10	11	9		8	5	6									12
	2	3	4		14		7						1		12	10	**11**	9		8	5	6									13
	2	3	4		14		7		**9**			8	1		12	10	11				5	6									14
	2	3	4	S	7							8	1		S	10	11				5	6	9								15
	2	3	12		7				14			8	1	**4**		10	11				5	6	9								16
	2	3	4		7		8		12				1			10		9	S		5	6	**11**								17
	2	12	14	4	3		8			**11**			1			10	7	9			5	6									18
	2	**7**		4	3					11		8	1	S		10	12	9			5	6									19
	2	7	14	4	3					11		8	1			10	12	**9**			5	6									20
		11	4	2	3				12	9		8	1	S		10	7				5	**6**									21
		9	4	6	3				12	2		8	1	**11**		10	7				5			14							22
	S	9	**4**	8	3		7		11	2			1		12	10					5			6							23
		11	4	9	3		S		12	8			1			10	**7**				5	2		6							24
		11	4	9	3				12	8			1	14		10	**7**				5	2		6							25
		11	4	9					8	3			1	14	12	10	**7**				5	2		6							26
		11	4	8						3			1	6	12	10	**7**				5	2			9		S				27
		11	4	8						3			1	6	12	10	**7**		14		5			2	9						28
		3	8	2					12	11		4	1			10	**7**		S		5	6			9						29
	2	3	8						**7**	11		4				10	12				5	6			9	1	S				30
	2	3							7			4				10	12		14*		6	11			9	1	5	8			31
	3	11		4	S				7			8	1			10	12				5	2			**9**			6			32
	3	11		4	S				**7**			8	1			10	12				5	2			9			6			33
		11		4	3				**7**			8	1			10	12			14	5	2			9			6			34
		11		4	3				9	14		8	1		12	10	7				5	2						**6**			35
	3	11		4	6					7		**8**	1		12	10					5	2			9				S		36
	3	11		4	6					7		8	1		12	10					5	2			**9**				S		37
	3	11	14	4	6					**7**		**8**	1		12	10					5	2			9						38
	6	11	4		3	12			S	7		**8**	1		10						5	2			9						39
	6	11	4		3		12			**7**			1		10	14					5	2			9				**8**		40
		11	4		6		S			7			1		10	3					5	2			9		S		8		41
		11	4		6				S	**7**			1		10	**3**				12	5	2			9				8		42
		11	4	14	6				12	7			1		**10**	3					5	2			9				8		43
		11	4	3	6		S			**7**			1		10					12	5	**2**			9				8		44
	2	11	4	**3**	6					7		8	1			10				12	5				9				14		45
	2	11	4	3	6					**7**		**8**	1			10				12	5				9				14		46
	31	45	24	28	32	5	17	2	12	34	-	23	42	12	12	41	19	11	-	4	38	32	3	5	19	2	1	5	5		A
	-	1	8	1	2	1	1	2	11	1	2	-	-	2	11	1	11	-	4	7	-	-	-	1	-	-	-	-	2		S
	1	3	5	2	1	1	-	-	-	2	-	2	-	-	3	4	6	3	-	-	-	1	-	-	5	-	-	1	1		G

atty	Newson	Pike	Skinner	Eckhardt	Thomas	Baker	Kelly	Joseph	Milton	Marshall	Cole	Scott	Stannard	Ferney	Haag	Brazil	Davies	Rosenior	Langley	Cobb	North	Morgan	Gray	Nebbeling	Stant	Parks	Finch	Talbot	Onwere	Gore	
	2	3	4		7				12			8	1	14	**9**	10				11	5	6									1
	2	3	4		7		8		12				1			10	**11**	9	S		5	6									2
	2	**3**	4	12	7		8			14						10	11	9			5	6									R

atty	Newson	Pike	Skinner	Eckhardt	Thomas	Baker	Kelly	Joseph	Milton	Marshall	Cole	Scott	Stannard	Ferney	Haag	Brazil	Davies	Rosenior	Langley	Cobb	North	Morgan	Gray	Nebbeling	Stant	Parks	Finch	Talbot	Onwere	Gore	
	2	3	14	5	6	7	8	10		11	**9**	4							12												1/1
	2	3		6	5	12	7	9	10	11		4			14															8	1/2

0 points v	Bolton W, Cambridge U, Stoke C, Wigan A	0 points
1 point v	Birmingham C, Bournemouth, Grimsby T, Huddersfield T, Leyton O, Reading, Southend U, Tranmere R	8 points
2 points v	Bradford C, Swansea C	4 points
3 points v	Brentford, Chester C, Preston NE, Rotherham U	12 points
4 points v	Bury, Crewe A, Mansfield T, Shrewsbury T	16 points
6 points v	Exeter C	6 points

Simon Morgan, Fulham's Player of the 1990s, made his debut in October 1990.

1991-92

Division Three

	P	W	D	L	F	A	Pts
Brentford	46	25	7	14	81	55	82
Birmingham City	46	23	12	11	69	52	81
Huddersfield Town	46	22	12	12	59	38	78
Stoke City	46	21	14	11	69	49	77
Stockport County	46	22	10	14	75	51	76
Peterborough United	46	20	14	12	65	58	74
West Bromwich Albion	46	19	14	13	64	49	71
Bournemouth	46	20	11	15	52	48	71
Fulham	46	19	13	14	57	53	70
Leyton Orient	46	18	11	17	62	52	65
Hartlepool United	46	18	11	17	57	57	65
Reading	46	16	13	17	59	62	61
Bolton Wanderers	46	14	17	15	57	56	59
Hull City	46	16	11	19	54	54	59
Wigan Athletic	46	15	14	17	58	64	59
Bradford City	46	13	19	14	62	61	58
Preston North End	46	15	12	19	61	72	57
Chester City	46	14	14	18	56	59	56
Swansea City	46	14	14	18	55	65	56
Exeter City	46	14	11	21	57	80	53
Bury	46	13	12	21	55	74	51
Shrewsbury Town	46	12	11	23	53	68	47
Torquay United	46	13	8	25	42	68	47
Darlington	46	10	7	29	56	90	37

Manager: Alan Dicks / Don Mackay

Did you know that?

The FA Cup defeat by Hayes was Fulham's first by a non-League club since the League was extended to four divisions just after World War One

5	A Cole debut
11	Marshall's 300th game
19	Farrell debut
24	Hails debut
46	Scott finale

No		Date	V	Opponents	R	H-T	F-T	Scorers	Att
1	A	17	A	Chester C	L	0-1	0-2		1,4
2		24	H	Birmingham C	L	0-1	0-1		4,7
3		31	A	Torquay U	W	0-0	1-0	Onwere	3,2
4	S	3	H	West Bromich A	D	0-0	0-0		4,5
5		7	H	Swansea C	W	1-0	3-0	Pike 2, Brazil	3,4
6		14	A	Stoke C	D	0-1	2-2	Cole, Newson	10,5
7		17	A	Bury	L	1-2	1-3	Thomas	2,2
8		21	H	Leyton O	W	1-1	2-1	Eckhardt, Haag	4,9
9		27	A	Bournemouth	D	0-0	0-0		6,4
10	O	5	H	Brentford	L	0-1	0-1		7,7
11		12	A	Bradford C	W	3-1	4-3	Newson, Onwere, Brazil, Haag	5,1
12		19	A	Bolton W	W	1-0	3-0	Brazil 2, Cole	5,1
13		26	H	Preston NE	W	1-0	1-0	Morgan	4,0
14	N	2	H	Hull C	D	0-0	0-0		3,3
15		6	A	Huddersfield T	L	1-1	1-3	Onwere	5,0
16		9	A	Hartlepool U	L	0-0	0-2		2,9
17		23	H	Stockport C	L	0-0	1-2	Cole	3,6
18		30	A	Darlington	L	0-1	1-3	Brazil	2,6
19	D	21	A	Birmingham C	L	0-1	1-3	Brazil	8,8
20		26	H	Torquay U	W	2-1	2-1	Farrell, Morgan	4,1
21		28	H	Chester C	D	0-0	2-2	Thomas, Scott	3,7
22	J	1	A	West Bromich A	W	2-1	3-2	Farrell 3	16,4
23		11	A	Peterborough U	L	0-1	1-4	Newson	4,9
24		18	H	Shrewsbury T	L	0-0	0-1		3,4
25		25	A	Exeter C	D	0-1	1-1	Brazil	4,0
26		28	H	Wigan A	D	0-1	1-1	Morgan	2,4
27	F	1	H	Bolton W	D	1-0	1-1	Kelly (M)	3,8
28		8	A	Preston NE	W	2-0	2-1	Brazil, Farrell	3,8
29		11	H	Darlington	W	1-0	4-0	Brazil 2, Farrell, Eckhardt	2,9
30		15	A	Reading	W	1-0	2-0	Eckhardt, Farrell	4,3
31		22	H	Peterborough U	L	0-1	0-1		5,2
32		28	A	Wigan A	W	1-0	2-0	Eckhardt, Farrell	2,2
33	M	3	A	Shrewsbury T	D	0-0	0-0		2,1
34		7	H	Exeter C	D	0-0	0-0		3,9
35		10	H	Huddersfield T	W	0-0	1-0	Eckhardt	3,1
36		14	A	Hull C	D	0-0	0-0		3,7
37		20	H	Hartlepool U	W	1-0	1-0	Haag	4,3
38		27	A	Stockport C	L	0-1	0-2		4,6
39		31	H	Stoke C	D	1-0	1-1	Haag	5,7
40	A	4	A	Swansea C	D	0-1	2-2	Hails, Eckhardt	3,3
41		7	H	Reading	W	0-0	1-0	Eckhardt	3,4
42		11	H	Bury	W	3-0	4-2	Brazil 2, Thomas, Haag	4,0
43		18	A	Leyton O	W	0-0	1-0	Farrell	7,0
44		20	H	Bournemouth	W	0-0	2-0	Brazil, Farrell	7,6
45		26	A	Brentford	L	0-4	0-4		12,0
46	M	2	H	Bradford C	W	2-1	2-1	Brazil, Haag	8,6
									Ap
									S
									Go

FA Cup

1	N	15	H	Hayes	L	0-0	0-2		6,4

Rumbelows League Cup

1/1	A	21	A	Charlton A	L	0-2	2-4	Brazil 2	3,0
1/2		27	H	Charlton A	D	1-1	1-1	Browne	3,5

Stannard	Marshall	Pike	Newson	Eckhardt	Thomas	Scott	Onwere	Haag	Brazil	Morgan	Milton	Cobb	Baker	Georgiou	Browne	Cole	Kelly M	Nebbeling	Finch	Farrell	Byrne (L)	Hails	Kelly P	Tucker	
1	2	3	4	5	6	7	8	9	10	11	12	14													1
1	2	3		5	6	7	8	9	10	11		4	12	14											2
1	2	3	4	5	6	14	8		10			12	7	9	11										3
1	2	3	4	5	6	11	8	9	10	S		12	7												4
1	2	3	4	5	6	11	8	12	10	14			7			9									5
1	2	3	4	5	6	11	8		10	S				12		9	7								6
1	2	3	4	5	6	11	8		10	S				12		9	7								7
1	2	3	4	5	6	11	8	12	10	S		7				9									8
1	2	3	4	5	6	11	8	S	10	12		7				9									9
1	2	3	4	5	6	11	8	12	10			7				9		S							10
1	2	3	4	5	6	11	8	12	10	7		S				9									11
1	2	3	4	5	6	11	8	S	10	7		S				9									12
1	2	3	4	5	6	11	8	12	10	7		14				9									13
1	2	3	4		6	11	8	12	10	7						9	5	S							14
1	2	3	4		6	11	8	S	10	7		12				9		5							15
1	2	3	4		6	11	8	5	10	7		12				9		S							16
1	2	S	4	5	6	11	8		10	7		12				9		3							17
1	2	3	4	5	6	11	8	9	10	7		S							12						18
1	8	3	2	4	6	11	14	12	10	7									5	9					19
1	2	3	4	5	6	11	12	S	10	7									8	9					20
1	2	3	4	5	6	11	S	S	10	7									8	9					21
1	8	3	2	4	6	11	12	S	10	7									5	9					22
1	8	3	2	4	6	11	12	14	10	7									5	9					23
1	2	3		5	6		8	12	10	7							4			9	11	14			24
1	2	3		8	6		S	S	10	5							4			9		7	11		25
1	2	3		5	6	14		12	10	7							4			9		11	8		26
1	2	3		5	6	4		12	10	7							11			9	8	S			27
1	2	3		5	6	4		12	10	7							11			9	8	14			28
1	2	3		5	6	4		12	10	7							11			9	8	14			29
1	2	3		5	6	4		S	10	7							11			9	8		S		30
1	2	3		5	6	4		12	10	7							11			9		8	S		31
1	2	3		8	6	4		12	10								11	5		9		7	S		32
1	2	3		8	6	4		12	10	S							11	5		9		7			33
1	2	3		8	6	4		11	10	7								5		9		12	S		34
1	2	3		8	6	4		11	10	7								5		9		S	S		35
1	2	3		8	6		12	11	10	7								5		9		S	4		36
1	4	3		7	6			11	10								8	5		9		S	S	2	37
1	2	3		7	6		14	11	10	4							8	5		9		12			38
1	4	3		7	6		S	11	10	2							8	5				9		S	39
1	4	3		7	6	S		11	10	2							8	5		9		12			40
1	4	3		7	6	9		11	10	2							8	5				12		S	41
1		3		7	6	9	12	11	10	2							8	5				4		14	42
1		3	5	7	6	4	12	11	10	2										9		8		S	43
1		3	6	7		8	S	11	10	2							S	5		9		4			44
1		3	14	7	6	4		11	10	2							12	5		9		8			45
1	S	3	2	7	6	4		11	10								12	5		9		8			46
6	41	45	25	43	45	37	19	18	46	34	-	4	3	1	1	13	19	16	5	25	5	11	3	1	A
-	-	-	1	-	-	2	8	16	-	2	1	7	1	3	-	-	2	-	1	-	-	7	-	1	S
-	-	2	3	7	3	1	3	6	14	3	-	-	-	-	-	3	1	-	-	10	-	1	-	-	G

1	2	3	4		6	11	8	9	10	7		5					S	S							1

	2	3	4	5	6	7	8	9	10	11	12	14													1/1
1	2	3		5	6		8	S	10	11			7	9	4		12								1/2

0 points v	Birmingham C, Brentford, Peterborough U, Stockport C	0 points
1 point v	Chester C, Shrewsbury T	2 points
2 points v	Exeter C, Hull C, Stoke C	6 points
3 points v	Bury, Darlington, Hartlepool U, Huddersfield T	12 points
4 points v	Bolton W, Bournemouth, Swansea C, West Bromich A, Wigan A	20 points
6 points v	Bradford C, Leyton O, Preston NE, Reading, Torquay U	30 points

Striker Sean Farrell, signed from Luton Town in December 1991.

1992-93

Division Two

	P	W	D	L	F	A	Pts
Stoke City	46	27	12	7	73	34	93
Bolton Wanderers	46	27	9	10	80	41	90
Port Vale	46	26	11	9	79	44	89
West Bromwich Albion	46	25	10	11	88	54	85
Swansea City	46	20	13	13	65	47	73
Stockport County	46	19	15	12	81	57	72
Leyton Orient	46	21	9	16	69	53	72
Reading	46	18	15	13	66	51	69
Brighton & Hove Albion	46	20	9	17	63	59	69
Bradford City	46	18	14	14	69	67	68
Rotherham United	46	17	14	15	60	60	65
Fulham	46	16	17	13	57	55	65
Burnley	46	15	16	15	57	59	61
Plymouth Argyle	46	16	12	18	59	64	60
Huddersfield Town	46	17	9	20	54	61	60
Hartlepool United	46	14	12	20	42	60	54
Bournemouth	46	12	17	17	45	52	53
Blackpool	46	12	15	19	63	75	51
Exeter City	46	11	17	18	54	69	50
Hull City	46	13	11	22	46	69	50
Preston North End	46	13	8	25	65	94	47
Mansfield Town	46	11	11	24	52	80	44
Wigan Athletic	46	10	11	25	43	72	41
Chester City	46	8	5	33	49	102	29

Manager: Don Mackay

Did you know that?

Ara Bedrossian made his Fulham debut at Bolton in March 1993. He was the first (and still only) Cyprus international to play for the Cottagers.

10	Stannard's 300th game
42	Nebbeling finale
43	Jupp debut
44	Newson finale
46	Kelly finale

No		Date	V	Opponents	R	H-T	F-T	Scorers	Atten
1	A	15	A	Port Vale	D	0-0	0-0		6,74
2		22	H	Preston NE	W	1-0	2-1	Eckhardt, Pike	3,64
3		29	A	Mansfield T	W	1-0	3-2	Marshall, Farrell, Eckhardt	3,22
4	S	1	A	Wigan A	W	3-1	3-1	Eckhardt, Marshall, Farrell	1,59
5		5	H	West Bromich A	D	0-1	1-1	Farrell	9,14
6		12	A	Bournemouth	L	1-1	1-2	Pike	5,39
7		15	H	Swansea C	D	1-0	1-1	Ferney	4,26
8		19	H	Plymouth A	W	0-0	3-1	Brazil 2, Nebbeling	5,43
9		25	A	Stockport C	D	0-0	0-0		4,75
10	O	2	A	Reading	L	0-2	0-3		7,20
11		10	H	Hull C	D	1-3	3-3	Morgan, Brazil, Onwere	5,24
12		17	A	Burnley	L	1-4	2-5	Farrell 2	9,88
13		24	H	Chester C	W	0-0	1-0	(Preece og)	3,75
14		31	A	Exeter C	W	2-1	2-1	Farrell 2	3,28
15	N	3	H	Stoke C	D	0-0	0-0		5,90
16		7	A	Bradford C	L	1-3	2-3	Pike, (Blake og)	3,62
17		21	H	Bolton W	L	1-1	1-4	Eckhardt	4,04
18		28	A	Brighton & HA	W	0-0	2-0	Hails, Pike	7,89
19	D	5	H	Mansfield T	D	0-0	0-0		3,28
20		12	H	Rotherham U	L	0-1	0-1		3,62
21		20	A	Blackpool	D	1-0	1-1	McGlashan	3,80
22		26	A	Leyton O	D	0-0	0-0		8,43
23		28	H	Hartlepool U	L	1-1	1-3	Hails	4,40
24	J	9	A	Swansea C	D	0-1	2-2	Morgan, Hails	5,04
25		16	H	Stockport C	W	1-0	2-1	Pike, Nebbeling	3,51
26		23	A	Plymouth A	D	0-0	1-1	Morgan	5,70
27		30	A	Preston NE	W	0-1	2-1	Hails, Morgan	5,85
28	F	6	H	Port Vale	L	1-1	1-2	Eckhardt	4,90
29		13	A	West Bromich A	L	0-2	0-4		12,85
30		20	H	Wigan A	W	0-0	1-0	Eckhardt	3,50
31		27	A	Hull C	D	0-1	1-1	Morgan	3,64
32	M	2	H	Bournemouth	D	0-1	1-1	Pike	3,42
33		6	H	Reading	D	0-0	0-0		4,81
34		10	A	Huddersfield T	L	0-1	0-1		3,67
35		13	H	Bradford C	D	0-1	1-1	Hails	4,34
36		20	A	Stoke C	L	0-0	0-1		17,93
37		23	H	Brighton & HA	W	1-0	2-0	Farrell, Onwere	5,40
38		27	A	Bolton W	L	0-0	0-1		8,40
39	A	2	H	Huddersfield T	L	0-0	0-1		3,61
40		6	A	Rotherham U	D	1-0	1-1	Hails	3,06
41		10	H	Leyton O	W	0-0	1-0	Onwere	5,97
42		12	A	Hartlepool U	W	0-0	3-0	Morgan 2, Brazil	2,36
43		17	H	Blackpool	W	1-0	1-0	Brazil	4,63
44		24	H	Burnley	W	1-0	4-0	Kelly, Farrell 3	5,53
45	M	1	A	Chester C	W	1-0	3-2	Brazil 2, Morgan	2,01
46		8	H	Exeter C	D	0-0	1-1	Farrell	6,05
									App
									Su
									Goal

FA Cup

No		Date	V	Opponents	R	H-T	F-T	Scorers	Atten
1	N	14	A	Northampton T	L	0-2	1-3	Farrell	4,82

Coca Cola Cup

No		Date	V	Opponents	R	H-T	F-T	Scorers	Atten
1/1	A	18	H	Brentford	L	0-1	0-2		5,06
1/2		25	A	Brentford	L	0-0	0-2		4,80

	Stannard	Morgan	Pike	Bailey	Nebbeling	Thomas	Hails	Marshall	Farrell	Eckhardt	Kelly M	Newson	Baah	Ferney	Onwere	Archibald	Gough	Brazil	Lewis	Tierling	Cooper	McGlashan	Haag	Tucker	Bedrossian	Jupp	Kelly P	Haworth
1	1	2	3	4	5	6	7	8	9	10	11	14	S															
2	1	2	3	4	5	6	7	8	9	10	11	S		S														
3	1	2	3	12	5		7	8	9	10		6	11	**4**	14													
4	1	2	3		5	6	7	8	9	10		S	11	4	14													
5	1	2	3		5	6	7	8	9	4	S		11	S		10												
6		2	3		5	6	7	8	9		12		11	**4**		10	1	14										
7		2	3		5	6	7	8	9		12		**11**	4	S		1	10										
8		2	3		5	6	7	8	9		11		S	4	S			10										
9		2	3		5	6	7	8	9	4	11		S	S				10										
10		2	3		5	6	7	**8**	9	4	11		12	S				10										
11		2	3		5	6	7	8	9	4	**11**	14			12			10										
12		2	3		**5**	6	7	8	9	4		12	11					10	14									
13		2	3		5	6	7	8	9	4		S			S			10	11									
14		2	3		5	6	7	8	9	4					S			10	11	S								
15		**2**	3		5	6	7	8	9	4					12			10	11	S								
16		**2**	3		5	6	7	8	9	4					12			10	11	14								
17		2	3			**6**	7	8	9	4					11			10	12	S	5							
18			3		2	6	7	8	9	4					11					10	5			S			S	
19			3			6	7	8	9	4		2			11					10	5			S			S	
20			3			6	7	8	9	4		**2**	14		11					12	5	10						
21			3			6	7	8		4		2	9		11						5	10					S	S
22		S	3		5	6	12	8		4		2			11			**9**			7	10						
23		14	3		**5**	6	7	8		4		2			11					12	9	10						
24		2	3			6	7	8		4		5		12	11					S	9	**10**						
25		2	3		9	6	7	8		4		5		12	**11**			10		S								
26		2	3		5	6	7	8	12	9		4		14	**11**			10										
27		2	3		5	6	7	8	11	9		4		S	S			10										
28		2	3		11	6	7	8	9	4		5		S	14			10										
29		2	3				7	8	9	4	11	5	14	**6**	10						12							
30		2	3			6	7	8	9	4	11	5		S	10								14					
31		2	3		4	6	7	8			11	5	S	S	10								9					
32		2	3		4	6	7	8			11	5	14	10									9				S	
33		2	3		4	6	7	8	9	10	**11**	5		14				12										
34			3				10	2	8	6	9	5		**4**	12			**7**					14	11				
35		2	3			6	7	8	9	4	**11**	5		12				10						S				
36			**3**			6	7	8	9		11	5		12	4			10			S			2				
37		2	3			6	7	8	9		11	5	S	S	4								10					
38		2	3			6	7	8	**9**		11	5			4		1	12					10		14			
39		2	3		14	6	**7**	8			11	5			4			10					9		12			
40		2	3		14	6	7	**8**				5	11		4			10					12		9			
41		2	3		8	6	7				12	5	**11**		4			10					14		9			
42		2	3		8	6	7				14	5	11		4			10					12		**9**			
43		2	3			6	7		8		12		**11**		4			10					S		9	5		
44		2	3			6	7		8		11	5	S		4			10					S		9			
45		2	3			6	7	14	8		11		S	4				10							9	5		
46		2	3			6	7	S	9		14		11	4				10							8	5		
A	3	38	46	2	28	43	45	40	34	30	19	26	12	10	22	2	3	27	4	2	8	5	5	2	7	3		
S		1	-	1	2	-	1	1	1	-	6	3	4	6	7	-	-	3	2	3	1	-	5	-	2	-		
G		8	6	-	2	-	6	2	12	6	1	-	-	1	3	-	-	7	-	-	-	1	-	-	-	-		

	Stannard	Morgan	Pike	Bailey	Nebbeling	Thomas	Hails	Marshall	Farrell	Eckhardt	Kelly M	Newson	Baah	Ferney	Onwere	Archibald	Gough	Brazil	Lewis	Tierling	Cooper	McGlashan	Haag	Tucker	Bedrossian	Jupp	Kelly P	Haworth
1		2	3		**5**	6	7	8	9	4		14			12				11	10								

	Stannard	Morgan	Pike	Bailey	Nebbeling	Thomas	Hails	Marshall	Farrell	Eckhardt	Kelly M	Newson	Baah	Ferney	Onwere	Archibald	Gough	Brazil	Lewis	Tierling	Cooper	McGlashan	Haag	Tucker	Bedrossian	Jupp	Kelly P	Haworth
1/1		2	3		5	6	7	8	9	10	11	S	12	**4**														
1/2		2	3		5	6	7	8	9	10		S	11	4	14													

0 points v	Bolton W, Huddesfield T	0 points
1 point v	Bournemouth, Bradford C, Port Vale, Reading, Rotherham U, Stoke C, West Bromich A	7 points
2 points v	Hull C, Swansea C	4 points
3 points v	Burnley, Hartlepool U	6 points
4 points v	Blackpool, Exeter C, Leyton O, Mansfield T, Plymouth A, Stockport C	24 points
6 points v	Brighton & HA, Chester C, Preston NE, Wigan A	24 points

Julian Hails, a maths graduate and a bright prospect at the time with chairman Jimmy Hill.

1993-94

Division Two

	P	W	D	L	F	A	Pts
Reading	46	26	11	9	81	44	89
Port Vale	46	26	10	10	79	46	88
Plymouth Argyle	46	25	10	11	88	56	85
Stockport County	46	24	13	9	74	44	85
York City	46	21	12	13	64	40	75
Burnley	46	21	10	15	79	58	73
Bradford City	46	19	13	14	61	53	70
Bristol Rovers	46	20	10	16	60	59	70
Hull City	46	18	14	14	62	54	68
Cambridge United	46	19	9	18	79	73	66
Huddersfield Town	46	17	14	15	58	61	65
Wrexham	46	17	11	18	66	77	62
Swansea City	46	16	12	18	56	58	60
Brighton & Hove Albion	46	15	14	17	60	67	59
Rotherham United	46	15	13	18	63	60	58
Brentford	46	13	19	14	57	55	58
Bournemouth	46	14	15	17	51	59	57
Leyton Orient	46	14	14	18	57	71	56
Cardiff City	46	13	15	18	66	79	54
Blackpool	46	16	5	25	63	75	53
Fulham	46	14	10	22	50	63	52
Exeter City	46	11	12	23	52	83	45
Hartlepool United	46	9	9	28	41	87	36
Barnet	46	5	13	28	41	86	28

Manager: Don Mackay / Ray Lewington

Did you know that?

Fulham were relegated with 52 points, four more than they won to stay up three seasons earlier. Only three clubs (Swansea, Reading and Southend) have been relegated from this division with as many or more points since three points for a win was introduced in 1981–82.

1	Angus debut
14	Herrera debut
32	Onwere finale
46	Eckhardt, Farrell and Pike finales

No		Date	V	Opponents	R	H-T	F-T	Scorers	Atte
1	A	14	A	Hartlepool U	W	1-0	1-0	Brazil	3,13
2		21	H	Cardiff C	L	0-1	1-3	(Baddeley og)	5,69
3		28	A	Bristol R	L	0-1	1-2	Hails	5,26
4		31	H	Wrexham	D	0-0	0-0		3,68
5	S	4	H	Bradford C	D	0-1	1-1	Farrell	4,22
6		11	A	Burnley	L	0-1	1-3	Brazil	9,02
7		14	A	Barnet	W	2-0	2-0	Baah 2	3,06
8		18	H	York C	L	0-1	0-1		3,59
9		25	A	Huddersfield T	L	0-1	0-1		5,61
10	O	2	H	Leyton O	L	1-1	2-3	Farrell, Brazil	4,41
11		9	H	Bournemouth	L	0-0	0-2		4,00
12		16	A	Hull C	D	1-0	1-1	Farrell	6,08
13		23	H	Stockport C	L	0-1	0-1		3,61
14		30	A	Reading	L	0-0	0-1		7,02
15	N	2	A	Exeter C	L	2-3	4-6	Hails, Farrell, Eckhardt, Brazil	2,91
16		6	H	Brighton & HA	L	0-0	0-1		4,38
17		20	A	Rotherham U	W	1-1	2-1	Brazil 2	2,66
18		27	H	Swansea C	W	1-0	3-1	Morgan, Hails, Brazil	3,28
19	D	11	A	Cardiff C	L	0-0	0-1		5,12
20		17	H	Hartlepool U	W	1-0	2-0	Brazil, Farrell	2,99
21		27	H	Port Vale	D	0-0	0-0		5,76
22		28	A	Plymouth A	L	1-1	1-3	Morgan	15,60
23	J	1	H	Brentford	D	0-0	0-0		9,79
24		3	A	Cambridge U	L	0-1	0-3		4,55
25		8	A	Blackpool	W	1-0	3-2	Baah, Morgan, Farrell	3,37
26		15	H	Hull C	L	0-0	0-1		4,40
27		22	A	Bournemouth	W	1-1	3-1	Angus, Brazil, Eckhardt	5,46
28		30	H	Reading	W	0-0	1-0	Hails	6,91
29	F	5	A	Stockport C	W	2-1	4-2	Eckhardt 2, Brazil 2	5,48
30		12	H	Blackpool	W	0-0	1-0	Bedrossian	4,25
31		19	H	Bristol R	L	0-1	0-1		5,06
32		22	A	Wrexham	L	0-0	0-2		2,09
33	M	5	H	Burnley	W	1-2	3-2	Morgan, Eckhardt, Brazil	4,94
34		12	A	York C	L	0-0	0-2		3,57
35		15	H	Barnet	W	1-0	3-0	Brazil, Marshall, Baah	3,32
36		19	H	Huddersfield T	D	1-1	1-1	Angus	3,62
37		26	A	Leyton O	D	0-1	2-2	Herrera, Farrell	5,09
38		29	H	Cambridge U	L	0-1	0-2		3,44
39	A	2	A	Port Vale	D	2-1	2-2	Pike, Farrell	7,38
40		4	H	Plymouth A	D	1-0	1-1	Morgan	5,81
41		9	A	Brentford	W	2-1	2-1	Morgan, Haworth	6,63
42		13	A	Bradford C	D	0-0	0-0		5,01
43		16	H	Exeter C	L	0-2	0-2		4,60
44		23	A	Brighton & HA	L	0-1	0-2		10,60
45		30	H	Rotherham U	W	0-0	1-0	Farrell	5,21
46	M	7	A	Swansea C	L	0-1	1-2	Brazil	4,35
									App
									Su
									Goa

FA Cup

1	N	15	A	Yeovil T	L	0-0	0-1		6,18

Coca Cola Cup

1/1	A	16	H	Colchester U	W	0-1	2-1	(Betts og), Farrell	2,8
1/2		24	A	Colchester U	W	0-1	2-1	Brazil, Farrell	3,3
2/1	S	22	H	Liverpool	L	0-2	1-3	Farrell	13,5
2/2	O	5	A	Liverpool	L	0-2	0-5		12,8

Stannard	Morgan	Pike	Ferney	Jupp	Thomas	Hails	Cooper	Farrell	Brazil	Marshall	Angus	Harrison	Baah	Onwere	Eckhardt	Kelly	Mahorn	Tierling	Herrera	Bedrossian	Haworth	Mison	Bartley	
1	2	3	4	**5**	6	7	8	9	10	11	12	S	14											1
1	2	3	**4**	5	6	7	8	9	10	11		S	14	12										2
1	2	3	4	**5**		7	14	9	10	11	6	S	12	8										3
1	2	3	4		6	7	14	9	10	5	S	S	11	8										4
1	2	3	4	5	6	**7**	12	9	10	5	S	S	11											5
1	2	3	4		6	**7**		9	10	5	S	S	11	8	12									6
1	2	3	4		6	7		S	10	5	S	S	11	8	9									7
1	2	3		12		7		9	10	**5**	6	S	11	8	4	14								8
1	2	3	4	5	6	7		9	10		12	S	11	**8**			14							9
1	2	3	4	5	6			9	10		12	S	14	8		**7**	11							10
1	2	3	**4**	8	6	7		9	10		5	S	S		11		12							11
1		3	4	2	6	7		9	10		5	S	11		8	S		14						12
1	2	**3**	4	8	6	7		9	10		5	S			11	12		14						13
1	2		**4**	S	6	7		9	10		5	S		12	11				3	8				14
1			4		6	7		9	10		5	S	12	8	2			14	**3**	11				15
1			3	2	6	7		9	10		5	S	14	**11**	4			12		8				16
1			**8**	2	6	7		9	10		5	S	12		4			S	3	11				17
1	2			6		7		9	10		5	S	11		4	S		S	3	8				18
1	2			5	6	7		9	10		S	S	11		4			S	3	8				19
1	2			5	6	7		9	10		S	S	11		4			S	3	8				20
1	2			5	6	7		9	10		14	S	11		4			S	3	8				21
1	2			5		7		9	10		6	S	**11**	4				12	3	8	14			22
1	2			5	6	7		9	10		14	S	11	4				S	3	8				23
1	2			5	6	**7**		9	10		3	S	11	4				12		8	14			24
1	2			5	6	**7**		9	10		S	S	11	4					3	8	12			25
1				2	6	7		9	10		5	S	**11**	4	12				3	8	14			26
1		12		2	6	7			10		5	S	11	4	9			S	**3**	8				27
1		12		2	6	7			10		5	S	**11**	4	9			S	3	8				28
1		3		2	6	7			10		5	S	11	4	9			S		8		14		29
1		3		2	6	7			10		5	S	**11**	4	9			12		8		S		30
1	12	3			6	7			10	2	5	S	11	4	9			14		**8**				31
1	8	3			6	7			10	2	5	S	11	**4**	9			S		12				32
1	8	3			6	7			10	2	5	S	11		9			S		4		S		33
1	8	3		12	6	7			10	2	5	S	11		9			S		**4**				34
1	8	3		6		7		9	10	2	5	S	11		4			S		S				35
1	8	3		6		7		9	10	2	5	S	**11**		4			S		12				36
1	8	3	S		6			**9**	10	2	5	S			4			12	11	7				37
1	8	3	S		6			9	10	2	5	S			4				11	**7**	12			38
1	8	3	7	5	6			9	10	**2**	14	S			4				11	12				39
1	2	3	8	5	6			9	10		14	S			4			**7**	11	12				40
1	2	3	8					9	10		5	S			4			7	6	S	11	14		41
1	2	3	8						10		5	S			4			7	6	S	11	9	S	42
1	2	3	**8**						10	11	5	S			4			7	6	12	9	14		43
1	2	3	8		6				10	11	14	S			4			**7**	5	12	9			44
1	2	3	S		6	7		**9**	10	11		S			4				5	8	12			45
1	2	3	14		6	7		9	10	11		S			4				5	**8**	12			46
6	36	31	22	28	37	37	2	34	46	21	28		26	20	33	1	1	5	23	24	4	1		A
-	1	2	1	2	-	-	3	-	-	-	8		7	2	2	2	2	9	-	6	7	3		S
-	6	1	-	-	-	4	-	9	14	1	2		4	-	5	-	-	-	1	1	1	-		G

Stannard	Morgan	Pike	Ferney	Jupp	Thomas	Hails	Cooper	Farrell	Brazil	Marshall	Angus	Harrison	Baah	Onwere	Eckhardt	Kelly	Mahorn	Tierling	Herrera	Bedrossian	Haworth	Mison	Bartley	
1			3	2	6	7		9	10	11	5	S			4	S		S		8				1

Stannard	Morgan	Pike	Ferney	Jupp	Thomas	Hails	Cooper	Farrell	Brazil	Marshall	Angus	Harrison	Baah	Onwere	Eckhardt	Kelly	Mahorn	Tierling	Herrera	Bedrossian	Haworth	Mison	Bartley	
1	2	3	4	5	6	7	8	**9**	10	11	12	S	S											1/1
1	2	3	**4**	5	6	7	8	9	10	11		S	14	12										1/2
1	2	3	4	5	6	7		14	10		S	S	11	8	9									2/1
1	2	3	4	12	6			9	10		5	S	S	8	7	**11**								2/2

0 points v	Brighton & HA, Bristol R, Cambridge U, Cardiff C, Exeter C, York C	0 points
1 point v	Huddersfield T, Hull C, Leyton O, Plymouth A, Wrexham	5 points
2 points v	Bradford C, Port Vale	4 points
3 points v	Bournemouth, Burnley, Reading, Stockport C, Swansea C	15 points
4 points v	Brentford	4 points
6 points v	Barnet, Blackpool, Hartlepool U, Rotherham U	24 points

Too little too late, Gary Brazil's last minute goal in the last game at Swansea cannot save Fulham from relegation.

1994-95

Division Three

	P	W	D	L	F	A	Pts
Carlisle United	42	27	10	5	67	31	91
Walsall	42	24	11	7	75	40	83
Chesterfield	42	23	12	7	62	37	81
Bury	42	23	11	8	73	36	80
Preston North End	42	19	10	13	58	41	67
Mansfield Town	42	18	11	13	84	59	65
Scunthorpe United	42	18	8	16	68	63	62
Fulham	42	16	14	12	60	54	62
Doncaster Rovers	42	17	10	15	58	43	61
Colchester United	42	16	10	16	56	64	58
Barnet	42	15	11	16	56	63	56
Lincoln City	42	15	11	16	54	55	56
Torquay United	42	14	13	15	54	57	55
Wigan Athletic	42	14	10	18	53	60	52
Rochdale	42	12	14	16	44	67	50
Hereford United	42	12	13	17	45	62	49
Northampton Town	42	10	14	18	45	67	44
Hartlepool United	42	11	10	21	43	69	43
Gillingham	42	10	11	21	46	64	41
Darlington	42	11	8	23	43	57	41
Scarborough	42	8	10	24	49	70	34
Exeter City	42	8	10	24	36	70	34

Manager: Ian Branfoot

Did you know that?

In January 1995, Rory Hamill scored after seven seconds in the 4-2 home win over Mansfield, the fastest Fulham goal on record.

1	Moore and M Thomas debuts
LC1	Marshall's 400th game
7	G Thomas finale
8	Blake debut
LC2	Stannard's 400th game
14	Hails finale
15	Cusack debut
39	Morgan's 200th game
40	Stannard finale
42	Brazil's 50th goal
42	Ferney finale

No		Date	V	Opponents	R	H-T	F-T	Scorers	Atten
1	A	13	H	Walsall	D	0-1	1-1	Moore	5,30
2		20	A	Scunthorpe U	W	1-1	2-1	Cork 2	3,16
3		27	H	Wigan A	W	1-0	2-0	Morgan, Cork	4,24
4		30	A	Doncaster R	D	0-0	0-0		3,00
5	S	3	A	Torquay U	L	1-2	1-2	Moore	4,73
6		10	H	Preston NE	L	0-0	0-1		5,00
7		13	H	Scarborough	L	1-2	1-2	Hails	2,72
8		17	A	Walsall	L	0-3	1-5	Brazil	3,37
9		24	H	Hereford U	D	0-1	1-1	Brazil	3,74
10	O	1	A	Barnet	D	0-0	0-0		3,57
11		8	A	Rochdale	W	0-1	2-1	Brazil, Hurlock	2,57
12		15	H	Exeter C	W	2-0	4-0	Stallard 3, Morgan	4,31
13		22	A	Chesterfield	D	0-1	1-1	Moore	2,86
14		29	H	Carlisle U	L	0-2	1-3	Morgan	5,56
15	N	5	A	Northampton T	W	1-0	1-0	Adams	7,36
16		19	H	Lincoln C	D	1-0	1-1	Adams	3,95
17		26	A	Bury	D	0-0	0-0		3,32
18	D	10	H	Scunthorpe U	W	1-0	1-0	Morgan	3,35
19		17	A	Wigan A	D	0-1	1-1	Marshall	1,79
20		26	A	Gillingham	L	0-1	1-4	Morgan	4,67
21		27	H	Colchester U	L	1-1	1-2	Hamill	4,24
22		31	A	Hartlepool U	W	1-1	2-1	Cusack, Brazil	1,69
23	J	2	H	Mansfield T	W	1-1	4-2	Hamill, Cusack, Blake, Thomas	4,09
24		8	H	Chesterfield	D	0-1	1-1	Brazil	3,92
25		14	A	Darlington	D	0-0	0-0		2,11
26		28	A	Carlisle U	D	1-1	1-1	(Walling og)	6,89
27	F	4	H	Bury	W	0-0	1-0	Thomas	3,94
28		14	H	Northampton T	D	2-1	4-4	Morgan 2, Adams, Hamill	3,42
29		18	H	Darlington	W	1-0	3-1	Adams 2, Hamill	3,84
30		25	H	Barnet	W	3-0	4-0	Cusack, Marshall, Morgan, Hamill	6,19
31	M	4	A	Hereford U	D	1-0	1-1	Jupp	2,89
32		11	A	Preston NE	L	1-1	2-3	Jupp, Blake	8,60
33		18	H	Doncaster R	L	0-1	0-2		4,03
34		25	H	Torquay U	W	0-1	2-1	Adams, Cusack	4,94
35	A	1	A	Scarborough	L	0-0	1-3	Adams	2,05
36		8	H	Hartlepool U	W	0-0	1-0	Blake	3,46
37		11	A	Lincoln C	L	0-1	0-2		2,93
38		15	A	Colchester U	L	1-4	2-5	Morgan, Mison	3,44
39		17	H	Gillingham	W	0-0	1-0	Morgan	3,61
40		22	A	Mansfield T	D	0-1	1-1	Morgan	2,86
41		29	A	Exeter C	W	0-0	1-0	Brazil	3,38
42	M	6	H	Rochdale	W	3-0	5-0	Cusack 3, Thomas, Brazil	4,34
									App
									Su
									Goa

FA Cup

No		Date	V	Opponents	R	H-T	F-T	Scorers	Atten
1	N	12	A	Ashford T	D	0-1	2-2	Adams 2	3,36
R		22	H	Ashford T	W	2-1	5-3	Morgan, Adams 2, Blake, Cork	6,53
2	D	2	H	Gillingham	D	0-1	1-1	Hamill	6,25
R		13	A	Gillingham	L	0-1	1-2	Hamill	6,53

Coca Cola Cup

No		Date	V	Opponents	R	H-T	F-T	Scorers	Atten
1/1	A	16	A	Luton T	D	0-0	1-1	Moore	3,28
1/2		23	H	Luton T	D	1-0	1-1	Haworth (4-3 on penalties)	5,13
2/1	S	20	H	Stoke C	W	0-0	3-2	Moore, Haworth, Blake	3,72
2/2		28	A	Stoke C	L	0-1	0-1		7,44

Morgan	Marshall	Mison	Moore	Thomas G	Thomas M	Bedrossian	Cork	Brazil	Herrera	Haworth	Jupp	Ferney	Hurlock	Hails	Angus	Adams	Blake	Stallard	Finnigan	Cusack	Harrison	Hamill	Bartley	Gregory	Bolt	
2	3	4	5	**7**	7	8	9	10	11	12	14										S					1
2	3	4	5	6		S	9	10	3	11	8	14									S					2
2	7	11	5	6			9	10	3		8	S	4	14							S					3
2	7	11	5	6		S		10			8	S	4	9	3						S					4
2	**7**	11	5	6			9	10		12	8		4	14		3					S					5
2	7	S	5	6			9	10		12	8		4	**11**		3					S					6
2	12	7	5	6	14		9	10			**8**		4	11		3					S					7
2	7		5		**6**		9	10	3	12	8		4	11			14				S					8
2	7	4	5			S	9	12	**3**		8					10	6	11			S					9
6	3	4			11	**7**		10		14			8		12		5	9	2		S					10
6		8			11	**7**		10		12	2		4		3		5	9	S		S					11
8		7	5		11			10		S	2		4	S	3		6	9			S					12
8		7	5					10		**9**	2		4	11	3	12	6		14		S					13
8		7	5					10		**9**	2		4	11	3	12	6		14		S					14
8	4	7				S	12	**10**	3						5	11	6		2	9	S					15
8	10	7	5				S		3		2		4		S	11	6			9	13					16
8	7		5				10	S	3		2		4		S	11	6			9	S					17
8	7		5				11	10	3		2		4		S		6			9	S	14				18
8	7	4	5					10	3		2	14			S		6			9	S	11				19
8		14	5					10	3		2	**7**	4		12		6			9	S	11				20
8		S	5					10	S		2		4		3		6		7	9	S	11				21
8			5		7			10	S		2		4		3		6		S	9	S	11				22
8		S	5		7			10	12		2		4		**3**		6			9	S	11				23
8			5		7			10	3	14	2		4		S		6			9	S	11				24
8		S	5		7			10	3			4			S		6		2	9	S	11				25
8	S		5		7			10		S		4			3		6		2	9	S	11				26
8	4		5		7		S	10			2				3		6		S	9	S	11				27
8	4		5		7			10			2				3	14	6		S	9	S	11				28
8	4				7		S		3		2				5	**10**	6		12	9	S	11				29
8	4	14			7				3		2				5	**10**	6		12	9	S	11				30
8	7	14						12	3		2		4		5	**10**	6			9	S	11				31
8	7	**10**					12		3		2	S	4		5		6			9	S	11				32
8	7		5		14				3		2		4		S	10	6			9	S	11				33
8	S		5		7				3		2		4		S	10	6			9	S	11				34
8	11		5		7				S		2		4		3	10	6			9	S	14				35
8	**7**	S	5				12		3		2		4			10	6				1	11	9	13		36
8	14		5		7		9		3		2		4			10	6			12	1	**11**		S		37
8	7	14	5				12	**11**	3		2		4			10	6			9	1			S		38
8	7	14			4			**11**	3		2				5	10	6			9	1	12		S		39
8		4			7			**11**	3		2	S			5	10	6			9		12		S		40
8		14			7			11	3			4			5		6		2	9	1	S		S	10	41
8		14			7			11	3			4			5		6		2	9	1	12		S	**10**	42
42	25	17	31	7	21	3	11	30	26	3	35	5	27	6	21	18	34	4	7	26	6	18	1	-	2	A
-	2	7	-	-	2	-	4	2	1	7	1	2	-	2	2	3	1	-	4	1	1	5	-	1	-	S
11	2	1	3	-	3	-	3	7	-	-	2	-	1	1	-	7	3	3	-	7	-	5	-	-	-	G

Morgan	Marshall	Mison	Moore	Thomas G	Thomas M	Bedrossian	Cork	Brazil	Herrera	Haworth	Jupp	Ferney	Hurlock	Hails	Angus	Adams	Blake	Stallard	Finnigan	Cusack	Harrison	Hamill	Bartley	Gregory	Bolt	
8	4	7	5				9		3	10	12				S	11	6		**2**		S					1
8	10	7	5				9		3	14	2		4		S	11	6				S					R
8	7		5				11	10	3		2		4		S		6			9	1	14		S		2
8	7	4	5				11	10	3		2				S		6			9	S	14				R

Morgan	Marshall	Mison	Moore	Thomas G	Thomas M	Bedrossian	Cork	Brazil	Herrera	Haworth	Jupp	Ferney	Hurlock	Hails	Angus	Adams	Blake	Stallard	Finnigan	Cusack	Harrison	Hamill	Bartley	Gregory	Bolt	
2	7	4	5	6		S	9	10	3	11	8	S									S					1/1
2	7	4	5	6			9	10	3	**11**	8		12	14							S					1/2
2	7	S	5				9	10	3	11	8		4	S			6				S					2/1
2	7	4	5		11	14		10		12	8					3	6				S		**9**			2/2

0 points v	Colchester U, Preston NE, Scarborough	0 points
1 point v	Carlisle U, Doncaster R, Lincoln C, Walsall	4 points
2 points v	Chesterfield, Hereford U	4 points
3 points v	Gillingham, Torquay U	6 points
4 points v	Barnet, Bury, Darlington, Mansfield T, Northampton T, Wigan A	24 points
6 points v	Exeter C, Hartlepool U, Rochdale, Scunthorpe U	24 points

Alan Cork, one of the Crazy Gang, signed as a player in 1994, and was Micky Adams' assistant manager.

1995-96

Division Three

	P	W	D	L	F	A	Pts
Preston North End	46	23	17	6	78	38	86
Gillingham	46	22	17	7	49	20	83
Bury	46	22	13	11	66	48	79
Plymouth Argyle	46	22	12	12	68	49	78
Darlington	46	20	18	8	60	42	78
Hereford United	46	20	14	12	65	47	74
Colchester United	46	18	18	10	61	51	72
Chester City	46	18	16	12	72	53	70
Barnet	46	18	16	12	65	45	70
Wigan Athletic	46	20	10	16	62	56	70
Northampton Town	46	18	13	15	51	44	67
Scunthorpe United	46	15	15	16	67	61	60
Doncaster Rovers	46	16	11	19	49	60	59
Exeter City	46	13	18	15	46	53	57
Rochdale	46	14	13	19	57	61	55
Cambridge United	46	14	12	20	61	71	54
Fulham	46	12	17	17	57	63	53
Lincoln City	46	13	14	19	57	73	53
Mansfield Town	46	11	20	15	54	64	53
Hartlepool United	46	12	13	21	47	67	49
Leyton Orient	46	12	11	23	44	63	47
Cardiff City	46	11	12	23	41	64	45
Scarborough	46	8	16	22	39	69	40
Torquay United	46	5	14	27	30	84	29

Manager: Ian Branfoot / Micky Adams

Did you know that?

Third Division Fulham beat Second Division Swansea 7-0 in the First Round of the FA Cup at the Cottage. This is the biggest victory over a team from a higher division in the history of the competition. The attendance for the visit of Scunthorpe in January 1996 (2,196) was the lowest recorded attendance for a first class game at the Cottage and it happened days before Fulham sank to their lowest-ever placing (91st) in the Football League.

1	Conroy and Lange debuts
23	Scott debut
23	Brazil finale
44	Jupp finale
46	Moore finale

No		Date	V	Opponents	R	H-T	F-T	Scorers	Att
1	A	12	H	Mansfield T	W	1-1	4-2	Mison 2, Thomas 2	4,9
2		19	A	Scarborough	D	2-1	2-2	Brazil, Thomas	1,9
3		26	H	Torquay U	W	1-0	4-0	Barkus, Adams, Hamill, (Barrow og)	4,7
4		29	A	Darlington	D	1-0	1-1	Conroy	1,9
5	S	2	A	Leyton O	L	0-0	0-1		7,2
6		9	H	Doncaster R	W	2-1	3-1	Conroy, Blake, Cusack	4,9
7		12	H	Rochdale	D	1-1	1-1	Morgan	3,8
8		16	A	Exeter C	L	0-1	1-2	Moore	4,4
9		23	H	Preston NE	D	1-1	2-2	Thomas, Morgan	5,2
10		30	A	Northampton	L	0-0	0-2		5,7
11	O	7	A	Plymouth A	L	0-2	0-3		6,6
12		14	H	Bury	D	0-0	0-0		3,8
13		21	A	Chester C	D	0-1	1-1	Conroy	2,7
14		28	H	Hereford U	D	0-0	0-0		3,6
15		31	H	Colchester U	D	0-1	1-1	Cusack	2,8
16	N	4	A	Wigan A	D	1-1	1-1	Angus	2,3
17		18	H	Barnet	D	0-0	1-1	Brazil	4,3
18		25	A	Gillingham	L	0-0	0-1		7,7
19	D	9	A	Preston NE	D	1-0	1-1	Bolt	8,4
20		16	H	Northampton T	L	1-2	1-3	Angus	3,4
21		19	H	Cardiff C	W	1-2	4-2	Bolt, Mison, Morgan, (Harding og)	2,2
22		26	A	Lincoln C	L	0-2	0-4		3,6
23	J	13	H	Scarborough	W	1-0	1-0	Cusack	3,5
24		20	A	Mansfield T	L	0-0	0-1		2,0
25		30	H	Scunthorpe U	L	0-1	1-3	Blake	2,1
26	F	3	A	Torquay U	L	1-1	1-2	Conroy	2,5
27		10	H	Hartlepool U	D	1-0	2-2	Blake, (McGuckin og)	3,7
28		13	A	Cambridge U	D	0-0	0-0		2,2
29		17	A	Rochdale	D	1-1	1-1	Conroy	1,9
30		24	H	Exeter C	W	1-0	2-1	Scott 2	4,0
31		26	A	Doncaster R	W	2-0	2-0	Thomas, Cusack	2,3
32	M	2	H	Lincoln C	L	1-2	1-2	McAree	4,2
33		5	H	Darlington	D	0-2	2-2	Cusack, Mison	2,5
34		9	A	Cardiff C	W	1-0	4-1	McAree, Scott, Conroy 2	3,0
35		12	A	Hartlepool U	L	0-1	0-1		1,1
36		16	H	Cambridge U	L	0-1	0-2		3,8
37		23	A	Scunthorpe U	L	0-1	1-3	Blake	1,9
38		26	H	Leyton O	W	0-0	2-1	Blake, Brooker	3,6
39		30	H	Plymouth A	W	1-0	4-0	Scott, Morgan, Conroy, Brooker	5,6
40	A	2	A	Bury	L	0-2	0-3		3,7
41		6	A	Hereford U	L	0-1	0-1		3,2
42		8	H	Chester C	W	2-0	2-0	Scott, Morgan	3,7
43		13	A	Colchester U	D	1-1	2-2	Conroy, Morgan	3,7
44		20	H	Wigan A	W	0-0	1-0	Hamill	4,6
45		27	H	Gillingham	D	0-0	0-0		10,3
46	M	4	A	Barnet	L	0-1	0-3		4,3

Ap
S
Go

FA Cup

1	N	11	H	Swansea C	W	3-0	7-0	Conroy 3, Cusack, Jupp, Brooker, Thomas	4,7
2	D	2	H	Brighton & HA	D	0-0	0-0		8,0
R		14	A	Brighton & HA	W	0-0	0-0	(4-1 on penalties)	6,2
3	J	6	H	Shrewsbury T	D	0-0	1-1	Angus	7,2
R		16	H	Shrewsbury T	L	1-0	1-2	Hamill	7,9

Coca Cola Cup

1/1	A	15	H	Brighton & HA	W	1-0	3-0	Mison Conroy Barkus	4,3
1/2		22	A	Brighton & HA	W	0-0	2-0	Conroy Brazil	3,7
2/1	S	20	A	Wolverhampton W	L	0-1	0-2		20,3
2/2	O	3	H	Wolverhampton W	L	0-1	1-5	Cusack	6,6

	Lange	Jupp	Herrera	Mison	Angus	Blake	Thomas	Morgan	Conroy	Brazil	Adams	Barkus	Cusack	Hamill	Bolt	Moore	Finnigan	Taylor	Harrison	Bower	Brooker	Gray	Williams	Marshall	Scott	McAree	Barber	Simpson	Hamsher
1	1	2	3	4	5	6	7	8	9	**10**	11	12	14						S										
2	1	2	3	4	5	6	**7**	8	9	10	11	12	14						S										
3	1	2	3	4	5	6	7			9	11	**8**	10	12		S			S										
4	1	2	3	4	5	6	7	8	10	9	11		S	S					S										
5	1	2	3	4	5	6	7	8	10	**9**	11		14	12					S										
6	1	2	3	4	5	6	**7**	8	10	9			11		S	S			S										
7	1	2	3	4	5	6	**7**	8	10	9			11		12	S			S										
8	1	2	3	4	5	6		8	10	9			11		7	14	S		S										
9	1	2	3	4	5	6	7	8	**10**	9			11	12	S				S										
10	1	2	3	4	5	6	7	8	**10**				11	12			14	9	S										
11	1	2		4	5	6	7	8	10	9			14		12	11		**3**	S										
12				4	5		**7**	8	10	11		12	9		S		2	3	1	6	14								
13	1	2					7	8	10	**9**		12	11	13		5	S	3		6		4							
14	1	2	14				**7**	8	10	9		12	11	13		5		3		6		4							
15	1	2	3	6			7	8	12	9			11	**10**		5		S			14	4							
16	1	2	3		6		7	8	10	9		S	11	13		5		S				4							
17	1	2	3		6		12	8	10	9				11	14	5					**7**	4	S						
18	1	2	3		6		7	8	10	9			11		14*	5		S			12	4							
19	1	2	3	8	6	S			10			7		**9**	11	5		4			13		12						
20	1	2	3		6	14		8	10			**7**	9		11	5		4			12		13						
21	1	2	3	4	**6**	12	7	8	10				9		11	5					S		13						
22	1	2	3		6	14	7	8	10				**4**	12	11	5					13		9						
23		2	3		5	6	7	8		12			9	13	11	S			1					4	10				
24		2	3		**5**	6	7	8				14	9			12			1					4	10	13	11		
25		2	3		5	6	**7**	8					9	12		13			1					S	10	4	11		
26	1	2	3		S	6	7		9				4	13		5								14	10	8	11		
27	1	2	3		S	6			9				4	14		5							S	7	10	8	11		
28	1	2	3			6	S	4	12				9			**5**							14	7	10	8	11		
29	1	2	3			6		4	9				**5**	14		S							12	7	10	8	11		
30	1		3			6	7	4	9				5	14		S							13	2	10	8	11		
31	1		3	12		6	7	4	9				5			S							14	2	10	**8**	11		
32	1		3	14		6	7	4	9				5			S							S	2	10	8	11		
33	1		3	14		6	7	4	9				5			**2**					12		13		10	8	11		
34	1		3	S		6	7	4	9				5	14							13		2		10	8	11		
35	1	2	3	12		6	7	4	9				5	14										13	10	**8**	11		
36	1	2	3		14	6	**7**	4	9				5								13		12	8	10		11		
37	1	2	3		5	6	13	4	9			S	8		11						7			S	10				
38	1	2	3	14	5	6	13	4				S	8	9							**7**				10	11			
39	1	2	3	S	5	6		4	9				8	13							7				10	11		14	
40	1	2	3	14	**5**	6		4	9				8								**7**				10	11		12	13
41	1	2	3	**11**	5	6	13	4	9				8								12				10			7	14
42	1		3	S	5	6	7	4					9	S							8			2	10			11	S
43	1		3	S	5	6	7	4	9			S		13							8			2	10			11	
44		12	3		5	6	7		9				4	10					1	S	8		13	**2**				11	
45	1		3	14		6		4	9				8	10		5					12		13	2		**7**		11	
46	1		3			6	13	4	9				8	12		5				10	11			2		**7**		11	14
A	1	35	42	16	30	35	32	41	38	17	5	3	38	6	7	17	1	7	5	4	9	6	2	14	21	16	13	5	-
S	-	1	1	7	1	3	5	-	2	1	-	6	4	19	4	3	1	-	-	-	11	-	11	2	-	1	-	2	3
G	-	-	-	4	2	5	5	6	9	2	1	1	5	2	2	1	-	-	-	-	2	-	-	-	5	2	-	-	-

	Lange	Jupp	Herrera	Mison	Angus	Blake	Thomas	Morgan	Conroy	Brazil	Adams	Barkus	Cusack	Hamill	Bolt	Moore	Finnigan	Taylor	Harrison	Bower	Brooker	Gray	Williams	Marshall	Scott	McAree	Barber	Simpson	Hamsher
1	1	2	3		6		7	8	**10**	9		4	11	12	14	5					13								
2	1	2	3	4	6		7		10			**8**	11		9	5		S			12		14						
R	1	2	3	13	6	S			10			12	8	9	11	5		4			**7**								
3	1	2	3		5	6	7	8	**10**	9			12	14	11	13								4					
R	1	2	3		5	6	7	8	14			S	9	10	11	13								4					

	Lange	Jupp	Herrera	Mison	Angus	Blake	Thomas	Morgan	Conroy	Brazil	Adams	Barkus	Cusack	Hamill	Bolt	Moore	Finnigan	Taylor	Harrison	Bower	Brooker	Gray	Williams	Marshall	Scott	McAree	Barber	Simpson	Hamsher
1/1		2	3	4	5	6	7	8	9	**10**	11	12	14						S										
1/2	1	2	3	4	5	6	7		9	12	11	**8**	10			S			S										
1/2	1	2	3	**4**	5	6	7	8	10	9			12	11		S			S										
2/2	1	12	3	**4**	5	6	7	8	10	9			14	11			2		S										

0 points v	Lincoln C, Northampton T, Scunthorpe U	0 points
1 point v	Barnet, Bury, Cambridge U, Gillingham, Hartlepool U, Hereford U	6 points
2 points v	Colchester U, Darlington, Preston NE, Rochdale	8 points
3 points v	Exeter C, Leyton O, Mansfield T, Plymouth A, Torquay U	15 points
4 points v	Chester C, Scarborough, Wigan A	12 points
6 points v	Cardiff C, Doncaster R	12 points

Fulham's lowest ever gate, 2,176, saw them lose to Scunthorpe. Rory Hamill leads a rare Fulham attack.

1996-97

Division Three

	P	W	D	L	F	A	Pts
Wigan Athletic	46	26	9	11	84	51	87
Fulham	46	25	12	9	72	38	87
Carlisle United	46	24	12	10	67	44	84
Northampton Town	46	20	12	14	67	44	72
Swansea City	46	21	8	17	62	58	71
Chester City	46	18	16	12	55	43	70
Cardiff City	46	20	9	17	56	54	69
Colchester United	46	17	17	12	62	51	68
Lincoln City	46	18	12	16	70	69	66
Cambridge United	46	18	11	17	53	59	65
Mansfield Town	46	16	16	14	47	45	64
Scarborough	46	16	15	15	65	68	63
Scunthorpe United	46	18	9	19	59	62	63
Rochdale	46	14	16	16	58	58	58
Barnet	46	14	16	16	46	51	58
Leyton Orient	46	15	12	19	50	58	57
Hull City	46	13	18	15	44	50	57
Darlington	46	14	10	22	64	78	52
Doncaster Rovers	46	14	10	22	52	66	52
Hartlepool United	46	14	9	23	53	66	51
Torquay United	46	13	11	22	46	62	50
Exeter City	46	12	12	22	48	73	48
Brighton & Hove Albion	46	13	10	23	53	70	47
Hereford United	46	11	14	21	50	65	47

Manager: Micky Adams

Did you know that?

Just five days short of his 37th birthday, Glenn Cockerill becomes the oldest player to make his Fulham debut when he played against Southend on August 20th 1996. The six straight away wins recorded between 27th August and 19th October is a club record.

1 Cullip and Watson debuts
FLC2 Marshall finale
9 Carpenter debut
13 Davis debut
30 Lange and Parker finales
31 Lawrence debut
46 Angus finale

No		Date	V	Opponents	R	H-T	F-T	Scorers	Atter
1	A	17	H	Hereford U	W	0-0	1-0	Conroy	5,27
2		24	A	Hartlepool U	L	0-0	1-2	Scott	2,45
3		27	A	Rochdale	W	1-0	2-1	Cusack, Conroy	1,68
4		31	H	Carlisle U	W	1-0	1-0	Conroy	5,86
5	S	7	H	Colchester U	W	0-2	3-1	Conroy 2, Morgan	5,18
6		10	A	Exeter C	W	1-0	1-0	Freeman	2,38
7		14	A	Swansea C	W	0-1	2-1	Conroy, Morgan	3,79
8		21	H	Mansfield T	L	0-1	1-2	Morgan	5,74
9		28	A	Darlington	W	1-0	2-0	Watson, Carpenter	3,26
10	O	1	H	Torquay U	L	1-0	1-2	Scott	4,45
11		5	A	Northampton T	W	0-0	1-0	Conroy	6,17
12		12	H	Doncaster R	W	0-0	3-1	Conroy, Scott, Carpenter	5,51
13		15	H	Cambridge U	W	3-0	3-0	Conroy 2, Blake	5,79
14		19	A	Hull C	W	1-0	3-0	Freeman, Watson, Conroy	3,98
15		26	A	Brighton & HA	D	0-0	0-0		8,38
16		29	H	Scunthorpe U	W	1-1	2-1	Conroy, Freeman	4,56
17	N	2	H	Lincoln C	L	1-1	1-2	Carpenter	6,94
18		9	A	Cardiff C	W	2-0	2-1	Conroy, Blake	6,14
19		19	H	Barnet	W	1-0	2-0	Conroy, Morgan	4,42
20		23	A	Wigan A	D	0-0	1-1	Scott	5,03
21		30	H	Brighton & HA	W	1-0	2-0	Conroy, Blake	8,27
22	D	3	A	Chester C	D	0-0	1-1	Freeman	1,76
23		14	H	Leyton O	D	0-0	1-1	Watson	7,35
24		21	A	Scarborough	W	2-0	2-0	Conroy, Scott	2,01
25		26	H	Exeter C	D	1-1	1-1	Angus	7,89
26	J	11	H	Darlington	W	1-0	6-0	Scott, Carpenter, Cullip, Freeman, Brooker, Conroy	5,73
27		14	A	Colchester U	L	0-1	1-2	Morgan	3,82
28		18	A	Torquay U	L	1-0	1-3	Scott	3,38
29		25	A	Scunthorpe U	W	3-0	4-1	Cusack, Conroy, Blake, Scott	3,25
30		31	H	Cardiff C	L	0-1	1-4	(Eckhardt og)	6,45
31	F	8	A	Lincoln C	L	0-1	0-2		3,94
32		11	H	Swansea C	W	0-0	2-1	Freeman, Brooker	4,83
33		15	H	Wigan A	D	0-0	1-1	Blake	9,44
34		22	A	Barnet	D	1-1	2-2	Conroy, Scott	3,31
35	M	1	H	Chester C	D	0-1	1-1	Morgan	5,78
36		8	H	Scarborough	W	2-0	4-0	Cockerill, Freeman, Blake, Warren	6,08
37		16	A	Leyton O	W	0-0	2-0	Blake, Carpenter	7,12
38		22	H	Hartlepool U	W	1-0	1-0	Freeman	7,22
39		29	A	Hereford U	D	0-0	0-0		4,47
40		31	H	Rochdale	W	1-1	1-1	Conroy	8,76
41	A	5	A	Carlisle U	W	0-0	2-1	Conroy, McAree	9,17
42		8	A	Mansfield T	D	0-0	0-0		3,91
43		12	H	Northampton T	L	0-1	0-1		11,47
44		19	A	Doncaster R	D	0-0	0-0		2,92
45		26	H	Hull C	W	1-0	2-0	Morgan 2	10,58
46	M	3	A	Cambridge U	W	1-0	1-0	Freeman	7,21
									App
									Su
									Goa

FA Cup

1	N	16	A	Plymouth A	L	0-1	0-5		7,10

Coca Cola Cup

1/1	A	20	A	Southend U	W	1-0	2-0	Conroy, Watson	3,08
2/1	S	3	H	Southend U	L	0-2	1-2	Conroy	4,29
1/2		17	H	Ipswich T	D	1-0	1-1	Morgan	6,94
2/2		24	A	Ipswich T	L	1-1	2-4	Brooker, (Sedgley og)	6,82

Walton	Watson	Herrera	Cullip	Cusack	Blake	McAree	Mison	Conroy	Morgan	Scott	Hamill	Brooker	Thomas	Cockerill	Angus	Freeman	Lange	Adams	Marshall	Carpenter	Davis	Soloman	Parker	Lawrence	Hartfield	Stewart	Warren	
	2	3	4	5	6	7	8	9	10	11	S	13	14															1
	2	3	**4**	5	6	7		9	10	11			12	8	S	14												2
	2	3	4	5	6	**7**		9	10	11			13	8	14	12	1											3
	2	3	4	5	6		12	9	10	11			13	8	S	**7**	1											4
	2	3	4	5	6	S		9	10	11		S	S		8	7	1											5
	2	3	4	5	6	14		9	10	11		S	S		8	7	1											6
	2	3	4	5	6	S		9	10	**11**		12		14	8	7	1											7
	2	3	4	5	6	13		9	10	12		14		**8**	11	7												8
	2	3		4	6		12	**9**	10	7		14	13		5	11				8								9
	2	3	S	4	6			9	10	**7**		12	13		5	11				8								10
	2	3	14	4	6			9	10	7		S			5	11		S		8								11
	2	3		4	6			9	10	7		S	S		5	11		13		8								12
	2	3		4	6		S	9	10	7			S		5	11				8	13							13
	2	3		4	6		13	9	10	**7**		14	12		5	11				8								14
	2	3	S	4	6			9	10	7			13	14	5	11				8								15
	2	3	5	4	6		S	9	10	11			S	14		7				8								16
	2	3	5	4	S			9	10	11			S	14	6	7				8								17
	2	3	5	4	6			9	**10**	11		13		8	12	S	1			**7**								18
	2	3	14	4	6			9	10	11		S	12	**8**	5		1			7								19
	2	3	9	4	6				10	11		14	S	8	5		1			7		S						20
	2	3	S	4	6			9	10	11				8	5	12	1			**7**		S						21
	2	**3**	S	4	6			9	10	11				8	5	12	1			7		S						22
	2	3	14	4	6			9	10	12			S	**8**	5	11	1			7								23
	2		12	4	6	14		9	10	11				8	5	**7**	1	3				13						24
	2		S	4	6	S		9	10	11		12		8	5	7	1					**3**						25
	2	3	6					9	10	**11**		14	13	8	5	12	1			7			4					26
	2	3	6	14				9	10	11		13		8	5	12	1			7			4					27
	2	**3**	12	4	6			9	10	11		13		14	5	7	1			8								28
	2		5	4	6		S	9	10	11		S	13	8		7	1			3								29
			5	4	6	14		9	10	11		12	13			7	1	3		8			2					30
				4	6			9	10	11		13	3	8		14				5				2	7	12		31
	3			4	6			9	10	**11**		12	2	8		7				5				13		S		32
	3			4	6			9	10	11		12	2	**8**		7				5				S	14			33
	3			4	6			**9**	10	12		13	2	8		7				5				14		11		34
	3		S	4	6				10	14		13	2	8		7				5				9		11		35
	3		12	4	6				10	11		13	14	8		7				5				2			**9**	36
	3		8	4	6			12	10	**11**		13	14			7				5				2			9	37
	3			4	6			14	10	11		13	12		5	7				**8**				2			9	38
	3		S	4	6			14	10	11		13			5	7				8				2			9	39
	3		S	4	6			9	10	12		13			5	**7**				8				2			11	40
	3		6	4		7		9	10	14		S	12	8	5									2			**11**	41
	3		6	4		**7**		9	10	14		13	12	8	5									2			11	42
	3		6	4	14			9		7		13	12	8	5					10				**2**			11	43
	3		5	4	6			9				13	11	8	S	**7**				10				2			12	44
	3		5	4	6			9	10				12	8	14	**7**				11				2			13	45
	3		5	4	6			9	10				12	**8**	14	7				11				2			13	46
3	44	26	23	44	40	5	1	40	44	36	-	-	6	27	28	32	18	2	-	34	-	1	3	13	1	2	8	A
	-	-	6	1	1	4	3	3	-	7	-	26	20	5	4	7	-	1	-	-	1	1	-	2	1	1	3	S
	3	-	1	2	7	1	-	21	8	9	-	2	-	1	1	9	-	-	-	5	-	-	-	-	-	-	1	G

Walton	Watson	Herrera	Cullip	Cusack	Blake	McAree	Mison	Conroy	Morgan	Scott	Hamill	Brooker	Thomas	Cockerill	Angus	Freeman	Lange	Adams	Marshall	Carpenter	Davis	Soloman	Parker	Lawrence	Hartfield	Stewart	Warren	
	2	3	5	4	6			9	10	11		13	S	8	12		1			7								1

Walton	Watson	Herrera	Cullip	Cusack	Blake	McAree	Mison	Conroy	Morgan	Scott	Hamill	Brooker	Thomas	Cockerill	Angus	Freeman	Lange	Adams	Marshall	Carpenter	Davis	Soloman	Parker	Lawrence	Hartfield	Stewart	Warren	
	2	3	4	5	6	7	S	9	10	**11**			12	8	S													1/1
		3	4	5	6	S	13	9	10	11			2	8	14	7	1											1/2
	2	3	**4**	5	6	S		9	10	12		S		8	11	7												2/1
	2	3	4	5	6		12	9	10	7		13			11			**8**	14									2/2

0 points v	Lincoln C, Torquay U	0 points
1 point v	Mansfield T	1 point
2 points v	Chester C, Wigan A	4 points
3 points v	Cardiff C, Colchester U, Hartlepool U, Northampton T	12 points
4 points v	Barnet, Brighton & HA, Doncaster R, Exeter C, Hereford U, Leyton O, Rochdale	28 points
6 points v	Cambridge U, Carlisle U, Darlington, Hull C, Scarborough, Scunthorpe U, Swansea C	42 points

Striker Mike Conroy led the promotion charge with 21 League goals.

1997-98

Division Two

	P	W	D	L	F	A	Pts
Watford	46	24	16	6	67	41	88
Bristol City	46	25	10	11	69	39	85
Grimsby Town	46	19	15	12	55	37	72
Northampton Town	46	18	17	11	52	37	71
Bristol Rovers	46	20	10	16	70	64	70
Fulham	46	20	10	16	60	43	70
Wrexham	46	18	16	12	55	51	70
Gillingham	46	19	13	14	52	47	70
Bournemouth	46	18	12	16	57	52	66
Chesterfield	46	16	17	13	46	44	65
Wigan Athletic	46	17	11	18	64	66	62
Blackpool	46	17	11	18	59	67	62
Oldham Athletic	46	15	16	15	62	54	61
Wycombe Wanderers	46	14	18	14	51	53	60
Preston North End	46	15	14	17	56	56	59
York City	46	14	17	15	52	58	59
Luton Town	46	14	15	17	60	64	57
Millwall	46	14	13	19	43	54	55
Walsall	46	14	12	20	43	52	54
Burnley	46	13	13	20	55	65	52
Brentford	46	11	17	18	50	71	50
Plymouth Argyle	46	12	13	21	55	70	49
Carlisle United	46	12	8	26	57	73	44
Southend United	46	11	10	25	47	79	43

Manager: M Adams / R Wilkins / K Keegan

Did you know that?

With the club's transfer record broken almost on a weekly basis, Paul Peschisolido became Fulham's first £1 million signing in October 1997. It almost got to £2 million with the purchase of Chris Coleman the following month and in the summer of 1998 it reached £3 million when Lee Clark was signed from Sunderland.

1	Smith and Hayward debuts
1	Morgan's 300th game
11	Cusack finale
11	Bracewell debut
14	Peschisolido debut
16	Conroy finale
18	Taylor debut
20	Watson finale
21	Coleman and Trollope debuts
25	Cullip finale
26	Herrera finale
28	W Collins debut
29	Brevett debut
33	M Thomas and Carpenter finales
P/01	Blake finale

No		Date	V	Opponents	R	H-T	F-T	Scorers	Atte
1	A	9	H	Wrexham	W	1-0	1-0	Conroy	8,78
2		16	A	Walsall	D	0-0	1-1	(Keister og)	4,41
3		23	H	Luton T	D	0-0	0-0		8,14
4		30	A	Wycombe W	L	0-1	0-2		6,27
5	S	2	A	Bristol C	W	1-0	2-0	Newhouse Carpenter	10,29
6		9	H	Plymouth A	W	0-0	2-0	Moody 2	8,95
7		13	H	Grimsby T	L	0-1	0-2		6,87
8		20	A	Southend U	L	0-1	0-1		5,02
9		27	A	Wigan A	L	1-1	1-2	Hayward	4,95
10	O	4	H	Oldham A	W	1-0	3-1	Moody 2 (Sinnott og)	8,80
11		11	H	Blackpool	W	1-0	1-0	Conroy	7,76
12		18	A	AFC Bournemouth	L	0-1	1-2	(Vincent og)	7,60
13		21	A	Watford	L	0-1	0-2		11,48
14		25	H	Northampton T	D	1-0	1-1	Peschisolido	9,84
15	N	1	H	Chesterfield	D	1-0	1-1	Blake	7,99
16		4	A	Millwall	D	0-0	1-1	Peschisolido	10,29
17		8	A	Bristol R	W	1-0	3-2	Carpenter Scott 2	6,16
18		18	H	York City	D	0-1	1-1	Peschisolido	5,52
19		21	H	Gillingham	W	1-0	3-0	Peschisolido 2 Watson	8,27
20		29	A	Preston NE	L	1-1	1-3	Scott	9,72
21	D	2	H	Brentford	D	0-1	1-1	Peschilido	10,76
22		13	A	Carlisle U	L	0-0	0-2		4,57
23		19	H	Burnley	W	0-0	1-0	Cullip	5,09
24		26	A	Plymouth A	W	1-1	4-1	Moody 2 Hayward Trollope	9,46
25		28	H	Bristol C	W	0-0	1-0	Moody	13,27
26		10	A	Wrexham	W	1-0	3-0	Moody Trollope Peschisolido	5,33
27		17	H	Wycombe W	D	0-0	0-0		10,46
28		24	A	Luton T	W	2-1	4-1	Moody 3 Hayward	8,36
29		31	A	Grimsby T	D	0-0	1-1	Lightbourne	6,78
30	F	7	H	Southend U	W	1-0	2-0	Peschisolido Lightbourne	9,12
31		14	A	Oldham A	L	0-0	0-1		6,0
32		21	H	Wigan A	W	0-0	2-0	Hayward Peschisolido	7,79
33		24	H	AFC Bournemouth	L	0-1	0-1		7,7
34		28	A	Blackpool	L	1-0	1-2	Coleman	5,81
35	M	3	H	Bristol R	W	0-0	1-0	Thorpe	6,84
36		7	A	Chesterfield	W	0-0	2-0	Morgan Blake	5,1
37		14	H	Millwall	L	1-0	1-2	Thorpe	12,31
38		21	A	York C	W	0-0	1-0	Peschisolido	4,87
39		28	A	Gillingham	L	0-1	0-2		10,5
40	A	4	H	Preston NE	W	0-1	2-1	Brazier Collins	8,8
41		7	H	Walsall	D	0-1	1-1	Trollope	6,7
42		11	A	Brentford	W	1-0	2-0	Moody 2	10,5
43		13	H	Carlisle U	W	2-0	5-0	Peschisolido 3 Moody Thorpe	9,2
44		18	A	Burnley	L	1-1	1-2	Moody	9,7
45		25	A	Northampton T	L	0-0	0-1		7,4
46	M	2	H	Watford	L	0-1	1-2	Beardsley	17,11
P/O		9	H	Grimsby T	D	1-0	1-1	Beardsley (pen)	13,9
P/O		13	A	Grimsby T	L	0-0	0-1		8,6

Ap

S

Goa

FA Cup

1	N	16	A	Margate	W	1-1	2-1	Carpenter Scott	5,1
2	D	6	H	Southend U	W	0-0	1-0	Blake (pen)	8,5
3	J	5	A	Tottenham H	L	0-2	1-3	Smith	27,9

Coca Cola Cup

1/1	A	12	A	Wycombe W	W	1-0	2-1	Newhouse Conroy	4,3
2/1		26	H	Wycombe W	D	3-1	4-4	Newhouse 2 Carpenter Conroy	5,0
1/2	S	16	H	Wolverhampton W	L	0-1	0-1		5,9
2/2		24	A	Wolverhampton W	L	0-0	0-1		17,8

Walton	Watson	Herrera	Cullip	Smith	Blake	Newhouse	Hayward	Conroy	Morgan	Carpenter	Cockerill	Scott	Moody	Lawrence	McAree	Brooker	Thomas	Arendse	Cusack	McKenzie	Bracewell	Selly	Freeman	Peschisolido	Aggrey	Taylor	McAnespie	Coleman	Neilson	Trollope	Maher	Arnott	Lightbourne	Collins	Brevitt	Thorpe	Brazier	Beardsley	
1	2	3	4	5	6	7	8	9	10	**11**	12	13	14																										1
1		3	4	5		7	8	9	10	**11**	6	13		2	12	14																							2
1		3	4	5		7	8	9	10	**11**	12	13		2	S	6																							3
1		3	4	5	6	7	8	**9**	10	13	11		12	2		14																							4
1		3	4	5	6	7	8		10	12	**11**	13	9	2		14																							5
1		3	4	5	6	7	8		10	14	12	13	9	2		**11**																							6
1		3	4	5	6	7	8		10	S		13	9	2		11	14																						7
		3	4	5		14	8	12	10	**11**		7	9	2			13	1	6																				8
		3	5	14			8	9	10	2	7	12	**11**	6	4			1	S																				9
		3	2	7	5		11	**10**		4	8		9	6	S			1	S	12																			10
1		3	2	7	5		11	**10**		4		14	9	6					13	12	8																		11
1		3	2	**7**	5		11	10	13	12				6						9	8	4	14																12
1		3	2	7			11	10	5	S		13	9	6						S	8	4																	13
1	14	3	2	7			11		5	12		S	9	6							8	**4**		10															14
1	S	3		7	2		11	S	5	4	S		9	6							8			10															15
	S	3		7	2		11	**9**	5	4	S	12		6				1			8			10															16
1	4	3		7	2		11		5	4		12	9	6			S	1			8			**10**															17
	11	3	12	7	2		13		**5**	4		9		6			S				8			10		1													18
	11	3	5	7	2		S			4		9	S	6							8			10	S	1													19
S	11	3	5	7	2		6			4		9	14				S				8			10		1													20
		3	4	7	S					S		9	13								8			10		1	2	5	6	11									21
		3	4	7						13		9	14	**2**							8			10		1	12	5	6	11									22
		3	12	7			11			4			9	2			14				**8**			10		1	13	5	6										23
		3	S	7			11			S			9	2			S				8			10		1		5	6	4									24
		3	13	**7**			11			12			9	2			S				8			10		1		5	6	4									25
		3		7	S		11			13			9	2							8		12	**10**		1		5	6	4									26
				7	S		11							3			S				8		12	10		1	2	5	6	4			9						27
				2	S		11						7	3							8		14	**10**		1		5	6	4			9	12					28
				7			11						9	2		S					8			S		1		5	6	4			10	13	3				29
				7			S						9	2		14					8			10		1		5	6	4			11	13	3				30
			S	7			14			S			9	2							8			10		1		5	6	4				11	3				31
					S		11			12				2		**7**					8			10		1		5	6	4		S		9	3				32
					13		11			7				2			14				8			10		1		5	6	**4**		12		9	3				33
				7	13		11			S				2							8		12	10		1		5	6	4					3	**9**			34
				7	6		12		S					2				1			8		14	9				5		4				11	3	**10**			35
				7	6		11		3	S				2							8		S	9		1	S	5		4						10			36
				7	**6**		11		3	S				2							8		12	9		1	S	5		4						10			37
				7	6		11			S			12	2							8			9		1		5	3	4						**10**	14		38
				2			11						9	3		14					8			**10**		1		5	6	4						12	13	7	39
				12			S						9	2							8			10		1		5	6	**4**				11		13	3	7	40
				4	6		S						**9**	2							8			10		1		5		13				11		12	3	7	41
				4	6								9	2							8			10		1		5		13				11	3	14	S	**7**	42
				4	6								9	2							8			10		1		5		13				**11**	3	14	12	7	43
				4	6		S						9	2							8			10		1		5		13					3	14	11	7	44
				4	6				3				9	2							8			10		1		5		S				11		14	12	**7**	45
				4	6				S				9	2							8			10		1		5		13				11	3	14		7	46
				12	13				4				9	2							8			10		1		5		6				11	3	14		**7**	P/O
				S	S		7		4					2		14					8			10		1		5		6				9	3	11			P/O
2	4	26	18	42	24	7	33	10	20	15	5	6	28	45	1	4	-	6	1	1	38	3	-	34	-	30	2	28	17	21	-	-	4	12	13	6	3	9	A
-	2	-	3	3	3	1	3	1	1	9	3	11	6	-	1	6	4	-	1	2	-	-	7	-	-	-	2	-	-	5	-	1	-	3	-	9	4	-	S
-	1	-	1	-	2	1	4	2	1	2	-	3	15	-	-	-	-	-	-	-	-	-	-	13	-	-	-	1	-	3	-	-	2	1	-	3	1	2	G

Walton	Watson	Herrera	Cullip	Smith	Blake	Newhouse	Hayward	Conroy	Morgan	Carpenter	Cockerill	Scott	Moody	Lawrence	McAree	Brooker	Thomas	Arendse	Cusack	McKenzie	Bracewell	Selly	Freeman	Peschisolido	Aggrey	Taylor	McAnespie	Coleman	Neilson	Trollope	Maher	Arnott	Lightbourne	Collins	Brevitt	Thorpe	Brazier	Beardsley	
S	11	3	S	7	2		S		5	4		9		6			S	1			8			10	S														1
S	S	3	4	7	5		16			S		9!	12								8			10		1	**2**		6	11									2
S		3		7	S		11			S			9	2			S				8			10		1	S	5	6	4									3

Walton	Watson	Herrera	Cullip	Smith	Blake	Newhouse	Hayward	Conroy	Morgan	Carpenter	Cockerill	Scott	Moody	Lawrence	McAree	Brooker	Thomas	Arendse	Cusack	McKenzie	Bracewell	Selly	Freeman	Peschisolido	Aggrey	Taylor	McAnespie	Coleman	Neilson	Trollope	Maher	Arnott	Lightbourne	Collins	Brevitt	Thorpe	Brazier	Beardsley	
1		3	4	5		7	8	9	10	**11**	6	13	14	2	12																								1/1
1		3	4	5		7	8	9	10	**11**	12	13		2	14	6																							1/2
		3	4	**5**		7	8		10	11		13	9	2		12	S	1	6																				2/1
		3	5			12	8	9	10	2	7	13	**11**	6	4			1	14																				2/2

0 points v	Bournemouth, Watford	0 points
1 point v	Grimsby T, Millwall, Northampton T, Wycombe W	4 points
2 points v	Walsall	2 points
3 points v	Blackpool, Burnley, Carlisle U, Gillingham, Oldham A, Preston NE, Southend U, Wigan A	24 points
4 points v	Brentford, Chesterfield, Luton T, York C	16 points
6 points v	Bristol C, Bristol R, Plymouth A, Wrexham	24 points

Mohamed Al Fayed takes over.

1998-99

Division Two

	P	W	D	L	F	A	Pts
Fulham	46	31	8	7	79	32	101
Walsall	46	26	9	11	63	47	87
Manchester City	46	22	16	8	69	33	82
Gillingham	46	22	14	10	75	44	80
Preston North End	46	22	13	11	78	50	79
Wigan Athletic	46	22	10	14	75	48	76
Bournemouth	46	21	13	12	63	41	76
Stoke City	46	21	6	19	59	63	69
Chesterfield	46	17	13	16	46	44	64
Millwall	46	17	11	18	52	59	62
Reading	46	16	13	17	54	63	61
Luton Town	46	16	10	20	51	60	58
Bristol Rovers	46	13	17	16	65	56	56
Blackpool	46	14	14	18	44	54	56
Burnley	46	13	16	17	54	73	55
Notts County	46	14	12	20	52	61	54
Wrexham	46	13	14	19	43	62	53
Colchester United	46	12	16	18	52	70	52
Wycombe Wanderers	46	13	12	21	52	58	51
Oldham Athletic	46	14	9	23	48	66	51
York City	46	13	11	22	56	80	50
Northampton Town	46	10	18	18	43	57	48
Lincoln City	46	13	7	26	42	74	46
Macclesfield Town	46	11	10	25	43	63	43

Manager: Kevin Keegan

Did you know that?

Ever-present goalkeeper Maik Taylor set a new club record of 24 clean sheets in 46 League games. He also kept another four clean sheets in the club's 12 cup ties that season. Fulham set a record for the most points won (101) in a Second Division season. Francois Keller's 18 minutes as substitute at home to Burnley in December makes his the shortest on-pitch Fulham career.

1	Symons debut
1	Lawrence finale
13	Horsfield finale
17	Finnan and Hayles debuts
45	Bracewell finale
46	N Smith finale

No		Date	V	Opponents	R	H-T	F-T	Scorers	Atter
1	A	8	A	Macclesfield T	W	1-0	1-0	Salako	3,93
2		14	H	Manchester C	W	3-0	3-0	Lehmann 2, Beardsley	14,28
3		22	A	Colchester U	W	0-0	1-0	Collins	6,37
4		29	H	Bournemouth	D	0-0	0-0		12,10
5		31	A	Oldham A	D	0-0	1-1	Moody	4,74
6	S	8	H	Stoke C	W	0-0	1-0	Brevitt	12,05
7		12	A	Notts C	L	0-1	0-1		5,80
8		19	H	York C	D	2-1	3-3	Cornwall, Coleman, Symons	9,07
9		26	A	Lincoln C	W	0-0	2-1	Beardsley 2	4,73
10		29	H	Wycombe W	W	1-0	2-0	Coleman, Bracewell	7,44
11	O	3	H	Luton T	L	0-1	1-3	Neilson	11,86
12		17	A	Millwall	W	0-0	1-0	Symons	11,87
13		24	H	Walsall	W	1-0	4-1	Peschisolido, Symons, Hayward, Horsfield	8,45
14		31	A	Blackpool	W	3-1	3-2	Morgan, Hayward, Horsfield	5,90
15	N	7	H	Bristol R	W	1-0	1-0	Collins	11,57
16		10	A	Wrexham	W	2-0	2-0	Uhlenbeek, Peschisolido	3,48
17		21	H	Chesterfield	W	1-0	2-1	Peschisolido 2	10,00
18		28	A	Gillingham	L	0-0	0-1		7,61
19	D	1	A	Wigan A	L	0-0	0-2		3,95
20		12	H	Burnley	W	2-0	4-0	Morgan 2, Hayles, Peschisolido	9,98
21		19	A	Preston NE	W	0-0	1-0	Coleman	12,32
22		26	H	Colchester U	W	1-0	2-0	Smith, Hayles	12,43
23		28	A	Northampton T	D	0-0	1-1	Horsfield	7,31
24	J	9	H	Macclesfied T	W	0-0	1-0	Horsfield	10,15
25		16	A	Manchester C	L	0-2	0-3		30,25
26		26	H	Oldham A	W	1-0	1-0	Morgan	8,16
27		30	H	Northampton T	W	1-0	2-0	Hayles, Albert	11,64
28	F	6	A	Wycombe W	D	1-1	1-1	Symons	7,53
29		20	H	Notts C	W	1-0	2-1	Horsfield 2	11,90
30		23	H	Reading	W	0-1	3-1	Horsfield 2, Symons	11,24
31		27	A	York C	W	2-0	3-0	Horsfield, Hayles, Peschisolido	6,16
32	M	2	A	Bournemouth	D	0-0	1-1	Symons	9,92
33		6	H	Lincoln C	W	1-0	1-0	Horsfield	11,70
34		9	A	Luton T	W	1-0	4-0	Horsfield 2, Trollope, Hayles	7,42
35		12	A	Bristol R	W	2-1	3-2	Symons, Horsfield, Trollpe	8,01
36		16	A	Stoke C	W	1-0	1-0	Symons	12,29
37		20	H	Blackpool	W	1-0	4-0	Hayles, Horsfield, Finnan, Symons	12,86
38	A	5	A	Reading	W	0-0	1-0	Morgan	18,74
39		10	H	Wigan A	W	0-0	2-0	Albert, Symons	12,14
40		13	H	Gillingham	W	1-0	3-0	Hayles, Coleman, Horsfield	13,11
41		17	A	Chesterfield	L	0-1	0-1		5,80
42		21	H	Millwall	W	2-0	4-1	Betsy, Hayles, Symons, Finnan	11,26
43		24	H	Wrexham	D	1-1	1-1	Peschisolido	11,75
44	M	1	A	Burnley	L	0-0	0-1		13,08
45		4	A	Walsall	D	1-1	2-2	Smith (J), Hayward	8,32
46		8	H	Preston NE	W	0-0	3-0	Moody 3	17,17

App

Su

Goa

FA Cup

1	N	15	H	Leigh RMI	D		1-1	Lehmann	7,96
R		24	A	Leigh RMI	W	2-0	2-0	Peschisolido 2	7,50
2	D	5	H	Hartlepool U	W	1-1	4-2	Horsfield 2, (Di Lella og), Morgan	6,35
3	J	2	A	Southampton	D	1-0	1-1	Hayward	12,54
R		13	H	Southampton	W	0-0	1-0	Hayles	17,44
4		23	A	Aston Villa	W	2-0	2-0	Morgan Hayward	35,26
5	F	14	A	Manchester U	L	0-1	0-1		54,79

Worthington Cup

1/1	A	11	H	Cardiff C	W	1-1	2-1	Beardsley, Lehmann	4,30
2/2		18	A	Cardiff C	W	2-0	2-1	Salako, Morgan	4,76
2/1	S	15	H	Southampton	D	0-0	1-1	Coleman	9,62
2/2		23	A	Southampton	W	1-0	1-0	Lehmann	11,64
3	O	27	A	Liverpool	L	0-0	1-3	Peschisoldo	22,29

aylor	Lawrence	Brevett	Symons	Coleman	Morgan	Trollope	Bracewell	Lehmann	Collins	Salako	Neilson	Hayward	Beardsley	Brown	Uhlenbbek	Moody	Peschisolido	Arendse	Davis	Cornwall	Brooker	Scott	Smith (N)	Horsfield	Finnan	Hayles	Keller	Brazier	Albert	Betsy	McAnespie	Smith (J)	
	2	3	4	5	6	7	8	9	10	11	S	S	S																				1
		3	6	5	2		8	9	10	**11**	S	4	7		12	14																	2
		3	6	5	4		8	9	12	**11**		10	7		2	14	13																3
		3	6	5	4		8	9	2	11		10	7		S	14	13																4
		3	6	5	4		8		2	11	S	10	7		S	9	14																5
		3	6	5	4		8	14	**2**	11		10	7		12	9			13														6
		3	6	5	4		8	9	11		S	10	7		2				13	14													7
		3	6	5	4		8	9	2		S	10	**7**		12					11	14												8
		3	6	5	4	13	8	9	10		S	11	7		2							14											9
		3	6	5	4		8		2		13	11	**7**		12				**10**	14		9											10
		3	6	5			8	10	2		4	11	7		12				13	14		**9**											11
		3	6	5	2		8	9	**4**			11	**7**		12		10				S		S										12
		3	6	5	4		**8**	9	7			11	S		2		10						12	14									13
		3	6	5	4		8	14	7			11	S		2		10						S	9									14
		3	6	5	4		**8**	9	7	14		11	13		2		10						12										15
		3	6	5	4	S	**8**	9	7	S		11			2		10						12										16
		3	6	5	4		8					11	S		12		10						14	9	2	**7**							17
		3	6	5	4	11						S	S		S		10						8	9	2	7							18
		3	6	5	4	13	8					11	14		12		**10**							9	2	7							19
		3	6	5	4	S				14		7			2		10						**8**	9		11	12						20
		3	6	5	4		**8**	S				7			2		10						11	9	12	14							21
		3	6	5	4	12	**8**	13				7			2		10						11	9		14							22
		3	6	5	4	S	8		S			7			2		10						11	9		14							23
		3	6	5			8	14	S	13	2	4					10							9	**7**	11							24
		3	6	5			**8**	9			2	4					13						12	14	7	11		10					25
		3	6	5	4			S	13						12		**10**						**7**	9	2	11			8				26
		3		5		10	8	14	4								13						7	9	2	11	S		6				27
		3	6	5		11	8	S	12			7					10							9	2	13			**4**				28
		3	6			7		14		8		10			S								4	9	2	11			5	13			29
		3	6	5		12		14				7					**10**						4	9	2	11			8	13			30
		3	6	5		10						7					14						4	9	2	11		12	**8**	13			31
		3	6	5	4	10		9				7			S		13						8		2	11				S			32
		3	6	5	4	10						7			12		14						8	9	2	**11**				S			33
		3	6	5	4	10		14				7											**8**	9	2	11				13	12		34
		3	6	5	4	10						7			S		13						8	9	2	11				S			35
		3	6	5	4	10		S				7			S		S						8	9	2	11							36
		3	6	5	4	10						7			12		14						**8**	9	2	11			13				37
			6	5	4	10		14	S			7					13						8	9		11			3			2	38
		3	**6**	5	12	10						7					14						13	9	8	11			4			2	39
		3	6	5	12	10						7					14						13	9	8	11			**4**			2	40
		3	6	5	S			S				7					13						10	9	8	11			4			2	41
		3	6	5				S				7					10		12				S		8	11			4	**9**		2	42
		3	6	5	12							7					10		13				8	9		11			4	14		2	43
		3	6	5	4	8		12				7					10						14	9		11				13		2	44
		3	6	5		10	13	9	8			7				14							12			11					4	2	45
		3	6	5	4			9	10			7			13	14							8			11					12	2	46
	1	45	45	45	32	17	25	16	18	7	3	42	11	-	11	2	19	-	1	1	-	2	20	26	21	26	-	1	12	1	1	9	A
	-	-	-	-	3	4	1	10	3	3	1	-	2	-	12	5	14	-	5	3	1	1	9	2	1	4	1	1	1	6	2	-	S
	-	1	11	4	5	2	1	2	2	1	1	3	3	-	1	4	7	-	-	1	-	-	1	15	2	8	-	-	2	1	-	-	G

aylor	Lawrence	Brevett	Symons	Coleman	Morgan	Trollope	Bracewell	Lehmann	Collins	Salako	Neilson	Hayward	Beardsley	Brown	Uhlenbbek	Moody	Peschisolido	Arendse	Davis	Cornwall	Brooker	Scott	Smith (N)	Horsfield	Finnan	Hayles	Keller	Brazier	Albert	Betsy	McAnespie	Smith (J)	
		3	6	5	S	12		9	7	11		4			2		10	S	**8**				S	13									1
		3	6	5	4	11	8	S		12		13			2		**10**	S					*7*	9				14					R
		S	6	5	4	S	8			12		7			2		10	S					13	9		**11**		3					2
		3	6	5		14	**8**	13	12		4	7			S			S					10	*9*	2	11							3
			6	5			*8*	13		S	2	7			14		**10**	S					12	9	4	11		3					R
		3	6	5	4	S	8		2	S		7					**10**	S					12	9	11	S							4
		3	6	5		13		**9**	*7*	8		10			14			S					4		2	11		S		12			5

aylor	Lawrence	Brevett	Symons	Coleman	Morgan	Trollope	Bracewell	Lehmann	Collins	Salako	Neilson	Hayward	Beardsley	Brown	Uhlenbbek	Moody	Peschisolido	Arendse	Davis	Cornwall	Brooker	Scott	Smith (N)	Horsfield	Finnan	Hayles	Keller	Brazier	Albert	Betsy	McAnespie	Smith (J)	
	13	3	6	5	2	**10**	8	9	4	11	S	12	7	S								S											1/1
		3	6	5	4		8	9		11	S	10	7		2	12	13	S													S		1/2
		3	6	5	4	S	8	9	2		S	10	7		S			S	12	**11**													2/1
		3	6	5	4	12	8	9	**2**		13	10	7		11			S		S	S												2/2
		3	6	5	4			**9**	7		S	11	13		2		10	S	*8*				14							12			3

0 points v		0 points
1 point v		0 points
2 points v	Bournemouth	2 points
3 points v	Burnley, Chesterfield, Gillingham, Luton T, Manchester C, Notts C, Wigan A	21 points
4 points v	Northampton T, Oldham A, Walsall, Wrexham, Wycombe W, York C	24 points
6 points v	Blackpool, Bristol R, Colchester U, Lincoln C, Macclesfield T, Millwall, Preston NE, Reading, Stoke C	54 points

Champions.

1999-2000

Division One

	P	W	D	L	F	A	Pts
Charlton Athletic	46	27	10	9	79	45	91
Manchester City	46	26	11	9	78	40	89
Ipswich Town	46	25	12	9	71	42	87
Barnsley	46	24	10	12	88	67	82
Birmingham City	46	22	11	13	65	44	77
Bolton Wanderers	46	21	13	12	69	50	76
Wolverhampton W	46	21	11	14	64	48	74
Huddersfield Town	46	21	11	14	62	49	74
Fulham	46	17	16	13	49	41	67
Queen's Park Rangers	46	16	18	12	62	53	66
Blackburn Rovers	46	15	17	14	55	51	62
Norwich City	46	14	15	17	45	50	57
Tranmere Rovers	46	15	12	19	57	68	57
Nottingham Forest	46	14	14	18	53	55	56
Crystal Palace	46	13	15	18	57	67	54
Sheffield United	46	13	15	18	59	71	54
Stockport County	46	13	15	18	55	67	54
Portsmouth	46	13	12	21	55	66	51
Crewe Alexandra	46	14	9	23	46	67	51
Grimsby Town	46	13	12	21	41	67	51
West Bromwich Albion	46	10	19	17	43	60	49
Walsall	46	11	13	22	52	77	46
Port Vale	46	7	15	24	48	69	36
Swindon Town	46	8	12	26	38	77	36

Manager: Paul Bracewell / Karlheinz Reidle (c/t)

Did you know that?

Between December 4th and January 22nd, Fulham played eight League matches and the only goal credited to them was an own goal by Tranmere's Roberts (although they did score 11 goals in four cup games in this period).

1	Clark and Melville debuts
28	Goldbaek debut
46	Horsfield finale

No		Date	V	Opponents	R	H-T	F-T	Scorers	Att
1	A	7	A	Birmingham C	D	1-0	2-2	Horsfield 2	24,0
2		14	H	Manchester C	D	0-0	0-0		16,7
3		21	A	Grimsby T	D	1-1	1-1	Finnan	6,1
4		28	H	Charlton A	W	2-0	2-1	Neilson, Peschisolido	15,1
5		30	A	West Bromich A	D	0-0	0-0		17,1
6	S	11	A	Port Vale	W	1-0	2-0	Peschisolido, Coleman	6,1
7		18	H	Queen's Park R	W	1-0	1-0	Peschisolido	19,6
8		25	H	Crewe A	W	3-0	3-0	Horsfield, Hayles, Symons	12,1
9	O	2	A	Norwich C	W	0-1	2-1	Riedle, Hayles	16,3
10		16	H	Swindon T	W	0-0	1-0	Horsfield	13,1
11		19	H	Wolverhampton W	L	0-0	0-1		13,1
12		23	A	Huddersfield T	D	1-0	1-1	Vincent (og)	13,3
13		26	A	Crewe A	D	1-1	1-1	Coleman	5,4
14		30	H	Norwich C	D	1-0	1-1	Symons	13,5
15	N	6	A	Stockport C	L	0-2	1-2	Cadamarteri	7,2
16		9	H	Portsmouth	W	0-0	1-0	Collins	13,2
17		13	H	Barnsley	L	1-1	1-3	Riedle, Hayles	10,6
18		20	A	Blackburn R	L	0-1	0-2		18,5
19		23	H	Bolton W	D	1-1	1-1	Peschisolido	9,6
20		26	A	Walsall	W	1-1	3-1	Riedle, Horsfield 2	5,4
21	D	4	H	Birmingham C	D	0-0	0-0		12,2
22		15	A	Nottingham F	D	0-0	0-0		14,2
23		18	A	Crystal Palace	D	0-0	0-0		17,4
24		26	H	Ipswich T	D	0-0	0-0		17,2
25		28	A	Sheffield U	L	0-0	0-2		17,3
26	J	3	H	Tranmere R	W	1-0	1-0	Roberts (og)	11,3
27		16	A	Manchester C	L	0-1	0-4		30,0
28		22	H	Grimsby T	L	0-0	0-1		10,8
29	F	5	H	West Bromich A	W	0-0	1-0	Riedle	12,0
30		12	A	Portsmouth	W	0-0	1-0	Goldbaek	17,3
31		15	A	Charlton A	L	0-0	0-1		19,9
32		19	H	Walsall	W	0-0	2-0	Phelan, Clark	10,5
33		28	A	Queen's Park R	D	0-0	0-0		16,3
34	M	4	H	Port Vale	W	2-0	3-1	Clark 2, Melville	10,4
35		7	H	Stockport C	W	1-0	4-1	Hayles 2, Goldbaek, Finnan	8,6
36		11	A	Bolton W	L	0-1	1-3	Clark	12,7
37		18	H	Blackburn R	D	1-1	2-2	Hayles, Riedle	15,1
38		21	A	Barnsley	L	0-1	0-1		14,2
39		25	A	Ipswich T	L	0-0	0-1		20,1
40	A	1	H	Crystal Palace	W	1-0	1-0	Horsfield	16,3
41		9	A	Tranmere R	D	0-0	1-1	Melville	7,1
42		15	H	Sheffield U	W	1-0	4-0	Phelan, Clark 2, Melville	12,1
43		22	A	Swindon T	L	0-0	0-1		7,5
44		24	H	Nottingham F	D	1-1	1-1	Coleman	12,6
45		30	A	Wolverhampton W	L	0-0	0-3		19,9
46	M	7	H	Huddersfield T	W	1-0	3-0	Clark 2, Goldbaek	13,7
									Ap
									S
									Goa

FA Cup

3	D	11	H	Luton T	D	2-1	2-2	Horsfield, Davis	6,0
3R		21	A	Luton T	W	0-0	3-0	Hayles 2, Hayward	8,1
4	J	8	H	Wimbledon	W	2-0	3-0	Collins 2, Finnan	16,8
5		29	H	Tranmere R	L	1-1	1-2	Coleman	13,8

Worthington Cup

1/1	A	10	A	Northampton T	W	0-0	2-1	Davis, Horsfield	4,4
1/2		24	H	Northampton T	W	3-1	3-1	Horsfield 3	5,5
2/1	S	14	A	Norwich C	W	1-0	4-0	Peschisolido, Coote (og), Clark, Collins	11,7
2/2		21	H	Norwich C	W	1-0	2-0	Hayles, Davis	
3	O	3	A	West Bromich A	W	1-1	2-1	Peschisolido, Collymore	10,5
4	D	1	H	Tottenham H	W	2-1	3-1	Hayles, Collins, Horsfield	18,1
5	J	12	A	Leicester C	L	0-0	3-3	Peschisolido, Horsfield, Coleman	13,5

* The tie ended 3-3 after extra time. Leicester won 3-0 on penalties

Taylor	Finnan	Brevett	Melville	Coleman	Morgan	Hughes	Clark	Horsfield	Collymore	Davis	Trollope	Hayward	Peschisolido	Betsy	Symons	Neilson	Hayles	Collins	Uhlenbeek	Riedle	Cadamarteri	Ball	Goldbaek	Phelan	Lewis	Hahnemann	Selley	Brooker	Thompson	
1	2	3	4	5	6	**7**	8	9	10	11	12	13	S			S										S				1
1	2	3	4	5	6	**7**	8	9	10	11	S	S	12		S											S				2
1	2	3	4	5	6	7	8		**10**	11	13	14	9	*12*	S											S				3
1	2		4	5	6		8	**9**		*11*	13	7	10	12	14	3			S							S				4
1	2	12	4	5	S		8	9		11	14	7	*10*		6	**3**	13									S				5
1	2	3	4	*5*	14			9	13	11	8	**7**	**10**		6		12	S								S				6
1	2	3	4	5	S		8	9			7	11	**10**		6		12	13	S							S				7
1	**2**	3	4	5	S		8	9	13	14	11	*7*			6		10		12							S				8
1	2	**3**	4	5	S		8	9	13	14	7	11			6		12			*10*						S				9
1	2	**3**		5	4		8	13		14	7	11	*10*		6	S	12			9						S				10
1				5	4		8	9		S	7	11	12		6	3	13	14	*2*	**10**						S				11
1		3		5	4		8	9		12	7	11	10		6	S	13	S	**2**							S				12
1		3		5	4		8	9		S	7	11	**10**		6	S		13	2	12						S				13
1		3		5	4		8			10	**7**	11			6	S		12	2	9						S	S	S		14
1		3	S	5	4		8			**2**	7	11			6			12	13	9	10					S	S			15
1		**3**	4	5	S		8			S	7	11			6			12	2	9	10					S	S			16
1			4	5	S		8	7			3	11	12		6		13	S	2	**9**	10					S				17
1		3	*4*	5	S		8	9		11		*7*	10		6	**2**	13			14	12					S				18
1		3	4	5	S		8	**9**		11		7	10		6		12		*2*	13	14					S				19
1		3	4	5	S		8	9		11		7			6		12	13	2	**10**	S					S				20
1	2	3	4	5	S		8	**9**		11	14	7	12		6		10			*13*						S				21
1	**2**	3	4	5	12		8	9		11	S	7	10		6		12	S								S				22
1	2	3	4		6		8			**11**	S	7	9		5		10	12	S							S		S		23
1	2	*3*	4		6		8	**9**			S	11	12		5		10	7	14			13				S				24
1	2	3	4		6		8				S	*11*	9		5		10	7	S			S				S		S		25
1	2		4	S	6		8	12			7		13		5		**9**	11	3			10				S		S		26
1	2	**3**	4	6	S		8	9			12	S	10		5			7		13		11				S				27
1	2		4	6	S		8				S	S	10		5			7	S	9		11	3			S				28
1	2		4		6		8			S		S	13		5		10	12		9		11	7	**3**		S				29
1	2		4	5	**6**		8	9		S		S			12		10	S				11	7	3		S				30
1	2		4	5	6		*8*	9		14		13			S		10			12		11	**7**	3		S				31
1	2		4	5	6		8	9		S		S			S		10			S		11	7	3		S				32
1	2		4	5	6		8			S		S			S		10	S		9		11	7	3		S				33
1	2		4	5	6		8			S	S	10			S			S		9		11	7	3		S				34
1	2		4	5	6		**8**			12	S	9			S		10	13				11	7	3		S				35
1	2		4	5	**6**		8			12	S	9			S		10	S				11	7	3		S				36
1	2		4	5	6		**8**			12	S	7			S		10			9		11	3		S	S				37
1	2		4	5	*6*					11		9	12		S		10	13				8	**7**	3	14	S				38
1	2		4	5	**6**					14		7	8		S		10			9		*11*	12	3	13	S				39
1	2		4	5	**6**			*9*		14		11	10		S		12	13					7	3	8	S				40
1	*2*		4	5			8	**9**				11	12		S		10	7				13	14	3	6	S				41
1	2		4	5	S		8	9			14	*11*	12				10		13				7	*3*	**6**	S				42
1	2		4	5			8	9				*11*	12				10	14	13				7	3	**6**					43
1	6		4	5			8	12					13		S		10		2	**9**		S	**7**	3	11				S	44
1			4	**5**			8	9			14	7	10		6	12	13		*2*			11		3			S		S	45
1	2		4				**8**	9		12	13	11	S		5	S	10					14	7	3	6					46
46	35	22	40	40	26	3	42	28	3	15	13	34	18	-	27	4	21	6	11	15	3	15	16	17	6	-	-	-	-	A
-	-	1	-	-	2	-	-	3	3	11	9	3	12	2	2	1	13	13	5	6	2	3	2	-	2	-	-	-	-	S
-	2	-	3	3	-	-	8	7	-	-	-	-	4	-	2	1	5	1	-	5	1	-	3	2	-	-	-	-	-	G

Taylor	Finnan	Brevett	Melville	Coleman	Morgan	Hughes	Clark	Horsfield	Collymore	Davis	Trollope	Hayward	Peschisolido	Betsy	Symons	Neilson	Hayles	Collins	Uhlenbeek	Riedle	Cadamarteri	Ball	Goldbaek	Phelan	Lewis	Hahnemann	Selley	Brooker	Thompson	
1	2	3	4	5	S		8	9		**7**	13	11	S		6		10	12								S				3
1	2	3	**5**		4		8	9			12	11	S		6		10	7	S							S	S			3R
1	2	S	4	6	3		8	9			S	S	12		5		**10**	7				11				S				4
1	2		4	6	S		8			13		S	10		5		12	7		9		**11**	3			S				5

Taylor	Finnan	Brevett	Melville	Coleman	Morgan	Hughes	Clark	Horsfield	Collymore	Davis	Trollope	Hayward	Peschisolido	Betsy	Symons	Neilson	Hayles	Collins	Uhlenbeek	Riedle	Cadamarteri	Ball	Goldbaek	Phelan	Lewis	Hahnemann	Selley	Brooker	Thompson	
1		3	4	5	6	7	8	9	10	11	S	S	S		2	S										S				1/1
1	2	**3**	4	5	6		8	9		11	7	12	10	S	13				S							S				1/2
1	2	3	4	5	S		*8*	9	13		7	11	**10**		6		12	14								S				2/1
1	2	3	4	5	6		8	**9**		13	10	7				S	11	S	12							S				2/2
1	*2*	**3**		5	4		8		12	13	7	11	10		6	14	9	S								S				3
1	S	3	4	5	S		8	9			12	11	S		6		10	**7**	2							S				4
1	2	12	4	5	3			9			8	11	**10**		6			7	S							S	S	S		5

0 points v	Barnsley, Wolves	0 points
1 point v	Blackburn R, Bolton W, Ipswich T, Manchester C, Grimsby T	5 points
2 points v	Birmingham C, Nottingham F,	4 points
3 points v	Charlton A, Sheffield U, Stockport C, Swindon T	12 points
4 points v	Crewe A, Crystal P, Huddersfield T, Norwich C, Queen's Park R, Tranmere R, West Bromwich A	28 points
6 points v	Portsmouth, Port Vale, Walsall	18 points

Signed from Sunderland, defender Andy Melville played 175 times. With Coleman, Neilson, Symons and Trollope, he was one of five Welsh internationals in the squad.

2000-01

Division One

	P	W	D	L	F	A	Pts
Fulham	46	30	11	5	90	32	101
Blackburn Rovers	46	26	13	7	76	39	91
Bolton Wanderers	46	24	15	7	76	45	87
Preston North End	46	23	9	14	64	52	78
Birmingham City	46	23	9	14	59	48	78
West Bromwich Albion	46	21	11	14	60	52	74
Burnley	46	21	9	16	50	54	72
Wimbledon	46	17	18	11	71	50	69
Watford	46	20	9	17	76	67	69
Sheffield United	46	19	11	16	52	49	68
Nottingham Forest	46	20	8	18	55	53	68
Wolverhampton W	46	14	13	19	45	48	55
Gillingham	46	13	16	17	61	66	55
Crewe Alexandra	46	15	10	21	47	62	55
Norwich City	46	14	12	20	46	58	54
Barnsley	46	15	9	22	49	62	54
Sheffield Wednesday	46	15	8	23	52	71	53
Grimsby Town	46	14	10	22	43	62	52
Stockport County	46	11	18	17	58	65	51
Portsmouth	46	10	19	17	47	59	49
Crystal Palace	46	12	13	21	57	70	49
Huddersfield Town	46	11	15	20	48	57	48
Queen's Park Rangers	46	7	19	20	45	75	40
Tranmere Rovers	46	9	11	26	46	77	38

Manager: Jean Tigana

Did you know that?

Tigana's Fulham set a new club record by winning the first 11 games of the season. It also equalled the best-ever First Division start, by Tottenham in 1960-61 (in reality, that was the equivalent of the Premiership today) and Newcastle in 1992-93. But it was two short of Reading's all time record of 13, in Division Three in 1985-86. Curiously, both Newcastle (Kevin Keegan) and Reading (Ian Branfoot) were managed by men who would later manage Fulham.

1	Collins, Saha and Boa Morte debuts
WC1	Knight debut
WC2	Peschisolido finale
WC2	Hayward finale
25	Coleman finale
44	Goma debut
44	W Collins finale
45	Trollope finale

No		Date	V	Opponents	R	H-T	F-T	Scorers	Atten
1	A	12	H	Crewe A	W	0-0	2-0	Hayles, Saha	11,15
2		18	A	Birmingham C	W	3-1	3-1	Collins, Saha, Davis	21,65
3		26	H	Stockport C	W	1-1	4-1	Hayles 2, Collins, Boa Morte	11,00
4		28	A	Norwich C	W	0-0	1-0	Boa Morte	16,67
5	S	10	H	Barnsley	W	3-0	5-1	Saha 3, Hayles, Boa Morte	10,43
6		12	H	Burnley	W	0-1	3-1	Goldbaek, Saha 2	11,86
7		16	A	Nottingham F	W	0-0	3-0	Saha, Fernandes, Hayles	18,73
8		23	H	Gillingham	W	1-0	3-0	Hayles 2, Clark	13,03
9		30	A	Bolton W	W	1-0	2-0	Boa Morte 2	19,92
10	O	15	H	Blackburn R	W	1-1	2-1	Fernandes, Saha	15,24
11		18	H	Crystal Palace	W	2-1	3-1	Saha, Clark 2	16,04
12		21	A	Wolverhampton W	D	0-0	0-0		21,08
13		24	H	Preston NE	L	0-0	0-1		14,35
14		28	A	Sheffield W	D	0-1	3-3	Saha, Hayles, Melville	17,55
15	N	4	H	Huddersfield T	W	0-0	3-0	Saha, Goldbaek, Finnan	13,10
16		11	A	Wimbledon	W	1-0	3-0	Saha 2, Hayles	14,07
17		18	H	Portsmouth	W	1-1	3-1	Hayles 2, Clark	19,00
18		21	A	Sheffield U	D	1-1	1-1	Finnan	16,04
19		25	H	Grimsby T	W	0-0	2-1	Boa Morte, Saha	12,10
20	D	2	A	Preston NE	D	0-1	1-1	Davis	16,04
21		9	A	West Bromich A	W	2-0	3-1	Davis 2, Stolcers	23,30
22		16	H	Tranmere R	W	2-1	3-1	Clark, Boa Morte 2	13,15
23		23	A	Crewe A	W	0-1	2-1	Boa Morte, Hayles	6,92
24		26	H	Watford	W	2-0	5-0	Saha, Hayles 3, Stolcers	19,37
25	J	1	A	Stockport C	L	0-1	0-2		6,10
26		13	H	Norwich C	W	1-0	2-0	Saha, Boa Morte	16,06
27		20	A	Watford	W	0-0	3-1	Boa Morte 2, Saha	18,33
28		27	H	Birmingham C	L	0-0	0-1		17,07
29		31	A	Queen's Park R	W	1-0	2-0	Moller. Riedle	16,40
30	F	4	H	Sheffield U	D	1-1	1-1	Boa Morte	12,48
31		10	A	Barnsley	D	0-0	0-0		14,65
32		17	H	Nottingham F	W	1-0	1-0	Saha	17,42
33		20	A	Burnley	L	0-0	1-2	Hayles	15,73
34		24	A	Gillingham	W	0-0	2-0	Collins, Boa Morte	9,93
35	M	4	H	Bolton W	D	1-0	1-1	Hayles	16,46
36		10	H	Queen's Park R	W	1-0	2-0	Saha, Clark	16,02
37		17	A	Crystal Palace	W	1-0	2-0	Boa Morte 2	21,13
38		30	A	Tranmere R	W	2-0	4-1	Saha 2, Hayles, Clark	12,36
39	A	7	H	West Bromich A	D	0-0	0-0		17,79
40		11	A	Blackburn R	W	1-1	2-1	Saha, Davis	21,57
41		14	A	Huddersfield T	W	0-0	2-1	Saha, Boa Morte	15,88
42		16	H	Sheffield W	D	0-1	1-1	Davis	17,50
43		21	A	Portsmouth	D	0-1	1-1	Saha	17,65
44		24	H	Wolverhampton W	W	1-0	2-0	Saha 2	15,37
45		28	H	Wimbledon	D	0-0	1-1	Boa Morte	18,57
46	M	8	A	Grimsby T	L	0-1	0-1		8,70

App

Su

Goal

FA Cup

3	J	7	H	Manchester U	L	1-1	1-2	Fernandes	19,17

Worthington Cup

1/1	A	22	A	Northampton T	L	0-1	0-1		3,48
2/1	S	5	H	Northampton T	W	1-1	4-1	Davis, Fernandes, Saha 2	5,30
2/1		19	A	Chesterfield	L	0-0	0-1		3,71
2/2		27	H	Chesterfield	W	1-0	4-0	Hayward, Symons, Hayles, Boa Morte	4,80
3	N	1	H	Wolverhampton W	W	0-0	3-2	Boa Morte 2, Saha	6,76
4		28	H	Derby C	W	2-2	3-2	Saha 2, Lewis	11,76
5	D	13	A	Liverpool	L	0-0	0-3	(aet)	20,14

Taylor	Finnan	Brevett	Melville	Coleman	Lewis	Goldbaek	Clark	Saha	Collins J	Boa Morte	Fernandes	Betsy	Hayles	Davis	Hayward	Collins W	Trollope	Symons	Willock	Sahnoun	Stolcers	Phelan	Moller	Riedle	Neilson	Hahnemann	Goma	Morgan	Peschisolido	Cornwall	Knight	McAnespie	Hudson	Thompson	McCracken	Keevil	Hammond	
1	2	3	4	5	6	7	8	9	10	11	14	13	12			S										S												1
1	2	3	4	5		7	8	9	10	12	S		11	6		S		S								S												2
1	2	3	4	5		7	8	9	10	12	13	S	11	6		S										S												3
1	2	3	4	5	14	7	8	9	10	12	13		11	6				S								S												4
1	2	3	4	5	12	7	8	9		14	10		11	6	13	S										S												5
1	2	3	4	5	14	7	8	9		12	10		11	6		13										S					S							6
1	2	3	4	5	S	7	8	9		13	10		11			6	12								S	S												7
1	2		4	5	S	7	8	9	10	12	6		11			3		S							S	S												8
1	2		4	5	S	7	8		10	11	6		9			S	3	S								S											S	9
1	2		4	5	13	7	8	12	10	11	6		9			S	3	S								S												10
1	2			5	14	7	8	9	10	11	6		12	13		S	3	4								S												11
1	2	3	4	5		7	8	9	10	12	6		11	S			S	S								S												12
1	2	3	4	5		7	8	9	12	13	6		10	11			14	S								S												13
1	2	3	4	5		12	8	9	10	13	6		11	7			14	S								S												14
1	2	3	S	5		7	8	9	10		12		11	6		S		4	13							S												15
1	2	3	4	5		7	8	9	10	11	12		13	6			14	S								S												16
1	2	3	4	5		7	8	9		12	6		10	11		S		S		13						S												17
1	2	3	4	5		7	8	9		12	6		10	11			14	S		13						S												18
1	2	3	S	5		7	8	12		9	6		10	11		S		4		S						S												19
1	2	3	4	5	S	7	8	9		10	6		12	11				S		S						S												20
1	2	3	4	5		7	8	9	12	14	6		10	11				S			13					S												21
1	2	3	4	5		14	8	9		11	6		13	12				S		10	7					S												22
1	2	3	4	5	S	7	8	12		11			9	10		13		S			6					S												23
1	2	3	4	5		7	8	9		13	6		10	11				14		S	12					S												24
1	2	3	4	5		7	8	9		12	6		10	11				S		13	14					S												25
1	2	3	4			7		9		11		8		10				5		13	6	12		S	S	S												26
1	2	3	4			7	8	9		10	6			11				5		S	S			S	S	S												27
1	2	3	4		13	7	8				6			11			S	5			10		9	12	S	S												28
1	2	3	4			7	8	9			6			11				5		S	S		10	12	S	S												29
1	2	3	4			7	8	9		10	6			11				5		S			S	12	S	S												30
1	2		4			7	8	9		10	6			11			3	5		S			S	12	S	S												31
1	2	3	4			7	8	9	10	11				6				5			13		14	12	S	S												32
1	2	3	4			7	8		10	11	12		9	6				5					S	13	S	S												33
1	2	3	4			7	8	9	10	12			11	6				5					S	14	13	S												34
1	2	3	4			7	8	9	10	12			11	6				5					S	S	S	S												35
1	2	3	4			7	8	9	10	12			11	6				5			14			13	S	S												36
1	2	3	4			7	8	12	10	11			9	6				5			S			S	13	S												37
1	2	3	4				8	9	10			S	11	6				5			7		S	S	S									S				38
1	2	3	4			12	8	9	10				11	6				5			7		S	13	S	S												39
1	2	3	4			7	8	9	10				11	6				5		S	S			S	12	S												40
1	2	3	4			7	8	9		11				13				5		10	6		14	12	S	S												41
S	2	3	4			7	8	9	10	11			12	6				5			13			14		1	S											42
1	2	3	4			7	8	9	10	11		14		6				12			S			13		S	5											43
1		3	4				8	9	10			11		6		2		5		12			14	7	S	S		13										44
1	2		12		S	7	8	9	10	11				6			3	5			13			14		S	4											45
S	2		4			7	8	9		11		13	12	6			S	S			10	3				1	5											46
4	45	39	42	25	1	41	45	39	25	21	23	2	28	37	-	3	5	22	-	2	8	1	2	1	-	2	3	-										A
-	-	-	1	-	6	3	-	4	2	18	6	3	7	3	1	2	5	2	1	5	7	1	3	13	3	-	-	1										S
-	2	-	1	-	-	2	7	27	3	18	2	-	18	6	-	-	-	-	-	-	2	-	1	1	-	-	-	-										G

Taylor	Finnan	Brevett	Melville	Coleman	Lewis	Goldbaek	Clark	Saha	Collins J	Boa Morte	Fernandes	Betsy	Hayles	Davis	Hayward	Collins W	Trollope	Symons	Willock	Sahnoun	Stolcers	Phelan	Moller	Riedle	Neilson	Hahnemann	Goma	Morgan	Peschisolido	Cornwall	Knight	McAnespie	Hudson	Thompson	McCracken	Keevil	Hammond	
1	2	3	4		S	7	8	9		11	6						S	5		10	12				S	S												3

Taylor	Finnan	Brevett	Melville	Coleman	Lewis	Goldbaek	Clark	Saha	Collins J	Boa Morte	Fernandes	Betsy	Hayles	Davis	Hayward	Collins W	Trollope	Symons	Willock	Sahnoun	Stolcers	Phelan	Moller	Riedle	Neilson	Hahnemann	Goma	Morgan	Peschisolido	Cornwall	Knight	McAnespie	Hudson	Thompson	McCracken	Keevil	Hammond	
					6					11	7	8		12	9	4	S	5				3			2	1			10	13		S		S				1/1
		3			6		8	12		11	4		9	7	13	2	S								5	1					10	S		S				1/2
1					8					11					7			5	S						2				9	10	6	3	4	S	S	S	12	2/1
					6		8			9	14	10	12		11		3	5							4	S					7	13	2				S	2/2
1	13		4		7	2	8	9		11	12		S	10		6	3	5								S							S					3
1	S		4	S	11	7	S	9		S	6		10			2	3	5		8	7					S												4
1	2	3	4	5		7	8	9		13	6		10	11			S	S			12					S												5

0 points v		0 points
1 point v	Preston NE	1 point
2 points v	Sheffield U, Sheffield W	4 points
3 points v	Birmingham C, Burnley, Grimsby T, Stockport C	12 points
4 points v	Barnsley, Bolton W, Portsmouth, West Bromwich A, Wimbledon, Wolves	24 points
6 points v	Blackburn R, Crewe A, Crystal P, Gillingham, Huddersfield T, Norwich C, Nottingham F, Queen's Park R, Tranmere R, Watford	60 points

Hayles scored three in the 5-0 win over Watford on Boxing Day.

2001-02

Premiership

	P	W	D	L	F	A	Pts
Arsenal	38	26	9	3	79	36	87
Liverpool	38	24	8	6	67	30	80
Manchester United	38	24	5	9	87	45	77
Newcastle United	38	21	8	9	74	52	71
Leeds United	38	18	12	8	53	37	66
Chelsea	38	17	13	8	66	38	64
West Ham United	38	15	8	15	48	57	53
Aston Villa	38	12	14	12	46	47	50
Tottenham Hotspur	38	14	8	16	49	53	50
Blackburn Rovers	38	12	10	16	55	51	46
Southampton	38	12	9	17	46	54	45
Middlesbrough	38	12	9	17	35	47	45
Fulham	38	10	14	14	36	44	44
Charlton Athletic	38	10	14	14	38	49	44
Everton	38	11	10	17	45	57	43
Bolton Wanderers	38	9	13	16	44	62	40
Sunderland	38	10	10	18	29	51	40
Ipswich Town	38	9	9	20	41	64	36
Derby County	38	8	6	24	33	63	30
Leicester City	38	5	13	20	30	64	28

Manager: Jean Tigana

Did you know that?

Manager Tigana lifted the Fulham transfer record to £7 million when he signed Dutch international goalkeeper Edwin van der Sar from Juventus in August 2001. He raised the bar again a month later when he paid Lyon a reported £11.5 million for Steve Marlet.

1 Van der Sar and Malbranque debuts
3 Legwinski debut
5 Marlet debut
6 Symons finale
WC4 Taylor's 200th game

No		Date	V	Opponents	R	H-T	F-T	Scorers	Atte
1	A	19	A	Manchester U	L	1-1	2-3	Saha 2	67,53
2		22	H	Sunderland	W	0-0	2-0	Hayles, Saha	20,19
3		25	H	Derby C	D	0-0	0-0		18,60
4	S	9	A	Charlton A	D	1-1	1-1	Boa Morte	20,45
5		15	H	Arsenal	L	0-1	1-3	Malbranque	20,80
6		22	A	Leicester C	D	0-0	0-0		18,91
7		30	H	Chelsea	D	0-1	1-1	Hayles	21,15
8	O	14	A	Aston Villa	L	0-0	0-2		28,57
9		21	H	Ipswich T	D	1-0	1-1	Hayles	17,22
10		27	H	Southampton	W	2-1	2-1	Malbranque 2	18,77
11	N	3	A	West Ham U	W	1-0	2-1	Legwinski, Malbranque	26,21
12		17	H	Newcastle U	W	2-0	3-1	Saha, Legwinski, Hayles	21,15
13		24	A	Bolton W	D	0-0	0-0		23,84
14	D	2	H	Leeds U	D	0-0	0-0		20,91
15		8	H	Everton	W	1-0	2-0	Hayles 2	19,33
16		12	A	Liverpool	D	0-0	0-0		37,16
17		15	A	Tottenham H	L	0-2	0-4		36,05
18		26	H	Charlton A	D	0-0	0-0		17,90
19		30	H	Manchester U	L	1-2	2-3	Legwinski, Marlet	21,15
20	J	2	A	Derby C	W	0-0	1-0	Carbonari (og)	28,16
21		12	H	Middlesbrough	W	2-1	2-1	Saha, Marlet	18,97
22		19	A	Sunderland	D	1-0	1-1	Malbranque	41,30
23		30	A	Ipswich T	L	0-1	0-1		25,14
24	F	2	H	Aston Villa	D	0-0	0-0		20,04
25		9	H	Blackburn R	W	1-0	2-0	Hayles, Malbranque	19,58
26		19	A	Middlesbrough	L	0-1	1-2	Marlet	26,27
27		23	A	Arsenal	L	1-3	1-4	Marlet	38,02
28	M	2	H	Liverpool	L	0-1	0-2		21,10
29		6	A	Chelsea	L	1-2	2-3	Saha 2	39,74
30		16	A	Everton	L	0-2	1-2	Malbranque	34,63
31		24	H	Tottenham H	L	0-2	0-2		15,88
32		30	A	Southampton	D	1-1	1-1	Marlet	31,61
33	A	1	H	West Ham U	L	0-1	0-1		19,41
34		8	A	Newcastle U	D	0-1	1-1	Saha	50,01
35		20	A	Leeds U	W	0-0	1-0	Malbranque	39,81
36		23	H	Bolton W	W	1-0	3-0	Goldbaek, Marlet, Hayles	18,10
37		27	H	Leicester C	D	0-0	0-0		21,01
38	M	11	A	Blackburn R	L	0-0	0-3		30,48
									App
									Su
									Goa

FA Cup

3	J		A	Wycombe W	D	0-0	2-2	Legwinski, Marlet	9,92
3R		15	H	Wycombe W	W	0-0	1-0	Hayles	11,98
4		26	A	York C	W	1-0	2-0	Malbranque, Marlet	7,56
5	F	16	A	Walsall	W	1-0	2-1	Bennett (og), Hayles	8,76
6	M	9	A	West Bromich A	W	0-0	1-0	Marlet	24,81
SF	A	14	N	Chelsea	L	0-1	0-1	(at Villa Park)	36,14

Worthington Cup

2	S	11	A	Rochdale	W	1-0	2-2	Boa Morte, Brevett	6,30
3	O	10	H	Derby C	W	1-1	5-2	Hayles, Legwinski, Collins, Saha, Malbranque	9,21
4	N	29	H	Tottenham H	L	1-1	1-2	Hayles	17,00

Van der Sar	Finnan	Harley	Melville	Goma	Davis	Goldbaek	Collins	Saha	Hayles	Malbranque	Stolcers	Betsy	Ouaddou	Brevett	Symons	Legwinski	Clark	Boa Morte	Marlet	Knight	Willock	Taylor	Lewis	Trollope	Hahnemann	Neilson	
1	2	3	4	5	8	**7**	8	9	10	*11*	12	13	14		S							S					1
1	2	12	4	5	8	7	8	9	10	11		S		**3**	S	S						S					2
1	2	13	4	**5**	8	7	8	9	10	11		S		3	12	14						S					3
1	2		4		8	S	8	**9**	12	13			S	3	5	7	11	10				S					4
1	2		4		8		8	9	12	11			S	3	5	*7*	S	**10**	13			S					5
1	2		4		8		8	9	S	14				3	12	*13*	11	10	7	**5**		S					6
1	2		4		8	**7**	*8*	9	10	13				3	S		11	12	14	5		S					7
1	2		4	12	8		8	9	13	11				3		7	S	14	*10*	**5**		S					8
1	2		4	5	12		8	13	10	14				3		7	**6**	11	*9*	S		S					9
1	2	S	4	5		S	8	12	10	6				3		7		11	**9**	S		S					10
1	2		4	5	12	13	8	**9**	10	*6*	14			3		7		11		S		S					11
1	2		4	5	6	12	8	9	10	**11**	S		S	3		7	13					S					12
1	2		4	5	6	S	8	9	**10**	11				3	S	7	13	12				S					13
1	2		4	5	12		8	9	10	6	S		S	3		**7**	S	11				S					14
1	2		4	5	12		8	**9**	10	6	S		S	3		7	S	11				S					15
1	2		4	5	**6**		8	9	10	11	S			3		12	S	7		S		S					16
1	2		4	5	S		**8**	9	10	6	S			3		7	12	11		S		S					17
1	2		4	5	6		12	9	10	11	S		S	3		**7**	8	13				S					18
1	2		4	5	12		8	9	10	6	S		S	3		**7**		11	13			S					19
1	2	S	4	5	6		8	12	**10**	11	S		S	3					9	7		S					20
1	2	S	4	5	6		8	12	10	11	S			3		**7**			9	13		S					21
1	2	S	4	5		S	8		**10**	6	13			3		7		12	9	11		S					22
1	2		4	5		**8**	13	9	12	6	S		14	3		*7*			10	11		S					23
1	2	3	4	5		12		9	10	6			S			7			8	11	S	S		S			24
1	2	S	4	5	6		8	S	10	11			S	3		7			**9**		12	S					25
1	2	S	4	5	6		**8**	12	10	11			S	3		7			9		S	S					26
1	2	14	4	5			8	13	10	11			S	*3*		7		12	9	**6**		S					27
1	2		S	5	**6**		14	9	13	11			4	3		7	*12*	10	8			S					28
1	2	11	S	5		S	8	9	12	6			4	3				**7**	10	S		S					29
1	2	S	4	**5**		14	8	9	13	6			12	3		*7*		11	10			S					30
1	2	**3**	S	5	6		S	9	10	11			4	12		7		S	8			S					31
1	2	14	4	5	**6**		*8*	13	10	11				3		7		12	9	S		S					32
1	2	14	4	5	*6*		8	**9**	10	11				3		7		12	13	S		S					33
1	2	S	4	5	6		8	9	S	11			S	3		7		S	10			S					34
1	2		4	5	*6*	12		9	13	8			14	3		7		**11**	10	S		S					35
1	2		4	5	6	7	13	**9**	10	*11*	14			3		8			12	S		S					36
1	2		4	5	6	*7*	12	13	10	11	S			3		**8**			9	S		S					37
	2	3	4		6	7	S	9			13		**5**			8			*10*	12	14	1	11		S		38
7	38	5	35	32	25	8	29	28	27	33	-	-	4	34	2	30	5	15	21	8	-	1	1			-	A
-	-	5	-	1	5	5	5	8	8	4	5	1	4	1	2	3	4	8	5	2	1	-	-			-	S
-	-	-	-	-	-	1	-	8	8	8	-	-	-	-	-	3	-	1	6	-	-	-	-			-	G

Van der Sar	Finnan	Harley	Melville	Goma	Davis	Goldbaek	Collins	Saha	Hayles	Malbranque	Stolcers	Betsy	Ouaddou	Brevett	Symons	Legwinski	Clark	Boa Morte	Marlet	Knight	Willock	Taylor	Lewis	Trollope	Hahnemann	Neilson	
S	2	S	4	5	12		8	9	13	11	S			3		7			10	**6**		1					3
	2		4	5	8			**9**	10	7	13			3				11	12	6		1			S		3R
1	2		4	5		12	**8**	9		11	S		S	3		7			10	6	S	S					4
1	2	14	13	5	6		*8*	12	10	11			4	3		7			**8**		S	S					5
1	2	S	4	5		13	8	*9*	14	**6**			12	3		7		**11**	10			S					6
1	2		4	5	6		**8**	9	13	11			S	3		*7*		12	10	S		S					SF

Van der Sar	Finnan	Harley	Melville	Goma	Davis	Goldbaek	Collins	Saha	Hayles	Malbranque	Stolcers	Betsy	Ouaddou	Brevett	Symons	Legwinski	Clark	Boa Morte	Marlet	Knight	Willock	Taylor	Lewis	Trollope	Hahnemann	Neilson	
	2	**3**	13		6	*7*			9	11		S	5	12		14	8	10		4		1			S		2
S	2		4		6		8	13	10	12				3		*7*	**11**	14	9	5		1				S	3
S	2	3	S	5	6	**7**	8	13	10	12			4	S			11	9				1					4

0 points v	Arsenal, Manchester U, Tottenham H	0 points
1 point v	Aston V, Chelsea, Ipswich T, Liverpool	4 points
2 points v	Charlton A, Leicester C	4 points
3 points v	Blackburn R, Everton, Middlesbrough, West Ham U	12 points
4 points v	Bolton W, Derby C, Leeds U, Newcastle U, Southampton, Sunderland	24 points
6 points v		0 points

The biggest close season signing was goalkeeper Edwin Van der Sar from Juventus.

2002-03

Premiership

	P	W	D	L	F	A	Pts
Manchester United	38	25	8	5	74	34	83
Arsenal	38	23	9	6	85	42	78
Newcastle United	38	21	6	11	63	48	69
Chelsea	38	19	10	9	68	38	67
Liverpool	38	18	10	10	61	41	64
Blackburn Rovers	38	16	12	10	52	43	60
Everton	38	17	8	13	48	49	59
Southampton	38	13	13	12	43	46	52
Manchester City	38	15	6	17	47	54	51
Tottenham Hotspur	38	14	8	16	51	62	50
Middlesbrough	38	13	10	15	48	44	49
Charlton Athletic	38	14	7	17	45	56	49
Birmingham City	38	13	9	16	41	49	48
Fulham	38	13	9	16	41	50	48
Leeds United	38	14	5	19	58	57	47
Aston Villa	38	12	9	17	42	47	45
Bolton Wanderers	38	10	14	14	41	51	44
West Ham United	38	10	12	16	42	59	42
West Bromwich Albion	38	6	8	24	29	65	26
Sunderland	38	4	7	27	21	65	19

Manager: Jean Tigana / Chris Coleman

Did you know that?

Both Fulham goals in 2-0 win over Everton in the penultimate home game were own goals. It was the first time two opponents had scored in the same match for Fulham since Eddie Lowe's final match, against Birmingham, exactly 40 years all but a day earlier.

5	Hayles' 50th goal
10	Djetou debut
23	Brevett's 200th game
24	Brevett finale
FAC5	Goldbaek finale
38	Finnan's 200th game
38	Finnan and Collins finales
38	Taylor finale

No		Date	V	Opponents	R	H-T	F-T	Scorers	Atter
1	A	17	H	Bolton W	W	3-1	4-1	Saha, Legwinski 2, Marlet	16,33
2		24	A	Middlesbrough	D	0-1	2-2	Davis, Sava	28,58
3		31	A	West Bromich A	L	0-0	0-1		25,44
4	S	11	H	Tottenham H	W	0-2	3-2	Inamoto, Malbranque, Legwinkski	16,78
5		14	A	Sunderland	W	1-0	3-0	Inamoto, Hayles, Marlet	35,43
6		23	H	Chelsea	D	0-0	0-0		16,50
7		28	A	Everton	L	0-2	0-2		34,38
8	O	6	H	Charlton A	W	1-0	1-0	Sava	14,77
9		19	H	Manchester U	D	1-0	1-1	Marlet	18,10
10		23	H	West Ham U	L	0-0	0-1		15,85
11		27	A	Southampton	L	2-2	2-4	Clark, Malbranque	26,18
12	N	3	H	Arsenal	L	0-1	0-1		17,81
13		9	A	Aston Villa	L	0-1	1-3	Boa Morte	29,56
14		17	A	Birmingham C	D	0-0	0-0		26,16
15		23	H	Liverpool	W	2-0	3-2	Sava 2, Davis	18,14
16		30	A	Blackburn R	L	0-1	1-2	Marlet	21,09
17	D	7	H	Leeds U	W	1-0	1-0	Djetou	17,49
18		15	H	Birmingham C	L	0-1	0-1		14,69
19		21	A	Newcastle U	L	0-1	0-2		51,57
20		26	A	West Ham U	D	0-0	1-1	Sava	35,02
21		28	H	Manchester C	L	0-0	0-1		17,93
22	J	11	A	Bolton W	D	0-0	0-0		25,15
23		19	H	Middlesbrough	W	1-0	1-0	Davis	14,25
24		29	A	Manchester C	L	1-1	1-4	Malbranque	33,26
25	F	1	A	Arsenal	L	1-1	1-2	Malbranque	38,05
26		8	H	Aston Villa	W	2-1	2-1	Malbranque, Harley	17,90
27		19	H	West Bromich A	W	0-0	3-0	Saha, Wome, Malbranque	15,79
28		24	A	Tottenham H	D	1-1	1-1	King (og)	34,70
29	M	1	H	Sunderland	W	0-0	1-0	Saha	16,28
30		15	H	Southampton	D	1-0	2-2	Saha, Svensson (og)	18,03
31		22	A	Manchester U	L	0-1	0-3		67,70
32	A	7	H	Blackburn R	L	0-2	0-4		14,01
33		12	A	Liverpool	L	0-1	0-2		42,12
34		19	H	Newcastle U	W	0-1	2-1	Legwinski, Clark	17,90
35		22	A	Leeds U	L	0-1	0-2		37,22
36		26	A	Chelsea	D	0-1	1-1	Boa Morte	40,79
37	M	3	H	Everton	W	2-0	2-0	Stubbs (og), Wright (og)	18,83
38		11	A	Charlton A	W	1-0	1-0	Saha	26,08
									App
									Su
									Goa

FA Cup

3	J	5	H	Birmingham C	W	2-0	3-1	Sava, Goldbaek, Saha	9,20
4		26	H	Charlton A	W	0-0	3-0	Malbranque 3	12,20
5	F	16	H	Burnley	D	1-1	1-1	Malbranque	13,06
5R		26	A	Burnley	L	0-2	0-3		11,63

van Der Saar	Finnan	Brevett	Melville	Goma	Davis	Legwinski	Malbranque	Saha	Marlet	Boa Morte	Inamoto	Sava	Knight	Wome	Collins	Hayles	Ouaddou	Djetou	Stolcers	Clark	Golbaek	Willock	Taylor	Hammond	Harley	Herrers	Hudson	Leacock	Thompson	Hahnemann	
	2	3	4	5	6	7	**8**	9	10	11	12	13			S		S						S								1
	2	3	4	5	6	7	**8**	9	10	11	12	13			S		S						S								2
	2	3	**4**	5	6	7	13	14	10	11	8	*9*	12			S							S								3
	2		S	5	6	7	13	**9**		11	8	10	4	*3*	14	12							S								4
		3	S	5	6	7	11		9		8	12	4		13	**10**	2		S				S								5
			S	5	6	7	11		9	12	**8**	S	4	3		10	2			S						S					6
	2		12	**5**	6	7	11		9	13	8	14	4	3		*10*				S			S								7
		3	4		6	7	8		9	**11**	12	*10*	5	13		14	2						S								8
	7	3		5	6	8	11		9	S	S	**10**	4		S	12	2						S								9
	2		4			7	6		9	11	**8**		5	3	S	10	S	12	13				S								10
	2	3	S	5		7	11		9	10			**4**			13	12	6	S	8			S								11
	2	3	4	5		7	11		9	10	12		S			13	6	**8**		S			S								12
	7	3	4	5		8	11		9	*10*	12	14					2	**6**	13				S								13
	2	3	4	5		**8**	11		9	10	14	S	13					12		6	*7*		S								14
	2	3		5	6		11		9		12	**10**	4	S				8	S	13	7		S								15
	2	3	4	5	6	7	11		9	10	12	S						S		**8**	S		S								16
	2	3	4		6	8	9			10	S		S	11				5	S		7	S	S								17
	2	3	*4*	5	6	7	9			10	12			**11**				8		14	S	13	S								18
		3	4	5	6	8	**10**		9				S	11	S			2	S		7	12	15								19
	2	3	4	5	6	**8**	7		9			*10*	S	11				12			13		1	14		S					20
	2	3	S	5	6	12	11		9			10	4	S				**8**			7		1	13		S					21
	2	3	S	5	6	8	11	9		12		**10**			S			4			7		1	S		S					22
	2	3	S	5	6	8	11		9	12		**10**			S			4			7		1	S		S					23
	2	3	S	5	6	8	11		9	10	S	S						4			7		1		S	S					24
	2		12	5	6	**7**	8	13	9	11		10		S				4			S		1		3	S					25
	2		4	5	6		7	*9*	10	11	S	14	12					8			13		1		3	S					26
	2		4	**5**			11	9	7		8	10		3			12	6	13		S		1			S		S			27
	2				6	8	7	13	9	11		*10*	12	3			5	**4**					1			15					28
	2		4			6	7	9			**8**	*10*		11			12	5	13				1	14	3	S		S			29
			4	5		8	7	9	10		12	S		**11**			2	6	13						3	1		S	S		30
			4			8	7	9	10	11	S	S	5	S			2	6		S			1		3	S					31
	2		S	5		12	7	9	10	11		S	4					8		**6**			1	13	3	S					32
	2		4		6	8	7	9	*10*	11		14		**3**			12	5		S			1	13		S					33
	2		4		6	8	7	**9**		*11*			S		14	13		5		10			1	12	3	S					34
	2		4		6	7				11	8	S	12		S	13		**5**		10			1	9	3	S					35
	2		4	5	6	7	**8**			11		S	S		13	12				10			1	9	3						36
	2		4	5	6	7	8	12		11			S		S	13				10			1	**9**	3						37
	2		4	5	**6**	7	8	9		11					13	12		S		10			1	14	3						38
9	32	20	24	29	28	33	35	13	28	25	9	13	12	13	-	4	9	22	-	9	8	-	18	3	11	1	-	-	-	-	A
	-	-	2	-	-	2	2	4	-	4	10	7	5	1	5	10	4	3	5	2	2	2	1	7	-	1	-	-	-	-	S
	-	-	-	-	3	4	6	5	4	2	2	5	-	1	-	1	-	1	-	2	-	-	-	-	1	-	-	-	-	-	G

van Der Saar	Finnan	Brevett	Melville	Goma	Davis	Legwinski	Malbranque	Saha	Marlet	Boa Morte	Inamoto	Sava	Knight	Wome	Collins	Hayles	Ouaddou	Djetou	Stolcers	Clark	Golbaek	Willock	Taylor	Hammond	Harley	Herrers	Hudson	Leacock	Thompson	Hahnemann	
	2		S	5	6	**8**	11	9				10			12			4			7	S	1	S	3	S					3
			4	5	6	8	7		9	11	S	10	13					**2**			12		1	S	3	S					4
	2		4	5	6		11	9	12		13	10		S			S	8			**7**		1		3	S					5
	2		4		6	8	7	*9*		**11**	10	12		13			14	5	S				1		3	S					5R

0 points v	Arsenal, Blackburn R, Manchester C	0 points
1 point v	Birmingham C, Manchester U, Southampton, West Ham U	4 points
2 points v	Chelsea	2 points
3 points v	Aston V, Everton, Leeds U, Liverpool, Newcastle U, West Bromwich A	18 points
4 points v	Bolton W, Middlesbrough, Tottenham H	12 points
6 points v	Charlton A, Sunderland	12 points

It started to go wrong for Tigana with the signing of Steve Marlet for £11m.

2002-03

Cont.

No		Date	V	Opponents	R	H-T	F-T	Scorers	Atte
Worthington Cup									
3	N	6	H	Bury	W	1-0	3-1	Stolcers 2, Clark	6,7
4	D	4	A	Wigan A	L	0-2	1-2	Boa Morte	7,6

No		Date	V	Opponents	R	H-T	F-T	Scorers	Atte
Intertoto Cup									
2/1	J	6	H	FC Haka	D	0-0	0-0		7,9
2/2		14	A	FC Haka	D	0-0	1-1	Marlet	3,5
3/1		20	H	Egaleo	W	0-0	1-0	Saha	5,1
3/2		27	A	Egaleo	D	1-1	1-1	Marlet	2,0
SF/1		31	H	Sochaux	W	0-0	1-0	Davis	4,7
SF/2	A	7	A	Sochaux	W	0-0	2-0	Legwinski, Hayles	11,0
F/1		13	A	Bologna	D	0-0	2-2	Inamoto, Hayles	23,6
F/2		27	H	Bologna	W	1-1	3-1	Inamoto 3	13,7

No		Date	V	Opponents	R	H-T	F-T	Scorers	Atte
UEFA Cup									
1/1	S	19	A	Hajduk Split	W	0-0	1-0	Malbranque	25,0
1/2	O	3	H	Hajduk Split	D	2-2	2-2	Marlet, Malbranque	18,5
2/1		31	A	Dinamo Zagreb	W	1-0	3-0	Boa Morte, Marlet, Hayles	30,0
2/2	N	14	H	Dinamo Zagreb	W	0-0	2-1	Malbranque, Boa Morte	7,7
3/1		26	A	Hertha Berlin	L	0-0	1-2	Marlet	14,4
3/2	D	12	H	Hertha Berlin	D	0-0	0-0		15,1

Van Der Saar	Finnan	Brevett	Melville	Goma	Davis	Legwinski	Malbranque	Saha	Marlet	Boa Morte	Inamoto	Sava	Knight	Wome	Collins	Hayles	Ouaddou	Djetou	Stolcers	Clark	Golbaek	Willock	Taylor	Hammond	Harley	Herrers	Hudson	Leacock	Thompson	Hahnemann	
	2		*4*								**10**	12		3	8	9	5	13	11	6	**7**		1			S	14				3
					12					13	7	9	**5**	3	8		4	10	11	6	S		1			S	S	2			4
			4	5	6	S	*11*	8	*7*	13		**9**	S		10	12	2				14		1		3		S			S	2/1
S			4	5	6	**7**	*11*	9	8	12		S	13		10	S	2		S		14		1		3						2/2
1			S	5	6	12	*7*	13	8	11		9	4		10	14	**2**		S		S				3	S					3/1
1			4	5	6	**7**	*11*	9	8	10		S	S		S	13	2		14		12				3	S					3/2
1		3	4	5	6	**7**	*11*	9	8	10	12	S	13		S	14	2								S	S		S			SF/1
1		3	4	5	6	7	*11*	**9**	8	10	14	S	S			12	2									S					SF/2
1		3	4	5	6	7	**8**	13	9	11	12	S			S	10	2						S		S			S			F/1
1	2	3	S	5	*6*	7	13	12	**9**	11	8	10	4		14	S	S														F/2
1		**3**	4	5	6	7	11		*9*		8	14	S	12	S	10	2		S	13			S								1/1
1		3	4		6	7	8		9	**11**	12	10	5	S	S	13	2			S			S					S			1/2
1	7	3	4	5		8	11		9	*10*	12		S	S		13	2	**6**	14	S			S								2/1
1	2	3	4	5		*8*	13		12	10	11	**9**		S			S	14	S	**6**	7		S								2/2
1	2	3	4	5	6		11		9	12	13	10	S	S				8	S	S	**7**		S								3/1
	2	*3*	4	5	6	12	7		9	10	13		S	11				**8**		S	14	S	1			S					3/2

2003-04

Premiership

	P	W	D	L	F	A	Pts
Arsenal	38	26	12	0	73	26	90
Chelsea	38	24	7	7	67	30	79
Manchester United	38	23	6	9	64	35	75
Liverpool	38	16	12	10	55	37	60
Newcastle United	38	13	17	8	52	40	56
Aston Villa	38	15	11	12	48	44	56
Charlton Athletic	38	14	11	13	51	51	53
Bolton Wanderers	38	14	11	13	48	56	53
Fulham	38	14	10	14	52	46	52
Birmingham City	38	12	14	12	43	48	50
Middlesbrough	38	13	9	16	44	52	48
Southampton	38	12	11	15	44	45	47
Portsmouth	38	12	9	17	47	54	45
Tottenham Hotspur	38	13	6	19	47	57	45
Blackburn Rovers	38	12	8	18	51	59	44
Manchester City	38	9	14	15	55	54	41
Everton	38	9	12	17	45	57	39
Leicester City	38	6	15	17	48	65	33
Leeds United	38	8	9	21	40	79	33
Wolverhampton W	38	7	12	19	38	77	33

Manager: Chris Coleman

Did you know that?

Manager Chris Coleman (reluctantly) restored some balance to Fulham's transfer dealings when Manchester United paid £12.85 million for striker Louis Saha, Fulham's share of which was £11.5 million, the club's record incoming fee.

1	Volz debut
1	Marlet finale
5	Saha's 50th goal
21	Melville and Saha finales
22	Bocanegra debut
23	McBride debut
33	Hayles finale
38	Davis and Djetou finales

No		Date	V	Opponents	R	H-T	F-T	Scorers	Atter
1	A	16	H	Middlesbrough	W	1-1	3-2	Marlet, Inamoto, Saha	14,54
2		23	A	Everton	L	0-3	1-3	Hayles	37,60
3		30	A	Tottenham H	W	1-0	3-0	Hayles 2, Boa Morte	33,42
4	S	14	A	Birmingham C	D	1-1	2-2	Saha, Boa Morte	27,25
5		20	H	Manchester C	D	0-0	2-2	Malbranque, Saha	16,12
6		28	A	Blackburn R	W	1-0	2-0	Boa Morte, Saha	21,98
7	O	4	H	Leicester C	W	1-0	2-0	Boa Morte 2	14,56
8		18	H	Wolverhampton W	D	0-0	0-0		17,03
9		21	H	Newcastle U	L	2-1	2-3	Clark, Saha	16,50
10		25	A	Manchester U	W	1-1	3-1	Clark, Malbranque, Inamoto	67,72
11	N	2	H	Liverpool	L	1-1	1-2	Saha	17,68
12		8	A	Charlton A	L	0-1	1-3	Davis	26,34
13		24	H	Portsmouth	W	2-0	2-0	Saha 2	15,62
14		30	A	Arsenal	D	0-0	0-0		38,06
15	D	6	H	Bolton W	W	0-0	2-1	Davis, Sava	14,39
16		14	A	Leeds U	L	0-1	2-3	Saha 2	30,54
17		20	H	Chelsea	L	0-0	0-1		18,24
18		26	H	Southampton	W	1-0	2-0	Saha 2	16,76
19		28	A	Aston Villa	L	0-1	0-3		35,61
20	J	7	A	Middlesbrough	L	0-1	1-2	Hayles	27,86
21		10	H	Everton	W	1-0	2-1	Saha, Malbranque	17,10
22		19	A	Newcastle U	L	0-2	1-3	Davis	50,10
23		31	H	Tottenham H	W	1-1	2-1	Malbranque, McBride	17,02
24	F	7	A	Southampton	D	0-0	0-0		31,82
25		11	H	Aston Villa	L	1-2	1-2	Boa Morte	16,15
26		21	A	Wolverhampton W	L	0-1	1-2	Malbranque	28,42
27		28	H	Manchester U	D	0-1	1-1	Boa Morte	18,30
28	M	13	H	Leeds U	W	0-0	2-0	Davis, Boa Morte	17,10
29		20	A	Chelsea	L	1-2	1-2	Pembridge	41,14
30		27	A	Manchester C	D	0-0	0-0		46,52
31	A	3	H	Birmingham C	D	0-0	0-0		14,66
32		10	A	Leicester C	W	0-0	2-0	John 2	28,39
33		12	H	Blackburn R	L	2-1	3-4	John 2, Boa Morte	13,98
34		17	A	Liverpool	D	0-0	0-0		42,04
35		24	H	Charlton A	W	1-0	2-0	Malbranque, Davis	16,58
36	M	1	A	Portsmouth	D	0-0	1-1	McBride	20,06
37		9	H	Arsenal	L	0-1	0-1		18,10
38		15	A	Bolton W	W	1-0	2-0	McBride 2	27,38
									App
									Su
									Goal

FA Cup

3	J	4	H	Cheltenham T	W	1-1	2-1	Saha 2	10,30
4		25	A	Everton	D	0-0	1-1	Davis	27,86
4R	F	4	H	Everton	W	0-0	2-1	Inamoto, Malbranque	11,55
5		14	H	West Ham U	D	0-0	0-0		14,70
5R		24	A	West Ham U	W	0-0	3-0	McBride, Hayles, Boa Morte	27,93
6	M	6	A	Manchester U	L	1-1	1-2	Malbranque	67,61

Carling Cup

2	S	23	A	Wigan A	L	0-0	0-1		4,87

an der Sar	Volz	Bonnissel	Djetou	Goma	Clark	Legwinski	Inamoto	Saha	Marlet	Malbranque	Hayles	Boa Morte	Knight	Buari	Sava	Pembridge	Leacock	Crossley	Melville	Davis	Pratley	Harley	Green	Petta	Bocanegra	Pearce	McBride	John	Rehman	Stolcers	Besant	Hudson	
	2	3	4	5	6	7	8	**9**	10	11	12	13	S	S				S															1
	2	3	4	5	6	**7**	*8*	9		11	12	10	13	14				S															2
	2	3		5	6	7	8	12		11	**9**	10	4	S	S		S	S															3
	2	3	14	5	6	7	*8*	9		**11**		10	4		13	12		S	S														4
	2	3	S	5	6	7	8	9		11		**10**	4		S	12		S	S														5
	2	3	S	5	6		8	9		7		10	4	13		11	12	S	S														6
		3	13	5	6	12	**8**	*9*		7	14	10	4			11	2	S	S														7
	S	3	S	5	6	7	**8**	9		10	12		4			11	2	S	S														8
		3	S	5	6	7	13	9		8	12		4	**10**		11	2	S	S														9
	2	3	13	5	6	7	12	9		8	14	*10*	4			**11**		S	S														10
	2	3	12		6	7		9		8	13	10	4	S		**11**		1	5	S											S		11
	2	3			6	7	*8*	**9**		11	12	**10**	4					S	5	13	14												12
	2	3	S		6	7	12	9		11	**10**		4		13			S	5	8	S												13
	2	3	S	S	10	7	8	**9**		11	12		4		S			S	5	6													14
	2	3	14	S	10	7	8	**9**		11	12		4		13			S	5	*6*													15
	2		S	S	8	7		9		11	12	10	4		13			S	5	6		3											16
	2		12	S	8	7		9		11	13	10	4		S			S	5	**6**		3											17
	2	**3**	6	5	10		8	9		**7**	S	11	4		S			S	S			12											18
	2		6	5	10		**8**	9		7	12	11	4		13			S	S			3	S										19
			2		8	**7**	S	9		11	12	10	4					S	5	6			3	S								S	20
			2		8	7	S	9		11	S	**10**	4		S			S	5	6			3	12									21
	12		2	5	8	**7**				11	9	10	4		13			S		6			S	S	3								22
	2		7		8		S			11	**9**	10	4		S			S		6				13	3	5	12						23
	2		6		*10*	13	14			**7**		11	4					S		8				12	3	5	9						24
	2		7		**10**	S	S			8	13	11	4					S		6				12	3	5	9						25
	2		13			7	S			8	**10**	11	4					S		6			S	12	3	5	9						26
	2			4		7	13			8		10	S			12		S		6			3	**11**		5	9		S				27
	2		S			7	S			8	**9**	10	4			11		S		6			3	S		5	12						28
	2		S	S		7				8	9	10	4			**11**				6					3	4	13	12			S		29
	2		8	5			S			7	**9**	10	4		S	11				6					3		12		S		S		30
	2		8	5		7	S			11	**9**	10	4					S		6				S	3	12	13						31
	2		8	5		7				11	**9**	10	4					S		6				S	3	S	13	12					32
	2		8	5		7				11	14	10	4					S		**6**				12	3	S	13	*9*					33
	2		4	5		7	13			11		10						S						8	*3*	6	12	**9**	14				34
	2		4	5		7	14			11		*10*	S					S		12				**8**	3	6	13	9					35
	2		**8**	5		7	10			11		9						S		6				S	3	4	12	13				S	36
	2		8	5		7	**10**			11		9						S		6				S	3	4	12	13				S	37
	2		8	5		7	S			11		10						S		6				S	3	4	**9**	12				S	38
7	32	16	19	23	25	30	15	20	1	38	10	32	30	1	-	9	3	1	9	22	-	3	4	3	15	12	5	3	-	-			A
	1	-	7	-	-	2	7	1	-	-	16	1	1	2	6	3	1	-	-	1	1	1	-	6	-	1	11	5	1	-			S
	-	-	-	-	2	-	2	13	1	6	4	9	-	-	1	1	-	-	-	5	-	-	-	-	-	-	4	4	-	-			G

an der Sar	Volz	Bonnissel	Djetou	Goma	Clark	Legwinski	Inamoto	Saha	Marlet	Malbranque	Hayles	Boa Morte	Knight	Buari	Sava	Pembridge	Leacock	Crossley	Melville	Davis	Pratley	Harley	Green	Petta	Bocanegra	Pearce	McBride	John	Rehman	Stolcers	Besant	Hudson	
			2	**5**		7	8	9		10	13		4		S			S	12	6	S		3	11									3
	2		7	5	8		S			11	**9**	10	4		12			S		6			S	S	3								4
	2		7	5			8			11	**9**	10	4		12			S		6			S	13	3				S				4R
	2		S	5		7	S			8	10	**11**	4					S		6			S	12	3		9						5
	2		**4**	5		7				8	13	10	12			14		S		*6*				11	3		9						5R
	2			5	*11*	7				8	12	10	4			13		S		6			3	14			**9**						6

an der Sar	Volz	Bonnissel	Djetou	Goma	Clark	Legwinski	Inamoto	Saha	Marlet	Malbranque	Hayles	Boa Morte	Knight	Buari	Sava	Pembridge	Leacock	Crossley	Melville	Davis	Pratley	Harley	Green	Petta	Bocanegra	Pearce	McBride	John	Rehman	Stolcers	Besant	Hudson	
			5			11	**8**					13		7	9	4	2	1	6	S	14		3						12	*10*	S		2

0 points v	Aston V, Chelsea, Newcastle U	0 points
1 point v	Arsenal, Liverpool, Wolves	3 points
2 points v	Birmingham C, Manchester C	4 points
3 points v	Blackburn R, Charlton A, Everton, Leeds U, Middlesbrough	15 points
4 points v	Manchester U, Portsmouth, Southampton	12 points
6 points v	Bolton W, Leicester C, Tottenham H	18 points

Louis Saha, top scorer, moved to Manchester United for a Fulham record fee.

2004-05

Premiership

	P	W	D	L	F	A	Pts
Chelsea	38	29	8	1	72	15	95
Arsenal	38	25	8	5	87	36	83
Manchester United	38	22	11	5	58	26	77
Everton	38	18	7	13	45	46	61
Liverpool	38	17	7	14	52	41	58
Bolton Wanderers	38	16	10	12	49	44	58
Middlesbrough	38	14	13	11	53	46	55
Manchester City	38	13	13	12	47	39	52
Tottenham Hotspur	38	14	10	14	47	41	52
Aston Villa	38	12	11	15	45	52	47
Charlton Athletic	38	12	10	16	42	58	46
Birmingham City	38	11	12	15	40	46	45
Fulham	38	12	8	18	52	60	44
Newcastle United	38	10	14	14	47	57	44
Blackburn Rovers	38	9	15	14	32	43	42
Portsmouth	38	10	9	19	43	59	39
West Bromwich Albion	38	6	16	16	36	61	34
Crystal Palace	38	7	12	19	41	62	33
Norwich City	38	7	12	19	42	77	33
Southampton	38	6	14	18	45	66	32

Manager: Chris Coleman

Did you know that?

When Zesh Rehman made his Fulham debut at Villa Park in October 2004, he became the first Pakistani and British Asian to play in the Premiership. Although an England youth international, he played for Pakistan against Sri Lanka in Karachi in December 2005.

1	A Cole returns
1	Radzinski debut
17	Rosenior debut
38	Cole and Clark finales
38	Van der Sar finale

No		Date	V	Opponents	R	H-T	F-T	Scorers	Att
1	A	14	A	Manchester C	D	0-1	1-1	John	44,0
2		21	H	Bolton W	W	1-0	2-0	Cole 2	17,5
3		25	H	Middlesbrough	L	0-0	0-2		17,7
4		30	A	Portsmouth	L	2-3	3-4	Cole, Boa Morte, Bocanegra	19,7
5	S	11	H	Arsenal	L	0-0	0-3		21,6
6		18	A	West Bromich A	D	0-0	1-1	Cole	24,1
7		25	H	Southampton	W	1-0	1-0	Radzinski	19,2
8	O	4	A	Crystal Palace	L	0-0	0-2		21,8
9		16	H	Liverpool	L	2-0	2-4	Boa Morte 2	21,8
10		23	A	Aston Villa	L	0-1	0-2		34,4
11		30	H	Tottenham H	W	1-0	2-0	Boa Morte, Cole	21,3
12	N	7	A	Newcastle U	W	1-0	4-1	John, Malbranque 2, Boa Morte	51,1
13		13	H	Chelsea	L	0-1	1-4	Diop	21,8
14		20	A	Everton	L	0-0	0-1		34,7
15		27	H	Blackburn R	L	0-1	0-2		19,1
16	D	4	A	Norwich C	W	1-0	1-0	Cole	23,7
17		13	H	Manchester U	D	0-1	1-1	Diop	21,9
18		20	A	Charlton A	L	0-1	1-2	Radzinski	26,1
19		26	A	Arsenal	L	0-1	0-2		38,0
20		28	H	Birmingham C	L	1-2	2-3	Legwinski, Radzinski	18,7
21	J	1	H	Crystal Palace	W	1-1	3-1	Cole 2, Radzinski	18,6
22		5	A	Southampton	D	2-2	3-3	Diop. Malbranque, Radzinski	27,3
23		16	H	West Bromich A	W	0-0	1-0	Diop	16,1
24		22	A	Birmingham C	W	0-0	2-1	Cole, Diop	28,5
25	F	2	H	Aston Villa	D	0-0	1-1	Clark	17,6
26		5	A	Liverpool	L	1-1	1-3	Cole	43,5
27		26	A	Tottenham H	L	0-0	0-2		35,8
28	M	5	H	Charlton A	D	0-0	0-0		18,2
29		19	A	Manchester U	L	0-1	0-1		67,9
30	A	3	H	Portsmouth	W	0-1	3-1	Cole, McBride, Boa Morte	20,5
31		9	A	Bolton W	L	0-2	1-3	Boa Morte	25,4
32		16	H	Manchester C	D	0-1	1-1	Boa Morte	21,7
33		19	A	Middlesbrough	D	0-0	1-1	McBride	30,6
34		23	A	Chelsea	L	1-1	1-3	John	42,0
35		30	H	Everton	W	2-0	2-0	John, McBride	21,8
36	M	4	H	Newcastle U	L	0-1	1-3	Radzinski	19,0
37		7	A	Blackburn R	W	1-1	3-1	Malbranque 2, McBride	18,9
38		15	H	Norwich C	W	2-0	6-0	McBride 2, Diop, Knight, Malbranque, Cole	21,9
									Ap
									S
									Go

FA Cup

3	Jan	8	A	Watford	D	1-1	1-1	Knight	14,8
3R		18	H	Watford	W	1-0	2-0	Volz, Radzinski	11,3
4		29	A	Derby C	D	0-0	1-1	John	22,0
4R	F	12	H	Derby C	W	1-1	4-2	Diop, Boa Morte, John, Jensen	15,5
5		19	A	Bolton W	L	0-1	0-1		16,1

Carling Cup

2	S	22	A	Boston U	W	0-3	4-1	Radzinski 2, Malbranque, McBride	5,3
3	O	27	A	Birmingham C	W	0-0	1-0	Pembridge	26,3
4	N	10	A	Nottingham F	W	0-0	4-2	Radzinski 2, McBride, Cole	9,2
5		30	H	Chelsea	L	0-0	1-2	McBride	14,5

van der Sar	Volz	Bocanegra	Diop	Knight	Pearce	John	Jensen	Cole	Radzinski	Legwinski	McBride	Pembridge	Goma	Boa Morte	Green	Malbranque	McKinlay	Rehman	Crossley	Rosenior	Hammond	Clark	Fontaine	Buari	Bonnissel	Flitney	Watkins	Ehui	Timlim	
[illegible]	2	3	4	5	6	**7**	8	9	10	11	12	13	S					S	S											1
[illegible]	2	3	4	5	S	**7**	8	9	*10*	11	13	14	6	12					S											2
[illegible]	2	3	4	5		**7**	8	9	10	11	12	S	6	13					S						S					3
[illegible]	2	3	4	5		12	8	9	**10**	7	13	S	6	11			S		S											4
[illegible]	2	3	4	5	6	7		9	12	**11**	13	8	S	10			S		S											5
[illegible]	2		4	5	6	**7**		9	12	11	S	8	S	10	3	S			S											6
[illegible]	2			5	6	12			**8**	7	9	4	S	10	3	11	13	S	S											7
[illegible]	2	14		5	6	13			**8**		9	11	*12*	10	3	7	4	S	S											8
[illegible]	2	6	4	5		12	S		**8**		9	11		10	3	7	S	S	S											9
[illegible]	2	3	4	5	**6**	13	8	*9*		S	14	11		10		7	S	12	S											10
	2	3	4	5		**8**		9	12		S	11		10	S	7		6	1	S						S				11
S	2	3	4	5		**8**		9	12	S	S	11		10		7		6	1	S										12
S	2	3	4	5				9	**8**	S	12	11		10		7		6	1	S	S									13
S	2	3	4	5	S			9	8	12	13	11		**10**		7		6	1		S									14
5	2	3	4	5	S			9	10	**8**	12	11				7		6	1	S	S									15
[illegible]	2	3	4	S	5			9	S	8	10	11				7		6		S	S					S				16
[illegible]		3	4	S	5	13		9	12	**8**	10	11				7		6		2	S					S				17
[illegible]	S	3	4	S	5	13		9	12	8	10	11				**7**		6		2						S				18
[illegible]	2	3	4	5	6	7		**9**	10	S	12	11				13		8	S				S							19
[illegible]	2	3	4	5	**6**	7		9	8	11	*10*	S				14		12	S		13									20
[illegible]	**2**	3	4	5		14		9	8		S	11		*10*		7		6	S	12		13								21
[illegible]		3	4	5		12		*9*	**8**		14	11		10		7		6	S	2		S	13							22
[illegible]	2	3	4	5		9			8	S	13	11		10		**7**		6	S	S		12								23
[illegible]	2	3	4	5		S		**9**	8	S	12	11		10				6	S	S		7								24
[illegible]	2		4	5		12		9	**8**	S	13	11	S	10				6	S	3		7								25
[illegible]		3	4	5			S	9	8	S	S	11	S	10				6	S	2		7								26
[illegible]	S	3	4	5		12	10	**9**	8	S	13		6	11					S	2		7								27
[illegible]	S	3	4	5		12	**8**	9	S	S			6	10		11			S	2		7								28
[illegible]	S	3	**4**	5		S	8	9	13	12			6	10		11			S	2		7								29
[illegible]	2	14		5			**8**	9	13	7	12		6	10		11			S	3		*4*								30
[illegible]	2	S		5		13	8	9	12		10	S	6	11		**7**			S	3		4								31
[illegible]	2	S		5		13		9	12		10	11	6	8		**7**		S	S	3		4								32
[illegible]	2	S		5		**7**	S		8		9	11	6	10		12		S	S	3		4								33
[illegible]	2	S		5		7	S		8		9	**11**	6	10		12		S	S	3		4								34
[illegible]	2	S	4	5		**11**	13	12	8		9	S	6	10					S	3		7								35
[illegible]	2	S		5	S		12	**9**	7		10	11	6	8				S	S	3		4								36
[illegible]	2		S	5	S				8		9	11	6	10		7		S	S	3		4							S	37
[illegible]	2	3	4	5	S			12	8		9	S	6	**10**		11		S	S			7								38
3	31	26	29	35	11	13	10	29	25	13	15	26	15	29	4	22	1	15	5	16	-	15	-	-					-	A
[illegible]	-	2	-	-	-	14	2	2	10	2	16	2	1	2	-	4	1	2	-	1	1	2	1	-					-	S
-	-	1	6	1	-	4	-	12	6	1	6	-	-	8	-	6	-	-	-	-	-	1	-	-					-	G
[illegible]	S	3		5		7		9		**8**	S	4		10		11		S	S	2		12	6							3
[illegible]	2	3	4	5		14		9	8	11	13	12		*10*				6	S	S		**7**								3R
[illegible]	2			5	S	12	S	9	**8**	7	S	11	6	10					S	3		4								4
[illegible]		3	4	5		13	14	9	8	*11*	S		12	10				**6**	S	2		7								4R
[illegible]		3	4	5	S	13	12	*9*	8	**11**	14		6	10					S	2		7								5
						13			10		9		5	8	3	**11**	4	6	1	7				2		S	S	S	12	2
	2	3	4	5		12	**8**	9			13	11		10	S	7		6	1	S						S				3
S	2	3	**4**	5				9	*8*	13	12	11		10		7		6	1	14	S									4
[illegible]	2	3	4		5			**9**	S	8	10	11			S	7		6		S	12					S				5

0 points v	Arsenal, Chelsea, Liverpool	0 points
1 point v	Aston V, Charlton A, Manchester U, Middlesbrough	4 points
2 points v	Manchester C	2 points
3 points v	Birmingham C, Blackburn R, Bolton W, Crystal P, Everton, Newcastle U, Portsmouth, Tottenham H	24 points
4 points v	Southampton, West Bromwich A	8 points
6 points v	Norwich C	6 points

Andy Cole, on loan to Fulham as a youngster in 1991, returned for a season and was top scorer.

2005-06

Premiership

	P	W	D	L	F	A	Pts
Chelsea	38	29	4	5	72	22	91
Manchester United	38	25	8	5	72	34	83
Liverpool	38	25	7	6	57	25	82
Arsenal	38	20	7	11	68	31	67
Tottenham Hotspur	38	18	11	9	53	38	65
Blackburn Rovers	38	19	6	13	51	42	63
Newcastle United	38	17	7	14	47	42	58
Bolton Wanderers	38	15	11	12	49	41	56
West Ham United	38	16	7	15	52	55	55
Wigan Athletic	38	15	6	17	45	52	51
Everton	38	14	8	16	34	49	50
Fulham	38	14	6	18	48	58	48
Charlton Athletic	38	13	8	17	41	55	47
Middlesbrough	38	12	9	17	48	58	45
Manchester City	38	13	4	21	43	48	43
Aston Villa	38	10	12	16	42	55	42
Portsmouth	38	10	8	20	37	62	38
Birmingham City	38	8	10	20	28	50	34
West Bromwich Albion	38	7	9	22	31	58	30
Sunderland	38	3	6	29	26	69	15

Manager: Chris Coleman

Did you know that?

Beating Manchester City at the City of Manchester Stadium in April meant Fulham avoided going through the season without an away victory. As in 1927–28, they recorded just one victory on their travels, something they were to repeat again in 2006–07.

No	Date		V	Opponents	R	H-T	F-T	Scorers	Atte
1	A	13	H	Birmingham C	D	0-0	0-0		16,5
2		20	A	Blackburn R	L	0-1	1-2	McBride	16,9
3		24	A	Arsenal	L	1-1	1-4	C. Jensen	37,8
4		27	H	Everton	W	0-0	1-0	McBride	17,1
5	S	10	A	Newcastle U	D	1-0	1-1	McBride	52,2
6		17	H	West Ham U	L	0-0	1-2	Boa Morte	21,9
7		26	A	Tottenham H	L	0-1	0-1		35,4
8	O	1	H	Manchester U	L	2-3	2-3	John, C. Jensen	21,8
9		17	A	Charlton A	D	1-0	1-1	John	26,3
10		22	H	Liverpool	W	1-0	2-0	John, Boa Morte	22,4
11		29	A	Wigan A	L	0-0	0-1		17,2
12	N	5	H	Manchester C	W	2-1	2-1	Malbranque 2	22,2
13		20	A	Middlesbrough	L	1-0	2-3	John, Diop	27,5
14		27	H	Bolton W	W	2-0	2-1	McBride 2	19,7
15	D	3	A	West Bromich A	D	0-0	0-0		23,1
16		10	A	Birmingham C	L	0-0	0-1		27,5
17		17	H	Blackburn R	W	1-0	2-1	Diop, Boa Morte	20,1
18		26	A	Chelsea	L	1-2	2-3	McBride, Helguson	42,3
19		28	H	Aston Villa	D	2-1	3-3	McBride 2, Helguson	20,4
20		31	A	Portsmouth	L	0-1	0-1		19,1
21	Jan	2	H	Sunderland	W	1-1	2-1	John 2	19,3
22		14	H	Newcastle U	W	0-0	1-0	Malbranque	21,9
23		23	A	West Ham U	L	0-2	1-2	Helguson	29,8
24		31	H	Tottenham H	W	0-0	1-0	Bocanegra	21,0
25	F	4	A	Manchester U	L	2-3	2-4	McBride, Helguson	67,8
26		11	H	West Bromich A	W	2-0	6-1	Helguson 3, Radzinski, John 2	21,5
27		26	A	Bolton W	L	1-1	1-2	Helguson	23,1
28	M	4	H	Arsenal	L	0-2	0-4		22,3
29		11	A	Everton	L	2-0	1-3	John	36,5
30		15	A	Liverpool	L	1-2	1-5	John	42,2
31		19	H	Chelsea	W	1-0	1-0	Boa Morte 2	22,4
32		25	A	Aston Villa	D	0-0	0-0		32,6
33	A	1	H	Portsmouth	L	1-2	1-3	Malbranque	22,3
34		15	H	Charlton A	W	2-1	2-1	Boa Morte	19,1
35		24	H	Wigan A	W	1-0	1-0	Malbranque	17,1
36		29	A	Manchester C	W	0-0	2-1	John, Malbranque	41,1
37	M	4	A	Sunderland	L	0-1	1-2	Radzinski	28,2
38		7	H	Middlesbrough	W	0-0	1-0	Helguson	22,4
									Ap
									Su
									Goa

24 Legwinski finale
28 Goma finale
31 Boa Morte's 50th goal
38 Malbranque finale

FA Cup

3	J	8	H	Leyton O	L	0-2	1-2	John	13,3

Carling Cup

2	S	21	H	Lincoln C	W	2-0	5-4	Rehman, Helguson, Rosenior, Radzinski, McBride	5,3
3	O	25	H	West Bromich A	L	0-1	2-3	Boa Morte, Helguson	7,3

Warner	Volz	Jensen N	Malbranque	Knight	Rehman	Legwinski	Jensen C	McBride	Radzinski	Boa Morte	Elrich	John	Diop	Helgusson	Bocanegra	Christanval	Crossley	Goma	Rosenior	Leacock	Pearce	Niemi	Elliott	Bridge	Brown	Pembrige	Timlin	Batista	Drobney	Milsom	Green	
	2	3	4	5	6	_7_	8	9	**10**	11	13	12		S						S								S				1
	2	3	7	5	6		8	_9_	**10**	11	S	12	4	13						S								S				2
	2	3	7	5	6		8	**9**	10	11	S	12	4	S						S								S				3
	2	3	7	5	S		8	9	10	11	S	S	4	S	6													S				4
	2	3	7	5			8	_9_	**10**	11	S	12	4	13	6	S												S				5
	2	3	7	_5_			8	9	**10**	11	S	12	4	S	6	13												S				6
	2	3	7	5			8	**9**	10	11	S	12	4		6	S	S			S												7
	2	3	7				8	**9**	13	11	S	_10_	4	12	6		1	5		S												8
	2	3	7				8	13	12	10		_9_	4	S	6	**11**	1	5	S													9
5	2	**3**	7		S		8	13		11	_10_	9	4	S	6		*1*	5	12													10
	2	3	7				**8**	13	10	11	12	_9_	4	S	*6*			5	14									S				11
	2	3	7	S				**9**	8	10	S	11	4	12	6			5	S									S				12
	2	3	11	5	S	8		9	10			**7**	4	12				6	S		S							S				13
	2		7	S		12		9	8	**10**		_11_	4	13	6		1	5	3		S											14
	2		7	12		13		*9*	8	**10**		_11_	4	14	6		1	5	3													15
		S	7	5		8		9	10		S	11		S	3	4	1	6	2		S											16
				5		13		9	8	*10*	14	**11**	_4_	12		7	1	6	3	2	S											17
5				5		7		9	8	11	S	12		**10**	S	4	*1*	6	3	2	S											18
		12		5		_7_		9	8	11	13	14		*10*	6	4	1		3	**2**	S											19
		S		5		7		9	8	11	_4_	12		**10**	13			6	3	2	S								S			20
		14	13	5	S	7		9	8	11		_10_	**4**	12					*3*	2	6								S			21
	S	3	12	5		_7_		9	**8**	11		13		10				S	2		6	1	4									22
		S	**8**	5		7		_9_	12	11		13		10	6			S	2			1	4	3								23
		S	8	5		**7**		_9_	12	11		13		10	6			S	2			1	4	3								24
		S	7	5				9	12	11		13		_10_	6			S	2			1	4	3	**8**							25
	2	S	7	5		S		**9**	8	11		12		10	6			S				1	4	3								26
	2	S	7	5				**9**	_8_	11		12	13	10	6			S	S				4	3								27
	2	S	7	5				9	8	11	S	12		**10**	S		S	6	3				4									28
	2	S	7	5				9		11		13		_10_	6	12	S	S	3				**4**			8						29
		S	7	**5**				13	_8_	10		9		S		12	S		2		6			3	4	11						30
	2	S	_7_	5				9	S	11		**10**		12		13	1		3		6				4	8						31
	2	S	7	5				9	12	11		**10**				S	1	S	3		6				4	8						32
	2		7	5				9	14	11		_10_		13		12	1				**6**			3	4	*8*						33
	S		7	5				9	S	11		S	8	10		12	S		2		6	1	**4**	3								34
	S		7	5				9	12	11		S	4	**10**		13	S		2		6	1	_8_	3								35
	S		7	**5**				9	S	11		13	4	_10_		12	S		2		6	1	8	3								36
	S		7					_9_	12	**11**		13	4	10		5	1		2		*6*		8	3	14							37
	2		7					_9_	13			**10**	4	12	6	5	S	S	3			1	S	11	8							38
	23	14	32	29	3	10	11	34	23	35	2	16	21	15	20	7	13	13	22	5	10	9	12	12	6	5	-	-			-	A
	-	2	2	1	-	3	-	4	10	-	4	19	1	12	1	8	-	-	2	-	-	-	-	-	1	-	-	-			-	S
	-	-	6	-	-	-	2	9	2	6	-	11	2	9	1	-	-	-	-	-	-	-	-	-	-	-	-	-			-	G

Warner	Volz	Jensen N	Malbranque	Knight	Rehman	Legwinski	Jensen C	McBride	Radzinski	Boa Morte	Elrich	John	Diop	Helgusson	Bocanegra	Christanval	Crossley	Goma	Rosenior	Leacock	Pearce	Niemi	Elliott	Bridge	Brown	Pembrige	Timlin	Batista	Drobney	Milsom	Green	
		3		5	S	7			8	11	**9**	10						13	2		_6_		4				12		S	S		3

Warner	Volz	Jensen N	Malbranque	Knight	Rehman	Legwinski	Jensen C	McBride	Radzinski	Boa Morte	Elrich	John	Diop	Helgusson	Bocanegra	Christanval	Crossley	Goma	Rosenior	Leacock	Pearce	Niemi	Elliott	Bridge	Brown	Pembrige	Timlin	Batista	Drobney	Milsom	Green	
	14				*4*			13	12		7	_10_		9		6		5	2	**8**							11	1		S	3	2
			10	4	7	**8**				9	_6_	13	12	11	14			S	3	2	*5*							S				3

0 points v	Arsenal, West Ham U, Manchester U, Portsmouth	0 points
1 point v	Birmingham C	1 point
2 points v	Aston V	2 points
3 points v	Blackburn R, Everton, Tottenham H, Liverpool, Wigan A, Middlesbrough, Bolton W, Chelsea, Sunderland	27 points
4 points v	Newcastle U, Charlton A, West Bromwich A	12 points
6 points v	Manchester C	6 points

Steed Malbranque, possibly Tigana's best signing, left at the end of the season.

2006-07

Premiership

	P	W	D	L	F	A	Pts
Manchester United	38	28	5	5	83	27	89
Chelsea	38	24	11	3	64	24	83
Liverpool	38	20	8	10	57	27	68
Arsenal	38	19	11	8	63	35	68
Tottenham Hotspur	38	17	9	12	57	54	60
Everton	38	15	13	10	52	36	58
Bolton Wanderers	38	16	8	14	47	52	56
Reading	38	16	7	15	52	47	55
Portsmouth	38	14	12	12	45	42	54
Blackburn Rovers	38	15	7	16	52	54	52
Aston Villa	38	11	17	10	43	41	50
Middlesbrough	38	12	10	16	44	49	46
Newcastle United	38	11	10	17	38	47	43
Manchester City	38	11	9	18	29	44	42
West Ham United	38	12	5	21	35	59	41
Fulham	38	8	15	15	38	60	39
Wigan Athletic	38	10	8	20	37	59	38
Sheffield United	38	10	8	20	32	55	38
Charlton Athletic	38	8	10	20	34	60	34
Watford	38	5	13	20	29	59	28

Manager: Chris Coleman / Lawrie Sanchez

Did you know that?

In the final game of the season at the Riverside, 16-year-old Matt Briggs came on as substitute against Middlesbrough, not only the youngest Fulham player in the League but the youngest ever for any club in the Premiership.

18 Boa Morte finale
33 Coleman finale
36 Bocanegra's 100th game
38 Radzinski finale

No		Date	V	Opponents	R	H-T	F-T	Scorers	Atte
1	A	20	A	Manchester U	L	1-4	1-5	Helguson	75,1
2		23	H	Bolton W	D	0-0	1-1	Bullard	18,5
3		26	H	Sheffield U	W	1-0	1-0	Bullard	18,3
4	S	9	A	Newcastle U	W	0-0	2-1	McBride, Bocanegra	50,3
5		17	A	Tottenham H	D	0-0	0-0		36,1
6		23	H	Chelsea	L	0-0	0-2		24,2
7	O	2	A	Watford	D	0-1	3-3	McBride, Helguson, Francis (og)	17,9
8		16	H	Charlton A	W	0-0	2-1	McBride, Jensen	19,1
9		21	A	Aston Villa	D	1-1	1-1	Volz	30,9
10		28	H	Wigan A	L	0-0	0-1		22,8
11	N	4	H	Everton	W	0-0	1-0	Jensen	23,3
12		11	A	Portsmouth	D	0-0	1-1	Knight	19,5
13		18	A	Manchester C	L	0-3	1-3	John	35,7
14		25	H	Reading	L	0-1	0-1		22,6
15		29	H	Arsenal	W	2-1	2-1	McBride, Radzinski	24,5
16	D	2	A	Blackburn R	L	0-2	0-2		16,7
17		9	A	Liverpool	L	0-0	0-4		43,1
18		18	H	Middlesbrough	W	2-0	2-1	Helguson, McBride	16,9
19		23	H	West Ham U	D	0-0	0-0		22,4
20		27	A	Charlton A	D	1-2	2-2	McBride, Queudrue	25,2
21		30	A	Chelsea	D	1-1	2-2	Volz, Bocanegra	41,9
22	J	1	H	Watford	D	0-0	0-0		19,6
23		13	A	West Ham U	D	1-1	3-3	Radzinski, McBride, Christanval	34,9
24		20	H	Tottenham H	D	0-0	1-1	Montella	23,5
25		30	A	Sheffield U	L	0-2	0-2		27,5
26	F	3	H	Newcastle U	W	0-0	2-1	Helguson, McBride	24,3
27		11	A	Bolton W	L	0-1	1-2	Knight	24,9
28		24	H	Manchester U	L	1-1	1-2	McBride	24,4
29	M	3	H	Aston Villa	D	1-1	1-1	Bocanegra	24,5
30		17	A	Wigan A	D	0-0	0-0		16,0
31		31	H	Portsmouth	D	0-1	1-1	Pearce	22,8
32	A	6	A	Everton	L	1-3	1-4	Bocanegra	35,6
33		9	H	Manchester C	L	0-2	1-3	Bocanegra	22,4
34		14	A	Reading	L	0-1	0-1		24,0
35		21	H	Blackburn R	D	1-0	1-1	Montella	23,6
36		29	A	Arsenal	L	0-1	1-3	Davies	60,0
37	M	5	H	Liverpool	W	0-0	1-0	Dempsey	24,5
38		13	A	Middlesbrough	L	1-2	1-3	Davies	29,5
									Ap
									S
									Goa

FA Cup

No		Date	V	Opponents	R	H-T	F-T	Scorers	Atte
3	J	6	A	Leicester C	D	0-0	2-2	McBride, Volz	15,4
3R		17	H	Leicester C	W	1-2	4-3	McBride, Montella, (2), Routledge	11,2
4		27	H	Stoke C	W	2-0	3-0	Montella, McBride, Radzinski	11,0
5	F	18	H	Tottenham H	L	0-1	0-4		18,6

Carling Cup

No		Date	V	Opponents	R	H-T	F-T	Scorers	Atte
2	S	20	H	Wycombe W	L	0-2	1-2	Helguson	6,6
									Ap
									S
									Goa

Niemi	Rosenior	Christanval	Pearce	Queudrue	Brown	Diop	Bullard	Boa Morte	John	Helguson	Radzinski	McBride	Crossley	Volz	Bocanegra	Drobney	Knight	Routledge	Lastuvka	Runstrom	Jensen C	Zakuani	Batista	Omozusi	Montella	Warner	Dempsey	Davies	Smertin	Briggs	Timlin	Jensen (N)	
1	2	3	4	5	6	7	8	9	10	11	12	13	S	S	S																		1
1	2	3	4	5	6	7	8	9	12	10	13	11		S	S	S																	2
1	2	3	4	5	6	7	8	9	10	12	13	11		S	S	S																	3
1	2		4	5	6	7	8	9	10	S	14	11			13		3	12	S														4
1	2		4	5	6			9	11	12	13	10		7	8		3		S	14	S												5
1	2		4	5	6	9			11	12	S	13		7	8		3	10	S		S												6
1	2		4	5	6	9			11	10	14	13		7	8		3	12	S		S												7
1	2		4	5	6	7			S	11	9	10		13	14		3	8	S		12												8
1	2		4	5	6				12	S	11	10		7	8		3	S	S		9	S											9
1	2		4	5	6			13	S	S	11	10		7	8		3	12	S		9												10
1	2		4	5				6	13	14	11	10		12	7		3	9	S		8	S											11
1	2		4	5		13		6	14	S	11	10		9	7		3	12	S		8												12
1	2		4	5		8		9	12	13	14	11		6	7		3	S	S		10												13
1	2		4	5	8	14		9	11	S	6	10			12		3	13	S		7												14
1	5	3			6	9		7	S	13	8	11		2			4	12	S		10	S											15
	5	S	3		6	7		9	11	10	12	13		2			4	14	1		8		S										16
	5	12	4		7	8		10	13	14	6	11		2			3	S	1		9		S										17
1	2	3		5	7					11	9	10		8	12		4	6	S	S	S	S											18
1	2	4		5	7					10	6	11		8	3			9	S	S	S	S		S									19
1	2	3		5	8				12	10	9	11		7	4			6	S	S	13	S											20
1	2	3		5	8			12	11		9	10		7	4			6		S		S	S	S									21
1	2	3		5	7			13	14	10	9	11		8	4			6	12	S		S											22
	2	3	S	5	8					10	9	11		7	4		6		1	S				S	12	S							23
	2	3	4	5	8					11	9	10		6	7		S		1					S	12	S	13						24
1	2		4	5	8					12	9	11		7			3	13	S					S	10		14	6					25
	2	3		5	7	12				10	S	11		8	4		S	6	1						14		13	9					26
	2	3		5	7	8				11	13	10		6			4	S	1						14	S		9	12				27
	5	3			7	8			13	14	6	11		2	4			S	1							S	12	10	9				28
1	2		3	5	8	9			14	13	10	11			4			12	S								S	7	6				29
1	2		3	5	9	8			13	12	10	11			4			S	S								S	7	6				30
1	2		3	5	8	9			14	S	11	10			4			12	S						13			7	6				31
1	5	S			8				12^	13	10	11		2	4		3	6	S								S	7	9				32
1	5	3			8					11	12	10		2	4		S	6	S						13		14	9	7				33
1	2		3	5	8	7				10	S	11			4		12	6	S						14		13	9					34
1	2	4			7	8				S	9	11		13	5		3	12	S						10		14	6					35
1	2'	4			7	8				13	10	11		14	5		3		S		9				S		12	6					36
1	2	4			7	8				13	6	11		14	5		3	S	S						10		12	9					37
1	2	4		12					13	10	9	11		7	5		3		S		S						6	8		14			38
1	38	19	22	28	34	20	4	12	9	16	25	34	-	24	26	-	23	12	7	0	10	-	-	-	3	-	1	14	6	-	-	-	A
-	-	1	-	1	-	3	-	3	14	14	10	4	-	5	4	-	1	11	1	1	2	-	-	-	7	-	9	-	1	1	-	-	S
-	-	1	1	1	-	-	2	-	1	4	2	9	-	2	5	-	2	-	-	-	2	-	-	-	2	-	1	2	-	-	-	-	G

Niemi	Rosenior	Christanval	Pearce	Queudrue	Brown	Diop	Bullard	Boa Morte	John	Helguson	Radzinski	McBride	Crossley	Volz	Bocanegra	Drobney	Knight	Routledge	Lastuvka	Runstrom	Jensen C	Zakuani	Batista	Omozusi	Montella	Warner	Dempsey	Davies	Smertin	Briggs	Timlin	Jensen (N)	
	2		3		7				S	10	9	11		8	4			6	1	S		12		5	13	S							3
	2	3		5	8					10	9	11		7	4			6	S	S		S		S	12	1							3R
S	2	3		5	7						9	10		8	4		S	6	1		14				11		12	13					4
		3		5		7			13	10	6	11		2	S		4		1						12	S	14	9	8				5

Niemi	Rosenior	Christanval	Pearce	Queudrue	Brown	Diop	Bullard	Boa Morte	John	Helguson	Radzinski	McBride	Crossley	Volz	Bocanegra	Drobney	Knight	Routledge	Lastuvka	Runstrom	Jensen C	Zakuani	Batista	Omozusi	Montella	Warner	Dempsey	Davies	Smertin	Briggs	Timlin	Jensen (N)	
	13								14	11	9			2	4			6	1	10	7	3		12							8	5	2
-	3	3	1	3	3	1	-	-	-	4	5	4	-	5	4	-	1	4	4	1	1	1	-	1	1	1	-	1	1	-	1	1	A
-	1	-	-	-	-	-	-	-	2	-	-	-	-	-	-	-	-	-	-	-	1	1	-	1	3	-	2	1	-	-	-	-	S
-	-	-	-	-	-	-	-	-	-	1	1	3	-	1	-	-	-	1	-	-	-	-	-	-	3	-	-	-	-	-	-	-	G

0 points v	Manchester U, Manchester C, Reading	0 points
1 point v	Bolton W, Chelsea, Wigan A, Blackburn R	4 point
2 points v	Tottenham H, Watford, Aston V, Portsmouth, West Man U	10 points
3 points v	Sheffield U, Everton, Arsenal, Liverpool, Middlesbrough	15 points
4 points v	Charlton A	4 points
6 points v	Newcastle U	6 points

Fulham's League Records: 1903–2007

	Division One/Premier*	Division Two/One*	Division Three/Two*	Division Three*
Biggest victory				
Home				
	10–1 v Ipswich 1963–64	8–1 v Swansea 1937–38	10–2 v Torquay 1931–32	6–0 v Darlington 1996–97
Away				
	5–2 v Blackpool 1960–61	6–1 v Doncaster 1957–58	8–0 v Halifax 1969–70	4–1 v Cardiff 1996–97
	5–2 v Aston Villa 1965–66			4–1 v Scunthorpe 1996–97
Biggest defeat				
Home				
	1–6 v Sheffield W 1960–61	1–6 v Bradford 1913–14	0–6 v Port Vale 1986–87	1–4 v Cardiff 1996–97
Away				
	0–9 v Wolves 1959–60	0–7 v Nottingham F 1927–28	0–7 v Chester 1988–89	1–5 v Walsall 1994–95
Highest Attendance				
Home				
	47,270 v Man U 1966–67	49,335 v Millwall 1938–39	29,253 v Brentford 1931–32	11,479 v Northampton 1996–97
Away				
	75,115 v Man U 2006–07	63,962 v Newcastle U 1938–39	33,340 v Aston V 1970–71	9,171 v Carlisle 1996–97
Lowest Attendance				
Home				
	8,954 v Blackpool 1962–63	1,000 v Barnsley 1914–15	2,352 v Rotherham 1986–87	2,176 v Scunthorpe 1995–96
Away				
	8,260 v Huddersfield 1951–52	500 v Glossop 1914–15	1,074 v Chester 1990–91	1,198 v Hartlepool 1995–96
Victories				
Most Home Wins				
	13 2005–06	18 1958–59	19 1998–99	13 1996–97
Most Away Wins				
	6 1960–61/1962–63	14 2000–01	12 1998–99	12 1996–97
Most Wins				
	17 1959–60	30 2000–01	31 1998–99	25 1996–97
Fewest Home Wins				
	5 1951–52	6 1947–48/1968–69/1979–80	7 1993–94	10 1995–96
Fewest Away Wins				
	1 1964–65/2005–06/2006–07	1 1923–24/1927–28/1968–69	2 1990–91	2 1995–96
Fewest Wins				
	8 1951–52/2006–07	7 1968–69	10 1990–91	12 1995–96
Defeats				
Most Home Defeats				
	11 1967–68	11 1979–80	10 1993–94	5 1994–95/1996–97
Most Away Defeats				
	15 1960–61	20 1927–28	14 1930–31	11 1995–96
Most Defeats				
	25 1967–68	26 1985–86	22 1993–94	17 1995–96

Fewest Home Defeats	2 1963–64	1 1912–13/1948–49	1 1998–99	4 1995–96
Fewest Away Defeats	8 2003–04/2003–04	3 2000–01	6 1931–32/1998–99	4 1996–97
Fewest Defeats	14 2001–02/2003–04	5 2000–01	7 1998–99	9 1996–97

Draws

Most Home Draws	8 1960–61/1963–64	9 1947–48	9 1969–70/1981–82/1992–93	9 1995–96
Most Away Draws	8 1949–50	9 1934–35/1952–53	9 1986–87	9 1994–95
Most Draws	14 1949–50	16 1974–75	17 1986–87/1992–93	17 1995–96
Fewest Home Draws	3 1961–62/2002–03	0 1914–15	3 1928–29/1930–31/1931–32/ 1998–99	5 1994–95/1996–97
Fewest Away Draws	0 1960–61	0 1912–13/1927–28	2 1988–89	7 1996–97
Fewest Draws	6 2005–06	4 1956–57	7 1930–31	12 1996–97

Goals Scored

Most Home Goals Scored	49 1966–67	65 1958–59	72 1931–32	41 1996–97
Most Away Goals Scored	33 1960–61/1965–66	44 1957–58	41 1928–29	31 1996–97
Most Goals Scored	73 1959–60	98 1953–54	111 1931–32	72 1996–97
Fewest Home Goals Scored	18 2006–07	19 1979–80	20 1993–94	39 1994–95/1995–96
Fewest Away Goals Scored	13 1963–64	10 1920–21	14 1990–91	18 1995–96
Fewest Goals Scored	36 2001–02	39 1973–74	41 1990–91	57 1995–96

Goals Conceded

Most Home Goals Conceded	41 1967–68	39 1953–54	41 1986–87	26 1995–96
Most Away Goals Conceded	57 1967–68	67 1927–28	54 1930–31	37 1995–96
Most Goals Conceded	98 1967–68	92 1926–27	83 1930–31	63 1995–96
Fewest Home Goals Conceded	16 2001–02	8 1921–22	12 1970–71/1998–99	20 1996–97
Fewest Away Goals Conceded	25 2003–04	18 2001–01	20 1998–99	18 1996–97
Fewest Goals Conceded	44 2001–02	32 1922–23/2000–01	32 1998–99	38 1996–97

Points **

Most Home Points			
41 1963–64/2005–6	55 1958–59	60 1998–99	44 1996–97
Most Away Points			
22 1962–63	48 2000–01	41 1998–99	43 1996–97
Most Points			
61 1959–60	101 2000–01	101 1998–99	87 1996–97
Fewest Home Points			
22 1951–52/1967–68	22 1979–80	27 1993–94	38 1994–95
Fewest Away Points			
7 2005–06	3 1927–28	13 1930–31	14 1995–96
Fewest Points			
35 1951–52	32 1968–69	46 1990–91	53 1995–96

* Change of divisional name in 1992 following the setting up of the Premiership
** Three points for a win throughout

Cup Competitions (1907–2006*)

Rounds Eliminated

FA CupLeague Cup

Final	1	Final	-
Semi-final	5	Semi-final	-
6	5	5	5
5	5	4	7
4	23	3	9
3	38	2	18
2	5	1	8
1	8		

*Fulham's pre-1907 FA Cup record has been excluded because it is not possible to compare the status of non-League clubs. In that time Fulham reached the last eight once, the last 16 twice and the last 32 once. On each occasion they lost to teams from a higher division.

Opponents

	FA Cup		**League Cup**	
Opponents	Victories	Defeats	Victories	Defeats
Higher Division	21	35	13	24
Same Division	26	34	12	10
Lower Division	50	21	23	13

Football League Records

Total League Appearances

Johnny HAYNES	594
Eddie LOWE	473
Frank PENN	427
Les BARRETT	420
George COHEN	408
Len OLIVER	406
Arthur REYNOLDS	399
John MARSHALL	395
Jim STANNARD	391
Albert BARRETT	389
Arthur STEVENS	386
Les STRONG	370
Gordon DAVIES	366
Alan MULLERY	363
Stan BROWN	348
Tony MACEDO	346
Simon MORGAN	345
Gerry PEYTON	345
Bobby ROBSON	344
Jimmy TORRANCE	338
Jim LANGLEY	323
Jim HAMMOND	316
Jimmy CONWAY	312

Football League Scorers

Gordon DAVIES	159
Bedford JEZZARD	154
Johnny HAYNES	147
Jim HAMMOND	142
Graham LEGGAT	127
Arthur STEVENS	110
Steve EARLE	98
Maurice COOK	89
Frank NEWTON	77
Bobby ROBSON	77
Les BARRETT	75
Ronnie ROOKE	70
Jimmy CONWAY	67
Tosh CHAMBERLAIN	59
Jimmy TEMPLE	58
John ARNOLD	57
Dean CONEY	56
John MITCHELL	56
Bob THOMAS	56
Roy DWIGHT	54
Louis SAHA	53
Jack FINCH	50
Bill HALEY	50

FA Cup Records

FA Cup Appearances

Johnny HAYNES	44
George COHEN	33
Eddie LOWE	33
Frank PENN	32
Les BARRETT	31
Tony MACEDO	31
Alan MULLERY	31
Albert BARRETT	30
Len OLIVER	28
Les STRONG	28
Arthur STEVENS	27
Jack FRYER	26
Jim HAMMOND	26
Jimmy CONWAY	25
Gordon DAVIES	24
Jim LANGLEY	23
Willie GOLDIE	22
Gerry PEYTON	22
Jimmy HILL	21
Arthur REYNOLDS	21

FA Cup Scorers

Arthur STEVENS	14
Jimmy HILL	11
Jim HAMMOND	9
Johnny HAYNES	9
Gordon DAVIES	8
Ronnie ROOKE	8
Viv BUSBY	7
Joe CONNOR	7
Fred HARRISON	7
Steed MALBRANQUE	7
Frank PENN	7
Dean CONEY	6
Maurice COOK	6
Barry HAYLES	6
John ARNOLD	5
Albert BARRETT	5
Tosh CHAMBERLAIN	5
Allan CLARKE	5
Harry FLETCHER	5
Graham LEGGAT	5

League Cup Records

League Cup Appearances

Les BARRETT	36
John MARSHALL	34
Simon MORGAN	33
Stan BROWN	29
Gordon DAVIES	28
Gerry PEYTON	28
Fred CALLAGHAN	27
Ray LEWINGTON	27
Jeff HOPKINS	26
Les STRONG	26
Jim STANNARD	25
Dean CONEY	24
Tony GALE	24
Steve EARLE	22
Maik TAYLOR	22
Glen THOMAS	22

League Cup Scorers

Les BARRETT	12
Gordon DAVIES	11
Dean CONEY	10
Steve EARLE	10
Allan CLARKE	7
Micky CONROY	7
Luis BOA MORTE	6
Jimmy CONWAY	6
Geoff HORSFIELD	6
Louis SAHA	6
Peter SCOTT	6
Barry HAYLES	5
Johnny KEY	5
Tomas RADZINSKI	5

Total Appearances

Johnny HAYNES	658
Eddie LOWE	511
Les BARRETT	487
George COHEN	459
Frank PENN	459
John MARSHALL	447
Len OLIVER	434
Jim STANNARD	430
Les STRONG	424
Arthur REYNOLDS	420
Albert BARRETT	419
Gordon DAVIES	418
Arthur STEVENS	413
Alan MULLERY	411
Simon MORGAN	398
Gerry PEYTON	395
Stan BROWN	392
Tony MACEDO	391
Bobby ROBSON	370
Jimmy TORRANCE	357
Jimmy CONWAY	356
Jim LANGLEY	356
Jim HAMMOND	342
Fred CALLAGHAN	332
Steve EARLE	321
Tony GALE	318
Syd GIBBONS	318
Bedford JEZZARD	306
Joe BACUZZI	299
Robin LAWLER	299
Jimmy HILL	297
Peter SCOTT	297
Jack FINCH	295
Arthur 'Pat' COLLINS	279
Barry LLOYD	278
Jim TAYLOR	278
Ian BLACK	277
Graham LEGGAT	277
Glen THOMAS	277
Alex CHAPLIN	276
Ray LEWINGTON	271
Ted CHARLTON	267
Jeff ECKHARDT	265
Jeff HOPKINS	251
Maurice COOK	248
Dean CONEY	244
Robert WILSON	239
Kevin LOCK	233
Gary BRAZIL	229
Maik TAYLOR	227
Peter MELLOR	224
Mike KEEPING	217
Alf TOOTILL	214
John ARNOLD	213
Johnny PRICE	205
Tosh CHAMBERLAIN	204
Wattie WHITE	203
Martin PIKE	202
Rufus BREVETT	201
Steve FINNAN	200

Leading Scorers

Leading Scorers

Gordon DAVIES	178
Johnny HAYNES	158
Bedford JEZZARD	154
Jim HAMMOND	151
Graham LEGGAT	134
Arthur STEVENS	124
Steve EARLE	108
Maurice COOK	97
Les BARRETT	90
Frank NEWTON	81
Bobby ROBSON	80
Ronnie ROOKE	78
Jimmy CONWAY	76
Dean CONEY	72
Tosh CHAMBERLAIN	64
John ARNOLD	62
Louis SAHA	62
Jimmy TEMPLE	61
John MITCHELL	60
Bob THOMAS	58
Allan CLARKE	57
Roy DWIGHT	57
Barry HAYLES	55
Bill HALEY	54
Fred HARRISON	54
Gary BRAZIL	53
Simon MORGAN	53
Johnny PRICE	53
Luis BOA MORTE	52
Jimmy HILL	52
Frank PENN	52
Jack FINCH	51
Bert PEARCE	50

Internationals at Fulham

Many fine players have appeared for Fulham over the years and some of the best were internationals. Fulham fans have been lucky enough to watch many star players including Johnny Haynes, Alan Mullery, George Cohen, Graham Leggat and Gordon Davies. This chapter covers the details of some of the internationals who have represented their country while wearing the white shirt of Fulham.

ENGLAND

There have been 39 England internationals who have played for Fulham during the club's history, but only 10 of these were capped while playing for the club. Allan Clarke, Rodney Marsh, Malcolm MacDonald, Alan Mullery, Paul Parker and Bobby Robson played for England after leaving the Cottage, as did Andy Cole, who was on loan at the Cottage from Arsenal at the start of his career and then returned for a season 15 years later.

The first England international to play for Fulham was Albert Wilkes. He had joined the club from Aston Villa in August 1907 after gaining five caps as a Villa player. He later became a Villa director and ran a successful photographic agency. Frank Osborne was the first Fulham player to be capped for England while at the Cottage, and he, ironically, was born in South Africa. His teammates in the Fulham side of the early 1920s included former England internationals Andy Ducat and Danny Shea. He was centre-forward against Ireland at The Hawthorns in October 1922 and then on the right wing in his second international against France in Paris in May 1923, but he failed to score in either game. Frank was transferred to Spurs in January 1924 for a £3,000 fee and played twice more for his country at White Hart Lane.

The long-serving wing-half duo of Bert Barrett and Len Oliver both won one England cap and remarkably each played for England while Fulham were in the Third Division South. Oliver appeared at right-half for his country in a 5–1 victory in Belgium, in which George Camsell of Middlesbrough scored four goals, and Barrett played at left-half for England five months later in a 3–0 victory in Belfast over Ireland.

Just weeks after signing for Fulham from Southampton, John Arnold played for England against Scotland at Hampden Park in April 1933. He had starred in a trial match for the Possibles when they beat the Probables and earned a call-up to the full team. In the summer of 1931 Arnold had played for England in a Test Match at Lords against New Zealand, and so joined the select band that played for England at football and cricket. Scotland won at Hampden, and it was Arnold's only cap just as the Lord's match against New Zealand was his only Test appearance. Several other Fulham players came close to England honours in that era, none more so than Arnold's cricketing colleague Jim Hammond. In those pre-substitute days, he was 12th man for England in the thrilling win over Austria at Stamford Bridge in December 1932.

Fortunately for Jim Taylor, he did not play in England's disastrous World Cup matches in Brazil in 1950, although he was in the party. He had been Fulham's centre-half since 1946 (playing alongside Pat Beasley, an England player in the 1930s) and was one of the best defenders in an era when England was spoilt for choice. His turn eventually came in May 1951, in a Festival of Britain match against Argentina, the first side from outside the UK to play at Wembley. Taylor was 33 years old when he made his England debut in a half-back line that included Billy Wright and Harry Cockburn. Argentina took the lead through Boye after 18 minutes, but after great pressure Stan Mortensen equalised in the 79th minute and Jackie Milburn hit the winner for England for a 2–1 victory. A few days later, Jim won his second and last cap in a 5–2 victory over Portugal at Goodison Park. Taylor again performed well at centre-half, and England never looked back after debutant Billy Nicholson scored after just 18 seconds.

Jim Taylor.

Bedford Jezzard was the next Fulham player to be capped in May 1954 when he appeared in a horrendous performance in Budapest during which Puskas' mighty Magyars tore the England defence apart and won 7–1. Beddy hardly touched the ball, but he had a happier time in his second and last England appearance. He was alongside teammate Johnny Haynes when England beat Northern Ireland 3–0 at Wembley and two Fulham players represented England for the first time. Johnny Haynes had a superb match as Northern Ireland were beaten 3–0 at Wembley in November 1955. Beddy played his part in the second and third goals, but he was never selected again. Fulham provided two England players that day despite the fact they were a Second Division club.

Johnny Haynes had made his England debut in October 1954, and he scored in a 2–0 victory over Northern Ireland in Belfast. The Maestro went on to play 56 times for his country, which included the 1958 and 1962 World Cup Finals. The highlights of his early caps were a 4–2 victory over Brazil at Wembley in May 1956 and a marvellous 3–1 victory over the World Cup holders Germans in Berlin, in which he scored. England went out of the 1958 World Cup in Sweden in a group play-off match with the Soviet Union, losing 1–0 due to an outstanding performance by the Soviets goalkeeper Lev Yashin. England took revenge five months later when Haynes hit a hat-trick in a 5–0 victory over Russia at Wembley in what was probably Johnny's best display for his country. Another great moment was captaining his side to a 9–3 victory over the Scots at Wembley in April 1961. Johnny scored twice as England took the Home Championship title. England were again disappointing during the 1962 World Cup Finals in Chile. They scrapped through the group stage but lost to eventual winners Brazil 3–1 in the quarter-finals. This proved to be Johnny's last cap as he was involved in a car crash soon afterwards, and new manager Alf Ramsey never selected him again.

Jim Langley gained three caps in April and May of 1958 in the same side as Haynes (Fulham were again a Second Division side). His debut was a sad affair as it was the first game after the Munich air disaster in which four England and Manchester United players lost their life. One of these was full-back Roger Byrne, who Jim replaced against Scotland at Hampden Park, which England won easily by 4–0. Just two weeks later he helped England beat Portugal 2–1, but Langley missed a penalty when he hit the post from the spot. His last cap came in a 5–0 defeat in Yugoslavia, and although he played well Jim was not selected for Englands World Cup squad that went to Sweden soon afterwards.

After several Under-23 caps, George Cohen made his full England debut in May 1964 against Uruguay in a 2–1 victory at Wembley. He was to go on to play in a World Cup Final in July 1966 in the same side as West Ham's Bobby Moore, who later played for Fulham during the 1970s. After a 10–0 victory over the USA in New York in May 1964, England travelled to Brazil to play the World Champions and came unstuck, with Pele in great form inspiring Brazil to a 5–1 victory in the Maracana. Cohen, who was injured in a League game in the run up to the World Cup but regained fitness, played in every match in the '66 tournament and is probably best remembered for an incident at the end of their 1–0 quarter-final win over Argentina after a highly-controversial match. England manager Alf Ramsey stopped George from swapping his shirt with an Argentina player at the end of the match. England won the dramatic World Cup Final by 4–2, but the Germans still claim today that the third goal did not cross the line. Cohen's last cap came in November 1967 against Northern Ireland at Wembley, but within a month George received a terrible injury that was to eventually end his career.

Johnny Haynes is carried off after captaining England to a 9–3 win over Scotland, Wembley 1961.

It was another 38 years before another Fulham player wore an England shirt. This was Zat Knight who, during the summer of 2005, played for England against the USA and Columbia. In the game against the States in Chicago, Zat came on as substitute for Sol Campbell at half-time as England won 2–1 thanks to two goals from Kieron Richardson. His second cap came days later when England beat Columbia 3–2 in New Jersey thanks to a Michael Owen hat-trick.

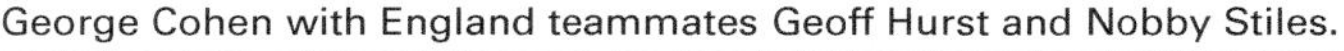

George Cohen with England teammates Geoff Hurst and Nobby Stiles.

Rodney Marsh, Malcolm Macdonald, Alan Mullery, Paul Parker and Bobby Robson all came through the ranks at Fulham and went on to play for England. Marsh was sold to Queen's Park Rangers and Macdonald went to Luton Town before they could reach their full potential. MacDonald scored five goals for England against Cyprus in a 5–0 victory at Wembley in September 1975. Mullery was the most successful and played for England 35 times; however, Paul Parker played in a World Cup semi-final in 1990 when his country lost to the Germans after a penalty shoot-out. Paul eventually made 19 appearances for his country. Allan Clarke also went on to play 19 times for his country, and Robson won 20 caps after moving to West Brom in 1956.

SCOTLAND

Fulham have had 22 Scottish internationals in their ranks since 1903, but only two played for the country while at the Cottage. Fulham managers Harry Bradshaw and Phil Kelso had signed a number of Scottish internationals during their time as manager of Fulham, including Mark Bell (from Hearts), Tom Fitchie (Queen's Park), Archie Gray (ex-Hibernian), Bobby Hamilton (Rangers), Willie Lennie (Royal Albert), Les Skene (Queen's Park), Wattie White (Everton) and the legendary Bobby Templeton (Kilmarnock). None of these was capped while at Craven Cottage, but it was rare for a Scot to be capped in those days unless they played in the Scottish League. Hamilton won 11 caps with Rangers and was one of the great centre-forwards of the Edwardian age, and Templeton loved to dribble and possessed great ball skills, gaining 11 caps. But only Jimmy Sharp played for Scotland in this era while a Fulham player. He gained his fifth and final cap in a 3–2 defeat by Wales in March 1909.

The only other player to be capped by Scotland while at the Cottage is Graham Leggat. He had already gained seven caps with Aberdeen, the first coming against England at Hampden Park in 1956. Leggat put Scotland ahead that day, but England equalised with only seconds remaining, through Johnny Haynes. As a Fulham player, Graham was first capped by Scotland against Wales in Cardiff in a 3–0 victory in October 1958. Leggat went on to score eight goals in 18 internationals for Scotland. His last cap came in June 1960 when the Scots drew 3–3 in Budapest against the Hungarians. Since then, Under-23 honours for Duncan Jupp in the 1990s is the closest a Fulham player has come to full Scottish honours.

WALES

In the same month that Jim Hammond was 12th man for England, December 1932, Billy Richards became the first Fulham player to gain a Welsh cap. He was outside-right in a 4–1 victory over Ireland at the Racecourse Ground, Wrexham. This proved to be his only cap for his country. The first Welsh international to sign for Fulham was Dicky Richards, who played for West Ham in the first Wembley FA Cup Final in 1923 and won nine caps for Wales in the 1920s. He failed to win a cap while at the Cottage but was capped when he moved on to play for Mold Town. Sid Thomas was Fulham's next Welsh cap. On 18 October 1947 he was selected to play against England at Ninian Park and ended on the losing side 3–0. He kept his place for the 2–1 victory over Scotland at Hampden Park and then completed the Home Championship matches, playing in a 2–0 victory over Northern Ireland at Wrexham in March 1948. Thomas played just once more for Wales in October 1948, a 3–1 defeat at Ninian Park against the Scots. The vastly-experienced Cliff Jones joined Fulham from Spurs in October 1968, and he was capped soon afterwards in a World Cup qualifier against Italy, and his second and final cap came against the Rest of the UK in July 1969. He won 59 caps in all for the Principality.

Jeff Hopkins in one of his Welsh caps.

Kit Symons, one of Fulham's more recent Welsh players.

Fulham had to wait another 11 years for their next Welsh cap when Gordon 'Ivor' Davies was selected to play against Turkey in Ismir on 21 November 1979. Davies went on to gain 15 caps while a Fulham player, and in one of these games he had a Fulham teammate as an international colleague. In May 1983 young Jeff Hopkins was called up to play for his country, along with Davies against Northern Ireland. Ivor scored the winner. Both Davies and Hopkins were in the Welsh side that beat England at Wrexham in May 1984, when Mark Hughes scored the winner in a 1–0 victory. Hopkins won 14 of his 16 caps while at the Cottage, appearing at right-back and as a central-defender.

In recent years there has been a substantial Welsh contingent at the Cottage. Chris Coleman, Matt Crossley, Andy Melville, Alan Neilson, Mark Pembridge, Kit Symons and Paul Trollope were Welsh teammates round the time they were also Fulham players. All but Neilson appeared for their country while on Fulham's books. Eddie Perry and Dave Roberts both went on to gain caps for Wales at other clubs after starting their careers at Fulham, and the club's most recent new cap is Welshman Simon Davies, who joined the club from Everton in January 2007.

IRELAND/NORTHERN IRELAND

Joe Connor was the first Fulham player to win an international cap when he played for Ireland against England at Belfast in March 1904. He had already been capped twice while at Griffin Park against Scotland and Wales. He was not even a first-team player at Fulham, and recent research has found that his name was O'Connor and he was born in Dublin not Dundee as previously thought. The next player to be capped for Ireland was Alex Steele. This was in February 1929 against Wales and Scotland. Steele had previously been capped twice while with Charlton Athletic. Between 1946 and 1950 four Fulham players won international honours with Northern Ireland. They were goalkeepers Ted Hinton and Hugh Kelly plus Johnny Campbell and Bobby Brennan. Hinton made his debut in a 0–0 draw against the Scots at Hampden Park in November 1946, and he went on to gain five caps while with Fulham. The best of these was a 2–0 victory over Scotland and a 2–2 draw with England at Goodison Park the following season. Poor Hugh Kelly's international experience was not so happy as he let in nine goals against England in November 1949 and six goals against Scotland a year later. Campbell gained two caps in the autumn of 1950, with both games ending in large defeats, 1–4 versus England and 1–6 against the Scots. Campbell was joined by Bobby Brennan, a £20,000 signing from Birmingham City, in the England game, his only cap while at the Cottage.

Ted Hinton.

REPUBLIC OF IRELAND

Nine Fulham players have won caps with the Republic of Ireland. The first was Robin Lawler, who would have won more than the eight caps that he won but for club commitments. During the 1960s Jimmy Conway, John Dempsey and Turlough O'Connor all played for Eire. Conway and Dempsey made their debuts in the same match in Valencia against the Spanish in a 2–0 defeat in December 1966. All three played in a shock victory over Czechoslovakia in Prague in November 1967. This was a World Cup qualifier and young O'Connor, who played just once for Fulham, scored the winner in a 2–1 victory. Jimmy Dunne gained just one cap for Eire in May 1971 in the same side as Jimmy Conway. This was a European Championship qualifier against Austria in Dublin which ended in a 4–1 defeat.

Gerry Peyton was the next Fulham player to be capped by Eire when he made his debut in a friendly against Spain in February 1977. He was the Republic's regular 'keeper until 1980 when he lost his place to Seamus McDonagh, although Peyton was later Eire's reserve goalkeeper in the 1990 World Cup Finals but did not play. Sean O'Driscoll won three caps on a tour of South America during the summer of 1983 when they played Chile and Brazil plus Trinidad and Tobago on the return trip. Steve Finnan made his debut for his country against Greece in April 2000 and later played in all of their games during the 2002 World Cup Finals in South Korea and Japan. They eventually lost to Spain on penalties in the second round. Terry Phelan gained four caps during his brief stay at the Cottage, three of these coming in a tournament in the US during the summer of 2000 when Eire met the USA, Mexico and South Africa.

Sean O'Driscoll.

Other Internationals

In recent years, particularly following the arrival of Mohamed Al Fayed and the club's rise to the Premiership, there has been an influx of foreign internationals at Craven Cottage. The list is now quite large and hard to track on a match-by-match basis for each individual player. However, the foreign internationals who have been Fulham players since 1990 are:

EUROPE:

Phillipe Albert (Belgium), Greg Saava (apprentice) and Ara Bedrossian (Cyprus), Bjarne Goldbaek, Claus Jensen, Niclas Jensen and Peter Moller (Denmark), Antti Niemi (Finland), Phillipe Christianval, Martin Djetou, Alain Goma, Steve Marlet and Louis Saha (France), Karl Heinz Riedle (Germany) Edwin van der Sar (Holland), Heider Helguson (Iceland), Vicenzo Montella (Italy), Andrejs Stolcers (Latvia), Luis Boa Morte (Portugal), Alex Smertin (Russia).

NORTH AMERICA AND THE CARIBBEAN:

Paul Psechisolido and Tomasz Radzinski (Canada), Kyle Lightbourne (Bermuda), Barry Hayles (Jamaica), Ronnie Mauge (Trinidad and Tobago), Carlos Bocanegra, Clint Dempsey, Marcus Hahnemann, Eddie Lewis and Brian McBride (USA), Callum Willock (St Kitts).

AFRICA:

Pierre Wome (Cameroon), Hassan Hegazi (Egypt), Elvis Hammond (Ghana), Abdes Ouaddou (Morocco) and Papa Bouba Diop (Senegal).

OTHER:

Ahmad Elrich (Australia), Junichi Inamoto (Japan), Chris James, Simon Elliott and Tommy Mason (New Zealand), and Zesh Rehman (Pakistan),

World Cup and European Championship Finals

Many internationals connected with Fulham have appeared in European Championship and World Cup Finals over the years. Of course, George Cohen and Bobby Moore played in England's World Cup-winning side of 1966, and the only other player to appear in a Final of a major international tournament is Vicenzo Montella, who was a playing substitute when Italy lost to France in the 2000 European Championship Final in Rotterdam. Edwin van der Sar, Louis Saha and Karl Heinz Riedler have come close to playing in a Final. Riedle was a 38th-minute substitute for Rudi Voller in the 1990 World Cup semi-final against England, which the Germans eventually won on penalties. However, he was not selected for the Final. Louis Saha appeared for the French as a substitute in the quarter-finals and semi-finals of the 2006 World Cup but again did not make an appearance in the Final. Edwin van der Sar has played in three losing semi-finals. He appeared in all of the Dutch games during the 2004 Euro Championships, but they lost at the semi-final stage to Portugal 2–1 in Lisbon. He also kept goal in the 1998 World Cup semi-final for Holland when they lost to Brazil on penalties in Marseille and again in the 2000

Euro Championship when they again lost on penalties in a semi-final against Italy after a 0–0 draw in their home country.

Other Fulham players who have appeared in the World Cup or European Championship Finals are Ray Houghton (Eire) 1990 and 1994, Philippe Albert (Belgium) 1994, Brian McBride (USA) 1998 and 2006, Pierre Wome (Cameroon) 1998, Alex Smertin (Russia) 2002, Vincenzo Montella (Italy) 2002, Papa Bouba Diop (Senegal) 2002, Junichi Inamoto (Japan) 2002, Luis Boa Morte (Portugal) 2006, and the American trio of Eddie Lewis, Carlos Bocanegra and Clint Dempsey in 2006.

Fulham International Player Records

ENGLAND

John Arnold (1)

Scotland	Apr 1933	Glasgow	1–2

Albert Barrett (1)

Northern Ireland	Oct 1929	Belfast	3–0

George Cohen (37)

Uruguay	May 1964	Wembley	2–1
Portugal	May 1964	Lisbon	4–3
Republic of Ireland	May 1964	Dublin	3–1
USA	May 1964	New York	10–0
Brazil	May 1964	Rio de Janeiro	1–5
Northern Ireland	Oct 1964	Belfast	4–3
Belgium	Oct 1964	Wembley	2–2
Wales	Nov 1964	Wembley	2–1
Netherlands	Dec 1964	Amsterdam	1–1
Scotland	Apr 1965	Wembley	2–2
Hungary	May 1965	Wembley	1–0
Yugoslavia	May 1965	Belgrade	1–1
West Germany	May 1965	Nurnberg	1–0
Sweden	May 1965	Goteborg	2–1
Wales	Oct 1965	Cardiff	0–0
Austria	Oct 1965	Wembley	2–3
Northern Ireland	Nov 1965	Wembley	2–1
Spain	Dec 1965	Madrid	2–0
Poland	Jan 1966	Liverpool	1–1
West Germany	Feb 1966	Wembley	1–0
Scotland	Apr 1966	Glasgow	4–3
Norway	Jun 1966	Oslo	6–1
Denmark	Jul 1966	Copenhagen	2–0
Poland	Jul 1966	Chorzow	1–0
Uruguay	Jul 1966	Wembley	0–0
Mexico	Jul 1966	Wembley	2–0
France	Jul 1966	Wembley	2–0
Argentina	Jul 1966	Wembley	1–0
Portugal	Jul 1966	Wembley	2–1
West Germany	Jul 1966	Wembley	4–2
Northern Ireland	Oct 1966	Belfast	2–0
Czechoslovakia	Nov 1966	Wembley	0–0
Wales	Nov 1966	Wembley	5–1
Scotland	Apr 1967	Wembley	2–3
Spain	May 1967	Wembley	2–0
Wales	Oct 1967	Cardiff	3–0
Northern Ireland	Nov 1967	Wembley	2–0

Johnny Haynes (56)

Northern Ireland	Oct 1954	Belfast	2–0
Northern Ireland	Nov 1955	Wembley	3–0
Spain	Nov 1955	Wembley	4–1
Scotland	Apr 1956	Glasgow	1–1
Brazil	May 1956	Wembley	4–2
Sweden	May 1956	Stockholm	0–0
Finland	May 1956	Helsinki	5–1
West Germany	May 1956	Berlin	3–1
Wales	Nov 1956	Wembley	3–1
Yugoslavia	Nov 1956	Wembley	3–0
Republic of Ireland	May 1957	Wembley	5–1
Denmark	May 1957	Copehagen	4–1
Republic of Ireland	May 1957	Dublin	1–1
Wales	Oct 1957	Cardiff	4–0
Northern Ireland	Nov 1957	Wembley	2–3
France	Nov 1957	Wembley	4–0
Scotland	Apr 1958	Glasgow	4–0
Portugal	May 1958	Wembley	2–1
Yugoslavia	May 1958	Belgrade	0–5
USSR	May 1958	Moscow	1–1
USSR	Jun 1958	Goteborg	2–2
Brazil	Jun 1958	Goteborg	0–0
Austria	Jun 1958	Goteborg	2–2
USSR	Jun 1958	Goteborg	0–1
Northern Ireland	Oct 1958	Belfast	3–3
USSR	Oct 1958	Wembley	5–0
Scotland	Apr 1959	Wembley	1–0
Italy	May 1959	Wembley	2–2
Brazil	May 1959	Rio de Janeiro	0–2
Peru	May 1959	Lima	1–4
Mexico	May 1959	Mexico City	1–2
USA	May 1959	Los Angeles	8–1
Northern Ireland	Nov 1959	Wembley	2–1
Yugoslavia	May 1960	Wembley	3–3

Spain*	May 1960	Madrid	0–3
Hungary*	May 1960	Budapest	0–2
Northern Ireland*	Oct 1960	Belfast	5–2
Luxembourg*	Oct 1960	Luxembourg	9–0
Spain*	Oct 1960	Wembley	4–2
Wales*	Nov 1960	Wembley	5–1
Scotland*	Apr 1961	Wembley	9–3
Mexico*	May 1961	Wembley	8–0
Portugal*	May 1961	Lisbon	1–1
Italy*	May 1961	Rome	3–2
Austria*	May 1961	Vienna	1–3
Wales*	Oct 1961	Cardiff	1–1
Portugal*	Oct 1961	Wembley	2–0
Northern Ireland*	Nov 1961	Wembley	1–1
Austria*	Apr 1962	Wembley	3–1
Scotland*	Apr 1962	Glasgow	0–2
Switzerland*	May 1962	Wembley	3–1
Peru*	May 1962	Lima	4–0
Hungary*	May 1962	Rancagua	1–2
Argentina*	Jun 1962	Rancagua	3–1
Bulgaria*	Jun 1962	Rancagua	0–0
Brazil*	Jun 1962	Vina del Mar	1–3

* Denotes Haynes as captain.

Bedford Jezzard (2)

Hungary	May 1954	Budapest	1–7
Northern Ireland	Nov 1955	Wembley	3–0

Zat Knight (1+1)

United States (sub)	May 2005	Chicago	2–1
Colombia	May 2005	New Jersey	3–2

Jim Langley (3)

Scotland	April 1958	Glasgow	4–0
Portugal	May 1958	Wembley	2–1
Yugoslavia	May 1958	Belgrade	0–5

Len Oliver (1)

Belgium	May 1929	Brussels	5–1

Frank Osborne (2)

Northern Ireland	Oct 1922	The Hawthorns	2–0
France	May 1925	Paris	4–1

Jim Taylor (2)

Argentina	May 1951	Wembley	2–1
Portugal	May 1951	Goodison Park	5–2

NORTHERN IRELAND

George Best (5)

Holland	Oct 1976	Rotterdam	2–2
Belgium	Oct 1976	Liege	0–2
West Germany	Apr 1977	Cologne	0–5
Iceland	Sep 1977	Belfast	2–0
Holland	Sep 1977	Belfast	0–1

Bobby Brennan (1)

England	Oct 1950	Belfast	1–4

Johnny Campbell (2)

England	Oct 1950	Belfast	1–4
Scotland	Nov 1950	Glasgow	1–6

Joe Connor (1)

England	Mar 1904	Belfast	1–3

Ted Hinton (5)

Scotland	Nov 1946	Glasgow	0–0
Wales	Apr 1947	Belfast	2–1
Scotland	Oct 1947	Belfast	2–0
England	Nov 1947	Goodison Park	2–2
Wales	Mar 1948	Wrexham	0–2

Hugh Kelly (2)

England	Nov 1949	Maine Road	2–9
Wales	Mar 1950	Wrexham	0–0

Jack McClelland (1)

Mexico	Jun 1966	Belfast	4–1

Alex Steele (2)

Wales	Feb 1929	Wrexham	2–2
Scotland	Feb 1929	Belfast	3–7

Maik Taylor (31+2)

Germany	Mar 1999	Belfast	0–3
Moldova	Mar 1999	Chisinau	0–0
Canada	Apr 1999	Belfast	1–1
Rep of Ireland	May 1999	Dublin	1–0
France	Aug 1999	Belfast	0–1
Turkey	Sep 1999	Belfast	0–3
Germany	Sep 1999	Dortmund	0–4
Finland	Oct 1999	Helsinki	1–4
Luxembourg (sub)	Feb 2000	Luxembourg	3–1
Malta (sub)	Mar 2000	Valletta	3–0
Hungary	Apr 2000	Belfast	0–1
Yugoslavia	Aug 2000	Belfast	1–2
Norway	Feb 2001	Belfast	0–4
Bulgaria	Jun 2001	Belfast	0–1
Czech Republic	Jun 2001	Teplice	1–3
Denmark	Sep 2001	Copenhagen	1–1

Iceland	Sep 2001	Belfast	3–0
Malta	Oct 2001	Valletta	1–0
Poland	Feb 2002	Limassol	1–4
Liechtenstein	Mar 2002	Vaduz	0–0
Spain	Apr 2002	Belfast	0–5
Cyprus	Aug 2002	Belfast	0–0
Spain	Oct 2002	Albacete	0–3
Ukraine	Oct 2002	Belfast	0–0
Finland	Feb 2003	Belfast	0–1
Armenia	Mar 2003	Erevan	0–1
Greece	Apr 2003	Belfast	0–2
Italy	Jun 2003	Campobasso	0–2
Spain	Jun 2003	Belfast	0–0
Ukraine	Sep 2003	Donetsk	0–0
Armenia	Sep 2003	Belfast	0–1
Greece	Oct 2003	Athens	0–1
Norway	Feb 2004	Belfast	1–4

SCOTLAND

Graham Leggat (11)

Wales	Oct 1958	Cardiff	3–0
Northern Ireland	Nov 1958	Glasgow	2–2
England	Apr 1959	Wembley	0–1
West Germany	May 1959	Glasgow	3–2
Holland	May 1959	Amsterdam	2–1
Northern Ireland	Oct 1959	Belfast	4–0
Wales	Nov 1959	Glasgow	1–1
England	Apr 1960	Glasgow	1–1
Poland	May 1960	Glasgow	2–3
Austria	May 1960	Vienna	1–4
Hungary	Jun 1960	Budapest	3–3

Jimmy Sharp (1)

Wales	Mar 1909	Wrexham	2–3

WALES

Chris Coleman (14+1)

Jamaica	Mar 1998	Cardiff	0–0
Malta	Jun 1998	Valletta	3–0
Tunisia	Jun 1998	Tunis	0–4
Italy	Sep 1998	Liverpool	0–2
Denmark	Oct 1998	Copenhagen	2–1
Belarus	Oct 1998	Cardiff	3–2
Switzerland	Mar 1999	Zurich	0–2
Belarus	Sep 1999	Minsk	2–1
Switzerland	Oct 1999	Wrexham	0–2
Qatar	Feb 2000	Doha	1–0
Finland	Mar 2000	Cardiff	1–2
Belarus	Sep 2000	Minsk	1–2
Norway	Oct 2000	Cardiff	1–1
Poland	Oct 2000	Warsaw	0–0
Germany (sub)	May 2002	Cardiff	1–0

Mark Crossley (1+1)

Scotland	Feb 2004	Cardiff	4–0
Latvia (sub)	Aug 2004	Riga	2–0

Gordon Davies (11+4)

Turkey	Nov 1979	Izmir	0–1
Iceland	Jun 1980	Reykjavik	4–0
Spain (sub)	Mar 1982	Valencia	1–1
France (sub)	Jun 1982	Toulouse	1–0
England	Feb 1983	Wembley	1–2
Bulgaria	Apr 1983	Wrexham	1–0
Scotland	May 1983	Cardiff	0–2
Northern Ireland	May 1983	Belfast	1–0
Brazil	Jun 1983	Cardiff	1–1
Romania (sub)	Oct 1983	Wrexham	5–0
Scotland (sub)	Feb 1984	Glasgow	1–2
England	May 1984	Wrexham	1–0
Northern Ireland	May 1984	Swansea	1–1
Iceland	Sep 1984	Reykjavik	0–1
Iceland	Nov 1984	Cardiff	2–1

Simon Davies

Jeff Hopkins (13+1)

Northern Ireland	May 1983	Belfast	1–0
Brazil	Jun 1983	Cardiff	1–1
Norway	Sep 1983	Oslo	0–0
Romania	Oct 1983	Wrexham	5–0
Bulgaria	Nov 1983	Sofia	0–1
Yugoslavia	Dec 1983	Cardiff	1–1
Scotland	Feb 1984	Glasgow	1–2
England	May 1984	Wrexham	1–0
Northern Ireland	May 1984	Swansea	1–1
Norway	Jun 1984	Trondheim	0–1
Israel	Jun 1984	Tel Aviv	0–0
Iceland	Sep 1984	Reykjavik	0–1
Iceland (sub)	Nov 1984	Cardiff	2–1
Norway	Jun 1985	Bergen	2–4

Cliff Jones (2)

Italy	Oct 1968	Cardiff	0–1
Rest of the UK	Jul 1969	Cardiff	0–1

Andy Melville (27)

Belarus	Sep 1999	Minsk	2–1
Qatar	Feb 2000	Doha	1–0
Finland	Mar 2000	Cardiff	1–2
Brazil	May 2000	Cardiff	0–3
Portugal	Jun 2000	Chaves	0–3
Belarus	Sep 2000	Minsk	1–2
Norway	Oct 2000	Cardiff	1–1
Poland	Oct 2000	Warsaw	0–0
Armenia	Mar 2001	Erevan	2–2
Ukraine	Mar 2001	Cardiff	1–1

Poland	Jun 2001	Cardiff	1–2
Ukraine	Jun 2001	Kiev	1–1
Armenia	Sep 2001	Cardiff	0–0
Belarus	Oct 2001	Cardiff	1–0
Argentina	Feb 2002	Cardiff	1–1
Czech Republic	Mar 2002	Cardiff	0–0
Germany	May 2002	Cardiff	1–0
Croatia	Aug 2002	Varazdin	1–1
Finland	Sep 2002	Helsinki	2–0
Italy	Oct 2003	Cardiff	2–1
Azerbaijan	Nov 2002	Baku	2–0
Bosnia	Feb 2003	Cardiff	2–2
Azerbaijan	Mar 2003	Cardiff	4–0
United States	May 2003	San Jose	0–2
Finland	Sep 2003	Cardiff	1–1
Russia	Nov 2003	Moscow	0–0
Russia	Nov 2003	Cardiff	0–1

Mark Pembridge (5)

Italy	Sep 2003	Milan	0–4
Finland	Sep 2003	Cardiff	1–1
Latvia	Aug 2004	Riga	2–0
Azerbaijan	Sep 2004	Baku	1–1
England	Oct 2004	Old Trafford	0–2

Bill Richards (1)

Northern Ireland	Dec 1932	Wrexham	4–1

Kit Symons (8+1)

Italy	Sep 1998	Liverpool	0–2
Denmark	Oct 1998	Copenhagen	2–1
Belarus	Oct 1998	Cardiff	3–2
Switzerland	Mar 1999	Zurich	0–2
Qatar (sub)	Feb 2000	Doha	1–0
Poland	Jun 2001	Cardiff	1–2
Armenia	Sep 2001	Cardiff	0–0
Norway	Sep 2001	Oslo	2–3
Belarus	Oct 2001	Cardiff	1–0

Sid Thomas (4)

England	Oct 1947	Cardiff	0–3
Scotland	Nov 1947	Glasgow	2–1
Northern Ireland	Mar 1948	Wrexham	2–0
Scotland	Oct 1948	Cardiff	1–3

Paul Trollope (2+1)

Jamaica (sub)	Mar 1998	Cardiff	0–0
Malta	Jun 1998	Valletta	3–0
Tunisia	Jun 1998	Tunis	0–4

REPUBLIC OF IRELAND

Jimmy Conway (17+1)

Spain	Oct 1966	Dublin	0–0
Turkey	Nov 1966	Dublin	2–1
Spain	Dec 1966	Valencia	0–2
Czechoslovakia	Nov 1967	Prague	2–1
Austria (sub)	Nov 1968	Dublin	2–2
Hungary	Jun 1969	Dublin	1–2
Scotland	Sep 1969	Dublin	1–1
Czechoslovakia	Oct 1969	Prague	0–3
Denmark	Oct 1969	Dublin	1–1
Hungary	Nov 1969	Budapest	0–4
Poland	May 1970	Dublin	1–2
West Germany	May 1970	Berlin	1–2
Italy	May 1971	Dublin	1–2
Austria	May 1971	Dublin	1–4
Uruguay	May 1974	Montevideo	0–2
Chile	May 1974	Santiago	2–1
Norway	Mar 1976	Dublin	3–0
Poland	May 1976	Poznan	2–0

John Dempsey (7)

Spain	Dec 1966	Valencia	0–2
Czechoslovakia	May 1967	Dublin	0–2
Czechoslovakia	Nov 1967	Prague	2–1
Poland	May 1968	Dublin	2–2
Poland	Oct 1968	Kotowice	0–1
Austria	Nov 1968	Dublin	2–2
Denmark*	Dec 1968	Dublin	1–1

* Abandoned after 51 minutes

Jimmy Dunne (1)

Austria	May 1971	Dublin	1–4

Steve Finnan (14+7)

Greece	Apr 2000	Dublin	0–1
Scotland	May 2000	Dublin	1–2
Portugal (sub)	Oct 2000	Lisbon	1–1
Estonia (sub)	Oct 2000	Dublin	2–0
Finland	Nov 2000	Dublin	3–0
Andorra (sub)	Mar 2001	Barcelona	3–0
Croatia (sub)	Aug 2001	Dublin	2–2
Holland (sub)	Sep 2001	Dublin	1–0
Cyprus	Oct 2001	Dublin	4–0
Iran	Nov 2001	Dublin	2–0
Iran	Nov 2001	Tehran	0–1
Russia	Feb 2002	Dublin	2–0
United States	Apr 2002	Dublin	2–1
Nigeria	May 2002	Dublin	1–2
Cameroon (sub)	June 2002	Niigata	1–1
Germany	June 2002	Ibaraka	1–1
Saudi Arabia	Jun 2002	Yokohama	3–0
Spain	Jun 2002	Suwon	1–1

Russia	Sep 2002	Moscow	2–4
Greece	Nov 2002	Athens	0–0
Norway (sub)	Apr 2003	Dublin	1–0

Robin Lawler (8)

Austria	Mar 1953	Dublin	4–0
Luxembourg	Oct 1953	Dublin	4–0
France	Nov 1953	Paris	0–1
Norway	Nov 1954	Dublin	2–1
Holland	May 1955	Dublin	1–0
Norway	May 1955	Oslo	3–1
West Germany	May 1955	Hamburg	1–2
Yugoslavia	Oct 1955	Dublin	1–4

Turlough O'Connor (1)

Czechoslovakia	Nov 1967	Prague	2–1

Sean O'Driscoll (2+1)

Chile	May 1982	Santiago	0–1
Brazil	May 1982	Uberlandia	0–7
Trinidad (sub)	May 1982	Port of Spain	1–2

Gerry Peyton (20+1)

Spain (sub)	Feb 1977	Dublin	0–1
Bulgaria	Oct 1977	Dublin	0–0
Turkey	Apr 1978	Dublin	4–2
Poland	Apr 1978	Lodz	0–3
Denmark	May 1979	Dublin	2–0
Bulgaria	May 1979	Sofia	0–1
West Germany	May 1979	Dublin	1–3
Argentina	May 1979	Dublin	0–0
Wales	Sep 1979	Swansea	1–2
Bulgaria	Oct 1979	Dublin	3–0
England	Feb 1980	Wembley	0–2
Cyprus	Mar 1980	Nicosia	3–2
Switzerland	Apr 1980	Dublin	2–0
Argentina	May 1980	Dublin	0–1
Cyprus	Nov 1980	Dublin	6–0
Belgium	Mar 1981	Brussels	0–1
Czechosolvakia	Apr 1981	Dublin	3–1
Holland	Sep 1981	Rotterdam	2–2
France	Oct 1981	Dublin	3–2
Trinidad	May 1982	Port of Spain	1–2
Wales	Mar 1986	Dublin	0–1

TERRY PHELAN (3+1)

Scotland (sub)	May 2000	Dublin	1–2
Mexico	Jun 2000	Chicago	2–2
United States	Jun 2000	Boston	1–1
South Africa	Jun 2000	New Jersey	2–1

Wartime Internationals

ENGLAND

Joe Bacuzzi (13)

Wales	Nov 1939	Cardiff	1–1
Wales	Apr 1940	Wembley	0–1
Scotland	Feb 1941	Newcastle	2–3
Wales	Apr 1941	Nottingham	4–1
Scotland	May 1941	Glasgow	3–1
Wales	June 1941	Cardiff	3–2
Scotland	Oct 1941	Wembley	2–0
Wales	Oct 1941	Birmingham	2–1
Scotland	Jan 1942	Wembley	3–0
Scotland	Apr 1942	Glasgow	4–5
Scotland	Oct 1942	Wembley	0–0
Wales	Feb 1943	Wembley	5–3
France	May 1946	Paris	1–2

Ronnie Rooke (1)

Wales	Oct 1942	Molineux	1–2

WALES

Eddie Perry (1)

England	Apr 1941	Nottingham	4–1

Viv Woodward (1)

England	June 1941	Cardiff	2–3

Football League

Joe Bacuzzi (1)

Scottish League	Oct 1941	Blackpool	3–2

Allan Clarke

Scottish League	Mar 1967	Glasgow	3–0
Belgian League	Sep 1967	Brussels	2–2

George Cohen

Scottish League	Mar 1964	Sunderland	2–2
Italian League	May 1964	Milan	0–1
League of Ireland	Oct 1965	Hull	5–0
Irish League	Sep 1966	Plymouth	12–0

Andy Ducat

The Army	Nov 1921	Leyton	4–1

Johnny Haynes (13)

Scottish League	Apr 1954	Chelsea	4–0
League of Ireland	Sept 1954	Dublin	6–0

Scottish League	Oct 1955	Sheffield	4–2
League of Ireland	Dec 1955	Liverpool	5–1
Irish League	Apr 1956	Belfast	2–5
Irish League	Oct 1956	Newcastle	3–2
Irish League	Oct 1956	Belfast	4–2
Irish League	Liverpool	Liverpool	5–2
League of Ireland	Dublin	Dublin	0–0
Italian League	Milan	Milan	2–4
League of Ireland	Bristol	Bristol	5–2
Italian League	Manchester	Manchester	0–2
Scottish League	Villa Park	Villa Park	3–4

Beddy Jezzard (3)

League of Ireland	May 1953	Dublin	2–0
Danish Combination	May 1953	Copenhagen	4–0
Scottish League	Apr 1954	Chelsea	4–0

Len Oliver (1)

The Army	Oct 1926	Millwall	4–1

Frank Penn (1)

The Army	Oct 1926	Millwall	4–1

Arthur Reynolds (1)

Southern League	Oct 1914	Highbury	2–1

Jim Taylor (1)

Scottish League	Mar 1948	Newcastle	1–1
Scottish League	Nov 1950	Glasgow	0–1
League of Ireland	Apr 1951	Dublin	1–0

Player Records

		Position	Fulham	Appearances			TOTAL	Goals			TOTAL
			Career	League	FA Cup	FL Cup	APPS	League	FA Cup	FL Cup	GOALS
ABEL	Sam	Centre-forward	1933–34	9	-	-	9	1	-	-	1
ACHAMPONG	Kenny	Forward	1984–89	68+13	1+1	8+1	77+15	15	-	1	16
ADAMS	Micky	Full-back	1994–97	25+4	2	4	31+4	8	4	-	12
AIMER	George	Full-back	1923–25	16	1	-	17	-	-	-	-
ALBERT	Philippe	Central-defender	1998–99	12+1	-	-	12+1	2	-	-	2
ALLEN	Albert	Outside-left	1934–37	11	-	-	11	-	-	-	-
ALLEN	Ralph	Inside-forward	1928–31	16	-	-	16	8	-	-	8
ANDERSON	Edward	Outside-left	1903–04	6	-	-	6	-	-	-	-
ANGUS	Terry	Central-defender	1993–97	107+15	6	7+2	120+17	5	1	-	6
ANGUS	William	Inside-left	1899–1900	1	-	-	1	-	-	-	-
ARCHER	Samson	Goalkeeper	1905–10	1	-	-	1	-	-	-	-
ARCHIBALD	Steve	Striker	1992–93	2	-	-	2	-	-	-	-
ARENDSE	Andre	Goalkeeper	1997–99	6	1	2	9	-	-	-	-
ARNOLD	John	Outside-left	1933–39	202	11	-	213	57	5	-	62
ARNOTT	Andy	Central-defender	1997–98	0+1	-	-	0+1	-	-	-	-
AVEY	Fred	Centre-forward	1928–32	62	6	-	68	28	1	-	29
AXCELL	Charlie	Utility player	1904–05	17	1	-	18	4	-	-	4
AYRES	Harry	Centre-forward	1946–50	38	5	-	43	8	3	-	11
BAAH	Peter	Midfield	1992–94	38+11	-	2+2	40+13	4	-	-	4
BACUZZI	Joe	Full-back	1936–56	283	16	-	299	2	-	-	2
BAGGE	Harry	Wing-half	1919–26	179	12	-	191	1	-	-	1
BAILEY	Danny	Midfield	1992–93	2+1	-	-	2+1	-	-	-	-
BAILLIE	James	Wing-half	1930–31	2	-	-	2	-	-	-	-
BAKER	Graham	Midfield	1990–92	8+2	-	2+1	10+3	1	-	-	1
BALL	Kevin	Midfield	1999–2000	15+3	2	-	17+3	-	-	-	-
BANKS	Billy	Inside-forward	1919–21	40	3	-	43	12	-	-	12
BANTON	Geoff	Centre-half	1978–82	37+1	6	2	45+1	3	-	-	3
BARBER	Phil	Midfield	1995–96	13	-	-	13	-	-	-	-
BARKUS	Lea	Midfield	1995–97	3+6	2+1	1+1	6+8	1	-	1	2
BARNETT	Gary	Midfield	1984–90	167+15	9+1	17	193+16	31	1	3	35
BARRETT	Albert	Right-half	1925–37	389	30	-	419	15	5	-	20
BARRETT	Les	Outside-left	1965–77	420+3	31+1	36	487+4	75	3	12	90
BARTLEY	Carl	Forward	1994–96	1	-	1	2	-	-	-	-
BARTON	Tony	Outside-right	1954–59	49	-	-	49	8	-	-	8
BATISTA	Ricardo	Goalkeeper	2005–07	-	-	1	1	-	-	-	1
BATTY	Laurence	Goalkeeper	1984–91	9	1	2	12	-	-	-	-
BEARDSLEY	Peter	Striker	1997–99	20+2	-	4+1	24+3	5	-	1	6
BEASLEY	Pat	Left-half	1945–50	152	11	-	163	13	-	-	13

		Position	Fulham Career	Appearances League	FA Cup	FL Cup	TOTAL APPS	Goals League	FA Cup	FL Cup	TOTAL GOALS
BECK	John	Midfield	1978–83	113+1	6	6	125+1	12	-	1	13
BEDROSSIAN	Ara	Midfield	1993–95	34+8	1	0+1	35+9	1	-	-	1
BEECHAM	Ernie	Goalkeeper	1925–32	174	13	-	187	-	-	-	-
BELFITT	Rod	Centre-forward	1974–75	6	-	-	6	1	-	-	1
BELL	Mark	Outside-right	1904–07	58	3	-	61	6	-	-	6
BELLAMY	James	Outside-right	1914–19	17	-	-	17	1	-	-	1
BENTLEY	Roy	Forward/half-back	1956–61	142	15	1	158	23	2	-	25
BERRY	Arthur	Outside-right	1909–10	12	-	-	12	-	-	-	-
BERTRAM	George	Inside-forward	1919–21	15	-	-	15	2	-	-	2
BEST	George	Outside-right	1976–78	42	2	3	47	8	-	2	10
BETSY	Kevin	Forward	1998–2002	3+12	0+1	2+1	5+14	1	-	-	1
BEVAN	Fred	Centre-forward	1907–08	5	-	-	5	1	-	-	1
BEWLEY	Dave	Left-half	1945–53	17	1	-	18	1	-	-	1
BIGGAR	Billy	Goalkeeper	1903–04	7	3	-	10	-	-	-	-
BINKS	Syd	Centre-half/forward	1929–30	27	2	-	29	-	-	-	-
BIRCH	Joe	Right-back	1931–38	185	10	-	195	-	-	-	-
BIRD	Sid	Left-back	1927–32	43	3	-	46	-	-	-	-
BLACK	Ian	Goalkeeper	1950–59	263	14	-	277	1	-	-	1
BLAKE	Mark	Central-defender	1994–98	133+8	10	10	153+8	17	2	1	20
BOA MORTE	Luis	Forward	2000–06	169+36	16+2	12+3	197+41	44	2	6	52
BOCANEGRA	Carlos	Defender	2003–07	87+7	11	4+1	102+8	7	-	-	7
BOLAND	Charles	Inside-left	1921–23	2	-	-	2	1	-	-	1
BOLAND	Dicky	Outside-left	1929–31	6	-	-	6	-	-	-	-
BOLT	Danny	Midfield	1994–96	9+4	4+1	-	15+5	2	-	-	2
BONNISSEL	Jerome	Left-back	2003–04	16	-	-	16	-	-	-	-
BOOT	Len	Goalkeeper	1925–26	9	-	-	9	-	-	-	-
BORLAND	Billy	Centre-half	1910–12	3	-	-	3	-	-	-	-
BOWER	Danny	Central-defender	1995–96	4	-	-	4	-	-	-	-
BOWERING	Ernie	Left-half	1912–13	1	-	-	1	-	-	-	-
BOWIE	Jimmy	Inside-forward	1951–52	34	4	-	38	7	-	-	7
BOYD	Gordon	Midfield	1978–79	1+2	-	0+1	1+3	-	-	-	-
BRACEWELL	Paul	Midfield	1997–99	63+1	8	4	75+1	1	-	-	1
BRADLEY	Robert	Full-back	1929–30	6	-	-	6	-	-	-	-
BRADSHAW	Joe	Outside-right	1904–08	7	-	-	7	-	-	-	-
BRADSHAW	Will	Outside-right	1904–05	5	-	-	5	2	-	-	2
BRATHWAITE	Roddy	Forward	1984–88	7+5	-	1	8+5	2	-	-	2
BRAZIER	Matthew	Full-back	1997–99	4+5	2+1	-	6+6	1	-	-	1
BRAZIL	Gary	Centre-forward	1990–96	207+7	9	13+1	229+8	48	1	4	53
BREMNER	Des	Midfield	1989–90	7+9	-	0+2	7+11	-	-	-	-
BRENNAN	Bobby	Inside-forward	1950–53	73	7	-	80	13	-	3	16
BREVETT	Rufus	Full-back	1997–2003	173+2	14	14+2	201+4	1	-	1	2
BRICE	Gordon	Centre-half	1952–56	87	6	-	93	1	-	-	1
BRIDGE	Wayne	Full-back	2005–06	12	-	-	12	-	-	-	-

		Position	Fulham	Appearances			TOTAL	Goals			TOTAL
			Career	League	FA Cup	FL Cup	APPS	League	FA Cup	FL Cup	GOALS
BRIGGS	Matthew	Midfield	2006–07	0+1	-	-	0+1	-	-	-	-
BROOKER	Paul	Midfield	1995–2000	13+43	1+3	1+2	15+48	4	1	1	6
BROOKS	John	Right-back	1924–26	9	-	-	9	-	-	-	-
BROOKS	Len	Goalkeeper	1934–37	2	-	-	2	-	-	-	-
BROWN	Arthur	Inside-forward	1910–12	41	5	-	46	9	3	-	12
BROWN	Bobby	Centre-forward	1960–61	8	-	-	8	4	-	-	4
BROWN	Harry	Inside-forward	1908–10	53	2	-	55	21	-	-	21
BROWN	Michael	Inside-forward	1962–63	4	-	1	5	-	-	1	1
BROWN	Michael	Midfield	2005–07	40+1	3	-	43+1	-	-	-	-
BROWN	Roger	Centre-half	1980–83	141	8	12	161	18	-	1	19
BROWN	Stan	Utility player	1959–72	348+5	15	29	392+5	16	2	1	19
BROWN	Tommy	Right-back	1926–27	11	2	-	13	-	-	-	-
BROWN	Willie	Inside-forward	1929–30	2	-	-	2	-	-	-	-
BROWNE	Corey	Midfield	1991–92	1	-	1	2	-	-	1	1
BUARI	Malik	Midfield	2003–05	1+2	-	2	3+2	-	-	-	-
BUCHANAN	Peter	Outside-right	1946–47	20	1	-	21	1	-	-	1
BUCKLEY	Ambrose	Left-back	1933–39	6	-	-	6	-	-	-	-
BULLARD	Jimmy	Midfield	2006–07	4	-	-	4	2	-	-	2
BULLIVANT	Terry	Midfield	1974–79	94+7	5	9	108+7	2	-	-	2
BURNS	Hugh	Right-back	1989–90	6	-	-	6	-	-	-	-
BURNS	Robert	Forward	1910–11	18	-	-	18	7	-	-	7
BURNS	Tommy	Full-back	1910–13	35	1	-	36	-	-	-	-
BURVILL	Glen	Midfield	1985–86	9	-	-	9	2	-	-	2
BUSBY	Viv	Centre-forward	1973–76	114+4	15	10	139+4	28	7	1	36
BYRNE	David	Winger	1991–92	5	-	-	5	-	-	-	-
BYRNE	Johnny	Forward	1968–69	16+3	-	-	16+3	2	-	-	2
CADAMARTERI	Danny	Striker	1999–2000	3+2	-	-	3+2	1	-	-	1
CAESAR	Bill	Centre-half	1925–26	1	-	-	1	-	-	-	-
CALLAGHAN	Fred	Left-back	1962–74	291+4	14	27	332+4	9	1	2	12
CAMP	Steve	Centre-forward	1975–77	4+1	-	-	4+1	-	-	-	-
CAMPBELL	Johnny	Inside-forward	1949–53	62	6	-	68	4	2	-	6
CANNON	George	Centre-forward	1914–15	6	-	-	6	5	-	-	5
CARLTON	David	Midfield	1970–73	5+4	-	2	7+4	-	-	-	-
CARPENTER	Richard	Midfield	1996–98	49+9	2	4	55+9	7	1	1	9
CARR	Cliff	Left-back	1982–87	136+9	4	13	153+9	14	-	2	16
CARTER	Bob	Inside-forward	1908–09	10	-	-	10	7	-	-	7
CAWLEY	Peter	Centre-half	1988–89	3+2	-	-	3+2	-	-	-	-
CHAMBERLAIN	Tosh	Outside-left	1951–65	187	13	4	204	59	5	-	64
CHAMPION	Percy	Outside-left	1912–14	2	-	-	2	-	-	-	-
CHAPLIN	Alex	Left-back	1919–26	259	17	-	276	1	-	-	1
CHARLTON	Ted	Right-back	1906–20	249	18	-	267	7	-	-	7
CHENHALL	John	Right-back	1953–58	91	4	-	95	-	-	-	-
CHRISTANVAL	Philippe	Central-defender	2005–07	26+9	3	1	30+9	1	-	-	1

		Position	Fulham	Appearances			TOTAL	Goals			TOTAL
			Career	League	FA Cup	FL Cup	APPS	League	FA Cup	FL Cup	GOALS
CLARK	Lee	Midfield	1999–2005	143+8	10+1	16	169+9	20	-	2	22
CLARKE	Allan	Centre-forward	1966–68	85+1	6	8	99+1	45	5	7	57
CLARKE	Bruce	Wing-half	1934–39	112	2	-	114	1	-	-	1
CLEMENT	Dave	Right-back	1980–81	17+1	2	-	19+1	-	-	-	-
CLIFFORD	Robert	Left-back	1911–12	8	-	-	8	-	-	-	-
CLUTTERBUCK	Henry	Goalkeeper	1904–05	3	-	-	3	-	-	-	-
COATES	Walter	Outside-right	1919–20	2	-	-	2	-	-	-	-
COBB	Gary	Midfield	1990–92	8+14	2	0+1	10+15	-	-	-	-
COCK	Donald	Inside-forward	1919–22	87	7	-	94	43	1	-	44
COCKERILL	Glenn	Midfield	1996–97	32+8	1	5+1	38+9	1	-	-	1
COHEN	George	Right-back	1956–69	408	33	18	459	6	-	-	6
COLE	Andrew	Centre-forward	1991–2005	42+2	5	3	50+2	15	-	1	16
COLE	Michael	Forward	1988–91	47+3	-	3	50+3	4	-	-	4
COLEMAN	Chris	Central-defender	1997–2001	138	11	13	162	8	1	2	11
COLEMAN	Tim	Inside-forward	1911–14	94	6	-	100	46	3	-	49
COLLINS	Arthur 'Pat'	Wing-half	1905–14	260	19	-	279	9	2	-	11
COLLINS	John	Midfield	2000–03	54+12	5+1	4	63+13	3	-	1	4
COLLINS	Ken	Full-back	1952–61	32	1	-	33	-	-	-	-
COLLINS	Wayne	Midfield	1998–2001	39+21	6+2	10+1	55+24	4	2	2	8
COLLYMORE	Stan	Striker	1999–2000	3+3	-	1+2	4+5	-	-	1	1
COLVILLE	George	Right-half	1903–04	6	-	-	6	-	-	-	-
CONEY	Dean	Centre-forward	1981–87	209+2	11	24	244	56	6	10	72
CONNOR	Joe	Centre-forward	1903–04	12	8	-	20	1	7	-	8
CONROY	Micky	Centre-forward	1995–98	88+6	5+1	11	104+7	32	3	7	42
CONWAY	Jimmy	Midfield	1966–76	312+4	25	19	356+4	67	3	6	76
CONWAY	John	Midfield	1971–75	30+8	3	4	37+8	6	1	-	7
COOK	Maurice	Centre-forward	1958–65	221	19	8	248	89	6	2	97
COOPER	Mark	Midfield	1992–94	10+4	-	2	12+4	-	-	-	-
COQUET	Ernest	Full-back	1913–20	47	2	-	49	-	-	-	-
CORK	Alan	Centre-forward	1994–95	11+4	4	3	18+4	3	1	-	4
CORNER	Brian	Midfield	1979–81	1+2	-	-	1+2	-	-	-	-
CORNWALL	Luke	Striker	1998–2001	1+3	-	2+1	3+4	1	-	-	1
COTTINGTON	Brian	Right-back	1983–88	67+6	1+2	8+1	76+9	1	-	-	1
COX	George	Centre-forward	1936–37	5	1	-	6	3	-	-	3
COX	Tommy	Centre-half	1929–31	5	-	-	5	1	-	-	1
CRAIG	Teddy	Inside-left	1924–30	151	10	-	161	29	2	-	31
CRANFIELD	Harry	Outside-left	1937–47	1	-	-	1	-	-	-	-
CROAL	Jimmy	Inside-forward	1922–24	36	-	-	36	6	-	-	6
CROCKFORD	Harold	Inside-forward	1917–22	26	-	-	26	9	-	-	9
CRONIN	Tommy	Inside-forward	1950–56	2	-	-	2	-	-	-	-
CROSS	Roger	Centre-forward	1971–72	39+1	3	3	45+1	8	2	-	10
CROSSLEY	Fred	Outside-left	1912–13	1	-	-	1	-	-	-	-
CROSSLEY	Mark	Goalkeeper	2003–07	19	-	4	23	-	-	-	-

		Position	Fulham Career	Appearances League	FA Cup	FL Cup	TOTAL APPS	Goals League	FA Cup	FL Cup	TOTAL GOALS
CROSSTHWAITE	Herbert	Goalkeeper	1907–09	2	-	-	2	-	-	-	-
CULLIP	Danny	Central-defender	1996–98	41+9	2	8	51+9	2	-	-	2
CUNNINGHAM	Hugh	Right-half	1966–68	0+1	-	-	0+1	-	-	-	-
CURTIS	Jock	Outside-right	1913–14	2	-	-	2	-	-	-	-
CUSACK	Nick	Utility player	1994–97	109+7	7+1	6+4	122+12	14	1	1	16
CUTBUSH	John	Right-back	1972–77	131+3	12	14	157+3	3	-	-	3
DALRYMPLE	Robert	Inside-right	1907–11	98	10	-	108	40	4	-	44
DARVILL	Harvey	Inside/outside-left	1921–24	69	6	-	75	10	-	-	10
DAVIDSON	Alex	Centre-forward	1903–04	1	1	-	2	-	-	-	-
DAVIDSON	Roger	Right-half	1970–71	1	-	0+1	1+1	-	-	-	-
DAVIES	Gordon	Forward	1978–91	366+30	24+1	28+1	418+32	159	8	11	178
DAVIES	Simon	Midfield	2006–07	14	1+1	-	15+1	2	-	-	2
DAVIS	Sean	Midfield	1998–2004	114+2	16+2	10+6	140+10	10	3	3	16
DAY	Clive	Midfield	1978–83	2+8	0+1	-	2+9	-	-	-	-
DEAR	Brian	Centre-forward	1968–69	13	-	-	13	7	-	-	7
DEMPSEY	Clint	Midfield	2006–07	1+9	0+2	-	1+11	1	-	-	1
DEMPSEY	John	Centre-half	1964–69	149	8	14	171	4	1	3	8
DENNISON	Bob	Utility player	1935–39	31	3	-	34	-	-	-	-
DEVAN	Charlie	Outside-right	1927–28	7	-	-	7	2	-	-	2
DIAPER	Bert	Wing-half	1933–35	3	-	-	3	-	-	-	-
DIGWEED	Perry	Goalkeeper	1977–81	15	-	-	15	-	-	-	-
DIOP	Papa Boupa	Midfield	2004–07	70+4	4	3+1	77+5	8	1	-	9
DIXON	Will	Outside-left	1909–10	1	-	-	1	-	-	-	-
DJETOU	Martin	Defender/midfield	2002–04	41+10	8	2+1	51+11	1	-	-	1
DODDS	Jock	Centre-forward	1934–36	1	-	-	1	-	-	-	-
DODGIN	Bill	Centre-half	1949–64	104	6	3	113	-	-	-	-
DOHERTY	John	Centre-forward	1954–62	49	2	-	51	7	1	-	8
DONNELLAN	Leo	Midfield	1985–90	54+25	5+1	2+4	61+30	4	-	-	4
DOWDEN	Bill	Centre-forward	1928–31	1	-	-	1	1	-	-	1
DOWIE	Iain	Striker	1989–90	5	-	-	5	1	-	-	1
DOWIE	John	Midfield	1973–77	32+5	8+3	2	42+8	2	1	-	3
DOWSON	Alan	Left-back	1989–90	4	-	-	4	-	-	-	-
DOYLE	Frank	Inside-forward	1923–26	30	1	-	31	9	-	-	9
DRAKE	Bobby	Right-back	1961–68	15	-	-	15	-	-	-	-
DREYER	John	Midfield	1985–86	12	-	-	12	2	-	-	2
DUCAT	Andrew	Right-half	1921–24	64	5	-	69	-	-	-	-
DUDLEY	John	Centre-half	1929–32	14	2	-	16	-	-	-	-
DUNCAN	David	Outside-left	1911–12	8	-	-	8	-	-	-	-
DUNNE	Jimmy	Left-half	1970–76	142+1	8	15	165+1	2	-	-	2
DWIGHT	Roy	Forward	1950–58	72	8	-	80	54	3	-	57
DYER	Reg	Right-back	1925–30	98	5	-	103	-	-	-	-
DYSON	Terry	Outside-left	1965–68	21+2	1	4	26+2	3	-	3	6
EARLE	Steve	Forward	1963–73	285+6	14	22	321+6	98	-	10	108

		Position	Fulham Career	Appearances League	Appearances FA Cup	Appearances FL Cup	TOTAL APPS	Goals League	Goals FA Cup	Goals FL Cup	TOTAL GOALS
EASSON	James	Inside-left	1938–39	3	-	-	3	-	-	-	-
ECKHARDT	Jeff	Utility player	1987–94	247+4	5+1	13	265+5	25	-	-	25
EDELSTON	Joe	Wing-half	1920–25	67	4	-	71	-	-	-	-
EDELSTON	Maurice	Inside-left	1935–37	3	-	-	3	-	-	-	-
EDGLEY	Frank	Centre-forward	1905–06	15	-	-	15	6	-	-	6
EDMONDS	George	Centre-forward	1923–26	66	7	-	73	23	3	-	26
EDWARDS-	Dave	Wing-half	1952–64	38	2	1	41	-	-	-	-
EDWARDS-	Tommy	Outside-left	1946–48	2	1	-	3	-	-	-	-
ELKINS	Gary	Full-back	1983–90	100+4	2+2	6	108+6	2	-	-	2
ELLIOTT	Frank	Goalkeeper	1954–56	25	1	-	26	-	-	-	-
ELLIOTT	Sid	Centre-forward	1927–28	42	1	-	43	26	-	-	26
ELLIOTT	Simon	Midfield	2005–07	12	1	-	13	-	-	-	-
ELRICH	Ahmad	Midfield	2005–07	2+4	1	2	5+4	-	-	-	-
EVANS	Jim	Right-half	1937–46	71	3	-	74	5	-	-	5
EVANS	Ossie	Goalkeeper	1946–47	1	-	-	1	-	-	-	-
EVANS	Ray	Right-back	1977–79	86	3	-	89	6	-	-	6
EVANSON	John	Midfield	1976–79	84+11	3	9	96+11	5	-	-	5
FABIAN	Howard	Outside-right	1934–35	3	-	-	3	-	-	-	-
FARNFIELD	Gilbert	Outside-left	1903–04	1	-	-	1	-	-	-	-
FARNFIELD	Herbert	Inside-left	1903–04	1	-	-	1	-	-	-	-
FARNFIELD	Percy	Centre-half	1903–04	1	-	-	1	-	-	-	-
FARRELL	Sean	Striker	1991–94	93+1	2	5+1	100+2	31	1	3	35
FERGUSON	Robert	Outside-left	1924–28	22	2	-	24	5	-	-	5
FERNANDES	Fabrice	Midfield	2000–01	23+6	1	4+2	28+8	2	1	1	4
FERNEY	Martin	Midfield	1990–95	49+11	1+1	6	56+12	1	-	-	1
FINCH	Jack	Forward	1930–39	280	15	-	295	50	1	-	51
FINCH	John	Central-defender	1990–92	6+1	-	-	6+1	-	-	-	-
FINNAN	Steve	Right-back	1998–2003	171+1	18	11+1	200+2	6	1	-	7
FINNIGAN	Tony	Defender	1994–96	8+5	2	-	10+5	-	-	-	-
FISHENDEN	Paul	Striker	1985–86	3	-	-	3	-	-	-	-
FISHER	Albert	Inside-left	1903–04	1	4	-	5	-	2	-	2
FISHER	George	Right-back	1954–55	8	-	-	8	-	-	-	-
FITCHETT	Jack	Right-half	1905–06	2	1	-	3	-	-	-	-
FITCHIE	Tom	Insie-forward	1912–13	8	-	-	8	2	-	-	2
FLACK	Doug	Goalkeeper	1938–53	54	1	-	55	-	-	-	-
FLANAGAN	Jack	Inside-forward	1909–10	11	1	-	12	1	-	-	1
FLEMING	Tom	Right-back	1922–25	111	3	-	114	-	-	-	-
FLETCHER	Harry	Inside-right	1903–04	40	7	-	47	14	5	-	19
FOLEY	Steve	Midfield	1983–84	2+1	-	-	2+1	-	-	-	-
FONTAINE	Liam	Central-defender	2004–05	0+1	1	-	1+1	-	-	-	-
FORBES	Alex	Wing-half	1957–58	4	-	-	4	-	-	-	-
FORREST	Sam	Centre-half	1912–15	8	-	-	8	-	-	-	-
FRASER	Alex	Inside-left	1904–08	79	12	-	91	24	4	-	28

		Position	Fulham	Appearances			TOTAL	Goals			TOTAL
			Career	League	FA Cup	FL Cup	APPS	League	FA Cup	FL Cup	GOALS
FRASER	John	Full-back	1971–76	55+1	8	2	65+1	1	-	-	1
FREEMAN	Darren	Forward	1996–98	32+14	-	2	34+14	9	-	-	9
FREEMAN	Harry	Right-back	1937–52	179	11	-	190	7	1	-	8
FREEMAN	Walter	Inside-forward	1906–09	57	6	-	63	22	3	-	25
FRIEND	Barry	Inside-forward	1973–76	2+1	-	-	2+1	-	-	-	-
FRYER	Jack	Goalkeeper	1903–11	142	26	-	168	-	-	-	-
GAGE	Larry	Goalkeeper	1948–50	3	-	-	3	-	-	-	-
GALE	Tony	Central-defender	1977–84	277	17	24	318	19	-	2	21
GARNISH	Tom	Outside-right	1925–26	1	-	-	1	-	-	-	-
GARVEY	William	Left-half	1913–14	2	-	-	2	-	-	-	-
GAVIGAN	Peter	Outside-right	1920–25	72	6	-	78	1	-	-	1
GAYLE	Howard	Outside-right	1979–80	14	-	-	14	-	-	-	-
GEORGIOU	George	Forward	1991–92	1+3	-	1	2+3	-	-	-	-
GIBBON	Sonny	Right-back	1929–34	114	13	-	127	1	-	-	1
GIBBONS	Syd	Centre-half	1930–38	299	19	-	318	13	2	-	15
GIBSON	Henry	Centre-half	1952–55	1	-	-	1	-	-	-	-
GILCHRIST	John	Right-back	1969–70	20+3	1	3	24+3	1	-	-	1
GILROY	Joe	Inside-forward	1967–68	23+1	2	2	27+1	8	1	2	11
GOLDBAEK	Bjarnie	Midfield	1999–2003	73+12	4+3	6	83+15	6	-	-	6
GOLDIE	Jock	Left-half	1908–11	31	2	-	33	-	-	-	-
GOLDIE	Willie	Left-half	1904–08	156	22	-	178	5	-	-	5
GOMA	Alain	Central-defender	2000–06	115+2	11+2	9	135+5	-	-	-	-
GOODLASS	Ronnie	Outside-left	1980–82	21+1	5	-	26+1	2	-	-	2
GORDON	Colin	Forward	1988–89	12+5	1	-	13+5	2	-	-	2
GORE	Shaun	Central-defender	1986–91	25+1	1+1	2+1	28+3	-	-	-	-
GOUGH	Alan	Goalkeeper	1992–93	3	-	-	3	-	-	-	-
GRAHAM	Bob	Inside-right	1904–05	24	8	-	32	-	1	-	1
GRANT	Cyril	Utility player	1946–48	14	1	-	15	4	-	-	4
GRAY	Archie	Full-back	1912–15	24	1	-	25	-	-	-	-
GRAY	Martin	Midfield	1995–96	6	-	-	6	-	-	-	-
GRAY	Peter	Centre-half	1903–05	43	9	-	52	1	-	-	1
GRAY	Phillip	Striker	1990–91	3	-	-	3	-	-	-	-
GREAVES	Steve	Right-back	1988–90	0+1	-	-	0+1	-	-	-	-
GREEN	Ellis	Centre-half	1903–04	9	4	-	13	-	1	-	1
GREEN	Adam	Full-back	2003–06	8	2	3	13	-	-	-	-
GREENAWAY	Brian	Midfield	1975–92	68+17	7+1	2	77+18	8	1	-	9
GREENWOOD	Ron	Centre-half	1955–56	42	-	-	42	-	-	-	-
GREGORY	Bob	Left-back	1925–28	37	1	-	38	-	-	-	-
GREGORY	John	Goalkeeper	1994–95	0+1	-	-	0+1	-	-	-	-
GREW	Mark	Goalkeeper	1985–86	4	-	-	4	-	-	-	-
GRIFFITHS	Lew	Centre-forward	1930–31	2	-	-	2	-	-	-	-
GUTHRIE	Chris	Centre-forward	1978–80	49+1	3	2	54+1	15	-	-	15
HAAG	Kelly	Forward	1990–93	35+32	2	1+1	38+33	9	-	-	9

		Position	Fulham	Appearances			TOTAL	Goals			TOTAL
			Career	League	FA Cup	FL Cup	APPS	League	FA Cup	FL Cup	GOALS
HADDLETON	Arthur	Centre-forward	1932–33	4	-	-	4	4	-	-	4
HAHNEMANN	Marcus	Goalkeeper	2000–01	2	-	2	4	-	-	-	-
HAILS	Julian	Midfield	1990–94	99+10	2	5+1	106+11	12	-	-	12
HALEY	Bill	Inside-forward	1928–31	93	8	-	101	50	4	-	54
HALL	Jack	Inside-left	1920–21	9	2	-	11	3	-	-	3
HALL	Joe	Inside-left	1951–56	1	-	-	1	-	-	-	-
HALL	William	Right-half	1917–20	1	-	-	1	-	-	-	-
HALOM	Vic	Forward	1968–71	66+6	2	8	76+6	22	-	3	25
HAMILL	Rory	Forward	1994–96	24+24	2+4	2	28+28	7	3	-	10
HAMILTON	Jock	Centre-half	1903–04	12	1	-	13	-	-	-	-
HAMILTON	Bobby	Centre-forward	1906–07	29	4	-	33	11	-	-	11
HAMMOND	Elvis	Striker	2000–05	3+8	-	0+2	3+10	-	-	-	-
HAMMOND	Jim	Inside-left	1928–39	316	26	-	342	142	9	-	151
HAMSHIER	John	Right-back	1996–97	0+3	-	-	0+3	-	-	-	-
HARLEY	John	Full-back	2001–04	19+6	4+1	2	25+7	1	-	-	1
HARRIS	George	Left-back	1926–28	8	-	-	8	1	-	-	1
HARRIS	Jack	Outside-right	1925–28	42	5	-	47	3	-	-	3
HARRISON	Fred	Centre-forward	1907–11	120	12	-	132	47	7	-	54
HARRISON	Lee	Goalkeeper	1993–96	11+1	1	-	12+1	-	-	-	-
HARTFIELD	Charlie	Midfield	1996–97	1+1	-	-	1+1	-	-	-	-
HARWOOD	Alf	Centre-forward	1903–06	14	4	-	18	2	-	-	2
HATTER	Steve	Centre-half	1976–83	25+1	5	0+1	30+2	1	-	-	1
HAWORTH	Robert	Right-half	1904–06	33	9	-	42	-	-	-	-
HAWORTH	Robert J.	Forward	1994–95	7+14	1+1	3+1	11+16	1	-	2	3
HAYLES	Barry	Forward	1998–2004	116+59	12+7	10+2	138+68	44	6	5	55
HAYNES	Johnny	Inside-left	1952–70	594	44	20	658	147	9	2	158
HAYWARD	Steve	Midfield	1997–2001	109+7	9+2	16+3	134+12	7	3	1	11
HEALEY	Bill	Right-back	1952–55	1	-	-	1	-	-	-	-
HEARD	Les	Inside-right	1923–25	19	-	-	19	3	-	-	3
HEBDEN	Jack	Right-back	1927–29	23	1	-	24	-	-	-	-
HEGAZI	Hassan	Inside-forward	1911–12	1	-	-	1	1	-	-	1
HELGUSON	Heidar	Striker	2005–07	31+26	3	3	37+26	13	-	3	16
HENDERSON	Jackie	Forward	1962–62	45	8	2	55	7	1	1	9
HENDERSON	Sam	Left-half	1929–30	18	5	-	23	-	-	-	-
HERRERA	Martin	Goalkeeper	2002–03	1+1	-	-	1+1	-	-	-	-
HERRERA	Robbie	Left-back	1993–98	143+2	13	15	171+2	1	-	-	1
HESFORD	Iain	Goalkeeper	1984–85	3	-	-	3	-	-	-	-
HEWKINS	Ken	Goalkeeper	1955–62	38	2	1	41	-	-	-	-
HICKIE	Bill	Left-back	1931–32	9	-	-	9	-	-	-	-
HICKS	Jim	Centre-half	1985–88	39+1	1	2	42+1	1	-	-	1
HIGGINS	Dennis	Outside-right	1935–39	30	2	-	32	12	-	-	12
HILES	Ernie	Centre-half	1934–48	49	-	-	49	-	-	-	-
HILL	Jimmy	Inside-right	1952–61	276	21	-	297	41	11	-	52

		Position	Fulham	Appearances			TOTAL	Goals			TOTAL
			Career	League	FA Cup	FL Cup	APPS	League	FA Cup	FL Cup	GOALS
HIND	Billy	Right-half	1907–08	3	-	-	3	-	-	-	-
HINDMARSH	James	Inside-left	1906–07	1	-	-	1	-	-	-	-
HINDSON	Jimmy	Right-back	1930–38	104	9	-	113	-	-	-	-
HINSHELWOOD	Wally	Outside-right	1946–52	19	-	-	19	1	-	-	1
HINTON	Ted	Goalkeeper	1946–49	82	4	-	86	-	-	-	-
HOARE	Gordon	Inside-left	1919–20	2	1	-	3	-	1	-	1
HODDY	Kevin	Midfield	1986–89	13+9	4	2+1	19+10	1	-	-	1
HOGAN	Cornelius	Inside-forward	1903–04	2	-	-	2	1	-	-	1
HOGAN	Jimmy	Outside-right	1905–08	18	1	-	19	5	-	-	5
HOLMES	Tom	Outside-left	1904–07	1	-	-	1	1	-	-	1
HOPKINS	Jeff	Defender	1981–88	213+6	12	26	251+6	4	-	2	6
HORLER	George	Left-back	1927–28	8	1	-	9	-	-	-	-
HORNE	Stan	Right-half	1969–73	73+6	2	5+1	80+7	-	-	-	-
HORNE	Will	Goalkeeper	1906–07	3	-	-	3	-	-	-	-
HORSFIELD	Geoff	Striker	1998–2000	54+5	8+1	6	68+6	22	3	6	31
HORTON	George	Centre-forward	1910–11	1	-	-	1	-	-	-	-
HOUGHTON	Jack	Left-back	1913–21	63	1	-	64	-	-	-	-
HOUGHTON	John	Centre-half	1919–20	2	-	-	2	-	-	-	-
HOUGHTON	Ray	Midfield	1982–85	129	4	12	145	16	3	2	21
HOWE	Ernie	Central-defender	1973–77	68+2	3	9+2	80+4	10	1	1	12
HOWFIELD	Bobby	Outside-left	1963–65	26	1	3	30	9	-	1	10
HOYLAND	Walter	Inside-forward	1927–28	22	1	-	23	4	-	-	4
HUBBARD	Archie	Inside-forward	1907–08	5	-	-	5	1	-	-	1
HUDSON	Albert	Inside-right	1937–47	1	-	-	1	-	-	-	-
HUDSON	Mark	Defender	2001–03	-	-	2+1	2+1	-	-	-	-
HUGHES	Jimmy	Right-half	1946–49	1	-	-	1	-	-	-	-
HUGHES	Stephen	Midfield	1999–2000	3	-	1	4	-	-	-	
HUNT	Fergus	Inside-right	1903–05	21	2	-	23	3	-	-	3
HURLOCK	Terry	Midfield	1994–96	27	2	1+1	30+1	1	-	-	1
ICETON	Jake	Goalkeeper	1930–35	90	9	-	99	-	-	-	-
INAMOTO	Junichi	Midfield	2002–04	24+17	3+1	3	30+18	4	1	-	5
JAMES	Tyrone	Right-back	1974–78	18+2	0+1	-	18+3	-	-	-	-
JENSEN	Claus	Midfield	2004–07	31+4	1+2	2	34+6	4	1	-	5
JENSEN	Niclas	Full-back	2005–07	14+2	-	1+1	15+3	-	-	-	-
JEZZARD	Bedford	Centre-forward	1948–56	292	14	-	306	154	-	-	154
JINKS	Jimmy	Centre-forward	1948–50	11	-	-	11	3	-	-	3
JOHN	Collins	Striker	2003–07	41+52	2+5	1+4	44+61	20	3	-	23
JOHNSON	Mike	Outside-left	1958–62	23	4	-	27	6	1	-	7
JOHNSON	Reg	Right-half	1926–29	4	-	-	4	1	-	-	1
JOHNSTON	Bert	Outside-right	1935–36	4	-	-	4	1	-	-	1
JOHNSTON	George	Forward	1970–72	33+6	1+1	0+1	34+8	12	1	-	13
JONES	Allan	Centre-forward	1958–61	7	-	-	7	3	-	-	3
JONES	Cliff	Outside-left	1968–70	23+2	-	1	24+2	2	-	-	2

		Position	Fulham	Appearances			TOTAL	Goals			TOTAL
			Career	League	FA Cup	FL Cup	APPS	League	FA Cup	FL Cup	GOALS
JONES	John	Inside-left	1947–50	1	1	-	2	-	-	-	-
JONES	Mike	Right-back	1963–64	-	-	1	1	-	-	-	-
JOSEPH	Francis	Forward	1990–91	2+2	-	2	4+2	-	-	1	1
JOY	Bernard	Centre-half	1931–35	1	-	-	1	-	-	-	-
JUMP	Stewart	Left-back	1976–77	3	-	-	3	-	-	-	-
JUPP	Duncan	Right-back	1993–96	101+4	9+1	10+2	120+7	2	1	-	3
KEEBLE	Albert	Centre-forward	1929–30	1	-	-	1	-	-	-	-
KEEN	Walter	Right-half	1930–32	-	1	-	1	-	-	-	-
KEEPING	Mike	Left-back	1933–39	205	12	-	217	7	-	-	7
KEETCH	Bobby	Centre-half	1959–66	106	4	10	120	2	-	-	2
KELLER	Francois	Midfield	1998–99	0+1	-	-	0+1	-	-	-	-
KELLY	Hugh	Goalkeeper	1949–50	25	2	-	27	-	-	-	-
KELLY	Mark	Midfield	1990–93	55+9	2	3+1	60+10	2	-	-	2
KELLY	Paul	Midfield	1992–94	4+2	-	1	5+2	-	-	-	-
KELLY	Tim	Inside-right	1930–32	1	-	-	1	-	-	-	-
KENNEDY	Sam	Centre-half	1924–26	6	-	-	6	1	-	-	1
KERRIGAN	Don	Inside-forward	1968–69	4+2	-	1	5+2	1	-	-	1
KERRINS	Wayne	Left-back	1983–89	51+15	4	5+1	60+16	1	-	-	1
KERSLAKE	Micky	Left-back	1975–78	1+2	-	-	1+2	-	-	-	-
KEY	Johnny	Outside-right	1956–66	163	8	10	181	29	3	5	37
KIMBLE	Garry	Left-back	1989–90	1+2	-	1+1	2+3	-	-	-	-
KINGABY	Bert	Outside-right	1906–07	33	4	-	37	3	-	-	3
KINGSLEY	Alf	Outside-right	1922–23	29	2	-	31	2	-	-	2
KIRBY	Conyers	Outside-right	1905–06	4	-	-	4	-	-	-	-
KIRKWOOD	Joe	Right-back	1910–11	1	-	-	1	-	-	-	-
KITCHEN	Peter	Forward	1979–80	21+3	-	-	21+3	6	-	-	6
KNIGHT	Zat	Central-defender	2000–07	137+10	15+2	9	161+12	3	1	-	4
LACY	John	Centre-half	1971–78	164+4	16	8	188	7	-	1	8
LAFFERTY	Hugh	Left-half	1923–25	4	-	-	4	-	-	-	-
LAMBERT	Jack	Centre-forward	1933–35	34	2	-	36	4	1	-	5
LAMPE	Derek	Centre-half	1954–64	88	7	1	96	-	-	-	-
LANGE	Tony	Goalkeeper	1995–97	59	5	5	70	-	-	-	-
LANGLEY	Jim	Left-back	1957–65	323	23	10	356	31	2	-	33
LANGLEY	Richard	Right-back	1986–91	43+7	2	4+1	49+8	-	-	-	-
LARGE	Frank	Centre-forward	1968–69	20+4	2	2	24+4	3	-	-	3
LASTUVKA	Jan	Goalkeeper	2006–07	7+1	3	1	11+1	-	-	-	-
LAWLER	Robin	Left-back/half	1949–62	281	18	-	299	-	-	-	-
LAWRENCE	Everard	Outside-left	1903–04	18	7	-	25	2	1	-	3
LAWRENCE	Matt	Right-back	1997–98	59+2	2	4+1	65+3	-	-	-	-
LAWS	Tommy	Left-back	1913–14	6	-	-	6	-	-	-	-
LAWSON	Tommy	Wing-half	1927–31	30	3	-	33	2	-	-	2
LEACOCK	Dean	Full-back	2002–06	8+1	-	4	12+1	-	-	-	-
LEE	Harry	Forward	1907–15	65	-	-	65	31	-	-	31

		Position	Fulham	Appearances			TOTAL	Goals			TOTAL
			Career	League	FA Cup	FL Cup	APPS	League	FA Cup	FL Cup	GOALS
LEE	Trevor	Forward	1984–85	1	-	-	1	-	-	-	-
LEGGAT	Graham	Forward	1958–67	251+3	18	8	277+3	127	5	2	134
LEGWINSKI	Sylvain	Midfield	2001–06	116+12	18	4+2	138+14	8	1	1	10
LEHMANN	Dirk	Striker	1998–99	16+10	2+2	5	23+12	2	1	2	5
LEIGH	Tommy	Full-back	1907–10	6	-	-	6	-	-	-	-
LENNIE	William	Outside-left	1904–05	17	9	-	26	3	1	-	4
LEWIN	Ron	Full-back	1946–50	41	1	-	42	-	-	-	-
LEWINGTON	Ray	Midfield	1980–90	230+4	14+1	27	271+5	21	1	2	24
LEWIS	Eddie	Midfield	1999–2002	8+8	-	6	14+8	-	-	1	1
LEWIS	Junior	Midfield	1992–93	4+2	1	-	5+2	-	-	-	-
LIGHTBOURNE	Carl	Striker	1997–98	4	-	-	4	2	-	-	2
LILLEY	Tom	Right-back	1930–31	7	1	-	8	-	-	-	-
LINDSAY	Archie	Left-back	1907–11	80	6	-	86	1	-	-	1
LINFOOT	Fred	Outside-left	1924–26	40	-	-	40	4	-	-	4
LIPSHAM	Bert	Outside-left	1908–10	56	3	-	59	5	-	-	5
LITTLEWORT	Harry	Centre-half	1909–10	4	-	-	4	-	-	-	-
LLOYD	Barry	Midfield	1969–76	249+8	8+2	21+2	278+12	29	-	1	30
LLOYD	Cliff	Left-back	1945–49	2	2	-	4	-	-	-	-
LLOYD	David	Inside-right	1899–1904	-	3	-	3	-	2	-	2
LOCK	Kevin	Defender	1978–85	210+1	10+1	13+1	233+3	27	-	2	29
LONDON	George	Right-back	1923–25	7	-	-	7	-	-	-	-
LOVELL	Mark	Midfield	1978–80	4+2	-	-	4+2	-	-	-	-
LOWE	Eddie	Defender	1950–63	473	33	5	511	8	2	-	10
LOWE	Harry	Centre-half	1927–30	3	-	-	3	-	-	-	-
LOWE	Reg	Left-back	1950–53	66	6	-	72	-	-	-	-
MCANESPIE	Steve	Right-back	1997–2000	3+4	1	1+1	5+5	-	-	-	-
MCAREE	Rod	Midfield	1995–98	22+6	-	2+2	24+8	3	-	-	3
MACAULAY	Archie	Right-half/inside-right	1950–53	49	4	-	53	4	-	-	4
MCBRIDE	Brian	Striker	2003–07	88+35	7+2	2+3	97+40	28	4	4	38
MCCLELLAND	Jack	Goalkeeper	1964–69	51	2	4	57	-	-	-	-
MCCORMICK	Jimmy	Inside-right	1945–47	9	1	-	10	2	-	-	2
MCCOURT	John	Inside-forward	1907–09	2	-	-	2	-	-	-	-
MCCREE	Jimmy	Outside-right	1925–26	2	-	-	2	-	-	-	-
MCCURDY	Colin	Centre-forward	1977–78	1	-	-	1	-	-	-	-
MCDERMOTT	Brian	Midfield	1982–83	0+3	-	-	0+3	-	-	-	-
MCDONALD	Billy	Outside-right	1919–23	75	4	-	79	2	1	-	3
MCDONALD	Hugh	Goalkeeper	1913–14	8	-	-	8	-	-	-	-
MCDONALD	Jack	Outside-left	1948–52	75	3	-	78	19	1	-	20
MACDONALD	Malcolm	Centre-forward	1968–69	10+3	-	-	10+3	5	-	-	5
MACEDO	Tony	Goalkeeper	1955–68	346	31	14	391	-	-	-	-
MCGIBBON	Doug	Centre-forward	1947–48	42	-	-	42	18	-	-	18
MCGLASHAN	John	Midfield	1992–93	5	-	-	5	1	-	-	1
MCINTOSH	William	Outside-left	1911–12	6	1	-	7	-	-	-	-

		Position	Fulham Career	Appearances League	FA Cup	FL Cup	TOTAL APPS	Goals League	FA Cup	FL Cup	TOTAL GOALS
MCINTYRE	Edward	Right-half	1906–07	5	-	-	5	-	-	-	-
MCINTYRE	Johnny	Inside-forward	1917–20	25	1	-	26	9	-	-	9
MCKAY	James	Centre-forward	1922–24	17	-	-	17	5	-	-	5
MCKENNA	Frank	Forward	1927–28	25	1	-	26	10	-	-	10
MCKENNA	Tom	Goalkeeper	1925–26	10	-	-	10	-	-	-	-
MCKENZIE	Leon	Forward	1997–98	1+2	-	-	1+2	-	-	-	-
MCKINLAY	Billy	Midfield	2004–05	1+1	-	1	2+1	-	-	-	-
MCLAUGHLIN	Pat	Centre-forward	1909–10	2	-	-	2	1	-	-	1
MCNABB	David	Centre-half	1925–30	158	11	-	169	21	-	-	21
MCQUEEN	Hugh	Inside-left	1903–04	10	4	-	14	-	1	-	1
MAHONEY	Tony	Centre-forward	1977–82	53+6	5+1	4	62+7	10	2	1	13
MAHORN	Paul	Midfield	1993–94	1+2	-	-	1+2	-	-	-	-
MALBRANQUE	Steed	Midfield	2001–06	160+12	17	6+2	183+14	32	7	2	41
MALCOLM	George	Inside-forward	1909–10	4	-	-	4	1	-	-	1
MALPASS	Sam	Left-back	1939–47	2	-	-	2	-	-	-	-
MANSLEY	Alan	Outside-left	1970–71	1	-	-	1	-	-	-	-
MARGERRISON	John	Midfield	1975–79	63+8	3+1	4	70+9	9	2	-	11
MARINELLO	Peter	Outside-right	1978–80	25+2	3	2	30+2	1	-	-	1
MARLET	Steve	Striker	2001–04	50+5	6+2	1	57+7	11	3	-	14
MARRABLE	Sid	Centre-half	1920–21	8	-	-	8	-	-	-	-
MARSH	Rodney	Centre-forward	1962–77	79	4	7	90	27	1	-	28
MARSHALL	Alf	Half-back	1909–20	100	7	-	107	-	-	-	-
MARSHALL	John	Utility player	1982–97	395+18	18+1	34+1	447+20	28	3	1	32
MARTIN	George	Left-half/inside-left	1916–25	48	2	-	50	-	-	-	-
MASON	Bill	Goalkeeper	1928–33	33	3	-	36	-	-	-	-
MASON	Tommy	Left-back	1978–81	6	1	-	7	-	-	-	-
MATTHEWSON	Reg	Centre-half	1968–73	156+2	7	9	172+2	1	-	-	1
MAUGE	Ronnie	Midfield	1988–90	49+3	1	4	54+3	2	-	-	2
MAUGHAN	William	Right-half	1914–15	22	2	-	24	1	-	-	1
MAVEN	Fred	Centre-half	1909–13	140	9	-	149	29	-	-	29
MAY	Hugh	Inside-left	1903–04	8	2	-	10	2	-	-	2
MAYBANK	Teddy	Forward	1976–80	46	2	2	50	17	-	2	19
MAYES	Ken	Inside-left	1935–37	2	-	-	2	-	-	-	-
MEADE	Tommy	Centre-forward	1900–05	7	2	-	9	1	4	-	5
MEALAND	Barry	Right-back	1961–68	28+1	3	3	34+1	-	-	-	-
MEESON	Arthur	Goalkeeper	1928–29	1	-	-	1	-	-	-	-
MELLOR	Peter	Goalkeeper	1972–77	190	17	17	224	-	-	-	-
MELVILLE	Andy	Central-defender	1999–2004	150+3	13+2	12+1	175+6	4	-	-	4
METCHICK	Dave	Inside-forward	1961–64	47	4	5	56	9	1	3	13
MIECZNIKOWSKI	Micky	Outside-left	1903–04	2	-	-	2	-	-	-	-
MILLER	Charles	Outside-right	1914–15	6	-	-	6	-	-	-	-
MILLER	John	Outside-left	1937–49	4	-	-	4	-	-	-	-
MILLINGTON	Ben	Inside-forward	1908–10	1	-	-	1	-	-	-	-

		Position	Fulham	Appearances			TOTAL	Goals			TOTAL
			Career	League	FA Cup	FL Cup	APPS	League	FA Cup	FL Cup	GOALS
MILLINGTON	Charlie	Inside-forward	1907–09	57	8	-	65	18	4	-	22
MILTON	Steve	Striker	1989–91	39+19	0+2	1+1	40+22	9	-	-	9
MISON	Michael	Midfield	1994–97	35+20	4+3	7	46+23	5	-	1	6
MITCHELL	John	Centre-forward	1972–78	158+11	11+1	11+2	180+14	56	2	2	60
MITTEN	Charlie	Outside-left	1952–56	154	6	-	160	32	1	-	33
MOLLER	Peter	Striker	2000–01	2+3	-	-	2+3	1	-	-	1
MOLLOY	Peter	Centre-half	1931–33	4	-	-	4	-	-	-	-
MONEY	Richard	Defender	1977–80	106	5	4	115	3	1	-	4
MONTELLA	Vincenzo	Striker	2006–07	3+7	1+3	-	4+10	2	3	-	5
MOODY	Paul	Striker	1997–99	30+11	1+1	2+2	33+14	19	-	-	19
MOORE	Kevin	Central-defender	1994–96	48+3	7+2	4	59+5	4	-	2	6
MOORE	Bobby	Left-half	1974–77	124	15	11	150	1	-	-	1
MORELINE	David	Left-back	1968–74	63+7	5+1	5+1	73+9	-	-	-	-
MORGAN	Simon	Utility player	1990–2001	345+10	20	33	398+10	48	3	2	53
MORRIS	Harry	Centre-forward	1919–21	6	1	-	7	2	-	-	2
MORRISON	Billy	Centre-half	1904–08	122	20	-	142	8	1	-	9
MORTON	Alan	Forward	1970–71	1	-	2+1	3+1	1	-	-	1
MOSELEY	Robert	Inside-right	1926–30	2	-	-	2	-	-	-	-
MOSS	Bobby	Inside-forward	1966–69	8+1	-	1	9+1	3	-	-	3
MOUNCHER	Fred	Outside-left	1907–11	42	9	-	51	9	1	-	10
MULLAN	Brendan	Inside-forward	1968–69	2+2	1	-	3+2	-	2	-	2
MULLERY	Alan	Right-half	1958–76	363+1	31	17	411+1	37	2	3	42
MURPHY	Jerry	Inside-forward	1929–31	13	-	-	13	2	-	-	2
MURRAY	Allan	Left-half	1933–35	1	-	-	1	-	-	-	-
MURRAY	Ivan	Right-half	1968–69	4+1	-	-	4+1	-	-	-	-
NASH	Bert	Outside-right	1919–20	3	-	-	3	-	-	-	-
NEBBELING	Gavin	Central-defender	1989–93	85+3	4	5	94+3	2	-	-	2
NEILSON	Alan	Defender	1997–2001	24+5	4	4+2	32+7	2	-	-	2
NELSON	Dave	Inside-forward	1946–47	23	1	-	24	3	-	-	3
NEWCOMBE	Bernard	Outside-left	1948–56	23	-	-	23	3	-	-	3
NEWHOUSE	Aidan	Forward	1997–98	7+1	-	3+1	10+2	1	-	3	4
NEWSON	Mark	Right-back	1990–93	98+4	4+1	3	105+5	4	-	-	4
NEWTON	Frank	Centre-forward	1931–35	83	5	-	88	77	4	-	81
NICHOL	James	Inside-left	1913–15	3	-	-	3	-	-	-	-
NICHOLS	Brian	Left-back	1963–68	50+1	1+1	4	55+2	1	-	-	1
NIDD	George	Left-back	1903–04	-	3	-	3	-	-	-	-
NIEMI	Antti	Goalkeeper	2005–07	40	-	-	40	-	-	-	-
NIXON	Wilf	Goalkeeper	1910–22	27	2	-	29	-	-	-	-
NORTH	Stacey	Central-defender	1990–92	38	3	-	41	-	-	-	-
OAKES	Keith	Central-defender	1986–88	76	5	3	84	3	1	-	4
O'CALLAGHAN	Taffy	Inside-forward	1937–39	39	3	-	42	6	1	-	7
O'CONNELL	Brian	Inside-forward	1958–66	152	10	8	170	26	-	2	28
O'CONNOR	Thurlough	Centre-forward	1966–68	1	-	-	1	-	-	-	-

		Position	Fulham	Appearances			TOTAL	Goals			TOTAL
			Career	League	FA Cup	FL Cup	APPS	League	FA Cup	FL Cup	GOALS
O'DONNELL	Peter	Goalkeeper	1909–10	3	-	-	3	-	-	-	-
O'DRISCOLL	Sean	Midfield	1979–84	141+7	11+1	12+1	164+9	13	-	-	13
O'LEARY	Danny	Inside-forward	1969–70	0+1	-	-	0+1	-	-	-	-
OLIVER	Len	Right-half	1924–35	406	28	-	434	3	-	-	3
OMOZUSI	Eliot	Defender	2006–07	-	0+1	1	1+1	-	-	-	-
ONWERE	Udo	Midfield	1990–94	66+19	1+1	4+2	71+22	7	-	-	7
ORR	William	Right-back	1903–04	26	7	-	33	-	-	-	-
OSBORNE	Frank	Forward	1921–24	67	3	-	70	18	-	-	18
O'SULLIVAN	Peter	Midfield	1981–83	45+1	2	7	54+1	1	-	-	1
OUADDOU	Abdes	Defender	2001–03	13+8	1+2	4	18+10	-	-	-	-
OVEREND	Alex	Outside-right	1912–13	3	-	-	3	-	-	-	-
PACKHAM	Fred	Outside-right	1923–26	5	-	-	5	-	-	-	-
PAPE	Albert	Centre-forward	1925–27	42	6	-	48	12	4	-	16
PAPWORTH	Jack	Centre-half/forward	1919–25	39	2	-	40	16	-	-	16
PARKER	Paul	Right-back	1982–97	143+14	11	16	170+14	2	-	1	3
PARKS	Tony	Goalkeeper	1990–91	2	-	-	2	-	-	-	-
PARMENTER	Terry	Outside-left	1964–69	18	1+1	1	20+1	1	-	1	2
PARSONAGE	George	Centre-half	1908–09	22	1	-	23	3	-	-	3
PAVITT	Bill	Centre-half	1946–52	50	2	-	52	1	-	-	1
PEARCE	Bert	Centre-forward	1911–15	90	7	-	97	48	2	-	50
PEARCE	Ian	Central-defender	2003–07	55+1	2	2	59+1	1	-	-	1
PEARSON	Mark	Midfield	1965–68	53+5	1+1	6	60+6	7	-	-	7
PEMBRIDGE	Mark	Midfield	2003–07	40+5	2+3	4	46+8	1	-	1	2
PENN	Frank	Outside-left	1915–34	427	32	-	459	45	7	-	52
PENTECOST	Mike	Right-back	1966–73	81+6	1	7	89+6	-	-	-	-
PERRY	Eddie	Centre-forward	1931–38	64	5	-	69	36	4	-	40
PESCHISOLIDO	Paul	Striker	1997–2001	71+26	9+1	7+1	87+28	24	2	4	30
PETERS	Frank	Outside-right	1932–33	1	-	-	1	1	-	-	1
PETERS	Gary	Right-back	1979–90	64+11	8	4	76+11	4	-	-	4
PETTA	Bobby	Midfield	2003–04	3+6	2+3	-	5+9	-	-	-	-
PEYTON	Gerry	Goalkeeper	1976–86	345	22	28	395	-	-	-	-
PHELAN	Terry	Full-back	1999–2001	18+1	-	1	19+1	2	-	-	2
PHILLIPSON	Tom	Inside-left	1904–05	1	-	-	1	-	-	-	-
PIKE	Chris	Forward	1985–90	32+10	-	3+1	35+11	4	-	1	5
PIKE	Martin	Left-back	1990–94	187+3	5	10	202+3	14	1	-	15
PIKE	Tot	Outside-right	1925–27	3	-	-	3	-	-	-	-
PILKINGTON	Fred	Right-back	1924–27	4	-	-	4	1	-	-	1
PINKNEY	Alan	Midfield	1972–73	11+1	-	-	11+1	-	-	-	-
PITTS	Harold	Right-back	1934–49	9	-	-	9	-	-	-	-
PORTER	Billy	Outside-left	1902–04	1	-	-	1	-	-	-	-
PRATLEY	Darren	Forward	2003–04	0+1	-	0+1	0+2	-	-	-	-
PRATT	Tom	Centre-forward	1904–05	4	-	-	4	-	-	-	-
PRICE	Johnny	Inside-forward	1928–37	190	15	-	205	49	4	-	53

		Position	Fulham	Appearances			TOTAL	Goals			TOTAL
			Career	League	FA Cup	FL Cup	APPS	League	FA Cup	FL Cup	GOALS
PROBERT	Bill	Left-back	1925–27	16	1	-	17	-	-	-	-
PROUD	Joe	Outside-right	1928–32	12	-	-	12	3	-	-	3
PROUSE	Bill	Inside-forward	1924–27	76	7	-	83	30	1	-	31
PROUT	Dick	Inside-forward	1907–10	7	1	-	8	-	-	-	-
QUEDRUE	Franck	Full-back	2006–07	28+1	3	-	31+1	1	-	-	1
QUESTED	Len	Right-half	1943–51	175	13	-	188	6	1	-	7
RADCLIFFE	Mark	Goalkeeper	1946–48	11	2	-	13	-	-	-	-
RADZINSKI	Tomas	Striker	2004–07	73+30	9	4+1	86+31	10	2	5	17
RAMPLING	Dennis	Outside-right	1942–48	2	2	-	4	-	1	-	1
REDWOOD	George	Left-back	1910–11	7	-	-	7	-	-	-	-
REEVES	John	Midfield	1981–85	9+5	2	1	12+5	-	-	-	-
REGAN	Ted	Right-half	1929–30	1	-	-	1	-	-	-	-
REHMAN	Zesh	Central-defender	2003–06	18+3	6	5	29+3	-	-	1	1
REID	George	Centre-forward	1923–24	2	1	-	3	-	-	-	-
REID	Joe	Full-back	1930–31	7	-	-	7	-	-	-	-
REIDLE	Karl Heinze	Striker	1999–2001	16+19	1	-	17+19	6	-	-	6
REYNOLDS	Arthur	Goalkeeper	1910–25	399	21	-	420	-	-	-	-
RICHARDS	Dicky	Outside-right	1924–25	21	2	-	23	2	1	-	3
RICHARDS	Billy	Outside-right	1931–35	76	6	=	82	14	1	-	15
RICHARDSON	John	Central-defender	1969–73	61+10	4	5	70+10	6	-	1	7
RICKETT	Harry	Goalkeeper	1944–46	-	2	-	2	-	-	-	-
RIDDELL	James	Left-half	1923–25	37	5	-	42	-	-	-	-
ROBERTS	Dave	Centre-half	1967–71	21+1	-	3	24+1	-	-	-	-
ROBOTHAM	Harry	Right-half	1903–05	34	5	-	39	-	1	-	1
ROBSON	Bobby	Inside-forward/wing-half	1950–67	344	14	12	370	77	2	1	80
RONSON	Brian	Goalkeeper	1953–56	2	-	-	2	-	-	-	-
ROOKE	Ronnie	Centre-forward	1936–46	105	5	-	110	70	8	-	78
ROSENIOR	Leroy	Centre-forward	1982–90	98+1	6	4	108+1	38	1	1	40
ROSENIOR	Liam	Full-back	2004–07	76+3	8	3+2	87+5	-	-	1	1
ROSIER	Bertie	Right-back	1928–30	52	5	-	57	-	-	-	-
ROSS	Harry	Right-back	1904–08	127	19	-	146	12	3	-	15
ROUGVIE	Doug	Central-defender	1988–89	20	-	-	20	1	-	-	1
ROUNCE	George	Centre-forward	1933–35	12	-	-	12	1	-	-	1
ROUTLEDGE	Wayne	Midfield	2006–07	12+11	3	1	16+11	-	1	-	1
ROWLEY	Arthur	Centre-forward	1948–50	56	3	-	59	26	-	-	26
RUNSTROM	Bjorn	Striker	2006–07	0+1	-	1	1+1	-	-	-	-
RUSSELL	Harry	Right-half	1913–23	138	4	-	142	7	-	-	7
RYAN	John	Full-back	1965–69	42+5	4	4	50+5	1	-	-	1
SAHA	Louis	Striker	2000–04	100+17	10+1	3+3	113+21	53	3	6	62
SAHOUN	Nicolas	Midfield	2000–01	2+5	1	1	4+5	-	-	-	-
SALAKO	John	Winger	1998–99	7+3	2+2	2	11+5	1	-	1	2
SALVAGE	Barry	Outside-left	1967–69	7	-	-	7	-	-	-	-
SAVA	Fecundo	Striker	2002–04	13+13	3+3	2+1	18+17	6	1	-	7

		Position	Fulham	Appearances			TOTAL	Goals			TOTAL
			Career	League	FA Cup	FL Cup	APPS	League	FA Cup	FL Cup	GOALS
SAYER	Andy	Centre-forward	1988–90	44+10	4	5	53+10	16	-	-	16
SCOTT	Peter	Midfield	1981–92	270+9	9	18+2	297+11	27	1	6	34
SCOTT	Rob	Forward	1996–98	65+19	3	3+5	71+24	17	1	-	18
SCRIVENS	Steve	Outside-left	1975–80	3+1	-	-	3+1	1	-	-	1
SCULLION	James	Centre-forward	1926–27	1	-	-	1	-	-	-	-
SEALY	Tony	Forward	1983–85	22+3	-	-	22+3	11	-	-	11
SELLEY	Ian	Midfield	1997–2000	3	-	-	3	-	-	-	-
SEYMOUR	Ian	Goalkeeper	1966–71	64	2	9	75	-	-	-	-
SHARP	Jimmy	Left-back	1904–20	114	11	-	125	1	-	-	1
SHEA	Danny	Inside-forward	1920–23	100	7	-	107	23	1	-	24
SHEPHERD	Ernie	Outside-left	1938–48	72	4	-	76	13	-	-	13
SHRUBB	Paul	Full-back	1972–75	1	-	-	1	-	-	-	-
SIMONS	Henry	Inside-forward	1914–15	9	-	-	9	4	-	-	4
SIMPSON	Gary	Central-defender	1995–96	5+2	-	-	5+2	-	-	-	-
SKENE	Leslie	Goalkeeper	1907–10	88	6	-	94	-	-	-	-
SKINNER	Justin	Midfield	1986–91	113+24	5+1	10+1	128+26	23	-	4	27
SLADE	Donald	Inside-forward	1914–15	17	-	-	17	5	-	-	5
SLOUGH	Alan	Midfield	1973–77	154	18	15	187	14	2	1	17
SMERTIN	Alexey	Midfield	2006–07	6+1	1	-	7+1	-	-	-	-
SMITH	Gary	Full-back	1986–87	0+1	-	-	0+1	-	-	-	-
SMITH	Jack	Centre-forward	1926–28	34	-	-	34	9	-	-	9
SMITH	James	Outside-right	1909–15	181	12	-	193	17	-	-	17
SMITH	James D.	Centre-forward	1922–23	5	-	-	5	1	-	-	1
SMITH	Jamie	Full-back	1998–99	9	-	-	9	1	-	-	1
SMITH	Neil	Midfield	1997–99	62+12	6+3	3+1	71+16	1	1	-	2
SMITH	Norman	Right-half	1948–60	60	3	-	63	-	-	-	-
SMITH	Trevor	Inside-right	1935–38	93	7	-	100	19	2	-	21
SOAR	Albert	Outside-right	1903–06	71	15	-	86	6	-	-	6
SOLOMON	Jason	Midfield	1996–97	1+3	-	-	1+3	-	-	-	-
SPACKMAN	Fred	Inside-left	1899–1904	-	2	-	2	-	-	-	-
SPARKE	Cecil	Outside-left	1927–29	2	-	-	2	-	-	-	-
SPINK	Thomas	Outside-right	1910–12	11	-	-	11	1	-	-	1
STALLARD	Mark	Forward	1994–95	4	-	-	4	3	-	-	3
STANNARD	Jim	Goalkeeper	1980–95	391	14	25	430	-	-	-	-
STANT	Phil	Forward	1990–91	19	-	-	19	5	-	-	5
STAPLETON	Joe	Half-back	1952–61	97	7	-	104	2	-	-	2
STEELE	Alex	Left-half	1927–30	49	4	-	53	-	-	-	-
STEGGLES	Kevin	Defender	1986–87	3	-	-	3	-	-	-	-
STEPHENSON	Alan	Centre-half	1971–72	10	-	-	10	-	-	-	-
STEPHENSON	Roy	Right-back	1903–04	1	-	-	1	-	-	-	-
STEVENS	Arthur	Outside-right	1943–59	386	27	-	413	110	14	-	124
STEWART	Simon	Central-defender	1996–98	2+1	-	-	2+1	-	-	-	-
STEWART	Tommy	Left-half	1912–14	15	-	-	15	-	-	-	-

		Position	Fulham	Appearances			TOTAL	Goals			TOTAL
			Career	League	FA Cup	FL Cup	APPS	League	FA Cup	FL Cup	GOALS
STOKES	Alf	Inside-right	1959–60	15	-	-	15	6	-	-	6
STOLCERS	Andres	Winger	2000–04	8+17	0+2	3+1	11+20	2	-	2	4
STOREY	George	Centre-forward	1903–04	3	-	-	3	-	-	-	-
STOREY	Peter	Defender	1976–78	17	-	2	19	-	-	-	-
STRATTON	Reg	Outside-left	1959–65	21	3	-	24	1	2	-	3
STRONG	Les	Left-back	1971–83	370+3	28	26	424+3	5	-	1	6
SUART	Bob	Centre-half	1908–11	97	5	-	102	1	-	-	1
SULLIVAN	Brian	Inside-forward	1959–62	2	-	-	2	1	-	-	1
SUMMERS	Johnny	Outside-left	1947–50	4	-	-	4	-	-	-	-
SYMES	Ernie	Right-half/outside-right	1917–23	6	-	-	6	-	-	-	-
SYMONS	Kit	Central-defender	1998–2001	96+6	12	14+1	122+7	13	-	1	14
TALBOT	Brian	Midfield	1990–91	5	-	-	5	1	-	-	1
TANNAHILL	Robert	Outside-right	1901–04	-	4	-	4	-	2	-	2
TAPLEY	Steve	Centre-half	1981–85	2	-	-	2	1	-	-	1
TARGETT	Alf	Left-half	1935–37	1	-	-	1	-	-	-	-
TAYLOR	Harry	Outside-right	1957–58	4	-	-	4	-	-	-	-
TAYLOR	Jeff	Inside-right	1951–54	33	2	-	35	14	4	-	18
TAYLOR	Jim	Centre-half	1938–53	261	17	-	278	5	-	-	5
TAYLOR	Maik	Goalkeeper	1997–2003	185+1	20	22	227+1	-	-	-	-
TAYLOR	Mark	Defender	1995–96	7	1	-	8	-	-	-	-
TAYLOR	Will	Inside-forward	1913–24	48	2	-	50	8	2	-	10
TEALE	Richard	Goalkeeper	1976–77	5	-	-	5	-	-	-	-
TEMPEST	Dale	Forward	1980–84	25+9	-	1	26+9	6	-	1	7
TEMPLE	Jimmy	Outside-right	1926–31	156	12	-	168	58	3	-	61
TEMPLETON	Bobby	Outside-left	1913–15	32	-	-	32	-	-	-	-
THOMAS	Andy	Forward	1982–83	3+1	-	-	3+1	2	-	-	2
THOMAS	Bob	Inside-forward	1947–52	167	9	-	176	56	2	-	58
THOMAS	Glen	Central-defender	1985–94	248+5	7	22	277+5	6	-	-	6
THOMAS	Len	Outside-right	1922–23	1	-	-	1	-	-	-	-
THOMAS	Louis	Inside-left	1905–06	1	-	-	1	-	-	-	
THOMAS	Martin	Midfield	1994–98	59+31	4	6+1	69+32	8	1	-	9
THOMAS	Sid	Inside-right	1938–50	57	4	-	61	4	-	-	4
THOMPSON	Benny	Outside-left	1906–08	8	-	-	8	2	-	-	2
THOMPSON	Edward	Left-back	1914–15	1	-	-	1	-	-	-	-
THOMPSON	Fred	Goalkeeper	1905–06	4	1	-	5		-	-	-
THOMPSON	Jimmy	Inside-forward	1930–31	4	1	-	5	2	-	-	2
THORPE	Harry	Left-back	1904–07	70	10	-	80	-	-	-	-
THORPE	Tony	Striker	1997–98	6+9	-	-	6+9	3	-	-	3
THRELFALL	Fred	Outside-left	1905–09	96	10	-	106	17	2	-	19
TIERLING	Lee	Midfield	1992–94	7+12	1	-	8+12	-	-	-	-
TILFORD	Arthur	Left-back	1932–34	41	1	-	42	-	-	-	-
TIMLIN	Stephen	Midfield	2004–07	-	0+1	2+1	2+2	-	-	-	-

		Position	Fulham Career	Appearances League	FA Cup	FL Cup	TOTAL APPS	Goals League	FA Cup	FL Cup	TOTAL GOALS
TOMPKINS	Jimmy	Left-half	1932–39	154	10	-	164	5	-	-	5
TONNER	Johnny	Inside-left	1926–27	28	2	-	30	13	2	-	15
TOOTILL	Alf	Goalkeeper	1932–38	203	11	-	214	-	-	-	-
TORRANCE	Jimmy	Utility-player	1910–26	338	19	-	357	33	-	-	33
TOWNSEND	Martin	Goalkeeper	1963–64	2	-	1	3	-	-	-	-
TRANTER	Wilf	Right-back	1969–72	20+3	0+1	1	21+4	-	-	-	-
TRAVERS	Barney	Centre-forward	1921–22	46	3	-	49	28	1	-	29
TROLLOPE	Paul	Midfield	1997–2002	56+23	3+5	9+2	68+30	5	-	-	5
TUCKER	Mark	Defender	1990–93	3+1	-	-	3+1	-	-	-	-
TUCKETT	Ernie	Centre-half	1938–39	1	-	-	1	-	-	-	-
TURNER	Hugh	Goalkeeper	1937–39	68	3	-	71	-	-	-	-
TURNER	Ted	Left-back	1903–04	29	6	-	35	-	-	-	-
TUTTHILL	George	Left-half	1899–1905	-	3	-	3	-	-	-	-
UHLENBEEK	Gus	Midfield	1998–2000	22+17	3+2	4+1	29+20	1	-	-	1
UNDERWOOD	Dave	Goalkeeper	1953–65	18	-	1	19		-	-	-
VAN DER SAR	Edwin	Goalkeeper	2001–05	126+1	15	1	142+1	-	-	-	-
VAUGHAN	John	Goalkeeper	1986–88	44	4	4	52	-	-	-	-
VERTANNES	Des	Left-back	1988–90	0+2	-	-	0+2	-	-	-	-
VOLZ	Moritz	Full-back	2003–07	110+6	11	4+1	125+7	2	2	-	4
WALKER	Clive	Outside-left	1987–90	104+7	4	5+1	113+8	29	1	1	31
WALKER	Harry	Left-half	1921–23	8	-	-	8	-	-	-	-
WALKER	Willie	Outside-left	1909–21	170	8	-	178	23	1	-	24
WALLBANKS	Harry	Right-half	1938–49	33	4	-	37	1	-	-	1
WALTERS	Charlie	Centre-half	1926–28	17	2	-	19	-	-	-	-
WALTON	Mark	Goalkeeper	1996–98	40	-	5	45	-	-	-	-
WARBOYS	Alan	Centre-forward	1976–78	19	-	2	21	2	-	-	2
WARBURTON	Arthur	Inside-forward/wing-half	1934–38	46	1	-	47	6	-	-	6
WARD	Felix	Outside-right	1907–08	4	-	-	4	-	-	-	-
WARDROPE	Willie	Centre-forward	1904–06	58	11	-	69	29	3	-	32
WARNER	Tony	Goalkeeper	2005–07	16+2	2	1	19+2	-	-	-	-
WARREN	Christer	Forward	1996–97	8+3	-	-	8+3	1	-	-	1
WATERSON	Fred	Right-back	1903–09	8	6	-	14	-	-	-	-
WATINS	Ernie	Centre-forward	1930–31	17	3	-	20	10	2	-	12
WATSON	Jack	Centre-half	1946–48	71	1	-	72	2	1	-	3
WATSON	John	Centre-forward	1989–90	12+2	2	4	18+2	-	1	1	2
WATSON	Paul	Full-back	1996–97	48+2	2	3	53+2	4	-	1	5
WATSON	Trevor	Outside-right	1956–64	17	-	-	17	1	-	-	1
WEBB	Harry	Left-half	1930–33	6	-	-	6	1	-	-	1
WEBSTER	Malcolm	Goalkeeper	1969–74	94	5	5	104	-	-	-	-
WEIR	Jimmy	Outside-left	1957–60	3	-	-	3	-	-	-	-
WEIR	Jock	Centre-forward	1912–13	1	-	-	1	-	-	-	-
WENT	Paul	Central-half	1972–73	58	1	8	67	3	-	2	5
WHALLEY	Fred	Goalkeeper	1924–25	8	1	-	9	-	-	-	-

		Position	Fulham	Appearances			TOTAL	Goals			TOTAL
			Career	League	FA Cup	FL Cup	APPS	League	FA Cup	FL Cup	GOALS
WHEATCROFT	Fred	Inside-left	1906–07	23	4	-	27	9	-	-	9
WHITE	Bert	Centre-forward	1925–26	7	1	-	8	1	1	-	2
WHITE	Wattie	Wing-half/inside-forward	1910–23	191	12	-	203	18	-	-	18
WILKES	Albert	Right-half	1907–09	16	-	-	16	1	-	-	1
WILLIAMS	Carl	Midfield	1995–96	2+11	-	0+1	2+12	-	-	-	-
WILLIAMSON	Brian	Goalkeeper	1968–69	12	2	-	14	-	-	-	-
WILLOCK	Callum	Striker	2000–03	0+5	-	-	0+5	-	-	-	-
WILSON	Robert	Midfield	1979–89	211+12	9	19+2	239+14	38	-	4	42
WILSON	Tom	Right-back	1950–57	45	4	-	49	-	-	-	-
WINSHIP	Thomas	Outside-left	1912–13	2	-	-	2	-	-	-	-
WOLFE	Tommy	Inside-left/left-half	1925–27	27	-	-	27	2	-	-	2
WOME	Pierre	Full-back	2002–03	13+1	0+1	2	15+2	1	-	-	1
WOOD	Albert	Inside-right	1931–35	21	2	-	23	9	-	-	9
WOOD	Arthur	Inside-forward-	1911–19	21	-	-	21	1	-	-	1
WOOD	Len	Inside-left	1924–26	4	-	-	4	2	-	-	2
WOOD	Willie	Inside-right	1905–06	9	2	-	11	2	-	-	2
WOODWARD	Viv	Inside-forward	1936–47	92	3	-	95	25	-	-	25
WORRALL	Ted	Right-back	1919–23	88	8	-	96	-	-	-	-
WORSLEY	Bert	Outside/inside-right	1935–39	106	6	-	112	15	1	-	16
WRIGHTSON	Frank	Inside-forward	1932–33	17	1	-	18	5	-	-	5
WYLLIE	David	Centre-forward	1908–09	7	-	-	7	-	-	-	-
ZAKUANI	Gabriel	Defender	2006–07	-	0+1	1	1+1	-	-	-	-

ND - #0172 - 090625 - C0 - 240/170/33 - PB - 9781780911328 - Gloss Lamination